Japan

Robert Strauss
Chris Taylor
Tony Wheeler

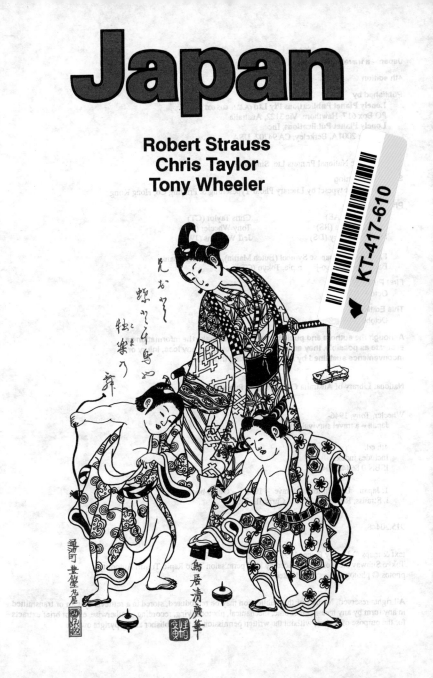

Japan – a travel survival kit

4th edition

Published by
Lonely Planet Publications Pty Ltd (A.C.N. 005 607 983)
PO Box 617, Hawthorn, Vic 3122, Australia
Lonely Planet Publications, Inc
PO Box 2001A, Berkeley, CA 94702, USA

Printed by
Singapore National Printers Ltd, Singapore

Script Typesetting
Kanji script typeset by Literary Photo-Typesetting & Printing Co, Hong Kong

Photographs by

Alan Elliott (AE)	Chris Taylor (CT)
Robert Strauss (RS)	Tony Wheeler (TW)
Deanna Swaney (DS)	Jeff Williams (JW)

Front cover: Japanese Symbol (Butch Martin), The Image Bank
Back cover: Senso-ji Temple, Tokyo (CT)

First Published
October 1981

This Edition
October 1991

Although the authors and publisher have tried to make the information as accurate as possible, they accept no responsibility for any loss, injury or inconvenience sustained by any person using this book.

National Library of Australia Cataloguing in Publication Data

Wheeler, Tony, 1946-
    Japan – a travel survival kit.

    4th ed.
    Includes index.
    ISBN 0 86442 104 4

    1. Japan – Description and travel – 1945 – – Guide-books.
    I. Strauss, Robert. II. Taylor, Chris. III. Title.

915.20448

Robert Strauss

In the early '70s Robert took the overland route to Nepal and then studied, taught and edited in England, Germany, Portugal and Hong Kong. For Lonely Planet Robert has worked on travel survival kits to *China* and *Tibet*. For Bradt Publications he wrote *The Trans-Siberian Rail Guide*. He has contributed photos and articles to other books, magazines and newspapers in the USA, Australia and Asia.

Delighted with Japan in most respects, he is still pondering the advice from a fortune-telling automat in Takayama: 'You will soon have a baby, but you will have trouble finding your way home!'.

Chris Taylor

Originally hailing from Bristol, England, Chris' vocational training includes a stint as a student psychiatric nurse, an eventful year as a clerk in the public service, a protracted period of neglect and grinding poverty while posing as a singer/songwriter and a year serving as a cultural missionary teaching English in Japan. Numerous trips around Asia and a BA later, Chris joined the Lonely Planet team to edit our phrasebooks. He is currently based in Taiwan.

Tony Wheeler

Tony Wheeler was born in England but spent most of his youth overseas. He returned to England to do a university degree in engineering, worked as an automotive design engineer, returned to university to complete an MBA, then dropped out on the Asian overland trail with his wife Maureen. They've been travelling, writing and publishing guidebooks ever since, having set up Lonely Planet Publications in the mid-70s. Travel for the Wheelers is now considerably enlivened by their daughter Tashi and their son Kieran.

From the Authors

From Robert The Japan National Tourist Organisation (JNTO) and TIC pulled out all the stops to provide a great variety of support. Special thanks to the following members of JNTO: Toshinobu Ikubo and Seiko Taniguchi in Tokyo; Sian Evans, Ms Mizuno, and Louisa Hooper in London. At Kyoto TIC, thanks are due to Tomoko Inuishi.

The following individuals should be mentioned for their help and inspiration without which my trip would have been much less rewarding: Peter Emerson, Sherry Disterheft, Irene Riese & Walter (the intrepid cycling duo), Anders Bohman, Marvin Breen, Todd Carlisle, Fujii Tadashi, Jonathan Morland, Susan Kreitman, Dave Lindberg, Nori & Junko Tokita, Andy Bain, Brian Sullivan, Suzanne Thomas, Michiko Yoshida, Takeo Shin, Yukio Tanaka, Fritz Ecknick, Barbara Hesse, Patricia Boertje, Audrey Magoun, Shinpei Koshika and Xiao Hong.

Michitaka Nakahara and family (Tokyo) were exceptionally generous with their offer of a base for operations, superb food, immense hospitality, a wealth of information and great patience with my unexpected arrivals and departures.

My slice of this book is dedicated to a number of close friends and relatives whose journeys came to an end in separate incidents whilst I was working on this book. And to my mum who keeps bouncing back and is probably out on the road at this moment – exceeding the speed limit as usual.

From Tony Thanks to Gene Trabich and Robert Glasser for pointing out the silver gorilla in Okayama, and the gang at the youth hostel on Iriomote Island for a most interesting afternoon tramping through leech-infested swamps to remote waterfalls and climbing telecommunication towers. Thanks to David Parry for his additional information on skiing in Japan, and to Richard Nebesky who wrote that section.

This Book

The first three editions of *Japan – a travel survival kit* were written by Ian L McQueen, a Canadian who has lived in Tokyo for many years. With this fourth edition it was time for a total rewrite and our three person team tackled the country from the northern reaches of Hokkaidō to the southern islands of Okinawa. All three writers visited Tokyo although it was Chris, a former resident of that city, who wrote most of the chapter.

Chris also handled the region around Tokyo and Osaka. Robert covered Kyoto and other parts of the Kinki District, Northern Honshū and Hokkaidō. Meanwhile, Tony headed west and south to cover Western Honshū, Shikoku, Kyūshū, Okinawa and the South-West Islands.

From the Publisher

This edition of Japan was edited by Miriam Cannell and Jeff Williams. Thanks to Lyn McGaurr, Sue Harvey and Sharan Kaur for copy editing and to Caroline Williamson and Alan Tiller for impeccable proof reading. A special thank you to Tom Smallman for editorial guidance and proofing. Thanks to Sharon Wertheim for preparing the index and to Chris Taylor and Felicia Zhang for their work on the Japanese script.

Peter Flavelle, assisted by Sandra Pietrolungo, produced the new maps for this edition and was helped by Chris Lee Ack, Greg Herriman and Glenn Beanland. Peter was also responsible for the cover design and colourwraps, and Margaret Jung for the illustrations. Greg and Peter were a formidable team in the design and layout of the book and were helped by Trudi Canavan, Ryan Taylor and Chris Hart.

Last, but not least, a special thanks to those travellers who took the time and energy to write to us. These people's names appear on page 725.

Warning & Request

Things change – prices go up, schedules change, good places go bad and bad places go bankrupt – nothing stays the same. So if you find things better or worse, recently opened or long since closed, please write and tell us and help make the next edition better!

Your letters will be used to help update future editions and, where possible, important changes will also be included as a Stop Press section in reprints.

All information is greatly appreciated and the best letters will receive a free copy of the next edition, or any other Lonely Planet book of your choice.

Contents

Map Legend

BOUNDARIES

—·—·—·—	........International Boundary
—··—··—··	................Internal Boundary
+++++++++	....National Park or Reserve
----------	.........................The Equator
·············	.........................The Tropics

SYMBOLS

◉ NEW DELHI	........................National Capital
● BOMBAY	.........Provincial or State Capital
● Pune	..............................Major Town
● Barsi	..............................Minor Town
⬔	..................................Post Office
✈	....Airport
𝑖	......................Tourist Information
◒	............Bus Station or Terminal
66	............Highway Route Number
☾ ✝ ⛪	......Mosque, Church, Cathedral
∴	......................Temple or Ruin
✚	.....................................Hospital
✳	......................................Lookout
⛺	...........................Camping Area
⛱	.............................Picnic Area
⌂	.............................Hut or Chalet
▲	.....................Mountain or Hill
	........................Railway Station
	.................................Road Bridge
	...........................Railway Bridge
	.................................Road Tunnel
	............................Railway Tunnel
	...............Escarpment or Cliff
	....Pass
	...........Ancient or Historic Wall

ROUTES

—————	.......Major Road or Highway
----------	.........Unsealed Major Road
—————	.........................Sealed Road
-·-·-·-·-	.....Unsealed Road or Track
	...........................City Street
▬▬▬▬	...........Railway, Shinkansen
	..................................Subway
—●—	..............................Tram Line
·············	.....................Walking Track
--------	...............................Ferry Route

HYDROGRAPHIC FEATURES

	.....................River or Creek
	............Intermittent Stream
	........Lake, Intermittent Lake
	.................................Coast Line
	....Spring
	......................................Waterfall
	....Swamp
	...............Salt Lake or Reef
	......................................Glacier

OTHER FEATURES

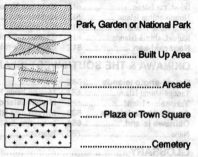

	Park, Garden or National Park
	...............................Built Up Area
	....Arcade
	.........Plaza or Town Square
	......................................Cemetery

Note: not all symbols displayed above appear in this book

Introduction

It's hardly surprising Japan inspires such a love-hate relationship in its visitors. The country seems to consist of a constant and often catastrophic series of collisions between opposites. Ancient history rubs shoulders with the 21st century; scenes of dazzling beauty suddenly give way to urban nightmares; you hurtle between cities on bullet trains only to be stuck in a logjam of people as soon as you emerge on the platform.

These juxtapositions are what make Japan such a fascinating place. The ancient temples, shrines and castles should be on every visitor's itinerary, but the modern factories are an equally important, and interesting, part of the Japan story. The traditional inns known as *ryokan* and *minshuku*

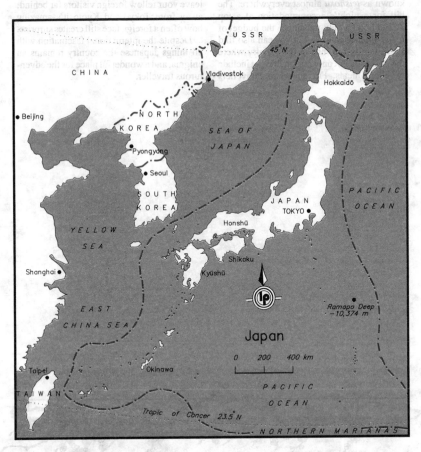

9

are delightful places to stay, but the adventurous visitor can also sample capsule hotels, love hotels and other exotica. A classic *kaiseki* meal can be a fine, albeit expensive, introduction to Japanese food at its best, but you can eat enjoyably, authentically and surprisingly cheaply at cosy, local 'red lantern' *aka-chochin* bars or in friendly, raucous *robatayaki* restaurants.

The clash of opposites can also provide you with some pleasant surprises. Japan can indeed be horrifically expensive but you can find bargain-priced lunch-time set meals known as *teishoku* almost everywhere. The bill for a night's accommodation at a top Tokyo hotel would unbalance the budget of many smaller nations. Yet you can also find small family-run inns in the country where the prices are not only reasonable but include excellent meals. For shoestring travellers

Japan not only offers a huge chain of youth hostels and other budget travel possibilities but also, if you're a native English speaker, good prospects for temporary employment.

Last, though far from least, Japan is a remarkably easy country to travel around. The fact that you probably cannot read the script makes little difference – finding your way around soon becomes second nature. Forget those tales of Japanese reserve as well: visitors quickly discover that there's always somebody on hand to offer directions to a lost *gaijin*. It's also wonderfully easy to leave your fellow foreign visitors far behind; away from Tokyo and Kyoto it's amazing how often a foreign face still creates surprise.

Despite the international fascination with all things Japanese the country remains an enigma, and a wonderful place for the adventurous traveller.

Facts about the Country

HISTORY
Prehistory
The origin of Japan's earliest inhabitants is obscure and uncertain: they may have come via land bridges that once connected Japan with Siberia and Korea but it is also thought that seafaring migrants from Polynesia may have landed on Kyūshū.

The first recorded signs of civilisation in Japan are found in the late Neolithic Age around 8000 BC. This is called the Jōmon (Cord Mark) period after the discovery of pottery fragments with cord marks. The people at this time lived as fishers, hunters and food-gatherers.

This period was gradually superseded by the Yayoi era, which dates from around 300 BC, and is named after the site where pottery fragments were found near modern Tokyo. The Yayoi people are considered to have had a strong connection with Korea and their most important developments were the wet cultivation of rice and the use of bronze and iron implements.

The period following the Yayoi era has been called the Kofun (Burial Mound) period by archaeologists who discovered thousands of grave mounds concentrated mostly on Kyūshū and in the Kansai region. Judging by their size and elaborate construction, these mounds must have required immense resources of labour. It seems likely that the custom of building these tombs was eclipsed by the arrival of Buddhism, which favoured cremation.

As more and more settlements banded together to defend their land, groups became larger until, by 300 AD, the Yamato Kingdom had loosely unified the nation through conquest or alliance. The Yamato leaders claimed descent from the sun goddess, Amaterasu, and introduced the title of emperor *(tennō)* around the 5th century.

Historical Periods	Date	Kanji Script
Jomon	800 - 300 BC	縄文時代
Yayoi	300 BC - 300 AD	弥生時代
Kofun	300 - 710	古墳時代
Nara	710 - 794	奈良時代
Heian	794 - 1185	平安時代
Kamakura	1185 - 1333	鎌倉時代
Muromachi	1333 - 1576	室町時代
Azuchi-Momoyama	1576 - 1600	安土桃山時代
Edo	1600 - 1867	江戸時代
Meiji	1868 - 1912	明治
Taisho	1912 - 1926	大正
Showa	1926 - 1945	昭和
Heisei	1945 - Present	平成

Introduction of Buddhism & Early Chinese Influence
In the mid-6th century Buddhism was introduced from China via the Korean kingdom of Packche. The decline of the Yamato court was halted by Prince Shōtoku (573-620) who set up a constitution and laid the guidelines for a centralised state headed by a single ruler. He also instituted Buddhism as a state religion.

Despite family feuds and coups d'état, subsequent rulers continued to reform the administration and laws. Previously, it had been the custom to avoid the pollution of a place through death by changing the site of the capital for each successive emperor, but in 710, this custom was altered and the capital was shifted to Nara where it remained for the next 75 years.

During the Nara period (710-794) there was strong promotion of Buddhism, particularly under Emperor Shōmu, who ordered construction of the Tōdai-ji Temple and the casting of its Daibutsu (Great Buddha) as supreme guardian deity of the nation. Both the temple and its image of Buddha can still be seen today in Nara.

Heian Period (794-1185) – Entrenchment of Japanese Values
By the end of the 8th century, Buddhism had

acquired such political strength in Nara that Emperor Kammu decided to sever the ties between Buddhism and government by moving the capital. The site eventually chosen was Heian (modern-day Kyoto). Like Nara, this city was modelled on Chang-an (present-day Xian), the capital of the Tang dynasty in China, and it was to continue as the capital of Japan until 1868. At first, this period saw great advances in art, literature and religion. Japanese masters started to branch out and interpret in their own fashion the ideas imported from China.

Rivalry between Buddhism and Shinto, the traditional religion of Japan, was reduced by presenting Shinto deities as manifestations of Buddha. Religion was assigned a role separated from politics and Japanese monks returning from China established two new sects, Tendai and Shingon, which became the mainstays of Japanese Buddhism.

With the conquest of the Ainu in the early 9th century, Japan's borders were extended to the tip of Northern Honshū. However, the emperors began to devote more time to leisure and scholarly pursuit and less time to government. This created an opening for a

Samurai

The prime duty of a samurai was to give faithful service to his feudal lord. In fact, the origin of the term samurai is closely linked to a word meaning 'to serve'. Over the centuries, the samurai established a code of conduct which came to be known as Bushidō (the Way of the Warrior). The components of this code were drawn from Confucianism, Shinto and Buddhism.

Confucianism required the samurai to show absolute loyalty to his lord; towards the oppressed he was expected to show benevolence and a belief in justice. Subterfuge was to be despised as were all commercial and financial transactions. A real samurai had endless endurance, total self-control, spoke only the truth and displayed no emotion. Since his honour was his life, disgrace and shame were to be avoided above all else; all insults were to be avenged.

From Buddhism, the samurai learnt the lesson that life is impermanent, a handy reason to face death with serenity. Shinto provided the samurai with patriotic beliefs in the divine status both of the emperor and of Japan, the abode of the gods.

Ritual suicide, *(seppuku* or *harakiri)* to which Japanese Buddhism conveniently turned a blind eye, was an accepted means to avoid dishonour. This grisly 'procedure' required the samurai to ritually disembowel himself before a helpful aide who then drew his sword and lopped off his head. One reason for this ritual was the requirement that a samurai should never surrender, always go down fighting. Since surrender was considered a disgrace, prisoners received scant mercy. During WW II this attitude was reflected in Japanese treatment of prisoners of war – still a source of bitter memories for those involved.

In slack moments when he wasn't fighting, the samurai dressed simply, but was easily recognisable by his triangular *eboshi*, a hat made from rigid black cloth.

The samurai's standard battle dress or armour (usually made of leather or lacquered steel) consisted of a breastplate, a similar covering for his back, a steel helmet with visor and more body armour for his shoulders and lower body. Samurai weaponry – his pride and joy – included bow and arrows (in a quiver), swords and a dagger; and he wasn't complete without his trusty steed.

Before entering the fray, a samurai was expected to be freshly washed and groomed – some even added a dash of perfume! The classic samurai battle took the form of duelling between individuals rather than the clashing of massed armies.

Not all samurai were good warriors adhering to the their code of conduct: portrayals of samurai indulging in double-crossing, subterfuge or outright cowardice became popular themes in Japanese theatre. ■

noble family called Fujiwara to hold all the important court posts and so ease its way into a dominant position of power which it held for several centuries.

Whilst court life concentrated on luxury, out in the provinces a new power was on the rise, that of the *samurai* or 'warrior class', which built up its own armed forces and readily turned to arms to defend its autonomy. Samurai families moved into the capital where they muscled in on the court.

The corrupt Fujiwara were eventually eclipsed by the Taira clan who ruled briefly before being ousted by the Minamoto family (also known as the Genji) at the battle of Dannoura (Shimonoseki) in 1185.

Kamakura Period (1185-1333) – Domination through Military Rule

After assuming the rank of *shogun* (military leader), Minamoto Yoritomo set up his headquarters in Kamakura whilst the emperor remained nominal ruler in Kyoto. Starting from this period, Japan was ruled by the samurai class supported by a feudal system until restoration of imperial power in 1868.

Yoritomo purged members of his own family who stood in his way, but after his death in 1199 (he fell from his horse), his wife's family (the Hōjō) eliminated all of Yoritomo's potential successors and became the true wielders of power behind the figureheads of shoguns and warrior lords.

During this era, the popularity of Buddhism spread to all levels of society. From the late 12th century, Japanese monks return-

ing from China introduced a new sect, Zen, which, through its austere characteristics, particularly appealed to the samurai.

The Mongols under Kublai Khan reached Korea in 1259 and sent envoys to Japan seeking Japanese submission. In response, the envoys were expelled and the Mongols reacted by sending an invasion fleet which arrived near present-day Fukuoka in 1274. This first attack was only just repulsed with a little help from a typhoon. Further envoys from Kublai Khan were promptly beheaded as a sign that the government of Japan was not interested in paying homage.

In 1281, the Mongols responded by dispatching a huge army of over 100,000 soldiers to Japan for a second attempt at invasion. After initial success, the Mongol fleet was almost completely destroyed by yet another typhoon. Ever since, this lucky typhoon has been known to the Japanese as the *kamikaze* (divine wind). In a vain attempt to repeat their luck, the Japanese tried using kamikaze pilots on suicide missions at the end of WW II.

Although the Kamakura government emerged victorious, it was unable to pay its soldiers and lost the support of the warrior class. Buddhist temples also put in a claim for prayer services rendered to whip up the divine wind. Emperor Go-Daigo led an unsuccessful rebellion against the government and was exiled to the Oki Islands near Matsue where he waited a year before having a go at another rebellion which successfully toppled the government.

Emperor Go-Daigo

Muromachi Period (1336-1576) – Country at War

Emperor Go-Daigo refused to reward his warriors and favoured the aristocracy and priesthood instead. This led to the revolt of Takauji Ashikaga who had previously changed sides to support Emperor Go-Daigo. Ashikaga defeated Go-Daigo at Kyoto then installed a new emperor and appointed himself shogun; the Ashikaga family later settled at Muromachi, a part of Kyoto. Go-Daigo escaped to set up a rival court at Yoshino in a mountainous region near Nara. Rivalry between the two courts continued for 60 years until the Ashikaga made a promise (which was not kept) that the imperial lines would alternate.

The Ashikaga ruled with gradually diminishing effect in a land slipping steadily into civil war and chaos. Despite this, there was a flourishing of those arts now considered typically Japanese such as landscape painting, classical Nō drama, flower arranging *(ikebana)* and the tea ceremony *(chanoyu)*. Many of Kyoto's famous gardens date from this period as do such well-known monuments as the Kinkaku-ji (Golden Temple) and Ginkaku-ji (Silver Temple). Formal trade relations were reopened with Ming China and Korea although Japanese piracy remained a bone of contention between both sides.

The Onin War, which broke out in 1467, developed into a full scale civil war and marked the rapid decline of the Ashikaga family. *Daimyō* (domain lords) and local leaders fought for power in bitter territorial disputes.

Momoyama Period (1576-1600) – Return to Unity

In 1568 Nobunaga Oda, the son of a daimyō, seized power from the imperial court in Kyoto and used his military genius to initiate the process of pacification and unification in central Japan. His efforts were cut short when he was assassinated by one of his own generals, Akechi Mitsuhide, in 1582.

Oda was succeeded by his most able commander, Toyotomi Hideyoshi, who was reputedly raised as the son of a farmer, although his origins are not clear. His diminutive size and pop-eyed features earned him the nickname of 'Saru-san' (Mr Monkey). Hideyoshi extended unification so that by 1590 the whole country was under his rule. He then became fascinated with grandiose schemes to invade China and Korea. The first invasion was repulsed in 1593 and the second was aborted on the death of Hideyoshi in 1598.

The arts of this period are noted for boisterous use of colour and gold-leaf embellishment. There was also a vogue for building castles on a flamboyant scale; the most impressive example was Osaka Castle which reputedly required three years of labour by up to 100,000 men.

The Christian Century (1543-1640)

In the mid-16th century when the Europeans first made their appearance, there was little authority over foreign trade. The first Portuguese to be shipwrecked off southern Kyūshū in 1543 found a most appreciative Japanese reception for their skills in making firearms which were soon spread throughout the region. The Jesuit missionary, Francis Xavier, arrived in Kagoshima in 1549 and was followed by more missionaries who quickly converted local lords keen to profit from foreign trade and assistance with military supplies. The new religion spread rapidly, gaining several hundred thousand converts, particularly in Nagasaki.

At first, Nobunaga saw advantages to trade with Europeans and tolerated the arrival of Christianity as a counterbalance to Buddhism. Once Hideyoshi had assumed power, however, this tolerance gradually gave way to the suspicion of subversion by an alien religion which was deemed a threat to his rule. Edicts against Christianity were followed in 1597 by the crucifixion of 26 foreign priests and Japanese believers.

Proscription and persecution of Christianity continued under the Tokugawa government until it reached its peak in 1637 with the ferocious quelling by the authorities of the Christian-led Shimabara Rebellion.

This brought the Christian century to an abrupt close, although the religion continued to be practised in secret until it was officially allowed to resurface at the end of the 19th century.

Edo or Tokugawa Period (1600-1867) – Peace & Seclusion

The supporters of Hideyoshi's young heir, Hideyori Hideyoshi, were defeated in 1600 by his former ally, Ieyasu Tokugawa, at the battle of Sekigahara. Ieyasu set up his field headquarters (*bakufu*) at Edo, now Tokyo, and assumed the title of shogun; the emperor and court continued to exercise purely nominal authority in Kyoto.

A strict division of government was introduced. The Tokugawa family, besides retaining large estates, also took control of major cities, ports and mines; the remainder of the country was allocated to autonomous daimyō. In descending order of importance, society consisted of the nobility, who had nominal power, the daimyō and their warriors (samurai), the farmers, and at the bottom of the list, artisans and merchants. To ensure political security the daimyō were required to make ceremonial visits to Edo every alternate year and their wives and children were kept in permanent residence in Edo as virtual hostages of the government. This constant movement and restriction kept up financial and social pressure on the daimyō to remain loyal. At the lower end of society, farmers were subject to a severe system of rules which dictated in minutest detail their food, clothing and housing. Social mobility from one class to another was blocked; social standing was determined by birth.

According to a standard parable, frequently trotted out by Japanese to elucidate the unification of Japan, the characters of Oda Nobunaga, Toyotomi Hideyoshi and Ieyasu Tokugawa can be imaginatively compared by their techniques for tackling a cuckoo which refuses to sing. Nobunaga, noted for his ruthlessness, would make a generous offer: sing or die. Hideyoshi, revered for his pragmatism, would insist on *making* the cuckoo perform; Ieyasu, renowned for his shrewd patience, would coolly wait until the bird decided to sing.

In the modern Japanese business world, managers reputedly seek inspiration from this comparison when calculating their style of command in a company.

Under Tokugawa rule, Japan entered a period of national seclusion (*sakoku*). Japanese were forbidden on pain of death to travel to or return from overseas or to trade abroad. Only the Dutch, Chinese and Koreans were allowed to remain under strict supervision; the Dutch were confined to De-jima Island near Nagasaki and their contacts restricted to merchants and prostitutes.

The rigid emphasis of these times on submitting unquestioningly to rules of obedience and loyalty has lasted to the present day. One effect of strict rule during the Tokugawa period was to create an atmosphere of relative peace and security in which the arts excelled. There were great advances, for example, in *haiku* poetry, *bunraku* puppet plays and *kabuki* theatre. Weaving, pottery, ceramics and lacquerware became famous for their refined quality.

Perhaps the most bizarre ruler of this period was the fifth Tokugawa shogun, Tokugawa Tsunayoshi, often referred to as the 'Dog Shogun' because of his preoccupation with canine welfare. After a priest advised Tsunayoshi that he had failed to produce a male heir because of mistreating a dog in a previous life, he determined to make amends. Orders were issued for the construction of special dog pounds and the provision of quality dinners for dogs which were to be addressed in honorific language only. Anyone caught mistreating canines faced severe punishment.

By the turn of the 19th century, the Tokugawa government was facing stagnation and corruption. Famines and poverty amongst the peasants and samurai further weakened the system. Foreign ships started to probe Japan's isolation with increasing insistence and the Japanese soon realised that their outmoded defences were ineffectual. Russian contacts in the north were followed by British and American visits. In 1853, Commodore Matthew Perry of the US Navy arrived with a squadron of 'black ships' to demand the opening of Japan to trade. Other countries moved in to demand the opening of treaty ports and relaxation of restrictions on trade barriers.

A surge of anti-government feeling amongst the Japanese followed. The Tokugawa government was accused of failing to defend Japan against the foreigners and of neglecting the national reconstruction necessary for Japan to meet the West on equal terms. In 1867 the ruling shogun, Keiki, resigned and the Emperor Meiji resumed control of state affairs.

Meiji Restoration (1868-1912) – Emergence from Isolation

The initial stages of this restoration were resisted in a state of virtual civil war. The abolition of the shogunate (military government) was followed by the surrender of the daimyō whose lands were divided into the prefectures that exist today. Edo became Japan's new capital and was renamed Tokyo (Eastern Capital). Government became centralised again with Western-style ministries

Emperor Meiji

appointed for specific tasks. A series of revolts by the samurai against the erosion of their status culminated in the Saigō Uprising when they were finally beaten and stripped of their power.

Despite nationalist support for the emperor under the slogan of 'sonnō-jōi' (revere the emperor, repel the barbarians), the new government soon realised it would have to meet the West on its own terms. Under the slogan 'fukoku kyōhei' (rich country, strong military) the economy underwent a crash course in Westernisation and industrialisation. An influx of Western experts was encouraged and Japanese students were sent abroad to acquire expertise in modern technologies. In 1889, Japan created a Western-style constitution which, like the renovation of the military, based itself on Prussian influences.

By the 1890s, government leaders were concerned by the spread of liberal Western ideas and encouraged a swing back to nationalism and traditional values.

Japan's growing confidence was demonstrated by the abolition of foreign treaty rights and in the ease with which it trounced China in the Sino-Japanese War (1894-5). The subsequent treaty recognised Korean independence and ceded Taiwan to Japan. Friction with Russia led to the Russo-Japanese War (1904-05) when the Japanese army attacked the Russians in Manchuria and Korea. The Japanese navy stunned the Russians by inflicting a crushing defeat on their Baltic fleet at the battle of Tsushima. For the first time, the Japanese were able to consider that they had drawn level with the Western powers.

Industrialisation & Asian Dominance

On his death in 1912, the Emperor Meiji was succeeded by his son, Yoshihito, whose period of rule was named the Taishō era. The later stages of his life were dogged by ill-health probably attributable to mental illness.

When WW I broke out, Japan sided against Germany but did not become deeply involved in the conflict. Whilst the Allies were occupied with war, the Japanese took the opportunity, through shipping and trade, to expand their economy at top speed. At the same time, a strong foothold was gained in China thereby giving Japan a dominant position in Asia.

Social unrest led the government to pursue a more democratic, liberal line; the right to vote was extended and Japan joined the League of Nations in 1920. Under the influence of the *zaibatsu*, financial cliques of industrialists and bankers, a moderate and pacific foreign policy was followed.

Nationalism & the Pursuit of Empire

The Showa era commenced when Emperor Hirohito ascended to the throne in 1926. He had toured extensively in Europe, mixed with European nobility and developed a liking for the British lifestyle.

A rising tide of nationalism was quickened by the world economic depression beginning in 1930. Popular unrest was marked by plots to overthrow the government and political assassinations. This led to a strong increase in the power of the militarists who approved the invasion of Manchuria in 1931 and the installation of a Japanese puppet regime, Manchukuo. In 1933, Japan withdrew from the League of Nations and, in 1937, entered into full-scale hostilities with China.

As the leader of a new order for Asia, Japan signed a tripartite pact with Germany and Italy in 1940. The Japanese military leaders saw their main opponents to this new order for Asia, the so-called 'Greater East Asia Co-prosperity Sphere', in the USA.

World War II

When diplomatic attempts to gain US neutrality failed, the Japanese launched themselves into WW II with a surprise attack on Pearl Harbor on 7 December 1941.

At first, Japan scored rapid successes, pushing its battle fronts across to India, down to the fringes of Australia and out into the mid-Pacific. The Battle of Midway opened the US counterattack, puncturing Japanese naval superiority and turning the tide of the war against Japan. By 1945, Japan had been driven back on all fronts and exhausted by submarine blockade and aerial bombing. In August of the same year, the declaration of war by the Soviet Union and the atom bombs dropped by the USA on Hiroshima and Nagasaki proved the final straws: Emperor Hirohito announced unconditional surrender.

After surrender, Japan was occupied by Allied forces under the command of General MacArthur. The chief aim was a thorough reform of Japanese government through demilitarisation, the trial of war criminals and the weeding out of militarists or ultra-nationalists from government. A new constitution was introduced which dismantled the political power of the emperor who completely stunned his subjects by publicly renouncing any claim to divine origins. This left him with the status of a mere figurehead.

The occupation was terminated in 1952, although the island of Okinawa was only returned to Japan in 1972.

Post-War Reconstruction

At the end of the war the Japanese economy was in ruins and inflation rampant. A programme of recovery provided loans, restricted imports and encouraged capital investment and personal saving.

By the late '50s, trade was again flourishing and the economy continued to expand rapidly. From textiles and the manufacture of labour-intensive goods such as cameras, the Japanese 'economic miracle' has branched out into virtually every sector of economic activity. Economic recession and inflation surfaced in 1974 and again in 1980, mostly as a result of steep price hikes for imported oil on which Japan is dependent.

Emergence as Economic Superpower

Despite these setbacks, the economy has become so successful at selling overseas and producing massive trade surpluses that it has aroused resentment in competing nations which face mounting import bills and unemployment. At present, Japan dominates such fields as electronics, robotics, computer technology, car production and banking – by the year 2000, it looks set to overtake the USA as the world's leading economy.

Post-war politics in Japan have been virtually monopolised by the conservatives, in particular (since 1955) by the Liberal Democratic Party (LDP). More recently, politics have been electrified by affairs such as the Lockheed corruption scandal which tainted the office of Tanaka in the '70s. This was followed in the '80s by a sex scandal when Prime Minister Ueno was denounced by his mistress and the Recruit Cosmos affair which implicated the government of Prime Minister Takeshita in the acceptance of complimentary shares in return for favours.

After the war, Emperor Hirohito kept out of the limelight, quietly following his passion for marine biology until his death in 1989. His role in WW II has recently been the subject of criticism by Japanese who felt he should bear more of the responsibility.

Emperor Hirohito was succeeded by his son Akihito in January 1989. The formal ceremonies of instalment, held in November 1990, sparked further heated political debate over the role of the emperor in modern Japan.

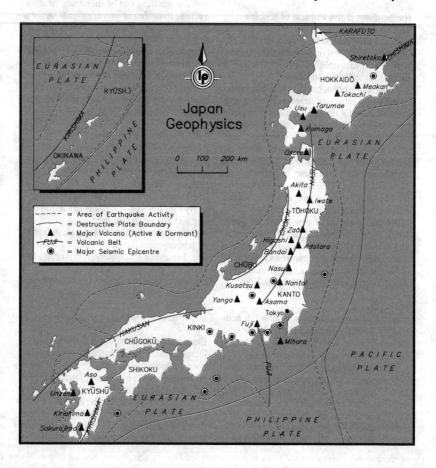

GEOGRAPHY

Japan is an island nation and, although much of its cultural heritage has been drawn from nearby Asian countries, its 'apartness' from the Asian mainland differentiates the Japanese from their neighbours. Both China and Korea are close enough to have been decisive influences, but at the same time, too distant to have actually dominated Japan.

Japan has not always been physically isolated. At the end of the last ice age, around 12,000 years ago, the level of the sea rose enough to flood the land bridge connecting Japan with the mainland. Today, Japan consists of a chain of islands that rides the back of a 3000 km long arc of mountains along the eastern rim of the Asian continent. It stretches from around 25°N at the southern islands of Okinawa to 45°N at the northern end of Hokkaidō; cities at comparable latitudes would be Miami or Cairo in the south and Montreal or Milan in the north. Japan's total land area is 377,435 sq km, more than 80% of it mountainous.

Japan consists of some 1000 small islands and four major ones: Honshū (slightly larger than Great Britain), Hokkaidō, Kyūshū and Shikoku. Okinawa, the largest and most significant of Japan's many smaller islands, is about halfway along an archipelago that runs almost all the way to Taiwan. It was far enough from the rest of Japan to have developed a culture that differs in many respects.

If Japanese culture has been influenced by isolation, it has equally been shaped by the country's mountainous topography. Many of the mountains are volcanic, more than 40 of them presently active, blessing the islands with numerous hot springs and spectacular scenery, and at the same time bringing the danger of frequent eruptions and intense seismic activity. Indeed, the rough and tumble of earthquakes, volcanic eruptions and tsunamis, along with a monsoonal climate, has perhaps contributed to Japanese industriousness. The Japanese are used to rebuilding their world every 20 or 30 years.

Japan has the dubious distinction of being one of the most seismically active regions of the world. It is calculated that the country gets around 1000 earthquakes a year, most of them too small to notice without sophisticated seismic equipment. This seismic activity is particularly concentrated in the Kantō region, in which Tokyo is situated. Tokyo is on the receiving end of a monster tremor about every 60 years. The last biggie measured 8.2 on the Richter scale and occurred in 1923, so another big one is overdue.

Geographical, Political & Administrative Divisions

Japan is divided up into nine political regions (see map) and further subdivided into 47 smaller divisions. Prefectures or *ken* make up 43 of these divisions, they are written as 'Okayama-ken' or 'Chiba-ken'. The remaining four are Hokkaidō which is a *do* (district), Tokyo-to which is a *to* (metropolis) and Osaka-fu and Kyoto-fu which are *fu* (urban prefectures). Each of the three city areas incorporates the named city but is otherwise similar in land area to a ken.

There are other traditional names for regions of the country. Thus, Chūgoku or Western Honshū, is often spoken of as the San-in or north coast region and the San-yō or south coast region. Other traditional names you may come across in tourist literature or other sources include Hokuriku (Fukui, Ishikawa and Toyama prefectures), Sanriku (Aomori, Iwate and Miyagi), Shinetsu (Nagano and Niigata) and Tokai (Aichi, Gifu, Mie and Shizuoka). In addition, the Tokyo area is often referred to as Kanto while the area around Osaka is often called Kansai.

CLIMATE

The combination of Japan's mountainous territory and the length of the archipelago (covering 22° of latitude) makes for a complex climate. There are big climatic differences between Hokkaidō in the north, which has short summers and long winters with heavy snowfalls, and the southern Ryūkyū Islands, which enjoy a subtropical climate. At the same time, Japan's proximity to the continental landmass also has significant climatic implications, producing a high degree of seasonal variation.

In the winter months, from December to February, cold, dry air masses from Siberia move down over Japan, where they meet warmer, moister air masses from the Pacific. The resulting precipitation results in huge snowfalls on Japan's western side. The eastern side of Japan receives less snow but can still get very cold; Tokyo has colder average January temperatures than Reykjavik in Iceland although snow, when it does fall on the capital, rarely lasts long.

The summer months, from June to August, are dominated by warm, moist air currents from the Pacific, and produce high temperatures and humidity throughout most of Japan. In the early part of summer there is a rainy season lasting a few weeks that starts in the south and gradually works its way northwards. Further heavy rains can occur in late summer when Japan is visited by typhoons bringing torrential rains and strong winds that can have devastating effects, particularly on coastal regions.

In contrast to the extremes of summer and

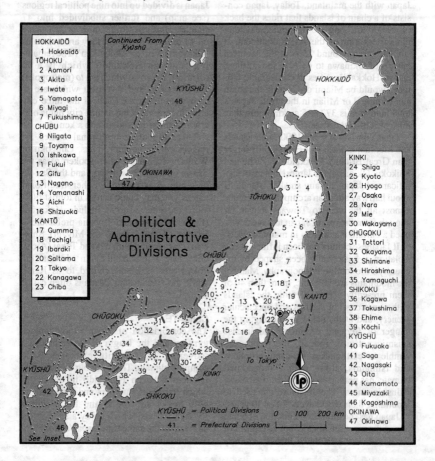

Political & Administrative Divisions

HOKKAIDŌ
1 Hokkaidō
TŌHOKU
2 Aomori
3 Akita
4 Iwate
5 Yamagata
6 Miyagi
7 Fukushima
CHŪBU
8 Niigata
9 Toyama
10 Ishikawa
11 Fukui
12 Gifu
13 Nagano
14 Yamanashi
15 Aichi
16 Shizuoka
KANTŌ
17 Gumma
18 Tochigi
19 Ibaraki
20 Saitama
21 Tokyo
22 Kanagawa
23 Chiba

KINKI
24 Shiga
25 Kyoto
26 Hyogo
27 Osaka
28 Nara
29 Mie
30 Wakayama
CHŪGOKU
31 Tottori
32 Okayama
33 Shimane
34 Hiroshima
35 Yamaguchi
SHIKOKU
36 Kagawa
37 Tokushima
38 Ehime
39 Kōchi
KYŪSHŪ
40 Fukuoka
41 Saga
42 Nagasaki
43 Oita
44 Kumamoto
45 Miyazaki
46 Kagoshima
OKINAWA
47 Okinawa

Continued From Kyūshū

KYŪSHŪ = Political Divisions
41 = Prefectural Divisions

0   100   200 km

See inset

To Tokyo

winter, spring and autumn are comparatively mild. Rainfall is relatively low and the days are often clear.

GOVERNMENT

Japan's government system is similar to the British parliamentary system rather than the American presidential one. Just as the British parliament has two houses so the Japanese Diet has the lower House of Representatives and the upper House of Councillors. The party that controls the majority of seats in the Diet is the party in power and has the right to appoint the prime minister, usually the party's president. The prime minister then appoints his cabinet, usually entirely constituted of Diet members.

Since its formation in 1955, the Liberal Democratic Party (LDP), the conservative party in Japanese politics, has been continuously in power, riding out every scandal which comes along. Democracy Japanese-style is indeed prone to scandals, meeting all the regular influence-buying and favour-repaying scandals of Western democracies and managing to add a few local versions of its own. The Lockheed scandal of the '70s (the prime minister took large bribes to ensure All Nippon Airways (ANA) bought Lockheed Tristar aircraft) was superseded by the Recruit Cosmos affair of the late '80s (all sorts of LDP politicians from the prime minister on down took all sorts of bribes).

The remarkable thing is that the party manages to survive these little problems every time they pop up. Part of it is a perennially unprepared opposition (the liberal Japan Socialist Party (JSP) seems set to be an eternal bridesmaid) and part of it is a glum acceptance that this is just the way politics works. A very large amount of political energy is expended on keeping all factions happy and ensuring there are plenty of jobs for the boys. Cabinet posts are traditionally handed out in strict proportion to the strengths of the various LDP factions and are usually held for only about a year, to ensure that these perks can be spread as widely as possible.

Like Britain's royal family, the emperor plays a ceremonial figurehead role but, perhaps even more than his British counterparts, he still commands a great deal of respect and deference. The emperor has a curious position in Japan. For centuries under the shogunate his role was purely symbolic. The Meiji Restoration 'restored' the emperor to real power, or at least it was supposed to, in actual fact it merely brought him out of the closet, dusted him off and gave him a new figurehead position. The close of WW II brought further changes when it was announced that the emperor was no longer divine; yet, despite this, he still has enormous importance in Japan.

ECONOMY

Japan is widely perceived as an economic powerhouse, utterly dominating world trade and with an enormous trade surplus being used to buy up industries and real estate in Western nations. Although that view has some truth, Japan's exports account for only 9% of its gross national product, a much smaller percentage than many European nations such as the UK (18%) or Germany (27%). Also, despite the huge Japanese investments overseas, these are still much smaller than the foreign investments of many other Western nations. Britain has far more industrial investment in the USA than Japan and the biggest foreign owners of real estate in the USA are not the Japanese but the Canadians.

The huge Japanese trade surpluses are chalked up not so much by massive exports as by a low level of imports. Japanese exports are highly visible – they're predominantly in consumer durables and their success in this field have made Japanese manufacturers (from Honda to Suzuki, Sony to Sanyo, Toshiba to National) familiar names throughout the world. The major Japanese imports are oil and energy resources, which are used frugally. Despite the limited land available for agricultural use, the Japanese manage to supply a large part of their food requirements by highly efficient and intensive land use.

Japanese farming policy is a continuing

stumbling block to trade negotiations. Although land use is highly efficient in terms of output to area, in terms of cost it is actually highly inefficient. It's frequently cited that Japanese rice growers produce far more per hectare than rice growers in, say, Indonesia. That's quite correct but, if the Indonesians spent as much per hectare of rice paddy, they too would grow a lot more rice but at a much higher cost per kg.

The Japanese would save themselves a great deal of money by simply buying their food overseas but the system won't change for two reasons. One is the public sentiment that, as far as possible, the nation should be self-sufficient and not at the mercy of foreign countries, particularly when it comes to food. The other and possibly more important reason is the blunt fact that the ruling LDP party's power base is in the country. An effective gerrymander gives country voters a much larger say than those in the cities. So city dwellers (working for efficient Japanese manufacturers) pay high food prices to keep the inefficient farmers rich, happy and voting LDP!

The high-cost farmers are not the only component of the Japanese economy contributing to sky-high prices. The Japanese distribution and retail system also jacks up prices making it even more difficult for foreign competitors to break in. Goods reach consumers via a layercake of intermediaries, each taking their slice out of the final price. Even the final stage, the retailer, is inefficient and costly by Western standards. Whoever called the British 'a nation of shopkeepers' had clearly never been to Japan where a huge proportion of retail sales are still made by tiny, hole-in-the-wall shops. Naturally, this is a very inefficient way of selling things but legislation protects these retailers and shackles any larger-scale competition.

Unfortunately for Western nations, simply opening up the Japanese market is not going to solve their trade problems at a stroke. Spending more on imports may reduce the imbalance but, in many fields, Japanese manufacturers have come to totally dominate the market, or create a market where none existed before. Motorcycles, cameras, video recorders and CD players are just a few

Imported Cars

Who says the Japanese don't import cars? It may be 'coals to Newcastle' and, compared to the local industry, the proportion of imported vehicles is indeed small, yet 5% of the Japanese market is still a lot of cars. As a group, Volkswagen-Audi were number one in 1990 but BMW is clearly the most common imported nameplate. Spend long enough on Japanese expressways and you'll come away with the impression that every BMW comes complete with an 'ignore all speed limits' permit so drivers can imagine they're zooming down the autobahn to Munich. It's popularly rumoured that BMW make more money in Japan than they do in the USA.

Other German makes – Mercedes, Porsche – get a good show and you'll also see Saabs, plenty of Volvos, a few Fiats, the odd Citroën, quite a few hot Peugeot 205 GTis and a surprising number of Jaguars, Bentleys and Rolls-Royces. Believe it or not, the other major-selling European car is the good old British Mini. Minis have a huge cult following in Japan, which has developed to such an extent that more Minis are now sold in Japan than in the UK (sales almost match the combined sales in Japan of all US cars!). In a country where cars seem to be redesigned every six months many of the Minis are sold as the 'Mini Thirty', with a notation on the side announcing that the design has barely altered since 1959.

All manner of oddities also find a market in Japan although, no doubt, they're only brought out for a drive on the odd sunny Sunday. I saw a Ferrari Testa Rossa in Kyoto and in Yamaguchi a flawless Lotus 7 complete with mini aero-screens and two samurai pilots in WW I leather flying helmets and aviator goggles.

Tony Wheeler ■

fields where Japan has become so utterly dominant that foreign competition is either minuscule, confined to specialist or esoteric corners of the market or simply nonexistent.

Beliefs in superlative Japanese efficiency and cautious Japanese investment policies are, however, just more examples of the myths about how things work in Japan. In terms of output per hour, Japan is not really that efficient, it's certainly a long way behind comparable levels in the USA. The difference is that Japanese workers put in many more hours than their counterparts in other advanced economies.

Don't believe that Japanese companies are models of financial circumspection either. In the go-go days of the '60s when Japan's economy was growing at a frantic pace, many Japanese firms had gearing (ratio of borrowings to investment) which would have given any Western banker sleepless nights. The difference between sky-high Japanese borrowings at that time and the sky-high borrowings which brought so many Western entrepreneurs crashing down in the late '80s and early '90s was that the Japanese firms made their borrowings work, they didn't simply buy, sell and take over.

Zaibatsu & Sogo Shosha
One of the curious factors in the Japanese industrial scene is the important role played by huge trading houses involved in a whole gamut of industrial and financial areas. Before the war they were known as zaibatsu and because it was felt that they played a major role in pushing Japan into conflict, they were broken up into their constituent companies. Like iron filings to a magnet many of them have regrouped to form mighty conglomerates like Mitsubishi or Mitsui.

When a Japanese consumer fills up his Mitsubishi car (financed by a Mitsubishi bank) it may well be in a Mitsubishi petrol station with fuel that came to Japan in a ship from the Mitsubishi shipyards. Kirin beer and Nikon cameras are two other products of the group. Many household Japanese names come under the umbrella of these holding companies or *keiretsu*, often with cross shareholdings so that one company may be part of more than one major holding company. Mitsukoshi, Toshiba and Toyota are part of Mitsui; Fuji Bank, Hitachi, Nissan and Marubeni are part of Fuyo; C Itoh, Kangyo Bank, Fujitsu, Isuzu and Kawasaki Steel come under the Dai-Ichi banner; Sanwa Bank, Daihatsu, Hitachi, Sharp and Kōbe Steel line up in the Sanwa group.

POPULATION
Japan has a population of around 120 million people and, with 75% of it concentrated in urban centres, population density is extremely high. Areas such as the Tokyo-Yokohama-Kawasaki conurbation are so densely populated that they have almost ceased to be separate cities, running into each other and forming a huge urban sprawl that, if counted together, would constitute the world's largest city.

While this high urban population density is tough on the Japanese, it has the advantage of leaving other parts of the country reasonably sparsely populated. Travellers visiting Japan are still able to enjoy large national parks, mountainous regions and, in places like Hokkaidō, near wilderness.

The other notable feature of Japan's population is its ethnic and cultural homogeneity. This is particularly striking for visitors from the USA, Australia and other nations whose countries are host to populations of considerable ethnic and cultural diversity. The Japanese have ensured that only a small number of foreigners settle in their country. Less than 1% of the population are of non-Japanese origin, the vast majority of these being Koreans.

For outsiders, Koreans are an invisible minority. Indeed, even the Japanese themselves have no way of knowing that someone is of Korean descent if he or she adopts a Japanese name. Nevertheless, Japanese-born Koreans, in some cases speaking no language other than Japanese, are required to carry thumb-printed ID cards at all times and face discrimination in the work place and other aspects of their daily lives.

Other ethnic groupings are the Chinese and a wide cross section of foreigners hitching a ride on the Japanese economic juggernaut. Groups such as the Ainu, the original inhabitants of Japan, have been reduced to very small numbers and are today found almost only in reservations on Hokkaidō.

Among the Japanese themselves, a traditional class of outcastes, the *burakumin*, still retain a certain degree of their untouchability. Traditionally, the burakumin belonged to communities whose work, such as leather-craft, was unclean according to the principles of Japanese Buddhism. While the conditions of modern Japan have long since rendered the burakumin distinction obsolete, it continues to exercise influence in such important aspects of Japanese social life as work and marriage. It is common knowledge, though rarely publicly alluded to, that information about any given individual's possible burakumin origin is available to anyone (generally employers and prospective fathers-in-law) who is prepared to make certain discreet investigations. This is not a

Japan & Ecology

In the ecologically conscious 'green' 1990s Japan is frequently cast as an international vandal, slaughtering whales and dolphins, hacking down rainforests and polluting the ocean and atmosphere, all in the name of the rising yen. There's more than a little truth to it.

There's a low level of concern in Japan about environmental issues, particularly when it comes to Japanese activities which do not have an effect on life within Japan itself. The international environmental organisation Greenpeace has made great efforts to focus world attention on whaling and driftnet fishing. In Japan itself, the Japan Tropical Forest Action Network (JATAN) at 801 Shibuya Mansions, 7-1 Uguisudani-cho, Shibuya-ku, Tokyo 150, is working hard to raise consciousness within the country about exploitation of tropical rainforests.

Driftnet Fishing For several years before it became an international *cause célèbre* the nations of the Pacific had been complaining bitterly about driftnet fishing; 'strip mining the ocean' as one critic described it. The technique is simple, the devastation dramatic – you simply drag a fine net between two boats. The net is typically about 15 metres deep and the two boats hauling it can be up to 50 km apart! It's been aptly named a 'wall of death' because the driftnets catch not only the tuna they're set for but everything else which gets in the way from turtles and dolphins to sea birds and sharks. Although these creatures are not wanted they die anyway.

It's been calculated that up to half of the catch in driftnets is unwanted and the effect on the balance of ocean life can be terrible. Following a storm of international protest, Japan has cut its driftnet fleet by one-third although Taiwan, the other chief culprit, is still using driftnets. There have been accusations that Japanese aid to the tiny South Pacific nations most at risk from the depredation of driftnet fishing has been used as a lever to silence complaints.

Ivory In late '89 Japan finally capitulated to international pressure to halt its trade in ivory. The African elephant population had declined disastrously in the 1980s as the price of their tusks climbed higher and higher. Japan used 40% of the world's ivory and 30,000 people were employed in processing it. Carvings, piano keys and chopsticks had all been made out of ivory but the number-one item was the humble *hanko* – the small name seal or 'chop' which is used like an official signature in Japan.

Packaging One example of Japan's lack of environmental concern which every visitor will soon be aware of, is the Japanese penchant for overpackaging. At a time when most Western subject, however, that most Japanese will feel happy about discussing with foreigners: they will often feign complete ignorance if the subject is raised.

PEOPLE

According to mythology, the origins of the Japanese people stretch back to a time when a pristine world was the playground of the gods. The Japanese themselves are, according to this scheme of things, divine in origin, being the issue of the sun goddess,

Amaterasu Omikami. In terms more familiar to the scientific frame of mind, the Japanese are not a distinct race but belong to the Mongoloid group, like the Koreans and Han Chinese.

The Japanese probably arrived from Korea via a land bridge that connected Japan to the continent prior to the end of the last ice age, 12,000 years ago. At that time, Japan was already inhabited by the Caucasian Ainu people but they were gradually displaced by the invaders through a policy of active suppression and assimilation. Today there are

---

nations are trying to cut back on packaging, in Japan it's full speed ahead to wrap things in the largest possible number of layers of paper, plastic and cardboard, all tied together with string and bows.

Rainforests Japan is the world's largest consumer of tropical rainforest timber. The terrible destruction wrought upon the rainforests of the Malaysian Borneo states of Sabah and Sarawak has principally been to supply Japan. Apart from the large-scale destruction of the forests (where minimal regeneration takes place), the logging also silts up rivers and kills fish.

Most of the logging activity is conducted by the big Japanese trading companies and 70% to 80% of the timber ends up as plywood, most of which is used for concrete formwork moulds and then destroyed. Rainforest and coastal mangrove forests have also been wiped out to supply Japanese woodchipping operations.

Recycling Recycling is a two sided coin in Japan. On one side, many household disposables, such as glass bottles, are efficiently recycled. On the other side, Japan is the throwaway society *par excellence*. The severe *shaken* vehicle inspection system encourages car owners to scrap their cars and buy new ones; cars more than a few years old are a rare sight on Japanese roads. There's little demand for second-hand goods and appliances, and consumer equipment is quickly scrapped to be replaced by the latest model. Stories abound of resident *gaijin* setting up house with Japanese throwaways. Around almost any big city railway station there will be tangled heaps of perfectly good bicycles, abandoned by their users.

Turtles Elephants, dolphins and whales are not the only creatures to fall prey to the Japanese economy. It's estimated that every year 30,000 hawksbill turtles, an endangered species, are killed to provide Japan with 30 tons of turtle shell.

Waribashi Japan's vast number of restaurants almost all provide their customers with disposable chopsticks or *waribashi*. Forests fall in order to supply these one-use only utensils.

Whales The international outcry against whaling has cut the whaling nations down to just three – Iceland, Norway and Japan. When the Japanese finally agreed to halt whaling they reserved the right to kill 300 minke whales a year for 'scientific research'. After they've been 'researched' they end up as restaurant whale meat. ■

only around 14,000 Ainu left, concentrated mainly in reservations on Hokkaidō.

Whatever the truth about their ancestry, the Japanese have developed a complex mythology concerning their origins and their uniqueness. To inhabitants of other parts of the globe, the Japanese curiosity about themselves and their differences is, at times, nothing short of obsessional. Books written about the Japanese by foreign writers frequently become bestsellers and the Japanese themselves contribute to the endless speculation with their own books. One of the more absurd theories gobbled up by a gullible Japanese public is the idea that the Japanese brain is unique. According to this theory, the 'Japanese brain' processes stimuli in the left hemisphere and is thus emotional and harmonious with nature, while the 'Western brain', with its right-hemisphere bias, is more rational and less harmonious. Where this leaves the rest of the world from Inuit to Zulus is not quite clear!

Theories like these, known as *nihonjinron* (theories about the Japanese), may to a large extent be a case of the public getting what it wants to hear – a recent example would be the huge sales of Ezra Vogel's book *Japan as Number One*. Clearly, however, this curiosity also points to a certain anxiety among the Japanese, both about who they are and what their place in the world is. Some see this as one of the major sources of the energy of modern Japanese society. Eager for praise, the Japanese can't help but harbour a sneaking suspicion that somewhere, people are sniggering behind their backs – an anxiety that only serves to goad them on to greater efforts.

Are the Japanese really different from the rest of us? As usual, the answer is 'yes ... and no'. If the question is whether the Japanese possess characteristics that are theirs alone (a unique brain, singular features, etc) the answer is obviously 'no'. On the other hand, the sum total of the culturally conditioned aspects of the 'typical' Japanese character can only be found in Japan. In short, it is Japanese culture not Japanese nature that is unique.

Of course, all cultures are unique. It is possible to feel the shock of entering another world simply by flying from Hamburg to Paris, or by driving from California to Texas. The difference is one of degree. Adapting from one European culture to another is a lot simpler than adapting from any of the cultures of the West to one of those of the East. In the case of Japan, the differences are such that some fairly major shifts have to take place in Westerners' thinking if they are to make sense of the Japanese world.

The Japanese & Gaijin

As a foreign visitor to Japan, you are a *gaijin*, literally an 'outside person'. Away from the gaijin-infested big cities you will often be a sufficiently unusual sight to warrant pointing out, so, at some point in your travels, you are sure to hear someone saying, 'Hey look, there's a gaijin'. One traveller, however, (who spoke some Japanese) preferred not to use the term gaijin himself and used, instead, *gaikoku gin* or 'foreign country person'.

Long-term visitors to Japan are prone to what has been called the 'Seidensticker syndrome', an ongoing love-hate relationship which frequently shifts sides. At one point, Japanese politeness and helpfulness may seem overwhelming, only to be overtaken by Japanese aloofness, disinterest and ethnocentricity a moment later. Fortunately for the short-term visitor, the polite and friendly nature of most contacts with Japanese is likely to be the main impression.

Despite the language barrier, it's hard to stay lost for long in Japan because somebody will always come over and inquire (politely!) if they can be of assistance. The best advice is to enjoy this side of the Japan experience and only worry about the flip side of the coin if you make the change from being a visitor to a long-term resident.

The Group

One of the most widely disseminated ideas regarding the Japanese is the importance of the group over the individual. The image of loyal company workers bellowing out the company anthem and attending collective exercise sessions has become a motif that is almost as powerful as Mt Fuji in calling to mind the Land of the Rising Sun.

It's easy to fall into the spirit of these kinds of images and start seeing the business-suited crowds jostling on the Yamanote line as so many ant-like members of a collectivised society that has rigorously suppressed individual tendencies. If this starts to happen, it's useful to remember that in some senses the Japanese are no less individual than their Western counterparts. The Japanese are not robotic clones, they experience many of the same frustrations and joys as the average Westerner and, given the opportunity, many will complain about their work conditions, the way their boss treats them and so on, just like any Westerner. The difference is, that while these individual concerns have a place in the lives of the Japanese, their principal orientation remains that of the group. The Japanese do not see their individual differences as defining.

For the Japanese, the individual has its rights and interests, but in the final analysis, these are subsumed under the interests of the group. Indeed the tension between group and individual interests and the inevitable sacrifices demanded of the latter has been a rich source for Japanese art. The Japanese see the tension as one between *honne*, the individual's personal views, and *tatemae*, the views that are demanded by the individual's position in the group. The same difference is expressed in the terms *ninjō*, which translates loosely as 'human feelings' or, looser still, as the 'dictates of the heart', and *giri*, which is the individual's social obligations. The salaryman who spends long hours at the office away from the family he loves is giving priority to giri over ninjō.

The precedence of the group is so important that it cannot be stressed too much in understanding Japanese culture. Among other things, it gives rise to the important *uchi* (inside) and *soto* (outside) distinction. For the Japanese all things are either inside or outside. Relationships, for example, are generally restricted to those inside the groups to which they belong. Mr Satō, who

works with Nissan, will have a social life comprised entirely of fellow Nissan workers and family. Mrs Satō, if she doesn't work (which is likely), will mix with members of the tea ceremony and jazz ballet clubs to which she belongs.

The whole of Japanese social life is an intricate network of these inside-outside distinctions. Of course, this is hardly unique to Japan; it's just that in Japan being inside a group makes such special demands on the individual. Perhaps foreigners who have spent many years in Japan learning the language and who finally throw up their hands in despair, complaining 'you just can't get inside this culture', should remember that to be 'inside' in Japan is to surrender the self to the priorities of the group – and not many foreigners are willing or able to do that.

Men & Women

Japan may be a modern society in many respects, but don't expect the same level of equality between the genders that you have come to expect in your own country. As everything else in Japan, male-female roles and relationships are strictly codified. Although there's some evidence that this is changing, it's definitely doing so at a much slower pace than it has done in the West. Part of the reason is that 'feminism' is a Western import and in a Japanese context tends to have a different resonance than it does in its culture of origin. Even the word 'feminist' has been co-opted so that a Japanese male can proudly declaim himself a *femunisuto* when he means that he is the kind of man that treats a woman as a 'lady', in the Walter Raleigh sense.

Anyone who visits Japan will be struck by the fact that Japanese women, like women in other parts of the world, are subordinate to men in public life. However, both sexes have their spheres of influence, domains in which they wield power. Basically women are *uchi-no* (of the inside) and men are *soto-no* (of the outside). That is, the woman's domain is the home, and here she will take care of all decisions related to the daily running of domestic affairs. The husband, on the other hand, while he may be the breadwinner, will still hand over his pay packet to his wife, who will then allocate the money according to domestic expenses and provide the husband with an allowance for his daily needs.

In public life, however, it is the men who rule supreme. In this world it is the role of women to listen, to cater to male needs and often to serve as vents for male frustrations. As any Western woman who tries hostessing will discover, women are expected to help men bear the burden of their public-life responsibilities not by offering advice – that would be presumptuous in the extreme – but by listening and making the appropriate sympathetic noises at the right moments.

Switch on a Japanese TV and you will see the same male-female dynamic at work. The male host invariably has a female shadow whose job it is to agree with everything he says, make astonished gasps at his erudition and to giggle politely behind a raised hand at his off-the-cuff witty remarks. These *sō desu* girls, as they're known, are a common feature of countless aspects of Japanese daily life. It's *de rigueur* for all companies to employ a bevy of nubile OLs, or 'office ladies', whose tasks include chiming a chorus of falsetto 'welcomes' to visitors, making cups of tea and generally adding a personal touch to an otherwise stolid male atmosphere.

Unfortunately, for many Japanese women, this is the sum of their job prospects. To make matters worse, it is considered that by the age of 25 they should be married, and in Japan married women are expected to resign from their work. This cut-off point of 25 years is a very serious one. Women who remain unmarried after this age are frequently alluded to as 'Christmas cake', this being a useless commodity after the 25th. By the time a woman is 26 and up, she will be regarded with suspicion by many men, who will wonder whether there isn't some flaw in her character that has prevented her from being swallowed up by the marriage market earlier.

Perhaps most disturbing for Western women visiting Japan, is the way in which women feature in so much of the male-oriented mass culture. It's not so much women being depicted as sex objects, which most Western women would at least be accustomed to in their own countries, but the fact that in comic strips, magazines and movies, women are so often shown being brutalised, passive victims in bizarre, sado-masochistic rites. Some disturbing conclusions could be drawn from much of the output of the Japanese media – at the very least it could be said that popular Japanese male sexuality has a very sadistic edge to it.

While these fantasies are disturbing, it is possible to take refuge in the thought that they *are* fantasies, and women are in fact a great deal safer in Japan than they are in other parts of the world. Harassment, when it does occur, is usually furtive, occurring in crowded areas such as trains; however, with direct confrontation, almost all Japanese men will be shamed into withdrawing the groping hand.

Education

Among the many things that surprise visitors to Japan is the leniency with which very young children are treated. Volumes have been written on this subject and the general consensus would seem to be that the Japanese see the early years of childhood as a kind of blissful Eden, a period of gloriously spoiled dependency that prefaces the harsh socialisation of the Japanese education system.

At an age as young as three or four, however, the party is over: children then enter the nurseries that start preparing them for one of the most gruelling education systems in the world. Competition is fierce from the beginning, since getting into the right school initially can mean an important head start when it comes to the university exams. These exams, of legendary difficulty, are so demanding that any student preparing for them and getting more than four hours sleep a night, is said to have no hope of passing.

To help coach students through the exams, evening schools have sprung up and are often more successful in teaching the school curriculum than the schools themselves. Students who fail to gain entry to the university of their choice frequently spend one or two years repeating the final year of school and sitting the exams again. These students, known as *rōnin*, or 'masterless samurai', are in a kind of limbo between the school education system and the higher education system, the key to employment in Japan.

The intense pressure of this system derives in no small part from the fact that 12 years of education culminates in just two examinations that effectively determine the future of the examinee. One exam is sat by all Japanese final-year high school students on the same day; the other exam is specific to the university the student wishes to attend.

Once exams have been completed and a student gains a university place, it is time to let loose a little. Basically, university or college is considered a transitional stage between the world of education and employment, a stage in which one spends more time in drinking bouts with fellow students than in the halls of higher learning. In a sense the university years, for those who make it, are similar to the early years of childhood. All kinds of antics are looked upon indulgently as the excesses of youth. Some have seen a pattern in this – an alternation between extreme pressure and almost complete relaxation – which is mirrored in many aspects of Japanese social life.

As in other parts of the world, the Japanese education system processes male and female students differently. The top universities are dominated by male students, with many female students opting for two-year college courses, often in topics seen as useful training for family life, such as child psychology.

According to one traveller, the best way to gain an understanding of the Japanese education system is to actually visit a school:

I think it is a good idea to pay a visit to an elementary or high school. It will tell you a great deal about Japanese society and you might get a chance to tell the students about your own country. You'll be a hit!
Inge Nielsen, Denmark

Work

Company life is very different for men and women. For men it is a lifetime commitment that will take up far more of their waking hours than will their family. For women, company-life experience is liable to be limited to four or five years of answering the phone and offering tea to visitors before retreating to a life of domesticity. Women who return to work after marriage, and more and more are doing so, are likely to be involved in small-scale industry that provides none of the benefits available for most Japanese workers. The gap between average female earnings and average male earnings is greater in Japan than any comparable advanced nation.

For the Japanese themselves, the issue is a difficult one. After all, Japanese companies make such excessive demands on their workers that many Japanese women have no desire to share the responsibilities that are, at present, almost entirely undertaken by men. Company life for most men is a non-stop commitment from graduation to retirement. Even their annual two-weeks holidays are often forfeited because it would look like disloyalty to want to have a holiday from the company.

Peter Tasker, in his book *Inside Japan* (Penguin, 1987), points to the story of the Bureau for the Promotion of the Forty Hour Week; so enormous was their task of persuading Japanese corporations to change their work practices, that members of the bureau were forced to put in long hours of overtime and weekend work. Before too long their efforts came to the attention of the authorities, who were unhesitating in praising them for their devotion to such a just cause!

Ageing Japan, Vacationing Japan

Foreign observers looking for signs of change in the Japanese economic powerhouse frequently focus their attention on the changing age make-up of the population. WW II left Japan with a very young population and, at that time, the average lifespan was also relatively short compared to advanced Western nations. A low birth rate and an average lifespan which is now the longest in the world is turning that age make-up right around. From being a nation of youngsters Japan is rapidly becoming a nation of oldsters. Other advanced nations are facing the same problem as the post-war baby boomers enter middle age, but nowhere is the change so dramatic as in Japan. Inevitably, such demographic change will have a major influence on the economy in coming decades.

Not only is the population ageing, it's also becoming, albeit rather slowly, less entranced with the Japanese workstyle with its long working hours and short vacations. Japanese workers are becoming increasingly keen on enjoying their mighty yen in other ways than new electronic gadgets. Still, although Japan's 16 vacation days and 20 holidays (a total of 36) are not as good as the best Western European levels, they're nowhere near as bad as the poor overworked Americans. The Germans get 40 days of vacation and holidays a year, the French 33.5, the British 33, and the downtrodden Americans just 23 miserable days. The Japanese are inclined not to take all their vacation; on average they utilise only nine of the 16 days, but that's gradually changing.

CULTURE & THE ARTS

The fascinating and intricate tapestry of contemporary Japanese culture can appear almost bewildering in the profusion of its components, but there is a recognisable trail of historical patterns which leads to the modern forms and tastes of Japanese society.

The Chinese influence on Japanese culture – particularly the introduction of Buddhism and the adoption of Chinese characters for the written Japanese language – runs long and deep from the 6th century to the present day. From imitation, the Japanese quickly progressed to assess the relevance of ideas and techniques to their own needs before adapting them. The policy of cultural enrichment through borrowing has been repeated throughout Japanese history.

During the Heian period, Japanese culture began to develop a more individual style. Life and love at the imperial court was described by Lady Murasaki in her classic novel *The Tale of Genji*. The Byōdō-in Temple at Uji (near Kyoto) has survived as a superb example of Heian architecture.

During the Kamakura period, the samurai were attracted by the austerity of Zen Buddhism which then became a strong and enduring part of Japanese culture. In return for complete subservience and loyalty, shoguns provided full protection and responsibility for their underlings. This freeing of subordinates from the burden of responsibility for decisions – a hotly disputed subject after WW II! – still pertains in Japanese society. Not surprisingly, the main literary themes of this bellicose period were war tales. The rise and fall of the Taira family is chronicled in the classic *Tales of Heike*.

The defeat of the Mongol invasions by divine winds (kamikaze) reinforced the Japanese assumption that they were a unique and superior race under divine protection. Not until WW II did Japan suffer occupation or defeat as a nation. Consequently, the invasion and surrender of Japan in WW II dealt a shattering blow to the Japanese psyche. However, the meteoric, post-war rise of Japan to its present status as an economic superpower appears to have revitalised the Japanese view of themselves as unique and superior.

In the Muromachi period, Japan refreshed its interest in Chinese culture and refined Zen Buddhism to a peak of elegant simplicity in aesthetic pursuits such as Nō theatre, tea ceremony (chanoyu), flower arranging (ikebana), gardening, calligraphy *(shodō)* and ink-painting.

The military rulers of the Momoyama period are renowned for their predilection for dazzling works of art and the construction of magnificent castles.

The Edo period was marked by the ideals of Confucianism – a hierarchical system which applied from the smallest family unit to the largest government institution. Harmony within society was only guaranteed if each member kept to his or her place and observed correct etiquette. Confucian origins can be ascribed to many aspects of modern Japanese life such as 'group behaviour' and rigid company allegiance, bowing, the dictates of loyalty and obligation, the emphasis on 'face' and the lesser status of women.

In the enforced idleness of peacetime, there was little demand for the martial skills of the samurai, who began to lose their role in society. The merchant classes, on the other hand, beavered their way to power through the acquisition of wealth and rose in social importance far beyond the bottom rung to which they had been traditionally assigned by Confucianist ethics. The founding of trading companies such as Mitsui, Sumitomo and Mitsubushi – now numbered among the corporate giants of Japan – dates from this period.

Entertainment districts, such as Yoshiwara in Edo (modern Tokyo), provided cultural

stimulation, both bawdy and refined, despite constant harassment by the authorities. Merchant classes provided financial support for such cultural developments as kabuki theatre and bunraku (puppet theatre), wood-block prints (ukiyo-e) and haiku poetry.

For a brief period, overlapping the Momoyama and Edo periods, Western trading nations were allowed to make contact with Japan. The Japanese were not bowled over by Western religion, but they soon grasped the practical application of Western firearms which they quickly copied and put to use. General suspicion of Western intentions prompted Japanese leaders to quell Christianity ruthlessly and seek isolation on their own terms, restricting the main trade and cultural contacts with the West to a tiny peephole at Nagasaki.

Towards the closing stages of the Edo period, new ideas seeping in from the outside world started to arouse curiosity in Japan. In

The Floating World

The Tokugawa era saw the flourishing of a culture that is referred to by the Japanese as *ukiyo* or 'floating world'. The term itself derives from Buddhism and refers to the transient world of fleeting pleasures. By Edo times, however, the term had come to signify the whole of a burgeoning popular culture that was much in evidence in the sprawling pleasure districts of Japan's major towns.

The floating world, centred in pleasure districts like Edo's Yoshiwara, was a topsy-turvy kingdom, an inversion of all the usual social hierarchies that were held in place by the power of the Tokugawa Shogunate. Here, money counted for more than rank, actors and artists were the arbiters of style, and prostitutes elevated their art to a level such that their social and artistic accomplishments matched those of the ladies of noble families. Added to this was an element of spectacle. Both kabuki and sumō, with their ritualised visual opulence found large popular audiences in this period.

Many of the features of this floating world can still be seen in Japanese popular culture today. Still, to get a glimpse of this world as it was in its heyday, it is best to turn to *ukiyo-e*, wood-block prints, or literally 'pictures from the floating world'. In keeping with the topsy-turvy world from which it issued, the ukiyo-e turned traditional Japanese graphic art upside down. For one, wood-block prints could be produced in quantity and made accessible to a large audience; and for two, ukiyo-e chose as its topics, not Chinese-style landscapes and mannered court scenes, but the people and scenes that filled the floating world. The ukiyo-e artist Utamarō, for example, depicted the lives of courtesans, sometimes depicting his subjects seminude, in a celebration of the female form. Other artists, such as Sharaku, turned their talents to depicting scenes from the kabuki theatre.

Ukiyo-e prints, ranging from around Y5000 upwards, are readily available in Japan, and make an excellent souvenir. ■

1853, Admiral Perry bluntly put an end to Japanese isolation and jolted the Japanese into reassessing the durability of their social values.

During the Meiji period, Japan pulled out all the stops for Westernisation and the instinct for survival prompted an immediate and often indiscriminate importation of Western knowledge, products and fashions. The government hired droves of foreign experts for tasks ranging from modernisation of the army to setting up a railway system, revamping the postal service and introducing telephones. Japanese nobility tried out frock coats, umbrellas, billiards and even Western-style fancy-dress parties which raised a few conservative eyebrows.

For the Japanese government, however, the main objective was to acquire the technology at the core of Western supremacy; the Japanese spirit was to remain untouched. Beneath the Western trappings, nationalist sentiments were hard at work, directing Japan towards the militarism and imperial expansion which was finally crushed in WW II.

The Allied occupation after WW II brought Japan into close contact with Western culture. The subsequent economic recovery of Japan, through the lean years of the '50s to the vast wealth of the '90s, has produced the interesting result that the economy, political structure and standard of living in Japan now bind the country closer to the West than to Asia. This may well account for the confusion and insecurity of contemporary Japanese culture, which derives a restless vitality from cultural see-sawing: zealously holding to Japanese traditions one moment, eagerly adapting to the latest Western crazes the next.

From the sporting leviathans of sumō wrestling to the giants of baseball; from the literary and calligraphic heights of haiku to the troughs of pornographic *manga* (comics); from the strange tones of *gagaku* (court music) to the blues of B B King 'live' at the Budokan Stadium; from the dainty dishes of kaiseki cuisine to the more mundane 'furaido poteto' at McDonald's;

from the pampered luxury of a Japanese inn *(ryokan)* to the claustrophobia of capsule hotels – a trip to Japan won't lack for weird and wonderful cultural experiences!

Japanese Theatre

Japanese theatre is certainly worth sampling, although it may take a while to acquire a taste for it. Even if you don't follow the plot, the scenery, dance, music and costumes are enough to appreciate the performance.

If you are not fluent in ancient or modern Japanese, and want to follow the plot, some theatres have programmes with a synopsis of the play in English and sometimes head-phones are available for a commentary in English.

The best source for details of performances is the Tourist Information Centre (TIC) in Tokyo or Kyoto. Some local publications such as *Tour Companion* in Kyoto and *Kansai Time Out* also publish theatre information. If you want to watch drama productions on TV in Tokyo, check the programme on channels 1 and 3. If you want to delve deeper into the subject the following publications may be useful:

The Kabuki Handbook by Aubrey & Giovanna Halford (Tuttle, New York, 1979)
The Nō Plays of Japan by Arthur Waley (Tuttle, Tokyo 1976)
A Guide to Nō by P G O'Neill (Hinoki Shōten, Tokyo & Kyoto, 1954)
A Guide to Kyōgen by Don Kenny (Hinoki Shōten, Tokyo & Kyoto, 1968)
The Bunraku Handbook by Shuzaburo Hironaga (Maison des Arts, Tokyo, 1976)

Kabuki The word kabuki was originally derived from the idea of something being extraordinary or avant-garde. It was later assigned Chinese characters to denote ka (song), bu (dance) and ki (skill). For many foreigners, the spectacular combinations of costume, make-up, scenery, action and music make kabuki the most enjoyable type of Japanese theatre.

The origins of kabuki can be traced back to the 17th century during the Tokugawa era

Kabuki

traitors, murderers, duellists, comics and female warriors.

For kabuki, the main theatres are the Kabuki-za and National theatres in Tokyo, the Minami-za Theatre in Kyoto and the Shin Kabuki-za Theatre in Osaka. Rather than staying for the whole performance, you can also buy a 'stand and watch' ticket (tachi-mi-seki) for one act.

Nō Nō developed in the Muromachi era (1336-1572) from several dances or semi-dramatic performances but especially from Shinto dances *(kagura)* and comic dance *(sarugaku)*.

Each Nō performance normally consists of six plays: the first about the gods; the second deals with battles and warriors; the third features a female heroine; the fourth recounts how spirits turn warriors to spiritual matters; the fifth relates human passions, moral responsibilities and daily life and the sixth is a celebration of some happy occasion. There is a certain similarity, in general structure and the use of a chorus and masks, between Nō and early Greek drama.

For Nō, the main theatres are the National Nō Theatre and Ginza Nō Stage in Tokyo and the Kongō Nō Stage in Kyoto.

Kyōgen This is a type of farce developed mainly as an interlude for Nō plays. The subjects of its satire are often samurai, depraved priests and faithless women – the performers are without masks and a chorus or chants are used.

Performances are often to be seen in major Nō theatres such as the Ginza Nō Stage in Tokyo, Kongō Nō Stage in Kyoto and Osaka Nō Kaikan in Osaka.

Bunraku Bunraku is traditional Japanese puppet theatre; some performances are full length plays but others offer a medley from various plays. Three puppeteers run operations, a presence which can seem obtrusive until one gets used to concentrating on the puppets rather than their manipulators. A narrator tells the story and supplies the voices for individual characters whilst

when female performers presented singing and dancing shows. The bawdy content of these performances became renowned, as did the easy virtue of the female performers who sometimes doubled as prostitutes. This aroused the displeasure of the Tokugawa government which promptly banned these women from the stage and called for all-male troupes with young boys playing the female roles. Sexual scandals continued in this male context and female roles were taken over by older males, known as *onnagata*, who impersonated females. To watch modern-day onnagata is to see the female role mimicked to such a fine level that the gender difference seems imperceptible.

The content of the play usually revolves around the themes of love, feudal loyalty or filial piety. Episodes from *The Tales of Heike* are common themes for the plays. The acting gives full scope for the lively and elaborate portrayal of such roles as suicidal lovers, musical accompaniment comes from the *shamisen* (a type of banjo) player.

For bunraku, the main theatres are the National Theatre in Tokyo, Gion Corner in Kyoto and the Asahiza Theatre and National Bunraku Theatre, both in Osaka.

Cinema

At the time cinema first developed in the West, Japan was in the throes of the Meiji Restoration, enthusiastically embracing every perceived new advance. It was scarcely surprising that cinema was also sucked into the Japanese vortex although, as usual, it was adapted in a peculiarly Japanese fashion. Early Japanese cinema had a live element in the form of the *benshi*, a commentator who interpreted and explained what was happening on the screen. This was necessary for foreign films but the benshi quickly became as important a part of the cinematic experience as the film itself.

At first, Japanese films were merely cinematic versions of traditional theatrical performances but the Tokyo earthquake in 1923 prompted a split between period films or *jidaigeki* and new *gendaigeki* films which followed modern themes. The more realistic storylines of the new films soon reflected back on the traditional films with the introduction of *shin jidaigeki* or 'new period films'. During this era, the movie samurai became an enduring staple of Japanese film.

As the government became increasingly authoritarian in the years leading up to WW II, cinema became much more constrained and eventually films were simply propaganda tools. After the war, feudal films with their emphasis on blind loyalty and martial ability were banned by the Allied authorities, but cinematic energy soon turned to new pursuits, including animated films, monster movies and comedies. In the '50s Japanese directors, in particular Akira Kurosawa, developed international reputations with films like *Rashomon* (1950) and *Seven Samurai* (1954); the latter gaining the ultimate accolade when it was shamelessly ripped off by the Hollywood blockbuster *The Magnificent Seven*.

In the '70s and '80s, however, Japanese cinema retreated before the onslaught of international movie making, in part because of the failure to develop new independent film-making companies in the era when big production companies were losing their clout worldwide. Recently, however, there have been a number of independently produced Japanese films which have had some art-house success in the West and make a good introduction, not just to Japanese cinema, but to modern Japan itself. Itami Juzo's *Tampopo* is a wonderful comedy about a Japanese noodle restaurant – 'Zen and the art of noodle making' as one critic described it. From the same director *A Taxing Woman* was an amusing insight into taxation, Japanese style.

Donald Richie's *Japanese Cinema – An Introduction* (Oxford University Press, Hong Kong, 1990) is brief, but useful for the beginner.

Painting

The techniques and materials used in the early stages of Japanese painting owed much to Chinese influence. The introduction of Buddhism to Japan in the 6th century also provided Japanese painting with a role as a medium for religious instruction.

Towards the end of the Heian period, after contacts between Japan and China had dwindled, the emphasis on religious themes painted according to Chinese conventions gave way to a purely Japanese style of painting. Known as *yamato-e*, this style covered indigenous subjects and was frequently used in scroll paintings and on screens.

Ink paintings *(suiboku* or *sumi-e)* by Chinese Zen artists were introduced to Japan during the Muromachi period and copied by Japanese artists who produced hanging pictures *(kakemono)*, scrolls *(emaki)* and decorated screens and sliding doors.

During the Momoyama period, the rulers demonstrated their opulence and prestige by commissioning artists to use flamboyant colours and copious gold leaf. The most popular themes were those depicting Japanese nature (plants, trees and seasons) or characters from Chinese legends. The outstanding school of painting in this period was that of the Kanō family.

Western techniques of painting, including the use of oils, were introduced during the 16th century by the Jesuits. Japanese painters who combined Western and Japanese styles sometimes produced interesting results: portraits of Westerners thoughtfully included an oriental incline to the eyes.

The Edo period was marked by an enthusiastic patronage for a wide range of painting styles. The Kanō school continued to be in demand for depictions of subjects connected with Confucianism, mythical Chinese creatures, or scenes from nature. The Tosa school, whose members followed the yamato-e style of painting, was kept busy with commissions from the nobility to paint scenes from the ancient classics of Japanese literature.

The Rimpa school not only absorbed the style of other schools (Chinese, Kanō and Tosa), but progressed beyond their conventions to produce strikingly original decorative painting. The works of art produced by a trio of outstanding artists from this school (Tawaraya Sōtatsu, Honami Kōetsu and Ogata Kōrin) must rank amongst the finest of this period.

Another genre of painting which developed at this time was the *ukiyo-e* wood-block print. If there is one art form which Westerners instantly associate with Japan, this is it. The name ukiyo-e or 'pictures of the floating world' refers to the 'floating world' concept used by Buddhists as a metaphor for human life, but the subjects of the 'pictures' were the colourful characters in the 'floating world' of the entertainment quarters of Edo (modern Tokyo), Kyoto and Osaka.

In the West, the vivid colours, novel composition and flowing lines of these prints caused great excitement, sparking a vogue which a French art critic dubbed 'Japonisme'. Ukiyo-e became a key influence on Impressionist (for example, Toulouse-Lautrec, Manet and Degas) and Post-Impressionist artists.

Amongst the Japanese, however, the prints were hardly given more than passing consideration – millions were produced annually in Edo (Tokyo). They were cheap items, often thrown away or used as wrapping paper for pottery. For many years, the Japanese continued to be perplexed by the keen interest foreigners took in this art form which they considered of ephemeral value.

Since the '70s, Japanese collectors have returned to buy back their own prints and now account for about half of the market in these works. The biggest auctions of ukiyo-e are held not in Japan, but in New York and London. If you want to see the best and largest collection of ukiyo-e in the world, pay a visit to the Boston Museum of Fine Arts.

In 1987, Yasuda Fire and Marine Insurance bought van Gogh's *Sunflowers* for US$39.9 million. More recently, Ryoei Saito (a Japanese business magnate) snapped up van Gogh's *Portrait of Dr Gachet* for a cool US$82.5 million. Van Gogh, who only sold one of his paintings in his lifetime, shortly before his death approached his brother Theo to fund a business venture which he thought would solve his constant money problems. Van Gogh's proposal was to set himself up as a dealer in ukiyo-e!

The first prints of ukiyo-e were made in black and white in the early 17th century; the technique for colour printing was only developed in the middle of the 18th century. The success of a publisher lay in close co-operation between the artist, engraver and printer through all stages of production.

The first stage required the artist *(eshi)* to draw a design on transparent paper and indicate the colouring needed. The engraver *(horishi)* then pasted this face down on a block of cherry wood and carved out the lines of the design in relief. The printer *(surishi)* inked the block and took a proof. Each colour required a separate block; it was up to the printer to use his skill to obtain accurate alignment and subtle colour effects which depended on the colour mixture and pressure applied.

The reputed founder of ukiyo-e is Iwa Matabei. The genre was later developed by Hishikawa Moronobu who rose to fame with his illustrations for erotic tales. His wood-block prints of scenes from the entertainment district of Yoshiwara introduced the theme of *bijin-e* (paintings of beautiful women) which later became a standard subject. Early themes also covered scenes from the theatre (including the actors) and the erotic *shunga* or 'spring pictures'. Kitagawa Utamaro is famed for his bijin-e which emphasise the erotic and sensual beauty of his subjects. All that is known about Tōshūsai Sharaku, a painting prodigy whose life is a mystery, is that he produced 145 superb portraits of kabuki actors between 1794 and 1795.

Towards the end of the Edo period, two painters produced outstanding works in this art genre. Katsushika Hokusai was a prolific artist who observed his fellow inhabitants of Edo (Tokyo) with a keen sense of humour. His most famous works include manga (cartoons), *Fugaku Sanjūrokkei* (Thirty-Six Views of Mt Fuji) and *Fugaku Hyakkei* (One Hundred Views of Mt Fuji). As Hokusai approached the end of his life – he died at the age of 89 – he delighted in signing his works with the pen name *gakyōrōjin* (literally, 'old man mad with painting').

Andō Hiroshige followed the lead of Hokusai and specialised in landscapes, although he also created splendid prints of plants and birds. His most celebrated works include *Tōkaidō Gojūsan-tsugi* (Fifty-Three Stations of the Tōkaidō); *Meisho Edo Hyakukei* (One Hundred Views of Famous Places in Edo); and *Omi Hakkei* (Eight Views of Omi) – Omi is now known as Lake Biwa-ko.

From the Meiji era onwards, painting in Japan focused on the twin poles of *nihonga* (Japanese-style painting) and *yōga* (Western-style painting).

Irezumi A more off-beat Japanese art form is the art of tattooing *(irezumi)*. In feudal times, the authorities tattooed criminals who then felt ashamed by the stigma of being 'branded'. In due course, those who had been tattooed exhibited a type of defiant pride in their markings which they considered almost as a status symbol setting them apart from others in society.

Japanese tattoos, usually completed in blue and red natural dyes, often cover the whole body with amazingly intricate designs based on fauna & flora, Buddhist deities or subjects drawn from Japanese myths. If you feel like it, you can have a dragon drawn down the length of your body – all the way from top to tail. When you're staying in shared accommodation, you can sometimes spot exotic markings amongst fellow bathers in o-furo (the bath).

As a sop to foreign sensibilities, tattooing was banned during the Meiji era, but was promptly reinstated after the Prince of Wales (later to become Britain's King George V) took a liking to the art and had a rampant dragon inscribed on his arm in 1881.

Nowadays, many ordinary Japanese shun tattoos; it is a fair assumption that any Japanese you see flaunting tattoos are either Yakuza (Japanese Mafia types) or have connections with the shady side of society.

Music
Ancient Music Gagaku is the 'elegant' music of the Japanese imperial court which was derived from Chinese models. It flourished between the 8th and 12th centuries, then declined for several centuries until it became part of a revival of interest in national traditions during the Meiji period.

Court orchestras were divided into two sections with formally prescribed functions. The orchestra of the 'right', dressed in green, blue or yellow and played Korean music. The orchestra of the 'left', dressed in red and played Chinese, Indian or Japanese music. The repertoire of an orchestra included *kangen* (instrumental) pieces and *bugaku* (dance) pieces.

Nowadays, a gagaku ensemble usually consists of 16 players performing on drums and kettle drums; stringed instruments such as the *biwa* (lute) and *koto* (plucked zither); and wind instruments such as the *hichiriki* (Japanese oboe) and various types of flute.

Traditional Japanese Instruments There

are several traditional Japanese instruments which continue to play a part in Japanese life, both publicly and privately. Some are used in orchestras or the theatre; others are used for solo performances or mastered by young ladies as an entrance card to the marriage stakes.

The *shamisen* is a three-stringed instrument resembling a banjo with an extended neck. It was very popular during the Edo period, particularly in the entertainment districts of Osaka and Edo (Tokyo). It is still used as formal accompaniment in the Japanese theatre (kabuki and bunraku) and the ability to perform on the shamisen remains one of the essential skills of a geisha.

The koto is a type of plucked zither with 13 strings. It was adapted from a Chinese instrument before the 8th century and gradually increased the number of strings from five to 13. Koto schools still operate, often catering to large numbers of young ladies keen to acquire this skill to improve their eligibility for marriage.

The biwa, which resembles a lute, was also derived from a Chinese instrument and appeared in Japan in the 8th century. It was played by travelling musicians, often blind, who recited Buddhist sutras to the accompaniment of the instrument. During the Heian period, the biwa was used in court orchestras. In the succeeding Kamakura period, story-tellers created a different style for the biwa to accompany tales from medieval war epics, the most famous being the *Tales of Heike*.

Although biwa ballads were in vogue during the 16th century, the instrument later fell out of favour. More recently, the composer Takemitsu Tōru has found a new niche for the biwa in a Western orchestra.

Modern Music Modern Japanese tastes in music range far and wide. At street level, pedestrians are often assaulted by gross electronic imitations of the sounds of nature – the apparatus which relentlessly spews out demented cuckoo sounds at street crossings definitely deserves shotgun treatment! In *karaoke* (empty orchestra) bars, where customers sing to taped music, tiddly singers favour sobbingly mournful *enka* (folk ballads). Coffee shops help you swill your American Blend with classical guitar, rhythm & blues, Richard Clayderman piano tinkling, or wallpaper muzak. Discos and live houses (live music venues) offer Jap rock, reggae, heavy metal, etc.

Sales of classical music recordings in Japan are amongst the highest in the world – another sound reason why Sony acquired CBS records in 1988. There is a constant stream of Japanese and foreign symphony orchestras dropping in and out of Japan for concerts.

Foreign jazz, pop and rock groups are continually jetting to and from Japan where promoters can offer huge fees for tours or one-off extravaganzas at venues like Tokyo's giant Budokan Stadium. The Japanese have also made a name for themselves in the field of synthesiser music, with composers such as Kitaro and Sakamoto Ryuichi. Watanabe is another Japanese musician well-known in jazz circles.

The Japanese seem to care very little about their own music. The medium operates a rigidly controlled system to which only a favoured few gain admittance. Record distribution is kept tightly in the hands of major labels, so recordings from independent producers are excluded from large record shops and thus limited to specialist outlets. A lot of Jap pop, in common with pop music elsewhere in the world, fits a rigidly formatted straitjacket to please teenyboppers.

The music from Okinawa has its own special sound. Two well-known names for this type of music are Kina Shokichi and Ueno Koji. The Tsugaru-hantō Peninsula, at the tip of Tōhoku (Northern Honshū), has its own brand of music called Tsugaru-jamisen which is a fun combination of racing banjos and wailing songs.

The music at the Bon summer festivals usually features a singer accompanied by drums and shamisen. The generic name for this type of music is Bon Odori, but there are several other kinds of Odori including

Kawachi Odori, which comes from a working-class district south of Osaka famous for its feisty dialect. The most famous exponent of Kawachi Odori was the gutsy singer, Asamaru, who died in 1985.

Japanese drumming is also worth a listen. The drumming group, 'Kodo', based on Sado Island off the north coast of Northern Honshū, has made several world tours.

For an interesting treatment of traditional Japanese instrumental music, you could look for the works of Tsuchitori Toshiyuki – one of his recordings features ancient bells dug from a tomb at Nara.

To find out what's happening in the music scene or to look for listings of events, you can consult newspapers, magazines such as *Tokyo Journal* or *Kansai Time Out* or call TIC. Prices for concert tickets start at around Y3000; most cities have specialist ticket agencies giving discounts.

If you want to buy music in Tokyo, the biggest selection of sound recordings is at Wave, a huge shop in the Roppongi district. In Kyoto, apart from the shops selling mainstream recordings, you can pick up recordings from independent labels either at Village Green (on the 1st floor of the Sanjo building, just east of Takakura) or at Junk Shop (on the 3rd floor of the LDC building, 50 metres north of Sanjo-Kawaramachi).

Ikebana

Ikebana, or the art of flower arranging, developed in the 15th century and can be grouped into four main styles: *rikka* (standing flowers); *nageire* (throwing-in); *shōkai* (living flowers); and *moribana* (heaped flowers). There are several thousand different schools at present – the top three being Ikenobō, Ohara and Sōgetsu – but they share one aim in common: to arrange flowers to represent heaven, earth and humanity. Ikebana displays were originally part of the tea ceremony but can now be found in private homes – in the tokonoma (alcove for displays) – and even in large hotels.

Apart from its cultural associations, ikebana is also a lucrative business – its schools have millions of students, including many eligible young ladies who view proficiency in the art as a means to improve their marriage prospects.

To find out more about courses for foreigners contact Ikebana International (tel 03-3293-8188), Ochanomizu Square Building, 1-6 Surugadai, Kanda, Chiyoda-ku, Tokyo. Some schools provide instruction in English; prices start around Y3000 per hour.

Chanoyu

The origins of the tea ceremony can be traced to the Nara period and the influence of Buddhism. By the 14th century, it had developed into a highly elaborate and expensive pursuit for the aristocracy. In the 16th century, the greatest exponent of the art was Sen no Rikyū. For reasons that have never been clearly established, he fell out with his patron, Hideyoshi, who condemned him to die. Sen no Rikyū retired to his teahouse for one last ceremonial cuppa, smashed his beloved tea-bowl and then committed seppuku. There are now many different schools of chanoyu, but most are connected with the traditions created by Sen no Rikyū. The three schools active in Kyoto today are: Ura Senke, Omote Senke, and Mushanokōji Senke.

The traditional setting is a thatched teahouse in a beautiful Japanese garden. The preparation and drinking of the tea is conducted according to a highly stylised etiquette and the mental discipline involved was once an essential part of the training of a samurai warrior. Foreigners can find their mental state tends towards fatigue as the ceremony progresses – connoisseurs maintain that full appreciation of the art takes years of reflection.

For a demonstration of chanoyu in Tokyo or Kyoto ask for details at TIC or check with the large hotels; prices for a session start at Y1000. A classic treatment of this subject, written with precision and devotion, is *The Book of Tea* (Dover Publications, New York, 1964) by Kakuzo Okakura.

Japanese Gardens

Japanese gardens aim to imitate nature as

opposed to the Western emphasis on reforming it. However, Japanese gardening with its strong Chinese influences, still has common motifs and standard conventions for different styles.

Although the real mecca for Japanese garden enthusiasts has to be Kyoto (which has dozens to choose from), Japan's three best gardens are said to be Okayama's Kōraku-en, Kanazawa's Kenroku-en and Mito's Kairaku-en. Other cities with renowned gardens are Tokyo, Yokohama, Nagoya, Nara, Hiroshima, Takamatsu, Kumamoto and Kagoshima.

Full-scale Japanese gardens can be roughly categorised into three types: *tsukiyama* or 'hill garden', the dry landscape of *kare-sansui* or 'waterless stream garden' and *chaniwa*, the 'tea garden'.

The hill garden usually contains a hill combined with a pond and a stream with islands and bridges. Viewing is done by strolling along paths or contemplating from an attached house. Examples of this type are the gardens of the Tenryū-ji Temple and Saihō-ji Temple, both in Kyoto.

The waterless stream garden features the dry landscape often associated with Zen meditation. The main elements are rocks and sand – the sea is symbolised by furrows in a layer of sand suggesting ripples; rocks suggest a waterfall. The Ryōan-ji Temple and Daitoku-ji Temple in Kyoto are representative of this type.

The tea garden surrounds a teahouse and features stepping stones. The Kinkaku-ji Temple in Kyoto is a typical example.

Most gardens charge admission fees varying between Y150 and Y500. Further information is given in a detailed leaflet entitled *Japanese Gardens*, published by the Japan National Tourist Organisation (JNTO), or contact TIC in Tokyo or Kyoto. For a thorough dig into Japanese gardens, try *The World of the Japanese Garden* (Weatherhill, Tokyo, 1968) by Lorraine Kuck.

The Japanese like to rank their gardens according to a traditional hit parade and patronise them accordingly, but many foreigners in search of peace and a break from hordes of people (who are presumably looking for the same thing!) opt to visit less famous gardens – preferably early in the morning or towards the end of the afternoon. Some technical knowledge about Japanese gardens is certainly an asset, but considerable pleasure and relaxation can be gained by simply wandering around and slowly absorbing the differences for investigation at a later date.

Bonsai

Bonsai, a skill imported from China during the Kamakura era (1192-1333), is the artificial dwarfing of trees or the miniaturisation of nature.

Bonsai trees are carefully clipped and their roots pruned to keep dwarf dimensions. Some specimens have been handed down over generations and are extremely valuable. A related art is *bonkei* which is the technique of reproducing nature on a small tray using moss, clay, sand, etc.

TIC offices can provide further information on where to find or practice bonsai. Large hotels or department stores often have bonsai displays. Devotees of the art should make the 30 minute trip outside Tokyo to visit the Bonsai Village at Bonsaimachi, Omiya, Saitama.

Ceramics & Pottery

Ceramic art in Japan is usually considered to have started around the 13th century with the introduction of Chinese ceramic techniques and the founding of a kiln in 1242 at Seto (Aichi Prefecture) by Tōshirō. The Japanese term for pottery and porcelain, *setomono* (literally, 'things from Seto'), clearly derives from this ceramic centre which still thrives.

During the following century, five more kilns were established (Tokoname, Shigaraki, Bizen, Echizen and Tamba). Together with Seto, these were known as the 'Six Ancient Kilns' and acquired a reputation for high quality stoneware.

The popularity of the tea ceremony (chanoyu) in the 16th century stimulated developments in ceramics. The great tea masters, Furuta Oribe and Sen no Rikyū, promoted production of exquisite Oribe and Shino wares in Gifu Prefecture. Hideyoshi, who thought nothing of smothering the walls of his tea room with gold, encouraged the master potter Chōjiro to create works of art from clay found near Hideyoshi's palace. Chōjiro was allowed to embellish the tea bowls he created with the character *raku* (enjoyment). This was the beginning of Kyoto's famous *raku-yaki* style of pottery. Tea bowls became highly prized objects commanding stupendous prices. Even today, connoisseurs of the tradition of the tea ceremony are happy to shell out as much as US$30,000 for the right tea bowl.

Hideyoshi's invasion of Korea at the end of the 16th century was a military disaster, but it proved to be a boon to Japanese ceramics when captured Korean potters introduced Japan to the art of manufacturing porcelain. In 1598, a Korean master potter, Ri Sampei, built the first porcelain kiln at Arita in Kyūshū.

During the Edo period, many daimyō encouraged the founding of kilns and the production of superbly designed ceramic articles. The climbing kiln *(noborigama)* was widely used. Constructed on a slope, the kiln had as many as 20 chambers and the capability to achieve temperatures as high as 1400 °C.

During the Meiji period, ceramics waned in popularity, but were later included in a general revival of interest in *mingeihin* (folk arts) headed by Yanagi Sōetsu who encouraged famous potters such as Kawai Kanjirō, Tomimoto Kenchiki and Hamada Shōji. The English potter Bernard Leach studied in Japan under Hamada Shōji and contributed to the folk art revival. On his return to Cornwall in England, Leach maintained his interest in Japanese ceramics and promoted their appreciation in the West.

There are now over 100 pottery centres in Japan with large numbers of artisans producing everything from exclusive tea utensils to souvenir badgers *(tanuki)*. Department stores regularly organise exhibitions of ceramics. Master potters are highly revered and the government designates the finest as 'living national treasures'.

TIC's useful *Ceramic Art & Crafts in Japan* leaflet is published by JNTO and provides full details of pottery centres, kilns and pottery fairs in Japan. Well-known pottery centres include:

Arita porcelain, Arita, Kyūshū – Arita porcelain is still produced in the town where the first Japanese porcelain was made. In the mid-17th century, the Dutch East India Company exported these wares to Europe where they were soon copied in ceramics factories such as those of the Germans (Meissen), the Dutch (Delft) and the English (Worcester). It is commonly known to Westerners as 'Imari' after the name of the port from which it was shipped. The Kakiemon style uses designs of birds and flowers in bright colours. Another popular style is executed in blue and white, incorporating scenes from legends and daily life.

Satsuma-yaki, Kagoshima, Kyūshū – The commonest style of this porcelain has a white, cloudy, cracked glaze enamelled with gold, red, green and blue.

Karatsu-yaki, Karatsu, Kyūshū – Karatsu, near Fukuoka in northern Kyūshū, produces tea ceremony utensils which are Korean in style and have a characteristic greyish, crackled glaze.

Hagi-yaki, Hagi, Honshū – The town of Hagi in Western Honshū is renowned for Hagi-yaki, a type of porcelain made with a pallid yellow or pinkish crackled glaze.

Bizen-yaki, Bizen, Honshū – The ancient ceramics centre of Bizen in Okayama Prefecture is famed for its chunky, unglazed bowls which turn red through oxidation. Bizen also produces roofing tiles.

Mashiko-yaki, Mashiko, Honshū – The town of Mashiko in Tochigi Prefecture, Northern Honshū, is renowned as a folk craft centre producing wares with a distinctive reddish glaze.

Mino-yaki, Toki, Honshū – From Toki in Gifu Prefecture in the Kinki district come pieces executed in the Oribe style which have a greenish glaze and are decorated with creatures and flowers; the Shino style, which is greatly prized by connoisseurs of tea utensils, employs a heavy white glaze.

Temmoku, Seto, Honshū – Seto city in Aichi Prefecture, Central Honshū, has a long tradition as a centre for ceramics. The standard product is ash-glazed, heavy stoneware but Seto also produces special ceramic wares such as *temmoku*, an ancient Chinese style which uses a brown and black glaze.

Kiyomizu-yaki, Kyoto, Honshū – The approach roads to the Kiyomizu-dera Temple in Kyoto are lined with shops selling Kiyomizu-yaki, a style of pottery which can be enamelled, blue-painted, or red-painted.

Kutani-yaki, Ishikawa, Honshū – The porcelain from Ishikawa Prefecture in Central Honshū is usually made as green kutani or painted kutani.

SPORT
Sumō

Sumō, Japanese wrestling, is a simple sport but a complicated ritual. The rules of the game are deceptively simple: the *higashi* (east) wrestler tries to either push his *nishi* (west) opponent out of the ring or unbalance him so that some part of his body other than his feet touch the ground. The 4.55 metre diameter ring *(dohyō)* is on a raised platform, much like a boxing ring, but there the similarity ends. Sumō matches do not go 10 rounds, they are brief and often spectacular and the ritual and build up to the brief encounter is just as important as the clash itself.

There are no weight classes in sumō, they're all big, and in lookalike Japan, sumō wrestlers certainly stand out. Gargantuan bulk is the order of the day and sumō wrestlers achieve their pigged-out look through diet (or lack of it from the weight watcher's point of view). Large quantities of an especially fattening stew called *chankonabe* are supplemented with esoteric activities such as masseurs who manipulate the wrestler's intestines so they can pack more food in. Would-be sumō wrestlers, usually 15 year olds from rural areas, traditionally join one of the 28 *heya* or stables of wrestlers, often run by retired fighters, and work their way up through the ranks.

Sumō still retains traces of its connections to shinto fertility rites including the shrine-like roof which hangs over the ring and the referee or *gyōji* in his wizard-like outfit. It's

said the dagger worn by the referee was to allow him to commit instant seppuku if he made a bad refereeing decision! The wrestlers wear a *mawashi* with a broad leather belt; it's rather like a *fundoshi*, the traditional loincloth drawn between the buttocks. A good grasp on the belt is a favourite hold but there are 48 recognised holds and throws.

The pre-game preliminaries often last far longer than the actual struggle as the opponents first hurl salt into the dohyō to purify it then put great effort into psyching each other out with malevolent looks and baleful stares. A series of false starts often follows before two immovable objects finally collide with an earth-shaking wallop. Sometimes that initial collision is enough to tip one of them out of the ring but usually there's a brief interlude of pushing, shoving, lifting and tripping. Sometimes neither opponent is able to get a grip on the other and they stand there, slapping at each other like two angry, and very overweight, infants.

Short though a sumō encounter may be, it can often be very exciting. In one match I saw a much smaller wrestler virtually lift up and hurl his enormous opponent out of the ring with such force that he, in turn, went flying out, right over the top of the defeated wrestler.

Tony Wheeler

The Tokyo sumō stables are in Ryōgoku, near the new Kokugikan sumō arena. Six major sumō tournaments *(basho)* are held each year: January (Tokyo – Kokugikan Stadium), March (Osaka – Furitsu Taiikaikan Gymnasium), May (Tokyo – Kokugikan Stadium), July (Nagoya – Aichi Kenritsu Taiikukan Gymnasium), September (Tokyo – Kokugikan Stadium) and November (Fukuoka – Kokusai Centre Sogo Hall).

At a basho, prices start at Y1000 for a basic bench seat at the back but, if you can afford Y7000 for a balcony seat you will not only be closer to the action, but will also be able to delve deep into the mysteries of the refreshment bag that comes with the ticket. Ringside seats are highly prized and virtually unobtainable unless you have inside contacts. Tune in to Far East Network (FEN) on 810 kHz for simultaneous radio coverage of the action in English. TV coverage is extensive and most of the English-language newspapers devote a section to sumō.

Each basho commences on the Sunday closest to the 10th of the month and lasts a fortnight, during which each wrestler competes in one bout per day. The big crowds arrive in the late afternoon to watch the top-ranking wrestlers; the earlier part of the day is reserved for the lower-ranking fighters.

If you want to see a sumō bout, but arrive in Japan at a time when no basho is being held, you can visit one of the sumō stables to watch training. JNTO publishes a leaflet entitled *Traditional Sports* which has a sumō section with full details of tournaments, purchase of tickets, visits to sumō stables and even a bibliography of books and magazines in English on the subject. Contact TIC for more information.

Wrestlers who reach the rank of *yokozuna* or 'grand champion' become celebrity figures in Japan. With the exception of several Hawaiians, very few foreigners have successfully made the big time in this sport. And what happens to a retired sumō wrestler? Well he loses weight, cuts his hair and returns to Japanese anonymity; many sumō wrestlers experience severe heart problems later in their lives.

Baseball

Sumō wrestling may be the most Japanese sporting activity, but baseball is Japan's number one sport both for spectators and participants. Baseball bounced into Japan in 1873 with a US teacher, Horace Wilson, who taught at Tokyo University. There have been professional teams since the 1930s and, just as in the USA, there are little league teams, school teams, work teams and 'bunch of friends in the local park' teams. At the professional level, however, baseball is big business and the nightly televised games draw huge audiences.

Despite the similarity to American baseball – even many of the terms (double play, first base, home run) are carried straight over without translation – baseball has been cleverly altered to fit the Japanese mood. Read Robert Whiting's *You've Got to Have Wa* (Macmillan, New York, 1989) for the full story on baseball Japanese style. Even the Japanese emphasis on the group over the individual has played its part in fitting baseball into the Japanese mould and *wa* means something like 'team spirit'.

Japanese professional baseball is divided into two leagues: Central and Pacific. Each league has six teams, usually given really original names such as Tigers or Giants (although the Hiroshima Carp do sound distinctly Japanese) and mostly supported or owned by big businesses. Each team is allowed two gaijin players, usually Americans past their prime or facing some sort of contractual difficulty in the USA. They often have trouble adapting to the Japanese requirements that they be just another member of the team, not rock the boat and definitely not show up the local stars!

The season lasts from April to October and is followed by the Japan Series, a seven-match contest between the top two teams. In Tokyo, the centre of the baseball universe is Korakuen Stadium. Expect to pay around Y700 for a basic seat.

The All-Japan High School Baseball Championship Tournaments, are taken very seriously in Japan as the major annual sporting events when the flower of youthful vitality goes on display. During August, when the summer tournament is in progress, baseball seems to be the only topic on everybody's mind.

Golf

Golf was introduced to Japan in 1903 when an intrepid English merchant named Arthur Goon set up the Kōbe Golf Club. More than 40 million Japanese now play the game, although golf is neither ritual like sumō or sport like baseball: to most Japanese it's a combination of business and prestige. The golf course is another place where business contacts are made and cultivated so, for the upwardly mobile salaryman, the ability to play golf (and equally important to look like

a real golfer) is a necessity. Since golf is expensive – anything requiring lots of real estate is expensive in Japan – playing golf also carries considerable prestige.

If you want to set foot on a green, a fat wallet and corporate clout are handy assets. Membership fees are rarely less than US$5000, easily reach US$25,000 and often soar higher. Of course it is usually the company that takes out corporate membership and thus pays for its employees to go golfing. Green fees usually start at around US$100 per day. Real golf courses have recently prompted an environmental backlash as Japanese non-golfers have raised a storm of protest against more and more of the countryside being converted to golf courses.

For most Japanese, golf time is principally time spent on one of the multi-tiered driving ranges which are a familiar sight in almost any Japanese city. It's easy to spot their green nets, often perched like aviaries on the tops of high-rise buildings.

The prohibitive cost of golfing in Japan means that it is often cheaper for Japanese to book a packaged golfing tour abroad – this explains the common sight at international airports of bevies of Japanese bent double under a huge bag of clubs. On the other hand, there seem to be plenty of Japanese carrying golf clubs to the fleshpots of Asia – it gives the right impression even if some might have a different intent.

Several years ago, foreigners were mystified to see young Japanese men outside sunbathing, but wearing gloves. The answer, of course, was that this resulted in the ultimate status symbol: suntanned arms and those lily-white hands which are the instantly recognisable and envied sign of a frequent golfer.

Tennis

Tennis was introduced to Japan in the late 19th century. A few years ago, it received a considerable boost in public esteem, particularly in the eyes of young ladies searching for the right marriage credentials, when it was discovered that the Crown Prince Akihito (who has since succeeded his father to become emperor) met his bride-to-be on the tennis court.

Early in this century, the Japanese came up with *nankyu*, a local adaptation which has its own rules and is only played as doubles using a soft, rubber ball. International championships are held regularly and, for unfathomable reasons, the game is quite popular in Zaire.

Skiing

Skiing developed in Japan in the 1950s and there are now more than 300 ski resorts, many with high-standard runs and snow-making equipment. The majority of resorts are concentrated on the island of Honshū, where the crowds are huge, the vertical drops rarely more than 400 metres and all runs start at altitudes of less than 2000 metres. Snow cover in southern and eastern Honshū is generally adequate, but can be sparse and icy.

Skiers on Hokkaidō, however, can look forward to powder skiing matching anything in the European Alps or North American Rockies. Niseko and Furano, two of Hokkaidō's best resorts, have excellent facilities (Niseko has 43 lifts) and neither suffer from extreme crowding.

JNTO's *Skiing in Japan* pamphlet covers 20 resorts on Honshū and Hokkaidō with travel information, ski season dates, accommodation details, resort facilities and costs. Japan Airlines offers special ski tour packages including air fares, transportation, meals and accommodation.

Skiing is normally possible from December to April, though the season can be shorter in some of Honshū's lower-altitude resorts. Akakura, within easy reach of Tokyo, is known for deep snow that thaws quickly by the end of March. Shiga and Zao, on Honshū, are best for early April skiing. The best time for cross-country skiing is March or April when the snow is firmer and deeper; January and February are often very cold and stormy.

Resort accommodation ranges from hostels to expensive hotels but is heavily booked during the ski season. Many resorts are sited at hot springs and double as *onsen* or bathing spas. Avoid weekends and holidays when lift lines are long and accommodation and transportation is heavily booked.

Lift passes cost Y2600 to Y4200 per day. Daily rental of skis, stocks and boots can cost up to Y5000 but finding larger-size ski boots may be difficult. Equipment can only be hired at resorts and is usually old and of a low standard; advanced equipment for the more experienced skier is rare. Since clothing cannot be hired, and second-hand gear is very hard to find, it's advisable to bring your own equipment. For those with plenty of cash it is possible to buy it in Japan – many ski shops hold sales from September to November and package-deal bargains can be found with skis, bindings and poles included. Tokyo's Jimbocho, Shinjuku, Shibuyu and Ikebukuro areas have good ski shops.

As well as downhill skiing, Japan also offers good terrain for cross-country skiing and touring, especially in the Hakodate region of Hokkaidō (a good way to get away from the crowds). The Japanese are very hospitable and foreigners are welcome to join in races and festivities organised by the local authorities – one of the most famous is the Sapporo Marathon cross-country ski race.

Martial Arts

Japan is renowned for its martial arts, many of which filtered through from China and were then adapted by the Japanese. During feudal times, these arts were highly valued by ruling families as a means to buttress their power.

After WW II, martial arts were perceived as contributing to the aggressive stance which had led to hostilities and their teaching was discouraged. Within a decade, however, they had returned to favour and are now popular both in Japan and abroad.

For more information contact TIC or the associations listed in the Martial Arts section of Studying in Japan in the Facts for the Visitor chapter. JNTO also publishes a leaflet entitled *Traditional Sports – MG088* which covers this subject.

Kendō *Kendō*, or the 'way of the sword', is the oldest of the martial arts and was favoured by the samurai to acquire skills in using swords as well as develop mental poise. Today, it is practised with a bamboo stave and protective body armour, gauntlets and face mask. The winner of a bout succeeds in landing blows to the face, arms, upper body or throat of an opponent.

Iaijutsu, the art of drawing a sword, is closely related to kendō. One of the few martial arts developed specially for women was the art of wielding *naginata*, a type of halberd.

Karate Karate originated in India and then spread via China to Okinawa in the 14th century only continuing on to the rest of Japan in the first half of this century.

The emphasis on unarmed combat is demonstrated by the name karate, which can be translated literally as 'empty hand'. Blows are delivered with the fists or feet. For optimum performance, all movements require intense discipline of the mind. There are two methods of practising karate. The first is *kumite*, when two or more people spar together. The second is *kata*, when one person performs formal exercises.

Aikidō The roots of this solely defensive art can be traced to the Minamoto clan in the 10th century, but the modern form of *aikidō* was started in the 1920's by Ueshiba Morihei.

Aikidō draws on many different techniques, including jūdō, karate and kendō. Breathing and meditation form an integral part of training, as does the concentration on movement derived from classical Japanese dance and the awareness of *ki* (life force or will) flowing from the fingertips.

Jūdō This is probably the most well-known martial art; it become a popular sport worldwide and regularly features in the Olympic Games.

The origins of this art are found in *jujitsu*, a means of self defence favoured by the samurai, which was modernised into jūdō

(the 'way of softness') by Kano Jigoro in 1882. The basic principles and subtle skills of the art lie in defeating an opponent simply by redirecting the opponent's strength against himself or herself.

RELIGION

Contemporary Japanese society may be materialistic, but religion still plays a strong, practical role in daily life. Since most Japanese view religion as a practical extension of everyday life, to be used as necessary, they find it quite natural to turn to whichever religion covers the area of spiritual life in question. Consequently, they see no contradiction in following two faiths at the same time. It's a bit like taking out two insurance policies for different events: one for now and one for later!

Shinto and Buddhism, the major religions in Japan, coexisted for many centuries in relative harmony. A notable break in this amicable relationship occurred during the Meiji period when nationalist fervour introduced 'State Shinto' as the national religion. Severe restraints were placed on Buddhism which came under attack by nationalist zealots. The balance was restored with the abolition of State Shinto after the Allied occupation in 1945.

Followers of Shinto turn to it to ensure the deities approve matters concerning life here and now: safe births, happy marriages, good luck in examinations, prosperity for a business venture, success in finding the right mate or safety from accidents in a new car. Similarly, followers of Buddhism will use it to take care of the 'life hereafter': funerals and the spirits of ancestors.

Since neither religion, as practised in Japan, is monotheistic, there have been few worries about shifting batches of Shinto gods into the Buddhist pantheon; priests of Buddhist temples have tended Shinto shrines in the same precincts. Buddhism has also proved quite amenable to the Shinto reverence for ancestors.

Whilst most Japanese draw spiritual support from Shinto and Buddhism, they also complement this with ethical principles derived from Confucianism. These principles – still taken very seriously in modern Japan – include unquestioning acceptance of one's position in a group or hierarchy, unswerving loyalty and respect for superiors and scrupulous observance of etiquette.

For those Japanese who want to specialise, there are numerous branches of Shinto and Buddhism. Zen Buddhism has a strong following and 'new religions' – particularly Sōka Gakkai – have also proved popular.

The appeal of Christianity to Japanese has had several handicaps. Insistence on monotheism leaves little leeway for the squads of Shinto deities; and it is hard to part Japanese from their supreme loyalty to an emperor descended from the gods.

Shinto

Shinto can loosely be called the traditional religion of Japan; it had no founder, developing naturally without fixed dogma into a code of values, customs and a way of thinking.

Although Shinto has no sacred scriptures, there are several highly venerated texts in which the Japanese see the essence of their identity. The Kojiki (Record of Ancient Matters), written in 712, relates the sequence of mythical creation, foundation and unification of the Japanese nation. The Nihonshoki (Chronicles of Japan), written in 720, cover further variants of the myths, the path to nationhood and the importance of ancestral spirit gods. In ancient times, the Japanese had no name for their ethnic religion, but later resorted to the Chinese-influenced term Shinto or 'way of the gods' as a means of distinction from Buddhism or Butsudō or 'way of the Buddha'.

The origins of Shinto lie in the worship of *kami* (spirit gods of natural phenomena) and Japanese are more familiar with the phrase *kami-no-machi* (the way of the kami).

Japanese Myths The mythology of Japan has much in common with neighbouring countries and the South-East Asian and Mongolian area. The creation of Japan is attributed to Izanami (The Male Who Invites) and Izanagi (The Female Who Invites) who alighted on the 'Floating Bridge to Heaven' before marrying and producing the islands and gods of Japan.

Izanami gave birth to 35 gods, but conception of the fire deity proved too hot to handle and she died. Izanagi ventured into the Land of the Dead (Yomi) to rescue his companion

Nyōō, King of Knowledge

but his deal with the King of Yomi fell through and he only managed to escape the Harpies of hell by hefting a huge boulder to block the passage between the lands of the living and the dead. On his return to the Land of the Living, Izanami purified himself in a stream. This act created more deities, the three most important being Amaterasu (the sun goddess, from whom the imperial family later claimed descent), Tsukuyomi no Mikoto (the moon god) and Susano-ō (the god of oceans).

The legend continues with Amaterasu ruling the High Plain of Heaven and Susano-ō given charge of the oceans. Susano-ō missed his mother and stormed around causing general destruction for which he was exiled by his father. In a fit of pique, Susano-ō visited his sister and they had such a quarrel that Amaterasu rushed off to hide in a cave. All the gods assembled round the cave entrance to find a way to make Amaterasu return.

Finally, Okame (the goddess of mirth) performed a ribald dance causing much laughter amongst the onlookers. Amaterasu, attracted by the commotion, peeped out of her cave and was quickly hauled out to restore light to the High Plain of Heaven. The site of these events is near Takachiho in Kyūshū. Susano-ō was deprived of his beard, toenails and fingernails and banished to earth where he landed in Korea before heading to Izumo in Japan.

Okuninushi, a descendant of Susano-ō, took control of Japan, but passed it on to Ninigi, a grandson of Amaterasu. Myth merges into history with Ninigi's grandson, Jimmu, who became the first emperor of Japan. Amaterasu is credited with having supplied the Three Treasures (mirror, sword and jewel) – symbols of the emperor's authority.

Shinto & the Introduction of Buddhism
With the introduction of Buddhism in the 6th century, the Japanese formed a connection between the religions by considering Buddha as a kami (spirit god) from neighbouring China. In the 8th century the kami were included in Buddhist temples as protectors of the Buddhas. Assimilation progressed with the belief that kami, like human beings, were subject to the suffering of rebirth and similarly in need of Buddhist intercession to achieve liberation from this cycle. Buddhist temples were built close to Shinto shrines and Buddhist *sutras* (collections of dialogues and discourses) recited for the kami.

Later, the kami were considered to be incarnations of Bodhisattvas (Buddhas who delay liberation to help others). Buddhist statues were included on Shinto altars or statues of kami were made to represent Buddhist priests.

The interweaving between Shinto and Buddhism continued with little resistance until the end of the Edo period, though a notable exception was the Grand Shrine at Ise.

Shinto as a State Religion During the Edo period, interpretative links were formed with Neo-Confucianism and there was a revival of interest in researching the ancient Japanese roots of Shinto. During the Meiji period, the government intervened to separate Buddhism from Shinto. Under state sponsorship, Shinto was elevated to an intensely nationalistic state religion with the divine emperor as its focus.

Within Shinto, 13 sects were formed. Some were based on mountain worship (for example, the cults of Mt Fuji or Mt Ontake) or on faith healing as the religious experience of a founder (Tenrikyō for example). Other sects followed a tradition of water purification (Misogikyō for example). Sects were also formed around the concepts of Confucianism and Revival Shinto.

After WW II, the Allied occupation issued the Shinto directive which broke the strong militaristic link between state and Shinto; the post-war constitution reinforced this division. Shinto no longer receives financial aid from the state and relies, instead, on donations from believers.

Shinto Shrines The most famous Shinto

shrines are the Meiji-jingū and Yasukuni-jinja in Tokyo, the Ise-jingū at Ise and the Izumo Taisha at Matsue. (See the Highlights section in the Facts for the Visitor chapter for more about the major shrines.)

Shrines differ in architectural styles, but follow a defined pattern. At the entrance to the shrine is the *torii* (gateway) marking the boundary of the sacred precinct. *Shimenawa*, plaited ropes, decorated with strips of white paper *(gohei)*, are strung across the top of the torii. They are also wrapped around sacred rocks or trees or above the actual shrine entrance. Flanking the main path are often pairs of stone dogs *(koma-inu)*, lions or archers. One of the koma-inu, called 'A', has its mouth open to represent the primeval Beginning; the other, called 'Un', has its mouth closed to signify the End.

Further along the approach is an ablution basin *(chōzuya)* where visitors use the ladle *(hishaku)* to rinse both hands before pouring water into a cupped hand to rinse their mouths.

In front of the *haiden* (hall of worship) is an offering box *(saisen-bako)*, above which hangs a gong and a long rope. Visitors lob a coin – Y5 or Y50 coins have an auspicious hole – into the box, then sound the gong twice, make two deep bows, clap loudly twice, bow again twice (once deeply, once lightly) and then step back to the side. Unlike Buddhist temples, no entrance fee is charged for entering a Shinto shrine.

Amulets are a popular buy at the shrine. *Omamori*, special talismans, are purchased at shrines to ensure good luck or ward off evil – taxi-drivers often have a 'traffic-safety' one dangling from the rear-view mirror. Votive plaques made of wood with a picture on one side and a blank space on the other are also common. On the blank side visitors write a wish – success in exams, luck in finding a sweetheart or safe delivery of a healthy child are good examples. Dozens of these plaques can be seen attached to boards. The horse plaques *(ema)*, depicting the divine steed, are favourites.

Fortunes *(omikuji)* are selected by drawing a bamboo stick at random from a box and picking out a fortune slip according to the number indicated on the stick. Luck is classified as *dai-kichi* (great good fortune); *kichi* (good fortune); *shō-kichi* (middling good fortune); and *kyō* (bad luck). If you like the fortune slip you've been given, you can take it home. If you've drawn bad luck, you can tie it to the branch of a tree in the shrine grounds – presumably some other force can then worry about it.

The *kannushi* (chief priest) of the shrine is responsible for religious rites and the administration of the shrine. The priests dress in blue and white; on special occasions they don more ornate clothes and wear an eboshi (a black cap with a protruding, folded tip). The *miko* (shrine maidens) dress in red and white. The ceremonial *kagura* dances performed by the miko can be traced back to shamanistic trances.

The main training centres for priests are Kokugakuin University in Tokyo and Kōgakukan University in Ise. Marriage is allowed and most of the posts are hereditary, mainly held by men.

Shinto Rites & Festivals These events are important components of Japanese life. For newborn children the first shrine visit occurs on the 30th or 100th day after birth. On 15 November, the Shichigosan rite is celebrated by taking children of seven (shichi), five (go) and three (san) to the shrine to be blessed. Seijin no Hi, the day of adulthood, is celebrated on 15 January by young people who have reached the age of 20.

Virtually all marriages are performed according to Shinto ritual by taking a vow before the kami. Funerals, however, are almost always Buddhist. Both religions coexist equably in a traditional Japanese home which has two altars: a Shinto *kamidana* or 'godshelf' and a Buddhist *butsudan* or 'Buddha stand'.

Shinto also plays a role in professional and daily life. A new car can be blessed for accident-free driving; a purification rite is often held for a building site or the shell of a new building; completed buildings are similarly blessed. One of the commonest purification rites is *oharai*, when the priest waves a wand to which are attached thin strips of paper.

Shinto *matsuri* or 'festivals' occur on an annual or occasional basis and are classed as grand, middle-size or minor. In divine processions, a ceremonial palanquin *(mikoshi)* is paraded on the shoulders of participants. Other rites include *misogi* (water purification), tug-of-war, archery, horse-racing, sumō (wrestling), gagaku (sacred music) and lion dances.

Although there are hundreds of Shinto festivals throughout the year, a selection of the most interesting or spectacular ones might include:

Onta Matsuri
    first Sunday in February at Asuka.
Tagata Hōnen-sai
    15 March at Tagata-jinja.
Hana-taue
    first Sunday in June at Chiyoda.
Osore-zan Taisai
    20-24 July on Mt Osore-zan.
Nachi-no Hi Matsuri
    14 July at Kumano Nachi Taisha.
Oyama-sankei
    first day of the eighth lunar month at Hirosaki.
Takachiho no Yo-Kagura
    late November to early February around Takachiho.
On-matsuri
    16-18 December in Nara.

Buddhism

Japanese Buddhism has adapted along individual lines with some decisive variances from other forms of the religion.

Origins of Buddhism The founder of Buddhism was Siddhartha Gautama, the son of King Suddhodana and Queen Mahamaya of the Sakya clan. He was born around 563 BC at Lumbini on the border of present-day Nepal and India.

In his 20s, Prince Siddhartha left his wife and newborn son to follow the path of an ascetic. Despite studying under several masters, he remained dissatisfied and spent another six years undergoing the severest austerities. During this period he gave a graphic account of himself: 'Because of so little nourishment, all my bones became like some withered creepers with knotted joints; my buttocks like a buffalo's hoof; my backbone protruding like a string of balls...' Realising that this was not the right path for him, he gave up fasting and decided to follow his own path to enlightenment. He placed himself cross-legged under a Bodhi tree at Bodhgaya and went into deep meditation for 49 days. During the night of the full moon in May, at the age of 35, he became 'the enlightened' or 'awakened one' – the Buddha (Nyorai in Japanese).

Shortly afterwards, Buddha delivered his first sermon, 'Setting in Motion the Wheel of Truth', at Deer Park near Sarnath. Then, as the number of his followers grew, he founded a monastic community and codified the principles according to which the monks should live. The Buddha continued to preach and travel for 45 years until his death at the age of 80 in 483 BC. To his followers, Buddha was also known as Sakyamuni (the sage of the Sakya clan or 'Shaka' in Japanese). Buddhists believe that he is one of the many Buddhas who appeared in the past – and that more will appear in the future.

Approximately 140 years after Buddha's death, the Buddhist community diverged into two schools: Hinayana (the Lesser Vehicle) and Mahayana (the Greater Vehicle). The essential difference between the two was that Hinayana supported those who strove for the salvation of the individual, whereas Mahayana supported those who strove for the salvation of all beings. Hinayana prospered in South India and later spread to Sri Lanka, Burma, Thailand, Cambodia, Indonesia and Malaysia. Mahayana spread to inner Asia, Mongolia, Siberia, Japan, China and Tibet.

The basis of Buddhism is that all suffering in life comes from the overindulgence of our desires. Suppression of our sensual desires will eventually lead to a state of nirvana where desire is extinct and we are free from its delusion.

Buddha, who was not a god and did not even claim to be the only enlightened one, felt that the way to nirvana was for our karma (central spirit) to follow the eight-fold path of right thinking, right behaviour and the like. For an over-affluent Western world, beginning to doubt the potency of the materialist concept of life, Buddhism has obvious charms.

Development of Buddhism in Japan Buddhism was introduced to Japan via Korea in the 6th century. Shōtoku Taishi, acknowledged as the 'father of Japanese Buddhism', drew heavily on Chinese culture to form a centralised state and gave official recognition to Buddhism by constructing temples in and around the capital. Horyū-ji, close to Nara, is the most celebrated temple in Japan from this period.

Nara Period The establishment of the first permanent capital at Heijōkyō (present-day Nara) in 710 also marked the consolidation of Buddhism and Chinese culture in Japan.

In 741, Emperor Shōmu issued a decree for a network of state temples (Kokubun-ji) to be established in each province. The centrepiece of this network was Tōdai-ji with its gigantic Vairocana Buddha (Daibutsu).

Nara Buddhism revolved around six schools (Ritsu, Jōjitsu, Kusha, Sanron, Hossō and Kegon) which covered the whole range of Buddhist thought as received from China. Three of these schools have continued to this day: the Kegon school, based at the Tōdai-ji Temple; the Hossō school, based at the Kōfuku-ji Temple and Yakushi-ji Temple; and the Ritsu school, based at the Tōshōdai-ji Temple.

Heian Period In 794, the capital was moved from Nara to Heian-kyō (present-day Kyoto). During the Heian period, political power drifted away from centralised government into the hands of aristocrats and their clans who became a major source of Buddhist support.

The new schools, which introduced Mikkyō (Esoteric Buddhism) from China, were founded by separate leaders on sacred mountains away from the orthodox pressures of the Nara schools.

The Tendai school (derived from a Chinese school on Mt Tian-tai in China) was founded by Saichō (762-822), also known as Dengyō Daishi, who established a base at the Enryaku-ji Temple on Mt Hiei-zan, near Kyoto.

Saichō travelled to Mt Tian-tai in China where he studied meditation and the Lotus Sutra. On his return, he expanded his studies to include Zen meditation and Tantric ritual. The Tendai school was only officially recognised a few days after his death, but the Enryaku-ji Temple developed into one of Japan's key Buddhist centres and was the source of all the important schools (Pure Land, Zen and Nichiren) in the following Kamakura period.

The Shingon school (derived from the Chinese term for mantra) was established by Kūkai (774-835), often referred to as Kōbō

17th Century Wood-block Print

Daishi, at the Kongōbu-ji Temple on Mt Kōya-san and at the Tō-ji Temple in Kyoto.

Kūkai trained for government service, but decided at the age of 18 to switch his studies from Confucianism and Taoism to Buddhism. He travelled as part of a mission to Chang-an (present-day Xian) in China where he immersed himself in Esoteric Buddhism. On his return, he made a broad impact on cultural life, not only spreading and sponsoring the study of Mikkyō, but also compiling the first Chinese-Japanese dictionary and the hiragana syllabary which made it much easier for Japanese to put their language into writing.

During this period, assimilation with Shinto continued. Many shrine temples *jingū-ji* were built for Buddhist rituals in the grounds of Shinto shrines. Theories were propounded which held the Shinto kami to be manifestations of Buddhas or Bodhisattvas. The collapse of law and order during these times inspired a general feeling of pessimism in society and encouraged belief in the Mappō or 'End of the Law' theory which predicted an age of darkness with a decline in Buddhist religion. This set the stage for subsequent Buddhist schools to introduce the notion of Buddhist saviour figures such as Amida.

Kamakura Period In this period, marked by savage clan warfare and the transfer of the capital to Kamakura, three schools emerged from Tendai tradition.

The Jōdo (Pure Land) school, founded by Hōnen (1133-1212), shunned scholasticism in favour of the Nembutsu, a simple prayer

---

Zen Buddhism

Probably the most widely known aspect of Japanese Buddhism in the West today was introduced as a separate school from Sung China. Its origins can be traced to Daruma, an Indian priest whose teaching spread to China in the 5th century. Daruma stressed meditation and striving for enlightenment from within, rather than seeking 'outside' help.

Japanese New Year dolls portray Daruma as a fierce, squat, lustrous red figure who is legless – his legs were reputed to have withered away after endless years of meditation.

Although Zen emphasises the direct, intuitive approach rather than rational analysis, there are dozens of books available on the subject. Two of my favourites are *Zen & Japanese Culture* (Princeton University Press, Princeton, New Jersey, 1971) by D T Suzuki and *Zen Flesh, Zen Bones* (Penguin Books, London, 1971) compiled by Paul Reps.

Two major schools of Zen were formed in Japan: Rinzai and Sōtō. Eisai (1141-1214), originally, a Tendai monk, visited China twice before returning to set up bases for the Rinzai school in Kamakura and Kyoto. Rinzai retained eclectic links with preceding Japanese schools and retained some esoteric Buddhism rituals in his teachings.

The main technique for enlightenment involved a dialogue between master and disciple which concentrated on *kōan* (topical riddles) usually culled from the experience of previous masters. The Rinzai school found support among influential samurai who were attracted to the spartan discipline. The meticulous attention to detail in all aspects of daily life found expression in components of Japanese culture such as Nō drama, flower arrangement *(ikebana)*, tea ceremony *(chanoyu)*, tea gardens *(tei-en)*, calligraphy *(shodō)* and martial arts *(budō)*.

Dōgen (1200-1253) introduced the Sōtō Zen school from China. The main technique of this school consisted of long sessions of *zazen* (sitting Zen) – practise itself was considered enlightenment.

Dōgen sought support for his school among provincial samurai and the common people. He settled first in Kyoto, but soon shifted his base to the rural setting of the Eihei-ji Temple (near Fukui) which is now the thriving headquarters and training centre of the Sōtō school. Sōtō has a larger membership than Rinzai and branches have flourished abroad, notably in the USA. ∎

that required the believer to recite Namu Amida Butsu or 'Hail Amida Buddha' as a path to salvation. This 'no-frills' approach – easy to practise, easy to understand – was popular with the common folk.

Shinran (1173-1262), a disciple of Hōnen, took a more radical step with his master's teaching and broke away to form the Jōdo Shin (True Pure Land) school. The core belief of this school considered that Amida had *already* saved everyone – hence to recite the Nembutsu was an expression of gratitude, not a petition for salvation.

The Nichiren School bears the name of its founder, Nichiren (1222-82), a fiery character who spurned traditional teachings to embrace the Lotus Sutra as the 'right' teaching. Followers learned to recite Namu Myōhō Rengekyō or 'Hail the Miraculous Law of the Lotus Sutra'. Nichiren's strident demands for religious reform of government caused antagonism all round and he was frequently booted into exile.

The Nichiren school increased its influence in later centuries; the famous Hokke-ikki uprising in the 15th century was led by Nichiren adherents. Many of the new religious movements in present-day Japan – Sōka Gakkai for example – can be linked to Nichiren.

Later Developments During the Tokugawa period (1600-1867), Buddhism was consolidated as a state institution. When the shogunate banned Christianity, a parallel regulation rigidly required every Japanese to become a certified member of the local temple.

During the Meiji period, Shinto was given priority and separated from Buddhism which suffered a backlash of resentment. Today, Buddhism prospers in Japan both in the form of traditional schools and in a variety of new movements.

Buddhist Gods There are dozens of gods in the Japanese Buddhist pantheon. Images vary from temple to temple, depending on the religious schools or period of construction, but three of the commonest images are those of Shaka (Sanscrit: Sakyamuni), the Historical Buddha; Amida (Sanskrit: Amitabha), the Buddha of the Western Paradise and Miroku (Sanskrit: Maitreya), the Buddha of the Future. For the optimistic follower, who is prepared to wait around a while, some sources schedule the appearance of Miroku in about 5670 million years.

Kannon (Sanskrit: Avalokitesvara) is the 'one who hears their cries' and is available in no less than 33 different versions, including the goddess of mercy, a female form popular with expectant mothers. When Christianity was banned, Japanese believers ingeniously kept faith with the Holy Virgin by creating a clone 'Maria Kannon'.

Jizō is often depicted as a monk with a staff in one hand and a jewel in the other. Pieces of clothing or red bibs draped around Jizō figures are an attempt to cover the souls of dead children. According to legend, this patron of travellers, children and expectant mothers helps the souls of dead children perform their task of building walls of pebbles on the banks of Sai-no-kawara, the river of the underworld. Believers place stones on or around Jizō statues as additional help.

Recently, there have been public murmurings about the maintenance of Jizō statues and the emotional blackmail involved when mothers of aborted babies receive demands from temples for donations.

Buddhist Temples Temples vary widely in their construction, depending on the type of school and the historical era of construction. A selection of the finest Buddhist temples would include many in and around Kyoto, Nara and Kōya-san plus the Eihei-ji (near Fukui) in Chūbu; the Chūson-ji (Hiraizumi) in Tōhoku; Zenkō-ji in Nagano; and, close to Tokyo, the temple complexes of Nikkō and Kamakura. (See the Highlights section in the Facts for the Visitor chapter for a list of major temples.)

An admission fee, ranging between Y200 and Y500, is usually charged at the entrance to these very important temples. Sometimes an additional fee is necessary to visit the museum of temple treasures, the temple gardens or for a cup of tea complete with ceremony. Talismans and fortunes (see the Shinto section) are often on sale near the entrance or in one of the halls. An attractive souvenir available for about Y1000 at many temples is the *shuenshu*, a cloth-covered, pocket-sized booklet with a concertina of folding pages. Railway stations, tourist attractions and temples provide ink pads and stamps for visitors to print souvenir logos in their booklet. For a small fee, you can ask a temple monk to give an artistic touch to your booklet by adding calligraphy.

The entrance is usually marked by a main gate, often of gigantic proportions and sometimes flanked by Niō, muscle-bound god kings from Hindu tradition, who are stripped for action as guardians. The central image, in the main hall, has offerings of smouldering incense sticks, food or flowers placed before it. Visitors stand in front of the image, press their palms together close to the chest and pray.

In the temple surroundings, there are often cemeteries – at Kōya-san there is a cemetery stretching for many hectares and spanning the centuries. Virtually all funerals in Japan are Buddhist.

Common Signs in Temples	Kanji Script
entrance	入口
exit	出口
follow the route	順路
garden	苑
gate	門
hall	堂
no admittance	立入禁止
pagoda	塔
palace	殿
palace/shrine	宮
pavilion	亭
pavilion	閣
pond	池
shrine	宮
teahouse	亭
temple	寺
temple	院
toilet	手洗
tower	楼
tower	塔

Shugendō

This somewhat offbeat Buddhist school incorporates ancient Shamanistic rites, Shinto beliefs and ascetic Buddhist traditions. The founder was En no Gyōja, to whom legendary powers of exorcism and magic are ascribed. He is credited with the enlightenment of kami (spirit gods), converting them to *gongen* (manifestations of Buddhas). Practitioners of Shugendō, called *yamabushi* (mountain priests), train both body and spirit with arduous exercises in the mountains.

Until the Meiji era, many of Japan's mountains were the domain of yamabushi who proved popular with the locals for their skills in sorcery and exorcism. During the Meiji era, Shinto was elevated to a state religion and Shugendō was barred as being culturally debased. Today, yamabushi are more common on tourist brochures than in the flesh, but Shugendō survives on mountains such as Dewa Sanzan and Omine-san.

Confucianism

Although Confucianism is essentially a code of ethics, it has exerted a strong enough influence to become part of Japanese religion. Confucianism entered Japan via Korea in the 5th century. To regulate social behaviour, Confucius took the family unit as his starting point and stressed the importance of the five human relationships: master and subject, father and son, elder brother and younger brother, husband and wife, friend and friend.

The strict observance of this social 'pecking order', radiating from individual families to encompass the whole of society, has evolved over centuries to become a core concept in Japanese life. The influence of Confucianism can be seen in such disparate examples as the absolute loyalty demanded in Bushidō (the code of the samurai), the extreme allegiance to the emperor in WW II, the low status of women and the hierarchical ties in a modern Japanese company.

Folklore & Gods

Japan has a curious medley of folk gods. Common ones include:

Shichifuku-jin are the seven gods of luck – a happy band of well-wishers plucked from Indian, Chinese and Japanese sources. Their images are popular at New Year when they are often depicted as a group on a treasure ship *(takarabune)*.

Ebisu is the patron of seafarers and a symbol for prosperity in business. He carries a fishing rod with a large red, sea bream dangling on the line and can be recognised by his beaming, bearded face.

Bishamon is the god of war. He wears a helmet, a suit of armour and brandishes a spear. As a protector of Buddhism, he can be seen carrying a pagoda.

Daikoku, the god of wealth, has a bag full of treasures slung over his left shoulder and a lucky mallet in his right hand.

Benzaiten is the goddess of art, skilled in eloquence, music, literature and wisdom. She holds a Japanese mandolin (biwa) and is often escorted by a sea snake.

Fukurokuju looks after wealth and longevity. He has a bald, dome-shaped head, dumpy body and wears long, flowing robes.

Jurojin also covers longevity. He sports a distinguished white beard and holds a cane to which is attached a scroll listing the life terms of all living beings.

Hotei, the god of happiness, is instantly recognisable (in Japan and elsewhere in Asia) by his large paunch and Cheshire-cat grin. Originally a Chinese beggar priest, he is the only god in this group whose antecedents can be traced to a human being. His bulging bag provides for the needy and is never empty.

A variety of fabulous creatures inhabit Japanese folklore and crop up regularly in shops, festivals and shrines:

Tanuki is a curious badger-like figure with a reputation for fickleness in bestowing favours. Statues usually depict this fellow in an upright position with straw headgear and clasping a bottle of saké. The scrotum deserves special respect for its legendary size which is reputed to have suffocated hapless hunters!

Kitsuné is a fox, but for Japanese it also has strong connections with the supernatural and is worshipped in Japan at over 30,000 Inari shrines as the messenger of the harvest god. The Fushimi Inari Taisha Shrine near Kyoto is the largest of its kind, crammed with fox statues.

Maneki-neko, the Beckoning Cat, is a very common sight outside shops or restaurants. The raised left paw attracts customers and their money. Cats were introduced to Japan from China and Korea and are believed to possess magical powers. Sailors favoured a three-coloured cat which protected against tempests; another type of cat was believed to be a monster intent on slaying and devouring humans. Corpses were often laid out with a sword beside them to protect against possession by malevolent cat spirits.

Tengu are mountain goblins with a capricious nature, sometimes abducting children, sometimes returning those that are missing. Their unmistakable feature is a lengthy nose, like a proboscis. The chief Tengu broke the Buddhist code and was condemned to vomit throughout the day.

A *kappa* is a boyish river sprite with webbed hands and feet. It has a reputation for mischief, such as dragging horses into rivers or stealing cucumbers. The source of its power is a depression on top of its head which must always contain water. A crafty method to outwit a kappa is to bow to it. When the kappa – Japanese to the core – bows back, it empties the water from its head and loses its power!

Christianity

Portuguese missionaries introduced Christianity to Japan in the 16th century. In 1549, Francis Xavier landed at Kagoshima, on Kyūshū. At first, the feudal lords (daimyō) seemed eager to convert together with their subjects. However, the motivation was probably less a question of faith and more an interest in gaining trade advantages.

The initial tolerance shown by Oda Nobunaga was soon reversed by his successor, Toyotomi Hideyoshi, who considered the Jesuits a colonial threat. The religion was banned in 1587 and 26 Christians were crucified in Nagasaki 10 years later. After expelling the remaining missionaries in 1614, Japan clammed up to the outside world for several centuries. During this time a small number of Christians kept their faith active as a type of 'back-room Buddhism'. Christian missions were allowed back at an early stage during the Meiji era to build churches and found hospitals and schools, many of which still exist.

Despite these efforts, Christianity has not met with wide acceptance amongst the Japanese who tend to feel more at home with

Shinto and Buddhism. The number of Christians in Japan is a very small portion of the population – possibly one million.

New Religions

A variety of new religions have taken root in Japan. They cover a wide range of beliefs from founder cults to faith healing. Easily the largest of these new religions is Sōka Gakkai (Creative Education Society). Founded in the '30s, it follows Nichiren's teachings and numbers over 20 million followers. (The Clean Government Party (Komeito) was founded in 1964 as a political offshoot of Sōka Gakkai, but now tends to play down the association. It is the second largest opposition party and, as its name implies, takes a dim view of corruption.)

HOLIDAYS & FESTIVALS

In 1873, the Japanese switched from the lunar calendar to the Gregorian calendar used in the West. They still follow the animal zodiac of the lunar calendar but indulge in an earlier celebration for the arrival of the zodiacal New Year on 1 January.

Years are counted in Japan according to two systems: Western and Imperial. The Western system sets the date from the birth of Christ. The Imperial system calculates the years from the accession of the emperor. The reign of each emperor is assigned a special name. The reign of the previous emperor, Hirohito (1926-89), is known as the Shōwa (Enlightened Peace) era. Thus 1988 was Shōwa 63. The present emperor, Akihito, reigns in the Heisei era, so 1989 was Heisei 1 and 1990, Heisei 2.

When a public holiday falls on a Sunday, the following Monday is taken as a holiday. You can expect a total sell-out for travel and lodging during the New Year (29 December to 6 January), Golden Week (27 April to 6 May) and mid-August.

Japan has hundreds of national and local festivals throughout the year. The biggest and most famous can attract thousands of spectators, but the smaller local ones can also be a lot of fun.

National Holidays

Ganjitsu (New Year's Day)
   1 January
Seijin-no-hi (Adult's Day)
   15 January
Kenkoku Kinen-no-bi (National Foundation Day)
   11 February
Shunbun-no-hi (Spring Equinox)
   21 March (approximately)
Midori-no-hi (Green Day)
   29 April
Kenpo Kinen-bi (Constitution Day)
   3 May
Kodomo-no-hi (Children's Day)
   5 May
Keiro-no-hi (Respect-for-the-Aged Day)
   15 September
Shubun-no-hi (Autumn Equinox)
   23 September (approximately)
Taiiku-no-hi (Sports Day)
   10 October
Bunka-no-hi (Culture Day)
   3 November
Kinro Kansha-no-hi (Labour Thanksgiving Day)
   23 November
Tennō Tanjōbi (Emperor's Birthday)
   23 December

National Festivals

O Shogatsu (New Year)
   1-3 January. New Year celebrations include much eating and drinking, visits to shrines or temples and the paying of respects to relatives and business associates.
Seijin-no-hi (Adult's Day)
   15 January. Ceremonies are held for boys and girls who have reached the age of majority (20). To celebrate the end of winter and drive out evil spirits the Japanese indulge in *setsubun* or bean throwing whilst chanting 'fuku wa uchi oni wa soto' (welcome good fortune, out with the devils).
Hina Matsuri (Doll Festival)
   3 March. During this festival old dolls are displayed and young girls are presented with special dolls *(hina)* which represent ancient figures from the imperial court.
Knickers Giving Day
   14 March. This is a slightly bizarre recent addition to the collection of festivals in Japan. The idea is that men should reciprocate the gift of chocolates on 14 February, St Valentine's Day, with a gift of panties for their lady!
Hanami (Blossom Viewing)
   February – April. The Japanese delight in the brief blossom viewing seasons. The usual sequence is plum in February, peach in March and cherry in late March or early April.

O Higan (Equinoctial Week)
> March and September. At this time, family graves are visited and temples hold memorial services for the dead.

Golden Week
> 29 April-5 May. Golden Week is so called because it bunches together Green Day (29 April), Constitution Day (3 May) and Children's Day (5 May). This is definitely not a time to be on the move since transport and lodging in popular holiday areas can be booked solid.

Kodomo-no-hi (Children's Day)
> 5 May. This is a holiday dedicated to children, especially boys. Families fly paper streamers of carp *(koi)* which symbolise male strength.

Tanabata Matsuri (Star Festival)
> 7 July. The two stars Vega and Altair meet in the Milky Way on this night. According to a myth (originally Chinese), a princess and a peasant shepherd were forbidden to meet, but this was the only time in the year when the two star-crossed lovers could sneak a tryst. Children copy out poems on streamers and love poems are written on banners which are hung out on display. An especially ornate version of this festival is celebrated 6-8 August in Sendai.

O Bon (Festival of the Dead)
> 13-16 July and August. According to Buddhist tradition, this is a time when ancestors return to earth. Lanterns are lit and floated on rivers, lakes or the sea to signify the return of the departed to the underworld. Since most Japanese try to return to their native village at this time of year, this is one of the most crowded times of year to travel or look for lodging.

Shichi-Go-San (Seven-Five-Three Festival)
> 15 November. Traditionally this is a festival in honour of girls who are three and seven and boys who are five. Children are dressed in their finest clothes and taken to shrines or temples where prayers are offered for good fortune.

Local Festivals

Japan has plenty of local matsuri (festivals) taking place throughout the year. Kyoto, Nara and Tokyo are especially famous for local festivals, but elsewhere too there are special matsuri which often involve the display of *mikoshi* (portable shrines). The religion section includes details of major Shinto matsuri.

Festival details are also provided throughout this book under relevant sections for individual cities or regions. TIC in Tokyo and Kyoto provide up-to-date listings of festivals and should be able to provide a useful JNTO leaflet entitled *Annual Events in Japan*. If you do base a visit around festivals, remember that accommodation can be swamped by visitors from all over the country, so book well in advance.

LANGUAGE

It is something of a cliché that Japanese spend years studying English at school and often at university or college without even being able to string a coherent English sentence together at the end of it all. This is at least partly due to the language-teaching techniques employed in Japanese classrooms, but part of the problem can also be attributed to translation difficulties. Structurally, Japanese and English are so very different that word-for-word translations will often produce almost incomprehensible sentences.

To English speakers, Japanese language patterns often seem to be back to front and lacking essential information. For example, where an English speaker would say 'I'm going to the shop' a Japanese speaker would say 'shop to going', omitting the subject pronoun (I) altogether and putting the verb at the end of the sentence. To make matters worse, many moods which are indicated at the beginning of a sentence in English occur at the end of a sentence in Japanese, as in the Japanese sentence 'Japan to going if' – 'if you're going to Japan'.

Fortunately for visitors to Japan, it's not all bad news. Unlike other languages in the region (Chinese, Vietnamese and Thai among others) Japanese is not tonal and the pronunciation system is fairly easy to master. In fact, with a little effort, getting together a repertoire of traveller's phrases ('this is the pen of my aunt' etc) should be no trouble – the only problem will be understanding what people say back to you.

The biggest problem for visitors to Japan who have never studied Japanese is the writing system. Japanese has one of the most complex writing systems in the world, using three different scripts (four if you include the increasingly used Roman script *romaji*). The most difficult of the three, for foreigners and

Japanese alike, is *kanji*, the ideographic script developed by the Chinese. Unfortunately for the Japanese, while this script works perfectly well for the Chinese language, the Japanese language does not fare so well. There is a kind of imperfect fit between the Japanese spoken language and kanji that results in a large number of variant readings (pronunciations) for any given character.

Even worse, because of the differences between the grammar of their language and that of Chinese, the Japanese were forced to supplement kanji with an alphabet of syllables, or a syllabary, known as *hiragana*. Finally, Japanese has a special script (another syllabary) that is used largely for representing foreign-loan words such as *terebi* (television) and *femunisuto* (feminist); this script is known as *katakana*.

The romaji used in this book attempts to follow the Hepburn system of romanisation with macrons being used to indicate long vowels. Most place names will use a combination of romaji and English - the romaji suffix will in most cases be separated from the proper name by a hyphen and followed by its English translation. For example: Tōdai-ji Temple (*ji* is the romaji word for temple); Shimabara-hantō Peninsula (*hantō* means peninsula) and Ise-jingū Shrine (*jingū* means shrine). These suffixes, however, will not be hyphenated when they are not followed by a direct English translation: for example, Suizenji Garden (the 'ji' for temple will not be hyphenated) and Ōshima-kōen Park (the *shima* for island will not be hyphenated).

If you're thinking of tackling the Japanese writing system before you go or while you're in Japan, your best bet would be to start with hiragana or katakana. The reasoning behind this is that there are around 2000 kanji in everyday use and it takes at least a year of pretty solid work before any real progress is made in learning them. Hiragana and katakana, on the other hand, only have 48 characters each and can be learned within a week. You can practise your katakana on restaurant menus, where such things as *kōhii*

(coffee) and *keiki* (cake) are frequently found and practise your hiragana on train journeys – station names are indicated in hiragana.

If all this seems a bit daunting, don't let it put you off. The Japanese are a very courteous people and will reward your attempts to make yourself understood in their language with liberal dollops of praise. Remember that the Japanese response to praise is a humble deprecation, not a big smile and 'thank you'. The expression *sono koto wa arimasen* ('not at all') is an appropriate response when someone flatters you.

The following selection of Japanese phrases will see you through some of the more common situations experienced by travellers to Japan. For a more comprehensive guide to making yourself understood in Japan, get a copy of Lonely Planet's *Japanese Phrasebook*. This book has all the phrases you need for travelling in Japan, charts for learning hiragana and katakana and Japanese script for all the phrases used in the book.

Pronunciation

a	as the 'a' in 'apple'
e	as the 'e' in 'get'
i	as the 'i' in 'macaroni'
o	as the 'o' in 'lot'
u	as the 'u' in 'flu'

Vowels that have a bar (or macron) over them (*ā, ē, ō, ū*) are pronounced the same as standard vowels except that the sound is held twice as long.

Consonants are generally pronounced as in English, with the following exceptions:

f	this sound is produced by pursing the lips and blowing lightly
g	as the 'g' in 'goal' at the start of a word; as the 'ng' in 'sing' in the middle of a word
r	more like an 'l' than an 'r'

Greetings & Civilities

The all-purpose title *san* is used after a name as an honorific, the equivalent of Mr, Miss, Mrs and Ms.

Good morning.
ohayō gozaimasu
おはようございます

Good afternoon.
konnichiwa
こんにちは

Good evening.
konbanwa
こんばんは

How are you?
o-genki desuka?
お元気ですか？

Fine.(appropriate response)
okagesamade
おかげさまで

Goodbye.
sayōnara
さようなら

See you later.
ja mata
じゃまた

Excuse me.
sumimasen
すみません

I'm sorry.
gomen nasai
ごめんなさい

I am disturbing you.(when entering a room)
o-jama shimasu
おじゃまします

Thank you.
arigatō gozaimasu
ありがとうございます

Thanks for taking care of me.(when leaving)
o-sewa ni narimashita
おせわになりました

Please.(when offering something)
dōzo
どうぞ

Please.(when asking for something)
onegai shimasu
お願いします

OK.
kekko desu
けっこです

Yes.
hai
はい

No.
iie
いいえ

No, it differs.
chigaimasu
違います

No, it differs somewhat.
chotto chigaimasu
ちょっと違います

Small Talk
I don't understand.
wakarimasen
わかりません

Please say it again more slowly.
motto yukuri mō ichidō itte kudasai
もっとゆっくりもう一度言って下さい

What is this called?
kore wa nan-to yomimasuka?
これは、何とよみますか？

My name is ...
watakushi no namae wa ... desu
私の名前は…です

What's your name?
o-namae wa nan desuka?
お名前は何ですか？

Where are you from?
dochira kara irasshaimasuka?
どちらからいらっしゃいますか？

It's up to you.(when asked to make a choice)
omakase shimasu
おまかせします

Is it OK to take a photo?
sasshin o toru ga, ii desuka?
写真を取るがいいですか？

Nationality
Australia
ōsutoraria
オーストラリア

Canada
kanada
カナダ

Denmark
denmāku
デンマーク

Germany
doitsu
ドイシ

France
furansu
フランス

Holland
oranda
オランダ

Italy
itarii
イタリー

Japan
nihon
日本

New Zealand
nūjirando
ニューシーランド

Sweden
sūeden
スウェーデン

Switzerland
suisu
スイス

UK
igirisu
イギリス

USA
amerika
アメリカ

Accommodation
Where is ...?
... wa doko desuka?
…はどこですか？

Do you have any vacancies?
aita heya wa arimasuka?
空いた部屋はありますか？

a single room
shinguru rūmu
シングルルーム

a double room
daburu rūmua
ダブルルーム

room with a bath
basu tsuki no heya
バス付きの部屋

I don't have a reservation.
yoyaku shite imasen
予約していません

Getting Around
How much is the fare to ...?
... made ikura desuka?
…までいくらですか？

Does this train go to ...?
kono densha wa ... e ikimasuka?
この電車は…へ行きますか？

Is the next station ...?
tsugi no eki wa ... desuka?
次の駅は…ですか？

Will you tell me when we get to ...?
... ga ketara oshiete kudasaimasuka?
…がけたら教えて下さいますか？

Where is the ... exit?
... guchi wa doko desuka?
…口はどこですか？

east/west/north/south
higashi/nishi/kita/minami
東/西/北/南

Do you have an English subway map?
eigo no chikatetsu no chizu ga arimasuka?
英語の地下鉄の地図がありますか？

Where is this address please?
kono jūsho wa doko desuka?
この住所はどこですか？

Excuse me, but can you help me please?
sumimasen ga, watashi o tasukeru ga yoroshi desuka?
すみませんが、私を助けるがよろしですか？

Emergencies

Help me!
tasukete!
助けて！

Watch out!
ki o tsukete!
気をつけて！

Thief!
dorobō!
どろぼう！

Call the police!
keisatsu o yonde kudasai!
警察を叫んで下さい！

Call a doctor!
isha o yonde kudasai!
医者を叫んで下さい！

Food

Do you have an English menu?
eigo no menyū ga arimasuka?
英語のメニューがありますか？

I'm a vegetarian.
watashi wa saishoku-shugisha desu
私は菜食主義者です

Do you have any vegetarian meals?
saishoku-shugisha no yō no ryōri wa arimasuka?
菜食主義者の用の料理はありますか？

What do you recommend?
o-susume wa nan desuka?
お勧めは何ですか？

Please bring the bill.
o-kanjō onegaishimasu
お勘定お願いします

Shopping

How much is this?
kore wa ikura desuka?
これはいくらですか？

It's too expensive.
taka-sugimasu
高過ぎます

I'll take this one.
kore o itadakemasu
これをいただけます

I'm just looking.
miru dake desu
見るだけです

Health

How do you feel?
kibun wa ikaga desuka?
気分はいかがですか？

I don't feel well.
kibun wa suguremasen
気分はすぐれません

It hurts here.
koko ga itain desu
ここが痛いんです

I have asthma.
watashi wa zenzoku desu
私はぜんぞくです

I have diarrhoea.
geri shite imasu
下痢しています

I have a toothache.
ha ga itamimasu
牙が痛みます

I'm allergic to antibiotics/penicillin.
kōsei busshitsu/penishirin ni arerugii desu
抗生物質/ペニシリンにアレルギです

Numbers

0	*zero*	〇
1	*ichi*	一
2	*ni*	二
3	*san*	三
4	*yon/shi*	四
5	*go*	五
6	*roku*	六
7	*nana/shichi*	七
8	*hachi*	八
9	*kyū/ku*	九
10	*jū*	十
11	*jūichi*	十一
12	*jūni*	十二
13	*jūsan*	十三
14	*jūyon*	十四
20	*nijū*	二十
21	*nijūichi*	二十一
30	*sanjū*	三十
100	*hyaku*	百
200	*nihyaku*	二百
223	*nihyaku nijūsan*	二百二十三
1000	*sen*	千
5000	*gosen*	五千
10,000	*ichiman*	一万
20,000	*niman*	二万
100,000	*jūman*	十万
1,000,000	*hyakuman*	百万

Facts for the Visitor

VISAS

Tourist and business visitors of many nationalities staying less than 90 days are not required to obtain a visa. Visits involving employment or other remunerated activity require an appropriate visa.

Like many other places in the world, the locals get much better treatment on arrival than the visitors. It's not unusual at Tokyo's Narita Airport for gaijin (foreigners) to be standing in line an hour after the last Japanese has been processed by immigration.

Reciprocal Visa Exemptions

Many visitors who are not planning to engage in any remunerative activities while in Japan are exempt from obtaining visas. Stays of up to six months are permitted for citizens of Austria, Germany, Ireland, Mexico, Switzerland and the UK. Stays of up to three months are permitted for citizens of Argentina, Belgium, Canada, Denmark, Finland, France, Iceland, Israel, Italy, Malaysia, Netherlands, New Zealand, Norway, Singapore, Spain, Sweden, the USA and a number of other countries.

Visitors from Australia and South Africa are amongst those nationals requiring a visa. This is usually issued free, but passport photographs are required and a return or onward ticket must be shown.

Embassies & Consulates

Australia
  112 Empire Circuit, Yarralumla, Canberra, ACT 2600 (tel 733-244); there are also consulates in Brisbane (tel 221-5188), Melbourne (tel 867-3244), Perth (tel 321-3455) and Sydney (tel 231-3455).
Canada
  255 Sussex Drive, Ottawa, Ontario K1N 9E6 (tel 236-8541); there are also consulates in Edmonton (tel 422-3752), Montreal (tel 866-3429), Toronto (tel 363-7038), Vancouver (tel 684-5868) and Winnipeg (tel 943-5554).
France
  7 Ave Hoche, 75008-Paris (tel 47-66-02-22)

Germany
  Bundeskanzlerplatz, Bonn-Center HI-701, D-5300 Bonn 1 (tel (0228) 5001)
Hong Kong
  25th Floor, Bank of America Tower, 12 Harcourt Rd, Central (tel 5-221184)
Ireland
  22 Ailesbury Rd, Dublin 4 (tel 69-40-33)
Israel
  Asia House, 4 Weizman St, 64 239 Tel-Aviv (tel 03-257-292)
New Zealand
  7th Floor, Norwich Insurance House, 3-11 Hunter St, Wellington 1 (tel 731-540); there is also a consulate in Auckland (tel 34-106)
Singapore
  16 Nassim Rd, Singapore 1025 (tel 235-8855)
Thailand
  1674 New Petchburi Rd, Bangkok 10310 (tel 252-6151)
UK
  43-46 Grosvenor St, London W1X OBA (tel 493-6030)
USA
  2520 Massachusetts Ave, NW Washington DC 20008-2869 (tel 939-6800); there are also consulates in Anchorage (tel 279-8428), Atlanta (tel 892-2700), Boston (tel 973-9772), Chicago (tel 280-0400), Honolulu (tel 536-2226), Houston (tel 652-2977), Kansas City (tel 471-0111), Los Angeles (tel 624-8305), New Orleans (tel 529-2101), New York (371-8222), Portland (tel 221-1811) and San Francisco (tel 777-3533).

Working Holiday Visas

Australians, Canadians and New Zealanders between the ages of 18 and 25 (the age limit can be pushed up to 30) can apply for a working holiday visa. This visa allows a six month stay and two six-month extensions. The visa's aim is to enable young people to travel extensively during their stay and for this reason employment is supposed to be part time or temporary, although in practice, many people work full time.

A working holiday visa is much easier to obtain than a proper visa and is popular with Japanese employers as it can save them a great deal of inconvenience. Applicants must have the equivalent of A$2000 of funds and an onward ticket from Japan, or A$3000 in funds without the ticket.

Working Visas

The ever-increasing number of foreigners clamouring for a role in the Asian economic miracle has prompted much stricter visa requirements for Japan. New immigration laws introduced in June 1990 designate legal employment categories for foreigners and specify standards of experience and qualifications. Working visas must be organised outside Japan.

It's unclear what this will mean for the many foreigners involved in freelance teaching and hostessing while on tourist visas, but those intending to work legally should try to organise their job and visa before they arrive.

Visa Extensions

It is usually possible to get a single 90 day extension on a tourist visa but further extensions require a letter of guarantee. The guarantor should preferably be Japanese, although a resident foreigner is acceptable. Processing can take some time so don't leave extending till the last minute. Many long-term visitors to Japan get around the extension problem by briefly leaving the country, usually going to Hong Kong, South Korea or Taiwan; however, the immigration officials can be very difficult when they return.

Aliens

Anyone, and this includes tourists, who stays more than 90 days is required to obtain an Alien Registration Card. The card can be obtained at the municipal office of the city, town or ward in which you're living but moving to another area requires that you re-register within 14 days.

You must carry your Alien Registration Card at all times as the police can stop you and ask to see the card. If you don't have the card, you will be taken back to the station and will have to wait there until someone fetches it for you.

WORKING IN JAPAN

The high value of the yen makes Japan a very attractive place for a working holiday. Many foreigners end up with a salary they could never command in their own country and stay for years. Others come to study and find themselves lingering ever longer as they struggle to master the spiralling complexities of the language or are confronted with the difficulties of parting with their egos through zazen meditation. By far the largest working group, however, are those that come for a six to 12 month stint as an English teacher, hostess, technical rewriter, model or itinerant pedlar of paintings, jewellery and other odds and ends.

There is still plenty of work for foreigners but the competition is fiercer, pay and conditions are getting worse and the government is clamping down on foreign workers. The main 'problem' is the many Asians involved in the 'water trade' (Japan's entertainment industry) but the government is also looking into areas like English-language teaching, which has long been the backpacker's standby.

The Japanese success story has attracted legions of guest workers in fields the Japanese themselves no longer have a taste for. Building sites and restaurants are just two areas that have become increasingly dominated by, often illegal, foreign workers. Most users of this book are more likely to be doing work the Japanese *can't* do – English teaching and foreign modelling for example – but these fields may also be swept up in the new regulations *if* the government decides to enforce them.

Finding casual work is certainly still possible, particularly if you look neat and tidy. Appearance are *very* important in Japan, suit and tie for the men please, businesslike dresses for the women. For most Japanese, arriving for work in casual clothes signifies a want of seriousness about the task at hand. If you are planning on working, make sure you have enough cash to last through to that first monthly pay cheque.

Once upon a time, blonde hair and blue eyes were all that was needed for an English-teaching job but nowadays, real qualifications are becoming increasingly important. Be wary of anyone who is prepared to employ you without qualifications – there are some very exploitative deals, especially in Tokyo. Nevertheless, if you fit the bill, it's still a seller's market in Japan.

English Teaching

Teaching has, for many years, been the easiest work for native-English-speaking foreigners to find. As more and more people arrive with real qualifications and as the Japanese themselves become more demanding, the market is getting tighter but it's unlikely the demand for unqualified people will disappear completely.

The reason for this is that much of what passes for teaching in Japan is actually nothing of the sort. Many qualified Teaching English as a Foreign Language (TEFL) teachers, for example, would be offended at being given a job that simply required them to sit in the 'lobby' of a school and wait for students to come and talk to them. Far from being teachers, they are, in fact, pet foreigners.

Another reason for the continuing need for unqualified teachers is the enormous size of the market for English 'conversation teachers'. In a country where English is as much a fashion accessory as Gucci handbags, it is possible to get paid quite handsomely for sitting with a small group of housewives or salarymen and chatting about who did what last week. At first the 'students' may put up with a 'teacher's' persistence in returning to the text book, but it won't be long before they implore the teacher to toss it away and concentrate on 'conversation practice'. Of course, finding work of this type is partly a matter of luck, and partly a matter of proving your experience by slowly working up your teaching hours.

Private Schools Japan abounds with private schools but formal qualifications are becoming increasingly necessary. Informal qualifications, that is, fitting the English-speaker stereotype of the blonde, blue-eyed Caucasian, also help. The Monday edition of the *Japan Times* is the best place to look for teaching jobs, although word of mouth is also useful and some larger schools simply rely on direct inquiries from would-be teachers.

Tokyo is the easiest place to find teaching jobs as even schools on other islands advertise or recruit in Tokyo. Osaka, with a sizeable population and smaller numbers of competing gaijin, is also a good bet.

Check the fine print carefully once you have an offer. Find out how many hours you will teach, whether class preparation time is included and whether you get sick leave and paid holidays. Find out how and when you will be paid and if the school will obtain your visa. It's worth checking with other foreign staff to find how they are treated.

Government Schools A recent programme opened 2000 teaching assistant positions for foreign teachers. The job operates on a yearly contract and will have to be organised in your home country. However, visiting different schools and classrooms means teachers are unable to establish an ongoing contract with one group of students; this can be less interesting than working at one of the private English-language schools.

International Schools Big cities like Tokyo and Yokohama with large foreign populations have a number of international schools for the children of foreign residents. Work is available for experienced, Western-trained teachers in all disciplines and the schools will usually organise your visa.

Rewriting

Since the general standard of translation in Japan ranges from bad to comical, transforming 'Japlish' into English has become a big industry. Technical documents and manuals pose particular problems and, ideally, visitors hoping to work as translators should also have some technical knowledge. Rewriting work is harder to come by than teaching but try the *Japan Times*. Office jobs usually pay Y2000 to Y3000 per hour.

Hostessing

Hostessing evolved from the geisha culture in which highly trained and cultivated women entertained powerful men with their repartee and artistic accomplishments. Geisha establishments are very expensive but most company expense accounts will stretch to the odd night at a hostess club where the women will pour drinks for the salarymen, listen to their troubles and generally provide an amiable atmosphere. Although hostessing has been described as 'psychological prostitution', there is no pressure to grant sexual favours; it's more a matter of slipping on the mask, making light conversation and giggling at the crude innuendos and general role playing.

Since working visas are not issued for hostessing, it's a mildly illegal activity to which the authorities seem to turn a blind eye. An introduction is usually required, but at any gaijin house there will usually be women working in this field. Rates typically range from Y2000 to Y3000 per hour with bonuses for bringing customers to the club. This only requires meeting the customer downstairs and escorting him through the door and most hostesses soon foster a small circle of admirers.

Modelling

Modelling jobs for foreigners are increasingly dominated by professional models so any hope of getting into the field will require a proper portfolio of photographs. Nonprofessionals are more likely to pick up casual work as extras in advertising or film and, once again, news of possible work circulates mainly by word of mouth.

On the Streets

In big cities, particularly Tokyo, you'll see Westerners busking or peddling everything from garish paintings to moving toy pandas. Although peddling is somewhat illegal, apologising and moving on is usually enough to defuse any unwanted police attention. The Yakuza (Japanese Mafia) may also show an interest since they often control the lively entertainment districts and will want a fee from any outsider who appears on their turf.

Buskers seem to work best as a team, while solo street selling can be tough work unless you know how to sell (the Japanese certainly have the money to spend). The business of selling horrible paintings on the street is controlled by Israelis, so you need to be an Israeli yourself or have an introduction from one if you want to get in on the act. It's said that Israelis are often intercepted at Narita Airport by others with connections in the street-selling game.

STUDYING IN JAPAN

The Japanese obsession for acquiring new skills and developing personal interests has resulted in schools and courses for almost every aspect of Japanese culture. The Tokyo Tourist Information Centre (TIC) has a wealth of information material available. Applicants for cultural visas should note that attendance at 20 class hours per week are required and the current dispensation to work 20 hours per week may be curtailed.

Japanese Language

Studying Japanese has become so popular that schools cannot keep up with demand and there are long waiting lists of foreign students. This has also led to many fly-by-night operations springing up. These tend to have poor facilities and teachers with limited training and experience (like us with English, most Japanese are deluded into thinking that being a native speaker automatically qualifies them for teaching the language). The TIC leaflet *Japanese & Japanese Studies* lists government-accredited schools that belong to the Association of International Education. The association can also be contacted directly (tel 3485-6827). *Nihongo Journal* is an excellent monthly language magazine for students of Japanese.

Costs at private Japanese-language schools vary enormously depending on the school's status and facilities. There is usually an application fee of Y5000 to Y30,000, an administration charge of Y50,000 to Y100,000 and annual tuition fees of

Y300,000 to Y600,000. Add accommodation and food, and it is easy to see that studying is not a viable option for most people unless they also have an opportunity to work.

Martial Arts

Aikidō, jūdo, karate and kendō can be studied in Japan as well as less popular fields such as *kyūdō* (Japanese archery) and sumo. Relevant addresses include:

International Aikidō Federation, 17-18 Wakamatsu-cho, Shinjuku-ku, Tokyo (tel 3203-9236)

All-Japan Jūdō Federation, c/o Kodokan, 1-16-30 Kasuga, Bukyō-ku, Tokyo (tel 3818-4199)

Japan Kendō Federation, c/o Nippon Budokan, 2-3 Kitanomaru-kōen, Chiyoda-ku, Tokyo (tel 3211-5804/5)

World Union of Karate-dō Organisation, 4th Floor, Sempaku Shinkokai Building, 1-15-16 Toranomon, Minato-ku, Tokyo (tel 3503-6637)

Nihon Sumō Kyokai, c/o Kokugikan Sumō Hall, 1-3-28 Yokoami, Sumida-ku, Tokyo (tel 3623-5111)

Amateur Archery Federation of Japan, Kishi Memorial Hall, 4th Floor, 1-1-1 Jinan, Shibuya-ku, Tokyo (tel 3481-2387)

CUSTOMS

Customs allowances include the usual tobacco products, three 760 ml bottles of alcoholic beverages, 57 grams of perfume and gifts and souvenirs up to a value of Y200,000 or its equivalent. Liquor is not cheap in Japan, so it's worth bringing some for personal consumption or as a gift; there is no possibility of reselling it for profit. The penalties for importing drugs are very severe.

Customs officers also confiscate literature, such as men's magazines, which shows pubic hair. Depictions of just about every kind of sexual liaison and contortion are readily available at newsagents in Japan, but all pubic hair is carefully erased.

There are no limits on the import of foreign or Japanese currency. The export of foreign currency is also unlimited but a Y5 million limit exists for Japanese currency.

MONEY

The currency in Japan is the *yen* (Y) and banknotes and coins are easily identifiable. There are Y1, Y5, Y10, Y50, Y100 and Y500 coins, Y1000, Y5000 and Y10,000 banknotes. The Y1 coin is an aluminium lightweight, the Y5 and Y50 coins have a hole in the middle.

USA	US$1	=	Y139
Australia	A$1	=	Y106
UK	UK£1	=	Y223
Germany	DM1	=	Y77
Canada	C$1	=	Y122
New Zealand	NZ$1	=	Y79
Singapore	S$1	=	Y79
Hong Kong	HK$1	=	Y18

The Japanese are used to a very low crime rate and often carry wads of cash for the almost sacred ritual of cash payment. Unfortunately, this habit also extends to trips abroad and greatly endears the Japanese tourist to the worldwide fraternity of muggers and rip-off artists. Foreign travellers in Japan can safely copy the cash habit, but should still take the usual precautions.

Changing Money

You can change cash or travellers' cheques at an 'Authorised Foreign Exchange Bank' (signs will always be displayed in English) or at some of the large hotels and stores. These are easy to find in cities, but much less common elsewhere. The safest and most practical way to carry your money is in travellers' cheques, preferably in US dollars, although other major currencies are acceptable. Exchanging Korean or Taiwanese currency in Japan is a fruitless task, so avoid bringing any if you're arriving from those countries.

Banking Hours

Banks are open Monday to Friday from 9 am to 3 pm and closed on Saturdays, Sundays and national holidays. Japan may be a hi-tech place, but to change money you have to show your passport, fill in forms and wait until

your number is called which can take anything up to half an hour. If you're caught cashless outside regular banking hours, try a large department store or major hotel.

Money Transfers

If you are having money sent to a bank in Japan, make sure you know *exactly* where the funds are going: the bank, branch and location. Telex or telegraphic transfers are much faster, though more expensive, than mail transfers. A credit card cash advance (see below) is a worthwhile alternative, American Express transfers require a trusty friend back home.

Bank & Post Office Accounts

Major changes are expected in banking operations in Japan in the next few years – good news for the customers who have had to put up with a creaky system. Surprisingly, for a hi-tech country like Japan, the present cosy arrangement between the banks discourages competition and encourages inefficiency and expensive bank charges for simple things like paying a bill. Interest rates on deposits – in most cases very low at present – are to be linked to market rates and raised to appropriate levels. Recently Japanese banks have even started to turn their ATMs on at weekends!

If you open a savings account at one of the major banks, you'll receive a savings book and a cash card which will allow you to draw cash at any branch of the bank or from a cash-dispensing machine. An easy option is to open a post office savings account *(yūbin chokin)* at the main post office in one of the major cities; this will allow you to withdraw funds from any post office. You should be able to get things started by using the following Japanese phrase: 'Yūbin chokin no kohza o tsukutte kudasai' (I would like to open a post office savings account).

The central post office in Tokyo took 10 minutes to open a post office savings account for me – I was even offered a choice of designs for my passbook and given two packs of tissues!

Robert Strauss

Credit Cards

The use of credit cards is becoming more widespread in Japan, but outside major cities, cash still reigns supreme. American Express, Visa, MasterCard and Diners Club are the most widely accepted international cards. The main offices are:

American Express
   Ogikubo Head Office, 4-30-16 Ogikubo, Suginami-ku, Tokyo (tel 3220-6000; 0120-376-100 toll free 24 hours)
Diners Club
   Senshu Building, 1-13-7 Shibuya, Shibuya-ku, Tokyo (tel 3499-1311; 3797-7311 emergency; 3499-1181 after hours)
MasterCard
   Union Credit Co, 1-10-7 Kaji-cho, Chiyoda-ku, Tokyo (tel 3254-6751)
Visa
   Sumitomo Credit Co, Taihei Building, 5-2-10 Shimbashi, Minato-ku, Tokyo (tel 3459-4800; 3459-4700 emergency)

Costs

Japan can be painfully expensive compared to other Asian countries, but this shouldn't be taken as an insuperable barrier to an enjoyable trip. A cup of coffee can indeed cost you Y600 (US$4) or more in an expensive place but it is equally possible to drop into one of the many chain coffee shops and pay Y150. If you want coffee, rather than a break in a coffee shop, it will cost just Y100 from one of the ubiquitous vending machines.

Similar comparisons could be made in the food or accommodation areas, but transport doesn't offer much latitude for savings – it's expensive whichever way you look at it.

A skeleton daily budget (assuming you stay at the cheapest places (Y2000 per night in a hostel), eat modestly (Y1500) and spend Y1500 on short-distance travel) would be Y5000 (US$35). Add at least Y1000 for extras like snacks, drinks, admission fees and entertainment. More expensive accommodation costs around Y3500 to Y5000 for a *minshuku* (Japanese-style B&B), cheap ryokan or business hotel.

Food costs can be kept within reasonable limits by taking set meals. A fixed 'morning service' breakfast (*mōningu sābisu* or *setto*) is available in most coffee shops for around Y350. At lunch time there are set meals (*teishoku*) for about Y650. Cheap noodle places, often found at stations or in department stores, charge around Y250 for a filling bowl of noodles. For an evening meal, there's the option of a set course again or a single order – Y600 should cover this. Average prices at youth hostels are Y450 for a Japanese breakfast and Y700 for dinner.

Transport is a major expense, although there are ways to limit the damage. The Japan Rail Pass is well worth the money if you intend to travel widely in a short space of time. Overnight buses are cheaper than the train, and enable you to save on accommodation. Hitching is not only easy, it also puts you in touch with a cross section of Japanese society. If you want to avoid emptying your wallet at an alarming rate, you should only use taxis as a last resort. Most cities in Japan have fast, efficient public transport, so you rarely need taxis anyway.

Foreigners approaching the zero budget in the urban wilderness can keep hunger at bay by cruising for free food samples in department stores but at the other extreme, high rollers will have no problems off-loading their cash. Japan specialises in establishments catering to the ostentatious flattery of business accounts – the higher the bill, the greater the prestige of the guests.

Tipping & Tax

The total absence of tipping does reduce costs a little; nobody expects a tip so it's best to keep it that way. However, if you feel your maid at a top-flight ryokan has given service surpassing that of a fairy godmother, you can leave her a small present, perhaps a souvenir from your home country. If you give cash, the polite way is to place it in an envelope.

Unfortunately, Japan does have a 3% consumer tax, introduced in 1989 and extremely unpopular with the Japanese public. If you eat at expensive restaurants and stay at 1st class accommodation you will encounter a service charge – a disguised form of tipping – which varies from 10% to 15%. A local tax of 3% is added for restaurant bills exceeding Y5000 or for hotel bills exceeding Y10,000. This means it is sometimes cheaper to ask for separate bills. At onsen (hot-spring) resorts, a separate onsen tax applies. This is usually 3% and applies at cheap accommodation, even youth hostels.

WHEN TO GO

The Japanese make a lot of fuss about the fact that Japan has four distinct seasons; indeed many young Japanese are genuinely surprised to hear that other parts of the world are also subject to seasonal change. For the Japanese, each of the seasons has its pleasures (though spring with its clear skies and cherry blossoms is probably the most celebrated), but for the visitor, the best times to visit are the more climatically stable seasons of spring and autumn.

Spring can be a magnificent season to visit Japan. The only drawback is that the cherry blossom season is a holiday period for the Japanese, and many of the more popular travel destinations tend to be flooded with Japanese tourists who head out of the cities in droves. Still, if you're not on too tight a budget, finding accommodation even at this time of the year won't be impossible.

Synchronising your trip with the cherry blossom season can be tricky, however. For one, the blossoms are notoriously fickle, blooming any time from early April to late April. Moreover, when the blossoms do come, their moment of glory is brief, lasting generally a mere week. Still, if you're going to be travelling in Japan during April, chances are you'll come across cherry blossoms somewhere, as they creep slowly across Japan beginning in the south and making their way northwards (their progress is followed obsessively on all the TV channels).

While a great deal is made of the cherry blossoms, spring remains a good time to be travelling in Japan whether you see them or not: temperatures are pleasant, rainfall is low and there is a high proportion of clear days.

Autumn (September to November) may lack the attraction of the cherry blossoms, but it is an equally good time to travel, with pleasant temperatures and the beautiful landscapes provided by russet shades of the forests and the carpets of red leaves on the ground. This is most certainly the time to visit historical centres such as Kamakura or Kyoto – the temples and shrines set against the backdrop of autumn leaves make a magnificent scene.

The extremes of the Japanese climate make travelling in either summer or winter less pleasant than at other times. The Japan Sea side of Honshū and Hokkaidō receive huge winter snowfalls and, from December to February, very cold temperatures prevail. On the other hand, summer (June to August) can be uncomfortably humid. Still, there are advantages that need to be considered. One thing to bear in mind is that both seasons are less popular with the Japanese and all the major travel destinations (with the exception of ski resorts in winter) will be less crowded than they would be in autumn or spring. Winter can be especially attractive, with temples and shrines blanketed in snow. However, traditional Japanese buildings are rarely heated so it can be miserably cold. In Hokkaidō, where temperatures really plummet over the winter months, there is the attraction of colourful festivals and the famous Sapporo ice sculptures where a small city is carved from ice.

All things considered, the ideal trip to Japan would see you in Hokkaidō and Northern Honshū during the height of summer, in southern Honshū, Kyūshū and Shikoku from late summer to early autumn and in Central Honshū during autumn. Peak holiday seasons, particularly the late April to early May 'Golden Week', can also cause travel problems. See the Holidays & Festivals section for details.

WHAT TO BRING

For the serious traveller, the number one rule

in Japan is much the same as anywhere else – travel light. There's nothing so useful as more space in your bag. The advantages of travelling light are even more important for rail travellers, as trains usually have little space for storing bags.

Clothing will depend very much on where and when you are in Japan and what you are doing. Japan extends a long way from north to south. The north of Hokkaidō can be under deep snow at the same time as the Okinawa Islands are basking in tropical sunshine. Japan also varies considerably in altitude, so, even at the height of summer, you'll need good, cold-weather gear if you're intent on climbing Mt Fuji. Generally, however, Japan's climate is somewhat similar to that of continental USA; while it can get very cold and icy in winter, high summer is definitely T-shirt weather and much of the year is pleasantly mild.

There is a distinct wet season between June and July, but rain seems to be possible at almost any time of year and an umbrella is well worth having. Almost every shop and hotel in Japan seems to have an umbrella stand outside, often with a neat locking arrangement so umbrellas can be stowed safely.

Unless you're in Japan on business, you are unlikely to meet situations where 'coat and tie' standards are enforced; casual clothing is all you'll need. Also, laundromats are reasonably common, so you can usually count on recirculating your wardrobe fairly regularly. Some hotels, hostels and other accommodation have laundry facilities for their guests' use. If you do need more clothes, only extra-large gaijin may have trouble finding big enough sizes; others should have no problems.

The same rule, but underlined, applies to shoes. If your feet are big, make sure your shoes will outlast your stay in Japan. Choose them carefully – you want shoes which are not only comfortable for walking but which are also easy to slip on and off for the frequent indoor occasions where they must be abandoned. Remember that slippers are almost always provided for indoor and bath-room use, so you don't need to bring anything other than your outdoor shoes.

Bring a towel – even in an expensive ryokan, a towel is not necessarily provided or it may be of a size Westerners will consider more like a washcloth. Most hotels and ryokan will supply a *yukata*, that all-purpose Japanese 'dressing gown', but not always and it's such a vital piece of apparel that you should buy yourself one as soon as possible. They make a fine souvenir of Japan.

TOURIST OFFICES

The Japan National Tourist Organisation (JNTO), which has both Japanese and overseas offices, produces a great deal of literature.

Tourist Information Centres (TIC)

JNTO operates three Tourist Information Centres; one at Narita International Airport (tel 047-632-8711), another in the Ginza in central Tokyo (tel 03-3350-21461) and the third near the railway station in Kyoto (tel 075-371-5649).

TIC offices do not make reservations or bookings, but will direct you to agencies which can, such as the Japan Travel Bureau (JTB) or the Nippon Travel Agency (NTA). TIC's Tokyo (tel 3503-2911) and Kyoto (tel 361-2911) offices operate 'Teletourist', a round-the-clock taped information service on current events in town. JNTO also operate Goodwill Guides, a volunteer programme with over 30,000 members who wear a blue and white badge with a dove and globe logo.

Japan Travel-Phone

JNTO operate a nationwide toll-free phone service available from 9 am to 5 pm, seven days a week. The main aim is to provide assistance for visitors unable to get to the TIC offices in Tokyo or Kyoto. To contact an English-speaking travel expert, call 0120-22-2800 for information on eastern Japan; 0120-44-4800 for western Japan. You can also use this service to help with language problems when you're stuck in a hopeless linguistic muddle. It's said that foreigners with Japanese dates, but minimal language skills, have even used the service to smooth the amorous path of acquaintance!

Other Information Offices

Away from Tokyo or Kyoto there are information offices *(annai-jo)* in almost all the major train stations but the further you venture into outlying regions, the less chance of finding English-speaking staff. If you want a licensed, professional tourist guide try TIC, a large travel agency such as JTB, or phone the Japan Guide Association in Tokyo on 3213-2706.

For any information on Japan Railways (JR) including schedules, fares, fastest routings, lost baggage and discounts on railway services, hotels and rent-a-cars call the JR East-Infoline in Tokyo on 3423-0111. The service is available from 10 am to 6 pm, Monday to Friday, but not on holidays.

Publications

JNTO's useful tourist literature is available both from its overseas and TIC offices. Publications include *Your Guide to Japan*, a handy booklet giving information on places of interest, calendar events and travel data; the *Tourist Map of Japan* and *Economical Travel in Japan*, which has money-saving tips on travel, accommodation and places to eat. *Explore Japanese Culture* offers information on cultural things to see and do throughout Japan. Most publications are available in English and, in some cases, other European and Asian languages. Separate brochures are available on a number of important tourist destinations.

JNTO Offices Overseas

Australia
    115 Pitt St, Sydney, NSW 2000 (tel (02) 232-4522)
Canada
    165 University Ave, Toronto, Ontario M5H 3B8 (tel (416) 366-7140)
France
    4-8 Rue Sainte-Anne, 75001 Paris (tel (01) 42-96-20-29)
Germany
    Kaiserstrasse 11, 6000 Frankfurt am Main 1 (tel (069) 20353

Hong Kong
    Suite 3606, Two Exchange Square, 8 Connaught Place, Central (tel 5255295)
South Korea
    10 Da-Dong, Chung-Ku, Seoul (tel (02) 752-7968)
Switzerland
    13 Rue de Berne, 1201 Geneva (tel (022) 731-81-40)
Thailand
    Wall Street Tower Building, 33/61, Suriwong Rd, Bangkok 10500 (tel (02) 233-5108)
UK
    167 Regent St, London W1 (tel (071) 734-9638)
USA
    Chicago: 401 North Michigan Ave, IL 60611 (tel (312) 222-0874)
    Dallas: 2121 San Jacinto St, Suite 980, LB-53, TX 75201 (tel (214) 754-1820)
    Los Angeles: 624 South Grand Ave, Suite 2640, CA 90017 (tel (213) 623-1952)
    New York: Rockefeller Plaza, 630 Fifth Ave, NY 10111 (tel (212) 757-5640)
    San Francisco: 360 Post St, Suite 401, CA 94108 (tel (415) 989-7140)

BUSINESS HOURS

Shops are typically open seven days a week from around 10 am to 8 pm. Department stores close slightly earlier, usually 6.30 or 7 pm, and also close one weekday each week. If a city has several major department stores, opening hours will probably be organised so that Mitsukoshi closes on Monday, Daimaru closes on Tuesday, and so on. Large companies usually work a 9 am to 5 pm five-day week, some also operate on Saturday mornings. (See the Money section for banking hours and the Post & Telecommunications section for post office hours.)

POST & TELECOMMUNICATIONS

The symbol for post offices is a white and red T with a bar across the top. Red mailboxes are for ordinary mail, blue ones for special delivery. The Japanese postal system is reliable and efficient and, for regular postcards and airmail letters, not markedly more expensive than other advanced countries. The airmail rate for postcards is Y70 to any overseas destination; aerograms cost Y80. Letters weighing less than 10 grams are Y80 to other countries within Asia, Y100 to North

America or Oceania (including Australia and New Zealand) and Y120 to Europe, Africa and South America.

Sending parcels overseas from Japan often works out 30% cheaper with Surface Airlift (SAL) and only takes a week longer.

District post offices (the main post office in a ward or *ku*), are normally open from 8 am to 7 pm on weekdays, 8 am to 3 pm on Saturdays and 9 am to 12.30 pm on Sundays and public holidays. Local post offices are open 9 am to 5 pm on weekdays and 9 am to 1 pm on Saturdays. Main post offices in the larger cities may have some counters open 24 hours a day.

Mail can be sent to Japan, from Japan or within Japan when addressed in our script (romaji) but it should, of course, be written as clearly as possible.

Receiving Mail

Although any post office will hold mail for collection, the poste restante idea is not well known and can cause confusion in smaller places. It is probably better to have mail addressed to you at a larger central post office. Letters are usually only held for 30 days before being returned to sender. When inquiring about mail for collection ask for *kyoku dome yūbin*.

American Express will hold mail for their cardholders or users of American Express travellers' cheques. Normally, mail will be held for 30 days only unless marked 'Please hold for arrival'. American Express offices in Japan are:

Naha, Okinawa
    Okinawa Tourist Service, 2-21-8 Maejima, Okinawa 900
    Okinawa Tourist Service, 1-2-3 Matsuo, Okinawa 900
Okinawa City, Okinawa
    Okinawa Tourist Service, 241 Aza-Yamazato, Okinawa 900
Osaka
    American Express, Umeda Mitsui Building, 2-5-10 Sonezaki, Kita-ku, Osaka 530
Tokyo
    American Express, Ginza 4-Star Building, 4-4-1 Ginza, Chūō-ku, Tokyo 104
    American Express, 5th Floor, Shuwa Kamiya-cho Building, 4-3-13 Toranomon, Minato-ku, Tokyo 105
    American Express, Shuwa Shiba Park Building, 2-4-1 Shiba-kōen, Minato-ku, Tokyo 100-91
    American Express, 3-8-1 Kasumigaseki, Chiyoda-ku, Tokyo 106

Some embassies will hold mail for their nationals, check before you depart. Hotels and youth hostels are another possibility.

Telephones

The Japanese public telephone system is very well developed; there are a great many public phones and they work almost 100% of the time. It would be very unusual to see a vandalised phone in Japan. Local calls cost Y10 for three minutes; long-distance or overseas calls require a handful of coins which are used up as the call progresses and any unused coins are returned.

Most pay phones will also accept prepaid phone cards. It's much easier to buy one of these, typically in Y500, Y1000, Y5000 denominations, rather than worry about having coins to hand. The cards (readily available from vending machines, telephone company card outlets and many shops) are magnetically encoded and, after each call, a small hole is punched to show how much value remains. The phone also displays the remaining value of your card when you insert it. Since you get a small discount on calls made with a card, phone card collecting is a popular activity.

Japanese telephone numbers consist of an area code plus a local code and the number. You do not dial the area code when making a call within that area.

International Calls The one problem with Japanese pay phones is the scarcity of phones which handle international calls. An overseas call (paid or operator-assisted) can only be made from a phone with a gold sign which specifically notes that it handles international calls. Although international pay phones will be quite plentiful in some towns, in others, you may have to search. Try big hotels, the main railway station, the main shopping arcade or Nippon Telegraph & Telephone (NTT) offices. (You can also try offices of NTT's international counterpart, Kokusai Denshin Denwa (KDD).) Once you've found one, calls are charged by the unit (there's no three minute minimum) so, if you talk fast enough, you could get a call through for Y100!

To place an international call through the operator, dial 0051 – international operators all seem to speak English. To make the call yourself, simply dial 001 then the international country code, the local code and the number. Another option is to dial 0039 for home country direct which takes you straight through to a local operator in the country dialled. You can then make a reverse-charge (collect) call or a credit card call with a telephone credit card valid in that country. In some hotels or other tourist locations, you may find a home country direct phone where you simply press the button labelled USA, UK, Canada, Australia, NZ or wherever to be put through to your operator.

Dialling codes include:

Country	Direct Dial	Home Country Direct
Australia	001-61	0039-611
Canada	001-1	0039-161
Hong Kong	001-852	0039-852
Netherlands	001-31	0039-311
New Zealand	001-64	0039-641
Singapore	001-65	0039-651
Taiwan	001-886	0039-886
UK	001-44	0039-441
USA	001-1	0039-111*

*for mainland USA you can also dial 0039-121, for Hawaii you can also dial 0039-181

Addresses
In Japan, finding a place from its address can be a near impossibility, even for the Japanese. The problem is twofold – firstly, the address is given by an area rather than a street and secondly, the numbers are not necessarily consecutive. Prior to the mid-50s numbers were assigned by date of construction! During the occupation after WW II, an attempt was made to bring some logic to Japanese addresses and many streets were assigned names, but the Japanese reverted to their own system as soon as the Americans left.

To find an address, the usual process is to ask directions and even taxi drivers often have to do this. The numerous local police boxes are there, in part, to give directions. Businesses often include a small map in their advertisements or on their business cards to show their location.

Starting from the largest area and working down to an individual address, first comes the ken (prefecture) as in Okayama-ken or Akita-ken. Four areas in Japan do not follow this rule – Tokyo-to, Kyoto-fu, Osaka-fu (those cities and the areas around them) and the island of Hokkaidō. After the prefecture comes the *shi* or city. Thus Okayama city in Okayama Prefecture is properly Okayama-shi, Okayama-ken. In country areas, there are also *gun*, which are like counties, and *mura* or 'villages'.

Large cities are then subdivided first into ku (wards), then into *cho* or *machi* and then into *chome*, an area of just a few blocks. The chome is the smallest division, so an address like 4-4 3-chome should locate the actual place you want. For the poor gaijin, the system often seems to be changed back and forth without rhyme or reason and an address like 2-4-8 Nishi Meguro can also be written 4-8 Nishi Meguro 2-chome. The building number is either a single numeric or a hyphenated double numeric. When there are three hyphenated numerics the first one is the chome, so 1-2-3 is building 2-3 in 1-chome.

You can buy maps which show every building in every chome and there are often streetside signs indicating building locations, but they are very hard to interpret.

TIME

Despite Japan's east-west distance, the country is all on the same time, nine hours ahead of Greenwich Mean Time (GMT). Thus, when it is 12 noon in Japan, it is 3 am in London, 11 am in Hong Kong, 1 pm in Sydney, 3 pm in Auckland, 10 pm the previous day in New York, 7 pm the previous day in San Francisco and 5 pm the previous day in Honolulu. Daylight-saving time is not used in Japan. Times are all expressed on a 24 hour clock.

ELECTRICITY

The Japanese electric current is 100 volts AC, an odd voltage found almost nowhere else in the world. Furthermore, Tokyo and eastern Japan are on 50 cycles, western Japan including Nagoya, Kyoto and Osaka is on 60 cycles. Most North American electrical items, designed to run on 117 volts, will function reasonably well on Japanese current. The plugs are flat two pin, identical to US and Canadian plugs.

BOOKS & MAPS

There's no need to stock up on books, particularly books about Japan, before you leave home. If you're passing through Tokyo there are bookshops with excellent selections of books on all aspects of Japanese culture. Outside Tokyo, the choice of foreign-language books is nowhere near as good, though many larger cities will have a branch of Kinokuniya and/or Maruzen with a foreign section. In the back blocks, however, you may be hard pressed to find anything in English other than the occasional newspaper and copy of *Time*.

Most of the following books should be available in Tokyo, often in paperback rather than in original hardbacks.

History

Inside Japan (Penguin, 1987) by Peter Tasker, is probably the best wide-ranging introduction to modern Japanese culture, society and the economy. Richard Storey's *A History of Modern Japan* (Penguin) is a concise and consistently interesting history of modern Japan.

The Japanese Achievement (Sidgwick & Jackson, 1990) by Hugh Cortazzi, provides a detailed yet highly readable survey of Japan's history and culture from earliest times to the present day. The biggest drawback is the hardback price.

Olive Statler's *Japanese Inn* traces the history of Japan through the comings and goings of visitors at an inn on the old Tōkaidō road. This engrossing book is available in paperback and makes excellent travel reading.

The Economic Superpower

As Japan elbows its way to the front of the industrial pack, the countries left behind have produced a flood of 'What was that?' and 'How did it happen?' style books. *The Enigma of Japanese Power* by Karel van Wolferen is an attack on the Japanese 'system' and a book for the finger pointers and accusers who reckon Japan got to the top by playing dirty.

Japan's most forceful recent reply was in *The Japan That Can Say No* by Akio Morita (chairman of Sony) and Shintaro Ishihara (former cabinet minister and politician). They argue that Japan is big enough to play a real role in world politics and need no longer be at the USA's beck and call, and that superior technology has made the USA dependent on Japan.

Other views on the growth of Japan as an economic superpower are found in *Trading Places: How America Allowed Japan to Take the Lead* (Charles E Tuttle) by Clyde V Prestowitz Jr and *The New Masters – Can the West Match Japan?* (Hutchinson Business Books, 1990) by Phillip Oppenheim. Ezra Vogel saw it coming more than 10 years ago in *Japan as Number One: Lessons for America* (Harvard University Press, 1979). Of course, Japan has hardly reached the top before someone is foreshadowing its descent – Bill Emmott describes it in *The Sun Also Sets*.

Culture & Society
Ruth Benedict's *The Chrysanthemum & the Sword* (available in paperback) is, in some ways, still regarded as the classic study of Japanese culture and attitudes. However, the fact that it was written in the USA during WW II, at a time when meeting the Japanese in Japan was clearly impossible, makes some of its conclusions a little questionable.

Japanese Culture (1973, now in paperback) by H Paul Varley is a slightly academic but nevertheless interesting account of the main currents in the development of Japan's culture. *Appreciations of Japanese Culture* (Kodansha, 1981) by Donald Keene is a readable, eclectic collection of essays by a renowned scholar of Japanese culture.

The Japanese Today (Belknap, 1988) by Edwin O Reischauer, is a recently revised standard textbook on Japanese society and a must for those planning to spend time in Japan. Ian Buruma's *A Japanese Mirror* (Penguin) provides an interesting examination of Japanese popular culture.

For a fascinating insight into the Japanese language and the position of women in Japanese society look for *Womansword – what Japanese words say about women* (Kodansha 1987) by Kittredge Cherry. *Japan as it Is* (Gakken, 1985; updated in 1990) is a collection of one-page essays on a whole range of matters relating to Japan, each one with its facing page in Japanese.

The two volumes of *Discover Japan – Words, Customs & Concepts* (Kodansha, 1987) were originally published as *A Hundred Things Japanese* and *A Hundred More Things Japanese* and consist of a series of short essays on things Japanese by a wide variety of writers.

Japanese Religion – A Survey by the Agency for Cultural Affairs (Kodansha, 1989) gives a good overall perspective of Japanese religions and their place in the lives of contemporary Japanese. (See the Religion section in the Facts about the Country chapter for more details.)

Travel & Places
Edward Seidensticker's *Low City, High City* (1983) traces the history of Tokyo from 1867 to 1923 – the tumultuous years from the Edo period to the great earthquake. He followed that book with *Tokyo Rising: The City Since the Great Earthquake* (Knopf, New York, 1990) which traces Tokyo's history from the '20s, through the destruction of WW II and the period of explosive growth to today's super city status. Much regret is expressed for the loss of the city's traditional elements and their replacement with faceless modern architecture; there is also a great deal of interest in Tokyo's freestyle entertainment possibilities.

If you're travelling along the San-yō coast of Western Honshū, or visiting Inland Sea islands between Honshū and Shikoku, you won't find a more enjoyable companion than Donald Richie's *The Inland Sea*. Originally published in 1971, it's now available in paperback and manages to be both amusing and educational.

Oliver Statler's *Japanese Inn* is an excellent introduction to the personalities of Japanese history; it was followed by *Japanese Pilgrimage* (available in paperback), the story of a walking tour of the Shikoku pilgrimage circuit. *The Roads to Sata* by Alan Booth (Penguin) is an account of a four month trip on foot from the tip of Hokkaidō to the southernmost point of Kyūshū.

Okubo Diary (Stanford University Press) by the British anthropologist Brian Moeran, is a memoir of his stay in a tiny Kyūshū village. *Unbeaten Tracks in Japan* (Virago Books, 1984) by Isabella Bird recounts the 'off the beaten track' travels of a doughty Victorian lady and includes an interesting account of the dying Ainu culture in Hokkaidō.

The Japan Travel Bureau (JTB) produces an illustrated book series with pocket-sized books covering various aspects of Japan including lifestyle, eating, festivals, the salaryman, Kyoto, Nikkō and other subjects in a bouncy, highly visual style.

Language

Japanese Phrasebook (Lonely Planet, 1989) offers a convenient collection of survival words and phrases for your trip to Japan. Tae Moriyama's *The Practical Guide to Japanese Signs* (Kodansha, 1987) is a convenient introduction to some commonly encountered Japanese signs. It not only identifies them but explains how they came about and has been followed by a second volume.

Literature

Murasaki Shikibu's *The Tale of the Genji*, translated by Edward Seidensticker, is the most famous classic of Japanese literature, and is available in paperback. This weighty tome is rather like a Japanese equivalent to *Beowulf*.

The Narrow Road to the Deep North is a famous travel classic by the revered Japanese poet Matsuo Bashō. *Kokoro*, by Natsume Sōseki, is a modern classic depicting the conflict between old and new Japan in the mind and heart of an aged scholar. The modern and the traditional also clash in the lives of two couples in *Some Prefer Nettles* by Tanizaki Junichirō.

The Makioka Sisters by Tanizaki Junichirō (Berkley Windhover, 1957) is a famous family chronicle that has been likened to a modern-day *Tale of the Genji*. Ibuse Masuji's *Black Rain* (Kodansha, 1969) is a response to Japan's defeat in WW II. (Although made into a film in Japan, the book bears no relation to the Hollywood movie of the same name.)

Snow Country by Kawabata Yasunari is a famous story set in Japan's northern regions. Endō Shūsaku's *Silence* is a historical story of the plight of Japanese Christians following Tokugawa Ieyasu's unification of the country.

Mishima Yukio's *The Golden Pavilion* reconstructs the life of a novice monk who burned down Kyoto's Golden Temple in 1950. Although Mishima is probably the most controversial of Japan's modern writers and is considered unrepresentative of Japanese culture by many Japanese, his work still makes for very interesting reading. Abe Kōbō's *Woman of the Dunes* is a classic tale by one of Japan's more respected avant-garde writers

Other Fiction

Of course not all Japanese fiction can be classified as literature. Ryu Murakami's *Almost Transparent Blue* is strictly sex and drugs and was a blockbuster in the Japan of the '70s. Haruki Murakami is another bestselling author and his recent novel *A Wild Sheep Chase* is available in English.

It's surprising that more Western novelists haven't used Japan as a setting for their books although James Clavell is an exception. His book *Shogun* has undoubtedly been a major influence on many people's perceptions of the country.

Guy Stanley's *A Death in Tokyo*, a reasonably gripping whodunit set in and around Tokyo, manages to reveal a fair bit about life in Japan along the way. Probably the most interesting use of Japan as a fictional backdrop is in US science fiction writer William Gibson's 'cyberspace' novels where Japan becomes almost a metaphor for the future: Japanese settings, technology, customs, language and slang are all heavily featured. *Mona Lisa Overdrive* and *Necromancer* are good examples of his work.

Maps

The Japanese word for map is *chizu*. For non-Japanese speakers, Japanese mapping is surprisingly unsatisfactory; most of the vast amount of mapping material available is in

Japanese. The JNTO's free *Tourist Map of Japan* is a reasonable 1:2,000,000 map of the whole country which is quite adequate for general route planning. However, it's difficult to find larger-scale maps of single islands or parts of islands.

The *Japan Road Atlas* (Shobunsha, Tokyo, Y2890) covers all of Japan at 1:250,000 except for Hokkaidō, which is covered at 1:600,000. Most towns are shown in kanji (Japanese script) as well as romaji (Roman script). However, mountains, passes, lakes, rivers and so on are only shown in romaji. Locating exactly where a small town or village is on the map is sometimes difficult and places are often left off. (Check the map of Iriomote-jima Island on page 14 of the atlas – none of the island's half-dozen little towns appears on the map!) Despite these drawbacks, the atlas is the best mapping available for detailed exploration of the country, both by car and rail, as every railway station is marked.

Japan Guide Maps (JGM) produce a series of maps covering the whole country area by area; the map of Kyūshū, at 1:500,000, is typical. Although they're not bad, these maps are not as good as equivalent Japanese-language maps, which are often free. Check the Service & Parking Area (SAPA) maps which are available free at expressway service centres.

Giveaway town maps may also have enough romaji detail to make them usable for non-Japanese speakers, however, much of this mapping is often wildly exaggerated in scale and appearance. Stylised maps, where all roads are completely straight and all corners right angles, are very common.

MEDIA

The insatiable Japanese hunger for information has given rise to an information industry equal to any in the world. Tokyo has seven television channels; cinemas do a roaring trade despite high admission charges; book-shops are overflowing with weekly magazines, newspapers and books; and a very efficient translation network allows the Japanese access to a wide range of foreign publications and films.

The Japanese are world leaders in tabloid consumption. There are more than 160 local and national newspaper companies in Japan, some of the larger ones producing morning and evening editions of the same paper. (What this must be doing for the world's forests doesn't bear thinking about.) Japan's most popular paper, the *Yomiuri Shimbun* has the largest daily circulation in the world, pulling in around 13 million readers daily.

Japan also produces a staggering range of weekly and monthly magazines. The enormous success of weekly tabloids such as *Focus* and *Friday*, with their uniquely lurid, gossip-column approach, has spawned racks of imitations.

The Japanese are also world leaders in the television field; 99% of all households have at least one TV set. No other group, except perhaps the Americans, embraces contemporary advertising-jingle culture as thoroughly as the Japanese do.

Newspapers & Magazines

In the major urban centres at least, you won't have any problem finding English-language newspapers and magazines. However, since English publications are produced in Tokyo, the further you get from the capital, the scarcer they become.

The *Japan Times*, with its good international news section and unbiased coverage of local Japanese news, is undoubtedly the best of the English-language newspapers. The paper's Monday edition also features an employment section which is the best place for anyone to start looking for work in Japan. The paper costs Y160 and in Kyūshū and other far-flung parts of Japan will usually be a day old when you get it.

The *Mainichi Daily News* and the *Yomiuri Daily* are a definite second place to the *Japan Times*. If you oversleep and miss the morning papers, the *Asahi Evening News* is not bad. All these newspapers can be picked up from newsstands in the major cities, particularly at railway stations, or at hotels that cater to foreign tourists and businesspeople.

Foreign magazines and newspapers are available in the major bookshops, though they tend to be three or four times more expensive than they would be in their country of origin. US magazines such as *Newsweek* and *Time* are popular and widely available despite a Y700 (US$4.70) cover price. For the more specialist magazines, you'll need to visit the big bookshops in Tokyo.

The Japanese also publish a number of magazines in English, mainly for their ever-growing English-speaking community. Most of these magazines are a kind of community service, providing what's-on information for theatres and cinemas, details about various cultural events as well as classifieds for anything from marriage partners to used cars. The Tokyo-based *Tokyo Journal* is the pick of the crowd with its comprehens-

Manga – Japanese Comics

It's a well-known fact that in comparisons of mathematical ability, Japanese high school students regularly show up better than their peers in other advanced nations. What is not so well known is that Japanese students would also come out well ahead in their consumption of comic books. In fact, the Japanese are the world's number one consumers of comic books *(manga)*.

Manga is a catch-all word covering cartoons, magazine and newspaper comic strips and the comic books which take up so much space in so many shops. A Japanese comic book is rarely a slim volume (weekly comics as thick as phone directories are not unusual) and there's a version to appeal to every market niche. The text will always be in Japanese but there's usually an English subtitle on the front cover announcing at whom it's aimed, whether it's a 'Lady's Comic', a 'Comic for Business Boys' or even an 'Exciting Comic for Men', (for 'exciting' read 'soft-core porn').

Japanese comic-strip artists (there are thousands of them to cater for the insatiable demand) are often as well known and wealthy as pop stars. There's no question that it's a big business: *Shōnen Jump*, the most popular comic, has weekly sales which top four million copies. It's also an inventive business. Japanese comic artists pioneered multi-panel movements, perspectives which brought the reader into the action, close-ups, curious angles and a host of movie-like techniques. Along with inventiveness came recognition in the form of annual awards, regular reviews and serious critiques.

The curious Westerner leafing through a manga may be somewhat surprised at the explicitness of the action. Japanese censors may black out the pubic hairs in imported copies of *Playboy* but it certainly all hangs out when it comes to comic books. Even those genteelly titled 'Lady's Comics' may give you a few surprises with their sexual activity but manga also tackle very serious subjects. *Jitsuma manga* ('practical comics') and *benkyō manga* ('study comics') actually set out to teach everything from high school subjects to international finance.

The ready acceptance of the dark side of so many manga would seem to indicate an avid interest in areas that are repressed in daily Japanese life. Of course (so the Japanese reasoning goes), it's only natural that adults should want to recapture something of their childhood by turning to comics after 11 hours in the office. And while we may level an accusing finger at the violence and sexual content of the manga, we also have to acknowledge that Japan is still probably the safest place in the world to walk the streets at night.

Those interested in Japanese comics can join the crowds leafing through recent issues in bookshops. Many smaller hotels, hostels and ryokan will have stacks of old issues for their guests' amusements. *Japan Inc* (University of California Press, Berkeley, 1988) by Shōtarō Ishinomori, is an English translation of a popular manga series on international finance and Japanese-US trade relations; it also contains an interesting introductory summation of the history of manga. ■

ive what's-on listings and informative, readable articles on local cultural and topical issues. Also based in Tokyo is the very similar *Tokyo Time Out*.

Kansai Time Out, produced in the Kansai region around Osaka, has excellent information about goings-on of interest to both foreign visitors and local residents. Like the *Tokyo Journal*, it also carries features on various aspects of life in Japan. In the same

region, *Discover Kinki*, is more tourist oriented, while in the Nagoya area *Eyes* is along the same lines.

If you're studying Japanese, *Nihongo Journal* and the *Hiragana Times* are monthly bilingual magazines for Japanese learners. The *Nihongo Journal* is particularly good, having an accompanying tape for pronunciation and listening comprehension practice and good listings of Japanese-language

schools. Both magazines require that you have acquired the rudiments of Japanese and can at least read hiragana and a smattering of kanji.

Radio

The common consensus is that Japanese radio is pretty dismal, mainly because it places far more emphasis on DJ jive than it does on music. Given the quality of Japanese pop music, this is probably just as well. For English-language broadcasts, the possibilities are pretty much limited to the appallingly banal US armed services' Far East Network (FEN).

Even the FM stations are fairly uninspiring although J-WAVE in Tokyo has recently tried to increase the music content and cut the talk. Bring a good supply of tapes and a Walkman if music is essential to your sanity.

Television

Like radio, most television is inaccessible to the non-Japanese speaker and, even if you do speak the language, most programmes seem to be inane variety shows. It's worth watching a few hours as a window into the culture, but it won't take long to figure out what the programmes are all about.

A typical show is hosted by a very elegant duo: he all-knowing, she all-coquettish smiles and gasps of wonderment at the pearls of wisdom he casts nonchalantly at her feet. The panel is a group of 'trendoids', the boys dressed in baggy suits and the girls in tight skirts – a couple of celebrities will also be included in this group but you won't know who they are. The group will be asked questions in response to which they will narrow their eyes, tilt their heads to one side as if pondering the nature of being and mutter 'Sō desu nē' (Really?). The camera will cut to the group of university students, who, in a great display of team spirit, will fall 20 metres from a narrow bridge (toppled by the cushions thrown at them by the other team) into a pool of untreated raw sewage, screaming 'Gambarimasu' (I'll try my hardest) all the way down. This is followed by uproarious laughter from the studio audience.

TVs can be fitted with an adapter so that certain English-language programmes and movies can be received in either Japanese or English. The Japanese Broadcasting Corporation (NHK) even broadcasts a nightly bilingual news report. Unfortunately, Japanese TV news is not the most informative in the world, often running extended reports on the daring rescue of a cat from a tree while the Middle East teeters on the brink of another all-out war. This, combined with the sometimes rather slow and halting simultaneous interpretation by an unusually laconic American, makes the evening news in English not quite the daily event it could be.

Finally, many Japanese hotel rooms will have a pay cable TV with video channels. It is unlikely that English-language movies will be available but the porn channel which is often available needs no translation.

FILM & PHOTOGRAPHY

The Japanese are a nation of photographers. No social occasion is complete without a few snaps and an exchange of the photos taken at the last get together. This, combined with the fact that the Japanese are major producers of camera equipment and film, means there is no problem obtaining photographic equipment or print film. Slide film is not as readily available and is best brought from home.

A 36 exposure Kodachrome 64 slide film costs about Y850 without processing. The very popular disposable cameras are even sold from vending machines. They typically cost from Y1000 to Y2000, more expensive ones have a built-in flash.

Processing

Processing print film is fast and economical in Japan, although the standards are not always the best. In the big cities it is usually possible to have Fuji or Sakura slide film processed within 24 hours and the results appear to be of a consistently high standard. Kodachrome slide film, however, can only be processed by the Imagica Kodak depot in Ginza, Tokyo but the processing is fast (24 hours) and the results are good. There is no problem honouring pre-paid Kodachrome film either. Away from Tokyo, send Kodachrome film to: Far East Laboratories Ltd, 2-14-1 Higashi Gotanda, Shinagawa-ku, Tokyo.

HEALTH

Travel health depends on your predeparture preparations, your day-to-day health care and how you handle any medical problem or emergency that develops. However, looking after your health in Japan should pose few problems since hygiene standards are high and medical facilities widely available, though expensive. The average life expectancy among the Japanese is now 80 years for women and 74 for men, a sure sign that they are doing something right.

Travel Health Guides

There are a number of books on travel health. *Staying Healthy in Asia, Africa & Latin America* (Volunteers in Asia) is probably the best all-round guide to carry as it's compact, very detailed and well organised. *Travellers' Health* (Oxford University Press) by Dr Richard Dawood, is comprehensive and easy to read. Although highly recommended, it's rather large to lug around. *Travel with Children* by Maureen Wheeler, (Lonely Planet Publications) provides basic advice on travel health for younger children.

Predeparture Preparations

No immunisations are required or necessary for Japan.

Health Insurance A travel insurance policy to cover theft, property loss and medical problems is a wise idea. With such a wide variety of policies available, it may be best to consult your travel agent for recommendations. The international student travel policies handled by the Student Travel Association (STA) or other student travel organisations are usually good value. Some policies offer a choice between lower and higher medical expense options; choose the high-cost option for Japan.

Medical Kit A small medical kit is a good thing to carry even though most items will usually be readily available in Japan. Your kit could include:

• Aspirin or panadol – for pain or fever.
• Antihistamine (such as Benadryl) – useful as a decongestant for colds, allergies, to ease the itch from insect bites or stings or to help prevent motion sickness.
• Kaolin preparation (Pepto-Bismol), Imodium or Lomotil – for stomach upsets.
• Antiseptic, mercurochrome and antibiotic powder or similar 'dry' spray – for cuts and grazes.
• Calamine lotion – to ease irritation from bites or stings.
• Bandages and band-aids – for minor injuries.
• Scissors, tweezers and a thermometer – mercury thermometers are prohibited by airlines.
• Insect repellent, sunblock cream (can be difficult to find in Japan), suntan lotion and chapstick.

Health Preparations Make sure you're healthy before you start travelling. If you're shortsighted bring a spare pair of glasses and your prescription. If you require a particular medication take an adequate supply as it may not be available locally. Take the prescription with the generic rather than the brand name which may be unavailable, as it will make getting replacements easier. It's a wise idea to have the prescription with you to show you legally use the medication.

Motion Sickness Eating lightly before and during a trip will reduce the chances of motion sickness. If you are prone to motion sickness, try to find a place that minimises disturbance – near the wing on aircraft, close to midships on boats or near the centre on buses. Fresh air usually helps, reading or cigarette smoke doesn't. Commercial anti-motion-sickness preparations, which can cause drowsiness, have to be taken before the trip commences; when you're feeling sick it's too late. Ginger is a natural preventative and is available in capsule form.

Food & Water

Food hygiene in Japan rarely causes complaints. Most of the raw food can be eaten without health worries although raw freshwater fish and raw wild boar meat should be avoided. The consumption of *fugu* (globefish) – for which you will need a fat wallet – is perhaps the one Japanese dish which can pose real dangers. (See the Food section for more details.)

When rare or endangered species arrive on a plate, make a point of eating something else. The trite Japanese argument that eating whale, dolphin or turtle is part of their culture is no reason to wipe them out.
Robert Strauss

Tap water is safe to drink all over Japan but drinking from mountain streams should be done with caution. On Rebuntō Island (Hokkaidō), travellers have been warned that the springs could be contaminated with fox faeces which contain tapeworm cysts. There have been reports of the schistosomiasis parasite still lurking in the countryside in rice paddies or stagnant water – avoid wading around barefoot in these places.

Medical Assistance

The TIC has lists of English-speaking hospitals and doctors in the large cities. Dental care is widely available at steep prices. If you need a medicine not readily available in Japanese pharmacies try the American Pharmacy (tel 3271-4034) close to the Yuraku-cho TIC in Tokyo. A peculiarity of the Japanese medical system is that most drugs are supplied not by pharmacies but by doctors. Critics say that as a result, doctors are prone to over-prescribe and choose the most expensive drugs.

Emergencies Emergency services in Japan will usually only react fast if you speak Japanese. Try the Tokyo English Lifeline (TELL) (tel 3403-7106) for emergency assistance in English. The Japan Helpline (tel 0120-461-997) is an emergency number which operates 24 hours a day, seven days a week. Don't clog the line unless you really do have an emergency.

Counselling & Advice Adjusting to life in Japan can be tough but there are several places to turn for help. The TELL phone service provides confidential and anonymous help. If they don't have the right answers at hand, they can pass you on to

Traditional Japanese Medicine

As in so many other fields, China has exerted a strong influence over traditional Japanese medicine. Acupuncture *(hari-kyū)* is well known in the West as an oriental medical technique using hair-thin needles (gold, silver, or steel) inserted at key points *(tsubo)* of the body to restore the flow of ki (loosely translated as 'life energy'). Closely associated with acupuncture is *okyū* (moxibustion) which stimulates the key points of the body by burning small amounts of *mogusa* (a powdered herb) over the points.

Shiatsu (acupressure) is also related to acupuncture, but uses the application of finger pressure on the key points of the body. *Kampo* is based on Chinese herbalism with Japanese additions. Several hundred drugs derived from animal, mineral or plant sources are used in small doses, sometimes mixed with water. Many of these remedies have been concocted after centuries of experimentation and can prove helpful, although bats, dragonflies or lizards may be amongst the ingredients.

Onsen (mineral baths) are an old favourite with the Japanese. Legend recounts how samurai warriors, injured in battle, would find their way to a remote mineral bath where they were revived by the waters and recouped their energy to return to the fray. Nowadays, you find mineral baths all over Japan, each one reputed to be beneficial for particular ailments. ■

someone who might. Tokyo Tapes (tel 3262-0224) has a wide variety of tapes available to help you deal with problems.

Contraception

Although oral contraceptives are available from clinics specialising in medical care for foreigners, it is preferable to bring adequate supplies with you. Only in 1990 was the marketing of oral contraceptives officially authorised in Japan. Meanwhile the condom reigns supreme and is the subject of much sniggering humour about the difference between 'regular size' and 'gaijin size'. Abortion remains a widely employed alternative to contraception.

MEETING THE JAPANESE

Your opportunities to meet the Japanese will depend a great deal on the way you travel. Obviously, anyone who is on a whirlwind tour of Japan, stopping in a different destination every night, is going to have far fewer opportunities to meet locals than the traveller who spends some months working in Tokyo or Osaka and then a month or so seeing the country. Nevertheless, even for those with limited time schedules, meeting the Japanese is not impossible due to the thoughtful provision of such programmes as the home visit system (described later in this section).

Shyness

Perhaps the most difficult aspect of getting to meet the Japanese is their almost chronic shyness. Young Japanese have generally been discouraged from taking individual initiative and consequently, visitors are much more likely to be surrounded by a gaggle of giggling school children chorusing 'haro' than having an interesting conversation with one or two Japanese. Many young Japanese will simply freeze in stunned and embarrassed silence if directly addressed by a foreigner. Unfortunately, the same applies to many adults if they have had little experience of gaijin.

Much of the Japanese shyness stems from the fear of making a mistake and somehow causing offence. The possibility of not responding appropriately often makes them extremely nervous in situations they've not been trained to deal with, such as a foreigner speaking to them in English or in halting Japanese. If you need to make casual contact with a Japanese, say, to ask directions, it is always best to appear calm and relaxed and smile as you talk.

I once had the experience of turning to a Japanese in frustration after wandering around Ikebukuro station looking for the north exit for what seemed an eternity, only to hear her screech in fear and scamper off. The harassed look on my face promised all kinds of potential communication problems that most Japanese would simply rather not deal with.

Tony Wheeler

Nowadays, particularly in the big cities, more and more Japanese are becoming accustomed to dealing with foreigners. The school system is using foreign teachers as assistants for teaching English and many students attend private English-language schools where they regularly have contact with gaijin. The result is that levels of foreign-language expertise and confidence in dealing with ambassadors from the outside world are on the rise in Japan.

Etiquette

One of the most enduring Western notions about Japan is that of Japanese courtesy and rigid social etiquette. With a little sensitivity, however, there is little chance of mortally offending anyone with your lack of social grace.

To be sure, many things are different: the Japanese bow and indulge in a ritualised exchange of *meishi* (business cards) when they meet; they exchange their shoes for uncomfortable plastic slippers before entering the home; and social occasions involve sitting on the floor in positions that will put the legs of an ill-bred foreigner to sleep within five minutes. But, overall, most of the really complex aspects of Japanese social interaction are functions of the language and only pose problems for the advanced student who's trying to get as close to the culture as possible.

Sitting When socialising with the Japanese or visiting them in their homes, sitting on the floor for extended periods of time can be a real nightmare for many foreigners. Sit with your legs beneath you for as long as possible and then, if you *must* stretch your legs out, do so discreetly without pointing them in anyone's direction. Pointing your feet (the lowest part of the body, literally) at people, even inadvertently, is bad form throughout Asia.

Bowing When you meet Japanese, it's polite to bow slightly from the waist and incline your head. Actually, the rule is that the deepness of a Japanese bow depends on the status (relative to oneself) of the person to whom one is bowing. When A has higher status than B (all this information is codified in the meishi), it is important that B's bow is deeper than A's. As the bows take place simultaneously, it is often incumbent on B to give a quick, surreptitious glance in the direction of A's exalted presence to determine that his or her bow is indeed lower than A's. Fortunately, no-one expects foreigners to carry on like this, and nowadays, many Japanese have taken to shaking hands, though the bow is still the most important mark of respect.

Business Cards If you're going to be working in Japan, get some business cards made up: without them, you'll be a nobody. All introductions and meetings in Japan involve an exchange of business cards – handing out yours to the right people can make things happen but not having a card will definitely look very bad. Cards should be handed over, and accepted, with some ceremony, studied carefully and referred to often. Do not simply stuff a proffered card into your pocket. Also, never write anything on a card you are given.

The Kimi Information centre in Tokyo (near the Kimi Ryokan in Ikebukuro) will make business cards for you, one side in English the other in Japanese, at a very reasonable price.

Gift Giving Reciprocity is an integral part of Japanese culture, and the exchange of gifts, the return of one kindness with another, is an important part of Japanese daily life. If you visit somebody at their home, you should bring them a gift. It needn't be anything big – chocolates or flowers, much the same things that are used as gifts in the West, will do. Ideally, it is nice to bring something from your own country. Gifts used for cementing friendships and for paying off small obligations are usually small and unostentatious. Where money is given it is presented in an envelope.

As a foreigner, it's quite likely that people will sometimes want to give you gifts 'for your travels'. You may not be able to reciprocate in these situations. The polite thing to do is to refuse a couple of times when the gift is offered. The other party will probably keep pushing as long as you keep refusing. A couple of refusals are enough not to seem too grasping before making off with your spoils.

Gift giving is so important in Japan that it has become institutionalised in many aspects of Japanese social life. If, for example, you are invited to a wedding, you are expected to bring a 'gift' of at least Y20,000 – consequently young Japanese with too many friends of a marriageable age can often have a very lean time of it if they all get married in the same year. One of the most notorious 'gifts', among foreign residents at least, is 'key money', the two month's rent that you must dole out to the owner of your new home. For many Westerners, this all seems like so much bribery; for the Japanese, these gift-giving rituals operate to show respect, to give face and to ensure smooth interpersonal relations.

Flattery What passes for flattery in the West is often perceived as quite natural in Japan. The Japanese recognise the importance of a bit of ego stroking and generally will never pass up the opportunity to praise each other in company. The foreigner who has made an effort to learn a few sentences of Japanese or to get by with chopsticks is likely to be regularly regaled with gasps of astonishment and unctuous praise. Don't feel anxious; the intent is not facetious, it's genuinely meant to make you feel good.

The correct response to praise is to decline it. Even if you do feel your dextrous manipulation of the chopsticks has reached a rarely achieved level of proficiency, the best response to exclamations of 'How skilful you are!' is to smile and say something like 'Not at all'. Importantly, don't forget to return a few compliments here and there – although there's no need to force yourself if it doesn't come naturally.

Directness One major difference between the Japanese and Westerners is that the Japanese do not make a virtue out of being direct. Indeed, directness is seen as vulgar; the Japanese prefer to resort to more vague strategies and to feel their way through a situation when dealing with others. The Japanese have a term for this that translates as 'stomach talk' – where both sides tentatively edge around an issue, feeling out the other's point of view until it is clear which direction negotiations can go. This can often result in what for many Westerners is a seemingly interminable toing and froing that only ever seems to yield ambiguous results. But don't be deceived, the Japanese can usually read the situation just as clearly as if both sides were clearly stating their interests.

Basically, when you're dealing with the Japanese, avoid direct statements that are likely to be perceived as confrontational. If someone ventures an opinion, however stupid it may seem, try not to crush it with a 'No, I disagree completely,' or something similar.

Go-Betweens The dislike of directness among the Japanese gives rise to another interesting phenomenon that residents are likely to come into contact with: the go-between. When the Japanese do have to confront someone with something unpleasant, it is customary to find a disinterested third party to do so. For example, if a misunderstanding arose between you and your concierge, he/she might contact your employer who, in turn, would represent his/her interests to you.

The thing to do in situations like this is not to become angry at the person meddling in your private affairs but to remember that the Japanese do this not so much from timidity as from a sense of being too close to an issue to be able to deal with it sensibly. The mediator plays an important role in all kinds of difficult social situations, the most famous of these being the *o-miai* or marriage go-betweens.

Calls of Nature It's not unusual to find men urinating in crowded streets, and public toilets are often unsegregated, but the public use of handkerchiefs for blowing your nose is definitely frowned upon. A Japanese student once related to me with an air of genuine disgust how, on a train, he had seen a beautiful Western girl take a hankie from her handbag and blow her nose into it. 'How could such a beautiful girl have such bad manners?' he wondered. The polite thing to do if you have a cold in public is to keep sniffing (an admirable sign of self-restraint in Japanese eyes) until you can get to some private place to do your business.

Home Visit System

The home visit system is publicised in JNTO pamphlets and gives visitors to some of Japan's larger cities the opportunity to visit a Japanese family in their home. Visits take place in the evening and, while dinner is usually not served, the hosts will often provide tea and sweets. It is polite to bring a small gift with you when you visit to show your appreciation of your hosts' thoughtfulness and hospitality.

Home visits can be organised in the following cities: Tokyo (tel 03-3502-1461), Yokohama (tel 045-641-5824), Kyoto (tel 075-752-0215), Osaka (tel 06-345-2189), Kōbe (tel 078-303-1010), Nagoya (tel 052-581-5678), Sapporo (tel 011-211-3341), Okayama (tel 0862-32-2255), Hiroshima (tel 082-247-6738), Fukuoka (tel 092-292-0777), Nagasaki (tel 0958-24-1111) and Kagoshima (tel 0992-24-1111).

Conversation Lounges

The conversation lounge is a uniquely Japanese institution that gives members an opportunity to meet foreigners in an informal setting. Generally, Japanese pay a fee to participate for an evening, while foreigners are admitted free. The lounge is usually a coffee-shop setup, though occasionally, as in Mickey House in Tokyo, alcohol is served. Lounges are almost always an excellent place to meet and talk with Japanese people who have an interest in the world outside their own country. For more information about conversation lounges, check the English-language magazines and the Tokyo chapter of this book.

WOMEN TRAVELLERS

Japan never gives you a chance to make your mind up firmly about anything. Just when you've decided something works one way, something happens to convince you the opposite is true. This policy of opposites applies to women travellers as well.

The crime rate in all categories is very low in Japan so the risk of rape or assault is minimal. Women should take normal precautions of course, but can travel by subway at night or wander the streets of the entertainment districts (dodging the reeling salarymen) with little concern.

The major concern of women travellers in many countries – 'Will I be physically safe?' – is not a worry in Japan, though jam-packed rush-hour subways or buses can still bring out the worst in the Japanese male. When movement is impossible, roving hands are frequently at work and women often put up with this interference because in Japan, it would simply be impolite or unseemly to make a fuss! Actually a loud complaint might have little effect in any case, since the usual Japanese reaction would be to look in the opposite direction and pretend this distasteful occurrence was not happening in their carriage. One woman visitor has suggested that it is not a Western woman's duty to reinforce Japanese mores and, if possible, the offending hand should be grabbed, held

up and the whereabouts of its owner inquired about (or better still, it should be bitten!).

There are some aspects of Japanese life which are not anti-female but certainly strike women as peculiar on first encounter. Public toilets, for example, are often not sex segregated although there may be doors labelled male and female. It can be a real shock to a Western woman when she enters the door marked 'women' and finds a row of urinals with men lined up at them! It's an equal shock to the unprepared Western male when he steps back from a urinal and finds women all around him.

Comic books (manga) and other mass media often portray women in wildly exploitative situations. Many of the manga themes would raise howls of protest from women's groups in the West but men openly read these comics in trains and other public places. The crime rate statistics would appear to indicate that they do not turn the readers into slavering brutes.

Women in Japan are, however, very much second class citizens. Pay levels for women relative to those for men are lower than any other advanced nation. In most companies, women are considered temporary workers, filling in a few years between school and marriage. They are referred to as OLs, office ladies, and it is considered highly unlikely that they will rise above the most menial ranks. The steady path to the top is strictly reserved for the salarymen. Many women work in occupations where they are purely decorative – they may be the smiling, bowing greeters at department store entrances or the coffee servers in big companies.

Many manual jobs, which, in the West would have a small but visible percentage of female workers, are strictly banned to women in Japan. Many manufacturing companies, for example, bar women from working on the assembly lines; one wonders if there is a female taxi or bus driver anywhere in Japan?

Yet, some of this is changing. Japan has been suffering a severe shortage of workers, particularly for those menial tasks the Japanese are simply no longer willing to undertake, and a blind eye is being turned to illegal immigration. In this situation, Japanese companies are being forced to relax male-only hiring policies.

The yuppie syndrome has also hit Japan in a big way and is changing the typical pattern where a woman works for only a few years and then devotes herself to raising a family. Furthermore, younger women are often the most affluent of Japanese consumers and much more attention is being paid to them by advertisers – young women do not have to squander a large part of their income on nightly circuits of the bars and entertainment districts the way an aspiring salaryman has to.

Finally, some observers feel that the very basis of women's deference to men is withering. For the past generation, the father figures to whom young children are taught to defer have simply not been there, they've been away winning the economic wars every day and consolidating the victory in the bars every night. A whole generation of women has grown up with that important, and superior, male figure hardly in sight.

DANGERS & ANNOYANCES
Theft
The low incidence of theft and crime in general in Japan is frequently commented on, though of course, theft does exist and its unlikelihood is no reason for carelessness. Airports and air terminals are reputed to be amongst the worst places in Japan for pickpockets and other sneak thieves, so take extra care in these places. It's probable the stolen goods are on their way overseas before the owner even realises their disappearance.

Lost and found services really do seem to work so, if you leave something behind on a train or other transport, it's always worth inquiring if it has been turned in.

Earthquakes
Japan is a very earthquake-prone country although most will only show up on instrumentation. If you experience a strong earthquake, look for a doorway or support-ing pillar. Small rooms, like a bathroom or cupboard, are often stronger than large rooms but even a table or desk can provide some protection from falling debris. Of course, it is better to be outside than inside, but keep away from buildings because of the danger of falling glass or other debris.

Fire
Although modern hotels are subject to high safety standards, traditional Japanese buildings with their wooden construction and tightly packed surroundings can be real fire traps. Fortunately, most old buildings are small places where you are unlikely to be trapped on the 40th floor but it's wise to check fire exits and escapes. Onsen (hot-spring/spa) centres, where buildings are often traditional in design with floors covered in grass tatami mats and where much drunken revelry takes place, can pose particular dangers.

Beaches & Swimming
Few public beaches have lifeguards and summer weekends bring many drowning accidents. Watch for undertows or other dangers. Severe sunburn is possible in Japan, just as in more obviously 'hot' places. However, as yet, the Japanese seem unaware of the dangers of overexposure. Bring a good sunblock lotion if you will be outdoors for long hours in the summer.

Noise
In Japanese cities, the noise assault on the auditory senses is spectacular, so it's no wonder so many pedestrians are plugged in to Walkmans. Pedestrian crossings are serenaded by electronic playtime music, loudspeaker systems broadcast muzak or advertisements, bus passengers are bombarded with running commentaries in Mickey Mouse tones and accommodation may include TVs turned up full volume in dining rooms or lounges. Earplugs can help.

Size
Even medium-sized foreigners need to mind their head in Japanese dwellings, though, in

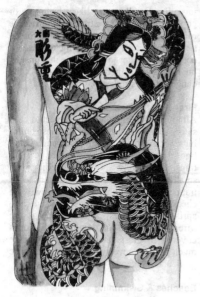

Yakuza Tattoos

some homes, padded bags attached to the top of door frames appear to acknowledge the problem. The Western frame may find it hard to fit into some seats and those with long legs will often find themselves wedged tight. Toilets in cramped accommodation necessitate contortions and careful aim. Sitting cross-legged takes a little practice to avoid the embarrassment of standing up only to find your legs so numb that you promptly topple over.

Some American physiotherapists told me that Asian people, many of whom spend a lifetime stretching their knee joints in the cross-legged position, suffer much less from knee problems than Westerners.

Wildlife

Japan is hardly a high danger region when it comes to wildlife although in Okinawa Prefecture, much fuss is made about the 'deadly *habu*' snake. To avoid an unhappy encounter with a deadly habu don't go traipsing barefoot through the undergrowth. Snake bites do not cause instantaneous death and antivenenes are available. Keep the victim calm and still, wrap the bitten limb tightly, as you would for a sprained ankle, and then attach a splint to immobilise it. Then seek medical help, if possible with the dead snake for identification. Don't attempt to catch the snake if there is any remote possibility of being bitten again. Tourniquets and sucking out the poison are now comprehensively discredited. On the mainland islands the *mamushi* is also poisonous.

There are still bears in remote areas of Hokkaidō and they can be fiercely protective of their cubs. Foxes, also found in Hokkaidō, can carry diseases and should be avoided. Japan also has wasps, mosquitoes and other biting or stinging insects but not in extraordinary numbers or of unusual danger. Jellyfish and other marine dangers also exist and local advice should be heeded before entering the water.

Smoking

One dangerous habit you're almost certain

The Yakuza

The Yakuza – the Japanese 'Mafia' – control or have major interests in the sex industry, *pachinko* (pinball) parlours and dog fighting. They seem to be accepted as a necessary evil and actually go out of their way to look the part. A yakuza will often drive a US *yakuzamobile* (nobody else fancies US cars very much), will affect an arrogant swagger *(iburi)* and a gruff manner of speech *(aragoto)*. The yakuza are also famed for their body tattoos; cherry blossom tattoos signify the brief but cheerful life of an ardent criminal. ∎

to indulge in while visiting Japan is passive smoking. Japan looks like being the last advanced nation to face up to the dangers of smoking – cigarettes are readily available and, at Y220 to Y240 for a pack from a vending machine, they're also cheap. Although the anti-smoking lobby is growing and there are now more nonsmoking seats on aircraft and more nonsmoking carriages on trains, Japan is still a long way behind California or Singapore.

HIGHLIGHTS

Visitors to Japan have few preconceptions of any highlight they definitely do not want to miss – there is no Taj Mahal, Statue of Liberty, Sydney Opera House or Eiffel Tower in Japan. Nevertheless there are numerous interesting things to see and areas of interest worth pursuing.

Castles

Although the Meiji Restoration was bad news for Japan's castles, the preceding Tokugawa Shogunate had not been good for their preservation either. The 'one kingdom, one castle' rule had resulted in many surplus castles being destroyed or dismantled. During the centuries of peace under the Tokugawas, castles were simply redundant; when they caught fire there was often no hurry to reconstruct them. Then, in 1873, the sixth year of the Meiji era, the government ordered the destruction of 144 of these feudal symbols and only 39 remained.

World War II further reduced Japan's castles and today only 12 original castle keeps remain. The '60s saw an enormous spate of castle reconstructions, but these were all rebuilt like Hollywood movie sets, very authentic looking from a distance but constructed from very 'unfeudal' concrete and steel.

Perhaps the greatest original castle is Himeji-jō, the huge and impressive 'White Egret' Castle. It's an easy day trip from Kyoto. The contrasting black Matsumoto-jō is also well preserved and in very original

Osaka Castle

condition. Hirosaki-jō Castle has some interesting surroundings including a samurai quarter. Conveniently near Kyoto are the pretty lakeside Hikone-jō and the small Inuyama-jō Castle.

Although Matsuyama-jō Castle was rebuilt only a few years before the Edo era ground to a halt, it has a spectacular setting overlooking the town and the appearance of a complete and battle-ready fortress. Shikoku's other original castles at Kōchi, Uwajima and Marugame are smaller, less impressive affairs. Maruoka-jō has the oldest surviving castle keep in Japan, though otherwise, it's not of great interest.

Matsue-jō Castle has a fine setting and some interesting nearby streets. Bitchu-Matsuyama Castle at Takahashi represents an earlier era, hidden away on a high hilltop rather than standing proudly at the centre of its town. Kumamoto-jō Castle is a modern reconstruction, but its design is very interesting; the museum has informative displays about castle construction. Edo Castle was once the largest castle in the world; today its huge moats and walls surround the Tokyo Imperial Palace.

Gardens

Japan is famed for its beautiful gardens and whether they are the larger Edo 'stroll gardens' or the small contemplative Zen gardens the emphasis is always on exquisite attention to detail. The Japanese love to rate things and the 'big three' in the garden category are the Kairaku-en (Mito), the Kenroku-en (Kanazawa) and the Kōraku-en (Okayama). Not all visitors are likely to agree with the official listings; Mito, for example, gets the nod principally because it has lots of lawn.

Kyoto has almost too many gardens to mention, including gardens that virtually define the rock garden and the Zen dry-landscape garden concepts. Among the best smaller Zen gardens outside Kyoto are the beautiful Kōmyō-ji at Dazaifu, the Jōei-ji in Yamaguchi and the Raikyū-ji at Takahashi.

Other large gardens include the Ritsurin-kōen in Takamatsu, the Suizenji-kōen with its miniature Mt Fuji in Kumamoto and the Iso-teien in Kagoshima with a real smoking volcano as borrowed scenery. Hikone has the very beautiful Genkyū-en Garden and also one of Japan's few surviving original castles. Close to Tokyo, the Sankei-en Park in Yokohama is also very fine.

History & Old Japan

Feudal castles are not the only symbols of 'old Japan' which have disappeared over the years. The destruction of WW II, the Japanese penchant for knocking down the old and putting up the new, plus the often flimsy and inflammable construction of so many old Japanese buildings have combined to leave few reminders of an earlier Japan. Apart from temples, shrines and castles there are, however, some intriguing reminders of the country's history.

Hakodate, in Hokkaidō is a fascinating old port town with some very interesting old buildings. Hakone, near Tokyo, was a post town on the Tōkaidō and preserves a short stretch of that historic road. Tsumago and Magome also maintain their old post town atmosphere.

Takayama, north of Nagoya, has many fine old buildings and a farmhouse village (Hida Folk Village) consisting of more than a dozen houses of the *gasshō-zukuri* or 'hands in prayer' architectural style. The houses were all dismantled and reconstructed as a village after a huge dam was built in the region. Similar farmhouse villages can be found at Kawasaki and Takamatsu. Kanazawa, which escaped bombing during WW II, is another town with many reminders of an earlier era.

Kurashiki is famed for its canal district and old warehouses, many of which have been converted into museums. A little further along the San-yō coast is Tomo no Ura, an interesting small port you can explore by bicycle. On the opposite San-in coast, the town of Hagi exemplifies the kind of contradiction so typical of Japan. While the town is famous for its role in the ending of the Edo era and the beginning of the Meiji Restoration, it is equally famous for its finely preserved Edo period buildings. Uchiko in Shikoku has a single old street where wealthy wax merchants once lived.

Nagasaki's atomic destruction distracts from its earlier history as a gateway between Japan and the outside world. During the centuries of seclusion under the Tokugawa Shogunate, Nagasaki was virtually the only peephole to the outside world and is still a remarkably cosmopolitan city today. The small town of Chiran, near Kagoshima in southern Kyūshū, has an old street of well-preserved samurai buildings and a more modern historic reminder in the form of a kamikaze museum.

Shrines

Japan's dual religions means there are two sets of indigenous religious structures – Shinto shrines and Buddhist temples. The shrines are known as *jinja, jingū* or *gū* and the arched torii is a positive indicator that you are entering a shrine rather than a temple.

The three great shrine centres are Ise, Nikko and Izumo Taisha. Ise has the imperial shrine to Amaterasu, the mythical ancestor of the Japanese imperial line. Nikko has the shrine to Ieyasu Tokugawa, founder of the Tokugawa Shogunate. Izumo Taisha has the largest and, it is claimed, oldest shrine hall in Japan. Kyoto is, of course, particularly well endowed with impressive shrines.

Other important or interesting shrines include the very popular Meiji-jingū Shrine in Tokyo, the Itsukushima-jinja with its much photographed floating torii on Miyajima Island and the hilltop Kotohira-gū Shrine in Shikoku. Kyūshū has two particularly interesting shrines. The Tenman-gū Shrine at Dazaifu near Fukuoka is dedicated to the legendary Sugawara no Michizane, who was exiled here from Kyoto. Just outside Takachiho the Ama no Iwato-jinja has the very cave where the sun goddess Amaterasu once hid.

In Northern Honshū, you can see shrines frequented by worshippers of Shugendō in the spectacular surroundings of the sacred mountains of Dewa Sanzan, near Tsuruoka.

Temples

Distinguishing a Buddhist temple from a Shinto shrine is simply a matter of examining the entrance. While shrines are entered through an arched torii, a temple or *ji* is entered through a gateway, usually flanked by guardian figures. The most important temples in Japan are concentrated in Kyoto and Nara and the surrounding Kinki District.

Important Kyoto temples include the Daitoku-ji, with its gardens; the ancient Kiyomizu-dera with its superb hillside site; the 13th century Sanjūsangen-dō and the Tō-ji, founded by Kōbō Daishi. Nara has the fine Tōshōdai-ji and the Tōdai-ji, with its Great Buddha. Also in the Kinki District is Kōbō Daishi's mountaintop Kōya-san, the wonderful Hōryū-ji and the Byōdō-in in Uji, one of the most famous buildings in Japan.

In Kamakura, the Kōtoku-in Temple has the best known giant Buddha statue in Japan. Although the 88 temples in Kōbō Daishi's circuit of Shikoku have no great significance individually, taken together, they make up the most important pilgrimage route in Japan. The Kōsan-ji, at nearby Setoda in the Inland Sea, is a Disneyland of temples – all modern reproductions of important temples crammed together in one location. Onomichi, on the Honshū coast near Setoda, has an interesting temple walk.

Scenery & Natural Attractions

Expressways, railways, factories, skyscrapers and a teeming population would scarcely seem to leave room for natural attractions. Yet, despite the population density, Japan is a mountainous country with many areas of great natural beauty.

Just as the Japanese rate the three best gardens, they also rate the three best views. These are the 'floating' torii of Miya-jima Island (see the Shrines section), the long sandspit of Amanohashidate and the bay of Matsushima, with its pine-covered islands. The misty, island-dotted waters of the Inland Sea would also have to be one of the most beautiful sights.

Some of the most spectacular mountain scenery in Japan is found in Nagano-ken

(Kamikōchi; Hakuba) and northern Gifu-ken (Takayama; Shōkawa Valley region).

Mt Fuji, the much climbed symbol of Japan, can actually seem like Tokyo Station at rush hour when you get close up, but from a distance, it's as beautiful as it has ever been. Mt Bandai-san and its lakes in the Tōhoku region offers more superb scenery.

Hokkaidō, the second largest but least densely populated island, offers wonderful mountain scenery around Mashu-ko Lake in the Daisetsuzan National Park and around Tōya-ko and Shikotsu-ko lakes in the west. The Shiretoko-hantō and Shakotan-hantō peninsulas have fine coastal scenery.

If you can possibly squeeze in an extra few days on Hokkaidō, the islands of Rishiritō and Rebuntō in the north offer superb hiking.

Kyūshū has some wonderful volcanic scenery, particularly in the immense caldera of Mt Aso, the bleak, volcano-studded Kirishima National Park, and rumbling Sakurajima near Kagoshima. At the extreme western end of the country, Iriomote-jima Island has dense jungle and good scuba diving.

Modern Japan

Ancient temples and shrines, feudal castles and Zen gardens are all very well but Japan is also the land of *pachinko* pinball parlours, love hotels, robot-operated production lines and multi-storey buildings filled with nothing but bars. It's also the first (and, thank God, still the only) place to have suffered atomic destruction. The atomic bomb museums at Hiroshima and Nagasaki are something no visitor to Japan should avoid.

Hiroshima is also a good place to see the modern Japanese industrial machine in peak form. It's easy to arrange a factory visit at many centres in Japan, but the huge Mazda car factory in Hiroshima is certainly worth a visit. After work, the Japanese salarymen head for the huge entertainment districts, where the neon burns bright and the bill at the end of the evening would bankrupt the average Third World country. Even if you don't venture inside a single bar, these col-ourful areas are fascinating to wander around. Interesting ones include Tokyo's up-market Roppongi area and, in the Shinjuku district, the decidedly raunchier Kabuki-cho area. Shinjuku in Tokyo is also 'modern Japan' at its most modern; with two million people passing through its railway station everyday, Shinjuku is probably the busiest place in the world.

Osaka's Namba district is another good example of a busy entertainment district, while Nakasu Island in Fukuoka is said to have a higher concentration of bars than anywhere else in Japan – hence the world?

If you travel north in search of bars and nightlife, then you should head for the Kokubun-cho district in Sendai and the Sus-ukino district in Sapporo, Hokkaidō.

The Japanese passion for hot springs is well documented and, in many places, is a very tasteful and ritualistic activity. In others, it is most definitely not. The spa town of Beppu in Kyūshū is the Las Vegas of onsen towns with bright lights and bad taste in full swing. Love hotels are another side of Japan and it's surprising that an enterprising publisher hasn't yet produced a coffee-table book on love hotel architecture. In some places there are major enclaves of love hotels, the Dōgenzaka area of Tokyo's Shibuya district is a good example.

ACCOMMODATION

Japan offers a wide variety of accommodation, Japanese-style and Western-style establishments catering to all budgets from shoestring to the ultra-rich.

Compared to the rest of Asia, Japanese budget places make a sizeable dent in the pocket, the lowest price per person per night being around Y1400. The average cost at a youth hostel is around Y1900, although there are slight seasonal variations. By staying at the cheapest places, you will conserve funds, but you will also cut yourself off from an essential part of the Japan experience – trying out different types of accommodation. You will considerably add to your enjoyment if you manage to vary your accommodation routine to include at least one night at a traditional ryokan (Japanese-style inn), *shukubō* (temple lodging) and minshuku (Japanese B&B).

Cheap places to stay are often further out of town which can mean an expensive taxi ride if you arrive late. If you get really stuck in the late hours, the nearest *kōban* (police box) should be able to point you in the right direction for a place to stay. Taxi drivers can also help, once you've explained the type and price of place you'd prefer. Business hotels are often conveniently close to the station. Capsule hotels or love hotels are useful late-night alternatives.

Reservations

Generally, it is quite feasible to look for a room when you arrive in a new town, though reservations are best made a few days in advance. During peak holiday seasons, you should book as far ahead as possible, particularly if you have a special choice. Out of season, calling a day in advance is usually sufficient.

The information office (annai-jo) at a main railway station can usually help with reservations, and is often open until about 6.30 pm or later. Even if you are travelling by car, the railway station is a good first stop in town for information, reservations and

Toilets

Western toilets are on the increase in Japan. On one trip aboard the bullet train, I was intrigued to see queues outside the Western toilet whilst the Japanese one remained vacant. A Dutch couple told me that back in the '70s, there were instructive diagrams on the correct use of Western toilets as part of a drive to dissuade toilet-goers from standing on the seat and aiming from on high.

It's quite common to see men urinating in public, typically in the evening in a bar district. In Shinjuku (Tokyo) I watched a tipsy, soberly suited salaryman slip behind a policeman and pee against the wall a couple of feet behind him. When the salaryman was finished, he turned round, thanked the policeman, exchanged bows and tottered into the station.

Japanese toilets are Asian style – level with, or in the floor. The correct position is to squat facing the hood, away from the door. This is the opposite to squat toilets in most other places in Asia. Make sure the contents of your pockets don't spill out. Toilet paper isn't always provided so carry tissues with you. Separate toilet slippers are often provided just inside the toilet door. These are for use in the toilet only, so remember to change out of them when you leave.

Mixed toilets also exist. Men and women often go through separately marked entrances, but land up in the same place. No-one feels worried and privacy is provided by cubicles and women are supposed to simply ignore the backs turned to them at the urinals. The kanji script for 'toilet' is 洗手間, for 'men' 男 and for 'women' 女

A recent newspaper article claimed that in about four years, research on the 'intelligent lavatory' would be complete. According to the article, these lavatories will use the latest microchip technology to check the user's waste products, weight, temperature and even blood pressure. Further research will also investigate the possibility of direct links between these smart conveniences and the closest hospitals so that suspicious symptoms are reported instantly and nipped in the bud. Of course, there are wide implications in this merging of private moments and public data. Perhaps, in the realms of litigation, constipation will be considered as the withholding of information!

My favourite establishment is a musical rest room at the remote tip of Sukoton Peninsula on Rebuntō Island, Hokkaidō. In the middle of nowhere stands this brand-new, windswept rest room. As you enter, an electric eye starts a tape, which plays classical guitar music or the recorded swishing of the sea which is outside the door.

Robert Strauss ■

even cheap car parking. The Japanese run their accommodation according to an established rhythm which favours checkouts at around 10 am and check-ins between 5 and 7 pm; unannounced latecomers disturb their pattern.

Making phone reservations in English is usually possible in most cities. Providing you speak clearly and simply, there will usually be someone around who can get the gist of what you want. However, once you head into the outlying areas, making telephone reservations in Japanese can be a major hassle for both sides. In practice, a combination of phrasebook consultation, memorised scraps of Japanese and your telephone partner's morsels of English usually get results. One way to avoid this linguistic jousting is to ask a passing Japanese for help or to ask the desk staff of your last place of accommodation to phone your reservation through.

Information on accommodation listings is provided in this section's accommodation categories. JNTO offices abroad and TIC offices in Tokyo and Kyoto also stock some of these publications as well as their own lists. JNTO publishes *Reasonable Accommodations in Japan (MG-085)*, a useful leaflet with details of 200 hotels, ryokan and business hotels in 50 major cities in Japan.

Gaijin Houses 外人ハウス

This is the cheapest category of accommodation, especially for long-term stays, but you should be prepared for basic dorms or shared tatami rooms and probably a communal kitchen. Prices for the cheapest houses start around Y1400 per night. Some places offer reductions for stays longer than a month.

Most of the gaijin houses are in Tokyo and Kyoto where listings are available from TIC. You can also find advertisements or listings of these places in publications such as *Tokyo Journal, Kansai Time Out* or *Kyoto Visitor's Guide*.

Youth Hostels ユースホステル

For anyone wanting to keep to a low budget,

youth hostels are the best option and it is quite feasible to plan an entire itinerary using them. By far the best source of information on hostels is the (Japan) *Youth Hostel Handbook* available for Y580 from the Japan Youth Hostel Association (JYHA) (tel 3269-5831), Hoken Kaikan, 1-2 Sadohara-cho, Ichigaya, Shinjuku-ku, Tokyo 162.

Branch offices in Tokyo which stock the handbook and can supply information are in the second level basement of Sogo department store, Yuraku-cho (two minutes on foot from TIC); the 4th floor of the Keio department store, Shinjuku; and the 7th floor of the Seibu department store, Ikebukuro. Many hostels throughout Japan also sell the handbook.

The *Youth Hostel Map of Japan* (approximately Y225) is a map with one-line entries for each hostel on the reverse. JNTO publishes *Youth Hostels in Japan*, a concise English listing of youth hostels.

The JYHA handbook is mostly in Japanese, though there is some English at the front in the symbol key and on the locator map keys. The hostels on each map are identified by name (in kanji) and a page number. Each hostel is accompanied by a mini-map, photo, address in Japanese, fax and phone details, a row of symbols, access instructions in Japanese, open dates, bed numbers and prices for bed and meals.

By looking at the photos and the symbols it is quite easy to single out hostels which might be interesting. The reversed swastika symbol means that the hostel is a temple. Pay careful attention to the closing and opening dates: many hostels – particularly those in rural areas – close over New Year or shut down in the winter. For the musically inclined, the handbook even has a page with the words and music for the 'Youth Hostel Song'.

The *Youth Hostel Map of Japan* has hostel addresses in English, but it can still be a struggle trying to work out a romaji version of the address. The *IYHF Handbook Vol II* has a ridiculously skimpy set of entries for Japan and is not worth considering for a Japan trip.

Youth Hostel Categories There are various categories of youth hostel in Japan: JYHA hostels, privately run and government-subsidised hostels, ryokan hostels and hostels run by youth organisations, shrines and temples. In general, the atmosphere is more relaxed at privately run hostels, ryokan and religious establishments; the other hostels can sometimes feel as if they are being run as military camps.

Membership & Regulations You can stay at the 75 municipal hostels without a youth hostel membership card. Elsewhere, you will need a JYHA membership card or one from an affiliate of the International Youth Hostel Federation (IYHF) otherwise you must pay an extra charge. It is much simpler if you join in your own country, as JYHA registration requires that members have lived in Japan for a year, have an Alien Registration Card and pay a Y2000 joining fee.

Nonmembers must pay an additional Y450 per night for a 'welcome stamp'. Six welcome stamps plus a photograph entitles you to a IYHF International Guest Card valid worldwide for the rest of the year. If you purchase all six stamps at once the price is reduced to Y2200, a saving of Y500.

Youth hostel membership has a minimum age limit of four years but no maximum age – you will meet plenty of Japanese wrinklies and often a few foreign ones approaching their 70s as well. When it comes to hostels, youth springs eternal!

Hostel charges currently average Y1900 per night; some also add the 3% consumption tax. Private rooms are available in some hostels at Y3500 per night. Average prices for meals are Y450 for breakfast and Y750 for dinner. Although official regulations state that you can only stay at one hostel for three consecutive nights, this probably depends on the season.

Almost all hostels require you to use a regulation sleeping sheet which you can rent for Y100 if you do not have your own. As a friendly gesture, some hostels have introduced a special reduction – sometimes as much as Y500 per night – for foreign hostellers.

Hostellers are expected to check in between 3 and 8 pm. Checkout is usually required before 10 am and dormitories are closed between 10 am and 3 pm. Bath time is usually between 5 and 9 pm, dinner time is between 6 and 7.30 pm, breakfast time is between 7 and 8 am.

Hostel Food The food at hostels varies widely: some places provide stodgy and unimaginative fare while others pull out all the stops to offer excellent value. At consecutive hostels in Hokkaidō, you may be served a luscious Jenghis Khan hotpot one night, sukiyaki the next and sashimi the following night – all accompanied by copious complimentary beer!

The hostel breakfast is usually Japanese style, for which it takes a little time to acquire a taste. I'll admit it, I sometimes skipped natto (fermented soybeans), seaweed and raw egg and went off in search of a setto (set breakfast) of coffee, toast and a boiled egg from a nearby coffee shop.

Robert Strauss

Youth hostel meals are not necessarily the cheapest. A morning coffee-shop setto or an evening teishoku (set meal) in a neighbourhood restaurant can work out more economical.

Many hostels now allow alcohol on the premises. Some require you to help with the washing-up, others prefer to keep you out of the kitchen.

Reservations Advance reservations are essential for the New Year holiday weeks, March, the late April/early May Golden Week, and July and August. You should state the arrival date and time, number of nights, number and sex of the people for whom beds are to be reserved and the meals required. When corresponding from abroad *always* include two International Reply Coupons.

In Japan, computer bookings can be made in Tokyo and Osaka and increasing numbers of youth hostels are plugging into the system. Many hostels also have fax numbers. For confirmation, return postage-paid postcards are available from post offices or to make things even simpler, use the pre-printed cards available from JYHA headquarters in Tokyo.

Telephone bookings are fine if you can handle enough Japanese. One way to simplify things is to ask a Japanese, perhaps a fellow hosteller or a member of the youth hostel staff, to make the booking.

Out of season you can probably get away with booking a day or so in advance. Hostels *definitely* prefer you to phone, even if it's from across the street, rather than simply rolling up without warning. If you arrive without warning, you shouldn't expect any meals.

The one time I turned up on a youth hostel's doorstep unannounced, I received a very sour reception and a long lecture in Japanese about phoning ahead – even though I later discovered that I was the only person staying in a completely empty hostel!
Robert Strauss

Advantages & Disadvantages Youth hostels are comfortable, inexpensive by Japanese standards, and usually good sources of information when used as a base for touring. They are also a good way to meet Japanese and other foreigners. By carefully studying the JYHA handbook, you can select interesting places and weed out possible duds. Many hostels have superb sites: some are farms, remote temples, outstanding private homes or elegant inns.

Standards obviously fluctuate from year to year and are open to subjective interpretation, but highlights on the youth hostel trail (the numbers in brackets are those in the JYHA handbook) would certainly include *Iwaobetsu* (0217), *Daisetsuzan Shirakabasō* (0119) and *Shikotsu-ko* (0330) on Hokkaidō, *Kinkazan-jinja* (1302) and *Towada-ko Hakubutsukan* (1111) in Tōhoku, *Kizō Inn* (5508) in Kansai, and *Ecchū Gokayama* (3208) in Central Honshū.

Some hostels, however, have very early closing hours, often 9 pm, and a routine strongly reminiscent of school or perhaps

even prison. In the high season you are likely to encounter waves of school children or throngs of students. Some hostels organise meetings in the evening with games, songs and dances, which any resident gaijin may find difficult to decline. The novelty of these can wear thin. If you are reliant on public transport, access to some youth hostels is complicated and time-consuming.

Shukubō 宿坊

Staying in a shukubō or temple lodging is one way to experience another facet of traditional Japan. Sometimes you are allocated a simple room in the temple precincts and left to your own devices. You may also be allowed to participate in prayers, services or zazen meditation. At many temples the meals are vegetarian *(shōjin ryōri)*.

The TICs in Tokyo and Kyoto both produce leaflets on temple lodgings in their regions. Kōya-san, a renowned religious centre, includes over 50 shukubō and is one of the best places in Japan to try this type of accommodation.

Over 70 youth hostels are temples or shrines – look for the reverse swastika symbol in the JYHA handbook. The suffix -ji or -in also provides a clue that the hostel is a temple. A few which proved interesting (the number in brackets refers to the JYHA handbook) include: Takayama (4101), Takaoka (3207), Otoyu (7404), Kinkazan (1302) and Yoshino (5508).

Toho & Mitsubachi ライダハウス

The Toho network is a diverse collection of places which have banded loosely together offering a more flexible alternative to youth hostels at a reasonable price. Most of the 70 places are in Hokkaidō, although there are a few in northern and central Japan. The emphasis seems to be on informal hospitality, outdoor pursuits, and accommodation with original architecture such as log cabins. Some members of Toho function as rider houses *(mitsubachi)* which offer reasonable accommodation to those touring on motorcycles.

Prices average Y2500 per person per night, without meals, or Y3700 with two meals. A list of Network members is available, in Japanese only, for Y150 plus postage. The list is published by Mr Shinpei Koshika (tel 011-271-2668), Sukkarakan, South 3 West 8, Chūō-ku, Sapporo 060, Hokkaidō. You will need to know some Japanese to make the most of this list.

Cycling Terminals
サイクリングターミナル

Cycling terminals (saikuringu terminaru) provide low-priced accommodation of the bunk-bed or tatami-mat variety and are usually found in scenic areas suited to cycling. If you don't have your own bike, you can rent one at the terminal.

At around Y2200 per person per night or Y3500 including two meals, terminal prices compare favourably with those of a youth hostel. For more information contact the Japan Bicycle Promotion Institute (tel 03-3583-5444), Nihon Jitensha Kaikan Building, 1-9-3 Akasaka, Minato-ku, Tokyo.

Campgrounds & Mountain Huts
カンピング

Camping is one of the cheapest forms of accommodation but official campgrounds are often only open during the Japanese 'camping season' (July to August) when you can expect an avalanche of students. Facilities range from bare essentials to de luxe. JNTO publishes Camping in Japan (MG-084), a selection of campgrounds which includes details of prices and facilities.

In some restricted areas and national parks, camping wild is forbidden, but elsewhere, foreigners have reported consistent success. Even if there is no officially designated campground, campers are often directed to the nearest large patch of grass. Provided you set up camp late in the afternoon and leave early, nobody seems to mind, though it would be common courtesy to ask permission first (assuming you can find the person responsible). Public toilets, usually spotless, and water are very common, even in remote parts of Japan.

The best areas for camping are Hokkaidō, the Japan Alps, Tōhoku and Okinawa.

Mountain huts are common in many of the hiking and climbing areas. Unoccupied huts

---

The Japanese Bath

The Japanese bath is another ritual which has to be learnt at an early stage and, like so many other things in Japan, is initially confusing but quickly becomes second nature. The all-important rule for using a Japanese bath is that you wash *outside* the bath and use the bath itself purely for soaking. Getting into a bath unwashed, or equally dreadful, without rinsing all the soap off your body, would be a major error.

One takes a bath in the evening, before dinner; a pre-breakfast bath is thought of as distinctly strange. In a traditional inn there's no possibility of missing bath time, you will be clearly told when it's time to head for o-furo (the bath) lest you not be washed in time for dinner! In a traditional inn or a public bath, the bathing facilities will either be communal but sex segregated, or there will be smaller family bathing facilities for families or couples.

Take off your yukata or clothes in the ante-room to the bath and place them in the baskets provided. The bathroom has taps, plastic tubs (wooden ones in very traditional places) and stools along the wall. Draw up a stool to a set of taps and fill the tub from the taps or use it to scoop some water out of the bath itself. Sit on the stool and soap yourself. Rinse thoroughly so there's no soap or shampoo left on you, then you are ready to climb into the bath. Soak as long as you can stand the heat, then leave the bath, rinse yourself off again, dry off and don your yukata. ■

provide a free roof over your head. Other huts, in the Japan Alps for example, are run privately and offer bed and board (two meals) at prices around Y4500 per person.

Kokuminshukusha 国民宿舎
Kokuminshukusha (people's lodges) are government institutions offering affordably priced accommodation in scenic areas. Prices average Y5000 per person per night including two meals.

Kokumin Kyukamura 国民休暇村
National vacation villages or *kokumin kyukamura* are also government sponsored and many offer camping or sports facilities in national parks. Prices are close to those of the people's lodges.

Kaikan 会館
Kaikan (literally 'meeting halls') are hotel-style accommodations sponsored by government or public organisations. Non-members are often accepted. A typical price per person per night is around Y5000, including two meals.

Minshuku 民宿
A minshuku is usually a family-run private home, rather like a B&B in Europe or the USA. Minshuku can be found throughout Japan and offer one way to peep into daily Japanese life. The average price per person per night with two meals is around Y5000. You are expected to lay out and put away your bedding and bring your own towel.

JNTO publishes a booklet, *Minshukus in Japan*, which lists details of about 300 minshuku. The Japan Minshuku Association (tel 03-3371-8120), New Pearl Building, Room 201, 2-10-8 Hyakunin-cho, Shinjuku, Tokyo, has a leaflet in English describing the minshuku concept and providing advice on staying at one; a list of minshuku is also available. The Japan Minshuku Center (tel 03-3216-6556), Tokyo Kotsu Kaikan Building, 21 Yuraku-cho, Chiyoda-ku, Tokyo 100 can help with computer bookings; a similar office operates in Kyoto. Some of the places listed in the Japanese Inn Group's handy little booklet (see the following Ryokan section) are really minshuku rather than ryokan. The line between the two accommodation categories can be fuzzy.

Ryokan 旅館
For a taste of traditional Japanese life, a stay at a ryokan is mandatory. Ryokan range from ultra-exclusive establishments (priced accordingly and available only to guests bearing a personal recommendation) to reasonably priced places with a homey atmosphere. There are corresponding fluctuations in what you get for your money, but the following description gives a rough idea of what to expect.

Staying at a Ryokan On arrival at the ryokan, you leave your shoes at the entrance steps, don a pair of slippers, and are shown by a maid to your room which has a tatami-mat floor. Slippers are taken off before entering tatami rooms. Instead of using numbers, rooms are named after auspicious flowers, plants or trees.

The interior of the room will contain an alcove *(tokonoma)*, probably decorated with a flower display or a calligraphy scroll. One side of the room will contain a cupboard with sliding doors for the bedding; the other side will have sliding screens covered with rice paper and perhaps open onto a veranda with a garden view.

The room maid then serves tea with a sweet on a low table surrounded by cushions *(zabuton)* in the centre of the room. At the same time you are asked to sign the register. A tray is provided with a towel, cotton robe (yukata) and belt *(obi)* which you put on before taking your bath. Remember to wear the left side over the right – the reverse order is used for dressing the dead. In colder weather, there will also be an outer jacket *(tanzen)*. Your clothes can be put away in a closet or left on a hanger.

Dressed in your yukata, you will be shown to the bath (o-furo). At some ryokan, there are rooms with private baths, but the communal ones are often designed with 'natural' pools or a window looking out into a garden. Bathing is communal, but sexes are segregated. Make sure you can differentiate between the bathroom signs for men and women – see the Aside before this section – although ryokan used to catering for foreigners will often have signs in English. Many inns will have family bathrooms for couples or families.

Dressed in your yukata after your bath, you return to your room where the maid will have laid out dinner – in some ryokan, dinner is provided in a separate room but you still wear your yukata for dining. Dinner usually includes standard dishes such as miso soup, pickles (tsukemono), vegetables in vinegar (sunomono), hors d'oeuvres (zensai), fish – either grilled or raw (sashimi), and perhaps tempura and a stew. There will also be bowls for rice, dips and sauces. Depending on the price, meals at a ryokan can become flamboyant displays of local cuisine or refined arrangements of *kaiseki* (a cuisine which obeys strict rules of form and etiquette for every detail of the meal and setting).

After dinner, whilst you are pottering around or out for a stroll admiring the garden, the maid will clear the dishes and prepare your bedding. A mattress is placed on the tatami floor and a quilt put on top. In colder weather, you can also add a blanket (*mōfu*).

In the morning, the maid will knock to make sure you are awake and then come in to put away the bedding before serving breakfast – sometimes this is served in a separate room. Breakfast usually consists of pickles, dried seaweed (nori), raw egg, dried fish, miso soup and rice. It can take a while for foreign stomachs to accept this novel fare early in the morning.

The Japanese tendency is to make the procedure at a ryokan seem rather rarefied for foreign comprehension and some ryokan

Shoes & Slippers

Knowing which shoes to wear where in a Japanese inn can initially be very confusing, but is a good thing to learn early on. Seeing gaijin take off their shoes as they arrive reassures the inn-keeper that they know what they're doing and will not make some truly awful faux pas like using soap in the bath.

When you enter a traditional inn there will be a *genkan*, a step up from street level, where you remove your shoes and put on slippers. There will usually be a series of pigeonholes where your shoes are stored and a large basket of assorted size slippers for you to select from. In the evening, the slippers will be lined up along the step, waiting for returning guests and new arrivals. In the morning, the process is reversed and guests' shoes will be lined up on the street side of the step. The sight of large numbers of waiting slippers is a good clue that an otherwise unidentified (in English at least) building is actually an inn of some type.

Wearing the slippers, you can now proceed to your room but must remove them again at the door, or on a small standing area just inside your room. You now go barefoot or in socks on the tatami matting which covers the floor. Further complications await if you head for the toilet, as there'll be another pair of slippers just inside the door for use only in that room. Toilet slippers are usually some garish colour, making it immediately obvious that you have committed a grave misdeed if you forget to change back to the regular slippers afterwards!

Shoes outside, slippers inside, bare or socked feet in your room and toilet slippers in the toilet still does not encompass all the possibilities. Some inns will provide wooden sandals or the traditional *geta* sandals at the front door so you can make short trips out of the inn without having to use your own shoes. In *onsen* (spa towns) or other holiday centres many guests will, after their evening bath, wander the town wearing their *yukata* (cotton robes) but shoes simply do not look right with a yukata; geta are far more appropriate. If there's a garden to wander in, yet another pair of sandals for that area may be awaiting you. ■

are wary of accepting foreign guests. However, once you've grasped the basics, it really isn't that hard to fit in.

Ryokan Prices Prices start around Y3800 (per person, per night) for a 'no-frills' ryokan without meals. For a classier ryokan, expect prices to start at Y8000. The really exclusive establishments – Kyoto is a prime centre for these – will charge Y25,000 and often much more, if you book way in advance and they like the look of your face.

Ryokan owners prefer to charge on a room and board (breakfast and dinner) per person basis. If, like many foreigners, you find yourself a bit overpowered by the fulsome and unusual offerings of a Japanese breakfast, it should be possible to have dinner only, but in many ryokan, opting out of both meals is unacceptable. The bill is reduced by about 10% if you decline breakfast.

A 10% to 20% service charge is added to your bill. If the total charge for accommodation, food, drink and other services per person per night is Y10,000 or less, a 3% tax applies – a bill over Y10,000 attracts 6% tax. Tipping is not expected.

Ryokan Guides & Addresses The Japanese Inn Group (tel 075-351-6748), c/o Hiraiwa Ryokan, 314 Hayao-cho, Kaminoguchi-agaru, Ninomiyacho-dōri, Shimogyo-ku, Kyoto 600, publishes an excellent listing of inexpensive ryokan, used to foreign guests, with full details on access, prices, facilities and mini-maps for each establishment. Prices start at Y3800 for a single room without meals.

JNTO publishes the *Japan Ryokan Guide*, a listing of government-registered members of the Japan Ryokan Association (JRA). Prices start around Y8000 and rise to astronomical heights. JRA produces a trilingual pamphlet called *Enjoy Japanese Home-Life at Ryokan* which uses cartoons and copious text to explain the intricacies of a ryokan stay.

Pensions ペンション
Pensions are usually run by young couples

offering Western-style accommodation based on the European pension concept and many offer sports and leisure facilities. They are common in rural areas and a considerable number operate in Nagano-ken. Pensions seem to specialise in quaint names like Pension Fruit Juice, Pension Pheasant or Pension Morning Salada and often have decidedly quaint décor as well, sometimes like a romantic Japanese dream of a European country cottage.

Prices average Y5000 per person per night or Y7500 including two meals. Food is often excellent, typically a French dinner and an American breakfast. JNTO publishes *Pensions in Japan*, a selection of pensions all over Japan.

Capsule Hotels カプセルホテル
In the '70s, the Japanese architect Kurokawa Kisho, came up with the idea of modifying a shipping container to hold a bed, bath and all 'mod cons'. A site was found for his construction which can still be seen in Tokyo's Ginza area.

Capsule hotels or 'capseru hoteru' have reduced the original concept to a capsule measuring two metres by one metre by one metre – about the size of a coffin. Inside is a bed, a TV, reading light, radio and alarm clock. Personal belongings are kept in a locker room.

This type of hotel is common in the major cities and often caters to travellers who have partied too hard to make it home or have missed the last train. There are a few for women only, but the majority are only for men. Some capsule hotels have the added attraction of a sauna.

An average price is Y3800 per night or Y1400 for a three hour stay. You could try one as a novelty, but it's not an experience recommended to those who easily become claustrophobic.

Business Hotels ビジネスホテル
These are economical and practical places geared to the single traveller, usually lesser-ranking business types who want somewhere

close to the station. Rooms are clean, Western style, just big enough for you to turn around in and include a miniature bath/WC unit. A standard fitting for the overstressed businessman is a coin-operated TV with a porno channel. Vending machines replace room service.

Cheap single rooms can sometimes be found for Y4000, though the average rate is around Y5000; some business hotels also have twin rooms. Cheaper business hotels usually do not have a service charge, though places costing Y6000 or more often add a 10% charge.

The Japan Business Hotel Association at 43 Kanda-Higashi, Matsusita-cho, Chiyoda-ku, Tokyo, publishes the *Business Hotel Guide*, a handy pamphlet which lists business hotels throughout Japan along with phone numbers, prices, addresses and access details. Ask for a copy at JNTO or TIC. The Japanese version is useful if you need to give directions to a taxi-driver – match up the phone numbers in the Japanese and English versions. Popular business hotel chains include the Green Hotels found near so many railway station, Sun Route, Washington,

Tōkyū Inns and Hokke Club. The Hokke Club hotels are unusual in their conveniently early check-in and late checkout times. Most Japanese hotels kick you out by 10 or 11 am and won't let you check in until 3 or 4 pm.

Hotels ホテル
De luxe and 1st class hotels offering the usual array of frills and comforts have sprung up in most of Japan's major cities and are comparable to the best in the USA and Europe. Singles start around Y6000 and rise to a cool Y20,000 or way beyond if you fancy a suite. The Japan Hotel Association has 389 government-registered members, all neatly listed in an informative JNTO leaflet, *Hotels in Japan*.

Some of the leading hotel chains, such as ANA Hotels, Holiday Inns, The New Otani Hotels, Prince Hotels and Tōkyū Hotels have overseas offices. Bookings can also be made through the overseas offices of major Japanese travel agencies such as Japan Travel Bureau (JTB), Kintetsu International, Tokyu Tourist Corporation, Nippon Travel Agency (NTA) and Japan Air Lines (JAL). Most of these agencies also have schemes for dis-

A Night in Capsuleland

My one experience of a capsule hotel was at Capsuleland in Fukuoka and, like much else in Japan, it was initially a little bewildering. Shoes were left at the entrance, just like in a traditional Japanese inn, but there the similarity ended. There was no space to take anything (apart from myself) into the capsule -a locker room was available for clothes and personal effects and, at the entrance, larger secondary lockers for bigger bags.

In the locker was a pair of pyjamas, emblazoned with the hotel's logo. Most of the other inmates seemed to wear their pyjamas all the time both in the hotel and outside in the neighbouring streets. (When I returned to the hotel later in the evening I realised I was getting close when, still a block or two away, I began to see men in blue and yellow short pyjamas!)

The hotel had a coffee bar, restaurant, TV lounge, sauna, massage room, toilets, washing facilities and a large communal bath. The capsules didn't lock (all my valuables were supposedly in the locker), and there was just a screen to pull down at the entrance. The capsule was exactly the length and width of the mattress but, also squeezed in, was a small shelf, a light, controls for a radio, alarm and the air-con and, mounted in the 'ceiling' of the capsule, a TV set complete with the obligatory porno channel. The capsules were stacked two high but were surprisingly quiet and, since the lighting was all artificial and there was no way of telling day from night, I slept way past my normal waking time.

Tony Wheeler ∎

count hotel coupons such as JTB's 'Sunrise Super Saver', NTA's 'NTA Hotel Pass' or JAL's 'Room & Rail'.

Expect to pay 10% or more as a service charge plus a 3% consumer tax; add another 3% local tax if the bill exceeds Y10,000. Asking for separate bills for meals can sometimes reduce the tax paid.

Love Hotels アベクホテル

Love hotels are one of the wild cards in Japanese accommodation. Their primary function is to serve as a short-time base for couples to enjoy some privacy. Customers are not necessarily unmarrieds in search of sex; the hotels are also used by married couples who often lack space at home for relaxing together. In Japanese they are known as *abecu hoteru*, from the French word *avec* for 'with'.

To find one on the street, just look for flamboyant facades with rococo architecture, turrets, battlements and imitation statuary. The design of the hotels emphasises discretion: entrances and exits are kept separate; keys are provided through a small opening without contact between desk clerk and guest; photos of the rooms are displayed to make the choice easy for the customer. There's often a discreetly curtained parking area so your car cannot be seen once inside.

The rooms can fulfil most fantasies with themes ranging from harem extravaganza to sci-fi. Further choices can include vibrating beds, wall-to-wall mirrors, bondage equipment and video recorders to recall the experience (don't forget to take the video cassette with you when you leave).

Charges on an hourly basis are at a peak during the day and early evening. Love hotels are of more interest to foreign visitors after 10 pm, when it's possible to stay the night for about Y5000 per room (rather than per person), but you should check out early enough in the morning to avoid a return to peak-hour rates. Outside love hotels there will usually be a sign in English announcing the rates for a 'rest' (usually two hours) or a 'stay' (overnight).

Long-Term Accommodation

If you're intending to stay longer in Japan, a job offer which appears lucrative at first sight may seem markedly less so when you work out your rent and other living costs. Ideally, you can avoid many hassles by negotiating decent accommodation as part of your work contract.

If at all possible, get a Japanese to help you with your search and negotiations since Japanese landlords are notoriously wary of foreign tenants and often prefer to do business with a go-between of their own kind. If you are on good terms with a Japanese friend, this person may offer to act as a *hoshō-nin* (guarantor). This represents considerable commitment and the guarantor's *hanko* (seal) is usually required on your rental contract.

A pitfall which is often overlooked is that you may have to lay out four, possibly as much as seven months' rent *in advance*. For starters, there's one to two months' rent payable as *reikin* (key money). This is non-refundable and a form of extortion to line the wallets of landlords. Then there's a *shikikin* (damage deposit) of one to three months' rent. This is refundable at a later date as long as both sides agree there's no damage. Avoid later squabbles over shikikin by making duplicate inventories, signed by both parties, before you move in. The *fudōsan-ya* (estate agent) will of course want *tesūryō* – one month's rent as a non-refundable handling fee. Finally, you have to pay *maekin* which is one month's rent in advance and is also non-refundable.

These high up-front costs are cogent reasons why foreigners looking for long-term employment in Japan should arrive with a sizeable financial float. This will allow more time to choose a decent job and avoid the scenario – assuming your stay was mostly motivated by financial gain – of leaving Japan with very little to show for your stay and an embittered feeling about the place.

Standard contracts often run for two years and some *ōya-san* (landowners) may require the additional payment of maintenance fees and fire insurance. When *kōshin* (renewal) comes up, you should expect a raise in your *yachin* (monthly rent). When you decide to move on, make absolutely sure you give notice *at least* one month in advance. Otherwise you will be landed with payment of an extra month's rent.

What to Look For It's usually best for budget travellers to find their feet in a gaijin house before putting out feelers for other accommodation. Inner city rentals are obviously high, as are those for chic suburban areas. Commuting costs often reduce the apparent gain of lower rental costs outside town and you may not like your nightlife being curtailed by transport timetables.

At the top end of the housing market are *manshon* which are modern concrete condominiums or rental apartments. At the lower end are *danchi*, functional concrete blocks of public flats, which are sought after by those with moderate or low incomes.

Japanese are often amazed at the spaciousness of Western housing since the average Japanese family in the city makes do with much less space in their apartment. If you want a house or apartment similar to urban sizes in the West, you can expect to pay several million yen a month.

In major cities like Tokyo and Kyoto, gaijin houses are the cheapest options for long-term stays, but you should be prepared for basic dorms or shared tatami rooms and a communal kitchen. Prices for the cheapest houses start around Y1400 per night. If you negotiate for a monthly price, you may be able to reduce the rent to Y30,000 per month.

Once you move up a bracket to your own room with separate facilities (kitchen, bathroom) in an apartment with easy access to the city centre, you can expect monthly rental to start around Y55,000. If you share facilities in this type of set-up with one other flat mate, the monthly rental is about Y10,000 cheaper.

Where to Look There are several methods to hunt for housing – it depends what you want and how long you intend to stay.

Asking other foreigners at work or play in schools, clubs, bars, gaijin houses, etc is one way of locating long-term accommodation. If you strike it really lucky, you may find somebody leaving the country or moving on who is willing to dump their job contacts, housing and effects in one friendly package.

Notice boards are another good source and are often found at tourist information offices, international clubs, conversation clubs, etc. Even if there's nothing on the board, ask someone in charge for a few tips.

Regional and city magazines aimed at foreigners often have classified ads offering or seeking accommodation. For Tokyo, you should look at *Tokyo Journal* or *Weekender*; for the Kansai area (Osaka, Kōbe, Kyoto, Nara) you should peruse *Kansai Time Out*; and further afield in Ishikawa Prefecture (Kanazawa for example) you could buy *Suimairu-Ishikawa* which is a monthly magazine devoted to house rental. There are plenty of other magazines all over Japan with suitable ads. TIC or the local tourist office should know which publications are best, particularly if you decide to live somewhere more remote like Hokkaidō or Okinawa.

Newspapers also have classified ads for rentals. The Friday edition of the *Japan Times* is a good example. If you want to get an idea of long-term accommodation costs before travelling to Japan, pick up a copy of this edition. JNTO offices and Japanese embassies usually have back copies lying around.

Common abbreviations in rental ads include K – kitchen, D – dining room, L – living room, UB – unit bath (combined bath and toilet). An ad specifying 3LDK, for example, means three bedrooms and one living room combined with dining kitchen. The size of rooms is usually given in standard tatami mat measurements, known as *jō*. There are several tatami sizes, but as a general rule of thumb, one tatami mat equals one jō which is 1.8 metres by 0.9 metres (1.62 sq metres). A room decribed as being 4.5 jō, for example, is 7.29 sq metres: a medium-sized room by Japanese standards but poky by Western standards.

Using a fudōsan-ya (estate agent) is the

most expensive option and really only feasible if you intend to stay a long time and need to determine exactly the type and location of your housing. English-language magazines such as *Tokyo Journal* and *Kansai Time Out* carry ads from estate agents specialising in accommodation for foreigners.

Additional Costs Before you sign your contract, ask the landlord for precise details about gas, electricity and water. Check if a telephone is already installed since installation of a new telephone is a costly business. You can expect to pay around Y75,000 but you've then purchased the right to have a phone line anywhere in Japan. This right is negotiable, either privately or through private agencies which deal in phone rights. If you move and want to take your phone line with you, the charge for transferral is around Y13,000.

Japan is introducing schemes for recycling garbage: in some cities residents are asked to separate it into *moeru-gomi* (burnable), *moenai-gomi* (non-burnable), and *shigen-gomi* (recyclable). If you hear a noisy truck grinding through your area with a loudspeaker announcing 'chirigami kōkan', your area will have a system to save used newspapers and magazines. In return for your used newspapers and magazines, you will be given rolls of toilet paper and garbage liners.

FOOD
With its obvious influence on nouvelle cuisine, Japanese food has been receiving more and more attention from food connoisseurs in the West over recent years. Japanese restaurants are becoming increasingly common in Western cities, and consequently more Westerners are coming to Japan with some idea of what to expect.

It is unlikely, however, that Japanese restaurants outside Japan could possibly prepare the visitor for the sheer diversity of cuisine inside Japan. For one, there is an enormous range of regional cuisines, some of which are variations on Japanese standards and others unique to the localities in which they're found. The Japanese are also

adept at modifying foreign dishes and making them their own; the pizza you order at the little 'Italian' place on the corner in Tokyo will probably be unlike any pizza you've had before.

This diversity in Japanese cuisine is increasing as Japanese eating habits, like everything else in Japan, continue to change in response to foreign influences. A Japanese today is just as likely to breakfast on toast or cereal as on the traditional breakfast of pickles and watery rice. A Japanese lunch might be anything from pasta, to Chinese noodles, to a British pub meal. Many young Japanese claim they can't eat rice and say that they'd rather have McDonald's for dinner than sushi.

The Western influence on Japanese eating habits began just before the turn of the century. From the 7th century through to this time the Japanese were not eaters of red meat, restricting their diet, in accordance with Japanese Buddhist precepts, to rice, fish and vegetables. The change came with the Meiji Restoration, when meat-eating was embraced, along with a vast range of other barbaric practices, as part of the national policy of strengthening Japan. The reasoning was, that if the Japanese were to become as strong as the barbarians apparently poised to overrun their country, they would have to adopt, among other things, the barbarians' carnivorous ways.

Today, in the big cities, almost any cuisine that takes your fancy is available. Outside these centres, the only non-Japanese food you're likely to come across is the occasional Chinese restaurant or a McDonald's, Kentucky Fried Chicken or Shakey's Pizza. Fast food has taken off in a big way across Japan, but to be honest it's not such a great bargain. Usually the Chinese noodle shops will give you a healthier and cheaper meal than the fast-food outlets.

If you're on a real budget, many of the coffee shops do very good set breakfasts, known as *mōningu sābisu* (morning service) from around Y350. They generally include two pieces of incredibly thick toast, a dollop of jam and butter, a hard-boiled egg, a small salad and a cup of coffee. For lunch, a noodle or *soba* shop will fill you up for around Y400. For dinner, you may have to push your budget up to around Y600 to Y700 for a decent meal to include both meat and vegetables.

The bakeries which are found everywhere in Japan (there's almost always one in larger railway stations) are another good place for an economical breakfast or a cheap snack at any time of day. They often have tables and chairs or a bar so you can have a cup of coffee or cold drink with your baked goods.

Even within this fairly basic price range, there will usually be an enormous selection of restaurants and cuisines to choose from. Because of the long hours they work, many Japanese are forced to eat most of their meals outside. Consequently, railway stations, business districts and shopping areas will usually have a large number of fast and reasonably priced restaurants.

Unlike Japanese restaurants in the West, Japanese restaurants in Japan tend to specialise in a particular kind of dish or cuisine. The following sections describe some of the restaurants and dishes you are likely to encounter in Japan.

Okonomiyaki お好みやき
This is an inexpensive Japanese cuisine, somewhat like a pancake or omelette with anything that's lying around in the kitchen thrown in. The dish is usually prepared by the diner on a hotplate on the table. Typical ingredients include vegetables, pork, beef and prawns.

Rāmen ラーメン
This is a Chinese cuisine that has been taken over by the Japanese and made their own. These restaurants are generally the cheapest places to fill yourself up in Japan. Rāmen dishes are big bowls of noodles in a chicken stock with vegetables and or meat and are priced from around Y350 upwards.

chāshūmen 叉焼メン
  rāmen with roasted pork

gomokumen 五目メン
  rāmen with a combination of five ingredients (meat, egg and vegetables)
gyōza 餃子
  Chinese fried meat and vegetable dumpling
miso rāmen みそラーメン
  rāmen with miso

Soba そば
This is a traditional Tokyo noodle dish, made with buckwheat noodles. The noodles come in a hot or cold fish-stock soup with various other ingredients.

kake かけそば
  soba with slices of spring onion
kamo-namban かもなんばんそば
  soba with spring onion and chicken
kitsune きつねそば
  soba with thinly sliced tōfu
tempura 天ぷらそば
  soba with prawn tempura
tsukimi 月見そば
  soba with a raw egg on top (literally 'moon viewing')

Udon うどん
This Osaka dish is similar to soba, except that the noodles are white and thicker.

kake-udon かけうどん
  udon with spring onions
kamo-namban かもなんばんうどん
  udon with chicken and spring onions
nabeyaki-udon なべやきうどん
  udon with tempura

Sukiyaki & Shabu-Shabu すき焼としゃぶしゃぶ
Restaurants usually specialise in both these dishes. Sukiyaki is generally cooked on the table in front of the diner. It is prepared by cooking thinly sliced beef, vegetables and tōfu in a slightly sweetened soya sauce broth. The difference between sukiyaki and shabu shabu is in the broth that is used. Shabu-shabu is made with a stock-based broth.

Sushi

Sushi & Sashimi すしとさしみ

These are probably the most famous of Japanese dishes. The difference between them is that sashimi is thin slivers of raw fish served with soy sauce and *wasabi* (hot horseradish), while for sushi, the raw fish is set atop a small pillow of lightly vinegared rice.

amaebi 甘海老
    sweet prawn (raw)
awabi あわび
    abalone
ebi 海老
    prawn or shrimp
hamachi はまち
    yellowtail
ika いか
    squid
ikura いくら
    salmon roe
kappa maki かっぱ巻
    cucumber in *norimaki* (seaweed roll)
maguro まぐろ
    tuna
tai たい
    sea bream
tamago たまご
    sweetened egg
toro とろ
    fatty tuna
uni うに
    sea urchin roe

Tempura 天ぷら

This dish has controversial origins, some maintaining that it is a Portuguese import. Tempura is what fish & chips might have been – fluffy, non-greasy batter and delicate, melt-in-your mouth portions of fish, prawns and vegetables.

Yakitori 焼き鳥

Various parts of the chicken, skewered on a stick and cooked over a charcoal fire. Yakitori is great drinking food and the restaurants will serve beer and saké with the food. Some common yakitori dishes:

kawa やきとり
    chicken skin
negima ねぎま
    chicken and spring onion
piiman ピーマン
    green capsicum
rebā レバー
    liver
sei-niku せい肉
    dark chicken meat
sasami ささみ
    chicken breast
tsukune つくね
    chicken meat balls

Robatayaki ろばた焼

Robatayaki restaurants are celebrated as the noisiest in the world. Enter and you will be hailed by a chorus of welcoming *irasshaimases*, as if you were some long-lost relative. Orders are made by shouting. The food, a variety of things including seafood, tōfu and vegetables, is cooked over a grill. Again, this is a drinking cuisine. Both sashimi and yakitori are popular robatayaki dishes – others include:

agedashi-dōfu 揚げ出し豆腐
    deep fried tōfu in a fish-stock soup
jagabatā じゃがバター
    potatoes grilled with butter
niku-jaga 肉じゃが
    broiled meat and potato
shio-yaki 塩焼
    a whole fish grilled with salt
tōmorokoshi とうもろこし
    corn on the cob
yaki-onigiri 焼おにぎり
    broiled rice balls

When Japan was getting me down, a robatayaki was always my favourite choice of a place to eat. The noisy bonhomie may simply be part of the background décor but it certainly made me feel better. The food was familiar and recognisable, and ordering was never any problem at all as everything was either out on view and you could simply point or the menu was illustrated.

Tony Wheeler

Nabemono　なべもの
This winter cuisine consists of a stew cooked in a heavy earthenware pot. Like sukiyaki, it is a dish cooked on the table in front of the diner.

Fugu　ふぐ
Only the Japanese could make a culinary speciality out of a dish which could kill you. The fugu, pufferfish or globefish, puffs itself up into an almost spherical shape to deter its enemies. Its delicate flesh is highly esteemed and traditionally served in carefully arranged fans of thinly sliced segments. Eat the wrong part of the humble pufferfish, however, and you drop dead. It's said a slight numbness of the lips indicates you were close to the most exciting meal of your life but fugu fish chefs are carefully licensed, and losing customers is not encouraged. Every year there are a few deaths from pufferfish poisoning but they're usually from home-prepared fish. Fugu can only be eaten for a few months each year and the very best fugu restaurants, places which specialise in nothing else, close down for the rest of the year. It's said that the fugu chef who loses a customer is honour bound to take his own life.

Unagi　うなぎ
This is Japanese for 'eel'. Cooked Japanese style, over hot coals and brushed with soy sauce and sweet saké, this is a popular and delicious dish.

Kaiseki　懐石料理
The origins of kaiseki are in the tea ceremony, where a number of light and aesthetically prepared morsels would accompany the proceedings. True kaiseki is *very* expensive – the diner is paying for the whole experience, the traditional setting and so on.

Etiquette
When it comes to eating in Japan, there are quite a number of implicit rules, but they're fairly easy to remember. If you're worried about putting your foot in it, relax – the Japanese almost expect foreigners to make fools of themselves in formal situations and are unlikely to be offended as long as you follow the standards of politeness of your own country.

Among the more important eating 'rules' are those regarding chopsticks. Sticking them upright in your rice is considered very bad form, that's how rice is offered to the dead! So is passing food from your chopsticks to someone else's – another Buddhist death rite involves passing the bones of the cremated deceased amongst members of the family using chopsticks.

When eating with other people, the general practice is to preface actually digging into the food with the expression *itadakimasu*, literally 'I will receive'. Similarly, at the end of the meal someone will probably say *gochisōsama deshita*, a respectful way of saying that the meal was good and satisfying. When it comes to drinking, remember that you're expected to keep

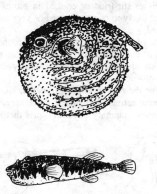

Fugu

the drinks of your fellow drinkers topped up. Don't fill your own glass: wait for someone to do this for you.

In Japan, there is a definite etiquette to bill-paying. If someone invites you to eat or drink with them, they will be paying. Even amongst groups eating together it is unusual for bills to be split. Generally, at the end of the meal, something of a struggle will ensue to see who gets the privilege of paying the bill. If this happens, it is polite to at least make an effort to pay the bill – it is extremely unlikely that your Japanese 'hosts' will acquiesce. Exceptions to this rule are likely amongst young Japanese such as students.

When eating Japanese food, it's worth considering that a great deal of effort has gone into its preparation; don't pour soya sauce over it and mix it up with your chopsticks. The accompanying sauces are for dipping food into. Finally, don't forget to slurp your noodles: the Japanese claim that it enhances the flavour.

Chopsticks Nowadays, more and more Westerners are getting used to the idea of chopsticks, which is just as well because you're going to have a hard time of it in Japan if you don't learn. The Japanese, for the most part, remain convinced that foreigners are unable to use *hashi*, as chopsticks are known in Japan, and dextrous wielding of this wooden 'cutlery' will invariably prompt admiring exclamations of 'Jōzu nē!' (So skilful!) from nearby diners.

Japanese chopsticks are longer than their Chinese equivalents and are pointed. Almost every restaurant uses disposable wooden chopsticks, although, at last, there seems to be a move away from the use of these due to ecological considerations. If you feel strongly about this, travel with your own chopsticks.

Ordering Ordering at a Japanese restaurant is made easier by the fact that many restaurants display plastic replicas of their dishes in the front window. Rather than point randomly at an indecipherable menu, you can drag one of the serving staff outside and point to the dish in the window. Another alternative is to ask what's recommended: 'O-susume wa nan desuka?'

Eating on the Cheap

Like anywhere else, the cheapest way to fill yourself up in Japan is to cook for yourself. Unfortunately, however, apart from some youth hostels, there are not many places where you can do this.

Those of the carnivorous persuasion will be pleased to hear that meat is not always as horrendously expensive in Japan as outsiders are led to believe. If you are cooking your own food and can abstain from *biifu* (beef), buying meat needn't leave you particularly out of pocket. One of the best options is to go to the meat section of one of the department store food halls and ask for *ramu* (lamb). Lamb is not a very popular meat with the Japanese and consequently is very cheap. The other cheap option is pork. As most meat is either stir-fried or cooked in broths it's most likely to come chopped or very thinly sliced.

Yasaiya (vegetable shops) can be found on almost every street corner of the more suburban areas. Prices are generally quite reasonable.

For the real shoestring traveller, another popular eating alternative is the bakery. The Japanese, naughty boys and girls that they

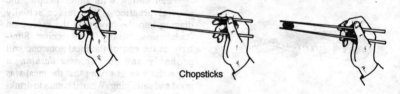

Chopsticks

are, have never learnt to eat their crusts – sandwiches and slices of bread are served with these horrid, chewy appurtenances neatly trimmed off. This means that if you ask for *pan no mimi* at the bakery you can buy yourself a whole bag of crusts for next to nothing. If you get fed up with your diet of crusts, you can always spend a pleasant afternoon at the park feeding the ducks.

Cheapest of all is to eat for free. Every supermarket and department store food floor seems to be continuously offering sample titbits and a judicious circuit will often provide some interesting free snacks!

DRINK
Alcoholic Drinks
Japanese culture features a serious interest in drinking and, unlike most other Asian countries, drinking is a popular pastime for both sexes. It is routinely taken to excess, presumably as a release from the straitjacket of proper conduct at work. Office workers are expected to join their group boozing sessions to promote bonding inside the group.

By 11 pm in Tokyo, it can seem that everyone on the streets is in various stages of inebriation. Fortunately, the Japanese are fairly good-natured drunks and it's extremely rare to see any trouble – though it does happen, especially in the hot summer months. A recent survey estimated that around 12% of the male population gets drunk every day, whilst nearly 70% get drunk once a week. Drunkenness is readily tolerated as an excuse for bad behaviour, but for those foolish enough to drink and drive, the police enforce very strict penalties.

Beer Introduced at the end of the last century, beer is now the favourite tipple of the Japanese. The quality is generally excellent and the most popular type is a light lager. The major brewers are Asahi, Suntory, Sapporo and Kirin. Beer is dispensed everywhere, from vending machines to beer halls and even in temple lodgings.

A standard can of beer from a vending machine is about Y220; elsewhere the price of your beer starts around Y500 and climbs upwards depending on the establishment. Draught beer *(nama biru)* is widely available and imported beers are common.

Saké Rice wine is a Japanese staple which has been brewed for centuries. Once restricted to imperial brewers, it was later produced at temples and shrines across the country. In recent years, consumption of beer has overtaken that of saké, but it's still a standard item in homes, in restaurants and in drinking dens. Large casks of saké are often seen piled up as offerings outside a shrine or temple and it plays a part in most celebrations or festivals. Although saké doesn't have quite the cultural significance that wine does in the West, it is still taken very seriously by many Japanese.

It takes about 20 days to ferment the brew from water, rice and malted rice. Ageing is not considered important for saké and most is drunk soon after processing.

There are cloudy, white and unrefined types of saké, but the commonest form is the clear one. The three grades of saké in descending order are tokkyū (premium), ikkyū (first grade) and nikyū (second grade). The latter is the routine choice. There is a further division of these grades into dry *(karakuchi)* and sweet *(amakuchi)*. Apart from national brewing giants, there are thousands of provincial brewers producing local brew *(jizake)*.

Saké is usually served warm *(atsukan)* but may be served cold *(hiyazake)* or *reishū* as a summer drink with ice. A different way to sample it cold, is in *masu* (little wooden boxes, traditionally used as measures) with a pinch of salt on the corner of the box. When served warm, saké enters the bloodstream extra fast – so don't underestimate its average alcohol content of 17%, which is slightly stronger than wine.

A variety of containers (ceramic pots, glass jars and bottles) are used, but bars and restaurants favour the slim, clay flask *tokkuri*, holding 180 ml, which usually costs around Y250 and provides several servings in miniature cups *(sakazuki)*. The flask and cups are sold in decorative sets which make inexpensive gifts. And remember, custom dictates that you never eat rice at the same time as you drink saké.

Shōchū For those looking for a quick and cheap escape route from the world of sorrows, *shōchū* is the answer. It's a distilled spirit (averaging 30% alcohol content) which has been resurrected from its previous low-class esteem – it was used as disinfectant in the Edo period – to the status of a trendy drink. You can drink it as *oyuwari* (with hot water) or as a highball *chūhai* (with soda and lemon). A bottle (720 ml) sells for about Y600 which makes it a relatively cheap option compared to other spirits.

Wine, Imported Drinks & Whisky Japanese wines are available from areas such as Yamanashi Prefecture, Nagano Prefecture, Hokkaidō and Tōhoku. Standard wines are often blended with imports from South America or Eastern Europe. The major producers are Suntory, Mann's and Mercian. Prices are expensive – expect to pay at least Y1000 for a bottle of something drinkable.

Imported wines are often stocked by large liquor stores or department stores in the cities. Bargains are sometimes available at around Y600, but most of the imports cost considerably more.

Prices for imported spirits such as brandy or cognac have been elevated to absurd levels by market gouging and customer pretentiousness. If you want imported spirits for your own consumption or as gifts, the simplest thing is to make full use of your duty-free allowance when entering Japan.

Whisky is available in most drinking establishments and is usually drunk *mizuwari* (with water) or *onzarokku* (on ice). Local brands, such as Suntory or Nikka, are sensibly priced and most measure up to foreign standards. The price of imported whisky reflects exploitation of the snob appeal of foreign labels. Expensive foreign labels are popular as gifts, since the greater the cost of the gift, the higher the esteem in which the recipient is held.

Drinking Customs The usual form when drinking in company is to fill your companion's glass and allow your own glass to be filled by your companion. Raise your glass slightly whilst it is being filled. Once everyone's glass has been filled, the usual starting signal is a chorus of *kanpai!* which means 'cheers!'. Constant topping up means you can be faced with a bottomless glass – just put your hand over the glass if you've had enough.

The Japanese make a habit of paying the bill for their foreign friends, particularly if they wish to make an impression or the acquaintance is slight. The custom of *warikan* (each person paying his own share) is common in a group where everyone knows each other well.

Drinking Places What you pay for your drink depends on where you drink, what you drink and especially if a hostess helps you drink it. Appearances can be misleading: swanky establishments imply high prices, but it is also quite possible for an outwardly drab-looking place to cater to an exclusive clientele who pay the requisite fortune. Avoid the painful shock of an unexpectedly hefty bill by asking about prices and cover charges *before* sitting down.

Izikaya and *yakitori-ya* are establishments with reasonable prices for standard drinks (beer, shōchū or whisky) and food in a casual atmosphere resembling that of a pub. *Aka-chochin*, which display a 'red lantern' (aka-chochin) outside the premises, are similar pubs for the working man – down-to-earth in price and décor.

In the summer, many department stores open up beer gardens on the roof. They are a popular spot to cool off with an inexpensive beer. Beer halls are affordable and popular places to swill your beer in the German tradition. The bars which are found in their hundreds jammed into tiny rooms on floor after floor of large buildings are often used by customers as a type of club – if you drop in without introduction from a regular, the reception may be cool.

In many bars you may find yourself

paying for *otsumami* (charms) which are minute snacks often served without being requested. To encourage regular patronage, bars also operate the 'keep bottle' system – you buy a bottle and keep it at the bar to consume whenever you visit. Apart from the initial cost of the bottle, you will also have to pay an 'ice charge' when you have a drink from your bottle.

Hostess bars are invariably expensive, often exorbitant. They cater mainly to those entertaining on business accounts. Shapely ladies pamper customers with compliments or bend a sympathetic ear to their problems. The best way to visit is in the company of a Japanese friend who knows the routine – and may pick up the tab!

Karaoke (literally 'empty orchestra') bars are a Japanese oddity, worth trying at least once, though after that, the experience might seem a bit empty. Customers sing to the accompaniment of taped music and, as the evening wears on, voices get progressively more ragged. Sobbingly mournful enka (folk ballads) are the norm, though foreigners might find tapes of *My Way* or *Let it Be* to exercise their vocal chords.

Non-Alcoholic Drinks

Most of the drinks you're used to at home, or at least varieties of them anyway, will be available in Japan. One convenient aspect of pounding city sidewalks, especially in warm weather, is the ubiquitous drink-dispensing machine. These have everything from hot coffee to that favourite soft drink, Pocari Sweat. Of course, if you're not gutsy enough for Pocari Sweat, you can always try the newly released Mucos – as the advertising puts it: 'If you feel that your body and skin become dry, try to drink Pokka's Mucos please'.

Coffee Coffee drinkers will find travelling in Japan difficult at times. Although there will be a coffee shop on every second street corner, in most instances the coffee they serve up is bitter and expensive – from Y350 to Y450 a cup. True, many of the machines dispensing drinks will provide the caffeine addict with a quick fix – but have you ever tried drinking hot coffee from a can? For one, how do you hold it? Two, how do you stop your lips getting stuck to the hot metal surface every time you take an anguished sip? Fortunately, a few chains of cheap coffee shops have opened up in the bigger cities. The most popular of these is Doutor; coffee here (five or six varieties) sells for Y150. The fast-food chains, Mister Donut for example, are also a good place for a cheap cup of coffee.

Tea & Other Drinks Of course, as everyone knows, the Japanese are tea drinkers. Unlike the tea Westerners drink, Japanese tea is green and does not contain caffeine. As a visit to the tea section of any Japanese

Hangovers

In Japan, just as in the West, hangovers *(futsukayoi)* have their popular remedies. Salted plums *(umeboshi)* in green tea *(sencha)* are one tip for the morning after. Tea made from boiled cloves is also used. Another herbal cure, recommended in rural Tōhoku, requires a handful of *senburi* (a herb) to be steeped for three hours in a cup of hot water – the resulting brew is revoltingly bitter. Less punishing options are a bowl of *rāmen* noodles, rice soup *(ochazuké)* or persimmons *(kaki)*.

Finally, if herbal cures don't help, you can always try evoking sympathy from the Japanese by cradling your head in your hands and moaning 'Kino o nomisugimashita' (Yesterday, I drank too much)!

Robert Strauss ■

department store will show, Japanese tea comes in a variety of forms: among these green leaf, ground green leaf and green leaf with bits of rice in it. During the summer many Japanese drink *mugicha*, a cold barley water drink.

THINGS TO BUY

The Japanese are obsessive shoppers, and consequently everything from tiny speciality shops to some of the world's largest and most luxurious department stores give visitors ample opportunity to empty their pockets before going home. True, some items are overpriced, but many things, including electronic gear like cameras and video cameras, are much cheaper than you might expect. In some instances, Japan's prices are competitive with those in other discount centres such as Hong Kong and Singapore.

As well as all the electronic gadgetry available in Japan, there are a wide range of traditional crafts to choose from, though for good stuff you're really going to be spending big money. It pays to shop around if you have anything particular on mind. The big department stores, which often have the best

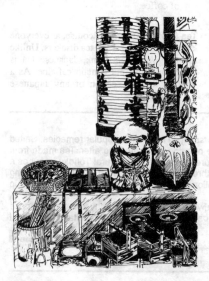

selections of Japanese gift items, can vary enormously in their prices from one store to another. In some shops, you are paying for extras such as the high level of service (a feature of all Japanese shops anyway), location and interior décor, all of which are very important to the well-heeled Japanese but lesser considerations to the traveller looking for a bargain.

Prices in Japan are fixed, though in some of the bargain electronic shopping areas, such as Akihabara in Tokyo, a certain amount of bargaining is usually required to get the best possible price. Generally, shops will only come down 10% to 15% from the original price. Don't push too hard, asking politely for a discount is enough in Japan – the sales clerk will tell you if one is available. In the big department stores, as in the West, the marked price is as low as you're going to get.

Tax Free

Shopping for tax-free goods in Japan may not necessarily give you the bargains you might expect. Although tax-free shops enable foreigners to get an exemption of the 10% to 30% sales tax levied on most items, these still may not always be the cheapest places to shop. Other bulk-buying shops are often a better deal. The best advice is to shop around and compare prices before making a purchase.

Photographic

Tokyo is an excellent hunting ground for photographic equipment. Almost all the big-name brands in camera equipment are Japanese, and for these locally produced items, prices can be very competitive. The prices for accessories, such as motor drives and flash units, can even be competitive with Singapore and Hong Kong. In addition, shopping in Japan presents the shopper with none of the rip-off risks that abound in other Asian discount capitals.

As always, be prepared to shop around. Tokyo's Shinjuku area (see the Tokyo chapter) is the best place for buying camera equipment, although Ginza too has a good selection of camera shops. If you're short of time, however, I'd suggest heading straight to Shinjuku's Yodobashi Camera, which is virtually a department store devoted to cameras, camera accessories and darkroom equipment. The range is enormous and prices generally compare well with elsewhere in Tokyo.

One possibility that few visitors consider is buying second-hand camera equipment. Both Shinjuku and Ginza have a fair number of second-hand shops where camera and lens quality is usually very good and prices are around half what you would pay for new equipment. Buying second-hand is a particularly good option if you are only in the market for lenses, which are much more easily tested in the shop.

Electronics & Hi-Fi

Real bargains can be picked up, but there are a few things to take note of before you rush into any purchases. The main problem is that much of the electrical gadgetry on sale in Japan is designed for Japan's curious power supply (100 volts at 50 or 60 Hz) and will usually require a transformer for use overseas. Other problems include the incompatibility of Japanese TVs, video recorders and FM radios with foreign models. The safest bet is to go for export models – the prices may be slightly higher, but in the long run you'll save the expense of converting the equipment to suit the conditions in your own country. Two places to look for export models are the International Arcade in Ginza and the big LAOX store in Akihabara, Tokyo.

For battery-operated items such as Walkmans and Diskmans, scout around the hundreds of electrical shops in Akihabara. A little bargaining (don't get too carried away – this is not Bombay) will generally bring the price down around 10% or so.

Computers

The computer market, both hardware and software, is one area in which the Japanese are lagging behind. Although Japanese manufacturers have grabbed a large part of the market for laptop computers, you're still better off looking in Hong Kong or Singapore for these and other computer goods.

Musical

From CDs to electric guitars, musical equipment can be a lot cheaper in Japan than elsewhere. At Tower Records in Shibuya, Tokyo, imported US CDs range between Y1800 and Y2100. Japanese CDs average around Y2100, although you can occasionally come across real bargains. Wave, located in Tokyo's Roppongi, Shibuya and Ikebukuro districts, has excellent selections of both Japanese and Western music in CD, LP and tape format.

The Japanese are great music lovers and, consequently, there are plenty of musical equipment shops in all the major cities. Bargains can usually be had on Japanese-made instruments, while foreign-made ones will generally be no cheaper than they are in other parts of the world. For example, a Japanese-assembled Fender guitar will be about half the price of the same US-assembled model. For musical equipment, it is usually possible to negotiate lower prices than those marked.

Pearls

The Japanese firm Mikimoto developed the technique of producing cultured pearls by artificially introducing an irritant into the pearl oyster. Pearls and pearl jewellery are still a favourite purchase for a visitor to Japan but it would be wise to check prices in your own country before buying. Size, quality and colour will all have a bearing on the price. Toba, in the Ise area (Kinki District) is a centre for the production of cultured pearls.

Cars, Motorcycles & Bicycles

Information on purchasing these vehicles can be found in the Getting Around chapter.

Clothes

Japanese-made clothes and shoes are excellent quality and needn't cost the earth. In well-heeled and fashionable districts, most of the clothes shops are exclusive boutiques with exclusive prices. In less fashionable areas, there are countless retail outlets for an industry providing economical, mass-produced versions of designer clothes. In such shops, it is possible to pick up a suit for around Y12,000 – perfect if you're a newly arrived English-language teacher with a backpack full of travel-soiled jeans and T-shirts.

Toys

Japanese toys are surprisingly disappointing, even dull; if you're on a business trip to Japan don't promise your children you'll bring them back some unimaginable technological wonder. Despite the numerous Japanese toy shops, the displays are unimaginative and the toys even more so. They're curiously uninvolving toys; a high percentage of them seem to be of the 'turn it on, sit back and watch it perform' type.

As in the West, there are many TV spin-off marketing ploys in Japan, but they're likely to be for TV programmes which have had no impact at all outside Japan, and hence have little interest to non-Japanese children. Teenage Mutant Ninja Turtles had not made an appearance in Japan long after they had swept the English-speaking children's world.

Japanese Arts & Crafts

As well as all the hi-tech knick-knacks produced by the Japanese, it is also possible to go home loaded down with Japanese traditional arts and crafts. Anything from carp banners to kimono can make good souvenirs for the converted Japanophile.

Ningyō *Ningyō* (Japanese dolls) are intended for display, not for playing with. Often quite exquisite, with coiffured hair and dressed in kimono, they make excellent souvenirs or gifts. Also available are the *gogatsu-ningyō*, dolls dressed in samurai suits used as gifts on Boy's Day. The most famous dolls are made in Kyoto and are known as *kyō-ningyō*.

Ningyō can be bought in tourist shops, department stores and special doll shops. In Tokyo (see the Tokyo chapter) Asakusa-bashi's Edo-dōri Ave is well known for its many doll shops.

Kasa *Kasa* (Japanese umbrellas) are another classic souvenir item. They come in two forms: *higasa*, which are made of paper, cotton or silk and serve as a sunshade; and *bangasa*, which are made of oiled paper and keep the rain off. Again, department stores and tourist shops are your best bet for finding kasa.

Koinobori *Koinobori* are the carp banners that you see flying from poles in Japan. The carp is much revered for its tenacity and perseverance, but you might like the banners for their simple elegance. They're available from Shibuya's Oriental Bazaar in Tokyo and are occasionally sold in tourist shops.

Katana *Katana* (Japanese swords) make a fantastic souvenir – it's just that good ones are going to cost more than all your other travel expenses put together! The reason for their expense is both the mystique attached to them as the symbols of samurai power and the great care that went into making them. Sword shops that sell the real thing will also stock *tsuba*, sword guards, and complete sets of samurai armour. Department stores, on the other hand, stock realistic (to the untrained eye at least) imitations at affordable prices.

Shikki *Shikki* (lacquerware) is another Japanese craft that has been mastered to a superlative degree. The lacquer-making process, involving as many as 15 layers of lacquer, is used to create objects as diverse as dishes to furniture. As you might expect, examples of good lacquerware cannot be had for a song, but smaller items can be bought at affordable prices from department stores. Popular, easily transportable items include bowls, trays and small boxes.

Washi *Washi* (Japanese paper) has been famous for more more than 1000 years as the finest hand-made paper in the world. Special shops stock sheets of washi and products made from it, such as notebooks, wallets and so on. As they're generally inexpensive and light, washi products make excellent gifts and souvenirs. Again, you'll find them in the big department stores. Tokyo's Ginza also has a large washi shop in the same building as the Contax Gallery (see the Central Tokyo map in the Tokyo chapter).

Stoneware & Porcelain The difference between stoneware and porcelain is in the firing process. Stoneware is fired at temperatures of between 600° and 900°C and is frequently admired for its earthiness and imperfections. Porcelain, on the other hand, is fired at much higher temperatures (1300° to 1400°C) and is transformed into a glass-like substance in the process. Imperfections in porcelain are considered just that – imperfections – and are discarded.

Numerous pottery villages still exist in various parts of Japan. Many of them feature pottery museums and working kilns which can be visited. Of course, it is also possible

to buy examples of stoneware and porcelain. Not too far from Tokyo is Mashiko (see the Around Tokyo section); in Western Honshū is Imbe, near Okayama, famed for its *bizen-yaki* pottery; in the Kansai region is Tamba Sasayama, with its Tamba pottery; in Kyūshū, the home of Japanese pottery, Koishiwara, Karatsu, Imari and Arita are all sources of different pottery styles.

Ukiyo-e Ukiyo-e wood-block prints (literally 'pictures from the floating world'), originally were not an art form. Wood-block printing originated in the 18th century as one of Japan's earliest manifestations of mass culture and, as such, was used in advertising and posters. The name derives from a Buddhist term indicating the transient world of daily pleasures, ukiyo-e uniquely depicting such things as street scenes, actors and courtesans.

Today, tourist shops in Japan stock modern reproductions of the work of famous ukiyo-e masters such as Hokusai whose scenes of Mt Fuji are favourites. It is also possible to come across originals by lesser-known artists at prices ranging from Y5000 to Y40,000. Try the Oriental Bazaar in Shibuya, Tokyo if you're looking for reasonably priced originals. In Ginza, Tokyo, there are a couple of galleries that stock contemporary wood-block prints – many of them deal with very modern themes and are strikingly innovative.

Kimono & Yukata Kimono are seldom worn by Japanese women nowadays. Indeed, most young Japanese women would have no idea how to dress themselves in a kimono. Still, they are worn occasionally, mostly on ceremonial occasions such as a school graduation or wedding day.

For most non-Japanese, the cost of a kimono is prohibitively expensive. For a 'bottom of the range' kimono, prices start at around Y60,000 and soar to Y1 million or more. The best option for those interested in owning their own kimono is to look for an antique silk kimono in places like Shibuya's

Oriental Bazaar in Tokyo. Alternatively, if you're in Japan during March or September, these are the months that the Daimaru store has sales of its rental kimono. Be warned, however: these sales are also popular with local Japanese.

For those not in the kimono league, another option might be to look for a yukata (the cotton bathrobes worn in ryokan). These have a distinctively Japanese look and are not only affordable (from around Y3500 up) but also highly useable.

Getting There & Away

Flying into Tokyo is only one of a diverse range of ways of getting to Japan and only a tiny part of the whole story. For a start there are many other airports in Japan, some of which make better entry points than Tokyo's inconvenient Narita International Airport. It's also possible to arrive in Japan by sea from a number of nearby countries, particularly South Korea. Japan also serves as the starting or finishing point for the popular Trans-Siberian Express trip across the USSR.

AIR

There are flights to Japan from all over the world, usually to Tokyo but also to a number of other Japanese airports. Although Tokyo may seem the obvious arrival and departure point in Japan, for many visitors this may not be the case. If, for example, you were travelling from Tokyo to western Japan then out to Hong Kong or Australia, it could be much more convenient to fly out of, say, Fukuoka rather than backtrack all the way to Tokyo.

Arriving in Japan

Airports There are international airports on the main island of Honshū (Nagoya, Niigata, Osaka and Tokyo), Kyūshū (Fukuoka, Kagoshima, Kumamoto and Nagasaki), Okinawa (Naha) and Hokkaidō (Sapporo).

Tokyo Despite having more international flights than any other airport in Japan, Tokyo is far from the best place to make your first landfall. For a start, Narita International Airport is 60 km from central Tokyo and a rush-hour traffic jam can mean a two hour drive to the city. Even the airport bus services take 1½ hours at the best of times.

Train services are faster, particularly since the JR Narita and private Keisei lines were extended all the way to the airport terminal. (Until the lines were completed in March 1991, visitors had to take a bus the short distance between the terminal and the Narita railway station.)

Unless you've got direct access to a major bank's central vault, don't even consider taking a taxi between the airport and central Tokyo. (See the Getting Around section of the Tokyo chapter for more details on airport transport.)

Airport transport isn't the end of the Tokyo horror story. Narita is not a particularly user-friendly airport and immigration formalities can be extremely slow and tedious. When you finally do reach Tokyo, the city itself is big, expensive and may seem overwhelmingly confusing. All in all, if you can plan your arrival elsewhere in Japan, then do so.

There is one exception to this tale of woe. When Narita International Airport opened, China Airlines (along with most domestic airlines flights) stayed at the convenient old Haneda Airport. This was because Air China (mainland China) did not want to fly to the same airport as China Airlines (Taiwan). Consequently, visitors preferring to make Tokyo their entry point can avoid the hassles of Narita International Airport by flying China Airlines to Haneda Airport instead.

Osaka Osaka, Japan's second largest city, has many international flights. Its airport is conveniently close to the town and there are direct bus services between the airport and nearby Kyoto, Japan's number one tourist destination. International connections include Canada, the USA and many countries in Europe, Asia and Australasia.

Nagoya Nagoya may have few attractions in its own right, but the town is conveniently located between Tokyo and Osaka and the airport is reasonably close. From Nagoya, flights connect with Australia, Canada, Guam, Hong Kong, Indonesia, the Philippines, Singapore, South Korea, Taiwan, Thailand and the USA.

Air Travel Glossary

Apex Apex, or 'advance purchase excursion' is a discounted ticket which must be paid for in advance. There are penalties if you wish to change it.

Bucket Shop An unbonded travel agency specialising in discounted airline tickets.

Bumped Just because you have a confirmed seat doesn't mean you're going to get on the plane – see Overbooking.

Cancellation Penalties If you have to cancel or change an Apex ticket there are often heavy penalties involved, insurance can sometimes be taken out against these penalties. Some airlines impose penalties on regular tickets as well, particularly against 'no show' passengers.

Check In Airlines ask you to check in a certain time ahead of the flight departure (usually 1½ hours on international flights). If you fail to check in on time and the flight is overbooked the airline can cancel your booking and give your seat to somebody else.

Confirmation Having a ticket written out with the flight and date you want doesn't mean you have a seat until the agent has checked with the airline that your status is 'OK' or confirmed. Meanwhile you could just be 'on request'.

Cross-Border Tickets Sometimes it is cheaper to fly to countries A, B, C rather than just B to C, usually because country A's airline is desperate to sell tickets or because the currency in A is very weak. Authorities in B can get very unhappy if you turn up for the flight from B to C without having first flown from A to B. Be cautious about discounted tickets which have been issued in another city, particularly in Eastern European cities.

Discounted Tickets There are two types of discounted fares – officially discounted (see Promotional Fares) and unofficially discounted. With unofficially discounted tickets you usually get what you pay for and the lowest prices often impose drawbacks like flying with unpopular airlines (Eastern European or Middle Eastern airlines for example), inconvenient schedules (only one flight a week and it leaves at 1 am) or unpleasant routes and connections (you get from A to B by a roundabout route and have to change airlines half way with a long wait at the airport). A discounted ticket doesn't necessarily have to save you money – an agent may be able to sell you a ticket at Apex prices without the associated Apex advance booking and other requirements. Discounted tickets only exist where there is fierce competition, they are rarely available on domestic routes if the country only has one or two domestic airlines or in similarly tightly controlled regions.

Freedoms An airline's right to take passengers between various cities is defined by six 'freedoms'. Unofficially discounted tickets are often associated with fifth freedom flights – where an airline from country A has the right to fly passengers between country B and country C – or sixth freedom flights – where the airline in country B can fly passengers from A to C as long as the flight goes through B.

Full Fares Airlines traditionally offer first class (coded F), business class (coded J) and economy class (coded Y) tickets. These days there are so many promotional and discounted fares available from the regular economy class that few passengers pay full economy fare.

Lost Tickets If you lose your airline ticket an airline will usually treat it like a travellers' cheque and, after inquiries, issue you with another one. Legally, however, an airline is entitled to treat it like cash and if you lose it then it's gone forever. Take good care of your tickets.

Maximum Permitted Mileage (MPM) Between city A and city Z there is an officially defined MPM and so long as you do not exceed that distance you can fly via B, C, X, Y and points in between if you have a full fare, unlimited stopover ticket. These days, however, full-fare tickets are rather rare.

No Shows No shows are passengers who fail to show up for their flight, sometimes due to unexpected delays or disasters, sometimes due to simply forgetting, sometimes because they made more than one booking and didn't bother to cancel the one they didn't want.

On Request An unconfirmed booking for a flight, see Confirmation.

Open Jaws A return ticket where you fly out to one place but return from another. If available this can save you backtracking to your arrival point.

Overbooking Airlines hate to fly empty seats and since every flight has some passengers who fail to show up (see No Shows) airlines often book more passengers than they have seats. Usually the excess passengers balance those who fail to show up but occasionally somebody gets bumped. If this happens guess who it is most likely to be? The passengers who check in late of course.

Promotional Fares Officially discounted fares like Apex fares which are available from any travel agent or direct from the airline.

Reconfirmation At least 72 hours prior to departure time of an onward or return flight you must contact the airline and 'reconfirm' that you intend to be on the flight. If you don't do this the airline can delete your name from the passenger list and you could lose your seat. You don't have to reconfirm the first flight on your itinerary or if your stopover is less than 72 hours. It doesn't hurt to reconfirm more than once.

Restrictions Discounted tickets often have various restrictions on them – advance purchase is the most usual one (see Apex). Others are restrictions on the minimum and maximum period you must be away, such as a minimum of 14 days or a maximum of one year. See Cancellation Penalties.

Standby A discounted ticket where you only fly if there is a seat free at the last moment. Standby fares are usually only available on domestic routes.

Tickets Out An entry requirement for many countries is that you have an onward or return ticket, in other words, a ticket out of the country. If you're not sure what you intend to do next, the easiest solution is to buy the cheapest onward ticket to a neighbouring country or a ticket from a reliable airline which can later be refunded if you do not use it.

Transferred Tickets Airline tickets cannot be transferred from one person to another. Travellers sometimes try to sell the return half of their ticket, but officials can ask you to prove that you are the person named on the ticket. This is unlikely to happen on domestic flights but can easily happen on an international flight where tickets may be compared with passports.

Travel Agencies Travel agencies vary widely and you should ensure you use one that suits your needs. Some simply handle tours while full-service agencies handle everything from tours and tickets to car rental and hotel bookings. A good one will do all these things and can save you a lot of money but if all you want is a ticket at the lowest possible price, then you really need an agency specialising in discounted tickets. A discounted ticket agency, however, may not be useful for other things, like hotel bookings.

Travel Periods Some officially discounted fares, Apex fares in particular, vary with the time of year. There is often a low (off-peak) season and a high (peak) season. Sometimes there's an intermediate or shoulder season as well. At peak times, when everyone wants to fly, not only will the officially discounted fares be higher but so will unofficially discounted fares or there may simply be no discounted tickets available. Usually the fare depends on your outward flight – if you depart in the high season and return in the low season, you pay the high-season fare. ■

Fukuoka Fukuoka, at the northern end of Kyūshū, is the major arrival point on Japan's western end. The airport, conveniently located near the city, has flight connections with Australia, North America and a number of Asian destinations.

Naha Okinawa Island, south-west of the main islands of Japan, is a convenient arrival or departure point for Hong Kong and Taiwan. There are also connections with Guam and the USA.

Niigata Niigata, north of Tokyo, is connected with Seoul in South Korea and with Khabarovsk in the USSR. From Khabarovsk, the Trans-Siberian Express and Aeroflot operate to Moscow. A *shinkansen* (bullet train) line connects Niigata with Tokyo.

Other Airports On the island of Kyūshū, Kagoshima Airport has flights to Hong Kong, Kumamoto Airport has flights to South Korea, and Nagasaki has flights to Shanghai and Seoul.

On Hokkaidō, Sapporo Airport has connections with South Korea.

To/From Europe

All direct flights between Europe and Japan fly into Tokyo but some continue to Osaka. Flight times vary widely depending on the route taken. The most direct route is across Scandinavia and the USSR and, since the Soviet Union became hard up for cash, there have been far more flights taking this route (the Russians charge hefty fees for crossing their airspace).

The fastest nonstop London-Tokyo flights on the USSR route take just under 12 hours. Flights that stop in Moscow take an extra 2½ hours. Finnair's Helsinki-Tokyo flight over the North Pole and the Bering Strait takes 13½ hours. Before the Russians opened their skies, the popular route was via Anchorage, Alaska. Some flights still operate that way and take about 17 hours,

including the Anchorage stopover. Finally, there are the old trans-Asian routes across the Middle East and South Asia, which take anything from 18 to 30 hours depending on the number of stops en route.

Return economy air fares between London and Tokyo are around UK£1000 and are valid for 14 days to three months. A ticket valid for a year away costs about £1300. Although a wide variety of cheaper deals are available, generally, the lower the price, the less convenient the route. Expect to pay around £900 to £1000 for a one-year valid return ticket with a good airline via a fast route. For a less convenient trans-Asian route, count on £700 or lower and about half that for one-way tickets.

In London, STA Travel (tel (071) 937-9962) at 74 Old Brompton Rd, London SW7 or 117 Euston Rd, London NW1; Trailfinders (tel (071) 938-3366) at 46 Earls Court Rd and at 194 Kensington High St, London W8 7RG (tel (071) 938-3444) and Travel Bug (tel (061) 721-4000) all offer rock-bottom return flights to Tokyo and can also put together interesting Round-the-World routes incorporating Tokyo on the itinerary. The weekly 'what's on' magazine *Time Out* or the various giveaway papers are good places to look for travel bargains but take care with shonky bucket shops and prices that seem too low to believe. The really cheap fares will probably involve cash-strapped Eastern European or Middle Eastern airlines and may involve complicated transfers and long waits along the way.

The Far East Travel Centre (FETC) (tel (071) 734-9318) at 3 Lower John St, London W1A 4XE, specialises in Korean Airline ticketing and can fly you from London Gatwick via Seoul to your choice of Nagasaki, Nagoya, Osaka, Sapporo and Tokyo. This is a good option for visitors who don't want to take the conventional Tokyo route.

The Japan Centre (tel (071) 437-6445) 66-68 Brewer St, London W1R 3PJ, handles all sorts of ticket permutations. Its basement has a shop section (tel (071) 439-8035) with books and assorted Japanese paraphernalia as well as a Japanese restaurant with reasonable prices. It's worth a visit for a taste of Japan.

An alternative route to Japan from Europe is to fly to Hong Kong and buy an onward ticket from one of Hong Kong's very competitive travel agencies. London-Hong Kong flights are much more competitively priced than London-Tokyo ones. If you have to go to Hong Kong en route to Tokyo, a London-Hong Kong-London ticket plus a Hong Kong-Tokyo-Hong Kong ticket can work out much cheaper than a London-Hong Kong-Tokyo-London ticket.

London remains one of the best places in Europe to purchase keenly priced airline tickets although Amsterdam is also very good.

To/From North America

West coast flights to Japan go straight across the Pacific and take about 10 hours. From the east coast, flights usually take the northern route over Alaska – the new nonstop flights take about 13 hours. The big time change on the trans-Pacific flights is a sure-fire recipe for jet lag and there's also a date change as you cross the International Date Line.

Seven-day advance purchase return fares are US$910 to US$1125 from the west coast (depending on the season) and US$1156 to US$1370 from the east. Regular economy fares are much higher – US$874 to US$935 (one way) from the west coast, US$1195 to US$1279 from the east coast.

Better deals are available if you shop around. From the east coast, return fares as low as US$759 to US$879 and one-way fares of US$749 are possible. From the west coast fares can drop to US$559 and US$689 with Korean Airlines. There are also good deals available via Vancouver with Canadian Airlines International. From San Francisco or Los Angeles, fares to Tokyo range from US$629 to US$769 or to Nagoya from US$579 to US$779. Check the Sunday travel sections of papers like the *Los Angeles Times* or the *New York Times* for travel bargains. Council Travel and STA Travel are two good discount operations specialising in

student fares and other cheap deals. They have offices all across North America.

Fares from Canada are similar to those from the USA. Canadian Airlines International, which operates out of Vancouver, often matches or beats the best fares available from the USA. Travel Cuts, the Canadian student travel organisation, offers one-way Vancouver-Tokyo flights from C$800 and returns from C$1000 or more depending on the season.

To/From Australasia

Japan Airlines (JAL), All Nippon Airways (ANA) and Qantas all have direct flights between Australia and Japan. You can fly from most Australia state capitals to Tokyo, Osaka, Nagoya and Fukuoka. There's only a one hour time change between Australia and Japan and a direct Sydney-Tokyo flight takes about nine hours.

A return excursion Sydney-Tokyo fare is around A$1500. Discount deals will involve round about routes via other Asian capitals like Kuala Lumpur or Manila. If you shop around, you can find one-way flights from Sydney or Melbourne for around A$750, return flights for A$1100. STA travel offices or the numerous Flight Centres International are good places to look for discount ticket deals.

From New Zealand, Auckland-Tokyo return excursion fares are around NZ$1900 in the low season rising to NZ$2500 in the high.

To/From Asia

Most Asian nations have air links with Japan. South Korea is particularly popular because it's used by many travellers as a place to take a short holiday from Japan when their visas are close to expiring. The immigration authorities treat travellers returning to Japan after a short break in South Korea with great suspicion. Hong Kong is popular because it is such a bargain basement for airline ticketing.

South Korea Numerous flights link Seoul and Pusan with cities in Japan but the cheapest travel is by ferry. (See the following Sea section for information on sea-travel bargains between Korea and Japan.)

Hong Kong There are direct flights between Hong Kong and a number of cities in Japan, though the biggest choice and best deals will be to Tokyo. Agents like the Hong Kong Student Travel Bureau or Phoenix Travel can offer one-way tickets from around HK$2000 to HK$2400, and return tickets from HK$2800 to HK$4500, depending on the period of validity.

Taiwan Agents handling discounted tickets advertise in the English-language *China Post*. There are flights from Taipei to Fukuoka, Naha, Osaka or Tokyo.

Flights also operate between Kaohsiung and Osaka or Tokyo.

Other Asian Centres There are regular flights between Japan and other major centres like Manila, Bangkok, Kuala Lumpur, Singapore and Jakarta. Some of the cheapest deals between Europe and Japan will be via South Asia – Bangladesh Biman will fly you from London to Dhaka to Tokyo at about the lowest price going.

To/From Other Regions
There are also flights between Japan and South America, Africa and the Middle East.

Round-the-World & Circle Pacific Tickets
Round-the-World (RTW) fares are put together by two or more airlines and allow you to make a circuit of the world using their combined routes. A typical RTW ticket is valid for one year, allows unlimited stopovers along the way and costs about UK£1400, A$3500 or US$2700. An example, including Tokyo in Japan, would be a British Airways/United Airways combination flying London, New York, Tokyo, Singapore, London. A South Pacific version might take you London, New York, Los Angeles, Tahiti, Sydney, Tokyo, London. There are many versions involving different

combinations of airlines and different routes. Generally, routes which stay north of the equator are usually a little cheaper than routes that include countries like Australia or South America.

Circle Pacific fares are a similar idea and allow you to make a circuit of the Pacific. A typical combination would involve Qantas and Japan Airlines flying Los Angeles, Tahiti, Sydney, Tokyo, Los Angeles. Circle Pacific fares are around A$2900 or US$2300.

Enterprising travel agents put together their own RTW and Circle Pacific fares at much lower prices than the joint airline deals but, of course, the cheapest fares will involve unpopular airlines and less popular routes. It's possible to put together a RTW from London for as little as UK£700. RTW or Circle Pacific fares from Australia start from around A$2100. Travel agents in London have also come up with another variation on these combination fares – the Circle Asia fare. A possible route would be London, Hong Kong, Tokyo, Manila, Singapore, Bangkok, London.

Leaving Japan
Japan is not a good place to look for discounted tickets, in fact flying from Japan to country A or Z is almost certainly more expensive than flying from country A or Z to Japan. If you have to buy a ticket in Japan there are often ads for specialist travel agents in the English-language papers and magazines aimed at resident foreigners. Council Travel (tel 3581-7581) has an office at the Sanno Grand Building, Room 102, 2-14-2 Nagata-cho, Chiyoda-ku, Tokyo 100. STA Travel (tel 3221-1733) is at Sanden Building, 3-5-5 Kojimachi, Chiyoda-ku, Tokyo.

SEA
To/From South Korea
South Korea is the closest country to Japan and a very popular visa-renewal point. Many long-term visitors to Japan who are teaching English or who are engaged in some other kind of work, drop over to Korea when their

permitted period of stay in Japan is about to expire, then come back to start a fresh stay. Expect to have your passport rigorously inspected.

Pusan-Shimonoseki This popular ferry service is the cheapest route between South Korea and Japan. Daily departures with the Kampur Ferry Service's vessels *Kampu* or *Pukwan* leave Pusan at 5 pm and arrive in Shimonoseki at 8.30 am the next morning. One-way fares start from about US$50 for students, continue up through US$60 for an open tatami-matted area and peak at between US$75 and US$100 for a cabin. There's a 10% discount on return fares and children under six travel free. Fares for children aged six to 12 are half price. (See the Shimonoseki section of the Western Honshū chapter for more details.)

Pusan-Osaka Services between Pusan and Osaka take nearly 24 hours and operate four times a week. One-way fares start at about US$80 for students in the larger cabins. Regular fares range from about US$100 for the multi-berth cabins or from US$125 per person for a two-berth cabin. Children under six travel free, children aged six to 12 qualify for half fare. The services are operated by a Korean and a Japanese ship. You cannot use Korean currency on the Japanese ship so, if you're leaving Korea on that boat, make sure you've disposed of all your *won* before boarding.

To/From Taiwan
A weekly ferry operates between Taiwan and Okinawa via Ishigaki and Miyako in Okinawa Prefecture. The Taiwan port alternates between Keelung (about US$110 economy class) and Kaohsiung (about US$130). Fares seem to be slightly cheaper from Taiwan than from Japan. The trip takes one day and travel agents in both Keelung and Kaohsiung will handle the tickets.

To/From Other Places
For travellers intending to take the Trans-Siberian Railway to Moscow, there's a weekly ferry service between Yokohama and the Soviet port of Nakhodka near Vladivostok.

A weekly service to Shanghai, China departs on alternate weeks from Osaka and Kōbe.

TRANS-SIBERIAN RAILWAY
Japan's position on the edge of Asia provides an intriguing opportunity for travellers to use the Trans-Siberian Railway when approaching or leaving Japan. Negotiating the procedures takes time but, compared to a tedious flight, the train ride is competitively priced and provides much more scope for meetings and adventures – particularly now that the USSR, Eastern Europe and even Mongolia are undergoing speedy change.

There are three Trans-Siberian Railway routings: one is directly across the USSR by rail followed by a final hop across to Japan by sea or air: this is expensive. The marginally cheaper, but more complicated, Chinese Trans-Mongolian and Russian Trans-Manchurian routes traverse the USSR before taking different routes into China – from China you can choose between a ship or a plane to continue to Japan. Obviously, you can follow these routes in either direction.

The Direct Trans-Siberian Route
The original Moscow-Khabarovsk-Nakhodka Trans-Siberia route takes you directly to Japan; from the Soviet port of Nakhodka near Vladivostok there are boats to Yokohama and to Hong Kong. You should probably allow about seven days for the Nakhodka-Hong Kong boat journey. Your Intourist rail ticket will be timed to connect with a specific sailing.

The *Rossia* express departs Moscow's Yaroslav Station every morning and the trip to Nakhodka takes about 8½ days. It is also possible to travel part of the route by air, stopping at Irkutsk, Bratsk or Khabarovsk, where you usually stay overnight before picking up the train connection to Nakhodka and Japan.

During the winter, or if the Nakhodka-Yokohama boat is fully booked, a more expensive alternative is a connecting flight between Khabarovsk (USSR) and Niigata (Japan) for Y62,000 (US$480).

Prices for the complete rail/ship journey from Moscow to Yokohama start from about US$900 for a 2nd class sleeper on the train and a four berth cabin on the ship. Intourist recommends a minimum of four weeks' notice to take care of visas, hotel bookings and train reservations. Further details are available in a special Intourist folder, *Independent Travel to the USSR – The Trans-Siberian Railway*.

In the opposite direction, the ship/rail journey from Yokohoma to Moscow costs around US$1000 and tickets are sold by the Japan Soviet Tourist Bureau (JSTB).

The Indirect Trans-Siberian Route

Moscow-Beijing prices for both the Trans-Manchurian and Trans-Mongolian route start at about US$640 for a 2nd class sleeper in a four berth compartment.

The Moscow-Manzhouli-Beijing Trans-Manchurian route is the Russian service which skirts Mongolia. The train departs Moscow on Saturdays at 1.20 am and arrives in Beijing the following Friday, early in the morning. Between June and November there is an additional weekly departure on Sundays at 1.20 am.

The Moscow-Ulan Bator-Beijing Trans-Mongolian route is the Chinese service which passes through Mongolia. Trains depart Moscow every Wednesday at 12.30 am and arrive in Beijing the following Monday afternoon. In terms of overall comfort, it is generally rated as preferable to the Russian train.

Onward China-Japan Connections

Air China has several flights a week from Beijing to Tokyo and Osaka, via Shanghai. Japan Airlines flies from Beijing and Shanghai to Tokyo, Osaka and Nagasaki.

There is a regular boat service between Shanghai and Osaka/Kōbe taking two days and costing around Y23,000 (US$175). A 10% student discount is available for 2nd class only. The ship departs once weekly: one week to/from Osaka and the next week to/from Kōbe.

Visas

If you apply for a Soviet visa through a Soviet embassy you must supply a confirmed Intourist itinerary and timetable. If you're applying through Intourist you must have an appropriate visa for your country of destination.

Intourist will process visa and ticket applications together; they require four to five weeks. During summer, ticket reservations are essential because trains – especially the Trans-Mongolian which runs only once a week – are quickly booked out. If you want to travel in September, for example, you should consider booking before April!

A Soviet transit visa is much cheaper than a tourist visa which requires a full itinerary and pre-booked accommodation. (Expect to pay US$135 per night for a two-star hotel inside Moscow or US$65 elsewhere. Hardly a bargain.)

Chinese and Polish tourist or transit visas and Mongolian transit visas are readily obtainable from the appropriate embassies, but prices are often high.

Information & Tickets

Travelling between Moscow and Japan varies considerably in cost depending on the route you take and the direction you travel. Cheapest is westbound via China – US$175 for the Osaka/Kōbe-Shanghai ship, US$50 for the Shanghai-Beijing train and US$250 for the Beijing-Moscow train – a total of US$475. Eastbound, the Moscow-Beijing fare jumps to US$640, raising the total cost to US$865.

The Moscow-Nakhodka train and Nakhodka-Yokohama boat route costs US$900 eastbound or US$1000 westbound.

In Europe For the latest information, contact specialist agencies or national tourist agencies such as the Japanese National Tourist Organisation (JNTO), China International Travel Service (CITS), Intourist (USSR) or Ibusz (Hungary).

London to Beijing via Berlin, Moscow and Ulan Bator, including one night's accommodation in Moscow, costs from about US$1300. Intourist provides an excellent timetable of the international passenger routes with rail prices. The most expensive section per km is usually the connection between Europe and Moscow, so you may want to save money by starting your trip closer to Eastern Europe. There are itineraries from Berlin or Helsinki or you could fly straight to Moscow and start from there.

Tickets from Hungary cost around US$500 from Budapest to Beijing. For more details contact the Hungarian state travel company (Ibusz), Tanacs Korut 3/C, Budapest V.

Several readers have recommended the Scandinavian Student Travel Service (SSTS), 117 Hauchsvej, 1825 Copenhagen V, Denmark. This organisation has branch offices in Europe, Hong Kong and North America and provides a range of basic tours for student or budget travellers (mostly in the summer). Prices start at US$1095 for a 20 day trip from Helsinki to Yokohama via Leningrad, Moscow, Novosibirsk, Irkutsk, Khabarovsk and Nakhodka.

In Japan The Japan-Soviet Tourist Bureau (JSTB) publishes a highly informative brochure which gives prices, routings, visa requirements, etc. The TIC in Tokyo also stocks this leaflet. The STA Travel office (tel 3221-1733) in Tokyo may have information on the SSTS tours. JSTB offices are:

JSTB Head Office, Kamiyacho Building, 3rd Floor, 5-12-12 Toranomon, Minato-ku, Tokyo 105 (tel 3432-6161)
JSTB Osaka Office, Takeda Building, Ground Floor, 1-12-20 Awaza, Nishi-ku, Osaka 550 (tel 06-531-7416)

In China If you want to save on Japanese prices, tickets can be obtained in Beijing from the China International Travel Service (CITS) office in the Chongwenmen Hotel. During peak season, seats are booked solid, so try to make your reservations far in advance and leave yourself time to negotiate bureaucratic hurdles.

The unofficial budget travellers' centre in Beijing is the Qiaoyuan Hotel. This is where you can check the notice board for offers of even cheaper Trans-Siberian tickets or meet up with wheeler-dealers in these tickets. You should check the validity of these offers carefully before parting with your money.

In Hong Kong Hong Kong is also a good place to organise tickets. Travellers have reported fast and efficient service and competitive prices for tickets arranged through Monkey Business (tel 7231376) at Grand House, 9th Floor, B-Block, Chungking Mansions, Tsimshatsui, Kowloon. The same company also has an office in Beijing (tel 3012244, ext 716) at the Qiaoyuan Hotel (new building, room 716) but it is preferable to use the Hong Kong office for bookings.

Predeparture Preparations
US dollars in small denominations are essential. Take food with you to supplement dining-car meals. Alcohol is not sold on Trans-Siberian trains, so bring your own if you want to initiate Siberian train parties.

Books
For in-depth information on the Trans-Siberian trip, see Robert Strauss' *Trans-Siberian Rail Guide* (Bradt Publications, England, 1987) or Bryn Thomas' *Trans-Siberian Handbook* (Lascelles, London, 1988). Updated editions of both books will be available from 1991. *China – a travel survival kit* (Lonely Planet, 1991) will help you traverse China and includes a section summarising Trans-Siberian procedures. Consult *USSR – a travel survival kit* (Lonely Planet) to see what might appeal en route in the USSR.

Getting Around

Japan has an enormous variety of travel possibilities and, like everything else in Japan, its transport network is extremely well organised. The Japanese are used to departures and arrivals timed to the minute and they plan trips with schedules that require split-second timing.

Timetables

In many popular areas of Japan, transport schedules are so frequent that timetables hardly matter – does it really make any difference if the train departs at 10.30 or 10.40 am? If, however, you really want to know what goes where and when, then you need a *jikokuhyō* or 'book of timetables'.

These come in a variety of forms including a completely comprehensive monthly *ōki-jikokuhyō* which lists just about everything that moves and takes passengers in and around Japan. This can be useful if you're really exploring the back blocks of Japan and need to know about buses to remote villages or ferries between small islands. Most travellers find it's altogether too much of a good thing since it's the size and weight of a telephone directory and is completely in Japanese. Deciphering a 1000 page kanji timetable is not most people's idea of fun travel! In any case, the ōki-jikokuhyō is always available at stations (often tied to the ticket-office counter with a piece of string) and at most ryokan, youth hostels, minshuku and other accommodation.

An easier alternative is JTB's *Mini-Timetable* which costs Y310 and is issued monthly. It's about the size of a pocket dictionary and lists JR shinkansen services, limited and ordinary expresses, intercity and express trains in the Tokyo, Nagoya and Osaka areas, limited express services on the main private lines, expressway buses and all the domestic airline schedules. Other advantages of the mini guide are that it has some explanations in English and places names are shown in romaji on maps and main timetables. You're still going to have to do some deciphering of kanji but even a short-stay visitor should find this no problem.

Travel Agencies

Information and tickets can also be obtained from travel agencies of which there are a great number in Japan. Virtually every train station of any size will have at least one travel agency in the station building to handle all sorts of bookings in addition to train services. The Japan Travel Bureau (JTB) is the big daddy of Japanese travel agencies.

Discount Tickets

There are some agencies that deal in discounted tickets both for international and domestic travel. Typical savings on shinkansen tickets are around 20%, which is good news for long-term residents who are not eligible for Japan Rail Passes. Discount ticket agencies are found in the major cities and these agencies sometimes advertise in the English-language journals produced for long-term residents. (See the Tokyo section for details of discounters in that city.)

Baggage Forwarding

In Japan, it's important to travel light, particularly on trains. However, if you have too much baggage, there are highly efficient forwarding services which you can use to send your baggage ahead to a final destination.

AIR

Rail travel has such a pervasive image in Japan that it's easy to forget there's a dense network of air routes. In many cases, flying can be much faster than even shinkansen rail travel and not that much more expensive. Flying is also an efficient way to travel from the main islands to the many small islands around the coast of Japan. As well as numerous small local operators, there are five major domestic airlines.

Japan Air Lines (JAL) is the major international carrier and also has a domestic network linking the major cities. All Nippon Airways (ANA) is the second largest international carrier and operates a more extensive domestic system. Japan Air Systems (JAS) only does a couple of overseas routes but flies to many destinations in Japan. Air Nippon Koku (ANK) and South-West Airlines (SWAL) are smaller domestic carriers. ANK links many smaller towns all over Japan while SWAL is particularly good for connections through Okinawa and the other South-West Islands.

The chart shows some of the major connections and the one-way fares. There's a 10% discount on round-trip fares if the return flight is made within seven to 10 days. The airlines have some weird and wonderful discounts if you know what to ask for. JAL, for example, has a women's group discount available for groups of three or more women.

Or a husband and wife discount if their combined age totals 88 or more!

If you're flying to or from Tokyo, note that most domestic airlines use the convenient Haneda Airport, while all international flights, except those with China Airlines, use Narita. If you're flying to Tokyo to make an international connection out of Narita it would be rather embarrassing to end up at Haneda – make sure you're on one of the less frequent domestic Narita flights or that you have plenty of time to make the transfer from Haneda to Narita.

TRAIN

As in India, rail is *the* way to travel in Japan but there are few other similarities. Japanese rail travel is usually fast, frequent, clean, comfortable and often very expensive. The services range from small local lines to the shinkansen super-expresses or 'bullet trains'

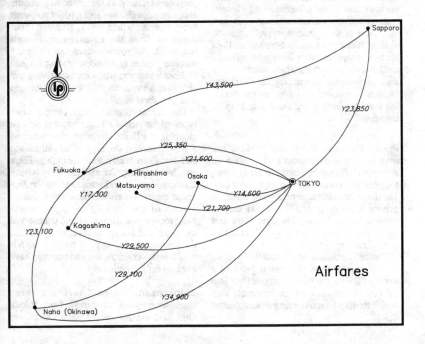

which have become a symbol of modern Japan.

Railway Systems

Japan Railways Japan Railways (JR) is actually a number of separate private railway systems which provide one linked service. For the railway user, JR gives every impression of being a single operation which indeed it was for more than a century. Then in 1987, it was decided that the accumulated losses of the government-run JNR (JR's predecessor) had simply gone too far and the government privatised it. To most Japanese, JR is known as *kokutetsu* – *koku* means 'national', *tetsu* means 'line' or literally 'iron', short for 'iron road'.

The JR system covers the country from one end to the other and also provides local services around major cities like Tokyo and Osaka. There are over 20,000 km of railway line and over 20,000 services daily. In many cities, the JR central station forms the hub of the town centre, and is surrounded by hotels, restaurants, entertainment areas, bus services, car rental agencies, travel agencies, airline offices and the like. Shinkansen lines are totally separate from the regular railways and, in some places, the shinkansen stations are a fair distance from the regular JR station. JR also operate buses and ferries and ticketing can combine more than one form of transport.

Private Railways The private railway lines usually operate over short routes, often no more than 100 km in length. In many cases, they extend to resort areas from a major city. The local commuter services are often on private railway lines. The Kinki district around Kōbe, Kyoto, Nagoya, Nara and Osaka is an area particularly well served by private railway lines.

Unlike JR stations, the private line stations do not usually form the central focus of a town. In Tokyo, the various private lines into the city all terminate on the Yamanote loop which forms a neat outer ring around central Tokyo.

Shinkansen

The fastest and best known train services in Japan are the 'bullet trains'. Nobody knows them by that name in Japan, they're simply the shinkansen or super-expresses. Shinkansen translates as 'new trunk line'. The shinkansen reach speeds of up to 240 km/h, running on continuously welded lines which totally eliminate the old railway clickety-clack of wheels rolling over joints. A new series of shinkansen running at even higher speeds will come into use in the early '90s. These will still not be as fast as the high-speed trains in France, but the Japanese service has established an incredible record for speed, reliability and safety. In more than 30 years of operation, there has never been a fatality.

The shinkansen service efficiency starts even before you board the train. Your ticket indicates your carriage and seat number, and platform signs indicate where you should stand for that carriage entrance. The train pulls in precisely to the scheduled minute and, sure enough, the carriage door you want is right beside where you're standing. Your departure from the train is equally well organised. As you approach the station, a recorded voice announces, in English and Japanese, that you will soon be arriving and should make your way to the door as the stop will be a short one.

On each shinkansen route, there are two types of services: a faster express service stopping at a limited number of stations and a slower service stopping at all shinkansen stations. There is no difference in fare. There are, however, regular and 1st class 'Green Car' carriages. If you want to avoid the Japanese cigarette passion, there are a limited number of non-smoking carriages *(kin-en-sha)*; request one when booking. Unreserved carriages will always be available, even on the shinkansen, but at peak holiday periods they can be very crowded and you may have to stand for the entire trip.

Shinkansen Routes There are three shinkansen routes, all starting from Tokyo. One runs via Nagoya, Kyoto, Osaka and

Hiroshima to Shimonoseki at the western end of Honshū and on to Fukuoka/Hakata on the northern coast of Kyūshū. Another runs via Sendai to Morioka, almost at the north-eastern end of Honshū. The third line runs north from Tokyo to Niigata on the north coast of central Honshū.

Tokyo-Osaka-Hakata The Tōkaidō line runs from Tokyo to Osaka and continues to Fukuoka/Hakata as the San-yō line. Two types of trains run on this route – the Hikari (Light) and the Kodama (Echo). The difference is purely in the number of stops – while the Hikari stops only at Nagoya and Kyoto on the Tokyo-Osaka run, the Kodama stops at all the shinkansen stations. From Tokyo to Kyoto, the Hikari service takes two hours 40 minutes, the Kodama four hours. All the way to Hakata from Tokyo takes six hours.

Most westbound Hikari services continue beyond Osaka but stops vary from one departure to the next, so check your schedule carefully. There's a similar pattern eastbound from Hakata: some Hikari services terminate in Osaka, others continue on to Tokyo. Kodama services usually operate shorter segments along the Tokyo-Osaka-Hakata route. For example, Tokyo-Osaka, Osaka-Hakata, Osaka-Hiroshima, Hiroshima-Hakata, or the reverse.

Departures from Tokyo or Osaka are generally every 10 to 15 minutes from around 6 am to 11 pm, and all arrivals are before midnight. Services use the Tokyo central station. On a clear day, the Tokyo-Kyoto shinkansen run provides fine views of Mt Fuji – the shinkansen train passing by with Mt Fuji in the background being a favourite travel brochure picture.

Tokyo-Sendai-Morioka The Tōhoku line would have continued all the way to Sapporo on Hokkaidō if costs had not aborted that plan. There are two services – the Yamabiko, which is the express and the Aoba which is the local train. The difference is once again in the number of stops. Depending on the stops, Yamabiko trains take as little as 1¾ hours to Sendai or 2½ to three hours 20

minutes to Morioka. Except for a few late evening services which terminate at Fukishima, the Aoba services all terminate in Sendai and take about 2½ hours.

There are more than 50 departures from Tokyo's Ueno station every day, roughly half going all the way to Morioka and the rest terminating at Sendai or Fukishima. The scenery on this route is not as impressive as on the Tokyo-Osaka-Hakata route.

Tokyo-Niigata The Jōetsu line is frequently held up as a prime example of Japanese political corruption. Niigata is not really of sufficient importance to require a shinkansen railway line so passenger usage has always been relatively low. To make matters worse, the route had to tunnel straight through the mountainous spine of Honshū, which made it a very expensive project. So why did it get built? Because Niigata was the home town of Prime Minister Kakuei Tanaka, whose political activities also included taking a couple of million US dollars in bribe money from Lockheed Aircraft !

There are about 40 departures a day from Tokyo's Ueno station, more than 30 going all the way to Niigata. The express services are known as Asahi (Sunrise), the slower ones as Toki (Crane). The Tokyo-Niigata trip takes from one hour 50 minutes to two hours 20 minutes.

Travellers on the Trans-Siberian Railway through the USSR will arrive at Niigata if flying to Japan from Khabarovsk in the USSR.

Other Trains

While the shinkansen routes run most of the length of Honshū, a network of JR lines, supplemented by a scattering of shorter private lines, cover much of the rest of Japan. Although these services are efficient, they are nowhere near as fast as the shinkansen, and typically take about twice as long. (See the following section on Service Levels for more information about non-shinkansen trains.)

Even slower than the regular trains, but enormously popular nevertheless, are JR's steam locomotive (SL) services. After retiring its last steam trains in 1975, JR has now revived several services as special holiday attractions. On the Yamaguchi line from Ogōri to Tsuwano in Western Honshū, there's a steam train service operating throughout the summer and autumn months. Other SL services operate on the Hōhi line from Kumamoto to Mt Aso in Kyūshū and on the private Oigawa line from Kanaya, near Shizuoka, about 200 km south-west of Tokyo, to Senzu. SL services are very popular, so make inquiries and reservations well ahead of time.

Tickets & Fares

Service Levels All JR trains, including the shinkansen, have regular and 1st class (Green Car) carriages. The seating is slightly more spacious in 1st class, but most people will find the regular carriages quite OK.

The slowest trains stopping at all stations are called *futsū*. A step up from this is the 'ordinary express' or *kyūkō* which stops at only a limited number of stations. A variation on the kyūkō trains is the *kaisoku* or 'rapid' services. Finally, the fastest regular (non-shinkansen) trains are the *tokkyū* or 'limited express' services.

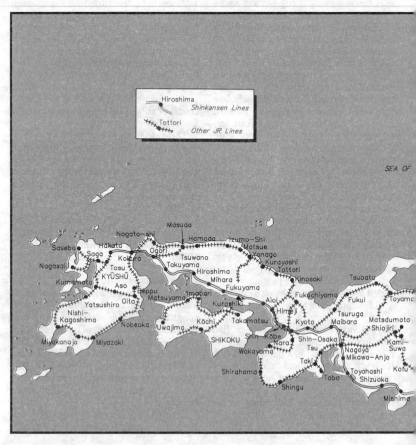

The longer the route, the more likely you are to find faster train services. Local futsū trains are mainly limited to routes of less than 100 km. In the back blocks of Japan these local trains are called *donko* and may well operate with older equipment than the main-line trains.

Tickets & Reservations Tickets can be bought at any JR station to any other JR station. Tickets for local services are usually dispensed from a vending machine but for longer distances you must go to a ticket window. For reservations, complicated tickets, Japan Rail Pass validations and the like, you will need a JR Travel Service Centre. These are found at Narita Airport and at the main JR stations in Hakata, Hiroshima, Kyoto, Kumamoto, Nagoya, Niigata, Nishi-Kagoshima, Osaka, Sapporo, Sendai, Shimonoseki, Tokyo and Yokohama. Large stations that don't have a Travel Service Centre will have a Green Window ticket counter – (Midori-no-Madoguchi or Guriin Uindō). Any major station should have these counters with their green band across the glass.

Major travel agencies in Japan also sell

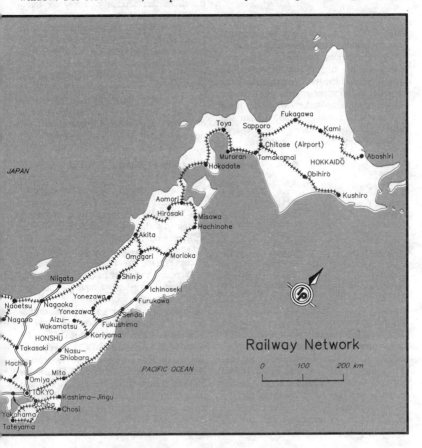

Railway Network

0   100   200 km

reserved-seat tickets and you can buy shinkansen tickets through JAL offices overseas if you will be flying JAL to Japan.

On futsū services, there are no reserved seats. On the faster kyūkō, tokkyū and shinkansen services you can choose to travel reserved or unreserved. However, if you travel unreserved, there's always the risk of not getting a seat and having to stand, possibly for the entire trip. This is a particular danger at weekends, peak travel seasons and on holidays. Reserved-seat tickets can be bought any time from a month in advance to the day of departure.

Fares Basic fares can easily be calculated from a straightforward distance/fare table in the JNTO *Railway Timetable*. Rural lines have a slightly higher fare structure than trunk lines. Shinkansen fares are simply the basic fare plus a super-express distance surcharge. Shinkansen tickets show the three figures – total, basic fare and shinkansen surcharge. (See the following Surcharge section.) Typical basic fares include:

Tokyo or Ueno to	Distance km	Futsū	Shinkansen
Nagoya	366	Y5970	Y10,380
Kyoto	514	Y7830	Y12,970
Osaka	553	Y8340	Y13,480
Okayama	733	Y9990	Y16,050
Hiroshima	895	Y11,120	Y17,700
Shimonoseki	1089	Y12,570	Y20,690
Hakata	1177	Y13,180	Y21,300
Fukushima	273	Y4530	Y8330
Sendai	352	Y5670	Y10,190
Morioka	535	Y8030	Y15,370
Niigata	334	Y5360	Y9880

Surcharges Various surcharges are applied to the base level fares, starting with a Y500 fee for a reserved seat. The shinkansen fares include this fee, so deduct Y500 for the cost of travelling by shinkansen in an unreserved carriage. Some surcharges vary with the season – see the Travel Seasons section. Above the basic futsū fare, the surcharge for kyūkō (ordinary express) and tokkyū (limited express) services are:

Up to	Kyūkō Surcharge	Tokkyū Surcharge
50 km	Y520	Y720
100 km	Y720	Y1130
150 km	Y930	Y1750
200 km	Y1030	Y2060
300 km	Y1240	Y2270
400 km	Y1240	Y2470
600 km	Y1240	Y2780
600 km +	Y1240	Y3090

The express surcharges (but not the shinkansen super-express surcharge) can be paid to the train conductor. There's an additional surcharge for Green Car (1st class) travel. Further surcharges apply for overnight sleepers and these vary with the berth type from Y5150 for a regular three-tier bunk, Y6180 to Y10,300 for various types of two-tier bunks, up to Y13,100 to Y16,850 for a standard or 'royal' compartment. Note that there are no sleepers on the shinkansen services as none of these run overnight. Japan Rail Pass users must still pay the sleeper surcharge. Sleeper services mainly operate on trains from Tokyo or Osaka to destinations in Western Honshū and Kyūshū.

Discounts & Special Fares If you buy a return ticket for a trip which is more than 600 km each way, you qualify for a 20% discount on the return leg. You can also get coupons for discounted accommodation and tours combined with your rail travel. There's even a JR prepaid card which you can use for ticket vending machines to gain a 6% or 7% discount on the larger denomination cards.

There are a number of excursion tickets, known as *shūyū-ken* or *furii* (sounds like 'free') *kippu*. A *waido shūyū-ken* or 'wide excursion ticket' takes you to your destination and back and gives you unlimited JR local travel in the destination area. There are waido shūyū-ken available to travel from Tokyo to Hokkaidō and then around Hokkaidō for up to 20 days. A Kyūshū or Shikoku waido shūyū-ken gets you to and from either island and gives you 20 days of travel around them. You can even go to Kyūshū one way by rail and one way by ferry.

Variations include a *mini shūyū-ken* (a shorter time span, smaller area waido shūyū-ken), a *rutō shūyū-ken* (a multi-stop ticket along a certain route) and an *ippan shūyū-ken* (a sort of do-it-yourself return ticket with certain stops). Or try a five day *seisban 18 kippu*. These tickets can quickly get very complicated but TIC offices have information sheets in English.

Validity & Stopovers Your ticket is valid for two days for a 100 to 200 km trip, with an extra day for each extra 200 km. During that time, you can make as many stopovers as you want so long as the ticket distance is more than 100 km. You cannot stop in Fukuoka, Hiroshima, Kitakyūshū, Kōbe, Kyoto, Nagoya, Osaka, Tokyo, Sapporo, Sendai or Yokohama if your ticket also starts or finishes in one of those cities. In other words, if you bought an Osaka-Kitakyūshū ticket you could not stop at Hiroshima but you could stop at other smaller stations along the way. Additional surcharges are on a per-trip basis, so that every time you break your journey, you must pay the relevant surcharge for the next sector. Therefore, if you're planning a multi-stop trip, you're better off getting a simple futsū ticket and paying express surcharges to the conductor as you go along.

Japan Rail Pass One of Japan's few travel bargains is the unlimited travel Japan Rail Pass. The pass lets you use any JR services for seven days for Y27,800, 14 days for Y44,200 or 21 days for Y56,600. Green Car (1st class) passes are Y37,000, Y60,000 and Y78,000 respectively. Children aged six to 11 get a 50% discount. The only additional surcharge levied on the Japan Rail Pass is for overnight sleepers. Since a reserved seat Tokyo-Kyoto shinkansen ticket costs Y12,970, you only have to travel Tokyo-Kyoto-Tokyo to make a seven day pass come close to paying off.

The pass can only be bought overseas and cannot be used by foreign residents in Japan. The clock starts to tick on the pass as soon as you validate it, which can be done at

certain major railway stations or even at the JR counter at Narita Airport if you're intending to jump on a JR train immediately. Don't validate it if you're just going into Tokyo and intend to hang around the city for a few days. The pass is valid *only* on JR services, you will still have to pay for private railway services.

Schedules & Information The most complete timetables can be found in the jikokuhyō (book of timetables) but JNTO produce a handy English-language *Railway Timetable* booklet which explains a great deal about the railway services in Japan and gives timetables for the shinkansen services, JR limited expresses and major private lines. If your visit to Japan is a short one and you will not be straying far from the major tourist destinations, this booklet may well be all you need.

The TIC offices at Narita Airport, Tokyo and Kyoto can also supply information on specific schedules. Major JR stations all have JR train information centres, however, you can only be certain of finding someone who speaks English at the really big foreign tourist points, like Tokyo station.

If you need to know anything about JR – time schedules, fares, fastest routings, lost baggage, discounts on rail travel, hotels and car rental – call the JR East-Infoline in Tokyo on 3423-0111. The service is available in English and operates between 10 am to 6 pm, Monday to Friday, but not on holidays.

Travel Seasons Some of the fare surcharges are different during the off-peak and peak seasons as opposed to the rest of the year. Off-peak dates are between 16 January and 28 February, all of June and September, and from 1 November to 20 December, excepting Fridays, Saturdays, Sundays, national holidays and the day before national holidays. Peak season dates are 28 April to 6 May (Golden Week), 21 July to 31 August, 25 December to 10 January and 21 March to 5 April. During these peak seasons, travelling is very difficult and trains are heavily booked. The rest of the year is 'normal season'! On shinkansen services, for example, you get a Y200 discount during the off-peak season or pay a Y200 surcharge during the peak season.

General Information

Meals The Japanese railway system is not renowned for its high-class cuisine, though you may find that the shinkansen dining cars turn out pretty good food. Anyway, you certainly won't starve, as apart from the dining cars, there are snacks, drinks, ice creams and meals sold from the aisles. A good bet is to come prepared with a *bentō* (boxed lunch). At almost every station there will be a shop selling bentō, typically for Y1000 or less. Some towns and stations have a particular bentō speciality.

Baggage Japanese trains are not designed for large quantities of baggage. There's no way you can load a dozen bags on to a shinkansen in the 120 seconds it stands stationary. There's unlikely to be anybody there to help you either, since station porters are rare creatures and inside the train there's little room to store bags. Travel light or see the Baggage Forwarding section earlier in this chapter.

Railway Stations Stations in Japan are usually very well equipped. The main station is often literally the 'town centre' and in many cases will be part of a large shopping centre with a wide variety of restaurants, bars, fast-food outlets and other facilities.

Only major stations have left-luggage facilities but there are almost always coin-operated storage lockers which cost Y100 to Y500 per day, depending on their size. The lockers work until midnight (not for 24 hours) so, after that time, you have to insert more money before your key will work. If your bag is simply too large to fit in the locker look suitably dumbfounded and ask *'Tenimotsu azukai doko desuka?'* (Where is the left-luggage office?) If you are directed

back to the lockers, just point at your over-sized luggage, shake your head and say *'Kore wa ōki sugi masu!'* (It's too big for the locker!).

BUS

In addition to its local city bus services, Japan also has a comprehensive network of long-distance buses. These 'highway buses' are nowhere near as fast as the shinkansen and heavy traffic can delay them even further, but the fares are comparable with those of the local train (futsū) without any reservation or express surcharges. The trip between Tokyo and Sendai, for example, takes about two hours by shinkansen, four hours by limited express and nearly eight hours by bus. Tokyo-Kyoto is less than three hours by shinkansen and more than eight hours by bus.

Bus services have been growing in recent years, partly because of the gradual extension of the expressway network, partly because of the closing of uneconomical JR lines and partly because of escalating rail fares. Of course, there are also many places in Japan where railways do not run and bus travel is the only public transport option.

The main intercity bus services run on the expressways and usually stop at expressway bus stops where local transport is available to adjacent centres. The main expressway bus route runs between Tokyo, Nagoya, Kyoto and Osaka and stops are made at each city's main railway station. There are also overnight services and the comfortable reclining seats are better for a night's sleep than sitting up in an overnight train. Bookings can be made through JTB offices or at the Green Window in large JR stations. The Japan Rail Pass is valid on highway buses although, of course, the shinkansen would be far preferable! Note, however, that the storage racks on most buses are generally too small for backpacks. Other popular bus services include routes from Tokyo to Sendai, Yamagata and Hirosaki in Northern Honshū and to Niigata and areas around Mt Fuji in Central Honshū. There are extensive networks from Osaka and Hiroshima into areas of Western Honshū and around the smaller islands of Hokkaidō, Kyūshū and Shikoku.

CAR

One of the common myths about travel in Japan is that it's virtually impossible for a gaijin to travel by car: the roads are narrow and congested making travel incredibly slow; getting lost forever is a constant fear since we cannot read the signs; the driving is suicidal; fuel is prohibitively expensive; parking is impossible and we're altogether better off sticking to the trains.

None of these myths is necessarily true. Of course, driving in Tokyo *is* a near impossibility but not many visitors rent cars to get around New York or London either. The roads are actually fairly well signposted in English so, on the major roads, getting lost is unlikely. The minor roads are more likely to test your navigational ability but as Japan is compact, you can never be lost for long. The driving is a long way from suicidal — polite and cautious is probably a better description. Fuel is expensive but no more so than most of Europe, in fact it's cheaper than many countries in Europe. As for parking, it is rarely free, but neither is it impossibly expensive.

All in all, driving in Japan is quite feasible, even for the mildly adventurous. In some areas of the country it can prove much more convenient than other forms of travel and, between a group of people (two adults and a couple of children for example), it can also prove quite economical. You will certainly see more of the country than all but the most energetic public transport users.

Vehicles

Car Rental There are a great many car rental companies in Japan and although you'll find many of them represented at Narita Airport, renting a car at Narita to drive into Tokyo is absolutely not a good idea. Heading off in the opposite direction towards Hokkaidō makes a lot more sense. Car rental offices cluster round railway stations and the best way to use rent-a-cars in Japan is to take a

train for the long-distance part of your trip, then rent a car when you get to the area you want to explore. For example the northern (San-in) coast of Western Honshū is a good place to drive — but don't drive there from Tokyo, take the train to Kyoto and rent a car there.

Japanese car rental companies are set up for this type of operation and offer lots of short-term rates — such as for people who just want a car for half a day. However, they're not much good at one-way rentals; you're always going to get hit for a repositioning charge and if the car has to be brought back from another island, the cost can be very high indeed. Typical one-way charges within the island of Honshū are Y6000 for 100 km and Y2400 for each additional 50 km. It makes a lot of sense to make your trip a loop one and return the car to the original renting office.

Some of the main Japanese car rental companies and their Tokyo phone numbers are:

Budget	tel 03-779-0543
Japaren	tel 03-352-7635
Nippon	tel 03-469-0919
Nissan	tel 03-587-4123
Toyota	tel 03-264-0100

Rental costs are generally a flat rate including unlimited km. Typical rental rates for a small car (a Toyota Starlet or Mazda 121 — one step up from the Japanese microcars) is Y7000 to Y8000 for the first day and Y4500 to Y6000 per day thereafter. Move up a bracket (a Mazda 323 or Toyota Corolla) and you're looking at Y9000 to Y12,000 for the first day and Y6000 to Y7000 thereafter. On top of the rental charge there's a Y800 per day insurance cost. Of course, you can also rent luxury cars, sports cars, even imported cars, but why give yourself headaches you don't need? Something easy to park is probably the best thing to have in Japan.

Communication can be a major problem when renting a car, although waving your driving licence and credit card and pointing at a picture of the type of car you want to rent usually makes it pretty clear what you want. Some of the offices will have a rent-a-car phrasebook with questions you might need to ask in English and Japanese – 'The cassette deck has jammed and my favourite Dylan tape is stuck in it'. Nippon Rent-a-Car even has an 'English-speaking desk' where you can ring for assistance in English (tel 03-3468-7126).

Check over your car carefully – perhaps it's an expectation that cars will only be used locally, but rental cars in Japan don't seem to be checked as thoroughly as those in the West. Check all the tyres are in good order and that the jack and tool kit are all in place.

I once rented a car with a radio that didn't work until I'd succeeded in unjamming the cassette mechanism, and when I had a puncture, I discovered the spare was totally unusable since some previous renter had hit a kerb hard enough to make it pretzel shaped.
Tony Wheeler

Apart from maps and a phrasebook, other essentials are a compass (see the Maps & Navigation section) and your favourite cassette tapes. Non-Japanese speakers will find very little to listen to on Japanese radio and the cassettes will help pass time in traffic jams. A Japanese-language tape is a good idea if you're keen to learn some Japanese as you drive.

Your rented car will, incidentally, almost certainly be white. Like refrigerators and washing machines, cars in Japan seem to be looked upon as white goods – 80% or 90% of the cars on the road are white. A few hot shots have red sports cars, a few members of the avant-garde drive black or grey cars, but apart from that it's white-white-white.

Buying a Car Since few foreign tourists drive themselves around Japan, the manufacturers have never promoted the overseas delivery options which are so popular with expensive European cars. Presumably, it could be done if you really wanted to. Long-term visitors or residents are more likely to be looking for a second-hand vehicle to use while in Japan and sell on departure. However, think carefully before making this decision. There are so many drawbacks to running a car in Japan's crowded cities that the alternative of renting a car on the odd

Kyoto to Kyoto, 4386 km

While researching this edition I rented a Mazda 323 (a Familia in Japan) in Kyoto. It was white (of course) and already carried dents on every corner (which I figured was ideal for a gaijin). In the next 27 days I added 4386 km to the 40,000 km it had already covered, an average of no less than 162 km a day! After various long-term rental discounts and the addition of the 3% tax and the insurance fee, the total cost worked out to about Y6000 a day, approximately US$40 a day. Fuel averaged about Y125 a litre and I used about Y50,000 (US$330) worth. So, all up, the cost came out to a bit over US$50 a day. I probably spent about another US$100 on tolls for various expressways, toll roads and skyline drives, bridge fees and a couple of ferry crossings.

Parking did not present as much of a problem as I'd expected. A lot of the places I stayed had a parking space, a few charged Y500 to Y1000 for a day's parking but many were free. Apart from that, it was a case of Y200 here, Y300 there for parking. Only a few times did I find parking meters and these typically cost Y100 for a half hour or hour. Railway stations usually offered the best parking deals and the first hour was often free. I did collect one parking ticket but couldn't figure out what to do with it, so I still have it.

The car ran faultlessly, apart from the one puncture when I discovered the spare was useless. At the next major town, the Nippon Rent-a-Car agency put a new spare in, washed the car, vacuumed out the interior, cleaned out the empty Pocari Sweat cans from under the seat and even chucked out all the junk in the glovebox which had been there when I picked it up.

Tony Wheeler ∎

occasion when you really need one may be preferable.

Buying cars in Japan is subject to the same pitfalls as in most other places in the world – a Tokyo used car salesman would sell his grandma-san just like anywhere else – but the stringent safety inspections mean that you're unlikely to buy an unsafe vehicle. Once it's three years old, every car has to go through a *shaken* (inspection) every two years which is so severe that it quickly becomes cheaper to junk your car and buy another. The shaken costs about Y100,000 and once the car reaches nine years of age it has to be inspected every year. This is the major reason you see so few old cars on the road in Japan. A car approaching an unpassable shaken drops in value very rapidly and, if you can find one, could make a good short-term purchase.

Another obstacle to buying a car in Japan is that you must have an off-street parking place before you can complete the registration formalities. Exemption from this requirement is one reason why the little microcars are so popular in Japan. To qualify as a microcar, a vehicle must have an engine of less than 660 cc, be less than 140 cm wide and less than 330 cm long.

Language is likely to be the major handicap in buying a car, so it's very useful to have a Japanese speaker to help with the negotiations. Foreign residents often sell their cars through the various English language papers.

A recent report noted that the latest status symbol in Japan is a suntanned left arm, a sure sign that the owner drives a foreign-made left-hand drive car!

Roads

When & Where to Drive If you're going to drive yourself in Japan, do it sensibly. There's absolutely no reason to drive in the big cities or to drive in the heavily built-up areas like the San-yō coast of Western Honshū. If you're simply going from town A to town B and then stopping for a while, you're much better off taking the train.

In the less urbanised areas, however, a car can be useful. The northern San-in coast of Western Honshū, for example, is a world apart from the congested southern coast and slow public transport makes a car much more feasible. Hokkaidō is another good area for a drive-yourself trip. There are many areas where a car can be useful for a short excursion into the surrounding countryside, such as the loop from Kagoshima in Kyūshū down to Chiran and Ibusuki on the Satsuma Peninsula or for a couple of days to make a circuit of (say) Okinawa Island. Car rental companies cater to this with short rental periods of a day or half day.

Expressways The expressway system will get you from one end of the country to another but it is not particularly extensive. Also, since all the expressways charge tolls, it is uniformly expensive – about Y27 a km. Tokyo to Kyoto, for example, will cost about Y9000 in tolls. This does have the benefit of keeping most people off the expressways so they are often delightfully uncrowded. The speed limit on expressways is 80 km/h but seems to be uniformly ignored. At a steady 100 km/h, you will still find as many cars overtaking you as you overtake, some of them going very fast indeed.

There are good rest stops and service centres at regular intervals. A prepaid highway card, available from tollbooths or at the service areas, saves you having to carry so much cash and gives you a 4% to 8% discount in the larger card denominations. Exits are usually fairly well signposted in romaji but make sure you know the name of your exit as it may not necessarily be the same as the city you're heading towards.

Other Roads On Japan's lesser roads, the speed limit is usually 50 km/h, and you can often drive for hours without ever getting up to that speed! The roads are narrow, traffic is usually heavy, opportunities to overtake are limited and no-overtaking restrictions often apply in the few areas where you could overtake safely. Sometimes you never seem to get out of built-up areas and the heavy traffic and frequent traffic lights can make covering

300 km in a long day's drive quite a feat. It's worth contemplating that just after WW II, only 1.5% of the roads in Japan were sealed.

Generally, however, the traffic does keep moving, slow though that movement may be. The further you travel from the main highways, the more interesting the country-side becomes. Occasionally you'll come to stretches which are a wonderful surprise. Along a beautiful winding mountain road without a car in sight, it's easy to appreciate why the Japanese have come to make such nice sports cars.

On the Road

Licence You'll need an International Driving Permit backed up by your own national licence. The international permit is issued by your national automobile association and costs around US$5. Make sure it's endorsed for cars and motorcycles if you're licensed for both.

Foreign licences and International Driving Permits are only valid in Japan for six months. If you are staying longer you will have to get a Japanese licence from the licence office (shikenjo). You need your own licence, passport photos, Alien Registration Card or Certificate of Residence, the fee and there's also a simple eyesight test to pass.

Even when driving, the Japanese manage to convey respect towards others, sometimes with near disastrous results. I was being driven by a Japanese lady out in the rural parts of Wakayama Prefecture, when we met another car at a junction. My friend bowed regally, and waited. The other driver bowed equally regally, and waited. Suddenly, both drivers shot forwards at the same instant, then lurched to a violent halt.

This sequence continued: more bows, more lurching forwards until we were within a few feet of each other. Just as I was bracing myself for impact, my friend bowed even deeper and longer over the steering wheel. When she raised her head again, the other car had driven off. Highway code?

Robert Strauss

Fuel There's no shortage of petrol (gas) stations, the cost of petrol is about Y125 per litre (about US$3.50 per US gallon) and the driveway service will bring a tear to the eye of any driver who resents the Western trend to self-service. In Japan, not only does your windscreen get washed but you may even find your floor mats being laundered and the whole staff coming out, at the trot, to usher you back into the traffic and bow respectfully as you depart.

Maps & Navigation Get a copy of the *Japan Road Atlas* (Shobunsha, Tokyo, 1990, Y2890). It's all in romaji (Roman script) with sufficient names in kanji (Japanese script) to make navigation possible even off the major roads. If you're really intent on making your way through the back blocks, a Japanese map will prove useful even if your knowledge of kanji is nil. When you really get lost, a signposted junction will offer some clues if you've got a good map to compare the symbols.

These days, there is a great deal of signposting in romaji so getting around is not a great feat. Road route numbers also help; for example, if you know you want to follow Route 9 until you get to Route 36 the frequent roadside numbers make navigation child's play. If you are attempting tricky navigation, use your maps imaginatively – watch out for the railway line, the rivers, the landmarks. They're all useful ways of locating yourself when you can't read the signs. Bring a compass, you'll often find it useful and, if you really get lost, Japan's compact size will always come to the rescue – 'If I head generally north I'm going to hit the main road or the coast in 20 km'.

If you're a member of an automobile association in your home country you're eligible for reciprocal rights at the Japan Automobile Federation (JAF). Its office is directly opposite the entrance to the Tokyo Tower at 3-5-8 Shiba-kōen, Minato-ku, Tokyo 105. The JAF has a variety of publications, including a useful *Rules of the Road* book and will make up strip maps for its members.

Road Rules & the Police
Driving in Japan is on the left – like most other countries in the region stretching from India, through South-East Asia and down

through Australia and the Pacific. One of the minor curiosities about this is that when the Japanese buy imported cars they like them to be really different – ie to have the steering wheel on the left side. This might have some sort of logic to it with German or US cars (they drive on the right) but none whatsoever with British cars (like the Japanese, the British drive on the left). Nevertheless, most Jaguars, Rolls-Royces and Minis sold in Japan will be left-hand drive.

Apart from being on the wrong side of the road from the European or North American perspective, there are no real problems with driving in Japan. There are no unusual rules or interpretations of them and most signposts follow international conventions. The Japan Automobile Federation (JAF) has an English-language *Rules of the Road* book for Y1860 (slightly discounted if you're a member of an overseas association). See the Maps & Navigation section for more about the JAF.

You see very little evidence of the police on Japanese roads, they're simply not there most of the time. I did see a taxi driver grabbed for running a red light in Kyoto once, but I never saw a speed trap and on most roads, there's very little opportunity to break the speed limit anyway. On the expressways, lots of cars exceed the speed limit and on one occasion I saw a police car cruising sedately along the inside lane at more-or-less the limit, while cars whizzed by at something above it. When speed traps *are* used, they will probably be on the one nice open stretch of road where the speed limit is way below the speed most people will be inclined to travel.

Tony Wheeler

Speed traps, however, are notorious in Hokkaidō and their presence is advertised in a strange manner: the incredibly rusty hulk of what was once a police car is simply mounted on a pedestal beside the road. Passing drivers nonchalantly activate their hi-tech radar detector defence systems and accelerate. Hokkaidō is definitely one of those places in Japan where you not only need to make use of a car, but you can also really enjoy yourself.

Robert Strauss

A blind eye may be turned to moderate speeding but for drinking and driving you get

locked up and the key is thrown away. Don't do it.

Parking

Along with congestion and navigational difficulties, the impossibility of finding a parking space is the other major myth about driving in Japan. While there are few places you can park for free and roadside parking is virtually nonexistent, finding a place to park is usually not too difficult and the cost is rarely excessive.

Parking meters are rare and when they do exist are often a distinct technological step beyond what we have in the West. One type has an electronic 'eye' to detect if your car is still sitting there when your time is up. If so, a light on top of the meter then starts to flash to alert a passing meter inspector to come and issue the ticket! Even more sinister are the meters which lock your car in place. When your time's up a barrier rises up between the front and back wheels and you cannot move the car until you've paid the fine directly into the meter! Under normal circumstances, meters usually cost Y100 for each half hour.

Off-street parking is usually in car parks – often very small ones with an attendant in a booth who records your licence plate number on arrival and charges you when you leave. Sometimes you have to leave the keys with the attendant. The charge might be Y200 or Y300 an hour but if you can read the small print, you may get a pleasant surprise or a nasty shock. Sometimes the first half hour or hour is free, particularly at railway station car parks. At some car parks the rate increases dramatically after, say, three hours to discourage long-term car parking. Unfortunately, it takes a lot of Japanese small print to discover these regulations. Even in big city multistorey car parks, the charges are rarely as high as in equivalent car parks in, say, Australia or the USA.

Railway station car parks are usually a good bet, as they are conveniently central and reasonably priced. Watch for interesting car parking technology, particularly the rotating vertical conveyer belts where your car disappears into a sort of filing cabinet.

Car parking spaces seem to be zealously guarded and many daytime car parks are chained up at night to prevent anyone getting a free space for the evening.

In one city I saw a series of meters which operated from 7 am to 7 pm. So they were free after 7 pm, right? No way, for no visible reason, after 7 pm it was 'no parking'!

Tony Wheeler

MOTORCYCLE

Japan is the home of the modern motorcycle and you certainly see a lot on the road. Once upon a time they were all small displacement machines but now there are plenty of larger motorcycles as well. During the holidays you will see many groups of touring motor-cyclists and, as usual in Japan, they will all be superbly equipped with shiny new motor-cycles, efficient carriers and panniers, expensive riding leathers and, when the inevitable rain comes down, excellent rain-proof gear.

Buying or Renting a Motorcycle

If you enjoy motorcycles and you're staying long enough to make buying and selling a motorcycle worthwhile, then this can be a great way of getting around the country. A motorcycle provides the advantages of your own transport without the automotive draw-back of finding a place to park. Nor do you suffer so badly from the congested traffic.

Although Japan is famed for its large-capacity road burners, these bikes are less popular in Japan for a number of reasons including outright restrictions on the sale of machines over 750 cc. The motorcycle

licence-testing procedure also varies with the size of machine and before you can get a licence for a 750 cc motorcycle, you must prove you can lift one up after it has fallen over! Not surprisingly, this cuts down on the number of potential big motorcycle riders.

The 400 cc machines are the most popular large motorcycles in Japan but, for general touring, a 250 cc machine is probably the best bet. Apart from being quite large enough for a compact country like Japan, machines up to 250 cc are also exempt from the expen-sive shaken (inspections). Also, motorcycles over 250 cc are not allowed on main city streets from 11 pm to 6 am! This curious law is to stop motorcycle gangs *(bososuku)* cruis-ing late at night but it's another reason sub-250 cc bikes are so popular. Smaller machines are banned from expressways and are generally less suitable for long-distance touring but people have ridden from one end of Japan to another on little 50 cc 'step-thrus'. An advantage of these is that you can ride them with just a driving licence, and don't need to get a motorcycle licence.

Buying a new machine from Japan's mul-titude of motorcycle dealers is no problem, though you will find a better choice of large capacity machines in the big cities. Used motorcycles are often not much cheaper than new ones and, unless you buy from another gaijin, you will face the usual language prob-lems in finding and buying one. Because of the small demand for large motorcycles, their prices tend to drop more steeply than small ones, but on the other hand, the popu-larity of the 250 cc class means these machines hold their value better. As with everything else in Japan, you rarely see a motorcycle more than a couple of years old. There are numerous used motorcycle dealers around Ueno station in Tokyo, on the streets parallel to Showa-dōri Ave and north of the Ueno subway station. Some of these larger dealers actually employ gaijin salespeople who speak Japanese and English. Corin Motors (tel 03-3841-4112), 7-8-15 Ueno, is a collection of nearly 20 motorcycle shops along Corin-cho Rd, a block from the Dis-neyland bus exit. They're open from 9 am to

7 pm, Monday to Saturday. As with used cars the English-language papers and magazines are a good place to look for a foreigner's motorcycle for sale.

Renting a motorcycle for long-distance touring is not as easy as renting a car although small scooters are available in many places for local sightseeing.

On the Road

As with car driving, your overseas licence and International Driving Permit are all you need to ride a motorcycle in Japan. Crash helmets are compulsory and you should also ensure your riding gear is adequate to cope with the weather, particularly rain. For much of the year the climate is ideal for motorcycle touring but when it rains it really rains.

Touring equipment – bags, panniers, carrier racks, straps and the like – are all readily available from dealers. Remember to pack clothing in plastic bags to ensure it stays dry, even if you don't. An adequate supply of tools and a puncture repair outfit can prove invaluable.

Riding in Japan is no more dangerous than anywhere else in the world, which is to say it is not very safe and great care should be taken at all times. Japan has the full range of worldwide motorcycle hazards from single-minded taxi drivers to unexpected changes in road surface, heedless car-door openers to runaway dogs.

BICYCLE

If you're keen about long-distance bicycle touring, exploring Japan by bicycle is perfectly feasible. Although the slow average speed of traffic on Japanese roads is no problem for a bike rider, pedalling along in a constant stream of heavy traffic is no fun at all. Reportedly, the Japan Cycling Association warns cyclists not to ride more than 100 km per day because of the danger from car exhaust fumes. Japanese cyclists seem to have a higher tolerance of heavy traffic and doggedly follow routes down recommended major highways. Tunnels can be an unnerving experience at first.

The secret of enjoyable touring is to get off the busy main highways and onto the minor roads. This requires careful route planning, good maps and either some ability with kanji or the patience to decipher country road signs, where romaji is much less likely to be used. Favourite touring areas for foreign cyclists include Kyūshū, Shikoku, the Japan Alps (if you like gradients!), the Noto-hantō Peninsula and definitely Hokkaidō. Valiant Japanese cyclists have been known to ride as far up Mt Fuji as the road permitted and then shouldered their

---

Foreign & Unusual Motorcycles

Just as expensive European cars have carved out a lucrative market in Japan, so have foreign motorcycles. The occasional Italian Ducati or Moto-Guzzi, German BMW or British Triumph can be seen amongst the throngs of Kawahondazukis, but the real foreign standout is the Harley-Davidson. Japanese motorcyclists have a real passion for 'hogs' and many HD riders even have their bikes kitted out like the California Highway Patrol and ride them in what looks like a US police uniform!

Old motorcycles also have a following, though you rarely see them on the road. There are Japanese magazines for vintage motorcycle enthusiasts and from the number of for-sale advertisements for old motorcycles, there must be many carefully restored machines hidden away – older Japanese ones as well as European and US collectors' items. Corin Motors in Ueno (see Buying or Renting a Motorcycle) have a small museum of old motorcycles and the Honda showroom, beside the Aoyama Itchōme subway station, displays some old Honda racing motorcycles including Mike Hailwood's beautiful six cylinder Honda of the mid-60s. ■

steeds so that they could conquer the peak together.

There's no point in fighting your way out of big cities by bicycle. Put your bike on the train or bus and get out to the country before you start pedalling. To take a bicycle on a train you may be required to use a bicycle carrying bag: they're available from good bicycle shops.

The Maps & Navigation section for car travel also applies to bicycles but there is also a series of Bridgestone *saikuringu mapu* (cycling maps). They identify many places in romaji as well as kanji but, as yet, only cover part of the country in Central Honshū. The cycling maps show where bicycles can be rented, identify special bicycle tracks and accommodation which is popular with cyclists and even show steep road gradients.

Information

The Japan Bicycle Promotion Institute (Nihon Jitensha Kaikon Biru) (tel 03-3583-5444) is also known as the Bicycle Cultural Centre and is across from the US Embassy at 1-9-3 Akasaka, Minato-ku, Tokyo. The institute has a museum and is a useful source of information about the special inns for cyclists (cycling terminals or saikuringu terminaru), maps, routes and types of bicycles suitable for foreign dimensions. Useful phrases for cyclists include *'Kana-zawa...yuki wa kono michi deska?'* (Is this the route to...Kanazawa?) and *'Chizu o kaite kudasai'* (Draw a map, please).

Getting a Bicycle

If you already have some experience of bicycle touring you will, no doubt, have your own bicycle and should bring this with you. Most airlines these days will accommodate bikes, sometimes as part of your baggage allowance, sometimes free. Often, all you have to do is remove the pedals before handing it over.

If you want to buy a bicycle in Japan, it is possible but nowhere near as simple as you might think. A glance at the bicycle park besides any big railway station – or simply at the bicycle-clogged streets and sidewalks

around the station – will reveal that lots of Japanese ride bikes. But very few of them are anything you would want to ride more than a few km. Despite all the high-tech Japanese bicycle equipment exported to the West, 10-speed touring bikes and modern mountain bikes are conspicuous by their absence in Japan. The vast majority of bicycles you see around the cities are utilitarian single-speed machines; cleaner and more modern versions of the heavy single-speed clunkers you find all over China or India.

This doesn't mean you can't find bicycles suitable for touring, it's just that you have to search them out. Even when you find an outlet handling multi-geared bikes, you should buy with care since they're likely to be built for the average-size Japanese rather than the average-size gaijin. If you're short to average it may not be a problem, but a tall gaijin is liable to have real trouble finding a big enough machine. Specialist dealers are one place to look, bicycle shops near US military bases are another but easiest of all is to bring your own bicycle with you.

A number of adventure travel companies operate bicycle tours in Japan. It is not easy to rent a touring bike for a long trip but, in a great many towns, you can rent bicycles to explore the town. Look for bicycle-rental outlets near the railway station; typical charges are around Y200 per hour or Y800 for a day. In many towns, a bicycle is absolutely the ideal way to get around. In the mountain town of Tsuwano in Western Honshū, for example, it seems like there are more bicycles available for rent than there can ever be visitors to rent them. Also in Western Honshū, between Okayama and Kurashiki, there's an excellent half day cross country bicycle path and a one-way rental system.

Many youth hostels have bicycles to rent – there's a symbol identifying them in the (Japan) *Youth Hostel Handbook*. The cycling inns found in various locations around the country (see the Accommodation section in the Facts for the Visitor chapter) also rent bicycles.

We don't recommend the following

reader's method of obtaining a bicycle but it's certainly true that Japan is the throwaway society and bicycles get thrown away like everything else:

The best way to get around Japan is to check out the abandoned bicycle racks. Any city of reasonable size has one of these, usually in the corner of the railway station car park. They are easy to recognise – the bikes are covered with dust and the tyres are usually flat. Find one you like, wheel it to a bike shop for tyre repairs and you're set for less than Y2000. We've set ourselves up with a number of bikes in this way.

Anytime someone moves house in Japan, they dump their bike, but sometimes the police get a little weird about a foreigner pushing a bike through the streets. The solution to this is to buy a lock and loop it around the seat; if they ask if it's your bike show them you can open the lock. Just be careful that you really are in the abandoned-bike section; lack of a lock is not proof that the owner is not coming back to collect it. Go for bikes where the tyres are flat and the dust and spider webs are thick.

Ed Henderson

On the Road

The following is an account of one couple's experiences during a six week bicycling tour of Japan:

Monkey Cycles (tel 03-3985-5663) at 3-13-6-102 Tokada, Toshima-ku did a lot of work on our bikes and we were amazed when the bill came to just under Y5000; we had expected to pay a lot more. Many of the bike shops all over Japan had an extensive range of bikes at prices which would be hard to beat in the West.

We wasted a lot of time in Tokyo looking for a good road map with both kanji and romaji but once on the road we discovered we could get detailed regional maps free from petrol stations. These varied in size and quality but normally covered an area of around 10,000 sq km and gave route numbers and other information including places of interest, youth hostels and camp sites. Though often only in Japanese, these maps, combined with the *Tourist Map of Japan* we'd got from the TIC, gave us all the information we needed.

The edges of busier roads had often become ridged and rutted by heavy trucks but there were usually cycle paths on these roads and on roads through towns. However, if these weren't full of pedestrians and potholes, they were covered in glass, overgrown or involved lengthy detours or footbridges, so we usually opted to take our chances with the traffic. Many of the roads featured tunnels, even in fairly flat areas. These were generally well lit but a lot of them

had very little room for cyclists and no alternative route around the tunnel. Large bridges, like those connecting islands, were usually for motor vehicles only and cyclists were often forced to take a ferry. You can generally expect to pay almost as much for your bike as for yourself on short ferry journeys.

There were quite a few toll roads, especially in scenic areas, and we were surprised to find we had to pay to ride on them. The fees ranged from Y30 to Y150, sometimes for very short stretches.

Camping wild was no problem at all. Many of the small towns and villages seemed to have an unofficial camp site near a river that locals happily directed us to. At other times we just found what looked like wasteland and pitched there. No-one ever objected to our presence, in fact more often than not, local people would come over for a chat and bring gifts of food and drink. We were invited into peoples' houses several times, particularly when the weather was bad, and were often given superb meals, lots of beer and a comfortable place to sleep.

We did check out a couple of camp sites, though many of these were closed because it was 'out of season'. The sites were generally pretty basic with simple toilets (a hole in the ground) and no washing facilities apart from a tap in the corner of the field. Most of them cost around Y500 per person. We also spent one night in a cycling terminal, which was like a cross between a youth hostel and a hotel. There are currently 50 of these around the country and the ultimate aim is to have one every 100 km or so. Terminals usually cost around Y3500 per person, including dinner and breakfast (Y2600 without meals) but, like youth hostels, are virtually deserted in the off season and we managed to get half price after haggling.

Most petrol stations had excellent toilet and washroom facilities, and were usually spotlessly clean and often quite luxurious. Some featured the latest in toilet technology – heated toilet seats, rotating seat covers, small hoses that appeared at the push of a button and squirted a jet of water straight to where it would give you the biggest shock and, to finish off, musical toilet-roll dispensers! The staff at these garages were usually only too willing to help, supplying us with fresh drinking water, giving us maps, directions and advice about routes and sometimes even photocopying pages from their road atlases!

For eating cheaply, we relied heavily on *pan no mimi* (bread crusts) from bakeries which cost nothing or up to Y50 for a big bag. These we supplemented with cheap food from supermarkets to make some very interesting and unusual sandwiches. In the colder areas we ate a lot of noodles. Most of the shops where we bought the noodles were happy to supply hot water for us to make them and many even supplied additional titbits to add to them. We found cycling and camping in Japan a great way to see the country and

meet the people. We often managed to get by on only US$5 each per day and we had a wonderful time.
Ruth & Leslie Isaacs, England

HITCHING

Japan can be an excellent country for hitch-hiking, though this may partly be because so few Japanese hitchhike and gaijin with their thumbs out are also a very rare sight. Nevertheless, there are many hitchhikers' tales of extraordinary kindness from motorists who have picked them up. There are equally numerous tales of motorists who think the hitchhiker has simply lost his or her way to the nearest railway station, and accordingly takes them there!

The rules for hitchhiking are similar to anywhere else in the world. Make it clear where you want to go – carry cardboard and a marker pen to write in kanji the name of your desired destination. Write it in romaji as well, as a car-driving gaijin may just be coming by. Look for a good place to hitch: it's no good starting from the middle of town, though unfortunately, in Japan, many towns only seem to end as they merge into the next one. Expressway entrance roads are probably your best bet. A woman should never hitch alone, even in Japan.

Truck drivers are particularly good bets for long-distance travel as they often head out on the expressways at night. If a driver is exiting before your intended destination, try and get dropped off at one of the expressway service centres. The Service Area Parking Area (SAPA) guide maps (tel 03-3403-9111 in Tokyo) are excellent for hitchers. They're available free from expressway service areas and show full details of each interchange (IC) and rest stop – important orientation points if you have a limited knowledge of Japanese.

In Japan, as anywhere else in the world, it's a hitchhiker's duty to entertain. Although the language gap can make that difficult, get out your phrasebook and try and use at least *some* Japanese. Finally, be prepared to reciprocate kindnesses. You may find your driver will insist on buying you food or drinks at a rest stop and it's nice if you can offer fruit, rice crackers or even cigarettes in return.

WALKING

There are many opportunities for hiking and mountain climbing in Japan but few visitors set out to get from place to place on foot.

Hitching in the Snow
Even in Japan, hitching ain't always plain sailing, as this traveller discovered when trying to hitch from Kamitono, near Hiroshima:

All the traffic going through the tollgates had come from the nearby ski fields to the west. We stood by the tollgate at the side of the road for five hours with our destination written in kanji. Intermittent bouts of sleet and sunshine had worn our patience thin so, in frustration, we climbed some embankments out of view of the tollgate attendant and clambered over a two metre fence lining the expressway.

It was a sorry sight – three unshaven foreigners hitching in the snow on a Japanese expressway. Sorrier still, however, when the highway patrol appeared and spotted us trying to hide our bulging packs from view. They drove past in disbelief, stopped, reversed back and stared at us. We were casually leaning against a rail. We nervously looked back at the policemen and, after what seemed like an eternity, my friend said 'konnichiwa'.

Although we knew we shouldn't have been hitching on the expressway we feigned ignorance and escaped with a warning. We were told to return to the tollgate if we wanted to hitch. I've hitched in several countries and have come to the conclusion that skiers will never stop to pick you up – skiers seem to be a different species from the rest of us.
Peter Moorhouse ■

Alan Booth did, all the way from Hokkaidō to Kyūshū and wrote of the four month journey in *The Roads to Sata*.

It would be quite feasible to base an itinerary on walks, preferably out of season to avoid the daytrippers. JNTO publishes a *Combined Mini-Travel Series* with ideas on walks in Japan including: *Walking Tour Courses in Tokyo (036)*; *Walking Tour Courses in Nara (053)*; and *Walking Tour Courses in Kyoto (052)*. *Hiking in Japan* by Paul Hunt (Kodansha, Tokyo & London, 1988) has excellent walking suggestions throughout the country.

The Oirase Valley walk, near Lake Towada-ko (Tōhoku) is very pleasant. In the Japan Alps region, Kamikōchi is one of several bases for walks; and Takayama has a pleasant extended walking trail for several hours round the temple district. In the Kiso Valley, there's a good walk between Magome and Tsumago.

In the Japan Alps and Hokkaidō, it's quite easy to break down hikes into smaller walks. On Rebuntō Island, at the northern tip of Hokkaidō, there is plenty of scope to spend several days doing different walks in spectacular scenery; the same applies to the other Hokkaidō national parks, especially Daisetsuzan. Shikoku has some fine walks, particularly up Mt Ishizuchi-san. In Kyūshū there are some excellent walks through areas of volcanic activity, such as on the Ebino-kōgen Plateau near Mt Kirishima-yama.

FERRY

Japan is an island nation and there are a great many ferry services both between islands and between ports on the same island. Ferries can be an excellent way of getting from one place to another and seeing parts of Japan you might otherwise miss. Taking a ferry between Osaka (Honshū) and Beppu (Kyūshū), for example, is a good way of getting to Kyūshū and (if you choose the right departure time) seeing some of the Inland Sea on the way.

The routes vary widely from two-hour services between adjacent islands to 1½-day

trips in what are really small ocean liners. The cheapest fares on the longer trips are in tatami-mat rooms where you simply unroll your futon on the floor and hope, if the ship is crowded, that your fellow passengers aren't too intent on knocking back the booze all night. In this basic class, fares will usually be lower than equivalent land travel but there are also more expensive private cabins. Bicycles can always be brought along and most ferries also carry cars and motorcycles.

There are long-distance routes from Hokkaidō to Honshū and many services from Osaka and Tokyo to ports all over Japan, but the densest network of ferry routes connects Kyūshū, Shikoku and the southern (San-yō) coast of Western Honshū, across the waters of the Inland Sea. Apart from services connecting A to B, there are also many cruise ships operating in these waters. Ferries also connect the mainland islands with the many smaller islands off the coast and those dotted down to Okinawa and beyond to Taiwan.

Information on ferry routes, schedules and fares can be found in the comprehensive monthly ōki-jikokuhyō and on information sheets from TIC offices. Ask for a copy of the the Japan Long Distance Ferry Association's excellent English-language brochure. Some ferry services and their lowest fares include:

Hokkaidō to Honshū

Muroran to Oarai	¥9570
Otaru to Maizuru	¥6590
Otaru to Niigata	¥5150
Otaru to Tsuruga	¥6590
Tomakomai to Nagoya	¥15,450
Tomakomai to Oarai	¥9570
Tomakomai to Sendai	¥8850

Routes from Tokyo

to Kōchi (Shikoku)	¥13,910
to Kokura (Kyūshū)	¥12,000
to Kushiro (Hokkaidō)	¥14,420
to Nachi-Katsuura (Honshū)	¥9060
to Naha (Okinawa)	¥19,670
to Tokushima (Shikoku)	¥8200
to Tomakomai (Hokkaidō)	¥11,840

Routes from Osaka

to Beppu (Kyūshū)	Y5870
to Hyuga (Kyūshū)	Y7620
to Imabari (Shikoku)	Y3810
to Kagoshima (Kyūshū)	Y10,300
to Kōchi (Shikoku)	Y4530
to Matsuyama (Shikoku)	Y4430
to Naha (Okinawa)	Y15,450
to Shin-Moji (Kyūshū)	Y4840
to Takamatsu (Shikoku)	Y2370

Other Routes from Honshū

Hiroshima to Beppu (Kyūshū)	Y3600
Kawasaki to Hyuga (Kyūshū)	Y17,720
Kōbe to Hyuga (Kyūshū)	Y7620
Kōbe to Kokura (Kyūshū)	Y4840
Kōbe to Matsuyama (Shikoku)	Y3500
Kōbe to Naha (Okinawa)	Y15,450
Kōbe to Oita (Kyūshū)	Y5050
Nagoya to Sendai (Honshū)	Y9580

Other Routes from Kyūshū

Hakata to Naha (Okinawa)	Y12,970
Kagoshima to Naha (Okinawa)	Y11,840
Kokura to Matsuyama (Shikoku)	Y3500

LOCAL TRANSPORT

All the major cities offer a wide variety of public transport. In many cities you can get day passes for unlimited travel on bus, tram or subway systems. The pass is called a 'one day open ticket' or a *furii* (free) *kippu*, though, of course, it's not free! If you're staying for an extended period in one city, commuter passes are available for regular travel.

Bus

Almost every Japanese city will have a bus service but it's usually the most difficult public transport system for gaijin to use. The destination names will almost inevitably be in kanji (the popular tourist town of Nikkō is a rare exception) and often, there are not even numbers to identify which bus you want. Buses are also subject to the usual traffic delays.

Fares are either paid to the driver on entering or as you leave the bus and usually operate on one of two systems. In Tokyo and some other cities, there's a flat fare irrespec-

tive of distance. In the other system, you take a ticket as you board which indicates the zone number at your starting point. When you get off, an electric sign at the front of the bus indicates the fare charged at that point for each starting zone number. You simply pay the driver the fare that matches your zone number. Drivers usually cannot change more than Y1000 but there is often a change machine in the bus.

In almost any town of even remote tourist interest, there will be *teiki kankō* tour buses, usually operating from the main railway station. The tour will be conducted entirely in Japanese and may well go to some locations of little interest. However, in places where the attractions are widespread or hard to reach by public transport, tours can be a good bet.

Subway & Local Train

Several cities, in particular Osaka and Tokyo, have mass transit rail systems comprising a loop line around the city centre and radial lines into the central stations. In Tokyo, these *kokuden* trains are operated by 11 private railways which connect with the Yamanote loop. Kokuden services are also often directly connected with subway services. Subway systems operate in Fukuoka, Kōbe, Kyoto, Nagoya, Osaka, Sapporo, Sendai, Tokyo and Yokohama. They are usually the fastest and most convenient ways of getting around the city.

For subways and local trains you will probably have to buy your ticket from a machine. Usually they're relatively easy to understand even if you cannot read kanji since there will be a diagram explaining the routes and from this you can find what your fare should be. However, if you can't work the fare out, an easy solution is to simply buy a ticket for the lowest fare on the machine. When you finish your trip, go to the *ryōkin seisanjo* or fare adjustment office before you reach the exit gate and they will charge you the additional fare. JR train and subway stations not only have their names posted above the platform in kanji and romaji but also the names of the preceding and following stations.

Tram

A number of cities have tram routes – particularly Nagasaki, Kumamoto and Kagoshima in Kyūshū, Kōchi and Matsuyama in Shikoku and Hakodate in Hokkaidō. These are excellent ways of getting around as they combine many of the advantages of bus travel (particularly the good views) with those of subways (it's easy to work out where you're going). Fares work on similar systems to bus travel and there are also unlimited-travel day tickets available.

Taxi

Taxis are convenient but expensive and are found in even quite small towns; the railway station is the best place to start looking. Drivers are often reluctant to stop and pick you up near a station taxi stand, so either wait at the correct spot for a taxi off the rank or walk a couple of streets away. Fares vary very little throughout the country – flagfall (posted on the nearside windows) is Y540 for the first two km, after which it's Y80 for each 395 metres (slightly further outside Tokyo). There's also a time charge if the speed drops below 10 km/h. A red light means the taxi is available, a green light means there's an additional night time surcharge, a yellow light means the cab is on a call.

Don't whistle for a taxi, a straightforward wave should bring one politely to a halt. Don't open the door when it stops, the driver does that with a remote release. He (if there are women taxi drivers in Japan they are very rare) will also shut the door when you leave.

Drivers are normally as polite as anybody else in Japan but, like the majority of Japanese, are not linguists. If you can't tell him where you want to go, it's useful to have the name written down in Japanese. At hotel front desks there will usually be business cards complete with name and location, which are used for just this purpose. Note that business names, including hotels, are often quite different in Japanese and English.

Taxi drivers have just as much trouble finding Japanese addresses as anyone else. Just because you've gone round the block five times does not necessarily mean your driver is a country boy fresh in from the sticks. Asking directions and stopping at police boxes for help is standard practice.

Tipping is not a standard practice unless you've got a lot of bags or your destination has been particularly difficult to find. A 20% surcharge is added after 11 pm at night or for taxis summoned by radio.

Like many other places in the world, taxis in Japan seem to dissolve and disappear when rained upon. Late at night, particularly in the big cities, can be a difficult time to find taxis. Public transport stops relatively early but, as the salarymen reel out of the bars taxis, become increasingly difficult to find and also become mysteriously reluctant to pick up foreigners. The reason is quite simple, the drunken carousers will be heading home to some far distant suburb while the poor gaijin will probably be heading for a hotel just a few km away. At times of severe taxi shortage, the Japanese custom is to hold up fingers to indicate how many times the meter fare you are willing to pay.

Tokyo is such a huge, sprawling city that you could spend a lifetime exploring it and still make new discoveries. At first glance, it can seem an exceptionally ugly city: an unending sea of bleak concrete housing estates and office blocks traversed by overhead express-ways crowded with trucks, buses and commuting drivers. Nevertheless, it doesn't take long to realise that, like all great cities, Tokyo is a bizarre conundrum, a riddle of contradictions that springs from the tension between the large-scale ugliness and the meticulous attention to detail that meets the attentive eye at every street corner; the ten-sions between the frantic rhythms of 20th century consumer culture and the quiet moments of stillness that are the legacy of other, older traditions.

While Tokyo sports some of the world's biggest and most lavish department stores, the average Tokyo suburb hasn't fallen prey to supermarket culture: the streets are lined with tiny specialist shops and restaurants, most of which stay open late into the night. Close to the soaring office blocks in the business districts and commercial centres are entertainment quarters, mazes of narrow alleys that blaze with neon light by night and offer an intoxicating escape from the '12 hours a day' working regimen that is the lot of Tokyo's surging crowds of office workers. In the shadow of the overhead expressways and the office blocks exist pockets of another Tokyo: an old wooden house, a kimono shop, a Japanese inn, an old lady in kimono and geta sweeping the pavement outside her home with a straw broom.

As might be expected of a city that has established itself as one of the economic powerhouses of the modern world, what confronts the visitor more than anything else is the sheer level of energy in Tokyo. Rush hour seems to begin with the first train of the day, sometime after 5 am, when drunken hordes of revellers from the night before start the two or three hour journey back to the so-called 'bedroom suburbs' in which they live.

On the busy train lines, even at 11 pm on a Monday evening there is standing room only. Crowds sweep you up, carry you in their wake, and a barrage of noise assaults you at every turn you make. Train drivers assume strange, masked voices to advise you of the stops. On escalators, female announc-ers who sound like chirping birds ask you to stand within the yellow lines. Shops blare out their personal anthems into the crowded streets, traffic lights and vending machines play digitised melodies, and politicians drive the streets in cars specially fitted with loud-speakers, thanking constituents for having voted for them in the recent elections.

In fact, some of the best sights Tokyo has to offer are often not the kind of things you can put in a guidebook. They jump out at you unexpectedly on a crowded street: the woman dressed in traditional kimono buying a hamburger at McDonald's; and the Bud-dhist monk with an alms bowl, standing serenely in the midst of jostling crowds of shoppers in Ginza. Tokyo is a living city. It is less a collection of sights than an experi-ence.

HISTORY

Tokyo is something of a miracle; a city that has literally risen from the ashes (the result of US aerial bombing at the end of WW II) to become one of the world's leading eco-nomic centres.

Before Tokyo was Tokyo (Eastern Capital), it was known as Edo (Estuary), so named for its location at the mouth of the Sumidagawa River. Edo first became histor-ically significant in 1603, when Tokugawa Ieyasu established his shogunate (military government) there. From a sleepy backwater town, Edo grew into a city from which the Tokugawa clan governed the whole of Japan and which, by the late 18th century, had become the most populous city in the world.

When the Tokugawas fell from power and the authority of the emperor was restored in 1868, the emperor and the capital were moved from Kyoto to Edo, which was renamed Tokyo.

After 250 years of isolation imposed by the Tokugawa Shogunate, Tokyo set about transforming itself into a modern metropolis. Remarkably, it has been successful in achieving this in spite of two major disasters that, in both cases, practically levelled the whole city: the great earthquake and ensuing fires of 1923, and the US air raids of 1944 and 1945.

Not much of the old Japan is left in Tokyo; indeed, given the violence of the city's history – the periodic conflagrations (known to the locals as the 'flowers of Edo'), the earthquakes and the destruction brought about through war – it's a wonder that anything is left at all. What you find today is a uniquely Japanese version of a 21st century city: a weaving of the remnants of a shattered past with Blade Runneresque cityscapes peopled by Orwellian legions of business-suited office workers. In short, if you're looking for traditional Japan you're better off heading for Kyoto or Kamakura, where recent history has been kinder to the traditional past. Tokyo is a place you visit to see the Japanese success story in action.

ORIENTATION

Tokyo is a conurbation spreading out across the Kantō Plain from Tokyo-wan Bay. Nevertheless, for visitors, nearly everything of interest lies either on or within the JR Yamanote line, the rail loop that circles central Tokyo. In Edo times, Yamanote referred to 'Uptown', the estates and residences of feudal barons, the military aristocracy and other members of the elite of Edo society in the hilly regions of Edo. Shitamachi, or 'Downtown', was home to the working classes, merchants and artisans. Even today the distinction persists, with the areas west of Ginza being the more modernised, housing the commercial and business centres of modern Tokyo, and the

areas east of Ginza, centred in Asakusa, retaining more of the character of old Edo.

Essential for finding your way around Tokyo is a map of Tokyo's subway and Japan Railways (JR) network (included in the Tokyo chapter). The JR Yamanote line does a loop through Tokyo, above ground, that takes you through most of the important centres of the city, both Yamanote and, to a lesser extent, Shitamachi. It is actually possible to do the trip very cheaply, because buying a ticket to the next station for Y120 doesn't stop you going in the less direct of the two possible directions and taking in the whole city on the way.

Starting in Ueno, which is where the Keisei Skyliner from Narita Airport is most likely to deposit you, two stops to the south is Akihabara, the discount electronics capital of Tokyo. Continuing in the same direction, you come to Kanda, which is near Tokyo's second-hand bookshop district, Jimbō-cho. The next stops are Tokyo and Yūraku-cho stations, the latter being a short walk from Ginza. From there, trains continue through to the teen-oriented, fashionable shopping areas of Shibuya and Harajuku. Another two stops on is Shinjuku, a massive shopping, entertainment and business district. Between Shinjuku and Ueno the train passes through Ikebukuro (really a down-market version of Shinjuku) and Nippori, one of the few areas left in Tokyo where you can find buildings that have survived Tokyo's 20th century calamities.

INFORMATION
Tourist Office

Practically on top of Hibiya subway station on the Hibiya, Chiyoda and TOEI Mita lines is the Tourist Information Centre, (TIC) (tel 3502-1461), the single best source of information about Tokyo and the rest of Japan available in Tokyo. The Japan National Tourist Organisation (JNTO) has two other TICs: in Kyoto and at Narita International Airport. The Tokyo centre is arguably the best, having an enormous range of information for travellers who know how to ask the right questions and, unlike the Kyoto centre,

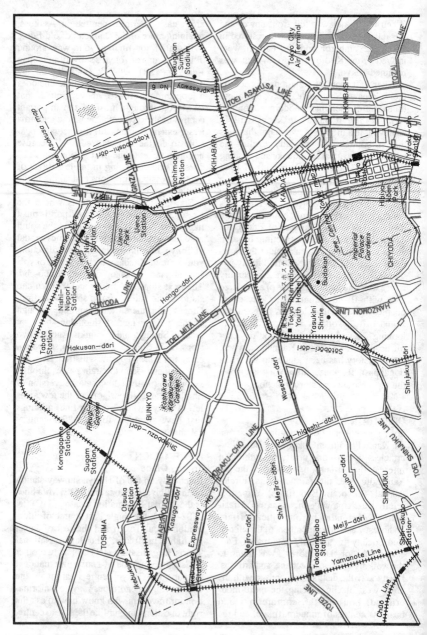

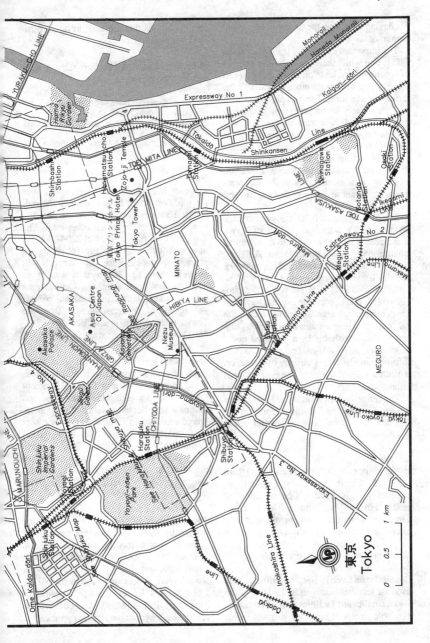

not having a limit on the time you can spend harassing the staff.

The important thing to bear in mind at the TIC is that while there are a limited number of brochures available on racks that you can take for yourself, much more is available for those who ask for it. The pamphlet you need will very likely be tucked away in a dusty cabinet or a drawer somewhere and will remain there unless you can prompt one of the TIC staff members to search it out for you. The centre also has information for those with specialised interests in Japan: anything from martial arts to the tea ceremony or Japanese paper making – all you have to do is ask.

One of the most useful things you can pick up at the centre is the *Tourist Map of Tokyo*. It includes a large map of Tokyo as well as smaller maps of Shinjuku, Ueno, Asakusa, central Tokyo, the transportation network and the Tokyo subway network.

The Tokyo TIC is at 1-6-6 Yūraku-cho, Tokyo 100, just beyond the expressway from the central Ginza area. To get there take the A2 exit of Hibiya subway station – the centre, distinguishable by a large red question mark and a sign reading 'Tourist Information Office', is directly opposite, on the other side of the road running towards Hibiya-kōen Park.

The centre is open Monday to Friday from 9 am to 5 pm and on Saturdays from 9 am to 12 noon. It is closed on Sundays and public holidays.

Money
Banks are open Monday to Friday from 9 am to 3 pm. Those that change travellers' cheques usually have a sign outside that reads 'Foreign Exchange'. The foreign-exchange counter is usually upstairs, and the exchange procedure can take up to 15 minutes. Money can be changed more quickly at many of the larger hotels.

Credit Cards Even in Tokyo, credit cards are used far less frequently than they are in the West. Credit card facilities will often not be available except at major department stores

and operations that are used to doing business with foreigners.

American Express There are three American Express offices in Tokyo:

American Express Tower, 4-30-16 Ogikubo, Suginami-ku (tel 3220-6000)
Toranomon Mitsui Buiding, 3-8-1 Kasumigaseki, Chiyoda-ku (tel 3508-2400)
Ginza 4-Star Building, 4-4-1 Ginza, Chūō-ku (tel 3564-4381)

Post
Look for the red and white T with a bar across the top. Post boxes have two slots: the red-lettered slot is for Tokyo mail and the blue-lettered one is for all other mail. The Tokyo central post office (tel 3284-9527) is next to Tokyo station in the Tokyo station plaza, Chiyoda-ku. Poste restante mail will be held there for 30 days: it should be addressed to Poste Restante, Central Post Office, Tokyo, Japan. International parcels and registered mail can be sent from the Tokyo international post office (tel 3241-4891) next to Otemachi subway station.

Telephone
Tokyo public telephones are the same as those everywhere else in Japan. All except the pink phones take telephone cards, and international phones are labelled in English. Tokyo also has an English-language directory assistance service (tel 3201-1010) available Monday to Saturday from 10 am to 7 pm. Some of the discount travel agencies (see the following Travel Agencies section) also offer 5% to 10% discounts on other items, such as telephone cards.

Japan Travel-Phone This is a service offered by JNTO for travellers having language or general travel problems anywhere in Japan. While you are in Tokyo ring 3502-1461; in Kyoto ring 371-5649; elsewhere, for information on eastern Japan ring 0120-222-800, and for information on western Japan ring 0120-444-800. Your coin will be returned after you have finished your call to either of the latter two numbers. In Tokyo and Kyoto you will be charged for a local call. The service is offered seven days a week from 9 am to 5 pm.

Fax

Japan may be an economic miracle but sending a fax from there can be a real hassle. Most post offices do not offer a fax service, and large hotels generally do not allow you to use their facilities unless you are a guest. The Kokusai Denshin Denwa (KDD) international telegraph office (tel 3270-511), one block north of Otemachi subway station, has fax and telex facilities.

Budget travellers, particularly those staying at the Kimi Ryokan, can use the Kimi Information Centre, around the corner from the ryokan. You have to pay a registration fee of Y2000, but after this you pay the fax charges individually. The centre will also receive faxes for you.

Visas & Embassies

Immigration Office The Tokyo Regional Immigration Bureau is best reached from Otemachi subway station on the Chiyoda line. Take the C2 exit, cross the street at the corner and turn left. Walk past the Japan Development building; the immigration bureau is the next building on your right.

Foreign Embassies Most countries have embassies in Tokyo, though visas are generally expensive in Japan.

Australia
    1-1-12 Shiba-kōen Park, Minato-ku (tel 3435-0971)
Austria
    1-1-20 Moto Azabu, Minato-ku (tel 3451-8281)
Belgium
    5-4 Niban-cho, Chiyoda-ku (tel 3262-0191)
Burma
    4-8-26 Kita Shinagawa, Shinagawa-ku (tel 3441-9291)
Canada
    7-3-38 Akasaka, Minato-ku (tel 3408-2101)
China
    3-4-33 Moto Azabu, Minato-ku (tel 3403-3380)
Denmark
    29-6 Sarugaku-cho, Shibuya-ku (tel 3496-3001)

France
    4-11-44 Minami Azabu, Minato-ku (tel 3473-0171)
Germany
    4-5-10 Minami Azabu, Minato-ku (tel 3473-0151)
India
    2-2-11 Kudan Minami, Chiyoda-ku (tel 3262-2391)
Indonesia
    5-2-9 Higashi Gotanda, Shinagawa-ku (tel 3441-4201)
Ireland
    No 25 Kowa Building, 8-7 Sanban-cho, Chiyoda-ku (tel 3263-0695)
Israel
    3 Niban-cho, Chiyoda-ku (tel 3264-0911)
Italy
    2-5-4 Mita, Minato-ku (tel 3453-5291)
Laos
    3-3-21 Nishi Azabu, Minato-ku (tel 3408-1166)
Malaysia
    20-16 Nanpeidai-cho, Shibuya-ku (tel 3770-9331)
Nepal
    7-14-9 Todoroki, Setagaya-ku (tel 3705-5558)
New Zealand
    20-40 Kamiyama-cho, Shibuya-ku (tel 3467-2270/1)
Norway
    5-12-2 Minami Azabu, Minato-ku (tel 3440-2611)
Philippines
    11-24 Nanpeidai-cho, Shibuya-ku (tel 3496-2731)
Singapore
    5-12-3 Roppongi, Minato-ku (tel 3586-9111)
South Korea
    1-2-5 Minami Azabu, Minato-ku (tel 3452-7611)
Spain
    1-3-29 Roppongi, Minato-ku (tel 3583-8531)
Sri Lanka
    1-14-1 Akasaka, Minato-ku (tel 3585-7841)
Sweden
    25 Mori Building, 1-4-30 Roppongi, Minato-ku (tel 3582-6981)
Switzerland
    5-9-12 Minami Azabu, Minato-ku (tel 3473-0121)
Taiwan (Association of East Asian Relations)
    5-20-2, Shirogane-dai, Minato-ku, Tokyo (tel 3280-7800)
Thailand
    3-14-6 Kami Osaki, Shinagawa-ku (tel 3441-7342)
UK
    1 Ichiban-cho, Chiyoda-ku (tel 3265-5511)
USA
    1-10-5 Akasaka, Minato-ku (tel 3224-5000)

USSR
   2-1-1 Azabudai, Minato-ku (tel 3583-4224)
Vietnam
   50-11 Moto Yoyogi-cho, Shibuya-ku (tel 3466-3311)

Cultural Centres

For the homesick, Tokyo has no shortage of Japanese and foreign-sponsored cultural institutes and libraries. The National Diet Library (tel 3581-2331) is the largest library in Japan, with over 1.3 million books in Western languages. Books have to be requested on a special form. The library is close to Nagata-cho subway station on the Yūraku-cho and Hanzomon lines and is open Monday to Saturday from 9.30 am to 5 pm.

The library at the American Center (tel 3436-0901) has books and magazines concerning the USA. It's close to Shiba-kōen subway station on the TOEI Mita line, and is open Monday to Friday from 10.30 am to 6.30 pm.

The library at the Australia-Japan Foundation (tel 3498-4141) has around 8000 volumes published in Australia and a large number of magazines. The foundation, close to Omote-sando subway station on the Ginza, Chiyoda and Hanzomon lines, is open from 11 am to 12.30 pm and from 1.30 to 6 pm.

The British Council (tel 3235-8031) has a library, and you can also inquire about other cultural activities. The office is close to Iidabashi subway station on the Yūraku-cho line. The library is open Monday to Friday from 10 am to 8 pm.

Finally, a nice place to get away from it all in Ginza is the World Magazine Gallery (tel 3545-7227). The gallery has a huge selection of magazines from all over the world and a coffee shop on the same floor. It's in a big modern building behind the Kabuki-za Theatre in Ginza. It's open Monday to Saturday from 10 am to 7 pm.

Travel Agencies

Getting cheap tickets in Tokyo is no easy task. Discounts are available if you shop around, but they're nowhere near as cheap as they are elsewhere in Asia. One of the best places to look is among the classified advertisements in the *Tokyo Journal*. Discounts are available on foreign and domestic air tickets, on JR tickets (particularly shinkansen), and on other items like telephone cards.

Most of the discount travel agencies will have English-speaking staff, but service tends to be rushed and the bargains are generally only displayed in Japanese. Places to try in Tokyo include:

Arch, 1st Floor, New Shimbashi Building, 2-16-1 Shimbashi, Minato-ku (tel 3595-1491)
Fuji Coin, 3-2-4 Kanda Kajimachi, Chiyoda-ku (tel 3241-0005)
Just Travel, 1st Floor, Koike Building, 2-13-7 Takadanobaba, Shinjuku-ku (tel 3348-6303)
Kennedy Stamp, 1-9 Yotsuya, Shinjuku-ku (tel 3353-5443)
Kinokuniya Gift, 3-31-5 Shinjuku, Shinjuku-ku (tel 3352-7011)
Number One Travel, 3rd Floor, Shoritsu Building, 7-8-12 Nishi Shinjuku, Shinjuku-ku (tel 3366-2481)
Sakura Coin, 4-3 Nihombashi Muromachi, Chūō-ku (tel 3241-4553)
Across Traveller's Bureau, Haneda Building, 2-5-1 Yoyogi, Shibuya-ku (tel 3374-8721)

You can call the Across Traveller's Bureau in English, Urdu, Tagalog, Chinese, Hindi, Bengali or Japanese. There is also an STA Travel office (tel 3221-1733) in Tokyo with Western, Chinese and Japanese staff. Ring the office and someone there will tell you how to find the office, which is in the Sanden Building, 3-5-5 Kojimachi, Chiyoda-ku. Council Travel (tel 3581-7581) is also a student-travel specialist and can be found at Room 102, Sanno Grand Building, 2-14-2 Nagata-cho, Chiyoda-ku.

Books & Maps

There are plenty of books available on Tokyo, the history of the city and how to get around the 20th century metropolis it has become.

People & Society For those intending to live in Tokyo, the bilingual Japanese-English publication *Your Life in Tokyo* (The Japan Times, 1987) has a lot of useful information. There are two volumes, *Daily Life* and *Leisure*, and they're readily available in Tokyo.

History For an interesting history of Tokyo from 1867 to 1923, look for Edward Seidensticker's *Low City, High City* (1983). *Tokyo Rising: The City Since the Great Earthquake* (Knopf, 1990), by the same author, continues the story to the present day.

Guidebooks The pick of the guidebooks specifically about Tokyo is the *Tokyo City Guide* (Kodansha International, 1984) by Judith Connor and Mayumi Yoshida. The book is somewhat out of date now, but the basics are all covered thoroughly.

Probably the most fun book to come out on Tokyo is Don Morton and Naoko Tsunoi's *The Best of Tokyo* (Charles E Tuttle, 1989). The book has a comprehensive list of 'best ofs', from 'best garlic restaurant' and 'best traditional Japanese dolls' to 'best toilet'. It's a good companion with which to explore a more idiosyncratic side of the city.

The *City Source English Telephone Directory* is useful for long-term visitors. It has over 500 pages of telephone numbers and a wealth of useful practical information. The Nippon Telegraph & Telephone (NTT) English Information Service (tel 3201-1010) will tell you the address of the nearest NTT office, where you can pick up a free copy.

Jean Pearce's *Footloose in Tokyo* (John Weatherhill, 1976) and *More Footloose in Tokyo* (John Weatherhill, 1984) are excellent guides to exploring Tokyo on foot. Even if you don't follow Pearce's routes, her introductions to some of Tokyo's most important areas make for interesting background reading. The first book contains most of the important areas in Tokyo.

Gary Walters' *Day Walks Near Tokyo* (Kodansha International, 1988) covers 25 countryside trails, most of which can be reached from central Tokyo in an hour.

Bookshops The English-language sections of several of the larger Tokyo bookshops would put entire bookshops in many English-speaking cities to shame.

The big bookshop area in Tokyo is Jimbō-cho, and although most of the bookshops there cater only to those who read Japanese, there are a couple of foreign-language bookshops. The best among these is Kitazawa Shoten (tel 3263-0011), which has an excellent academic selection on the ground floor and second-hand books on the 2nd floor, many of them hardback and not all that cheap. If you exit from Jimbō-cho subway station on Yasukuni-dōri Ave and set off westwards in the direction of Ichigaya, Kitazawa is about 50 metres away on the left.

Kinokuniya (tel 3354-0131) in Shinjuku (see the Shinjuku map) has a good selection of English-language fiction and general titles on the 6th floor, including an extensive selection of books and other aids for learning Japanese. There is also a limited selection of books in other European languages – mainly French and German. Kinokuniya is a good place to stock up on guidebooks if you are continuing to other parts of the world. It's closed on the third Wednesday of every month.

Maruzen (tel 3272-7211) in Nihombashi near Ginza has a collection of books almost equal to Kinokuniya's and it is always a lot quieter. This is Japan's oldest Western bookshop, having been established in 1869. Take the Takashimaya department store exit at Nihombashi subway station and look for Maruzen on the other side of the road. It's closed on Sunday.

The 3rd floor of Jena (tel 3571-2980) in Ginza doesn't have quite the range of some other foreign-language bookshops but it does have a good selection of fiction and art books and stocks a large number of newspapers and magazines. Take the Sukiyabashi Crossing exit of Ginza subway station and walk along Harumi-dōri Ave towards the Kabuki-za Theatre. Jena is on the third block on your right. It's closed on public holidays.

Maps A *Tourist Map of Tokyo* is available

from the TIC (see the earlier Tourist Office section of this chapter).

Newspapers & Magazines

See the Media section in the Facts for the Visitor chapter for information about newspapers. Most of the jobs advertised in the Monday edition of the *Japan Times* are in English. This is the best place to look for teaching and rewriting work.

Tokyo has a wealth of English-language magazines covering local events, entertainment and cultural listings. The pick of the pack is undoubtedly the *Tokyo Journal*; the Cityscope section alone is worth Y500 a month for its comprehensive listings of movies, plays, concerts, art exhibitions and unclassifiable 'events'. The *Tokyo Journal's* classified advertisements are particularly useful for those basing themselves in Tokyo for some time. Sections include housing, employment and education. There are also general advertisements for things like moving house on a budget and furniture rental. The *Tokyo Journal* is available in bookshops with English-language sections.

An excellent source of information about more tourist-oriented events is the *Tokyo City Guide*, a free, twice-monthly magazine. However, its listings are nowhere near as comprehensive as those in the *Tokyo Journal*, and it is pitched at well-heeled visitors. The magazine has some good features on places to visit in Tokyo, and the shopping and dining out advertisements should give you some ideas on how to get rid of your money quickly. You can find it in the TIC, hotels and travel agencies. The monthly *Tokyo Time Out* magazine takes a slice of the *Tokyo Journal* cake. It also costs Y500 and seems a bit less jaded and less critical of Japan than its competitor.

Infozine, produced by the International Rockers, is an English-Japanese bilingual publication put together by musicians and artists, both gaijin and Japanese. The magazine includes short articles on environmental and community issues as well as listings of alternative music in Tokyo live houses.

Some of the advertised bands are very good, and this is one way you can find genuine alternatives to Japanese mainstream pop. *Infozine* is free and can be found at some of the live houses listed in the magazine as well as at the Kimi Ryokan. For more information, contact the International Rockers, 2-18-35-202 Minami-cho, Kokubunji-shi, Tokyo 185, or phone Steven on 3042-324-0536.

If you're studying Japanese, all the articles in the *Hiragana Times* are in English and Japanese and all the kanji include *furigana* (Japanese script used to give pronunciation for kanji) readings – great for improving your reading skills. The magazine has some good features on restaurants and events around Tokyo.

Medical Services

For general health problems, there are a number of clinics in Tokyo where English is spoken. The International Clinic (tel 3583-7831) in Azabudai has been running for some time, though it is by no means the final word on Tokyo clinics. Call the clinic for instructions on how to find it. English is also spoken at the Tokyo Medical & Surgical Clinic (tel 3436-3028) and King's Clinic in Shibuya (tel 3400-7917).

American Pharmacy If you're having trouble finding what you want in Japanese pharmacies, try the American Pharmacy (tel 3271-4034). It's at 1-8-1 Yūraku-cho, Chiyoda-ku, just around the corner from the TIC, near Yūraku-cho station and Hibiya subway station, and is open Monday to Saturday from 9 am to 7 pm.

Emergencies

The police can be contacted by telephoning 110, and the fire brigade and ambulance by telephoning 119. For general hospital information, telephone 3212-2323.

Japan Helpline This service (tel 0120-461-997) provides emergency information in the event of travel or life crises: you shouldn't use it unless you really have to. It's available seven days a week, 24 hours a day.

Earthquakes These are a risk throughout Japan, but the Tokyo region is particularly prone to them. Since major earthquakes occur every 60 years on average, a big one is overdue. There is no point in being paranoid, but it is worthwhile checking the emergency exits in your hotel and being aware of earthquake safety procedures (see the Earthquakes section in the Facts for the Visitor chapter). If an earthquake occurs, Nihon Hoso Kyokai (NHK) (the Japanese Broadcasting Corporation) will broadcast information and instructions in English on all its TV and radio networks. Tune to channel 1 on your television, or to NHK (639 AM) or FEN (810 AM) on your radio.

Clubs & Conversation Lounges

When millions of people compete for limited amounts of recreational space and facilities, membership of a club brings privileges denied to outsiders: the right to hit hundreds of small balls against a net on top of a building for example. Even studying at a language school, as any newly arrived 'English teacher' will soon discover, is not simply a matter of paying for the classes you attend. Students actually pay for a package that includes such things as the right to use the school's lounge for chatting with other students and the teachers. Not surprisingly, clubs have sprung up to give Japanese the opportunity to meet and talk to foreigners. Generally, activities centre around a lounge or a coffee shop, entry to which costs foreigners little or nothing – it is the Japanese who pay.

Mickey House (tel 3209-9686) is an 'English bar' that offers free coffee and tea as well as reasonably priced beer and food. Entry is free for foreigners and it's a good place to meet young Japanese as well as long-term gaijin residents. It's a lively place with a fairly regular crowd, but it is definitely not a closed scene. This can be a good place to make contacts and pick up tips on living in Tokyo.

Mickey House is close to the JR Takadanobaba station on the Yamanote line. Facing towards Shinjuku station, take the exit on the left side of the station. Keeping the Big Box building to your right, walk straight up Waseda-dōri Ave. Look for the Tōzai line subway station entrance on your left; Mickey House is on the 4th floor of the Yashiro building, several doors on. The bar is open Monday to Friday from 3 to 11 pm. Every Saturday night from 7 to 11 pm is party night, when a Y1000 entry fee will also get you a drink and some food.

The Japan International Friendship Club (tel 3341-9061) offers a wide range of activities for its Japanese members, including the opportunity to meet and exchange ideas with foreigners from many different countries. On Fridays the club has get-togethers that foreign nonmembers can attend free of charge. The location of the parties varies, but if you ring the club someone will meet you at Shimbashi station and take you by the hand.

Associations

Tokyo has a large number of associations for foreigners with special interests:

Buddhist English Academy has lectures every Friday at a location near Shinjuku (tel 3342-6605)

Ikebana International has monthly meetings (tel 3295-0720)

International Friends of Kabuki meets monthly: ask for Ursula Imadegawa (tel 3724-5858)

Japan Foundation has, among other things, library classes and free screenings of Japanese films with English subtitles – a real rarity in Japan (tel 3263-4503)

Corn Popper Club is very much an American affair, but if you're from the USA and into popcorn, coffee, tea, billiards and the occasional party, this could be just the club for you (tel 3715-4473)

International House of Japan is a prestigious association that runs academic seminars and is able to provide accommodation to its members at reasonable rates, although membership is expensive (Y200,000) and requires two nominations from members (tel 3470-4611)

Japan Afro-American Friendship Society meets monthly (tel 3557-2383)

Japan-Ireland Society meets monthly (tel 3561-1491, ask for Mr Nishi)

St Andrew's Society is a Scottish social and cultural association (tel 3264-2171)

Tokyo British Club (tel 3443-9083, after 5 pm)

Tokyo Canadian Club has a pub night on the first Thursday of every month at Zest in Nishi Azabu (tel 3581-5765)

Association of Foreign Teachers in Japan meets monthly (tel 3238-3909)

Foreign Correspondents Club (tel 3211-3161)

Japan Association of Translators (tel 3385-5709)

International Lesbians meets monthly – write for a newsletter to IWG GPO Box 1780, Tokyo 100-91

CENTRAL TOKYO 東京中心

Imperial Palace

The Imperial Palace is the home of Japan's emperor and the imperial family, but there's very little to see. The palace itself is closed to the public for all but two days of the year: 2 January (New Year's) and 23 December (the emperor's birthday). Nevertheless, it is possible to wander around its outskirts and visit the gardens, from which you can at least get a good view of the palace with the Nijū-bashi Bridge in the foreground.

The present palace is a fairly recent construction, having been completed in 1968. Like much else in Tokyo, the original palace, built at the time of the Meiji Restoration, was a victim of the bombing in WW II. Before the construction of the Meiji Imperial Palace, the site was occupied by Edo-jō Castle, the seat of power of the Tokugawa Shogunate. In its time the castle was the largest in the world, though apart from the massive moat and walls, little remains to mark its former existence.

It is an easy walk from Tokyo station, or Hibiya or Nijū-bashi-mae subway stations, to the Nijū-bashi Bridge. The walk involves crossing Babasaki Moat and the expansive (for Tokyo at least) Imperial Palace plaza. The vantage point, which is popular with photographers, gives you a picture-postcard view of the palace peeking over its fortifications, with the Nijū-bashi Bridge in the foreground.

Imperial Palace East Garden

This is the nicest spot in the immediate vicinity of the Imperial Palace. Enter through the Ote-mon Gate, a 10 minute walk north of the Nijū-bashi Bridge. This was once the principal gate of Edo-jō Castle, while the garden is situated at what was once the centre of the old castle. Remarkably, there is no entry fee for the park, which is open daily except Mondays and Fridays from 9 am to 4 pm (last entry at 3 pm).

Kitanomaru-kōen Park

The park itself is fairly average, but it is home to a few museums and the Budokan, if you're in the mood to pay homage to the venue at which so many live recordings have been produced over the years. The park is reached most easily from Kudanshita or Takebashi subway stations. Alternatively, if you're walking from the Imperial Palace East Garden, take the Kitahanebashi-mon Gate, turn left and look for Kitanomaru-kōen Park on your right.

Science Museum There's little in the way of English explanations but the museum does give out an excellent booklet in English when you buy your ticket. There are displays dealing with space development, nuclear energy and 'bikecology' ('Man and Bicycle', as the booklet helpfully explains). The staff even put on a 'variety show', which gives you the somewhat dubious privilege of being witness to the 'interfacial condensation of nylon': apparently 'a great deal of carbon dioxide is generated and foam is produced'. All this for a mere Y515. The museum is open Monday to Friday from 9.30 am to 4.50 pm.

National Museum of Modern Art The emphasis here is on Japanese art from the Meiji period onwards. Admission is Y360, and it is open Tuesday to Sunday from 10 am to 5 pm.

Craft Museum Actually an annex of the National Museum of Modern Art, this museum houses crafts such as ceramics, lacquerware and dolls. Admission is Y360, and it is open Tuesday to Sunday from 10 am to 5 pm.

Yasukuni-jinja Shrine

If you take the Tayasu-mon Gate exit (just past the Budokan) of Kitanomaru-kōen Park, across the road and to your left is the Yasukuni-jinja Shrine, literally 'Peaceful Country Shrine'. Given that the shrine is actually a memorial to Japan's war dead, the title is something of a misnomer.

In the years leading up to and during WW II, Yasukuni was the most important shrine for state Shinto in Tokyo. Not surprisingly, it's a subject of controversy today. Despite a Japanese constitutional commitment to a separation of religion and politics and a renunciation of militarism, in 1979 a group of class-A war criminals were enshrined there. Also, the shrine has become the object of yearly visits by leading Liberal Democratic Party (LDP) politicians on the anniversary of Japan's defeat in WW II (15 August). Whatever your personal feelings about honouring Japanese war dead, it's an interesting shrine to have a look at. In the vicinity of the shrine, you may see rather evil-looking black vans that broadcast right-wing propaganda from speakers mounted on their roofs.

Yūshūkan Museum Next to the Yasukuni-jinja Shrine is the Yūshūkan Museum, with treasures from the Yasukuni-jinja Shrine and other items commemorating Japanese war dead. There are limited English explanations, but there is an English pamphlet. Interesting exhibits include the long torpedo in the large exhibition hall which is actually a *kaiten*, or 'human torpedo', a submarine version of the kamikaze. There are displays of military uniforms, samurai armour and a 'panorama of the Divine Thunderbolt Corps in final attack mode at Okinawa'. Admission is Y200, and the museum is open daily from 9 am to 5 pm.

Ginza

Ginza is the shopping area in Tokyo that *everyone* has heard of. Back in the 1870s, Ginza was one of the first areas to modernise, featuring a large number of novel – for Tokyoites of that time – Western-style brick buildings. Ginza was also home to Tokyo's first department stores and other Western emblems of modernity such as gas lamps.

Today, other shopping districts rival Ginza in opulence, vitality and popularity, but Ginza retains a distinct snob value. Ginza is still the place to go to if you want to lighten the weight of your wallet. If you are an impecunious traveller, on the other hand, this is still an interesting area to browse through, full of galleries and display rooms, most of which are free; and you can at least afford a cup of coffee at one of the discount coffee shops that materialise from among the exclusive boutiques every block or so.

The best starting point for a look at Ginza is the Sukiyabashi Crossing, which is a 10 minute walk from the Imperial Palace. Alternatively, take the Sukiyabashi Crossing exit at Ginza subway station.

Sony Building Right on the Sukiyabashi Crossing is the Sony building, which has fascinating displays of Sony's many products. You're free to fiddle with many of the items. The high-definition television display is particularly interesting, and there is a viewing room where you can watch the technology in action. Shows take place at regular intervals during the day.

Galleries Ginza is overflowing with galleries, many of them so small that they can be viewed in two or three minutes. Others feature work by unknown artists who have hired the exhibition space themselves. Wander around and visit any galleries that seem particularly interesting. They are scattered throughout Ginza but are concentrated in the area south of Harumi-dōri Ave, between Ginza-dōri Ave and Chūō-dōri Ave.

If you have an interest in ukiyo-e woodblock prints, a few minutes south-west of the Sukiyabashi Crossing, next to the railway tracks, is the Riccar Art Museum (tel 3571-3254). Admission is Y300, and it is open Tuesday to Sunday from 11 am to 6 pm. Do not enter by the Riccar building's main door but through another entrance at the side. The gallery is on the 7th floor.

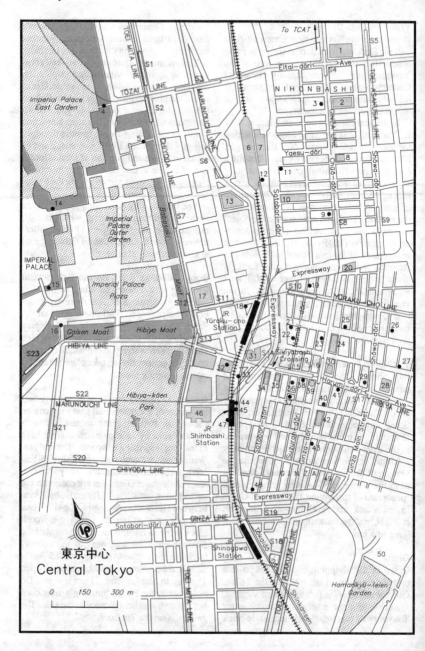

東京中心
Central Tokyo

Central Tokyo

1	Tōkyū Department Store	39	Mitsubishi Building
2	Takashimaya Department Store	40	Gandhara Pakistani Restaurant
3	Maruzen Bookshop	41	Maharaja Indian Restaurant
4	Ote-mon Gate	42	Matsuzakaya Department Store
5	Wadakura-mon Gate	43	Lion Beer Hall
6	JR Tokyo Station	44	Riccar Art Museum
7	Daimaru Department Store	45	Nishiginza Electric Centre
8	Bridgestone Art Museum	46	Imperial Hotel
9	Meidi-ya International Supermarket	47	International Arcade
10	Yaesu Bookshop	48	Ginza Nikkō Hotel
11	Airport Limousine Bus Stop	49	Ginza Dai-Ichi Hotel
12	JR Highway Bus Terminal	50	Tsukiji Fish Market
13	Central Post Office		
14	Sakashita-mon Gate		**SUBWAY STATIONS**
15	Nijū-bashi Bridge		
16	Sakadura-mon Gate	S1	Otemachi (Chiyoda Line)
17	Imperial Theatre & Idemitsu Art Museum	S2	Otemachi (TOEI Mita Line)
18	Sogo Department Store	S3	Otemachi (Tōzai Line)
19	American Express Travel Service Office	S4	Nihombashi
20	Hotel Seiyo Ginza	S5	Edobashi
21	Printemps Department Store	S6	Tokyo-Otemachi
22	Kodak Imagica (Kodachrome Processing)	S7	Nijū-bashi-mae (Chiyoda Line)
		S8	Kyobashi
23	Nikon Gallery	S9	Takara-cho
24	Matsuya Department Store	S10	Ginza-Itchome
25	Kaiten-zushi Sushi	S11	Yūraku-cho
26	Chichibu Nishiki Nomiya Saké Pub	S12	Hibiya (TOEI Mita Line)
27	World Magazine Gallery	S13	Hibiya (Hibiya & Chiyoda Lines)
28	Kabuki-za Theatre	S14	Ginza (Marunouchi Line)
29	Nair's Indian Restaurant	S15	Ginza (Hibiya Line)
30	Mitsukoshi Department Store	S16	Ginza (Ginza Line)
31	Hankyū & Seibu Department Stores	S17	Higashi-Ginza
32	Tourist Information Centre (TIC)	S18	Shimbashi (TOEI Asakusa Line)
33	Yakitoris	S19	Shimbashi (Ginza Line)
34	Toshiba Building	S20	Kasumigaseki (Chiyoda Line)
35	Sony Building	S21	Kasumigaseki (Hibiya Line)
36	Yoseido Gallery	S22	Kasumigaseki (Marunouchi Line)
37	Torigin Restaurant	S23	Sakuradamon
38	Jena Bookshop		

The Idemitsu Art Museum holds Japanese and Chinese art and is famous for its collection of work by the Zen monk Sengai. It's a five minute walk from either Hibiya or Yūraku-cho stations, on the 9th floor of the Kokusai building, next door to the Teikoku Gekijō Theatre (the Imperial Theatre). Admission is Y550, and it is open Tuesday to Sunday from 10 am to 5 pm.

Probably the best of the photographic galleries in the area are the Nikon Gallery (tel 3572-5756) and the Contax Gallery (tel 3572-1921). They're sponsored by the respective camera companies and have free, changing exhibits. The Nikon Gallery is on the 3rd floor of the Matsushima Gankyōten building, opposite the Matsuya department store on Chūō-dōri Ave, and is open Tuesday to Sunday from 10 am to 6 pm. The Contax Gallery is on the 5th floor of the building next door to the Sanai building on Chūō-dōri Ave; there is no English sign at ground level. Admission is free, and it is open Tuesday to Sunday from 10.30 am to 7 pm.

Central Tokyo

1	東急百貨店	39	三菱ビル
2	高島屋百貨店	40	ガンダーラ
3	丸善書店	41	マハラジャ
4	大手門	42	松坂屋百貨店
5	和田倉門	43	ライオンビルホール
6	東京駅	44	リッカー美術館
7	大丸百貨店	45	西銀座電力センター
8	ブリヂストン美術館	46	帝国ホテル
9	明治屋	47	イントナショナルアーケード
10	八重洲ブックセンター	48	銀座日光ホテル
11	空港リムジン、バスの停	49	銀座第一ホテル
12	ハイウェイバスタミナル	50	東京中央卸売市場
13	中央郵便局		
14	坂下門		**SUBWAY STATIONS**
15	二重橋		
16	桜田門		
17	帝国劇場/出光美術館	S1	大手町(千代田線)
18	そごう百貨店	S2	大手町(都営地下鉄三田線)
19	アメリカンエクスプレス	S3	大手町(東西線)
20	ホテルセイヨ銀座	S4	日本橋
21	プランタン	S5	江戸橋
22	コダック現像所	S6	東京大手町
23	ニコンギャラリー	S7	二重橋前(千田線)
24	松屋銀座	S8	京橋
25	かいてんずし	S9	宝町
26	ちちぶにしきのみやパーブ	S10	銀座一丁目
27	ワールドマガジンギャラリー	S11	有楽町
28	歌舞伎座	S12	日比谷(都営地下鉄三田線)
29	ナイア	S13	日比谷(日比谷線と千代田線)
30	三越百貨店	S14	銀座(丸内線)
31	阪急と西武有楽町	S15	銀座(日比谷線)
32	TIC	S16	銀座(銀座線)
33	焼き鳥	S17	東銀座
34	東芝ビル	S18	新橋(都営地下鉄浅草線)
35	ソニビル	S19	新橋(銀座線)
36	よせいどビル	S20	霞ケ関(千代田線)
37	鳥ぎんレストラン	S21	霞ケ関(日比谷線)
38	イエナ書店	S22	霞ケ関(丸内線)
		S23	桜田門

Kabuki-za Theatre Further east, in Harumi-dōri Ave, is the Kabuki-za Theatre (tel 3541-3131). Even if you don't plan to attend a kabuki performance, it's worth wandering down and taking a look at the building. Performances usually take place twice daily and tickets range from Y2000 to Y14,000, depending on the seat. If you only want to see part of a performance you can ask about a restricted ticket for the 4th floor. For Y600, plus a deposit of Y1000, you can get an earphone guide that explains the kabuki performance in English as you watch it. However, the earphone guide is not available with restricted tickets. For phone bookings, ring at least a day ahead; the theatre won't take bookings for the same day.

Tsukiji Fish Market

This is where all that sushi and sashimi turns up after it has been fished out of the sea (preferably as far away from the murky waters surrounding Japan as possible). The day begins very early, with the arrival of fish and its wholesale auctioning. The wholesale market is not open to the general public, which is probably a blessing, given that you'd have to be there before 5 am to see the action. You are free to visit the outer market and wander around the stalls that are set up by wholesalers and intermediaries to sell directly to restaurants, retail stores and other buyers. It is a fun place to visit, and you don't have to arrive *that* early: as long as you're there sometime before 8 am there'll be something going on. Watch out for your Reeboks – there's a lot of muck and water on the floor.

The done thing is to top off your visit with a sushi breakfast in one of the nearby sushi shops. There are plenty of places on the right as you walk from the market back to Tsukiji subway station. The market is closed on Sundays and public holidays.

AKIHABARA　秋葉原

Akihabara is the discount electrical and electronics centre with countless shops ranging from tiny specialist stores to electrical department stores. You could go there with no intention of buying anything and within

half an hour find half a dozen things that you couldn't possibly live without.

The range of products is mind boggling; but before you rush into making any purchases, remember that most Japanese companies use the domestic market as a testing ground. Many products end their days there without ever making it onto overseas markets. This may pose difficulties if you take something home and later need to have a fault repaired. Also, the voltage for which the product was made may not be the same as that available in your home country. Some larger stores (Laox is a reliable option) have tax-free sections with export models for sale.

Many of the prices can be quite competitive with those you are used to at home, though it's unusual to find prices that match those of dealers in Hong Kong or Singapore. You should be able to knock another 10% off the marked prices by bargaining. To find the shops, take the Electric Town exit of Akihabara station. You'll see the sign on the platform if you come in on the JR Yamanote line.

UENO　上野

Ueno Hill was the site of a last-ditch defence of the Tokugawa Shogunate by about 2000 Tokugawa loyalists in 1868. They were duly dispatched by the imperial army and afterwards the new Meiji government decreed that Ueno Hill would be transformed into one of Tokyo's first parks.

Today, Ueno-kōen Park is Ueno's foremost attraction. The park has a number of museums, galleries and a zoo that, by Asian standards at least, is pretty good. The park is also famous as Tokyo's most popular site for *hanami* (cherry blossom viewing) when the blossoms come out in early to mid-April.

Ueno is an interesting area to stroll around. Opposite the station is the Ameyoko-cho arcade (look for the large romaji sign over the entrance), a market area where you can buy anything from dried fish to imitation Rolex watches. Only two stops away on the Ginza subway line is Kappabashi-dōri Ave, the place you go to if

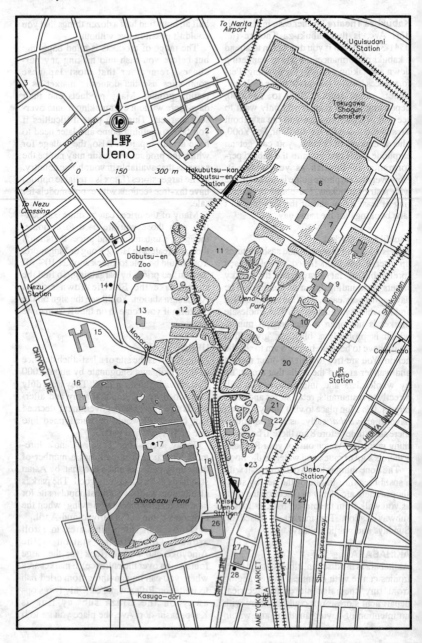

上野
Ueno

0   150   300 m

To Narita
Airport

Uguisudani
Station

Tokugawa
Shogun
Cemetery

To Nezu
Crossing

Hakubutsu-kan
Dōbutsu-en
Station

Keisei Line

Ueno
Dōbutsu-en
Zoo

Nezu
Station

Ueno-kōen
Park

Shinkansen

CHIYODA LINE

Monorail

Com-cho

JR
Ueno
Station

HIBIYA LINE

Shinobazu Pond

Ueno
Station

Keisei
Ueno
Station

AMEYOKO MARKET
AREA

GINZA LINE

Shuto Expressway

Kasuga-dōri

Ueno	
1	Kane-ji Temple
2	Tokyo University of Fine Arts
3	Ryokan Sawanoya
4	Ryokan Katsutaro
5	Gallery of Hōryū-ji Treasures
6	Tokyo National Museum
7	Gallery of Eastern Antiquities
8	Rinno-ji Temple
9	National Science Museum
10	National Museum of Western Art
11	Tokyo Metropolitan Museum of Art
12	Five Storeyed Pagoda
13	Tōshō-gū Shrine
14	Suigetsu Hotel
15	Children's Zoo
16	Aquarium
17	Benzaiten Temple
18	Ueno Station Hotel
19	Kiyomizu-dō Temple
20	Tokyo Metropolitan Festival Hall
21	Japan Art Academy
22	Ueno no Mori Art Museum
23	Saigō Takamori Statue
24	Ameyoko-cho Arcade
25	Marui Department Store
26	Shitamachi History Museum
27	Ameyoko Centre Building
28	Samrat Indian Restaurant

Ueno	
1	寛永寺
2	東京芸術大学
3	澤の屋旅館
4	旅館勝太郎
5	法隆寺宝物殿
6	東京国立博物館
7	東洋館
8	りんの寺
9	国立科学博物館
10	東京国立西洋美術館
11	東京都美術館
12	五重塔
13	東照宮
14	水月ホテル
15	こどもの動物園
16	水族館
17	弁天堂
18	上野スティションホテル
19	清水堂
20	東京文化会館
21	日本美術協会
22	上野の森美術館
23	西郷隆盛銅像
24	アメ横
25	丸井百貨店
26	下町風俗資料館
27	アメ横センタビル
28	サムラート

you want to buy as a souvenir some of the plastic food used for window displays.

Ueno-kōen Park

Saigō Takamori Statue This slightly unusual statue of a samurai walking his dog, near the southern entrance to the park, is a favourite meeting place. Saigō Takamori's history is a little complicated. He started out by helping the cause of the imperial forces of the Meiji Restoration yet ended his life by committing seppuku after having been frustrated in his attempts to defeat them. The turnabout in his loyalties occurred when the Meiji government withdrew the powers of the military class to which he belonged. See Kagoshima in the Kyūshū chapter for more about Saigō Takamori.

Tokyo National Museum The Tokyo National Museum (Kokuritsu Hakubut-

sukan) is the one museum in Tokyo that it is worth going out of your way to visit. Not only is it Japan's largest museum, it also has the world's biggest collection of Japanese art. Only a portion of the museum's huge collection is displayed at any one time. Admission is Y350, and it is open Tuesday to Sunday from 9 am to 4.30 pm.

The museum has four galleries, the most important of which is the Main Gallery. It's straight ahead as you enter and houses a very impressive collection of Japanese art, from sculpture and swords to lacquerware and calligraphy. The Gallery of Eastern Antiquities, to the right of the ticket booth, has a collection of art and archaeological finds from all of Asia east of Egypt. The Hyōkeikan, to the left of the ticket booth, has a collection of Japanese archaeological finds. There is a room devoted to artefacts used by the Ainu, the indigenous ethnic group of Japan now found only in Hokkaidō.

Finally, there is the Gallery of Hōryū-ji Treasures, which is only open on Thursdays, and then only 'weather permitting'. The exhibits (masks, scrolls, etc) are from the Hōryū-ji Temple in Nara. Because they are more than 1000 years old, the building often remains closed if it's raining or humid.

National Museum of Western Art The National Museum of Western Art (Kokuritsu Seiyō Bijutsukan) has quite an impressive collection, although it seems a bit absurd to go all the way to Japan to see it. There is a special emphasis on the French impressionists, with originals by Rodin, including *The Thinker*, and paintings and sketches by, among others, Renoir and Monet. Admission is Y360, and it is open Tuesday to Sunday from 9.30 am to 5 pm.

Tokyo Metropolitan Museum of Art The Metropolitan Museum of Art (Tokyo-to Bijutsukan) has a number of different galleries that run temporary displays of contemporary Japanese art. Galleries feature both Western-style art such as oil paintings and Japanese-style art such as ink brush and ikebana. The admission charge varies according to the exhibition, but entry to the museum itself is free, and there are often interesting displays with no admission charge. It's open Tuesday to Sunday from 9 am to 5 pm.

National Science Museum The National Science Museum (Kokuritsu Kagaku Hakubutsukan) may be of more interest to Japanese than to foreigners. As well as a wide range of general scientific displays, there are displays on the origin of the Japanese people, on Japanese technology and so on. Not all the exhibits are labelled in English, but an English pamphlet is available for Y300. Admission is Y360, and it is open Tuesday to Sunday.

Shitamachi History Museum The Shitamachi History Museum (Fūzoku Shiryōkan) is away from the other museums, at the south-eastern corner of Shinobazu Pond. It re-creates life in Edo's Shitamachi, the plebeian downtown quarters of old Tokyo, through an exhibition of typical Shitamachi buildings. The buildings include a merchant's shop, a sweet shop, the home and business of a copper-boiler maker, and a tenement house. You can take off your shoes and look around inside. Upstairs, the museum has many utensils and items from the daily life of the average Shitamachi resident. You are free to pick many of them up and have a closer look. Admission is Y200, and it is open Tuesday to Sunday from 9.30 am to 4.30 pm.

Ueno Zoo There's nothing in this zoo (Ueno Dōbutsu-en) to get particularly excited about. Among the Japanese the zoo is very popular for its pandas (not on view on Fridays). Admission is Y400, and it is open Tuesday to Sunday from 9.30 am to 4 pm.

Tōshō-gū Shrine Dating from 1651, this is a shrine, like its counterpart in Nikkō, to Tokugawa Ieyasu, who unified Japan. There is a Y100 entrance fee to the shrine, which is open from 9 am to 5.30 pm except in winter, when it's open from 9 am to 4.30 pm.

Ameyoko-cho Arcade
This area, opposite Ueno station, was famous as a black-market district after the war and is still a lively shopping area, where many bargains can be found. Shopkeepers there are much less restrained than those in other shopping areas in Tokyo, calling to prospective customers in the crowded alleyways. This is a good area in which to wander and get something of the feeling of Shitamachi. Look for the big romaji sign opposite Ueno station.

AROUND UENO 上野の附近
Corin-cho Rd

See the Motorcycle section of the Getting Around chapter for information about the busy Corin-cho Rd motorcycle centre near Ueno station, and the interesting motorcycle museum on the 3rd and 4th floor of the clothing shop of Corin Motors.

Kappabashi-dōri Ave

Just two stops from Ueno subway station on the Ginza line is Kappabashi-dōri Ave. This is where you go if you're setting up a restaurant. You can get flags that advertise the food in your restaurant, personalised cushions, crockery and of course, most importantly, all the plastic food you need. Whether you want a plate of bolognese complete with an upright fork, a steak and chips, a lurid pizza or a bowl of rāmen, it's all there. Items aren't particularly cheap, but some of them are very convincing and could make unusual Japanese mementoes.

Kappabashi-dōri Ave is about five minutes from any of the Tawaramachi subway station's exits.

ASAKUSA 浅草

Asakusa's most famous attraction is the Sensō-ji Temple, also known as the Asakusa Kannon Temple. Like Ueno, though, Asakusa is an interesting area just to look around. It has long been the very heart of Shitamachi. In Edo times, Asakusa was a halfway stop between the city and its most infamous pleasure district, Yoshiwara. In time, however, Asakusa developed into a pleasure quarter in its own right, eventually becoming the centre for that most loved of Edo entertainments, kabuki. In the very shadow of the Sensō-ji Temple a fairground spirit prevailed and a whole range of very secular entertainments were provided, from kabuki theatres to brothels.

When Japan ended its self-imposed isolation with the commencement of the Meiji Restoration, it was in Asakusa that the first cinemas opened, in Asakusa that the first music halls appeared and in Asakusa's Teikoku Gekijo Theatre (Imperial Theatre) that Western opera was first performed before Japanese audiences. It was also in Asakusa that another Western cultural export

---

Shitamachi

Today there is little left of Shitamachi and the only way to get some idea of the circumstances in which the lower classes of old Edo lived is by visiting somewhere like Ueno's Shitamachi Fūzoku Shiryōkan (History Museum). In its time, Edo was a city of wood, and the natural stained-wood frontages and dark tiled roofs gave the city an attractiveness that is little in evidence in modern Tokyo. Nevertheless, the common people lived in horribly crowded conditions, in flimsy wooden constructions often with earthen floors. Conflagrations regularly swept great swaths across the congested wooden buildings of the city. In a perverse attempt to make the best of misfortune, Edo dwellers almost seemed to take pride in the fires that periodically purged their city, calling them *Edo no hana*, or 'the flowers of Edo'.

The flowers of Edo occurred with such frequency that it has been estimated that any Shitamachi structure could reckon on a life span of around 20 years, often less, before it would be destroyed by fire. Preventive measures included building houses that could be completely sealed: with the approach of a fire, the house would be sealed and left with candles burning inside, starving the interior of oxygen. Private fire brigades operated with standard bearers who would stake their territory close to a burning building and exact payment if they managed to save it.

Modern building techniques have eliminated Edo's flowers, but you can still see the occasional wooden structure that has miraculously survived into the late 20th century.

Chris Taylor ∎

Asakusa	
1	Banryo-ji Temple
2	Asakusa View Hotel
3	Sukeroku-no-yado Sadachiyo Bekkan
4	Hanayashiki Amusement Park
5	Sensō-ji Temple
6	Five Storeyed Pagoda
7	Hozo-mon Gate
8	Restaurant Bell
9	Ryokan Mikawaya Bekkan
10	Tatsumiya Restaurant
11	Matsuya Department Store
12	Sumidagawa River Cruise
13	Kamiya Bar
14	Tonkyu Restaurant
15	Real Italian Gelato
16	Kaminari-mon Gate
17	Ichimatsu Restaurant
18	Post Office

Asakusa	
1	ばんりょ寺
2	浅草ビューホテル
3	助六の宿貞千代別館
4	花やしき遊園地
5	浅草寺
6	五重塔
7	宝蔵門
8	レストランベル
9	三河屋別館
10	東南屋
11	松屋百貨店
12	隅田川水上バスの停
13	神谷バー
14	とんきゅレストラン
15	イタリャンジェラト
16	雷門
17	一松レストラン
18	郵便局

to the Japanese – the striptease – was introduced. A few clubs still operate in the area.

Unfortunately, Asakusa never quite recovered from the bombing at the end of WW II. Although the Sensō-ji Temple was rebuilt, other areas of Tokyo assumed Asakusa's role of pleasure district. Asakusa may be one of the few areas of Tokyo to have retained something of the spirit of Shitamachi, but the bright lights have shifted elsewhere – notably, to Shinjuku.

Sensō-ji Temple

The Sensō-ji Temple enshrines a golden image of the Buddhist Kannon, goddess of mercy, which according to legend was miraculously fished out of the nearby Sumidagawa River by two fishermen in 628. In time, a temple was built to house the image, which has remained on the spot ever since, through successive rebuildings of the temple.

If you approach the Sensō-ji Temple from Asakusa subway station, you'll enter through the Kaminari-mon Gate (Thunder Gate). The gate houses a couple of wild-looking gods: Fūjin, the god of wind, on the right; and Raijin, the god of thunder, on the left.

Straight ahead through the gate is Nakamise-dōri Ave, a street of shops within the temple precinct where everything, from tourist trinkets to genuine Edo-style crafts, is sold. There's even a shop selling wigs to be worn with a kimono. You can at least buy some of the *sembei* (crackers) that a few shops specialise in – you'll have to queue, though, as they are very popular with the Japanese.

Nakamise-dōri Ave leads to the main temple compound, but it's hard to say if the long surviving Kannon image really is inside, as you cannot see it – not that this stops a steady stream of worshippers making its way up the stairs to pay respect. In front of the temple is a large incense cauldron where people go to rub smoke against their bodies to ensure good health. If any part of your body (as far as modesty permits) is giving you trouble, you should give it particular attention when 'applying' the smoke.

The temple itself is, of course, a post-1945 concrete reproduction of the original, but the

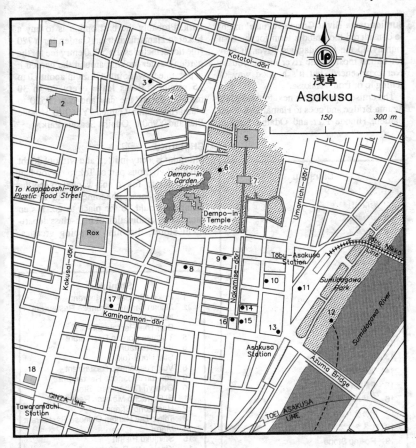

浅草
Asakusa

0   150   300 m

temple is not the reason people go there. It's the sheer energy of the place, with its gaudy, almost fairground atmosphere lingering from Asakusa's past, that is the real attraction.

Around Sensō-ji Temple

If you turn to the left when you reach the temple, you'll find the Hanayashiki Amusement Park on your right. It hasn't got a lot to recommend it, unless you are overcome by a hankering to risk your life on one of the fairly rickety-looking rides. Near the playground are many interesting little shops selling kimono, yukata and assorted traditional accessories. This area is all that's left of Asakusa's old cinema district, but the only cinemas remaining seem to restrict their screenings almost exclusively to Japanese pornography – at least they all carry the familiar lurid posters depicting naked women trussed up and hanging from the ceiling, their meek eyes casting plaintive looks at the tattooed torturers standing over them.

Sumidagawa River Cruise 'Cruise' might be considered too grand a term for the boat journey up the Sumidagawa River. It may not be the most scenic river cruise you've ever experienced, but it's a good way of getting to or from Asakusa.

The cruise departs from next to Asakusa's Azuma Bridge and goes to Hamarikyū-teien Garden, Hinode Pier and Odaiba Seaside

Park. Probably the best option is to buy a ticket to Hamarikyū-teien Garden for Y720 (the ticket includes the Y200 entry fee for the garden). After looking around the garden it is possible to walk into Ginza in about 10 to 15 minutes. Boats leave every 20 to 30 minutes during the day and cost Y520 to Hamarikyū-teien Garden, Y560 to Hinode Pier and Y960 to Odaiba Seaside Park.

SHINJUKU 新宿

Shinjuku is a city in itself and without doubt the most vigorous part of Tokyo. If you had only a day in Tokyo and wanted to see the modern Japanese phenomenon in action, Shinjuku would be the place to go. It's an incredible combination of high-class department stores, discount shopping arcades,

---

Shinjuku

1 北京レストラン
2 台南担仔麺
3 コマ劇場
4 バンタイレストラン
5 東海苑
6 いぶき
7 スターホテル
8 ボルガレストラン
9 とりじゅんレストラン
10 小田急百貨店
11 エルボラチョレストラン
12 花園神社
13 東京大飯店
14 丸井百貨店
15 Pit Inn 新宿
16 紀伊國屋書店
17 伊勢丹本店
18 イスタンブルレストラン
19 Rolling Stone
20 三越百貨店
21 My City 百貨店
22 小田急駅
23 京王百貨店
24 空港のリムジンバスの停
25 郵便局
26 ヨドバシカメラ
27 ハイウェイバスのタミナル
28 カメラのさくらや
29 ホテルサンルート
30 新宿ワシントンホテル

Shinjuku

1 Pekin Chinese Restaurant
2 Tainan Taami Taiwanese Restaurant
3 Koma Theatre
4 Ban Thai Restaurant
5 Tōkaien Korean Restaurant
6 Ibuki Restaurant
7 Star Hotel Tokyo
8 Volga Japanese Restaurant
9 Tori-jun Japanese Restaurant
10 Odakyū Department Store
11 El Borracho Mexican Restaurant
12 Hanazono Shrine
13 Tokyo Dai Hanten Chinese Restaurant
14 Marui
15 Shinjuku Pit Inn
16 Kinokuniya Bookshop
17 Isetan Department Store
18 Istanbul Turkish Restaurant
19 Rolling Stone
20 Mitsukoshi Department Store
21 My City Department Store
22 Odakyū Department Store & Station
23 Keio Department Store
24 Airport Limousine Bus Stop
25 Post Office
26 Yodobashi Camera
27 Highway Bus Terminal
28 Sakuraya Camera
29 Hotel Sun Route
30 Shinjuku Washington Hotel

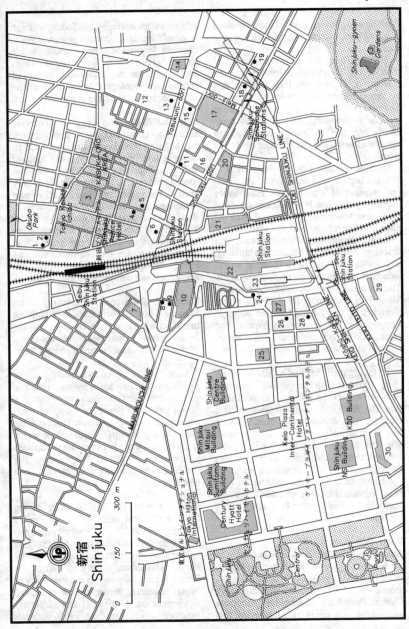

新宿
Shinjuku

flashing neon, government offices, stand-up drinking bars, hostess clubs and sleazy strip bars.

Shinjuku is such a huge business, commercial and entertainment centre that the place never seems to stop. It is calculated that up to two million people a day pass through Shinjuku station, making it one of the busiest stations in the world. The station is commonly regarded by foreign residents and visitors alike as the most confusing in the world.

On the western side of the station is Tokyo's highest concentration of skyscrapers, several of which have reasonably interesting interiors. It is the eastern side of the station, however, that is far and away the most lively part of Shinjuku to visit.

From Shinjuku station's eastern exit, your first sight will be of the Studio Alta building, with its huge video screen showing advertisements and video clips all day and night. The sheltered area underneath the screen is Shinjuku's most popular meeting place, though like the Almond coffee shop in Roppongi, it has become so popular that finding the person you're meeting is something of an ordeal – gaijin at least stand out in the crowd.

To the right of the Studio Alta building, about 100 metres up Shinjuku-dōri Ave and on your left, is the Kinokuniya bookshop (see the Books & Maps section of this chapter). The sheltered area here is also a popular meeting place. All around Kinokuniya there are shops selling discounted clothes and shoes. There are also some cheap second-hand camera shops on the backstreets. The area abounds in fast-food restaurants, cheap noodle shops, reasonably priced Western food, and some of the best Chinese food in Japan.

West Side

Shinjuku's west side does have a couple of attractions. If you're after camera equipment, it's home to Tokyo's largest camera stores: Yodobashi Camera and Sakuraya Camera. Yodobashi Camera has practically everything you could possibly want that relates to photography, including a huge stock of film, darkroom equipment, tripods, cameras, lenses and other accessories. It's prices are usually very reasonable. Yodobashi even has a limited selection of second-hand photographic equipment. The stores are behind the Keio department store.

Shinjuku NS Building If you're in the mood for a bit of eccentric high tech, the interior of this building is hollow, featuring a 1600 sq metre square from which you can look up and see sunlight coming in through the glass roof. Overhead, at 110 metres, is a 'sky bridge'. The square itself features a 29 metre pendulum clock that is listed by the *Guinness Book of Records* as the largest in the world. The 29th and 30th floors have a large number of restaurants, including a branch of the Spaghetti Factory. On the 5th floor, you can browse through the showrooms of the Japanese computer companies in the OA Centre.

Shinjuku Sumitomo Building The Sumitomo building bills itself as 'a building that's actually a city', a concept that the Japanese seem to find particularly appealing (Sunshine City in Ikebukuro is another 'city' building).

Like the Shinjuku NS building, the Sumitomo building has a hollow core. The ground floor and the basement feature a 'jewel palace' (a jewellery shopping mall) and a general shopping centre. There is a free observation platform on the 51st floor, which is a good deal when you consider the inflated prices being charged by Tokyo Tower and the Sunshine building for entry to their observatories.

Pentax Forum On the 1st floor of the Shinjuku Mitsui building is the Pentax Forum (tel 3348-2941), a must for photography buffs. The exhibition space has changing exhibits by photographers sponsored by Pentax. Undoubtedly, the best part of the Pentax Forum, however, is the vast array of Pentax cameras, lenses and other optical equipment on display. It is completely hands-on – you can snap away with the cameras and use the huge 1000 mm lenses to look through the windows of the neighbouring buildings. Admission is free, and it's open daily from 10.30 am to 7 pm.

East Side

Shinjuku's east side is an area to wander through and get lost in rather than an area in which to search out particular sights. There's plenty to see.

Kabuki-cho Tokyo's most notorious red-light district is the area next to the Seibu Shinjuku station, north of Yasukuni-dōri Ave. To get there, head north from the eastern exit of Shinjuku station; Kabuki-cho starts on the other side of the first major intersection you come to. It's still a safe area to stroll around, but most of what goes on is pretty much off limits to foreigners. There are, however, several strip clubs in the area that are frequented by foreigners, and gaijin males are likely to be approached by touts offering to take them to one. These places will have a straight Y3500 to Y4000 door charge and no other hidden costs. Further explorations of Kabuki-cho's seedy delights will require a Japanese escort or exceptional Japanese-language skills.

This is one of the more imaginative red-light areas in the world, with 'soaplands' (massage parlours), love hotels, no-pants coffee shops (it's the waitresses who doff their undies, not the customers), peep shows, so-called pink cabarets ('pink' is the Japanese equivalent of 'blue' in English), porno video booths and strip shows that involve audience participation. As you walk through streets lined with neon signs and crowded with drunken salarymen, high-pitched female voices wail out invitations to their establishments through distorting sound systems, and Japanese punks earn a few extra yen passing out advertisements for telephone clubs, where young Japanese men pay an hourly fee for a room, a telephone and a list of girls' telephone numbers: if the two like the sound of each other, they can make a date to meet.

Kabuki-cho is not wall-to-wall sex; there are also some very straight entertainment options, including cinemas and some of the best restaurants in Tokyo.

Shinjuku-gyoen Park This park is one of Tokyo's best escapes, with a Japanese garden, a French garden, a hothouse containing tropical plants and, near the hothouse, a pond containing giant carp. Admission is Y200, and it's open Tuesday to Sunday from 9 am to 4.30 pm.

IKEBUKURO 池袋

Poor old Ikebukuro. Although it's home to the world's largest department store (Seibu), the tallest building in Asia (the Sunshine City building) and the second busiest station in Tokyo, it remains unmistakably déclassé. It is almost like a Shinjuku waiting to happen, but for some reason the bright lights and the revellers never arrive. Ikebukuro's few sights are on the eastern side of the station. The western side is notable only for a sleazy red-light area and some discount clothes shops.

Sunshine City

What a monstrosity! Billed as a city in a building, this 'workers' paradise', as it's referred to in the promotional literature, is basically 60 floors of office space and shopping malls, with a few overpriced cultural and entertainment options thrown in. If you've got Y620 to burn, you can take a lift (apparently the fastest in the world) to the observatory on the 60th floor and gaze out on Tokyo's murky skyline.

Not in the Sunshine City building itself but in the Bunka Kaikan building of Sunshine City is the Ancient Orient Museum. Admission is Y400. It's open Tuesday to Sunday from 10 am to 5 pm and is strictly for those with a special interest in ancient odds and ends such as coins and beads.

Seibu Department Store

Seibu has branches all over Tokyo, but the Ikebukuro branch is the biggest. You can easily spend an entire afternoon just wandering around the basement food floor sampling

Ikebukuro

1 Kimi Ryokan
2 Post Office
3 Cinema Rosa
4 Sumitomo Bank
5 Horindo Bookshop
6 Marui Department Store
7 McDonald's
8 Western Exit
9 Tōbu Hope Centre
10 Hotel Metropolitan
11 Wave Record Shop
12 Seibu Department Store
13 Eastern Exit
14 Hotel Sun Route
15 Hotel Grand Business
16 Hotel Plaza Inn Ikebukuro
17 Tōkyū Hands Store
18 Sunshine City Building
19 Prince Hotel

Ikebukuro

1 貴美旅館
2 郵便局
3 シネマロサ
4 住友銀行
5 芳林堂書店
6 丸井百貨店
7 マクドナルド
8 西口
9 東武ホープセンタ
10 ホテルメトロポリタン
11 Wave
12 西武百貨店
13 東口
14 ホテルサンルート
15 ホテルグランドビジネス
16 ホテルプラザインイケブクロ
17 東急ハンズ
18 サンシャインビル
19 プリンスホテル

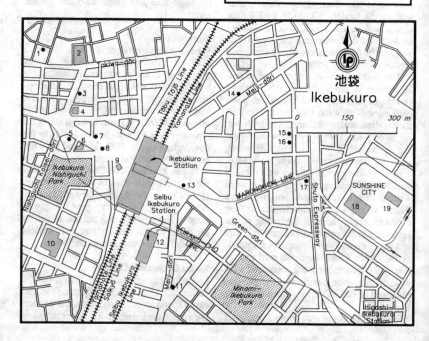

池袋
Ikebukuro

the little titbits on offer. The 12th floor has an art museum and the top floor is restaurant city, with something like 50 restaurants, many of them with great lunch specials. Across the road from the Seibu annex is a Wave record shop. Seibu is open daily except Thursday from 10 am to 6 pm.

Sezon Museum of Art In the annex of the Seibu department store is the Sezon Museum of Art, which has changing art exhibits, usually of a very high standard.

AROUND IKEBUKURO 池袋の附近
Rikugi-en Garden

Just three stops from Ikebukuro, near the JR Komagome station on the Yamanote line, is the Rikugi-en Garden, a very pleasant place for a walk, with landscaped views unfolding at every turn of the pathways that crisscross the grounds. The garden is rich in literary associations; its name is taken from the six principles of Japanese *waka* poetry (poems of 31 syllables), and the garden itself recreates in its landscaping famous scenes from Chinese and Japanese literature (good luck finding them). The garden was established in the late 17th century by Yanagisawa Yoshiyasu, and after falling into disuse was restored by the founder of the Mitsubishi group, Iwasaki Yataro. Admission is Y200, and it is open Tuesday to Sunday from 9 am to 5 pm.

HARAJUKU & SHIBUYA 原宿、渋谷

Harajuku and Shibuya are the up-and-coming fashion centres of Tokyo. Harajuku is probably somewhat younger in its orientation than Shibuya, but it's difficult to pin the area down, as there are all kinds of surprises in the backstreets and in the basements of unlikely buildings. Harajuku has many shops catering to Tokyo teenagers on the lookout for fashion alternatives – second-hand, punk and '50s and '60s fashions to name a few possibilities. Shibuya, on the other hand, is like Ginza with a bit more energy. The atmosphere there is vibrant but more mainstream than that in Harajuku. It's where young fashionable Japanese go to do some shopping and hang out.

Harajuku

You can go to Shibuya any time, but the day to visit Harajuku is Sunday, when Tokyo's subcultures put themselves on public display in the nearby Yoyogi-kōen Park, performing anything from avant-garde theatre to Sex Pistols-style punk.

The activity starts at 1 pm, when the road through the park is closed to traffic. Just five minutes from the park, on Takeshita-dōri, are the shops that serve as the source of the bizarre fashions you see in Harajuku. The streets can be like rush hour on the Yamanote line, but it is still worth exploring Takeshita-dōri and the surrounding area on a Sunday.

Late on Friday and Saturday nights, you can see another side of Japanese youth culture, when car enthusiasts parade up and down Kōen-dōri between NHK and Shibuya station.

Meiji-jingū Shrine The Meiji-jingū Shrine is without a doubt Tokyo's, if not Japan's, most splendid Shinto shrine. It is difficult to believe that it is so close to the crowds in Harajuku. Completed in 1920, the shrine was built in memory of Emperor Meiji and Empress Shōken, under whose rule Japan ended its long isolation from the outside world. Unfortunately, like much else in Tokyo, the shrine was destroyed in the bombing at the end of WW II. Rebuilding was completed in 1958.

The Meiji-jingū Shrine might be a reconstruction of the original, but unlike so many of Japan's postwar reconstructions, it has been rebuilt with all the features of a Shinto shrine preserved. The shrine itself was built with Japanese cypress, while the cypress for the huge torii gates came from Ali Shan in Taiwan.

Meiji-jingū-gyoen Park The English explanation on the entry ticket to the park points out that this park was originally part of the garden of a 'feudal load' and that the garden itself has 'spots in it'. Don't let this put you

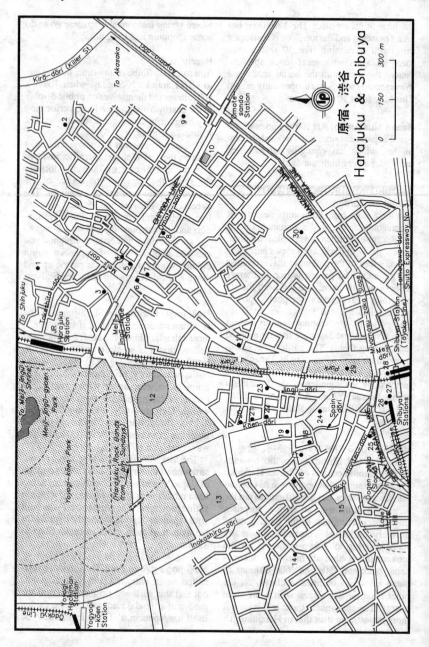

原宿、渋谷

Harajuku & Shibuya

	Harajuku & Shibuya
1	Tōgō-jinja Shrine
2	Myoen-ji Temple
3	Ota Memorial Art Museum
4	Kiku Japanese Restaurant
5	Haagen Dazs Ice Cream
6	Lotteria
7	Oh God Bar
8	Oriental Bazaar
9	Zenko-ji Temple
10	Hanae Mori Building
11	Crocodile Live House
12	Yoyogi National Stadium
13	NHK Broadcasting Centre
14	Kanze Nō-gakudō Theatre
15	Tōkyū Department Store
16	Tower Records
17	Tōkyū Hands Store
18	Parco Part III
19	Parco Part II
20	Pizza Hut
21	Siam Thai Restaurant
22	Tobacco & Salt Museum
23	Tepco Electric Energy Museum
24	Seibu Department Store
25	109 Building
26	Hachikō Statue
27	Tōkyū Department Store
28	Tōkyū Department Store (East)
29	Shibuya Tōkyū Inn
30	Children's Castle

	Harajuku & Shibuya
1	東郷神社
2	みよえん寺
3	太田記念美術館
4	きくレストラン
5	ハーゲンダーズ
6	ロッテリア
7	オーゴドバー
8	オリエンタルバザー
9	ぜんこ寺
10	ハナエモリビル
11	Crocodile ライブハウス
12	代々木ナショナルスティデアム
13	NHK 放送センター
14	観世能楽堂
15	東急百貨店東横店
16	タワーレコード
17	東急ハンズ
18	パルコパート3
19	パルコパート2
20	Pizza Hut
21	サイアム レストラン
22	たばこと塩の博物館
23	電力館
24	西武百貨店
25	109 ビル
26	ハチコ像
27	東急百貨店
28	東急百貨店(東)
29	渋谷東急イン
30	こどもの城

off, however: the park has some very peaceful walks and is almost deserted on weekdays. It's particularly beautiful in June, when the irises are in bloom, but entry is a somewhat steep Y400. The entrance is on the left before you reach the shrine; the garden is open daily from 9 am to 4.30 pm.

Meiji-jingū Treasure Museum As you approach the Meiji-jingū Shrine, there are so many signs indicating the way to the treasure museum that you tend to feel obligated to go there. In fact, the collection of items from the lives of the emperor and empress is pretty unexciting. It includes official garments, portraits and other imperial odds and ends. Admission is Y200, and it is open daily from 9 am to 4.30 pm, except on the third Friday of each month, when it is closed.

Yoyogi-kōen Park The park has nothing in particular to recommend it, apart from the Sunday afternoon crowds of Japanese youth, rock bands, mime troupes and assorted alternatives to mainstream culture. There's no need to be coy about photography; everyone goes there to be seen, and being photographed is like achieving momentary star status.

Ota Memorial Art Museum The Ota Memorial Art Museum (Ota Kinen Bijutsukan) has an excellent collection of ukiyo-e woodblock prints and offers a good opportunity to see works by Japanese masters of the art, including Hiroshige. To get there, walk away from the JR Harajuku station down Omotesando (the big boulevard opposite the entrance to the Meiji-jingū Shrine) and take the first turn to your left. The museum is a few doors down and is open daily from 10.30 am to 5.30 pm, except from the 25th to the end of the month, when it is closed. Entry is very expensive at Y800.

Shibuya

Shibuya is one of the most trendy shopping areas in Tokyo, but its appeal is predominantly to the young – it's one of those areas in Tokyo notable for an absence of old people. It's not an area rich in sights, but there's plenty to see if you take the time to explore.

The best place to start is Shibuya station. Take the Hachikō exit to see the bronze statue of the dog Hachikō. The statue is Shibuya's most popular meeting place, although as with other Tokyo meeting places, its popularity sometimes makes it less than an ideal spot to meet someone. The story goes that Hachikō waited for his master every day at the railway station for 10 years, unable to come to terms with the fact that his master had died one day at work and wouldn't be coming home again...ever. It's a touching tale, and the dog was much admired throughout Japan for its uncompromising loyalty, a quality that still plays a big part in Japanese social life.

Opposite Hachikō, roads radiate in a number of directions. If you take the largest of the roads, cross at the first set of traffic lights and bear left at the second, you come to the enormous Seibu department store complex. On the first small street on your left is the Wave record shop and Loft, also run by Seibu. Loft is like a youth-oriented department store – lots of junk and interesting oddments.

Further up the road from Seibu are the Parco I, II and III department stores (three branches), touted by some as the ultimate in shopping splendour and convenience in Tokyo. The upper floors of all the stores provide some great lunch specials.

Next is Tōkyū Hands, a wonderful store full of do-it-yourself and hobby equipment, hardware, toys and bizarre oddments.

If you continue away from Parco and turn right at the end of the road, on your left is Tower Records, another great record shop and the place to pick up imported US CDs.

Near Parco III, look for Spain-dōri, so named because many of the shops in it have, independently, adopted a Spanish flavour.

Love Hotel Hill Take the main road to the left of the Hachikō plaza, and at the top of the hill, on the sidestreets that run off the main road, is a concentration of love hotels catering to all tastes. The buildings alone are interesting, as they represent a broad range of architectural pastiches, from miniature gothic castles to Middle-Eastern temples. It's OK to wander in and take a look. Just inside the entrance there should be a screen with illuminated pictures of the various rooms available. You select a room by pressing the button underneath a room's picture and proceeding to the cashier. This is not an area for cheap love hotels, however. Prices for an all-night stay start at around Y7000.

Tobacco & Salt Museum The Tobacco & Salt Museum (Tobako To Shio No Hakubutsukan) is another in Japan's long list of quirky museums. There are diagrams and exhibits explaining the history of tobacco use and production (salt gets the same treatment) and a display of cigarette packets from around the world.

There's not much in the way of English explanations, but you get a useful English pamphlet when you pay your Y100 admission fee. There's a cheap coffee shop on the ground floor. The museum is open Tuesday to Sunday from 10 am to 6 pm.

Tepco Electric Energy Museum The Tepco Electric Energy Museum (Tokyo

Denryoku Enerugiikan) is the building in Jingū-dōri with the bulbous silver roof, but it's of no real interest. There are no English explanations. Admission is free, and it's open Thursday to Tuesday from 10.30 am to 6.30 pm.

AKASAKA　赤坂

East of Shibuya and Harajuku and north of Roppongi is exclusive Akasaka, with expensive restaurants and clubs and a thriving cultural scene. Near the Akasaka-Mitsuke subway station are the Suntory Art Museum, which is open Tuesday to Sunday from 10 am to 5 pm (to 7 pm on Friday), and the Sannō Hie-jinja Shrine.

Aoyama-dōri Ave leads from there to Shibuya, running beside the Akasaka Palace grounds. The Sōgetsu Kaikan building is, believe it or not, devoted to flower arrangement. A little further along, beside the Aoyama-Itchome subway station, is the Honda showroom, in which classic Honda Grand Prix motorcycles and Formula I cars are displayed. Near Gaien-mae subway station is Kirā-dōri, better known as 'Killer St', the location of fashionable boutiques and restaurants. The Noh Institute and the Nezu Art Museum (see the Museums & Galleries section later in this chapter) are near Omote-sando subway station.

ROPPONGI　六本木

Playground of the rich, the beautiful and hordes of lecherous off-duty English teachers, Roppongi comes to life with the setting of the sun. There's no reason to go there by day, but by night it is the glittering disco capital of Tokyo. Actually, the way you feel about the whole Roppongi scene is going to depend a lot on how you feel about discos and the kind of crowds they attract. See the Places to Eat and Entertainment sections for more information on Roppongi. There are, however, some attractions in the vicinity of Roppongi that can be visited before nightfall and the onset of disco fever, and these are discussed in the following section.

AROUND ROPPONGI　六本木の附近
Tokyo Tower

This Eiffel Tower lookalike is really more impressive from a distance; up close the 330 metre tower is the familiar tourist rip-off. The Grand Observation Platform (Y750) is only 150 metres high; if you want to peer through the smog at Tokyo's uninspiring skyline from 250 metres up, it will cost you a further Y520 to get to the Special Observation Platform. The tower also features an overpriced aquarium (Y800), a wax museum (Y750), the Holographic Mystery Zone (Y300) and showrooms.

The tower is a fair trudge from Roppongi: take the Hibiya subway line one stop to Kamiya-cho station. The observation platforms are open daily from 9 am to 6 pm. They close at 8 pm from 16 March to 15 November, except in August, when they are open until 9 pm.

Zōjō-ji Temple

Behind the Tokyo Tower is this former family temple of the Tokugawas. It has had a calamitous history, even by Tokyo's standards, having been rebuilt three times in recent history, most recently in 1974. It's still a pleasant place to visit if you're in the vicinity of the tower. The main gates date from 1605 and are included among the nation's 'Important Cultural Properties'. On the grounds there is a large collection of statues of Jizō, the patron saint of travellers and the souls of departed children.

OTHER ATTRACTIONS
Parks & Gardens

Although the Japanese purport to be ardent lovers of nature and see this as one of the qualities that distinguishes them from other races, Tokyo, like many other Japanese cities, is not particularly green and has a shortage of park space. If you've been hitting the bitumen and haven't seen a tree for days, try the following parks.

Hibiya-kōen Park This park is not one of Tokyo's best but it is close to Ginza and makes a reasonably quiet retreat from the boutiques and department stores.

Roppongi

1. Hotel Ibis
2. Haiyū-za Building
3. Doutor (Coffee Shop)
4. Tainan Taami Taiwanese Restaurant
5. Square Building (Birdland & Java Jive Nightclubs)
6. Lexington Queen Disco
7. Maggie's Revenge
8. Charleston Bar
9. Déjà Vu Bar
10. Henry Africa Bar
11. Revolving Sushi Shop
12. Jazz Puis After 6
13. Pips Disco
14. Mister Donut
15. Roy Building
16. Hard Rock Café
17. Spago's Californian Restaurant
18. Almond
19. Serendip Bookshop
20. Raja Indian Restaurant
21. Meidiya International Supermarket
22. Moti Restaurant
23. Wave Building
24. Bengawan Solo Indonesian Restaurant
25. Bodaiju Vegetarian Restaurant

Koishikawa Kōraku-en Garden Next to the Kōraku-en amusement park and baseball stadium, this has to be one of the nicest and least-visited (by foreigners at least) gardens in Tokyo. Established in the mid-17th century, it incorporates elements of Chinese and Japanese landscaping. Admission is Y200, and it is open Tuesday to Sunday from 9 am to 4.30 pm.

Hamarikyū-teien Garden This is the Detached Palace Garden. It can be combined either with a visit to Ginza or, via the Sumidagawa River Cruise, with a visit to Asakusa (see the Asakusa section of this chapter). The garden has walks, ponds and teahouses. Admission is Y200, and it is open Tuesday to Sunday from 9 am to 4.30 pm.

Museums & Galleries

There's an enormous number of museums and galleries in Tokyo. In many cases their exhibits are small and specialised and the admission charges prohibitively expensive for travellers with a limited budget and a tight schedule. For an up-to-date and more complete listing, get hold of the TIC's *Museums & Art Galleries* pamphlet.

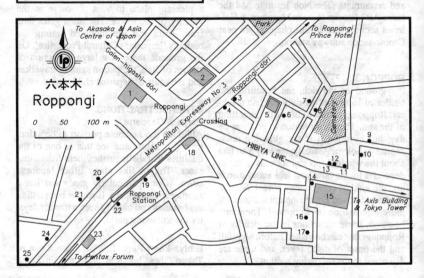

六本木
Roppongi

0   50   100 m

To Akasaka & Asia Centre of Japan

To Roppongi Prince Hotel

Gaien-higashi-dōri

Roppongi-dōri

Metropolitan Expressway No 3

Roppongi Crossing

HIBIYA LINE

Roppongi Station

To Axis Building & Tokyo Tower

To Pentax Forum

Nezu Art Museum This well-known collection of Japanese art includes paintings, calligraphy and sculpture, and there are also Chinese and Korean art exhibits, and teahouses where tea ceremonies are performed. From Omote-sando subway station, walk down Omote-sando away from Harajuku. Turn right at the end of the road and look for the museum on the left. Admission is Y550, and it is open Tuesday to Sunday from 9.30 am to 4.30 pm.

Bridgestone Art Museum Contemporary art by Japanese and European artists is displayed in this museum, five minutes from Tokyo, Nihombashi and Edobashi stations.

Admission is Y550, and it is open Tuesday to Sunday from 10 am to 5.30 pm.

Sumō Museum The Kokugikan Sumō Stadium, where the museum is located, is a hop, skip and a jump from Ryōgoku station on the Sobu line. Admission is free, and it is open Monday to Friday from 9.30 am to 4.30 pm.

Japanese Sword Museum For corporate warriors with a hankering for Japan's samurai past, the Sword Museum has a collection of over 6000 swords. Entry is Y550, and it is open Tuesday to Sunday from 9 am to 4 pm. The nearest station is Sangubashi station on the Odakyū line.

Lookouts
The expensive lookouts in the Tokyo Tower and the Sunshine building are covered in the previous Roppongi and Ikebukuro sections. Less well known and considerably cheaper (it's free) is the view from the 36th floor of the Kasumigaseki building in Kasumigaseki. Even a look through a telescope there is free.

Amusement Parks
Tokyo Disneyland Only the Japanese signs reveal that you're a long way from Orange County; Tokyo Disneyland is a near-perfect replica of the Anaheim, California, original. A few rides may be in slightly different locations, but basically you turn left from the entrance to the African Jungle, head straight on to Fantasyland or turn right to Tomorrowland.

It's open varying hours (usually from 9 am to 7 pm at least, but phone 3366-5600 for details) every day, except for about a dozen days a year (most of them in January) when it is closed all day. A variety of tickets are available, including an all-inclusive 'passport' which gives you unlimited access to all the rides for Y4440 (children aged 12 to 17, Y4000; those aged 4 to 11, Y3000). As at the original Disneyland, there are often long queues at popular rides (30 minutes to one hour is normal). Crowds are usually lighter in the mornings and heavier on weekends and holidays.

To get to Tokyo Disneyland, take the Tōzai subway line to Urayasu station. Follow the 'direct bus to Disneyland 340 m' sign out of the station. A shop-lined laneway leads to the Disneyland bus station. A ticket on this bus costs Y200. Alternatively, take the Yūraku-cho subway line to Shin-kiba station and the JR Keiyo line to Mahihama station, which is right in front of Disneyland's main gate. A variety of shuttle buses also run from Tokyo (Y600), Ueno (Y600) and Yokohama (Y1000) stations, from Narita (Y2000) and Haneda (Y700) airports and from the various nearby Disneyland hotels.

Kōraku-en Amusement Park Next to Kōraku-en subway station on the Marunouchi subway line is an amusement park that gets good reports from some travellers. It's nowhere near as big or glossy as Disneyland, but that's part of the attraction. The roller coaster is the popular ride. The park is open Tuesday to Sunday from 10 am to 7 pm.

FESTIVALS

Tokyo has many festivals worth seeing if you're in town at the right time of year.

Ganjitsu (New Year's Day)
1 January. This is the one day in the year (well, the night before is, anyway) that the trains run all night. It is customary for Japanese to visit Buddhist and Shinto shrines to pray for luck in the coming year. For a look at the action, head to Meiji-jingū Shrine, Sensō-ji Temple or the Yasukuni-jinja Shrine. The day after New Year's Day is one of the two occasions each year when the Imperial Palace is open to the public and the imperial couple display themselves before adoring crowds. Enter the inner gardens by the Nijū-bashi Bridge between 9 am and 3.30 pm.

Dezome-shiki
6 January. Firemen dressed in Edo-period costumes put on a parade involving acrobatic stunts on top of bamboo ladders. The parade takes place on Chūō-dōri Ave in Harumi from 10 am onwards.

Seijin-no-hi (Adult's Day)
15 January. Those who turn 20 get a national

holiday for reaching the age when they are legally able to drink and smoke. A traditional display of archery is held at Meiji-jingū Shrine.

Setsubun
3 or 4 February. Throughout Japan, beans are scattered from the inside of a building outwards, which is the direction it is hoped the 'devils' will take, and from the outside inwards, which is the direction that good luck is meant to take. In Tokyo, ceremonies are held at Zōjō-ji Temple, Kanda-jinja Shrine and Sensō-ji Temple. Sensō-ji Temple offers the added attraction of a classical dance.

Hari-kuyō
Early February. Check with the TIC for the dates of this typically quirky Japanese festival held for pins and needles that have been broken in the preceding year. At Sensō-ji Temple, women lay their pins and needles to rest by 'burying' them in tōfu and radishes.

Hina Matsuri (Doll Festival)
3 March. Throughout Japan, girls display miniature imperial figures on shelves covered with red cloth. From about mid-February onwards, a doll fair is held in Asakusabashi – check with the TIC for exact details.

Kinryū No Mai
18 March. A golden dragon dance is held at Sensō-ji Temple to celebrate the discovery of the golden image of Kannon that now rests there. Two or three dances are performed during the day.

Hanami (Blossom Viewing)
Early to mid-April. This is one festival you can't help hearing about if you happen to be in Japan when the blossoms come out. Interest in the progress of the sakura (cherry blossoms) verges on a national obsession, with panoramic views of famous cherry blossom viewing parks and close ups of the blooms themselves taking up as much TV viewing time as major sports do in other parts of the world. In Tokyo, *the* place to go for hanami is Ueno-kōen Park. Other famous spots around Tokyo include Yasukuni-jinja Shrine and Koishikawa Kōraku-en Garden.

Hana Matsuri (Buddha's Birthday)
8 April. Celebrations are held at Buddhist temples all over Japan. In Tokyo, celebrations take place at Sensō-ji Temple and Zōjō-ji Temple, among others.

Ueno Tōshō-gū Taisai
17 April. Ceremonies, traditional music and dance are held at Ueno's Tōshō-gū Shrine in memory of Tokugawa Ieyasu.

Kanda Matsuri
Mid-May. This festival is held on odd-numbered years on the Saturday and Sunday closest to 15 May and is a traditional Edo festival that cele-

brates a Tokugawa battle victory. A whole range of activities take place at Kanda-jinja Shrine.

Sanja Matsuri

May. On the 3rd Friday, Saturday and Sunday of May, at Sensō-ji Temple in Asakusa, up to 100 mikoshi carried by participants dressed in traditional clothes are paraded through the area in the vicinity of the temple.

Sannō-sai

10 to 16 June. Street stalls, traditional music and dancing, and processions of mikoshi are all part of this Edo Festival, held at Sannō Hie-jinja Shrine, near Akasaka-Mitsuke subway station.

O Bon

13 to 15 July. This festival takes place at a time when, according to Buddhist belief, the dead briefly revisit the earth. Dances are held and lanterns lighted in their memory. In Tokyo *bon odori* dances are held in different locations around town.

Sumidagawa Hanabi Taikai

Last Saturday of July. The biggest fireworks display of its kind in Tokyo is held on the Sumidagawa River in Asakusa.

Tsukudajima Sumiyoshi-jinja Matsuri

Sunday closest to 7 July. There are several three-day festivals that take place in Tokyo every three years. In this one, activities centre around the Sumiyoshi-jinja Shrine, with dragon dances and mikoshi parades among other things. The next festival will take place in 1992. The Sumiyoshi-jinja Shrine is across the Sumidagawa River (via the Tsukuda-ōhashi Bridge) from Tsukiji subway station on the Hibiya line.

Fukagawa Hachiman Matsuri

15 August. In this, another tri-annual, three day Edo festival, foolhardy mikoshi-bearers charge through eight km of frenzied crowds who dash water on them. The action takes place at Tomioka Hachiman-gū Shrine, next to Monzen-Naka-cho subway station on the Tōzai line. The next festival will be held in 1992.

Ningyō-kuyō

25 September. Childless couples make offerings of dolls to Kannon in the hope that she will bless them with children. More interesting for spectators is the ceremonial burning by priests of all the dolls that remain from previous years. It takes place at Kiyomizu-dō Temple in Ueno Park from 2 pm to 3.30 pm.

Furusato Tokyo Matsuri (Metropolitan Citizen's Day)

First Saturday and Sunday in October. A wide range of activities are held at different locations around town. In particular, check out Asakusa's Sensō-ji Temple and Ueno-kōen Park.

Oeshiki

12 October. This festival is held in commemoration of Nichiren (1222 to 1282), founder of the Nichiren sect of Buddhism. On the night of the 12th, people bearing large lanterns and paper flower arrangements make their way to Hommon-ji Temple. The nearest station is Ikegami station on the Tōkyū Ikegami line.

Kanda Furuihon Ichi

27 October to 3 November. A huge sale of second-hand books is held in the Jimbō-cho area. There are 30% reductions on books. Go to the Jimbō-cho intersection and start your explorations there (see the Books & Maps section of this chapter).

Meiji Reidaisai

30 October to 3 November. A series of events is held at Meiji-jingū Shrine in commemoration of the Meiji emperor's birthday. Particularly interesting to watch are displays of horseback archery in traditional clothes. Other events include classical music and dance.

Shichi-go-san (Seven-Five-Three Festival)

15 November. As the title implies, this is for children aged seven, five and three. The children (boys aged five and girls aged three and seven) make a colourful sight, as they are dressed in traditional clothes and taken to different shrines around town, notably Meiji-jingū Shrine, Yasukuni-jinja Shrine and Sannō Hie-jinja Shrine.

Gishi-sai

14 December. The day's events commemorate the deaths of the 47 rōnin (masterless samurai) who committed seppuku after avenging the death of their master. The activities involve a parade of warriors to Sengaku-ji Temple – the rōnin's burial place – and a memorial service from 7.30 pm onwards. The temple is directly west of Sengaku-ji subway station on the TOEI Asakusa line.

PLACES TO STAY

Accommodation in Tokyo tends to be expensive. Central Tokyo would be an ideal place to be based but the only possibilities in that part of town are five-star hotels. If your budget doesn't reach five-star levels you can find cheaper accommodation with easy access to central Tokyo by staying somewhere on the Yamanote line.

Around the line, business and entertainment districts like Shinjuku or Ikebukuro will have capsule hotels from around Y3000 per night or business hotel singles from Y5000 to Y6000 per night. For the same price, a couple could even find a room in a love hotel from 10 or 11 pm.

The cheapest short-term accommodation will be in a youth hostel, from around Y2000 per person. For long-term visitors, there are also gaijin houses, a form of accommodation restricted to Tokyo, Kyoto and Osaka. In Tokyo, they're scattered all over the city, almost always outside the Yamanote line and often a good 30 to 40 minutes away from central Tokyo. Gaijin houses are cheap but are generally only an option for long-term visitors.

For those who'd like a taste of traditional Japan, there are a number of ryokan. As elsewhere in Japan, they tend to be divided into those that are reasonably priced and accustomed to foreigners and those that cost the earth and turn foreigners away if they do not have an introduction. Ueno and Asakusa – older areas with their own tourist attractions as well as direct subway connections with central Tokyo – have a number of ryokan that can cope with foreign guests. Other ryokan are scattered around town and can even be found in bustling commercial centres like Shinjuku. Prices can often be very reasonable, from around Y4500 per person.

Other traditional accommodation options, such as minshuku, are more rustic and are not available in Tokyo. There are, however, some shukubō (temple lodgings) available out of town for those who want to offset the frantic rhythms of the big city with the calming influence of a Buddhist temple. Staying in a temple requires a high degree of sensitivity to the rules and etiquette that prevail, and many temple lodgings refuse to accept foreigners on the grounds of bad experiences in the past.

Places to Stay – bottom end

The accommodation situation in Tokyo is not what it is in other cities around Asia. If you're happy spending from Y5000 to Y6000 or more a night for a single room, there's no shortage of accommodation but things are definitely harder if you are travelling on a budget.

The problem for shoestring travellers is

that Japan is *the* place in Asia in which to stay while making a few bucks before hitting the road again. Most people fly into Tokyo and stay there until they have enough money to leave. Unfortunately for other travellers, this influx of long-term gaijin means that a lot of Tokyo's longer-term budget accommodation is booked out for weeks or even months at a time.

Youth Hostels The cheapest short-term accommodation options in Tokyo are the youth hostels in Iidabashi and Yoyogi. The only problem is the usual youth hostel stuff – you have to be out of the building between 10 am and 3 pm (10 am and 5 pm at Yoyogi) and you have to be home by 10 pm in the evening – a real drawback in a city like Tokyo. Finally, there's a three night limit to your stay and the hostels can often be booked right out during peak holiday periods.

If you can handle these drawbacks, the common consensus is that the *Yoyogi Youth Hostel* is the better option of the two. The Iidabashi branch might be a showcase for Japan's youth hostels (it's on the 18th floor of a towering office block, giving you great views of Tokyo), but the staff and the general atmosphere are much more businesslike and officious.

The *Tokyo International Youth Hostel* (Iidabashi) (tel 3235-1107) doesn't require that you be a member but does ask that you book ahead and provide some identification (a passport will do) when you arrive. To get there, exit from Iidabashi station (either JR or subway) and look for the tallest building in sight (it's long, thin and glass fronted). There is a basic charge of Y2250 per person per night, and a sleeping sheet costs Y150 for three nights. The Narita Airport TIC has a step-by-step instruction sheet on how to get to the hostel from the airport most cheaply.

The *Yoyogi Youth Hostel* (tel 3467-9163) requires that you be a youth hostel member to stay. There are no meals available, but there are cooking facilities. To get there, take the Odakyū line to Sangubashi station and walk towards the Meiji-jingū Shrine gardens. The hostel is enclosed in a fenced compound – not a former prison camp but the National Olympics Memorial Youth Centre – in building No 14. Staff may let you exceed the three night limit if it is not crowded.

Ryokan & Other Budget Accommodation

The *Kimi Ryokan* (tel 3971-3766) deserves a special mention in any listing of Tokyo's budget accommodation. The Kimi is in Ikebukuro, which isn't a bad location from which to see Tokyo: 10 minutes from Shinjuku; 20 minutes from Ginza. The rooms are cheap by Tokyo standards, nicely designed in Japanese style (tatami mats and futons) and the place is friendly, clean and

relaxed about the hours you keep – just remember to take your room key with you if you're going to be out after 11.30 pm.

The Kimi lounge area is a good meeting place, with an excellent notice board; the Kimi bulletin board has metamorphosed into the nearby Kimi Information Centre. Some of the people who come to the lounge are actually staying elsewhere, but the Kimi lounge is still the place in which to hang out and discover what's new in town. If you're planning to stay at the Kimi, phone and book a few weeks ahead, as there's nearly always a waiting list. Alternatively, arrive early in the morning and wait for someone to leave.

To get to the Kimi, turn left at the eastern exit of Ikebukuro station, go to the police box at the corner of the station and say 'Kimi

---

The Kimi Ryokan

The Kimi Ryokan is rapidly turning into a Tokyo institution; a refuge for all kinds of enterprising characters looking for an opportunity to get a bit-part in the Tokyo success story. Like the collection of characters gathered together in a hotel at the moment of a crime in a detective story, these were people with mysterious backgrounds who all seemed to be living an alibi – the stories just seemed too incredible to be true.

There was the Paris-based Canadian reporter who had met so many Japanese reporters covering the events in Germany and Eastern Europe that he had decided to come and have a look at the place they were all coming from. On the top floor was a tall, lanky ex-racing driver who seemed to spend all his time at expensive lunches and late-night drinking sessions trying to convince well-heeled Japanese to buy European sports cars. There was the girl from Harvard (the illustrious institution's name was emblazoned across every article of clothing in her possession just in case we should forget) who had come to lecture the Japanese on child abuse. And a mysterious importer of quail eggs seemed to spend a lot of time skulking in the meeting room until he went crazy and had to be dragged off by the police.

The bottom floor of the Kimi was enlivened by the arrival of a group of Black rap dancers from New York. They were slowly busking their way around Asia and were a great source of graphic information as to the sexual mores of the cultures they had spent some time observing. Another musician from New York who had also worked as a Wall St trader turned up with a demo tape, long hair and a trendy suit, an image that, he patiently explained to the doubters among us, was going to take Japanese rock audiences by storm. Within a week his hair was shorn and he was wearing the suit to an office where he commenced a career rewriting business documents.

The mysterious Mr Brittanica, freelance English-Japanese translator who gave a different name depending on the nationality of the person talking to him, could be heard one night conversing in some obscure dialect of the upper Ukraine, the next talking French, and the next regaling the rotund importer of fabrics from Bombay in Hindi. Meanwhile the Englishman with an MA in child psychology and a huge collection of gaijin-sized condoms stumbled home in the early hours of the morning in ever-worsening states of lassitude after fruitless nights on the prowl.

Chris Taylor ■

Ryokan' to the policeman on duty. He'll give you a map. Prices range from Y2600 to Y3500 for singles, from Y5000 to Y5500 for doubles and from Y5500 to Y6000 for twins.

The *Asia Centre of Japan* (tel 3402-6111), near Aoyama-Itchome subway station on the Ginza line, is a popular option in the upper-budget category. This is another place that attracts many long-term stayers, and even though it's a lot bigger than the Kimi, it's still often fully booked. The station is under the easily recognisable Aoyama Twin Tower building on Aoyama-dōri Ave. Walk past the building towards Akasaka-Mitsuke, turn right (towards Roppongi) and the Asia Centre is a short walk up the third street on the left. Rooms have pay TVs, and singles cost Y4430, or Y5240 with bathroom. Twins cost from Y5600 to Y6700, or from Y8900 to Y9400 with bathroom. Doubles cost from Y6900 to Y8200 with bathroom. Triples cost from Y9450 to Y11,550.

There are a number of less popular but still good-value alternatives around town. If you want to be based in Shinjuku, the *Inabaso Ryokan* (tel 3341-9581) has plenty of foreigners. It provides breakfast (Japanese or continental) and the rooms include bathrooms, TVs and fridges. Take the eastern exit of Shinjuku station and follow Yasukuni-dōri Ave. Cross the two major intersections – the Inabaso Ryokan is just around the corner, on the left-hand side of the seventh street on your left. Prices for singles/doubles are Y4400/8000; triples cost Y10,500.

An easy place to get to from Narita Airport is the *Suzuki Ryokan* (tel 3821-4944) in Nippori. Some of the rooms there have private bathrooms and all include TVs. Take the Keisei line from Narita and get off at Nippori station, the last stop before Ueno station. Walking in the direction of Ueno, go to the end of the station and turn right. After you've crossed the tracks straight ahead, there's a flight of stairs that takes you up to a road. The Suzuki Ryokan is a few doors down on the right – look for the English sign. Rooms cost Y3500 per person, or Y4000 with private bathrooms.

Close to the JR Gotanda station on the Yamanote line is the *Ryokan Sansuisō* (tel 3441-7475). This is not the greatest of locations, but it's only a few stops from Shibuya, the nearest main railway terminus. Take the exit furthest away from Shibuya and exit on the left-hand side. Turn right, take the first right after the big Tōkyū department store and then the first left. Turn left and then right, walk past the bowling centre and look for the sign on the right directing you down the sideroad to the ryokan. Prices for singles/doubles are Y4000/7000; triples cost Y9600.

In Ueno, which is a good place to be based for sightseeing, even if it is a bit of a trek from the bright lights, there are several budget ryokan. The cheapest is *Sawanoya Ryokan* (tel 3822-2251) – Nezu subway station on the Chiyoda line is the closest station. Take the Nezu Crossing exit and turn right into Kototoi-dōri Ave. Turn left at the fourth street on your left – the Sawanoya Ryokan is a couple of minutes down the road on your right. If you're coming from Narita International Airport, it would probably be easier and just as cheap if there are more than one of you to catch a taxi from Ueno station. Singles/doubles cost Y3800/7000; triples cost Y9300.

A bit closer to Ueno station is *Ryokan Katsutaro* (tel 3821-9808). If you follow the road that runs alongside Shinobazu Pond for about 10 minutes, you'll see the ryokan on the right. Singles/doubles/triples cost Y3900/7000/9600. On the left, before you get to Ryokan Katsutaro, is the larger *Suigetsu Hotel* (tel 3822-9611), which has a laundrette and rooms with private bathrooms. You can also change money there. Singles/doubles cost Y5000/8800; triples cost Y10,800.

One stop away from Ueno on the JR Yamanote line (Uguisudani station) is the *Sakura Ryokan* (tel 3876-8118). Take the southern exit and turn left. Pass the Iriya subway station exits on the left – the Sakura Ryokan is on the right-hand side of the second street on your left. If you're exiting from Iriya subway station on the Hibiya line, take the No 1 exit and turn left.

Singles/doubles cost Y4500/8400; triples cost Y12,000.

Three stops away from Ueno on the Ginza line is Asakusa, which also has a few reasonably priced ryokan. *Ryokan Mikawaya Bekkan* (tel 3843-2345) is just around the corner from the Sensō-ji Temple in an interesting area. It's on a sidestreet off the shop-lined street leading into the temple. From the Kaminari-mon Gate, the street is a few streets up on the left – there's a toy shop and a shoe shop on the corner. The ryokan is on the left-hand side of the road. Singles/doubles cost Y4800/9200.

Just outside the Sensō-ji Temple precinct is the *Sukeroku-no-yado Sadachiyo Bekkan* (tel 3842-6431). Singles/doubles/triples with private bathrooms and air-con cost Y5500/9000/12000.

In Nishi Asakusa (near Tawaramachi subway station, which is one stop away on the Ginza line from Asakusa station) is the *Kikuya Ryokan* (tel 3841-6404). It's just off Kappabashi-dōri Ave and prices are Y4000/7000 for singles/doubles; triples cost Y9000.

There are several other budget alternatives worth checking out, although they are popular with long-term visitors and often full. In Ikebukuro, *House Ikebukuro* (tel 3984-3399) has singles/doubles/triples for Y3090/5150/6180. Near Kotake-Mukaihara subway station, a few stops out of Ikebukuro on the Yūraku-cho line, is the *Rikkō Kaikan Guest Room*, with singles/doubles from Y3605/7210. Near Shin-Nakano subway station on the Marunouchi line is the *Shin-Nakano Lodge* (tel 3381-4886), which has singles from Y3500 to Y4000 and doubles from Y6500 to Y7000.

The *YMCA Asia Youth Centre* (tel 3233-0631) takes both men and women but is pretty expensive for what it offers. It's halfway between Suidobashi and Jimbō-cho subway stations. Rooms with bathroom cost Y6180/10,300 for singles/doubles; triples cost Y13,905. The *Japan YWCA Hostel* (tel 3264-0661) is a bit cheaper but only accepts women. It's a few minutes from the Kudan exit of Ichigaya subway station and costs Y4738 per person. The *Tokyo YWCA Sadohara Hostel* (tel 3268-4451), near the Ichigaya exit of Ichigaya subway station, accepts couples and is cheaper. Singles/doubles with toilet cost from Y4635/9785.

Capsule Hotels Capsule hotels are a strictly male domain and you find them wherever there are large numbers of salarymen, bars, hostess clubs and other drains for company expense accounts. Close to the western exit of Ikebukuro station is the *Ikebukuro Puraza* (tel 3590-7770), which costs Y3800 per night.

Gaijin Houses Although a few gaijin houses quote daily or weekly rates, they are generally not an option for short-term visitors. If you are planning a long stay, a gaijin house may be the only affordable option, but the shortage of cheap accommodation means they often have long waiting lists. Typically prices range from Y30,000 to Y60,000 a month for a bed in a shared room, with no deposits or key money required.

While you wait for a room to become available, you may have to book into a cheaper ryokan or a youth hostel. There have been reports of travellers paying nearly Y1000 a night for the privilege of sleeping in a car parked outside a gaijin house. The proprietors had the nerve to class it as one of their rooms.

Gaijin house conditions often leave much to be desired. Rooms are usually very small and chances are you're going to be sharing one to keep expenses down. Facilities are often pretty limited – one shower and toilet for 40 people is a typical shock-horror story. This kind of thing is OK for a while, but if you're going to be based in Tokyo for an extended period, you'll probably want to start looking for something better.

If you ring a gaijin house, there is always someone who speaks English. Generally someone will be able to meet you at the station and take you to the house. Unless otherwise indicated, the prices given here are per person per month.

Aardvark Villa: share Y40,000; private Y75,000; five minutes from Kichijō-ji station (tel 0422-48-0550)

ABC House: share Y30,000; private singles/doubles Y46,000/75,000; three minutes from Kamata station on the Keihin Tōhoku line (tel 3736-2311)

Ajima House: near Nakano and Musashisakai stations (tel 3331-4607)

Bilingual House: share from Y38,000 to Y40,000; private from Y43,000 to Y60,000; three houses – near the Seibu Shinjuku line, the Keio line and the JR line (tel 3200-7082)

Bronte House: share Y38,000; near Sugamo station (tel 3984-0207)

Friendship House: share from Y8750 to Y9950 per week; three locations – near Higashi-Koenji subway station on the Marunouchi line, and near Hachimanyama and Oimachi stations (tel 3327-3179)

Fuji House: share Y36,000; near Shimura-Sanchome subway station on the TOEI Mita line (tel 3967-4046)

Green Peace: near Kaminakazato station (tel 3915-2572)

Guest House Fantasy Villa: near Kugayama station (tel 3334-6293)

House California: share Y41,000; private Y55,000; two houses – near Takadanobaba and Kamikitazawa stations (tel 3209-9692)

International House: share Y38,000; private Y58,000; couple Y68,000; near Musashisakai station on the Chūō line (tel 3326-4839)

International Guest House: share Y40,000; private Y70,000 (tel 3623-8445)

Japan House: share from Y29,000; two locations – near Senkawa subway station on the Yūraku-cho line and Kamata station on the Keihin Tōhoku line (tel 3962-2495)

Lily House Mansion: share Y40,000; private Y70,000; near Kawaguchi station on the Keihin Tōhoku line (tel 0482-23-8205)

Maharaja Palace: private singles Y52,000; doubles Y63,000; near Ishikawadai station on the Ikegami Line (tel 3748-0568)

Marui House: near Ikebukuro station (tel 3962-4979)

Midori House: private singles Y46,000; doubles Y86,000; near Nishi-Magome station (tel 3754-3112, ask for Mary)

Miracle House: private singles Y60,000; doubles from Y87,000 to Y90,000; near Omorimachi station on the Keihin Kyūkō line (tel 3761-8099)

Oriental House: share Y50,000; private Y90,000; near Shin-Koenji subway station on the Marunouchi line (tel 3354-0607)

Privilege Guest House: share from Y30,000 to Y38,000; private from Y50,000 to Y70,000; two locations – near Shimura-Sakaue subway station on the TOEI Mita line and Akabane station on the Saikyo line (tel 3558-0721)

Stone House: share Y27,500: private Y39,000 (tel 0474-38-8664)

Sun Academy: private Y58,000; near Motosumiyashi station (tel 0444-34-4450)

Taihei English House: share Y36,000; private Y40,000; near Tokiwadai station (tel 3940-4705)

Tokyo English Centre: share Y42,000; near Higashi-Nakano station (tel 3360-4781)

Tokyo House from Y33,500; three locations – in Ogikubo (tel 3391-5577), Shakuji-kōen (tel 3995-5306) and Otsuka (tel 3910-8808)

Toyama House: two locations – near Nerima and Nakano stations (tel 0422-49-8938)

YTC House: share Y33,000; near Nishi-Sugamo station on the TOEI Mita line (tel 3946-5266, 3942-2887)

Places to Stay – middle

Hotels The middle price bracket in Tokyo principally comprises business hotels. There's very little to distinguish one from another, and their main attraction is usually convenience. Every district in Tokyo has numerous business hotels with singles/doubles from about Y6000/10,000. Generally, each room will have a built-in bathroom with shower, bath and toilet, a telephone, pay TV and other features like disposable toothbrushes and shaving equipment.

An interesting late-night alternative is a love hotel. There are plenty of these in any of Tokyo's entertainment districts but particularly in Shinjuku, Shibuya, Roppongi and Ikebukuro. All-night rooms range in price from about Y6000 to Y7000, but 'all night' doesn't start until 10 or 11 pm, when the regular hour-by-hour customers have run out of energy.

One of the major problems with accommodation in Tokyo is actually finding the place you've decided you want to stay at. Although the following is a very selective list of mid-range hotels, they do at least have English-speaking staff who'll give you instructions over the phone on how to get to the hotel from the nearest station.

Central Tokyo Any hotels in this area tend to be expensive, simply because real estate values are so high. Nevertheless, there are a few mid-range places.

Hotel Ginza Dai-ei: singles Y8750; doubles or twins Y13,000; one minute from Higashi-Ginza subway station (tel 3545-1111)

Hotel Atamise: singles Y8724; twins Y16,995; two minutes from Higashi-Ginza subway station (tel 3541-3621)

Ginza Capitol Hotel: singles Y6800; twins Y11,800; two minutes from Tsukiji subway station (tel 3543-7888)

Ginza Nikkō Hotel: singles/doubles Y13,526/21,572; four minutes from Shimbashi station (tel 3571-4911)

Ginza International Hotel: singles/doubles Y11,310/15,295; twins Y16,428; two minutes from Shimbashi station (tel 3574-1121)

Sun Hotel Shimbashi: singles Y6700; twins Y10,500; three minutes from Shimbashi station (tel 3591-3351)

Tokyo Hotel Urashima: singles Y6798; twins Y12,463; get there on the No 03 bus from Ginza (tel 3533-3111)

Tokyo Station Hotel: singles Y7930; doubles or twins Y13,590; in the JR Tokyo station (tel 3231-2511)

Tokyo City Hotel: singles/doubles Y6901/10,300; twins Y10,815; two minutes from Mitsukoshi-mae station (tel 3270-7671)

Yaesu Terminal Hotel: singles/doubles Y8446/13,390; one minute from the JR Tokyo station (tel 3281-3771)

Ueno The cheaper ryokan in the Ueno area are better value, but if they're all full, the business hotels there are generally cheaper than those in other areas around Tokyo.

Hokke Club Ueno – Ikenohata: singles Y5356; twins Y9270; 10 minutes from Ueno station, five minutes from Yushima subway station (tel 3822-3111)

Ikenohata Bunka Centre: singles Y5098; twins Y10,097; three minutes from Yushima subway station (tel 3822-0151)

Hotel Pine Hill Ueno singles Y7500; doubles and twins Y14,000; three minutes from Yushima or Okachimachi stations (tel 3836-5111)

Shinjuku Shinjuku is a good hunting ground for business hotels that cater for foreigners.

Shinjuku Park Hotel: singles Y6000; twins Y10,500; seven minutes from Shinjuku station (tel 3356-0241)

Lions Hotel Shinjuku: singles/doubles Y8157/14,162; eight minutes from Shinjuku station (tel 3208-5111)

Star Hotel Tokyo: singles/doubles Y7477/14,955; three minutes from Shinjuku station (tel 3361-1111)

Shinjuku New City Hotel: singles/doubles Y7390/15,300; twins Y13,600; 15 minutes from Shinjuku station (tel 3375-6511)

Shinjuku Washington Hotel: singles/doubles Y8858/14,935; 10 minutes from Shinjuku station (tel 3343-3111)

Business Hotel Shinjuku Inn: singles Y6500; doubles or twins Y9800; five minutes from Shinjuku-gyoen-mae station (tel 3341-0131)

Shinjuku Sun Park Hotel: singles/doubles Y6490/8760; five minutes from Shin-Okubo and Okubo stations (tel 3362-7101)

Taisho Central Hotel: singles/doubles Y6180/14,420; twins Y11,330; two minutes from Takadanobaba station (tel 3232-0101)

Shibuya The following hotels are all within easy striking distance of Shibuya station.

Shibuya Tōkyū Inn: singles Y11,024; doubles or twins Y15,965; one minute from the station (tel 3498-0109)

Shibuya Business Hotel: singles/doubles Y7810/10,530; two minutes from the station (tel 3409-9300)

Hotel Sun Route Shibuya: singles Y6231; twins Y12,349; five minutes from the station (tel 3464-4611)

Hotel Ivy Flat: singles Y9579; twins Y14,832; five minutes from the station (tel 3770-1122)

Aoyama Shanpia Hotel: singles/doubles Y8960/13,490; five minutes from the station (tel 3407-8866)

Taishin Hotel: singles/doubles Y8990/13,900; 13 minutes from the station (tel 3469-1511)

Roppongi This is a good area to be based in if you want access to central Tokyo and a lively nightlife. The following list includes hotels in areas adjacent to Roppongi.

Hotel Yoko Akasaka: singles/doubles Y7550/10,000; three minutes from Akasaka subway station (tel 3586-4050)

Hotel Tōkyū Kankō: singles/doubles Y7364/14,729; seven minutes from Akasaka subway station (tel 3583-4741)

Akasaka Shanpia Hotel: singles Y7550; twins Y13,590; four minutes from Akasaka subway station (tel 3583-1001)

Toshi Centre Hotel: singles Y6839; twins Y10,690; triples Y17,150; seven minutes from Akasaka-Mitsuke subway station (tel 3265-8211)

Hotel Ibis: singles/doubles Y12,000/15,000; two minutes from Roppongi subway station (tel 3403-4411)

Ikebukuro There are innumerable business and love hotels in the Ikebukuro area, as well as some of the most popular cheaper ryokan.

Hotel Grand Business: singles Y5500; twins Y9200; five minutes from Ikebukuro station (tel 3984-5121)

Business Hotel Three Star Ikebukuro: singles Y5200; twins Y8800; eight minutes from Ikebukuro station (tel 3982-3331)

Hotel Ohedo: singles/doubles Y5000/8000; five minutes from Ikebukuro station (tel 3971-0288)

Otsuka Sun First: singles Y5200; doubles and twins Y8800; two minutes from Otsuka station (tel 3944-4141)

Places to Stay – top end

Although Tokyo is one of the world's most expensive cities, its top-end hotels are no more expensive than similar hotels anywhere else, and you get Japan's legendary high standard of service.

The real top-notch hotels in Tokyo are reportedly the *Hotel Seiyo Ginza*, which is the most expensive, the *Akasaka Prince*, the *New Otani* and the *Hotel Okura*. The New Otani has the cheapest singles, from Y17,500; if, on the other hand, you wanted the same hotel's best suite, you'd be looking at a cool Y450,000 a night. The *Imperial Hotel* in Central Tokyo is probably the best known hotel in the city. The following prices are for the cheapest rooms available in each hotel.

Akasaka Prince Hotel: singles Y19,000; twins Y28,000; next to Nagata-cho subway station (tel 3234-1111, 3262-5163)

Akasaka Tōkyū Hotel: singles Y16,000; twins Y24,500; next to Nagata-cho subway station (tel 3580-2311)

ANA Hotel Tokyo: singles Y19,500; twins Y26,000; near Akasaka subway station (tel 3505-1111/1155)

Asakusa View Hotel: singles Y13,000; twins Y20,000; 10 minutes from Ueno station (tel 3847-1111, 3842-2132)

Capitol Tōkyū Hotel: singles Y20,500; twins Y27,000; near Nagata-cho subway station (tel 3581-4511/5822)

Century Hyatt Tokyo: singles Y17,000; twins Y23,000; near Shinjuku station (tel 3349-0111, 3344-5575)

Ginza Dai-Ichi Hotel: singles Y12,500; twins Y16,000; near Higashi-Ginza and Shimbashi stations (tel 3542-5311/3030)

Ginza Tōkyū Hotel: singles Y13,000; twins Y24,000; near Higashi-Ginza station (tel 3541-2411/6622)

Hotel Grand Palace: singles Y12,000; twins Y19,000; near Kudanshita subway station (tel 3264-1111, 3230-4985)

Hotel Seiyo Ginza: singles Y38,000; twins Y52,000; 10 minutes from Higashi-Ginza subway station (tel 3535-1111)

Imperial Hotel: singles Y22,500; twins Y26,500 (tel 3504-1111/1258)

Keio Plaza Inter-Continental Hotel: singles Y17,000; twins Y21,000; near Shinjuku station (tel 3344-0111, 3345-8269)

Hotel Metropolitan: singles Y12,500; twins Y16,500; near Ikebukuro station (tel 3980-1111/5600)

Miyako Hotel: singles Y16,000; twins Y20,000; near Shinagawa station (tel 3447-3111/3133)

Hotel New Otani: singles Y17,500; twins 24,000; near Nagata-cho subway station (tel 3265-1111, 3221-2619)

Hotel Okura: singles Y23,000; twins Y26,000; near Kamiya-cho subway station (tel 3582-0111/3707)

Hotel Pacific Meridian: singles Y17,500; twins Y20,000; near Shinagawa station (tel 3445-6711/5733)

Palace Hotel: singles Y17,000; twins Y23,500; near Tokyo station (tel 3211-5211/6987)

Takanawa Prince Hotel: singles Y17,000; twins Y20,000; near Shinagawa station (tel 3447-1111, 3446-0849)

Tokyo Hilton International: singles Y21,000; twins Y25,000; near Shinjuku station (tel 3344-5111, 3342-6094)

Tokyo Prince Hotel: singles Y18,000; twins Y20,000; near Onarimon subway station (tel 3432-1111, 3434-5551)

PLACES TO EAT

Food is one area where Tokyo really comes into its own. Everywhere you go there are restaurants, many of them very good value for money. The best place to look is around railway stations, but in many big commercial centres every sidestreet harbours a multitude of eateries, ranging from exclusive Japanese and foreign restaurants to inexpensive places where you slurp your noodles standing at the counter. Generally, you won't have any trouble distinguishing the cheap places from the expensive – the plastic food in the window is almost always marked with a price.

Another place to look is in department stores and office blocks. Department stores often have branches of famous Tokyo restaurants offering special lunch-time prices.

For the best cheap eats, try to be a bit adventurous: avoid the Western-style fast-food barns and experiment with the Japanese and Chinese restaurants that are popular with local office workers for lunch and after work. You can usually get a large bowl of noodles for between Y350 and Y450. Other budget options that are popular with the Japanese are the curry rice shops and the revolving sushi shops where three sushi pieces on a plate will set you back between Y100 and Y150.

During the day, the best eating areas are the big shopping districts like Shibuya, Shinjuku, Harajuku and Ginza. Shinjuku could well take the prize as Tokyo's best daytime gourmet experience, with rows of restaurants in the big department stores and, at street level, an endless selection of reasonably priced restaurants and the best affordable Chinese food in Tokyo. Shinjuku is the busiest commuter junction in Tokyo, and there are a vast number of restaurants around the station and in the frenetic entertainment area. There are also many restaurants underground, along the 1½ km of shopping streets which run from around the station.

At night, Shinjuku is again in the running with the best Chinese food in Tokyo at affordable prices, plus a fantastic selection of Japanese, Korean and various 'ethnic' (Thai, Turkish, Mexican, etc) restaurants. Places in central Tokyo, on the other hand, are really too expensive for evening meals. A couple of exceptions include *Nair's* Indian restaurant and a hole-in-the-wall Pakistani restaurant. The Ueno and Ikebukuro areas, where many travellers stay, abound in small Japanese and Chinese noodle bars, though Ikebukuro has a few up-market alternatives including a Greek and an Italian restaurant or two. Another good eating area is

Roppongi, ideal if you're planning on hitting the bright lights in Tokyo's international nightlife centre.

For a serious restaurant crawl get Rick Kennedy's *Good Tokyo Restaurants*. Many of the places recommended are too expensive for travellers on a budget, but if you're planning a longer stay the book is definitely a worthwhile investment.

The following cuisine guide first describes restaurants serving Japanese food by area. Places serving international cuisine are listed by area in the Other Cuisines section and are then described more fully under separate cuisine sections.

Japanese

Of course there are more Japanese restaurants in Tokyo than all those offering other national cuisines put together. Many of them specialise in a particular type of Japanese food. At one extreme, the simple neighbourhood okonomiyaki and yakitori places found on every corner are often very economical. At the other extreme there are very exclusive restaurants with very high prices; you may not even get in without an introduction. Some individual recommendations follow in the area descriptions.

Central Tokyo & Ginza Restaurants in the central area are not all glossy and expensive. There are some great lunch-time bargains in department stores and plenty of small night-time food stalls. *Restaurant City* on the 8th floor of the Matsuya department store has a wide variety of restaurants with not too outrageous prices. It's conveniently close to the centre of Ginza on Ginza-dōri Ave and is open until 9 pm daily except Thursdays. The store itself closes at 6 pm but the restaurant floor has its own elevator.

Another floor of restaurants can be found in the 2nd basement level of the Matsuzakaya department store, also on Ginza-dōri Ave but just the other side of Harum-dōri Ave. A little further along Ginza-dōri is the *Lion Beer Hall*, where you'll find beer and cheap food.

Also just south of Harum-dōri Ave is

Torigin, hidden away down a very narrow back alley but signposted in English and quite easy to find. There's a menu in English and this authentic, very popular little place does excellent food including yakitori at Y120 to Y200 per stick and the steamed rice dish known as *Kamameshi* at Y700. A complete meal with a beer costs about Y1500.

Almost behind the TIC office, in the shadow of the elevated expressway and railway lines, is a host of popular and budget priced little yakitori stalls. *Chichibu Nishiki* is a traditional *nomiya* (saké pub) with good cheap food in a very authentic setting. It's tucked away behind the Kabuki-za theatre.

Ueno & Asakusa In these older areas, the Shitamachi or 'low' city of pre-Meiji Tokyo, you find fewer foreign restaurants and more traditional Japanese food. The Ameyoko shopping area near the station is packed with small Japanese places.

Right across from Asakusa station is *Kamiya*, claimed to be the oldest bar in Japan. There's a beer hall on the ground floor where you order and pay for beer and food as you enter. Upstairs, both Western and Japanese food are served. The Kamiya is closed on Tuesdays.

Tonkyu, on the entranceway to the Asakusa Kannon Temple, is a nice little place – good value at lunch time. 'Tonkatsu' (pork cutlets) are the speciality. The restaurant is closed on Thursdays.

A block over from the entranceway to the Sensō-ji Temple in Asakusa, *Tatsumiya* (tel 3842-7373) is an old fashioned looking place where you can try kaiseki ryōri (the traditional Japanese high cuisine) without breaking the bank.

Shinjuku Shinjuku is the busiest and most energetic commuter junction in Tokyo and there are a vast number of restaurants around the station and in the frenetic entertainment area.

A number of restaurants in Shinjuku specialise in suki-yaki and shabu-shabu. *Ibuki* has great suki-yaki and shabu-shabu starting at around Y1500 per head. Next door

is a pleasant sushi restaurant. To get there, take the eastern exit of Shinjuku station and look for the Alta building with its huge video screen. Cross the road and turn left, following the road round as it turns to follow the railway tracks. After you've turned, turn again into the second lane on your right. Ibuku is a few doors on your left but unfortunately the sign is only in kanji.

Just west of the station *Tori-jun* and *Volga* are two popular yakitoris, on the same little block. Tori-jun has good tempura and an English menu.

There are some good-value eating places in department stores and hotels at lunch time. The North-South building or NS Bil is on the west side of the station and the top two floors are entirely devoted to restaurants. The Tokyo Hilton International, also on the west side, has a bargain weekday lunch-time curry and salad buffet in its *St George's Bar*. There are also many restaurants underground, along the 1½ km of shopping streets which run from around the station.

Harajuku & Shibuya For a special meal in a traditional Japanese setting, *Kiku* (tel 3408-4919) in Harajuku is a popular spot with foreign residents. There's a sampling of different Japanese dishes here rather than the usual specialisation. To get there, walk straight down Omote-sando from Harajuku Station, cross over Meiji-dōri Ave (the first major intersection you come to) and continue down the hill and take a left (down a flight of stairs) shortly after the Haagen Dazs ice cream parlour. Kiku is in a wooden building about 50 metres on your left.

Akasaka & Roppongi The Japanese restaurants in Akasaka and Roppongi are usually expensive, though there are some great Chinese, Indian, Indonesian and Japanese restaurants there. (See the Other Cuisines section which follows.)

Ikebukuro The *Tobu Hope Center*, by the Tobu department store on the west side of Ikebukuro station, has a floor of restaurants.

Top: Cherry blossoms (CT)
Middle: Shin-kyō Bridge, Nikkō (CT)
Bottom: Temple doors, Tokyo (CT)

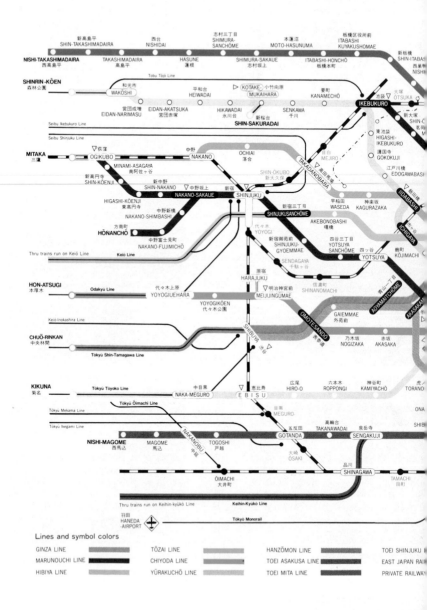

Lines and symbol colors

GINZA LINE

MARUNOUCHI LINE

HIBIYA LINE

TŌZAI LINE

CHIYODA LINE

YŪRAKUCHŌ LINE

HANZŌMON LINE

TOEI ASAKUSA LINE

TOEI MITA LINE

TOEI SHINJUKU

EAST JAPAN RAIL

PRIVATE RAILWAY

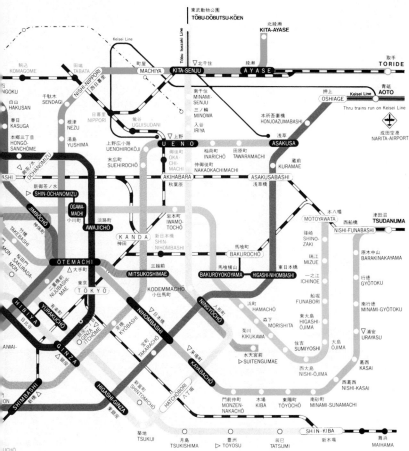

東武動物公園
TŌBU-DŌBUTSU-KŌEN

北綾瀬
KITA-AYASE

Keisei Line

町屋
MACHIYA

北千住
KITA-SENJU

綾瀬
A Y A S E

取手
TORIDE

駒込
KOMAGOME

田端
TABATA

Tōbu Isezaki Line

押上
OSHIAGE

青砥
AOTO

Keisei Line

Thru trains run on Keisei Line

千駄木
SENDAGI

白山
HAKUSAN

NISHI-NIPPORI
西日暮里

南千住
MINAMI-SENJU

本所吾妻橋
HONJOAZUMABASHI

成田空港
NARITA-AIRPORT

春日
KASUGA

根津
NEZU

日暮里
NIPPORI

三ノ輪
MINOWA

浅草
ASAKUSA

本郷三丁目
HONGŌ-
SANCHŌME

湯島
YUSHIMA

鶯谷
UGUISUDANI

入谷
IRIYA

御茶ノ水
OCHANOMIZU

上野広小路
UENOHIROKŌJI

UENO
上野

御徒町
OKA-
CHI-
MACHI

稲荷町
INARICHŌ

田原町
TAWARAMACHI

蔵前
KURAMAE

新御茶ノ水
SHIN-OCHANOMIZU

末広町
SUEHIROCHŌ

仲御徒町
NAKAOKACHIMACHI

ASAKUSABASHI
浅草橋

JIMBŌCHŌ

OGAWA-
MACHI

AKIHABARA
秋葉原

本八幡
MOTOYAWATA

津田沼
TSUDANUMA

TAKEBASHI

小川町

淡路町
AWAJICHŌ

岩本町
IWAMO-
TOCHŌ

西船橋
NISHI-FUNABASHI

SAKURADA-
MON.

KANDA
神田

新日本橋
SHIN-
NIHOMBASHI

篠崎
SHINO-
ZAKI

原木中山
BARAKINAKAYAMA

ŌTEMACHI

大手町

三越前
MITSUKOSHIMAE

馬喰町
BAKUROCHŌ

東日本橋
瑞江
MIZUE

行徳
GYŌTOKU

東京
TŌKYŌ

二重橋前
NIJŪBASHI-
MAE.

馬喰横山
BAKUROYOKOYAMA

東日本橋
HIGASHI-NIHOMBASHI

一之江
ICHINOE

南行徳
MINAMI-GYŌTOKU

KODEMMACHŌ
小伝馬町

船堀
FUNABORI

HIBIYA
日比谷

YURAKUCHŌ

銀座一丁目
GINZA-
ITCHŌME

NIHOMBASHI
日本橋

NINGYŌCHŌ

浜町
HAMACHŌ

東大島
HIGASHI-
ŌJIMA

浦安
URAYASU

京橋
KYOBASHI

森下
MORISHITA

大島
ŌJIMA

AIWAI-

G I N Z A

宝町
TAKARACHŌ

菊川
KIKUKAWA

住吉
SUMIYOSHI

葛西
KASAI

新富町
SHIN-TOMICHŌ

KAYABACHŌ

水天宮前
SUITENGUMAE

西大島
NISHI-ŌJIMA

西葛西
NISHI-KASAI

SHIMBASHI

HATCHŌBORI
八丁堀

八丁堀

門前仲町
MONZEN-
NAKACHŌ

木場
KIBA

東陽町
TŌYŌCHŌ

南砂町
MINAMI-SUNAMACHI

HIGASHI-GINZA
東銀座

ION

築地
TSUKIJI

月島
TSUKISHIMA

豊洲
TOYOSU

辰巳
TATSUMI

SHIN-KIBA
新木場

舞浜
MAIHAMA

UCHŌ

Types of stations

GINZA   Junctions of subway lines.

KANDA   Junctions of Subway, East Japan Railway and Private Railway lines.

▽   Stations with a Pass Office.

- - - - -   Streetcar

©: Apr, 1991 TRTA.

Patterns

Ikebukuro has two floors of restaurants in the Sunshine 60 building.

Other Cuisines

The following restaurant recommendations do not include many real budget-priced places – they are simply too numerous and too similar in standard to make recommendations worthwhile. Anyway, finding a restaurant and experimenting a little with the menu is half the fun of eating out. Most of the places that follow are good for a special meal. Even so, many of them shouldn't be too expensive: from around Y700 for a lunch-time special and about Y1200 (not including drinks) for dinner. (See the following cuisine sections for more information about each restaurant.)

Central Tokyo & Ginza For international cuisine Ginza has some of the best subcontinental curries to be found in Tokyo:

Indian – *Maharaja, Nair's*
Pakistani – *Gandhara*

Ueno & Asakusa If you're determined to avoid Japanese food there are plenty of fast-food specialists, but fewer foreign restaurants in the Ueno and Asakusa areas. *Samrat* serves good Indian food.

Shinjuku As well as a wide variety of Japanese restaurants and fast-food centres there are also some superb places for foreign food in Shinjuku; the Kabuki-cho area to the east of the station has countless restaurants of all types.

Cambodian – *Angkor Wat* (in Yoyogi)
Chinese – *Tainan Taami, Pekin, Tokyo Kaisen Ichiba, Tokyo Dai Hanten*
Korean – *Tokaien*
Thai – *Ban Thai*
Turkish – *Istanbul*

Harajuku & Shibuya Harajuku and Shibuya are crowded crossroads on the Yamanote Line with numerous fast-food restaurants and places serving a wide variety of international cuisines. Places to try here include:

Indian – *Maharaja, Samrat*
Chinese – *Tainan Taami*
Thai – *Siam Thai*
Italian – *Capricciosa*
International – *Shibuya*

Roppongi *Hard Rock Café* (see Entertainment) is a Tokyo institution and just behind it is *Spago's*, an up-market Californian restaurant. Burgers and other beef dishes plus a good salad bar can be found at the *Victoria Station* chain. The Roppongi branch is in the Haiyū-za Building, on the other side of Roppongi Crossing from Almond.

Some other less expensive international possibilities include:

Indian – *Moti, Raja, Samrat*
Indonesian – *Bengawan Solo*
Chinese – *Tainan Taami*
Italian – *Capricciosa*
Vegetarian – *Bodaiju*

Ikebukuro There's good Italian food at the *Faggio Ristorante*.

Fast Food

Most of the budget-priced Japanese and Chinese restaurants serve their food just as quickly and often more cheaply than the fast-food chain places, but if you simply can't do without a Big Mac or a Shakey's pizza, you can rest assured that Tokyo won't deprive you of the pleasure: these places can be found all over the city.

It seems that almost all the major fast-food chains in the world are trying to muscle in on the lucrative Japanese market. *Shakey's Pizza*, *Kentucky Fried Chicken* and *McDonald's* seem to have a branch next to every railway station in Tokyo. Others, such as *El Polo Loco* and *Pizza Hut*, also have a shop here and there. In another interesting move, the McDonald's phenomenon has spawned some Japanese variations on the same theme: *Mos Burger*, *Lotteria* and *Love Burger*, to name a few.

The fast-food places are particularly popular with teenagers, so eating in them may mean being squeezed onto a table with a contingent of giggling high-school kids. Some of the chains offer pretty good lunch-time specials – Y550 for all the Shakey's pizza you can eat is an example.

The budget-priced coffee shop, of which there is an ever-increasing number, is one good fast-food option. The major chain is *Doutor* (look for the big yellow and brown signs). Doutor sells coffee for Y150 and German hotdogs for Y170. You can put together a good lunch, including a Y120 piece of cake, for around Y450 – not bad in Tokyo. The *Mister Donut* places are good for an economical donut, orange juice and coffee breakfast.

Indian

Ginza has a couple of good Indian restaurants. *Maharaja* (tel 3572-7196), which has branches all over Tokyo, is a bit pricey in the evening, but it has good lunch-time specials from Y700 and an excellent tandoori mixed grill for Y1100. The Ginza branch is opposite the Mitsukoshi department store, about 50 metres down Harumi-dōri Ave towards the Kabuki-za Theatre. Maharaja is in the basement – look for the plastic sample dishes in a glass cabinet at floor level. The Shibuya branch is on the 8th floor of the 109 building.

If you continue towards the Kabuki-za Theatre along Harumi-dōri Ave and turn left at the first major intersection, not far up on your left is *Nair's*, a Tokyo institution. It's almost impossible to get in for lunch, but dinner is also good value. The curries are very reasonably priced and made to Nair's unique recipe. It's closed on Thursdays.

Moti has one branch in Roppongi (tel 3479-1939) and two in Akasaka (tel 3582-3620, 3584-6640). It's almost universally applauded as the best Indian restaurant in Tokyo, and although the Roppongi branch is the most popular, the food is great in all three. The only problem is that you often have to queue for up to half an hour to get a seat – a common occurrence in good Tokyo restaurants. The food and atmosphere make the wait worthwhile. You can expect to pay about Y2000 per head.

Directly opposite Moti in Roppongi is *Raja* (tel 3408-6175). Although it doesn't match the standards set by Moti, it's an alternative if you can't face the long queues there. Like Moti, Raja seems to attract a sizeable Indian clientele and has an English menu.

Another Indian restaurant with several branches is *Samrat*. If you're sightseeing in the Ueno area, Samrat (tel 3568-3226) has a good lunch-time special of chicken, mutton or vegetable curry with rice and nan for Y850. Other branches are in Shibuya (tel 3496-9410) and Roppongi (tel 3478-5877). Main courses average Y1500.

Pakistani

Gandhara (tel 3574-9289) in Ginza claims to bring you the 'peculiar world-famous delicious taste of Pakistan'. Actually the food isn't *that* peculiar, but the management do take great pains to distance their cuisine from that of their great neighbour on the subcontinent, maintaining that Pakistani food is quite different and is the 'choice of billions all over the world'. Bold claims, but Gandhara is a good place for a Y750 lunch-time set meal; the dinner menu is pretty reasonable too. To get there, take Harumi-dōri Ave towards the Kabuki-za Theatre, turn right at the San-ai building and left at the next set of traffic lights. Gandhara is upstairs on the left, but there's a sign at ground level.

Cambodian

There's not much else to do in Yoyogi by night (one stop from the JR Shinjuku station on the Yamanote line), but it's worth a special trip to visit *Angkor Wat* (tel 3370-3019). This place has been around for some time, and despite a move to more spacious (but less atmospheric) quarters, the food is as good as ever. The staff are friendly and speak Japanese, Mandarin, Khmer and some English, so there should be someone who can help you with the Japanese menu.

The food has much in common with Thai cuisine, including spicy salads and great coconut-based curries. To get to Angkor Wat, take the Yamanote line to the JR Yoyogi station. Walk in the opposite direction to

Shinjuku station to the end of the platform, exit the station on the left-hand side, cross the road, walk straight ahead and after about 100 metres look for Angkor Wat in a lane on your right.

Indonesian

Bengawan Solo (tel 3403-3031) in Roppongi is deservedly the most popular of Tokyo's Indonesian restaurants. The atmosphere is great, and the food is delicious and not particularly expensive. You can find Bengawan Solo across the road from the Wave building.

Chinese & Taiwanese

Just as in Chinatowns all over the world the food has been modified for Western palates, so has most Chinese food in Japan been changed to suit Japanese tastes. Fortunately, there are still a number of places in Tokyo (there's probably not much hope for the rest of Japan) where you can find genuine Chinese food. In these places most of the people eating in the restaurant are likely to be Chinese.

Some of the most authentic Chinese food you're likely to come across (there's no sweet & sour pork here) outside China or Taiwan is at the Taiwanese restaurant *Tainan Taami*. There are branches in Roppongi (tel 3408-2111), Suidobashi (tel 3263-4530), Shinjuku (tel 3232-8839) and Shibuya (tel 3464-7544), but the pick of them is the Shinjuku branch. The menu is complete with photographs of the dishes to make ordering easy. Most of the dishes are small serves ranging in price from Y300 to Y600 – try as much as possible and whatever you do don't order rice. If you want rice, the restaurant is famous for its zongzi – sticky rice, pork and other oddments wrapped in a lotus leaf and steamed. Delicious!

To get there, walk through Kabuki-cho past the Koma Theatre and turn left at the end of the road. Tainan Taami is a few doors down from the corner of the last street on the right before the end of the road. Look for the red sign above the door and the queue snaking out of the entrance; don't worry about the queue – the food is worth the wait.

Just two doors down from Tainan Taami is *Pekin* (tel 3208-8252), a very down-to-earth Chinese noodle shop that is always crowded with Chinese. The décor may leave a lot to be desired and the staff may be surly, but you can get a good bowl of noodles there for around Y550. Unfortunately, there's no English sign, so look for the glass front window through which you can see the chefs at work.

On the same road in the other direction, away from the Seibu Shinjuku station, is a unique Chinese restaurant known as the *Tokyo Kaisen Ichiba* (tel 35273-8301), literally the 'Seafood Market'. You can't miss the building, a girder and glass construction with a fish market downstairs. Upstairs you get to eat the fish. This place has slightly up-market prices but simply picking the cheapest things on the menu at random (around Y1200 per serve) will provide some delicious surprises. Japanese, Mandarin and Cantonese are spoken, but not English.

For yum cha or dim sum, one of the few possibilities in Tokyo is at the multi-storey (12 floors) *Tokyo Dai Hanten* (tel 3202-0121) in Shinjuku. Most of the food is overpriced and not particularly special, but the yum cha service is not bad, if a bit more expensive than in other parts of the world. This is one of the few places in Tokyo where correct yum cha form is observed by having the food brought around on trolleys.

Korean

Korean restaurants are very popular in Japan, and Tokyo is full of them. A lot of the Korean barbecue restaurants that you find on every second street corner are great places at which to have a few beers and sizzle food with some friends. If you want to go somewhere a little up-market, there's a huge (nine floors) Korean restaurant on Yasukuni-dōri Ave in Shinjuku called *Tōkaien* (tel 3200-2924). The staff there are very helpful to stupid gaijin who don't know what they're doing. Mandarin is spoken as well as Japanese and Korean, but not much English. Reckon on about Y1500 per head on any of the first four floors. The upper floors have banquets and are more exclusive.

Thai

Like elsewhere in the world, Thai restaurants seem to be becoming increasingly trendy in Tokyo. This puts many of them out of the price range of budget travellers, but there are a number of reasonably priced ones around. One of the most popular is *Ban Thai* (tel 3207-0068) in Shinjuku. The food is excellent, but as usual you're going to have to wait for it – the queues can be very long. The menu has pictures to help you order, and there's a very good banquet, although it's rather expensive at Y3500 per person. The restaurant lies in the heart of Shinjuku's Kabuki-cho red-light area, on the 3rd floor of the Dai-Ichi Metro building.

The *Siam Thai Restaurant* (tel 3770-0550) in Shibuya is not a particularly big place, but it's nicely laid out, with rough-hewn wooden tables and chairs. The food's comparable with that of Ban Thai and the meals are a bit less expensive. There's a good lunch-time set menu for Y750. To get there, walk straight ahead from the pedestrian crossing at the Hachikō exit of Shibuya station, turn left at the second major intersection and look for the Siam on your right about 100 metres before you reach the Pizza Hut.

Turkish

Near Shinjuku's gay quarter is *Istanbul* (tel 3226-5929), a great little Turkish restaurant. It can be difficult to locate this hole in the wall, but there's an English menu there and you can sample a few different dishes for around Y1500. Take the eastern exit at Shinjuku station, walk along Shinjuku-dōri Ave past the Isetan department store, cross the main road that intersects Shinjuku-dōri Ave at Isetan and take the second lane on your left. The Istanbul is a few doors down on your right.

Italian

Tokyo abounds in Italian restaurants. The top floor of almost every department store has one, and every shopping district has a myriad of places serving up spaghettis and pizzas. Many of them alter dishes to suit the idiosyncrasies of Japanese palates. This isn't to say they're no good, it's just that what you get may come as a bit of a surprise.

In Ikebukuro, the *Faggio Ristorante* (tel 3988-5816) has reasonable prices and fairly authentic dishes. The interior is a bit stuffy, but this might be a plus for those who like to eat in fairly formal surroundings. To get there, take the western exit of Ikebukuro station and walk straight ahead to the corner with a McDonald's on it. Continuing straight ahead, the Faggio is across the road and a few doors up.

For great cheap Italian food in a lively atmosphere, try the *Capricciosa* restaurants (there are 12 branches in the Tokyo region). They are very popular with students and young people in general and a good alternative to the run-of-the-mill Italian places. It's easy to order too much, as the food comes in enormous servings that are enough for two or three people. If there are three of you, two dishes at about Y1300 will be more than enough. To get to the Roppongi branch (tel 3423-1171), turn right just before the Hard Rock Café and look for the restaurant on your left. Other branches are in Shimokitazawa (tel 3487-0461) (a popular area with students) and Shibuya (tel 3407-9482).

African

There are undoubtedly other African restaurants in Tokyo, but at the *Osun Ghana House Africa* (tel 3463-4734) English is spoken and there's a really warm atmosphere. This restaurant, as well as having cheap and tasty dishes, has the added distinction of offering daily conversation classes. If you're a collector of unusual languages this could be just the place to hang out – sample phrases on the restaurant's business card include 'I love you', 'kiss me' and 'you are my sun'. The lessons could lead to some interesting experiences.

British

You're probably thinking *British!?* but British-style pubs are a popular import and Tokyo has no shortage of them. The *1066* (tel 3719-9059) in Naka-Meguro has hearty English food (roast lunch on Sundays) and British beer on tap. There is also live folk music regularly – the entrance fee includes a banquet.

French

French restaurants in Tokyo are generally not very affordable, but *Pas A Pas* (tel 3357-7888 is a tiny, informal place that resembles a living room more than a restaurant; it has a great atmosphere and great food. You can order any combination of starter, main course and dessert for Y2500. To get there, take the Marunouchi line to Yotsuya-Sanchome subway station, take the Yotsuya-Sanchome exit, turn right, walk past the Marusho bookshop, cross the road and take the second street on the left. Pas A Pas is a few doors down on the left on the 2nd floor.

Vegetarian

Eating out in Japan can be a hassle for strict vegetarians. Most people working in Japanese restaurants won't really understand the concept of vegetarianism – simply taking the meat out of a dish that has been cooked in a meat stock is the standard response to customers who profess to be noncarnivorous. There are some vegetarian restaurants springing up around town, however, and there are always Indian restaurants that are used to catering for vegetarians. For those who find this to be a particular problem, the TIC has a list of Tokyo's natural food restaurants that includes some vegetarian possibilities.

For a real vegetarian treat, try *Bodaiju* (tel 3423-2388) in Roppongi for Chinese vegetarian temple food. Given that meat plays such an important part in Chinese cuisine, Chinese vegetarians have over the centuries become adept at preparing vegetables so that they look and taste like meat. It's easy to spend Y3000 a head, but Bodaiju is unique.

It's opposite and a bit down the road (away from Roppongi Crossing) from the Wave building. There's another branch near Mita subway station (tel 3456-3257).

Other Restaurants

Tokyo has some great restaurants which defy categorising, including *Ninnikuya* (tel 3446-5887), literally the 'Garlic Restaurant'. If you're not fond of garlic this is not the place for you, since the chefs, who work behind the bar in front of the customers, ladle generous dollops of it onto every dish served. The food ranges from Italian to Thai, the single unifying theme being the humble garlic clove. Keep your distance from friends the next day. Ring the restaurant from Ebisu station for instructions on how to get there (there are English speakers on the premises) and be prepared to queue for half an hour or more.

The kanji outside *Sunda* (tel 3465-8858) in Shibuya says *mukokuseki ryōri*, or 'no nationality cuisine'. The food is an interesting fusion of Thai, Indonesian, Chinese, French and Italian cuisines. The interior is quite incredible, featuring slate floors, muted colours, ambient music and a gurgling stream that runs through the centre of the restaurant. Count on spending around Y3000 per person for a starter, main course and dessert. Sunda's main drawback is the difficulty of finding the place. From the Hachikō exit of Shibuya station, take the shopping street with the arched entrance between the 109 building and the Seibu department store. Continue walking up this road until you leave the shops behind and the road dwindles down to the size of a laneway. Keep walking, passing children's swings (you're in the suburbs now) until the lane forms a V with another lane that flows into it. Sunda is straight ahead on the right – be careful or you'll mistake it for a house. If you have problems with this route, ring them up; they'll be only too happy to help.

Right beside the Kaminari-mon Gate near Sensō-ji Temple in Asakusa is a place with an English sign announcing that it has 'real

Italian gelato'. It's very popular, and deservedly so.

Just behind the *Hard Rock Café* (a Tokyo institution – see the Entertainment section of this chapter) is *Spago's*, the up-market Californian restaurant.

Burgers and other beef dishes plus a good salad bar can be found at the *Victoria Station* chain. The Roppongi branch is in the Haiyūza building, on the other side of Roppongi Crossing from Almond.

ENTERTAINMENT

Tokyo is a fascinating city by night, and many of the memories that are likely to stay with you longest will be of the bright lights, neon kanji and huge video screens or the backstreet red lanterns strung up in front of bustling eating and drinking spots. The only real problem with hitting the bright lights in Tokyo is that entry prices and drink prices tend to be much higher than in most Western countries. There's really no way of doing nightlife centres like Roppongi on a shoestring. Areas like Shinjuku can be cheaper, but even there clubs often have a nominal entry fee, and a bottle of beer may cost, say, Y800.

As well as all the nightlife attractions you'd expect to find in any big city, Tokyo offers the more traditional Japanese entertainment options.

Kabuki

The best place to see kabuki in Tokyo is the *Kabuki-za Theatre* (tel 3541-3131) in Ginza. Performances and times vary from month to month, so you'll need to check with the TIC or with the theatre directly for programme information. Earphone guides providing 'comments and explanations' in English are available for Y600 for those who find themselves becoming disoriented and confused during the performance. Prices for tickets vary from Y2000 to Y14,000, depending on how keen you are to see the stage. One distraction you may encounter is a large group of school children on a school outing – the excitement of the proceedings gives rise to a lot of chatting and giggling.

Kabuki performances can be quite a marathon, lasting from 4½ to five hours. If you're not up to it, you can get tickets for the 4th floor for less than Y1000 and watch only part of the show but earphone guides are not available in these seats. Fourth floor tickets can be bought on the day of the performance. There are generally two performances daily, starting at around 11 am and 4 pm.

Japan's national theatre, *Kokuritsu Gekijō Theatre* (tel 3265-7411), also has kabuki performances, with seat prices ranging from Y1200 to Y7200. Again, earphone guides are available. Check with the TIC or the theatre for performance times.

Nō

Nō performances are held at various locations around Tokyo. Tickets will cost between Y3000 and Y10,000, and it's best to get them at the theatre itself. Check with the TIC or the appropriate theatre for times.

The *Kanze Nō-gakudō Theatre* (tel 3469-6241) is a 10 to 15 minute walk from Shibuya station. From the Hachikō exit, turn right at the 109 building and follow the road straight ahead past the Tōkyū department store. The theatre is on the right, a couple of minutes down the third street on the left after Tōkyū.

The *Ginza Nō-gakudō* (tel 3571-0197) (Ginza Nō Stage) is about a 10 minute walk from Ginza subway station. Turn right into Sotobori-dōri Ave at the Sukiyabashi Crossing and look for the theatre on the left.

The *Kokuritsu Nō-gakudō* (tel 3423-1331) (National Nō Theatre) is in Sendagaya. Exit Sendagaya station in the direction of Shinjuku on the left and follow the road which hugs the railway tracks; the theatre is on the left.

Bunraku

Osaka is the bunraku centre, but performances do take place several times a year at the *Kokuritsu Gekijō Theatre* (tel 3265-7411). Check with the TIC or the theatre for information.

Sumō

Sumō may not be in the same league, culturally speaking, as the preceding entries, but there are definite connections: sumō is actually a highly ritualised and quite fascinating event that is as much a spectacle as it is a sport. The actual jostling in the ring can be over very quickly and great importance is attached to the pomp that precedes and follows the action.

Sumō tournaments at Tokyo's *Ryōgoku Kokugikan Stadium* (tel 3866-8700) in Ryōgoku take place in January, May and September and last 15 days. The best seats are all bought up by those with the right connections, but balcony seats are usually available from Y6000 and bench seats at the back for about Y1000. If you don't mind standing, you can get in for around Y500. Tickets can be bought up to a month prior to the tournament, or simply turn up on the day. The stadium is adjacent to Ryōgoku station on the northern side of the railway tracks.

Tea Ceremonies

A few hotels in Tokyo hold tea ceremonies which you can observe and occasionally participate in for a fee of about Y1000. The *Hotel New Otani* (tel 3265-1111) has ceremonies on its 7th floor on Thursday, Friday and Saturday from 11 am to 12 noon and 1 to 4 pm. Ring them before you go to make sure the show hasn't been booked out. The *Hotel Okura* (tel 3582-0111) and the *Imperial Hotel* (tel 3504-1111) also hold daily tea ceremonies.

Music

There's a lot of live music in Tokyo, ranging from big international acts to lesser known performers from the West who end up playing in clubs and other small venues. And, of course, there are many local bands. On any night there are hundreds of performances around town.

Live music in Tokyo has its drawbacks. Apart from in some of the more alternative 'live houses', entry charges and drinks prices are very high. Another catch is that the quality of the local music often leaves a lot to be desired. Like many other aspects of popular culture, music is almost completely dominated by the mainstream. Cute girls with insipid backing bands churning out sticky sweet melodies are the order of the day. Even the alternatives are far too often nothing more than unimaginative derivatives of Western heavy metal bands.

Look for information about what's happening in the mainstream music scene in *Pia*, a weekly what's-on-in-Tokyo Japanese magazine, or in the *Tokyo Journal*, the English-language magazine. Both have information on all the high-culture stuff (operas, philharmonics, etc) as well as details about jazz and rock. For information on alternative rock music, check *Infozine*.

Live Houses A number of live houses have reasonable entry charges and drink prices and provide good opportunities to hear interesting live music. The crowds in these places tend to be a mixture of local foreign residents and eccentric Japanese. Unfortunately, some very interesting local bands are supported far more by gaijin living in Tokyo than they are by the local Japanese.

A place that should be high on any list of live houses in Tokyo is *Club Z* (tel 3336-5841). (Despite the recent name change to Club Z, many people still refer to it by the old name, Lazy Ways.) This place is fairly roomy by Tokyo standards and usually has something interesting happening on Saturday nights. The club is next to Koenji station on the Chūō line. Facing in the direction of Shinjuku, exit on the left side of the station and make a sharp right. Follow the road beside the railway tracks for about 50 metres and then cross the road. Club Z is opposite the railway tracks, next to Nippon Rent-a-Car, in the basement.

Also in Koenji, not far from Club Z, is a very special bar, *Inaoiza* (tel 3336-4480), with a small stage for live music. The people who run the bar are musicians and often, if no-one is booked to perform, there'll just be an impromptu jam session. Live music has to stop at 10.30 pm because of the neighbours, but the action continues with lots of local English teachers, hostesses and out-of-the-ordinary Japanese dropping in after work for a few drinks. Inaoiza also has good food – ask for their menu – and a great, friendly atmosphere. The only problem is finding it. Your best bet is to ask someone at Club Z, as most of that crowd also frequent Inaoiza. You really need someone to lead you by the hand the first time you go.

In Harajuku, *Crocodile* (tel 3499-5205) has something happening seven nights a week. To get there from the JR Harajuku station, walk down Omote-sando and turn right at Meiji-dōri Ave. Cross the road and continue straight ahead, passing an overhead walkway. Crocodile is on your left, in the basement of the New Sekiguchi building.

Also in Harajuku is *Petite Rue* (tel 3400-9890), where all kinds of things happen, from acid house parties to avant-garde rock music. To get there, walk down Omote-

sando from the JR Harajuku station, cross the intersection at Meiji-dōri Ave and take the next right. Petite Rue is on your left a few doors down.

Another good live house is *Rock Mother* (tel 3460-1479) in Shimokitazawa. The whole area around there is worth a look: it's a kind of down-market Harajuku or a youth-oriented Shinjuku with lots of cheap places to eat and drink – very popular with students. To get to Rock Mother, take the Odakyū line to Shimokitazawa station and exit via the southern exit (Minami-guchi). After you leave the station, turn left, then right, then left again. Follow the road around to the right and look for the club on your left.

Jazz Jazz is very big in Tokyo, although some places seem to take it rather too seriously. Quiet, solemn audiences hanging on the musicians' every note: that's the Japanese for you – a serious lot when it comes to enjoying themselves. Still, if you're interested in jazz, there are a lot of places to try, and all the big names who are visiting Tokyo will have listings in the *Tokyo Journal*.

An old standard is the *Shinjuku Pit Inn* (tel 3354-2024). The cost of the cover charge depends on who's playing, but it should include a drink.

In Roppongi, there's another *Pit Inn* (tel 3585-1063), where the music is reportedly less traditional than that played at its Shinjuku counterpart. Walking away from Roppongi subway station, turn right at Almond, cross over the road and look for the Pit Inn on your left, about 100 metres down the road.

Another Roppongi jazz club is *Birdland* (tel 3478-3456), in the basement of the Square building, the hub of all the disco activity in Roppongi. Admission is around Y3000. Cross the intersection at Almond, continue walking away from Roppongi subway station, take the second right turn and you'll bump into the Square building. Look for all the beautiful people lounging around outside waiting to see where the happening spot is tonight.

Other Nightlife

There's so much happening that it's difficult to make recommendations. Most people seem to find their own favourite watering holes wherever they happen to be, but some areas have high concentrations of pubs, clubs and discos which are popular among both foreigners and Japanese. At bars that have gained some notoriety as the hang-outs of wild and crazy gaijin, there will also be plenty of Japanese who come along for the thrill.

Shinjuku Shinjuku's nightlife opportunities are underrated by many of Tokyo's residents. There's actually plenty there, but you have to know where to look for it. Just wandering under the bright lights of Kabuki-cho and ducking into one of the revolving sushi shops or one of the yakitori bars for a bite to eat is a good prelude to a night of debauchery.

If you'd like to have a few drinks and some yakitori to the accompaniment of karaoke in very strange surroundings, try *Yamagoya*. Feel free to participate with the patrons who are on stage, singing to the accompaniment of taped music, (karaoke literally means 'empty orchestra') but don't worry, no-one's going to drag you on stage. You enter Yamagoya by a narrow flight of stairs and end up in what seems like the hull of an old wooden ship. Huge wooden beams, every inch of them carved with names and graffiti, crisscross overhead, and wooden stairs continue down two more levels. The bottom level is the gloomiest and most dungeon-like and definitely the most fun.

It's a cheap place in which to eat and drink and very popular with students, but watch your head, particularly after a couple of beers. To get there, walk along Shinjuku-dōri Ave away from Shinjuku station and turn left after the Isetan department store. Cross the road and turn right into the lane next to the cinema. You'll pass an advertisement for a Tokyo Playboy club; afterwards take the first left. Yamagoya is down the road a little, on your right – a wooden sign hangs outside with kanji written on it. Look for the stairs going down into the building.

Just down the road from Yamagoya is the *Rolling Stone* (tel 3354-7347). It has been around for years but is definitely not for the faint-hearted. The music is rock & roll from the '70s onwards (with a heavy emphasis on Stones material), and it's a hang-out for Tokyo's heavy metal kids – lots of leather jackets, outrageous hairdos and cool posing. It's actually a good place to meet young Japanese who are outside the mainstream, as long as you don't go on a Friday or Saturday night, when the place is packed out. There's a Y200 cover charge and a sign announcing: 'we know it's shit but the police keep busting this place so please no dancing' – people do anyway. To get there, walk along Shinjuku-dōri Ave past the Isetan department store, cross the main road and keep walking until you come to the next main road; turn left and take the next left. The Rolling Stone is a few doors down, next door to a soapland.

Back across the main road and five lanes down from Shinjuku-dōri Ave, on the far left corner of the first street you come to, is *Sazae* (tel 3354-1745). This is another low-life bar, in Shinjuku's gay quarter, but it's a bit more fashionable and up-market than the Rolling Stone. It's also open late – until 6 am – and is a popular spot to while away the night for those who have missed the last train. On Fridays and Saturdays after 1 am, it's a circus.

Harajuku Harajuku is one of those rare areas in Tokyo that are more active by day than by night. *Oh God* (tel 3406-3206) is popular with foreign residents; in fact some people rave about it. It has a bar, pool tables and movie screenings every night, and the food gets very good reports. Walk down Omotesando and take the first lane on the right after Meiji-dōri Ave. Oh God is in the basement of the building at the end of the lane.

Roppongi Roppongi is undoubtedly the nightlife capital of Tokyo. It's where the beautiful people go, and in order to ensure that they keep going, a lot of the discos let anyone who claims to be a model in for free. (Your looks are going to have to back up this little fib.) Roppongi is one place in Tokyo other than the English-language classrooms where Japanese make a point of mingling with foreigners, although it is often the case that the only things that get exchanged are lascivious leers on the dance floor.

Not everyone has a negative reaction to Roppongi, and it is worth seeing by night. Most of the action centres around discos, but there are also a few interesting bars and clubs featuring live dance music.

The main point of orientation is the Roppongi Crossing, with the Almond Coffee Shop – a favourite meeting spot – on the corner. Follow the road under the metropolitan expressway in the opposite direction to the Wave building, take the second turn to the right and on the first corner on the right is the *Square* building, which has eight floors of discos. They all charge Y3000 to Y4000 (Y500 less for women) for entry and a couple of drinks. Most discos ban males unaccompanied by representatives of the opposite sex, but this is rarely enforced as long as there isn't a big crowd of you. It makes little difference which disco you choose, although the most popular is *Java Jive* (tel 3478-0087), where a reggae band is alternated with recorded music throughout the night.

In the basement, just around the corner from the Square building, is the *Lexington Queen* (tel 3401-1661), a disco for name-droppers and high-society voyeurs. It probably typifies all that is worst about Roppongi – you won't even get in if you don't look the part.

Not in the same high-class league as the Lexington, on the right if you walk in the direction of Tokyo Tower is *Hot Co-Rocket* (tel 3583-9409), with a cover charge of around Y2000 and live reggae music. It can be pretty dead during the week but it hots up on Friday and Saturday nights.

Heading back in the other direction, towards Roppongi Crossing, are a few more bars with much more casual standards. *Henry Africa* (tel 3405-9868) is a popular spot with both foreigners and Japanese, where a beer and some popcorn will set you back Y800.

Just around the corner to the right, on the left side, is *Déjà vu* (tel 3403-8777), one of the liveliest bars in Roppongi. It's very popular and drinkers spill out of the open-fronted entrance into the street.

It's the kind of place to meet people like the Japanese girl who told me she was majoring in 'international relationships', a field for which Roppongi no doubt provides rich research opportunities.

Chris Taylor

Go back onto the main road and turn right. A few doors down on the right, opposite Mister Donut, is *Pip's* (tel 3470-0857). This place is in the basement and entry is theoretically free – you just have to buy a drink ticket (Y800 for a beer) at the door. With a disco juke box and a few pin-ball machines, it's a bit of a dive; the atmosphere gets fairly rowdy by the time the last train has chuffed off in the evening.

A tour of late-night hang-outs can be completed with a visit to the *Charleston* (tel 3402-0372), labelled as 'the best sleaze pick-up bar' in Tokyo in the book *The Best of Tokyo*. It's rapidly losing its legendary status in the pick-up/sleaze stakes to the nearby Déjà vu, but if you turn up late on a Saturday night you won't be disappointed – things get fairly desperate. Take the next right turn after Pip's and follow the road down the hill, looking for the Charleston on your left.

Finally, Tokyo has its own *Hard Rock Café* (tel 3408-7018), with a ready supply of hamburgers, rock music and expensive cocktails. You can't miss the King Kong figure clambering up its exterior, near Roppongi Crossing, in a lane beside the Roy building.

Ikebukuro Your nightlife options in Ikebukuro are on the whole limited to karaoke and seedy nightclubs that won't be all that hospitable to gaijin. Nevertheless, *One Lucky* (tel 3985-0069) is a favourite among foreign residents and guests of the nearby Kimi Ryokan. 'One Rucky', as it's affectionately called by its Japanese patrons, is a one-man show where the master-san prepares all the food (a delicious set-menu dinner for Y700), pours the drinks (a beer is Y500) and, most importantly, takes a photograph of everyone who visits his establishment. There's a bookcase of photo albums containing the master's social shots, dated so that you can see how you looked when you last visited.

One Lucky is quite close to Kaname-cho subway station – turn left into the lane next to the park on Yamate-dōri Ave and look for it on the right after the second bridge. From the Kimi Ryokan, turn left, left again and then right. Follow this road straight ahead for about 10 minutes (you'll pass a bakery on the right) until you come to a brick-paved road with a bridge. Turn left there and look for One Lucky on the left just before the second bridge.

Also on Ikebukuro's west side is *Ultra*, a friendly karaoke bar that is popular with the staff of the Kimi Information Centre. If you're in the area and haven't experienced karaoke before, this is a good place to check out.

Cinemas

Foreign movies are screened with their original soundtracks and Japanese subtitles. There is usually a fairly good selection of alternative movies playing around town.

Japanese cinemas have a bad reputation for doing things like letting the audience for the next screening into the cinema 10 minutes before the end so that they can claim the good seats. Fortunately, things are steadily improving, although even now it is common only to dim the house lights, not to turn them off – maybe it's to discourage members of the audience from misbehaving. If things like this matter, stick to the arthouse cinemas, where a lot more attention is paid to these kinds of details. Tickets average Y1600.

Pia, the weekly Japanese-language Tokyo guide, and the English-language *Tokyo Journal* list what's playing where, complete with maps showing you how to find the cinemas.

THINGS TO BUY

Although Tokyo is an expensive city, certain things can be considerably cheaper there than they would be at home (wherever that is). Many electrical items, for example, can be very reasonably priced – check the Akihabara section of this chapter for more information. The Ueno section of this chapter has information on where to buy some mouth-watering plastic food.

Almost all the big department stores in Tokyo have good selections of things like Japanese dolls, ceramics, lacquerware, fans, etc. The problem with these places is that their goods are often way overpriced. You're likely to find less glamorous but possibly more interesting souvenirs in Tokyo's flea markets, where you can buy Japanese antiques and all kinds of curiosities from daily life.

There are a number of markets worth visiting. The Tōgō-jinja Shrine has a flea market from 4 am to 4 pm on the first and second Sundays of each month. To get there from the JR Harajuku station, turn left and take the next right after Takeshita-dōri.

A market operates at the Nogi-jinja Shrine from dawn to dusk on the second Sunday of each month. You get there from Nogi-zaka subway station on the Chiyoda line – the shrine is on the other side of Gaien-higashi-dōri.

Sunshine City also has a flea market, in the Alpa shopping arcade. It runs from 8 am to 10 pm on the third Saturday and Sunday of each month. It's five minutes from the western exit of Ikebukuro station.

The Ramura building plaza has a market from 6 am to sunset on the first Saturday of each month. It's next to Iidabashi subway station.

Folkcrafts & Antiques

Not far from Ikebukuro station's eastern exit, on the 1st floor of the Satomi building (tel 3980-8228), there are more than 30 antique dealers. They are open Friday to Wednesday from 10 am to 7 pm.

Another place to look is in the basement of the Hanae Mori building (tel 3406-1021) in Harajuku. There are more than 30 antique shops there, open daily. Walk straight down Omote-sando past the Tokyo Union Church and look for the Hanae Mori building on the right.

The Oriental Bazaar (tel 3400-3933) is open every day except Thursdays and is an interesting place to rummage through. It has a wide range of good souvenirs – fans, folding screens, pottery, etc. The bazaar is on the right in Omote-sando (walking away from the JR Harajuku station), not far past Meiji-dōri Ave.

The Tokyo Antique Fair takes place three times a year and brings together more than 200 antique dealers. The schedule for this event changes annually, but for information on this year's schedule you can ring Mr Iwasaki (tel 3950-0871) – he speaks English.

Japanese Dolls

Edo-dōri Ave, next to Asakusabashi station, is the place to go if you're interested in Japanese dolls. Both sides of the road have large numbers of shops specialising in traditional Japanese dolls as well as their contemporary counterparts. *Kawaii ne*!

Photographic Equipment

Check the Shinjuku section for information on the big camera stores there. Many places deal in second-hand photographic equipment; foreign-made large-format equipment is usually ridiculously expensive, but Japanese equipment can often be bought at very good prices. One of the best places to look, surprisingly, is in Ginza. If you walk along

Harumi-dōri Ave, there's a place opposite the Sony building on the Sukiyabashi Crossing. On the same side as the Sony building, towards the Kabuki-za Theatre, there are a couple more places. They're all on ground level and the windows are full of cameras and lenses.

Clothes

Areas like Ginza aren't ideal for clothes shopping: the high prices take all the fun out of buying things! Generally, the big department stores, with the exception of their sale floors and big annual sales, are also expensive. The best places for clothes are the smaller discount shops that abound in areas such as Shinjuku, Harajuku and Ikebukuro.

Reasonably priced clothing stores are scattered all over the east side of Shinjuku – there are quite a few around the Kinokuniya bookshop. In Harajuku, Omote-sando and Takeshita-dōri make good hunting grounds, although it's likely to be pretty much youth oriented. In Ikebukuro, around the western exit of the station, there is a large number of discount fashion shops.

The prohibitively high prices asked for new kimono and other traditional Japanese clothing items make second-hand shops the best option. The Oriental Bazaar and the basement of the Hanae Mori building in Harajuku are good places to look. (See the preceding Folkcrafts & Antiques section for more information.) If you've got money to burn and are set on getting a new kimono or similar item, check the big department stores like Isetan and Seibu. In March and September, there are big sales of rental kimono at Daimaru.

GETTING THERE & AWAY
Air

With the exception of China Airlines, all international airlines touch down at Narita Airport rather than at the more conveniently located Haneda Airport. Narita Airport has had a controversial history, its construction having met with considerable opposition from farmers it displaced and from student radicals. Even today, it is very security conscious, which can slow down progress in and out of the airport.

Arrival Immigration and customs procedures are usually straightforward, although they can be very time consuming for non-Japanese. Everything is clearly signposted in English and you can change money in the customs hall after having cleared customs or in the arrival hall. The rates will be the same as those offered in town.

The airport Tourist Information Centre (TIC) (tel 0476-32-8711) is an important stop. (There are only three TICs in the country, the others being in Tokyo and Kyoto.) It has a wealth of invaluable information – at the very least, pick up a subway map and the *Tourist Map of Tokyo*. The office is open Monday to Friday from 9 am to 8 pm and on Saturdays from 9 am to 12 noon; it is closed on Sundays and public holidays. The centre is to the right as you exit the customs hall, between the main building and the southern wing.

In the middle of the central block there is a JR office where you can make bookings and exchange your Japan Rail Pass voucher for a pass if you're planning to start travelling straight away.

Airline Offices Following is a list of the major airline offices in Tokyo.

Aeroflot
   No 2 Matsuda Building, 3-4-8 Toranomon, Minato-ku (tel 3434-9671)
Air China (formerly CAAC)
   AO1 Building, 3-2-7 Akasaka, Minato-ku (tel 3505-2021)
Air India
   Hibiya Park Building, 1-8-1 Yūraku-cho, Chiyoda-ku (tel 3214-7631)
Air Lanka
   Dowa Building, 7-2-22 Ginza, Chūō-ku (tel 3573-4261)
Air New Zealand
   Shin Kokusai Building, 3-4-1 Marunouchi, Chiyoda-ku (tel 3287-1641)
Alitalia
   Tokyo Club Building, 3-2-6 Kasumigaseki, Chiyoda-ku (tel 3580-2181)

All Nippon Airways (ANA)
   Kasumigaseki Building, 3-2-5 Kasumigaseki, Chiyoda-ku (tel 3272-1212, international; 3552-6311, domestic)
American Airlines
   201 Kokusai Building, 3-1-1 Marunouchi, Chiyoda-ku (tel 3214-2111)
Bangladesh Biman
   Kasumigaseki Building, 3-2-5 Kasumigaseki, Chiyoda-ku (tel 3593-1252)
British Airways
   Sanshin Building, 1-4-1 Yūraku-cho, Chiyoda-ku (tel 3593-8811)
Canadian Airlines International
   Hibiya Park Building, 1-8-1 Yūraku-cho, Chiyoda-ku (tel 3281-7426)
Cathay Pacific
   Toho Twin Tower Building, 1-5-2 Yūraku-cho, Chiyoda-ku (tel 3504-1531)
China Airlines
   Matsuoka Building, 5-22-10 Shimbashi, Minato-ku (tel 3436-1661)
Continental Airlines
   Suite 517, Sanno Grand Building, 2-14-2 Nagata-cho, Chiyoda-ku (tel 3592-1631)
Delta Airlines
   Kokusai Building, 3-1-1 Marunouchi, Chiyoda-ku (tel 3213-8781)
Finnair
   NK Building, 2-14-2 Kojimachi, Chūō-ku (tel 3222-6801)
Garuda Indonesian Airways
   Kasumigaseki Building, 3-2-5 Kasumigaseki, Chiyoda-ku (tel 3593-1181)
Japan Airlines (JAL)
   Tokyo Building, 2-7-3 Marunouchi, Chiyoda-ku (tel 3457-1121, international; 3456-2111 domestic)
Japan Air System (JAS)
   No 18 Mori Building, 2-3-13 Toranomon, Minato-ku (tel 3507-8036)
KLM
   Yūraku-cho Denki Building, 1-7-1 Yūraku-cho, Chiyoda-ku (tel 3216-0771)
Korean Air
   Shin Kokusai Building, 3-4-1 Marunouchi, Chiyoda-ku (tel 3211-3311)
Lufthansa
   3-2-6 Kasumigaseki, Chiyoda-ku (tel 3580-2111)
Malaysian Airlines (MAS)
   3rd Floor, No 29 Mori Building, 4-2 Shimbashi, Minato-ku (tel 3432-8501)
Northwest Orient Airlines
   5-12-12 Toranomon, Minato-ku (tel 3432-6000)
Philippine Airlines
   Sanno Grand Building, 2-14-2 Nagata-cho, Chiyoda-ku (tel 3593-2421)

Qantas
  Tokyo Shoko Kaigisho Building, 3-2-2 Marunouchi, Chiyoda-ku (tel 3211-4482)
Sabena Belgian World Airlines
  Address Building, 2-2-19 Akasaka, Minato-ku (tel 3585-6151)
Scandinavian Airlines (SAS)
  Toho Twin Tower Building, 1-5-2 Yūraku-cho, Chiyoda-ku (tel 3503-8101)
Singapore Airlines
  Yūraku-cho Building 709, 1-10-1 Yūraku-cho, Chiyoda-ku (tel 3213-3431)
Swissair
  Hibiya Park Building, 1-8-1 Yūraku-cho, Chiyoda-ku (tel 3212-1011)
Thai Airways International
  Asahi Seimei Hibiya Building, 1-5-1 Yūraku-cho, Chiyoda-ku (tel 3503-3311)
United Airlines
  Kokusai Building, 3-1-1 Marunouchi, Chiyoda-ku (tel 3817-4411)
Virgin Atlantic Airways
  3-13 Yotsuya, Shinjuku-ku (tel 5269-2680)

Train

Arriving in Tokyo by train is a simple affair. Most of the major train lines terminate at either Tokyo or Ueno stations, both of which are on the JR Yamanote line. As a general rule of thumb, trains for the north and north-east start at Ueno station and southbound trains start at Tokyo station. For day trips to areas such as Kamakura, Nikkō, Hakone and Yokohama, the most convenient means of transport is usually one of the private lines. With the exception of the Tōbu Nikkō line, which starts in Asakusa, all of them start from somewhere on the Yamanote line.

Shinkansen There are three shinkansen lines that connect Tokyo with the rest of Japan: the Tōkaidō line passes through Central Honshū, changing name along the way to the San-yō line before terminating at Hakata in Northern Kyūshū; the Tōhoku line runs north-east via Utsunomiya and Sendai as far as Morioka; and the Jōetsu line runs north to Niigata. Of these lines, the one most likely to be used by visitors to Japan is the Tōkaidō line, as it passes through Kyoto and Osaka in the Kansai region. The Tōkaidō line starts at Tokyo station, while the Tōhoku and Jōetsu lines start at Ueno station.

Other JR Lines As well as the Tōkaidō shinkansen line there is a Tōkaidō line servicing the same areas but stopping at all the stations that the shinkansen zips through without so much as a toot of its horn. Trains start at Tokyo station and pass through Shimbashi and Shinagawa stations on their way out of town. There are express services to Yokohama and the Izu-hantō Peninsula, via Atami, and from there trains continue to Nagoya, Kyoto and Osaka.

If you are keeping expenses down and travelling long distance on the Tōkaidō line, there are some late-night services that do the Tokyo to Osaka run, arriving early the next morning. One of them will have sleepers available.

Travelling in the same direction as the initial stages of the Tōkaidō line, the Yokosuka line offers a much cheaper service to Yokohama and Kamakura. Like the Tōkaidō line, the Yokosuka line starts at Tokyo station and passes through Shimbashi and Shinagawa stations on its way out of Tokyo.

Northbound trains start in Ueno. The Takasaki line goes to Kumagaya and Takasaki, with onward connections from Takasaki to Niigata. The Tōhoku line follows the Takasaki line as far north as Omiya, from where it heads to the far north of Honshū via Sendai and Aomori. Getting to Sendai without paying any express surcharges will involve changes at Utsunomiya and Fukushima. Overnight services also operate for those intent on saving the expense of a night's accommodation.

Private Lines The private lines generally service Tokyo's sprawling suburbia and very few of them go to any areas that visitors to Japan would care to visit. Still, where private lines do pass through tourist areas, they are usually a cheaper option than the JR lines. Particularly good bargains are the Tōkyū Toyoko line, running between Shibuya station and Yokohama; the Odakyū line, running from Shinjuku to Odawara and the Hakone region; the Tōbu Nikkō line, running from Asakusa to Nikkō; and the

Seibu Shinjuku line from Ikebukuro to Kawagoe.

Bus

There are buses plying the expressways between Tokyo and various other parts of Japan. Generally they are little or no cheaper than the trains but are sometimes a good alternative for long-distance trips to areas serviced by expressways. The buses will often run direct, so that you can relax instead of watching for your stop as you would have to do on an ordinary train service.

There are a number of express buses running between Tokyo, Kyoto and Osaka. Overnight buses leave at 10 pm from Tokyo station and arrive at Kyoto and Osaka between 6 and 7 am the following morning. They cost from Y8000 to Y9000. The buses are a JR service and can be booked at one of the Green Windows in a JR station. Direct buses also run from Tokyo station to Nara and Kōbe. And from Shinjuku station there are buses running to the Fuji and Hakone regions, including, for Mt Fuji climbers, direct services to the fifth stations, from where you have to walk.

Ferry

A ferry journey can be a great way to get from Tokyo to other parts of the country. Fares are not too expensive (by Japanese standards anyway) and there is the advantage that you save the expense of a night or two's accommodation.

From Tokyo, there are long-distance ferry services to Kushiro in Hokkaidō (Y14,420), to Kōchi (Y13,910) and Tokushima (Y8200) in Shikoku, to Kokura in Northern Kyūshū (Y12,000) and to Naha in Okinawa (Y19,670).

Departures may not always be frequent (usually once every two or three days for long-distance services) and ferries are sometimes fully booked well in advance, so it pays to make inquiries early. Unless you have some Japanese-language skills, phoning the ferry companies directly may not always yield the best results. If you have problems, contact the TIC at Narita or in Tokyo.

GETTING AROUND

Tokyo has an excellent public transport system. There are very few worthwhile spots around town that aren't conveniently close to a subway or JR station. When the rail network lets you down, there are generally bus services, though these are harder to use if you can't read kanji.

Most residents of and visitors to Tokyo find themselves using the railway system far more than any other means of transport. In fact, the only real drawback with the Tokyo railway network is that it shuts down somewhere between 12 midnight and 1 am and doesn't start up again until 5 or 6 am. Subway trains have a habit of stopping halfway along their route when closing time arrives. People who get stranded face the prospect of an expensive taxi ride home or of waiting the rest of the night for the first morning train.

Undoubtedly, the most useful line in Tokyo is the JR Yamanote line, which does a loop around the city, taking in most of the important areas. You can do the whole circuit in an hour for the Y120 minimum fare – a great introduction to the city. Another useful above-ground JR route is the Chūō line.

Apart from the JR Yamanote and Chūō lines, there are 10 subway lines, of which seven are TRTA lines and three are TOEI lines. This is not particularly important to remember, as the subway services are essentially the same, have good connections from one to the other and allow for ticket transfer between the two systems.

Avoiding Tokyo's rush hour is a good idea, but unfortunately almost impossible. Things tend to quieten down between 10 am and 4 pm, when travelling around Tokyo can actually be quite pleasant, but before 9.30 am and from about 4.30 pm onwards there are likely to be cheek-to-jowl crowds on all the major train lines. The best advice for coping with the late evening crowds is probably to be as drunk as everyone else.

To/From Narita Airport

Narita International Airport is used by almost all the international airlines but only by a small number of domestic operators. The airport is 66 km from central Tokyo, which means that getting into town is going to take from 50 minutes to 1½ hours, depending on your mode of transport.

The JR Narita express (JR NEX) costs Y2890 to Tokyo central station while a rapid train (kaisoku) on the same line costs Y1260. A train on the private Keisei line, which runs to Ueno station, will cost Y910 or Y1630. A taxi to Tokyo will cost about Y20,000. The so-called limousine buses are Y2500 or Y2700.

Train In March 1991, two Narita Airport railway stations opened under the terminal buildings, providing direct access to the Keisei and JR Narita railway lines. (Prior to their opening, visitors wishing to take a train to Tokyo had to use a five minute shuttle bus service to reach Narita station.)

The JR Narita line has express services (JR NEX) to Tokyo central station (Y2890, 53 minutes); to Shinjuku station (Y3050, 80 minutes); to Ikebukuro station (Y3050, 90 minutes) and Yokohama station (Y4100, 90 minutes). The rapid train (kaisoku) takes 90 minutes and costs Y1260 to Tokyo central.

On the private Keisei line, there are three trains running between Narita Airport and Ueno stations: the Skyliner, which runs nonstop and takes one hour (Y1630); a limited express (tokkyū) service, which takes 70 minutes (Y910); and an express service, which takes 85 minutes. You can buy tickets at the Keisei ticket office in the northern wing of the arrival lounge at Narita Airport or at the station. Ueno is the final destination of the train and is on the JR Yamanote line and on the Hibiya and Ginza subway lines.

Going to the airport from Ueno, the Keisei station is right next to the JR Ueno station. You can buy advance tickets for the Skyliner service at the ticket counter, while limited express and express tickets are available from the ticket dispensing machines. From the JR station on the Yamanote line, take the southern exit (you should come out under the railway bridge, more or less opposite the

Ameyoko market area) and turn right. The station is about 50 metres away on your right.

Limousine Bus Ticket offices, marked with the sign 'limousine', can be found in both wings of the arrival building. The limousine buses are just ordinary buses and take 1½ to two hours (depending on the traffic) to travel between Narita Airport and a number of major hotels around Tokyo. Check departure times before buying your ticket, as services are not all that frequent. The fare to hotels in eastern Tokyo is Y2500, while to Ikebukuro, Akasaka, Ginza, Shiba, Shinagawa, Shinjuku or Haneda Airport it is Y2700. There is also a bus service straight to Yokohama, which costs Y3100. The trip to Yokohama City Air Terminal (YCAT) takes at least two hours.

There are also buses every 20 minutes to the Tokyo City Air Terminal (TCAT), costing Y2500. The TCAT is inconveniently located in Nihombashi, about a 15 minute walk from the nearest subway stations at Ningyō-cho and Kayaba-cho. There is a frequent shuttle bus service between the TCAT and Tokyo station, costing Y200 and departing from the Yaesu side at Tokyo station (look for the signs). If you are leaving Tokyo, you can check in your luggage at the TCAT before taking the bus out to the airport. Allow some extra time if you plan to do this.

To/From Haneda Airport

Most domestic flights and China Airlines (Taiwan) flights use the convenient Haneda Airport.

Getting from Haneda Airport to Tokyo is a simple matter of taking the monorail to Hamamatsu-cho station on the JR Yamanote line. The trip takes just under 20 minutes; trains leave every 10 minutes and cost Y270. Taxis to places around central Tokyo will cost around Y6000. There's a regular bus service between Haneda and the YCAT that takes around 30 minutes.

There is a direct bus service between Haneda and Narita which can take up to two hours, depending on the traffic. The alternative is to take the monorail in to Tokyo, then the Yamanote line to Ueno and the Keisei line from there, but this is much more time consuming.

Train

The Tokyo train system can be a bit daunting at first, but you soon get the hang of it. All the subway lines are colour coded, so even if you can't read a thing you soon learn that the Ginza line is orange. For all local journeys, tickets are sold by vending machines called *jidō kippu uriba*. Above the vending machines will be a rail map with fares indicated next to the station names. Unfortunately for visiting illiterates, the names are almost always in kanji only. Probably the best way around this problem is to put your money in the machine and push the lowest fare button (usually Y120). This will get you on the train and when you get to your destination you can correct the fare at the fare adjustment office. You can get your money back before you press the ticket button by pressing the button marked *torikeshi*.

If you get tired of fumbling for change every time you buy a ticket, the JR system offers the option of 'orange cards'. The cards are available in denominations of Y1000, Y3000 and Y5000. Fares are automatically deducted from the cards when you use them in the orange-card vending machines.

For long-term residents, passes called *teiki-ken* are available between two stops over a fixed period of time, but you really have to use the ticket at least once a day for it to pay off. The incentive for buying one is as much for the saving in time spent queuing for tickets as for any pecuniary advantage.

Also available are the so-called furii kippu, tickets for a day's unlimited travel on either the subway system or the JR system, within the bounds of the Yamanote line. These tickets are not 'free' at all, and given that you generally need to use both systems, are quite difficult to get your money's worth from.

Bus

Many Tokyo residents and visitors spend a considerable amount of time in the city without ever using the bus network. This is partly because the train services are so good and partly because the buses are much more difficult to use. In addition, buses are at the mercy of Tokyo's sluggish traffic. Services also tend to finish fairly early in the evening, making buses a pretty poor alternative all round.

When using the buses, it's useful to have the name of your destination written in Japanese so that you can either show the driver or match up the kanji yourself with that on the route map. Fares are paid as you enter the bus.

Taxi

Taxis are so expensive that you should only use them when there is no alternative. Rates start at Y540 and rise by Y80 every 370 metres. You also click up Y80 approximately every two minutes while you relax in a motionless taxi in a typical Tokyo traffic jam.

If you have to get a taxi late on a Friday or Saturday night and are able to find one, be prepared for delays and higher prices. At these difficult times, gaijin may find themselves shunned like lepers because their ride is likely to be a short one, whereas the drunken salaryman holding up two fingers (to indicate his willingness to pay twice the meter fare) is probably bound for a distant suburb.

Tram

There is a lone tram (streetcar) service operating between two rather uninteresting spots close to Ikebukuro.

Tours

Guided tours of Tokyo are a very expensive way of seeing places that you could see much more cheaply on your own. If you simply *must* join a tour, check with the TIC.

Japan Grey Line (tel 3433-5745) runs typical day and part-day tours. A full-day tour with lunch will set you back Y9200. The company also offers night tours that take in such things as Kabuki, a geisha show, dinner and a 'modern revue' – a variety show featuring girls covered in feathers and dressed in sequenced swimming costumes. The night tours range from Y10,200 to Y14,320 depending on what debaucheries are included in the itinerary.

Unfortunately, the no-pants coffee shop sukiyaki dinner followed by the soapland 'super-pleasure' course and topped off with a group-encounter session at the Meguro Emperor Love Hotel is no longer available as a night-tour option with any of the Tokyo tour companies. You'll have to organise this one on your own.

Around Tokyo 東京の附近

Tokyo itself may be a tangle of expressways and railway lines, an ugly sprawl of office buildings and housing estates, but an hour or so on the train will take you to some of Japan's most interesting travel destinations. Apart from the Ogasawara Islands, all the places in this chapter can be visited as day trips from Tokyo, although in several cases it would be worth staying away overnight.

Foremost among the attractions around Tokyo are Kamakura and Nikkō. If you have limited time and are interested primarily in Japan's important historical sites, these are the places you should visit, along with Kyoto and Nara. If you've got a bit more time, visit Hakone or the Mt Fuji region, where you will get magnificent views of Mt Fuji if the weather is in your favour.

Most of the other places around Tokyo are less interesting to short-term visitors, despite heavy promotion by the Tourist Information Centre (TIC). For long-term residents, places like the Izu-hantō Peninsula and Dogashima are pleasant retreats from Tokyo, but they are geared to Japanese tourists: they have entry fees, roped walkways and orderly queues.

This chapter begins with places to the far west of Tokyo and moves clockwise, finishing with the Izu Seven Islands to the east and the Ogasawara Islands further south.

Izu-hantō Peninsula 伊豆半島

The Izu-hantō Peninsula, west of Tokyo, is noted for its abundance of hot springs, but unless you have a particular interest in hot-spring resorts – an extremely popular holiday option for the Japanese – there's nothing to take short-term visitors there except for some very pleasant scenery. No destination is particularly exciting, and

travel costs to and around the area can be high.

Although you can get around the peninsula in one long and hurried day, it's better to stay overnight at a halfway point, such as Shimoda. If you do this, try to find accommodation at a hot-spring hotel – cooking yourself in a hotel's steaming hot-spring pool can be very relaxing once you've become accustomed to the heat.

A suggested itinerary for circuiting the peninsula is to start at Atami – a hot-spring resort town whose name means 'hot sea' – and travel down the east coast to Shimoda; from there you can cut across to Dogashima on the west coast and travel up to Mishima or Numazu, where there are railway stations with direct access to Tokyo. There are frequent and reliable bus services between all the main towns on the peninsula, and some of the towns are also serviced by ferries.

ATAMI 熱海
Atami has more appeal to Japanese couples for weekend hot-spring affairs than it has to Westerners for its sightseeing potential. Its easy access from Tokyo by shinkansen and its fame as a hot-spring resort make it an expensive place to spend the night, so Itō or Shimoda are better for accommodation on the peninsula.

MOA Art Museum
Atami's prime attraction is the MOA Art Museum. There's a free shuttle bus from the station, but admission is a very hefty Y1500. The museum, housed in the world headquarters of the Church of World Messianity, has a collection of Japanese and Chinese art that includes a few 'national treasures' and a good number of 'important cultural properties'. The museum is open Friday to Wednesday from 9.30 am to 4 pm.

Getting There & Away
An ordinary Tōkaidō line train from Tokyo

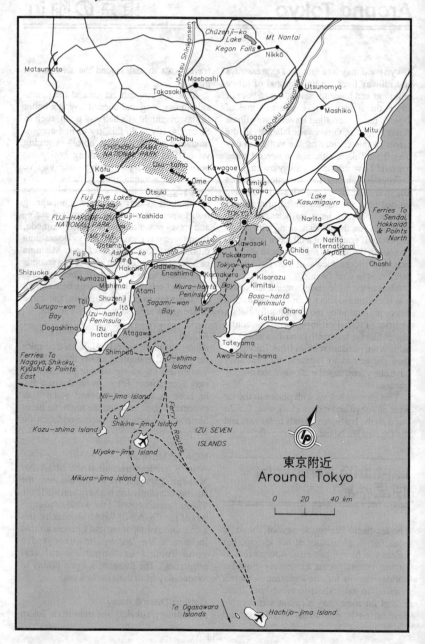

Chūzenji-ko Lake
Kegon Falls
Mt Nantai
Nikkō
Matsumoto
Utsunomya
Takasaki
Maebashi
Mashiko
Jōetsu Shinkansen
Tōhoku Shinkansen
Mitu
Chichibu
Koga
CHICHIBU-TAMA NATIONAL PARK
Kawagoe
Kōfu
Oku-Tama
Ōme
Omiya
Urawa
Lake Kasumigaura
Ōtsuki
Tachikawa
Narita
Fuji Five Lakes
Fuji-Yoshida
TOKYO
Narita International Airport
FUJI-HAKONE NATIONAL PARK
Tōkaidō Shinkansen
Kawasaki
MT FUJI
Gotemba
Yokohama
Chiba
Goi
Choshi
Ferries To Sendai, Hokkaidō & Points North
Fuji
Ashino-ko Lake
Hakone
Odawara
Tokyo-wan Bay
Shizuoka
Numazu
Tōkaidō
Kamakura
Kisarazu
Mishima
Enoshima
Kimitsu
Tōi
Shuzenji
Atami
Miura-hantō Peninsula
Bōsō-hantō Peninsula
Suruga-wan Bay
Itō
Sagami-wan Bay
Miura
Izu-hantō Peninsula
Izu
Inatori
Ōhara
Dogashima
Atagawa
Katsuura
Tateyama
Shimoda
Ō-shima Island
Awa-Shira-hama
Ferries To Nagoya, Shikoku, Kyūshū & Points East
Nii-jima Island
Kōzu-shima Island
Shikine-jima Island
Ferry Routes
IZU SEVEN ISLANDS
Miyake-jima Island
東京附近
Around Tokyo
Mikura-jima Island
0   20   40 km
To Ogasawara Islands
Hachijō-jima Island

station will get you to Atami in one hour 45 minutes for Y1850. The shinkansen takes only 50 minutes but costs Y4000. Ordinary trains leave Tokyo every 40 minutes during the day.

ITO 伊東

Itō is another hot-spring resort and is famous as the place where Anjin-san (William Adams), the hero of James Clavell's *Shogun*, built a ship for the Tokugawa Shogunate. Among the sights around the town are the gourd-shaped Ippeki-ko Lake, the Cycle Sports Centre and the Izu Cactus Garden (ask for Izu Shaboten-kōen), which is 35 minutes by bus from Izu station and costs a mere Y1550 for admission.

In the event of some catastrophe leaving you stranded in Itō, you could continue on to Atagawa by rail and visit the Atagawa Banana & Crocodile Park.

Ikeda 20th Century Art Museum

The Ikeda 20th Century Art Museum has a collection of paintings and sculptures by Matisse, Picasso, Dali and others. The museum is 25 minutes from Itō station and is open daily from 10 am to 4.30 pm. Admission is Y720.

Izu Ocean Park

The Izu Ocean Park (ask for Izu Kaiyō-kōen) has 12 natural swimming pools as well as opportunities for snorkelling and scuba diving. It's 45 minutes by bus from Itō. Admission is Y1550 in July and August, the peak months, and Y550 during the rest of the year.

Festivals

On the first Sunday of July, Itō holds the Tarai-nori Kyoso, although what this race, which involves paddling down the Matsukawa River in washtubs using rice scoops as oars, is in aid of, no-one seems to know.

Places to Stay

The *Itō Youth Hostel* (tel 0557-45-0224) costs Y1980 or Y2180 depending on the

season, and is 15 minutes out of town by bus. The *Tōtaru Youth Hostel* (tel 0557-45-2591) costs Y1900 and is 30 minutes out. The *Izu Okawa Youth Hostel* (tel 0557-23-1063) is similarly priced but easier to find. To get there, go to Izu Okawa station, which is about a third of the way to Shimoda, and exit on the far right-hand side of the station, facing away from Itō. Turn to your left when you come out of the station and turn left again at the T junction. Follow the road till it separates into two roads going in opposite directions and bear to the right. Look for the YH sign on a tree on your left.

Getting There & Away

Itō is about 25 minutes from Atami station on the JR Itō line. When you arrive at Atami station, a sign on the platform in romaji tells you when and from which platform the next train for Itō leaves. There is also a JR limited express (tokkyū) service from Tokyo station to Itō, taking 1 hour 50 minutes and costing Y4000. Direct ordinary trains from Tokyo station are quite a bit cheaper at Y2160 and take about 2 hours 10 minutes.

SHIMODA 下田

If you only have time for one town on the peninsula, make it Shimoda, the most pleasant of the hot-spring resorts. It's a peaceful place with a few historical sites as well as the usual touristy stuff.

Shimoda is famous as the residence of the American Townsend Harris, the first Western diplomat to live in Japan. The Treaty of Kanagawa, which resulted from Commodore Perry's visit, ended Japan's centuries of self-imposed isolation by opening the ports of Shimoda and Hakodate to US ships and establishing a consulate in Shimoda in 1856.

Ryōsen-ji & Chōraku-ji Temples

About a 25 minute walk from Shimoda station is Ryōsen-ji Temple, famous as the site of another treaty, supplementary to the Treaty of Kanagawa, signed by Commodore Perry and representatives of the Tokugawa Shogunate. Today the temple is less interest-

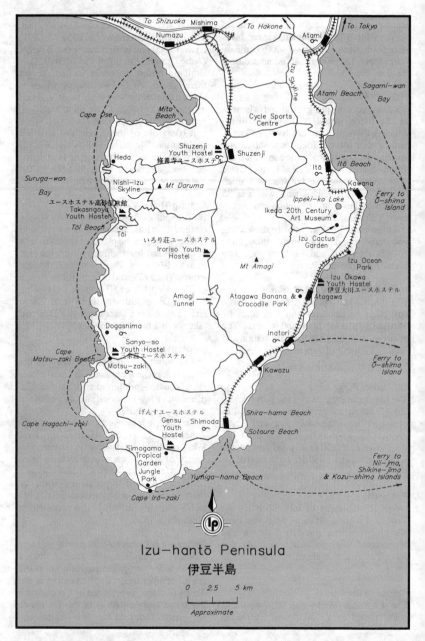

To Shizuoka Mishima
Numazu
To Hakone
Atami
To Tokyo

Izu Skyline

Atami Beach

Sagami-wan
Bay

Cape Ose

Mito
Beach

Cycle Sports
Centre

Shuzenji
Youth Hostel
修善寺ユースホステル

Shuzenji

Heda

Itō
Itō Beach

Kawana

Ferry to
Ō-shima
Island

Suruga-wan
Bay

Nishi-Izu
Skyline

▲ Mt Daruma

Ippeki-ko Lake

ユースホステル高砂屋旅館
Takasngoya
Youth Hostel

Ikeda 20th Century
Art Museum

Tōi Beach

Tōi

いろり荘ユースホステル
Iroriso Youth
Hostel

▲ Mt Amagi

Izu Cactus
Garden

Izu Ocean
Park

Amagi
Tunnel

Atagawa Banana &
Crocodile Park

Izu Ōkawa
Youth Hostel
伊豆大川ユースホステル

Atagawa

Dogashima

Sanyo-so
Youth Hostel
三余荘ユースホステル

Inatori

Cape
Matsu-zaki Beach

Matsu-zaki

Kawazu

Ferry to
Ō-shima
Island

Cape Hagachi-zaki

げんすユースホステル
Gensu
Youth
Hostel

Shimoda

Shira-hama Beach

Sotoura Beach

Simogamo
Tropical
Garden
Jungle
Park

Ferry to
Nii-jima,
Shikine-jima
& Kozu-shima Islands

Yumiga-hama Beach

Cape Irō-zaki

Izu-hantō Peninsula

伊豆半島

0   2.5   5 km

Approximate

ing than its next-door neighbour, Chōraku-ji Temple, which has a collection of erotic knick-knacks – pickled turnips with suggestive shapes and stones with vagina-like orifices in them. Admission to this odd museum is Y200.

The small sex museum also has a series of pictures depicting the tragic life of the courtesan Okichi-san. The story goes that Okichi-san was forced to give up the man she loved in order to attend to the needs of the barbarian Harris, and was thereafter stigmatised by her relationship with him, a situation that drove her to drink and culminated in her suicide. The pictures show the Japanese feeling that their old way of life had been compromised in the confrontation with the West, and Okichi-san is regarded as a kind of sacrifice to internationalism, a symbol of the defilement of Japanese culture by contact with things foreign.

To get to the temples, turn right from the square in front of Shimoda station with the bus ranks. Bear left after you cross the bridge and follow the road around in the same direction as you were walking in before. The temples are to your left, on the opposite side of the road, at the T junction.

Hōfuku-ji Temple
On the way to Ryōsen-ji Temple is Hōfuku-ji Temple, which has a museum that memorialises the life of Okichi-san and includes scenes from the various movie adaptations that have been made of her life.

Mt Nesugata-yama
Cablecars lurch their way up Mt Nesugata-yama every 10 minutes, parking at the top of what is less a mountain than a hill. The park has a photography museum, a small temple, good views of Shimoda and Shimoda Bay and a reasonably priced restaurant. A return cablecar trip, including admission to the park, costs Y820. It's impossible to miss the 'mountain', as it's directly in front of the Shimoda station square.

Festivals
From 16 to 18 May, the Kuro-fune Matsuri (Black Ship Festival) is held in Shimoda. It commemorates the first landing of Commodore Perry with parades and fireworks displays.

Places to Stay
As in the other peninsula resort towns, there is a wealth of accommodation in Shimoda, most of it well out of the price range of mere mortals. The *Gensu Youth Hostel* (tel 05586-2-0035) is 25 minutes by bus from the town and has beds for Y2100. The hostel is opposite a bus stop and a post office.

Staff at the information counter across the square from the station will book accommodation. If you want a cheap room, ask for a minshuku or kokuminshukusha (people's lodge); you should be able to get a room for Y4000 to Y5000. If you want to find something yourself, the best hunting ground is the area that fronts onto Shimoda Bay. Turn right as you leave the station square, take the second left and cross the bridge. Follow this road around and bear left when it approaches the bay. The left-hand side of the road is crowded with hotels, ryokan and minshuku for more than a km.

The *Kinsei Hotel* (tel 05582-2-1253) on the waterfront has singles/doubles for Y8000/15,000. During the week, when it is almost deserted, you can have the hot-spring pool all to yourself.

Getting There & Away
Shimoda is as far as you can go by train on the Izu-hantō Peninsula; the limited express from Tokyo station takes two hours 45 minutes and costs Y5560. Alternatively, take an Izu Kyūkō line train from Itō station for Y1340; the trip takes about an hour. There are a few express services each day from Atami station, but the express surcharges makes them expensive.

Bus platform No 5 in front of the station is for buses going to Dogashima, while platform No 7 is for those bound for Shuzenji.

CAPE IRO-ZAKI 石廊崎
Cape Irō-zaki, the southernmost point of the peninsula, is noted for its cliffs and light-

house. It also has a jungle park and a tropical garden; if that sounds appealing, you can get to the cape by bus or boat from Shimoda.

DOGASHIMA 堂ケ島

From Shimoda, it's a very scenic bus journey to Dogashima, on the other side of the peninsula. There are no breathtaking views, but the hilly countryside and narrow road that winds its way past fields and small rural townships make for an interesting trip. Along the way is Cape Matsu-zaki, recommended for its traditional-style Japanese houses and quiet sandy beach.

The main attractions at Dogashima – a touristy but pleasant place to wander around – are the unusual rock formations that line the seashore. The frequent boat trips available include a visit to the town's famous shoreline cave which has a hole in the roof that lets in light. A 20 minute trip costs Y720, while two hour tours cost Y1680. Paths from the right of the jetty follow the cliffs to the hole in the cave roof.

Getting There & Away

Buses to Dogashima from platform No 5 in front of Shimoda station take about an hour and cost Y1200.

To complete your peninsula circuit, there are a number of bus stops in Dogashima on the road opposite the jetty. The fare to Shuzenji from stop No 2 is a pretty outrageous Y1910. A more interesting and not that much more expensive alternative is to catch a ferry to Numazu, on the Tōkaidō line which can take you back to Tokyo. Boats also go to Toi, where the Takasagoya Youth Hostel is near the harbour. From Toi, you could continue to Heda and Shuzenji by bus or take another boat to Numazu.

HEDA 戸田

Further up the west coast of Dogashima is the small town of Heda, which has a pleasant beach and fewer tourists. Heda is currently pushing to get a bit more of the peninsula's tourist action with a promotional pamphlet that features the mysterious English slogan 'come on your Heda'. To get to Heda from

Dogashima, you may have to change buses at Toi or take the boat from Dogashima and change to a bus at Toi.

SHUZENJI 修善寺

Shuzenji is just another hot-spring resort with overpriced accommodation, but there is a rail connection with the Tōkaidō line in this town, which serves, along with Mishima and Atami, as one of the three rail entry points to the peninsula.

MISHIMA 三島

Mishima is another of the Tōkaidō line entry points to the Izu-hantō Peninsula. The Rakuju-en Garden is a short walk from the station, while Mishima-taisya Shrine is a five minute bus journey away.

Festivals

Mishima-taisya Shrine is the venue for an annual festival involving horseback archery and parades of floats from 15 to 17 August.

Getting There & Away

A Tōkaidō line shinkansen from Tokyo takes one hour five minutes to get to Mishima and costs Y4310. Ordinary trains take twice as long and cost Y2160. From Mishima station, it's half an hour on the private Izu Hakone line to Shuzenji.

It's only 10 minutes by train from Mishima to Numazu, from where it is possible to continue your journey by boat or by bus (see the Dogashima section of this chapter for details).

OKITSU 興津

In the days when feudal lords were required to make regular visits to Edo (Tokyo today), Okitsu was the 17th stop on the old Tōkaidō Highway between Kyoto and Edo. Many visitors to Japan will already be familiar with the town's famous inn, a survivor from the feudal era, as it plays the key role in Oliver Statler's popular book *Japanese Inn*. The Seiken-ji Temple with its attractive garden is about a km west of the station.

SHIMIZU & SHIZUOKA　清水、静岡
A little further west are the towns of Shimizu
and Shizuoka. Tokugawa Ieyasu 'retired' to
Shizuoka and the Kunōzan Tōshō-gū Shrine
in Shimizu has a number of his possessions
in its treasure house. Only moats and ram-
parts mark the site of Shizuoka Castle,
destroyed during WW II, but the town also
boasts the interesting prehistoric site of Toro
Iseki which dates from the Yayoi period (see
the History section in the Facts about the
Country chapter). The site museum displays
the artefacts excavated here and there are
reconstructions of Yayoi dwellings. The site
is about 2½ km south-east of the JR station.

Hakone　箱根

If the weather co-operates and Mt Fuji is
clearly visible, the Hakone region can make
a wonderful day trip out of Tokyo. You can
enjoy cablecar rides, visit an open-air
museum, poke around smelly volcanic hot-
water springs and cruise Ashino-ko Lake.
The weather, however, is crucial, for without
Mt Fuji hovering in the background, much
of what Hakone has to offer is likely to
diminish in interest. Visibility permitting, a
one day circuit of the region offers some of
the best opportunities for a glimpse of
Japan's most famous mountain.

An interesting loop through the region
takes you from Tokyo by train and toy train
to Gōra; then by funicular and cablecar up
Mt Soun-zan and down to Ashino-ko Lake;
by boat around the lake to Moto-Hakone
where you can walk a short stretch of the Edo
era Tōkaidō Highway; and from there by bus
back to Odawara, where you catch the train
to Tokyo. (If you're feeling energetic, you
can spend 3½ hours walking the old
highway back to Hakone-Yumoto, which is
on the Tokyo line.)

ODAWARA　小田原
Odawara is billed in the tourist literature as
an 'old castle town', which it is; the only
problem is that the castle, like many of

Japan's castles, is an uninspiring reconstruction of the original. If you're still interested,
it's a 10 minute walk from Odawara station
and admission is Y250. There is very little
else of interest in the town, which is principally a transit point for Hakone.

HAKONE OPEN-AIR ART MUSEUM
彫刻の森美術館
Between Odawara and Gōra on the Hakone-
Tōzan line is the Chōkoku-no-mori
Bijutsukan. The museum is next to
Chōkoku-no-mori station, a little before
Gōra station, the final stop on the line. The
museum itself features sculptures by
Western artists such as Rodin and Moore in
a 30 sq km park. There are also a couple of
indoor exhibits, including a collection of
Picassos.

Admission is a hefty Y1300, and the
Hakone furii pasu or 'free pass' (see the
following Getting Around section for
details) is *not* accepted. The museum is open
from 9 am to 5 pm between March and
October; during the rest of the year it closes
at 4 pm.

GORA　強羅
Gōra is the terminus of the Hakone-Tōzan
line and the starting point for the funicular
and cablecar trip to Togendai on Ashino-ko
Lake. The town also has a couple of its own
attractions, which may be of minor interest
to travellers.

Gōra-kōen Park
Just a short walk beside the funicular tracks
up Mt Soun-zan is Gōra-kōen Park. For
Y800 you can enjoy the French Rock
Garden, along with a collection of 'seasonal
flowers, alpine plants and tropical plants'.
The park is open from 9 am to 9 pm from 21
July to 21 August; during the rest of the year,
it closes at 5 pm.

Hakone Art Museum
Further up the hill (sorry, mountain), 10
minutes from Gōra station, is the Hakone
Bijutsukan, which has a moss garden and a

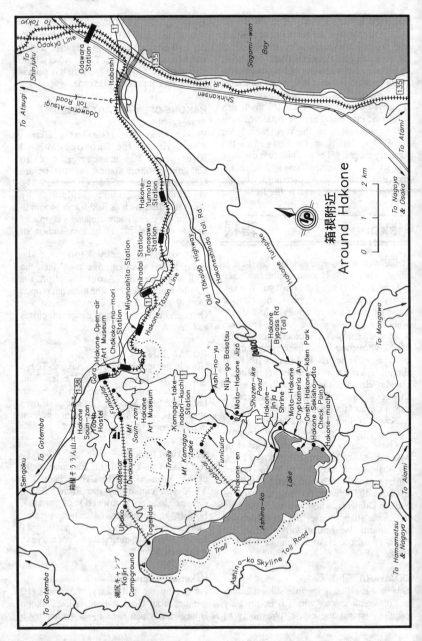

Around Hakone
箱根附近

collection of ceramics from Japan and other Asian nations. It is open Friday to Wednesday from 9.30 am to 4 pm, and admission is Y500.

MT SOUN-ZAN & OWAKUDANI

Almost everyone going to Gōra will continue to the top of Mt Soun-zan on the funicular. If you don't have an Hakone furii pasu (see the following Getting Around section), you'll need to buy a ticket at the booth to the right of the platform exit. You could walk to the top but it's a steep climb and the funicular does it in a mere 10 minutes for only Y280.

Mt Soun-zan is the starting point for what the Japanese refer to as a 'ropeway', a 30 minute, four km cablecar ride to Togendai by Ashino-ko Lake. On the way, the gondolas pass through Owakudani, giving you a chance to get out and have a look at the volcanic hot springs; the gondolas pass by every 52 seconds. If the weather is fine, there are great views of Mt Fuji, both from the gondolas and from Owakudani. The journey from Gōra to Togendai costs Y1560; keep the ticket if you pause at Owakudani.

The volcanic activity at Owakudani includes clouds of steam, bubbling mud and mysterious smells but hopefully no walls of rapidly advancing molten lava. The black, boiled eggs on sale there are cooked in the boiling mud, which it is believed results in certain medicinal properties being imparted. Buy a couple if you feel in need of a volcanic pick-me-up. Next to the cablecar stop, there's a building with restaurants, shops selling tourist junk and a reasonably priced stand-up noodle bar. If you want to sit down, the restaurant has a good lunch selection (the katsudon is not bad, at Y850) with a view of Mt Fuji thrown in (weather permitting).

The Owakudani Natural Science Museum has displays relating to the geography and natural history of Hakone. It's open daily from 9 am to 5 pm, and admission is Y350.

ASHINO-KO LAKE 芦ノ湖

Ashino-ko Lake is touted as the primary attraction of the Hakone region, and although it's actually nothing to get excited about, the majestic form of Mt Fuji does rise over the surrounding hills, its snow-clad slopes reflected on the waters of the lake. That is, if the venerable mount is not hidden behind a dirty grey bank of clouds. If so, you have the consolation of a ferry trip across the lake and a postcard of the view.

At Kojiri, Moto-Hakone and Hakone, you can hire rowing boats (Y500 to Y600 per half hour) or pedal boats (Y1500 per half hour). The truly indolent can take chauffeur-driven motor boats for a Y6000 jaunt around the lake. See the following Getting Around section for more details about lake transport.

MT KOMAGA-TAKE

Mt Komaga-take is a good place from which to get a view of the lake and Mt Fuji. From Togendai, boats run to Hakone-en, from where a cablecar (Y600) goes to the top. You can leave the mountain by the same route or by a five minute funicular descent (Y300) to Komaga-take-nobori-kuchi. Buses run from there to Odawara for Y910.

MOTO-HAKONE 元箱根

Moto-Hakone is a pleasant spot with a few places at which you can eat or get an overpriced cup of coffee. There are a couple of interesting sights within easy walking distance of the jetty.

Hakone-jinja Shrine

It's impossible to miss Hakone-jinja Shrine, with its red torii rising from the lake itself. Walk around the lake towards the torii; huge cedars line the path to the shrine, which is in a wooded grove. The well-maintained shrine is nothing special, but the general effect is quite atmospheric.

Cryptomeria Ave

Cryptomeria Ave or 'Sugi-namiki' is a two km path between Moto-Hakone and Hakone-machi lined with cryptomeria trees planted more than 360 years ago. The path runs behind the lakeside road used by the buses and other traffic.

Old Tōkaidō Highway
Up the hill from the lakeside Moto-Hakone bus stop is the old Tōkaidō Highway, the road that once linked the ancient capital Kyoto with Edo, today the modern capital of Tokyo. You can take a 3½ hour walk along the old road to Hakone-Yumoto station, passing the Amazake-jaya Teahouse, the Old Tōkaidō Road Museum and Soun-ji Temple along the way.

Rock Carvings
The Buddhas and other figures carved in relief at the foot of Mt Futago-jaya can be reached by a 10 minute bus ride to the Futago-jaya bus stop. They date from the Kamakura era (1192 to 1333) and are in a fine state of preservation. On one side of the road is the Niju-go Bosatsu, a rock carved with numerous figures of the Buddha. Across the road, the Moto-Hakone Jizō figure of the patron saint of travellers and souls of departed children is the largest of a number of rock carvings.

HAKONE-MACHI　箱根町
Hakone-machi is further around the lake beyond Moto-Hakone. Known in Japanese as Hakone Sekisho-ato, the Hakone Check Point was operated by the Tokugawa Shogunate from 1619 to 1869 as a means of controlling the flow of anything unwanted – from people and arms to ideas, in and out of Edo. The present-day check point is a recent reproduction of the original. Further back towards Moto-Hakone is the Hakone Sekisho Shiryōkan (Hakone History Museum), which has some samurai artefacts. It's open daily from 9 am to 4.30 pm, and admission is Y200.

FESTIVALS
The Ashino-ko Kosui Matsuri, held on 31 July at Hakone-jinja Shrine in Moto-Hakone, features fireworks displays over Ashino-ko Lake. On 16 August, in the Hakone Daimonji-yaki Festival, torches are lit on Mt Myojoga-take so that they form the shape of the Chinese character for 'big' or 'great'. The Hakone Daimyō Gyoretsu on 3 November is a re-enactment of a feudal lord's procession by 400 costumed locals.

PLACES TO STAY
Hakone's local popularity is reflected in the high price of most accommodation in the area. The *Hakone Soun-zan Youth Hostel* (tel 0460-2-3827) costs the standard Y2100. The hostel is on the left-hand side of the road that goes off to the right of the cablecar. Look for the wooden sign with Japanese writing and the YHA triangle outside the hotel.

The Japanese Inn Group has a comfortable, clean and reasonably priced guesthouse in the area. The *Fuji Hakone Guest House* (tel 0460-4-6577) has singles from Y4500 to Y5000 and twins from Y8000 to Y9000. It is a 45 minute bus journey from stop No 4 at Odawara to the Senkyoro-mae bus stop. When you get off the bus, turn back and take the first right, then turn left into the road opposite the swimming pool (there's a sign on the corner advertising the guesthouse).

If you want the best, the *Fujiya Hotel* (tel 0460-2-2211) is famous as one of Japan's earliest Western-style hotels and has basic doubles from Y12,000. Prices vary with the season. The hotel is near Miyanoshita station on the Hakone-Tōzan line; if you ring from the station, someone will give you instructions in English as to how to get to the hotel.

GETTING THERE & AWAY
There are basically three ways of getting to the Hakone region: by the Odakyū express bus service from the Shinjuku bus terminal on the western side of Shinjuku station; by JR from Tokyo station; and by the private Odakyū line from Shinjuku station.

Train
JR trains run on the Tōkaidō line between Tokyo station and Odawara. Ordinary trains take 1½ hours, cost Y1420 and run every 15 minutes or so. Shinkansen do the journey in 42 minutes, cost Y3570 and leave Tokyo station every 20 minutes.

Trains also service Odawara from Shinjuku station on the Odakyū line. Quickest and most comfortable is the Romance

Car, which takes one hour 25 minutes, costs Y1490 and leaves every half hour. There's also an express service, taking one hour 35 minutes, which at Y610 is by far the cheapest way of reaching Odawara.

At Odawara, it is possible to change to the Hakone-Tōzan line, which takes you to Gōra. Alternatively, if you are already on the Odakyū line, you can continue on to Hakone-Yumoto and change to the Hakone-Tōzan line there simply by walking across the platform.

For those coming from or continuing on to the Kansai region, Kodama shinkansen run between Odawara and Shin-Osaka station. The journey takes three hours 20 minutes, costs Y11,380 (you can use your Japan Rail Pass) and runs every 20 minutes.

Bus

The Odakyū express bus service has the advantage of running directly into the Hakone region, to Ashino-ko Lake and to Hakone-machi for Y1650. The disadvantage is that the bus trip is much less interesting than the combination of Romance Car, toy train (Hakone-Tōzan line), funicular, cablecar (ropeway) and ferry.

GETTING AROUND
Train

The Odakyū line offers an Hakone furii pasu (Hakone free pass), which costs Y4520 and allows you to use any mode of transport within the Hakone region for four days. The fare between Shinjuku and Hakone-Yumoto is also included in the pass, although you will have to pay a Y620 surcharge if you want to take the Romance Car. This is a good deal for a Hakone circuit, as the pass will save you at least Y1000 even on a one day visit to the region.

You can get to Gōra from Odawara or Hakone-Yumoto stations on the the Hakone-Tōzan line (literally the 'Hakone climb mountain line'). The ride itself is very enjoyable, involving several switchbacks in a small train that heaves and puffs against the steep gradient. The journey takes around an hour from Odawara (Y500) or 45 minutes from Hakone-Yumoto (Y380).

Bus

Buses run between Moto-Hakone and Odawara. The trip takes one hour and costs Y1000. At Moto-Hakone, the buses depart from the stop next to the jetty.

Ferry

Ferry services crisscross Ashino-ko Lake, running between Togendai, Hakone-machi and Moto-Hakone for Y870 every 30 minutes or so. Ferries also go to Hakone-machi and Moto-Hakone from Kojiri for Y820.

There are also frequent ferries between Togendai and Moto-Hakone.

Mt Fuji Area
富士山の附近

Curiously, in a country where people have had such an impact on the landscape, Japan's most familiar symbol is a natural one. The perfectly symmetrical cone of Mt Fuji is the most instantly recognisable symbol of the country; combine it with a shinkansen hurtling past and there is absolutely no way of missing that it's Japan you're talking about. Apart from the mountain itself, the Mt Fuji area also has a series of attractive lakes around its northern side.

MT FUJI 富士山
Japan's highest mountain stands 3776 metres high, and when it's capped with snow in winter, it's a picture-postcard perfect volcano cone. Fuji-san, as it's reverently referred to, last blew its top in 1707, when streets in Tokyo were covered in volcanic ash. On an exceptionally clear day, you can see Mt Fuji from Tokyo, 100 km away, but for much of the year you'd be pushed to see it from 100 metres away. Despite those wonderful postcard views, Mt Fuji is a notoriously reclusive mountain, often

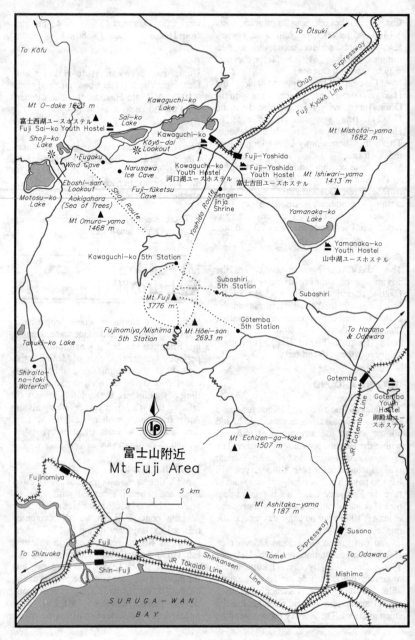

To Ōtsuki

To Kōfu

Chūō Expressway

Fuji Kyūkō Line

Mt O-dake 1623 m

Kawaguchi-ko Lake

Sai-ko Lake

富士西湖ユースホステル
Fuji Sai-ko Youth Hostel

Kōyō-dai Lookout

Shoji-ko Lake

Kawaguchi-ko

Mt Mishotai-yama 1682 m

Fugaku Wind Cave

Narusawa Ice Cave

Fuji-Yoshida

Eboshi-san Lookout

Kowaguchi-ko Youth Hostel
河口湖ユースホステル

Fuji-Yoshida Youth Hostel
富士吉田ユースホステル

Mt Ishiwari-yama 1413 m

Motosu-ko Lake

Aokigahara (Sea of Trees)

Fuji-fūketsu Cave

Sengen-jinja Shrine

Shoji Route

Yoshida Route

Yamanaka-ko Lake

Mt Omuro-yama 1468 m

Kawaguchi-ko 5th Station

Yamanaka-ko Youth Hostel
山中湖ユースホステル

Subashiri 5th Station

Mt Fuji 3776 m

Subashiri

Tanuki-ko Lake

Gotemba 5th Station

To Hadano & Odawara

Fujinomiya/Mishima 5th Station

Mt Hōei-san 2693 m

Shiraito-no-taki Waterfall

Gotemba

Gotemba Youth Hostel
御殿場ユースホステル

富士山附近
Mt Fuji Area

Mt Echizen-ga-take 1507 m

JR Gotemba Line

0   5 km

Fujinomiya

Mt Ashitaka-yama 1187 m

Susono

To Shizuoka

Fuji

Shin-Fuji

JR Tōkaidō Line

Shinkansen Line

Tomei Expressway

To Odawara

Mishima

SURUGA-WAN BAY

hidden by cloud. The views are usually best in winter, when a snow cap adds to the spectacle.

Information

Climbing Mt Fuji and *Mt Fuji & Fuji Five Lakes* brochures are available from the TIC and provide exhaustive detail on transport to the mountain and how to climb it, complete with climbing schedules worked out to the minute. There is a tourist information office in front of the Kawaguchi-ko station.

Fuji Views

You can get a classic view of Mt Fuji from the shinkansen as it passes the city of Fuji. There are also good views from the Hakone area and from the Nagao Pass on the road from Hakone to Gotemba. The road that encircles the mountain offers good views, particularly near Yamanaka-ko and Sai-ko lakes.

Climbing Mt Fuji

Officially the climbing season on Fuji is July and August, and the Japanese, who love to do things 'right', pack in during those busy months. The climbing may be just as good either side of the official season but transport services to and from the mountain are less frequent then and many of the mountain huts are closed. You can actually climb Mt Fuji at any time of year, but a mid-winter ascent is strictly for experienced mountaineers.

Although everybody – from small children to grandparents – makes the ascent in season, this is a real mountain and not to be trifled with. It's just high enough for altitude sickness symptoms to be experienced, and as on any mountain, the weather on Mt Fuji can be viciously changeable. On the summit it can quickly go from clear but cold to cloudy, wet, windy, freezing cold and not just miserable but downright dangerous. Don't climb Mt Fuji without adequate clothing for cold and wet weather: even on a good day at the height of summer, the temperature on top is likely to be close to freezing.

The mountain is divided into 10 'stations' from base to summit but these days most climbers start from one of the four fifth stations, which you can reach by road. From the end of the road, it takes about 4½ hours to climb the mountain and about 2½ hours to descend. Once you're on the top, it takes about an hour to make a circuit of the crater. The Mt Fuji Weather Station on the south-western edge of the crater is on the actual summit of the mountain.

You want to reach the top at dawn – both to see the *goraiko* (sunrise) and because early morning is the time when the mountain is least likely to be shrouded in cloud. Sometimes it takes an hour or two to burn the morning mist off, however. To time your arrival for dawn you can either start up in the afternoon, stay overnight in a mountain hut and continue early in the morning, or climb the whole way at night. You do not want to arrive on the top too long before dawn, as it's likely to be very cold and windy, and if you've worked up a sweat during the climb, you'll be very uncomfortable.

Although nearly all climbers start from the fifth stations, it is possible to climb all the way up from a lower level. These low-level trails are now mainly used as short hiking routes around the base of the mountain, but gluttons for punishment could climb all the way on the Yoshida Route from Fuji-Yoshida or on the Shoji Route from near Shoji-ko Lake.

There are alternative sand trails on the Kawaguchi-ko (Yoshida), Subashiri and Gotemba routes which you can descend very rapidly by running and *sunabashiri* (sliding), pausing from time to time to get the sand out of your shoes.

Fifth Stations There are four fifth stations around Fuji, and it's quite feasible to climb from one and descend to another. On the northern side of Fuji is the Kawaguchi-ko Fifth Station, at 2305 metres, which is reached from the town of Kawaguchi-ko. This station is particularly popular with climbers starting from Tokyo. The Yoshida route, which starts much lower down, close to the town of Fuji-Yoshida, is the same as

Climbing Mt Fuji

I'd started out on a hot August night; at 10 pm the temperature had been in the mid-20°Cs (80°F) but by 4 am it was below freezing and the wind was whistling past at what felt like hurricane speed. With a surprising number of other gaijin and a huge number of Japanese, I'd reached the top of Mt Fuji.

Climbing Fuji-san is definitely not heroic: in the two month 'season' as many as 180,000 people get to the top – 3000-odd every night. Nor is it that much fun – it's a bit of a dusty slog and when you get to the top it's so cold and windy that your main thought is about heading down again. But with Fuji the climb and the views aren't really what you do it for. To Japanese Fuji climbers, it's something of a pilgrimage; to gaijin, it's another opportunity to grapple with something uniquely Japanese.

Like many other climbers, I made my Fuji climb overnight. Although seeing the sunrise from mountaintops is a 'must do' in many places, on Fuji it is almost imperative that you arrive at dawn, as this is the one time of day when you have a good (but not guaranteed) chance of a clear view: most of the time, the notoriously shy mountain is discreetly covered by a mantle of cloud.

So at 9.30 pm I got off the bus at the Kawaguchi-ko Fifth Station, which is where the road ends and you have to start walking. I'd bought some supplies (a litre of 'Pocari Sweat' and a packet of biscuits) at a Seven-11 in the town of Kawaguchi-ko, and wearing a shirt and a coat, I was all set. The night was clear but dark, and I was glad I'd got some new batteries for my flashlight before I'd left Tokyo.

My experience of climbing holy mountains is that you always get to the top too early: you work up a real sweat on the climb, and then you freeze waiting for dawn. So I hung around for awhile before starting out. Surprisingly, about half my fellow passengers on the bus had been gaijin, most of them a group of Americans planning on converting the Japanese to Mormonism!

By the time I reached a marker at 2390 metres I'd already stopped to unzip the lining from my coat, but on the rest of the climb to the top I put on more and more clothes.

Despite the daily hordes climbing the mountain, I still managed to lose the path occasionally, but by 11 pm I was past 2700 metres and thinking it was time to slow down even more if I wanted to avoid arriving too early. By midnight I was approaching 3000 metres – virtually halfway – and at this rate I was going to be at the top by 2.30 am, just about in line with the four hours 35 minutes it was supposed to take, according to the tourist office leaflet! In Japan, even mountain climbing is scheduled to the minute.

It was also getting much cooler. First I added a T-shirt under my shirt, then a hat on my head, then gloves. Next I zipped the jacket lining back in place, and finally, I added a sweater to the ensemble. Although I'd started on my own, some of the other faces I met at rest stops were becoming familiar by this point, and I'd fallen in with two Canadians and a Frenchman.

Huts are littered up the mountainsides, but their proprietors have been fairly cavalier about matching huts with stations: some stations have a number of huts, while others have none. The proprietors are very jealous of their facilities, and prominent signs in English as well as Japanese announce that even if it is pouring with rain, you can stay outside if you aren't willing to fork over the overnight fee. Fortunately, at 1.30 am we were virtually swept into one hut, probably in anticipation of the numerous bowls of rāmen (noodles) we would order. We hung out in this comfortable 3400 metre hideaway until after 3 am, when we calculated that a final hour and a bit of a push would get us to the top just before the 4.30 am sunrise.

We made it and looking back from the top, we suddenly saw hordes of climbers heading up towards us. It was no great surprise to find a souvenir shop (there is absolutely no place in Japan that tourists might get to where a souvenir shop is not already waiting for them). The sun took an interminable time to rise but eventually it poked its head through the clouds, after which most climbers headed straight back down. I spent an hour walking around the crater rim but I wasn't sorry to wave Fuji-san goodbye. The Japanese say you're wise to climb Fuji, but a fool to climb it twice. I've no intention of being a fool.

Tony Wheeler ∎

Food & Drink

Signs & Symbols

the Kawaguchi-ko route for much of the way.

The Subashiri Fifth Station is at 1980 metres, and the route from there meets the Kawaguchi-ko one just after the eighth station. The Gotemba Fifth Station is reached from the town of Gotemba and, at 1440 metres, is much lower than the other fifth stations. From the Gotemba station it takes seven to eight hours to reach the top, as opposed to the 4½ to five hours it takes on the other routes. The Fujinomiya or Mishima Fifth Station, at 2380 metres, is convenient for climbers coming from Nagoya, Kyoto, Osaka and western Japan. It meets the Gotemba route right at the top.

Equipment Make sure you have plenty of clothing suitable for cold and wet weather, including a hat and gloves. Bring drinking water and some snack food. If you're going to climb at night, bring a torch (flashlight). Even at night it would be difficult to get seriously lost, as the trails are very clear, but it's easy to put a foot wrong in the dark.

Mountain Huts There are 'lodges' dotted up the mountainside but they're expensive – Y4000 for a mattress on the floor squeezed between countless other climbers – and you don't get much opportunity to sleep anyway, as you have to be up well before dawn to start the final slog to the top. No matter how miserable the nights, don't plan to shelter or rest in the huts without paying. The huts also prepare simple meals for their guests and for passing climbers. Camping on the mountain is not permitted.

Getting There & Away
See the following Fuji Five Lakes and Gotemba sections for transport details to Kawaguchi-ko and Gotemba, the popular arrival points for Tokyo Fuji climbers. Travellers intending to head west from the Fuji area towards Nagoya, Osaka and Kyoto can take a bus from Kawaguchi-ko or Gotemba to Mishima on the shinkansen line.

Kawaguchi-ko Route From Kawaguchi-ko, there are bus services up to the fifth station from April to mid-November. The schedule varies considerably during that period. The trip takes 55 minutes and costs Y1570. During the peak climbing season there are buses until quite late in the evening – ideal for climbers intending to make an overnight ascent. Taxis also operate from the railway station to the fifth station for around Y7210 plus tolls – not much different from the bus fare when divided amongst four people.

There are also direct buses from the Shinjuku bus terminal to the Kawaguchi-ko Fifth Station. These take 2½ hours and cost Y2160. This is by far the fastest and cheapest way of getting from Tokyo to the fifth station. If you take two trains and a bus, the same trip can cost nearly Y6000.

Subashiri Route From Subashiri, buses take 55 minutes and cost Y1040 to the Subashiri Fifth Station. They start from or finish at the Gotemba station.

Gotemba Route From Gotemba, buses to the Gotemba Fifth Station operate four to six times daily, but only during the climbing season. The 45 minute trip costs Y930.

Fujinomiya or Mishima Route The southern route up the mountain is most popular with climbers from western Japan approaching the mountain by shinkansen. There are bus services from the Shin-Fuji (Y2410) and Mishima railway stations (Y2270) to the fifth station, taking just over two hours. The Shin-Fuji bus goes by the Fujinomiya station, taking 1½ hours and costing Y2000.

FUJI FIVE LAKES 富士五湖
The five lakes arced around the northern side of Mt Fuji are major attractions for Tokyo day-trippers, offering water sports and some good views of Mt Fuji. Yamanaka-ko is the largest of the lakes. On Kawaguchi-ko Lake is a town of the same name which, like Gotemba, is a popular departure point for climbing Mt Fuji. It has two museums: the Fuji Hakubutsukan Museum is near the Fuji

Lake Hotel, a 10 minute walk from the station, and has exhibits on the local area's people and natural history; the Yamanashi-ken Visitors' Centre, a 15 minute walk from the station, has displays about Mt Fuji.

At Fuji-Yoshida is Sengen-jinja Shrine, which dates from 1615 and is dedicated to the kami of the mountain. In the days when climbing Mt Fuji was more of a pilgrimage and less of a tourist event, a visit to this shrine was a necessary preliminary to the ascent. The entrance street to the shrine still has some Edo era pilgrims' inns. Until the Meiji Restoration, women were only allowed to climb Fuji once every 60 years, as the mountain kami was female and would have been jealous of other women.

The area around the smaller Sai-ko Lake is less developed than the areas around the larger lakes. There are good views of Mt Fuji from the western end of the lake and from the Kōyō-dai lookout near the main road. Close to the road are the Narusawa Ice Cave and the Fugaku Wind Cave, both formed by lava flows from a prehistoric eruption of Mt Fuji. There's a bus stop at both caves, or you can walk from one to the other in about 20 minutes. The Fuji-fūketsu Cave, further to the south, is often floored with ice.

The views of Mt Fuji from further west are not so impressive, but tiny Shoji-ko Lake is said to be the prettiest of the Fuji Five Lakes. Continue to Mt Eboshi-san, a one to 1½ hour climb from the road to a lookout over the Aokigahara (the Sea of Trees) to Mt Fuji. Next is Motosu-ko Lake, the deepest of the lakes, while further to the south is the wide and attractive drop of the Shiraito-no-taki Waterfall.

Places to Stay

The *Marimo (Yamanaka-ko)* (tel 0555-62-4210), *Kawaguchi-ko* (tel 0555-72-1431) and *Fuji Sai-ko* (tel 0555-82-2616) youth hostels are by their namesakes. The first two cost Y2100 a night, while the Sai-ko is Y2250 or Y2450, depending on the season. The Sai-ko is also about two km off the main road, which can make getting to it a little difficult. The *Fuji-Yoshida Youth Hostel* (tel

0555-22-0533) in the town of the same name is also Y2100.

There are numerous hotels, ryokan, minshuku and pensions around the Fuji Five Lakes, particularly at Kawaguchi-ko. The tourist information office at the Kawaguchi-ko station can make reservations. The Japanese Inn Group is represented by the *Hotel Ashiwada* (tel 0555-82-2321), at the western end of Kawaguchi-ko Lake. Rooms are Y4000 per person or Y5000 with attached bathrooms.

Getting There & Away

Fuji-Yoshida and Kawaguchi-ko are the two main travel centres in the Fuji Five Lakes area. Buses operate directly to Kawaguchi-ko from the Shinjuku bus terminal in the Yasuda Seimei 2nd building, beside the main Shinjuku station in Tokyo. The trip takes one hour 45 minutes and there are departures up to 16 times daily at the height of the Fuji climbing season. The fare is Y1520. Some buses continue to Yamanaka-ko and Motosu-ko lakes.

You can also get to the lakes by train, although it takes longer and costs more. JR Chūō line trains go from Shinjuku to Otsuki (one hour and Y2890 by limited express; Y1260 by local train or futsū). At Otsuki you cross the platform to the Fuji Kyūkō line local train which takes another 50 minutes at a cost of Y1070 to Kawaguchi-ko. The train actually goes to Fuji-Yoshida first, then reverses out for the final short distance to Kawaguchi-ko. On Sundays and holidays from March to November there is a direct local train from Shinjuku which takes two to 2½ hours and costs Y2200.

From Fuji-Yoshida and Kawaguchi-ko, buses run north to Kofu, from where you can continue north-west to Matsumoto.

Getting Around

There's a comprehensive bus network in the area, including regular buses from Fuji-Yoshida station that pass by the four smaller lakes and around the mountain to Fujinomiya on the south-western side. From Kawaguchi-ko, there are nine to 11 buses daily making the two hour trip to Mishima on the shinkansen line.

GOTEMBA 御殿場

Gotemba is an unexciting town – just an arrival point for Mt Fuji climbers. Views of the mountain from the Gotemba area are unexceptional until you get north near Yamanaka-ko Lake.

Places to Stay

The *Gotemba Youth Hostel* (tel 0550-82-3045) is Y2100 a night.

Getting There & Away

From Shinjuku station in Tokyo, it takes about one hour 45 minutes to get to Gotemba via the JR Gotemba line and then the private Odakyū line. The cost is Y1950. There's one service daily direct from Tokyo station to Gotemba, which would be good for Japan Rail Pass holders. Regular Tomei buses from Tokyo station to the Tomei Gotemba bus stop cost Y1350 and take one hour 45 minutes. This bus stop is on the Tomei Expressway, about a km from Gotemba station.

Getting Around

Buses run 15 to 17 times daily between Gotemba and Kawaguchi-ko from where services continue west via the lakes. Services from Kawaguchi-ko to Mishima, which is on the shinkansen line, operate via Gotemba.

North of Tokyo
東京の北部

North of Tokyo are the Saitama and Tochigi prefectures, which include numerous places of interest, such as the old town of Kawagoe, the Chichibu-Tama National Park and the temple and shrine centre of Nikkō, one of Japan's major tourist attractions.

KAWAGOE 川越

The principal attraction in Kawagoe (population 294,000) is a number of *kurazukuri*

(clay-walled stores), many of them have been designated as 'national treasures'. The clay-walled buildings, built by wealthy merchants, are significant mainly for the fact that they are fireproof. Most of them were built after a disastrous fire swept the town in 1893, and several are now operated as museums. The buildings are strung out along one street, and once you've walked up it there's very little else to do.

Getting There & Away

The Seibu Shinjuku line from Tokyo's Seibu Shinjuku station operates to the conveniently located Hon-Kawagoe station. From the station, take the middle of the three roads that radiate out – most of the old buildings are along this road or on sideroads off it. The Tōbu Tojo line also runs to Kawagoe but the station is inconveniently situated a Y1000 taxi ride from the old part of town.

CHICHIBU-TAMA NATIONAL PARK
秩父国立公園

Hikes in the Chichibu-Tama National Park are more likely to appeal to Tokyo residents than to short-term visitors to Japan. The park is divided into the Chichibu and the Oku-Tama regions – these are connected by a hiking trail that goes via Mt Mitsumine.

Chichibu Region

The Chichibu region has two walks and the famous Chichibu-jinja Shrine, which is near Chichibu and Seibu Chichibu stations. The shorter walk starts from Yokoze station, one stop before Seibu Chichibu station. You can walk the trail as a circuit via Mt Buko-san or turn off to the Urayama-guchi station via the Hashidate Stalactite Cavern.

From Urayama-guchi station it is possible to continue to Mitsumine-guchi station, the starting point for the longer 10 km walk which connects Chichibu with Oku-Tama. There is reasonably priced accommodation available on the trail at the Mountain Hut Kumitori San-sō. The trail goes past Mitsumine-jinja Shrine, about a 40 minute walk from the station. The shrine was founded some 2000 years ago and has long

Chichibu-Tama National Park

1 秩父長瀞SLホテル
2 西中旅館
3 ちくじゅかん旅館
4 秩父ユースホステル
5 山小屋雲取山荘
6 国民宿舎鳩ノ巣荘
7 ユースホステル御嶽
8 駒鳥山荘

been favoured as a mountain retreat by members of the Tendai Buddhist sect. The walk takes about eight hours to Kamozawa, from where buses run to Oku-Tama station.

Nagatoro Near Nagatoro station there is a rock garden and the Nagatoro Synthetic Museum, which houses a collection of rocks and fossils. From mid-March to mid-November, boats leave from Oyahana-bashi Bridge, 700 metres from Kami-Nagatoro station, to shoot the Arakawa River rapids. The trip lasts 50 minutes and costs Y2600.

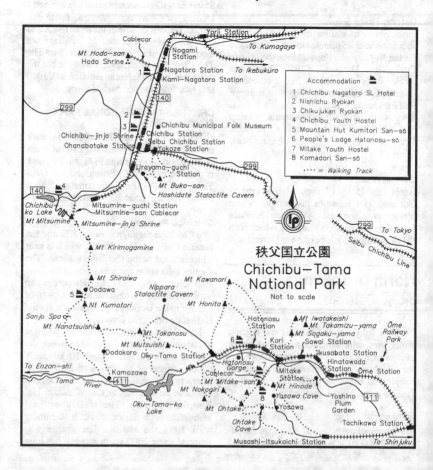

Cablecar
Mt Hodo-san
Hodo Shrine
Yorii Station
To Kumagaya
Nogami Station
Nagatoro Station   To Ikebukuro
Kami-Nagatoro Station

Accommodation
1 Chichibu Nagatoro SL Hotel
2 Nishichu Ryokan
3 Chikujukan Ryokan
4 Chichibu Youth Hostel
5 Mountain Hut Kumitori San-sō
6 People's Lodge Hatonosu-sō
7 Mitake Youth Hostel
8 Komadori San-sō

···· = Walking Track

Chichibu-jinja Shrine
Ohanabatake Station
Chichibu Municipal Folk Museum
Chichibu Station
Seibu Chichibu Station
Yokoze Station
Urayama-guchi Station
Mt Buko-san
Hashidate Stalactite Cavern
Chichibu ko Lake
Mt Mitsumine
Mitsumine-guchi Station
Mitsumine-san Cablecar
Mitsumine-jinja Shrine
Mt Kirimogamine
Mt Shiraiwa
Oodawa
Nippara Stalactite Cavern
Mt Kawanori
Mt Honita
Hatonosu Station
Mt Iwatakeishi
Mt Takamizu-yama
Ome Railway Park
Nt Kumotori
Sanjo Spa
Mt Nanatsuishi
Mt Takanosu
Mt Mutsuishi
Dodokoro
Oku-Tama Station
Kori Station
Mt Sogaku-yama
Sawai Station
Ikusabata Station
Hinatawada Station
Ome Station
To Enzan-shi
Kamozawa
Tama River
Hatonosu Gorge
Cablecar
Mitake Station
Mt Hinode
Yoshino Plum Garden
Oku-Tama-ko Lake
Mt Nokogiri
Mt Mitake-san
Yasawa Cave
Yosawa
Mt Ohtake
Ohtake Cave
Tachikawa Station
Musashi-Itsukaichi Station
To Shinjuku
To Tokyo
Seibu Chichibu Line

秩父国立公園
Chichibu–Tama National Park
Not to scale

Places to Stay *Chichibu Youth Hostel* (tel 0494-55-0056) is about a 15 minute walk from Chichibu-ko Lake bus stop and costs Y1800. The *Chichibu Nagatoro SL Hotel* (tel 0494-66-3011) is good value. It charges Y3800 per person, including two meals, and is close to the Mt Hodo-san cablecar and to Nagatoro station.

Not far from Chichibu station is the *Nishichu Ryokan* (tel 0494-22-1350), costing Y3500 per person or Y5000 with two meals. Down the road towards Chichibu station is the more expensive *Chikujukan Ryokan* (tel (0494-22-1230), which costs Y5000 per person or Y8000 with two meals.

Getting There & Away The cheapest and quickest way of getting to the Chichibu area is via the Seibu Ikebukuro line from Seibu Ikebukuro station. The limited express Red Arrow service goes direct to Seibu Chichibu station in 1½ hours for Y1170. If Ikebukuro is not a convenient spot to commence your trip, JR trains depart from Ueno station to Kumagaya station on the Takasaki line, where you will have to change to the Chichibu Tetsudō line to continue to Chichibu station.

Oku-Tama Region
Like the Chichibu region, Oku-Tama has some splendid mountain scenery and a few good hiking trails.

Ome Railway Park Steam locomotives are on display, and there is a memorial hall housing model trains in the railway museum, about a 15 minute walk from Ome station. It is open Tuesday to Sunday from 9 am to 4.30 pm and admission is Y100.

Mitake From Mitake station it is possible to walk via Mt Sogaku-yama and Mt Takamizu-yama back to Kori station. A shorter (one hour) walk to Sawai station takes in Mitake Gorge and the Gyokudo Art Museum.

Mt Mitake-san Buses run from Mitake station to the Mt Mitake-san cablecar termi-nus, from where a cablecar (Y430) takes you close to the summit. About 30 minutes on foot from the cablecar terminus on Mt Mitake-san is Mitake-jinja Shrine, said to date back some 1200 years.

Other Attractions Buses run from Oku-Tama station to the nearby artificial Oku-Tama-ko Lake. The Nippara Stalactite Cavern is 40 minutes by bus from Oku-Tama station.

Places to Stay The *Mitake Youth Hostel* (tel 0428-78-8501) is very close to the Mt Mitake-san cablecar terminus and charges the usual Y1900 per person. About a 15 minute walk from the cablecar terminus in the opposite direction from the youth hostel is the *Komadori San-sō* (tel 0428-78-8472), which costs Y3500 per person or Y5000 with meals. The *People's Lodge Hatonosu-sō* (tel 0428-85-2340) charges Y2600 per person or Y4800 with two meals, and is a short walk from Hatonosu station.

A good alternative if you're in the mood for hiking is the *Mountain Hut Kumitori San-sō* (tel 0485-23-3311), with a per person charge of Y2300 without meals or Y4000 with them. The hut is a few hours up the trail that connects the Chichibu and Oku-Tama regions.

Getting There & Away You can get to Oku-Tama by taking the JR Chūō line from Shinjuku station to Tachikawa station (Y430) and changing there to the JR Ome line, which will take you on to Oku-Tama station (Y590). The first leg takes 40 minutes, the second, 70 minutes.

NIKKO 日光
Nikkō is not only one of the most popular day trips from Tokyo, it's also one of Japan's major tourist attractions due to the visual splendour of its shrines and temples. Visitors must contend with the jostling crowds found at any of Japan's big-name attractions, but Nikkō should be included on even the most whirlwind tour of Japan.

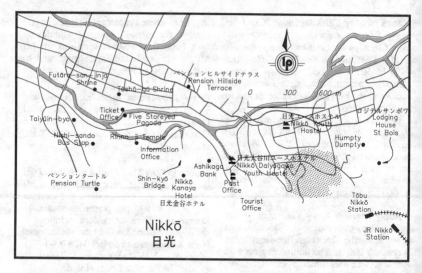

Nikkō
日光

History

Nikkō's history as a sacred site stretches back to the middle of the 8th century, when a Buddhist priest established a hermitage there. For many years it was a famous training centre for Buddhist monks. By the 17th century the area's significance had seriously declined. Nevertheless, it was chosen as the site for the mausoleum of Tokugawa Ieyasu, the warlord who took control of all Japan and established the shogunate which ruled for 250 years until the Meiji Restoration ended the feudal era.

Tokugawa Ieyasu was laid to rest among Nikkō's towering cedars in 1617, but it was his grandson Tokugawa Iemitsu who commenced work in 1634 on the shrine that can be seen today. The original Tōshō-gū Shrine was completely rebuilt using a huge army of some 15,000 artisans from all over Japan.

The work on the shrine and mausoleum took two years to complete and the results continue to receive mixed reviews. In contrast with the simplicity, the minimalism, that is generally considered the essence of Japanese art, every available space of Ieyasu's shrine and mausoleum is crowded with detail. Animals, mythical and other-

wise, jostle for your attention from amongst the glimmering gold-leaf and red lacquerwork. The walls are decorated with intricate patterning, coloured relief carvings and paintings of, among other things, flowers, dancing girls, mythical beasts and Chinese sages. The overall effect is more Chinese than Japanese but don't let this put you off – Tōshō-gū Shrine, despite continuing accusations of vulgarity and that it goes against the grain of all that is quintessentially Japanese, remains a grand experience.

It is worth bearing in mind that what you see at Nikkō was constructed as a memorial to a warlord who devoted his life to conquering Japan. Tokugawa Ieyasu was a man of considerable determination in this respect and was not above sacrificing a few scruples in order to achieve his aims. He is attributed with having had his wife and eldest son executed because at a certain point it was politically expedient to do so in order to ingratiate himself with other feudal powers. More than anything else, the grandeur of Nikkō is intended to inspire awe; it is a display of wealth and power by a family that for nearly three centuries was the supreme arbiter of power in Japan.

Information

First stop in Nikkō (after the cheesecake shop next to the Tōbu Nikkō line railway station of course) should be the excellent tourist information office on the road up to Tōshō-gū Shrine. The office has a wealth of useful pamphlets and maps, as well as up-to-date information on how not to get completely ripped off and pissed off by the highly unusual ticketing arrangements that are in force at Nikkō's shrines and temples. The office even has a resident gaijin dispensing information to bewildered travellers.

Tickets Every shrine has its own admission fee, but there are also tickets available which allow you entry to all the shrines. These multiple-entry tickets are substantially cheaper than paying individual entry fees. However, within a couple of shrines there are further charges for special sights that aren't covered by the multiple-entry tickets but *are* included in the individual entry tickets. The best option is probably to go to one of the ticket offices and ask for the Y750 *nisha ichiji kyōkutsuken* (two-shrines-one-temple ticket), which gets you into Tōshō-gū Shrine, Rinnō-ji Temple and Futāra-san-jinja Shrine, Nikkō's major attractions. (Separately, entry to these three would come to Y2010.) However, once in the shrines and temples, you will have to make decisions about whether to pay extra for other sights, such as Ieyasu's Tomb and the Sleeping Cat (Y430) at Tōshō-gū Shrine.

Shin-kyō Bridge

If you take the road from the Tōbu Nikkō line station to Tōshō-gū Shrine area, the first point of interest you come to is the Shin-kyō Bridge. The story goes that the monk, Shōdō Shōnin, who first established a hermitage in Nikkō in 782, was carried across the river at this point on the backs of two huge serpents. Today's bridge is a 1907 reconstruction of the mid-17th century original. It costs Y300 to cross the bridge on foot.

Rinnō-ji Temple

The original temple on this site was founded 1200 years ago by Shōdō Shōnin and it remains a temple of the Buddhist Tendai sect. The Sambutsu-dō (Three Buddha Hall) has huge gold-lacquered images, the most impressive of which is the *senjū* (1000 armed Kannon). The central image is Amida Nyorai, flanked by *batō* (a horse-headed Kannon), whose special domain is the animal kingdom.

The Hōmutsu-den (Treasure Hall), also on the temple grounds, has a collection of treasures associated with the temple, but admission (Y250) is not included in the two-shrines-one-temple ticket.

Tōshō-gū Shrine

A huge stone torii marks the entrance to Tōshō-gū Shrine, while to the left is a five storeyed pagoda, originally dating from 1650 but reconstructed in 1818. The building is remarkable for its lack of foundations: the interior is said to contain a long suspended pole that swings like a pendulum in order to restore equilibrium in the event of an earthquake.

The true entrance to the shrine is through the torii at the Omote-mon Gate, protected on either side by Deva kings. Through the entrance to the right is the Sanjinko (Three Sacred Storehouses), the upper storey of which is renowned for the imaginative relief carvings of elephants by an artist who had never seen the real thing. To the left of the entrance is the Sacred Stable, a suitably plain building housing a carved white horse. The stable's only adornment is an allegorical series of relief carvings depicting the life-cycle of the monkey. They include the famous 'hear no evil, see no evil, speak no evil' threesome that has become emblematic of Nikkō.

Just beyond the stable is a granite water font at which, in accordance with Shinto practice, worshippers can cleanse themselves by washing their hands and rinsing their mouths. Next to the gate is a sacred library containing 7000 Buddhist scrolls and books; it's not open to the public.

Pass through another torii, climb another

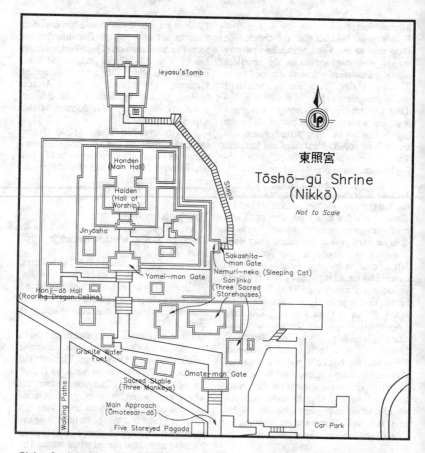

 leyasu's Tomb

Honden
(Main Hall)

Haiden
(Hall of
Worship)

Jinyōsha

東照宮
Tōshō-gū Shrine
(Nikkō)

Not to Scale

Steps

Sakashita-
mon Gate

Nemuri-neko (Sleeping Cat)

Yomei-mon Gate

San jinko
(Three Sacred
Storehouses)

Honji-dō Hall
(Roaring Dragon Ceiling)

Granite Water
Font

Omote-mon Gate

Walking Paths

Sacred Stable
(Three Monkeys)

Main Approach
(Ōmotesar-dō)

Five Storeyed Pagoda

Car Park

flight of stairs, and on the left and right are a drum tower and a belfry. To the left of the drum tower is the Honji-dō Hall, which has a huge ceiling painting of a dragon in flight known as the Roaring Dragon. There's a queue to stand beneath the dragon and clap hands in order to hear it roar.

Next comes the Yōmei-mon Gate, which is covered with a teeming multitude of reliefs of Chinese sages, children, dragons and other mythical creatures. So much effort and skill went into the gate that its creators worried that its perfection might arouse envy in the gods, so the final supporting pillar on

the left-hand side was placed upside down as a deliberate error.

Through the Yōmei-mon Gate and to the right is the Nemuri-neko (Sleeping Cat). The Sakashita-mon Gate here opens onto a path that climbs up through towering cedars to Ieyasu's tomb, a relatively simple affair. If you are using the two-shrines-one-temple ticket it will cost an extra Y430 to see the cat and the tomb. To the left of the Yōmei-mon Gate is the Jinyōsha, a storage depot for Nikkō's mikoshi (portable shrines), which come into action during the May and October festivals. The Honden (Main Hall) and the Haiden (Hall of Worship) can also be seen in the enclosure.

Futāra-san-jinja Shrine

Shōdō Shōnin founded this shrine. It's dedicated to the mountain Nantai, to the mountain's consort Nyotai and to their mountainous progeny Tarō.

Taiyūin-byō

The Taiyūin-byō enshrines Ieyasu's grandson Iemitsu (1604-51) and is very much a smaller version of Tōshō-gū Shrine. The smaller size gives it a less extravagant air and it has been suggested that it is more aesthetically worthy than its larger neighbour – this is best left for the experts to quibble over. Many of the features to be seen in the Tōshō-gū are replicated on a smaller scale: the storehouses, drum tower and Chinese gate for example. The shrine also has a wonderful setting in a quiet grove of cryptomeria.

Chūzenji-ko Lake

On a quiet day it's a 50 minute bus trip up to Chūzenji-ko Lake along a winding road complete with hairpin bends. There's some beautiful scenery, including the 97 metre Kegon Waterfall and the lake, but don't cut short a visit to the shrine area just so as to fit in Chūzenji-ko Lake. The waterfall features an elevator (Y300) down to a platform where you can observe the full force of the plunging water. Also worth a visit is the third of the Futāra-san-jinja shrines, complementing the ones in Tōshō-gū Shrine area and on Mt Nantai.

Buses run from Tōbu Nikkō station to Chūzenji Onsen at 10 to 20 minute intervals from 6.20 am to 7.30 pm and cost Y900. Returning buses depart only once an hour. The cablecar at the lake costs Y650 one way.

The wonderful little *Guide in Nikkō* points out that the Kegon Waterfall is 'greatly noted for committing suicide', and that nowadays 'more than one hundred people are coming here every year, intending to commit suicide'. The Kegon Waterfall has an historical pedigree as a destination for those set on doing away with themselves, having first been used for this purpose by a Tokyo high school student 'who jumped down from the top for the first time' in 1893. It's actually not clear whether he committed suicide from being 'too much absorbed in philosophy', as the guidebook suggests, or whether he was suffering from a chronic complex about his height. His final words read: 'How long the time is! How spacious the heaven and earth! I am going to measure the greatness with my body, which is only five feet tall'.

Festivals

The Gōhan Shiki on 2 April is a rice-harvesting festival held at Rinnō-ji Temple in which men (in days past, samurai lords) are forced to eat great quantities of rice in a tribute to the bounty supplied by the gods. Sacred dances are also performed by the priests as an accompaniment to the ceremonial pig-out.

On 16 and 17 April, the Yayoi Matsuri – a procession of portable shrines – is held at Futāra-san-jinja Shrine.

The Tōshō-gū Shrine Grand Festival on 17 and 18 May is Nikkō's most important annual festival. It features horseback archery and a 1000-strong costumed re-enactment of the delivery of Ieyasu's remains to Nikkō.

The Tōshō-gū Shrine Autumn Festival is held on 17 October and needs only the equestrian archery to be an autumnal repeat of the performance in May.

Places to Stay

Because of Nikkō's importance as a tourist attraction, it is one of the few places in Japan, apart from Tokyo and Kyoto, where travellers on a budget actually get some choice as to where to stay. If you're willing to spend Y1000 or so over the standard youth hostel rates, there are some very good accommodation options close to the central shrine and temple area.

Youth Hostels The *Nikkō Daiyagawa Youth Hostel* (tel 0288-54-1974) is the more popular of the town's two hostels. It costs Y1900 per night and is just behind the post office. A 10 minute walk away is the *Nikkō Youth Hostel* (tel 0288-54-1013); it is slightly cheaper, at Y1800, but meals there are a little more expensive.

Pensions Nikkō's proliferating pensions offer very reasonable rates and clean, comfortable surroundings. Per person costs are around Y5000 but in many cases you can reduce expenses by sharing rooms with other travellers. Nikkō is very popular so book ahead. All of the following pensions have someone who can answer your questions in English.

Far and away the most popular of Nikkō's pensions is the *Pension Turtle* (tel 0288-53-3168), with rooms from Y3300 per person. It's by the river, beyond the shrine area. Also justifiably popular is the *Lodging House St Bois* (tel 0288-53-0082). This place touts itself as a mountain lodge and has both Western and Japanese-style singles/doubles starting at Y4500/9200 for rooms without baths. It's across the river, north of the station.

Other pensions around Nikkō are a little more expensive, but feature extra touches such as Italian-trained chefs. Recommended is the *Pension Hillside Terrace* (tel 0288-54-3235), which charges Y5000 per person or Y6500 for rooms with attached bathrooms. *Humpty Dumpty* (tel 0288-53-3168) is similarly priced and is near the Lodging House St Bois.

Hotels Not far from the Shin-kyō Bridge is the *Nikkō Kanaya Hotel* (tel 0288-54-0001), where singles without bathrooms cost Y6500 and twins without bathrooms cost Y7500; the price is very reasonable for a hotel that combines classiness with a great location. Not quite in the same historical league as the nearby shrines and temples, this hotel has nevertheless been running since the 1870s. During peak holiday periods – Golden Week and the summer holidays for example – room prices soar to nearly double the normal rates.

Places to Eat

Eating options are mainly noodle and rice dishes. There are a few places on the road from the railway stations to the shrine area. In the shrine area itself there are a couple of shops selling tourist trinkets and quite rea-sonable food – they'll even provide an English menu if you look like you are having difficulties.

Next to the Tōbu Nikkō station is a tiny coffee and cheesecake shop, which is a nice place to hang out while waiting for the next train.

For an up-market lunch or dinner, the restaurant at the *Nikkō Kanaya Hotel* is recommended both for its atmosphere and for its meals, which cost from Y1500 to Y3000.

Getting There & Away

The best way to visit Nikkō is via the Tōbu Nikkō line from Asakusa station in Tokyo. The station, which is separate from Asakusa subway station, is in the basement of the Tōbu Department Store, but is well signposted and easy to find from the subway. Limited express trains cost Y2200 and take one hour 55 minutes. These trains require a reservation (on a quiet day you'll probably be able to organise this before boarding the train) and run every 30 minutes or so from 7.30 to 10 am; after 10 am they run hourly. Rapid trains require no reservation, take 15 minutes longer than the limited express and cost Y1100. They run once an hour from 6.20 am to 4.30 pm.

As usual, travelling by JR trains works out to be more time consuming and more expensive and is only really of interest to those on a Japan Rail Pass. The quickest way to do it would be to take the shinkansen from Ueno to Utsunomiya (Y4400, 50 minutes) and change there for an ordinary train (no other options) for the 45 minute, Y700 journey to Nikkō. The trains from Utsunomiya to Nikkō leave on average only once an hour.

A limited express service taking 1½ hours and costing Y3600 and an ordinary service taking one hour 50 minutes and costing Y1800 also run between Ueno and Utsunomiya.

MASHIKO 益子

Mashiko is a centre for country-style pottery, with about 50 potters, some of whom you can see working at their kilns. The town achieved fame when the potter Hamada Shōji settled there and, from 1930, produced his Mashiko pottery. Today he is designated as a 'living national treasure' and has been joined in Mashiko by a legion of other potters. The noted English potter Bernard Leach also worked there for several years.

Getting There & Away
It is possible to combine Mashiko with a visit to Nikkō if you set off from Tokyo very early and use the JR route. See the Nikkō Getting There & Away section for travel details to Utsunomiya. From Utsunomiya, buses run regularly during the day to Mashiko, taking one hour and costing Y1000 one way.

East of Tokyo
東京の東部

East and south-east of Tokyo much of Chiba-ken is suburbs or market gardens. There are few compelling reasons to visit the area. However, a large majority of visitors to Japan will arrive or depart from Narita Airport, and if you have a few hours to kill at the airport, there are some points of interest in the town of Narita.

NARITA　成田
If you're not going to the airport, the only real reason to go to Narita is to visit Narita-san Shinshō-ji Temple. It was founded some 1000 years ago, though the main hall is a 1968 reconstruction. The temple itself remains an important centre of the Shingon sect of Buddhism and attracts as many as 10 million visitors a year. Taxis and buses run to the temple from the JR and Keisei Narita stations.

If you've got to kill time in the airport area, there's also the Museum of Aeronautical Sciences and the Chiba Prefectural Botanical Garden, both right beside the airport. There's a brochure *For Passengers Transiting at Narita* about the airport vicinity attractions, and tours are operated from the airport.

Festivals
The main festivals centred around Narita-san Shinshō-ji Temple are Setsubun, on 3 or 4 February, and the Year End Festival, on 25 December. Things get very hectic at the temple on both these occasions and a high tolerance level for crowds is a must.

Places to Stay
If you have to stay at Narita – perhaps because you are catching an early flight – there are several accommodation options in the vicinity, though none in the real budget category.

Not far from Narita-san Shinshō-ji Temple is the *Kirinoya Ryokan* (tel 0476-22-0724) with singles/doubles for Y4000/7000. To get there, leave the temple by the front gate and turn left; the ryokan is about five minutes down the road on the left.

Not much further from the temple is the *Business Hotel Teradai* (tel 0476-23-0744), with singles from Y4000 to Y4500 and doubles from Y7000 to Y8000. To get there, continue walking straight ahead from the Kirinoya Ryokan and cross the bridge and an intersection; the hotel is on your right.

Getting There & Away
From Narita Airport there are buses going into the city of Narita every 20 minutes or so from bus gate No 5. The trip takes 25 minutes and costs Y370. The easiest way to get to Narita is via the Keisei line, which starts in Ueno. For information on using this service, see the Tokyo Getting There & Away section.

BOSO-HANTO PENINSULA　房総半島
The Boso-hantō Peninsula's attractions are almost certainly only for long-term residents, although the displays by women divers at Shira-hama and Onjuku beaches may be of interest to foreign visitors. The women dive to the sea bottom in search of edible goodies such as shellfish and seaweed.

The peninsula's main attraction is its beaches, most of which are easily accessible by train. The tourist literature promises a number of unusual activities at the beaches, including 'houseback rising', 'summering', 'sand bath' and 'dragnet fishing'.

Places to Stay

The Boso-hantō Peninsula is a very popular resort for Japanese, so there are many minshuku and youth hostels. Youth hostels, all at Y1900 per person, include the *Kujūkurihama Youth Hostel* (tel 0475-33-2254) at Awa-Amatsu, the *Tateyama Youth Hostel* (tel 0470-28-0073) at Cape Nojima-zaki and the *Hiranoya Youth Hostel* (tel 0439-87-2030) at Kisarazu.

Getting There & Away

Train The Boso-hantō Peninsula can be reached on either the Sotobō line or the Uchibō line, both running from Tokyo station. From Tokyo to Ohara Beach costs Y3020 and takes one hour 25 minutes via the Sotobō line. A cheaper option is to go to Goi on the Uchibō line, which costs Y930 and takes one hour five minutes. Onward travel from this point will be expensive.

Ferry An unusual approach to the peninsula is to take a ferry from Kawasaki's Ukushima Port. One leaves every 30 minutes, taking 70 minutes to Kisarazu and costing Y1000.

Getting Around

The transport network around the peninsula is very good. Most of the beaches are serviced by JR trains; there is also a private line that cuts across the peninsula from Goi to Ohara, as well as a good network of local buses.

South-West of Tokyo
東京の南西部

South-west of Tokyo are the cities of Kawasaki and Yokohama, which have virtually merged with the capital to create one immense urban corridor. Beyond this huge city is the fascinating old town of Kamakura and the Miura-hantō Peninsula.

KAWASAKI 川崎

Kawasaki (population one million) is a fairly uninteresting industrial city. However, it does have the colourful Horinouchi entertainment district, an interesting enclave of Love Hotels and the Nihon Minka-en Garden.

Nihon Minka-en Garden

The Nihon Minka-en Garden is an open-air museum with 22 traditional Japanese buildings collected from the surrounding country and reassembled on one sight to give visitors a glimpse of the way of life of an older Japan.

Most of the structures are farmhouses, although there are also a Shinto shrine and a kabuki stage. The oldest of the buildings dates back to 1688.

The garden is open Tuesday to Sunday from 9.30 am to 4 pm, except over New Year, when it is closed. Admission is Y300. The garden is about a 10 minute walk from Mukōgaoka-yuen station on the Odakyū line.

Festivals

Kawasaki hosts the famous Jibeta Matsuri. Processions of costumed people carry wooden phalluses to celebrate the vanquishing of a sharp-toothed demon with an appetite for male sexual organs. The demon had taken up residence in a fair maiden and had already emasculated two bridegrooms before a local blacksmith came up with the ingenious idea of deflowering the maiden with an iron phallus. This scheme can't have been particularly appealing to the maiden but defeat of the demon gave rise to much celebration and an annual re-enactment of the forging of the metal phallus.

The festival takes place in the late afternoon of 15 April, commencing with a procession, followed by a re-enactment of the forging and rounded off with a banquet. The action takes place close to Kawasaki Taishi station.

Getting There & Away

Take the Odakyū line from Tokyo's Shinjuku station to Mukōgaoka-yuen station. From the southern exit, look for the start of the monorail and follow the line until it bears left, when you must bear right. The Nihon Minka-en is up the hill and on the right-hand side, opposite a parking lot.

YOKOHAMA 横浜

The site of present-day Yokohama (population three million) was little more than mud flats 150 years ago, but with the end of Japan's long isolation from the outside world the city was the closest port to Tokyo open to foreign traders. Since then Yokohama has grown to be the second largest city in Japan, sprawling outwards from its original small-town beginnings at the water's edge and forming a vast continuous conurbation with Tokyo.

Unfortunately, Yokohama is like a dull extension of Tokyo, lacking the bright lights, historical sites and vibrant, international-city atmosphere of the capital. Yokohama has always had a relatively large foreign population, including a large Chinese community, but the city's only real attractions are a fairly uninteresting harbour, an unexceptional Chinatown and the Sankei-en Garden.

Information

The Yokohama International Tourist Association (tel 045-641-5824) and the Kanagawa Prefectural Tourist Association (tel 045-681-0007) are both next door to the Silk Museum. Both offices have at least one staff member who speaks English and useful brochures including the *Tourist Map of Yokohama*.

Sankei-en Garden

The Sankei-en Garden is not particularly old, having been established in 1906 by a Yokohama silk merchant, but it is beautifully landscaped and features a three storeyed pagoda that is 500 years old. The pagoda, along with an old villa and farmhouses, was moved to the garden and reconstructed there.

There are separate Y200 admission charges to the outer and inner gardens. The inner one is a fine example of traditional Japanese garden landscaping. The garden is open daily from 9 am to 4.30 pm. The No 8 bus, from the road running parallel to the harbour behind the Marine Tower, operates with less than commendable frequency. If one does happen along, ask for the Sankei-en-mae bus stop.

Marine Tower

Viewing towers seem to be a popular feature of almost every major Japanese city. Basically the idea is to queue for 15 minutes, fork out Y600, catch a crowded lift commanded by a chirping hostess in a silly hat to the top floor of the 106 metre high tower and then peer through the smog at the sea on one side and an apparently infinite expanse of concrete on the other.

Chinatown

About a five to 10 minute walk from the Marine Tower and away from the harbour is Chinatown, or 'Chukagai', as it is known in Japanese. Even if you've seen plenty of Chinatowns before, the gaudy colours and the liveliness on the streets of this district are a welcome respite from the rest of Yokohama.

Other Attractions

The Silk Museum deals with every possible aspect of silk and silk production with characteristic Japanese thoroughness. Entry is Y300 and it's closed on Mondays. About five minutes from the Silk Museum is the harbourfront Yamashita-kōen Park. Moored in the harbour next to the park is the *Hikawa Maru*, a passenger liner that you can board and explore. In summer, the boat stays open till 9 pm and has a beer garden. Admission is Y700.

Harbour cruises operate from the pier next to the *Hikawa Maru* and take from 40 minutes (Y750) to 1½ hours (Y2000). Close to the Marine Tower is the Yokohama Doll Museum, which has 1200 dolls from around the world. Admission is Y300 and it is open from 10 am to 5 pm. Just beyond the expressway is the Harbour View Park and the nearby Foreigner's Cemetery, containing the graves of more than 4000 foreigners.

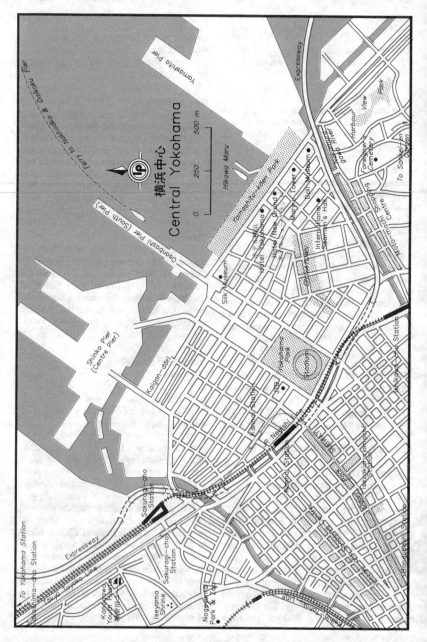

横浜中心
Central Yokohama

Places to Stay

The *Kanagawa Youth Hostel* (tel 045-241-6503) costs Y2000. From Sakuragi-cho station, exit on the opposite side to the harbour, turn right and follow the road alongside the railway tracks. Cross the main road, turn left into the steep street with a bridge and a cobblestoned section and the youth hostel is up the road on the right.

Most other accommodation in Yokohama is aimed at business travellers but the *Yokohama International Seamen's Hall* (tel 045-681-2358) is slightly cheaper, with singles/doubles for Y4600/8800. Walk away from the harbour along the road beside the Marine Tower to the third intersection and turn right.

Opposite Yamashita-kōen Park, the expensive *Hotel Yokohama* (tel 045-662-1321) is an up-market option by the waterfront, offering singles/doubles for Y12,000/22,000. The marginally cheaper *Hotel New Grand* (tel 045-681-1841) has singles/doubles for Y11,700/20,450.

Places to Eat

Chinatown is undoubtedly the place for a meal in Yokohama although, as usual, the food has been modified to suit Japanese tastes. Front window displays are common in the many restaurants, and long queues of patient Japanese pinpoint the best places.

Getting There & Away

Train There are numerous trains from Tokyo, the cheapest being the Tōkyū Toyoko line from Shibuya station to Yokohama station for Y160. The trip takes 40 minutes and continues from Yokohama station to Sakuragi-cho station, a bit closer to the harbour area.

The Keihin Tōhoku line from Tokyo station is a bit more convenient, going through to Kannai station, but at Y610 it's considerably more expensive. If you only want to go as far as Yokohama station, take the Tōkaidō line from Tokyo station or Shinagawa station; the 30 minute trip costs Y470.

It is convenient to continue on to Kamakura on the Yokosuka line from Yokohama station. There is also a shinkansen connection for those continuing to the Kansai region.

Ferry Ships from Nakhodka in the USSR, the eastern end of the line for the Trans-Siberian Railway, arrive at Yokohama's Osanbashi Pier. There's an information office on the pier and another in the nearby Silk Museum building.

Getting Around

To/From the Airport Buses run from Narita and Haneda airports to the Yokohama City Air Terminal (YCAT) (tel 045-459-4800) by the eastern exit of Yokohama station. It's only 30 minutes to Haneda but it takes 2½ hours and costs Y3200 to get to Narita.

KAMAKURA 鎌倉

Kamakura may not have as much to offer historically as Kyoto or Nara but a wealth of notable Buddhist temples and Shinto shrines make this one of Tokyo's most interesting day trips. The town has some relaxing walks and a peacefulness that is hard to come by in locations such as Kyoto that are particularly popular with tourists.

History

Kamakura is a bit of a backwater today, although its moment of glory included a spell as the capital from 1192 to 1333. In the 10th century the power of the emperor was restricted to ceremonial and cultural affairs, while real power had for some time been in the hands of the Fujiwara clan. As the Fujiwaras themselves declined, other clans became increasingly powerful, until the Taira, led by Taira Kiyomori, and the Minamoto, led by Minamoto Yoshitomo, commenced an all-out struggle for supreme power. The struggle culminated in a battle in 1159 that completely routed the Minamoto forces.

In the executions that followed, by chance Yoshitomo's third son's life was spared and the boy was sent to spend his days in an Izu-hantō Peninsula temple. However, as

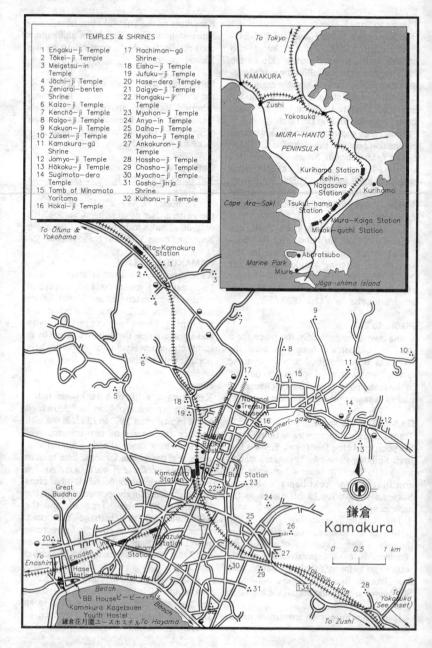

TEMPLES & SHRINES

1 Engaku–ji Temple
2 Tōkei–ji Temple
3 Meigetsu–in Temple
4 Jōchi–ji Temple
5 Zeniarai–benten Shrine
6 Kaizo–ji Temple
7 Kenchō–ji Temple
8 Raigo–ji Temple
9 Kakuon–ji Temple
10 Zuisen–ji Temple
11 Kamakura–gū Shrine
12 Jomyo–ji Temple
13 Hōkoku–ji Temple
14 Sugimoto–dera Temple
15 Tomb of Minamoto Yoritomo
16 Hokai–ji Temple
17 Hachiman–gū Shrine
18 Eisho–ji Temple
19 Jufuku–ji Temple
20 Hase–dera Temple
21 Daigyo–ji Temple
22 Hongaku–ji Temple
23 Myohon–ji Temple
24 Anyo–in Temple
25 Daiho–ji Temple
26 Myoho–ji Temple
27 Ankokuron–ji Temple
28 Hossho–ji Temple
29 Chosho–ji Temple
30 Myocho–ji Temple
31 Gosho–jinja Shrine
32 Kuhonu–ji Temple

鎌倉
Kamakura

0   0.5   1 km

Kamakura Temples & Shrines

1	円覚寺	17	鶴岡八幡宮
2	東慶寺	18	英勝寺
3	明月院	19	寿福寺
4	浄智寺	20	長谷寺
5	銭洗弁天	21	大巧寺
6	海蔵寺	22	本覚寺
7	建長寺	23	妙本寺
8	来迎寺	24	安養院
9	覚園寺	25	大宝寺
10	瑞泉寺	26	妙法寺
11	鎌倉宮	27	安国論寺
12	浄明寺	28	法性寺
13	報国寺	29	長勝寺
14	杉本寺	30	妙長寺
15	源頼朝の墓	31	五所神社
16	宝戒寺	32	九品寺

soon as the boy, Minamoto Yoritomo, was old enough, he began to gather support for a counterattack on his clan's old rivals. In 1180 he set up his base at Kamakura, an area that shared the advantages of being far from the debilitating influences of Kyoto court life, close to other clans loyal to the Minamoto and naturally easy to defend, being enclosed by the sea on one side and densely wooded hills on the others.

A series of victories over the Taira led to Minamoto Yoritomo being appointed shogun of Japan in 1192 and governing the country from Kamakura. The lack of an heir after Yoritomo's death, however, gave power to the Hōjos, the family of Yoritomo's wife.

The Hōjo clan ruled Japan from Kamakura for more than a century, until finally in 1333, weakened by the cost of maintaining defences against threats of attack from Kublai Khan in China, the Hōjo clan fell from power at the hands of the forces of Emperor Go-daigo. Though the restoration of imperial authority was somewhat illusory, real power reverting to another of Japan's clans, the capital nevertheless shifted back to Kyoto and Kamakura disappeared from the history books.

Orientation & Information

The sights in Kamakura are spread over a fairly wide area, and although most of them can be seen on foot, there are times when it is necessary to catch a bus. Fortunately there's not much chance of getting lost, as the temples are well signposted in both English and Japanese. You can either start at Kamakura station and work your way around the area in a circle or start north of Kamakura at Kita-Kamakura station and visit the temples between there and Kamakura on foot. The latter route is preferable, and the following itinerary moves south from Kita-Kamakura station.

The useful TIC booklet *Sightseeing in Kanagawa* covers Kamakura and other sights in the region. The Kamakura station information counter sells a great map which includes walking routes as well as opening hours and prices for the shrines and temples around Kamakura. If you arrive at Kita-Kamakura station, there are vendors as you exit the station selling very similar maps with points of interest marked in both English and Japanese.

Engaku-ji Temple

Engaku-ji Temple is on the left as you exit Kita-Kamakura station. It is one of the five main Rinzai Zen temples in Kamakura. Rinzai is distinguished from the other major school of Zen Buddhism in Japan, Sōtō, by its use among other things of riddles, stories concerning the lives of Zen masters and formal question-and-answer drills as aids to attaining enlightenment. Sōtō, on the other hand, relies more exclusively on meditation.

Engaku-ji Temple was founded in 1282,

allegedly as a place where Zen monks might be able to pray for soldiers who had lost their lives defending Japan against the second of Kublai Khan's invasion attempts. Today the only real reminder of the temple's former magnificence and antiquity is the San-mon Gate, which is a 1780 reconstruction. At the top of the long flight of stairs through the gate is the Engaku-ji bell, the largest bell in Kamakura, which was cast in 1301. The Main Hall inside the San-mon is quite a recent reconstruction, dating from the mid-60s.

The temple has a Y200 entry fee and is open from 8 am to 5 pm from April to September and from 8 am to 4 pm during the rest of the year.

Buddhism in Kamakura

The Buddhism that established itself in Japan during the 6th century belonged to the Mahayana (Greater Vehicle) school. Basically this school maintained that enlightenment, or release from the cycle of birth and death, was available not only to those special few with the ability to unswervingly follow Buddhist precepts (the eight-fold path) but to all sentient beings. This it was claimed had been disclosed by the Buddha (Gautama) himself in his last sermon, the *Lotus Sutra*.

It was not until some five centuries later, during the Kamakura period, that Buddhism spread to all of Japan. Initially the Kamakura period was marked by disillusionment with the institutions of Buddhism and the monastic orders, and a widespread belief that history had entered the Mappō (Later Age), a period of Buddhist decline, during which individuals would no longer be able to achieve enlightenment through their own efforts. This led to the flourishing of several alternatives to established Buddhist doctrine – notably Zen and the Pure Land school of Buddhism.

Adherents of the Pure Land school preached that in the Later Age salvation could only be achieved through devoting oneself to the transcendent Buddha Amida. Such, it was believed, was the infinite mercy of the Amida, that all who called on him sincerely would achieve salvation in the Pure Land after death. This denial of responsibility for one's own enlightenment was, in a sense, a 'soft option' and thus accounted for the sect's popularity among the lower orders of society who did not have the 'luxury' of devoting themselves to the rigours of pursuing personal enlightenment. This also contrasted with Zen, a Chinese import that strove to bring out the Buddhahood of the individual through meditative practice that sought out the empty centre of the self.

Zen, which literally means 'meditation', with its rigorous training and self-discipline, found considerable support among an ascendant warrior class and has been seen as having made a considerable contribution to the evolution of a samurai ethic. Doctrinal differences on the question of whether *satori* (enlightenment) could be attained suddenly or whether it was a gradual process accounted for Zen breaking into the Rinzai and Sōtō sects.

The contending schools of Pure Land and Zen, along with the views of charismatic leaders such as Nichiren, led to revitalisation of Buddhism within Japan during the Kamakura period. All the major Buddhist sects active in Japan today can trace their antecedents back to that period. ■

Tōkei-ji Temple

Tōkei-ji Temple, across the railway tracks from Engaku-ji Temple, is notable for its grounds as much as for the temple itself. On weekdays, when visitors are few, it can be a pleasantly relaxing place. Walk up to the cemetery and wander around.

Historically, the temple is famed as having served as a kind of women's refuge. Women could be officially recognised as divorced after three years as nuns in the temple grounds. Today no nuns live in the temple precincts; the grave of the last abbess can be found in the cemetery. The temple is open daily from 8.30 am to 5 pm and entry is Y50.

Jōchi-ji Temple

A couple of minutes further on from Tōkei-ji Temple is Jōchi-ji Temple, another temple with pleasant grounds. Founded in 1283, this is considered one of Kamakura's five great Zen temples. It is open daily from 9 am to 4.30 pm, and admission is Y100.

Kenchō-ji Temple

Kenchō-ji Temple is about a 10 minute walk beyond Jōchi-ji Temple. It is on the left after you pass through a tunnel. This is not only Kamakura's most important Zen temple but something of a showcase generally. The grounds and the buildings are well maintained and still in use. The first of the main buildings you come to, the Buddha Hall, was moved to its present site and reassembled in 1647. The second building, the Hall of Law, is used for Zazen meditation. Further back is the Dragon King Hall, a Chinese-style building with a garden to its rear. The temple bell, the second largest in Kamakura, has been designated a 'national treasure'. The temple is open daily from 9 am to 4.30 pm and admission is Y200.

Ennō-ji Temple

Across the road from Kenchō-ji Temple is Ennō-ji Temple, distinguished primarily by its collection of statues depicting the judges of hell. The temple is open daily from 10 am to 4 pm.

Hachiman-gū Shrine

Further down the road, where it turns towards Kamakura station, is Hachiman-gū Shrine. The shrine was founded by Minamoto Yoriyoshi, of the same Minamoto clan that was later to rule Japan from Kamakura. There is some debate as to whether Hachiman, the deity to which the shrine is dedicated, has always been regarded as the god of war; his dedication may simply be a reflection of the fact that Hachiman is also the guardian deity of the Minamoto clan. Whatever the case, this Shinto shrine presents the visitor with a drastically different atmosphere to the repose of the Zen temples clustered around Kita-Kamakura station.

If you enter the shrine from the direction of Kita-Kamakura station, you are actually entering from the rear and not by the proper entrance gates. This is not a problem; after taking a look at the shrine, follow the stairs down to the square below the shrine. To your right is a gingko tree beneath which it is said that a famous political assassination was carried out in 1219, making the tree very old indeed.

At the foot of the stairs you will find a dancing platform and the main avenue which runs to the entrance of the shrine. At the entrance on the left is an arched bridge, which in times past was designated for the passage of the shogun and no-one else. The bridge is so steep that every crossing must have been quite a test of shogunate athletic prowess.

National Treasure Museum To the left of the dancing platform (assuming you're continuing to walk away from the shrine) is the Kokuhōkan. This is one museum which is recommended, as it provides your only opportunity to see Kamakuran art, most of which is hidden away in the temples. The museum is open Tuesday to Sunday from 9 am to 4 pm, and admission is Y150.

Kamakura Station Area

It is possible to continue on to Kamakura station by exiting through the big torii gates at the entrance to Hachiman-gū Shrine and walking straight ahead down Wakamiya-dōri Ave. The avenue has a green centre strip, complete with sakura trees and a pathway. Kamakura station is on the right-hand side, down the first main street you come to after the second torii gate, and is a good place to get some food before continuing.

Apart from Hachiman-gū Shrine, there are no sites of historic importance in the immediate vicinity of the station; most places require a short bus trip from one of the bus stops in front of the station.

Great Buddha

The Daibutsu (Great Buddha) was completed in 1252 and is Kamakura's most famous sight. Once housed in a huge hall, the statue today sits in the open, its home having been washed away by a tsunami in 1495. Cast in bronze and weighing close to 850 tonnes, the statue is 11.4 metres tall. Its construction is said to have been inspired by Yoritomo's visit to Nara (where there is another, even bigger Buddha statue) after the Minamoto clan's victory over the rival Taira clan. Even though Kamakura's Great Buddha doesn't quite match Nara's in stature, it is commonly agreed that it is artistically superior.

The Buddha itself is the Amida Buddha, worshipped by the followers of the Jodō and Shinshū sects of Japanese Buddhism. These sects continue to attract followers, particularly from among ordinary people who find the monastic discipline and obscure rites of Zen inaccessible. The statue remains the figurehead of Japan's most popular Buddhist sects.

To get to the Great Buddha, take a bus from the No 7 bus stop in front of Kamakura station and get off at the Daibutsu-mae bus stop. The Great Buddha can be seen daily from 7 am to 5.30 pm, and admission is Y120.

Hase-dera Temple

If you walk back towards Kamakura station and turn right at the intersection where the bus goes left, this small street will take you to Hase-dera Temple, also known as Hase Kannon Temple. The pleasant grounds have a garden and an interesting collection of statues of Jizō, the patron saint of travellers and souls of departed children. Ranked like a small army of urchins, the statues are clothed to keep them warm by women who have lost children by abortion or miscarriage. The main point of interest in the grounds, however, is the Kannon statue.

Kannon, the goddess of mercy, is a Boddhisattva – a Buddha who has put off enlightenment in order to help others along the same path. This altruism has given Kannon a reputation for compassion and mercy, leading people to call on her for help in times of trouble. The nine metre wooden carved jūichimen (11 faced Kannon) here is believed to be very ancient, dating from the 8th century. The 11 faces are actually one major face and 10 minor faces, the latter representing 10 stages of enlightenment. However, in keeping with her reputation for mercy and compassion, it is also commonly believed that the 11 faces allow Kannon to cast an eye in every direction and maintain an unrelenting vigilance for those in need of her assistance.

From October to February, Hase-dera Temple is open from 7 am to 4.40 pm. During the rest of the year it closes at 5.40 pm. Admission is Y200.

Other Shrines & Temples

If you're still in the mood for temple tramping, there are plenty more in and around Kamakura. There are said to be about 70 temples and shrines in the area.

From the vicinity of the Great Buddha it is best to return to Kamakura station by bus and take another bus out to the temples in the western part of town. These have the advantage of being even less popular with tourists than the temples in Kita-Kamakura, though they tend to be smaller and lack the grandeur of the more famous temples. What they lack in grandeur they more than make up in charm, and there's a delightfully restful village-like atmosphere in the town's outer fringes.

Egara Ten-jin Shrine You can take a bus from stop No 6 in front of Kamakura station to Egara Ten-jin Shrine; get off the bus at the Ten-jin-mae stop. This Shinto shrine is nothing to get excited about, but it attracts a fair amount of attention because of its perceived association with education. Students write their academic aspirations on ema (small wooden plaques) which are hung to the right of the shrine. In the grounds there's another ancient gingko tree said to be around 900 years old.

Zuisen-ji Temple The grounds of this secluded Zen temple are very pleasant to walk in and include Zen gardens laid out by the Musō Kokushi, the temple's founder. The temple is open daily from 9 am to 5 pm and has a Y100 admission charge. You can get there from Egara Ten-jin Shrine on foot in about 10 to 15 minutes; turn right where the bus turns left in front of the shrine, take the next left and keep following the road.

Sugimoto-dera Temple This interesting little temple is reputed to be the oldest in Kamakura, founded in 734. Ferocious temple guardians are poised on either side of the entrance, while around the temple grounds and the thatch-roofed temple itself you can see white banners with the kanji characters reading: 'Jūichimen Sugimoto Kannon' (the 11 faced Kannon of Sugimoto). The temple houses three Kannon statues, though they are not in the same league as the famous statue at Hase-dera Temple.

The temple is open daily from 8.30 am to 4.30 pm and admission is Y100. To get to the temple, take a bus from the No 5 stop in front of Kamakura station and getting off at the Sugimoto Kannon bus stop.

Hōkoku-ji Temple Down the road (away from Kamakura station) from Sugimoto-dera Temple, on the right-hand side, is Hōkoku-ji Temple. This is a Rinzai Zen temple with quiet landscaped gardens where you can relax under a red parasol with a cup of Japanese tea. This is also one of the more active Zen temples in Kamakura, regularly holding Zazen classes for beginners. The temple is open from 9 am to 4.30 pm and entry is Y100.

Festivals
Setsubun is the bean-throwing ceremony held throughout Japan on 3 or 4 February. The best celebrations in Kamakura are at Hachiman-gū Shrine.

The Kamakura Matsuri is a week of celebrations held from the second Sunday to the third Sunday in April. It includes a wide range of activities, most of which are centred around Hachiman-gū Shrine.

During the Bonbori Matsuri, held from 7 to 9 August, hundreds of lanterns are strung up around Hachiman-gū Shrine.

The Hachiman-gū Matsuri is held from 14 to 15 September. Festivities include a procession of mikoshi and, on the 16th, a display of horseback archery.

The Menkake-gyōretsu, on 18 September, is a masked procession held at Goryō-jinja Shrine.

Places to Stay
The *Kamakura Kagetsuen Youth Hostel* (tel 0467-25-1238) has beds at Y2100. You can walk to the hostel from Hase-dera Temple by continuing to walk away from the Great Buddha along the road that runs in front of the temple. When you reach the T junction, turn right and look for the hostel on the corner of the next road on the left. Hase station is also a five minute walk away in the direction of Hase-dera Temple.

Just around the corner from Kamakura station is the *Ryokan Ushio* (tel 0467-22-7016), which has singles from Y4200. Follow the road next to McDonald's parallel to the train lines and take the next left. Ryokan Ushio is on the left.

Not far from the youth hostel is *BB House* (tel 0467-25-5859), which provides accommodation for women only and costs Y5000 per person, including breakfast. It's past Hase-dera Temple entrance, at the end of the road that runs past the Great Buddha.

The *Kamakura Hotel* (tel 0467-22-0029) has Western-style rooms from Y7000 per person and Japanese-style rooms from Y14,000 per person. It's not far from Hase station and there are English-speaking staff to tell you how to get there.

Places to Eat

Around the square facing the station is a *McDonald's*, a *Love Burger* and other fast-food places. For real food, the best hunting ground is in Wakamiya-dōri Ave towards Hachiman-gū Shrine, or in the road next to the station that runs parallel with Wakamiya-dōri Ave in the same direction. There is a large number of budget-to-medium priced places on both of these streets, ranging from noodle shops to Italian restaurants.

Getting There & Away

Trains on the Yokosuka line that are blue with a white stripe operate from Tokyo, Shimbashi and Shinagawa stations – take your pick. The trip takes about 55 minutes and fares are Y930 from Tokyo and Shimbashi and Y880 from Shinagawa. It is also possible to catch a train from Yokohama on the Yokosuka line. If you're planning to get off at Kita-Kamakura station, it is the stop after Ofuna.

A cheaper but more complicated option begins with a one hour 15 minute ride on the Odakyū line from Shinjuku in Tokyo to Katase-Enoshima station. (This will cost Y460 by express.) When you leave the station, cross the river and turn left. Enoshima station is a 10 minute walk away, and there you can catch the Enoden line to Kamakura. (This will cost Y170.)

It is possible to continue on to Enoshima, either via the Enoden line from Kamakura station or by bus from stop No 9 in front of Kamakura station. The train is the simpler and cheaper option, taking 36 minutes and costing Y170.

ENOSHIMA 江ノ島

Avoid this popular beach on weekends, when it's packed with day-trippers. At the end of the beach is a bridge to Eno-shima Island where the Enoshima-jinja Shrine is reached by an 'outdoor escalator'. It houses a *hadakabenzaiten* – a nude statue of the Indian goddess of beauty. Other sights around the island include the Enoshima Shokubutsu-en (Enoshima Tropical Garden).

Getting There & Away

Buses and trains run frequently between Kamakura and Enoshima (see the Kamakura Getting There & Away section). The Tōkaidō line goes to Ofuna station from Tokyo station, at a cost of Y780. At Ofuna, change to the Shonan monorail to Shonan Enoshima station, a trip costing Y260. Alternatively, trains run on the Odakyū line from Shinjuku station to Katase-Enoshima station. The Romance Car takes one hour 10 minutes and costs Y870, while an express takes five minutes longer and costs Y460.

MIURA-HANTO PENINSULA
三浦半島

Strictly for long-term residents suffering from boredom, the Miura-hantō Peninsula has beaches and the usual collection of over-priced, touristy marine parks, harbours and tropical gardens.

Aburatsubo Marine Park

This park has around 6000 fish in an aquarium that surrounds the viewer. It also offers 'synchronised swimming with girls and dolphins and laser light shows all put to music'. If this is your scene, start saving for the Y1600 entry charge. The park is a 15 minute bus trip from Misaki-guchi station.

Joga-shima Island

Excursion boats to nearby Joga-shima Island depart from the pier a 10 minute walk from the Aburatsubo bus stop. The 35 minute trip costs Y850. It's said that on a clear day you are able to see Mt Fuji from the boat but you'd have to be *very* lucky. The island is actually connected to the mainland by a bridge, and buses go there from Misaki-guchi station.

Other Attractions

Cape Ara-saki, about five km north of Joga-shima Island, has beaches with unusual rock formations. Take a bus from Misaki-guchi station to the Nagai bus stop and change for a bus to the Ara-saki bus stop. It takes about an hour to walk the Mito-hama Beach Hiking Course from Misaki-guchi station and back. The path takes you past a fishing village, beaches and a small shrine.

Getting There & Away

The cheapest and easiest way to the Miura-hantō Peninsula is to take the Keihin Kyūkō line from Tokyo station or Shinagawa station through to Misaki-guchi station, from where buses go to different places around the peninsula. From Shinagawa the train takes one hour 20 minutes and costs Y730.

An alternative point of entry to the peninsula is Yokosuka, which is serviced by the Yokosuka line (it passes through Kamakura) from Tokyo and Shinagawa stations. The fare is Y1090.

Izu Seven Islands
伊豆諸島

The Izu Seven Islands are peaks of a submerged volcanic chain that projects out into the Pacific from the Izu-hantō Peninsula. There is still considerable volcanic activity: in November 1986 the residents of O-shima Island were evacuated to Tokyo when Mt Mihara-yama erupted.

Until recently the chain was considered more appropriate as a place of exile than of scenic beauty, but today it's a popular holiday destination for Tokyo residents. To escape the crowds, avoid holidays and head for the remoter islands. See the earlier Around Tokyo map.

O-SHIMA ISLAND   大島
The main attraction of O-shima Island – at 91 sq km the largest of the group – is the active volcano Mt Mihara-yama. Buses run to the summit from Motomachi Port.

Oshima-kōen Park has a natural zoo and a campground.

Information
The Izu Seven Islands Tourist Federation (tel 03-436-6955) in Tokyo has information on minshuku, and there is also the Oshima Tourist Association (tel 04992-2-2177), which offers help to depressed travellers.

Places to Stay
The *Oshima-kōen Park* and *Umi no Furusatsu-mura* campground are the cheapest places at which to stay, the latter having pre-pitched tents at Y4000 for seven people. The *Mihara Sansō Youth Hostel* (tel 04992-2-1111) charges Y2800 per person, while the *Izu Oshima People's Lodge* (tel 04992-2-1285) costs Y4800 per person, including two meals.

Getting There & Away
Air There are three flights a day from Tokyo to O-shima Island with Air Nippon Koku (ANK) (tel 03-552-6311). The 40 minute flight costs Y6550 one way and Y11,800 return.

Ferry Ferry services run twice daily to O-shima Island from Tokyo's Takeshiba Pier (10 minutes from Hamamatsu-cho station), Atami and Itō. The trip from Tokyo takes seven hours and costs Y2840. From Atami it takes two hours and costs Y2030, while from Itō it takes 1½ hours and costs Y1770. High speed services taking about one hour are available from Atami (Y4590) and Itō (Y4050).

For information about departure times, contact Tokai Kisen (tel 03-432-4551). The TIC also has up-to-date information on getting to O-shima Island.

TO-SHIMA ISLAND   利島
To-shima Island, 27 km south-west of O-shima Island, is the smallest of the Izu Seven Islands, with a circumference of only eight km. The island is mountainous, although its volcano is now dormant, and there are no swimming beaches. Much of the island is

used for the cultivation of camellias, which makes it a picturesque place to visit between December and February, when the flowers are in bloom.

Places to Stay
The island has a few ryokan and minshuku – for information contact the Izu Seven Islands Tourist Federation (tel 03-436-6955).

Getting There & Away
Ferries leave from Tokyo's Takeshiba Pier. The trip takes around nine hours and fares start at Y3160 in 2nd class.

NII-JIMA ISLAND 新島
Nii-jima Island has an area of 23 sq km, and its beaches have made it so popular that there are now over 200 minshuku on the island. Even with this abundance of accommodation, it's a good idea to ring the Niijima Tourist Association (tel 04992-5-0422) if you're visiting during a holiday.

Getting There & Away
The 10 hour boat trip from Tokyo's Takebashi Pier costs Y3810 in 2nd class.

SHIKINE-JIMA ISLAND 式根島
Six km south of Nii-jima Island is tiny Shikine-jima Island, with an area of only 3.8 sq km. The island has swimming beaches, hot springs and plenty of accommodation. Contact the island's tourist information office (tel 04992-7-0170) for accommodation details.

Getting There & Away
Ferries to Shikine-jima Island depart from Takeshiba Pier daily, take 10 hours and cost Y3810 in 2nd class.

KOZU-SHIMA ISLAND 神津島
This 18 sq km island is dominated by an extinct volcano, Mt Tenjo. The island also has good beaches, Tokyo-ji Temple and a cemetery for former exiles, including 57 feudal warriors, from the days when the island served as a resort for Japanese unwanted by their compatriots on the mainland.

Places to Stay
There are around 200 minshuku on the island and bookings can be made through the Kozushima Tourist Association (tel 04992-8-0321).

Getting There & Away
Ferries leave from Takeshiba Pier and cost Y4040 2nd class.

MIYAKE-JIMA ISLAND 三宅島
Known as Bird Island due to the 200 species of birds that live there, the island is 180 km south of Tokyo and is the third largest of the Izu Seven Islands, with a circumference of 36 km. It has a volcano, which last erupted in 1962, some good beaches, a couple of small lakes and an onsen. You can either explore the island in a hired car or on a rented bicycle or make use of the local bus services.

Places to Stay
For reasonably priced minshuku, contact the Village Office (tel 04994-6-1324). There are campgrounds at Sagiga-hama, Okubo-hama and Miike-hama beaches.

Getting There & Away
By boat from Tokyo costs Y4280 in 2nd class. There are also two flights a day with Air Nippon (tel 03-552-6311) for Y8210 one way or Y14,780 return.

MIKURA-JIMA ISLAND 御蔵島
Mikura-jima Island is only 20 km from Miyake-jima Island but is not of great interest. Accommodation is limited, camping is not allowed and transport connections are infrequent.

HACHIJO-JIMA ISLAND 八丈島
Hachijo-jima Island, 290 km south of Tokyo, is the southernmost and second largest of the Izu Seven Islands. It has a pleasant semitropical climate and is becoming increasing popular among young Japanese. Sights include the now dormant volcano, some

good beaches, a botanical garden, Tametomo-jinja Shrine and Sofuku-ji Temple. Bicycles and cars can be rented.

There are some interesting local customs which are now maintained as tourist attractions, including a form of bull fighting found throughout Asia in which two bulls try to push each other out of a ring. Bull fights are held daily at Jiyugaoka and admission is Y800. The Runin Matsuri (Exile Festival) is held from 28 to 30 August, with a costumed procession, drum beating and folk dancing.

Places to Stay

For accommodation information, ring the local tourist association (tel 04996-2-1377).

Getting There & Away

Ferries from Tokyo, via Miyake-jima Island, taking around 10½ hours, cost Y5340 and depart six days a week. Alternatively, there is a more frequent air service (six flights a day) between Haneda Airport and the island.

The flight takes one hour and costs Y11,110 one way, Y20,160 return.

Ogasawara Islands
小笠原諸島

Although technically part of Tokyo-to, these islands are far to the south of the Izu Seven Islands. They have a climate similar to that of the Okinawa islands. Like those islands, they were occupied by US forces long after they had left the mainland islands.

The main group of islands include Chichi-jima, Haha-jima and Ani-jima islands, on which you will find a number of minshuku and where scuba diving is popular. Further south are the Kazan (Volcano) Islands which include Iwo-jima Island, one of the most famous battle sites of WW II. The island is still off limits to visitors because it contains live ammunition.

Northern Honshū　　　　　　　　　東北地方

The northern part of Honshū, often referred to as Tōhoku, includes Fukushima, Miyagi, Iwate, Aomori, Akita and Yamagata prefectures. For ease of reference, Niigata Prefecture and Sado-ga-shima Island have been included in this chapter.

The region is mostly mountainous and was originally inhabited by a people known in previous centuries as Ezo. The Ezo are believed to have been related to the Ainu who now only remain on Hokkaidō. Although the Ezo were conquered and pushed back during the Kamakura period, it wasn't until the 17th century that extensive and powerful government was established in Tōhoku.

During the Meiji era, the region suffered from years of neglect. This trend was only reversed after WW II with a drive for development which was based heavily on industrial growth. Despite this development, the region retains a strong reliance on agriculture and many Japanese still consider it as a place in the back of beyond – an economic laggard compared to the rest of Japan.

For those who want to see the traditional ways of rural life and enjoy vast areas of unspoilt natural scenery, this lack of development is a real bonus and provides a strong reason to visit Tōhoku.

Transport in the region focuses around three major railway lines: two of these run north-south down the east and west coasts and the third snakes down between them in the centre. The Tōhoku shinkansen line links Tokyo (Ueno) with Morioka in the lightning time of 2½ hours.

Exploration of the remoter parts of Tōhoku, particularly if you're following an east-west route, requires a greater amount of time chugging patiently along local railway lines or winding up mountains on local bus services.

The major cities, few in number, generally merit no more than a cursory stop before heading off into the back country to try some hikes in volcanic and mountainous regions or along spectacular rocky coastlines. Tōhoku has scores of hot springs tucked away in the mountains and there are also cultural sights such as temples, festivals and folkcrafts. Several excellent ski resorts benefit from the long and severe winters with accompanying heavy snowfalls.

This coverage of Northern Honshū starts with a few sights north of Tokyo which are just beyond the day trips covered in the Around Tokyo chapter, then moves north along the east side of Tōhoku, continues round the northern tip, and descends the west side to Niigata and Sado-ga-shima Island.

Since Tōhoku is less travelled by foreigners and sources of information are less common outside major cities, you may well find your queries are answered more easily by phoning Japan Travel-Phone, toll free on 0120-22-2800 between 9 am and 5 pm.

Exploring Tōhoku (Weatherhill, 1982) by Jan Brown is a guide to the region which provides solid and very detailed background information including useful indices with place names in kanji.

For some literary refreshment en route you could dip into *The Narrow Road to the Deep North & Other Travel Sketches* (Penguin, 1970) which contains classic haiku penned by Bashō (1644-94), perhaps the most famous Japanese poet, on his travels in Tōhoku and elsewhere. To bring yourself up to date, you could also read *The Narrow Road to the Deep North: Journey into Lost Japan* (Jonathan Cape, 1990) by Lesley Downer. This is a well-written account of her walk which retraced one of Bashō's trips through the central and southern parts of Tōhoku.

The Japan National Tourist Organisation (JNTO) publishes a glossy brochure entitled *Tōhoku* which includes a map and brief details for sights, festivals and transport in Northern Honshū. JNTO also publishes leaflets for separate parts of Tōhoku and these

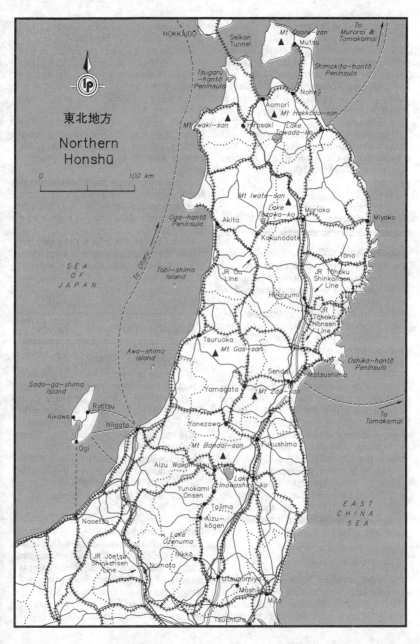

東北地方

Northern
Honshū

are mentioned in the appropriate places in this chapter.

Tourist information offices in the northern prefectures of Tōhoku (Iwate, Aomori and Akita) can provide a very useful timetable entitled *Kita Tōhoku Kankō Jikokuhyō*. Although it's in Japanese, it has a map in romaji which makes the checking of details relatively easy.

The same tourist offices also provide a large map of northern Tōhoku entitled *Kita Tōhoku Kankō Chizu* which is in Japanese and on a scale of 1:500,000.

Ibaraki-ken 茨城県

TSUCHIURA 土浦

Tsuchiura was originally a castle town and post town. It is now a major city which draws large numbers of visitors to its annual firework display.

The Hanabi Matsuri (Firework Festival) takes place on the first Saturday in October and pyromania grips the city as firework maestros from all over Japan compete for the biggest sparkle or bang.

JNTO publishes a leaflet entitled *Tsuchiura & Tsukuba (MG-025)* which has basic information for Tsuchiura. The tourist information office (tel 0298-21-4166) at Tsuchiura station is open from 10 am to 6 pm but closed every second Thursday.

An inexpensive place to stay is *Tsuchiura Masuo Youth Hostel* (tel 0298-21-4430), 20 minutes on foot from the station.

The JR Joban line links Tokyo (Ueno) with Tsuchiura in under an hour by limited express (tokkyū). From Tsuchiura to Mito takes 45 minutes by limited express on the same line.

MITO 水戸

The major attraction of Mito, an otherwise unremarkable destination, is Kairaku-en Garden which the Japanese include in their 'trinity' of top gardens – the other two are in

Kanazawa (Kenroku-en Garden) and Okayama (Koraku-en Garden).

Kairaku-en is a stroll garden which was laid out in 1842. The top ranking it receives in terms of visual splendour probably only applies between late February and mid-March when the apricot trees bloom – not surprisingly, this is also a time when the grounds are packed with visitors. The Kobuntei Pavilion in the garden is a reproduction, but worth a stop to look at the genteel interior and enjoy the peaceful setting.

Admission to the garden is free and admission to Kobuntei costs Y160. It's open from 7 am to 6 pm (16 September to 31 March); during the rest of the year it's open from 6 am to 7 pm.

From Mito station, take a 12 minute bus ride to the Kairakuen-mae bus stop. From Tokyo (Ueno), it takes about 80 minutes to Mito by limited express on the JR Joban line.

Tochigi-ken 栃木県

LAKE OZENUMA 尾瀬沼湖

This lake and its swampy surroundings is on a plateau about 70 km north of Nikkō (see the Around Tokyo chapter for details about Nikkō). The area is a popular destination for hikers who wish to follow trails along boardwalks and admire the mountain flora. There are plenty of mountain huts providing basic accommodation – prices start around Y5500 per person and include two meals. *Oze Tokura Youth Hostel* (tel 0278-58-7421) is opposite the bus stop in Oze Tokura.

Getting There & Away

There are buses running from JR Nikkō station via Chūzenji to Yumoto Onsen. From Yumoto Onsen there are infrequent buses to Kamata (Y1250, 75 minutes) where you change to a bus for Oze Tokura. From Oze Tokura, there are infrequent and separate bus services – both take about 20 minutes – to

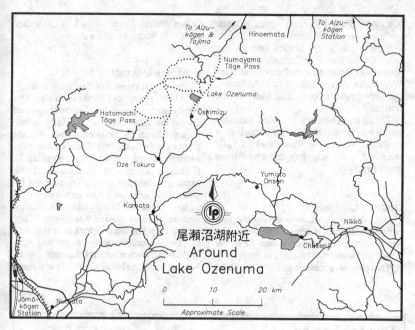

尾瀬沼湖附近
Around
Lake Ozenuma

0   10   20 km

Approximate Scale

the two major trailheads (Hatomachi Tōge Pass and Oshimizu).

See the section on Numata (Gumma-ken) for transport between Numata and the trailheads for Lake Ozenuma.

If you're heading down from Fukushima-ken, the lake can be reached by taking a bus from Aizu-kōgen station (Aizu line) to Numayama Tōge Pass (Y2050, two hours) where trails lead into the swamp.

Gumma-ken　群馬県

NUMATA　沼田
Numata is a convenient staging point for transport if you're travelling across from Nikkō with a sidetrip to Lake Ozenuma and then continuing to Kusatsu and across to Nagano-ken. Numata is on the JR Jōetsu

line. It can also be reached with a 30 minute bus ride from Jōmō-kōgen station on the JR Jōetsu shinkansen line.

If you want to visit Lake Ozenuma with its surrounding network of hiking trails (often slippery and boggy), there are buses running from Numata station via Kamata to Oze Tokura (about 95 minutes, Y1900). From Oze Tokura, there are infrequent and separate bus services – both take about 20 minutes – to the two major trailheads (Hatomachi Tōge Pass and Oshimizu).

Fukushima-ken　福島県

TAJIMA　田島
Tajima was formerly a post town on the Nikkō Kaidō Highway. You can stop here to visit the Oku-Aizu Minzoku Shiryōkan

254 Northern Honshū

(Oku-Aizu Folk Museum) which exhibits crafts and household utensils.

From Aizu-Tajima station (the correct name for the station at Tajima), there is, in addition to the train, a bus service to Aizu Wakamatsu – if you want to visit Ouchijuku, the appropriate stop is Yunokami Onsen station.

There are also bus services (usually requiring a bus change en route) to a trailhead (Numayama Tōge Pass) for Lake Ozenuma – the trip requires about three hours (Y2370).

OUCHIJUKU 大内宿
Once a thriving post town during the Edo period, Ouchijuku is remarkable because it has preserved 40 thatched houses from that period and some still function as inns.

The closest access point is Yunokami Onsen station. From there, you can either walk (1½ hours) or take a taxi.

AIZU WAKAMATSU 会津若松
During feudal times, this castle town developed into a stronghold for the Aizu clan. The family later remained loyal to the shogunate during the Edo period then briefly defied imperial forces in the Boshin Civil War (at the start of the Meiji era). The resistance was swiftly crushed and the town went up in flames – the heroic 'last stand of the samurai', complete with mass suicides by young warriors, has found its way into the annals of Japanese history and attracts many Japanese visitors to Aizu Wakamatsu.

Two loop bus lines – clockwise and anticlockwise – conveniently circle from Aizu Wakamatsu station around the main sights. Bicycle rental is also available at the station.

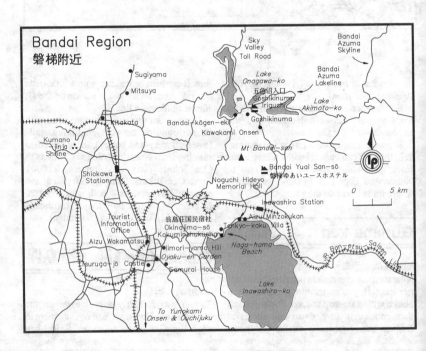

Bandai Region 磐梯附近

Information

Aizu Wakamatsu tourist information office (tel 0242-32-0688) is inside Aizu Machikata Folklore Museum, a short walk south of the station. Large, detailed maps of the area in English are available – excellent for orientation. The office is open from 9 am to 6 pm but closed on Mondays. If you want to visit nearby saké museums and breweries (tastings available!) or a hall exhibiting local lacquerware, the English-speaking staff can give you directions.

JNTO publishes a leaflet entitled *Aizu Wakamatsu & Bandai (024-MG)* which has maps and brief details for sights, transport and accommodation in Aizu Wakamatsu and the surrounding region.

Iimori-yama Hill

This hill is renowned as the spot where teenage members of the Byakkotai (White Tigers Band) retreated from the imperial forces and committed ritual suicide in 1868. The standard account of this tragedy maintains that the youngsters self destructed when they looked down from the hilltop and saw the town and its castle go up in flames; another version maintains that it was just the town that was alight – the Meiji government did not get around to torching the actual castle until 1874.

The graves of 19 Byakkotai members are lined up on the hill – one member of the group survived his suicide attempt and is reported to have felt ashamed for the rest of his life. The event has received attention not only from Japanese admirers of loyalty, but also from foreigners with similar sentiments. Close to the graves are two monuments: one from a German military attaché and another from Italian fascists.

One tourist brochure saw a link between the tragedy of the Byakkotai in 1868 and the opening of the first transcontinental railroad across the USA one year later; puzzling indeed.

Apart from a museum housing Byakkotai memorabilia, there's also the Sazae-dō Hall, a hexagonal building dating from the 18th century, which has an intricate set of stairs

arranged as a double spiral. Admission to the hall costs Y200 and it's open from 8 am to sunset.

The hill is a 15 minute bus ride from the railway station and can be climbed on foot – or use the hillside elevator.

Oyaku-en Garden

This is a splendid garden complete with tea arbour, large central pond (and huge carp) and a section devoted to the cultivation of medicinal herbs which was encouraged by former Aizu lords.

In the souvenir shop you can sample herbal tea, and packets of daimyō herbal brew are on sale.

Admission costs Y300 and it is open from 8 am to 5 pm (April to October) and 8.30 am to 4.30 pm (November to March). The garden is a 15 minute bus ride from the station – get off at the Oyaku-en Iriguchi bus stop.

Samurai House

Aizu Buké-yashiki is an interesting, large-scale reconstruction of the lifestyle of opulent samurai in the Edo period. An English leaflet and map are provided for you to guide yourself around dozens of rooms, which range from the kitchen to the principal residence. Don't miss the rice mill, where 16 grinding stones driven by water power are capable of producing 900 kg of rice in a day. The toilet has a special sandbox for medical advisers to inspect their lord's daily deeds!

One irritation is the mass of souvenir shops scattered around the grounds which are geared to huge numbers of visitors. The house is open from 8.30 am to 5.30 pm (April to October) and 9 am to 4.30 pm (November to March). Admission costs a whopping Y770. To reach the residence, take a 15 minute bus ride from the station and get off at the Buké-yashiki-mae bus stop.

Tsuruga-jō Castle

The present castle is a reconstruction from 1965 and contains a historical museum. Admission costs Y300 and it's open from 8.30 am to 5 pm.

Festivals

Aizu Aki Matsuri Festival, held from 22 to 24 September, features a large parade with participants dressed as daimyō and their retainers, and there are performances of folk dances.

Places to Stay

The tourist information office has lists of accommodation and can help with reservations.

Aizu-no-Sato Youth Hostel (tel 0241-27-2054) is a 10 minute walk from Shiokawa station which is 10 km from Aizu Wakamatsu and a little closer to Kitakata. Bicycle rental is available at the hostel.

Getting There & Away

From Tokyo (Ueno), the quickest route is to take the JR Tōhoku shinkansen line to Koriyama then change to the JR Ban-etsu-Saisen line to Aizu Wakamatsu – total time for the trip is about 2½ hours.

From Nikkō, there's the option of combining train rides from Shimo-Imaichi to Kinugawa Onsen on the Tōbu Kinugawa line, then changing to the Aizu-Kinugawa line. To get a closer look at the countryside and rural architecture in the valleys on this route, you can also take buses part of the way from Kinugawa Onsen before hopping back onto the train.

KITAKATA AREA 喜多方

Kitakata, just 20 minutes by train from Aizu Wakamatsu, is famed for its thousands of *kura* or mud-walled storehouses which come in all sorts of colour schemes and function not only as storehouses, but also as living quarters, shops and workshops.

The information office at the station can provide a map in English which outlines walking routes – allow three hours at an easy pace. Bicycle rental is also available near the station (Y250 per hour) and a horse-drawn tourist carriage (a sort of double-decker 'kuramobile') does the rounds in two hours (Y1200) – Japanese commentary only.

Brick-built, Western-style kura can be seen at Mitsuya, nine km north of Kitakata (15 minutes by bus from Kitakata station) on Route 121. The tiny community of Sugiyama, six km further north from Mitsuya, is almost solid with kura.

Kumano-jinja Shrine, six km west of Kitakata (25 minutes by bus from Kitakata station), is renowned for its Nagatoko Hall which was built over 900 years ago and has neither walls nor doors – more than 40 massive columns support the roof.

LAKE INAWASHIRO-KO 猪苗代湖

This is a large lake – the fourth largest in Japan – and is popular with the Japanese as a place to take ferry rides and go camping. However, the terrain around the lake is mostly flat and the town of Inawashiro is best used as a staging point to visit the more scenic area around Mt Bandai-san.

Noguchi Hideyo Kinenkan (Noguchi Hideyo Memorial Hall) is close to Lake Inawashiro-ko (10 minutes by bus from Inawashiro station). The hall honours Noguchi Hideyo, a medical pioneer famed for his research into snake poison, syphilis and yellow fever – the latter disease terminated his life at the age of 52 in Africa. Admission costs Y250. It's open daily from 8.30 am to 4.45 pm (April to October) and 9 am to 4 pm (November to March).

Close to this memorial hall is Aizu Minzokukan, a folk museum which includes two farmhouses from the Edo period, a mill, and a candle-making shop. Admission costs Y500 and it's open daily – except Thursdays – from 8 am to 5 pm (April to October) and 8.30 am to 4.30 pm (November to March).

About 12 km further west along the lake is Naga-hama Beach which is accessible by bus from Inawashiro station. Perched on a hill behind the beach is Tenkyo-kaku Villa, built by an imperial prince in 1908 as a summer residence. It has fine views across the lake.

Places to Stay

Next door to Tenkyo-kaku Villa (and sharing its view) is *Okinajima-sō Kokuminshukusha*

Top: Suizenji-kōen Garden, Kumamoto (TW)
Left: Stone garden, Tōfuku-ji Temple, Kyoto (RS)
Right: Carp pond, Matsue (TW)

Top: Temple garden, Takayama (RS)
Left: Ichikan-tei Garden, Niigata (RS)
Right: Tōkō-en Garden, Okayama (CT)

(tel 0242-65-2811), a comfortable place to stay. Prices start around Y5000 per person and include two meals.

Just north of the lake, there's the *Bandai Yūai San-sō Youth Hostel* (tel 0242-62-3424) which is 15 minutes by bus from Inawashiro station.

MT BANDAI-SAN & BANDAI-KOGEN PLATEAU
磐梯山、磐梯高原

Mt Bandai-san erupted on 15 July 1888 and in the course of the eruption it destroyed dozens of villages and their inhabitants. At the same time it completely rearranged the landscape to create a plateau and dam local rivers which then formed numerous lakes and ponds. Now designated as a national park, the whole area offers spectacular scenery with ample scope for walks or long hikes.

The most popular walk – sometimes jammed with hikers from end to end – takes about an hour and follows a trail between a series of lakes known as Goshikinuma (Five Coloured Lakes). The trailheads for the Goshikinuma walk are at Goshikinuma Iriguchi and at Bandai-kōgen-eki – the main transport hub – on the edge of Lake Hibara-ko. As can be expected of a main transport hub, Bandai-kōgen-eki is geared to the tourist circus – souvenir shops, restaurants and a vast asphalt expanse to accommodate the tour buses. The pleasure boat rides can safely be skipped, but there are various walking trails along the eastern side of the lake. Nearby are several other lakes, including Lake Onagawa-ko and Lake Akimoto-ko, which also offer scope for walks along their shores.

Ura Bandai Youth Hostel is very close to Goshikinuma Iriguchi and makes a convenient base for extended hikes. The hostel has maps in Japanese which outline routes and approximate times for hikes in the areas.

The most popular hiking destination is Mt Bandai-san which can be climbed in a day – start as early as possible and allow up to nine hours. A popular route for this hike starts from Kawakami Onsen (about 10 minutes by

bus from the youth hostel) and climbs up to Mt Bandai-san, looping around the rim of the crater before descending to Bandai-kōgen-eki.

Places to Stay

There are numerous kokuminshukusha, pensions, minshuku and hotels in the area. There's a tourist information office at Idemitsu, between Goshikinuma Iriguchi and Bandai-kōgen-eki, but if you need help with booking accommodation (and you don't speak Japanese) it's probably easier to use the tourist office in Aizu Wakamatsu which has English-speaking staff.

Ura Bandai Youth Hostel (tel 0241-32-2811) seems a little the worse for wear, but it's in a quiet spot next to one of the trailheads for the Goshikinuma walk. It's also a good base for longer mountain hikes. The hostel manager can provide maps and basic information for hikes in the area. Bicycle rental is also available – much cheaper than the rental at Lake Hibara-ko.

Take the bus bound for Bandai-kōgen from Inawashiro station and get off 30 minutes later at the Goshikinuma Iriguchi bus stop. The hostel is seven minutes on foot from the bus stop.

Getting There & Away

There are buses from Aizu Wakamatsu station and Inawashiro station to the trailheads for the Goshikinuma walk. Buses from Aizu Wakamatsu to Lake Hibara-ko take 1½ hours (Y1450) and from Inawashiro to Hibara-ko Lake 25 minutes (Y750).

Between Bandai-kōgen-eki and Fukushima there is a bus service along two scenic toll roads – Bandai Azuma Lakeline and Bandai Azuma Skyline. The trip provides great views of the mountains and is highly recommended if you are a fan of volcanic panoramas.

The bus makes a scheduled stop (30 minutes) at Jōdodaira, a superb viewpoint, where you can climb to the top of Mt Azumakofuji (1705 metres) in 10 minutes and, if you still feel energetic, scramble down to the bottom of the crater. Across the road is Mt Issaikyō-yama which belches steam in dramatic contrast to its passive neighbour – a steepish climb of 45 minutes is needed to reach the top with its sweeping views.

The bus fare between Fukushima and Bandai-kōgen-eki is Y2560; the trip takes about three hours. This service only operates between late April and late October.

Between Bandai-kōgen-eki and Yone-zawa there is another bus service along the scenic Sky Valley toll road. The trip takes two hours and the fare is Y1590. This service only operates between late April and late October.

Miyagi-ken   宮城県

SENDAI 仙台

The dominant figure in Sendai's history is Date Masamune (1567-1636) who earned the nickname 'one-eyed dragon' after he caught smallpox as a child and went blind in his right eye. Date adopted Sendai as his base and used his military might and administrative skills to become one of the most powerful feudal lords in Japan. An accomplished artist and scholar, Date also developed Sendai as a cultural focus for Tōhoku.

During WW II, Sendai was demolished by bombing. The city was later rebuilt with streets and avenues laid out in a grid pattern. Despite its lack of historical sights, the tree-lined avenues and parks provide a pleasing ambience which makes Sendai convenient if only as a staging post or 'refuelling' stop whilst travelling through Tōhoku.

Orientation

Sendai station is within easy walking distance of the city centre and the grid layout of the streets makes orientation relatively simple. From the station, the broad sweep of Aoba-dōri Ave, lined with many of the major department stores, banks and hotels, leads west to Aoba-yama Hill. The main shopping areas are along Higashi Ichibanchō-dōri Ave

and a roofed section of Chūō-dōri Ave. Kokubunchō-dōri is west of Higashi Ichibanchō-dōri and is claimed to be the largest entertainment district in Tōhoku with thousands of bars and eateries.

Information

Sendai tourist information office (tel 022-222-4069), on the 2nd floor of JR Sendai station, has English-speaking staff who can help with information not only for Sendai, but also for other parts of Tōhoku. If you give advance notice, Goodwill Guides and home visits can be arranged. The office is open daily from 8.30 am to 8 pm. The Sendai English Hotline (tel 022-224-1919) also offers travel information and advice to foreigners.

The JR Travel Service Centre in the station deals with the exchange of Japan Rail Pass vouchers.

JNTO publishes a leaflet entitled *Sendai, Matsushima & Hiraizumi (023-MG)* which has a schematic map of Sendai and brief details for sights, transport and accommodation.

English guidebooks about Sendai, such as *In & Around Sendai* and *Everyone's Sendai* (two volumes), are available in bookshops in the city and sometimes in the station bookshops.

Aoba-jō Castle

Aoba-jō Castle was built on Aoba-yama Hill in 1602 by Date Masamune. Its partial destruction during the Meiji era was completed by bombing in 1945. The castle ruins – a restored turret and that's about it – lie inside Aobayama-kōen Park where you can pause for a look at Gokoku-jinja Shrine or walk south to Yagiyama-bashi Bridge which leads to a zoo. Admission costs Y400. It's open from 9 am to 4.15 pm. From Sendai station, take bus No 9 for the 15 minute ride to the Aoba-jōshi Uzumi-mon bus stop.

Zuihō-den Hall

This is the mausoleum of Date Masamune originally built in 1637, but later destroyed by bombing in WW II. The present building

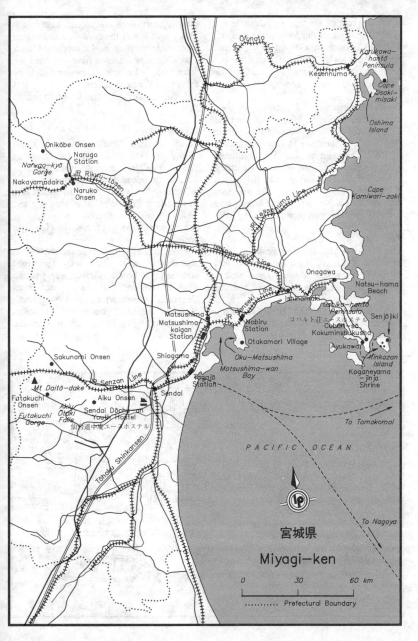

宮城県

Miyagi-ken

is an exact replica – faithful to the ornate and sumptuous style of the Momoyama period. The hall is open from 9 am to 4 pm and admission costs Y500. From Sendai station, take either bus Nos 11 or 12 for the 15 minute ride to the Otamaya-bashi stop.

Osaki Hachiman-jinja Shrine
The original shrine building dates from the 12th century and was moved from outside Sendai to its present site by Date Masamune in 1607. The main building is a luxurious, black-lacquered edifice with eye-catching carved designs. Admission to the shrine costs Y300 and it closes at sunset. From Sendai station, take bus No 10 for the 15 minute ride to the Hachiman-jinja-mae stop.

Festivals
The Tanabata Matsuri (Star Festival), held from 6 to 8 August, is the big annual event in Sendai. Several million visitors ensure that accommodation is booked solid at this time.

According to a myth (originally Chinese), a princess and a peasant shepherd were forbidden to meet, but 7 July – the time when the two stars Vega and Altair meet in the Milky Way – was the only time in the year when the two star-crossed lovers could sneak a tryst. Sendai seems to have stretched the dates a bit, but celebrates in grand style by decorating the main streets, holding parades and rounding off the events with a fireworks finale.

Places to Stay
Youth Hostels *Sendai Dōchu-an Youth Hostel* (tel 022-247-0511), just south of Sendai in an old farmhouse, has a high reputation for hospitality to foreigners – it's twinned with a youth hostel in Meiringen, Switzerland. Bicycle rental is available and there may still be a discount on the price of accommodation offered to foreign hostellers.

From Sendai station, take the subway to Tomizawa station then walk for eight minutes to the hostel. Alternatively, you can walk to the hostel in 18 minutes from Nagamachi station which is one stop south of Sendai station. If you get lost, the hostel manager can give you directions over the phone.

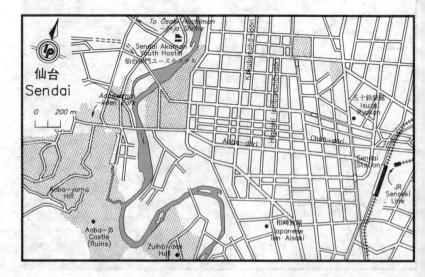

Sendai Onnai Youth Hostel (tel 022-234-3922) is north of Sendai station. Take bus No 24 bound for Shihei-cho (the stop is in front of the Sendai Hotel, opposite the station) and get off after about 15 minutes at the Tōhokukai Byō-in Shigakubu-mae stop. The hostel is two minutes walk away. Bicycle rental is available at Y200 for the day.

Sendai Akamon Youth Hostel (tel 022-264-1405) is north-west of Sendai station – about 15 minutes by bus No 16 to the Nakanose-bashi bus stop then five minutes on foot.

Ryokan *Isuzu Ryokan* (tel 022-222-6430), a member of the Japanese Inn Group, is five minutes on foot from Sendai station. Prices for singles/doubles start at Y3400/6000; triples cost from Y8400.

Japanese Inn Aisaki (tel 022-264-0700), also a member of the Japanese Inn Group, is right behind the post office which is a 12 minute walk from Sendai station. Prices for singles/doubles start at Y4000/7000.

Places to Eat
If you stroll around the main shopping areas – Higashi Ichibanchō-dōri Ave and the roofed section of Chūō-dōri – you can take your pick from dozens of restaurants serving Western or Japanese food. If you want to loosen your wallet and combine eating with evening entertainment, the district around Kokubunchō-dōri Ave has the bright lights.

Things to Buy
If you have time to spare in the morning, there's the *asa-ichi* (morning market) close to the station which features rows of stalls offering wild plants and seafood. One enthusiastic brochure mentions 'sea squirts' – sounds perilous!

The tourist information office can direct you to shops specialising in arts and crafts. Perhaps the most renowned craft items in Tōhoku are *kokeshi*, which are cylindrical, wooden dolls with decorated heads. There are at least 10 different types which can be distinguished by their variation in facial features.

If your backpack is becoming threadbare, you might be interested in Sendai Tansu, massive chests made from *keyaki* (zelkova elm) and decorated with blackened ironwork.

Sendai Dagashi, local cakes made from rice, soybean flour and sugar, are produced in many different varieties – edible crafts!

Getting There & Away
Air From Sendai Airport there are flights to Osaka, Sapporo Airport (Chitose Kūko), Nagoya, Fukuoka, Komatsu (Kanazawa) and Okinawa. To get to and from Tokyo, the shinkansen is so fast, it's not really sensible to take a plane.

Train The JR Tōhoku shinkansen line provides a super-fast connection between Tokyo (Ueno) and Sendai – there are dozens of trains daily and the fastest ones do the run in a mere two hours. The same line connects Fukushima with Sendai in 26 minutes and continues north to Morioka in 50 minutes.

The JR Senzan line connects Sendai with Yamagata in one hour. The JR Senseki line links Sendai with Matsushima in 40 minutes.

Bus The Tōhoku Kyūkō (express night bus) runs between Tokyo and Sendai (Y5300 one way, 7¾ hours) and reservations are necessary.

Ferry Sendai is a major port with daily ferries operating to Tomakomai (Hokkaidō). The trip takes just under 17 hours and the passenger fare is Y8600. There are also ferries operating every second day to Nagoya (Y9300, 21 hours).

To get to Sendai-futō Pier from Sendai station, take the JR Senseki line to Tagajō station and then a 10 minute taxi ride.

Getting Around
To/From the Airport Sendai Airport is a 40 minute bus ride (Y730) south of Sendai.

Bus Sendai has a huge – and initially confusing – network of bus services. Most of the sights can be reached by bus direct from

Sendai station. The tourist information office provides a bilingual leaflet with relevant bus numbers, bus destinations and the names of the appropriate bus stops. If you want to save time or avoid complicated bus routes whilst crossing between the sights, short hops by taxi are inexpensive.

Subway The present subway system runs from north to south. Apart from the subway station close to JR Sendai station, it's not really useful for sightseeing. An extension of the subway is planned to run from east to west.

AKIU ONSEN   秋保温泉

This hot-spring resort, 50 minutes by bus west of Sendai, is a good base for sidetrips further into the mountains to see Akiu Otaki Falls and, further still, Futakuchi Gorge with its rock columns known as Banji-iwa. There are hiking trails along the river valley and there's a trail leading from Futakuchi Onsen to the summit of Mt Daitō-dake (about a three hour walk).

SAKUNAMI ONSEN   作並温泉

This is another hot-spring resort, west of Sendai, which can be reached from Sendai by bus (70 minutes) or by train on the JR Senzan line (40 minutes). Sakunami is renowned for its open-air hot springs and the production of kokeshi dolls.

SHIOGAMA

Shiogama is a thriving fishing port which has a famous shrine and cruises to Matsushima-kaigan. To reach Shiogama from Sendai, take the 30 minute ride on the JR Senseki line to Hon-Shiogama station. On 5 August, Shiogama celebrates its Port Festival with a parade of colourful boats decked out with streamers and banners.

Shiogama-jinja Shrine stands on a wooded hill above Shiogama, 15 minutes on foot from Hon-Shiogama station; there are pleasant views across the bay.

The boat dock for the cruises to Matsushima-kaigan is about 10 minutes on foot from Hon-Shiogama station – turn right at the station exit.

Cruises between Shiogama and Matsushima-kaigan usually take about 50 minutes and operate from 8 am to 4 pm. There are hourly departures between April and November – less frequent departures during the rest of the year – and the one-way fare costs Y1400. The loudspeakers on the boat are cunningly placed so that there is no escape from the full-blast Japanese commentary. You may want to use ear plugs (or a Walkman) to minimise the audio assault.

Apart from the standard boats, there are also more expensive ones shaped like peacocks or dragons. All the boats loop around the islands of Matsushima-wan Bay between Shiogama and Matsushima-kaigan.

MATSUSHIMA   松島

Matsushima and the islands in Matsushima-wan Bay are meant to constitute one of the 'three great sights' of Japan – the other two are the floating torii of Miya-jima Island and the sandspit at Amanohashidate. Besides the islands, there's also a lot of unprepossessing industrial scenery. Bashō (yes, Bashō was here too!) was reportedly so entranced by the surroundings in the 17th century that, according to a local brochure, his flow of words was reduced to: 'Matsushima, Ah! Matsushima! Matsushima!'.

It's certainly a picturesque place which merits a half-day visit, but there are also impressive and less-touristed seascapes further east which are worth visiting.

Orientation & Information

Matsushima-kaigan station and the main sights of Matsushima are within easy walking reach of the dock for the cruise boats.

Matsushima Tourism Association (tel 022-354-2618) is next to the dock and has a few brochures – no English is spoken.

JNTO publishes a leaflet entitled *Sendai, Matsushima & Hiraizumi (023-MG)* which has maps of Matsushima and the vicinity and brief details relating to sights, transport and accommodation.

Zuigan-ji Temple
Founded in 828, the present buildings of Zuigan-ji were constructed in 1606 by Date Masamune to serve as a family temple. This is one of Tōhoku's finest Zen temples and well worth a visit to see the painted screens and interior carvings of the main hall and the Seiryūden (Treasure Hall), which contains works of art associated with the Date family.

Admission costs Y500 and includes an English leaflet. The temple is open from 7.30 am to 5 pm from April to mid-September, though for the rest of the year, opening hours vary almost month by month; the core opening hours are from 8 am to 3.30 pm. The temple is five minutes on foot from the dock and is approached along an avenue lined with tall cedars.

Godai-dō Hall
This is a small wooden temple reached by two bridges, just a couple of minutes on foot to your right as you get off the boat. The interior of the hall is only opened every 33 years – so you'll probably have to be content with the weatherbeaten exterior and the view out to sea.

Kanran-tei Pavilion
This pavilion is about five minutes on foot from the dock; bear left after leaving the boat. Kanran-tei is claimed to have been presented to the Date family by Toyotomi Hideyoshi in the late 16th century and served as a genteel venue for tea ceremonies and moon-viewing. The garden includes a small museum housing a collection of relics from the Date family.

Admission to the pavilion costs Y200 and includes entrance to the museum. It's open from 8.30 am to 5.30 pm (April to October) but closes an hour earlier during the rest of the year.

O-jima Island
About five minutes on foot, south of Kanran-

tei, you'll see this island connected with the mainland by a red, wooden bridge. It's a pleasant spot for a stroll. The island was once a retreat for priests, and women were forbidden entry until late last century.

Festivals
Seafood lovers will be interested in the Matsushima Oyster Festival which is held on the first Sunday in February – fresh oysters are sold near the boat dock.

The Tōrō Nagashi Festival, held on 15 August, honours the souls of the departed with the Bon ritual of floating lighted lanterns out to sea. A fireworks display adds zip to the occasion.

Places to Stay
Matsushima has dozens of ryokan, minshuku and hotels catering for the tidal waves of visitors. The Sendai tourist information office and the Matsushima Tourist Association can help with booking accommodation.

One useful option, close at hand, but further removed from the madding crowds is *Matsushima Youth Hostel* (tel 022-588-2220) which is at Oku-Matsushima to the east of Matsushima Bay, near Nobiru station.

OKU-MATSUSHIMA 奥松島
On the eastern curve of Matsushima-wan Bay, Oku-Matsushima is less touristed and offers scope for exploration by bicycle or on foot along several hiking trails.

To reach Oku-Matsushima, take the JR Senseki line east from Matsushima-kaigan to Nobiru station (two stops). From Nobiru station, it's a 10 minute bus ride to Otakamori village where a 20 minute climb up the hill provides a fine panorama of the bay.

Matsushima Youth Hostel is about 20 minutes on foot from Nobiru station. Bicycle rental is available and the manager can provide directions for the hiking trails.

Oshika-hantō Peninsula
牡鹿半島

The gateway to this beautiful, secluded peninsula is Ishinomaki, about 30 minutes from Matsushima-kaigan by limited express on the JR Senseki line.

From Ishinomaki station there are buses (Y1430, 90 minutes) to Ayukawa at the base of the peninsula – you may be able to get a Y100 discount by asking for a shūyū-ken or block of tickets. There is also a boat connection between Ishinomaki and Ayukawa which leaves at 9.50 am (Y1850, two hours).

The bus ride down the peninsula is particularly enjoyable as the bus repeatedly climbs across forested hills before dropping down into bays and inlets where tiny fishing villages are surrounded by mounds of seashells and the ocean is full of rafts and poles for oyster and seaweed cultivation.

On my trip to Ayukawa, I noticed that the other passengers in the bus were businessmen travelling in a group, but they seemed to show no interest in looking out of the window. A quick glance soon indicated why. They all had their noses glued to the steamy action in their manga – Japanese bimbos in revealing poses on the front cover and Western bimbos in amazing positions between the covers. Female anatomy was definitely winning their attention at the expense of Japanese seascapes!

Robert Strauss

AYUKAWA 鮎川
Ayukawa was once a major whaling centre and is now reliant on other types of fishing and tourism. The tourist information office, close to the dock for boats to Kinkazan Island, has helpful staff – only Japanese spoken – who will sit you down with a cup of coffee and arrange accommodation if you miss the last ferry to Kinkazan Island.

Just beside the tourist information office is the Ayu Whaling Museum. If the Japanese continue their whaling policies, museums will probably be the only place left for them to see whales. The museum is interesting, but steel yourself for pickled whale foetuses, diabolical harpoons, gruesome pictures of old whaling methods in open boats and giant diagrams where whales are compared in size to a bus or a shinkansen train. Admission costs Y260.

The souvenir shop next door appears to be selling pendants, carvings and other souvenirs made from whale products such as balleen – so where does this stuff come from? Who wants to buy these things and contribute to the extinction of whales – so lovingly cited by the Japanese as a tasty part of their culture?

Festivals
On 4 August, Ayukawa celebrates a whale festival with a parade of fishing boats and a fireworks display.

Places to Stay
An excellent place to stay is *Cobalt-sō Kokuminshukusha* (tel 022-545-2281). This modern people's lodge is in a superb position on a forested hilltop opposite Kinkazan Island. The lodge's minibus operates a 15 minute shuttle service to and from Ayukawa. For Y5000 you get two meals and a well-maintained room. A variety of seafood is included in the evening meal.

Getting There & Away
Ferries to Kinkazan Island depart hourly between 8 am and 3.30 pm; the trip takes 25 minutes (Y780 one way, Y1550 return). The daily ferry from Ayukawa to Ishinomaki leaves at 8 am.

KINKAZAN ISLAND 金華山
For those in search of peace and quiet an overnight stay on Kinkazan Island is highly recommended. The island features a pyramid-shaped mountain (445 metres), an impressive and drowsy shrine, a handful of houses around the boat dock, no cars, droves of deer and monkeys and mostly untended trails.

The island is considered one of the three holiest places in Tōhoku – women were banned until late last century – and you should respect the ban on smoking. On the first and second Sundays in October, there's a deer-horn cutting ceremony to stop the deer from causing injury to each other during the mating season.

From the boat dock, it's a steep 20 minute walk up the road to Koganeyama-jinja Shrine which has several attractive buildings in its forested precincts. Below the shrine are grassy expanses where crows delight in hitchhiking on the back of deer which know a trick or two when it comes to cadging titbits from visitors. At ground level, the deers' droppings provide busy times for large numbers of iridescent dung beetles.

A steep trail leads from the shrine up the thickly forested slopes, via several wayside shrines, to the summit in about 50 minutes. From the shrine at the summit, there are magnificent views out to sea and across to the peninsula. On the eastern shore of the island is Senjōjiki or '1000 Tatami Mats Rock', a large formation of white, level rock.

A map of the island on green paper is provided by the shrine or the tourist information office in Ayukawa. It has neither contour lines nor scale and its only use is to demonstrate that there *are* trails and to provide the kanji for various places on the island (this may be useful when you come across one of the weatherbeaten trail markers).

I spent a full eight hours tramping around without meeting another person; the only sounds were crows cawing, frogs burping and boats hooting in the far distance. Deer danced across the bracken into the undergrowth and a huge male monkey suddenly barred my path with a belligerent baring of teeth and as a final comment proffered a close-up display of his ugly pink bum before retreating behind a rock.

Before setting off for an extended hike, stock up on food and drink either at the dock or at the shrine shop. Apart from the route up to the summit shrine, the trails are mostly untended and you should be cautious with some of the wooden walkways along the summit which are collapsing into rotten pulp. If you do get lost, head downhill towards the sea – there's a dirt road around all but the northern part of the island.

Robert Strauss

Places to Stay

Koganeyama-jinja Shrine (tel 022-545-2264), 15 minutes on foot up the steep hill from the dock, has spartan rooms set aside for hostellers and basic meals are served. You can supplement the meals with food purchased from the shop outside the shrine – careful, the deer can mug the unwary! If you get up before 6 am you may be allowed to attend morning prayers. Most Japanese visitors seem to be day-trippers – this means the island is virtually deserted in the early morning and late afternoon.

The shrine also has a lodge for pilgrims which provides classier accommodation and food. Near the dock are a couple of unexciting minshuku.

Getting There & Away

Ferries to Ayukawa depart hourly between 9 am and 5 pm and take 25 minutes (Y780 one way, Y1550 return).

A variation in routing is provided by the ferry – a high-speed catamaran – between Kinkazan Island and Onagawa which is the eastern gateway to the peninsula. There are four daily departures in both directions; the first ferry leaves between 9 and 10 am and the last leaves between 2 and 3 pm (Y1600 one way, Y3020 return; half an hour).

ONAGAWA 女川

This fishing town serves as a gateway for the Oshika-hantō Peninsula. Having enjoyed the pristine scenery of the peninsula, you might like to know that the authorities have plonked an atomic power plant on the eastern coast, close to Natsuhama Beach. If you are interested, this plant has an Atomic Power Plant Superintending Centre which 'facilitates a proper understanding of atomic power generation' with the help of models and pictures. In Onagawa itself, there's the Atomic Power PR Centre which is described as an 'atomic museum' – this PR operation cost the regional power company Y800 million. Now it is understandable why the scenic highway down the peninsula is called 'Oshika Cobalt Line'.

Onagawa is the terminus for the JR Ishinomaki line, 30 minutes from Ishinomaki where you can either catch a train south-west towards Sendai or west towards

Furukawa (a change of train may be necessary, en route, at Kogota).

If you arrive at Onagawa Pier from Kinkazan Island, turn right as you leave the pier, continue for 200 metres, then turn left and proceed straight ahead for about 100 metres to the station.

KESENNUMA 気仙沼

North of Onagawa there is a road winding along the rugged coastline past the eroded rock formations of Cape Kamiwari-zaki (there's a campground nearby) up to Kesennuma and the Karukawa-hantō Peninsula.

Kesennuma serves as a base to visit the peninsula and O-shima Island which is 30 minutes by boat from Kesennuma Port. The port, 10 minutes by bus from Kesennuma station, is also worth a morning visit to witness the busy fish market – Kesennuma is the largest fishing town in the prefecture.

At the tip of Karukawa-hantō Peninsula, one hour by bus from Kesennuma, is Cape Osaki-misaki which has a campground, a kokuminshukusha and the Tsunami Hakubutsukan (Tsunami Museum) – the latter demonstrates the horrifying effects of the *tsunami* or tidal wave with simulated earthquakes, films and scary wind effects.

Karakuwa Youth Hostel (tel 02263-2-2490) is on the peninsula and can be reached by bus or boat from Kesennuma in about an hour. Special guest rooms and bicycle rental are also available.

Kesennuma is connected with Ichinoseki (Iwate-ken) by train on the JR Ofunato line in about 1¾ hours.

NARUKO ONSEN 鳴子温泉

This is a major hot-spring resort in the northwestern corner of Miyagi-ken. Those interested in kokeshi dolls might want to visit the Nihon Kokeshikan (Nihon Kokeshi Museum) which is within walking distance of Naruko station. The entrance to Narugokyō Gorge is a 10 minute drive from Narugo station in the direction of Nakayama-daira. From the entrance there is a 50 minute walk along the river valley to Nakayama-daira.

From Narugo station, there is a bus service which heads north for 30 minutes to reach more hot springs at Onikōbe Onsen which is also a popular ski resort in winter.

Naruko Onsen is one hour by train from Furukawa on the JR Rikuu-tōsen line.

Iwate-ken 岩手県

HIRAIZUMI 平泉

Of the few cultural sights in Tōhoku, Hiraizumi is one that should not be missed.

From 1089 to 1189, three generations of the Fujiwara family created a political and cultural centre in Hiraizumi which was claimed to approach the grandeur and sophistication of Kyoto. This short century of fame and prosperity was brought to an end when the last Fujiwara leader, Fujiwara Yasuhira, displayed such greed and treachery that he incurred the distrust of Minamoto Yoritomo who ordered the annihilation of the Fujiwara clan and the destruction of Hiraizumi.

Only a couple of the original temple buildings now remain as the rest have been restored or added over the centuries.

Orientation & Information

Hiraizumi is now a small town and orientation is straightforward. The tourist information office is on your right as you exit Hiraizumi station. JNTO publishes a leaflet entitled *Sendai, Matsushima & Hiraizumi (023-MG)* which has a schematic map of Hiraizumi and brief details for sights, access and accommodation.

Gouverneur Mosher, who has written a sensitive guide to Kyoto (see the Kyoto section of the Kinki District chapter), also wrote about Hiraizumi in a book entitled *Japan Caught Passing*, but it appears that this is out of print.

Chūson-ji Temple

Chūson-ji Temple was originally established in 850, but it was the first lord of the Fujiwara clan who decided in the early 12th century

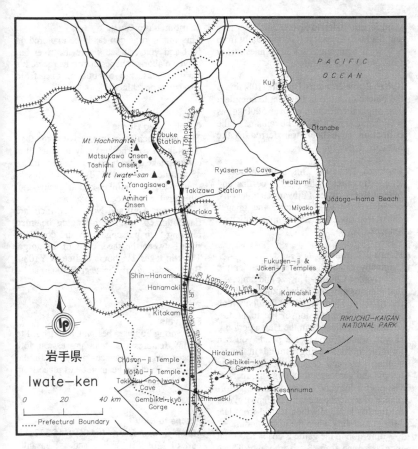

岩手県
Iwate-ken

0   20   40 km

..... Prefectural Boundary

to expand the site into a complex with over 40 temples and hundreds of residences for priests. A massive fire in 1337 destroyed most of the complex – even so, what you can see now is still most impressive.

The steep approach to the temple follows a long, tree-lined avenue past the Hondō (Main Hall) to an enclosed area with the splendid Konjiki-dō (Golden Hall) and several less interesting buildings.

Golden Hall Built in 1124, the Konjiki-dō is small but packed with gold ornamentation, black lacquerwork and inlaid mother-of-pearl. The centrepiece of the hall is a statue of Amida with attendants. Beneath the three side altars are the mummified remains of three generations of the Fujiwara family. The fourth and last lord of the family, Fujiwara Yasuhira, was beheaded at the order of Minamoto Yoritomo who further required the severed head to be sent to Kyoto for inspection before returning it for interment next to the coffin of Yasuhira's father.

During the '60s, the protective shelter for the hall was renewed and the interior decoration was given a complete restoration.

Admission costs Y500 – the ticket is also

valid for admission to Kyōzō Sutra Treasury and Sankōzō Treasury. It is open daily from 8.30 am to 5 pm but closes 30 minutes earlier from November to March.

Kyōzō Sutra Treasury Built in 1108, this is the oldest structure in the temple complex. The original collection of over 5000 sutras was damaged by fire and the remains of the collection have been transferred to the Sankōzō Treasury.

Sankōzō Treasury This building houses temple treasures including the coffins and funeral finery of the Fujiwara clan, scrolls, swords of the Fujiwara clan and images transferred from halls and temples which no longer exist.

Mōtsū-ji Temple
Originally established in 850, this temple once rivalled Chūson-ji in size and fame. All that remains now are foundation stones and the attractive Jōdo (Paradise) Garden which gives a good impression of the luxurious, sophisticated lifestyle in the Heian period – as you wander around the pond, you can imagine nobles lazing around in boats, sipping saké and composing verses. The temple and gardens attract large numbers of visitors for Jōgyōdō Hatsukayasai, a performance of ancient dances on 20 January; and for the Iris Festival which is held from late June to mid-July when the irises bloom.

Admission to the gardens costs Y500 and they are open from 8 am to 5 pm. Those staying at the youth hostel in the grounds do not have to pay for admission.

Takkoku-no-Iwaya Cave
A few km south-west of Mōtsū-ji Temple is a temple built into a cave and dedicated to Bishamonten, the Buddhist guardian deity of warriors. The present structure is a reproduction dating from 1961.

The cave is open from 8 am to 5 pm but closes half an hour earlier from November to March. Admission costs Y200. The cave can be reached in 10 minutes by bus or taxi; or you can cycle if you like.

Gembikei-kyō Gorge
This small gorge can easily be explored on foot and you can see where the river has carved elaborate shapes out of the rocks. It's easily accessible by bus or taxi from Hiraizumi or Ichinoseki.

Geibikei-kyō Gorge
This is a much more impressive gorge than Gembikei-kyō. The best way to reach it is either to take a taxi from Hiraizumi or take a 45 minute bus ride (Y570) from Ichinoseki station to the Geibikei-kyō Iriguchi stop, which is the entrance to the gorge.

Between April and November, there are flat-bottomed boats with singing boatmen ferrying their passengers up and down the river between the sheer cliffs of the gorge. The trip takes 1½ hours and costs Y1030. Boats depart hourly between 8.30 am and 4 pm.

Festivals
The Spring Fujiwara Festival, held from 1 to 5 May, features a costume procession, folk dances and performances of Nō. A similar Autumn Fujiwara Festival takes place from 1 to 3 November.

Places to Stay
Mōtsū-ji Youth Hostel (tel 0191-46-2331) is part of Mōtsū-ji Temple and a pleasantly peaceful place to stay – guests at the hostel are not charged admission to the gardens. The temple is eight minutes on foot from Hiraizumi station.

Getting There & Away
To reach Hiraizumi from Sendai, take a JR Tōhoku shinkansen to Ichinoseki (35 minutes) then the bus which goes via Hiraizumi station to Chūson-ji Temple (Y320, 26 minutes). You can also take a JR Tōhoku Honsen line train from Sendai to Hiraizumi station, but a change of trains is

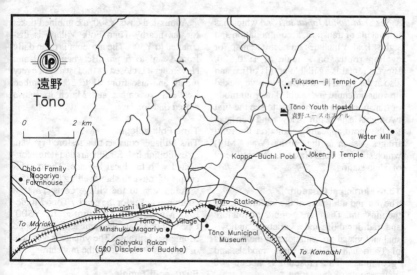

遠野
Tōno

0   2 km

Fukusen—ji Temple

Tōno Youth Hostel
遠野ユースホステル

Water Mill

Kappa—Buchi Pool   Jōken—ji Temple

Chiba Family
Magariya
Farmhouse

JR Kamaishi Line   Tōno Station

To Morioka   Tōno Folk Village
Minshuku Magariya   Tōno Municipal
Gohyaku Rakan   Museum
(500 Disciples of Buddha)   To Kamaishi

usually necessary at Ichinoseki and the trip takes about two hours.

From Morioka to Ichinoseki on the JR Tōhoku shinkansen line takes 43 minutes. Trains between Ichinoseki and Morioka on the JR Tōhoku Honsen line are less frequent and take about 1¾ hours.

Getting Around

Frequent buses run from Ichinoseki station via Hiraizumi station to Chūson-ji Temple; the 20 minute walk from Hiraizumi station to Chūson-ji Temple is not particularly appealing. From the station, Mōtsū-ji Temple is an easy 10 minute walk. Bicycle rental is available outside the station.

KITAKAMI   北上

Kitakami is renowned for its Michinoku Kyodo Geino Matsuri Festival. This is held from 7 to 9 August and features folk-art performances not only from the Kitakami region, but also from many other parts of Tōhoku.

TONO   遠野

Tōno excited attention at the beginning of this century when a collection of regional folk tales were compiled by Kunio Yanagida and published under the title *Tōno Monogatari*. During the '70s, this work was translated into English by Robert Morse under the title *The Legends of Tōno* – it should still be available in specialist foreign-language bookshops like Kinokuniya or Maruzen in Tokyo. The tales cover a racy collection of topics from supernatural beings and weird occurrences to the strange ways of the rustic folk in traditional Japan.

The present city of Tōno was formed out of a merger of eight villages in the '50s and is not uniformly interesting – just a few sights scattered around the more appealing rural fringes. The region still has some examples of the local style of farmhouse, known as *magariya*, where farmfolk and their prized horses lived under one roof – but in different sections.

Information

The tourist information office in Morioka has details about Tōno. The Tōno tourist information office (tel 0198-62-3030) is outside JR Tōno station. The staff can provide an English brochure entitled *Come*

& *See Traditional Japan in Tōno* which has full details of transport, accommodation and sights. It also includes an accurate map for cycling routes on a scale of 1:70,000. Bicycle rental is available at this office and also at the youth hostel. Once you've picked up your brochure and decided on your mode of transport, you might want to see the first two sights in the centre of town and then head for the more appealing sights on the rural fringes – such as the Suisha (Water Mill) which still functions about 10 km north-east of Tōno station.

Tōno Municipal Museum
The 3rd and 4th floors of the building house the museum. There are exhibits of folklore and traditional life and a variety of audiovisual and visual presentations of the legends of Tōno using slides, films, models and 'georamas'. The museum is about 500 metres south of the station.

Admission costs Y300; a combined ticket for the nearby Tōno Folk Village is discounted to Y500. The museum is open daily from 9 am to 5 pm. Between April and November it is closed on the last day of every month and also from 21 to 30 September. Between November and March it is also closed on Monday.

Tōno Folk Village
This 'village' consists of a restored ryokan, an exhibition hall for folk art and items connected with the local legends. There are a couple of souvenir shops selling local crafts.

Admission to the village costs Y300; a combined ticket for the nearby Tōno Municipal Museum is discounted to Y500. Opening hours are the same as for the Tōno Municipal Museum. The village is a couple of minutes on foot from the museum.

Fukusen-ji Temple
This temple lies north-east of Tōno station, about 30 minutes by bicycle. Founded as recently as 1912, its major claim to fame is the wooden Fukusen-ji Kannon statue – 17 metres in height – which is claimed to be the tallest of its type in Japan. Admission costs Y300.

Jōken-ji Temple & Kappa-Buchi Pool
Jōken-ji Temple is about one km south of Fukusen-ji. Outside the temple is a distinctive lion statue; inside the temple is a famous image which some believe will cure their illness if they rub the part on its body which corresponds to the part where their own body ailment is.

Behind the temple is a stream and the Kappa-Buchi Pool. Kappa are considered to be mischievous, mythical creatures but legend has it that the kappa in this pool once put out a fire in the temple. The lion statue was erected as a gesture of thanks to honour the kappa. See the Folklore & Gods section of the Facts About the Country chapter for more details about kappa.

Gohyaku Rakan
On a wooded hillside, about three km south-

west of Tōno station, are the Gohyaku Rakan (500 Disciples of Buddha). These rock carvings were fashioned by a priest to console the spirits of those who died in a disastrous famine in 1754.

Chiba Family Magariya Farmhouse
Just over 10 km west of Tōno station is this magariya which has been restored to give an impression of the traditional lifestyle of a wealthy farming family in the 18th century. The farmhouse is open from 8 am to 5 pm and admission costs Y300.

Places to Stay
The tourist information office can help with booking accommodation – there are a couple of hotels and ryokan and at least a dozen minshuku.

Minshuku Magariya (tel 0198-62-4564), about two km south-west of the station, is a popular place where you can stay inside a traditional farmhouse. Prices start around Y6000 per person and include two meals.

Tōno Youth Hostel (tel 0198-62-8736) provides a base for cycling or walking around the area. From Tōno station, take a bus bound for Iwate-Yamaguchi and get off at the Nitagai stop (about 12 minutes). From there it's 10 minutes on foot to the hostel. Bicycle rental is available at Y500 for the day.

Getting There & Away
Train On the JR Kamaishi line, it takes an hour to get from Tōno to Hanamaki (which is on the JR Tōhoku line) and an hour to Shin-Hanamaki (which is on the Tōhoku shinkansen line).

Bus There are buses departing four times a day from Kitakami to Kamaishi via Tōno. The trip to Tōno takes 70 minutes.

Getting Around
The sights in Tōno can't be adequately covered on foot and the bus services can be inconvenient. The best method is either to take a taxi or, even better, rent a bicycle for the day (about Y500). The cycling course map in the tourist brochure is accurate and detailed in its coverage of three different routes.

MORIOKA 盛岡
From its origins as a castle town in the late 16th century, Morioka has developed into one of the largest cities in Tōhoku.

Although there are very few sights in the city, it is a terminus for the JR Tōhoku shinkansen line and this makes it a useful staging post for visiting the northern part of Tōhoku.

Information
Kita Tōhoku Sightseeing Centre (tel 0196-25-2090) inside Morioka station has English-speaking staff and a good supply of information material. It's open from 8.30 am to 8 pm.

JNTO publishes a leaflet entitled *Morioka & Rikuchū-kaigan National Park (022-MG)* which has basic details for sightseeing, transport and accommodation and includes a small map of Morioka.

Iwate-kōen Park
This park, in the centre of town, is really only of interest as a useful point for orientation. In the grounds are the ruins of the city's original castle. From Morioka station, the park is five minutes by bus or 20 minutes on foot.

Hachiman-gū Shrine
This shrine is dedicated to Hachiman, the tutelary deity of Morioka. The Hachiman Festival, held here from 14 to 16 September, features processions with floats, portable shrines and drummers. The shrine is about 20 minutes on foot from Iwate-kōen.

Just south of the shrine, about 10 minutes on foot, are the Jūroku Rakan (16 Disciples) – large stone statues with interesting expressions which were carved by a compassionate priest early last century as a mark of respect for the souls of those who had died in a famine.

Morioka Hashimoto Art Museum

This is perhaps the most worthwhile sight in Morioka. The museum is perched halfway up the slope of Mt Iwate-yama and combines various architectural styles including a magariya (traditional farmhouse). Hashimoto Yaoji (1903-79), a local artist, built the museum during his lifetime and according to his own fancy, rather than using blueprints from an architect. Some of his own sculptures and paintings are on display amongst the many other exhibits of folk art and crafts; his taste as a collector included both Western and Japanese works of art. The museum is open from 10 am to 5 pm and admission costs Y700.

From Morioka station, take bus No 12 for the 30 minute ride to the museum.

Festivals

The Chagu-Chagu Umakko festival, held on 15 June, features a parade of brightly decorated horses through Morioka to Hachiman-gū Shrine.

Places to Stay

The tourist information office at the station has lists for moderate or inexpensive accommodation and can help with reservations.

Morioka Youth Hostel (tel 0196-62-2220) is large and a bit bland, but the manager is helpful. From Morioka station, take a bus from terminal No 11 – not all buses are suitable so check first – and get off after 15 minutes at the Takamatsu-no-ike-guchi stop. It's a three minute walk from here to the hostel.

Ryokan Kumagai (tel 0196-51-3020), a member of the Japanese Inn Group, is eight minutes on foot from the station. Singles/doubles start at Y3700/6800; triples from Y9000.

Another Japanese Inn Group member, *Tamaya Ryokan* (tel 0196-22-8500), is 10 minutes by bus from Morioka station and close to the Hachiman-gū Shrine. Singles/doubles start at Y4000/7000; triples cost from Y10,000.

Places to Eat

The local speciality is 'wanko soba' which consists of buckwheat noodles served in tiny, bite-sized portions in lacquer bowls (wanko). Waitresses hover around you waiting to serve a fresh bowl as soon as you've slurped down your previous one. Groups of diners will often indulge in a contest when matchsticks are used to keep count of numbers of bowls consumed; a diner only admits defeat by successfully placing the lid back on the bowl. A local tourist leaflet had some advice that is sure to please fellow diners: 'if you just can't get another bowl down, you throw up your white flag'!

The Fezan department store, adjacent to Morioka station, has a food floor with a variety of restaurants serving Western and Japanese dishes.

Things to Buy

The region around Morioka is famous for the production of Nambu Tetsubin (Nambu Ironware) which includes items such as tea kettles, flower pots and wind chimes. These ironware items make popular souvenirs and are on sale at many shops in the station and in the city centre.

Getting There & Away

From Morioka to Tokyo (Ueno) on the JR Tōhoku shinkansen line, the fastest trains take a mere 2¾ hours. If you are heading further north to Aomori by train, you should change to the JR Tōhoku line for the 2½ hour trip.

Lake Tazawa-ko, just west of Morioka, is reached via the JR Tazawa-ko line. To visit the Hachimantai area, north-west of Morioka, take the JR Hanawa line to either Obuke station or Hachimantai station, then continue by bus. To reach Miyako, on the eastern coast of Tōhoku, take the JR Yamada line.

Getting Around

Buses leave from the station and from the bus terminal, close to Iwate-kōen Park.

MT IWATE-SAN

The volcanic peak of Mt Iwate-san is a dominating landmark, north-west of Morioka, and a popular destination for hikers. From Morioka station, you can take a bus north-west to Amihari Onsen (Y1240, 65 minutes) which is the start of one of the main trails to the summit. Another popular approach is to take the train north on the JR Tōhoku line to Takizawa station then change to a bus for Yanagisawa where you can join the steep trail to the summit.

MIYAKO 宮古

Miyako is a small city in the centre of the Rikuchū-kaigan National Park (which extends 180 km along the eastern coastline of Tōhoku from Kesennuma in the south to Kuji in the north). This huge coastal park does have some interesting rock formations and seascapes, but it really isn't necessary to devote too much time to them – the boat tours may seem like a good idea, but are often marred by an incessant, full-blast commentary hammering out of loudspeakers.

Information

Miyako tourist information office (tel 0193-62-3574) is on your right as you exit the station. The staff speak a little English and can provide maps and timetable details.

Jōdoga-hama Beach

This is a very attractive beach with white sand, dividing rock formations and a series of walking trails through the forests of pine trees on the steep slopes leading down to the beach.

From the concrete souvenir centre opposite the bus stop, a path leads down to the dock for excursion boats. A 40 minute boat trip (Y820) to a few rock formations should be enough to introduce you to the loudspeakers and gluttonous seagulls. These seagulls seem to be such a source of amazement to sightseers that local souvenir shops now sell rubber versions of them.

You can skip the boat excursion and escape some of the crowds by leaving the tarmac road beyond the bus stop and climbing up trails into the hills where there are good views across the beach.

There are frequent buses to the beach from Miyako station (Y150, 15 minutes).

A daily excursion boat links Jōdoga-hama Beach with Otanabe. It stops at a couple of fishing ports and passes several rock formations en route. The trip (Y2200) takes nearly three hours, and is not, in my opinion, an outstanding outing.

Places to Stay

Suehiro-kan Youth Hostel (tel 0193-62-1555) is just three minutes on foot from Miyako station. Walk straight out of the station exit and continue 30 metres to the intersection with the main street, turn right and walk about 20 metres to the hostel which is on the right-hand side of the street – there's a youth hostel sign next to the door.

Miyako Kimura Youth Hostel (tel 0193-62-2888) is seven minutes on foot from the station. Walk straight out of the station exit and continue for 30 metres until you reach the intersection with the main street. Turn right and the hostel is down the fifth side-street on the left-hand side of the main street. There have been reports that hostellers are encouraged to sing and dance here in the evenings!

Getting There & Away

Train Morioka is linked with Miyako on the JR Yamada line (2¼ hours) which continues south from Miyako down the coast for another 75 minutes to Kamaishi.

The JR Kita-Rias line runs north from Miyako along the coastline to Kuji in about 1¾ hours – the scenery is mostly obscured by tunnels.

Bus Between Morioka station and Miyako station, there's a fast bus service with hourly departures for the 2¼ hour trip (Y1850). There are several bus services linking

Miyako with Kamaishi via the southern coastline of Rikuchū-kaigan National Park.

RYUSEN-DO CAVE   龍泉洞
Close to Iwaizumi (north-west of Miyako), is Ryūsen-dō Cave, one of the three largest stalactite caves in Japan. It contains a huge underground lake – the clearest in the world – which is 120 metres deep.

From Iwaizumi station, it's a 10 minute bus trip to the cave. There are bus services from Morioka station direct to the cave and also buses from Miyako to the cave.

Aomori-ken   青森県

HACHINOHE   八野辺
Travellers to Hokkaidō can take the ferry from Hachinohe-kō Port to either Tomakomai or Muroran.

The ferry for Tomakomai leaves three times daily at 8.45 am, 1 and 10 pm. The trip takes about nine hours and the cheapest passenger fare is Y3900.

The ferry for Muroran departs twice daily at 5.45 am and 5.30 pm. The trip takes about eight hours and the cheapest passenger fare is Y3900.

To reach the port, take a bus from Hon-Hachinohe station.

MISAWA
Misawa has a huge contingent of foreigners employed at Misawa Air Force Base which is run by US and Japanese military authorities. Avid plane spotters may want to join a tour of the base to see the latest hardware such as F-16 and P-3 Orion combat planes. The tours take place every Friday afternoon and last 2½ hours. Prior permission is required from base officials – check first with the Sightseeing Section of the Misawa City Office (tel 0176-53-5111).

Aviation pilgrims will probably also want to trek to Sabishiro Beach, just north of the air base, where the US flyers Pangborn and Herndon took off in 1931 and successfully coaxed their doughty monoplane, *Miss Veedol*, through the first nonstop trans-Pacific crossing. The flight took just over 41 hours and the pilots were able to claim the US$25,000 prize offered by the Japanese newspaper, *Asahi Shimbun*. The memories may be a bit faded by now, but an annual 'Miss Veedol' festival is still held here in September.

NOHEJI   野辺地
Noheji is a staging post for travel to the Shimokita-hantō Peninsula and also provides the option of a ferry connection to Hokkaidō.

From Noheji station, there are buses (Y1180, 95 minutes) to Mutsu bus terminal which is the best access point for Mt Osore-zan.

There are three daily sailings from Noheji-kō Port to Hakodate (Hokkaidō), departing at 0.35 am, 12.30 pm and 5 pm. The trip takes 4¾ hours and the passenger fare is Y1400.

MT OSORE-ZAN   恐山
This volcano has been held in awe as a mysterious, sacred place for many centuries – probably long before the founding of the Entsū-ji Temple on its slopes in the 9th century.

As you approach Osore-zan by road, the stench of sulphuric gas intensifies – it's definitely the mountain, not the passengers! Rhododendrons are the only plants that can hack it in this environment. After paying Y300 admission, you can walk through the temple grounds, past the bathhouses and crunch your way along the trails of volcanic rock crisscrossed by rivulets of green and yellow sludge.

The scene is reminiscent of a Hitchcock movie as clouds of steam rise from hissing vents in the ground and flocks of ravens swarm over shrines dotted across the barren slopes The shrines are surrounded with garishly coloured toys and children's whirligigs spin in the breeze. Paths lead down to the leaden waters of the lake that has formed in the caldera. The small statues of Jizō, the Buddhist deity in charge of the spirits of departed children, are covered with bibs and sweets.

Whatever your beliefs, it would be hard to deny that there is a strong, sinister feeling here of other-worldly power.

Robert Strauss

Information

The information office inside Mutsu bus terminal can help with transport information and leaflets in Japanese.

Festivals

Osore-zan Taisai, a festival held from 20 to 24 July, attracts huge crowds of visitors keen to consult *itako* or 'mediums'. The itako are blind women who act for the visitors and make contact with dead family members. A similar, but smaller festival is held from 9 to 11 October.

Places to Stay

The staff at the information office inside Mutsu bus terminal don't speak English, but they will do their best to help you book

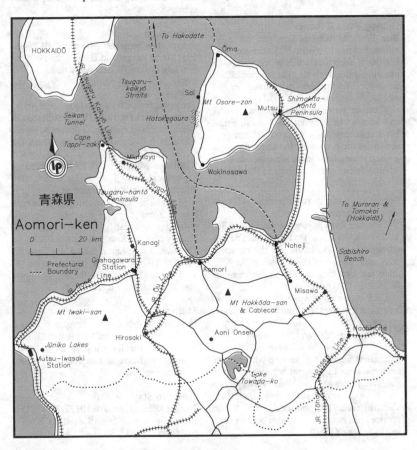

accommodation. There are plenty of minshuku in the drab confines of Mutsu and there are more expensive hotels and ryokan at Yagen Onsen, a scenic hot-spring resort in the mountains, about 80 minutes by bus from Mutsu.

Of the two youth hostels on the peninsula – both in remote locations – you might find that the most useful one is *Wakinosawa Youth Hostel* (tel 0175-44-2341). This hostel is well-placed for an excursion along Hotokegaura, the spectacular western coast of the peninsula, and for the ferry connection to Aomori.

Getting There & Away
Bus From Mutsu bus terminal, it's a 35 minute bus ride (Y640) to Mt Osore-zan. The last bus to the mountain is at 3.20 pm, 4.45 pm during the festivals. The service closes down for the winter between November and April.

There are buses running between Aomori and Mutsu bus terminal via Noheji. From Mutsu bus terminal – the centre of transport action for the peninsula, but a real dump of a place otherwise – there are buses to Oma where you can catch the ferry to Hokkaidō.

Ferry From Oma, there are ferries to Hakodate and Muroran on Hokkaidō.

There are three daytime departures (6.30, 11.25 am and 5.25 pm) to Hakodate. The trip takes just over 1½ hours and the cheapest passenger fare is Y1000. During August, there are also two sailings in the evening (8.35 and 10.20 pm).

There is one daily departure to Muroran at 3 pm. The trip takes five hours and the cheapest passenger fare is Y1400. During June and July there is usually an extra sailing at 9.20 am.

There is also a ferry service which takes about an hour for the trip between Aomori and Wakinosawa. From Wakinosawa, there are boat excursions via Hotokegaura to Sai. The trip takes 1½ hours (Y2160). A bus service links Sai with the Mutsu bus terminal in 2¼ hours (Y1960).

AOMORI 青森
Aomori is the prefectural capital and an important centre for shipping and fishing. It was bombed heavily during WW II and has since been completely rebuilt – as a result, it's of limited appeal to the passing tourist.

Prior to the opening of the Seikan Tunnel linking Honshū and Hokkaidō, Aomori did booming business with its ferry services to Hokkaidō. Although this no longer applies, Aomori still serves as a useful transport hub for visits to Lake Towada-ko, the scenic region around Mt Hakkōda-san, the Shimokita-hantō and Tsugaru-hantō peninsulas.

Information
A tourist information office (tel 0177-35-5311) is on the ground floor of the ASPAM building next to JR Aomori station.

Things to See
The prime reason for a visit to Aomori would be the Nebuta Festival. Those interested in folkcrafts could visit the Keikokan Museum which is a five minute bus ride from the station. In addition to folkcrafts, the Aomori Kyōdokan Museum also displays archaeological exhibits. This museum is a five minute bus ride from the station.

Munakata Shikō Memorial Museum houses a collection of wood-block prints, paintings and calligraphy by Munakata Shikō who was a famous artist from Aomori. To reach the museum, take a bus from JR Aomori station bound for Tsutsui and get off after about 15 minutes at the Bunka Sentamae stop near the cultural centre.

Festivals
The Nebuta Matsuri, held in Aomori from 2 to 7 August, is renowned throughout Tōhoku and Japan for its parades of colossal illuminated floats accompanied by thousands of dancers.

Places to Stay
Aomori Kokusai Hotel (tel 0177-22-4321) is a five minute walk from the station. Singles cost from around Y5000.

Aomori Green Hotel (tel 0177-23-2001) is a three minute walk from the station. Prices for singles/doubles start at Y4700/9000.

Getting There & Away
Air JAS operates frequent flights to Tokyo, Osaka and Sapporo. From Aomori station, it's a 35 minute bus ride to the airport (Aomori Kūkō) just south of the city.

Train Aomori is connected with Hokkaidō by the JR Tsugaru Kaikyō line which runs via the Seikan Tunnel beneath the Tsugaru Straits to Hakodate in 2½ hours.

The JR Tōhoku Honsen line links Aomori with Morioka in just over two hours by limited express. From Morioka, you can zip back to Tokyo in 2½ hours on the shinkansen.

The JR Ou line runs from Aomori, via Hirosaki, to Akita then continues down to Yamagata and Fukushima. From Akita, the JR Uetsu Honsen line runs down to Niigata.

Bus JR operates a frequent bus service between mid-April and mid-November from Aomori to Lake Towada-ko (Y2470, three hours). One hour out of Aomori, the bus reaches Hakkōda cablecar (ropeway), then continues through a string of hot-spring hamlets to the lake.

For a visit to Mt Osore-zan (Shimokita-hantō Peninsula), you can take a direct bus from Aomori via Noheji to the Mutsu bus terminal in 2¾ hours.

Ferry For a ferry connection to Shimokita-hantō Peninsula, you could take the one hour trip (Y2160) between Aomori and Wakinosawa.

MT HAKKODA-SAN　八甲田山
Just south of Aomori is a scenic region around Mt Hakkōda-san which is popular with hikers, hot-spring enthusiasts and skiers.

A bus service from Aomori reaches Hakkōda cablecar in 70 minutes then continues to Lake Towada-ko. The cablecar whisks you up to the summit of Mt Tamoyachi-yama

in nine minutes (Y980 one way). From there you can follow a network of hiking trails. Some trails in this area are covered in *Hiking in Japan* by Paul Hunt.

TSUGARU-HANTO PENINSULA 津軽半島
If you fancy a sidetrip out to the extremity of this peninsula above Aomori, take the 1¾ hour ride on the JR Tsugaru line from Aomori station to Miumaya. From there, a bus service (Y630, 45 minutes) follows the road around the coastline to Cape Tappi-zaki which has superb views across the Tsugaru Straits. Just a couple of km east of this cape is the spot where the Seikan Tunnel wends its way underground, leaving the mainland and heading under the sea.

HIROSAKI　弘前
Founded in the 17th century, the castle town of Hirosaki developed into one of the leading cultural centres in Tōhoku. With the exception of its dreary modern centre – which can be avoided – it has retained much of its original architecture including a large portion of its castle area, temple districts and even a few buildings from the Meiji era. Hirosaki is recommended for its pleasing atmosphere and just a few sights that can be covered in a day at an easy walking pace.

Orientation & Information
The main station is JR Hirosaki station. All bus connections for destinations outside Hirosaki are made at Hirosaki bus terminal, a concrete monster of a building just a few minutes up the street from the JR station. Hirosaki is compact in size and easily covered on foot. To give yourself a quick start – and avoid the drab town centre – take a bus or a taxi from the station for a 15 minute ride to Neputa-mura where you can start your circuit of the castle and the other sights.

The information office at the station can provide an English brochure with a very sketchy map of the town.

Neputa-mura Museum
This museum is set up as a type of 'village'

(mura) which allows visitors to follow a circuit through several sections devoted to different topics. There is a fine display of floats used in the Neputa festival and a man dutifully pops out every 10 minutes to give a drumming demonstration. After passing through the garden with its pond full of greedy carp, you enter a crafts section where you can watch the production of pots, kokeshi and kites – or even have a go at making them yourself. On the 2nd floor is a room filled with a mind-boggling variety of figurines. There is also a souvenir shop where you can buy the professional product to compare with your own creation. (See the later section on Things to Buy.)

The museum is open from 9 am to 5 pm (April to mid-November) but closes an hour earlier during the rest of the year. Admission costs Y500.

Samurai Quarter

Just north of the Neputa-mura Museum, you can walk around the residential district once reserved for samurai. The traditional layout of the district now contains mostly modern buildings, but a couple of samurai houses have been restored and opened to the public.

Hirosaki-jō Castle

Construction of the castle was completed in 1611, but the main keep burnt down in 1627 after being struck by lightning. It was rebuilt in 1810 and this attractive structure has survived – a relative rarity today when most of Japan's remaining castle structures are replicas. The castle grounds have been turned into a splendid park which is a magnet for thousands of cherry blossom devotees in April.

Saishō-in Temple

About a 15 minute walk south of the castle, this temple is worth a visit to see the Gojū-no-tō Pagoda, a splendid five storeyed example constructed in 1667.

Chōshō-ji Temple

About 20 minutes on foot, north of the pagoda, you come to an avenue – flanked by temples on either side – which leads to Chōshō-ji Temple. After passing through the impressive temple gate, you can continue

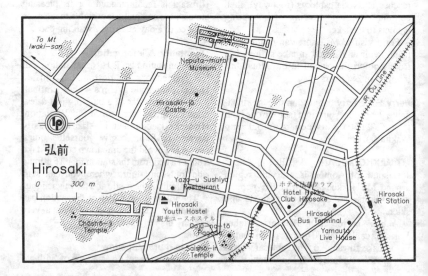

past a large, 14th century bell to the main hall which dates from the 17th century. Keeping to the left of the hall, you can follow a path through the trees to several timeworn shrines.

This peaceful temple district is a pleasant place to walk in the early morning or late afternoon.

Festivals

From 1 to 7 August, Hirosaki celebrates Neputa Matsuri, a festival famous throughout Japan for its beautifully painted floats which are illuminated from within. These are paraded in the evenings on different routes through the town to the accompaniment of flutes and drums. Like its more rowdy counterpart held in Aomori, this festival attracts thousands of visitors – book accommodation well in advance if you plan to visit at this time.

Places to Stay

Hirosaki Youth Hostel (tel 0172-33-7066) is in a good location for the sights, but it's a bit drab. From Hirosaki station, take a bus from bus stop No 3 and get off after about 15 minutes at the Daigaku-byōin stop. Walk straight up the street for five minutes and the hostel is on your left down an alley.

Hotel Hokke Club Hirosaki (tel 0172-34-3811) is in the centre, 10 minutes on foot from the station. Most of the rooms are Western style and prices for singles start around Y6000.

Places to Eat

Close to the youth hostel is *Yazo-u Sushiya*, a sushi restaurant which does good teishoku (set-menu lunches) at prices starting from Y1000. The boss and his wife are friendly – the fish is picked up fresh from the market every morning.

Walk out of the youth hostel door and up the alley to the main street, then turn right and walk for about five minutes – the restaurant is on the other side of the road.

Entertainment

If you want to combine food and entertainment then why not splurge on a visit to *Yamauta Live House*, a wooden-fronted building just five minutes on foot from the station. The place is run by a family which serves the drinks and food, then picks up musical instruments and launches into local music, known as 'tsugaru-jamisen'.

The players lay down a fast rhythm using large plectrums on banjo-like instruments and are accompanied in a wailing, sometimes quavering voice by the well-proportioned lady of the house who is encouraged by the audience shouting the Japanese equivalent of 'right on'! It's infectious music – the old lady sitting next to me was bouncing up and down like a steamhammer!

Robert Strauss

There is an extensive menu. If you order one of the teishoku and a couple of beers, you can expect to pay around Y2500. The music starts around 8 pm.

Things to Buy

Neputa-mura has a shopping section where you can purchase kokeshi (wooden dolls), paper goldfish, tiny figurines, spinning tops that perform nifty stunts and *tako* (kites), a regional art form produced in bold designs and bright colours at prices from around Y550. Hirosaki is famed for its apples and you can buy cans of unadulterated apple juice here at Y100 each.

Hirosaki is also known for its exceptionally hard Tsuruga Nuri lacquerware, *kogin* embroidery and wickerwork using *akebi* (vine).

Getting There & Away

Train Hirosaki is connected with Aomori on the JR Ou line (35 minutes by limited express). On the same line, trains south from Hirosaki to Akita take about 2½ hours by limited express.

Bus Between mid-April and early November, there are up to six buses from Hirosaki bus terminal to Lake Towada-ko.

Morioka is linked with Hirosaki by a JR bus service which takes 2¼ hours (Y2880).

From mid-April to late October, there are buses from the Hirosaki bus terminal to Mt Iwaki-san.

AONI ONSEN   青荷

The bus from Hirosaki to Lake Towada-ko climbs through the mountains and passes a series of remote hot-spring hamlets. One is Aoni Onsen (tel 0172-52-3243), a rustic group of ryokan that prefer oil lamps to electricity and serve wholesome mountain food. To get there you'll have to get off the bus at Aoni Onsen Iriguchi then walk about an hour up the track. Advance reservations are necessary and you should expect to pay around Y6000 per person which includes two meals.

The bus makes a short stop at Taki-no-zawa, a scenic lookout across the lake, before descending to Nenokuchi beside the lake.

MT IWAKI-SAN   岩木山

Soaring above Hirosaki is the sacred volcano of Iwaki-san which is a popular climb for both pilgrims and hikers.

From mid-April to late October, there are buses from the Hirosaki bus terminal to Mt Iwaki-san. The trip takes 80 minutes to Hachigōme at the foot of the cablecar below the summit. After a seven minute ride (Y350) on the cablecar, it then takes another 45 minutes to climb to the summit (1625 metres). This route is the shortest and easiest – the youth hostel in Hirosaki has maps showing other climbing routes and times.

An autumn festival known as Oyama-sankei is celebrated on the mountain, usually in September. A colourful procession of local farmers wends its way from Iwaki-san-jinja Shrine to the summit to complete ancient harvest thanksgiving rites.

KANAGI   金木

North of Hirosaki is Kanagi, a town which attracts thousands of Japanese 'literary groupies' to the residence of the Tsushima family. Tsushima Shūji (1909-48) was one of Japan's famous writers, better known by his pen name of Dazai Osamu. Stung by a feeling of guilt at his wealthy origins, Dazai hung out with social movements and dropped out of university. After a series of unsuccessful attempts at suicide, Dazai finally brought his life to an early conclusion by jumping into a river with his mistress.

Several of his books have been translated into English, the best known titles being *The Setting Sun (Shayō)* and *No Longer Human (Ningen Shikkattu)*.

The Tsushima family residence, known as Shayōkan (after the novel mentioned above), has been preserved as a ryokan where guests can stay amidst bizarre furnishings from the Meiji era and ponder the short life span of this cult figure. The residence is a 10 minute walk from Kanagi station.

To reach Kanagi, take the train from either Aomori or Hirosaki to Goshogawara station. From there, it's a 30 minute ride by bus or train (Tsugaru Dentetsu line).

JUNIKO LAKES   十三湖

If you are passing from Aomori towards Akita down the west coast of Tōhoku, you might like to make a short detour to spend a few hours hiking around this collection of lakes scattered inside a forest park and nod respectfully to the nearby Nihon Canyon – not the grandest in terms of size.

From Mutsu-Iwasaki station on the JR Gonō line, buses run five times daily and take about 10 minutes to reach the trailheads for the lakes. This service is stopped between early November and late April.

Akita-ken   秋田県

LAKE TOWADA-KO   十和田湖

This is a large crater lake with impressive scenery. It is rated by Japanese as the top tourist spot in Tōhoku which means you can expect lots of company! The main town on the lake is Yasumiya which is nothing special, just a staging post and centre for boat trips around the lake. Unfortunately, however, the loudspeaker babble and hazy conditions may spoil the trip for you.

Nenoguchi, a small tourist outpost on the eastern shore of the lake, marks the entrance to the Oirase Valley. The 3½ hour hike up this valley to Ishigedo (refreshment centre and bus stop) is the most enjoyable thing to do around the lake. You can, of course, do the hike in the opposite direction. The path winds through thick deciduous forest following the Oirasekawa River, with its mossy boulders, plunging waterfalls and tumbling tracts of white water. Early morning might be the best time to do the hike, particularly if you go during the peak viewing season in autumn.

There are frequent buses from mid-April to early November which link the valley with Aomori and Hirosaki. You can take a boat or a bus between Yasumiya and Nenoguchi.

Places to Stay

Hakubutsukan Youth Hostel (tel 0176-75-2002) is tucked away *inside* the Grand Hotel, a few metres from the pier at Yasumiya.

I spent a frustrating quarter of an hour trying to find the hostel, as each time I asked, I was pointed in the direction of the Grand Hotel. Finally it dawned on me that the Grand Hotel has a quota of rooms reserved for hostellers – you just front up at the reception desk and receive the keys to a comfortable room for the price of a bunk bed elsewhere.

The dinner was plentiful, included a cook-your-own stew and was enlivened by a large group of handicapped kids firing food missiles and devoting themselves to disobedience with great gusto – a rare sight. Later that evening, the kids pinched my slippers outside the bathroom, and then screamed around the corridors until midnight when there was a one hour pause for sleep, followed by more bedlam until 5 am when they all started preparing for breakfast! At 8 am, the entire staff of the hotel lined up outside with banners and flags to wave goodbye to their young guests – I also joined the line to wave a cherished goodbye to treasured memories of a sleepless night.
Robert Strauss

The *Oirase Youth Hostel* (tel 0176-74-2031) is at Yakeyama, just north of Ishigedo. It

charges a very reasonable Y1500 per person between April and September and Y1900 during the rest of the year.

There's nothing much to do in Yasumiya. You can walk along the lake shore past the Donald Duck boats, to a beach with a statue officially entitled 'Maidens by the Lake'; though, in the early morning mist or befuddled by a sleepless night, you might think you've run into two pudgy ladies playing 'pat-a-cake'! Some of the smart hotels have restaurants and terrace cafés. One menu offered 'smorked salmon' and 'crub meet salad'.

Getting There & Away

There are two bus centres in Yasumiya: one for JR buses and one for other services. Both are a couple of minutes on foot from the pier.

Between mid-April and early November, there are up to six buses from Hirosaki bus terminal to Lake Towada-ko – more details

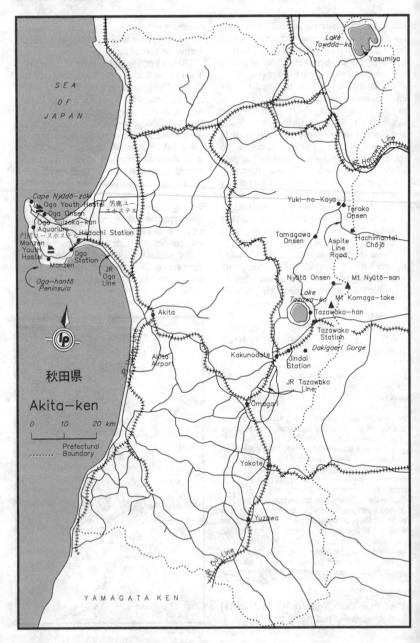

SEA
OF
JAPAN

Lake Towada-ko

Yasumiya

JR Hanawa Line

Cape Nyūdō-zaki
Oga Youth Hostel
Oga Onsen
男鹿ユー
スキステル
Oga Suizoku-kan
Aquarium
門前ユースホステル
Monzen Youth Hostel
Monzen
Hadachi Station
Oga Station
JR Oga Line

Yuki-no-Koya
Toroko Onsen
Tamagawa Onsen
Aspite Line Road
Hachimantai Chōjō

Nyūtō Onsen
Mt Nyūtō-san
Mt Komaga-take
Lake Tazawa-ko
Tazawako-han
Tazawako Station
Dakigaeri Gorge

Akita

Akita Airport

Kakunodate
Jindai Station
JR Tazawako Line

Oga-hantō Peninsula

JR Ou Line

秋田県

Akita-ken

0   10   20 km

········ Prefectural
Boundary

Omagari

Yokote

Yuzawa

JR Ou Line

YAMAGATA KEN

are provided in the Getting There & Away section for Hirosaki.

Between mid-April and mid-November, JR operates a frequent bus service from Aomori to Lake Towada-ko (Y2470, three hours) – more details are provided in the Getting There & Away section for Aomori.

There are also direct buses from Odate (Y1570, two hours) and Morioka (2¼ hours, Y2380).

If you want to visit the region around Mt Hachimantai, there are buses from Lake Towada-ko to Hachimantai Chōjō bus stop, the main point of access to the summit. This service only operates three times a day from May to late October; the trip takes about 2¾ hours and the ticket costs Y2260 – a reserved seat costs Y210 extra. From Hachimantai you can continue east to Morioka by bus or take the bus south to Lake Tazawa-ko.

HACHIMANTAI 八幡平

Further south from Lake Towada-ko, is the mountain plateau region of Hachimantai which is popular with hikers, skiers and onsen enthusiasts.

The Aspite Line Highway, open from late April to November, runs east to west across the plateau. Transport connections revolve around Hachimantai Chōjō, the main access point and car park for the summit. Although the views are nice, the walks around the ponds on the summit only take an hour or so and are rather tame. Longer hikes are possible over a couple of days, for example, from nearby Tōshichi Onsen to Mt Iwate-san.

West of the summit, the road winds along the Aspite Line Highway past a number of hot-spring resorts before joining Route 341 which leads south to Lake Tazawa-ko and north towards Lake Towada-ko.

Places to Stay

Yuki-no-Koya (tel 0186-31-2118) is a member of the Toho network and functions as an alternative youth hostel and mountain lodge – it has been highly recommended by some travellers. Prices start at Y3900 per person including two excellent meals.

The lodge is on a major bus route, one km from the bus stop at Toroko Onsen which is on Route 341, just north of the turn-off for the Aspite Line Highway to Hachimantai.

Kyoun-sō (tel 0195-78-2256), a member of the Japanese Inn Group, is at Matsukawa Onsen which is 50 minutes by bus from Obuke station on the JR Hanawa line; or 1¾ hours by bus direct from Morioka JR station. Visitors can use the open-air hot spring. Prices for singles/doubles start at Y3800/7200 and for triples, from Y10,200.

Hachimantai Youth Hostel (tel 0195-78-2031) is east of the summit, 23 minutes by bus to Hachimantai Kankō Hoteru-mae bus stop. If you're coming by bus from Obuke station, the ride to this stop takes about 50 minutes.

Getting There & Away

From Morioka, there are buses which take about 2¼ hours (Y1230) to Hachimantai Chōjō bus stop – this service only operates between late April and October. Another option is to take the train on the JR Hanawa line from Morioka to Obuke or Hachimantai stations, then change to the bus service.

For bus connections with Lake Towada-ko, see the earlier Getting There & Away section for that lake.

A bus service connects Hachimantai via Tamagawa Onsen with Lake Tazawa-ko in about 2½ hours (Y2060).

TAMAGAWA ONSEN 玉川温泉

This hot-spring resort, 41 km north of Lake Tazawa-ko on Route 341, has a variety of hot springs, baths and treatments. A paved path leads up the ravine through the steam and bubbling vents to open-air baths. Serious soakers who'd like to organise a stay can check rates and availability with the resort office (tel 0187-49-2352).

LAKE TAZAWA-KO AREA 田沢湖

Tazawa-ko is the deepest lake in Japan and a popular place for Japanese tourists keen on watersports. The foreign traveller may find more enjoyment by using the lake as a staging point for hikes along the trails of Mt

Komaga-take and perhaps combining these with a stay in one of the remote hot-spring ryokan scattered around Nyūtō Onsen.

Orientation & Information

The main centre of activity on the east side of the lake is known as Tazawako-han – from there it's a 15 minute bus ride south to Tazawako bus terminal which is next to Tazawako station. A tourist information office stands to your left as you exit the station. You can get leaflets and the staff will help with accommodation bookings.

The bus station at Tazawako-han has an information office where you can sort out timetables and pick up a map of the area – though the map is more useful for its bilingual Japanese/English place names than for its accuracy. Even if they don't want to stay, prospective hikers may want to visit the youth hostel to request a look at the plastic folder with its detailed hiking maps.

Things to Do

The lake offers boat excursions, swimming beaches, row boats and a road around the lake shore which can be followed by bus, car or on a bicycle rented at Tazawako-han.

If you're interested in hiking around Mt Komaga-take there are many options. The easiest way to start would be to take a bus from Lake Tazawa-ko for the 50 minute ride to Komagatake-Hachigōme (Komagatake Eighth Station). From there it takes about an hour to climb up to the summit area where you can choose trails circling several peaks. One trail leads across to Nyūtō Onsen where there is another trail climbing up to the peak of Mt Nyūtō-san. Make sure you are properly prepared – see the comment earlier about the map folder in the youth hostel. The bus service operates from June to October only – during July and August there are departures three times a day and during the rest of the year the service only operates on Saturdays, Sundays and national holidays.

Hot-spring enthusiasts will want to try some of the places around Nyūtō Onsen which is 40 minutes by bus from Lake Tazawa-ko.

Places to Stay

The staff in the information office at Tazawako-han bus station don't speak much English, but will try to help with accommodation bookings.

Tazawako Youth Hostel (tel 0187-43-1281) is about five minutes on foot from the bus station at Tazawako-han. If you're arriving by bus, ask to get off at the Kōen Iriguchi bus stop which is virtually opposite the hostel's front door.

When I visited the Tazawako Youth Hostel it was a total shambles and seemed almost derelict. I was ushered next door to the kokuminshukusha which had also obviously seen better days. The owner was friendly enough, but water was dripping through the roof in the hall and there was a dead, musty feel to the place. The sukiyaki evening meal was good value and the folder with detailed hiking maps was useful.
Robert Strauss

To really get away from it all, you can stay in one of the hot-spring ryokan around Nyūtō Onsen. There are at least half a dozen to choose from, but *Tsurunoyu Onsen Ryokan* (tel 0187-46-2814) and *Kuroyu Onsen Ryokan* (tel 0187-46-2214) are rustic, traditional places with thatched roofs and a variety of open-air baths. If you book basic accommodation only – some guests cook for themselves – you can expect to pay around Y2000 per person. However, you'd be missing out on well-prepared meals which usually include succulent mountain greens and fresh fish. Prices for accommodation and two meals start around Y7500. The ryokan close from early November until late April.

Getting There & Away

Train Morioka is connected with Tazawako station in 40 minutes by limited express on the JR Tazawako line. Kakunodate, a short distance south-west of Lake Tazawa-ko, is reached in 20 minutes by local train on the same line. Connections to Akita take about 1½ hours and usually require a change to the JR Ou line at Omagari.

Bus A bus service connects Lake Tazawa-ko via Tamagawa Onsen with Hachimantai in about 2½ hours (Y2060). From Hachimantai you can then catch a bus north to Lake Towada-ko or east to Morioka. There are also direct buses running from Lake Tazawa-ko to Morioka in 1¾ hours.

From the bus station at Tazawako-han, there's a bus service for the 40 minute ride to Nyūtō Onsen. Ask the driver to let you off at the stop closest to your ryokan but then be prepared to walk a couple of km.

KAKUNODATE 角館

This small town with its well-preserved samurai district and avenues of cherry trees is well worth a visit. You can cover the main sights in a few hours or devote a lazy day to browsing around town. There are half a dozen samurai houses open to the public along a couple of the main streets north-west of Kakunodate station – 15 minutes on foot. The cherry tree promenade beside the river is a major tourist attraction when the trees bloom in April.

Just outside Kakunodate, about 25 minutes away by bus or train (Jindai station), is Dakigaeri Gorge with a pleasant four km nature trail.

Orientation & Information

JNTO publishes a leaflet entitled *Towada-Hachimantai, Akita & Oga Peninsula (MG-021)* which has a map of Kakunodate and brief details for the sights.

The tourist information office (tel 0187-54-2995) is on your right as you leave the station. The staff can help with reservations, lists of minshuku and provide a rough map which is good enough to keep one on the right track.

The town is small and easily covered on foot in three or four hours. Bicycle rental is available at the station.

Kawarada-ke House

The interior of the house can be viewed from a path leading through the garden. Next door is the Samurai Shiryōkan, a cramped museum with an interesting assortment of martial equipment. Admission is Y300 and it's open from 8.30 am to 4.30 pm.

Denshōkan Museum

This museum houses exhibits of armour, calligraphy, ceramics and a large section devoted to the tools and products of the

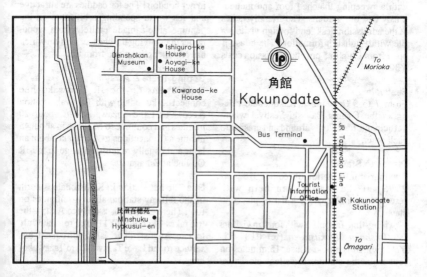

cherry-bark craft. In a room to the side is an artisan demonstrating the craft.

The museum is open daily from 9 am to 5 pm (April to October) and closes 30 minutes earlier and all day Thursdays during the rest of the year. Admission costs Y300.

Aoyagi-ke House

Aoyagi-ke is really a large conglomeration of mini-museums, intriguing in their higgledy-piggledy presentation. One museum focuses on folk art, a treasure house exhibits heirlooms from the Aoyagi family and a 'new-fangled gadget' museum displays all the things that seemed so modern in the Meiji era. A flea market is crammed into the ground floor. In the middle of the grounds, a small restaurant sells decent soba for Y500. It's curious watching the Japanese tourists ogling an old Bell & Howell ciné camera that was once such a novelty. The tide has long since turned and Japan now leads the world with innovative video equipment. Admission costs Y500. It's open from 9 am to 5 pm.

Ishiguro-ke House

This is a fine example of a samurai house with a sweeping thatched roof and meticulously laid out gardens. The friendly ladies at the admission desk lend foreign visitors a file with English information. The house is open from 9 am to 5 pm and admission costs Y300.

Festivals

From 7 to 9 September, Kakunodate celebrates the Oyama Bayashi Festival where participants haul floats around and crash into each other.

Places to Stay

The tourist information office (tel 0187-54-2995) at the station can help with reservations and provide a list of places to stay.

A long-time favourite with foreign visitors is *Minshuku Hyakusui-en* (tel 0187-55-5715) which is an old house, 15 minutes on foot from the station. Excellent meals are

served around an *irori* (open hearth). The owner believes that beer and saké should flow freely and guests are seated next to each other so there's less isolation and more chat.

One of my neighbours, an enterprising fellow from Nagoya, explained that he'd come specially to Kakunodate to buy an ancient Japanese toilet. He later proudly unwrapped and showed it to me – truly a thunderbox worthy of the samurai!

Robert Strauss

Prices start around Y4500 per person without meals or Y7000 with two meals. A couple of rooms behind the irori have been turned into a musty, cobwebby museum – admission costs Y200.

Things to Buy

Kakunodate is renowned for *kabazaiku*, a craft which uses cherry bark to cover household or decorative items. You can see the production process in the Denshōkan Museum and there are numerous shops selling the finished products. The canny merchants of Kakunodate have got just about everything covered with the bark – from cigarette lighters to geta (sandals) and even tissue boxes for the lady who has everything in her boudoir! The tea caddies are attractive and it's worth spending a bit more on the genuine article made entirely from wood, rather than buying the cheaper version which has an inner core made from tin.

Getting There & Away

Train Trains on the JR Tazawako line connect Kakunodate with Tazawako station (access to Lake Tazawa-ko) in about 20 minutes and continue to Morioka in about 45 minutes. Connections to Akita take about an hour and usually require a change to the JR Ou line at Omagari.

Bus The bus station in Kakunodate is north of the railway station, about 10 minutes on foot. There are six buses daily to Akita – the trip takes 1¾ hours (Y1190). From late July to late August, there is an infrequent bus service round Lake Tazawa-ko to Tazawako-han.

AKITA 秋田

Akita is the prefectural capital and a large commercial and industrial city. It has few sights of special interest to foreign travellers and is best used as a staging point for visits to Kakunodate, Lake Tazawa-ko or the Oga-hantō Peninsula. The tourist information office at the station provides maps and details for transport and sightseeing.

If you have time to kill, it's just 10 minutes on foot from the station to Senshū-kōen Park which was once the site of Kubota-jō Castle. The park provides the locals with greenery and contains the castle ruins. Also inside the park is Hirano Masakichi Art Museum (Hirano Masakichi Bijutsukan) which houses both Western and Japanese works of art.

Festivals

From 4 to 7 August, Akita celebrates the Kantō Matsuri which is one of the most famous festivals in Tōhoku. During the festival, there's a parade with over 160 men balancing giant poles, hung with illuminated lanterns, on their heads, chins, hips and shoulders. The poles can be 10 metres tall and weigh 60 kg.

Places to Stay

Kohama Ryokan (tel 0188-32-5739), a member of the Japanese Inn Group, is five minutes on foot from Akita station. Prices for singles/doubles start at Y4000/7600; triples start from Y11,400.

Places to Eat

The local food specialities include two types of hotpot – 'kiritampo' (made with chicken, rice cakes and chicken) and 'shottsuru' (made from a local fish). Just 15 minutes walk west of the station is Kawabata-dōri, the main street for eateries, which is packed with hundreds of pubs, restaurants and bars.

Getting There & Away

Air There are flights between Akita and Tokyo, Osaka, Nagoya and Sapporo. Akita's airport (Akita Kūkō) is south of the town, 50 minutes by bus (Y790) from JR Akita station.

Train Akita is linked with Morioka via the JR Tazawako line – two hours by limited express. This line is also useful to visit Kakunodate and Lake Tazawa-ko. The JR Uetsu line connects Akita with Niigata in four hours.

The JR Oga line links Akita with the Oga-hantō Peninsula in about an hour.

Bus A convenient bus service runs from Akita station via Kakunodate to Tazawako station.

OGA-HANTO PENINSULA 夏泊半島

This peninsula juts out for about 20 km and is worth visiting to see the contrasts in its rugged coastlines and grassy slopes. Most of the transport shuts down between November and late April as do the sights. Both local buses and sightseeing buses operate to the sights at other times during the year, but the sightseeing commentary in Japanese can be intrusive.

The Oga Suizokukan (Oga Aquarium) is the largest one in northern Japan and has a huge variety of species on display. Admission costs Y800 and it's open from 9 am to 4 pm. A 50 minute boat cruise (Y1500) operates along the spectacular coastline between the aquarium and Monzen.

Cape Nyūdō-zaki, at the northern tip of the peninsula, has wide cliff-top lawns, fine seaviews and, to complete the picture, a striped lighthouse.

Festivals

A curious festival called Namahage is celebrated here on 31 December. The *namahage* are men dressed as fearsome demons complete with a straw cape over the body, a terrifying mask over the face and equipped with a wooden pail and knife. The demons roam around villages and visit houses where there are children and then admonish the youngsters against idleness. The house owners do their bit to welcome the demons and mollify the threats by giving the namah-age rice cakes and saké.

This type of festival is common in northern Japan, but the one on this peninsula is particularly famous.

Places to Stay

Monzen Youth Hostel (tel 0185-27-2823) is part of a temple and a useful base for exploring the peninsula. From Akita, take the train on the JR Oga line to Oga station, then change to a bus to reach the bus terminus at Monzen; from there it's a seven minute walk to the hostel.

Oga Youth Hostel (tel 0185-33-3125) is right next to the sea at Oga Onsen, one of the gateways for visits to the peninsula. Bicycle rental is available. From Akita, take the train on the JR Oga line to Hadachi station; then take a 50 minute bus ride to Oga Onsen and get off at the Oga Grand Hoteru-mae stop – the hostel is 200 metres down the street, above the seashore. There is also a direct bus which takes 1¾ hours from Akita station to Oga Onsen.

Getting There & Away

Trains on the JR Oga line connect Akita with the peninsula in about an hour. Buses leave from the terminal at JR Oga station for Monzen where there is an excursion boat to Oga Suizokukan (Oga Aquarium). From Hadachi station, one stop before Oga station, there are buses to Oga Onsen, Cape Nyūdō-zaki and Oga Suizokukan.

Yamagata-ken 山形県

JNTO publishes a brochure entitled *Yamagata Prefecture* which gives details on sights and festivals and includes a useful map of the prefecture.

SAKATA 酒田

This large port city has a couple of interesting sights and is a useful staging point for boat trips on the Mogami River or an island hop to Tobi-shima Island.

The Homma Art Museum (Homma Bijutsukan) is a couple of minutes on foot from the station. In the museum grounds is an impressive residence of the Homma family and a delightful rock garden.

Homma Kyū Hontei is another imposing residence built by the Homma family in 1769 to receive visiting dignitaries from the Edo government. The residence is a five minute bus ride from the station.

Domon Ken Kinenkan Museum (Domon Ken Memorial Museum) contains the photographs of the renowned Japanese photographer, Domon Ken. It's worth a visit both for the sensitive photographic portrayal of Japan and for a look at the sleek, modern lines of the museum building. The museum is a 15 minute ride south of the station by taxi.

From 15 to 17 February, the *Kuromori Kabuki* festival features performances of kabuki by farmers.

Sakata is on the JR Uetsu line: 1½ hours by limited express north to Akita or 2½ hours by limited express south to Niigata.

TOBI-SHIMA ISLAND 飛島

You might like to try a trip to this island – a mere 2½ sq km in size – which is accessible by ferry from Sakata. The main attractions are rugged cliffs, sea caves, black-tailed gulls and other feathered friends and, reportedly, excellent fishing. You can also organise boat trips out to smaller islands.

There are over a dozen ryokan and minshuku. The *Sawaguchi Ryokan* (tel 0234-95-2246) also operates as the island's youth hostel – seven minutes on foot from the ferry pier.

Ferries run daily from Sakata-kō Port to the island. The trip takes 1½ hours and the passenger fare is Y1750.

MOGAMI-KYO GORGE 最上峡

Boat tours are operated through the Mogami-kyō Gorge on a section of the Mogami River between Sakata and Shinjō. It's harmless fun complete with a boatman singing a selection of the top 10 local folk hits – recent reports indicate that the boatmen have been extend-

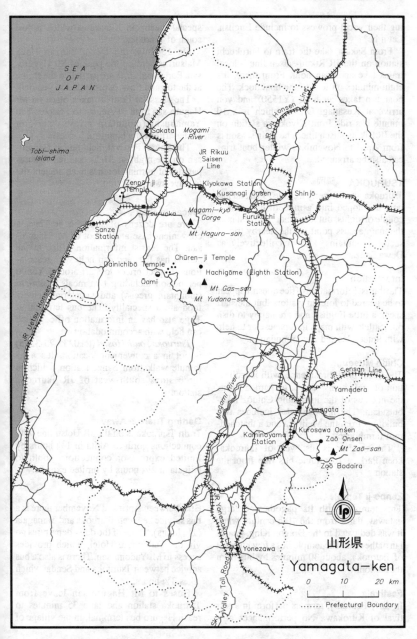

SEA
OF
JAPAN

Tobi-shima Island

Sakata

Mogami River

JR Rikuu Saisen Line

JR Ou Honsen Line

Kiyokawa Station

Kusanagi Onsen

Shinjō

Zenpō-ji Temple

Tsuruoka

Mogami-kyō Gorge

Furukuchi Station

Sanze Station

Mt Haguro-san

Chūren-ji Temple

Dainichibō Temple

Hachigōme (Eighth Station)

Ōami

Mt Gas-san

Mt Yudono-san

JR Uetsu Honsen Line

Mogami River

JR Senson Line

Yamadera

Yamagata

Kaminoyama Station

Kurosawa Onsen

Zaō Onsen

Mt Zaō-san

Zaō Bodaira

JR Yoneskao Line

Yonezawa

Sky Valley Toll Road

山形県

Yamagata-ken

0   10   20 km

.... Prefectural Boundary

ing their vocal prowess to include English. Let it be?

From Sakata, take the train to Furukuchi station on the JR Rikuu-saisen line – local trains take about an hour. From there, it's eight minutes on foot to the boat dock. The boat trip takes an hour (Y1550) and you arrive at Kusanagi Onsen which is a 10 minute bus ride from Kiyokawa station on the JR Rikuu-saisen line. The main season is from April to November; winter boat trips can also be arranged.

TSURUOKA　鶴岡

Tsuruoka was formerly a castle town and has now developed into a modern city with a couple of sights, but its primary interest is as the main access point for the nearby trio of sacred mountains, known collectively as Dewa Sanzan.

Information

The tourist information office doesn't appear to be geared to foreign visitors, but the staff speak a little English and are happy to dish out leaflets with maps in Japanese or to help with timetables and accommodation.

Chidō Museum

The Sakai family residence, with its collection of craft items, and large garden forms the nucleus of the intriguing Chidō Hakubutsukan. The museum also includes two buildings from the Meiji era and a thatched-roof farmhouse.

The museum is just west of Tsuruoka-kōen Park, a 10 minute bus ride from the station.

Zenpō-ji Temple

This temple, with its pagoda and large gateway, dates from the 10th century when it was dedicated to the Dragon King, guardian of the seas. The temple lies a few km west of Tsuruoka, about 30 minutes by bus from the station.

Festivals

In early February, farmers perform in a festival of Kurokawa Nō performances at a special theatre in Kurokawa which is just south of Tsuruoka.

On 15 July, the Dewa Sanzan Hana Matsuri is held on the peak of Mt Haguro-san. Portable shrines are carried to the shrine at the top and flowers presented to visitors.

The Hassaku Festival takes place on Mt Haguro-san from 31 August to 1 September. Yamabushi (mountain priests) perform ancient rites for a bountiful harvest.

The Shōrei Festival, held on Mt Haguro-san on the night of 31 December, features parades of burning torches in an ancient rite to drive away affliction.

Places to Stay

There are dozens of shukubō at Tōge, a convenient base at the foot of Mt Haguro-san. The tourist information office at the station has lists and can help with reservations. Expect prices to start around Y5500 per person including two meals – san-cai (mountain greens) and vegetarian temple food are a speciality. The bus terminal at Tōge also has an information office which can help with accommodation.

Tsuruoka Youth Hostel (tel 0235-73-3205) is not in a convenient location. It's a 15 minute walk from Sanze station, which is three stops south-west of JR Tsuruoka station.

Getting There & Away

Train Tsuruoka is on the JR Uetsu line with connections north to Akita in 1¾ hours by limited express or connections south to Niigata in 2¼ hours by limited express.

Bus Between April and November there is a bus service between Tsuruoka and Yamagata (1¾ hours). Three of the daily departures go via the Yudonosan Hotel, which provides access to Mt Yudono-san. There is also a bus service between Tsuruoka and Sendai which takes 3¾ hours.

Buses to Mt Haguro-san leave from Tsuruoka station and take 35 minutes to reach Haguro bus terminal, in the village of

Tōge, then continue for 15 minutes to the terminus at Haguro-sanchō. From July to October, there are a couple of buses which save the sweat of pilgrims by allowing them to travel from this terminus towards the peak of Mt Gas-san, as far as Hachigōme (Eighth Station) in 50 minutes (Y660).

Between June and late October there are infrequent buses direct to Sennin-Zawa on Mt Yudono-san. The trip takes 80 minutes (Y1390).

DEWA SANZAN 出羽三山

Dewa Sanzan (Three Mountains of Dewa), is the collective title for three sacred peaks (Mt Haguro-san, Mt Gas-san and Mt Yudono-san) that have been worshipped for centuries by yamabushi (mountain priests) and followers of the Shugendō sect. (See the Shugendō section under Religion in the Facts about the Country chapter.) During the pilgrimage seasons you can see many pilgrims (equipped with wooden staff, sandals and straw hat) and the occasional yamabushi (equipped with conch shell, check jacket and voluminous white pantaloons) stomping along mountain trails or sitting under icy waterfalls as part of the arduous exercises intended to train both body and spirit. You can also see plenty of older pilgrims happy to pay easy cash and avail themselves of the bus services and other labour-saving devices provided.

For details of access to the individual mountains, refer to Getting There & Away under Tsuruoka.

Mt Haguro-san

This mountain has several attractions and easy access, thus ensuring a busy flow of visitors. From Tsuruoka station, there are buses to Tōge, a village consisting mainly of shukubō at the base of the mountain. The orthodox approach to the shrine on the summit of the mountain requires the pilgrim to climb hundreds of steps from here but the less tiring approach is to take the bus to the top. The climb is well worth the trouble and can be done at a very leisurely pace in about

50 minutes – take your time and enjoy the woods.

From the bus terminal at Tōge, walk straight ahead through an entrance gate and continue across a bridge into beautiful cryptomeria woods with trees forming a virtual canopy overhead. En route you pass a marvellous, weatherbeaten, five storeyed pagoda which dates from the 14th century. Then comes a long slog up hundreds of stone steps arranged in steep sections. Pause halfway at a teahouse for refreshment and a view across the hills to the sea.

As you continue up the steps, you come to a small water font on your right. You can make a pleasant excursion away from the main track by taking the path branching off to the right. At the end of the path you'll find a peaceful glade with a simple pavilion and a pond full of fat, crimson-bellied newts, water lilies and croaking frogs. To return to the main track, you'll need to retrace your steps.

The scene at the top is a slight anticlimax. There are several shrines, often crowded with visitors, and a history museum. The museum charges Y200 admission to see statues, scrolls, plastic replicas of temple food and a large model of Dewa Sanzan.

Mt Gas-san

Mt Gas-san (1980 metres), the highest peak of the three, attracts pilgrims to Gassan-jinja Shrine on the peak itself. The peak is linked by a trail from Mt Haguro-san to Mt Yudono-san. The usual hiking route starts from Hachigōme (the Eighth Station on Mt Haguro-san), passes through the alpine plateau of Midagahara to the Ninth Station (Kyūgōme) in 1¾ hours and then requires an uphill grind for 70 minutes to the shrine. The trail between Hachigōme and Gassan-jinja Shrine is *only* open between 1 July and 10 October.

The descent on the other side to Yudonosan-jinja Shrine takes another 2½ hours. After about 40 minutes of this descent, you also have the choice of taking the trail to Ubazawa, the main ski resort on Mt Gas-san, which has its own cablecar.

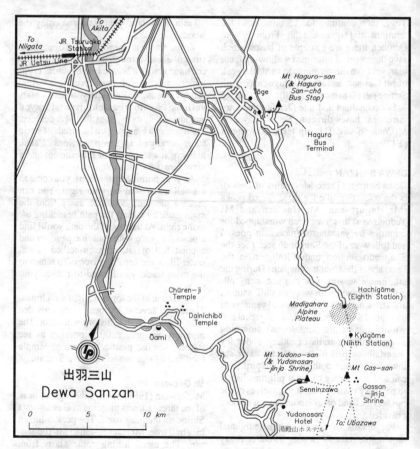

出羽三山
Dewa Sanzan

0   5   10 km

Mt Yudono-san

The mountain is approached via a three km toll road from Yudonosan Hotel to Senninzawa. From there, you can either walk uphill for another three km or pay Y150 to take the convenient bus (a nice little earner for the shrine management) to the shrine approach. The shrine is then a 10 minute hike further up the mountain.

Yudonosan-jinja, the sacred shrine on this mountain is not a building, but a large orange rock continuously lapped by water from a hot spring. Admission costs Y300 – another nice little earner! Take off your shoes and

socks, pay the fee, receive your blessing with a type of feather duster, deposit your prayer slip into a nearby channel of water and then proceed into the inner sanctum where you perform a barefoot circuit of the rock, paddling through the cascading water. You should respect the signs outside the shrine prohibiting photos.

CHUREN-JI & DAINICHIBO TEMPLES
注蓮寺、大日坊

These two temples can be visited if you get off the bus at Oami – about an hour from Tsuruoka or 20 minutes from Mt Yudono-san. Take the small road uphill for a 20 minute walk to the crossroads at the village centre where a grocery shop doubles as a bus stop. To reach Chūren-ji, turn left immediately after the grocery shop and traverse the hills for about 25 minutes. To reach Dainichibō continue straight up the road for about 20 minutes.

Chūren-ji is an attractive temple which is renowned for its 'mummified priest'. Admission costs Y300 and a helpful leaflet in English provides pointers for males on 'how to become a living Buddha'. It helps if you restrict your diet to nothing but nuts and roots of plants, and no wives are allowed. The mummy is to your left as your enter the temple. The crab-like hands have a deep-brown, polished gloss and the grimace of the priest is emphasised by a drooping jaw. The adjoining rooms have some eye-popping art on the ceilings: one room has dozens of panels in pop-art style with clowns, Asians, Westerners, priests and even a character looking like Andy Warhol; another room has panels devoted to startling fish and nubile ladies!

Dainichibō also has its own mummified priest on display. There are infrequent buses to Tsuruoka from the bus stop at the grocery shop.

YAMAGATA 山形

Yamagata is the prefectural capital and a thriving industrial city. For the foreign traveller, the city is not a sightseeing destination but a useful gateway to the sacred mountains of Dewa Sanzan, Yama-dera Temple and the skiing and hiking region around Zaō Onsen.

Information

The Yamagata tourist information office, in front of Yamagata station, has started an English Hot Line (tel 0236-31-7865) for foreign travellers. The office is open from 10 am to 6 pm.

Festivals

The Hanagasa Festival, held in Yamagata from 6 to 8 August, is one of Tōhoku's major events. Large crowds of dancers wearing *hanagasa* (straw hats) cavort through the streets in the evenings.

Places to Stay

Yamagata Youth Hostel (tel 0236-88-3201) is at Kurosawa Onsen, a 25 minute bus ride from Yamagata station.

Yamagata Business Hotel (tel 0236-23-7300) is a five minute taxi ride from the station. Prices for singles/doubles start at Y3800/7200.

Getting There & Away

Air There are flights from Yamagata to Tokyo and Osaka. Buses run from Yamagata to the airport (Yamagata Kūkō) in 40 minutes (Y620).

Train The JR Tōhoku shinkansen line will be extended to Yamagata in 1992. The travel time between Yamagata and Tokyo will then be 2½ hours. At present, you have to take the JR Ou line to Fukushima then change to the JR Tōhoku shinkansen line.

The JR Senzan line runs from Yamagata via Yamadera to Sendai in about 70 minutes.

The JR Yonesaka line links Yamagata with Niigata in 3¼ hours by limited express and a change to the JR Uetsu line is usually necessary at Sakamachi.

Tsuruoka is connected with Yamagata via the JR Ou line, JR Rikuu- saisen line and JR Uetsu line in about three hours – the direct connection is infrequent.

The JR Ou line runs north from Yamagata along the centre of Tōhoku to Omagari (with easy access to the region around Lake Tazawa-ko) in 2½ hours by limited express.

Bus For details of buses to Dewa Sanzan and Tsuruoka, see the section on Getting There & Away under Tsuruoka. There are frequent buses from Yamagata to Zaō Onsen (Y740, 45 minutes), more services to Yama-dera Temple and Sendai and night buses to Tokyo.

MT ZAO-SAN 蔵王山

The region around this mountain is very popular with skiers in the winter (the main skiing season is from December to April) and also a pleasant hiking destination at other times of the year. The main ski resorts are centred around Zaō Onsen and Zaō Bodaira. There is an extensive network of ropeways and lifts, and night skiing is available until 9 pm.

The local scenic wonders, called *juhyō* or 'ice monsters', are conifers laden with ice and snow which look vaguely monstrous.

Information
Zaō Onsen tourist information office (tel 0236-94-9328) can help with maps and advice on transport and accommodation.

Places to Stay
There are plenty of minshuku, pensions and ryokan, but advance reservations are essential if you visit during the peak season or at weekends. You might want to try one of the two minshuku at Zaō Onsen: *Lodge Chitoseya* (tel 0236-94-9145) or *Yugiri-Sō* (tel 0236-94-9253) which have prices starting around Y5500 per person including two meals.

At Zaō Bodaira, you could try *Pension Alm* (tel 0236-79-2256) or *Pension Ishii* (tel 0236-79-2772) which have prices starting around Y7500 per person including two meals.

Getting There & Away
There is a frequent bus service from Yamagata to Zaō Onsen (Y740, 45 minutes). Buses also run to Zaō Onsen from Kaminoyama station, just south of Yamagata. To cope with demand during the winter – over a million visitors – there is a regular bus service direct from Tokyo.

YAMADERA 山寺
The main attraction is Yama-dera Temple, also known as Risshaku-ji Temple, which was founded here in 860 as a branch of the Enryaku-ji Temple near Kyoto. The temple buildings are laid out on wooded slopes. From the Konponchū-dō Hall, a few minutes on foot from the station, you continue past a treasure house and start a steep climb up hundreds of steps through the trees to the

Niō-mon Gate. The trail continues a short distance uphill to the Okuno-in (Inner Sanctuary); trails lead off on either side to small shrines and lookout points. The temple is open from 8 am to 5 pm and admission is Y200. Yamadera tourist information office (tel 0236-95-2816) provides maps and help with finding accommodation.

Pension Yamadera (tel 0236-95-2240) is just a one minute walk from the station.

Trains on the JR Senzan line link Yamagata with Yamadera station in 15 minutes and then take another hour to Sendai. There are also direct buses to Yamadera from Yamagata.

YONEZAWA 米沢
During the 17th century, the Uesugi clan built their castle in this town which later developed into a major centre for silk weaving. The town's production of rayon textiles has now eclipsed the previous role of silk.

The town is quiet and unpretentious – worth a brief stopover if you are passing through this part of the prefecture.

Things to See
Matsugasaki-kōen Park, a 10 minute bus ride from JR Yonezawa station, contains the castle ruins and the Uesugi-jinja Shrine. The shrine's Keishō-den (Treasure House) displays armour and works of art belonging to many generations of the Uesugi family.

Just south of the shrine is the Uesugi Kinenkan (Uesugi Memorial Hall) which is a fine residence from the Meiji era with more relics from the Uesugi family.

The Uesugi-ke Byō Mausoleum is further west from the park, about 15 minutes on foot. A dozen generations of the Uesugi clan are interred here in a gloomy row of individual mausoleums overshadowed by tall trees.

Places to Stay
Yonezawa Green Hotel (tel 0238-23-3690) is a business hotel, five minutes from the station by taxi. Prices for singles/doubles start at Y4300/7400.

Getting There & Away

Train The JR Ou line connects Yonezawa with Yamagata in 45 minutes and trains run east from Yonezawa on the same line to Fukushima in about an hour. The JR Yonesaka line links Yonezawa with Niigata via the JR Uetsu line.

Bus Between Yonezawa and Bandai-kōgen (Fukushima Prefecture) there is a bus service along the scenic Sky Valley toll road (Y1590, two hours). This service only operates between late April and late October.

Niigata-ken 新潟県

NIIGATA  新潟
Niigata, the capital of the prefecture, is an important industrial centre and functions as a major transport hub. The city itself has few sights and most foreign visitors use Niigata as a gateway for Sado-ga-shima Island or as a connection with Khabarovsk (USSR) as part of a trip on the Trans-Siberian Railway. See the Trans-Siberian Railway section in the Getting There & Away chapter for more details.

Information
The tourist information office (tel 025-241-7914), on your left as you exit on the north side of Niigata station, has to win top marks for friendly service. There is usually an English-speaking member of staff available to load you with city maps and leaflets and to assist with reservation of accommodation or transport queries – including queries relating to Sado-ga-shima Island.

JNTO publishes a glossy brochure entitled *Japan Niigata Prefecture* which has excellent maps and copious information on sights, transport and regional specialities. Also published by JNTO is a leaflet entitled *Niigata & Sado Island (MG-041)* which has specific information for these two destinations.

For literary companionship you might want to dip into *Yukiguni*, a novel written by the celebrated Japanese writer Kawabata Yasunari. It is available in an English translation under the title *Snow Country* and is the story of an affair between a geisha and a Tokyo dabbler, set in Echigo Yuzawa Onsen, on the southern border of Niigata Prefecture.

Things to See
Dotted around the outskirts of Niigata are several fine residences known as Gono-no-Yakata (Landlord Mansions) – highly recommended for those who like peering into noble pads and pottering around their gardens.

These can be visited on a bus tour, but you may prefer to skip the packaged approach which sometimes spoils the atmosphere. The tourist information centre can provide full details and explain the best means of transport. You can see the lot in a full day, but it might be more rewarding to cover less at a slower pace.

Ito-tei House contains, in its attractive gardens, several farmhouses, individual tea arbours and an art collection displayed in a traditional warehouse (Northern Culture Museum).

Ichishima-tei House is an elegant mansion, built in 1897, with an extensive and relaxing garden – except for a bird which makes a persistent burping sound! After your visit to this residence, you are close to Shibata, a small town which has another pleasant garden known as Shimizu-en.

Festivals
Kite-flyers may be interested in Shirone Takogassen, held in Shirone (about 15 km south of Niigata) for five days in early June. The festival features flying demonstrations of huge kites, kite battles and a kite market.

From 7 to 9 August, Niigata celebrates Niigata Matsuri Festival, the major annual bash with boat parades, thousands of folk dancers, a costume parade and a bumper fireworks display.

Places to Stay
The tourist information office can suggest accommodation to suit most budgets. There are plenty of business hotels around the

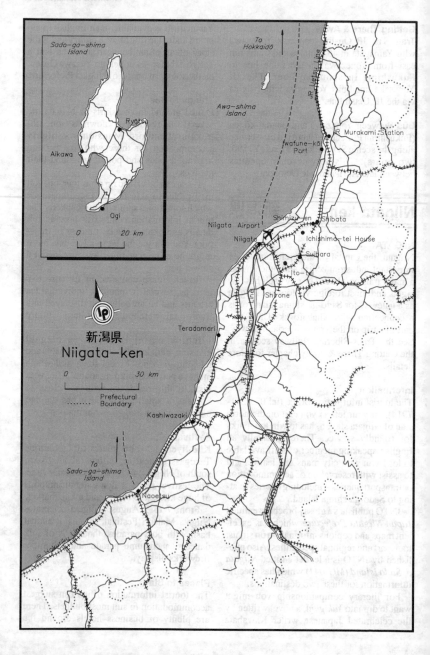

Sado-ga-shima Island

Ryōtsu

Aikawa

Ogi

0   20 km

新潟県
Niigata-ken

0   30 km

········· Prefectural Boundary

To Hokkaidō

Awa-shima Island

JR Uetsu Line

JR Murakami Station

Iwafune-kō Port

Shimizu-en   Shibata

Niigata Airport

Ichishima-tei House

Niigata

Suibara

Ito-tei

Shirone

Teradomari

JR Shin-etsu Line

Kashiwazaki

To Sado-ga-shima Island

Naoetsu

JR Hokuriku Line

station. *Ben Cougar Hotel – No 3* (tel 025-243-3900) has singles/doubles from Y3800/5900. Similar hotels, with slightly higher prices, in the same area are *Green Hotel* (tel 025-246-0341) and *Hotel Rich Niigata* (tel 025-243-1881).

Ryokan Furukawa-tei Honten (tel 025-062-2013), a member of the Japanese Inn Group, is on the outskirts of Niigata in the town of Suibara. Prices for singles/doubles start at Y4000/7000; triples cost from Y9000. The ryokan is 15 minutes on foot from Suibara station on the JR Uetsu line.

Getting There & Away
Air Niigata has flights to Khabarovsk (USSR) which connect with departures on the Trans-Siberian Railway. The Aeroflot office (tel 025-244-5935) is a couple of minutes on foot from the station. Flights link Niigata with Ryōtsu on Sado-ga-shima Island in 25 minutes (Y7400). There are also flights to Tokyo, Osaka, Nagoya, Sendai and Sapporo.

Niigata Airport (Niigata Kūkō) lies north-east of Niigata, 30 minutes by bus from Niigata station.

Train Niigata is connected with Tokyo by the JR Jōetsu shinkansen line in 96 minutes (the Asahi express train) or 2¼ hours (the Toki local train).

Travelling north, Niigata is linked via the JR Uetsu line with Tsuruoka (two hours) and Akita (four hours). Travelling south-west on the JR Hokuriku line, it takes four hours to Kanazawa, and direct trains also continue to Kyoto and Osaka. To travel from Niigata to Matsumoto requires a routing via Nagano which takes 3¾ hours.

Bus There are long-distance buses to Tokyo (Y5150, five hours) and a night bus to Kyoto (Y8750, 8¼ hours) and Osaka.

Ferry The Shin-Nihonkai Ferry from Niigata to Otaru (Hokkaidō) is excellent value at Y5000 for a passenger ticket. The trip takes 18 hours and there are six sailings per week.

The appropriate port is Niigata-kō which is 20 minutes by bus from Niigata station.

The ferry to Ryōtsu on Sado-ga-shima Island takes 2½ hours, the cheapest passenger fare is Y1780 and there are between five and seven departures daily. The hydrofoil (also known as the 'jet foil') zips across in a mere hour, but costs a hefty Y5460. There are at least five departures daily between April and early November and only two or three daily during the rest of the year.

The appropriate port is Sado Kisen terminal which is 10 minutes (Y160) by bus from the station.

AWA-SHIMA ISLAND 粟島
This is a small island, roughly 21 km in circumference, which has a couple of villages offering minshuku accommodation. There are also campgrounds for cyclists and hikers. It's a popular spot for fishing and you can also arrange boat trips.

The ferry departs from Iwafune-kō Port, close to Murakami station (JR Uetsu line), 60 km north-east of Niigata. The ferry trip takes 55 minutes and the cheapest ticket costs Y1570. There are between three and 10 sailings daily, according to the season.

NAOETSU ナオエツ
The port town of Naoetsu, 111 km south-west of Niigata, provides ferry and hydrofoil services to Ogi, a small port in the south-west of Sado-ga-shima Island. Further details are provided in the following Sado-ga-shima Island section under Getting There & Away.

SADO-GA-SHIMA ISLAND 佐渡島
In medieval times, this was a place of exile for intellectuals who had lost favour with the government. Among those banished here were the Emperor Juntoku and Nichiren, the founder of one of the most influential sects of Buddhism in Japan. When gold was discovered near Aikawa in 1601, there was a sudden influx of gold-diggers who were often vagrants shipped from the mainland as prisoners and made to work like slaves. Nowadays, the island relies on fishing, rice farming and tourism.

The two mountain ranges of this island in the south and north are connected by a flat, fertile plain. The best season to visit is between late April and early November – during the winter, the weather can be foul, much of the accommodation is closed and transport is reduced to a minimum.

It is possible to do a two day tour which hits all the sights, but the real attractions of the island are its unhurried pace of life and natural scenery. A minimum of three or four days would be preferable to visit the rocky coastlines and remote fishing villages, or to wander inland to the mountains and their temples.

Information

Sado tourist information office (tel 0259-52-3163) at 176 Kawaharada-Honcho, Sawata, provides pamphlets, books and advice for foreign visitors. It's open from 1 to 8 pm from Monday to Saturday but is closed on Sundays.

Niigata Kotsū Information Centre (tel 0259-27-5164) is in front of the pier at Ryōtsu. They have timetables for tour buses and local buses, but only minimal English is spoken.

The Sado Association publishes a glossy brochure entitled *Japan Sado Island* which has information on sights and transport, and an excellent map. JNTO publishes a leaflet entitled *Niigata & Sado Island (MG-041)* which has specific information for these two destinations.

The Sado Kisen Ferry Company (tel 025-245-1234) publishes an annual magazine in English which has excellent timetables, some sightseeing and transport information and a good map. These are available at the ferry terminal offices or you can contact the company's head office at 9-1, Bandaijima, Niigata City, 950.

Festivals

The annual magazine published in English by the Sado Kisen Ferry Company has a detailed list and brief descriptions for many of the festivals on the island. There seem to be festivals happening almost every week

although some seem engineered for tourists, rather than locals. The island is famed for its *okesa* (folk dances), *ondeko* (demon drum dances) and *tsuburosashi* (a phallic dance with two goddesses). The following are a brief selection.

Sado Geino Matsuri
   28 to 29 April. The festival is held in Mano with ondeko, folk songs and performances of tsuburosashi.
Kozan Festival
   25 to 27 July. The festival is celebrated in Aikawa with okesa, ondeko and fireworks.
Ogi Matsuri
   28 to 30 August. Celebrated in Ogi, this festival features lion dances, folk songs and tub-boat frolics.
Mano Matsuri
   15 to 16 October. This festival takes place in Mano and includes performances of local art forms and lion dances.

As a special favour to tourists, between April and November there are nightly performances of okesa and ondeko dances in Ryōtsu, Aikawa, Ogi and Sawata. The tourist information office in Sawata has exact details.

Ryōtsu

This is the main town and tourist resort and a base to pick up information before travelling to more interesting places on the island. At Ryōtsu Ferry Terminal you can stop at the tourist information office for maps and timetables. The business and restaurant part of town is a 10 minute walk north of the terminal. Between April and November, there are daily performances of Ondeko and Okesa at 8.30 pm at the Ryōtsu Kaikan Hall which is in the same area. Admission costs Y600, but a Y100 discount is applied if the ticket is bought by guests at a ryokan in the town.

Sawata

The town of Sawata, 16 km west of Ryōtsu, is on the main road between Ryōtsu and Aikawa. If you get off the bus at Shimonogaki, about one km east of the town, you can then walk for about 30 minutes up into the hills to Myōshō-ji Temple. This

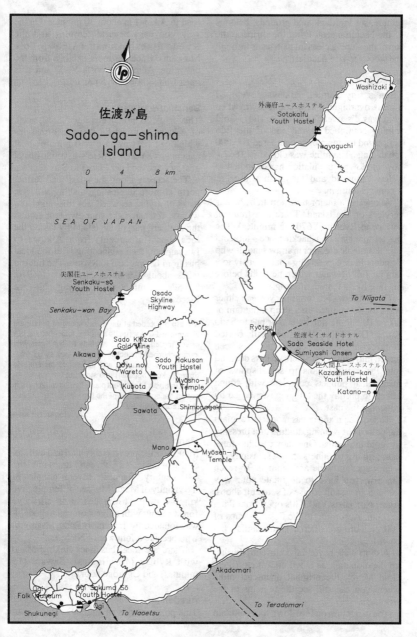

佐渡が島
Sado-ga-shima
Island

0   4   8 km

SEA OF JAPAN

Senkaku-wan Bay

尖閣荘ユースホステル
Senkaku-sō
Youth Hostel

Osado
Skyline
Highway

外海府ユースホステル
Sotokaifu
Youth Hostel

Washizaki

Iwayaguchi

To Niigata

Ryōtsu

佐渡セイサイドホテル
Sado Seaside Hotel
Sumiyoshi Onsen

Sado Kinzan
Gold Mine

Aikawa

Dōyu no
Wareto

Sado Hakusan
Youth Hostel

Myōsho-ji
Temple

佐久間ユースホステル
Kazashima-kan
Youth Hostel

Katano-o

Kubota

Sawata

Shimonagaki

Mano

Myōsen-ji
Temple

Akadomari

To Teradomari

Ogi
Folk Museum

Ogi Sakuma Sō
Youth Hostel

Shukunegi

Ogi

To Naoetsu

temple, set in dilapidated grounds, belongs to the Nichiren sect. From the shrine at the top of the steps, a pleasant path leads through the woods to rice paddies.

Aikawa

From a tiny hamlet, Aikawa developed almost overnight into a boom town when gold was discovered nearby in 1601. Gold mining continued to the end of the Edo period and the town once numbered 100,000 inhabitants. The mine was closed in 1867 – now the town's population has dwindled to a few thousand and the main source of income is tourism.

Aikawa is a major transport hub for bus services on the island. There is a frequent service to Ryōtsu (Y670, 55 minutes). The bus terminal is a ramshackle place – look out for the amiable dreamer in straw sandals who wanders in circles talking continuously to a jam jar full of water which he holds before his face like a temple offering.

From Aikawa bus terminal, you can either walk for 40 minutes up a steep mountain or take a 10 minute ride by taxi or bus to Sado Kinzan Gold Mine. The mine finally ceased working in 1989 and one section has been turned into a museum where visitors descend into the chilly depths to see displays of mechanical puppets complete with sound effects to portray the tough existence led by miners in the past.

The museum annex has models to explain the process of refining, trading and pressing the gold into coins. One showcase has miniature figures of miners shown splashing out their wages on wine and women. To reach the exit, you have to negotiate your way through an assault course of souvenir shops. Admission costs Y600. It's open from 8 am to 6 pm. According to the ticket, groups of 300 or more are offered a substantial discount!

A short walk beyond the museum, further up the mountain, is Dōyu no Wareto (Sado Gold Mine), the original open-cast mine where you can still see the remains of the workings.

You can return on foot down the mountain

road to Aikawa in about 30 minutes. On the way you pass several temples and the Kyōdo Hakubutsukan (Aikawa Folk Museum) which has more exhibits from the old mine. Admission costs Y300 and it is open from 8.30 am to 5 pm.

Senkaku-wan Bay

This bay, a 20 minute bus ride (Y270) north of Aikawa, is noted for its rock formations which can be viewed on 40 minute boat excursions (Y600). There's a youth hostel nearby – see the later Places to Stay section.

The scenery along the coast road further north is more interesting: fishing villages, racks of drying seaweed, sea mist and calm waters. You can make your own tour around the northern part of the island by taking the local bus (infrequent) from Aikawa to Iwayaguchi, then connecting with the local bus from Iwayaguchi to Ryōtsu. The full trip takes about 3½ hours and costs Y1970. There's a youth hostel at Iwayaguchi – see Places to Stay.

My trip proceeded at the stately speed of maximum 20 km/h and was virtually a private tour – just the bus driver, myself and a little old lady from Niigata who karate-chopped the ticket machine, took swigs from a bottle in a paper bag and fast-talked the amiable driver (a keen botanist) into stopping the bus at frequent intervals to point out plants of interest. After she got off the bus, the rest of the trip was like riding in a chauffeur-driven bus!

Robert Strauss

Mano

Mano was the provincial capital and cultural centre of the island from early times until the 14th century. There are several temples in the vicinity of Mano. Myōsen-ji Temple, five km east of the town, lies in an attractive forest setting with a five storeyed pagoda. It was founded by Tamemori Endo, a samurai who became a follower of Nichiren.

There are local bus lines linking Mano with Ryōtsu (40 minutes), Sawata (15 minutes) and Ogi (one hour).

Akadomari

This port provides an alternative ferry connection with Niigata. A local bus line links Akadomari with Ogi (35 minutes) and Sakata (70 minutes).

Ogi

Ogi is a drowsy port which has been kept in business by the ferry connection with Naoetsu. The big tourist attraction, next to the ferry terminal, is a ride in a *taraibuné* or 'tub boat' which is poled by a lady in traditional fisherwoman's costume – well, nobody wears it nowadays, it's just for the photos. The tub boats were once commonly used as a means to collect seaweed and shellfish but they are no longer a common sight. A 15 minute spin in the tub costs Y400 – you can fit in several passengers and the lady in charge may let you make a fool of yourself trying to steer.

On the hill overlooking the harbour there is a park with some fine views across the sea; the park is circled by an overgrown path.

Shukunegi

This is a tiny fishing village with a drowsy temple, a few weather-beaten rows of wooden houses and a cove where a couple of old tubs moulder on the harbour. On the hill, just at the entrance to the village, you should definitely pop in to see the quirky Ogi Minzoku Hakubutsukan (Ogi Folk Museum) with its higgledy-piggledy (and dusty) collection of dolls, clocks, tools, ceramics, old TVs, radios, projectors and even thermos flasks! The hall at the back contains fishing paraphernalia, snapshots of countless generations of the village community – from babes in arms to aged pensioners – and a collection of postcards depicting the island belles of past decades as well as the island's sights – before the tourist boom. The museum is open from 8 am to 4 pm and admission costs Y300.

There is an infrequent bus service running west from Ogi via Shukunegi to the museum, though since it's only four km, you could also walk or rent a bicycle in Ogi.

Places to Stay

The island is well supplied with minshuku, ryokan, kokuminshukusha, hotels and youth hostels. There are several campgrounds as well. You can get help with booking accommodation from the tourist information offices in the towns and villages described earlier as well as from the Sado Kisen Ferry Company offices at the ferry terminals. The following are a few suggestions in the budget and middle-range category.

Senkaku-sō Youth Hostel (tel 0259-75-2011) is in the touristy area of Senkaku-wan Bay, close to Aikawa. If you like, you can upgrade your accommodation since this youth hostel is part of a ryokan. It's open only from April to the end of October. From Aikawa, take the Kaifu-sen bus line for the 20 minute ride north to the Himezu bus stop.

Sado Hakusan Youth Hostel (tel 0259-52-4422) is open only from March to October. Take the bus from Ryōtsu bound for Aikawa, but get off after about 40 minutes at Kubota (about two km west of Sawata). Then it's a 25 minute walk up the sideroad virtually opposite the bus stop. If you phone the hostel, they'll fetch you at the bus stop. Guests can use a nearby hot spring.

Sotokaifu Youth Hostel (tel 0259-78-2911) is in a tiny fishing hamlet in the middle of nowhere. Bicycles and scooters are available for rental so you might want to explore by this method of transport. To get there from Ryōtsu, take the Sotokaifu-sen bus line which runs via Washisaki, continues round the northern tip of the island and deposits you at the Iwaya-guchi bus stop – in front of the hostel door. This service operates two or three times a day (Y1070, 1¾ hours) – late April to late November only. A separate bus service continues down the coast to Aikawa in an hour.

Ogi Sakuma-sō Youth Hostel (tel 0259-86-2565) is 20 minutes on foot from Ogi, in the far south of the island. It is open only between March and November. Guests can use a nearby hot spring.

Kazashima-kan Youth Hostel (tel 0259-29-2003) is on the south-eastern side of the island. From Ryōtsu, take the Higashi Kaigan-sen line to Katano-o and get off after 45 minutes at the Yūsu-hosuteru-mae bus stop.

Sado Seaside Hotel (tel 0259-27-7211) is at Sumiyoshi Onsen about two km (25 minutes on foot) from Ryōtsu Port. A free shuttle service is available to and from the port, and for the dance and music performances in Ryōtsu in the evening. The hotel has its own hot-spring bath which you can use any time. Seafood dinners are a speciality and good value with prices from Y1800 to Y2800. Prices for singles/doubles start at Y3500/6000; triples cost from Y9000.

The Sado Seaside Hotel is not an architectural delight, but a good stopgap place to stay and the efficient staff are keen to help. Take a look at the information folder in your room which cautions guests 'not to bring in firearms or swords' and to desist 'from twisting, distorting or otherwise changing the shape of the facilities'. A section entitled 'How to Cope with Potential Disaster' covers the fear of personal distortion from earthquakes with the comforting advice to 'obey the instructions we will be a worker'.
Robert Strauss

Things to Buy
There are shops all over the island selling Mumyoi-yaki, pottery made from the clay rich in iron-oxides from the mines of Aikawa. Culinary souvenirs include Marudai miso and many of the things you may see hanging up to dry on the seashore – wakame seaweed and ika (dried cuttlefish). For the latter, the best advice is to keep chewing, you'll get there in the end.

Getting There & Away
Air Flights link Ryōtsu on Sado-ga-shima Island with Niigata in 25 minutes (Y7400).

Ferry The ferry from Ryōtsu on Sado-ga-shima Island to Niigata takes 2½ hours and the cheapest passenger fare is Y1780; there are between five and seven departures daily. The hydrofoil (also known as the 'jet foil') zips across in a mere hour, but costs a hefty Y5460. There are at least five departures daily between April and early November; just two or three during the rest of the year.

From Naoetsu (south-west of Niigata), there are ferry and hydrofoil services to Ogi, a small port in the south-west of Sado-ga-shima Island. Between April and late November, there are four or more ferry departures daily; during the rest of the year the service is considerably reduced. The cheapest passenger fare is Y1960 and the trip takes 2½ hours. The hydrofoil operates twice daily from April to late November and the ticket costs Y5460. From Naoetsu station, it's a 10 minute bus ride (Y130) to the port.

From Teradomari (a short distance below Niigata), there is a ferry service to Akadomari, on the southern edge of Sado-ga-shima Island. The cheapest passenger ticket is Y1220 and the trip takes two hours. Between April and late September, there are two or three departures daily; only one departure daily during the rest of the year.

Getting Around
Bus Local buses are fine on the main routes between Ryōtsu and Aikawa, for example. However, services to other parts of the island are often restricted to two or three a day. If you plan to make extended use of local buses, a vital piece of paper is the Sado-ga-shima Basu Jikokuhyō, the island's bus timetable (in Japanese) which is available from bus terminals and tourist information offices. The timetable has a map showing the numbered bus routes for you to match up to the individual timetables.

Taxi A group of travellers could put together their idea of an itinerary, then approach the Sado Hired Car Service Association (tel 0259-27-6962) in Ryōtsu. The *Sado Kisen* magazine has a list of sample itineraries ranging from Y10,820 for a 2½ hour tour, to Y40,690 for the 9½ hour blockbuster circuit.

Car This might make sense for a small group since it frees the visitor from the hectic schedules of tour buses and the infrequency of local buses. Sado Kisen Ferry Company in Ryōtsu provides car rental (tel 0259-27-5195) at prices from Y9790 for 24 hours. See the company's magazine for more details.

Bicycle This is quite feasible and an enjoyable way to potter off the beaten track. The tourist information offices can provide details for bicycle rental in Ryōtsu, Aikawa and Ogi. Sotokaifu Youth Hostel has bicycles and scooters available for hire.

Hitching This is not a very reliable method because most drivers are going short distances and traffic away from the main roads can be very limited. Time and patience are required.

Tours *Teiki kankō* (sightseeing buses) are available in neatly packaged itineraries –

ultra-convenient, sanitised, hectic and brassy. Tickets and departures are arranged at Sado Kisen offices or tourist information offices where you can pick up the appropriate *teiki kankō jikokuhyō* (sightseeing bus timetable). The one itinerary that merits a recommendation is the Skyline Course because it follows the spectacular Osado Skyline Highway from Ryōtsu to Aikawa – there is no local transport alternative for this particular highway. The trip takes about three hours and costs Y3700. The 'Free Pass' costs Y5150 and is valid for travel on all the regular sightseeing buses for two days.

Hokkaidō is the northernmost of Japan's islands and although it accounts for over one fifth of Japan's land area, only 5% of the Japanese population lives there. The real beauty of the place lies in the unpopulated, wilderness regions where – in contrast to Honshū – there are no cultural monuments, but superb opportunities for outdoor activities such as hiking, camping, skiing, sampling of hot springs and observing wildlife.

Without hesitation I'd rate Hokkaidō as my favourite destination in Japan for outdoor pursuits. Sapporo and Hakodate are the only cities worth a brief stop before visiting the rest of the island, especially the five major national parks: Daisetsuzan, Rishiri-Rebun-Sarobetsu, Shiretoko, Akan and Shikotsu-Tōya – given in my order of preference!

Robert Strauss

History & Development
The prehistory and early history of Hokkaidō, or Ezo as it was once known, was of a time when the island was more or less ignored by the Japanese on Honshū. The indigenous people on the island, in particular the Ainu, were related to Siberian tribes but their exact origins are still unclear.

In the 16th century, the Matsumae clan arrived from Honshū to establish a foothold on the tip of the south-western part of the island, but the rest of Hokkaidō continued to be the domain of the Ainu who lived mostly from fishing, hunting and gathering wild plants. The Meiji Restoration in 1868 was also a turning point in policy for Hokkaidō. The government took a strong interest in the opening of this frontier region and set up a colonial office to encourage settlers from all over Japan – the name Hokkaidō was adopted at this time. Foreign advisors were called in to help with development: Sapporo was designed by a US architect, and US agricultural experts also introduced farm architecture which has endured as a characteristic of Hokkaidō's landscape.

The island's developmental path started with agriculture (grain, rice and vegetables), fisheries and mining before its inhabitants moved on to dairy farming and, most recently, forestry, pulp and paper industries and steel production. Although some hi-tech electronics industries have been attracted by the lack of pollution, the growth in the number and size of cities on the island has created some ugly blots on the landscape and may lead to a decline in the purity of the environment.

Another noticeable feature of the landscape is the increasing number of abandoned farmsteads; as farming proves less profitable, the communities split up and individuals move into towns to find work. In contrast, Hokkaidō also attracts small numbers of Japanese who seek to escape the overcrowded, polluted life elsewhere in the country and set themselves up as residents rather than tourists. Tourism has become a major source of income, particularly for remote communities which would otherwise find it hard to make a living, for example from fishing or agriculture.

When to Go
The season between May and October attracts hikers and campers to Hokkaidō – the peak months for tourism are June, July and August. This is also the period when transport services are more frequent and extensive. However, it's often possible to escape crowds and enjoy the last of the autumn weather from October to early November. After that, the winter sets in for five months of heavy snowfalls and subzero temperatures. Skiers then form the bulk of the tourists, many of whom head for the ski resorts of Niseko or Furano, though some skip skiing to see Sapporo's Ice Festival in February. Whatever time of year you visit, don't underestimate the weather – take proper clothing to stay warm and dry.

Planning Your Itinerary

Even if you only want to skim the surface of Hokkaidō, the absolute minimum would be a week. There is no pressing need to spend more than a day in Sapporo – that is, to pick up information, organise transport, make bookings and change money – before heading into remoter parts. If you cut out a visit to Rishiri-Rebun-Sarobetsu National Park, you could visit the other four national parks at a comfortable pace in a fortnight. If you include this park, you'll need an extra week. It would also be feasible to devise a trip which devotes a full week, for example, to exploring Daisetsuzan National Park.

To keep to a comfortable and enjoyable itinerary, it's best to remember that the less time you have available, the less you should try and pack into it – otherwise the transport costs simply soar and the fun factor plummets. It is also essential that you check the operating dates for transport services which vary each year and can be ascertained from timetables or by consulting the information sources given in this chapter.

This chapter on Hokkaidō begins in Hakodate, then moves up to Sapporo in a loop north via the Shakotan Peninsula. From Sapporo the route leads straight to the northernmost tip of Hokkaidō and works round in a clockwise direction via Daisetsuzan National Park and Shiretoko National Park to the region south of Sapporo.

Information

The best sources of information for Hokkaidō are given under the Sapporo section of this chapter. Bear in mind also that you can always use the Japan Travel-Phone, a nationwide toll-free phone service provided by the Japan National Tourist Organisation (JNTO). To contact an English-speaking travel expert call 0120-222800 between 9 am and 5 pm, any day of the week, for information on eastern Japan. You can also use this service to help with language problems when you're stuck in a hopeless linguistic muddle!

JNTO publishes two useful leaflets entitled *Sapporo & Vicinity (MG-011)* and *Southern Hokkaidō (MG-012)* and a glossy brochure, *Japan Hokkaidō*, which provides an overview of sights. Pocket-sized timetables for Hokkaidō are published in Japanese and are available in several versions at station newsagencies on Hokkaidō – ask for *Hokkaidō Jikokuhyō*.

Hiking in Japan by Paul Hunt has a chapter devoted to hikes in Hokkaidō. Skiers might want to pick up a copy of JNTO's skiing leaflet entitled *Skiing in Japan* which has some details for Hokkaidō's two major ski resorts: Furano and Niseko.

Unbeaten Tracks in Japan (Virago Books, 1984) by Isabella Bird recounts the off-the-beaten-track travels of a doughty Victorian lady and includes an interesting account of dying Ainu culture in Hokkaidō.

Festivals

The Sapporo Yuki Matsuri (Sapporo Ice Festival) held in early February is a major event on Hokkaidō. Thousands of visitors arrive to see dozens of large ice sculptures. Various Ainu festivals are also celebrated, though many seem to be presented more as a freak show for tourist consumption.

Accommodation & Food

Hokkaidō has a good selection of places to stay, particularly for those on a budget. The island has the largest concentration of youth hostels in Japan, many are in superb surroundings and offer excellent food, advice on hiking and, generally, a more relaxed approach to house routine than in some hostels on Honshū. In common with other accommodation on Hokkaidō, an additional heating charge of about Y200 is levied during the winter.

A diverse collection of places have banded loosely together to form the Toho network which offers a more flexible alternative to youth hostels and at a reasonable price. There are over 50 members in Hokkaidō and they seem to concentrate on informal hospitality, outdoor pursuits and original architecture, such as log cabins.

You should not expect owners of the Toho places to speak much (if any) English and

北海道

Hokkaidō Island

RISHIRI–REBUN–SAROBETSU
NATIONAL PARK

Rebuntō
Island

Mt Rishiri-zan

Rishirito
Island

Sarobetsu Natural
Flower Garden

Wakkanai

Horonobe

JR Sōya Line

Yagishiritō
Island

Teuritō
Island

Haboro

SEA   OF   JAPAN

Rumoi

Asahikawa

Takikawa

Purano

JR Furano Line

Yobetsu

Shakotan
Peninsula

JR Chitose
Line

Otaru

Okadamo
Airport

Sapporo

Kamoenai

SHIKOTSU–TOYA
NATIONAL PARK

Iwanai

Mt Nisekoannupuri

Mt Yōtei-zan

Mt Eniwa-dake

Hidaka

Konbu
Onsen

Niseko

Lake
Shikotsu-ko

Chitose

Chitose
Airport

Mt
Tarumae-dake

Mt Shōwa
Shin-zan

Lake
Toya-ko

Oshamambe

Shiraoi

Tomakomai

Setana

Noboribetsu
Onsen

JR Muroran
Line

Muroran

Okushiritō
Island

Okushiri

JR Hakodate Line

Mt Komaga-dake

Onuma

ONUMA QUASI-
NATIONAL PARK

Esashi

JR Esashi Line

Hakodate

Tsugaru Kaikyō Straits   The Seikan Tunnel

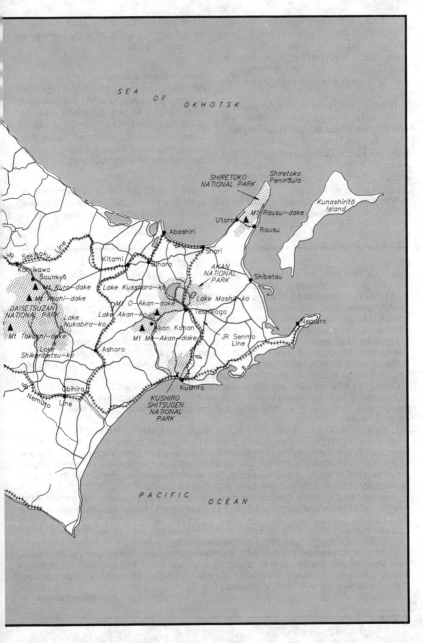

you should *definitely* phone ahead to make reservations. Even if you are phoning from down the street, the common courtesy is appreciated – don't just turn up on the doorstep. See under Places to Stay in the Sapporo section for more details on a list (in Japanese) of Toho.

Food available on Hokkaidō includes dairy products (especially ice cream and cream toffee), seafood ad infinitum (especially salmon, scallops and hairy crab), Sapporo rāmen (local noodle dish), and sweet corn (often sold on the street). To accompany the meals, you can try Sapporo beer, the island's own brew.

Many of the youth hostels specialise in slap-up dinners which provide excellent value and include dishes such as 'Jingis Khan Hotpot' – a stew of lamb and vegetables, cooked at the table.

Getting There & Away

Air There are numerous flights operated daily by Japan Airlines (JAL), All Nippon Airways (ANA) and Japan Air Systems (JAS) between Hokkaidō and the rest of Japan; a network of internal flights also makes it easier for those in a hurry to bridge the large distances on Hokkaidō.

Train Two of the fastest rail connections from Tokyo are the Hokutōsei Express, which is a direct sleeper to Sapporo in 16

Ainu

The indigenous population of Hokkaidō originally included a variety of ethnic groups, but they are now generally referred to collectively as Ainu. In Ainu language, the word 'Ainu' means man (male or human being). There is a possible link between the Ainu and the people known in ancient records as 'hairy people' who once lived in Tōhoku. Although there is a heavier growth of body hair and a tendency towards lighter skin colouring, the physical differences between Ainu and Japanese are slight; intermarriage has further reduced these differences.

From the Meiji period onwards, the Ainu rapidly lost out to a policy of colonisation and assimilation. The old ways of life based on hunting, fishing and plant gathering were replaced with a reliance on commercial fishing and agriculture. Their housing, dress and language gave way to the substitutes of Japanese culture.

During the '80s, the Ainu population was estimated to be around 25,000; almost half of this number lived in the Hidaka district, south-east of Sapporo. Intermarriage with Japanese has become so common, it's calculated that there are now probably less than 200 pure-blooded Ainu left.

Culturally, the Ainu have suffered a fate similar to the American Indians. The Ainu have made some efforts recently to rekindle pride in their culture, but the absence of a written language means that when the old folks die they also take with them a rich tradition of *yukar* or 'epic poems', folktales and songs. The Japanese still exercise racial discrimination against the Ainu (most of whom speak Japanese). The Ainu, however, lack the land or the finance to compete with the Japanese who have settled on Hokkaidō.

Japanese tourists seem comfortable at seeing the Ainu culture debased by pseudo 'Ainu villages' with Disneyland surroundings and souvenir shops selling tacky carvings. The old Ainu festivals and shamanic rites are 'acted' by listless, elderly Ainu. I found these tourist circuses intensely depressing – they are often combined with caged bears in zoos, a sight I find equally depressing, symbolic of the freedom lost by the Ainu.

If you want to see how the Ainu wish to portray themselves, make a point of visiting the Ainu Museum (not the souvenir shop ghetto) in Shiraoi which has excellent displays and sells a catalogue sensitively compiled by the Shiraoi Institute for the Preservation of Ainu Culture, Wakakusa 2-3-4, Shiraoi, Hokkaidō 059-09.

Robert Strauss ■

hours, and a combination of the shinkansen to Morioka followed by a limited express (tokkyū) via Aomori and Hakodate to Sapporo in 11 hours.

The trains cross from Honshū to Hokkaidō via the Seikan Tunnel, the world's longest undersea tunnel, which is an eerie 53.85 km in length. Travellers who can't stand the idea of being underground, and under the sea, for so long can still take a ferry from Aomori.

JR offers special round-trip deals for Hokkaidō which include a return ticket to Hokkaidō plus unlimited travel on JR buses and trains whilst you're there. For example, a 10 day pass of this kind commencing in Tokyo costs Y23,000 – there are more permutations available. Check details for these discount tickets with travel agencies, JR Travel Service Centres (found in major JR stations – see the Tickets & Reservations section in the Getting Around chapter), or call the JR East-Infoline in Tokyo on 3423-0111. The JR East-Infoline service is available from 10 am to 6 pm, Monday to Friday, but not on holidays.

Ferry If you have the time, the cheapest way to visit Hokkaidō is on one of the many long-distance ferries from Honshū – if you travel overnight, you also save on accommodation costs too. The main ferry ports on Hokkaidō are Otaru, Hakodate, Muroran, Tomakomai and Kushiro. These are connected with major ports on Honshū such as Tokyo, Niigata, Nagoya, Sendai, Maizuru and Tsuruga. From Northern Honshū (Tōhoku) there are short-hop ferry routes to several of the major ports on Hokkaidō.

Getting Around
When planning a route around Hokkaidō it's essential to remember the time (and expense) required because of the sheer size of the place. By way of illustration: the train journey from Hakodate in the extreme southwest to Wakkanai at the northernmost tip will take over nine hours by limited express; a flight from Sapporo to Wakkanai takes only 50 minutes but the round trip ticket costs

Y24,220; the ferry from Otaru to the islands of Rishiritō and Rebuntō, close to Wakkanai takes 11 hours and costs Y7720.

To/From the Airport The main airport for Sapporo is Chitose Kūkō which is south of the city. Sapporo has a subsidiary airport at Okadamo Kūkō which is north of the city. Ask, if you're not certain, which airport is stated on your ticket.

Train The rail network on Hokkaidō has a couple of major lines with fast and frequent services whilst the remainder have slow or infrequent services. Many of the unprofitable lines have been phased out – several lines shown on old maps are no longer in operation – and more are due to be axed.

Bus Cities like Sapporo and Hakodate have excellent transport infrastructures, but the bus lines to remoter regions tend to run infrequently, or only during the peak tourist season. Some of the national parks have efficient bus services which do a circuit of the individual sights.

Car Hire If you can afford the extra expense, or can find passengers to share the costs, driving on Hokkaidō is highly recommended because this cuts out the problems with the slow or infrequent transport described above. It also provides you with the mobility to reach remote areas at your own pace. Most of the large cities have car rental agencies such as Nippon or Budget Rent-a-Car. Rates for the smallest type of car start around Y7500 for 24 hours, but bear in mind the expressway tolls and fuel costs.

Bicycle This is a popular mode of transportation; many of the roads around the coastline have low gradients and there are plenty of cycling terminals and youth hostels which cater for cyclists.

Hitching The residents on Hokkaidō – and even tourists passing through – seem happy to oblige with a ride. In more remote regions, and especially during the off season for tourism, there may simply be a lack of traffic. If you ask around, it's sometimes possible to arrange a ride with other guests at youth hostels – the hostel manager usually knows who's going where.

Ferry The ferry from Otaru to the islands of Rebuntō and Rishiritō, close to Wakkanai, is a slow but inexpensive way of reaching the northernmost part of Hokkaidō.

HAKODATE 函館

Hakodate is a convenient gateway for Hokkaidō and is perhaps the most interesting and appealing city on the island. In contrast to Sapporo which emphasises sleek modernity, Hakodate has retained architectural influences from the last century when it was chosen as an international trading port and attracted foreign communities.

It's worth spending a day here to ride the trams (introduced in 1913), or stroll around the Motomachi district with its assortment of Western-style buildings, and if the weather's good, go to the summit of Mt Hakodate-yama for a spectacular view – day or night.

Orientation

Hakodate is not complicated when it comes to orientation. The western part of the city, within easy reach of Hakodate station by tram and bus, is the area with the bulk of the historical sights and is spread out below the slopes of Mt Hakodate-yama. Just east of the station is the sprawling city centre and a couple of km to the north are the mildly interesting remains of Goryōkaku fort.

Information

The Hakodate Tourist Information Office (tel 0138-23-5440) is to the right as you exit the station. It's open from 9 am to 7 pm but closes at 5 pm in the winter. The office has

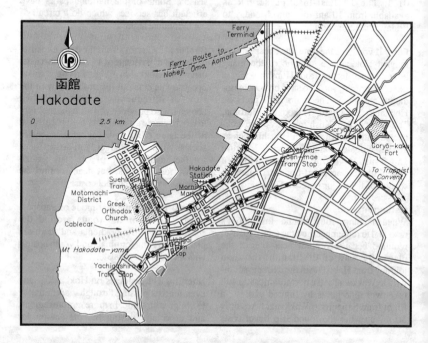

plenty of detailed maps and brochures in English.

JNTO publishes a leaflet entitled *Southern Hokkaidō (MG-012)* which has a basic map and details the sights, transport and accommodation in Hakodate.

Mt Hakodate-yama

The star attraction of Hakodate is the view from the summit of this mountain, preferably enjoyed on a clear night. A cablecar (the Japanese call these 'ropeways') whisks you up to the top in a few minutes and relieves you of Y1130 for the return trip. Operating hours extend into the evening: from 9 am to 9 pm (1 February to 20 April), 9 am to 10 pm (21 April to 10 October), 10 am to 9 pm (11 October to 10 November) and 10 am to 8 pm (11 November to 31 January). To reach the cablecar station from JR Hakodate station, take tram Nos 2, 3 or 5 and get off at the Jūjigai tram stop (about a six minute ride). The base station is then a seven minute walk uphill. Just to the right of the base station, take a look at the telephone booth shaped like a church!

If you feel fit, there's a mountain trail winding up the mountain, though it's closed from late November to late April. From Hakodate station, you can also take a 20 minute bus ride (Y280) direct to the summit, but this service is suspended from late October until late April.

Motomachi District

This district, at the base of Mt Hakodate-yama, has retained several Western-style buildings from the turn of the century and is a pleasant place to stroll around.

The easiest building to recognise is the Greek Orthodox Church, an attractive reconstruction dating from 1916. The sounds of choral harmony issuing from the church – presumably taped – are in stark contrast to the sounds of boogie music belted out from the Cha-cha Café, placed strategically on the hillside above the church!

To reach Motomachi, take tram Nos 3 or 5 from Hakodate station to the Suehirocho tram stop, then walk uphill for about 10 minutes.

Goryōkaku Fort

Japan's first Western-style fort was built here in 1864 in the shape of a five pointed star. Four years later, forces loyal to the Tokugawa Shogunate held out for a month before surrendering to the attacking troops of the Meiji Restoration. All that's left now are the outer walls and the grounds have been made into a park with the obligatory squads of cherry trees. Inside the grounds, keen historians or militarists can pay Y100 admission to visit the Hakodate Museum (Hakodate Hakubutsukan) which displays the hardware used in the battle and the inevitable blood-stained uniforms. The fort is a favourite destination for school outings, presumably with the aim of instilling in pupils an appreciation for past heroics.

Haematologists will probably be interested in a tourist pamphlet which notes that a monument was set up below Mt Hakodate-yama to commemorate the dead from this battle and given the name 'Monument of Green Blood'. According to Chinese folklore, if soldiers die for a just cause, three years after death their blood turns green. This poses the follow-up question: 'What colour is produced by dying for an unjust cause?'

Close to the park's entrance is the Goryōkaku tower which provides a bird's-eye view of the ruins and the surrounding area. The tower is open from 8 am to 8 pm and admission is Y520.

To reach the fort, take tram Nos 2, 3 or 5 for a 15 minute ride to the Goryōkaku-kōen-mae tram stop. From there, it's a 10 minute walk to the fort.

Trappist Convent

This convent, founded in 1898, is on the outskirts of Hakodate, close to Yunokawa Onsen. Visitors come to see the architecture and gardens, but the real drawcard is the shop which sells delicious home-made biscuits, sweets and butter.

From Hakodate station, take bus No 19 for the 35 minute ride to the Yunokawa-danchikitaguchi bus stop. From there, it's a 15 minute walk to the convent.

Markets

If you're an early bird, the asa-ichi (morning market) is open from 5 am to 12 noon; closed on Sundays. It's a two minute walk from the west exit (nishi-guchi) of Hakodate station.

Festivals

In the middle of May, the festival of Hakodate Goryōkaku Matsuri features a parade with townsfolk dressed in the uniforms of the soldiers who took part in the Meiji Restoration battle of 1868.

Places to Stay

The tourist information office outside the station can provide details of ryokan, minshuku and hotels. There are plenty of business hotels in the centre of town.

Station Area Hotel Ocean (tel 0138-23-2200) is an efficient business hotel with helpful staff. Singles start at Y4800. There are two hotels of this name in the station area. To reach this one, walk out of the station exit to the main road, then turn right and continue for about 100 metres until you see the neon sign – the walk takes about three minutes.

Minshuku Ryorō (tel 0138-26-7652) is a member of the Toho network. Prices start at Y4500 per person including two meals, Y3000 without any meals or an additional Y500 if you only want breakfast.

To reach the minshuku – close to the morning market – take the west exit from the station then walk for six minutes keeping to the left of the street until you come to the seventh sidestreet. Go left down the sidestreet and the minshuku is about 30 metres on your right.

Akai Boshi (tel 0138-26-4035) is a popular minshuku, 13 minutes on foot from the station. Prices start at Y2500 per person without meals. English is spoken.

Mt Hakodate-yama Area Free Station (tel 0138-26-6817), a member of the Toho network, is in a quiet location below Mt Hakodate-yama. Prices start at Y3600 per person including two meals or from Y2000 without the meals. Use of the nearby hot spring is included in the price. Special dishes can be ordered between July and September. From Hakodate station, take tram No 2 for the 15 minute ride west to the terminus at Yachigashira; the Free Station is about 15 minutes walk away.

North of Hakodate If you want to stay out of Hakodate in some fine scenery, you could consider Ikusanda Onuma Youth Hostel (tel 0138-67-3419) – see the section on Onuma.

Places to Eat

For a meal with a view, there's the restaurant on Mt Hakodate-yama. At the foot of the mountain, in the Motomachi district, there are plenty of trendy eateries in converted Western-style buildings. Below the cablecar station is a curious restaurant with a pink exterior, American-style trimmings and a sign outside saying 'Jolly Jellyfish'. Neither the atmosphere nor the food seemed set to make a jellyfish jolly!

Getting There & Away

Train Hakodate is connected with Aomori by the JR Tsugaru Kaikyō line which runs via the Seikan Tunnel beneath the Tsugaru Kaikyō Straits to Hakodate in 2½ hours.

Sapporo is linked with Hakodate in 3¾ hours by limited express via Chitose Kūkō Airport and Tomakomai.

Bus An overnight bus service links Hakodate with Sapporo in 6½ hours (Y4600).

Ferry Ferries link Hakodate with ports on Honshū such as Oma (Y1000, 1¾ hours), Noheji (Y1400, 4¾ hours) and Aomori (Y1400, 3¾ hours).

Hakodate-kō Port is not convenient for access to the centre of the city. The taxi ride to the JR station costs Y1140. The closest bus stop, Hokkudai-mae, is a seven minute walk from the ferry terminal; from there you can catch bus Nos 1 or 19 to the station.

Getting Around

To/From the Airport A bus service links Hakodate Kūkō Airport with the city in 30 minutes (Y290).

Bus & Tram One-day (Y900) and two-day (Y1500) open tickets, which entitle you to unlimited bus and tram travel, are available from the tourist information centre or on buses or trams.

The trams were my favourite means of transport. On one tram ride, I was so busy concentrating on my proposed stop that I completely forgot to pay as I got off. After I had been standing at the tram stop, looking at my map for a few minutes, I suddenly realised the tram hadn't moved. The driver and the passengers were patiently watching and waiting for me to pay!

Robert Strauss

ONUMA 大沼

This small town, just north of Hakodate, is the gateway to Onuma Quasi-National Park which contains a trio of lakes beneath Mt Komaga-dake, the volcano that formed the lakes when it erupted. There are several campgrounds on the shores of the lakes as well as a network of hiking trails.

Places to Stay

Ikusanda Onuma Youth Hostel (tel 0138-67-3419) is a 10 minute walk from JR Onuma station. Bicycle rental is available at the hostel and there are hot springs nearby.

Takeda-sō (tel 0138-67-2522) is a reasonably priced minshuku, three minutes on foot from Onuma-kōen station. Prices start at Y5500 per person including two meals.

Getting There & Away

Onuma station is about 40 minutes by local train (futsū) from Hakodate on the JR Hakodate line. There's also a bus service from Hakodate station to Onuma station (1¼ hours, Y660).

ESASHI & OKUSHIRITO ISLAND
江差、奥尻島

Esashi is a major fishing town, 67 km west of Hakodate. The town is renowned for its annual festival, Ubagami Taisha Matsuri,

which is held from 9 to 11 August and features a parade of more than a dozen ornate floats. Esashi can be reached from Hakodate by bus (2¼ hours, Y1700) or by train in about three hours (infrequent service) on the JR Esashi line.

From Esashi, there is also a ferry service to Okushiritō Island. The ferry departs twice daily and the trip takes 2¼ hours (Y2060). A bus service operates on the island, connecting the main town of Okushiri with several fishing villages, hot-spring resorts and the island's small airfield (there are flight connections to Hakodate). Another ferry service operates from Okushiri to Setana which is further north from Esashi. Ferries depart once or twice daily and the trip takes 1¾ hours (Y1540). From Setana there is a bus service across to Oshamambe (1¾ hours, Y1150) which is on the JR Hakodate line.

NISEKO ニセコ

Niseko lies between Mt Yōtei-zan and Mt Nisekoannupuri and functions as a year-round resort: one of Hokkaidō's prime ski resorts during the winter and a hiking base during the summer and autumn. Numerous hot springs in the area are also popular.

Places to Stay

Lodge Ururi (tel 0136-58-2957) is a member of the Toho network. Prices start at Y4500 per person including two meals. From Niseko station, take the 15 minute ride on the bus bound for Konbu Onsen – ask to get off at the Moiwa Ski-jo stop which is two minutes on foot from the lodge.

Pension Asauta (tel 0136-44-2943) is five minutes by taxi from Niseko station. Prices start at Y7500 per person including two meals.

Fuji Kankō Hotel (tel 0136-58-2221), a member of the Japanese Inn Group, charges resort prices. From Niseko station, take the 15 minute ride on the bus for Konbu Onsen – the hotel is a minutes walk from the bus stop. Singles/doubles are Y5000/9000 while triples cost from Y12,000. The bill will be amply elevated by a 15% service charge and three types of tax.

Getting There & Away

Niseko is 2¾ hours from Sapporo by limited express on the JR Hakodate line. There are also regular bus services connecting Niseko with Sapporo, Chitose Kūkō Airport and Otaru.

SHAKOTAN PENINSULA   積丹半島

This peninsula is renowned for its rugged coastline, steep cliffs and spectacular rock formations.

Places to Stay

Bikuni Youth Hostel (tel 0135-44-2610) and *Shakotan Youth Hostel* (tel 0135-46-5051) are convenient for the northern side of the peninsula, while *Shakotan Kamoi Youth Hostel* (tel 0135-77-6136) is close to the terminus of the bus route on the southern side.

Getting There & Away

On the northern side of the peninsula, a sightseeing bus runs from Otaru around the tip of the peninsula to Yobetsu in 2¼ hours (Y1300). On the southern side of the peninsula, a bus service runs from Iwanai to a lookout just beyond Kamoenai in about an hour (Y770).

OTARU   小樽

Otaru is a major ferry port with services south to Honshū and north to the islands of Rishiritō and Rebuntō. Apart from its function as a transport hub, Otaru doesn't have much else to attract travellers.

Information

The tourist information office (tel 0134-29-1333), at the entrance to JR Otaru station, is open from 10 am to 6 pm daily, except on Saturdays and Sundays, when the opening hours are from 9.30 am to 5.30 pm. A useful leaflet with maps and detailed information about Otaru in English is available there.

Places to Stay

The tourist information office at the station can provide suggestions and help with bookings for accommodation.

The *Otaru Green Hotel* (tel 0134-33-0333) is a business hotel, four minutes on foot from Otaru station. Prices for singles/doubles start at Y3500/7000.

Otaru Tengu-Yama Youth Hostel (tel 0134-34-1474) is close to the Tengu-Yama cablecar, a 10 minute bus ride from the station.

Getting There & Away

Train Otaru is 36 minutes from Sapporo on the JR Hakodate line.

Bus A regular bus service runs directly between Otaru and Sapporo in 55 minutes (Y470).

Ferry Long-distance ferries link Otaru with ports on Honshū such as Niigata (Y5000, 18 hours), Tsuruga (Y6400, 30 hours) and Maizuru (Y6400, 30 hours). There is also a service to the islands of Rishiritō and Rebuntō off the northern tip of Hokkaidō. The overnight trip takes about 11 hours and the cheapest passenger ticket costs Y7210.

The Otaru Katsunai-futō Pier is a 20 minute walk from Minami Otaru station.

SAPPORO   札幌

Sapporo is the capital of Hokkaidō and the island's focal point for administration, culture and transportation. The city was founded in 1871 on the site of an Ainu village and foreign advisors contributed to the precision of its design.

For the foreign visitor, the ordered streets provide easier orientation at the expense of architectural variety. The city has few sights and is best used briefly as a staging post to pick up information or mail, organise transport, make bookings and change money before heading into the wilder parts.

Yet, the residents of Sapporo are as good a reason as any to visit the city: they seem to be more open towards outsiders than in many other parts of Japan, and they certainly know how to have a good time, whether in the bright lights of Susukino – the largest nightlife district north of Tokyo – or during the February ice festival.

Orientation

The precise grid pattern of the streets makes it easy to get within reach of your required address, but you'll still have to ask a couple of times to pin down the exact building on the street.

From Sapporo station, the city centre extends south to Odōri-kōen Park, which despite its name, is in fact a wide, tree-lined boulevard running from east to west. If you continue further south from this boulevard, you cross Tanuki-kōji (shopping arcade) before reaching Susukino, the entertainment district. A straight walk from the station to Susukino only takes 20 minutes.

Information

There are several tourist offices in Sapporo, including the Sapporo Tourist Association (tel 011-211-3341) and the Sapporo City

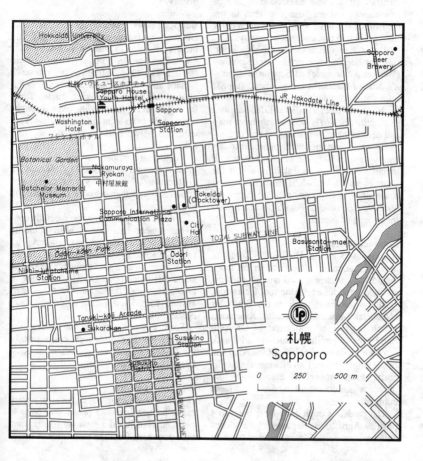

Government's tourist section (tel 011-211-2376); both have English-speaking staff.

However, perhaps the most useful place is the Sapporo International Communication Plaza (tel 011-211-2105) on the 3rd floor of the MN building, just opposite the clocktower. This is an excellent source of information and a great place for meetings with Japanese – impromptu or organised. English-speaking staff can arrange home visits if you give advance notice. There is a notice board with messages, teaching advertisements and invitations to 'Free Talk Parties'. There's also a selection of foreign newspapers and magazines to read in the comfort of the large lounge. It's open daily from 9 am to 5 pm, except on Sundays.

A subsidiary office with English-speaking staff has been opened in the Nishi Konkōsu (Western Concourse) of Sapporo station – it's next to the kankō annai-kauntā (tourist information counter).

JNTO publishes a leaflet entitled Sapporo & Vicinity (MG-011) which has a basic map and details the sights, transport and accommodation in and around Sapporo. Another handy item is Welcome to Sapporo, which includes maps and useful information for Sapporo and Hokkaidō. If you plan to spend some time in Sapporo, pick up copies of Monthly Hokkaidō or What's On in Sapporo for listings of events.

Botanical Garden

If you want a look at Hokkaidō's flora, the botanical garden or shokubutsuen has more than 5000 varieties spread around 14 hectares and provides a relaxing spot for a stroll.

In the garden grounds is the Batchelor Memorial Museum (Batchelor Kinenkan) which houses the collection of Dr John Batchelor, an English missionary who took a keen interest in the culture of the Ainu and tribes from Siberia. Exhibits include handicrafts, tools, household utensils and old photos which document the demise of these cultures.

The garden is open daily from 9 am to 4 pm (29 April to 30 September) but closes half an hour earlier from October to early November and is closed on Mondays. Admission is Y360. Between 4 November and 28 April, only the greenhouse is open (10 am to 3 pm); admission is Y50 and it is closed on Sundays.

Clocktower

The clocktower or 'tokedai' was constructed in 1878 and has now become a cherished landmark for the residents or a useful orientation point for visitors. It's not particularly stunning, but you can enter the building and wander round a small museum of local history.

Sapporo Beer Brewery

Beer enthusiasts may like to visit this brewery, the first in Japan, which dates from 1878. Tours are free, but you should phone (tel 011-731-4368) before you go, to reserve a place and increase your chances of being allotted an English-speaking guide. Tours lasting about 80 minutes are given throughout the year from 9 am to 5 pm; the hours are extended between June and August from 8.40 am to 6 pm.

Visitors are guided around the factory, given some time at the Sapporo Museum – a collection of bibulous souvenirs and antiques – and then allowed to sample the product.

In the brewery's garden, the specially constructed beer hall caters, with Teutonic finesse, for the more serious drinkers who can take advantage of 'all you can eat and drink' offers which start around Y3000. The standard dish is 'Jingis-Khan Hotpot' – prices for other dishes on the menu start around Y1000 and a mug of draught beer costs Y450.

From the north exit of the station, the brewery is a 15 minute walk east – or take the Higashi 63 bus and get off at the Kitahachi Higashi-nana bus stop.

Susukino District

If you like bars, cabarets, nightclubs, restaurants, hostess bars and places that cater to nocturnal fancies of a steamier nature, then take your pick from the thousands of establishments in Susukino. Helpful 'guide' maps are available in Japanese which show the location of the establishments and provide the vital statistics of who or what is on offer. The best way to enjoy the place is to go with locals; you are unlikely to spend less than Y3000/4000 for just a couple of hours of drinking – that depends on what you drink and who helps you drink it. One place in the district that has been recommended for its friendly, jazz-loving owner is *American Melody House* (tel 011-512-4388), 2nd Floor, Liberty Building, Minami 5 jō, Nishi 5 chome.

Festivals
The Sapporo Yuki Matsuri (Sapporo Ice Festival), held in Odōri-kōen Park in early February, is a major event on Hokkaidō. Since 1950 when the festival was first held, it has developed into a mass display of snow sculptures, many of which are very intricate buildings complete with internal illumination. If you plan to visit at this time, you should book accommodation well in advance.

Places to Stay
Youth Hostels Although there are three hostels in Sapporo, only one (Sapporo House) has convenient access, but it's hardly a place to rave about. The hostels are more of an option if you are stuck or don't mind the institutional atmosphere.

Sapporo House (tel 011-726-4235) is a seven minute walk from the station. Not a memorable place to stay – drab and prison-like. When leaving the station, take the south exit *(minami-guchi)*, turn right down the main street and keep walking until you reach the Keio Hotel at the third intersection. Turn right here, continue under the bridge and the hostel is about 20 metres further ahead on your right.

Sapporo Miyagaoka Youth Hostel (tel 011-611-9016) is close to Maruyama-kōen Park in the west of Sapporo, but it's open from July to late September only. *Sapporo Lions Youth Hostel* (tel 011-611-4709) is further west, close to the Miyanomori Ski Jump. Transport from the station to both of these hostels is a bit complicated – a combination of subway, bus and walking – and neither is particularly appealing anyway.

Toho Network *Sukarakan* (tel 011-271-2668), Minami 3, Nishi 8, Chūō-ku, Sapporo 060 is a basic hostel and coffee room run by Mr Shinpei Koshika. He keeps track of individual members of the Toho network – for more details on this group, see the section on Accommodation & Food in the introduction to this chapter. A list of network members is available, in Japanese only, for Y150 plus postage from this address. You will need to know some Japanese to make the most of this list.

Sukarakan has a cheery crashpad atmosphere: nothing fancy and no curfew. Prices start at Y2500 per person; breakfast costs an additional Y500.

Friendly Mr Shinpei knows more English than you might, at first, think and doles out coffee and toast in the morning for foreigners he's directed to or around Susukino the night before; he has a mountain of tapes to play for fans of Japanese or other music on all sorts of levels. He also has a liberal attitude towards his dogs, one of which delights in making surprise attacks on unsuspecting passers-by (foreign hostel guests seem to be forbidden fodder). The other dog, despite being called Torro ('bull' in Spanish), is addicted to potato chips, not passers-by.

From Sapporo station, take the subway (Y160) to Susukino station – Sukarakan is then eight minutes on foot. From the station, walk west following the tram lines for a couple of minutes until they curve sharp left. Turn right here and continue for about 100 metres past a school until you reach an intersection where you turn left; turn left again at the next intersection – Sukarakan is tucked in an alley halfway down the first street on your right. It's much easier to find the second time!

Ryokan *Nakamuraya Ryokan* (tel 011-241-2111) is a member of the Japanese Inn Group. Prices are relatively high at around

Y7000/13,000 for singles/doubles and Y18,000 for triples, though discounts are sometimes available on polite request. The ryokan is a seven minute walk west of the station.

Places to Eat

There are plenty of restaurants and eateries in shopping arcades such as Tanuki-kōji, the underground shopping centres beneath the station and Odōri-kōen Park, and most of the major department stores have at least one floor with inexpensive restaurants.

Local housewives, secretaries and students fill up on inexpensive food by visiting the basement of the Sapporo City Hall (opposite the clocktower) between 1 and 2 pm for the canteen lunch. An excellent bowl of soba (noodles) costs Y360 or you can choose from the plastic models in the window before buying your coupon which you exchange for the food. If you like sweet corn, this inexpensive snack is sold by street vendors in Odōri-kōen Park.

In Susukino, there's *rāmen-yokochō* which is an alley full of tiny restaurants dishing up rāmen (noodle dishes); rāmen makes an inexpensive and filling meal. Another touristy option is the Sapporo Beer Brewery described earlier in the section on sights – well, yes, the place and the diners can indeed look a sight towards the end of the evening!

Things to Buy

Shoppers will be interested in shopping arcades such as Tanuki-kōji and the underground shopping centres below Odōri-kōen Park and the station. To escape the severe winter weather, you can traverse much of central Sapporo by walking through these underground shopping complexes.

Getting There & Away

Air Sapporo has flight connections with most of the major cities on Honshū and even Okinawa. There are dozens of flights daily from Tokyo – round-trip fares start at Y43,100. The principal airlines offering services to Hokkaidō are JAS, ANA and JAL.

Air Nippon Koku (ANK) also operates on internal routes for Hokkaidō. See the later Getting Around section for details on transport to/from the airport.

Train Two of the fastest rail connections from Tokyo include the Hokutōsei Express which is a direct sleeper to Sapporo in 16 hours, and a combination of the shinkansen to Morioka followed by a limited express via Aomori and Hakodate to Sapporo in 11 hours. If you are using a Japan Rail Pass, you will have to pay the sleeper supplement.

From Sapporo to Hakodate takes 3¾ hours by limited express via Chitose Kūkō Airport and Tomakomai.

The trip from Sapporo to Otaru on the JR Hakodate line takes 36 minutes. There are frequent trains running north-east on the JR Hakodate line to Asahikawa in 90 minutes (limited express). From Sapporo to Wakkanai, there's a sleeper service that leaves Sapporo around 10 pm and arrives in Wakkanai around 6 am, nicely timed to take the early ferry across to Rishiritō or Rebuntō islands. If you're travelling on a Japan Rail Pass, you'll need to pay about Y7400 in supplementary charges.

Bus Sapporo is linked with the rest of Hokkaidō by an extensive network of long-distance bus services such as those for Wakkanai (6¼ hours, Y5850), Asahikawa (two hours, Y1750), Kushiro (night bus – seven hours, Y5700), Obihiro (4¾ hours, Y3800), Kitami (4½ hours, Y3400) and Hakodate (night bus – six hours, Y4600). The night bus option is worth considering if you are backtracking, short on time or wish to save money on accommodation costs. However, it isn't exactly restful, and if you aren't backtracking you may lose out on some spectacular scenery.

Getting Around

To/From the Airport The main airport for Sapporo is Chitose Kūkō, a 35 minute train ride (Y900) or 70 minute bus ride (Y750) south of the city. Sapporo has a subsidiary airport at Okadamo Kūkō which is a 35 minute bus ride (Y170) north of the city. If you're not certain which airport is stated on your ticket, ask.

Bus There are several bus terminals in Sapporo, but the main one is next to the station.

Subway This is the most efficient way to get around Sapporo. There are three lines, the two most useful being the Nanboku line, which runs on a north-south axis and the Tozai line, which runs on an east-west axis. Special one day passes for sightseeing are available for Y700 and are also valid for buses and trams.

ASAHIKAWA 旭川
Asahikawa is an unimpressive urban sprawl, one of the largest cities on Hokkaidō. For the traveller, it is really only useful as a transport hub: to the north, it's a long haul to Wakkanai; to the south, there are the attractions of Daisetsuzan National Park.

Places to Stay
There probably won't be any reason to stay here unless your transport arrangements go wrong.

Asahikawa Green Hotel Annex (tel 0166-26-1414) is a reasonable business hotel, just a five minute walk from the station. Prices for singles/doubles start at Y4400/8000.

Asahikawa Youth Hostel (tel 0166-61-2751) is four km from the station. You can either take a 15 minute bus ride or hop in a taxi (Y1000). Bicycle rental is available at the hostel and there are hot springs nearby.

Getting There & Away
Train Asahikawa is linked with Sapporo in 1¾ hours by limited express on the JR Hakodate line. The JR Furano line connects Asahikawa with Furano in an hour. The JR Sōya line runs north to Wakkanai – the trip takes just under four hours by limited express.

Bus There are several bus services running from Asahikawa into Daisetsuzan National Park. One service runs twice daily (three times daily from mid-June to mid-October) to Tenninkyō Onsen via Asahidake Onsen (see the Asahidake Onsen section later for more details, including the youth hostel ticket refund). Another bus service runs from Asahikawa via Kamikawa to Sōunkyō. The trip takes 1¾ hours and the ticket costs Y1800.

A frequent bus service also operates between Sapporo and Asahikawa (two hours, Y1750).

WAKKANAI 稚内
This windswept port on the northernmost fringe of Hokkaidō is visited by travellers heading for Rishiritō and Rebuntō islands. Wakkanai station has an information counter where you can ask for timetables and maps. From the station, it's a 10 minute walk to the ferry terminal. Wakkanai has few sights. Unless your transport arrangements strand you there overnight, there's no compelling reason to stay.

Places to Stay
Wakkanai Sun Hotel (tel 0162-22-5311) is next to the station. Singles/doubles start from Y5800/9500.

Wakkanai Youth Hostel (tel 0162-23-7162) is a 12 minute walk from the southern station for Wakkanai, known as 'Minami Wakkanai Eki'. It's open from June to late September only. Bicycle rental is available.

Wakkanai Moshiripa Youth Hostel (tel 0162-24-0180) is a five minute walk from Wakkanai station and eight minutes on foot from the Wakkanai-kō Port. Bicycle rental is available. It's closed during November.

Getting There & Away
Air There are two ways to fly with ANK from Sapporo to Wakkanai – both take about an hour; the one-way/round-trip ticket prices are Y13450/24220. There is one daily flight from Sapporo's Chitose Kūkō Airport and

two daily flights from Sapporo's Okadamo Kūkō Airport. Make sure you know which airport you are going to be using.

Train From Sapporo to Wakkanai, there's a sleeper service that leaves Sapporo at around 10 pm and arrives in Wakkanai around 6 am, nicely timed to take the early ferry across to Rishiritō or Rebuntō islands. If you're travelling on a Japan Rail Pass, you'll need to pay about Y7400 in supplementary charges. The journey south from Wakkanai to Asahikawa on the JR Sōya line takes just under four hours by limited express.

Bus A bus service runs from Sapporo via Asahikawa to Wakkanai in six hours and costs Y5850.

Ferry Wakkanai is linked by ferries with Rishiritō Island and Rebuntō Island. The ferry to Oshidomari on Rishiritō Island departs up to four times daily (between June and the end of August) and takes 90 minutes; the cheapest passenger ticket is Y1850. From Oshidomari and Kutsugata (infrequent) there are ferry connections (Y720, 45 minutes) to Rebuntō Island – these are linked to the arrivals/departures of the Wakkanai service.

There are direct ferries from Wakkanai to Kafuka on Rebuntō Island up to three times daily (between June and the end of August); the ride takes 2¼ hours (Y2060). There is only one daily service directly from Wakkanai to Funadomari on Rebuntō Island.

The port at Wakkanai is a 10 minute walk from the station – turn right as you exit the station.

Don't be surprised if you see huge Soviet car ferries in the harbour – locals mentioned that they load up here every year with hundreds of used Japanese cars which are then freighted back to the Soviet Far East for some lucrative sales.

Rishiri-Rebun-Sarobetsu National Park
利尻礼文サロベツ
国立公園

If you have the time available, a visit to Rishiritō and Rebuntō islands is a must. The best weather for hiking is during the tourist season which lasts from June to late September. You should plan on spending a minimum of four days if you want to visit both islands at an easy pace, including a hike or two.

RISHIRITO ISLAND   利尻島
This is an island dominated by the volcanic peak of Mt Rishiri-zan which soars majestically out of the sea. A road circles the island and a bus service links the small fishing communities. The main activity for visitors is hiking on the various trails and lakes below the summit of the mountain. Providing you have warm clothes and proper footwear, the hike to the summit can be comfortably completed in a full day. Oshidomari and Kutsugata are the main ports for the island.

Information
Information booths at the ferry terminals of these two ports provide maps and information on transport, sights and hiking as well as making reservations for accommodation. The booths are opened for the arrival or departure of ferries.

Mt Rishiri-zan Hike
There are three trails to the summit (1718 metres) but the most reliable ones lead from Oshidomari and Kutsugata. It doesn't make much difference which of these trails you take up, and which one you take down. Prepare properly for a mountain hike, aim for an early start and allow a total of 10 hours for the ascent and descent. Advice and maps in Japanese (excellent hiking details with contour lines) are available from the information booths at the ports and from the youth hostels.

People

Architecture

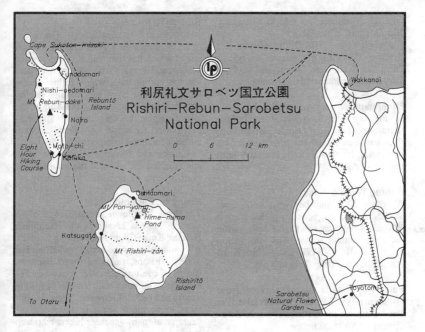

利尻礼文サロベツ国立公園
Rishiri–Rebun–Sarobetsu
National Park

Just below the summit is Rishiridake-Sangoya, an unstaffed mountain hut, which perches on the edge of a precipice and provides the bare minimum for a roof over your head. Take your own food (purchase it from shops in the ports) and water. If you stay here, be warned that it's bloody cold at night and the wind contributes generously to the drop in temperatures. If you can't sleep, the night views are absolutely amazing and, providing the clarity holds, the views during the day extend as far as Sakhalin Island (USSR).

There is severe erosion on the sections between the mountain hut and the summit where there is a small Shinto shrine containing a model boat. Although the shrine has been tethered with thick steel ropes, the ferocity of the wind is indicated by the fact that it has dislodged the shrine from its concrete plinth and smashed the contents.

If you don't feel like hiking to the summit, there are several enjoyable hikes which are less strenuous. One of these follows the trail from Oshidomari for an hour towards the summit, but branches left in thick forest, about 10 minutes after reaching a group of A-frame chalets at the end of a paved road. This trail leads to Hime-numa Pond in 1¾ hours with the option of a 30 minute sidetrip to Mt Pon-yama.

Places to Stay

The information booth at Oshidomari-kō Port is opened for the arrival and departure of ferries and can help with booking accommodation both on this island and on Rebuntō Island. There are plenty of minshuku and a couple of youth hostels.

Youth Hostels *Rishiri Youth Hostel* (tel 01638-4-2523) is a 15 minute walk from Kutsugata-kō Port. If you arrive on the other side of the island, at Oshidomari-kō Port, take the 20 minute bus ride to Kutsugata. Bicycle rental is available.

Rishiri Green Hill Youth Hostel (tel 01638-2-2507) is a five minute bus ride or 25 minute walk from Oshidomari-kō Port. Bicycle and scooter rental is available.

Minshuku *Herasano-ya* (tel 01638-2-2361) is a member of the Toho network and is three minutes on foot from Oshidomari-kō Port. Prices start at Y4500 per person including two meals. It's closed from November until the end of April.

Getting There & Away
Air It's a 20 minute hop with ANK from Wakkanai and the round-trip ticket costs Y10,580 – there are two flights daily during the peak summer season. The information office (tel 01638-2-1770) at Rishiri Kūkō Airfield is open from 9 am to 5 pm.

Ferry For details of the service from Oshidomari via Kafuka (Rebuntō Island) to Wakkanai, see the Getting There & Away section for Wakkanai.

A daily service connects Kutsugata with Otaru in about 11 hours and the cheapest ticket costs Y7210 – the same service also extends to Kafuka on Rebuntō Island.

Getting Around
Bus There are six buses daily which complete a 1¾ hour (Y1880) circuit of the island.

Taxi Taxis are available in Kutsugata and Oshidomari.

Bicycle Bicycles are a great way to get around the island and are available for rental at the youth hostels. You can complete a leisurely circuit (53 km) of the island in about five hours.

Hitching The island isn't exactly a hive of vehicular activity, but you can thumb a ride if you're patient – when a vehicle chugs in to sight, it's a rare enough event for everyone in the village to pass comment.

REBUNTO ISLAND 礼文島
In contrast to the conical heights of its neighbour, Rebuntō is a low, sausage-shaped island which has one major road down the east coast. The main attractions of the island are the hiking trails which follow routes along the west coast past remote fishing communities. Between June and August, the island's alpine flowers – over 300 species – pull out all the stops for a floral extravaganza: a memorable experience.

Kafuka and Funadomari are the main communities and ports, at the southern and northern ends of the island, respectively.

Hiking on Rebuntō Island
The classic hike down the entire length of the western coast is known as the Hachijikan Haiking Kursu (Eight Hour Hiking Course). It's a marvellous hike across varied terrain: grassy clifftops, fields of dwarf bamboo, forests of conifers, deserted, rocky beaches and remote harbours with clusters of fishing shacks and racks of seaweed. There doesn't seem to be much sense in following the example of many Japanese hikers who turn it into an endurance race – complete with certificate of survival! If you have the extra day, or simply want to pack less into the day, it would be more enjoyable to break the hike into two four-hour sections, known as Yonjikan Haiking Kursu (Four Hour Hiking Course) starting or finishing at Nishi-uedomari.

Information & Preparation All the youth hostels and other places to stay on the island provide information on hiking, transport to trailheads and assign hikers to groups.

Although the eight hour hike is not a death-defying feat, it has some tricky stretches, including steep slopes of loose scree and several km of boulder-hopping along beaches, which can become very nasty in the unpredictable weather of these northern regions. Much of the trail is several hours away from human habitation and, for the most part, those who slip off a cliff or twist an ankle will require rescue by boat. There's no need to be paranoid, but this is the reason why group hiking is encouraged. Beware of being marshalled into large groups because things can then become too regimented. The best group size is four.

You'll need proper footwear, warm clothes and some form of rainwear. The hostels often provide packed lunches which hikers affectionately refer to as 'the Japanese Flag' – an aluminium container of rice with an *umeboshi* stuck in the centre! Take water or soft drinks with you. Do *not* drink the water from the streams. During the '30s, foxes were introduced from the Kurile Islands (USSR) and their faeces now contaminate the streams – it may be tapeworm gunk or something else.

Rebun Youth Hostel in Kafuka has an excellent guide book in English entitled *Hiking Maps of Rebun*. The author details seven hikes and grades them according to difficulty and a really useful point is the inclusion of place names in kanji and romaji. The book is not for sale, but you can look through it and make notes, sketch maps and compile lists of place names.

Hiking Routes The eight hour hike runs from Cape Sukoton-misaki on the northern tip, down to Moto-chi on the southern tip. The Four Hour Hike starts or finishes at Nishi-uedomari, a small fishing village midway down the trail. You can follow the trails in either direction – most people seem to hike from north to south – but make sure you have got transport arranged and keep your timetable flexible to avoid spoiling things with the rush of a forced march.

Another popular hike is the one from Nairo, halfway down the east coast, to the top of Mt Rebun-dake. The peak is a tiddler at 490 metres, but it's a pleasant 3½ hour return hike.

Places to Stay

The information booth at the port can help find accommodation. There are many minshuku, a couple of hotels and a trio of youth hostels on the island.

Youth Hostels *Rebun Youth Hostel* (tel 01638-6-1608) in Kafuka is a very friendly place, 13 minutes on foot from Kafuka-kō Port. If you phone ahead, they'll pick you up at the port and when you leave, you may be given a lift back to the port by two staff members who insist on playing guitar and harmonica to serenade your departure!

Momoiwa-sō Youth Hostel (tel 01638-6-1421) is a 15 minute bus ride from Kafuka-kō Port. Take the bus bound for Moto-chi and get off at the Momoiwa Iriguchi stop; the hostel is about a seven minute walk from there, conveniently close to one of the trailheads for the eight hour hike. It's open from June to late September only.

Rebuntō Funadomari Youth Hostel (tel 01638-7-2717) is a 20 minute walk from Funadomari-kō Port. It's open from 10 May to the end of October only.

Minshuku *Seikan-sō* (tel 01638-7-2078) is a member of the Toho network, just a couple of minutes on foot from Funadomari-kō Port. Prices start at Y4120 per person including two meals. It's closed from October until the beginning of May.

Getting There & Away

Air It's a 20 minute hop with ANK from Wakkanai and the round-trip ticket costs Y12,080 – there are flights twice daily during the peak summer season. The information office (tel 01638-7-2175) at Rebun Kūkō Airfield is open from 9 am to 5 pm.

Ferry For details of the service from Kafuka providing connections to Oshidomari (Rishiritō Island) and to Wakkanai, see the Getting There & Away section for Wakkanai. There is one daily ferry between Funadomari and Wakkanai.

A daily service connects Kafuka via Kutsugata (Rishiritō Island) with Otaru in about 11 hours and the cheapest ticket costs Y7720.

Getting Around

Most of the time you'll be getting around the island on foot. Youth hostels and other accommodation will usually help with your transport arrangements on arrival or departure. Taxis are available, but careful attention to the bus timetables should be enough to get you to the key points for hiking. A couple of the minshuku also have bicycles to rent.

Bus The main bus service follows the island's one major road from Kafuka in the south, to Cape Sukoton-misaki in the north. En route it passes. Funadomari, the Kūkō-shita (airport) bus stop and Nishi-uedomari. Buses run on this route up to six times daily, but only four go to Cape Sukoton-misaki. Top marks must go to the solitary splendour of the hi-tech toilet on this cape where you can follow the needs of nature whilst listening to the recorded sounds of the waves outside! Another useful bus service runs five times daily from Kafuka to Moto-chi, a trailhead for the hiking trail along the western coastline of the island. Pick up a copy of the island's bus timetable at the information office in Kafuka-kō Port.

Hitching Since there is only one major road, hitching is relatively simple. The only problem is that most of the traffic seems to consist of fisherfolk commuting, at most, one km from the beach to their home.

SAROBETSU NATURAL FLOWER GARDEN
サロベツ花園

The Sarobetsu Gensai-kaen (Natural Flower Garden) is basically a visitor's centre with a series of wooden walkways across swamps. It is the most well-known part of the Sarobetsu plain, which lies a short distance south of Wakkanai, and is a vast swampy region famous for its flora. It's only worth visiting from June to late July when the vistas of rare plants will make a botanist's pulse race.

During the flowering season, there are buses running from Toyotomi station to the garden in 14 minutes (Y380).

YAGISHIRITO & TEURITO ISLANDS
焼尻島、天売島

Yagishiritō and neighbouring Teuritō lie off the west coast of Hokkaidō and are popular with naturalists and ornithologists who take boat trips out to the islands between June and August.

Excursion boats leave from Haboro and take 80 minutes (Y1300) to Yagishiritō before continuing for the 20 minute trip (Y600) to Teuritō Island. The service only operates between June and August.

A bus service connects Haboro with Horonobe, just south of the Sarobetsu Plain, and Rumoi, on the coast west of Asahikawa. Both Horonobe and Rumoi are also accessible by rail.

Daisetsuzan National Park
大雪山国立公園

This is Japan's largest national park consisting of several mountain groups, volcanoes, lakes and forests. It is spectacular hiking and skiing territory and the main centres of interest are Sōunkyō, Asahidake Onsen, Tenninkyō Onsen, Furano and Tokachidake Onsen. You can pick up maps and information (in English) about the park in Sapporo or try the tourist information offices locally. Only a couple of hikes on the more well-trodden trails have been mentioned here, but there are many more routes leading to more remote regions if you have several days or even a week to spare.

The main gateways to the park are Asahikawa and Kamikawa in the north, Kitami in the east and Obihiro in the south. Bus services through the park are restricted to routes between Kitami and Kamikawa (continuing to Asahikawa) via Sōunkyō and a service between Asahikawa and Tenninkyō Onsen via Asahidake Onsen.

KAMIKAWA 上川
Kamikawa is a useful gateway to Sōunkyō

in Daisetsuzan National Park. Local trains from Asahikawa take about 1¼ hours to Kamikawa on the JR Sekihoku line. Buses run from Kamikawa to Sōunkyō in 32 minutes (Y600).

Places to Stay

Yuwanto-Mura (tel 01658-2-2772), a member of the Toho network, is about four km from JR Kamikawa station. From the station, take the bus bound for Sōunkyō and get off after six minutes at the Rubeshibe-bashi stop; from there, it's about 20 minutes

on foot. It might be easier either to take a taxi or to phone from the station and inquire if you can be picked up. Prices start at Y3600 per person including two meals. Yuwanto-Mura is closed in November.

ASAHIDAKE ONSEN 旭岳温泉

This unspoilt hot-spring resort consists of several houses surrounded by forest, which lie at the foot of Mt Asahi-dake (2290 metres) – the highest mountain on Hokkaidō. The nearby cablecar runs in two stages (12

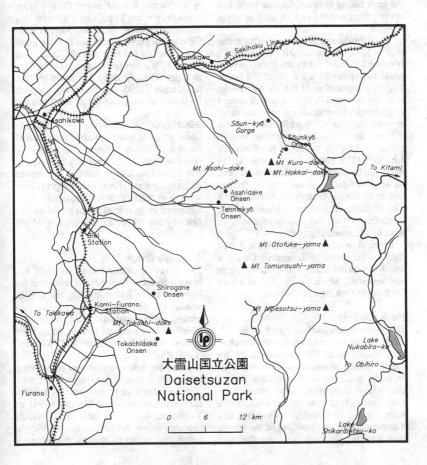

大雪山国立公園
Daisetsuzan
National Park

0   6   12 km

minutes, Y1300) to a point within easy hiking distance of the peak.

The base station of the cablecar has a restaurant and shop where you can buy *Daisetsuzan Attack* (Y1500), a very detailed map in Japanese. The youth hostel can provide advice on hiking and will loan you a hiking map together with a compass and a jingle-bell. There are rotemburo (open-air, natural hot springs) at Yudoku Onsen and Nakadake Onsen along the trails over the peaks. Take warm clothing, appropriate footwear, and sufficient food and drink. During the peak hiking seasons, cablecars and lifts operate from as early as 6 am until as late as 7.30 pm.

There are dozens of hiking options in this region; the most popular hike follows trails from the Mt Asahi-dake cablecar via several peaks to Sōunkyō – allow about 6½ hours. From the top station of the Mt Asahi-dake cablecar, it takes 1¾ hours to climb along a ridge overlooking steaming, volcanic vents to reach the peak of Mt Asahi-dake.

From there, you can continue via Mt Hokkai-dake (1½ hours) to Mt Kurodake Ishimuro (1½ hours) for a pause at the mountain hut and then continue via the peak of Mt Kuro-dake (30 minutes) to the top station of Sōunkyō chair lift (40 minutes). The lift takes 15 minutes to connect with a cablecar which whisks you down to Sōunkyō in seven minutes.

From Asahidake Onsen there's a trail through the forest to Tenninkyō Onsen, a small hot-spring resort with a scenic gorge and waterfall, which can be used as a base for extended hiking into the park.

Places to Stay

Daisetsuzan Shirakaba-sō (tel 0166-97-2246) is an outstanding youth hostel at Asahidake Onsen. The evening meals are excellent and sometimes include fish caught from the mountain stream outside. There's an indoor hot-spring bath, an outdoor rotemburo where you can soak under the stars, a beautiful Canadian log cabin with a Japanese tatami-mat interior and the couple who run the place are well travelled and genuinely hospitable. From the hostel – maps and advice are provided – you can hike up and over Mt Asahi-dake, or do more hiking towards Tenninkyō Onsen. Cross-country skiing is popular here in the winter too. As a further inducement to visit this beautiful spot, the hostel even refunds the price of your return bus ticket from Asahikawa. Please be gentle with the place; that way, it will remain as it is for many years to come.

Getting There & Away

A bus service runs twice daily from Asahikawa to Tenninkyō Onsen via Asahidake Onsen; from mid-June to mid-October the service increases to three times daily. The last bus to Asahidake Onsen is at 3 pm; the last bus from Asahidake Onsen is at 5 pm. The trip takes 1½ hours and the ticket costs Y1180 – see the previous section for details of the youth hostel ticket refund.

SOUNKYO   層雲峡温泉

Sōunkyō is the touristic hub of the park and consists of Sōunkyō Onsen, the hot-spring resort with an array of brutally ugly hotels, and Sōun-kyō Gorge itself – *kyō* means gorge in Japanese. For hikers, the gorge may seem a secondary attraction, rather tame compared to the role of Sōunkyō Onsen as a gateway for hikes into the interior of the park.

Sōun-kyō Gorge

The gorge stretches for about eight km beyond Sōunkyō Onsen and is renowned for its waterfalls – Ryūsei-no-taki and Gingano-taki are the main ones – and for two sections of perpendicular columns of rock which give an enclosed feeling, hence their names: 'Obako' (Big Box) and 'Kobako' (Little Box).

Since the view from the road is restricted by tunnels, a separate cycling path has been constructed and local entrepreneurs derive a sizeable income from bicycle rental at Y1200 per day – the local youth hostels probably offer the best deals for bicycle rental. You could also speed things up by taking a taxi to Obako (20 minute ride) and walking back in a couple of hours.

Hiking Routes

The combination of a cablecar (seven minutes, Y750) and a chair lift (15 minutes, Y220) provides fast access to Mt Kuro-dake for skiers and hikers. Discounts are given to youth hostellers and for return tickets.

The most popular hike is the one across to Mt Asahi-dake – see the section on Asahidake Onsen for details. You can arrange to leave your baggage at either end and pick it up later after making the tedious loop back through Asahikawa by bus, or simply restrict your baggage to the minimum required for an overnight stay and return on foot by a different trail.

If you want to do simple day hikes from Sōunkyō Onsen and return there at the end of the day, you could climb from the chair lift station to the peak of Mt Kuro-dake in an hour and then descend in about 20 minutes to the mountain hut called Kurodake Ishimuro which provides basic accommodation and food during the peak hiking season. The return trip to this hut from Sōunkyō Onsen takes about four hours at a leisurely pace.

Places to Stay

Ginsenkaku Youth Hostel (tel 01658-5-3003) is a five minute walk from the bus terminal at Sōunkyō. As you leave the terminal, cross over the bridge to the right-hand side of the river and continue up the steep hill to another bridge below the cablecar – the hostel is down the road on your right. Hot-spring baths are available for an additional fee of Y150.

There is another youth hostel in Sōunkyō, but judging by reports, the attitude of the manager towards foreigners doesn't make for a pleasant stay.

Getting There & Away

Buses run from Sōunkyō to Kamikawa in 32 minutes (Y600). The bus service from Sōunkyō to Kitami takes about two hours. The price is a hefty Y2400, but you get to

ride in a deluxe sightseeing bus with plush seats, chandeliers!, headphones, etc – a bizarre contrast with the wild scenery outside, especially if you've been out there hiking for a few days.

If you want to head south towards Obihiro, you'll have to use Route 273 which follows a scenic route via Lake Nukabira-ko, but which has *no* bus services – hitch or hire a car. From Obihiro, there's a bus (1¾ hours, Y1600) to Lake Shikaribetsu-ko which is about 15 km from Lake Nukabira-ko. Incidentally, Obihiro will delight park bench enthusiasts: it has the world's longest bench at 400 metres! Plenty of room for those who need to sit and think for a while.

FURANO 富良野

This is one of Japan's most famous ski resorts with over a dozen ski lifts and excellent facilities for powder skiing considered by some to be amongst the best in the world.

The JR Furano line links Asahikawa with Furano in 1¼ hours. There is also a railway line from Sapporo via Takikawa to Furano and trains takes 2¼ hours. Buses also run directly from Sapporo to Furano in 2½ hours (Y1800).

Places to Stay

There are plenty of minshuku, ryokan, hotels and pensions – the information centre at Furano station can provide help with accommodation. For an inexpensive place to stay, you could try *Furano White Youth Hostel* (tel 0167-23-4807) which is a 10 minute bus ride from Furano station. Bicycle and scooter rental is available.

TOKACHIDAKE & SHIROGANE ONSEN
十勝岳、白金温泉

A short distance north-east of Furano are the remote hot spring villages of Tokachidake Onsen and Shirogane Onsen which are bases for hiking and skiing. You can climb Mt Tokachi-dake in a day; some trails extend as far as Tenninkyō Onsen or Mt Asahi-dake, but these require between three and four days of hiking. An inexpensive place to stay at

Shirogane Onsen is *Shirogane Center* (tel 0166-94-3131) which is a youth hostel.

From Kami Furano station on the JR Furano line, it's a 35 minute bus ride (Y490) to Tokachidake Onsen – up to three buses daily. From Biei station on the JR Furano line, it's a 30 minute bus ride (Y600) to Shirogane Onsen – up to four buses daily.

BIHORO 美幌

Bihoro lies east of Asahikawa, and north of Akan National Park. If you're not going to Shiretoko National Park, you can head south from here into Akan National Park.

From Bihoro, sightseeing buses follow a scenic route to the park, pausing after 50 minutes at Bihoro Pass which provides a superb view across Lake Kussharo-ko. The buses then continue around all the sights of the park for another 2¾ hours before reaching the terminus at Akan Kohan. It's best to use this expensive service in small doses – the incessant, babbling commentary and 'packaged' feel can be oppressive. The trip from Bihoro to Kawayu Onsen on the shore of Lake Kussharo-ko takes 65 minutes (Y2590).

Places to Stay

Bihoro Youth Hostel (tel 0152-73-2560) is close to the town centre. From Bihoro station it's a six minute bus ride followed by a 10 minute walk. A Y500 discount may still be offered to overseas hostellers. Bicycle rental is available and there are hot springs nearby.

ABASHIRI 網走

Abashiri is of primary interest to travellers as a transport hub for access to Shari and the Shiretoko Peninsula.

The tourist information office in Abashiri station has details about the few sights around Abashiri which can be reached by bus from the station. There's an observation point at Mt Tento-san, about four km from the station, which also features Okhotsk Ryu-hōkan (Museum of Ice Floes) and another museum, Oroke Kinenkan, which displays items from the culture of the Oroke,

a nomadic tribe of Siberian origins, but now close to extinction.

Places to Stay

Minshuku Chokodai (tel 0152-44-5343) is a 10 minute bus ride from Abashiri station. Prices start around Y5500 per person including two meals.

Minshuku Hokui Yonjū-Yondo (tel 0152-44-4325), a member of the Toho network, is a 30 minute walk from Abashiri station or a five minute bus ride followed by a three minute walk. Prices start at Y3300 per person including two meals. The hot springs can be used for an additional fee of Y200.

The nearest youth hostel is *Gensei-Kaen* (tel 0152-46-2630) which is a 15 minute walk from Kitahama station – three stops east of Abashiri. The coastal strip close to the hostel is worth a visit between June and July when it is covered for many km with a blanket of flowers.

Getting There & Away

Abashiri is the terminus for the JR Sekihoku line which runs across the centre of Hokkaidō to Asahikawa – the fastest trains take about 3¾ hours.

It is also the terminus for the JR Senmō line which runs via Shari to Kushiro. From Abashiri to Shari takes 2¼ hours. It's hard to make good use of this line because trains are slow and infrequent. You might prefer to take the 65 minute bus ride (Y980) from Abashiri to Shari – there are up to four buses daily.

Shiretoko National Park
知床国立公園

This remote park features a peninsula with a range of volcanic peaks leading out to the rugged cliffs around Cape Shiretoko-misaki. Two roads run along each side of the peninsula, but they peter out well before the tip which can be viewed as part of a long boat excursion from Utoro. Another road crosses

from Shari to Iwaobetsu takes 70 minutes (Y1600). Buses to Rausu operate twice daily from July to mid-October.

Places to Stay
Kaze-no-Ko (tel 01522-3-1121) is a member of the Toho network. From Shari station, take the bus bound for Utoro and get off after 10 minutes. Prices start at Y3800 per person including two meals.

UTORO　ウトロ
Although Utoro is the largest resort on the peninsula, the boat excursions are about the only things it has to offer. There's a tourist information office just behind the bus centre. *Shiretoko Youth Hostel* (tel 01522-4-2764) is a massive place ready to cater for large numbers. Bicycle rental is available.

Between May and early September, two boat excursions operate from Utoro: one runs once daily out to the soaring cliffs of Cape Shiretoko-misaki (Y4910, 3¾ hours); the other runs up to five times daily for a short cruise along the coastline as far as Kamuiwakka-no-taki Falls (Y1900, 90 minutes).

IWAOBETSU　岩尾別
Iwaobetsu is a hamlet, further up the coast from Utoro, and *Iwaobetsu Youth Hostel* (tel 01522-4-2311) deserves recommendation as a friendly and convenient base for exploration of the peninsula. The hostel runs 'briefing' sessions every evening to outline hikes and trips available on the peninsula; organised outings are also arranged. Bicycle rental is available at Y300 per day.

The hostel is closed from late October until the beginning of June. If you are fortunate enough to arrive when the hostel opens for the season, you can expect three consecutive nights of slap-up dinners and partying.

To reach the hostel, either take a direct bus from Shari via Utoro to Iwaobetsu (70 minutes, Y1600), or change at Utoro for the bus bound for Shiretoko Goko (Shiretoko Five Lakes) and get off after about 20 minutes – just ask the bus driver to drop you off at the hostel. If you've missed the bus

the peninsula from Rausu to Utoro. Transport is restricted to infrequent buses and bicycle rental; hitching can prove quite successful. The main season for visitors is from mid-June to mid-September – most of the hikes are not recommended outside this season.

From Shari, the gateway to the peninsula, there is an efficient bus service to the large and rather bland resort of Utoro. However, as Iwaobetsu Youth Hostel is more convenient as a base for hiking, details about sights and hiking on the peninsula are concentrated in the Iwaobetsu section.

SHARI　斜里
Shari functions as the gateway to Shiretoko peninsula. A tourist information office at the station can provide timetables and leaflets in Japanese. The bus centre is to your left as you exit the station. There are up to eight buses daily from Shari to Utoro, but only three or four continue to Iwaobetsu – the full trip

from Utoro, either hitch (it's only nine km) or phone the cheery and long-suffering hostel manager who has been known to fetch stranded foreigners.

A road almost opposite the youth hostel leads four km uphill to Iwaobetsu Onsen, a hot-spring hotel, at the start of the trail up Mt Rausu-dake. The hotel is a bit frayed at the edges; a shop in the lobby sells tins of sea-lion meat (Y550), bear meat and venison and, unless you're an uninhibited carnivore, you'll probably be more interested in the rotemburo (open-air baths) just below the hotel's car park.

Shiretoko Peninsula Attractions

About 10 minutes by bus from Iwaobetsu Youth Hostel are the Shiretoko Goko (Shiretoko Five Lakes) where wooden walk-ways have been laid out for visitors to stroll around the lakes in an hour or so.

Another 45 minutes by bus down the rough road towards the tip of the peninsula, you come to Ohashi Bridge just below the spectacular rotemburo (natural, open-air hot springs) which form part of Kamuiwakka-

no-taki Falls. It takes about 20 minutes to climb up the rocky bed of the stream until you come to cascades of hot water emptying into a succession of pools. Bathers simply strip off and soak in the pools which command a superb panorama across the ocean. A special sightseeing bus service operates to the lakes and the rotemburo once a day between mid-June and mid-September – passengers are given time to take a dip in the pools.

There are several hikes on the peninsula: Iwaobetsu Youth Hostel can provide more

Japan's Northern Territories

Japan and the Soviet Union have spent almost half a century at loggerheads over a group of islands, one of which is less than four km from Cape Nosappu-misaki, just east of the town of Nemuro. The disputed islands are Kunashiritō, Etorofutō, Shikotantō and Habomaishotō. On 3 September 1945, the Soviet Union completed a swift occupation of these islands and chose to ignore previous international agreements. Since then, the Soviets have kept their grip on one of the richest fishing grounds in the world and the Japanese have maintained a frosty demeanour in their relations, keeping up pressure for the return of the territories and restricting their investment in the Soviet Union to minuscule levels.

On Hokkaidō, this topic is highlighted by annual rallies and appeals for signatures. In Hakodate, I was standing outside the station when a large truck roared into view. The sides of the truck were covered with huge maps of Hokkaidō with the Northern Territories, of course, highlighted; on the roof of the truck was an array of loudspeakers churning out martial music. As I watched, the rear doors flew open and several young men wearing the Japanese flag as a bandanna round their heads and dressed in military fatigues, clambered onto the roof of the truck and commenced a thunderous verbal assault. Nobody in the station entrance even stopped to look...except for me, and I couldn't understand a word!

The good news is that the Soviets have recently been making comments about mending political fences with Japan and discussing a shift in security priorities for the region; the Japanese have also been hinting at an interest in investment in Siberia...assuming something happens with the Northern Territories.

Robert Strauss ■

detailed advice on routes, trail conditions and the organisation of transport. Proper footwear and warm clothes are essential.

The hike to the top of Mt Rausu-dake starts from the hotel at Iwaobetsu Onsen. There's only one bus a day out to the hotel, so you'll probably have to walk for an hour up the road from Iwaobetsu Youth Hostel to reach the start of the trail – allow 4½ hours from there to reach the top (1660 metres) at a comfortable pace.

The hike to the summit of Mt Iō-zan (1562 metres) starts about 500 metres beyond Ohashi Bridge and requires about eight hours for the return trip.

The youth hostel owner also recommended another short hike from Shiretoko Pass – midway between Utoro and Rausu – to Lake Rausu-ko.

RAUSU 羅臼

This is an unimpressive fishing village which Japanese travellers seem to like to visit to try the culinary delights of *todo* (sea lion) meat.

Places to Stay

Rausu Youth Hostel (tel 01538-7-2145) is reached by infrequent bus services either from Shibetsu to the south, or from Utoro to the west.

Akan National Park
阿寒国立公園

This large park in eastern Hokkaidō contains several volcanic peaks, some large caldera lakes and extensive forests.

The main gateways on the fringe of the park are Bihoro in the north and Kushiro in the south. The major centres inside the park are the towns of Teshikaga, Kawayu Onsen and Akan Kohan. The main sights have been included with the descriptions of the last two towns as they provide the most convenient bases from which to see them.

The only efficient and speedy transport in the park is provided by sightseeing buses which get you to the sights but also have the disadvantages of 'packaged' travel – see the comments in the Bihoro section. Bus services are most frequent between June and October. Kushiro would be a convenient choice to rent a car – ask at the tourist information office in Kushiro station. The JR Senmō line runs from Shari to Kushiro but trains are slow and infrequent. Hitching is a viable alternative.

KAWAYU ONSEN 川湯温泉

This hot-spring resort is a convenient base for visiting the nearby sights of Lake Kussharo-ko, Mt Iō-zan and Lake Mashū-ko.

About three km from Kawayu Onsen is Lake Kussharo-ko, the largest inland lake in Hokkaidō and a popular spot for swimming and camping. At Sunayu Onsen on the eastern shore, the hot springs warm the sand on the beach and at Wakoto Onsen on the southern shore, there are hot springs bubbling into open-air pools.

Mt Iō-zan, just outside Kawayu Onsen, is unmistakable for its steam and distinctive smell. A pleasant nature trail leads from the bus centre through dwarf pines to the mountain and takes 35 minutes. The scene is certainly impressive with hissing vents, billowing clouds of steam and bright yellow sulphur deposits. The egg business is big here, crates of them are boiled over the vents and sold at Y350 for five – although the whole place provides an eggy whiff for free anyway!

There are other aspects to the scene: hordes of tourists are disgorged from tour buses and greeted by loudspeakers playing a 'welcome cassette' which is endlessly repeated to entice customers into the souvenir shops. Meanwhile, an emaciated and badly crippled Siberian fox drags itself out of a rubbish bin to line up for the cameras in the hope of food.

Lake Mashū-ko is about 15 km south-east of Kawayu Onsen. Known to the Ainu as the 'Lake of the Devil', there is certainly an unusual atmosphere to this lake which is surrounded by steep rock walls. If you are fortunate enough to visit when the lake is not wreathed in mist, the clarity of the water and its intense blue colour is quite startling. Visitors view the lake from two observation points which are equipped with souvenir stands and stalls selling sweet corn.

In the corner of the coach park, I noticed an old Ainu gentleman with a flowing white beard and dressed in crumpled Ainu garb. He was slumped on a chair and stared glumly away from the sacred lake. Next to him was a photographer, busy encouraging tourists to pose with the old man.

Robert Strauss

Places to Stay

Kussharo-ko Youth Hostel (tel 01548-3-3539) is part of a large ryokan on the shore of the lake and hostellers are given comfort-

able rooms in the ryokan. For an additional fee of Y150 you can use the hot-spring bath on the premises. It is lined with smooth rocks and offers a view across the lake. There is a shuttle service operated by the ryokan to transport guests the four km to the bus terminal in Kawayu Onsen. The hostel is open from May to late October.

Sanzoku-no-Ie (tel 01548-3-2725), a member of the Toho network, is a small minshuku about six minutes on foot from Kawayu Onsen station. Prices start at Y3800 per person including two meals. It's open from May to late October.

Mashumaro (tel 01548-2-2027), a member of the Toho network, is a five minute walk from JR Biruwa station – the stop between Kawayu Onsen and Teshikaga. Prices start at Y3800 per person including two meals. It's closed during November and April.

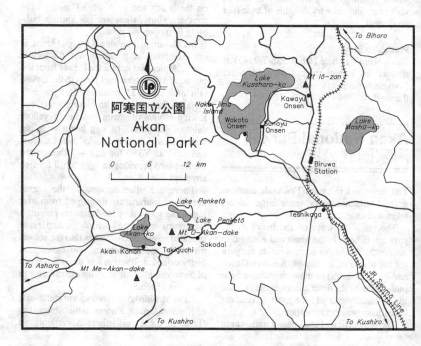

Getting There & Away

The JR Senmō line links Kawayu station with Shari in 55 minutes and with Kushiro in 1½ hours. Kawayu Onsen bus centre is a 10 minute bus ride from Kawayu station.

A sightseeing bus service operates from Kawayu Onsen via the main sights in the park to Akan Kohan (2½ hours, Y3160).

TESHIKAGA 弟子屈

Teshikaga lies in the centre of the park and is a useful transport hub, but there's no pressing reason to stay here.

The sightseeing buses all pass through Teshikaga which is 15 minutes south of Kawayu Onsen, on the JR Senmō line. Between Lake Akan-ko and Teshikaga is a particularly scenic stretch on Route 241 with an outstanding lookout at Sokodai which overlooks Lake Penketō and Lake Panketō.

AKAN KOHAN 阿寒湖畔

This is a hot-spring resort on the edge of Lake Akan-ko. You can safely skip the boat trips on the lake and the atrocious tourist facilities that purport to be part of an Ainu village, but I'd still recommend using this resort as a base for doing some interesting mountain hikes in the area.

On the eastern edge of the resort is a tourist information office where you can pick up information and hiking maps for the region – mostly in Japanese. The centre also has tanks where you can come face to face with *marimo*, a globe-shaped algae which is peculiar to the lake. These green fuzzballs can take 200 years to grow to the size of a baseball and have the ability to rise to the surface or sink to the bed of the lake, depending on the weather. They are interesting items, but severely overdone as a tourist attraction.

Behind the centre is a nature trail which leads through the woods to Bokke, a collection of spluttering mudholes beside the lake, and then returns to the town.

In town, you can stock up on food if you're going hiking or simply browse along the rows of souvenir stalls. Early in the evening, an obnoxious loudspeaker van roams around

and booms out a twangy, Jew's harp type music before advertising the time of the evening's entertainment: Ainu dance tailored to the needs of Japanese tourists.

Hiking

Mt O-Akan-dake (1371 metres) is about six km north of the town. The hiking trail starts at Takiguchi and the ascent takes about three hours, the descent about two hours. From the peak there are fine views of Lake Penketō and Lake Panketō. One local claimed that bears were a common sight at the base of the mountain in late spring and autumn – the same source claimed the bears were small and timid. Hiking maps are available from the visitor's centre and the owner of Akan Angel Youth Hostel can provide more details.

Mt Me-Akan-dake (1499 metres) is an active volcano and the highest mountain in the park. Keep a close watch on the weather which can change very fast. When hiking around the crater, watch out for the noxious effects of the sulphur fumes from the vents. There is a clear trail up the mountain which requires about 4½ hours for the ascent and 3½ hours for the descent if you return by the same trail. It's also possible to descend by a different trail on the west side of the mountain which joins the road leading to Nonaka Onsen Youth Hostel. Hiking maps are available from the tourist information office and the owner of Akan Angel Youth Hostel can provide more details.

Places to Stay

Akan Angel Youth Hostel (tel 0154-67-2309) is a 12 minute walk from the bus terminal at Akan Kohan. If you phone ahead, the friendly owner may offer to fetch you and will give you a lift to the terminal when you leave. He can also provide advice on hiking in the area and often takes groups himself. Bicycle rental and a hot-spring bath (Y150 additional fee) are also available.

Akan-Kohan Youth Hostel (tel 0154-67-2241) is a four minute walk from the bus terminal at Akan Kohan. Bicycle rental and a hot-spring bath are available. It's open from June to late October.

Nonaka Onsen Youth Hostel (tel 01562-9-7454), about 20 km west of Lake Akan-ko, also provides a base for climbing Mt Me-Akan-dake. The hostel is reached by a very infrequent direct bus service or you can use the more frequent bus service between Akan Kohan and Ashoro station – get off at the Noboriyama-guchi stop (about 55 minutes from Akan Kohan) then take the sideroad south for the 45 minute walk to the hostel. It is located in a nice position beside a small lake. For an additional fee of Y75 you can use the hot-spring bath.

Getting There & Away
Sightseeing buses run north-east from Akan Kohan to the main sights in the rest of the park as far as Kawayu Onsen. Other services connect with Ashoro and Obihiro (2¾ hours, Y3500) to the south-west, Bihoro (1¼ hours, Y1950) and Kitami to the north and Kushiro (2¼ hours, Y2440) to the south.

KUSHIRO 釧路
Kushiro is the industrial and economic centre of eastern Hokkaidō and one of the main gateways to Akan National Park.

If you have time to spare, you might want to visit the nearby Kushiro Shitsugen (Kushiro Marshlands Park), a swampy area famed for its flora and dwindling numbers of *tancho-zuru* (red-crested white cranes).

Places to Stay
Kushiro Makiba Youth Hostel (tel 0154-23-0852) is a 15 minute walk from the station. Bicycle and scooter rental is available.

Kushiro Youth Hostel (tel 0154-41-1676) is a 15 minute bus ride from the station on a No 8 or No 15 bus and then a two minute walk.

Charanke-sō (tel 0154-41-2386) is 12 minutes by bus from Kushiro station. Prices at this minshuku start at Y5500 per person including two meals.

Getting There & Away
Air Flights connect Kushiro with Sapporo

(40 minutes) and Tokyo (1¾ hours). Kushiro Kūkō Airport is a 45 minute bus ride (Y800) from Kushiro station.

Train The JR Senmō line runs north through Akan National Park to Shari. The JR Nemuro line runs west to Sapporo (4¾ hours by limited express).

Bus There are bus services from Kushiro to Akan Kohan (2¼ hours, Y2440) and to Rausu (3½ hours, Y2730) on the Shiretoko Peninsula. There's also a night bus to Sapporo (seven hours, Y5700).

Ferry A regular ferry service connects Kushiro with Tokyo in 32 hours – the cheapest passenger fare is Y14,000. Kushiro Nishi-kō Port is a 15 minute bus ride from Kushiro station.

CHITOSE KUKO AIRPORT & CHITOSE 千歳空港
Chitose Kūkō Airport, the main airport for Sapporo and Hokkaidō, is just a few minutes by bus from the actual city of Chitose which is an expanding industrial centre.

The airport has its own station and bus centre so you can normally make your onward transport connections and speed up your exit from Chitose. The information desk and car rentals counter are next to the exit on the 1st floor of the airport terminal. Ask at the information desk for a brochure called *Chitose* which is in English and Japanese and includes useful phone numbers, details of bus services and maps of the region. The bus centre is outside the exit.

Getting There & Away
Sapporo is a 35 minute train ride (Y900) by limited express on the JR Chitose line. There are convenient bus services to many destinations on Hokkaidō. Some useful ones include Sapporo (70 minutes, Y750), Lake Shikotsu-ko (47 minutes), Lake Tōya-ko (2¼ hours), Noboribetsu Onsen (70 minutes) and Niseko (three hours).

TOMAKOMAI 苫小牧

This is a city renowned for its multitude of paper-making factories and its rapidly expanding vistas of industrial zones. For the foreign traveller, probably the most useful facet of Tomakomai is its port which is the hub for ferry links with Honshū.

Places to Stay

Business Hotel Okuni (tel 0144-34-6441) is five minutes by taxi from Tomakomai station. Prices for singles/doubles start at Y3900/7800.

Getting There & Away

Buses run between Shiraoi and Tomakomai in 35 minutes (Y300) and between Tomakomai and Lake Shikotsu-ko in 45 minutes (Y540). The JR Chitose line links Tomakomai with Sapporo in one hour by limited express; Tomakomai to Hakodate takes three hours.

Ferry services link Tomakomai with Sendai (Y8600, 16½ hours), Nagoya (Y15,000, 39½ hours), Tokyo (Y11,500, 31 hours) and Hachinohe (Y3900, 8½ hours). The Tomakomai Kaihatsu-futō Pier is a 15 minute bus ride from Tomakomai station.

SHIRAOI 白老

The big attraction in this small town is the reconstructed Ainu village, known as 'Poroto Kotan', and the Ainu Minzoku Hakubutsukan which is an excellent museum of Ainu culture in a modern building inside the village.

The lacklustre and highly commercial village consists of a huge arcade of souvenir shops with about half a dozen model huts. For some reason, it has been thought necessary to keep the bears here in cramped cages barely large enough for them to be able to move. One adult bear is clearly psychotic and there is also a small pen containing a couple of listless bear cubs lying in their own urine. Perhaps the Japan Animal Welfare Society (JAWS) could help these miserable animals find a more dignified home.

The museum, however, deserves a recommendation for its presentation and description (in English) of exhibits – definitely worth a visit. The museum guide (Y400), written in English and Japanese, is also an interesting read. Admission costs Y515 and the museum is open from 8 am to 5.30 pm, April to October, and from 8.30 am to 4.30 pm, November to March. The village is a 10 minute walk from JR Shiraoi station – turn left when you walk out of the south side of the station. Most bus services drop passengers off at the Poroto Kotan bus stop opposite the approach road to the village.

Places to Stay

Shiraoi Youth Hostel (tel 0144-82-2302) is a 12 minute walk from Shiraoi station. If you are arriving by bus, get off at the Poroto Kotan stop adjacent to the hostel. Bicycle rental is available.

Getting There & Away

Shiraoi is on the JR Muroran line, 25 minutes from Noboribetsu station and 30 minutes from Tomakomai. Buses run between Shiraoi and Tomakomai in 35 minutes (Y300).

Shikotsu-Tōya National Park 支笏洞爺国立公園

This park in southern Hokkaidō is centred around Lake Shikotsu-ko, Lake Tōya-ko and Noboribetsu Onsen. The lakes have the added attractions of mountain hikes or close-up encounters with volcanoes while Noboribetsu Onsen will appeal to hot-spring enthusiasts. Fast and easy access to the park from Sapporo or Chitose Kūkō Airport makes it a favourite with visitors who have only a short time to spend in Hokkaidō.

JNTO publishes a leaflet entitled *Southern Hokkaidō (MG-12)* which provides a map of the park with information on sights, transport and accommodation.

LAKE SHIKOTSU-KO 支笏湖

Lake Shikotsu-ko is a caldera lake surrounded by several volcanoes. The main centre for transport and information is Shikotsu Kohan which consists of a bus terminal, a tourist information office, a pier for boat excursions and assorted souvenir shops, restaurants and places to stay.

The information office (tel 01232-5-2453), close to the bus terminal, is open from 9.30 am to 4.30 pm and has maps and other information. From the boat pier, there are rather tame sightseeing cruises which stop

off at a couple of places around the lake before returning to the pier (1½ hours, Y1580). If you cross the bridge on your far left as you walk down to the lake shore, you can follow a nature trail around the forested slopes for an hour or so. The youth hostel provides bicycle rental (Y250 per hour or Y800 per day) and this is a good way to follow the road around the edge of the lake as there is no bus service.

Hiking

The mountain hikes are perhaps the most

interesting activities to do around the lake. The youth hostel or tourist information office can give more advice on access, routes and timings.

Mt Eniwa-dake (1320 metres) lies on the western side of the lake. The start of the trail is about 10 minutes on foot from Poropinai – the Eniwadake Yamaguchi bus stop is nearby. It takes about 3½ hours to hike to the summit where there is a fine panorama of the surrounding lakes and peaks. Don't bother with this hike if it rains – some of the steeper

sections of the trail become dangerously slippery.

Mt Tarumae-dake (1038 metres) lies on the southern side of the lake and offers the rugged delights of wandering around the crater of an active volcano. The crater is an easy 40 minute hike from the seventh station which can be reached from Shikotsu Kohan in three hours on foot – or in 20 minutes if you use the bus service that seems to run only on Sunday. From the crater, you can either return to the seventh station, or follow the

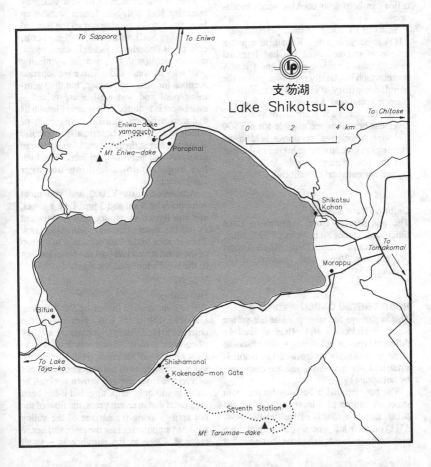

支笏湖
Lake Shikotsu-ko

To Sapporo
To Eniwa
To Chitose
0   2   4 km
Eniwa-dake yamaguchi
Mt Eniwa-dake
Poropinai
Shikotsu Kohan
To Tomakomai
Morappu
Bifue
To Lake Tōya-ko
Shishamonai
Kokenodō-mon Gate
Seventh Station
Mt Tarumae-dake

trail north-west down the mountain for 2½ hours to Kokenodō-mon, a mossy gorge, which is 10 minutes from the car park at Shishamonai on the lake shore. From Shishamonai you'll have to walk or hitch the 15 km to Shikotsu Kohan.

Places to Stay
There are over a dozen minshuku, ryokan and hotels on the edge of the lake; campgrounds are also available at Morappu, Poropinai and Bifue. The tourist information office can help with booking accommodation.

Shikotsu-ko Youth Hostel (tel 0123-25-2311) is at Shikotsuko Kohan, and just a couple of minutes from the bus terminal there. This is a well-organised and friendly hostel which has family rooms as well as the usual dormitory-style accommodation. Bicycle rental and a hot-spring bath (additional fee of Y150) are also available. Overseas hostellers are eligible for a Y500 discount. A 'briefing' session is held in the evenings to give advice on hiking in the area and the hostel may be able to help with organising transport to trailheads.

Getting There & Away
The bus service from Sapporo to Lake Shikotsu-ko takes 80 minutes (Y990); other bus services run from Chitose Kūkō Airport (47 minutes, Y660) and Tomakomai (45 minutes, Y540).

NOBORIBETSU ONSEN　登別温泉
This is perhaps the most popular hot-spring resort in Hokkaidō and offers at least 11 different types of hot-spring water to soothe ailments or simply invigorate. The resort is small and worth a visit if you are fascinated by hot springs.

The bus terminal is halfway up the main street. A couple of minutes further up the street, there's a tourist office (tel 0143-84-3311) on your left where you can pick up a pink brochure in English about the resort, but very little English is spoken. The main sights are all accessible on foot from the main street.

Dai-ichi Takimoto-kan
Dai-ichi Takimoto-kan is a hotel, recently refurbished, with one of the largest bath complexes in Japan. Guests of the hotel are allowed to use the bath for free (it costs enough to stay there anyway), but visitors are admitted on payment of a large admission fee.

Plan to make the most of your ticket by spending half a day or longer wandering from floor to floor trying out all the mineral pools (very hot!), waterfalls, walking pools, cold pools (freezing!), jacuzzi, steam room, outdoor pool (with bar) and the swimming pool with its water slide. There are separate sections for men and women, but the swimming pool and water slide are mixed – swimwear is required. There are at least half a dozen different mineral pools each of which is considered beneficial for specific ailments such as rheumatism, blood pressure disorders and nervous problems. The bath has huge windows looking out over Jigokudani.

Admission costs Y2000 and you must enter between 9 am and 3 pm. Take a towel, and you'll need swimming gear if you want to use the water slide and swimming pool. The entrance to the bath section is at the top of the main street, just past the ramp leading to the hotel's lobby on the right.

Hell Valley
A five minute walk further up the hill from Dai-ichi Takimoto-kan, you reach the entrance to Hell Valley (Jigokudani), a valley of volcanic activity. A pathway leads up the valley close to steaming and sulphurous vents with streams of hot water bubbling out of vivid red, yellow and brown rocks. The scene is still quite imposing, but it has been suggested that in recent years, the flow of the hot springs along the surface of the valley has been siphoned off for the town and hence reduced. Close to the entrance is a small

shrine where visitors can sample hot mineral water – rather vinegary.

If you continue up the valley and bear left, you cross a road and come out on a point overlooking Oyu-numa Pond with its water bubbling violently and steam rising from the sickly coloured surface. If you have time to continue, the area is crisscrossed by a network of hiking trails.

Lake Kuttara-ko

About six km from Noboribetsu Onsen is this small caldera lake with exceptionally clear water which turns an intense blue colour on fine days. Buses run three times a day from Noboribetsu Onsen to the lake.

Mt Kuma-yama

About 50 metres uphill from the bus terminal, a road leads off to the right to the cablecar for Mt Kuma-yama (Bear Mountain). The cablecar ticket costs a whopping Y1900 and includes admission to the 'sights' on the mountain: a motley collection of Ainu huts, a bear museum and utterly repulsive concrete enclosures with over 130 depressed, bored, heavily scarred bears begging for food, fighting with each other or attempting to escape being sprayed by a hose.

Every hour or so, a bevy of elderly Ainu accompanied by a frisky bear cub do a weary performance of the Iomante Festival – once the most sacred Ainu festival. From the roof of the bear museum, there are fine views across to Lake Kuttara-ko and the surrounding mountains – probably the one good thing I could say about my visit to the mountain. As I returned on the ropeway, I still couldn't fathom why this subjugation and humiliation of human and beast was necessary.
Robert Strauss

Places to Stay

Youth Hostels *Kannon-ji Youth Hostel* (tel 0143-84-2359) is part of a modern temple; you'll receive a friendly reception when you arrive and a ceremonial send-off with a gong when you depart. The food is excellent. From the bus terminal walk uphill for five minutes until you reach a junction next to a shrine; take the road to the left and walk for

another three minutes until you see the temple (large insignia on the front wall) on your right. A hot-spring bath is available if you pay an extra Y100.

Akashiya-sō Youth Hostel (tel 0143-84-2616) is a couple of minutes walk downhill from the bus terminal and on your left after the fire station. A hot-spring bath is available for an additional fee of Y100.

Kanefuku Youth Hostel (tel 0143-84-2565) is a 15 minute walk from the centre of Noboribetsu Onsen. It's on the left-hand side of the road if you're arriving on the bus from Noboribetsu station.

Ryokan *Ryokan Hanaya* (tel 0143-84-2521), a member of the Japanese Inn group, is next to the Hanaya-mae bus stop, five minutes on foot from the bus terminal. Singles/doubles cost Y3500/7000 and triples, Y10,000.

Ryokan Kiyomizu (tel 0143-84-2145), also a Japanese Inn group member, is three minutes on foot uphill from the bus terminal. Prices for singles/doubles start at Y4500/7000, while triples cost from Y10,500.

Getting There & Away

Between 1 June and late October, a bus service operates five times daily from Noboribetsu Onsen on a scenic route via Orofure Pass to Tōyako Onsen, on Lake Tōya-ko (Y850, 1¼ hours). The bus service from Sapporo to Noboribetsu Onsen takes 2¾ hours (Y1600) and runs via Tomakomai.

From Noboribetsu station on the JR Muroran line, it's a 13 minute bus ride to Noboribetsu Onsen.

LAKE TOYA-KO   洞爺湖

Although Lake Tōya-ko is a large and attractive lake, most foreign visitors who come here concentrate on seeing the 'upstart' volcanoes nearby. The centre of activity for the lake is Tōyako Onsen, a hot-spring resort on the south shore of the lake.

Mt Shōwa Shin-zan & Mt Usu-zan

In 1943, after a series of earthquakes, Mt Shōwa Shin-zan was first formed as an upstart dimple in some vegetable fields and then continued to surge upwards for two more years to reach its present height (406 metres). It is still an awesome sight as it sits there, hissing and issuing steam and keeping the locals guessing about its next move.

At the base of the mountain is a large car park with tourist facilities. At the lower end of the car park is the Shōwa Memorial Museum (Shinzan Kinenkan). It's an intriguing museum which displays many items collected by the postmaster who actually owned the ground that turned into a volcano. For many years the old man kept possession of his land, but finally let it pass into the hands of the government.

Among all the photos and paintings, look out for the articles taken from English newspapers. Apparently, the Japanese government was keen to hush up the volcanic eruption which it thought might be misinterpreted and thereby hamper the progress of WW II. The postmaster was even requested to find a way to shield the volcanic glare or extinguish it so that the volcano couldn't be used by enemy aircrew for orientation! Admission to the museum costs Y300 and it's open from 8 am to 5 pm.

At the top end of the car park is the cablecar for Mt Usu-zan which operates from May to the end of September. The ride takes six minutes and the return ticket costs Y1350. Those who stay at the Shōwa Shinzan Youth Hostel are eligible for a 10% discount.

Mt Usu-zan (725 metres) is a frisky volcano which has erupted frequently and was the force behind the creation of Mt Shōwa Shin-zan. The last eruption in 1977 destroyed the previous cablecar and rained down rocks and some 30 cm of volcanic ash onto Tōyako Onsen – you can see film clips of this eruption in the volcano museum in the resort. From the top station of the cablecar, there are superb views across the lake to the cone of Mt Yōtei-zan. A short trail leads up to a lookout where you can look into the desolate crater and keep an eye on the emission of smoke and fumes.

Getting There & Away The volcanoes are a 15 minute bus ride south-east of Tōyako Onsen and about three km from Shōwa Shinzan Youth Hostel. Between May and late October buses run hourly between 9 am and 5 pm.

Toyako Onsen Attractions

If you have time to spare after seeing the volcanoes, the following are a few ideas for things to see or do.

On the floor above the bus terminal is the Abuta Kazan Kagakukan (Abuta Volcano Museum) which charges Y400 for admission to displays explaining the origins and activities of volcanoes with special emphasis on Mt Usu-zan. Visitors can sit in a special room and experience the visual and aural fury of an eruption – the 16-woofer speakers will certainly clean your ears out! It's worth a visit and is open from 9 am to 5 pm.

Hot-spring enthusiasts could fork out Y2000 (Y2500 on Sundays) and indulge in the bathing pleasures of the Sun Palace Hotel which is a 30 minute walk from the bus terminal and has facilities considered by some to be even more sophisticated than those of the Dai-ichi Takimoto-kan Hotel in Noboribetsu Onsen – see the earlier Noboribetsu Onsen section. The Sun Palace Onsen is open to visitors from 9 am to 4 pm.

Apart from boat trips out to islands in the lake, and daily fireworks displays every evening during the summer, the resort doesn't have many other attractions. If you hire a bicycle, you can pedal around the lake in 2½ hours.

Places to Stay

Shōwa Shinzan Youth Hostel (tel 0142-75-2283) is at the beginning of the steep road leading uphill to Mt Usu-zan and Mt Shōwa Shin-zan. To get there take an eight minute bus ride from Tōyako Onsen to the Noboriyama-guchi stop. The hostel is not particularly appealing, just a place to stay.

Hostellers are eligible for a 10% discount on the Mt Usu-zan cablecar ticket. For an additional fee of Y100 you can use the hot-spring bath. Bicycle and scooter rental is also available – a convenient way to pop into Tōyako Onsen for the evening fireworks display or to pedal around the lake.

Getting There & Away

The bus service between Tōyako Onsen and Noboribetsu Onsen is described under Getting There & Away in the Noboribetsu Onsen section. Bus services also operate from Sapporo (2¾ hours, Y2550) and from Muroran (1¾ hours, Y1000).

From Tōya station on the JR Muroran line, it's a 15 minute bus ride to Tōyako Onsen.

MURORAN 室蘭

Muroran is a huge industrial hub, not worth a special visit unless you want to tour factories or use one of the city's handy ferry links with Honshū.

Places to Stay

Muroran Youth Hostel (tel 0143-44-3357) is a 15 minute walk from Wanishi station. Foreign hostellers are eligible for a Y500 discount. Bicycle rental is available.

Business Hotel Muroran Royal (tel 0143-44-8421) is five minutes on foot from Higashi Muroran station. Singles/doubles start at Y3800/7200.

Getting There & Away

Train A direct limited express between Muroran and Hakodate on the JR Muroran line takes 2¼ hours; the loop north to Sapporo takes 1¾ hours.

Ferry Ferry services link Muroran with Oma (Y1400, five hours), Hachinohe (Y3900, eight hours) and Aomori (Y3400, seven hours). Muroran-futō Pier is a three minute walk from Muroran station.

Central Honshū 中部地方

Central Japan, often referred to as Chūbu, extends across the area sandwiched between Tokyo and Kyoto.

This chapter concentrates on the prefectures at the heart of the Chūbu region: Aichi-ken, Gifu-ken, Nagano-ken, Toyama-ken, Ishikawa-ken and Fukui-ken. Niigata-ken and Sado-ga-shima Island have been included in the Northern Honshū chapter and Shizuoka-ken and Yamanashi-ken are described in the Around Tokyo chapter.

Chūbu divides into three geographical areas with marked differences in topography, climate and scenery. To the north, the coastal area along the Sea of Japan features rugged seascapes. The central area inland encompasses spectacular mountain ranges and

highlands which are dominated by the Japan Alps, whilst in the south, the Pacific coast area is heavily industrialised, urbanised and densely populated.

Transport in the southern area is excellent, with Nagoya functioning as the major transport hub and southern gateway to the region. The mountainous inland area is served by the JR Takayama line and JR Chūō line which both run roughly parallel from north to south. The main transport hubs and gateways for this area are Takayama and Matsumoto. Another useful rail connection is provided by the JR Shin-etsu line which links Tokyo with Nagano. Transport in the northern area centres around the JR Hokuriku line which follows the coast along the Sea of Japan, providing an efficient link between the main transport hubs of Kanazawa and Toyama.

Bear in mind that transport outside main cities in Chūbu, especially around the Japan Alps, is severely restricted between November and May. Access to ski resorts is an obvious exception.

The attractions of Chūbu lie in the central and northern areas, each of which can be skimmed in five days, but preferably give yourself two weeks for both. In terms of variety and interest, these areas of Chūbu are amongst the star attractions of Japan.

The central area includes highlights such as well preserved traditional architecture (Takayama and the Kiso Valley), superb mountain scenery and hiking (most of Nagano-ken, especially Kamikōchi) and remote rural communities such as those in the Shōkawa Valley.

The northern area highlights include the cultural and artistic centre of Kanazawa, the seascapes and rural relaxation of the Noto-hantō Peninsula and Eihei-ji Temple in Fukui-ken.

Aichi-ken

NAGOYA 名古屋

Nagoya rose to power as a castle town during the feudal age. All three of Japan's great

historical heroes, Oda Nobunaga, Toyotomi Hideyoshi and Tokugawa Ieyasu were born in the town or nearby. Tokugawa Ieyasu built Nagoya-jō Castle for one of his sons in 1612.

During WW II, the city's role as a major manufacturer of aircraft and munitions made it a prime target. The castle, along with the rest of the city, was obliterated by US bombing.

Nagoya has bounced back to become Japan's fourth largest city and, with a population of more than two million, contributes as one of the country's major industrial and commercial centres.

Nagoya offers few sights, but is a very convenient transport hub for trips to Ise-jingū Shrine and the Kii Peninsula further south or, if you head north, for excursions to Gifu and Inuyama or longer trips into the Japan Alps.

Orientation
The city was completely rebuilt after WW II on a grid system with expansive avenues and sidestreets connecting in straight lines. This makes it easy to find one's way around the central part of the city.

As you exit Nagoya station to the east, the colossal TV tower looms straight ahead in Sakae, the core area of the city for shopping and entertainment. To the north-east is the castle.

Nagoya station is vast, a city in itself. The shinkansen platforms are on the west side of the station. The Meitetsu and Kintetsu lines are on the east side of the station which is the part you want for the tourist information office, for connections with the subway system, the Meitetsu bus centre and the city centre.

Information
As you exit on the east side of Nagoya station, the tourist information office (tel 052-541-4301) is on your left. Open from 8.30 am to 6.45 pm, this office will provide maps and basic information.

A much better source is the Nagoya International Centre (tel 052-581-5678, ext 24/25) which is on the 3rd floor of the Inter-

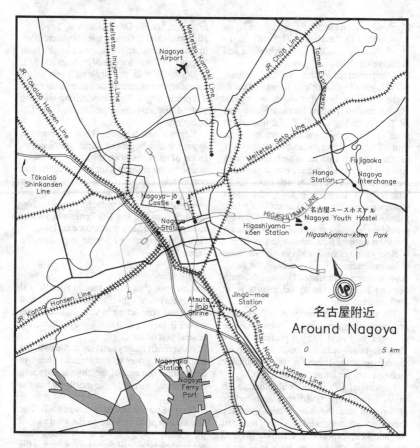

Nagoya Airport

Meitetsu Inuyama Line

Meitetsu Komaki Line

JR Chūō Line

Tōmei Expressway

JR Tōkaidō Honsen Line

Meitetsu Seto Line

Fujigaoka

Tōkaidō Shinkansen Line

Hongo Station

Nagoya Interchange

Nagoya-jō Castle

HIGASHIYAMA LINE 名古屋ユースホステル Nagoya Youth Hostel

Nagoya Station

Higashiyama-kōen Station

Higashiyama-kōen Park

JR Kansai Honsen Line

Atsuta-jinja Shrine

Jingū-mae Station

名古屋附近
Around Nagoya

Meitetsu Nagoya Honsen Line

0   5 km

Nagoyako Station

Nagoya Ferry Port

national Centre (Kokusai Centre) – a 10 minute walk east along Sakura-dōri Ave. It's open daily from 9 am to 8.30 pm and is staffed by foreigners or English-speaking Japanese.

The staff provide you with an armful of sightseeing literature and a free copy of the monthly *Nagoya Calendar* which provides an exhaustive list of what's bopping in Nagoya in cultural, artistic and other circles.

Useful brochures include the Japan National Tourist Organisation's (JNTO's) *Japan: Nagoya & Inuyama*, and another JNTO leaflet entitled *Nagoya & Vicinity*.

These are available at the Tourist Information Centre (TIC) in Kyoto or Tokyo and at JNTO offices abroad. There's also a library, TV newscasts from the USA and a bulletin board.

Post Office The main post office is a couple of minutes on foot, north of Nagoya station; it's open 24 hours.

Emergencies Nagoya International Centre (tel 052-581-5678, ext 24/25) can provide advice needed for dealing with emergencies. There's a medical clinic (tel 052-201-5311) in the same building.

Home Visits

Nagoya International Centre (tel 052-581-5678, ext 24/25) can put you in touch with Japanese families willing to invite you to their homes for a few hours for tea and a chat.

Planning Your Itinerary

There are just a couple of significant sights in Nagoya which can be seen in half a day or less. Inuyama, Gifu and Seki are within easy reach by train. Ise-jingū Shrine and Takayama are feasible as a day trip if you make an early start.

Nagoya-jō Castle

Tokugawa Ieyasu built the original castle for one of his sons in 1612. It was destroyed in WW II and replaced in 1959 with a ferroconcrete replica topped with gilded dolphins. The interior houses a museum with armour and family treasures which escaped the bombing. The castle also boasts an elevator to save you all the puff of climbing stairs. The Ninomaru Garden has a teahouse in an attractive setting in the castle grounds. Admission costs Y400 and it's open from 9.30 am to 4.30 pm.

The castle is a five minute walk from Shiyakusho station on the Meijo subway line.

Tokugawa Art Museum

The collection of the Tokugawa Art Museum (Tokugawa Bijutsukan) includes prints, calligraphy, painted scrolls, lacquerware and ceramics which previously belonged to the Tokugawa family. A special exhibition is mounted in November, at which time you may feel you are getting your money's worth for the high admission charge. The museum is open from 10 am to 5 pm but is closed on Mondays; admission costs Y1000.

To reach the museum from the castle, take bus No 16 from Shiyakusho subway station and get off at the Shindeki stop.

Atsuta-jinja Shrine

This shrine, one of the most important in Japan, dates from the 3rd century and is dedicated to the Kusanagi-no-Tsurugi (Grass-Mowing Sword), one of the 'Three Sacred Treasures' of the imperial family.

From Shiyakusho subway station (close to the castle), take the Meijo line south to Jingū-nishi station (seven stops). To reach the shrine from Nagoya station, take the Meitetsu Nagoya Honsen line to Jingū-mae (four stops) and then walk for five minutes.

Higashiyama-kōen Park

If you need a break from the concrete jungle

The Owls of Mt Hōraiji-san

Tourist literature all over the world provides surprises and I was particularly impressed by an item in a glossy brochure about Aichi-ken. According to the brochure, there is something quite amazing in the remote north-eastern regions of the prefecture which border on Shizuoka-ken. Midway up Mt Hōraiji-san is Hōrai-ji Temple which is well known for owls which cry 'bupposo'. Since they resemble the sounds of 'bup', 'po' and 'so' which stand for 'Buddhism', 'ways' and 'priest' respectively, the birds are considered holy.

To an irreverent foreigner it might seem that the birds are suffering from a dose of hiccups or indigestion. I'll definitely look forward to readers' feedback on this destination.

Robert Strauss ■

and want to amble around some extensive greenery, this vast park contains a zoo, a botanical garden and an amusement centre.

From Nagoya station, take the Higashiyama subway line and get off at Higashiyama-kōen station (16 minutes). It's open from 9.30 am to 4.30 pm but is closed on Mondays.

Festivals
The Atsuta Festival, held on 5 June at the Atsuta-jinja Shrine, features displays of martial arts and fireworks.

On the first Saturday and Sunday of June, the Tenno Matsuri Festival takes place in Deki-machi. Large *karakuri* (mechanical puppets) are paraded on floats in the precincts of the Susano-o-jinja Shrine.

Nagoya Matsuri Festival, held in mid-October, is the big event of the year. Displays include costume parades, processions of floats with karakuri, folk dancing, music and a parade of decorated cars.

Places to Stay
The areas around Nagoya station, the castle

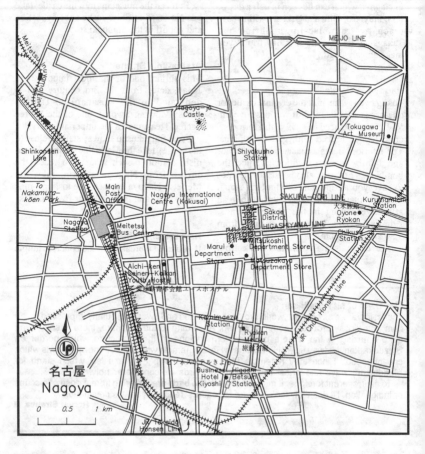

and the Sakae district have a large number of hotels, business hotels and ryokan. The information office at the station and the staff at the Nagoya International Centre have extensive lists and may help with reservations if you're stuck. The following are a few budget places to get you started.

Aichi-ken Seinen-Kaikan Youth Hostel (tel 052-221-6001) is in a popular location close to Nagoya station. As a result, it's the first budget place to be booked out – reserve in advance if you want to make sure of a bed. The hostel charges Y2100 per night. Japanese-style family rooms and guest rooms are available from Y3500 per night. From Nagoya station (eastern exit), the hostel is a 20 minute walk south-east. Alternatively, you can take bus No 20 from the stop in front of the Toyota building and get off at the Nayabashi stop. From there, it's three minutes south on foot.

Oyone Ryokan (tel 052-936-8788) is a member of the Japanese Inn Group and charges Y3500/7000 for singles/doubles. A Western breakfast is available for Y500. From Nagoya station, take the subway on either the Higashiyama line or the Sakuradōri line. If you take the Higashiyama line, get out at Chikusa station and take the No 1 western exit. If you take the Sakura-dōri line, get out at Kurumamichi station and take the No 4 exit. If you are coming from Matsumoto on the JR Chūō line, get out at Chikusa station which is a couple of minutes on foot from the ryokan.

Nagoya Youth Hostel (tel 052-781-9845) is further out to the east of town near Higashiyama-kōen Park. The charge is Y1980 per night. From Nagoya station, take the subway on the Higashiyama line to Higashiyama-kōen station. From there, it's eight minutes on foot to the hostel.

Ryokan Meiryu (tel 052-331-8686) is also a member of the Japanese Inn Group and charges Y4000/7500 for singles/doubles. It's three minutes on foot from Kamimaezu station on the Meijo subway line.

Business Hotel Kiyoshi (tel 052-321-5663) provides basic rooms in the business hotel mould. Singles/doubles cost Y4000/7000. The hotel is adjacent to the second exit of Higashi-Betsuin station on the Meijo subway line.

Places to Eat

Nagoya is renowned for several regional specialities such as 'kishimen' (noodles in soup stock), dishes made with local miso soybean paste, 'unagi' (eel, usually grilled) and 'tōfu-dengaku' (grilled bean curd with miso).

The Sakae district is full of places to eat, drink and shop – above and below the ground.

Nagoya station has a similar warren of establishments at ground level or below. The 9th floor of the Meitetsu department store, close to the station, has a bunch of restaurants offering a variety of inexpensive dishes from tempura or noodles to the more pricey unagi (eel).

Entertainment

The best source of information for sports, film, ballet, dance, drama, music, etc is the monthly *Nagoya Calendar* which is available free at the Nagoya International Centre. The centre can also provide tips on the latest 'in' bars and nocturnal hotspots from amongst the hundreds in Sakae.

Things to Buy

Nagoya and the surrounding area are known for various arts and crafts such as *arimatsu-narumi shibori* (elegant tie-dying), cloisonné (enamelling on silver and copper), ceramics and seki blades (swords, knives, scissors, etc). Nagoya International Centre can provide details on tours of specific factories or museums as well as shopping.

The major shopping centres are in Sakae and around Nagoya station. The Radio Centre Ameyoko building in Sakae is crammed from top to bottom with shops selling camera, hi-fi and electrical goods. For souvenir items (handmade paper, pottery, tie-dyed fabric, etc) you can browse in Sakae in the giant department stores such as Matsuzakaya, Maruei and Mitsukoshi, or try Meitetsu, an equally vast department store, next to the station.

Getting There & Away

Air Nagoya is served with domestic flights by All Nippon Airways (ANA), Japan Airlines (JAL) and Japan Air Systems (JAS) for cities such as Tokyo (Narita), Sapporo, Sendai, Fukuoka and Naha. As the bus takes 45 minutes from Nagoya's Komaki Airport to the city centre, the shinkansen from Tokyo is much quicker.

An increasing number of international flights are using Nagoya's Komaki Airport which does not suffer from the chronic congestion of Tokyo's Narita Airport. This is definitely an option to be considered since direct flights are now available to Nagoya from Hong Kong, Seoul, Manila, Singapore, Vancouver and Sydney.

Train The JR shinkansen is the fastest rail service for Nagoya. The journey on the Hikari shinkansen takes one hour and 52 minutes from Tokyo, one hour and 2 minutes from Shin-Osaka station and 50 minutes from Kyoto.

Ise-shima National Park is connected with Nagoya on the Kintetsu line which runs via Ise-shi station and Toba to Kashikojima. Nagoya to Ise takes one hour and 20 minutes. If you want to use JR, you will need to take the JR Kisei line to Taki and then change for Ise.

Nara is connected with Nagoya on the Kintetsu line. Nagoya to Nara takes two hours and 16 minutes.

For the Japan Alps and related sidetrips, you can take the JR Chūō line to Nagano via Matsumoto. To reach Takayama from Nagoya, you should take the Meitetsu Inuyama line to Inuyama (Unuma station) and then change to the JR Takayama line.

Inuyama is connected with Nagoya station on the Meitetsu Inuyama line. The trip takes about 30 minutes.

Gifu is connected with Nagoya station on the JR Tōkaidō Honsen line. The trip takes about 30 minutes.

Bus A JR bus operates between Tokyo and Osaka with stops in Nagoya and Kyoto. The approximate times and prices for Nagoya are as follows: from Tokyo (six hours, Y4500); from Kyoto (2¾ hours, Y2000); from Osaka (3½ hours, Y2400). The Nagoya International Centre will have up-to-date details.

Ferry The Taiheiyo Ferry (tel 03-661-7007) runs between Nagoya and Tomakomai (Hokkaidō) via Sendai. Ferries depart from Nagoya-futō Pier which is 40 minutes by bus from the Meitetsu bus centre or you can take the Meijo subway south to its terminus at Nagoya-ko station.

The passenger fare from Nagoya to Sendai is Y9300 and the trip takes 21 hours. There are evening departures every second day. The fare from Nagoya to Tomakomai is Y15,000 and the full trip takes about 40 hours.

Hitching To hitch east from Nagoya to Tokyo, or west to Kyoto or Osaka, your best bet is the Nagoya Interchange on the Tomei Expressway. Take the subway on the Higashiyama line from Nagoya station to Hongo station (13 stops) – one stop before the terminus at Fujigaoka. The interchange is a short walk east of the station.

Getting Around

To/From the Airport Express bus services run between the airport and the Meitetsu bus centre (3rd floor, stop No 5). The trip takes 45 minutes and the one-way fare is Y640. Taxis take about 10 minutes less and cost about Y2500.

Bus There is an extensive bus system but the subway is easier to handle for those with a limited grasp of Japanese. The main bus centre is the Meitetsu bus terminal on the 3rd floor of the Meitetsu department store on the south side of Nagoya station.

Subway Nagoya has four subway lines in an excellent system with station names written in English and Japanese. The most useful lines for visitors are probably the Meijo line,

Higashiyama line and the brand-new, Sakura-dōri line. The last two run via Nagoya station. The JNTO brochure entitled *Japan: Nagoya & Inuyama* has a subway map. If you intend to do a lot of travel by bus and subway, you can save money with a one day pass which is available at subway stations.

Taxi There is no shortage of taxis around the station and in Sakae, but the subway system should meet your needs unless you stay out until the wee hours.

Southern Gifu-ken
岐阜県の南部

The Gifu Prefecture consists almost entirely of mountains, with the exception of the plain around the city of Gifu, the prefectural capital. In the south of the prefecture the two cities of interest to travellers are Gifu and Inuyama which are famed for ukai (cormorant fishing) and easily visited as sidetrips from Nagoya.

SEKI 関

Seki is renowned as an ancient centre for swordsmiths. It still produces a few swords, but there isn't much growth in the sword market so the emphasis of production has been switched to cutlery.

Swordsmithing demonstrations are given on the first Sunday of each month (five times daily), on 2 January and during the second weekend in October. The best source of information on swordsmithing displays is the Seki Tourism Association (tel 0575-22-3131). There are several minshuku and ryokan around Seki and some visitors combine a stay with an evening dinner on a boat whilst watching ukai.

From Gifu (Noisshiki station), the train runs on the Meitetsu Minomachi line to Seki in 50 minutes. There are also buses from Gifu to Seki which take about half an hour.

GIFU 岐阜
In the past, Gifu was laid waste by a colossal earthquake in 1891 and later given a thorough drubbing in WW II. The city is overlooked by Mt Kinka-zan which is topped by a postwar reconstruction of Gifu Castle. A cablecar runs from Gifu-kōen Park to the top of the mountain.

Gifu is not wildly attractive from an architectural viewpoint and most tourists go there for ukai and for handicrafts.

There's a tourist information office (tel 0582-63-7291) at the JR station which provides maps and leaflets. The Meitetsu and JR stations are close to each other in the southern part of the city.

Cormorant Fishing
The ukai (cormorant fishing) season in Gifu lasts from 11 May to October. Boats depart every evening, except after heavy rainfall, or on the night of a full moon. For details on ukai see the Western Kyoto section in the Kinki District chapter.

Tickets are sold by hotels or, after 6 pm, at the booking office (tel 0582-62-0104 for advance reservations) just below the Nagarabashi Bridge. During the peak season (June to August) tickets cost Y2800 but during the rest of the year, tickets are Y200 less.

The fishing takes place around Nagarabashi Bridge, a short tram ride from Gifu JR and Meitetsu stations. If you don't want to join the partying on the boats, you can get a good view of the action by walking along the shingle to the east of the bridge.

Shōhō-ji Temple
The main attraction of this orange and white temple is the papier-mâché Daibutsu (Great Buddha) which is nearly 14 metres tall and was created from a tonne of paper sutras (prayers). Completed in 1747, the Buddha took 38 years to make. The temple is a short walk south-west of Gifu-kōen Park.

Arts & Crafts
Gifu is famous for its kasa (oiled paper parasols) and *chōchin* paper lanterns which are stocked in all the souvenir shops.

Zenshō-ji Temple

Gero

NAGANO-KEN

FUKUI-KEN

Nagaragawa Railway

JR Takayama Line

GIFU-KEN

Gujō Hachiman

Mino

Meitetsu Minomachi Line

Seki

Mino Ōta

Gifu

Noisshiki Station

JR Chūō Line

Meitetsu Komaki Line

Inuyama

Gakuden Station

Meiji-mura Village

Ōagata-jinja Shrine

Tajimi

Tagata-jinja Shrine

Tagata-jinja-mae Station

AICHI-KEN

岐阜県南部
Southern Gifu-ken

If you want to see a shop that not only sells but also makes kasa, you should visit Sakaida Honten (tel 0582-71-6958). It's a 12 minute walk south-east of JR Gifu station.

If you want to see a lantern factory, you should visit Ozeki Shōten (tel 0582-63-0111). Take the tram from Gifu station and get off at the Daigaku-byō-in stop which is at the junction of the road leading to the tunnel. From there, it's a short walk east down the main road to the factory. A guided tour takes visitors through the processes of frame building, pasting and painting. Lanterns are also on sale here.

Both Sakaida and Ozeki are closed on Sundays.

Places to Stay

Gifu commands the elevated prices of a prime tourist centre and has plenty of ryokan and hotels. The information office at the station can provide accommodation details. The following are a couple of places at the lower end of the price range.

Gifu Youth Hostel (tel 0582-63-6631) is perched close to the cablecar station on top of Mt Kinka-zan. If the cablecar is not operating, the hostel has to be reached via a circuitous ramble up the mountain. The recompense for getting lost is the low Y1380 it costs for a bed for the night.

If the cablecar is not operating, or you simply prefer to walk, take the tram from Gifu station (15 minutes) and get off at the Yana-ga-se stop. Then walk east down the main road and turn left at the second crossroads. A short distance down this street, there's a path to your right which leads up the mountain to the hostel (about a 20 minute walk).

Alternatively, take the tram from Gifu station (20 minutes) and get off at the Daigaku Byō-in stop. Walk east down the main road towards the tunnel and just before the entrance, take the path to the right which leads uphill to the hostel, a walk which also takes about 20 minutes.

Gifu Dai Ichi Hotel (tel 0582-51-2111) is a five minute walk from Gifu station. Singles/doubles cost Y5280/9350.

Hotel Shinanoya (tel 0582-62-0328) is a seven minute walk from Gifu Meitetsu station. Japanese-style rooms are available at prices between Y4500 and Y7000 per person.

Getting There & Away
From Nagoya station take the Meitetsu Honsen (Main) line (30 minutes) to Gifu. If you are going to watch ukai, you should then take the tram to Nagarabashi.

Gifu is also served by the JR Takayama line and the JR Tōkaidō line.

INUYAMA 犬山
The highlights of Inuyama are its castle and activities such as ukai and river running. The riverside setting of the castle is quite attractive, but it's stretching the imagination a bit to claim that it's the 'Japanese Rhein', as claimed in some tourist brochures. Many of the sights have been moulded or hyped into tourist attractions which are of specific appeal to Japanese. For foreigners, probably the most interesting items are the castle, the teahouse, ukai and shooting the Kisogawa River rapids.

The Meiji-mura Village Museum should appeal to those interested in Western architecture; it requires at least half a day if you want to give it thorough attention.

Orientation & Information
The castle and the ukai area are within easy walking distance of Inuyama-yuen station which is one stop north of Inuyama station. Inuyama City Hall's international section (tel 0568-61-1800, ext 233) is open on weekdays from 9 am to 5 pm and from 9 am to 12 noon on Saturdays. The city hall is a couple of minutes on foot south-west of JR Inuyama station. Explanatory leaflets and maps are available and staff can help you find accommodation. There is another tourist information office at Inuyama-jō Castle.

Inuyama-jō Castle
Dating from 1440, this is Japan's oldest castle and is preserved in its original state – a relative rarity in Japan. From the top storey of the castle, there's a fine view across the Kisogawa River.

The castle is a 15 minute walk west of Inuyama-yuen station. Admission costs Y300 and it's open from 9 am to 5 pm but closes half an hour earlier between December and February.

Uraku-en Garden & Jo-an Teahouse
Uraku-en Garden is 300 metres east of Inuyama Castle in a corner of the grounds of the Meitetsu Inuyama Hotel.

The centre of attention in the garden is the Jo-an Teahouse which is rated as one of the finest in Japan. It was constructed in 1618 in Kyoto by Oda Urakusai, a younger brother of Oda Nobunaga. Urakusai was a renowned tea master who founded his own tea ceremony school.

Admission to the teahouse costs Y800. It's open from 9 am to 5 pm but closes an hour earlier between December and February.

Cormorant Fishing
Ukai takes place close to Inuyama-yuen station at Inuyama Bridge; the boat dock and booking office is just east of the bridge. Tickets cost Y2600 during July and August;

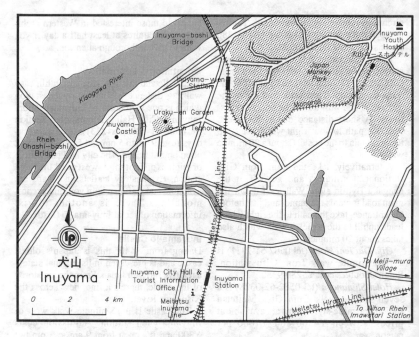

Y200 less during June and September. Book your ticket in Inuyama in the morning or call ahead and reserve tickets at the dock office (tel 0568-61-0057).

The boats go fishing every night from 1 June to 30 September except after heavy rainfall or on the night of a full moon. For details on ukai see the Western Kyoto section of the Kinki District chapter.

Kisogawa River Trip

Flat-bottomed, wooden boats shoot the rapids on a 13 km section of the Kisogawa River. The trip takes about an hour and entails little risk although you might get dampened by spray. If you want a slightly faster and noisier ride, you can take a motorised boat but for a quieter ride, choose a boat without a motor.

From Nagoya station take the Meitetsu line via Inuyama along the Meitetsu Hiromi line to Nihon Rhein Imawatari station. From there it's a five minute bus ride to the boat dock. The fare for the boat trip is Y2900. Call Nihon Rhein Kankō (tel 0574-26-2231) for more details.

Japan Monkey Park

Unless you are interested in the commercial exploitation of monkeys, you can skip this. Apart from the Japan Monkey Research Centre, a zoo and a botanical garden, there's also a collection of handicrafts related to monkeys.

Admission to the park costs Y1100. It's open from 9.30 am to 5 pm daily but closes an hour earlier from early December to mid-February. A monorail zips you from Inuyama-yuen station to the park in four minutes.

The Little World Museum of the World

This is a bizarre exhibition of modes of living in Africa, Asia, Europe and America. Compared with the cost of a Round-the-World

Colourful Characters, Yoyogi-kōen Park, Tokyo (CT)

Statues & Sculptures

airline ticket, the admission to this place seems cheap.

The museum is open daily from 9.30 am to 6 pm but closes at 4.30 pm from 16 September to 15 March; admission costs Y1000. To get there, take a bus from Inuyama station (25 minutes) or take a bus from the Meitetsu bus station in Nagoya (allow one hour).

Festivals

On the Saturday and Sunday closest to 7 and 8 April, the Inuyama Matsuri takes place at the Haritsuna-jinja Shrine. This festival dates back to 1650 and features a parade of 13, three-tiered floats decked out with lanterns. Mechanical puppets perform to music on top of the floats.

Places to Stay

If you intend to stay in Inuyama, perhaps as an extension of an ukai jaunt, you should check with the information office in the Nagoya International Centre (see the earlier Nagoya section) or the Inuyama City Hall information office.

The cheapest option in Inuyama, and one of the cheapest in Japan, is *Inuyama Youth Hostel* (tel 0568-61-1111) which is a 20 minute walk east of Inuyama-yuen station. The charge for a bed for the night is a bargain at Y1000.

Getting There & Away

Inuyama is connected with Nagoya station via the Meitetsu Inuyama line. The ordinary express takes 35 minutes.

AROUND INUYAMA　犬山の附近
Meiji-mura Village Museum

In Meiji-mura, 20 minutes by bus from Inuyama, you can see more than 60 buildings which were transported here from all over Japan during the Meiji era. The juxtaposition of Western and Japanese buildings gives an idea of the play of contradictions during the late Meiji period when Japan was intent on transformation. The destruction of WW II and the frenetic building activity in modern Japan have left few buildings of this era

standing so this open-air museum offers a chance to see what's left.

Notable buildings include a section of Frank Lloyd Wright's original Imperial Hotel, the mansion of the Japanese statesman, Saigō Tsugumichi, the summer house of Lafcadio Hearn, a hall for martial arts, a bath house, a brewery, a kabuki theatre, a prison, two churches and dozens more spread over 100 hectares.

Even if you chug around on the village locomotive or tram, you'll still need at least half a day to enjoy the place at an easy pace.

The village is open from 10 am to 5 pm daily but closes an hour earlier between November and February. Admission costs Y1240.

A bus departs every 15 minutes from Inuyama station for the 20 minute trip to Meiji-mura. You can also take a one hour bus ride from Meitetsu bus station in Nagoya direct to Meiji-mura. Buses leave twice an hour. The round-trip fare, including admission to Meiji-mura, is Y3000.

Oagata-jinja Shrine

This shrine is dedicated to Izanami, the female Shinto deity, and draws women devotees who are seeking marriage or the birth of children. The precincts of the shrine contain rocks and other items resembling female genitalia.

Oagata-jinja is a 15 minute walk east of Gakuden station, just south of Meiji-mura, on the Meitetsu Komaki line.

The Hime-no-Miya Grand Festival takes place on the first two Sundays in March at Oagata-jinja Shrine. The local populace pray for good harvests and prosperity by parading through the streets bearing a portable shrine with replicas of female genitals.

Tagata-jinja Shrine

This shrine is dedicated to Izanagi, the Shinto deity who is the male counterpart of Izanami. The main hall of the shrine has a side building containing a collection of phalluses of all dimensions, left as offerings by grateful worshippers.

Tagata-jinja is at Tagata-jinja-mae station,

one stop further south from Gakuden station, on the Meitetsu Komaki line.

The festival of Tagata Hōnen Sai takes place on 15 March at the Tagata-jinja Shrine. Replicas of male genitals are carted around in this male counterpart of the Hime-no-Miya Festival.

Tajimi

Those interested in ceramics might want to visit Tajimi which has over a thousand potteries and is one of the largest porcelain producing centres in Japan.

Tajimi is connected with Nagoya on the JR Chūō line.

GERO 下呂

Gero is favoured by Japanese tourists for its spas, but there is little appeal in its sprawl of concrete buildings. The waters of the spas are reputedly beneficial for a woman's complexion and some male visitors are attracted by 'adult' entertainments.

Apart from its numerous spas, including several communal open-air ones, Gero boasts its own 'hot-spring temple' – Onsen-ji Temple – overlooking the town. Other minor attractions include the Mine-ichigo Relics Park, Takehara Bunraku Puppet Theatre and Zenshō-ji Temple which is next to the station of the same name, one stop north of Gero.

To get there, take a Takayama line train from Gifu station.

GUJO HACHIMAN 郡上八幡

The main claim to fame of this town is its Gujō Odori Folk Dance Festival, held from the first 10 days of July through to the first 10 days in September, when the townsfolk continue nearly four centuries of tradition and let their hair down for some frenzied dancing. During the four main days of the festival (from 13 August to 16 August) the dancing goes on through the night.

From Gifu, take a train to Mino Ota, then change to the Nagaragawa Railway for the 70 minute trip to Gujō Hachiman.

Northern Gifu-ken
岐阜県の北部

The major attractions of the mountainous Gifu Prefecture lie to the north in the Hida district which is part of the Japan Alps. Takayama, the administrative centre of Hida, retains much of its original architecture and small-scale charm. From Takayama, you can make sidetrips to the spectacular mountain regions around Kamikōchi to the east (where there are numerous hot-spring resorts and excellent scope for short walks or long hikes) or you can visit the Shōkawa Valley for a look at rural life and architecture in remote farming villages to the west. If you go east from Takayama you can cross the Japan Alps to Matsumoto and Nagano and if you head west, you can continue to Kanazawa.

Access to the remoter parts of Hida is restricted by severe weather conditions which often last from November to mid-May. Check first with Japan Travel-Phone, (tel 0120-444800, toll free) or the Takayama tourist office if you plan to visit during the winter.

More details about the Japan Alps region can be found in the Nagano-ken section of this chapter (Kamikōchi, Norikura and Shirahone Onsen).

TAKAYAMA 高山

Takayama lies in the ancient Hida district tucked away between the mountains of the Japan Alps. From early times, the inhabitants were known for their woodworking skills and Hida carpenters were in demand to construct imperial palaces and temples in the Kyoto and Nara regions. The tradition continues to this day with the production of furniture and wood carvings.

From the late 16th century to the late 17th century, the Kanamori family used Takayama as an administrative centre for the district and the present layout of the town dates from this period.

Takayama should be a high priority on any visit to Central Honshū and the Japan Alps.

Give yourself two days to enjoy the place and add a few more if you use it as a base to visit the mountains.

The town – particularly the centre (Sanmachi Suji) with its traditional inns, shops and saké breweries – has retained much of the traditional architecture and intimacy that is mostly lacking in other cities in Japan. It's also an ideal size for walking or cycling around the sights without being swamped by asphalt and traffic.

The Takayama Festival, held in April and October, is rated as one of the three great festivals in Japan and attracts over half a million spectators. If you go to the festival and want to stay in Takayama then book your accommodation well in advance.

Orientation

All the main sights, except Hida Folk Village, are in the centre of town, a short walk from the station. The streets are

arranged in a grid pattern, similar to Kyoto or Nara, and this makes it easy to get around town. From the centre, you can continue east for 10 minutes along Kokubunji-dōri St, which is the main street, until you reach Teramachi (Temple District) and Shiroyama-kōen Park in the Higashiyama (Eastern Mountain) district.

Hida Folk Village is a 10 minute bus ride west of the station.

Information

The fount of all brochures, maps, reservations and knowledge on Takayama and the surrounding region is the Hida tourist information office (tel 0577-32-5328) which is in front of the station.

The office is open from 8.30 am to 6.30 pm between 1 April and 31 October. During the rest of the year it closes at 5 pm. If you want to arrange a home visit, a home stay or would like to arrange for a volunteer inter-

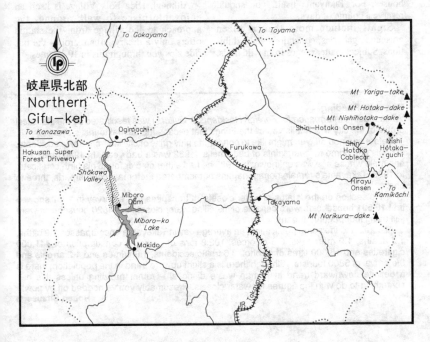

岐阜県北部
Northern Gifu-ken

To Gokayama
To Toyama
To Kanazawa
Hakusan Super Forest Driveway
Ogimachi
Furukawa
Shōkawa Valley
Miboro Dam
Miboro-ko Lake
Makido
Takayama
Mt Yariga-take
Mt Hotaka-dake
Mt Nishihotaka-dake
Shin-Hotaka Onsen
Shin Hotaka Cablecar
Nishi Hotaka-guchi
Hirayu Onsen
To Kamikōchi
Mt Norikura-dake
Takayama Line

preter for non-Japanese languages (or even sign language) ask at this office or call the International Affairs Office (tel 0577-32-3333, ext 212). There's also a video machine if you want a preview of the sights.

Useful publications are *Japan: Hida Takayama* and *Takayama & Vicinity (MG-044)* both published by JNTO. Those interested in the Takayama festivals should ask for a pale green booklet called *Background of Takayama Festival* which has full details. Encyclopaedic coverage of Takayama is provided in *Information for Foreign Residents & Visitors* which has over 50 pages of facts, figures and information which are not only extremely useful but also a riveting read.

Planning Your Itinerary

Takayama makes a good base for trips into the mountains (Kamikōchi, Hirayu Onsen, Shin-Hotaka cablecar or Norikura), or to the Shōkawa Valley with its traditional farmhouses. For Takayama itself, you should reserve a couple of days.

Sights include more than a dozen museums, galleries, collections and exhibitions. Subject matter ranges from wild birds, toys and lion masks to folkcraft and archaeology. A small sampling is provided in this section, but check with the information office if you have a special interest.

The Hida Takayama Tenshō-ji Youth Hostel (tel 0577-32-6345) can provide details of a nearby Zen temple run by a priest who speaks a little English and is willing to help genuinely interested people.

Walking Tour

From the station, you can complete a circular walking tour of the main sights in an hour. A walking tour of the Higashiyama district which passes through Teramachi and Shiroyama-kōen Park is also highly recommended. This walk takes about two hours and is particularly enjoyable in the early morning or late afternoon. The tourist information office in front of the station has a small, green booklet entitled *Temples & Shrines in Higashiyama Preserved Area* which gives details for many of the temples.

Although Hida Folk Village is itself an enjoyable place to walk around, the approach to the village from the station offers only a dreary, urban stroll – the bus ride zips you through this in 10 minutes.

Bed-time Reading

While reading *Information for Foreign Residents & Visitors* I was fascinated by the statistical profile of the city which tells you all the things that escape the casual tourist's eye.

Before you nod off, you might like to ponder the nitty gritty of city life from traffic accidents, schools and crime to 'complaints of bad smells' (1982 was a bad year). In 1980, there was one male whose age was unknown; by 1985 he had either died or found his birth certificate. In 1985, Takayama's female nonagenarians outnumbered their male counterparts, three to one.

In the section on the 'status of water closets', it transpires that a survey in 1987 showed that 10,601 households were capable of installing water closets but 4820 households were still using independent means.

According to the same publication, an average day in Takayama encompasses 1.9 births, 1.2 deaths, 1.9 marriages, 0.3 divorces, 102.9 tons of garbage, consumption of 441,000 cigarettes and 16,300 litres of alcohol, 3.5 traffic accidents, 1.6 crimes and 1.2 arrests and the arrival of 5800 tourists. Although there is a slight upward trend in the population, there is a definite downward trend in human waste disposal – rather puzzling unless this has something to do with the figures for water closets. Presumably you've nodded off by now!

Robert Strauss ∎

Takayama-jinya

Originally built in 1615 as the administrative centre for the Kanamori clan, Takayama-jinya (Historical Government House) is worth visiting to see how the authorities governed at that time. The present buildings are reconstructions dating from 1816.

Apart from government offices, a rice granary and a garden, there's a torture chamber with explanatory detail. For foreigners who have the misfortune to tour this place during school holidays, a variation on this theme can be provided by dozens of raucous schoolkids mouthing 'gaijin'.

Admission costs Y300 and it's open from 8.45 am to 5 pm, April to October, and closes half an hour earlier during the rest of the year.

Sanmachi Suji

This is the centre of the old town which consists of three streets (Ichino-machi, Nino-machi and Sanno-machi) lined with traditional shops, breweries, restaurants, museums and private homes. The saké breweries are easily recognised by the round basket of cedar fronds hanging above the entrance. The best plan is to stroll around without trying to see everything and thus avoid risking an overdose of museums.

On the subject of overdoses, the saké breweries provide samples of the product. There are a lot of them: breweries and samples. I took a strong interest in quality control and no sooner had I wobbled off on my bike than I collided with a passing pedestrian tourist, or perhaps it was vice-versa!

Robert Strauss

Hida Archaeology Museum
The Hida Archaeology Museum (Hida Minzoku Kōkokan) displays craft items and archaeological objects in a traditional house. The house was constructed with secret passages and windows in case the owners needed to make a quick exit. Admission costs Y300 and it's open from 8 am to 5 pm.

Fujii Folkcraft Museum
This museum (Fujii Bijitsu Mingeikan) is close to the archaeology museum and displays folkcraft from Japan, China and Korea. It's in an old merchant's house. Admission costs Y300 and opening hours are from 9 am to 5 pm.

Hirata Folk Art Museum
The Hirata Folk Art Museum (Hirata Kinenkan) is a merchant's house dating from the turn of the century. The displays include items from everyday Japanese life. Admission costs Y200 and it's open from 9 am to 5 pm.

Gallery of Traditional Japanese Toys
This gallery (Kyōdo Gangukan) is the place to go if you are keen on dolls and folk toys from the 17th century to the present day. The gallery is open from 9 am to 5 pm and entry costs Y200.

Takayama Local History Museum
This museum (Takayama-shi Kyōdokan) is devoted to the crafts and traditions of the region. Pride of place is allotted to rustic images carved by Enshū, a woodcarving priest who wandered around the region in the 17th century. Admission costs Y200. It's open from 9 am to 4.30 pm, closed on Mondays.

Wild Bird Museum
The Wild Bird Museum (Oita Yachokan) is devoted to the wild birds of the Japan Alps and surrounding areas. It's probably of interest to avid 'twitchers'. Admission costs Y150 and it's open from 9 am to 5 pm daily except Wednesdays.

Hachiga Folk Art Gallery
The Hachiga Minzoku Bijitsukan is a merchant house containing more folk arts and antiques, some of which depict Christian themes. Admission to the gallery costs Y200 and it's open from 8.30 am to 5 pm but closed on Wednesdays in January and February.

Kusakabe Heritage House

The Kusakabe Heritage House (Kusakabe Mingeikan) is a fine example of a wealthy merchant's home with the living quarters in one section and warehouse in another. It is fitted out as it would have been if you'd walked in to talk business in the late 1890s.

Takayama

1 Festival Floats Exhibition Hall
2 Lion Mask Exhibition Hall
3 Lacquerware Exhibition Hall
4 Yoshijima-ke House
5 Kusakabe Heritage House
6 Ryokan Kinkikan
7 Miyagawa Market
8 Hachiga Folk Art Gallery
9 Hida Kokubun-ji Temple
10 Wild Bird Museum
11 Hida Takayama Tenshō-ji Youth Hostel
12 Fujii Folkcraft Museum
13 Suzuya Restaurant
14 Hirata Folk Art Museum
15 Takayama Local History Museum
16 Hida Archaeology Museum
17 Gallery of Traditional Japanese Toys
18 Tourist Information Office
19 Takayama Post Office
20 Takayama-jinya
21 Jinya-mae Market
22 Shōren-ji Temple
23 Takayama-jō Castle

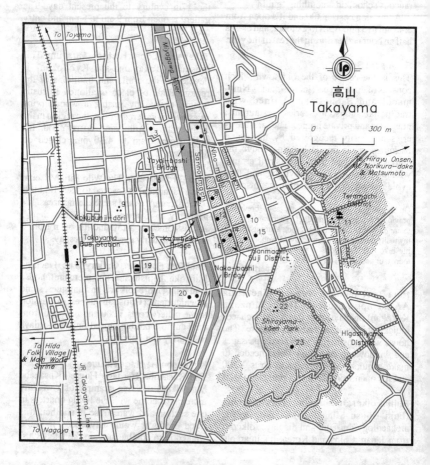

高山
Takayama

Admission costs Y309 – the extra Y9 is tax! It's open from 9 am to 4.30 pm.

Yoshijima-ke House
This house is on the same street as the Kusakabe Heritage House. Although Yoshijima-ke is also a merchant's house, it has more refined architectural details such as lattice windows which provide a lighter atmosphere. It is certainly worth a visit.

The house is open from 9 am to 4.30 pm but is closed on Tuesdays; admission costs Y250.

Festival Floats Exhibition Hall
If you can't be in Takayama for the big festivals, you can still see four of the *yatai* (festival floats) which are displayed in this hall (Takayama Yatai Kaikan) in seasonal rotation. The hall is adjacent to the grounds of the Sakurayama Hachiman-gū Shrine where the autumn festival begins. Those yatai which are not on display are stored in tall *yatai-kura* (yatai storehouses) which can be seen in the town. For the technically minded – a collapsible top tier allows the yatai to pass through the doors.

The yatai, some of which date from the 17th century, are spectacular creations with flamboyant carvings, metalwork, and lacquerwork. The complex marionettes, manipulated by eight experts using 36 strings, are capable of amazing tricks and acrobatics. The marionettes on the Hotei Tai float perform astounding feats. Life-size figures standing next to the floats are dressed in the costumes worn in the festival parade.

Admission to the hall costs Y460 and includes a glossy leaflet with information about the yatai. It's open from 9 am to 4.30 pm. At the ticket desk you will be offered a cassette recorder to guide you around the display or you may be assigned to a guide.

If you are near visiting tour groups, you can expect your ears to be blown off by flag-waving guides vying to drown each other's commentaries with bullhorns. There's a side room on the upper storey used for showing videos of the festival; it offers a convenient escape.

Lion Mask Exhibition Hall
Just below the Yatai Kaikan is the Shishi Kaikan (Lion Mask Exhibition Hall) which has a display of over 800 lion masks and musical instruments connected with *shishi* (lion) dances which are commonly performed at festivals in central and northern Japan. There are also frequent displays of ancient mechanical puppets – a good chance for a close-up view of these marvellous gadgets in action.

Admission costs Y430 and this includes the mechanical puppet show (displays every 15 minutes). The hall is open from 8.30 am to 5 pm.

At the exit from the hall are souvenir shops and a machine that tells your fortune in

English. Put Y100 in the slot and a mechanical priestess toddles out from her shrine and drops your fortune into the tray below. If you want to continue feeling happy and secure in life, don't even open 'Written Oracle No 27: Excellent Luck'!

Hida Kokubun-ji Temple

The original temple was built in the 8th century, but the oldest of the present buildings dates from the 16th century. The old ginko tree beside the three storeyed pagoda is impressively gnarled and in remarkable good shape considering it's believed to have stood there for 1200 years. Admission costs Y200 and it's open from 9 am to 4 pm. The temple is a five minute walk from the station.

Teramachi & Shiroyama-kōen Park

The best way to link these two areas in the Higashiyama district is to follow the walking trail. Teramachi has over a dozen temples (the youth hostel is in Tenshō-ji Temple) and several shrines which you can wander round at your leisure before continuing to the lush greenery of the park. Various trails lead through the park and up the mountainside to the ruins of Takayama-jō Castle. As you descend, you can take a look at Shōren-ji Temple which was transferred to this site from the Shirakawa Valley when a dam was built there in 1960. Admission to the main hall costs Y200.

From the temple it's a 10 minute walk back to the centre of town.

Hida Folk Village

The Hida Minzoku-mura (Hida Folk Village) is a large open-air museum with dozens of traditional houses which once belonged to craftspeople and farmers in the Takayama region. The houses were dismantled at their original sites and rebuilt here. You should definitely include this museum in your visit to Takayama.

The admission charge (Y500) is good value since it admits you to both the eastern and western sections of the village which are connected part of the way by a pleasant walk through fields. Allow at least two hours if you want to explore the village on foot at a leisurely pace. On a fine day, there are good views across the town to the peaks of the Japan Alps. The village is open from 8.30 am to 5 pm.

Hida Minzokukan The eastern section of the village is centred around the Hida Minzokukan (Hida Folklore Museum) at the Minzokukan-mae bus stop. There are four buildings in the museum complex: Wakayama House, Nokubi House, Go-kura Storehouse (used for storage of rice as payment of taxes) and the Museum of Mountain Life.

Wakayama House is of interest for its heavily slanted gasshō-zukuri roof which is typical of the Hida area as it was used to prevent the accumulation of heavy snowfall on the roof. 'Gasshō-zukuri' is a descriptive term that compares the roof style to 'hands

---

Written Oracle No 27: Excellent Luck

I was blessed with Written Oracle No 27: Excellent Luck. Here's a sample of how lucky I was: 'wish' – at first it appears to be realised very soon, but later it will be alright; 'missing thing' – it will be difficult to find, it will pass into another's hands; 'illness' – it will be a heavy illness, but take it easy; and 'travel' – it will do you less good, you will have much difficulty in finding your way to your home.

The last item was depressing news for someone writing about travel, but I hate to think what sort of fortune lies in store for those who get 'Poor Luck'. Still, the general prognosis was vaguely heartening: 'you'll have good luck in the near future, to get it you must be moderate in anything and abide your time without being tired'.

Robert Strauss ∎

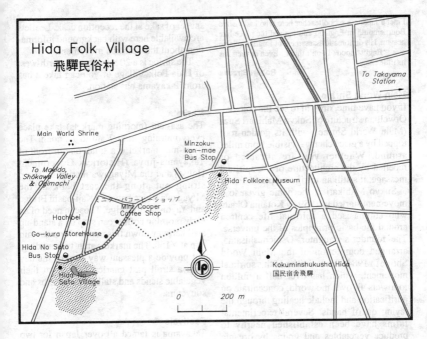

Hida Folk Village
飛驒民俗村

To Takayama
Station

Main World Shrine

Minzoku-
kan–mae
Bus Stop

Hida Folklore Museum

To Matido,
Shōkawa Valley
& Ogimachi

ミニクーパーショップ
Mini Cooper
Coffee Shop

Hachibei

Go-kura Storehouse

Hida No Sato
Bus Stop

Hida No
Sato Village

Kokuminshukusha Hida
国民宿舎飛驒

0   200 m

folded in prayer'. The interior gives a good
idea of a farmer's lifestyle in the 18th
century. The 2nd and 3rd floors were used
for rearing silkworms and have been filled
with household implements of that era.

Nokubi House is a standard farmhouse –
the interior is arranged around a central
earthen floor and fireplace.

The Museum of Mountain Life is a
random collection of mountaineering memorabilia: old skis, boots, stuffed roosters,
swans and assorted feathered friends and
pickled-looking fish.

To reach the western section of the Hida
Folk Village, continue uphill from the
Museum of Mountain Life along a pleasant
path, which winds past fields until you rejoin
the road. Keep walking uphill on the road
until you reach the rows of souvenir shops
and the ticket office for Hida No Sato Village
which is on your left at the top of the hill.

Hida No Sato Village The western section
of the village is centred round Hida No Sato
Village at the Hida No Sato bus stop.

Hida No Sato stretches over 10 hectares
and is divided into two parts: a village of 12
traditional old houses and a complex of five
traditional buildings with artisans demonstrating folk arts and crafts. It takes about
two hours, at a leisurely pace, to follow the
circular route. The displays are well presented and offer an excellent chance to see
what rural life was like in previous centuries.

Hida Folk Village is only a 20 minute walk
from Takayama station, but the route through
the urban sprawl is not enjoyable. Either hire
a bicycle in town, or take the Hida Minzoku-
mura bus from the bus station which takes
10 minutes to reach Hida No Sato (the
western section of the village) and then continues downhill for a couple of minutes to
Minzokukan-mae (the eastern section).

I met a Japanese schoolteacher here who had visited Bournemouth in England and praised the place like heaven. His diplomatic assessment of English cuisine was : 'English food? I don't think'. Even heaven has its little snags.

Robert Strauss

Main World Shrine

If you have time, drop in to see the colossal, Orwellian structure of Sukyo Mahikari Suza (Main World Shrine), with its golden roof topped by a glacé cherry – visible from miles around. Whether you are attracted or repelled by the architecture or the spiritual message, it's still an intriguing place.

Sukyo Mahikari is the name given to a movement started in 1959 by Kotama Okada who emphasised a spiritual life centred around the basic principles of the universe. The founder's daughter, Oshienushisama, arranged completion of the Main World Shrine in 1984. The activities of this spiritual movement, which has over half a million followers all over the world, concentrate on purification and include healing through the laying on of hands. Several experimental farms have been established nearby to produce vegetables and grains by organic methods. There are four major ceremonies held annually and smaller ceremonies are held every month.

From the massive bus station at the base of the building, you ascend to the visitors' hall and continue to a vast platform with fine views of the Japan Alps. A long flight of stone steps leads up to the main hall. As you go, notice the Quetzalcoatl Fountain and the Towers of Light, standing like obedient spaceships with reversed swastika motifs.

Inside the doors of the main hall is a reception desk where you are required to deposit any cameras or daypacks. The main hall has seating for at least 1000 people in front of a gigantic shrine which is traversed by a shimmering blue aquarium complete with fish. At the rear of the hall is a giant pipe organ from Denmark. A courteous attendant will probably give you instructions in Japanese, helping you through the motions of praying, bowing and clapping.

When you leave, you will be offered a saucer of saké at the reception desk. Leaflets are available here with background information about this spiritual movement.

The shrine is a 20 minute walk north-west of Hida Folk Village or you can take a bus from Takayama bus station.

Markets

The asa-ichi (morning markets) take place every morning from 7 am to 12 noon. The Jinya-mae market is a small one in front of Takayama-jinya (Historical Government House) and the Miyagawa market is larger, strung out along the east bank of the Miyagawa River, between Kaji-bashi Bridge and Yayoi-bashi Bridge. Those in need of an early morning coffee, can stop by a stand-up stall halfway down this market for a bargain cup at Y150. The markets aren't astounding, but provide a pleasant way to start the day with a stroll past gnarled farmers at their vegetable stands and stalls selling herbs and souvenirs.

Festivals

Takayama is famed all over Japan for two major festivals which attract over half a million visitors. Book your accommodation well in advance.

Sannō Matsuri Festival takes place on 14 and 15 April. The starting point for the festival parade is Hie-jinja Shrine. A dozen *yatai* (festival floats), decorated with carvings, dolls, colourful curtains and blinds, are drawn through the town. In the evening the floats are decked out with lanterns and the procession is accompanied by sacred music. A famous feature of the floats are the marionettes which perform amazing antics.

Hachiman Matsuri Festival, which takes place on 9 and 10 October, is a slightly smaller version of Sannō Matsuri.

Places to Stay

If you are going to stay in Takayama for the big festivals in April or October, you must book months in advance and expect to pay up to 20% more than you would at any other time. Alternatively, you could stay elsewhere in the region and commute to Takayama for the festival.

The information office outside Takayama station can help with reservations either in Takayama or elsewhere in the region. It has a list of places to suit all budgets. There are dozens of ryokan and minshuku; prices for the cheapest ryokan start at Y8000 per person, including two meals. The cheapest minshuku and kokuminshukusha charge Y5000 per person, including two meals.

Youth Hostel *Hida Takayama Tenshō-ji Youth Hostel* (tel 0577-32-6345) is a temple in the pleasant surroundings of Teramachi but hostellers should be prepared to stick to a rigid routine. To get there from the station, it takes about 20 minutes to walk across town. A bed for the night costs Y1900. You receive strict instructions on bath times and there are signs warning you that slippers must not be worn beyond a certain point. Punctually at 10 pm you are lulled to sleep by music and at 7 am you are awakened by the recorded twittering of birds.

Minshuku *Hachibei* (tel 0577-33-0573) is a pleasantly faded, rambling place close to Hida No Sato Village. Take a bus to the Hida No Sato bus stop; from there it's an eight minute walk to the north. Prices start at Y5500 per person and include two meals.

Business Hotel The *New Alps Hotel* (tel 0577-32-2888) is just a minutes walk from the station. Singles/doubles start at Y4200/8000.

Kokuminshukusha Close to Hida Folk Village is *Kokuminshukusha Hida* (tel 0577-32-2400). It's about 10 minutes on foot south-east of Hida Minzokukan. Prices start at Y5500 per person and include two meals. This place is popular with Japanese tourists so advance reservations are recommended.

Ryokan The architecturally modern *Ryokan Seiryu* (tel 0577-32-0448) is close to the town centre. Prices start at Y7000 per person including two meals.

If you want nothing but the finest, classical ryokan and are willing to dig really deep into your bank account, then you should stay at *Ryokan Kinkikan* (tel 0577-32-3131) in the centre of town which has antique furnishings and a delightful garden in immaculate Japanese taste. Prices start around Y16,000 per person.

Places to Eat
Takayama is known for several culinary treats. These include 'Hida soba' (buckwheat noodles with broth and vegetables), 'hoba miso' (vegetables cooked with miso) and 'san-cai' (mountain greens). You might also want to try 'midarashi-dango' (skewers of grilled rice balls seasoned with soy sauce) or 'shio-senbei' (salty rice crackers).

Bunched around the old part of town are eight saké breweries with pedigrees dating back to the Edo period. Formerly, the production processes for this jizake (local saké) were closed to visitors, but the breweries have recently started to arrange tours and tastings from early January to the end of February only. The information office at the station can arrange for prospective foreign imbibers to join these tours.

Central Takayama There are numerous restaurants and teahouses in the Sanmachi Suji area, which serve the constant flow of tourists but these have slightly elevated prices.

Suzuya (tel 0577-32-2484) is a well-known restaurant with rustic décor in the centre of town, but is on the other side of the river from Sanmachi Suji. It serves all the local specialities and its teishoku lunches are good value – prices start from around Y1000. Opening hours are from 11 am to 8 pm, but it's closed on Tuesday. To help you order, there's also an English menu.

For a complete change, you could try *Tom's Bellgins Bell* (tel 0577-33-6507) at 24 Asahi-machi, a couple of blocks west of Yayoi-bashi Bridge. The best way to find it is to phone for directions from the amiable Swiss owner, Tom Steinmann, who fulfils all those cravings for things like rösti or fondue. Pizzas are a speciality and prices start around

Y1200. Tom has spent several years in the area and done plenty of mountain hikes.

Finally, jetsetters might like to try the 'plane yoghurt' at the *Bagpipe Coffee Shop* which is next to the eastern end of the Nakabashi Bridge in the centre of town.

Teramachi Area The Tenshō-ji Youth Hostel supplies a small map which shows cheap eateries in the area. The *Daikokuya* is an unpretentious noodle shop run by a lady who cooks standard buckwheat noodle dishes. The san-cai soba is delicious and comes in various versions which cost about Y700. If you walk down the steps from the hostel and turn left along the road, you come to a junction about 30 metres later. Take the road downhill to the right and you'll see the Daikokuya on your left, next to the river.

Hida Folk Village Area If you are walking from the Hida Minzokukan (Folklore Museum) via the path to Hida No Sato Village, you eventually join the road leading uphill. About 30 metres up this road, you will see the curiously named *Mini Cooper Coffee Shop* with its requisite sign on your right. It's a cheap place for a snack and a cup of coffee.

Things to Buy
Takayama is renowned for several crafts. *Ichii ittobori* (wood carvings) are fashioned from yew and can be seen as intricate components of the Yatai floats or as figurines for sale as souvenirs. The craft of Shunkei lacquerware was introduced from Kyoto several centuries ago and is used to produce boxes, trays and flower containers. Pottery is produced in three styles ranging from the rustic Yamada-yaki to the decorative ceramics of Shibukusa-yaki. If your house feels empty, local makers of traditional furniture can help you fill it.

The Sanmachi Suji area has many shops selling handicraft items or you can browse in handicraft shops along the section of Kokubun-ji dōri St between the river and the station.

If lacquerware is a specific interest, you should visit Shunkei Kaikan (Lacquerware Exhibition Hall) which is north-east of the station, a couple of blocks before Yayoibashi Bridge. More than 1000 lacquerware items are on display with an exhibit showing production techniques. The hall is open from 8.30 am to 5 pm; admission costs Y200.

Hida Folk Village is full of shops selling souvenirs, but you might like to browse in the Gokura antiques shop which is 20 metres uphill from the Mini Cooper Coffee Shop. A venerable old lady presides over a dusty selection of antiques and bric-a-brac with long lines of zeros on the price tickets.

Getting There & Away
Train Takayama is connected with Nagoya on the JR Takayama line. The fastest limited express (tokkyū) takes two hours and 50 minutes.

Express trains run from Osaka and Kyoto to Gifu or Nagoya and continue on the JR Takayama line to Takayama. The trip takes about five hours from Osaka and half an hour less from Kyoto.

Toyama is connected with Takayama on the JR Takayama line. The fastest express from Toyama takes around 1½ hours whereas the local train (futsū) rambles to Takayama in just under three hours.

A bus/train combination runs from Takayama via Kamikōchi to Matsumoto. You take a bus from Takayama to Kamikōchi then change to another bus for Shin-Shimashima station on the Matsumoto Dentetsu line and continue by rail to Matsumoto.

Bus Staff from several tourist offices in the Japan Alps go to great lengths to warn travellers that many roads in this region close in the winter. This means that bus schedules usually only start from early May and finish in late October. For exact opening or closing dates either phone Japan Travel-Phone (0120-444800 toll free) or the tourist offices.

A bus service connects Takayama with Hirayu Onsen (one hour) and takes another hour to reach Kamikōchi. Direct buses run from Takayama via Hirayu Onsen to Shin-

Hotaka Onsen and the nearby cablecar (ropeway).

Another bus route runs on the spectacular Norikura Skyline Road connecting Norikura with Takayama in 1¾ hours.

Details for the bus/train connection between Takayama and Matsumoto via Hirayu Onsen are given in the preceding section on rail connections.

The bus service between Kanazawa and Nagoya runs via Takayama and Shirakawa-gō, but only operates midsummer.

Hitching Providing you are equipped for mountain conditions, hitching is quite feasible in the Japan Alps between May and late September.

I had several good hitches between Shirakawa-gō and Takayama and from Kamikōchi down to Matsumoto. On one occasion I was picked up by a petrol tanker and soon discovered that the only form of communication between myself and the driver was via his mania for foreign sports cars. We swapped names of sports cars in a type of monosyllabic, verbal ping-pong. When I mentioned I'd once driven an Austin Healey 3000 the driver almost went off the road in delirium.

Robert Strauss

Getting Around

With the exception of Hida Folk Village, the sights in Takayama can be easily covered on foot. You can amble from the station across to Higashiyama on the other side of town in 25 minutes.

Bus The bus station is on your left as you exit the station. There is a circular bus route around the town and bus passes are available for one day (Y890) or two days (Y1350).

Although the main sights in town are best seen on foot or by bicycle, the walk to Hida Folk Village is tedious and unattractive. It's preferable to use the frequent bus service which takes 10 minutes.

Taxi There are plenty of taxis at the station. If you want to arrive in style at the temple youth hostel, the taxi ride across town costs Y560.

Bicycle There are several bicycle rental places near the station and in town. Rates are high at Y250 for the first hour, Y200 for each additional hour and Y1250 for the day. The youth hostel charges Y80 per hour or Y600 for the day and is probably the best deal available.

Rickshaw For those who want a change from the shinkansen, there are several tourist rickshaws available for hire at prices which approach those of the shinkansen. A two hour ride costs Y5000 per person and a half day ride costs Y10,000 per person.

Ask at the tourist office if you want to arrange a ride or you can negotiate direct with the rickshaw-pullers who are usually found posing for photos in the streets of Sanmachi Suji.

SHOKAWA VALLEY REGION 荘川

This is one of the most interesting regions in Japan and highly recommended as a day trip from Takayama or as a stopover en route between Takayama and Kanazawa. Although much of what you see here has been specially preserved for, and supported by tourism, it still presents a view of rural Japan far removed from the usual images of Japan as a giant urban factory or a genteel collection of temples. If you want to avoid large contingents of tourists, bear in mind that the peak seasons for this region are May, August and October.

In the 12th century, the remoteness and inaccessibility of the area is claimed to have attracted a few stragglers from the Taira clan who sought hideaways here and on Kyūshū after their clan was virtually wiped out by the Genji clan in a brutal battle at Shimonoseki in 1185.

In the present century, construction of the gigantic Miboro Dam in the '60s submerged many of the villages and the attention this attracted to the region also drew tourists interested in the unusual architecture of the remaining villages and their remote mountain surroundings.

There are many villages and hamlets

spread around the Shokawa Valley region, but Shirakawa-gō and Gokayama are two districts with dozens of specially preserved houses and are the two concentrations of villages most commonly visited by travellers.

SHIRAKAWA-GO DISTRICT & OGIMACHI 白川郷

The Shirakawa-gō district consists of several clusters of houses in villages stretching for several km. Ogimachi, the central cluster, is the most convenient place for bus connections, tourist information and orientation. When arriving by bus, ask to get off at the Gasshō-shuraku bus stop.

Information

The tourist information office (tel 05769-6-1751/1013) is next to the Gasshō-shuraku bus stop in the centre of Ogimachi. It's open from 9 am to 5 pm. The office has a Japanese

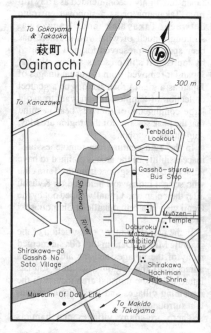

map of the whole region including a detailed map of Ogimachi itself. An English leaflet is also available.

Tenbōdai Lookout

To get your bearings on the village, climb up to the Tenbōdai lookout; from here, you'll obtain the view seen on most tourist brochures. From the Gasshō-shuraku bus stop, walk north down the main road for about 10 minutes and on your right you will see a wooded hill beside the road with a sideroad leading around the foot of the hill.

You can either follow the sideroad to the top of the hill, or, after walking about 10 metres down the sideroad, take the steep path on your right which gets you to the top in about 15 minutes.

Shirakawa-gō Gasshō No Sato Village

This is a well-presented collection of over a dozen gasshō-zukuri buildings which have been largely collected from the surrounding region and reconstructed in this open-air museum. Several of the houses are used for demonstrating regional crafts such as woodworking, straw handicrafts, ceramics and painting in Chinese ink – most of these items are on sale either from the artisans or at the ticket office.

You can wander away from the houses for a pleasant stroll through the trees further up the mountain. If you don't take a picnic, you can stop at the rest house near the exit which is run by a chatty lady who offers tea, biscuits and home-made mochi (rice cakes) toasted over the irori (open hearth).

Admission costs Y500. The village is open from 8.30 am to 5 pm between April and November, from 8 am to 6 pm during August and from 9 am to 4 pm between December and January. To reach the entrance, you have to walk west from the main road, cross a suspension bridge over the river, and continue through a dimly lit tunnel dripping with moisture.

Myōzen-ji Temple

This temple, in the centre of Ogimachi, is

combined with a museum displaying the traditional paraphernalia of daily life.

Admission costs Y200 and it's open from 7 am to 5 pm. There are shorter opening hours during the winter.

Doburoku Matsuri Exhibition Hall

This exhibition hall (Doburoku Matsuri no Yakata) is very close to Shirakawa Hachiman-jinja Shrine. The hall contains displays and a video show devoted to the Doburoku Matsuri Festival, an event clearly not lacking in liquid refreshment (doburoku is a type of unrefined saké), which is held in mid-October at the shrine.

Admission costs Y310 and it's open from 8.30 am to 4.30 pm (9 am to 4 pm during winter).

Museum of Daily Life

If you walk for about 15 minutes from the centre of Ogimachi back along the road towards Takayama, you'll reach the Museum of Daily Life (Seikatsu Shiryōkan) which is on your right, just beyond the second bridge. On display are agricultural tools, rural crafts, equipment for the cultivation of silkworms and various household items from the past. Admission costs Y200 and the museum is open from 8 am to 5 pm.

Places to Stay

If you want to stay in a typical gasshō-zukuri house, the tourist information office has lists of those places which operate as ryokan or minshuku and will make reservations. Ryokan prices start at Y7000 per person

including two meals and minshuku prices, for the same deal, start at Y5500. *Juemon* (tel 05769-6-1053) is one minshuku which has received consistently favourable comments from foreign visitors.

If you want the cheapest option in the area, you'll have to travel to *Etchū Gokayama Youth Hostel* which is a gasshō-zukuri house in a more remote location (about two km on foot from the bus stop on the main road) and close to Gokayama.

Places to Eat

Breakfast and dinner are usually included in the price for your ryokan or minshuku. The main street in Ogimachi has several restaurants.

Getting There & Away

If you plan to travel in this region during the winter, you should check first on current road conditions by phoning Japan Travel-Phone (tel 0120-444800, toll free) or the tourist office in Takayama.

Bus *Nagoya* There are direct JR buses, running twice daily, between Nagoya and Ogimachi during the following peak seasons: from 28 April to 10 May, from 20 July to 31 August, from 10 October to 3 November and from 28 December to 15 January. The price for a one-way ticket is about Y4500 and the trip takes 5½ hours. Advance bookings are recommended. Slight alterations are made to these dates every year so you should check exact details before travelling.

Gasshō-zukuri Architecture
The most striking feature of the villages are houses built in the *gasshō-zukuri* style. The poorest peasants had ramshackle hovels, but the leading families crammed several generations into massive buildings with up to four storeys.

The ground floor was used for communal living in open rooms and – not surprisingly, considering the bitter winters – the focal point was the *irori* (open hearth). The smoke from the fire drifted up into the upper storeys which were used for storage and, from the 18th century onwards, for the cultivation of silkworms which provided extra income. The acutely slanted thatched roof repelled heavy snowfall and its shape was considered to resemble 'hands in prayer' (gasshō-zukuri). See the earlier Hida Folk Village section. ■

Another bus service is operated once a day by Nagoya Tetsudō and runs between Nagoya and Kanazawa via Ogimachi between 1 July and 12 November. The price for a one-way ticket on this service from Ogimachi to Kanazawa costs about Y2200 and the trip takes about three hours.

Takayama Bus connections with Ogimachi run four times daily and are made in two stages. The first stage is a bus service operated by Nohi bus company between Takayama and Makido (Y1800, one hour).

The second stage is a connecting bus service operated by JR between Makido and Ogimachi. The trip takes about an hour and a one-way ticket costs Y1200 – unless, of course, you have a Japan Rail Pass.

Kanazawa If you are not able to use the Nagoya Tetsudō bus described earlier, there are other options. One is to take the train from Kanazawa on the JR line to Takaoka, then from Takaoka station, take a bus to Ogimachi via Gokayama (two hours).

Another option is to take the train on the

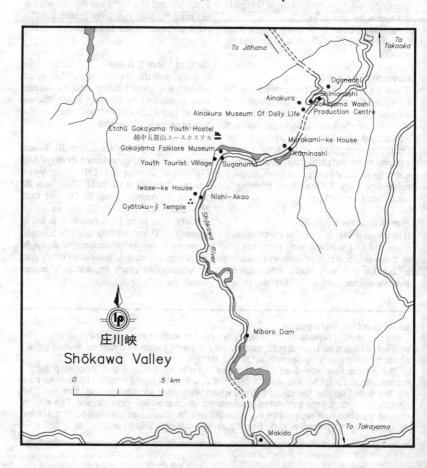

To Jōhana

To Takaoka

Ogimachi

Shimonashi

Ainokura

Gokayama Washi Production Centre

Ainokura Museum Of Daily Life

Etchū Gokayama Youth Hostel
越中五箇山ユースホステル

Gokayama Folklore Museum

Murakami-ke House

Youth Tourist Village

Kaminashi

Suganuma

Iwase-ke House

Nishi-Akao

Gyōtoku-ji Temple

Shōkawa River

庄川峡
Shōkawa Valley

0   5 km

Miboro Dam

To Takayama

Makido

Jōhana line from Takaoka to Jōhana. From Jōhana there's a bus service to Ogimachi.

Getting Around

Ogimachi is easily covered on foot. If you want to visit Gokayama, you will have to wait for infrequent buses or simply hitch.

GOKAYAMA DISTRICT 五箇山

Gokayama is just inside the boundaries of Toyama-ken, a short distance north of Ogimachi. Prior to the Edo period, the feudal lords of Kanazawa used the isolated location of Gokayama as a centre for the secretive production of gunpowder. Many of the houses open to the public in this region have displays of equipment for making gunpowder. The construction of a road to Gokayama and the provision of electricity only took place in 1925.

In the Gokayama area, gasshō-zukuri houses are scattered in small groups along the valley. The following is a brief description of the sights as you travel north from Shirakawa-gō and Ogimachi. There are bus stops at each group of houses.

Nishi-Akao

Nishi-Akao is about 20 minutes by bus from Ogimachi. The two attractions here are Gyōtoku-ji Temple and Iwase-ke House which was once the local centre for the production of gunpowder.

Suganuma

Suganuma is four km beyond Nishi-Akao and lies just below the main road. The Gokayama Minzokukan (Gokayama Folklore Museum) consists of two houses: one displays items from traditional life; and across the path, the other is devoted to exhibits which explain the traditional techniques for gunpowder production. The combined admission charge is Y300 and it's open from 9 am to 5 pm between May and November. For Y1000 you can buy cassettes of the local music – a haunting combination of twanging stringed instruments and mournful wailing.

Just south of these houses is a Youth Tourist Village. If you cross the bridge over the river and take the road to the right, you'll eventually puff your way uphill to the youth hostel (see Places to Stay).

Kaminashi

Kaminashi is on the main road, four km beyond Suganuma. Murakami-ke House dates from 1578 and has now become an interesting museum well maintained by the proud and enthusiastic owner who conducts visitors on a tour of the exhibits then sits them down around the irori and sings local folksongs. He provides a musical accompaniment for the songs using two curious musical instruments: a string of wooden blocks flicked expertly to produce a prolonged rattling sound and two bamboo sticks which are deftly twirled together to produce a rhythmic 'clack' sound. The owner also sells suiboku (water and black ink) paintings which he dashes off at great speed. Admission costs Y300. A detailed leaflet is provided in English.

Shimonashi & Ainokura

Shimonashi is on the main road, four km beyond Kaminashi. Just beyond the bus stop, there's a road on your left leading up a steep hill towards Ainokura. About 100 metres up this road, you reach Gokayama Washi Production Centre on your left. The production of washi (Japanese paper) has been a speciality of the region for several centuries and you can see the production process here. If you pay Y350, you can even have a go at it yourself and keep your work of art. If you want to buy some of the elegant paper products, you can do so in the small shop. The centre is open daily from 8.30 am to 5 pm from April to November.

From here it takes another 25 minutes on foot, winding up the hill to reach the sideroad leading off to the left to Ainokura, an impressive village of gasshō-zukuri houses with fine views across the valley. The Ainokura Minzokukan (Ainokura Museum of Daily Life) is in the village and charges Y200 admission.

If you are here when the tour buses are absent, or if you stay here in one of the minshuku, it should be possible to appreciate the slow, measured pace of village life. Frogs croak in flooded fields, farmers tramp through the mud and women in headscarves fan out across the fields to attack weeds and chat.

Places to Stay
Several gasshō-zukuri houses in the Gokayama area function as minshuku. Expect to pay around Y5000 per person for a bed and two meals. The youth hostel near Suganuma offers the most inexpensive way to stay in accommodation of this kind.

The tourist information offices in Takayama and Ogimachi can help with reservations and there is an information office in the centre of Ainokura. Advance reservations are highly recommended particularly during the peak seasons of May, August and October.

Etchū Gokayama Youth Hostel (tel 07636-7-3331) is a fine old gasshō-zukuri farmhouse and a great place to stay; it's only a few km off the main road.

A bed for the night costs Y1900. For Y700 you get a fine dinner which includes broiled trout, pickles, san-cai (mountain greens), a huge slab of tōfu, tempura vegetables and rice. The owner and his family sit around a large irori as the smoke from the fire curls up through the rafters.

The hostel is not easy to find. The closest bus stop is at Suganuma which is only 12 minutes by bus from Kaminashi bus stop or 25 minutes by bus from Ogimachi. A sign in the Suganuma bus shelter warns hostellers arriving during the snowy season not to attempt the walk to the hostel before phoning from a nearby house to make sure the road is not blocked!

From the Suganuma bus stop on the main road, walk down the sideroad through the cluster of houses by the river and cross the large bridge. At the other end of the bridge, turn right and wind your way for several km uphill until you come to the hostel which is in a small cluster of houses perched on the mountainside. The total distance is about two km from the bus stop to the hostel.

In Suganuma itself, you could also try *Yohachi* (tel 0763-67-3205), a rambling minshuku close to the river.

In Ainokura, you have a choice of several minshuku; check with the *minshuku annai-sō* (minshuku information office) which can help with reservations.

Getting There & Away
Gokayama is just inside the boundaries of Toyama-ken, about 20 minutes by infrequent bus from Ogimachi. Hitching is a good way to avoid long waits for buses. Gokayama is also served by the buses running between Kanazawa and Nagoya via Ogimachi, but only from July to November. For details, refer to the Getting There & Away section under Ogimachi. Remember that many roads in this region are closed during the winter.

HIRAYU ONSEN   平湯温泉
This is a hot-spring resort in the Japan Alps and of primary interest to visitors as a hub for bus transport in the region. The information office opposite the bus station has leaflets and information on hot-spring ryokan and nature trails in the area. If you have time, perhaps while waiting for a bus connection, the trail to Hirayu-ōtaki Falls is quite enjoyable – allow 1½ hours in total for the hike. Ask for the *Hirayu-ōtaki Kursu Chizu* which is a decent map with some details in English and includes directions to the nearby campground.

Getting There & Away
There are frequent bus connections between Hirayu Onsen and Kamikōchi, but *only* from late April to late October. The trip takes 65 minutes (Y1400) and runs via Nakanoyu. The section on Kamikōchi has more details regarding combined bus/rail connections with Matsumoto.

Buses to Norikura, Kamikōchi and Shin-Hotaka Onsen all run via Hirayu Onsen. Consequently, there are frequent bus connections between Takayama and Hirayu Onsen (Y1080, one hour).

There are bus connections approximately three times a day between Norikura and

Hirayu Onsen. The trip takes 45 minutes. The Norikura Skyline Road is *only* open from 15 May to 31 October.

There are frequent bus connections between Hirayu Onsen and Shin-Hotaka Onsen (Y770, 35 minutes). If you want to continue to Toyama, there are bus connections twice daily (four hours).

SHIN-HOTAKA ONSEN　新穂高温泉

This is a hot-spring resort with the added attraction of the Shin-Hotaka cablecar, reportedly the longest of its kind in Asia, which whisks you up close to the peak of Mt Nishi Hotaka-dake (2908 metres) for a superb mountain panorama. The cablecar consists of two sections and a combined ticket costs Y1240 one way and an extra Y300 if you take your backpack.

If you are fit, properly equipped and give yourself ample time, there are a variety of hiking options from Nishi Hotaka-guchi (the top cablecar station). One option which takes a bit less than three hours, would be to hike over to Kamikōchi.

Getting There & Away There are frequent bus connections with Hirayu Onsen (Y770, 35 minutes) and Takayama (Y1850, 95 minutes). From Shin-Hotaka Onsen to Toyama there are buses twice daily (3½ hours).

FURUKAWA　古川

Furukawa, on the route between Takayama and Toyama, was originally a castle town. It's quite a pleasant place to visit, particularly if you like strolling around areas with white storehouses, old residences and shops; the old streets are arranged in the traditional grid pattern. The main draw for Furukawa is the festival in April. If you want to attend, you should stay in Furukawa and reserve your accommodation well in advance.

Information
Information can be obtained at the station, but you may find it easier to use the tourist information office in Takayama which can also provide maps and leaflets, and arrange reservations.

Festivals
The major annual festival is Furukawa Matsuri which is held on 19 and 20 April. The festival features squads of young men, who, dressed in loincloths (the event is also referred to as the Hadaka Matsuri or 'Naked Festival'), parade through town with a giant drum. There are also processions with large yatai (festival floats) similar to those used in the Takayama festivals.

Places to Stay
Hida Furukawa Youth Hostel (05777-3-6177) is about three km west of the station (40 minutes on foot) and lies close to a ski field. Only 14 beds are available. To avoid disappointment make an advance reservation. A dorm bed costs Y2100 and bicycles are available for hire.

Things to Buy
Furukawa is famous for handmade candles. In the centre of town, you can visit Mishimaya, a shop which has specialised in traditional candle-making techniques for over two centuries.

Getting There & Away
Furukawa is three stops north of Takayama on the JR Takayama line. The trip takes 15 minutes. There are also hourly buses from Takayama station to Furukawa station (30 minutes).

Nagano-ken　長野県

Most of Nagano-ken consists of the northern, central and southern ranges of the Japan Alps – hence its claim to being the 'Roof of Japan'.

Nagano-ken is one of the most enjoyable regions to visit in Japan, not only for the beauty of its mountainous terrain, but also for its traditional architecture and culture which exist in many parts of the prefecture

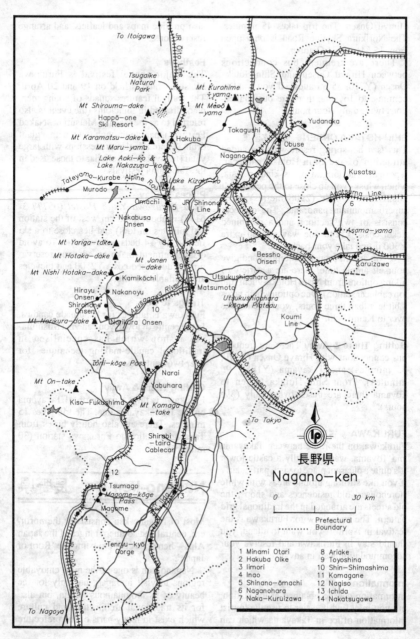

長野県
Nagano-ken

0   30 km

········· Prefectural
         Boundary

1 Minami Otari   8 Ariake
2 Hakuba Oike   9 Toyoshina
3 Iimori   10 Shin-Shimashima
4 Inao   11 Komagane
5 Shinano-ōmachi   12 Nagiso
6 Naganohara   13 Ichida
7 Naka-Kuruizawa   14 Nakatsugawa

and which have been spared the industrial zoning often seen elsewhere in Japan. Agriculture is still a major source of income for this prefecture, but the lack of pollution has also attracted growing numbers of companies from the electronics and precision industries and they are leaving their mark on the landscape.

Included in this prefecture are numerous national parks and quasi-national parks which attract large numbers of campers, hikers, mountaineers and hot-spring aficionados. Several hikes in this prefecture are covered in *Hiking in Japan* by Paul Hunt. Skiers can choose from dozens of resorts during the skiing season which lasts from late December to late March.

Travel in the prefecture relies mainly on the JR lines which run parallel to the Japan Alps from south to north and it is this axis which dictates the itinerary for most visitors. There are two scenic routes which traverse the Japan Alps: one runs from Matsumoto via Kamikōchi to Takayama (Gifu-ken) and the other runs from Shinano-ōmachi via the Kurobe Dam to Tateyama (Toyama-ken). When making travel plans for the mountains, bear in mind that many roads are closed and bus services are stopped due to heavy snow-

fall from mid-October to early May. If possible try and avoid major sights and trails during peak tourist seasons (early May, July and August) when they tend to become clogged with visitors.

JNTO publishes *Japan Nagano Prefecture*, a brochure which provides concise details and mapping.

KARUIZAWA 軽井沢

Karuizawa lies at the foot of Mt Asama-yama and lays claim to being Japan's trendiest summer resort or 'holidayland'. Originally a prosperous post town on the Nakasen-dō Highway linking Tokyo and Kyoto, it was 'discovered' by Archdeacon A C Shaw in 1896 and quickly became a favourite summer retreat for the foreign community.

Since then many affluent urbanites, both foreign and Japanese, have set up summer residences and turned the place into a booming centre for outdoor pursuits such as golf, tennis, horse riding and walking. Naturally, the pursuit of shopping has received due attention in the shape of a 'Ginza' street duplicating all the fashionable boutiques, restaurants, shops and crowds which no city-dweller can do without. In comparison with the other attractions of Nagano-ken, this place gets a low rating.

Orientation & Information

Karuizawa extends over a large area. Kyu-Karuizawa (Old Karuizawa) is the core part which is close to Karuizawa station. Naka-Karuizawa (Central Karuizawa) is several km further east.

There are tourist information offices at JR Karuizawa station (tel 0267-42-2491), Naka-Karuizawa station (tel 0267-45-6050), and on Karuizawa Ginza (tel 0267-42-5538). Office hours are from 9 am to 5 pm or for longer during peak season.

The JNTO brochure, *Karuizawa Heights (MG-046)*, has concise details and maps. The tourist offices can help with queries about day trips, hiking trails, transport and accommodation.

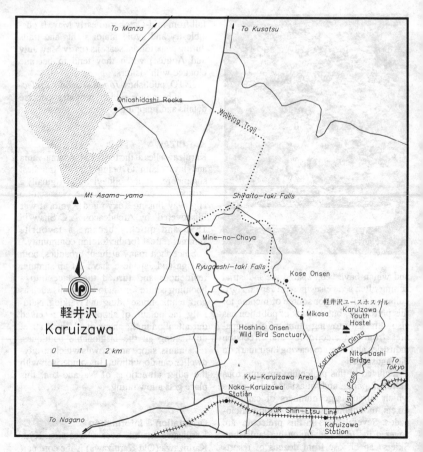

To Manza

To Kusatsu

Onioshidashi Rocks

Walking Trail

Mt Asama-yama

Shiraito-taki Falls

Mine-no-Chaya

Ryugaeshi-taki Falls

Kose Onsen

軽井沢ユースホステル
Karuizawa
Youth
Hostel

Mikasa

Hoshino Onsen
Wild Bird Sanctuary

軽井沢
Karuizawa

0   1   2 km

Kyu-Karuizawa Area

Naka-Karuizawa
Station

Karuizawa Ginza

Usui Pass

Nite-bashi
Bridge

To
Tokyo

JR Shin-Etsu Line

To Nagano

Karuizawa
Station

Mt Asama-yama

Climbing is currently prohibited on this mountain for good reason: it is known to have erupted at least 50 times and has recently become active again.

For a close look, you can visit Onioshidashi Rocks, a region of lava beds on the northern base of the mountain, where there are two gardens with lookout platforms. Both gardens are open from 8 am to 5 pm and entry is Y300.

There are buses from Karuizawa and Naka-Karuizawa stations to the lookouts (55 minutes).

Usui Pass & Lookout

In Kyu-Karuizawa, a walking trail (allow 80 minutes) leads from Nite-bashi Bridge at the end of Karuizawa Ginza to this pass and a lookout with fine views of the surrounding mountains.

Hoshino Onsen Wild Bird Sanctuary

If you are interested in birds, you could stroll for a couple of hours along the bird-watching route. For dedicated 'twitchers' there are two observation huts.

Take a five minute bus ride from Naka-

Karuizawa station to Nishiku-iriguchi. From there it's a 10 minute walk to the sanctuary.

Mine-no-Chaya to Mikasa Hike

If you have four or five hours to spare, this is a pleasant forest amble along a 10 km trail.

Take the bus from Naka-Karuizawa station to Mine-no-chaya (25 minutes). From there a trail leads to Shiraito-taki Falls, continues to Ryugaeshi-taki Falls and then leads via Kose Onsen to Mikasa. The JNTO brochure *Karuizawa Heights (MG-046)* has a map which shows the trail.

Places to Stay

As can be expected for a fancy summer resort, there is no shortage of accommodation ranging from luxury hotels, ryokan, minshuku and pensions to youth hostels and campgrounds. The tourist information office has lists to help with reservations. If you fancy a taste of the high life, you can arrange to rent a villa.

One of the cheapest options is *Karuizawa Youth Hostel* (tel 0267-42-2325) which is on the northern fringe of Kyu-Karuizawa. Take the four minute bus ride from Karuizawa station to Kyu-Karuizawa. Walk to the end of Karuizawa Ginza, cross Nite-bashi Bridge, take the first road on your left, and then follow the first road on your right to the hostel. From Karuizawa Ginza to the hostel takes about 20 minutes on foot.

Getting There & Away

Karuizawa is on the JR Shin-etsu Honsen line and can be reached in two hours from Ueno station in Tokyo. The rail connection with Nagano on the same line takes two hours.

Getting Around

Bus For both local and regional destinations, there is an extensive network of bus services radiating from both Karuizawa and Naka-Karuizawa stations.

Bicycle This is a pleasant way to get around the town. There are bicycle shops in front of Karuizawa station, Naka-Karuizawa station

and in the centre of Kyu-Karuizawa. Rental rates start around Y500 per hour or Y1500 for the day.

BESSHO ONSEN　別所温泉

This town was established around the hot springs during the Heian period. It flourished as an administrative centre during the Kamakura period and this cultural influence encouraged the construction of several temples, notably Anraku-ji Temple which is renowned for its octagonal pagoda, Chūzen-ji Temple and Zenzan-ji Temple. Anraku-ji Temple is 10 minutes on foot from Bessho Onsen station. If you have a couple of hours to spare for a five km rural hike, you can continue east to visit the temples of Chūzen-ji and Zenzan-ji.

If you want an inexpensive place to stay in Bessho Onsen, the *Ueda Mahoroba Youth Hostel* (tel 0268-38-5229) is eight minutes on foot from the station.

To reach Bessho Onsen, take the JR Shin-etsu Honsen line to Ueda then change to the Ueda Railway for the 30 minute ride to Bessho Onsen.

NAGANO　長野

Nagano is the capital of the prefecture, a thriving industrial centre and transport hub. The star attractions are Zenkō-ji Temple (which attracts millions of pilgrims every year) and the superb recreational facilities in the surrounding region.

Information

There's an information office at the station which supplies a leaflet in English with a map. JNTO publishes *Japan Nagano Prefecture*, a brochure which includes concise details and mapping for this city.

Zenkō-ji Temple

The Zenkō-ji Temple is believed to have been founded in the 7th century, but there are several different stories concerning the main image which was, at times, either the subject of disputes, lost, rediscovered and finally, installed again. Although the temple buildings have frequently been destroyed by fire, donations for reconstruction have always been provided by believers throughout Japan. The immense popularity of this temple stems from its liberal acceptance of believers, including women, from all Buddhist sects.

The approach to the temple passes from the Dai-mon Gate up a flight of steps to the Niō-mon Gate and then continues past shops selling religious paraphernalia to the immense San-mon Gate. Straight ahead lies the Hondō (Main Hall) with its inner sanctum.

Once you've entered the inner sanctum, you'll see ticket machines on your right. Buy a ticket (Y300), take off your shoes (and place them in the bag provided) then proceed through the ticket collector's entrance. As you continue to the back of the hall, you'll see a large image of Buddha on your left. At the back of the hall, you descend a flight of steps into complete darkness – the absence of light is intentional and mandatory. Keep groping your way along the right-hand side of the tunnel until you feel something heavy, movable and metallic – the key to salvation! Continue to fumble your way along the tunnel until you see light again.

Although the temple is usually thronged with lines of pilgrims passing through the tunnel, I was completely on my own during my 10 minute fumble for the key to salvation and found the experience quite eerie. There is a strong feeling of religious power in the temple – a feeling that was reinforced when I revisited the illuminated temple precincts later in the evening.
Robert Strauss

The temple is about 1½ km from JR Nagano station, at the northern end of Chūō-dōri Ave. It's not a pleasant walk through the urban snarl and it's much easier to use one of the frequent buses from the station. The 10 minute bus ride to Dai-mon Gate costs Y190. A taxi ride costs about Y700. Another option is to take the Nagano Dentetsu line from the station and get off at the third stop – Zenkōzishita station. From there it's a 10 minute walk westward to the temple.

Festivals

The Gokaichō Festival is held at Zenkō-ji Temple once every seven years from 10 April to 20 May. Millions of pilgrims attend this extravaganza when a sacred image of Buddha, given to the emperor by a Korean king in 552, is put on display – the next is in 1992.

Places to Stay

Kyōju-in Youth Hostel (tel 0262-32-2768) is a temple in a sidestreet a couple of minutes on foot, east of Zenkō-ji Temple. Matronly guidance from the manager ensures an amicable, but strict regime. Keep things amicable by making an advance reservation.

Shukubō (temple lodgings) are available around Zenkō-ji Temple (tel 0262-34-3591). Either call direct and make reservations in Japanese, or ask the tourist office to help.

Hotel New Nagano (tel 0262-27-7200) is a couple of minutes on foot from the station. It's a standard Western-style hotel with prices for single rooms starting around Y5500.

Places to Eat

The *Midori Store*, immediately on your right as you exit the station, has a cluster of inexpensive restaurants on the 5th floor.

Nagano is famed for its soba (buckwheat noodles) and there are many restaurants around Zenkō-ji Temple which make and serve their own soba.

If you walk downhill from Dai-mon Gate along the left-hand side of Chūō-dōri Ave, after about 300 metres you'll see a shop window with a mill grinding flour. This is *Ohtaya*, a restaurant which specialises in homemade soba. Prices for a soba teishoku (set meal) start at around Y600.

Getting There & Away

Trains from Ueno station in Tokyo via the JR Shin-etsu Honsen line take three hours. The JR Shinonoi line connects Nagano with Matsumoto in 55 minutes.

Getting Around

See under the earlier Zenkō-ji Temple

section for information about getting around Nagano.

TOGAKUSHI 戸隠

Togakushi lies north-west of Nagano and is a popular destination for hikers, particularly in late spring and during autumn. In the winter, skiers favour the slopes around Mt Menō-yama and Mt Kurohime-yama. The one hour hike to Togakushi-Okusha Sanctuary includes a pleasant section along a tree-lined approach.

For an inexpensive place to stay, there's *Togakushi Kōgen Yokokura Youth Hostel* (tel 0262-54-2030) which is a couple of minutes from the bus stop.

There are frequent buses from Nagano station to Togakushi which take about an hour for the trip and run via the scenic Togakushi Birdline Highway.

OBUSE 小布施

If you are interested in ukiyo-e, then you should make the short trip to Obuse, north-east of Nagano, and visit the Hokusaikan Museum. This museum displays a collection of ukiyo-e works by the great master of this art form, Hokusai. The display consists of 30 paintings and two festival floats. Admission costs Y400 and it's open from 9 am to 5 pm from April to October. During the rest of the year the opening hours are from 9.30 am to 4.30 pm. Souvenir sets of ukiyo-e postcards are on sale at the ticket counter.

To reach Obuse, take the Nagano Dentetsu line from Nagano (Y600, 20 minutes). The museum is eight minutes on foot from the station. Exit the station building and walk straight ahead, crossing a small intersection, until you reach the main road. Turn right here and continue down the main road past two sets of traffic lights. About 50 metres after the second set of lights, take the sidestreet to your right which leads to the museum.

YUDANAKA 湯田中

This town is famous for its hot springs, particularly those known as Jigokudani Onsen (Hell Valley Hot Springs) which attract monkeys keen to escape the winter chill by having a leisurely immersion.

Uotoshi Ryokan (tel 0269-33-1215), a member of the Japanese Inn Group, charges Y4000 per person per night. The ryokan owner may offer to demonstrate kyūdō (Japanese archery) on request. You can either arrange to be picked up at the station or walk from there to the ryokan in seven minutes.

From Nagano, take the Nagano Dentetsu line for the 40 minute ride to Yudanaka.

KUSATSU 草津

From Yudanaka, there's a scenic route (closed in winter) across Shiga Heights to Kusatsu, one of Japan's most renowned hot-spring resorts, just inside the borders of Gumma-ken.

If you want to stay and sample the waters, there are dozens of ryokan. The *Kusatsu Kōgen Youth Hostel* (tel 0279-88-3894) is about 25 minutes on foot from the centre of town, which is itself clustered round the Yuba hot-spring area. The youth hostel has bicycles for rent.

From Kusatsu, it takes 25 minutes by bus to Naganohara railway station which is on the Agatsuma line.

HAKUBA 白馬

The town of Hakuba is used as a staging point for access to outdoor activities in the nearby mountains. Skiing in the winter and hiking or mountaineering in the summer attract large numbers of visitors. The hiking trails tend to be less clogged during September and October. Even in midsummer you should be properly prepared for hiking over snow-covered terrain. For information in English about Hakuba and the surrounding region, contact the tourist information office in Matsumoto.

Mt Shirouma-dake

The ascent of this mountain is a popular hike, but you should be properly prepared. There are several mountain huts which provide meals and basic accommodation along the trails.

From Hakuba station there are buses

which take 40 minutes to reach Sarakura-sō (Sarakura Mountain Hut) which is the trailhead. From here, you can head west to climb the peak in about six hours and note that there are two huts on this route. If you don't feel like climbing to the peak, you can follow the trail for about 1¾ hours as far as the Daisekkei (Snowy Gorge).

You could also take the trail south-west of Sarakura-sō and do the three hour climb to Yari Onsen. There's an open-air hot spring here with a mountain panorama and another mountain hut, in case you feel compelled to stay.

Tsugaike Natural Park

Tsugaike Natural Park (Tsugaike Shizen-en) lies below Mt Norikura-dake in an alpine marshland. A three hour hiking trail takes in most of the park which is renowned for its alpine flora.

From Hakuba Oike station it takes an hour by bus to reach the park. Between June and late October there's also a bus from Hakuba station which takes about 1½ hours.

Happō-one Ski Resort

This is a busy ski resort in the winter and a popular hiking area in the summer. From Hakuba station, a five minute bus ride takes you to Happō; from there it's an eight minute walk to the cablecar base station. From the top station of the cablecar you can use two more chair lifts, and then hike along a trail for an hour or so to Happō-ike Pond on a ridge below Mt Karamatsu-dake. From this pond you can follow a trail leading to Mt Maru-yama (one hour), continue for 1½ hours to the Karamatsu-dake San-sō (mountain hut) and then climb to the peak of Mt Karamatsu-dake (2696 metres) in about 30 minutes.

Nishina Three Lakes

While travelling south from Hakuba, there are three lakes (Nishina San-ko), which provide scope for short walks. Lake Nakazuna-ko and Lake Aoki-ko are close to Yanaba station and Lake Kizaki-ko is next to Inao station.

Salt Road

In the past, Hakuba lay on the route of the Shio-no-Michi (Salt Road) which was used to carry salt on oxen from the Japan Sea to Matsumoto. Parts of this road still exist and there's a popular three hour hike along one section which starts at Otari Kyodokan (Otari Folklore Museum) – three minutes on foot from Minami Otari station – and continues via Chikuni Suwa Shrine before finishing at Matsuzawa-guchi. From there, it's a 15 minute bus ride to Hakuba Oike station which is two stops north of Hakuba station.

If you are thirsting for more background on salt, you could take the train further down the line to Shinano-ōmachi station and visit the Shio-no-Michi Hakubutsukan (Salt Museum).

Places to Stay

Hajimeno Ippo (tel 0261-75-3527) is a minshuku which is a member of the Toho network. You'll probably need to know some Japanese and it's small, so advance reservations are a necessity. For a bed and two meals, prices vary between Y4300 and Y4600 according to the season. The minshuku is 12 minutes on foot from Iimori station (one stop south of Hakuba) and is usually closed in June and November.

Lavenue Sakae (tel 0261-72-2212) is a minshuku close to Hakuba – seven minutes by bus from Hakuba station. Prices start at Y5500 per person and include two meals.

Getting There & Away

Train Hakuba is on the JR Oito line. From Matsumoto the trip takes about 1½ hours. From Shinano-ōmachi station allow 35 minutes.

If you continue north, the Oito line eventually connects with the JR Hokuriku Honsen line at Itoigawa, which offers the options of heading north-east towards Niigata or south-west to Toyama and Kanazawa.

OMACHI 大町

The city of Omachi has several stations, but

the one to use is called Shinano-ōmachi which has tourist information facilities. The main reason for visiting Omachi is to start or finish the Tateyama-Kurobe Alpine Route which is an expensive but impressive jaunt by various means of transport across the peaks between Nagano-ken and Toyama-ken. If you have time to kill in Omachi whilst waiting for connections, the Shio-no-Michi Hakubutsukan (Salt Museum) is just five minutes on foot from the station.

Places to Stay

An inexpensive place to stay is the *Kizaki-ko Youth Hostel* (tel 0261-2-1820) which is 15 minutes on foot from Inao station (next to Lake Kizaki-ko) three stops north of Shinano-ōmachi station.

Poppo Minshuku (tel 0261-23-1700) is a member of the Toho network. You'll probably need to know some Japanese and it's small, so advance reservations are a necessity. Prices start at Y3800 for a bed and two meals. The minshuku is close to Omachi ski area, several km east of Inao station. You can also take a bus from Shinano-ōmachi station and get off after 15 minutes at the stop for the Omachi ski area. It's closed during June.

Getting There & Away

Local trains on the JR Oito line connect Omachi with Matsumoto in one hour. For connections with Hakuba on the same line allow 35 minutes. The main approach or departure is, of course, via the Tateyama-Kurobe Alpine Route – see the Toyama-ken section of this chapter for more details.

HOTAKA   穂高

Hotaka is a small town with a couple of interesting sights, but it's especially popular with hikers and mountaineers who use it as a base to head into the mountains. Both the station and bicycle rental place (to your right as you exit on the east side of the station) have basic maps of the town. You can either walk around the area or rent a bicycle at Y200 per hour. If you're staying at the youth hostel, you can also rent a bicycle there.

Rokuzan Art Museum

The Rokuzan Art Museum (Rokuzan Bijutsukan) is 10 minutes on foot from the station and worth a visit. On display are sculptures by Rokuzan Ogiwara, a master sculptor whom the Japanese have claimed as the 'Rodin of the Orient'. Admission costs Y400 and it's open from 9 am to 5 pm between April and October but closes an hour earlier during the rest of the year. It is also closed on Mondays except during May and August.

Horseradish Farms

Even if you're not a great fan of green horse-radish, a visit to the Gohōden Wasabi-en (Horseradish Farm) is a good excuse to cycle or walk through fields crisscrossed with canals. The farm is the largest of its kind in Japan. Notice the *dōsojin* (roadside guardians) carved on stones which usually depict a contented couple. The basic map provided at the station or at the adjacent bicycle rental is sufficient for orientation.

Nakabusa Onsen

These remote hot springs are reached by bus (70 minutes) from Ariake station, one stop north of Hotaka. From here, there are several trails for extended mountain hikes.

Mt Jonen-dake

From Toyoshina station, two stops south of Hotaka, it takes 10 minutes by taxi to reach Kitakaidō which is the start of a trail for experienced hikers to climb Mt Jonen-dake (2857 metres) – the ascent takes about eight hours. There are numerous options for mountain hikes extending over several days in the region, but you must be properly prepared.

Places to Stay

Azumino Youth Hostel (tel 0263-82-4265) is four km west of Hotaka station. Bicycles are available for hire.

Shalom Hutte (tel 0263-83-3838) is a member of the Toho network. You'll probably need to know some Japanese and, as it's very small, advance reservations will be necessary. Prices start at Y3000 for B&B. It's 10 minutes by car from Hotaka station, but there's also an infrequent bus from the station which stops nearby. It's closed from 7 January to 15 March.

MATSUMOTO 松本

Matsumoto is worth a visit for its superb castle and as a convenient base for exploration of the Japan Alps.

One curious thing I've noticed at Matsumoto station is the musical delight of the station announcer who intones the name of the station like a muezzin calling from a mosque – 'Matsumoootooo'. The musical infatuation extends from the station to the city centre where every street seems to be lined with loudspeakers piping music at the pedestrians.

Robert Strauss

Information

Matsumoto tourist information office (tel 0263-32-2814) is on your right at the bottom of the steps leading from Matsumoto station's eastern exit. The English-speaking staff can provide maps and leaflets, help with accommodation and give plenty of other travel information. The office is open daily from 9.30 am to 6 pm and 9 am to 5.30 pm during the winter.

JNTO publishes two colour brochures: *Japan Matsumoto* which has good maps; *Japan Matsumoto & the Japan Alps* which provides wider regional coverage and a concise leaflet entitled *Matsumoto & Kamikōchi*. Despite its English title, the *Tourist Map of Matsumoto* is only useful for orientation if you read Japanese.

The main attraction of Matsumoto is the castle which is just 15 minutes on foot from the station.

Matsumoto-jō Castle

Even if you only spend a couple of hours in Matsumoto, make sure you see this splendid castle.

The main attraction in the castle grounds is the original three turreted castle keep (donjon), built circa 1595, in contrasting black and white. Steep steps and ladders lead you up through six storeys. On the lower

floors there are displays of guns, bombs and gadgets to storm castles – complete with technicolour graphics which are useful for those who can't read the Japanese descriptions. At the top, there's a fine view of the mountains. The structure includes slits and slots for archery and firearms, slatted boards to provide basic ventilation (or a means to bombard attackers) and a Tsukimi Yagura or 'Moon-Viewing Pavilion' which was used as a dainty retreat for those lighter moments when the castle was not under attack.

The castle is flood-lit at night and the park adjoining the castle moat is open to the public who stroll around here in the evenings. Opening hours are from 8.30 am to 4.30 pm daily but it is closed from 29 December to 3 January.

Admission to the castle costs Y500. You may buy your ticket at the Japan Folklore Museum – keep your ticket because it is also valid for the museum. The castle is 15 minutes on foot from the station, or, if you take a bus, the stop for the castle is Shiyakusho-mae.

Japan Folklore Museum

To the right of the entrance to the castle grounds is the Nihon Minzoku Shiryōkan (Japan Folklore Museum) which has exhibits on several floors relating to the archaeology, history and folklore of Matsumoto and the surrounding region. One floor is devoted to flora & fauna, including ducks, owls, beetles and extremely anaemic-looking bottled fish. Another floor displays the superb Honda Collection of clocks and watches from the East and West. There are some fascinating timepieces, including a Rolls-Royce clock, a banjo clock and an elephant clock.

Admission to the museum is included in the price of the castle admission ticket (Y500). Opening hours for the museum are the same as those for the castle.

Japan Ukiyo-e Museum

Tourist brochures delicately refer to the 'ultra-modern' architecture of the Nihon Ukiyo-e Hakubutsukan (Japan Ukiyo-e Museum) though some have described it as 'an ugly metallic box'. Anyway, this shouldn't deter you from entering for a look at the Sakai collection of Japanese wood-block prints inside. If you have an interest in ukiyo-e, this museum should be on your list. Several generations of the Sakai family collected over 100,000 prints, paintings, screens and old books – the largest private collection of its kind in the world.

The displays are kept small in number, approximately 100 prints at a time, and frequently changed. This small-scale method of display allows the visitor to sustain interest without being swamped by large numbers of exhibits. English labelling is minimal, but an explanatory leaflet in English is provided, and there's a slide show upstairs which has an English commentary. Ukiyo-e postcards are also on sale. Admission is Y600 and opening hours are from 10 am to 5 pm daily, closed Mondays.

Access to the museum is a real pain unless you take the eight minute taxi ride (Y1000) from the station.

A more complicated route is to go from Matsumoto station on the Matsumoto Dentetsu line and get off at the fourth stop, Oniwa (Y160). Turn left out of the tiny station office and walk about 50 metres up the street to a main road. Bear left again and continue for about 300 metres, passing under an overpass, and then turn right at the road mirror. Carry on down this street to the traffic lights then continue straight across for another 100 metres. The Japan Ukiyo-e Museum is on your left, just beyond the Japan Judicature Museum. (The latter is only really worth a visit (Y500 admission) if you like judicial documents and police weapons and uniforms from the Edo and Meiji periods.) The walk from Oniwa station to the Japan Ukiyo-e Museum takes about 20 minutes.

Matsumoto Folkcraft Museum

The Matsumoto Folkcraft Museum (Matsumoto Mingeikan) has a collection of Japanese folk art with a few items from other parts of Asia and the rest of the world. Admission costs Y200. It's open from 9 am to 5 pm but is closed on Mondays. The museum is 15 minutes by bus from Matsumoto. Take a bus in the direction of Utsukushigahara and get off at the Shimo-Kanai-Mingeikan-guchi bus stop.

Utsukushigahara-kōgen Plateau

From April to mid-November, this alpine plateau is a popular excursion from Matsumoto. Buses stop at Sanjiro Bokujo (Sanjiro Ranch) which offers pleasant walks and the opportunity to see cows in pasture (a source of Japanese fascination) and Utsukushi-gahara-kōgen Bijutsukan (an open-air museum) which charges about Y1000 for admission. It has a bizarre series of 120 sculptures, including 'Venus of Milo in the Castle of Venus' and 'Affection Plaza'. There is also a two day hiking trail to Kirigamine. The bus trip from Matsumoto to the plateau takes 80 minutes.

Alps-kōen Park

For those interested in speed thrills, this park includes the 'Alps Dream Coaster', a 600 metre dry-sleigh run. Each ride costs Y300. There's an exhibition hall with displays on the flora & fauna of the Japan Alps and the history of Japanese mountaineering. There's also a small zoo. The park is 20 minutes by bus from Matsumoto. It's open daily from 9 am to 5 pm but is closed on Mondays.

Suzuki Education Hall

Those interested in the Suzuki method of teaching musical skills to children may want to watch lessons or listen to concerts. The hall (Suzuki Saino Kyoiku Kaikan) is in the centre of the city, about 15 minutes on foot from the station. The tourist information office can help with arrangements.

Festivals

During the Heso Matsuri (Navel Festival), held from 6 to 7 June, revellers demonstrate that Matsumoto is the navel of Japan by prancing through the streets wearing costumes that appropriately reveal their navels.

During August, the Takigi Nō Festival features Nō theatre, by torch light, which is performed outdoors on a stage in the park below the castle. For those interested in phallic festivals, the Dōsojin Festival is held in honour of dōsojin (roadside guardians) on 23 September at Utsukushigahara Onsen. On 3 and 4 October, Asama Onsen celebrates the Asama Hi-Matsuri, a fire festival with torchlit parades which is accompanied by drumming. At the beginning of November, Matsumoto celebrates the Oshiro Matsuri (Matsumoto Castle Festival) which is a cultural jamboree including costume parades, puppet displays and flower shows.

The tourist information office has precise dates and more information.

Places to Stay

The tourist information office at the station has lists of accommodation and can help with reservations. If your main objective is to use Matsumoto as a staging point to visit the Japan Alps, there's no real reason to stay in the town itself unless you get stranded here late in the day. Even if you do, there are several rural places within easy reach of the station.

Asama Onsen Youth Hostel (tel 0263-46-1335) is a bit distant, regimented and drab, but it's cheap. It closes at 9 pm and lights go out punctually at 10 pm.

The hostel manager proudly showed me a glowing letter from the author of another guide book. When I left at the crack of dawn and headed at a smart pace for the bus stop, I soon had the feeling that a mystery person had been pursuing me for several blocks. On turning round, I was confronted by the breathless manager who just wanted to say goodbye!
Robert Strauss

To reach Asama Onsen by bus from the Matsumoto bus terminal, there are two options: either take bus No 6 to Shita Asama or bus No 7 to Dai-ichi Koko-mae. The bus ride takes 20 minutes, and the hostel is then five minutes on foot. The bus ride provides the latest in technology with a video screen at the front of the bus which shows pictures of the next stop (useful at night!) interspersed with bizarre advertising for brooms

and weddings. For a foreign audience this can quickly become confusing!

Utsukushigahara Sanjiro Youth Hostel (tel 0263-31-2021) is on an alpine plateau, nearly an hour's bus ride from Matsumoto. It's closed from December to April. Take the bus bound for Utsukushigahara Bijutsukan and get off after 50 minutes at the Sanjiro bus stop. The hostel is two minutes on foot from there.

Enjoh Bekkan (tel 0263-33-7233) is a member of the Japanese Inn Group. Prices at this ryokan start at Y4800/9000 for singles/doubles – excluding meals. The total bill will include an additional 3% consumption tax, 3% local consumption tax and Y150 spa tax per person. The hot-spring facilities are available day and night. A Western-style breakfast is available for Y800. From Matsumoto, take the 20 minute bus ride to Utsukushigahara Onsen and get off at the terminal. From there it's 300 metres to the ryokan.

Hotel Ikkyu (tel 0263-35-8528), 10 minutes on foot from Matsumoto station, provides functional rooms and meals; prices start around Y5000.

Places to Eat

Matsumoto is renowned for its 'Shinshu soba' (buckwheat noodles) which are either eaten hot or cold (zaru-soba) with wasabi (horseradish) and soy sauce. The local 'okashi' are sponge cakes filled with bean paste. Other specialities more peculiar to the region include raw horsemeat, bee larvae, pond snails and zazamushi (crickets).

The *McDonald's* opposite the station opens early and does a set breakfast for Y470 which you can digest to the sounds of classical music.

The 2nd floor of the station has an arcade with various restaurants offering inexpensive set meals. In the basement of the bus terminal there are also various cheap eateries. The 7th floor (known as *Palette*) of the department store above the bus terminal consists of several restaurants with set meals at around Y800.

Just around the corner from the Asama

Onsen Youth Hostel is a student eatery, the *Tambien Coffee Shop*, which does inexpensive teishoku (set meals).

For natural foods you could try *Naja* (tel 0263-36-9096), a small restaurant offering inexpensive set meals from Y600; note that it's closed on Sundays. It's 15 minutes on foot from the station – the tourist office has a detailed map on which the staff will mark the precise alley.

Things to Buy
The region around Matsumoto is known for Matsumoto Tsumugi (a fabric made from floss silk), Matsumoto Mingei Kagu (furniture and household items mostly made from cherry wood), Matsumoto Shikki (decorative lacquerware), Misuzu Zaiku (basketware), and Azumino-yaki and Asama-yaki (pottery from Azumino and Asama).

Other traditional crafts include the production of Tanabata Ningyō (unique dolls used in the Tanabata Festival), Oshie-bina (padded figurines) and Temari (embroidered balls of silk).

The tourist information office can supply more details on shopping and arrange for visits to a saké brewery, a karate centre or a shop which produces dolls.

Getting There & Away
Air JAS operates flights twice a day between Osaka and Matsumoto. There's a bus service connecting Matsumoto Airport with the city centre in 25 minutes.

Train & Bus From Tokyo (Shinjuku station), there are Azusa limited express services which reach Matsumoto in 2¾ hours. The fastest services on the JR Chūō Honsen line from Nagoya take 2½ hours. From Osaka, the fastest trip takes 3½ hours and usually requires a change of trains at Nagoya. The JR Shinonoi line connects Matsumoto with Nagano in 55 minutes. The trip from Matsumoto to Hakuba on the JR Oito line takes about 1½ hours.

Both train and bus travel have to be combined for the connection between Matsumoto and Kamikōchi. From Matsumoto, take the Matsumoto Dentetsu line to Shin-Shimashima station – don't confuse this with the station called Shimojima. The trip takes 30 minutes and the fare is Y650. From Shin-Shimashima station take the bus via Nakanoyu to Kamikōchi (Y1950, 75 minutes). From Kamikōchi you can continue by bus via Hirayu Onsen to Takayama.

There are regular buses from Tokyo (3¼ hours), Osaka (5½ hours) and Nagoya (3½ hours).

Getting Around
The castle and the city centre are easily covered on foot. Matsumoto bus terminal is diagonally across the main street to the right as you leave the east exit of the station. The terminal is part of a large department store and this means you have to negotiate your way down to the basement before choosing your exit door, climbing the steps, and finding the bus stop back at ground level.

SHIRAHONE ONSEN　白骨温泉
This is a classic hot-spring resort which has retained some traditional inns with open-air, hot-spring baths in a mountain setting. Since it is close to Shin-Shimashima station, it could be visited as part of a trip to Kamikōchi, although you may not want to observe the old saying that you'll avoid a cold for three years if you bathe here for three days. Shirahone Onsen is also popular with hikers as a base for trails around Norikura-kōgen Plateau.

For a place to stay, you could try *Oishi-kan Youth Hostel* (tel 0263-93-2011) which is part of a ryokan, just a couple of minutes on foot from the bus terminal.

From Matsumoto, travel by rail on the Matsumoto Dentetsu line to Shin-Shimashima station, then take the bus (one hour) to Shirahone Onsen. Bus connections are infrequent, so check carefully.

KAMIKOCHI　上高地
Kamikōchi lies in the centre of the northern Japan Alps and has some of the most spec-

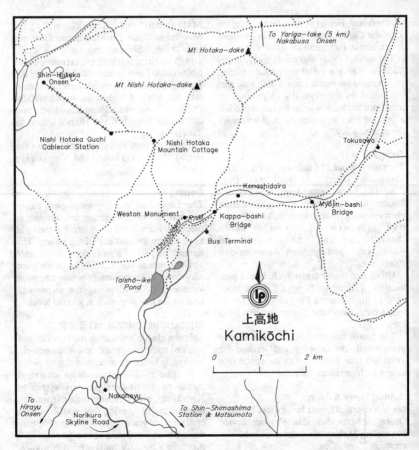

上高地
Kamikōchi

0   1   2 km

tacular scenery in Japan. In the late 19th century, foreigners 'discovered' this mountainous region and coined the term 'Japan Alps'. A British missionary, Reverend Walter Weston, toiled from peak to peak and sparked Japanese interest in mountaineering as a sport. He is now honoured with his own annual festival and Kamikōchi has become a base for strollers, hikers, and climbers. Remember, Kamikōchi is *closed* from November to May.

Despite the thousands of visitors, Kamikōchi has so far resisted the commercial temptation of development that might –

as has happened elsewhere in Japan – destroy the original attractions. Let's hope it stays that way.

Orientation

On a fine day, the final stages of the approach to Kamikōchi on the road from Nakanoyu provide a superb mountain panorama: Taishō-ike Pond on your left; and a series of high peaks ranged in the background. From here, the road continues a short distance to the bus terminal which is the furthest point to which tourist traffic is officially allowed in this valley. A short distance on foot beyond the bus terminal, the Azusa-gawa River is spanned by Kappa-bashi Bridge – at peak season, you probably only need to follow the sound of clicking shutters to find this photogenic subject! From this bridge, you can choose to follow a variety of trails.

Information

Tourist Office At the bus terminal, there is an information office (tel 0263-95-2405) which is open from late April to mid-November only. It's geared mostly to booking accommodation, but also has leaflets and maps. It's preferable to make prior use of the tourist information offices in Takayama or Matsumoto which have English-speaking staff.

Books & Maps JNTO publishes a leaflet entitled *Matsumoto & Kamikochi (MG-042)* which has brief details and a map for Kamikōchi. The tourist offices also have several large maps (covering Kamikōchi, Shirahone Onsen and Norikura Kōgen Plateau) which show mountain trails, average hiking times, mountain huts and lists of tourist facilities. However, they are all in Japanese. *Hiking in Japan* by Paul Hunt covers some trails in the area.

Emergencies Strollers are unlikely to suffer mishap, but those heading off on long hikes or climbs should be properly prepared.

There are medical facilities at the bus terminal and a helicopter is called in for heavy duty search & rescue operations. The mountain huts should be able to pass on messages via telephone or radio links. Some also have basic medical facilities.

Accidents can happen, but in many cases they occur through poor judgement of weather conditions, inadequate clothing and miscalculation of physical fitness. When I was in Kamikōchi, the season had hardly started before a rapid change of weather stranded a climber traversing an ice-bound ridge below Mt Yariga-take. When the weather cleared, a helicopter search revealed he'd dropped over the edge.

Robert Strauss

Planning Your Itinerary

If you want to avoid immense crowds, don't plan to visit between late July and late August, or during the first three weeks in October. Between June and mid-July, there's a rainy season which makes outdoor pursuits depressingly soggy.

It's perfectly feasible to visit Kamikōchi from Matsumoto or Takayama in a day, but you'll miss out on the pleasures of staying in the mountains and the opportunity to take early morning or late evening walks before the crowds appear.

Day Walks If you want to do level walking for short distances, without any climbing, then you should stick to the river valley. A sample three hour walk (round trip) of this kind would proceed east from Kappa-bashi Bridge along the right-hand side of the river to Myōjin-bashi Bridge (45 minutes) and then continue to Tokusawa (45 minutes) before returning. For variety, you could cross to the other side of the river at Myōjin-bashi Bridge.

West of Kappa-bashi Bridge, you can amble along the right-hand side of the river to Weston Monument (15 minutes) or keep to the left-hand side of the river and walk to Taishō-ike Pond (20 minutes). A bridge across the river between Weston Monument and Taishō-ike Pond provides variation for the walk.

Hiking There are dozens of long-distance options for hikers and climbers, varying in duration from a couple of days to a week. *Hiking in Japan* by Paul Hunt provides some ideas. The large Japanese maps of the area show routes and average hiking times between huts, major peaks and landmarks – but you've got to be able to read Japanese or get someone reliable to help decipher them. Favourite trails and climbs (which can mean human traffic jams on trails during peak seasons!) include Mt Yariga-take (3180 metres) and Mt Hotaka-dake (3190 metres) – also known as Mt Okuhotaka-dake. Other more distant popular destinations include

Nakabusa Onsen and Murodō which is on the Tateyama-Kurobe Alpine Route.

If you want to hike between Kamikōchi and Shin-Hotaka Onsen (see Shin-Hotaku under the Gifu-ken section of this chapter), there's a steep trail which crosses the ridge below Mt Nishi Hotaka-dake (2909 metres) at Nishi Hotaka San-sō (Nishi Hotaka Mountain Cottage) and continues to Nishi Hotaka Guchi, the top station of the cablecar for Shin-Hotaka Onsen. The hike takes nearly four hours (because of a steep ascent). Softies might prefer to save an hour of sweat and do the hike in the opposite direction!

Festivals
On the first weekend in June, the climbing season opens with the Weston Festival which honours Walter Weston, the British missionary and alpinist.

Places to Stay
Accommodation is relatively expensive, advance reservations are essential during the peak season and the whole place shuts down from November to May. You'd be well advised to make reservations before arriving in Kamikōchi; the tourist information offices at Takayama and Matsumoto are convenient since they have English-speaking staff.

There is a handful of hotels, mostly around Kappa-bashi Bridge, which is a short walk from the bus terminal. *Gosenjaku Lodge* (tel 0263-95-2221) and *Kamikōchi Nishiitoya San-sō* (tel 0263-95-2206) provide a bed and two meals at prices starting from Y9000. For a bed only, you may get a reduction to around Y6000.

Dotted along the trails and around the mountains are dozens of mountain cottages or mountain huts *(san-sō* or *yama-goya)* which provide two meals and a bed for an average cost of around Y6000. Given the usually lower standards of the food and lodging in such mountain accommodation, these prices are expensive. However, the proprietors have to contend with a short season and difficult access and most hikers are prepared to pay the premium for somewhere out of the cold.

Campgrounds are provided at Konashidaira (about 10 minutes beyond Kappa-bashi Bridge) and Tokusawa (about two hours from Kamikōchi).

The closest youth hostels are at Shirahone Onsen and on Norikura-kōgen Plateau, both within easy reach of Kamikōchi.

Places to Eat
Most visitors either take their meals as part of their accommodation package or bring their own. Several of the hotels around Kappa-bashi Bridge have restaurants. The bus terminal has vending machines and limited facilities for buying food.

Getting There & Away
Bus services for Kamikōchi cease from mid-November to late April and the exact dates can vary. If you plan to travel at the beginning or end of this period, check first with a tourist office or call Japan Travel-Phone (tel 0120-222800, toll free).

The connection between Kamikōchi and Matsumoto involves travel by train and bus. For more details, see the Getting There & Away section for Matsumoto in this chapter.

Between Takayama and Kamikōchi there are frequent bus connections but *only* from April to October. The bus runs via Nakanoyu and you have to change to another bus at Hirayu Onsen. The whole trip takes just over two hours (Y1480).

Between Norikura and Kamikōchi there are buses running via Hirayu Onsen approximately three times a day (two hours). The Norikura Skyline Road is *only* open from 15 May to 31 October.

There is also an infrequent bus service between Kamikōchi and Shirahone Onsen.

Getting Around
Once you've arrived in Kamikōchi, you're restricted to getting around on foot.

The road between Nakanoyu and Kamikōchi is closed to private cars between late April and early May, between late July and late August, from early October for about three weeks and on Sundays and public holidays between late April and early November. Parking charges are also high.

This policy leaves a few inches of space between the bumpers of the buses and taxis. It also gives an idea of the incredible numbers of visitors crammed into these peak visiting times and, conversely, the likelihood of lesser numbers of visitors and more tranquillity on the main trails at other times.

NORIKURA-KOGEN PLATEAU & NORIKURA ONSEN
乗鞍高原、乗鞍温泉

This alpine plateau below Mt Norikura-dake (3026 metres) is popular with hikers and famous for the Norikura Skyline Road (closed from November to May), a scenic bus route which leads to the Tatami-daira bus stop at the foot of the mountain. From there, a trail leads to the peak in about 1½ hours. Norikura Onsen is a hot-spring resort on the plateau and a base for skiing and hiking which is open all year round.

Places to Stay

There is a choice of accommodation including ryokan, pensions and mountain huts. An inexpensive place to stay near the ski lifts is *Norikura Kōgen Youth Hostel* (tel 0263-93-2748).

Getting There & Away

The bus between Norikura and Takayama operates along the Norikura Skyline Road between May and October and usually runs via Hirayu Onsen. The ride takes about 1½ hours.

From July to mid-October, there's a bus between Norikura and Shin-Shimashima station. The trip takes about an hour.

There are infrequent buses between Norikura and Shirahone Onsen and Kamikōchi.

KISO VALLEY REGION　木曽川

A visit to this region is highly recommended if you want to see several small towns with architecture carefully preserved from the Edo period. As a bonus, there's the opportu-

nity to combine your visit to Magome and Tsumago with an easy walk.

The thickly forested Kiso Valley lies in the south-west of Nagano-ken and is surrounded by the Japan Alps. It was traversed by the Nakasen-dō Highway, an old post road which connected Edo (present day Tokyo) with Kyoto and provided business for the post towns en route. With the introduction of new roads and commercial centres to the north, and the later construction of the Chūō railway line, the region was effectively bypassed and the once prosperous towns went into decline. During the '60s, there was a move to preserve the original architecture of the post towns and tourism has become a major source of income.

JNTO publishes a leaflet entitled *Kiso Valley (MG-047)* which has details and maps for the region. Magome was the birthplace of a famous Japanese literary figure, Shimazaki Tōson (1872-1943). If you're interested in reading a novel appropriate to the area, you should find a copy of *Ie* (published in English in 1976 and entitled *The Family*) which draws on his experiences here.

On 23 November, the Fuzoku Emaki Parade is held along the old post road in Tsumago and features a procession by the townsfolk who are dressed in costume from the Edo period.

THE MAGOME TO TSUMAGO WALK
馬篭至妻籠
Magome

Magome is a small post town with rows of traditional houses and post inns (and souvenir shops!) lining a steep street. The tourist information office (tel 0264-59-2336) is a short way up, on the right-hand side of the street. The office is open from 8.30 am to 5 pm and dispenses tourist literature as well as reserving accommodation. Close by is a museum devoted to the life and times of Shimazaki Tōson.

To walk from Magome to Tsumago, continue toiling up the street until the houses eventually give way to a forest path which winds down to the road leading up a steep hill to Magome-kōge Pass. This initial walk from Magome to the pass takes about 45 minutes and is not particularly appealing because you spend most of your time on the road. You can cut out this first section by taking the bus between Magome and Tsumago and getting off after about 12 minutes at the pass.

There's a small shop-cum-teahouse at the top of the pass where the trail leaves the road and takes you down to the right along a pleasant route through the forest. From the teahouse to Tsumago takes just under two hours – allow time to stop at waterfalls or ponder the Latin names thoughtfully labelled on plants beside the trail.

Tsumago

Tsumago is so geared to tourism and well preserved, it feels like an open-air museum. Designated by the government as a protected area for the preservation of traditional buildings, no modern developments such as TV aerials or telephone poles are allowed to mar the picture. The tourist information office (tel 0264-57-3123), open from 8.30 am to 5 pm, is half way down the main street. Tourist literature on Tsumago and maps are available and the staff are happy to make reservations for accommodation.

Just down the street from the tourist information office, you can pop into the post office which sells an interesting assortment of commemorative stamps and postcards depicting life on the old post road.

About 50 metres beyond the post office, on the same side of the street, is the Okuya Kyōdokan Folk Museum which is part of a magnificent house built like a castle. During the Edo period, felling of trees in the Kiso region was strictly controlled. In 1877, following the relaxation of these controls, the owner decided to rebuild using *hinoki* (cypress trees).

If you continue from this house up the main street, the bus terminal can be reached by taking any of the sidestreets on your left.

Baggage Forwarding

As a special service for walkers on the trail between Magome and Tsumago, the tourist offices in both villages offer a baggage-forwarding service. For a nominal fee of Y300 per piece of luggage, you can have your gear forwarded. The deadline for the morning delivery is 9 am and for the afternoon delivery, it's 1 pm. The service operates daily from 20 July to 31 August but is restricted to Saturday, Sunday and national holidays between 1 April and 19 July and throughout September and November.

Places to Stay & Eat

Both tourist information offices specialise in helping visitors find accommodation – telephone inquiries can only be dealt with in Japanese. There are many ryokan and minshuku. Prices for a room and two meals at a ryokan start around Y8000 while minshuku prices for a similar deal start around Y5500. *Minshuku Daikichi* (tel 0264-57-2595) is a friendly place just four minutes on foot from the bus terminal.

Magome and Tsumago have several restaurants on their main streets. The local specialities include 'gohei-mochi' (a rice dumpling on a stick coated with nut sauce) and san-cai (mountain greens) which can be ordered as a set meal (san-cai teishoku) for about Y800.

Getting There & Away

The main railway stations on the JR Chūō line which provide access to Magome and Tsumago are Nakatsugawa station and Nagiso station respectively. Some services do not stop at these stations which are about 12 minutes apart by limited express – check the timetable. By limited express, the trip between Nagoya and Nakatsugawa takes 55 minutes; between Nakatsugawa and Matsumoto it takes 85 minutes. Direct buses also operate between Nagoya and Magome and the trip takes just under two hours.

Buses leave hourly from outside Nakatsugawa station for Magome (30 minutes). There's also an infrequent bus service between Magome and Tsumago (30 minutes). If you decide to start your walk from the Magome-kōge Pass, take this bus and get off at the bus stop at the top of the pass.

From Tsumago, either walk to Nagiso station (1½ hours) or take the bus (nine minutes).

KISO-FUKUSHIMA & MT ONTAKE
木曽福島、御岳

Kiso-Fukushima was an important barrier gate and checkpoint on the old post road. From the station, it takes about 20 minutes on foot to reach several old residences, museums and temples.

Mt Ontake (3063 metres) is an active volcano – entry to the crater area is prohibited. For centuries the mountain has been considered sacred and an important destination for pilgrims.

There are several trails to the summit. One popular trailhead is at Nakanoyu, 80 minutes by bus from Kiso-Fukushima station. From the trailhead, it takes about 3½ hours to hike to the summit. Another trailhead is at Tanohara, 1¾ hours by bus from Kiso-Fukushima station; from here the hike to the summit takes about three hours.

An inexpensive place to stay is *Kiso Ryōjōan Youth Hostel* (tel 0264-23-7716) which is a short bus ride from Kiso-Fukushima station. Take the 25 minute bus ride to Ohara bus terminal – the hostel is three minutes on foot from there and provides a useful base for hiking or sightseeing in the area.

Kiso-Fukushima is on the JR Chūō line and limited expresses run to Nagoya in 1½ hours or to Matsumoto in 40 minutes.

NARAI   奈良井

Narai is another town on the old post road with a high proportion of traditional buildings from the Edo period. It seems less exposed to large-scale tourism than Magome and Tsumago.

Orientation & Information

Narai's main street extends for about one km and lies to your left as you exit the railway station.

The station office is run by local senior citizens who go out of their way to load you down with Japanese brochures.

Things to See

About a five minute walk down the main street, and beneath a blue 'Shiseido' shop sign, is an interesting automat. Put Y100 in the slot and you receive a neatly packaged old Japanese coin or opt for a foreign one if you like.

At intervals along the street there are five old wells which were used by thirsty travellers during the Edo period. The saké brewery is easily recognised by its basket of fronds hanging from the roof above the entrance. Continuing down the street, there are side-streets on the right-hand side which lead to tranquil temples.

Many of the houses lining the main street originally functioned as inns during the heyday of the old post road; most have been turned into museums though some still operate as ryokan. Nakamura-tei House was once a shop specialising in lacquer and is now a museum run by a friendly proprieter. Admission costs Y150.

At the end of the main street, you pass a temple on your left and just beyond is the Narai Minzoku Shiryōkan (Local History Museum) with a cart propped up against the wall. The energetic custodian does her best to guide you round the exhibits with a rapid-fire Japanese commentary and skilful mime to bridge the linguistic gap. On the upper floor, there's a delightful assortment of old implements and paraphernalia such as ice skates attached to geta (clogs), travelling lanterns, money boxes, local combs and bowls for tooth blacking powder, a collapsible candlestick, a large display of festival banners and dolls, straw snow shoes and a belt made out of leather with a design curiously similar to a bicycle chain! On the ground floor, there are antique household gadgets such as a kettle stand, a mochi (rice cake) pestle, a rice winnower and a staircase with drawers integrated into the steps. Admission costs Y150.

If you feel like following the old post road, continue uphill for four km (about 1¾ hours) to Torii-kōge Pass. From there, it's another four km (1¾ hours) to the station at Yabuhara.

Getting There & Away
Narai is on the Chūō line, about 45 minutes by local train from Matsumoto.

TENRYU-KYO GORGE & MT KOMAGA-TAKE
天竜峡、駒ヶ岳

Both Tenryū-kyō Gorge and Mt Komaga-take lie east of the Kiso Valley and are easily reached via the JR Iida line which runs roughly parallel to the Chūō line.

The main sightseeing approach for Tenryū-kyō Gorge is a 1½ hour boat trip down the Tenryū River and through the gorge. Boats leave from the dock close to Ichida station.

Mt Komaga-take (2956 metres) is a popular hiking destination. From Komagane station, a 55 minute bus ride takes you up to the base station of the cablecar at Shirabi-taira. The eight minute cablecar ride whisks you up to Senjōjiki. From there, the hike to the peak takes about 2½ hours.

There are numerous pensions, minshuku and ryokan around the town, and several mountain huts along the trails. If you stay at *Komagane Youth Hostel* (tel 0265-83-3856), you need to take a 15 minute bus ride from the station, then walk for 12 minutes.

Toyama-ken   富山県

The main attractions of this prefecture are two alpine routes across the northern Japan Alps and the mountain villages in the Gokayama region, to the south of the prefecture on the border with Gifu-ken. Toyama serves as a transport hub for trips into the northern Japan Alps and Takaoka is a conve-

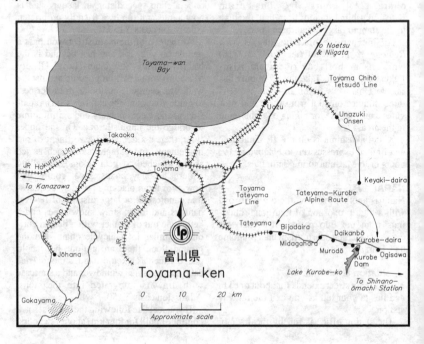

nient staging post for a visit to Noto-hantō Peninsula or to Gokayama.

TOYAMA 富山
This heavily industrialised city has few attractions for the tourist, but it provides a convenient access point for a visit to the northern Japan Alps.

Information
The information office in Toyama station has maps and leaflets.

Places to Stay
If you have to stay in Toyama, there are plenty of business hotels just a few minutes on foot from the station. The *Toyama Station Hotel* (0764-32-4311) is 100 metres down the street on your right as you exit the station. Prices for singles/doubles start at Y4800/10,000.

Toyama Youth Hostel (tel 0764-37-9010) lies way out to the north-east of the city, 45 minutes by bus from the station (bus terminal Nos 7 and 8).

Getting There & Away
Air Daily flights operate between Toyama and Tokyo.

Train The JR Takayama line links Toyama with Takayama in about 1¾ hours. The Toyama Tateyama line links Toyama with Tateyama which is the starting (or finishing) point for those travelling the Tateyama-Kurobe Alpine Route. The Toyama Chihō Tetsudō line links Toyama with Unazuki Onsen which is the starting point for a trip up the Kurobe-kyō Gorge.

The JR Hokuriku line runs west via Takaoka (15 minutes) to Kanazawa (40 minutes), Kyoto (3½ hours) and Osaka (four hours). The same line runs north-east via Naoetsu (75 minutes) to the ferry terminal for Sado-ga-shima Island and Niigata (three hours) to Aomori at the very tip of Northern Honshū.

TATEYAMA-KUROBE ALPINE ROUTE
立山黒部アルペンルート

Information
Before giving more details, it should be stressed that this route is closed from late November to early May. For the precise dates, which vary each year, check with a tourist office or call Japan Travel-Phone (tel 0120-222800, toll free). The season for heavy crowds of visitors lasts between August and late October and reservations are advised for travel in these months.

JNTO publishes a leaflet entitled *Tateyama, Kurobe & Toyama (MG-038)* with details for the route which is divided into nine sections, using various modes of transport, between Toyama and Shinano-ōmachi. The best place to take a break, if only to escape the Mickey Mouse commentaries and enjoy the tremendous scenery, is Murodō. Transport buffs will want to do the lot, but some visitors find a trip from Toyama as far as Murodō is sufficient – and skip the expense of the rest. The following route description runs from Toyama to Shinano-ōmachi, but travel in either direction is possible.

The Route
From Toyama station, take the chug-a-lug Toyama Tateyama line for the 50 minute ride (Y1010) through rural scenery to Tateyama (at an altitude of 454 metres). Very close to Tateyama station is *Sugita Youth Hostel* (tel 0764-82-1754), a convenient place to stay if you are making an early start or a late finish on the route.

From Tateyama, take the seven minute ride (Y620) in the cablecar to Bijodaira. From here, it's a 55 minute ride (Y1620) by bus via the alpine plateau of Midagahara to Murodō (altitude 2450 metres). You can break the trip at Midagahara and do the 15 minute walk to see Tateyama caldera – the largest non-active crater in Japan. The upper part of the plateau is often covered with deep snow until late into the summer – the road is kept clear by piling up the snow to form a virtual tunnel.

At Murodō, the natural beauty of the surroundings has been requited by a monstrous bus terminal to service the annual flood of visitors. From here, there are various options for short hikes. To the north, just 10 minutes away on foot is Mikuriga-ike Pond and 20 minutes further on is Jigokudani (Hell Valley Hot Springs). To the east, you can hike for about two hours – including a very steep final section – to the peak of Mt O-yama (2992 metres) for an astounding panorama. For the keen long-distance hiker, who has several days or even a week to spare, there are fine routes south to Kamikōchi or north to Keyaki-daira in the Kurobe-kyō Gorge.

Continuing on the route from Murodō, there's a 10 minute bus ride to Daikanbō via a tunnel dug through Mt Tate-yama. The ticket for this claustrophobic experience costs the hefty sum of Y2060.

At Daikanbō you can pause to admire the view before taking the cablecar for the seven minute ride (Y1240) to Kurobe-daira where another cablecar whisks you down in five minutes (Y820) to Kurobeko beside the vast Kurobe Dam. For the technically minded, this is the largest formed dome arch dam in Japan (492 metres long and 186 metres high).

At the dam, you can descend to the water for a cruise or climb up to a lookout point before taking the trolley bus from Kurobe Dam to Ogisawa (16 minutes, Y1240). From there, a 40 minute bus ride (Y1400) takes you down to Shinano-ōmachi station – at an altitude of 712 metres.

For the technically minded, the trip from Toyama to Shinano-ōmachi covers 88.7 km and requires just over Y10,000 in transport expenses for an adult.

KUROBE-KYO GORGE & UNAZUKI ONSEN
黒部峡、宇奈月温泉

From Unazuki Onsen, there's a tramcar line which provides a superbly scenic alpine run past hot-spring lodges and continues up the Kurobe-kyō Gorge to Keyaki-daira. Here you can hike to an observation point for a panorama of the northern Japan Alps. Keyaki-daira is also linked with Hakuba and

Murodō by trails which are suitable for seasoned hikers, properly prepared and with several days to spare.

Getting There & Away

Take the train on the Toyama Chihō Tetsudō line from the separate terminus (next to Toyama station) to Unazuki Onsen. The trip from Toyama takes 1½ hours and the fare is Y1550. If you're arriving on the JR Hokuriku line from the north, change to the Toyama Chihō Tetsudō line either at Kurobe (the stations are separate) or at Uozu (the stations are together).

When you arrive at the railway station at Unazuki Onsen, you then have to walk for five minutes to the station for the Kurobe Kyōkoku Tetsudō (tramcar line). The tramcar line only operates from early May to late November and open carriages are used on most runs. The fare from Unazaki Onsen to Keyaki-daira is Y1300 and the trip takes 1½ hours. A surcharge is payable for travel on the daily run with enclosed carriages.

GOKAYAMA 五箇山

This remote region, famous for its gasshō-zukuri architecture, lies next to the southern border of Toyama-ken with Gifu-ken. Details for Gokayama are given in the section on Shōkawa Valley in Gifu-ken.

TAKAOKA 高岡

Takaoka is known for its Daibutsu (Great Buddha) statue and the local skill in producing bells. It's a useful staging post for travellers heading north-west to Noto-hantō Peninsula or south-east to Gokayama and Takayama. There's an information office at the JR Takaoka station and the bus station is on your right as you exit the station.

Just 10 minutes on foot from the station is Zuiryū-ji Temple (tel 0766-22-0179) which also functions as a youth hostel. Take the south exit (minami-guchi) from the station and walk straight ahead for 500 metres to the second intersection, then turn right and continue for 300 metres to the temple.

Getting There & Away

Train The JR Hokuriku line runs south-west via Kanazawa (25 minutes) and Kyoto (3¼ hours) to Osaka. The same line runs east to Toyama (15 minutes) and continues to Aomori at the very tip of northern Honshū.

Bus To visit Gokayama, you can either take a bus from Takaoka station (one hour and 50 minutes to Suganuma, Y1600) or you can take a Jōhana line train from Toyama to Jōhana (50 minutes) and continue from there by bus (one hour to Suganuma). Several of the buses on these services run further, linking Gokayama with Ogimachi and Shirakawa-gō. From Ogimachi you can take buses to Takayama.

Ishikawa-ken　石川県

KANAZAWA　金沢

During the 15th century, Kanazawa came under the control of an autonomous Buddhist government, but this was ousted in 1583 by Maeda Toshiie, head of the powerful Maeda clan, which continued to rule for another three centuries. The wealth acquired from rice production allowed the Maeda to patronise cultural and artistic pursuits – Kanazawa is still one of the key cultural centres in Japan.

During WW II, the absence of military targets in Kanazawa spared the city from destruction and preserved several historical and cultural sites. As the capital of Ishikawa-ken, Kanazawa has its fair share of functional urban architecture. However, it has retained some attractive features from the old city, including the famous Kenroku-en Garden.

The main sights can be seen in a day or so and sidetrips to the Noto-hantō Peninsula and Eihei-ji Temple in Fukui-ken are highly recommended.

Orientation

Kanazawa has an excellent bus service which makes it easy to get to the sights in each district; these areas can then be covered on foot. A short bus ride south of the station is the Katamachi district which is the commercial and business hub of Kanazawa. From there it's a short walk east to Kenroku-en Garden and surrounding sights and museums. The samurai houses in the Nagamachi district are a short walk west from Kōrimbō 109 shopping plaza, a useful orientation point in the centre of Katamachi.

Just south of Katamachi, across the river, is the temple district of Teramachi which can be covered on foot.

On the eastern side of Kanazawa , the hills rising behind Higashiyama district are popular with those who want to escape urban streets for a stroll in the park or to enjoy the view across the city.

Information

For a quick trawl of maps and leaflets, you could use the small tourist information office at the eastern exit of Kanazawa station. The office is open from 8 am to 8 pm and from 8.30 am to 7.30 pm during winter.

For really extensive information on the whole of Ishikawa-ken, there's the excellent Kanazawa tourist information office (tel 0762-22-1500) on the ground floor of Kōrimbō 109 shopping plaza in the centre of the city – thread your way through all the sales counters to find the information desk. This office has English-speaking staff and is open daily from 10 am to 7 pm but closed on Wednesdays. The staff will help with reservation of accommodation and most other queries.

The Society to Introduce Kanazawa to the World (tel 0762-22-7332) specialises in organising home visits, Goodwill Guides, language courses and home stays – if you give advance notice. Visitors with specific cultural interests can arrange to visit workshops, craft centres and theatres through the society.

Kanazawa has a network of groups promoting international exchange and friendship. The Kanazawa International Exchange Foundation (KIEF) (tel 0762-20-2522) functions as an advisory centre for

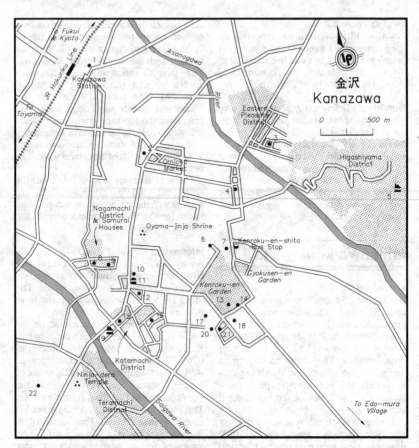

金沢
Kanazawa

0   500 m

Kanazawa

1 Hokutetsu Kankō Bus Company
2 Meitetsu Marukoshi Department Store
3 Yōgetsu Minshuku
4 Terajima Samurai House
5 Kanazawa Youth Hostel
6 Ishikawa-mon Gate
7 Ishikawa Prefectural Museum of
   Handicrafts
8 Nomura Samurai House
9 Yūzen Silk Centre
10 Daiwa Department Store
11 Post Office
12 Kōrimbō 109 Shopping Plaza
13 Seison-kaku Villa
14 Prefectural Museum for Traditional
   Arts & Crafts
15 Murataya Ryokan
16 Nakamuraya Ryokan
17 Ishikawa Prefectural Art Museum
18 Nōgaku Bunka Kaikan
19 Matsui Youth Hostel
20 Nakamura Memorial Museum
21 Honda Museum
22 Kutani Kosen Gama Kiln

Kanazawa

1　兆鉄観光バス
2　名鉄丸越デパート
3　民宿湯月
4　寺島応養邸
5　金沢ユースホステル
6　石川門
7　石川県立伝統産業工芸館
8　野村家
9　彩筆庵シルクセンタ
10　大和デパート
11　郵便局
12　Kōrimbō 109 Shopping Plaza
13　成巽閣
14　県立美術工芸館
15　むらたや旅館
16　中村旅館
17　石川県美術館
18　能楽文化会館
19　三井ユースホステル
20　中村記念美術館
21　木多蔵品館
22　九谷光仙窯

Post Office The most convenient post office is in Kōrimbō, close to Kōrimbō 109 shopping plaza. This post office is open from Monday to Friday from 9 am to 6 pm.

Bookshops For a limited selection of foreign books, you can try Maruzen or Kinokuniya which are both in the centre of the city, near Kōrimbō 109 shopping plaza.

Walking Tour

A suggested walking route for a full day of sightseeing could start with a 10 minute bus ride (for example, bus Nos 20, 21 or 22) from the station to the Kōrimbō bus stop.

From there it's a 10 minute walk to the samurai houses in Nagamachi. You can then return to Kōrimbō and walk east for 15 minutes to Kenroku-en Garden and Seison-kaku Villa. A five minute walk south of the garden is the Ishikawa Prefectural Art Museum which is also close to the Honda Museum. From here you can continue uphill for five minutes to the Ishikawa Prefectural Museum for Traditional Arts & Crafts then follow the road east down the hill to the Ishikawa Prefectural Museum of Handicrafts. Close by is the Kenroku-en-shita bus stop – bus Nos 11 or 12 will take you back to the station.

Nagamachi Samurai Houses

The Nagamachi district, once inhabited by samurai, has retained a few of its winding streets and tile-roofed mud walls. Nomura Samurai House, though partly transplanted from outside Kanazawa, is worth a visit for its decorative garden. Admission costs Y400 and it's open from 8.30 am to 5 pm.

Close by is Saihitsu-an (Yūzen Silk Centre) where you can see the silk-dyeing process. Admission costs Y500 and includes an English leaflet, tea and a sweet. It's open from 9 am to 12 noon and from 1 to 4.30 pm but is closed on Thursdays.

Oyama-jinja Shrine

This shrine is not worth a special trip, but have a look if you are in the centre of the city and have time to spare. The shrine was

foreigners and organises a variety of services and activities which are of interest to the long-term or short-term visitor. KIEF has published a detailed guide book to living in Kanazawa entitled *Hello Kanazawa* (Y900) which is full of explanations and practical tips for foreigners.

JNTO publishes a leaflet entitled *Kanazawa (MG-043)* which has concise information on sights, maps, timetables and lists of places to stay for Kanazawa.

The Kanazawa Tourist Association has published *Kanazawa: The Other Side of Japan* by Ruth Stevens. It's rather outdated now but still provides immense and affectionate detail for Kanazawa and the surrounding area. It's available in bookstores in Tokyo, Kyoto and Osaka as well as in Kanazawa.

dedicated to Maeda Toshiie in 1599. In the Meiji period, a couple of Dutchmen helped to design the three storeyed gate with a stained-glass window on the top storey.

Kenroku-en Garden

Usually billed as the star attraction of Kanazawa, Kenroku-en Garden is also ranked by Japanese as one of their three top gardens – the other two are Kairaku-en in Mito and Kōraku-en in Okayama.

The name of the garden (*kenroku* translates as 'combined six') refers to a renowned Chinese garden from the Sung dynasty which required six attributes for perfection: seclusion, spaciousness, artificiality, antiquity, abundant water and broad views. In its original form, Kenroku-en formed the outer garden of Kanazawa Castle, but from the 17th century onwards it was enlarged until it reached completion in the early 19th century. The garden was opened to the public in 1871.

Using the explanatory leaflet and map which are provided at the entrance booth, you can spend a couple of hours wandering around the grounds (100.74 hectares!) admiring the paths, bridges, trees (5000), shrubs (3500), waterfalls and stone lanterns. Each season brings with it some special botanical attraction: winter, for example, sees the use of *yuki-tsuri*, intricate umbrella-like structures which protect the trees from snow damage. The exits are clearly marked on the map.

Kenroku-en is certainly attractive, but its fame has attracted enormous crowds which, by sheer weight of numbers, make severe inroads into the intimacy and enjoyment of the place as a garden. To escape the rush hours, try and visit early in the morning or late in the afternoon.

Admission costs Y300 and it's open daily from 6.30 am to 6 pm. From 16 October to 15 March opening hours are from 8 am to 4.30 pm.

Seison-kaku Villa

This retirement villa, on the south-eastern edge of Kenroku-en Garden, was built in 1863 by a Maeda lord for his mother. A visit to this stylish residence with its elegant chambers and furnishings is recommended. Admission costs Y500 and includes a detailed explanatory leaflet in English. It's open daily from 8.30 am to 4.30 pm, closed Wednesdays.

Ishikawa Prefectural Art Museum

This museum (Ishikawa Kenritsu Bijutsukan) specialises in antique exhibits of traditional arts with special emphasis on Kutani ceramics, Japanese painting, Yūzen fabrics and costumes. The English caption for one art exhibit: 'Awake from a Dream by Honking' sounds like advice for a drowsy motorist! The exhibits are rotated throughout the year. Admission costs Y350 but more is charged for special exhibitions. It's open from 9.30 am to 5 pm.

Nakamura Memorial Museum

The Nakamura Memorial Museum (Nakamura Kinen Bijutsukan) is reached via a narrow flight of steps below the Ishikawa Prefectural Art Museum. The museum displays the collection of a wealthy saké brewer, Nakamura Eishun. Exhibits are changed throughout the year, but usually include tea-ceremony utensils, calligraphy and traditional crafts. Admission costs Y300 and includes green tea and a Japanese titbit. It's open from 9 am to 4.30 pm daily except Tuesdays.

Honda Museum

Members of the Honda family were chief retainers to the Maeda clan and this museum (Honda Zōhinkan) exhibits the family collection of armour, household utensils, and works of art. One cogent reason to visit this museum is the detailed, descriptive catalogue in English; the bullet-proof coat and the family vase are particularly interesting.

Admission costs Y500. It's open from 9 am to 5 pm but is closed on Thursdays between November and February. A sprightly, elderly guide sometimes conducts free tours in English.

Nō Theatre

Regular Nō performances are held at the Nō Theatre (Nōgaku Bunka Kaikan) at 12.30 pm on the first Sunday of each month, on the second Sunday in April and on 15 January.

Museum for Traditional Arts & Crafts

This museum (Dentō Sangyō Kōgeikan) is an interesting shop window for the crafts of the region, ranging from ceramics, lacquerware and woodcarving to metalwork and the extraordinary precision of gold leaf techniques. Nothing is on sale, but prices are indicated for individual exhibits. For your own Buddhist altar, you'll need to shell out nearly three million yen but by contrast, the lacquered phone is a snip at Y88,000. Of course, for the person with everything, there's always the gold-plated phone. Anglers will be entranced by the fly-tying exhibit where the heads of artificial flies get the gold leaf treatment.

Admission costs Y250 and a detailed leaflet is provided in English. It's open daily from 9 am to 5 pm but closed every Thursday (December to March) and every third Thursday between April and November.

Gyokusen-en Garden

If you want to visit a delightful garden with more intimacy and less crowds than Kenroku-en, Gyokusen-en is definitely recommended. The garden dates from the Edo period and consists of several gardens rising on two levels up a steep slope. You can take tea here for an additional Y400.

Admission costs Y400 and includes a very detailed leaflet in English. The garden is open from 9 am to 4 pm but is closed in the winter.

Ishikawa Prefectural Museum of Handicraft

This museum (Kankō Bussankan) is a commercially oriented establishment with only the third floor functioning as a museum, which is, in fact, called the Hall of Traditional Arts & Crafts. Here you can observe demonstrations of the processes for making Japanese cakes, lacquerware, gold leaf, pottery and Yūzen silk. It's worth a visit as a change from gawping at static exhibits in a museum. Admission to the hall costs Y200 and includes an English leaflet about the handicrafts. It's open from 9 am to 6 pm but opens an hour later between 21 November and 20 March. It's also closed on Thursdays.

Ishikawa-mon Gate

This elegant gate with its lead tiles (useful if ammunition ran short!) is all that's left of Kanazawa Castle which suffered many fires.

Terajima Samurai House

This is the residence of a middle-class retainer of the Maeda and was built in 1770. There's a peaceful garden and tea is available for Y400 in the tea-ceremony room. Admission costs Y300 and includes a detailed pamphlet in English. It's open from 9 am to 5 pm but is closed on Thursdays.

Eastern Pleasure District

If you follow the main road north from Terajima Samurai House and cross the Asanogawa River, you reach the Eastern Pleasure District which was established early in the last century as a centre for geisha to entertain opulent patrons. There are several streets still preserved with the slatted, wooden facades of the geisha houses.

A former geisha house which is open to the public is Shima. Admission (including the enclosed garden) costs Y300. It's open from 8.30 am to 4.30 pm but is closed on Mondays. Yōgetsu is another former geisha house in this district which now functions as a minshuku – see Places to Stay.

Teramachi District

Teramachi stretches beside the Saigawa River, just south of the city centre. This old neighbourhood was established as a first line of defence and still contains dozens of temples and narrow backstreets: a good place for a peaceful stroll.

Ninja-dera Temple, also known as Myōryū-ji Temple, is about five minutes on foot from the river. Completed in 1643, this temple resembles a labyrinthine fortress with dozens of stairways, corridors, secret chambers, concealed tunnels and trick doors – the Maeda lords did not want to be caught napping! The popular name of Ninja-dera refers to the temple's connection with *ninjutsu* (the art of stealth) and the *ninja* (practitioners of the art). Although the gadgetry is mildly interesting, mandatory reservation and a tour (conducted in Japanese) can make the visit unduly time-consuming.

Admission costs Y500 and is by reservation (tel 0762-41-2877) only. It's open from 9 am to 4.30 pm but closes half an hour earlier between December and February. The entrance ticket enjoins visitors to 'Refrain from amoking in the precincts'. For more information on the activities of the elusive ninja see the Iga-Ueno section of the Kinki District chapter.

Those interested in the production of Kutani ceramics might like to visit the nearby Kutani Kosen Gama Kiln which is open to the public. There is no charge for admission and it's open daily from 8.30 am to 12 noon and from 1 to 5 pm. The kiln is in an area of the city that was once known as the Western Pleasure District, a precinct which had similar functions to its counterpart in the eastern part of the city.

Edo-mura Village

This is an open-air museum of transposed buildings dating from the Edo period – it's a long way from Kanazawa and you should allow at least half a day for your visit.

There are 20 buildings on display, including an inn, farmhouses, a samurai mansion and a pawnshop. One of the farmhouses has a tiny room above the entrance which housed the servants and at night the stairs were removed to stop them doing a flit!

Minibuses shuttle between Edo-mura Village and Danpūen which is a similar but smaller open-air museum concentrating on crafts.

Admission to the village costs a hefty Y1100 and the ticket includes free transport to and from Danpūen. An explanatory English leaflet and map are provided. The

village is open daily from 8 am to 6 pm between April and October but closes an hour earlier between November and March.

To reach Edo-mura Village, take bus No 12 (Y520, 45 minutes) from Kanazawa station. The bus goes via Yuwaku Onsen and climbs uphill for a few more minutes before dropping you off at the palatial Hakuunrō Hotel. Walk for about 10 minutes up the hill in front of the hotel and then climb the steps on the left to reach the entrance office for Edo-mura. The minibus for Danpūen leaves from this office every 20 minutes.

Markets

Omichō market lies on the main bus route between the station and the Kōrimbō area in the centre of the city. The most convenient bus stop for the market is Musashi-ga-tsuji. Omichō market is a warren of several hundred shops many of which specialise in seafood. Take a break from sightseeing and just wander around here to watch market life.

Festivals

Kagatobi Dezomeshiki
6 January. Scantily clad firemen brave the cold, imbibe saké, and demonstrate ancient firefighting skills on ladders.

Dekumawashi (Puppet Theatre Festival)
10 to 16 February. Displays of Jōruri, a traditional form of puppet theatre, are held in the evening at the village of Oguchi.

Asano-gawa Enyūkai
Early April. Performances of traditional Japanese dance and music are held on the banks of the Asonagawa River.

Hyakumangoku Matsuri
13 to 15 June. This is the main annual festival in Kanazawa and the highlight is a huge parade of townsfolk dressed in costumes from the 16th century. Other events include Takigi Nō (torchlit performances of Nō drama), Tōrō Nagashi (lanterns floated down the river at dusk) and a special tea ceremony at Kenroku-en Garden.

Bon Odori (Folk Dancing Festival)
Mid-August. Folk dancing festivals are held in several places including the Futamata area, and the village of Hatta where the festival is called Sakata Odori.

Places to Stay

The tourist information office in the 109

Kōrimbō shopping plaza can help with reservations for accommodation.

Katamachi District *Matsui Youth Hostel* (tel 0762-21-0275) is small and relaxed. The regulations exhort you to 'be good frieds...be cosmopolites despite differences...and remember you are cosmopolitants'. The hostel closes at 10 pm.

From the station, take a bus from terminal Nos 7, 8 or 9 for the 14 minute ride to the city and get off at the Katamachi kingeki-mae bus stop. Walk a few metres back up the street to a large intersection. Turn right here then take the second sidestreet on your right. The hostel is half way down this street.

Murataya Ryokan (tel 0762-63-0455) is a member of the Japanese Inn Group. The helpful manageress is used to dealing with foreigners' queries on things to see and do in Kanazawa. Prices for singles/doubles start at Y4200/8000; triples cost from Y10,500. Western breakfast costs Y400. To find this ryokan, follow the directions for Matsui Youth Hostel. Having turned right at the large intersection, take the first sidestreet on your left and continue about 20 metres until you see the ryokan sign on your left.

Nakamuraya Ryokan (tel 0762-31-1806) is another popular ryokan with prices for a single starting at Y4000 including breakfast.

To reach Nakamuraya ryokan, follow the directions for Matsui Youth Hostel. Having turned right at the large intersection, take the second sidestreet on your left, then continue about 20 metres to another junction. Turn right here and take the next street on your left and cross the bridge over a stream. The ryokan is about 10 metres further down the street on your right.

Higashiyama District *Yōgetsu Minshuku* (tel 0762-52-0497) is a geisha house dating from the previous century. Prices start around Y5500 per person including two meals. The minshuku is close to Enkō-ji Temple, about 20 minutes on foot from the station; or 10 minutes by bus.

Kanazawa Youth Hostel (tel 0762-52-3414) is way up in the hills to the east of the city and commands a superb position. Unfortunately, this also means that access to the hostel is mighty inconvenient, unless you have your own transport – bus services are infrequent.

A dorm bed costs Y2100, but foreigner hostellers are given a Y200 discount. Private rooms are a good deal at Y3500 per person. The doors close at 10 pm and loudspeakers marshal the slumbering troops for reveille in the morning. During peak season, the hostel takes members only. Bicycle rental is available. If you hear early morning whoops and shrieks, they are probably issuing from the zoo in 'Kiddyland' – an amusement park/aquarium opposite the hostel.

To reach the hostel from the station, take bus No 90 for Utatsuyama-kōen Park and get off after about 25 minutes at the Suizokukan-mae bus stop which is virtually opposite the hostel.

Places to Eat

The 4th floor of Kōrimbō 109 shopping plaza has a variety of inexpensive places to eat. Similar restaurants are found on the upper floors of Daiwa department store, diagonally opposite Kōrimbō 109 plaza, and in Meitetsu Marukoshi department store which is on the major intersection next to Omichō market. Connoisseurs consider the sushi restaurants in this market serve the freshest and best sushi in town.

The *Takanoha* restaurant on the 2nd floor of the Ishikawa Prefectural Museum of Handicrafts does standard set meals at prices starting around Y1400 and set meals which include local specialities at prices starting around Y2000.

A short walk from the Kanazawa Youth Hostel are a couple of chic and pricey places to eat, such as the quaintly named *Birds House*.

My favourite breakfast place – for people, not décor – is in the station. Take the stairs below the UCC coffee shop sign at the side of the main concourse and squeeze onto a stool at the counter of this minuscule coffee shop which is run by a friendly couple. The set breakfast costs Y420. I met a few of the regulars: a blind man accompanied by his guide dog; and a secretary, bound for the office, stopping for a quick shot of caffeine to clear her head after a night's carousing!

Robert Strauss

Things to Buy

Kanazawa is a centre for traditional crafts such as Kaga Yūzen (silk dyeing), Kutani-yaki (colourful ceramics), Kaga maki-e (lacquerware with raised lacquer design work), woodcarving using *kiri* paulownia and *kinpaku* (gold leaf) – a tiny gold leaf in your tea is meant to be good for rheumatism.

For a quick view or purchase of these crafts, you can visit Kankō Bussankan (Ishikawa Prefectural Museum of Handicrafts). The tourist information office can set up visits to workshops or direct you to museums of specific interest such as the one close to the station which specialises in the production of gold leaf.

Getting There & Away

Air Kanazawa Airport (Komatsu Kūkō) has air connections with Tokyo, Sendai, Fukuoka and Sapporo. There's also an international connection with Seoul (Korea).

Train Kanazawa is linked to south-western destinations by the JR Hokuriku line: Fukui (55 minutes), Kyoto (2¾ hours) and Osaka (3¼ hours). The same line runs north-east to Takaoka (45 minutes), Toyama (one hour), Naoetsu (2¼ hours) and Niigata (3¾ hours). To travel to Takayama (2½ hours), you need to change to the JR Takayama line at Toyama.

The JR Nanao line connects Kanazawa with Wajima (Noto-hantō Peninsula) in 2¼ hours.

Bus There are regular bus services between Kanazawa and Tokyo, Kyoto and Nagoya. The Meitetsu bus service between Kanazawa and Nagoya operates from July to early November via Gokayama and Shirakawa-gō.

Getting Around

To/From the Airport A bus service connects Kanazawa Airport (Komatsu Kūkō) with Kanazawa station in 55 minutes (Y1000).

Bus The bus network is extensive and fares start at Y170. From the station, bus Nos 10 and 11 will take you to the Kenroku-en-shita bus stop, a useful point if you just want to visit the main sights around Kenroku-en Garden. To ride from the station to the centre of the city, you can choose from several buses, including bus Nos 20, 21 and 30, and get off at the Kōrimbō bus stop.

The office of the Hokutetsu Kankō bus company outside the station sells kaisūken (discount tickets) and teikiken (discount commuter passes) if you want to travel frequently by bus for a day or more.

Bicycle Rental is available (Y1000 for the day or Y600 for four hours) at the station, but the hills and the urban traffic snarls aren't particularly inviting. The Kanazawa Youth Hostel also has bicycles for rent (cheaper prices), but it's quite a puff returning up the hill. The tourist information office in Kōrimbō 109 has details of bicycle rental places in the city centre.

Noto-hantō Peninsula
能登半島

For an enjoyable combination of rugged seascapes, traditional rural life and a light diet of cultural sights, this peninsula is highly recommended. Noto-hantō is easily accessible from Kanazawa, Takaoka or Toyama. The wild, unsheltered western side of the peninsula contrasts with the calm and indented coastline of the eastern side.

Information

Kanazawa tourist information office (tel 0762-22-1500) on the ground floor of Kōrimbō 109 can help reserve accommodation and deal with most other queries regarding the Noto-hantō Peninsula.

The Society to Introduce Kanazawa to the

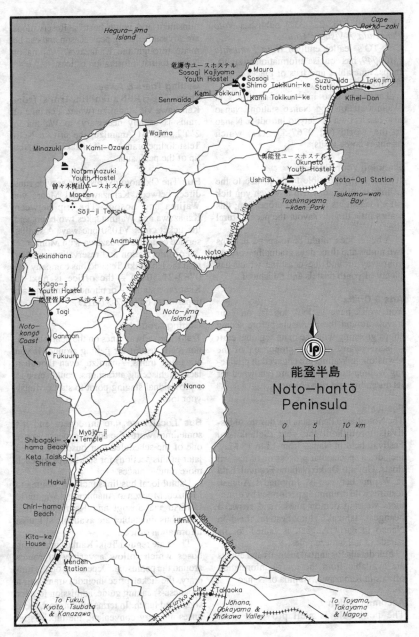

Cape
Rokkō-zaki

Hegura-jima
Island

竜護寺ユースホステル
Sosogi Kajiyama
Youth Hostel

Maura
Sosogi
Shimo Tokikuni-ke

Suzu-Iida
Station

Takojima

Kami Tokikuni
Kami Tokikuni-ke

Kihei-Don

Senmaida

Wajima

奥能登ユースホステル
Okunoto
Youth Hostel

Minazuki

Kami-Ōzawa

Notominazuki
Youth Hostel
曽々木梶山ユースホステル
Monzen

Sōji-ji Temple

Ushitsu

Noto-Ogi Station

Toshimayama
-kōen Park

Tsukumo-wan
Bay

Anamizu

Noto

Sekinohana

Ryūgo-ji
Youth Hostel
能登管見ユースホステル

Togi

Noto-jima Island

Noto-
kongō
Coast

Ganmon

Fukuura

Nanao

能登半島
Noto-hantō
Peninsula

0   5   10 km

Myōjō-ji
Temple

Shibagaki-
hama Beach

Keta Taisha
Shrine

Hakui

Chiri-hama
Beach

Kita-ke
House

Menden
Station

Himi

Jōhana
Line

To Fukui,
Kyoto, Tsubata
& Kanazawa

Line Takaoka

Hokuriku Line

Jōhana,
Gokayama &
Shōkawa Valley

To Toyama,
Takayama
& Nagoya

World (tel 0762-22-7332) publishes *Noto Peninsula, A Visitors' Guide.*

JNTO's leaflet entitled *Noto Peninsula (MG-049)* has concise information on sights, maps, timetables and lists of places to stay for the Noto-hantō Peninsula.

There are also information offices at Wajima station and Nanao station; Nanao also has its own Society to Introduce Nanao to the World (tel 0767-53-1111) which arranges home visits.

Planning Your Itinerary

It's not really possible to do justice to the peninsula with a day trip in which you tick off all the sights in hurried procession; this leaves little time to savour the pace of rural life.

A better idea might be to spend perhaps two nights and three days gradually working your way around the coastline which has plenty of youth hostels and minshuku.

Arts & Crafts

You won't have to look too far on your travels around the peninsula before seeing shops groaning with the main regional craft – lacquerware. A large proportion of the townsfolk in Wajima are engaged in producing Wajima-nuri, lacquerware renowned for its durability and rich colours.

Festivals

The Noto-hantō Peninsula has dozens of festivals throughout the year. Seihaku-sai Festival, held in Nanao from 13 to 15 May, includes a spectacular procession of festival floats. Gojinjō Daikō Nabune Festival, held in Wajima between 31 July and 1 August, features wild drumming performed by drummers wearing demon masks and seaweed headgear. Ishizaki Hoto Festival, held in Nanao in early August, is famed for its parade of tall lantern poles.

Full details for annual festivals and events are available from the tourist information offices in Kanazawa, Wajima or Nanao.

Accommodation

The peninsula is well provided with minshuku and youth hostels. Reservations are advisable during peak season and can be made through the Kanazawa, Wajima or Nanao tourist information offices.

Getting There & Away

Train The JR Nanao line runs from Kanazawa via Anamizu (where a change of trains is usually necessary) to Wajima in 2¼ hours. At Anamizu, the private Noto Tetsudō line branches off to Takojima on the tip of the peninsula.

Bus The Okunoto express bus service runs direct between Kanazawa and Maura via Wajima and Sosogi. The trip between Kanazawa and Wajima takes two hours and the ticket costs Y1050 one way. A similar service connects Kanazawa with Monzen.

For information and reservations, call or visit the Hokuriku Tetsudō bus company (tel 0762-21-5011) – the office is next to Kanazawa station – or phone the appropriate department on 0762-37-8111.

Getting Around

Train The railway lines on the peninsula are not really useful for getting around. If you are using trains, Anamizu, even though it lacks sightseeing attractions, could serve as a provisional staging point to start or finish your tour.

Bus Local buses are infrequent and it's sometimes worth the added expense to use one of the scheduled tour buses (described later in this section) for short hops to reach more remote places.

Useful local bus lines include: Wajima to Monzen, Monzen to Anamizu and Wajima to Ushitsu via Sosogi and Kami Tokikuni. Local bus timetables are available at tourist information offices.

There are regular Teiki Kankō sightseeing buses which follow a variety of routes around the peninsula. Depending on the itinerary, the ticket price includes transport, a Japanese-speaking guide, admission fees for sights and lunch. In terms of transport, these buses are very convenient, the lunch is no great shakes and any pauses in the rapid-fire commentary from the guide are filled with recorded sounds ranging from jungle noises to songs and breaking waves. Ear plugs are advised.

There are many permutations, but most of the itineraries use Kanazawa or Wajima as a starting or finishing point. Some tours operate throughout the year, others only operate between March and November.

For example, by placing two itineraries back to back, you could construct your own two day tour with an overnight in Wajima (make your own reservation for accommodation). On the first day you could take the bus tour which goes from Kanazawa via Chiri-hama Beach, Myōjō-ji Temple, and Ganmon to Wajima. The bus leaves Kanazawa station at 9.10 am and arrives at Wajima station at 3.25 pm and the ticket costs Y5050. The next day you could take the bus tour (Y5350) which goes from Wajima station (9.20 am) via Kami Tokikuni and Cape Rokkō-zaki to Tsukumo-wan Bay (4.10 pm). From there, you can return by train to Kanazawa.

The advantage of these tours is that you get to see all the major sights including those which are in more remote places. It's also worth noting that you can hop on or off the buses en route: a good way to shorten your exposure to the 'package'. A distinct disadvantage, apart from the cost and haste, is that you may well find the 'guided tourist missile' approach extremely wearing on the nerves.

Bicycle The peninsula should appeal to cyclists as its coastal terrain is flat and inland there's only an occasional gradient. The campgrounds and youth hostels are spread out at convenient intervals. The tourist information offices (Kanazawa, Wajima, Nanao) have a very good map (in Japanese) entitled *Noto Hantō Rōdo Matsupu* which covers the area on a scale of 1:160,000.

KITA-KE HOUSE 喜多家
This residence of the Kita, a wealthy family which once administered over 100 villages in the region, is on the coast, about 30

minutes by bus north of Kanazawa. Kita-ke is built in local farmhouse style, and inside there are displays of weapons, ceramics, farming tools, folk art and documents. There is also a fine garden.

Admission costs Y700 and includes a detailed leaflet in English. It's open from 8.30 am to 5 pm. To get there by train, take the JR Nanao line to Menden station then walk for 20 minutes.

CHIRI-HAMA BEACH 千里浜
This long beach has become an attraction for motorists and at times it resembles a sandy motorway with droves of buses, motorbikes and cars roaring past the breakers. Without the motorised invasion the beach would be attractive, but the hyperactive circus leaves behind the usual detritus of plastic, fast-food wrappings and dead sea birds.

An ugly tourist office sells souvenirs and medicines such as dried snake and what looked like small turtles. Outside, there's the pungent smell of fried squid and a stone plaque where chic bikers and their metal steeds queue up for a standard photo against the beach backdrop.

KETA TAISHA SHRINE けた大社
This shrine, set in a wooded grove close to the sea, is believed to have been founded in the 8th century, but the architectural style of the present building dates from the 17th century. The shrine is open from 8.30 am to 4.30 pm and is 10 minutes by bus from Hakui station. Admission costs Y100.

MYOJO-JI TEMPLE 妙成寺
Myōjō-ji was founded in 1294 by Nichijō, a disciple of Nichiren, as the main temple of the Myōjō-ji school of Nichiren Buddhism. The temple complex is composed of several buildings including the strikingly elegant *gojū-no-tō* (five storeyed pagoda) which has just undergone extensive renovation. The grounds are relatively quiet – just one loudspeaker grinding out its message – and the structures have a pleasantly unembellished, weather-beaten feel.

Admission costs Y350 and includes an

excellent English leaflet with map. It's open from 8 am to 5 pm. To reach the temple from Hakui station, take the bus for 15 minutes and then walk for 15 minutes.

From the temple, it takes about 25 minutes on foot to reach Shibagaki-hama Beach with its small fishing community.

NOTO-KONGO COAST 能登金剛

The stretch of rocky shoreline known as Noto-kongō extends for about 16 km between Fukuura and Sekinohana and includes a variety of rock formations such as Ganmon which resembles a large gate. Buses from Hakui station to Noto-kongō take just under an hour. There are pleasant sea views as the road winds along the coast passing fishing villages with their protective concrete breakwaters.

Ryūgo-ji Youth Hostel (tel 0767-42-0401) is part of Ryūgo-ji Temple and you may, on request, be allowed to take part in a Zen meditation session. To reach the hostel, take a 20 minute bus ride from Togi in the direction of Monzen. Get off at the Sakami Ryūgoji-mae bus stop, then follow the road across the bridge to the hostel (about seven minutes).

Close to Monzen, there's the famous Sōji-ji Temple which was established in 1321 as the head temple of the Sōtō school of Zen. After a fire severely damaged the buildings in 1898, the temple was restored, but it now functions as a branch temple; the main temple has been transferred to Yokohama. Admission costs Y300 and it's open daily from 8 am to 5 pm. To reach the temple from Anamizu station, take a 40 minute bus ride to the Sōji-ji-mae bus stop.

Notominazuki Youth Hostel (tel 0768-46-2022) is at Minazuki which is 35 minutes by bus from Monzen. There's a coastal hiking trail (about 2½ hours) between Minazuki and Kami-ōzawa.

WAJIMA 輪島

Wajima is a small town, but it has long been renowned as a centre for the production of lacquerware and has now become a major centre for tourism.

The tourist information office at Wajima station provides English leaflets, maps and timetable information and the staff will help you book accommodation.

Wajima Lacquerware Hall

This hall (Wajima Shikki Kaikan) is in the centre of town and will appeal to craft enthusiasts who can go straight to the 2nd floor to see demonstrations of lacquerware production techniques. They can then admire the finished products in a museum section, and afterwards, descend to make purchases in the shop.

Admission to the hall costs Y300 and includes a shopping bag, a leaflet and a pair of chopsticks.

Wajima Honten

Wajima Honten is another lacquerware emporium which is worth an evening visit for Gojinjō Daikō Drumming – a dramatic performance by a group of masked, demonic drummers beating rhythms singly and in groups. The 30 minute show is held between April and October at 8.30 pm on Friday and Saturday, and daily during the peak season. Admission is free. The honten is opposite the Wajima Lacquerware Hall.

Market

The morning market (asa-ichi) takes place daily between 8 and 11 am – except on the 10th and 25th of each month. Despite its touristy trappings, the market might appeal for its array of chuckling old crones dangling seaweed, fish or ridiculous tourist tat in front of shoppers and drawing attention to their wares with a cheery 'Do deska?' (How about it?). Take your pick from tiny whitefish, large-finned fat fish, dried squid or comic toys resembling beetles, crabs or fish complete with tails, pincers or legs that wiggle.

Kiriko Kaikan

This is a hall housing the huge lacquered floats used in the regional festivals. Admission costs Y350. It's open from 8 am to 5 pm. From the station, the hall is 20 minutes on foot or you can take the six minute bus ride from the station and get off at the Tsukada bus stop.

Hegura-jima Island

Those interested in a day trip to an island can take the ferry to Hegura-jima Island which boasts a lighthouse, several shrines and no traffic. Birdwatchers flock to the island in spring and autumn. The main industries which support the islanders are fishing and tourism. If you want to extend your island isolation by staying overnight there are plenty of minshuku. Reservations can be made in Japanese by calling 0768-22-4961.

From early April to late October, the ferry departs Wajima at 8.30 am and reaches the island at 10.20 am. The return ferry leaves at 2.30 pm. During the winter, weather conditions can cause cancellation of the trip and the return ferry departs at 1 pm. A return ticket costs Y3000.

Places to Stay

The tourist information office at Wajima station can help you find accommodation. Wajima has dozens of minshuku with prices starting at around Y5500 per person and these include two meals (copious and delicious seafood). *Wajima Chōraku-ji Youth Hostel* (tel 0768-22-0663) is 15 minutes on foot from the station.

Getting There & Away

Wajima is a major transport hub for the peninsula. The bus station is opposite the railway station – for transport details see under Getting Around at the beginning of the Noto-hantō Peninsula section.

SENMAIDA　千枚田

Senmaida (literally '1000 rice paddies') is an attractive terraced slope and, in fact, there are more than 2000 small paddies. It's about 30 minutes by bus north-east of Wajima.

SOSOGI　曽々木

The village of Sosogi, about 10 minutes by bus from Senmaida, has a couple of attractions. After the Taira were defeated in 1185, one of the few survivors, Tokitada Taira, was exiled to this region. The Tokikuni family, which claims descent from this survivor, eventually divided into two parts and established separate family residences here.

Shimo Tokikuni-ke (Lower Tokikuni Residence), built in 1590, is a smaller version of its counterpart, but it has an attractive garden. Admission costs Y300 and includes an English leaflet. The residence is open from 8 am to 6 pm.

Kami Tokikuni-ke (Upper Tokikuni Residence), with its impressive thatched roof and elegant interior, was constructed early in the 19th century. Admission costs Y310 and includes an English leaflet. It's open from 8 am to 5 pm. From Wajima station, the bus ride to Kami Tokikuni-ke takes about 40 minutes.

Close to the turn-off for Sosogi is *Sosogi Kajiyama Youth Hostel* (tel 0768-32-1145) – seven minutes on foot from the Sosogi-guchi bus stop. The hostel is a convenient base for walking along the nearby coastal hiking trail.

CAPE ROKKO-ZAKI　禄剛崎

The road east from Sosogi passes Cape Rokkō-zaki and winds round the tip of the peninsula to the less dramatic scenery of its eastern coast. At the cape, you can amble up to Noroshi Lighthouse where a nearby signpost marks the distances to Vladivostok, Shanghai and Tokyo. A coastal hiking trail runs west along the cape.

There is an infrequent local bus service which takes about an hour between Sosogi and the cape.

KIHEI-DON　喜兵衛どん

Farming implements and household utensils which belonged to wealthy farmers during the Edo period are displayed in this mildly interesting museum, which is about 45 minutes by bus from Cape Rokkō-zaki. Admission costs Y400. It's open from 8 am to 6 pm. The museum is a 10 minute walk from Suzu-Iida station.

TSUKUMO-WAN BAY　九十九湾

Tsukumo-wan Bay, heavily indented and dotted with islands, is mildly scenic, but it's not really worth spending Y610 on the boat tour despite the boat's glass bottom. From the bay, it's five minutes on foot to Noto-Ogi station and rail connections via Ushitsu to Kanazawa. If you want an inexpensive place to stay right next to the water, *Tsukumo-Wan Youth Hostel* (tel 0768-74-0150) is only 15 minutes on foot from the station.

USHITSU 宇出津

The limited attractions of Ushitsu are around Toshimayama-kōen Park which has good views out to sea. Close to the park is *Okunoto Youth Hostel* (tel 0768-62-0436) where bicycle rental is available. Take the five minute bus ride in the direction of Ogi and get off at the Kōen-shita bus stop. The hostel is seven minutes on foot from the bus stop.

Fukui-ken 福井県

FUKUI 福井

Fukui is the prefectural capital and a major textile centre. It has few places of interest, but it is useful as a staging point to visit sights in the prefecture. Between 19 and 21 May, Fukui celebrates the Mikuni Festival with a parade of giant warrior dolls.

If you need to stay in Fukui, there's the rather drab *Fujin Seinen Kaikan Youth Hostel* (tel 0776-22-5625) or the *Hotel Akebono Bekkan* (tel 0776-22-0506) which is a member of the Japanese Inn Group. Both are close to the station.

Fukui lies on the JR Hokuriku Honsen line: 55 minutes east is Kanazawa and 40 minutes south-west is a major railway junction at Tsuruga which provides convenient access to Nagoya, Kyoto and Osaka.

EIHEI-JI TEMPLE 永平寺

Founded in 1244 by Dōgen, Eihei-ji is now one of the two head temples of the Sōtō sect of Zen Buddhism and is ranked amongst the most influential centres of Zen in the world.

The temple is geared to huge numbers of visitors who come either as sightseers or for Zen training. Admission tickets can be bought from automats outside the temple, and plastic covers for shoes and umbrellas are doled out as you pass through the hall in the modern administration centre and are marshalled into groups. Foreigners are equipped with a detailed English leaflet (including a list of rules for visitors) and groups are then led into a hall for an introductory talk in Japanese before being unleashed on the circuit of the complex.

The complex has about 70 buildings, but the standard circuit usually concentrates on the seven major buildings: *tosu* (toilet), Sanmon Gate, *yokushitsu* (bath), *daikuin* (kitchen), Butsuden (Buddha Hall), Hattō (Dharma Hall) and the Sō-dō (Priests' Hall).

Foreigners can apply for training in Zen and accommodation is also provided. If you apply in person, you should do so at least two weeks in advance – be prepared for a rigorous routine. By mail, applications must be made one month in advance, should include reply postage (from outside Japan, enclose international reply coupons) and should contain the following information: name, address, phone number, age, sex and preferred training dates. Apply to Kokusaibu Eihei-ji (International Department), Eihei-ji-cho, Yoshida-gun, Fukui-ken, 910-12.

Note, however, that the temple does not admit *sanrosha* (trainees) on the following dates: 1, 2, 3, 7, 26 January; 1 to 8, 15 February; 13, 21 to 29 April; 6, 17 May; 15 June; 2 July; 9 August; 13, 21 to 29 September; 5 October; 6, 17 November and 1 to 10, 22 December, plus on other days when special services are held.

Fees are Y7000 for each overnight stay and two meals are provided.

Normal daily admission costs Y400. The temple is open from 5 am to 5 pm; however, note that the temple is frequently closed for periods varying from a week to 10 days – before you visit, check with a tourist information office or use Japan Travel-Phone (tel 0120-222800).

Places to Stay

A convenient youth hostel is *Eihei-ji Monzen*

Yamaguchi-sō (tel 0776-63-3123) which is five minutes on foot from Eihei-ji station.

Getting There & Away

From Fukui, take the Keifuku Dentetsu Eihei-ji line to Eihei-ji station (Y710, 35 minutes). If you don't catch a direct train, you'll need to change trains at Higashi-Furuichi.

The temple is about 10 minutes from Eihei-ji station. Turn right as you exit the station and plod uphill past the souvenir shops.

ECHIZEN ONO DISTRICT   越前

The town of Ono is known for its castle (a very recent reconstruction) and the morning market held on Shichiken-dōri St between 21 March and 31 December. Further east from Ono is the scenic Kuzuryū-kyō Gorge. From Fukui, the Etsumi Hokusen line provides convenient rail access to Ono and the gorge.

About 10 km north of Ono is the town of Katsuyama and the nearby Heisen-ji Temple with its moss garden in an attractive forest setting. Trains on the Echizen Honsen line link Katsuyama with Fukui in just under an hour.

TOJINBO 東尋坊

About 25 km north-east of Fukui, are the towering rock columns and cliffs at Tōjinbō which is a popular tourist destination. Visitors can take a 30 minute boat trip to view the rock formations or travel further up the coast to O-jima Island.

The Keifuku Mikuni Awara line connects Fukui with Mikuni-minato station. From there, it's a few minutes by bus to Tōjinbō.

TSURUGA 敦賀

The city of Tsuruga, just north of Lake Biwa-ko, is a thriving port and major rail junction. The Shin Nihonkai ferry company operates four sailings a week between Tsuruga and Otaru (Hokkaidō). The trip takes 30 hours and passenger fares are good value at Y6400 (2nd class, one way). Tsuruga-kō Port is 20 minutes by bus from Tsuruga station.

The Wakasa Bay region, south-west of Tsuruga, has fine seascapes and coastal scenery. Close to Mikata station are the Mikatago-ko (Mikata Five Lakes). See the Wakasa Bay section in the Western Honshū chapter for details.

Kinki District 近畿地方

The term *kansai* (west of the barrier) is loosely used to describe the core area around Kōbe, Osaka, Kyoto and Nara. This chapter concentrates on the Kinki District, a geographical division in the heart of Kansai, which covers the prefectures of Shiga, Mie, Nara, Kyoto, Wakayama, Osaka, Kōbe and Hyōgo. Much of Japan's history and tradition has its roots here: a prime reason to visit.

Kyoto, with its hundreds of temples and gardens, was the imperial capital between 794 and 1868 and is now a magnet for domestic and international tourism. It continues to function as the major cultural centre of Japan, but business and industry are closing in on the traditional architecture. Nara predates Kyoto as an imperial capital and has an impressive array of temples, burial mounds and relics from early times.

Osaka and Kōbe are part of a large indus-

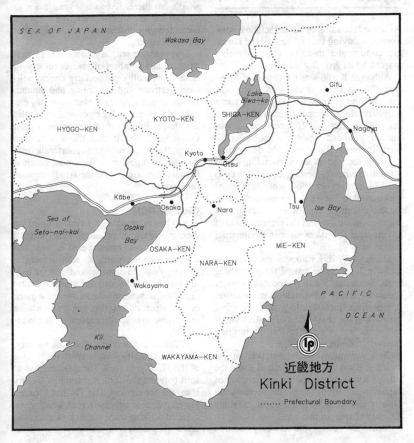

SEA OF JAPAN

Wakasa Bay

Gifu

Lake Biwa-ko

KYOTO-KEN

SHIGA-KEN

HYOGO-KEN

Nagoya

Kyoto

Ōtsu

Kōbe

Osaka

Nara

Tsu

Ise Bay

Sea of Seto-nai-kai

Osaka Bay

OSAKA-KEN

MIE-KEN

NARA-KEN

Wakayama

PACIFIC OCEAN

Kii Channel

WAKAYAMA-KEN

近畿地方
Kinki District

······· Prefectural Boundary

trial belt and are of limited interest to travellers. Himeji, just east of Kōbe, is famed for its castle.

In Mie Prefecture the main attractions are Ise-jingū, one of Japan's most important Shinto shrines, and the seascapes around the Shima-hantō Peninsula. In Wakayama Prefecture, the temple complex of Kōya-san, one of the major centres of Japanese Buddhism, is a pleasant place to stay in the mountains.

Kyoto　京都

A visit to Japan simply *has* to include Kyoto, a city embodying the key qualities of Japanese culture and tradition yet undeniably marked by its growing industrial role.

Although Kyoto was the capital of Japan from 794 to 1868, at times its power was usurped and it remained capital in name only. The city's fortunes fluctuated dramatically: in the 15th and 16th centuries, it was virtually pounded to rubble in ferocious civil wars. Toyotomi Hideyoshi welded the nation back together and set about rebuilding Kyoto – much of what one sees today dates back to the 17th century. In 1868, when the capital was moved to Tokyo, Kyoto retained its role as the country's repository of traditional culture and the arts and the enthronement of the emperor still takes place in the imperial palace here.

During WW II, Kyoto was one of the few cities in Japan to be spared from bombing raids. Since the '50s, it has become a major industrial centre (specialising in precision engineering, biotechnology and electrical goods) and the heavy hand of modern architecture is laying siege to fast diminishing oases of traditional buildings.

To complement the information on the sights in Kyoto or for more detail about the role of Kyoto in the history and religion of Japan, refer to the separate sections on History and Religion in the Facts about the Country chapter of this book.

Most visitors to Kyoto seriously question the much vaunted beauty of the city when they arrive in the station area or wander downtown only to be confronted with glaring urban ugliness. Yet, despite this flaw, you'll see why it has a strong claim to being one of the world's most attractive cities if you seek out the surrounding districts; the infrastructure of streets is studded with some stunning sights.

Kyoto has more than 2000 temples and shrines, a trio of palaces, dozens of gardens, plenty of museums and the finest cultural and artistic choices in Japan. The attractions covered in this chapter are a small slice of what's out there. Kyoto is a great place to wander off the tourist track, combing the backstreets for obscure shops, old houses or hidden temples.

One problem with Kyoto's fame is that it attracts huge numbers of visitors (nearly 40 million annually), particularly during holidays, festivals and the spring and autumn foliage seasons. An early start to the day can help, but sooner or later you will encounter the masses in pursuit of the famous sights. One consolation is that the less famous sights, though perhaps just a short walk from the famous ones, may be almost deserted because they are not on the standard group itinerary.

ORIENTATION

Kyoto has retained a grid system based on the classical Chinese concept. This system of numbered streets running east to west and avenues running north to south makes it relatively easy to move around with the help of a map from the Tourist Information Centre (TIC). Addresses are indicated with the name of the closest intersection and their location north (*agaru*) or south (*sagaru*) of that intersection.

Efficient bus services crisscross the city. There's a simplified bus map on the reverse of the TIC Kyoto map. The quickest way to shift between the north and south of the city is to take the subway. The TIC has a leaflet, *Walking Tour Courses in Kyoto*, which gives detailed walking maps for major sightseeing areas (Higashiyama, Arashiyama, north-

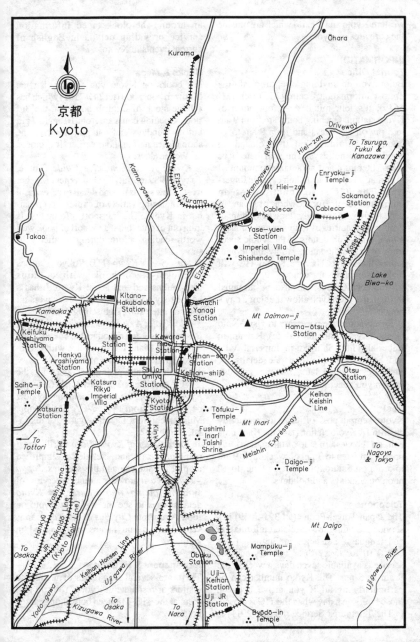

western Kyoto and Ohara) which are outside the core area of Kyoto.

INFORMATION
Tourist Office
Before you do anything else, drop into the Tourist Information Centre (TIC) (tel 371-5649); it's four minutes on foot north of Kyoto station. Opening hours are from 9 am to 5 pm on weekdays and from 9 am to 12 noon on Saturdays but it is closed on Sundays and holidays. The staff here have maps, literature and an amazing amount of information on Kyoto at their capable fingertips. The TIC also functions as an information centre for the whole of Japan. To cope fairly with the daily flood of visitors, it deals with inquiries by numbers and imposes a time limit. Full details of the whole spectrum of accommodation are available and, unlike the Tokyo TIC, the Kyoto TIC will make reservations for you.

Volunteer Guides can also be arranged through the TIC if you allow the staff a day's notice.

Reservations are necessary to visit Kyoto Gosho (Kyoto Imperial Palace), Katsura-in Imperial Villa, Shūgaku-in Imperial Villa and Saihō-ji Temple. Separate details for each are provided later, but the TIC can inform you about the procedures.

Post
Kyoto central post office is conveniently close to JR Kyoto station (take the Karasuma exit, on the western side of the station). It's open from 9 am to 7 pm on weekdays, 9 am to 5 pm on Saturdays and from 9 am to 12 noon on Sundays and holidays.

Telephone
The Japan Travel-Phone (tel 371-5649) is a service providing travel-related information and language assistance in English. Calls cost Y10 for every three minutes and the service is available seven days a week, from 9 am to 5 pm. The Kyoto number can be particularly useful if you arrive between those hours on a day when the TIC is closed.

The Teletourist Service (tel 361-2911) is an around-the-clock taped information service providing details in English of current events in Kyoto.

Books & Maps
For books on Kyoto you should visit the Maruzen bookshop (tel 241-2161) which has a large stock of English books on the 3rd floor. Opening hours are from 10 am to 7 pm but on Sundays and national holidays the shop closes half an hour earlier. It is closed on Wednesdays.

Kyoto: A Contemplative Guide (Tuttle, Tokyo, 1989 reprint) by Gouverneur Mosher treats a few sights in fond detail to give a taste of the amazing variety of exploration possible in Kyoto. The transport information is long out of date, but it's the sort of book well worth reading before, during or after your stay.

Must-See in Kyoto (JTB, Tokyo, 1988) is a pocket-sized book with copious illustrations and text about Kyoto. It has a bouncy style, is easy to read and covers all sorts of interesting sightseeing details.

Old Kyoto: A Guide to Traditional Shops, Restaurants & Inns (Kodansha, Tokyo, 1989 reprint) by Diane Durston helps with exploration in the backstreets of Kyoto.

For those anticipating a longer stay, the YWCA publishes *The Resident's Guide to Kyoto* (Y980). An updated edition may now be available from the YWCA Thrift Shop, Muromachi-dōri, Demizu-agaru, Kamikyo-ku, Kyoto 602.

Tourist Map of Kyoto, Nara fulfills most mapping needs and includes a simplified map of the subway and bus systems. *Japan – Kyoto, Nara* provides a quick overview of sights. *Walking Tour Courses in Kyoto* details ways to see the sights in Kyoto on foot. A separate *City Bus & Subway* map is very detailed and names are supplied in kanji.

Newspapers & Magazines
There are several magazines of interest to visitors or residents in Kyoto. You can find them at the TIC, Maruzen bookshop or large hotels.

Kyoto Visitor's Guide is a free, English-language publication which is readily available in Kyoto. It is crammed with maps and information on accommodation, restaurants, shopping, entertainment, festivals, etc. If you want to get a copy before you arrive in Kyoto, try your local JNTO office or make direct contact: Kyoto Visitor's Guide (tel 256-2412), Nippo Karasuma Building, 4th Floor, Oike Sagaru Higashi-no-toin Nakagyo-ku, Kyoto.

Kyoto Monthly Guide is published by the Kyoto City Government to provide news of current events and general information. Copies are often available from the TIC.

Monthly Guide Kyoto provides lists of events and general accommodation and sightseeing information. Most large hotels have copies.

Kansai Time Out is an English-language, monthly 'what's on' magazine (Y300) which covers not only Kyoto, but also Nara, Kōbe and Osaka. Apart from all the lively articles, it has a large section of small ads for employment, travel agencies, clubs, lonely hearts, etc. It's all in there: from the 'Kinki Macintosh Users Group' (it's OK, they're into computers) to Japan Animal Welfare Society (JAWS).

Discover Kinki!, with exclamation mark included, is aimed more at the tourist market. It provides maps as well as information on local cuisine, handicrafts, folk traditions, sports and entertainment.

Emergencies

If you need to use English and want help finding the closest suitable service, you should try the Japan Travel-Phone (tel 371-5649) or Japan Helpline (tel 0120-461-997).

If your Japanese is proficient, the police phone number is 110, and for an ambulance dial 119.

For an emergency clinic you could try Kyoto Holiday Emergency Clinic (tel 811-5072); for emergency dental problems call Kyoto Holiday Emergency Dental Clinic (tel 441-7173).

Sakabe International Clinic (tel 231-1624) provides 24 hour emergency service;

the Japan Baptist Hospital (tel 781-5191) usually has some US doctors on its staff.

Home Visits

If you would like to meet a Japanese family at home, you can make arrangements at least one day, preferably two days in advance through: Tourist Section (tel 752-0215), Department of Cultural Affairs & Tourism, Kyoto City Government, Kyoto Kaikan, Okazaki, Sakyo-ku, Kyoto.

WHEN TO GO

The ephemeral cherry blossom season usually starts in April and lasts about a week. The Japanese become besotted with 'cherry blossom mania' and descend on favourite spots in hordes. The top spots for spectacular displays of blossom include the Path of Philosophy, Maruyama-kōen Park and Heian-jingū Shrine (see the eastern Kyoto section), Arashiyama (see under western Kyoto) and the Imperial Palace Park (see the central Kyoto section).

Autumnal tints are similarly spectacular and attract huge numbers of 'leaf-gazers'. Popular viewing spots include Ohara and Shūgaku-in Imperial Villa (see under northeastern Kyoto), Sagano and Takao (western Kyoto) and Tōfuku-ji temple (see the southeastern Kyoto section).

PLANNING YOUR ITINERARY

Kyoto is worth considering as a base for travel in Japan. It is within easy reach of Osaka Airport which has none of the acute overcrowding problems experienced at Tokyo's Narita International Airport.

It is difficult to advise on a minimum itinerary for Kyoto – you should certainly consider it a 'must-see' in Japan and allocate as much time as possible for it. Take your time: there's no point in spoiling the quality of enjoyment by overdoing the quantity of sights visited. Quite apart from the sensory overload, overintensive sightseeing also entails heavy outlay on admission fees. Kyoto is particularly suited to random rambling through the backstreets.

The absolute minimum for a stay in Kyoto

would be two days in which you could just scratch the surface by visiting the Higashiyama area in eastern Kyoto. Five days will give you time to add Arashiyama, western Kyoto and central Kyoto. Ten days would allow you to cover these areas plus northern Kyoto, southern and south-eastern Kyoto and leave a day or so for places further afield (from Kyoto you have easy access for day trips to Nara, Yoshino, Lake Biwa-ko, Ise, Himeji and Osaka) or for in-depth exploration of museums, shops and cultural pursuits.

Kyoto is also the place to indulge your special interests in Japanese culture, whether it be in the arts, in daily life or even industrial tours.

Your first line of inquiry should be the TIC which is used to dealing with both ordinary and extraordinary requests. For example, details are available on Zen temples which accept foreigners, specialist museums, Japanese gardens and villas, Japanese culinary arts and natural food outlets, traditional crafts (silks, basketry, ceramics, pottery, temple paraphernalia, paper making, etc), Japanese drama, chanoyu (tea ceremony) and ikebana (flower arranging).

MARKETS

On the third Saturday of each month, there is a flea market and general get-together of foreigners at the YWCA Thrift Shop, Muromachi-dōri, Demizu-agaru, Kamikyo-ku, Kyoto 602.

On the 21st of each month, there is a market fair, Kōbō-san, at Tōji Temple. On the 25th of each month, there's another market fair, Tenjin-san, at Kitano Tenmangū Shrine. Arrive early and prepare to bargain.

FESTIVALS

There are hundreds of festivals (matsuri) spread throughout the year. Listings can be found at the TIC or in *Kyoto Visitor's Guide*, *Monthly Guide Kyoto* and *Kyoto Monthly Guide*. The following are some of the major or most spectacular festivals. These attract hordes of spectators from out of town, some-

times twice as many as the resident population, so you need to book accommodation well in advance.

Aoi Matsuri (Hollyhock Festival)
15 May. This festival dates back to the 6th century and commemorates the successful prayers of the people for the gods to stop calamitous weather. Today, the procession involves imperial messengers in oxcarts and a retinue of 600 people dressed in traditional costume hollyhock leaves are carried or used as decoration. The procession leaves around 10 am from the imperial palace and heads for Shimogamo-jinja Shrine where ceremonies take place. It sets out from here again at 2 pm and arrives at Kamigamo-jinja Shrine at 3.30 pm.

Gion Matsuri
16-17 July. Perhaps the most renowned of all Japanese festivals, this one reaches a climax on these days with a parade of over 30 floats depicting ancient themes which are decked out in incredible finery.

Daimon-ji Gozan Okuribi
16 August. This is a festival to bid farewell to the souls of ancestors. Enormous fires are lit on five mountains in the form of Chinese characters or other shapes. The fires are lit at 8 pm and it is best to watch from the banks of the Kamogawa River or pay for a rooftop view from a hotel.

Kurama-no-Himatsuri
22 October. The origins of this festival are traced back to a rite using fires to guide the gods of the nether world on their tours around this world. Portable shrines are carried through the streets and accompanied by youths with flaming torches. The festival climaxes around 10 pm at Yuki-jinja Shrine in the village of Kurama which is 30 minutes by train from Kyoto station.

Jidai Matsuri (Festival of the Ages)
22 October. This festival is of recent origin, dating back to 1895. More than 2000 people, dressed in costumes ranging from the 8th century to the 19th century, parade from the imperial palace to Heian-jingū Shrine.

CENTRAL KYOTO
京都中心

The centre of Kyoto is predominantly a concrete jungle, clogged with traffic and the attendant bustle of commercial and business life. This is the area for shopping, errands and evening entertainment. There are a few sights in the area such as the imperial palace, Nijō-jō Castle and several museums.

The area around Kyoto station (just below

the city centre) is another hub of commercial activity. For information, be sure to use the TIC which is a couple of minutes on foot, just north of the station. Interesting sights in the station area include Nishi Hongan-ji Temple and Tō-ji Temple.

Kyoto Imperial Palace

The original Kyoto Imperial Palace (Kyoto Gosho) was built in 794 and was replaced numerous times after destruction through fires. The present building, on a different site and smaller than the original, was constructed in 1855. Enthronement of a new emperor and other state ceremonies are still held there.

The tour guide explains details while you are led for about 30 minutes past the Shishin-den Hall, Ko Gosho (Small Palace), Tsune Gosho (Regular Palace) and the Oike-niwa (Pond Garden).

Foreigners are privileged to be given preferential access – Japanese visitors have to wait months for permission – but the imperial palace rates low in comparison with other attractions in Kyoto.

Reservation & Admission This is organised by the Imperial Household Agency (Kunaichō) (tel 211-1215) which is a short walk from Imadegawa subway station. You will have to fill out an application form and show your passport; children should be accompanied by adults over 20 years of age. Permission is usually granted for the same day for the imperial palace. English guided tours are given at 11 am and 2 pm; you should arrive no later than 20 minutes beforehand at the Seisho-mon Gate. Admission is free.

The office is open weekdays from 8.45 am to 12 noon and 1 to 4 pm but note that on the first and third Saturdays of the month it 's open from 8.45 am to 12 noon. There are no afternoon tours on the first and third Saturdays, no tours on the second and fourth Saturdays, Sundays, national holidays, during the New Year holiday (25 December to 5 January) or from 14 to 17 May.

This is also the place to make advance reservations to see the Sentō Gosho, Katsura-in and Shūgaku-in (the latter are imperial villas). If you want to arrange reservations from abroad or from outside of Kyoto, the application forms are available from JNTO offices, the TIC or direct from the Imperial Household Agency – remember to include return postage or international reply coupons.

To reach the imperial palace, take the subway to Imadegawa or a bus to the Karasuma-Imadegawa stop.

Sentō Gosho Palace

This is close to the Kyoto Imperial Palace. Visitors must obtain advance permission from the Imperial Household Agency and be over 20 years old. Tours (in Japanese) start at 11 am and 1.30 pm. The gardens, which were laid out in 1630 by Kobori Enshū, are the main attraction.

Nijō-jō Castle

This castle was built in 1603 as the official Kyoto residence of the first Tokugawa shogun, Ieyasu. The ostentatious style of construction was intended as a demonstration of Ieyasu's prestige and to signal the demise of the emperor's power. To safeguard against treachery, Ieyasu had the interior fitted with 'nightingale' floors (intruders were detected by the squeaking boards) and concealed chambers where bodyguards could keep watch.

After passing through the grand Karamon Gate, you enter Ninomaru Palace which is divided into five buildings with numerous chambers. Access to the buildings depended on rank – only those of highest rank were permitted into the inner buildings. The Ohiroma Yon-no-Ma (Fourth Chamber) has spectacular screen paintings. Don't miss the excellent Ninomaru Palace Garden, designed by the tea master and landscape architect Kobori Enshū.

The neighbouring Honmaru Palace dates from the middle of last century and is only open for special viewing in the autumn.

Admission for Ninomaru Palace and garden is Y500; it's open daily from 8.45 am

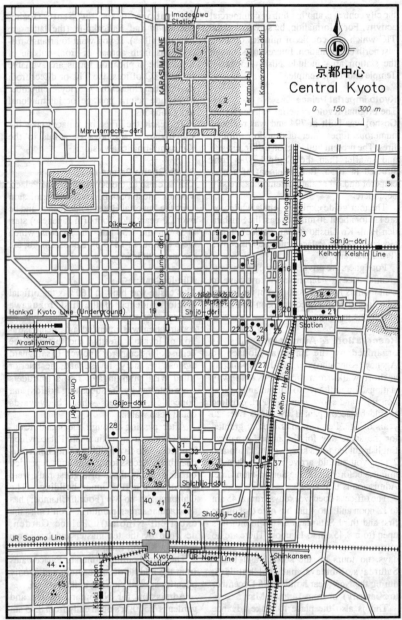

京都中心
Central Kyoto

0   150   300 m

Central Kyoto

1	Imperial Palace	24	Takashimaya Department Store
2	Sentō Gosho Palace	25	Fujii Daimaru Department Store
3	Uno House	26	Ninomiya
4	Ippō-dō Teashop	27	Ryokan Hinomoto
5	Kanze Kaikan Nō Theatre	28	Costume Museum
6	Nijō-jō Castle	29	Nishi Hongan-ji Temple
7	Kerala	30	Kungyoku-dō
8	Nijō-jinya	31	Matsubaya Ryokan
9	Hiiragiya Ryokan	32	Ryokan Kyōka
10	Tawaraya Ryokan	33	Ryokan Murakamiya
11	Ristorante Chiaro	34	Kikokutei Shōsei-en Garden
12	Kyoto Royal Hotel	35	Yuhara Ryokan
13	Taka Jyo Noodle Restaurant	36	Ryokan Hiraiwa
14	Ukiya Noodle Restaurant	37	Riverside Takase & Annex Kyōka
15	Tani House Annex	38	Higashi Hongan-ji Temple
16	Pontochō	39	Pension Station Kyoto
17	Far East Bar & Restaurant	40	Kintetsu Department Store
18	Gion	41	TIC
19	Kongō Nō Theatre	42	Kyoto Minshuku Reservation Centre
20	Yamatomi	43	Porta Shopping Centre
21	Gonbei	44	Kanchi-in Temple
22	Kinmata Ryokan	45	Tō-ji Temple
23	Hankyū Department Store		

Central Kyoto

1	京都御所	24	高島屋
2	仙洞御所	25	大丸
3	うのハウス	26	にのみや
4	一保堂	27	旅館ひのもと
5	カンゼ会館能座	28	服装博物館
6	二条城	29	西本願寺
7	ケララ	30	くんこょくどう
8	二条陣屋	31	松葉屋旅館
9	柊屋旅館	32	旅館京花
10	俵屋旅館	33	旅館むらかみや
11	リストランテチャロ	34	渉成園
12	京都ロヤルホテル	35	ゆはら旅館
13	高城麵店	36	平岩旅館
14	うきや麵店	37	リバサイドたかセアネクス
15	谷ハウスアネクス	38	東本願寺
16	先斗町	39	ペンションステーション京都
17	ファーイーストバー	40	金鉄デパート
18	祇園	41	TIC
19	こんごう能座	42	民宿予定センター
20	やまとみ	43	ポータショッピングセンター
21	ごんべい	44	観智院
22	近又旅館	45	東寺
23	阪急デパート		

until last admission at 4 pm (gates close at 5 pm). Also, it's closed from 26 December to 4 January. A detailed fact sheet in English is provided. The Ninomaru Palace is so inundated with visitors that you have to choose your exit according to the numbered location of your shoes!

To reach the palace, take bus Nos 9, 12, 50, 52, 61 or 67 to the Nijō-jō-mae stop. Alternatively you can take the subway to Oike and then walk for 12 minutes.

Nijō-jinya

Nijō-jinya (tel 841-0972) was built in the 17th century as the home of a wealthy merchant and eventually functioned as an inn. It was fitted with a variety of contrivances to guard against fire and intruders. The house contains trap ladders, trap doors, concealed chambers for bodyguards and special screens to deter attackers.

Tours are conducted in Japanese and are only possible with advance reservation. Check with the TIC. The house is a 10 minute walk, south of Nijō-jō Castle.

Pontochō

Pontochō is a traditional centre for night entertainment in a narrow street running between the river and Kawaramachi-dōri St. It's a pleasant place for a stroll in the summer if you want to observe Japanese nightlife. Many of the restaurants and teahouses which have verandahs over the river tend to prefer Japanese customers. The geisha houses usually control admittance of foreigners with a policy of introductions from Japanese only and astronomical charges. Many of the bars also function along similar lines, like a club. Don't bother with bars that use touts outside to entice you inside for fleecing.

KYOTO STATION AREA
京都駅の附近
Nishi Hongan-ji Temple

In 1591, Hideyoshi Toyotomi built this temple, known as Hongan-ji Temple, as a new headquarters for the Jōdo Shin (True Pure Land) school of Buddhism which had accumulated immense power. Later,

Tokugawa Ieyasu saw this power as a threat and sought to weaken it by encouraging a breakaway faction of this school to found Higashi Hongan-ji (*higashi* means 'east') in 1602. The original Hongan-ji Temple then became known as Nishi Hongan-ji Temple (*nishi* means 'west'). It now functions as the headquarters of the Hongan-ji branch of the Jōdo Shin school with over 10,000 temples and 12 million followers worldwide.

The temple contains five buildings featuring some of the finest examples of architecture and artistic achievement from the Momoyama period. The Daisho-in Hall has sumptuous paintings, carvings and metal ornamentation. A small garden and two Nō stages are connected with the hall. The dazzling Kara-mon Gate has intricate ornamental carvings. Both the Daisho-in Hall and the Kara-mon were transported here from Fushimi-jō Castle.

Reservations (preferably several days in advance) for tours should be made either at the temple office or through the TIC. The tours (in Japanese) cover some but not all of the buildings and are conducted from Monday to Friday at 10 and 11 am and then 1.30 and 2.30 pm. On Saturday the tours are at 10 and 11 am. The temple is a 12 minute walk north-west from JR Kyoto station.

Higashi Hongan-ji Temple

When Tokugawa Ieyasu engineered the rift in the Jōdo Shin school, he founded this temple as a competitor against Nishi Hongan-ji Temple. Rebuilt in 1895 after a fire, it is certainly monumental in its proportions, but less impressive artistically than its counterpart. A curious item on display is a length of rope, made from hair donated by female believers, which was used to haul the timber for the reconstruction. It is now the headquarters of the Otani branch of the Jōdo Shin school.

Admission is free and the temple is open from 9 am to 4 pm. It's a five minute walk north of Kyoto station.

Kikokutei Shōsei-en Garden

Kikokutei Garden is just east of Higashi

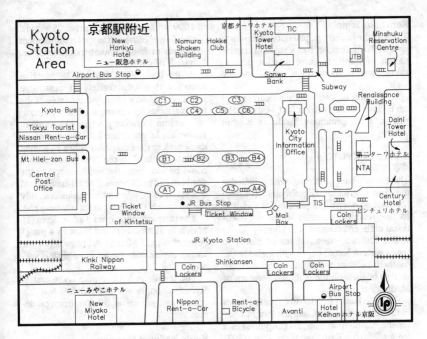

Hongan-ji Temple and dates back to 1657. The landscaped garden arranged around a lake is gently falling into disrepair – a pleasant spot for a quiet stroll. Ask at the Nishi Hongan-ji Temple office for permission to enter.

Costume Museum

This museum displays traditional costumes from early times to the Meiji era. It's on the 5th floor of the Izutsu building, opposite the north-eastern corner of Nishi Hongan-ji Temple. The museum is open from 9 am to 5 pm daily except Sundays; admission costs Y300.

Tō-ji Temple

This temple was established in 794 by imperial decree to protect the city. In 818, the emperor handed over the temple to Kūkai, the founder of the Shingon school of Buddhism. Many of the temple buildings were destroyed by fire or fighting during the 15th century; most of those that remain today date from the 17th century.

The Lecture Hall (Kōdō) contains 21 images representing a Mikkyō (Esoteric Buddhism) mandala. The Main Hall (Kondō) contains statues depicting the Yakushi (Healing Buddha) trinity. In the southern part of the garden, stands the five storeyed pagoda which, despite having burnt down five times, was doggedly rebuilt in 1643 and is now the highest (57 metres) pagoda in Japan.

Kōbō-san market fair is held here on the 21st of each month. Those held in December and January are particularly vigorous.

Admission to the temple costs Y400 and there is an extra charge for entry to special exhibitions. An explanatory leaflet in English is provided. It's open from 9 am to 4 pm. The temple is a 15 minute walk southwest of Kyoto station.

Kanchi-in Temple

The Kanchi-in Temple, just outside the north gate of Tō-ji Temple, has a striking combination of gardens, good interior design, statues and tearoom on a small, intimate scale.

Admission is Y400 and it's open from 9 am to 5 pm. For an extra Y500, you can take part in a tea ceremony inside an elegant tearoom.

EASTERN KYOTO
京都の東部

The eastern part of Kyoto, which includes the core district of Higashiyama (Eastern Mountains), merits top priority for a visit to its fine temples, peaceful walks and traditional night entertainment in Gion.

The following descriptions of places to see in eastern Kyoto begin with sights in the southern section; the sights in the northern section begin with the National Museum of Modern Art.

Allow at least a full day to cover the sights in the southern section, and another full day for the northern section. JNTO publishes a leaflet, *Walking Tour Courses in Kyoto (MG-052)*, which covers the whole of eastern Kyoto.

Sanjūsangen-dō Temple

The original temple was built in 1164 at the request of the retired Emperor Go-shirakawa. After it burnt to the ground in 1249, a faithful copy was constructed in 1266.

The temple's name refers to the 33 *(sanjūsan)* spaces between the columns in this long, narrow building which houses 1001 statues of Kannon (the Buddhist goddess of mercy). The large Senjū Kannon (1000 armed Kannon) is flanked on either side by 500 smaller Kannon images, neatly lined up in rows.

There are an awful lot of arms, but if you are picky and think the 1000-armed statues don't have the required number, then you should remember to calculate according to the nifty Buddhist mathematical formula which holds that 40 arms are the equivalent of 1000 arms, because each saves 25 worlds. Visitors also seem keen to spot resemblances to friends or family members amongst the hundreds of images.

At the back of the hall are 28 guardian statues with a great variety of expressive poses. The gallery at the western side of the hall is famous for the annual Tōshi-ya Festival, held on 15 January, when archers shoot arrows the length of the hall. The ceremony dates back to the Edo period when an annual contest was held to see how many arrows could be shot from the southern end to the northern end in 24 hours. The all-time record was set in 1686, when an archer successfully landed over 8000 arrows at the northern end.

The temple is open from 8 am to 5 pm (16 March to 31 October) and 8 am to 4 pm (1 November to 15 March). Admission is Y400 and an explanatory leaflet in English is supplied.

The temple is a 15 minute walk east of Kyoto station, or you can take bus Nos 206 or 208 and get off at the Sanjūsangen-dō-mae stop.

Kyoto National Museum

The Kyoto National Museum, (Kokuritsu Habukutsan), is housed in two buildings opposite Sanjūsangen-dō Temple. There are excellent displays of fine arts, historical artefacts and handicrafts.

Admission costs Y300 but note that a separate charge is made for special exhibitions. It's open daily from 9 am to 4 pm and closed on Mondays.

Kawai Kanjirō Memorial Hall

This museum was once the home and workshop of one of Japan's most famous potters, Kawai Kanjirō. The house is built in rural style and contains examples of his work, his collection of folk art and ceramics and his kiln.

The museum is open daily from 10 am to 5 pm but closed on Mondays, from 10 to 20 August and from 24 December to 7 January. Admission costs Y700. The hall is a 10 minute walk north of the Kyoto National Museum or you can take bus Nos 206 or 202 from Kyoto station and get off at the Umamachi stop.

Kiyomizu-dera Temple

This temple was first built in 798, but the present buildings are reconstructions dating from 1633. As an affiliate of the Hossō school of Buddhism which originated in Nara, it has successfully survived the intrigues of local Kyoto schools of Buddhism through the centuries and is now one of the most famous landmarks of the city.

The temple management recently bought a large tract of land beneath the temple and thereby saved the famed hilltop view of the city from being obliterated by an ugly high-rise development.

The main hall has a huge verandah, supported on hundreds of pillars, which juts out over the hillside. Just below this hall is the Otawa waterfall where visitors drink or bathe in sacred waters which are believed to have therapeutic properties. Dotted around the precincts are other halls and shrines. At the Jishu Shrine, visitors try to ensure success in love by closing their eyes and walking about 18 metres between a pair of stones – if you miss the stone, your love won't be fulfilled!

The steep approach to the temple, known as 'Teapot Lane', is lined with shops selling Kyoto handicrafts, local snacks and souvenirs. Shopkeepers hand out samples of *yatsuhashi*, a type of dumpling filled with a sweet bean paste.

Admission to the temple costs Y300 and it's open from 6 am to 6 pm. To get there from Kyoto station take bus Nos 207, 206 or 202 and get off at either the Kiyomizu-michi or Gojō-zaka stops. Plod up the hill for 10 minutes to reach the temple.

Sannenzaka & Ninnenzaka Walk

One of the most enjoyable strolls around the backstreets and temples of Kyoto follows a winding route between Kiyomizu-dera Temple and Maruyama-kōen Park.

If you walk down from the entrance of Kiyomizu-dera Temple along the right-hand road (Kiyomizuzaka) for about 200 metres,

you'll see a small street on your right down a flight of steps. This is Sannenzaka, a street lined with old wooden houses and shops selling local pottery, foods and souvenirs. There are also pleasant teahouses with gardens and its a good place to relax over a bowl of noodles.

Half way down Sannenzaka, the road bears sharp left. Follow it a short distance, then go right down a flight of steps into Ninnenzaka, another street lined with historic houses, shops and teahouses. At the end of Ninnenzaka, zig-zag left then right and continue north for five minutes to reach the entrance for Kōdai-ji Temple entrance.

Kōdai-ji Temple

Kōdai-ji Temple was founded in 1605 by Kita no Mandokoro in memory of her late husband, Toyotomi Hideyoshi. The extensive grounds include gardens designed by the famed landscape architect, Kobori Enshū, and teahouses designed by the renowned master of the tea ceremony, Sen no Rikyū. The temple was only recently opened to the public and is worth a look. It's open from 9 am to 5 pm and admission costs Y500. An explanatory leaflet in English is provided.

Maruyama-kōen Park

This park is a favourite spot for locals and visitors to escape the bustle of the nearby city centre and amble round the gardens, ponds, souvenir shops and restaurants. Peaceful paths meander through the trees up the hill.

Yasaka-jinja Shrine

This shrine is right next to Gion, west of Maruyama-kōen Park. This is a busy, colourful shrine which sponsors the Gion Matsuri Festival (for details, see the later section on Festivals).

Gion District

Gion is the famous entertainment and geisha district on the eastern bank of the Kamogawa River. Modern architecture, congested traffic and contemporary nightlife establishments have cut a swathe through the

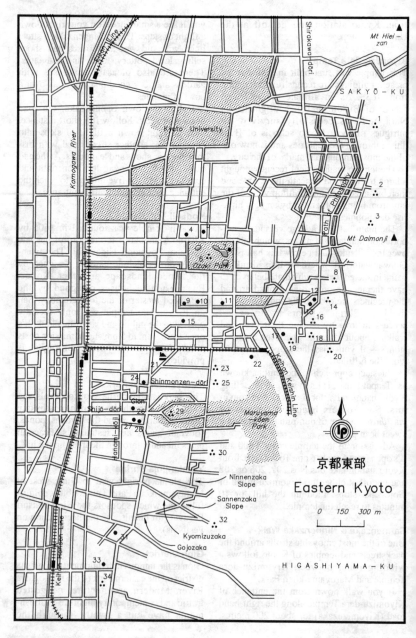

SAKYŌ-KU

Shirakawa-dōri

Mt Hiei-zan ▲

Eizan Line

Kyoto University

Kamogawa River

Path of Philosophy

Mt Daimonji ▲

4

6 Ozaki Park

9 10   11

15

21

24 Shinmonzen-dōri

23

25

22

Keihan Keishin Line

8

12

13   16

14

17

19   18

20

Gion

26

27 28

29

Maruyama kōen Park

Shijō-dōri

Hanami-kōji

30

Ninnenzaka Slope

Sannenzaka Slope

京都東部

Eastern Kyoto

0   150   300 m

31

32

Kyomizuzaka

Gojozaka

33

34

HIGASHIYAMA-KU

Keihan Honsen Line

Keihan Honsen Line

	Eastern Kyoto
1	Ginkaku-ji Temple
2	Hōnen-in Temple
3	Anraku-ji Temple
4	Kyoto Handicraft Centre
5	YWCA
6	Heian-jingū Shrine & Time Paradox Eatery
7	Three Sisters Inn
8	Eikan-dō Temple
9	Museum of Traditional Industry
10	National Museum of Modern Art
11	Kyoto Municipal Museum of Art
12	Nomura Museum
13	Okutan Restaurant
14	Chōshō-in Temple
15	Kanze Kaikan Nō Theatre
16	Nanzen-ji Temple
17	Yachiyo Ryokan
18	Tenju-an Temple
19	Konchi-in Temple
20	Nanzen-in Temple
21	Higashiyama Youth Hostel
22	Miyako Hotel
23	Shōren-in Temple
24	Iwanami Ryokan
25	Chion-in Temple
26	Kyoto Craft Centre
27	Gion Kōbu Kaburenjō Theatre
28	Gion Corner
29	Yasaka-jinja Shrine
30	Kōdai-ji Temple
31	Kawai Kanjirō Memorial Hall
32	Kiyomizu-dera Temple
33	Kyoto National Museum
34	Sanjūsangen-dō Temple

	Eastern Kyoto
1	銀閣寺
2	法然院
3	安楽寺
4	京都工芸館
5	YWCA
6	平安神宮
7	洛東荘
8	永観堂
9	伝統産業会館
10	国立近代美術館
11	市立美術館
12	野村美術館
13	奥丹
14	ちょうしょう院
15	かんぜ会館能台
16	南禅寺
17	八千代旅館
18	天授庵
19	金地院
20	南禅院
21	東山ユースホステル
22	都ホテル
23	青蓮院
24	岩波旅館
25	知恩院
26	京都工芸センター
27	祇園甲部歌舞練所
28	祇園甲部
29	八坂神社
30	高台寺
31	河井寛次郎記念館
32	清水寺
33	京都国立博物館
34	三十三間堂

historical beauty, but there are still some places left for an enjoyable walk.

Hanami-Kōji St is a street running north to south which bisects Shijō-dōri St. The southern section is lined with 17th century, traditional restaurants and teahouses many of which are exclusive establishments for geisha entertainment. If you wander around here in the late afternoon or early evening, you can often glimpse geisha or *maiko* (apprentice geisha) on their way to or from appointments.

At the bottom of this street you reach Gion Corner and the adjoining Gion Kōbu Kaburenjō Theatre. For more detail on these two places, see the section on Entertainment later.

If you walk from Shijō-dōri St up the northern section of Hanami-Kōji St, you will reach Shinmonzen-dōri St running east to west at the fourth intersection. Wander in either direction along this street which is packed with old houses, art galleries and shops specialising in antiques – but don't expect flea-market prices here.

For more historic buildings in a beautiful waterside setting, wander down Shirakawa Minami-dōri St which is roughly parallel with, and one block south of the western section of Shinmonzen-dōri St.

Chion-in Temple

Chion-in Temple was built in 1234 on the site where Hōnen had taught and eventually fasted to death. Today it is still the headquarters of the Jōdo school, which was founded by Hōnen, and a hive of religious activity.

The oldest of the present buildings date back to the 17th century. The two storeyed San-mon Gate at the main entrance is the largest in Japan and prepares the visitor for the massive scale of the temple. The immense main hall contains an image of Hōnen and is connected with the Dai Hōjō Hall by a 'nightingale' floor constructed to 'sing' (squeak) at every step.

The garden attached to the abbot's quarters is good for a quiet stroll.

The giant bell, cast in 1633 and weighing 74 tonnes, is the largest in Japan. The combined muscle-power of 17 monks is required to make the bell budge for the famous ceremony which rings in the new year.

Admission costs Y300 and it's open from 9 am to 4.30 pm (April to October) and from 9 am to 4 pm (November to March). The temple is close to the north-eastern corner of Maruyama-kōen Park. From Kyoto station take bus Nos 18 or 206 and get off at the Chion-in-mae stop.

Shōren-in Temple

Shōren-in was originally the residence of the chief abbot of the Tendai school. The present building dates from 1895, but the main hall has sliding screens with paintings from the 16th and 17th centuries. The gardens are the most compelling reason to visit.

Admission costs Y400 and it's open from 9 am to 5 pm. An explanatory leaflet in English is provided. The temple is a five minute walk north of the Chion-in temple.

National Museum of Modern Art

This museum is renowned for its collection of contemporary Japanese ceramics and paintings. Exhibits are changed on a regular basis. Admission costs Y500 and it's open from 10 am to 5 pm daily except Mondays.

Kyoto Museum of Traditional Industry

If you want a break from temple gazing, you could pop in to the Kyoto Dentō Sangyō Kaikan (Kyoto Museum of Traditional Industry) for exhibitions, demonstrations and sales of Kyoto handicrafts. For more details, refer to the later Things to Buy section.

Heian-jingū Shrine

The Heian-jingū Shrine was built in 1895 to commemorate the 1100th anniversary of the founding of Kyoto. The buildings are gaudy replicas, reduced to a two-thirds scale, of the imperial palace of the Heian period.

The spacious garden, with its large pond and Chinese-inspired bridge, is also meant to represent the kind that was popular in the Heian period.

Two major events, Jidai Matsuri (22 October) and Takigi Nō (1 to 2 June), are held here. Jidai Matsuri is described later in the Festivals section, while details for Takigi Nō are under Dance & Theatre in the later Entertainment section.

Entry to the shrine precincts is free but admission to the garden costs Y500. It's open from 8.30 am to 5.30 pm (15 March to 31 August) though closing time can be an hour earlier during the rest of the year.

Nanzen-ji Temple

The Nanzen-ji Temple began as a retirement villa for Emperor Kameyama, but was dedicated as a Zen temple on his death in 1291. Civil war in the 15th century destroyed most of the temple; the present buildings date from the 17th century. It operates now as headquarters for the Rinzai school of Zen.

At the entrance to the temple stands the

massive San-mon Gate. Steps lead up to the 2nd storey which has a fine view over the city. Beyond the gate is the Hōjō Hall with impressive screens painted with a vivid depiction of tigers and a classic Zen garden called 'Leaping Tiger Garden'.

Admission to the temple costs Y350 and it's open from 8.20 am to 5 pm. A brief explanatory leaflet in English is provided. The temple is a 10 minute walk south-east from the Heian-jingū Shrine; from Kyoto station take bus No 5 and get off at the Eikan-dō-mae stop.

Dotted around the grounds of Nanzen-ji Temple are several subtemples which are often skipped by the crowds and consequently easier to enjoy.

Nanzen-in Temple This subtemple is on your left when leaving the Hōjō Hall – follow the path under the aqueduct. It has an attractive garden designed around a heart-shaped pond. Admission costs Y350.

Tenju-an Temple This stands at the side of the San-mon Gate, a four minute walk west of Nanzen-in Temple. Constructed in 1337, the temple has a splendid garden. A detailed leaflet in English is provided. Admission costs Y350.

Konchi-in Temple When leaving Tenju-an Temple, turn left and continue for 100 metres – Konchi-in Temple is down a small side-street on the left. The stylish gardens fashioned by the master landscape designer Enshū are the main attraction. Admission costs Y400. It's open from 8.30 am to 5 pm (March to November) but closes half an hour earlier during the rest of the year.

Nomura Museum
The Nomura Museum is a 10 minute walk north of Nanzen-ji Temple. Exhibits include scrolls, paintings, tea-ceremony implements and ceramics which were bequeathed by the wealthy business magnate Tokushiki Nomura. Admission costs Y500.

Eikan-dō Temple
Eikan-dō Temple, also known as Zenrin-ji Temple, is made interesting by its varied architecture and its gardens and works of art. It was founded in 855 by the priest Shinshō, but the name was changed to Eikan-dō in the 11th century to honour the philanthropic priest Eikan.

The best approach is to follow the arrows and wander slowly along the covered walkways connecting the halls and gardens.

In the Amida-dō Hall, at the southern end of the complex, is the famous statue of Mikaeri Amida (Buddha Glancing Backwards).

There are various legends about this statue. One version maintains that Eikan was doing a dance in honour of Amida Buddha when the statue stepped down and joined in. When Eikan stopped in amazement, the Buddha looked over his shoulder and told him to keep on jiving.

On the right of this statue, there's an image of a bald priest with a superb expression of intense concentration.

From the Amida-dō Hall, head north to the end of the covered walkway. Change into the sandals provided, then climb the steep steps up the mountainside to the Taho-tō Pagoda where there's a fine view across the city.

The temple is open from 9 am to 4 pm and admission costs Y350. An explanatory leaflet in English and a map are provided.

The Path of Philosophy
This walk, Tetsugaku-no-Michi, has long been a favourite with contemplative strollers who follow the traffic-free route beside a canal lined with cherry trees which come into spectacular bloom in April. It only takes 30 minutes to follow the walk which starts after Eikan-dō Temple and leads to Ginkaku-ji Temple. During the day, be prepared for crowds of tourists; a night stroll will definitely be quieter. A map of the walk is part of *Walking Tour Courses in Kyoto*, a leaflet available from the TIC or JNTO.

Anraku-ji Temple This is a temple of the

Jōdo school and honours two monks, Anraku and Juren, who were involved in a juicy scandal.

In 1206, two ladies of the imperial court went to hear the two monks preach and felt so moved – nobody knows whether it was a call to love or a call to religion – that they became nuns. Emperor Go-Toba, feeling mighty piqued, summoned the monks to court to make them recant their faith. When the monks defied this offer of clemency, the emperor exiled their leader, Hōnen, and had the monks executed in 1207. On hearing the news, the two ladies, with the quaint names of Suzumushi (Bell Cricket) and Matsumushi (Pine Beetle), are reputed to have taken their lives.

The two monks and their ladies are buried in the temple grounds – the burial site is a still place to ponder the events of long ago.

The temple lies on the eastern side of the canal, a short walk south of Hōnen-ji Temple.

Hōnen-in Temple This temple was founded in 1680 to honour Hōnen, the charismatic founder of the Jōdo school. This is a lovely, secluded temple with carefully raked gardens set back in the woods.

Entry is free. It's open from 7 am to 4 pm. The temple is a 12 minute walk from Ginkaku-ji Temple, on a sideroad just east off the Path of Philosophy. Cross the bridge over the canal and follow the road uphill.

Ginkaku-ji Temple

Ginkaku-ji Temple is definitely worth seeing, but be warned that it is often swamped with busloads of visitors jamming the narrow pathways.

In 1482, Shogun Ashikaga Yoshimasa constructed a villa here which he used as a genteel retreat from the turmoil of civil war. Although its name translates as 'Silver Pavilion', the plan to completely cover the building in silver was never carried out. After Yoshimasa's death, it was converted to a temple.

The approach to the main gate runs between tall hedges before turning sharply into the extensive grounds. Walkways lead through the gardens which include meticulously raked cones of white sand (probably symbolic interpretations of a mountain and a lake), tall pines and a pond in front of the temple. A path also leads up the mountainside through the trees.

Admission costs Y400 and it's open from 9 am to 5 pm. An explanatory leaflet in English is provided. From Kyoto station, take bus No 5 and get off at the Ginkaku-ji-mae stop.

NORTH-WESTERN KYOTO
京都の西北部

The north-western part of Kyoto is predominantly residential, but there are a number of superb temples with tranquil gardens in secluded precincts. For Zen fans, a visit to Daitoku-ji Temple and Ryōan-ji Temple is recommended. Kinkaku-ji Temple is another major attraction. The JNTO leaflet on walks also covers this area, but most of the walk is along unremarkable city streets.

Those who have the time and inclination to escape the tourist trail might consider a visit to the Takao district.

Daitoku-ji Temple

The precincts of this temple, which belongs to the Rinzai school of Zen, contain an extensive complex of 24 subtemples: two are mentioned below, but eight are open to the public. If you want an intensive look at Zen culture, this is the place to visit, but be prepared for temples which are thriving business enterprises and often choked with visitors.

My visit coincided with a ceremony marking the 400th anniversary of Sen no Rikyū's death. Dozens of smart geisha, some young, others a little long in the tooth, streamed through the grounds. The most incongruous foil to all this gentility were rows and rows of bright green, plastic porta-loos in precise lines on the path outside the subtemples. Zen and the art of porta-loo maintenance?

Robert Strauss

Daitoku-ji Temple is on the eastern side of the grounds. It was founded in 1319, burnt down in the next century, and rebuilt in the 16th century. The San-mon Gate contains an image of the famous tea master, Sen no Rikyū, on the 2nd storey.

According to some historical sources, Toyotomi Hideyoshi was so enraged when he discovered he had been demeaning himself by walking *under* Rikyū, that he forced the master to commit seppuku (ritual suicide) in 1591.

Daisen-in Subtemple The famous Zen garden in this subtemple is worth a look – that is, of course, if you can make any progress through the crowds. The jovial abbot posed for pictures, dashed off calligraphy souvenirs at lightning speed, held up his fingers in a 'V' for victory sign and completed the act with a regal bow and a rousing 'Danke schön' to each member of a German tour group. If you arrive at 9 am, you might miss the crowds.

Kotō-in Subtemple This subtemple is in the western part of the grounds. The gardens are superb.

Admission charges to the temples vary, but usually average Y350. Those temples

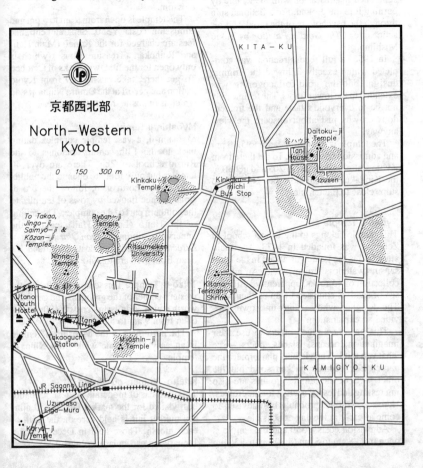

京都西北部

North–Western Kyoto

0   150   300 m

KITA–KU

Daitoku–ji Temple

谷ハウス Tani House

Izusen

Kinkaku–ji Temple

Kinkaku–ji michi Bus Stop

To Takao, Jingo–ji, Saimyō–ji & Kōzan–ji Temples

Ryōan–ji Temple

Ritsumeikan University

Ninna–ji Temple

Kitano Tenman–gū Shrine

Utano Youth Hostel

Keifuku Arashiyama Line

Takaoguchi Station

Myōshin–ji Temple

KAMIGYŌ–KU

JR Sagano Line

Uzumasa Eiga–Mura

Kōryū–ji Temple

which accept visitors are usually open from 9 am to 5 pm. The temple bus stop is Daitoku-ji-mae. Convenient buses from Kyoto station are Nos 205 and 206.

Kinkaku-ji Temple

Kinkaku-ji Temple, the famed 'Golden Temple', is one of the Japan's best known sights. The original building was constructed in 1397 as a retirement villa for Shogun Ashikaga Yoshimitsu. His son converted it into a temple. In 1950, a young monk consummated his obsession with the temple by burning it to the ground. For a fictional spin through the psychology of the monk and his actions, read *The Golden Pavilion* by Yukio Mishima.

In 1955, a full reconstruction was completed which exactly followed the original design, but the gold-foil covering was extended to the lower floors. The temple may not be to everyone's taste and the tremendous crowds just about obscure the view anyway.

The temple is open from 9 am to 5.30 pm and admission costs Y300. To get there from Kyoto station, take bus No 205 and get off at the Kinkaku-ji-michi stop; bus No 59 also stops close to the temple.

Ryōan-ji Temple

This temple belongs to the Rinzai school of Zen and was founded in 1473. The main attraction is the garden arranged in the kare-sansui (waterless stream) style. An austere collection of 15 rocks, apparently adrift in a sea of sand, is enclosed by an earthen wall. The designer, who remains unknown, provided no explanation.

This has encouraged others to use their imagination: oceans, islands, tigers – see what you think. The viewing platform for the garden can become packed solid but the other parts of the temple grounds are also interesting and less of a target for the crowds. Here too, you are probably best advised to come as early in the day as possible.

Admission costs Y350 and the temple is open from 8 am to 5 pm (8.30 am to 4.30 pm

from December to March). Bus No 59 is convenient for this temple.

Ninna-ji Temple

The original building was a palace for Emperor Omuro in the 9th century, but the present temple buildings, including a five storeyed pagoda, are from the 17th century. The extensive grounds are full of cherry trees. If you visit during the cherry blossom season, you may find the area full of drinkers, picnickers and tipsy ladies in flowing dresses dancing around in clouds of blossom.

The temple is open from 9 am to 5 pm and admission costs Y350. Separate entrance fees are charged for the Kondō (Main Hall) and Reihōkan (Treasure House) which is only open for the first two weeks of October. To get there, take bus No 59 from Kyoto station and get off at the Omuro Ninna-ji stop which is opposite the entrance gate.

Myōshin-ji Temple

Myōshin-ji, a vast temple complex dating back to the 14th century, belongs to the Rinzai school of Zen. There are over 40 temples but only four are open to the public.

From the north gate, follow the broad, stone avenue flanked by rows of temples to the southern part of the complex. The ceiling of the Hattō (Lecture Hall) features the unnerving painting *Dragon Glaring in Eight Directions*. Admission costs Y400 and it's open from 9.10 am to 3.40 pm.

Taizō-in Temple This temple is in the south-western corner of the grounds. The garden is worth a visit. Admission costs Y400 and it's open from 9 am to 5 pm.

The north gate of the Myōshin-ji Temple is an easy 10 minute walk from Ninna-ji temple.

Kitano-Tenman-gū Shrine

This shrine is of moderate interest, probably best visited for the market fair. The Tenjin-san market fair is held here on the 25th of each month. Those held in December and January are particularly colourful.

There's no charge for admission and it's open from 5.30 am to 6 pm. From Kyoto station, take bus No 50 and get off at the Kitano-Tenmangū-mae stop.

Kōryū-ji Temple

Kōryū-ji Temple was founded in 622 to honour Prince Shōtoku who was an enthusiastic promoter of Buddhism.

The Hattō (Lecture Hall), to the right of the main gate, houses a magnificent trio of 9th century statues: Buddha, flanked by manifestations of Kannon.

The Reihōkan (Treasure House) contains numerous fine Buddhist statues including the Naki Miroku (Crying Miroku) and the world renowned Miroku Bosatsu which is extraordinarily expressive. A national upset occurred in 1960 when an enraptured student clasped the statue and snapped off its little finger.

The temple is open from 9 am to 5 pm and admission costs Y500. To get there from JR Kyoto station, first take a No 59 bus to the Omuro Ninna-ji stop and walk to the southern gate of Myōshin-ji Temple. From here you can take bus Nos 61, 62 or 63 to the Uzumasa-Kōryū-ji-mae stop.

Toei Uzumasa Eiga-Mura

Toei Uzumasa Eiga-Mura (tel 881-7716/1011) is a huge film set inside Toei's Uzumasa studios. This will probably only appeal to film buffs who enjoy wandering around historical reconstructions and town sets of the Edo and Meiji eras. Be prepared to share your tour with swarms of Japanese kids. If you fancy yourself as a film star, you can have your picture taken dressed in a kimono or other historical costume.

The studios are open to visitors from 9 am to 5 pm (16 March to 15 November), from 9.30 am to 4 pm during the rest of the year and are closed 21 December to 1 January. Admission costs Y1550 per person. From the southern gate of Myōshin-ji Temple take bus Nos 61, 62 or 63 and ask to get off at the Uzumasa Eigamura stop.

Takao District

This is a secluded district tucked far away in the north-western part of Kyoto. It is famed for autumn foliage and the temples of Jingo-ji, Saimyō-ji and Kōzan-ji.

To reach Jingo-ji Temple, take bus No 8 from Shijō-Omiya station – allow one hour for the ride. The other two temples are within easy walking distance.

There are two options for bus services to Takao: there is the hourly JR bus which takes about an hour to reach the Takao stop from Kyoto station; the other is the hourly Kyoto bus from Keihan-sanjō station which also takes one hour to Takao.

Hozu River Trip

Between 10 March and 30 November, there are seven trips daily down the Hozu River. During the winter, the number of trips is reduced to three a day and the boats are heated.

The ride lasts two hours and covers 16 km between Kameoka and Arashiyama through occasional sections of choppy water – a scenic jaunt with minimal danger.

Prices start around Y3400 per person. The boats depart from a dock which is eight minutes on foot from Kameoka station. Kameoka is accessible by rail from Kyoto on the JR Sagano (San-in) line. The Kyoto TIC provides an English leaflet and a photocopied timetable sheet for rail connections.

WESTERN KYOTO
京都の西部

Arashiyama and Sagano are two districts worth a visit in this area if you feel like strolling in pleasant natural surroundings and visiting temples tucked into bamboo groves. The JNTO leaflet, *Walking Tour Courses in Kyoto*, has a rudimentary walking map for the Arashiyama area.

Bus Nos 71, 72 and 73 link Arashiyama with Kyoto station. Bus No 11 connects Keihan-sanjō station with Arashiyama. The most convenient rail connection is the 20 minute ride from Shijō-Omiya station on the Keifuku-Arashiyama line to Arashiyama station. There are several bicycle rental shops (Y600 for three hours, Y1000 for the day) near the station, but it's more enjoyable to cover the relatively short distances between sights on foot.

Togetsu-kyō Bridge

Togetsu-kyō Bridge is the main landmark in Arashiyama, a couple of minutes on foot from the station. In July and August, this is a good vantage point to watch ukai (cormorant fishing) in the evening. If you want to get close to the action, you can pay Y1300 to join a passenger boat. The TIC can provide a leaflet and further details.

Tenryū-ji Temple

Tenryū-ji Temple is one of the major temples of the Rinzai school of Zen. It was built in 1339 on the former site of Emperor Go-Daigo's villa after a priest had dreamt of a dragon rising from the nearby river. The dream was interpreted as a sign that the emperor's spirit was uneasy and the temple was constructed as appeasement – hence the name *tenryū* (heavenly dragon). The present buildings date from 1900, but the main attraction is the 14th century Zen garden.

Admission costs Y500 and it's open from 8.30 am to 5.30 pm (April to October) and has a 5 pm closing time during rest of the year.

Okōchi Sansō Villa

This is the lavish home of Denjiro Okōchi, a famous actor in samurai films. The extensive gardens provide fine views over the city and are open to visitors. Admission costs a hefty Y700 (including tea and a cake). The villa is a 10 minute walk through bamboo groves north of Tenryū-ji Temple.

Temples North of Okōchi Sansō Villa

If you continue north from Okōchi Sansō Villa, the narrow road soon passes stone steps on your left leading up to the pleasant grounds of Jōjakkō-ji Temple. A further 10 minutes on foot brings you to Nison-in Temple, which is in an attractive setting up the wooded hillside.

If you have time for a detour, there are several small temples west of Nison-in Temple. Adashino Nembutsu-ji Temple is a rather bizarre temple where the abandoned bones of paupers and destitutes without next

---

Cormorant Fishing

Ukai (cormorant fishing) is mentioned in historical documents in Japan as early as the 8th century. It is still common in Gifu and Kyoto prefectures although I wonder if the people fishing may make less out of selling fish and more out of taking passengers along on the boat ride. Whilst the cormorants and the crew do all the work, the passengers have a fun time with lots of drinking and eating.

The season lasts from May to September; the best times for fishing are moonless nights when the fish are more easily attracted to the glare of a fire in a metal basket suspended from the bow of the boat. Fishing trips are cancelled during and after heavy rain.

The cormorants, up to a dozen in number, sit on the boat and are attached to long leashes. Once they dive in to do some fishing, a small metal ring at the base of their necks stops them doing the sensible thing and guzzling their catch. After filling their gullets with fish, they are hauled on board and obliged to disgorge the contents.

Each boat usually has a crew of four to handle the birds, the boat and the fire.

The cormorant catch is usually *ayu*, a type of sweetfish, much prized by Japanese foodies. A nifty cormorant can catch several dozen fish in a night. After completing their night's work, the cormorants are loaded into bamboo baskets in a strictly observed order of seniority – cormorants are very conscious of social ranking and will protest if this is not respected. Life expectancy for a cormorant ranges between 15 and 20 years, so they probably do have a point about seniority. ■

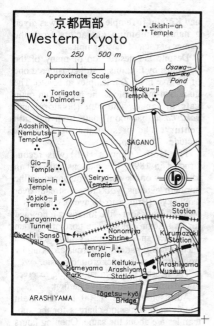

京都西部
Western Kyoto

0   250   500 m
Approximate Scale

•• Jikishi–an
   Temple

Ōsawa–
no–ike
Pond

Toriigata
Daimon–ji

Daikaku–ji
Temple

Adashino
Nembutsu–ji
Temple

SAGANO

Gio–ji
Temple

Nison–in
Temple

Seiryo–ji
Temple

Jōjakō–ji
Temple

Saga
Station

Ogurayanma
Tunnel

Ōkōchi Sansō
Villa

Nonomiya
Shrine

Kurumazaki
Station

Tenryu–ji
Temple

Keifuku–
Arashiyama
Station

Arashiyama
Museum

Kameyama
Park

ARASHIYAMA

Tōgetsu–kyō
Bridge

to Kyoto station and No 61 to Keihan-sanjō station).

SOUTH-WESTERN KYOTO
京都の西南部
Katsura Rikyū Imperial Villa
This villa is considered to be one of the finest examples of Japanese architecture. It was built in 1624 for the emperor's brother, Prince Toshihito. Every conceivable detail of the villa, the teahouses, the large pond with islets and the surrounding garden has been given meticulous attention.

Tours (in Japanese) start at 10 am and 2 pm and last about 40 minutes. You should be there 20 minutes beforehand. An explanatory video is shown in the waiting room and a leaflet is provided in English.

An imperial villa tour can evolve into an interesting cultural experience with Japanese sticking close to the guide whilst the foreigners hang back. Both groups eagerly jostle for camera positions: the Japanese want everyone *in* the picture whereas the foreigners want everyone *out*. Meanwhile, the harassed security man brings up the rear, nervously twiddling his earphone, trying to shepherd all the straggling foreigners.

To get to the villa from Kyoto station take bus No 33 and get off at the Katsura Rikyū-mae stop which is a five minute walk from the villa. The easiest access from the city centre is to take a Hankyū line train from Hankyū Kawaramachi station to Hankyū Katsura station which is a 15 minute walk from the villa.

Admission is free, but you *must* make reservations through the Imperial Household Agency (see earlier details for the Kyoto Imperial Palace) and usually several weeks in advance. Visitors must be over 20 years of age.

Saihō-ji Temple
The main attraction at this temple is the heart-shaped garden, designed in 1339 by Musō Kokushi. The garden is famous for its luxuriant mossy growth – hence the temple's other name: 'Koke-dera' (Moss Temple). Visiting the temple is recommended only if

of kin were gathered. Thousands of stone images are crammed into the temple grounds. These thousands of abandoned souls are remembered each year with candles here in the Sentō Kuyō ceremony held on the evenings of 23 and 24 August.

Daikaku-ji Temple
Daikaku-ji Temple is 25 minutes walk northeast of Nison-in Temple. It was built in the 9th century as a palace for Emperor Saga who converted it into a temple. The present buildings date from the 16th century, but are still palatial in style with some impressive paintings. The large Osawa no Ike Pond was once used by the emperor for boating.

The temple is open from 9 am to 4.30 pm and admission costs Y500. Close to the temple entrance are separate terminals for Kyoto-shi (Kyoto City) buses (No 28 goes to Kyoto station) and Kyoto buses (No 71 goes you have time and patience to follow the reservation rules.

Reservations Reservations are the only way you can visit. This is to avoid the overwhelming crowds of visitors who used to swamp the place when reservations were not required.

Send a postcard at least one week before the date you require and include details of your name, number of visitors, address in Japan, occupation, age (you must be over 18) and desired date (choice of alternative dates preferred). The full address is Saihō-ji Temple, 56 Kamigaya-cho, Matsuo, Nishikyō-ku, Kyoto. Enclose a pre-stamped return postcard for a reply to your Japanese address. You might find it convenient to buy an *ōfuki-hagaki* (send and return postcard set) at a Japanese post office.

You should arrive at the time and on the date supplied by the temple office. After paying your Y3000 'donation', you spend up to 90 minutes copying or chanting sutras or doing Zen meditation before finally being guided around the garden for 90 minutes.

Take bus No 73 from Kyoto station (45 minutes) or bus No 63 from Keihan-sanjō station (40 minutes).

SOUTH & SOUTH-EASTERN KYOTO
京都の南、東南部

The district to the south of Kyoto is mostly devoted to industry (also famed for saké breweries), but Tōfuku-ji Temple and the foxy Fushimi Inari Taisha Shrine are worth a visit.

To the south-east, Daigo-ji Temple is in rural surroundings and offers scope for a gentle hike to complement the architectural splendours. The city of Uji isn't exactly part of Kyoto, but it's easy to reach on a day trip, or as a convenient stop when travelling between Kyoto and Nara.

Tōfuku-ji Temple
Founded in 1236 by Jujo Michiie, Tōfuku-ji Temple now belongs to the Rinzai sect of Zen Buddhism. Since this temple was intended to compare with Tōdai-ji Temple

and Kōfuku-ji Temple in Nara, it was given a name combining characters from the names of each of these temples.

Despite the destruction of many of the buildings by fire, this is still considered one of the five main Zen temples in Kyoto. The huge San-mon Gate is the oldest Zen main gate in Japan. The *tosu* (lavatory) and *yokushitsu* (bathroom) date from the 14th century. The present temple complex includes 24 subtemples.

The Hōjō (Abbot's Hall) was reconstructed in 1890. The gardens, laid out in 1938, are worth a visit. As you approach the northern gardens, you cross a stream over Tsūtenkyō (Bridge to Heaven) which is a pleasant leafy spot – the foliage is renowned for its autumn colour. The northern garden has stones and moss neatly arranged in a chequerboard pattern; vigorous croaking by frogs provides the background music.

The nearby Reiun-in subtemple receives few visitors to its attractive garden.

Admission costs Y300 for the main temple and admission charges for the subtemples are about the same. Opening hours are from 9 am to 4 pm. English leaflets are provided.

To reach Tōfuku-ji Temple by train, you can either take a JR train on the Nara line or a train from Keihan-sanjō station on the Keihan Honsen line. Get off at Tōfuku-ji station. Bus No 208 also runs from Kyoto station via Tōfuku-ji Temple. Get off at the Tōfuku-ji-mae stop.

Fushimi-Inari Taisha Shrine
This intriguing shrine was dedicated to the gods of rice and saké by the Hata family in the 8th century. As the role of agriculture diminished, deities were enrolled to ensure prosperity in business. Nowadays, the shrine attracts hordes of tradespeople and businessfolk seeking blessings for their enterprises.

The entire complex, consisting of five shrines, sprawls across the wooded slopes of Mt Inari. A pathway wanders four km up the mountain and is lined with hundreds of red torii (arches). There are also dozens of Inari (fox deity) statues in stone. Inari is the messenger of the gods and a fickle character reportedly capable of being able to 'possess' humans – the favoured point of entry is under the fingernails. The key often seen in the fox's mouth is for the rice granary.

On 1 April, there is a festival at 11 am which features displays of flower arranging. On 8 April, there's a Sangyō-sai Festival with offerings and dances to ensure prosperity for national industry. During the first few days in January, thousands of festive believers pray at the shrine.

Local delicacies sold on the approach streets include barbecued sparrow and 'Inari-sushi' which is fried tōfu wrapped around sweetened sushi.

To get to the shrine from Kyoto station, take a JR Nara line train to Inari station. From Keihan-sanjō station on the Keihan Honsen line (honsen means 'main') and get off at Fushimi-Inari station. There is no admission charge for the shrine.

Daigo-ji Temple

Daigo-ji Temple was founded in 874 by the priest Shobo who gave it the name of Daigo (ultimate essence of milk). This refers to the five periods of Buddha's teaching which were often compared to the five forms of milk prepared in India – the highest form is called 'daigo' in Japanese.

The temple was expanded into a vast complex of buildings on two levels: Shimo Daigo (Lower Daigo) and Kami Daigo (Upper Daigo). During the 15th century, the buildings on the lower level were destroyed with the sole exception of the five storeyed pagoda. Built in 951, this pagoda still stands and is lovingly pointed out as the oldest of its kind in Japan and the oldest existing building in Kyoto.

In the late 16th century, Hideyoshi took a fancy to Daigo-ji Temple and ordered extensive rebuilding. It is now one of the main temples of the Shingon school of Buddhism.

To explore Daigo-ji Temple thoroughly and leisurely, mixing hiking with temple viewing, you will need at least half a day.

Hōkō Hanami Gyōretsu Parade On the second Sunday in April, a parade called Hōkō Hanami Gyōretsu takes place in the temple precincts. This re-enacts in full period costume the cherry-blossom party which Hideyoshi held in 1598. As a result of this party, the temple's abbot was able to secure Hideyoshi's support for restoration of the dilapidated temple complex.

Sampō-in Temple This was founded as a subtemple in 1115, but received a total revamp under Hideyoshi's orders in 1598. It is now a fine example of the amazing opulence of that period. The Kanō paintings and the garden are special features.

The garden is jam-packed with about 800 stones – the Japanese mania for stones goes back a long way. The most famous stone here is Fujito-no-ishi which is linked with deception, death and a fabulous price that was spurned; it's even the subject of a Nō play, Fujito. Admission to Sampō-in Temple costs Y500. It's open from 9 am to 5 pm (March to October) and closes one hour earlier during the rest of the year.

Hōju-in Treasure House This is close to the Sampō-in Temple, but is only open to the public from 1 April to 25 May and from 1 October to 25 November. Despite the massive admission fee of Y700, it really should not be missed if you happen to be there at the right time. The display of sculptures, scrolls, screens, miniature shrines and calligraphy is superb.

Climb to Kami Daigo From Sampō-in Temple in Shimo Daigo (Lower Daigo), walk up the large avenue of cherry trees, through the Niō-mon Gate and past the pagoda. From here you can continue for a pleasant climb through Kami Daigo (Upper Daigo), browsing through temples and shrines on the way. Allow 50 minutes to reach the top.

To get to the Daigo-ji Temple complex, take bus No 12 or bus 'Higashi' No 9 from central Kyoto to Rokujizo station (40 minutes). From there, it's an eight minute ride on the Toku (Special) No 12 bus to the Sampō-in-mae stop.

Mampuku-ji Temple

Mampuku-ji Temple was established as a Zen temple in 1661 by the Chinese priest Ingen. It is a rare example in Japan of a Zen temple built in the pure Chinese style of the Ming dynasty. The temple follows the Obaku school of Zen which is linked to mainstream Rinzai Zen, but incorporates a wide range of Esoteric Buddhist practices.

Admission costs Y400 and it's open from 9 am to 4.30 pm. The temple is a short walk from the two railway stations (JR Nara line and Keihan Uji line) at Obaku – about 30 minutes by rail from Kyoto.

Uji

Uji is a small city to the south of Kyoto. It's main claims to fame are the Byōdō-in Temple, tea cultivation and ukai (cormorant fishing). The stone bridge at Uji, the oldest of its kind in Japan, has been the scene of many bitter clashes in previous centuries – traffic jams seem to dominate nowadays.

Uji can be reached by rail in about 40 minutes from Kyoto on the Keihan Uji line or JR Nara line.

Byōdō-in Temple This temple was converted from a Fujiwara villa into a Buddhist temple in 1052. The Phoenix Hall (Hōō-dō), built in 1053, is the only original remaining building. The phoenix was a popular mythical bird in China and was revered by the Japanese as a protector of Buddha. The architecture of the building resembles the shape of the bird and there are two bronze phoenixes perched opposite each other on the roof.

Inside the hall is the famous statue of Amida and 52 Bosatsu (Bodhisattvas) dating from the 11th century and attributed to the priest-sculptor, Jōchō.

The temple, complete with its reflection in a pond, is indeed a stirring sight, but be warned that it's also a No 1 attraction in Japan and draws huge crowds. For a preview without the masses, take a look at the 10 yen coin. Admission costs Y300 and it's open from 8.30 am to 5 pm (March to November) and from 9 am to 4 pm during the rest of the year. English leaflets are provided.

The nearby Hōmotsukan Treasure House contains the original temple bell and door paintings and the original phoenix roof adornments. Admission to the house costs Y300 and it is only open from 10 April to 31 May and from 15 September to 3 November. Opening hours are from 9 am to 4 pm. A brief leaflet is supplied in English.

The approach street to the temple complex is lined with souvenir shops many of which roast local tea outside. A small packet of the tea is popular as a souvenir or gift.

Between 17 June and 31 August, ukai trips are organised in the evening around 7 pm on the river near the temple. Prices start at Y1500 per person. The TIC has a leaflet with up-to-date information on booking. More details about ukai are included in the Arashiyama section in Western Kyoto.

NORTHERN KYOTO
京都の北部

The area north of Kyoto provides scope for exploration of rural valleys and mountainous areas. Ohara makes a pleasant day trip, perhaps twinned with an excursion to Mt Hiei-zan and the Enryaku-ji Temple or Shūgaku-in Rikyū Imperial Villa.

Shūgaku-in Rikyū Imperial Villa

This villa was constructed for Emperor Go-Mizuno-o in the 1650s by the Tokugawa Shogunate to keep him distracted from ideas about a political role.

The villa grounds are divided into three large garden areas: lower, middle and upper. Each one has a teahouse.

The upper gardens are designed around a lake and 'borrow' the scenery of hills in the distance; the view from the Rinun-tei Teahouse at the top of these gardens is especially dramatic.

Tours (in Japanese) start at 9 and 10 am; 1.30 and 3 pm and the time required is about 50 minutes. You should be there 20 minutes beforehand. An English leaflet is provided.

Admission costs Y400 and it's open from 9 am to 5 pm. An English leaflet is provided. The house is a five minute walk from the Ichijoji-sagarimatsu-mae bus stop on the No 5 route.

Manshū-in Temple was originally founded by Saichō on Mt Hiei-zan, but was relocated here at the beginning of the Edo period. The architecture, works of art and garden are impressive.

The temple is open from 9 am to 5 pm and admission costs Y500; an English leaflet is provided. The temple is a 10 minute walk from Shūgaku-in Rikyū Imperial Villa.

Mt Hiei-zan & Enryaku-ji Temple

A visit to Hiei-zan and Enryaku-ji Temple is a good way to spend half a day hiking, poking around temples and enjoying the atmosphere of a key site in Japanese history.

In the 8th century, Emperor Kammu decided to protect Kyoto from evil influences traditionally believed to come from the north-east. He asked the priest, Saichō, to build a temple on Mt Hiei-zan to keep the evil spirits away.

Saichō founded the Tendai school of Buddhism which was only officially recognised after his death and the temple was given the new name of Enryaku-ji. The Tendai school quickly grew in size. For several centuries it dominated religious affairs and exerted strong pressures on government. At its peak, the temple complex numbered over 3000 buildings. To quash religious rivals or underline political disagreements, the temple 'army' regularly descended from the mountain to raid, slaughter and plunder in Kyoto and beyond.

During these times, an emperor ruefully commented that the only things which did not bend to his will were: 'the floods of the River Kamo, the dice in a game of sugoroku and the warrior monks (Sōhei) on the mountain'.

In 1571, Oda Nobunaga finally had enough of these antics and attacked Enryaku-ji. His orders regarding the priests were explicit: 'surround their dens and burn them, and suffer none within them to live!' The monks and the buildings were wiped out.

Some rebuilding took place in the 17th century, but the present buildings represent only a tiny fraction of what was once there.

Admission is free, but you must make reservations through the Imperial Household Agency – usually several weeks in advance (see the earlier Kyoto Imperial Palace section for details).

From Kyoto station, take bus No 5 and get off at the Shūgaku-in Rikyū-michi stop. The trip takes about an hour. From the bus stop it's a 15 minute walk to the villa.

Shisendō & Manshū-in Temples

Both these sights are in the vicinity of Shūgaku-in Rikyū Imperial Villa and both are less touristy than other major sights.

Shisendō (House of Poet-Hermits) was built in 1641 by Jōzan, a scholar of Chinese classics and a landscape architect, who wanted a place to retire at the end of his life. The garden provides relaxation – just the rhythmic 'thwack' of a bamboo *sōzu* (animal scarer) to interrupt your snooze. It was reputedly a favourite of Princess Diana when she visited Japan.

As it now stands, the temple area is divided into three sections: Tōdō, Saitō and Yokawa (of minimal interest). The Tōdō (Eastern

Section) contains the Kompon Chū-dō (Primary Central Hall) which dates from 1642. Admission costs Y400. It's open from 8.30 am to 4.30 pm (April to November) and from 9 am to 4 pm during the rest of the year. An English leaflet is provided. This part is heavily geared to group access with large expanses of asphalt for parking.

The Saitō (Western Section) contains the Shaka-dō (Shaka Hall) dating from the Kamakura period. The Saitō, with its stone paths winding through forests of tall trees, temples shrouded in mist and the sound of distant gongs, is less developed and more atmospheric than the other sections.

Getting There & Away *Train* If you want to go via Lake Biwa-ko, you can take a train from Kyoto to one of two stations (Sakamoto and Eizan) close to the base of Mt Hiei-zan. The most convenient of these two is Sakamoto which is near the base station of the cable railway which runs up Mt Hiei-zan to Enryaku-ji Temple.

To reach Sakamoto station, take the Keihan Kyozu line from Keihan-sanjō (in central Kyoto), then change to the Keihan Ishiyama line at Hama-ōtsu.

Eizan station is further from Sakamoto, but it's worth mentioning for Japan Rail Pass holders because it's on the JR Kosei line.

Although the views from the cable railway are excellent the rest of the train trip from Kyoto is unremarkable and tedious.

If you are starting from the north of Kyoto, you can also reach Yase-yuen by taking the train from Demachiyanagi station on the Eizan line.

Bus Bus Nos 17 and 18 run from Kyoto station to Ohara in about 50 minutes. Get off before Ohara at the Yase-yuenchi bus stop. From there it's a short walk to the cablecar station (departures every half hour) where you can ascend the mountain in two stages. A combined ticket (one way) for both sections costs Y820. The observatory at the top cablecar station has fine views across Lake Biwa-ko, though skip it if the weather is dull; entry costs Y300.

From Keihan-sanjō station in central Kyoto, you can take bus No 16 towards Ohara and get off at the Yase-yuenchi bus stop.

From Kyoto station there are direct buses to Enryaku-ji Temple and Mt Hiei-zan, at 9.50, 10.45 and 11.45 am and 1.50 pm (Y650, one hour 10 minutes). There are also direct buses from Keihan-sanjō station at 8.55, 9.35 and 11.06 am and 12.06, 1.05 and 3.05 pm (Y650, 52 minutes).

Ohara

Ohara is in a drowsy rural area with some fine temples – the most famous are Sanzen-in Temple and Jakkō-in Temple. The Oharame (Ohara damsels) who once dressed in distinctive costume and toted loads of twigs on their heads are still promoted on postcards or dressed up to parade for photos.

From Kyoto station, bus Nos 17 and 18 run to Ohara. The ride takes about 90 minutes. Allow half a day for a visit, possibly twinned with an excursion to Mt Hiei-zan and the Enryaku-ji Temple. JNTO includes a basic walking map for the area in its leaflet *Walking Tour Courses in Kyoto (MG052)*.

Sanzen-in Temple To visit this temple, walk out of the bus station up the road to the traffic lights. From there, take the small road to the right and turn left after the phone box. Then continue along a narrow path, lined with souvenir stalls, up the steep hill.

The oldest part of the temple is the main hall known as the 'Temple of Rebirth in Paradise' which was originally built in 985 by Eshin, a priest who retired from Mt Hiei-zan. The centrepiece of the hall is a set of statues – the Amitabha trinity.

The gardens are famous for their autumn colours. Part of the garden is jarringly modern compared with the venerable dignity of the classical section around the main buildings.

The temple is open from 8.30 am to 5.30 pm March to November and closes half an hour earlier during the rest of the year. Admission costs Y500 and an English leaflet is provided.

Jakkō-in Temple This temple lies to the west of Ohara. Walk out of the bus station up the road to the traffic lights, then follow the small road to the left; the temple is at the top of a steep flight of stone steps.

The history of this temple is exceedingly tragic – bring a supply of hankies. Founded in 594, the temple has become famous as the nunnery which harboured Kenreimon-in, a lady of the Taira clan. In 1185, the Taira lost their power completely when they clashed with the Minamoto clan in a sea battle. The entire Taira clan was slaughtered or drowned and Kenreimon-in threw herself into the waves with her son, the infant emperor, but she was fished out – the only member of the clan to survive.

She was returned to Kyoto where she became a nun living in a bare hut until it collapsed during an earthquake. Kenreimon-in was accepted into Jakkō-in Temple and stayed there, immersed in prayer and sorrowful memories, until her death 27 years later.

Jakkō-in is open from 9 am to 5 pm and admission costs Y500.

PLACES TO STAY

Kyoto has plenty of places to stay to suit all budgets. You have a choice ranging from the finest and most expensive ryokan in Japan to youth hostels or gaijin houses. Bear in mind that most of the cheaper places are further out of town. You can save time spent traversing the city if you organise your accommodation around the areas of interest to you. To help with planning, the following accommodation listings have been sorted according to location and price range. Gaijin houses usually offer reduced rates if you ask for weekly or monthly terms.

The TIC offers advice, accommodation lists and helps with reservations. Two useful TIC leaflets are *Reasonable Ryokan & Minshuku in Kyoto* and *Inexpensive Accommodations in Kyoto (Dormitory-Style)*.

Seven minutes walk from the TIC is the *Kyoto Minshuku Reservation Centre* (tel 351-4547), On Building, 7th Floor, Shimogyo-ku. The centre provides computer reservations for minshuku not only in Kyoto,

but all through Japan. Some English is spoken.

Kyoto is a mega-attraction for tourists so try and book in advance, particularly during holiday seasons.

Places to Stay – bottom end
Central Kyoto *Tani House Annex* (tel 211-5637) has doubles with bath and air-con for Y5500 per night. Take bus No 5 from Kyoto station (bus terminal A1) and get off at the Kawaramachi-sanjō-mae stop. The trip takes about 20 minutes.

Uno House (tel 231-7763) is another of the celebrated gaijin houses. Rates start at Y1400 for a dorm bed for the night and private rooms cost Y1600 per person.

Take bus Nos 205 or Toku 17 – make sure the kanji character for toku or 'special' (特) precedes the number – from Kyoto station (bus terminal A3) to the Kawaramachi-marutamachi-mae stop. The trip takes about 20 minutes.

Eastern Kyoto *Higashiyama Youth Hostel* (tel 761-8135) is a spiffy hostel which makes an excellent base very close to the sights of Higashiyama. For a dorm bed and two meals, the charge is Y3200. Private rooms are available for Y4600 per person (including two meals). There is a reduction in prices for foreign hostellers. Bicycle rental costs Y800 per day.

Less appealing aspects of the hostel are its regimentation – one traveller referred to it as Stalag 13 in a welcome note to his friends – and the 9.30 pm curfew. Meals are not a highlight, so you might prefer to skip them and find something more interesting in the town centre.

To get there, take bus No 5 from Kyoto station (terminal A1) to the Higashiyama-sanjō-mae stop (20 minutes).

Ise Dorm (tel 771-0566) provides basic accommodation (42 rooms) at rates between Y1350 and Y2600 per day; monthly terms range between Y27,000 and Y51,000 and yearly terms are also possible. Facilities on offer include phone, fridge, air-con, shower and washing machine.

Take bus No 206 from Kyoto station (bus terminal A2) to the Kumano-jinja-mae stop. Allow 30 minutes for the ride.

North-Western Kyoto *Utano Youth Hostel* (tel 462-2288) is a friendly, well-organised hostel which makes a convenient base for covering the sights of north-western Kyoto.

For a dorm bed and two meals, the charge is Y2250. Everything is ordered: 10 pm curfew, 10.30 pm lights-out and 6.30 am wakey-wakey. The men's bath is a large jacuzzi. There's an international phone just outside the front door. The buffet breakfast is good value for Y400. If you want to skip the hostel supper, turn left along the main road to find several coffee shops offering cheap set meals (teishoku).

Ask at the hostel's front desk about postage stamps, one-day travel passes, '11 bus tickets for the price of 10', postcards and discount entry tickets (to Sanzen-in Temple, Manshu-in Temple and Movieland). There's also a meeting room with bilingual TV news, but for many travellers, fond memories are reserved for the heated toilet seats!

Take bus No 26 from Kyoto station (bus terminal C1) to the Yūsu hosuteru-mae stop. The ride takes about 50 minutes.

Northern Kyoto *Aoi-Sō Inn* (tel 431-0788) charges Y2000 (without meals) per person. It's reported to be a quiet place with no evening curfew, and a coin laundry and kitchen are available. Dormitory-style accommodation costs Y1000 per person per night and a private room for two costs Y3000 per night. Rooms are available in another building at prices ranging between Y16,000 and Y43,000 per month.

The inn is near the old imperial palace, a five minute walk west from subway Kuramaguchi Shin-mei (exit 2) between the Kuramaguchi Hospital buildings. Call first to check directions and vacancies.

Tani House (tel 492-5489) is an old favourite for short-term and long-term visitors on a tight budget. There is a certain charm to this fine old house with its warren of rooms, jovial owners and quiet location

next to Daitoku-ji Temple. Costs per night are Y1400 for a space on the floor in a tatami room and Y3200 for a double private room. There's no curfew and free tea and coffee are provided. It can become crowded, so book ahead. Take the 45 minute ride on bus No 206 from Kyoto station (bus terminal B4) and get off at the Kenkun-jinja-mae stop.

Kitayama Youth Hostel (tel 492-5345) charges Y2200 for a dorm bed (without meals) or Y3200 with two meals. Take bus No 6 from Kyoto station (bus terminal B4) to the Genkoan-mae stop (allow 35 minutes for the trip). Walk west past a school, turn right and continue up the hill to the hostel (five minutes on foot). This hostel would be an excellent base to visit the rural area of Takagamine which has some fine, secluded temples such as Kōetsu-ji Temple, Jōshō-ji Temple and Shōden-ji Temple.

Green Peace, 14-1 Shibamoto-cho, Matsugasaki, Sakyo-ku (tel 791-9890) is a gaijin house offering dorm beds for Y1400. Twin rooms cost Y2800 per night, Y16,000 per week and Y42,000 per month. Facilities include a kitchen, shower and even a friendship room.

Take bus No 4 from Kyoto station (bus terminal A4) to the Nonogami-cho-mae stop. Allow 35 minutes for the ride.

Guest House Kyoto (tel 491-0880) has single rooms at Y2500 per day or Y40,000 for one month. Twin rooms are Y4000 per day or Y50,000 for one month. Take bus No 205 from Kyoto station (bus terminal B3) to the Senbon-kitaoji-mae stop (50 minutes).

Takaya (tel 431-5213) provides private rooms at Y2500 per day or Y45,000 for one month. Take the subway from Kyoto station to Imadegawa station (15 minutes).

Kyoto Ohara Youth Hostel (tel 744-2528) is a long way north out of town, but the rural surroundings are a bonus if you want to relax or dawdle around Ohara's beautiful temples. A dorm bed costs Y2100. From Kyoto station, you can take the subway to Kitaoji station and then take bus No 'north' 6 to Ohara (make sure the kanji for 'north' precedes the number or ask for *kita rokku*). Get off at the To-dera stop (near To-dera

Temple). The TIC can give precise details for other train or bus routes to get you there.

West of Kyoto Station *Tani Guest House,* 13 Inoguchi-cho, Kisshoin, Minami-ku (tel 681-7437, 671-2627) provides a dorm bed for Y1500 and single/double rooms for Y1800/3600. This is not connected with the management of the other Tani lodgings.

Take the JR line to Nishioji station (five minutes), then walk for 10 minutes.

Places to Stay – middle
Central Kyoto & Station Area *Ryokan Hiraiwa* (tel 351-6748), a member of the Japanese Inn Group, is used to receiving foreigners and offers basic tatami rooms. It is conveniently close to central and eastern Kyoto. Singles/doubles cost Y3500/7000 and facilities include bilingual TV, air-con and coin laundry. To get there from Kyoto station you can either walk (15 minutes) or take bus Nos 205, 42 or Toku (Special) 17 – make sure the kanji for toku precedes the number – from bus terminal A3. Get off at the third stop, Kawaramachi Shomen; from there it's a five minute walk.

Ryokan Kyōka (tel 371-2709), a member of the Japanese Inn Group, has 10 spacious, Japanese-style rooms. Singles/doubles cost Y3600/7200. If you give advance notice, a kaiseki dinner is available for Y3500. It's about eight minutes on foot from Kyoto station, close to the Higashi Hongan-ji Temple.

Matsubaya Ryokan (tel 351-4268) is a member of the Japanese Inn Group. Prices for singles/doubles are Y3800/7000; triples cost Y10,000. This ryokan is also close to Higashi Hongan-ji Temple.

Ryokan Murakamiya (tel 371-1260), also a member of the Japanese Inn Group, is seven minutes on foot from Kyoto station. Prices for singles/doubles are Y3500/7000; triples cost Y9000.

Riverside Takase (tel 351-7920) is a member of the Japanese Inn Group and has five Japanese-style rooms. The cost for singles/doubles starts at Y3100/5150; triples cost from Y7750. Take bus No 205 from

Kyoto station (bus terminal A3) and get off at the third stop, Kawaramachi Shomen.

The recently built *Pension Station Kyoto* (tel 882-6200) is a member of the Japanese Inn Group and a quiet place. Prices for singles/doubles are Y3600/7200; triples cost Y10,000. The pension is an eight minute walk from the station.

Yuhara Ryokan (tel 371-9583) has a family atmosphere and a riverside location popular with foreigners. Prices for singles/doubles are Y3500/7000. It's a 15 minute walk from Kyoto station.

Ryokan Hinomoto (tel 352-4563) is a member of the Japanese Inn Group with a position right in the centre of the city's action. Singles/doubles cost Y3500/7000; triples, Y9000. Take bus Nos 17 or 205 from Kyoto station (bus terminal A3) and get off at the Kawaramachi-matsubara-mae stop.

Eastern Kyoto *Ryokan Mishima (Mishima Shrine)* (tel 551-0033) operates as part of a Shinto shrine and is a member of the Japanese Inn Group. Singles/doubles cost Y4000/7000. On request, you can fulfil your photographic fantasy by dressing up in Shinto robes. Take bus No 206 (east-bound) from Kyoto station (bus terminal A2) and get off at the Higashiyama-umamachi-mae stop.

Pension Higashiyama (tel 882-1181) is a member of the Japanese Inn Group. It's a modern construction by the waterside and convenient for seeing the sights in Higashiyama. Prices for singles/doubles are Y3600/7200; triples cost Y10,000. For a break from Japanese breakfast, you could try the pension's American breakfast (Y800).

To get there, take bus No 206 from Kyoto station (bus terminal A2) for an 18 minute ride to the Chion-in-mae stop.

Three Sisters Inn (Rakutō-sō) (tel 771-0225) is a popular ryokan, at ease with foreign guests. Prices for singles/doubles start at Y7000/9000; family rooms start at Y12,000. Take bus No 5 from Kyoto station and get off at the Dobutsu-en-mae stop – the inn is just to the north of Heian-jingū Shrine. *The Three Sisters Annex* (tel 761-6333), close by, is run by the same management and has slightly cheaper room rates.

Iwanami (tel 561-7135) is a pleasant, old-fashioned ryokan with a faithful following of foreign guests. Book well in advance. Prices start at Y7200 per person including breakfast.

Kyoto Traveller's Inn (tel 771-0225) is a business hotel, very close to the Heian-jingū Shrine, offering both Western and Japanese-style rooms. Prices for singles/doubles start at Y5000/8600. There's no curfew and the Green Box restaurant on the 1st floor is open until 10 pm.

Northern Kyoto *Ryokan Rakucho* (tel 721-2174) is a member of the Japanese Inn Group. Prices for singles/doubles are Y3800/6600; triples cost Y8400.

The quickest way to get there is to take the subway from Kyoto station to Kitaoji station, walk east across the river and then turn north at the post office. To get there by bus, take bus No 205 from Kyoto station (bus terminal A3) and get off at the Furitsu-daigaku-mae stop.

Western Kyoto *Pension Arashiyama* (tel 881-2294) is a member of the Japanese Inn Group. Most of the rooms in this recently opened ryokan are Western style. Singles/doubles are Y3600/7200; triples cost Y10,000. An American breakfast is available for Y800.

To get there, take the 30 minute ride on Kyoto bus Nos 71, 72 or 73 and get off at the Arisugawa-mae stop.

Places to Stay – top end
Central Kyoto *Kinmata* (tel 221-1039) is a ryokan you should consider if you want to splurge on some traditional Japanese pampering. The inn started early in the last century and this is reflected in the original décor, interior gardens, antiques and hinoki (cypress) bathroom. Prices start at Y20,000 per person for a room and two meals. Advance reservation is essential. It's in the centre of town, very close to the Nishiki-kōji

market – if you can afford to stay here, the cost of a taxi will be a financial pinprick.

Hiiragiya (tel 221-1136) is another pinnacle of Japanese elegance favoured by celebrities from East and West. Reservations at this ryokan are essential. For a room and two meals, expect to pay at least Y25,000 per person.

Tawaraya (tel 211-5566) has been operating for over three centuries and is classed as one of the finest places to stay in the world. Guests at this ryokan have included the imperial family and royalty from overseas. It is a classic in every sense. Reservations are essential, preferably many months ahead. Expect to pay at least Y30,000 per person for a room and two meals.

Eastern Kyoto *Yachiyo* (tel 771-4148) is an elegant ryokan close to Nanzen-ji Temple. Prices per person for a room and two meals start at Y20,000.

Miyako Hotel (tel 771-7111) is a graceful, Western-style hotel perched up on the hills and a classic choice for visiting foreign dignitaries. The hotel surroundings stretch over 6.4 hectares of wooded hillside and landscaped gardens. For a change from Western-style rooms, you could try the Japanese wing. Prices for singles/doubles start around Y10,000/15,000.

Shukubō
Shukubō or temple lodgings are usually in peaceful, attractive surroundings with spartan tatami rooms, optional attendance at early morning prayer sessions and an early evening curfew. Guests use public baths near the temples. The Kyoto TIC has more details and a leaflet on the subject.

Myoren-ji Temple (tel 451-3527) charges Y3000 with breakfast. Take bus No 9 from Kyoto station (bus terminal B1) to the Horikawa-Teranouchi-mae stop.

Myoken-ji Temple (tel 414-0808, 431-6828) charges Y3500 per night with breakfast. It is close to Myoren-ji Temple (access details are given in the previous paragraph).

Hiden-in Temple (tel 561-8781) charges

Y4000 with breakfast. Take bus No 208 to the Sennyuji-michi-mae stop; another approach is to take the JR Nara line to Tōfuku-ji station.

Lodgings for Ladies
In Japan's male-oriented society, this might be an interesting option for female travellers to explore.

Ladies' Hotel Chōrakukan (tel 561-0001) is in Higashiyama, just south of Maruyama-kōen Park.

Also in Higashiyama is *Uemura* (tel 561-0377), a ryokan close to Kōdai-ji Temple.

Rokuō-in Temple (tel 861-1645) provides temple lodgings for women only – it's in western Kyoto, close to Rokuō-in station on the Keifuku Arashiyama line. Ask at the TIC for further information on these places and more ideas on the range of lodgings for women.

PLACES TO EAT
Kyoto is famed for *kyōryōri*, the local style of cooking, which closely follows *kaiseki* (stone on the stomach), the formal category of Japanese cuisine. Kaiseki evolved in Buddhist temples when the monks fended off hunger by holding warm stones against their stomachs whilst meditating. Gradually, the plain dishes which accompanied tea became part of a more and more complicated ritual.

Today, a kaiseki meal obeys strict rules of form and etiquette for every conceivable detail of the diner's surroundings and meal: it is the pinnacle of Japanese cuisine. A limited meal of this kind in a modest restaurant might cost Y6000 per person, a full spread easily costs Y15,000 and then there are exclusive establishments where you can shell out Y50,000 (if you are deemed fit to make a reservation). For lesser mortals with punier budgets, some restaurants do a kaiseki bentō (boxed lunch) at lunch time (11 am to 2 pm) at prices starting around Y2000.

Another style of cooking for which Kyoto is renowned is shōjin ryōri. This is a vegetarian cuisine (no meat, fish, eggs or dairy products are used) which was introduced from China and is now available in special

restaurants usually connected with temples. The emphasis is on tranquillity and precise presentation. Tōfu (bean curd) plays a prominent role in the menu and for a meal of this type, prices start at Y2000.

The TIC produces a food guide, *Kyoto Gourmet Guide* and has lists and maps for restaurants to suit all tastes and budgets. *Kyoto Visitor's Guide* has several pages with details for a wide selection of restaurants. *Old Kyoto: A Guide to Traditional Shops, Restaurants & Inns* would be a handy companion for extended exploration of Kyoto's culinary pleasures.

At the lower end of the food budget, there are plenty of fast-food eateries (*Shakey's Pizza, McDonald's, Kentucky Fried Chicken, Mr Donut,* etc) all over town.

Coffee shops and noodle restaurants are good for inexpensive meals or snacks. Good value is offered by the chain of *Doutor* coffee shops (big yellow and brown signs) which sell coffee for Y150 and inexpensive snacks.

Most of the major department stores have restaurants usually offering teishoku (set meals) which are good value at lunch time. Locals favour *Seven-Eight*, the 7th and 8th floors of Hankyū department store, which together form a large complex of inexpensive restaurants and are open until 10 pm. In the Porta shopping centre below Kyoto station there are also rows of restaurants with reasonable prices.

If you use the food section in the Facts for the Visitor chapter as a guide, you will soon develop your own skill at hunting for places to eat. It's usually more rewarding to make your own discoveries. The following places are but a brief sampling.

International Cuisine
Central Kyoto For Italian food, the *Ristorante Chiaro* (tel 231-5547) does reasonable lunches from Y850 (closed on Wednesday). It's opposite the Kyoto Royal Hotel on Kawaramachi-dōri St (just north of the intersection with Sanjō-dōri). Nearby is *Kerala* (tel 251-0141), a restaurant serving regional Indian dishes where lunch prices start at Y1500.

For Chinese food, *Gasshotei Gion* (tel 531-2100) has prices starting at Y800 and stays open until 3 am (closed on Sundays). It's on Tominagacho-dōri St, one block north of Shijō-dōri St.

Eastern Kyoto A couple of minutes walk north of the Heian-jingū Shrine is *Time Paradox* (tel 751-7531), a quirky eatery-cum-bar popular with university students and as a foreigners' den. The Western-style menu includes pizzas, omelettes, salads, soups, etc – prices start around Y800. It's open from 5 pm to 1 am daily except Thursdays.

Northern Kyoto *Knuckles Eatery* (tel 441-5849) was started by an American to provide Western-style foods (knuckle sandwiches, Bagels, cheesecake, etc). It's on the southern side of Kitaoji-dōri St at the Funaoka-kōen bus stop, two blocks east of Senbon-dōri St. It's open from 12 noon to 10 pm but closed on Mondays.

Japanese
Central Kyoto *Taka Jyo* (tel 751-7090) is open daily from 11 am to 9.30 pm and serves noodles from Y500 and a tempura bentō for Y650. It's on Sanjō-dōri St, about 100 metres east of Sanjō station. If you head west from this station along Sanjō-dōri St, cross over the bridge and continue for about 150 metres, you'll find *Ukiya* (tel 221-2978), a noodle restaurant on the right. Apart from inexpensive rice and noodle dishes (English menu), this place offers the free entertainment of daily noodle-making demonstrations between 2 and 4 pm. It's closed on Mondays.

Gonbei (tel 561-3350) is a well-known noodle restaurant in the heart of Gion, about 30 metres north of Shijō-dōri St on Kiridoshi St – look for the red lanterns outside. It is open until 11.30 pm but closed on Thursdays.

In the Pontochō area (a short walk north of Shijō-dōri St) on the western bank of the Kamogawa River, there are clusters of exclusive riverside restaurants. *Yamatomi* (tel 221-3268) is one of the cheaper places to sample a meal in this milieu. In the summer, there's a traditional dining platform outside, overlooking the river. The speciality of the house is 'teppin-age', a meal of vegetables, meat and seafood which you cook in a pot at your table. Set menus start at Y2500. It's open from 12 noon to midnight but is closed on Tuesdays.

Eastern Kyoto In the Higashiyama area, tucked inside the north gate of Maruyama-kōen Park, there's a traditional restaurant called *Hiranoya Honten* (tel 561-1603) in restful surroundings. The speciality of the house is 'imobō', a meal made from a type of sweet potato and dried fish. Prices for a set meal start at Y2000. It's open from 10.30 am to 8 pm.

If you walk north of Nanzen-ji Temple for a couple of minutes along the Path of Philosophy, you reach *Okutan* (tel 771-8709), a restaurant inside the luxurious garden of Chōshō-in Temple. This is a popular place which has specialised in vegetarian temple food for hundreds of years. A course of 'yutōfu' (bean curd cooked in a pot) together with vegetable side dishes costs Y3000. The restaurant is open from 10.30 am to 5.30 pm daily except Thursdays.

About five minutes walk from Ginkaku-ji Temple, and virtually opposite the Ginkaku-ji-mae bus stop, is *Omen* (tel 761-8926), a noodle shop named after the thick, white noodles (*omen*) it serves in a hot broth with vegetables. At Y850, the noodles are reasonable value and the folksy décor is interesting – one drawback is that the place is often packed solid. It's open from 11 am to 11 pm, closed on Thursdays.

North-Western Kyoto You can combine a visit to Daitoku-ji Temple with a shōjin ryōri meal at *Izusen* (tel 451-6665) inside the Daiji-in subtemple. It's open from 11 am to 5 pm and set meals start at Y2500.

ENTERTAINMENT
To find out what's on, check the listings at the TIC or look in *Kyoto Monthly Guide* or *Kansai Time Out*.

Dance & Theatre

Gion Corner (tel 561-1119) presents shows every evening at 7.40 and 8.40 pm between 1 March and 29 November; it's closed on 16 August. The presentation is definitely touristy, but you get a chance to see snippets of the tea ceremony, Koto music, flower arrangement, gagaku (court music), kyōgen (ancient comic plays), Kyōmai (Kyoto-style dance) and bunraku (puppet play). Tickets cost Y2500 and include an explanatory brochure. Photography is permitted. Be prepared for bursts of flash photography comparable to a wartime flak barrage.

The action starts on a stage on the far right-hand side – I spent the first five minutes studiously watching the stage in front and just as I was wondering why nothing was happening, realised I'd been missing the silent procedure of the tea ceremony on the far right!
Robert Strauss

Dance The Miyako Odori (Cherry Blossom Dance) takes place four times a day throughout April at the Gion Kōbu-Kaburenjō Theatre (tel 41-3391) which adjoins Gion Corner. Maiko (apprentice geisha) dress elaborately to perform a sequence of traditional dances in praise of the seasons. The performances start in the afternoon at 12.30, 2, 3.30 and 4.50 pm. The cheapest ticket is Y1650 (non-reserved on the tatami mat) and the Y3800 ticket includes participation in a tea ceremony.

A similar series of dances, Kamogawa Odori, takes place from 1 to 24 May and from 15 October until 7 November at Pontochō Kaburenjō Theatre (tel 221-2025). Ticket prices start at Y1650 (for a non-reserved seat on the 2nd floor).

Kabuki For a taste of kabuki, go to the Gion area in central Kyoto and visit Minami-za Theatre (tel 561-0160), the oldest kabuki theatre in Japan. The major event of the year is the Kao-misé Festival (1 to 26 December) which features Japan's finest kabuki actors.

Nō For performances of Nō, the two main theatres are Kanze Kaikan Nō Theatre (tel 771-6114) and Kongō Nō Stage (tel 221-

3049). Takigi-Nō is an especially picturesque form of Nō performed with lighting from blazing fires. In Kyoto, this takes place in the evenings of 1 and 2 June at Heian-jingū Shrine – tickets cost Y1800 if you pay in advance (ask at the TIC for the location of ticket agencies) or pay Y2500 at the entrance gate.

Bars

The main areas for nightlife in Kyoto are around Pontochō and Gion. Establishments with geisha entertainment are incredibly expensive – Y100,000 for a night is quite normal – and usually require an introduction from a patron. If you wander round Gion in the late afternoon or early evening, you can often catch sight of geisha or their apprentices (maiko) tripping off to an appointment. Pontochō has hundreds of drinking spots. To avoid an unpleasant surprise when presented with the bill, ignore pavement touts and hostess bars and always ask prices before imbibing. As a general rule of thumb, you can expect reasonable prices at aka-chochin – bars displaying a red lantern outside.

Far East (tel 252-2995) is a restaurant (open from 5 to 11 pm) and bar (open from 11 pm to 2 am), tucked down a sidestreet in the centre of town. (See the Central Kyoto map.) It's a popular meeting-point for locals and foreigners and prices start at Y500 for all sorts of snacks, including Chinese food. There is a selection of international bottled beers at about Y500 a bottle.

From Takashimaya department store, head north along Kawaramachi-dōri St for about 200 metres. Take the fourth sidestreet on the right and look for the Rex building (Reksu Biru) with a large flag outside.

Pig & Whistle Kyoto (tel 761-6022) is a pub on the 2nd floor of the Shobi building, opposite Keihan-sanjō station. It's an English-style pub, a favoured watering-hole for foreigners and reputed to be a pick-up joint. However, if you pop in for a quick pint of Kirin draught (Y600), the centre of attention is just as likely to be a darts game.

Kyoto Connection (tel 561-7557, 822-0898) holds an evening of music, poetry and performance on the last Saturday of each month. It's a meeting point with an open invitation to get on stage and share your talent.

Time Paradox near the Heian-jingū Shrine in eastern Kyoto, is another popular spot to meet foreigners and locals.

Concerts, Cinemas & Live Houses
Kyoto Visitor's Guide has extensive listings with venues and prices.

THINGS TO BUY
Kyoto offers probably the best shopping opportunities for traditional arts and handicrafts in Japan.

The TIC provide shopping maps and can help you track down specialist shops. *Old Kyoto: A Guide to Traditional Shops, Restaurants & Inns* is useful for finding unusual traditional items sold (and often produced) by elegant shops with vintage character.

There are several crafts which are specific to Kyoto. Kyō-ningyō are display dolls, Kyō-shikki is lacquerware with designs formed using gold or silver dust, Kyō-sensu are ritual fans made from bamboo and Japanese paper, Kyō-yaki are ceramics with elegant decorations, Zogan is a damascene technique laying pure gold and silver onto figures engraved on brass, Nishijin-ori is a special technique of silk textile weaving and Kyō-yūzen is a form of silk-dyeing.

The main shopping haunts in the centre of town are around Kawaramachi-dōri St, between Sanjō-dōri and Shijō-dōri. In the same area, Teramachi-dōri St is lined with shopping arcades. In eastern Kyoto, the paved streets of Ninnenzaka and Sannenzaka (close to Kiyomizū-dera Temple) are renowned for their crafts and antiques.

Kyoto's largest department stores (Hankyū, Takashimaya and Fujii Daimaru) are grouped on Shijō-dōri St, close to Kawaramachi station. Kintetsu department store is one block north of the TIC.

If you want to do all your shopping under one roof, the following places offer a wide selection of Kyoto handicrafts. Kyoto Municipal Museum of Traditional Industry (tel 761-3421), close to the Heian-jingū Shrine, holds exhibitions of Kyoto handicrafts and demonstrations of techniques. A selection of crafts is also on sale. Admission is free and it is open from 9 am to 4.30 pm but closed on Mondays.

The Kyoto Craft Centre (tel 561-9660) in Gion exhibits and sells handicrafts. It's open from 10 am to 6 pm daily except Wednesdays.

The Kyoto Handicraft Centre (tel 761-5080), just east of Kumano-jinja Shrine, is a huge co-operative which sells, demonstrates and exhibits crafts. It's open from 9.30 am to 6 pm.

If you are interested in seeing all the weird and wonderful foods required for cooking in Kyoto, wander through Nishiki-kōji market. It's in the centre of town, one block north of Shijō-dōri St and just behind Daimaru department store. For other monthly markets, see the information section at the beginning of the Kyoto chapter.

Ippō-dō (tel 211-4321) and Kungyoku-dō (tel 371-0162) are two shops which are particularly appealing. Ippō-dō is an old-fashioned teashop selling all sorts of teas. Some English is spoken. It's on Teramachi-dōri St, two blocks north of Kyoto City Hall and it's open from 9 am to 7 pm, closed on Sundays. Kungyoku-dō is a shop which has dealt in incense, herbs, spices and fine woods for four centuries. It's a haven for the olfactory senses, and is opposite the gate of the Nishi Hongan-ji Temple. It's open from 9 am to 7 pm but is closed on the first and third Sundays of each month.

For ideas about duty-free or discount items (cameras, hi-fi, watches, etc) you could try Ninomiya (tel 361-7767). It's open daily from 10 am to 7 pm; closed on Wednesdays.

GETTING THERE & AWAY
Air
Kyoto is served by Osaka Itami Airport – a major hub for domestic and international flights. There are frequent flights between Tokyo and Osaka – flight time is about 70 minutes but unless you are very lucky with

airport connections you'd probably find it almost as quick and more convenient to take the shinkansen. The airport is an hour by bus from central Kyoto.

Train

Kyoto to Osaka If you are loaded with money, or have a Japan Rail Pass you can take the JR shinkansen line between Kyoto and Shin-Osaka – the trip takes only 16 minutes. To connect between Shin-Osaka and central Osaka, you can either take the JR Tōkaidō (San-yō) line to Osaka station or switch to the Mido-suji subway line for Osaka's Namba district.

The Japan Rail Pass is also valid on the JR Tōkaidō (San-yō) line which runs via Osaka. The trip between Kyoto and Osaka station takes 45 minutes and is Y530 for a one-way ticket.

The Hankyū Kyoto line runs between Kyoto (Kawaramachi station) and Osaka (Umeda station – close to JR Osaka station). The fastest trip takes 47 minutes and is Y330 for a one-way ticket.

The Keihan line runs between Kyoto (Keihan-sanjō station) and Osaka (Yodobashi station). The fastest trip takes 40 minutes and costs Y330 for a one-way ticket.

Kyoto to Nara Unless you have a Japan Rail Pass, the best option is the Kintetsu line linking Kyoto and Nara (Kintetsu Nara station) in 33 minutes by limited express (tokkyū) (Y900 one way). If you take a local or express train on this line, the ticket price drops to Y500 for the 45 minute ride, but you will need to change at Yamato-Saidai-ji which is a five minute ride from Nara Kintetsu station.

The JR Nara line connects Kyoto with Nara JR station in one hour (Y740 one way).

Kyoto to Tokyo The JR shinkansen line is the fastest and most frequent rail link. The super-express takes two hours and 40 minutes from Tokyo station and a one-way ticket including surcharges costs Y12,970.

The TIC has a leaflet which gives examples of a cheap route using local trains for

eight hours on the JR Tōkaidō line between Tokyo and Kyoto. A one-way ticket should cost about Y8000.

Bus

A JR bus runs frequently during the day between Osaka and Tokyo via Kyoto and Nagoya. Passengers change buses at Nagoya. Travel time for the express buses between Kyoto and Nagoya is about 2½ hours (Y2200). The journey between Nagoya and Tokyo takes about 6¼ hours (Y5000).

The overnight bus (JR Dream Bus) runs between Tokyo and Kyoto (departures in both directions). The trip takes about eight hours and there are usually two departures at 10 and 11 pm. Tickets are Y8050 plus a reservation fee. You should be able to grab some sleep in the reclining seats. If you find sleep a bit of a struggle, you can console yourself with the thought that you are saving on accommodation and will be arriving at the crack of dawn to make good use of the day.

Hitching

For long-distance hitching, the best bet is to head for the Kyoto-Minami Interchange of the Meishin expressway which is about four km south of Kyoto station. Take the Toku No 19 bus (make sure the kanji for 'special' (toku) precedes the number) from Kyoto station and get off when you reach the Meishin expressway signs.

From here you can hitch east towards Tokyo or west to southern Japan.

GETTING AROUND
To/From the Airport
There's a limousine bus service every 20 minutes from early morning until early evening between Kyoto station and Osaka Itami Airport (Y830, one hour). The buses serve Kyoto station as well as the major hotels in Kyoto.

Bus
Kyoto has an intricate network of bus routes which provides an efficient way of getting around at moderate cost. Many of the bus

routes used by foreign visitors have announcements in English. The core timetable for buses is between 7 am and 9 pm though a few run earlier or later.

The main bus terminals are Kyoto station, Keihan-sanjō station, and Shijō-karasuma station. On the northern side of Kyoto station is a major bus terminus with departure terminals clearly marked with a letter of the alphabet and a number.

The TIC has two bus maps: a simplified map on the reverse of the *Kyoto, Nara* brochure and a bus route map, studded with kanji, for advanced bus explorers.

Bus stops throughout the city usually display a map of bus stops in the vicinity on the top section. On the bottom section there's a timetable for the buses serving that stop.

Entry to the bus is usually through the back door and exit is via the front door. Inner city buses charge a flat fare (Y180) which you drop into a machine next to the driver. The machine gives change for Y100 and Y500 coins or Y1000 notes, or you can ask the driver.

On buses serving the outer areas, you take a numbered ticket *(seiriken)* when entering. When you leave, an electronic board above the driver displays the fare corresponding to your ticket number.

To save time and money, you can buy a *kaisū-ken* (book of six tickets) for Y1000 at bus centres or from the driver. There is also a deal offering 11 tickets for the price of 10.

There's a one-day pass, *ichinichi jōshaken*, which is valid for unlimited travel on city buses, private Kyoto buses and the subway. It costs Y1050 and is available at bus centres and subway stations.

Bus No 59 is useful for travel between the sights of north-western Kyoto and Keihan-sanjō station. Bus No 5 connects Kyoto station with the sights of eastern Kyoto.

Three-digit numbers denote loop lines. No 204 runs round the northern part of the city and Nos 205 and 206 circle the city via Kyoto station.

Bicycle

Renting a bicycle makes sense in peripheral areas of Kyoto such as Higashiyama, Arashiyama or northern Kyoto. Dense traffic in central Kyoto makes cycling unpleasant. Compared with bus travel, the savings on bicycle rental are minimal, but you can stop as you please. On the other hand, many of the peripheral areas are easily and enjoyably covered on foot.

Both the youth hostels at Higashiyama and Utano provide bicycle rental. In Higashiyama you could try Taki Rent-a-Bicycle on Kaminokuchi St, east of Kawaramachi. Arashiyama station has several places for bicycle rental. Nippon Rent-a-Cycle is in front of Kyoto station, close to the Hachijo exit. The TIC has more information on bicycle shops and rental.

Subway

The quickest way to travel between the north and the south of the city is to take the subway which operates from 5.30 am to 11.30 pm. There are eight stops, though the most useful ones are those in the centre of town. The minimum fare is Y160.

Taxi

Kyoto is well-endowed with taxis. Fares start at Y430 for the first two km.

MK Taxi (tel 721-2237) provides a regular taxi service as well as tours with English-speaking drivers. For a group of up to four people, prices start at Y12,620 for a three hour tour.

Osaka 大阪

There's no way around it: Osaka (population 2.9 million) is another big, dirty city with little to offer the short-term visitor. Second only to Tokyo in economic importance (third, after Yokohama, in population), Osaka suffers from even more of a lack of open spaces, greenery and historical sites than the capital city. Unfortunately, even though Osaka has been around for some 1500 years and even had a brief spell in the 16th century as the nation's capital, there is

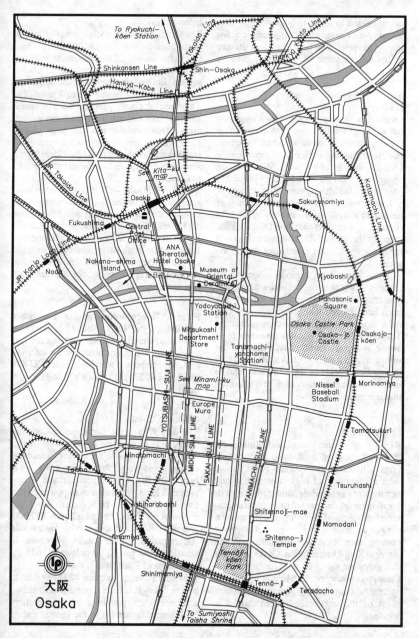

To Ryokuchi-kōen Station

Tokaidō Line

Hankyū Kyoto Line

Shinkansen Line

Shin-Osaka

Hankyū-Kōbe Line

JR Tokaidō Line

See Kita-ku map

Osaka

Temma

Sakuranomiya

Fukushima

Central Post Office

Katamachi Line

JR Kanjo Loop Line

Nakano-shima Island

ANA Sheraton Hotel Osaka

Noda

Museum of Oriental Ceramics

Kyobashi

Yodoyabashi Station

Panasonic Square

Mitsukoshi Department Store

Osaka Castle Park

Osaka-jō Castle

Osakajō-kōen

Tanimachi-yonchome Station

See Minami-ku map

Nissei Baseball Stadium

Morinomiya

YOTSUBASHI-SUJI LINE

Europe Mura

MIDO-SUJI LINE

SAKAI-SUJI LINE

TANIMACHI-SUJI LINE

Tamatsukuri

Minatomachi

Tsuruhashi

Taisho

Shitennoji-mae

Ashiharabashi

Momodani

Imamiya

Shitennō-ji Temple

Shinimamiya

Tennōji-kōen Park

Tennō-ji

Teradacho

大阪
Osaka

To Sumiyoshi Taisha Shrine

not much left to remind visitors of that long history. The one real compensation for having to spend time here is the opportunity to indulge in some of the best dining in Japan.

History

Osaka may have been around for a long time but it wasn't until the late 16th century that the city rose to prominence when Toyotomi Hideyoshi, having unified all of Japan, chose Osaka as the site for his castle. Merchants set up around the castle and the city quickly grew into a flourishing economic centre.

Even though the Toyotomi clan was defeated by the Tokugawas early in the 17th century, in a conflict that saw Osaka Castle razed to the ground, the Tokugawas rebuilt the castle and the city maintained its importance.

Today the Osaka region's economy is actually larger than that of entire developed countries like Canada and Australia. It has even been argued that, given the very real risks of another major earthquake levelling Tokyo, Osaka might one day take over from Tokyo as Japan's capital city. Whatever the future might hold for Osaka, its residents have a fierce pride in their city and tend to be a little contemptuous of all the attention that is received by Tokyo.

Orientation

Kita-ku, the northern ward, and Minami-ku, the southern ward each have distinct features. Kita-ku is the business part of town with a scattering of high-rises and trendy department stores, while Minami-ku, with its bustling entertainment quarters, great restaurants and discount shopping, is a living area.

Osaka station is in Kita-ku, but if you're coming from Tokyo by shinkansen you will arrive at Shin-Osaka station. Osaka station is two stops, or about 10 minutes from Shin-Osaka by subway on the Mido-suji line. The same line continues to Minami-ku, where most of the cheaper accommodation is located.

Information

The Osaka Tourist Association has offices at both Shin-Osaka (tel 06-305-3311) and Osaka (tel 06-345-2189) stations, though the main one is near the eastern exit of Osaka station. Both offices have English-speaking staff and are open from 8 am to 7 pm daily. Their useful *Osaka* map includes a small subway map and insets of the main tourist areas. Also available is a 200 page glossy book with extensive information on sights, restaurants, hotels and festivals – ideal if you are planning on spending the rest of your life in Osaka.

The TIC *Osaka – Kōbe* brochure has reasonable maps of the two cities along with effusive descriptions of their sights. *Osaka & Vicinity* has good maps of the Kansai region and of the railway lines radiating out from Osaka; stations are indicated in both kanji and romaji. See the Kyoto section for information on the magazines *Kansai Time Out* and *Discover Kinki!*.

Post & Telecommunications The main post office (tel 06-347-8034) is between Osaka and Umeda stations. For telex and fax services try the major hotels or the international telegraph and telephone office (KDD) (tel 06-343-2571) in Umeda's Shin-Hanshin building.

Osaka-jō Castle

The city's foremost attraction is unfortunately a 1931 concrete reproduction of the original. The castle's exterior retains a certain grandeur but the interior looks like a barn with lifts. The original castle, completed in 1583, was a display of power on the part of Toyotomi Hideyoshi. After he achieved his goal of unifying Japan, 100,000 workers toiled for three years to construct an 'impregnable' granite castle. However, it was destroyed just 32 years later in 1615 by the armies of Tokugawa Ieyasu.

Within 10 years the castle had been rebuilt by the Tokugawa forces, but it was to suffer a further calamity when another generation of Tokugawas razed it to the ground rather

Top: Sakurajima erupting (TW)
Middle: Fuji-san (CT)
Bottom: Chinoike Jigoku (Blood Pool Hell), Beppu (TW)

Advertising - Japanese style

than let it fall to the forces of the Meiji Restoration in 1868.

The interior of today's castle houses a museum of Toyotomi Hideyoshi memorabilia as well as displays relating the history of the castle. They are of marginal interest but the 8th floor provides a view over Osaka. The castle is open from 9 am to 5 pm daily and admission is Y400.

The Ote-mon Gate is about a 10 minute walk north-east of Tanimachi-yonchome station on the Chūō and Tanimachi subway lines. From the JR Kanjo line that circles the city, get off at Morinomiya station and look for the castle grounds a couple of minutes to the north-west. You enter through the back of the castle.

Shitennō-ji Temple

Shitennō-ji Temple, founded in 593, has the distinction of being one of the oldest Buddhist temples in Japan but none of today's buildings are originals. Most are the usual concrete reproductions but an exception, and a feature that is quite unusual for a Buddhist temple, is the big stone torii (entrance gate). It dates back to 1294, making it the oldest of its kind in Japan. Apart from the torii, there is little of real historical significance there, and the absence of greenery in the raked-gravel grounds makes for a rather desolate atmosphere.

The temple is open from 9 am to 5 pm daily and admission is Y500. It's most easily reached from Shitennō-ji-mae station on the Tanimachi line. Take the southern exit, cross to the left side of the road and take the small road that goes off at an angle away from the subway station. The entrance to the temple is on the left.

Tennō-ji-kōen Park

About a 10 minute walk from the temple with which it shares its name, this park can be combined with a visit to Shitennō-ji Temple, although its prime attraction, the Keitaku-en Garden, has rather irregular opening hours.

The park has a botanical garden, a zoo and a circular garden known as Keitaku-en. The latter is only open from 9 am to 4.30 pm on Tuesday, Thursday and Sunday. The park is a 10 minute walk from Tennō-ji station on the JR Kanjo line. To get there from the Shitennō-ji Temple, exit through the torii, turn left, then right, then left again into the main road and look for the park on your right.

Sumiyoshi Taisha Shrine

This shrine is dedicated to Shinto deities associated with the sea and sea travel, in commemoration of a safe passage to Korea by a 3rd century empress.

Having survived the bombing in WW II, the Sumiyoshi Taisha Shrine actually has a couple of buildings that date back to 1810. The shrine was founded in the early 3rd century and the buildings that can be seen today are faithful replicas of the originals. They offer a rare opportunity to see a Shinto shrine that predates the influence of Chinese Buddhist architectural styles.

The main buildings are roofed with a kind of thatch rather than the tiles on most later shrines. Other interesting features are a collection of more than 700 stone lanterns donated by seafarers and businesspeople, a stone stage for performances of bugaku and court dancing and the attractive Taiko-bashi Bridge, an arched bridge with park surroundings.

The shrine is next to both Sumiyoshi-taisha station on the Nankai line and Sumiyoshi-tori-mae station on the Hankai line.

Kita-ku

There's not a lot to do in Kita-ku and if you've passed through the area on your arrival that might be enough to get a feel for what the northern part of town is about. Basically, if you've been pining for concrete this is the place to get a fix.

Hankyū Grand Building This 32 storeyed building next to Osaka station is renowned for its restaurants which occupy the 27th to 31st floors – not a bad place to check out the lunch-time specials, though its prestige

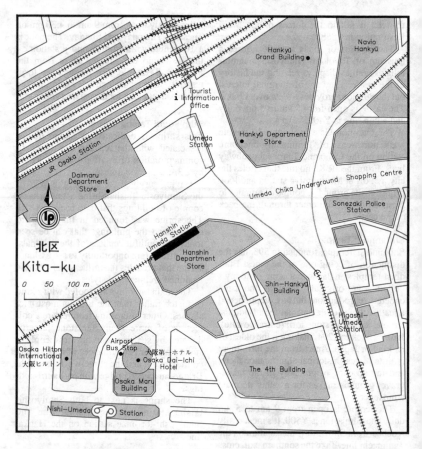

rating nudges the prices up a little. There is a free observatory on the 32nd floor.

Umeda Chika Centre This labyrinthine underground shopping complex can easily keep you occupied for a few hours with everything from cheap eats to antiques. The complex links Osaka station with Umeda station and can be entered from either.

Museum of Oriental Ceramics

With more than 1000 exhibits the museum is claimed to have one of the finest collections of Chinese and Korean ceramics in the world. Opening hours are from 9.30 am to 5 pm daily (closed on Mondays) and admission is Y400.

To get to the museum, go to Yodoyobashi station on either the Mido-suji line or the Keihan line (different stations). Walk north to the river and cross to Nakano-shima Island. Turn right, pass the city hall on your left, bear left with the road and the museum is on the left.

Panasonic Square

Billed as a 'Futuristic Electro-Fun Zone', Panasonic Square is a display forum for high-tech gadgetry developed by the Matsushita Electric Group of companies. It's very much hands-on and quite fun if you haven't already been to a similar place in Japan. Highlights include Adventure Space-ship where multi-screen video projectors give you the illusion of approaching earth from outer space and a CD jukebox that you enter and request songs from by punching in a number.

Panasonic Square is open from 10 am to 6 pm daily except Wednesdays and admission is Y200. The easiest way to get there is to take the Keihan line to Kyobashi station, take the southern exit, cross the river and turn right. Panasonic Square is on the 2nd floor of the Twin 21 Tower building.

Minami-ku

This part of town south of Shinsaibashi station is fun just to wander around but it really doesn't come into its own until night falls when the blaze of neon makes an incredible difference to the atmosphere. North of Dōtomburi, between Midosuji-dōri Ave and Sakaisu-ji-dōri Ave, the narrow streets are crowded with hostess bars, discos and pubs. Expensive cars clog the streets, hostesses dressed in kimono and geta trot a few steps behind flushed businessmen, and young salarymen stagger around in drunken packs.

Dōtomburi You can start by exploring the wall-to-wall restaurants along the south bank of the Dōtomburigawa Canal, though don't restrict your gaze to ground level – almost every building has three or four floors of restaurants with prices ranging from reasonable to sky-high.

National Bunraku Theatre Although bunraku, or puppet theatre, did not originate in Osaka, the art form was popularised there. The most famous bunraku playwright, Chikametsu Monzaemon (1653-1724), wrote plays set in Osaka concerning the classes that traditionally had no place in Japanese art: merchants and the denizens of the pleasure quarters. Not surprisingly, bunraku found an appreciative audience amongst

these people and a famous theatre was established to put on the plays of Chikametsu in Dōtomburi. Today's theatre is an attempt to revive the fortunes of bunraku.

Performances are only held at certain times of the year: check with the tourist information offices. Tickets normally start at around Y3500 and English programme guides and earphones are available.

Expo Memorial Park

This park is the legacy of Expo '70, and houses a few interesting attractions such as the National Museum of Ethnology, Expo Land and a Japanese garden. To get there take the Mido-suji line to Senri Chūō station and change to bus Nos 114 or 115 to the park, (that is, if the monorail from the station to the park is not already operating).

National Museum of Ethnology This museum features everyday items from cultures around the world and makes extensive use of audio-visual equipment. Admission is Y300 and it is open from 10 am to 5 pm but closed on Wednesdays.

Festivals
Sumiyoshi Taisha Odori
    1 to 3 January. Children stage traditional dances every 30 minutes from 10 am to 3 pm at Sumiyoshi Taisha Shrine.
Toka Ebisu
    9 to 11 January. Huge crowds of more than a million people flock to the Imamiya Ebisu Shrine to receive bamboo branches hung with auspicious tokens. The shrine is near Imamiya Ebisu station on the Nankai line.
Doya Doya
    14 January. Billed as a 'huge naked festival', this event involves a competition between young men, clad in little more than headbands and imitation Rolex wrist watches, to obtain the 'amulet of the cow god'. This talisman is said to bring a good harvest to farmers. The festival takes place at 3 pm at Shitennō-ji Temple.
Shōryō-e
    22 April. Shitennō-ji Temple holds night-time performances of bunraku.
Otaue Shinji
    14 June. Women and girls dressed in traditional costumes commemorate the establishment of the imperial rice fields. The festival is held at the Sumiyoshi Taisha Shrine.

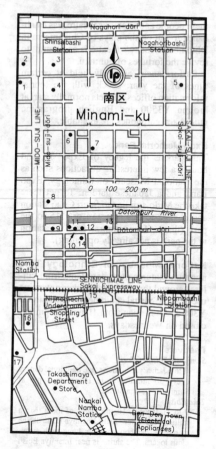

Minami-ku	
1	Hotel California
2	Hotel Nikko Osaka
3	Sogo Department Store
4	Daimaru Department Store
5	Minami Post Office
6	Pig & Whistle Pub
7	Shanghai Bar
8	Holiday Inn
9	Moti Indian Restaurant
10	Kirin Plaza Building
11	Kani Doraku Restaurant
12	Sawasdee Thai Restaurant
13	Ebi Doraku Restaurant
14	Kuidaore Restaurant
15	Printemps Namba
16	Shin Kabuki-za Theatre
17	Airport Bus Stop

Minami-ku	
1	ホテルカリフォルニア
2	ホテル日光大阪
3	そごうデパート
4	大丸デパート
5	南郵便局
6	ビッグ＆ホイッスル
7	上海
8	ホリディイン
9	モティレストラン
10	キリンプラザビル
11	かにどらくレストラン
12	サワスディレストラン
13	えびどらくレストラン
14	くいだおれレストラン
15	ブランタンなんば
16	新歌舞伎座
17	空港バス乗り場

Tenjin Matsuri

24 to 25 July. Processions of portable shrines and people in traditional attire start at Temmangu Shrine and end up in the Okawa River (in boats). As night falls the festival is marked with a huge fireworks display.

Places to Stay

The best place to stay when visiting Osaka is Kyoto. It's less than 20 minutes away by shinkansen, there'a a far better choice of accommodation (particularly in the budget bracket) and it's a much nicer place. Busi-

ness hotels in Osaka are concentrated in the central area and the cheaper places are inconveniently further out.

Youth Hostels *Osaka Shiritsu Nagai Youth Hostel* (tel 06-699-5631) near Nagai station on the Mido-suji line is only about 10 minutes from Minami-ku and costs Y1600 or Y1850 depending on the season. Further out, about 15 minutes from Kita-ku or 30 minutes from Minami-ku, is the *Osaka-fu Hattori Ryokuchi Youth Hostel* (tel 06-862-0600), where beds are Y1600. Take the Mido-suji line to Ryokuchi-kōen station and leave through the western exit. Enter the park and follow the path straight ahead past a fountain and around to the right alongside the pond. You will find the youth hostel a little further on the right.

Budget Hotels *Rinkai Hotel Dejimaten* (tel 0722-41-3045) and *Rinkai Hotel Kitamise* (tel 0722-47-1111) are close together and good for short or long-term stays; they're much cheaper by the month. Singles start from Y2500, or Y3000 with bathroom. For long-term stays, rooms are Y1800/3200 for singles/doubles. There are cooking facilities and dining areas. Take an express from platform 5 or 6 at Namba station, change to a Nankai line local train at Sakai and get off at the next stop, Minato station. Take the eastern exit, turn right, then left at the first intersection to the Dejimaten. Walk back along the road that the Dejimaten is on until you reach a T junction. The Kitamise is on the opposite side of the road, to the left.

The *Ebisu-sō Ryokan* (tel 06-643-4861) is a bit more expensive but more convenient and has singles/doubles from Y3800/7000. The rooms are small, but have a TV, heater and fan. The ryokan is a 10 minute walk from the No 4 exit of Namba station or from the No 1 exit of Ebisu-chō station.

Middle-Range Hotels Without a doubt, the best mid-range hotel in town is the wonderfully kitsch *Hotel California* (tel 06-243-0333). The bar downstairs is a very Japanese interpretation of California style, complete with garish wooden marlin, parrots and vertical ducks hanging on the walls. The huge potted plants give the lounge the supposedly appropriate 'everglade' feel. The rooms are slightly larger than those in an average business hotel and prices start at Y7000/10,000 for singles/doubles with bathroom. To get to the Hotel California, take the No 8 exit of Shinsaibashi station, turn right into the small street that runs off the main road next to the big Hotel Nikkō Osaka and the hotel is about 50 metres down on the left – you'll see the sign.

Other mid-range possibilities include the *Tennōji Miyako Hotel* (tel 06-779-1501), a fairly good standby at Y6000/11,000 for singles/doubles (Y8500/13,000 with private bathroom). It's located virtually on top of Tennō-ji station.

Expensive Hotels Close to the action in Minami-ku, the *Hotel Nikkō Osaka* (tel 06-244-1111) has all the international-class facilities and rooms from Y14,000/23,500 for singles/doubles. It's located above Shinsaibashi station. On the opposite side of the road, down towards Dōtomburi is the *Holiday Inn Nankai Osaka* (tel 06-213-8281) with rooms from Y11,500/18,000.

The highly rated *ANA-Sheraton Hotel* (tel 06-347-1112) is beautifully laid out; prices for singles/doubles start at Y14,000/23,000. It's about 10 minutes walk south of Osaka station. The *Osaka Hilton Hotel* (tel 06-347-7111), also close to Osaka station, is a 35 storeyed building with everything from shopping malls to a tennis court; singles/doubles cost from Y20,000/25,000.

Places to Eat
Kita-ku The eating options in Kita-ku are more expensive and not as exciting as in Minami-ku. Use Kita-ku as a lunch spot and reserve the more colourful and economical Minami-ku for your evening meal.

The *Food Park* in the Umeda Chika Centre has about 20 small restaurants with dishes ranging from noodles to sushi. Nothing is over Y500 and ordering is made easy by the colour photographs of dishes displayed by each restaurant. On the 27th to 31st floors of the Hankyū Grand building there are plenty of restaurants and although they're a bit pricey there are a few good lunch-time specials.

Minami-ku The place to eat in Minami-ku is the restaurant-packed street of Dōtomburi. If you pick somewhere that is doing brisk business you are unlikely to be disappointed. Dōtomburi has a couple of famous Japanese restaurants whose extensive menus feature some very reasonably priced dishes. You can't miss *Kuidaore* (tel 06-211-5300) as it has a mechanical clown posted outside its doors, attracting the attention of potential customers by beating a drum. The restaurant has eight floors serving almost every kind of Japanese food, and windows featuring a huge range of plastic replicas. Main-course meals cost from Y1000.

Down the road, giving a little competition to the drum-pounding clown, is a restaurant that sports a huge mechanical crab helplessly waving its pincers around. The *Kani Doraku* (tel 06-211-8975) (*kani* is Japanese for 'crab') specialises in crab dishes and they do all kinds of imaginative things to the unfortunate crustaceans. Most dishes are fairly expensive (over Y3000) although there are a few exceptions.

Not to be outdone by the clown and the crab, Dōtomburi's prawn restaurant features, yes you guessed it, a big mechanical prawn. *Ebi Doraku* (tel 06-211-1633) has all kinds of prawn dishes from around Y1500.

Dōtomburi also has a wide range of international restaurants including *Sawasdee* (tel 06-212-2301), a small Thai restaurant with friendly staff and great food. The restaurant is on the 2nd floor of the Shibata building, a short distance from Kani Doraku. Look for the English sign at ground level.

If you're in the mood for Indian food, the popular Tokyo restaurant *Moti* (tel 06-211-6878) has a branch in Osaka. The restaurant is on the 3rd floor a few doors down Dōtomburi from its intersection with Midosuji-dōri Ave. The food, prepared by Indian chefs, is not quite as good as in Tokyo but it's still pretty tasty; there are great curries from around Y1000.

Entertainment

Osaka has a very active nightlife with much of it pitched at businesspeople with fat expense accounts. Fortunately there are also many places whose clientele is composed largely of students with more moderate means. Osaka also has a smattering of nightspots that cater to Westerners and to Japanese who like to move in international circles.

If you're in Osaka for the night, forget Kita-ku and head for Minami-ku's Dōtomburi where there are many places for a drink and a bite to eat. The very popular *Kirin City Bar* on the 2nd floor of the Kirin Plaza building next to the river is a good place to meet young locals. The 1st floor has a coffee shop and the top floors have exhibition space for local and international cultural displays.

Cross the bridge next to the Kirin Plaza building, turn right and take the next left, a couple of streets down where, in the midst of all the hostess bars and exclusive clubs, on the right-hand side is *Shanghai*. It's easy to miss as the name is displayed only in kanji; look for a darkened doorway into a tiny bar whose walls are decorated with rock posters and the complete Keith Richard's guitar collection. This is a great place, especially late in the evening, to meet locals, both gaijin and Japanese. Shanghai gets *very* crowded from about midnight but that's part of the appeal.

Before heading off to Shanghai, most of the local gaijin and a lot of the more 'international' Japanese hang out at the *Pig & Whistle*, one of those ubiquitous English pubs. It's very popular among locals and very unusual, for a Japanese establishment of this kind, in that the staff are Westerners.

There's a friendly crowd at the Pig & Whistle, but be careful who you tell that you've just arrived in Osaka. A couple of young Osakan men, upon hearing that it was my first day in their city, decided that they would take me on a tour of their town's hottest nightspots; a tour that involved being plied with lots of scotch, exchanging pleasantries with coy Japanese hostesses and being dumped at my hotel shortly before daylight.
Chris Taylor

In the vicinity of the Pig & Whistle and Shanghai there are a number of discos, among which *Maharaja* and *Dynasty* are the most popular. They charge the usual Y4000 to Y4500 admission, which includes a few drink tickets.

Getting There & Away

Air As well as internal flights, Osaka is a major international air centre. Japan's first 24 hour airport is under construction off-shore from Osaka on an artificial island, connected to the mainland by a bridge. It's due to open in 1993 and will make Osaka a much more important international arrival and departure point. The present airport is a much more convenient arrival port than its international counterpart in Tokyo (Narita Airport)

Train Osaka is the centre of an extensive rail network that sprawls across the Kansai region. Kōbe is a mere 30 minutes away, even quicker by shinkansen, while Kyoto and Nara are each about 50 minutes from Osaka.

Shinkansen services operate between Tokyo station and Shin-Osaka station (just under three hours) via Kyoto, and from Shin-Osaka station on to Hakata in northern Kyūshū (about 3½ hours).

To get to Kyoto from Osaka, the quickest route, other than the shinkansen and which takes only 17 minutes, is with the private Hankyū line, departing from Umeda station. The trip takes around 40 minutes by limited express.

To get to Nara, your best bet is to take the JR Kansai line from Tennō-ji station and get off at Horyu-ji station. The trip takes around 30 minutes. The private Kintetsu line also operates between Namba station and Nara station, taking about 30 minutes.

It is possible to travel between Osaka and Koyasan from Shiomibashi station via the private Nankai-Kōya line.

Ferry Osaka has two international ferry services to and from Pusan (South Korea) and Shanghai (China). The ferries leave from the Nanko International Ferry Terminal, which can be reached by taking the 'New Tram' service from Suminoe-kōen station to Nankoguchi station. Information about Shanghai-bound ferries can be obtained by ringing 06-261-9924 and information about Pusan ferries can be obtained by ringing 06-263-0200.

Ferries also depart from Nanko, Kanome-futō and Benten-futō piers for various destinations around Honshū, Kyūshū and Shikoku. Inquire at the Osaka Tourist Association offices for more information on times and prices.

Getting Around

To/From the Airport There are frequent lim-ousine buses running between the airport and various parts of Osaka. To Shin-Osaka station buses run every 15 minutes from 6.50 am to 8.15 pm and cost Y320. The trip takes around 25 minutes. Buses run at about the same frequency to Umeda and Namba sta-tions (Y410, half an hour).

There are also direct airport buses to and from Kyoto (see the Kyoto section for details).

Train Osaka has a good subway network and, like Tokyo, a JR loop line that circles the city area. In fact, there should be no need to use any other form of transport while you are in Osaka unless you stay out late and miss the last train. Subway and JR stations are clearly marked in English as well as hiragana and kanji so finding your way is relatively easy.

If you're going to be using the rail system a lot on any day, it might be worth consider-ing a 'one-day free ticket'. For Y800 you get unlimited travel on any subway, the so-called New Tram and the buses but unfortunately you cannot use the JR line. You'd really need to be moving around all day to save any money but it might save the headaches of working out fares and where to buy tickets.

Bus Osaka has a bus system though it is nowhere near as easy to use as the rail network. Japanese language bus maps are available from the tourist offices.

Around Osaka
大阪の附近

SAKAI NINTOKU BURIAL MOUND
堺仁徳天皇陵

The history of Sakai's burial mound is a lot more interesting than its present reality. Today it merely looks like a mound. In its time, however, it is thought that some 800,000 workers laboured to fashion the final resting place of the 4th century Emperor Nintoku. To get to the mound, take the Hanwa line from Tennō-ji station in Osaka to Mozu station, from where it is about a five minute walk.

KOBE　神戸

Kōbe (population 1,450,000) is popular among young Japanese for its cosmopolitan atmosphere. The city has a relatively large foreign population and this is reflected in the city's many foreign restaurants and some of the things to be seen around town. Among the Japanese, Kōbe is renowned for Kōbe beef and for its foreign houses, the former being too pricey for the average traveller and the latter probably not too exciting to anyone that grew up in the West.

All things considered, Kōbe shouldn't be a high priority on your itinerary. Most of its sights are largely nonevents and with the exception of a few foreign restaurants, there's very little to do at night.

Information

There are two information offices in town, but very little English is spoken at either of them – you have to be a bit persistent if you want any help. One office is in Shin-Kōbe station, the other is on the 2nd floor of the Kōbe Kōtsū bus centre at Sannomiya station – it's a little difficult to find. The office at Sannomiya may be more helpful with questions regarding accommodation. Both offices have copies of the *Kobe: Guide Book*, a useful pocket-sized booklet with maps and practical information.

Kobe City Museum

This museum is known for its collection of *namban* art. The paintings were produced under the influence of the Spanish and the Portuguese in the 16th and 17th centuries. There are also displays of national treasures from the Yayoi period. The museum is open from 10 am to 5 pm, closed Mondays and admission is Y200.

Chinatown

Known as 'Nankinmachi' by locals, Kōbe's Chinatown is nothing to write home about if you've seen Chinatowns elsewhere. The restaurants all seem to offer the same Japanese/Chinese cuisine. Apart from eating and shopping in one of the little places selling kung fu shoes and silly silk hats decorated with tassels, there's little else to do. Chinatown is easy to find: a five minute walk south of Motomachi station.

Kitano Area

Kitano is the area where most of Kōbe's foreign architecture can be found. Among the places open to the public is a house with a kind of Tudor/Swiss architectural cross known as *kazamidori no yakata*. There are also a number of places of religious worship in the area: a Russian Orthodox church, a Moslem mosque, a synagogue and a Catholic church. If you're desperate for something to do or have an anthropological interest in Japanese sight-seeing rituals, you can get to Kitano by walking for about 10 minutes north of Sannomiya station along Kitanozaka St.

Port Island

An artificial island, this is touted as one of Kōbe's premier tourist destinations. A monorail does a circuit of the island from Sannomiya station, and sights along the way (which you may or may not want to stop and have a look at) include a container terminal, a science museum and an international trade show hall.

Other Attractions

Featured prominently in all the tourist literature is 931 metre Mt Rokko-san. It's a pleasant trip by cablecar to the top. To get there, take bus No 16 from Rokko station on the Hankyū line. Get off the bus at the Rokko cablecar station.

Fifteen minutes north of Motomachi station is the Japanese-style Soraku-en Garden with a pond and some old buildings. The garden is a pleasant enough place for a stroll. It is open from 9 am to 5 pm (closed Thursdays) and admission is Y150.

Places to Stay

Youth Hostels The *Kōbe Tarumi Youth Hostel* (tel 078-707-2133) has beds for Y1900, breakfast for Y450 and dinner for Y700, but it's a bit far out of town. Take a Tōkaidō line train from Kōbe station and get off after six stops at Tarumi station. The hostel is an eight minute walk to the east along the road that parallels the south side of the railway tracks.

The *Kōbe Mudō-ji Youth Hostel* (tel 078-581-0250) is a 10 minute bus journey north of Shin-Kōbe station, followed by a further

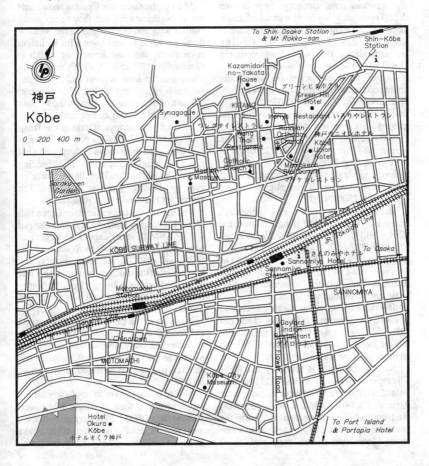

10 minutes on foot. A bed here costs Y1500, breakfast Y450 and dinner Y650.

Budget Accommodation Apart from the hostels there's not much in the way of cheap accommodation (even by Japanese standards) in the town itself except for the *Tor Ryokan* (tel 078-331-3590) where rooms start from Y4300 per person. Book ahead – it's small in size and its reasonable rates mean that this place is frequently booked out.

Hotels Middle-range places are almost all in the business hotel category; from around Y5500 you get a tiny room with a bathroom, coin-TV and fridge. If you go to the information offices for help in finding accommodation they will almost certainly direct you to one of these places.

Some of the cheaper places are on the main road to the north of Sannomiya station. The *Green Hill Hotel 1* (tel 078-222-1221) is past the pedestrian crossing at the first major intersection and charges from Y6000/12,000 for singles/doubles. The *Green Hill Hotel 2* (tel 078-222-0909) is further up the hill, on the road that runs behind and parallel to the main road north of Sannomiya station. It has slightly bigger rooms at Y7500/14,000.

Back down the hill towards Sannomiya station, on the other side of the road from the Green Hill hotels, is the *Kōbe Union Hotel* (tel 078-222-6500) where singles/doubles cost from Y6000/11,000. It's easy to find as it is next to a Lawson's 24 hour convenience store, the only splash of colour on an otherwise uninteresting main street.

If you want to be close to Sannomiya station, the *Sannomiya Terminal Hotel* (tel 078-291-0001) has comfortable rooms with all the usual features for Y7500/15,000; it's right next to the station.

Kōbe's top hotel is probably the *Kōbe Portopia Hotel* (tel 078-302-1111) on Port Island with nearly 800 deluxe rooms (prices start at Y8500/19,000 for singles/doubles) and no less than 15 restaurants. Near the waterfront, about 10 minutes walk south from Motomachi station, the *Hotel Okura*

Kōbe (tel 078-333-0111) has rooms from Y16,000/22,000.

Places to Eat

Kōbe is famous among Japanese for its restaurants. There *is* a fairly wide variety of cuisines available in Kōbe, but nothing mind boggling for travellers who come from countries where there is a greater degree of ethnic diversity than the Japanese are used to. The local speciality is the famous Kōbe beef, which to most foreigners may seem both too expensive and too fatty.

Most of the numerous Chinese restaurants are in Nankinmachi, but they're all pretty similar with plastic offerings in the window displays. Kōbe is well known for its Indian restaurants, the best known of which is *Gaylord* (tel 078-251-4359). It's not exactly cheap but the food is good and lunch-time set meals range from Y1200. The restaurant is south of Sannomiya station on the left side of Flower Rd and has an English sign.

North of Sannomiya station is the *Wang Thai* (tel 078-222-2507), a popular Thai restaurant. Again this is not a budget option but it is a nice place if you don't mind spending around Y2500 per head for dinner. There's a very good buffet lunch at that price. The restaurant is closed every Wednesday.

Just around the corner from the Green Hill Hotel 1 is the tiny *Marrakech Ethnic Bar* (tel 078-261-9464), an adjunct of the larger and more expensive *Marrakech Restaurant* (tel 078-241-3440). The restaurant is classy, but you can sit at the much more intimate bar and order food, which is brought from the nearby restaurant. You can eat well here for around Y2000.

If you're in the mood for some very good pub food, *Danny Boy* (tel 078-231-6566) has an excellent, very diverse and reasonably priced menu and a pleasant, quiet atmosphere. You can eat well here from around Y1000.

You're going to have to pay dearly for the privilege if you want to sample Kōbe beef. *Misono* (tel 078-331-2890), arguably Kōbe's most famous steakhouse, offers Kōbe steaks from Y11,000 up. Eating Kōbe beef with either sukiyaki or shabu shabu is probably a more reasonable option. You can do this at *Iroriya* (tel 078-2316777), where Kōbe beef sukiyaki costs from around Y4000.

Entertainment

Not much happens in Kōbe at night. *Danny Boy* is OK for a drink though rather boring. So is the nearby *Second Chance* (tel 078-391-3544) which is at least brightly lit and has a jukebox and a few pinball machines.

The *Garage Bar*, about 50 metres from Second Chance, has rather pricey food but the bar/restaurant area features live entertainment and there's a dimly lit, slightly Bohemian atmosphere and a small disco. This trendy spot has an equal mix of foreigners and locals.

Getting There & Away

Train By shinkansen it's about 15 minutes from Shin-Osaka station to Shin-Kōbe station, which in turn is five minutes from Sannomiya station in central Kōbe. From Osaka station rapid trains (kaisoku) only take about 10 minutes more than the shinkansen.

Ferry Ferries from Kōbe operate to destinations as diverse as Okinawa, Shikoku, Kyūshū and Awaji-shima Island. The departure point for the ferries is Naka Pier, next to the port tower. For information regarding departure times and prices call Japan Travel-Phone (tel 0120-444-800) or inquire at the TIC in Tokyo or Kyoto.

Getting Around

To/From the Airport It is possible to take a bus directly from Osaka International Airport to Kōbe. The buses leave the airport every 20 minutes and cost Y680 for the 40 minute trip.

Local Transport JR, Kankyū and Hanshin railway lines run east to west across Kōbe, providing fairly easy access to most of Kōbe's sights. A subway line also connects Shin-Kōbe station with Sannomiya station. Buses are frequent and reliable and because

of the fairly low level of traffic, taxis are often a reasonable option in Kōbe.

HIMEJI　姫路

If you see no other castles in Japan you should at least make an effort to visit Himeji Castle, unanimously acclaimed as the most splendid Japanese castle still standing. It is also known as the 'White Egret', a title which derived from its stately white form. The surrounding town itself has little to offer as a tourist attraction, but there are plenty of places to grab a meal on the way to the castle.

Himeji can be easily visited as a day trip from Kyoto. A couple of hours at the castle, plus the 10 to 15 minute walk from the station is all the time you need there. The only other attraction worth lingering for is Himeji's historical museum, which has some interesting exhibits on Japanese castles. Walk to the castle down one side of the main street and back on the other to see the statuary dotted along both sides.

Orientation & Information

There's a tourist information counter at the station. The castle is straight up the main road from the station, and clearly visible to the north if you're simply passing through Himeji. If you have luggage with you there are coin lockers at the station.

Himeji-jō Castle

Himeji-jō Castle is the most magnificent of the handful of Japanese castles which survive in their original (non-concrete) form. Although there have been fortifications in Himeji since 1333, today's castle was built in 1580 by Toyotomi Hideyoshi and enlarged some 30 years later by Ikeda Terumasa. Ikeda was awarded the castle by Tokugawa Ieyasu when the latter's forces defeated the Toyotomi armies. In the following centuries the castle was home to 48 lords.

The castle has a five storeyed main donjon and three smaller donjons, the entire structure being surrounded by moats and defensive walls punctuated with rectangular, circular and triangular openings for firing guns and shooting arrows at visiting tourists.

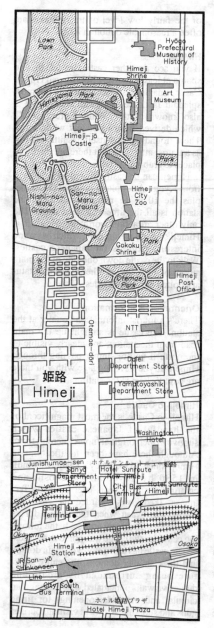

The walls of the donjon also feature *ishiotoshi* or openings that allowed defenders to pour boiling water or oil on to anyone that made it past the defensive slits and was thinking of scaling the walls. All things considered visitors are recommended to pay the Y500 admission charge and enter the castle by legitimate means.

It takes about 1½ hours to follow the arrowed route around the castle. The castle is open from 9 am to 6 pm (last entry 5 pm) in summer and it closes an hour earlier in winter.

Hyōgo Prefectural Museum of History
This well laid out museum has good displays on Himeji-jō Castle and other castles around Japan and, indeed, the whole world. If you're at the museum at 2 pm you can try on a suit of samurai armour or a kimono. In the event of competition for this singular honour, the museum staff resolve the conflict by the drawing of lots.

The museum is a five minute walk north of the castle. Admission is Y200, and it's open from 10 am to 5 pm daily except Mondays.

Festivals
The Mega-Kenka Festival, held on 14 and 15 October, involves a conflict between three *mikoshi* (portable shrines) which are battered against each other until one smashes. The festival is held about a five minute walk from Shirahamanomiya station (10 minutes from Himeji station on the Sanyō-Dentetsu line); just follow the crowds.

Places to Stay
There *are* some places to stay in Himeji, but in general they are overpriced and have little to recommend them. Basing yourself elsewhere and visiting Himeji as a day trip would be a far better option.

The *Tegarayama Youth Hostel* (tel 0792-93-2716) gets consistently bad reports from travellers even though beds are only Y1300 and the place does not require a youth hostel card. The hostel is a 10 minute walk south of Tegara station.

In town, *Hotel Sun Route New Himeji* (tel 0792-23-1111) has rooms with all the usual business-hotel features and costs from Y5500/11,000 for singles/doubles. It's a two minute walk from the station on the right-hand side of Otemae-dōri. The *Hotel Himeji Plaza* (tel 0792-81-9000) is also close to the station and has rooms from Y6000/10,500. See the map for other Himeji hotels.

Getting There & Away

The quickest way to get to Himeji is by shinkansen. From Shin-Osaka station the trip takes around 40 minutes, from Okayama it takes 30 to 40 minutes. JR trains also run between Osaka, Kyoto, Kōbe and Himeji, and the private Hankyū line runs between Kōbe and Himeji.

Nara-ken 奈良県

NARA 奈良

Prior to the 8th century, it had been the custom amongst the rulers of Japan to change the capital – perhaps to avoid the pollution of death which seemed to follow each successive emperor. In 710, this custom was changed when Nara was made the permanent capital under Empress Gemmyō. Permanent status, however, lasted a mere 75 years. Several decades later, after a few more moves, the capital was shifted to Kyoto where it remained until 1868.

Although brief, the Nara period was extraordinarily vigorous in the absorption of influences from China which set the foundations for Japanese culture and civilisation. The adoption of Buddhism as a national religion made a lasting impact on government, arts, literature and architecture. Once Nara had lost its role as a capital it was spared the subsequent destruction that occurred in Kyoto and a number of magnificent buildings have survived.

Orientation

Nara retains the grid pattern of streets laid out in Chinese style during the 8th century.

This makes it easy to cover the city centre and the major attractions in adjoining Nara-kōen Park on foot.

Information

If you are heading for Nara from Kyoto, the TIC in Kyoto has extensive material. In Nara, the best source of information is the Nara City Tourist Centre (tel 0742-22-3900) which is open from 9 am to 9 pm. It's a short walk from JR Nara and Kintetsu Nara stations. There's a plush lounge for relaxing, a display of handicrafts and helpful staff doling out stacks of maps and literature about transport, sights, accommodation, etc.

JNTO publishes a walking guide to Nara, *Walking Tour Courses in Nara (MG-053)*, which has maps and information on sights. The green *Japan: Nara City* map and red *Tourist Map of Kyoto & Nara*, also published by JNTO are useful. The staff has comprehensive listings of places to stay and, time permitting, will help you with reservations (Nara receives thousands of tourists, but they're mostly day-trippers).

The TIC can also put you in touch with volunteer guides who speak English and other foreign languages – try to book ahead. There are three such services: Goodwill Guides (tel 0742-22-3900), Student Guides (tel 0742-26-4753) and YMCA Guides (tel 0742-27-4858). These services are a pleasant way for a foreigner to meet the Japanese (often bright students keen to practise their foreign languages), but they are not not business ventures so you should offer to cover the day's expenses for your guide.

There are also information offices at both of Nara's stations which stock maps and whose staff can answer basic questions. The JR Nara station's office (tel 0742-22-9821) is open from 8 am to 6 pm; the Kintetsu Nara station information office (tel 0742-24-4858) is open from 9 am to 5 pm.

For a short, taped announcement in English about current festivals and events around Nara call 27-1313.

For a more academic look at Nara's sights, pick up a copy of *Historical Nara* by Herbert Plutschow (Japan Times, Tokyo, 1983).

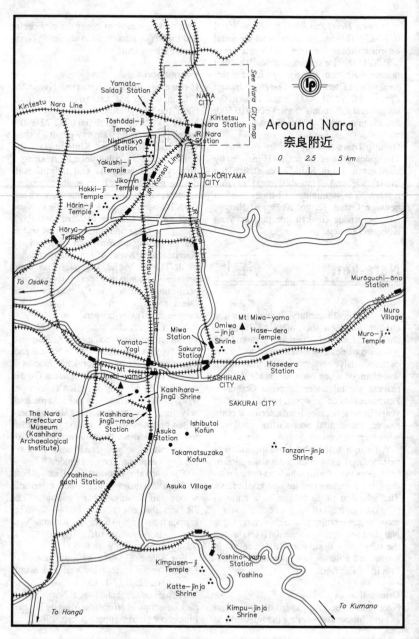

Around Nara
奈良附近

0   2.5   5 km

Planning Your Itinerary
Nara tends to be skimped by visitors in favour of Kyoto's huge choice of sights, but Nara's smaller scale does make it easier to concentrate on a smaller selection of attractions – some of the finest in Japan.

Although it's quite possible to pack most of Nara's sights into a full day, the pace is more enjoyable if you can spend at least two full days here. Allow a day for Nara-kōen Park and another day for the sights in western and south-western Nara.

Day Walks Traipsing around dozens of temples in quick succession can be tiring for mind and body. If you've got a day or half a day to spare, a walk in the forested hills around Nara is definitely recommended.

Take some food and drink and give yourself an easy schedule to get pleasantly lost, meet local farmers who confidently put you back on the wrong track, and keep following your nose and the erratic mapping until you reach Nara! It is the complete antithesis of a guided tour and the sort of disorganised Western fun that some Japanese find most puzzling.

The Nara City Tourist Centre can provide maps and transport details. The Takisaka-michi and the Yamanobe-no-michi are popular walks. The tourist centre probably won't have any English maps, but you can make do with the Japanese ones which are more detailed anyway. Ask the staff to circle a few of the key points on the route and write down the names in romaji.

The Takisaka-michi is the old highway leading from the Yagyū area to Nara city. It is cobblestone for part of the way, but most of it meanders through forests passing the occasional stone Buddhas and shrines by the wayside. I took an early bus from boarding bay 4 opposite Kintetsu station to Enjō-ji Temple. The ride took 30 minutes and cost Y520. Bus Nos 100, 101 and 102 all go via Enjō-ji Temple and take another 17 minutes (and an extra Y230) to reach Yagyū which is another possible place to start if you want a longer walk down the Takisaka-michi.

From Enjō-ji Temple you head off the road and down the hills through the forest. Together with my trail companion, who was half-Japanese but equally

stymied by the mapping, we soon strayed down a sidetrack and came to a dead end in a farmer's yard. The farmer was very helpful, but obviously a little thrown by the sight of foreigners stumbling into his backyard.

This probably accounted for his extreme care in accompanying us back to the trail and pointing us in the wrong direction. We later realised there had been a misunderstanding since he was presumably used to going *up* the trail to take the bus to market, and we wanted to go *down* the trail to Nara without transport.

After that, the trail was easy to follow. The official walking time from Enjō-ji to Nara is about three hours, but it took us about five hours including numerous breaks for lunch, tea, photos, etc.

About halfway down the trail, there's a delightful old teahouse and antique shop (worth a stop for tea, mochi cakes and a chat). Further on, you pass tea plantations complete with dozens of electric fans on poles to circulate the air around the plants. There are various shrines and stone Buddhas along the way. Tucked away on a side track, almost obscured by trees, is the Sunset Buddha, so named because the last rays of the sun light up its face.

The trail comes out near Shin-Yakushi-ji Temple. Shortly before the temple I saw a vandalised vending machine, a unique sight in Japan. If you are exhausted by the time you reach the temple, the No 2 bus will take you back to the city centre.

Robert Strauss

Nara-kōen Park Area
The park was created from wasteland in 1880 and covers a large area. JNTO publishes a leaflet called *Walking Tour Courses in Nara* which includes a map for this area. Although walking time is estimated at two hours, you'll need at least half a day to see a selection of the sights and a full day to see the lot.

The park is famous for its deer which provide a cutesy backdrop for photos and are fed by tourists who buy special packets of biscuits for Y100 from vendors. Although they look cute, these creatures, numbering over a thousand, have been spoilt rotten and can be a nuisance.

I was sitting in the park writing in my notebook when two deer approached. One deer distracted me from behind by breathing down my neck, whilst the other one stuffed its head into my daypack and tried to guzzle all my notes and books!

Robert Strauss

Kōfuku-ji Temple This temple was transferred here from Kyoto in 710 as the main temple for the Fujiwara family. Although the original temple complex had 175 buildings, fires and destruction through power struggles have only left a dozen still standing. There are two pagodas, a three storeyed one and a five storeyed one, dating from 1143 and 1426 respectively.

The National Treasure Hall (Kokuhōkan) contains a variety of statues and art objects salvaged from previous structures. A descriptive leaflet is provided in English.

Admission to the Kokuhōkan costs Y400 and it's open from 9 am to 5 pm.

Nara National Museum The Nara Kokuritsu Hakubutsukan (Nara National Museum) is devoted to Buddhist art and is divided into two wings. The western gallery exhibits archaeological finds and the eastern gallery has displays of sculptures, paintings and calligraphy. The galleries are linked by an underground passage.

A special exhibition is held in May and the treasures of the Shōsō-in Hall, which is part of the Tōdai-ji Temple, are displayed here in November only. The exhibits include priceless items from the cultures along the Silk Road. If you are in Nara at these times, you should make a point of visiting the museum.

Admission to the museum costs Y360 or Y720 for special exhibitions and it's open from 9 am to 4.30 pm.

Neiraku Art Museum & Isui-en Garden The art museum (Neiraku Bijutsukan) displays Chinese bronzes and Korean ceramics and bronzes. The garden, dating from the Meiji era, is beautifully laid out with abundant greenery and a fine view of Tōdai-ji Temple with the hills rising behind. It is recommended if you need a break.

Admission to the museum costs Y500. The same ticket allows entry into the garden. It is open from 10 am to 4.30 pm.

Tōdai-ji Temple This temple is the star attraction in Nara. It is the largest wooden building in the world and houses the Great Buddha – one of the largest bronze images in the world. It also deserves a place in the record books for the largest concentration of tour groups, including hundreds of uniformed kids wearing yellow baseball caps being herded by dozens of guides with megaphones and banners. Confronted at the entrance by that lot, it's not surprising to see a plaintive sign in English – 'Entrance is backward'!

Emperor Shōmu ordered construction of the temple and casting of the Great Buddha (Daibutsu) during the 8th century. Fires, earthquakes and civil wars necessitated reconstruction in subsequent centuries. The present gigantic structure dates from the Edo period and is still only two-thirds the size of the original.

Daibutsu-den The Daibutsu-den (Hall of the Great Buddha) is the largest wooden building in the world, but the actual structure is not remarkably ancient because it is a reconstruction dating from 1709.

After numerous attempts, the Daibutsu was successfully cast in 746. Over the centuries the statue took quite a beating from earthquakes and fires, losing its head a couple of times in the process. The present statue stands just over 16 metres high and consists of bronze, gold and several tons of vegetable wax. Big isn't necessarily beautiful, but it's still impressive – even more so if you consider that it is only two-thirds the size of the original.

As you circuit the statue towards the back, you'll see a wooden column with a small hole at the base. Popular belief maintains that those who can squeeze through are ensured of enlightenment. (You'll probably see a lot of disappointed, firmly wedged adults reluctantly giving way to streams of nimble kids making quick work of enlightenment!)

Admission to the Daibutsu-den costs Y300 and your ticket has a convenient list of the Daibutsu's vital statistics. Opening hours vary throughout the year. You might conceivably be able to reduce exposure to the hordes of visitors if you come very early or an hour before closing. Opening hours are as follows: January to February from 8 am to 4.30 pm; during March from 8 am to 5 pm; April to September from 7.30 am to 5.30 pm; during October from 7.30 am to 5 pm and between November and December from 8 am to 4.30 pm.

Shōsō-in The Shōsō-in (Treasure Repository) is a short walk north of Daibutsu-den. If you discount the slight curve to the roof, the structure is reminiscent of a log blockhouse from North America. The building was used to house fabulous imperial treasures and its wooden construction allowed precise regulation of humidity through natural expansion and contraction. The treasures have been removed and are shown twice a year, in spring and autumn, at the Nara National Museum. The Shōsō-in building is open to the public at the same time.

Kaidan-in Hall A short walk west of the entrance gate to the Daibutsu-den, you can visit this hall which was used for ordination ceremonies and is famous for its clay images of the Shi Tennō (Four Heavenly Guardians). The hall is open from 8 am to 4.30 pm and admission costs Y300.

Nigatsu-dō & Sangatsu-dō Halls If you walk east from the entrance to the Daibutsu-den, climb up a flight of stone steps, and continue to your left, you reach these two halls.

Nigatsu-dō Hall is famed for its Omizutori Festival (see the later section on Nara festivals for details) and a splendid view across Nara which makes the climb up the hill well worthwhile – particularly at dusk. The hall is open from 8 am to 5.30 pm and admission is free.

A short walk south of Nigatsu-dō is Sangatsu-dō Hall which is the oldest building in the Tōdai-ji Temple complex. This hall contains a small collection of fine statues from the Nara period. Admission costs Y300 and it's open from 8 am to 5.30 pm.

Kasuga Taisha Shrine This shrine was founded in the 8th century by the Fujiwara family and completely rebuilt every 20 years according to Shinto tradition, until the end of the 19th century. It lies at the foot of the hill in a pleasant wooded setting with herds of sacred deer waiting for hand-outs.

The approaches to the shrine are lined with hundreds of lanterns and there are many more hundreds in the shrine itself. The lantern festivals held twice a year at the shrine are a major attraction. For details about these and other festivals held at the nearby Wakamiya-jinja Shrine, see the later section on Nara festivals.

The Hōmotsu-den (Treasure Hall) is just north of the entrance torii for the shrine. The hall displays Shinto ceremonial regalia and equipment used in bugaku, Nō and gagaku performances. Admission costs Y300 and it's open from 9 am to 4 pm.

Shin-Yakushi-ji Temple

This temple was founded by Empress Kōmyō in 747 in thanks for her husband's recovery from an eye disease. Most of the buildings were destroyed or have been reconstructed, but the present main hall dates from the 8th century. The hall contains sculptures of Yakushi Nyorai (Healing Buddha) and a set of 12 divine generals. Admission costs Y400 and the temple is open from 8.30 am to 5.30 pm.

Hōryū-ji Temple

This temple was founded in 607 by Prince Shōtoku. It is renowned not only as the oldest temple in Japan, but also as a repository for some of the country's rarest treasures. Despite the usual fires and reconstructions in the history of the temple, several of the wooden buildings now remaining are believed to be the oldest of their kind in the world. The layout of the temple is divided into two parts: Sai-in (West Temple) and Tō-in (East Temple).

The entrance ticket costing Y700 allows admission to the Sai-in Temple, Tō-in Temple and Great Treasure Hall. A detailed map is provided and a guidebook is available in English. The JNTO leaflet called *Walking Tour Courses in Nara* includes a basic map

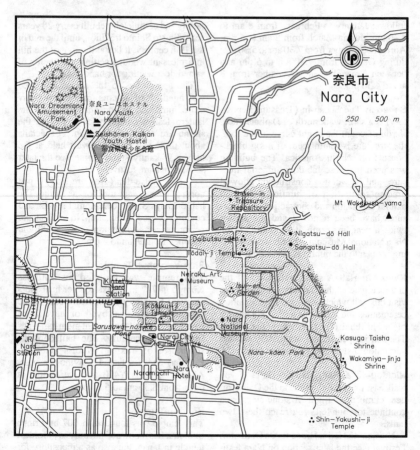

for the area around Hōryū-ji Temple. The temple is open from 8 am to 4.30 pm.

The main approach to the temple proceeds from the south along a tree-lined avenue and continues through the Nandai-mon Gate and Chū-mon Gate before entering the Sai-in Temple which contains the oldest buildings.

As you enter the Sai-in Temple, you see the Kondō (Main Hall) on your right, and a pagoda on your left. The Kondō houses several treasures, including the Shaka Trinity which is the central image on the altar.

The pagoda rises gracefully in five, finely tapered storeys. The inside walls are lined with clay images depicting scenes from the life of Buddha.

On the eastern side of the Sai-in Temple are the two concrete buildings of the Daihōzō-den (Great Treasure Hall) containing numerous treasures from Hōryū-ji Temple's long history. Renowned images in this hall include the Kudara Kannon and the Amida Trinity in the Lady Tachibana Shrine, but there are many other fine items.

If you leave this hall and continue east through the Tōdai-mon Gate you reach the Tō-in. The Yumedono (Hall of Dreams) in this temple is where Prince Shōtoku is believed to have meditated and been given help with problem sutras by a kindly, golden apparition.

At the rear of the Tō-in compound is the entrance to Chūgū-ji Nunnery which is drab in appearance, but contains two famous art treasures: the serene statue of Miroku Bosatsu (Buddha of the Future) and a portion of the embroidered Tenjukoku (Land of Heavenly Longevity) mandala which is believed to date from the 7th century and is the oldest remaining example of this art in Japan. Admission to this temple costs Y300 and it's open from 9 am to 4.30 pm.

To get to the Hōryū-ji Temple, take the JR Kansai line from JR Nara station to Hōryū-ji station (15 minutes). A bus service shuttles the short distance between the station and Hōryū-ji Temple. On foot it takes about 15 minutes.

Hōrin-ji Temple

Hōrin-ji Temple is about 10 minutes on foot from Chūgū-ji Nunnery. In the Kondō (Main Hall) of the temple there are several images including a fine statue of Yakushi Nyorai (Healing Buddha) with a radiant smile. The pagoda was frazzled by lightning in 1944, but reconstructed in 1975. Admission costs Y300 and an English leaflet is provided. It's open from 8 am to 5 pm daily but closes half an hour earlier between December and February.

Hokki-ji Temple

Hokki-ji Temple is a 10 minute walk from Hōrin-ji and instantly recognisable by its elegant three storeyed pagoda which dates back to the 8th century. The temple has a cosy garden with a small pond. Admission costs Y200. It's open from 8 am to 4.30 pm.

Jikō-in Temple

Jikō-in Temple is about 25 minutes on foot from Hokki-ji. This Zen temple was founded in 1663 by Sekishu Katagiri who had studied at Daitoku-ji Temple in Kyoto and then devoted himself to Zen and the tea ceremony. Although the gardens and buildings

are impressive, the Y800 admission fee is a bit steep even though it includes a free cup of matcha. The view from the tearoom ranges over the garden to the encroaching urban sprawl. The temple is open from 8.30 am to 5 pm but closes at 5.30 pm in the summer.

To return to Nara by bus, you should turn left when leaving the temple and go down the hill a short distance to the main road. Turn left again and walk about 100 metres along the road until you cross a bridge over a river. The bus stop is just beyond the bridge.

Yakushi-ji Temple

Yakushi-ji was established by Emperor Temmu in 680. With the exception of the East Pagoda, the present buildings either date from the 13th century or are very recent reconstructions.

The main hall was rebuilt in 1976 and houses several images including the famous Yakushi Triad dating from the 8th century.

The East Pagoda is a unique structure because it appears to have six storeys, but three of them are *mokoshi* (lean-to additions) which give a pleasing balance to its appearance.

Admission costs Y300 and a leaflet in English is provided. Ii's open from 8.30 am to 5 pm.

To get to Yakushi-ji take a Kintetsu line train from Nara Kintetsu station to Saidai-ji, then change to the southbound Kintetsu Kashihara line and get off at the second stop – Nishinokyō station – which is very close to Yakushi-ji Temple.

Tōshōdai-ji Temple

This temple was established in 759 by the Chinese priest Ganjin who had been recruited by Emperor Shōmu to reform Buddhism in Japan. Ganjin didn't have much luck with his travel arrangements from China to Japan: five attempts were thwarted by shipwreck, storms and bureaucracy. Despite being blinded by eye disease, he finally made it on the sixth attempt and spread his teachings to Japan. The lacquer sculpture in the Miei-dō Hall is a moving tribute to Ganjin: blind and rock steady. It is shown only once a year on 6 June – the anniversary of Ganjin's death (6 May in the lunar calendar).

The Shin Hōzō (Treasure Hall) has some fine sculptures and images. Admission costs Y100 and it's open during the same hours as the temple, but only from late March to late May, and from mid-September to early November.

Admission to the temple costs Y300 and a detailed leaflet is provided in English, including a precise map of the extensive temple grounds. It's open from 8.30 am to 4.30 pm.

Tōshōdai-ji Temple is a 10 minute walk from Yakushi-ji Temple; see the preceding section for transport details from Nara.

Festivals

Nara has plenty of festivals throughout the year. The following is a brief list of the more interesting ones. More extensive information is readily available from Nara tourist offices or from the TIC in Kyoto.

Yamayaki (Grass Burning Festival)
  15 January. To commemorate a feud many centuries ago between the monks of Tōdai-ji and Kōfuku-ji temples, Mt Wakakusa-yama is set alight at 6 pm with an accompanying display of fireworks. Arrive earlier to bag a good viewing position in Nara-kōen Park.

Mantōrō (Lantern Festival)
  2-4 February. Held at Kasuga Taisha Shrine at 6 pm, this is a festival renowned for its illumination with 3000 stone and bronze lanterns – a bugaku dance also takes place in the Apple Garden.

Omizutori (Water-Drawing Ceremony)
  1-14 March. The monks of Tōdai-ji Temple enter a special period of initiation during these days. On the evening of 12 March, they parade huge flaming torches around the balcony of Nigatsu-dō (on the temple precincts) and rain down embers on the spectators to purify them. The water-drawing ceremony is performed after midnight.

Kasuga Matsuri
  13 March. This ancient spring festival features a sacred horse, classical dancing (Yamato-mai) and elaborate costume.

Takigi Nō
  11-12 May. Open-air performances of Nō held after dark by the light of blazing torches at Kōfuku-ji Temple and Kasuga Taisha Shrine.

Mantōrō (Lantern Festival)
  14-15 August. The same as the festival held in February.

Shika-no-Tsunokiri (Deer Antler Cutting)
  Sundays & National Holidays in October. Those pesky deer in Nara-kōen Park are pursued in a type of elegant rodeo into the Roku-en (deer enclosure) close to Kasuga Taisha Shrine. They are then wrestled to the ground and their antlers sawn off. Tourist brochures hint that this is to avoid personal harm, though it's not clear whether they mean the deer fighting each other, or the deer mugging the tourists.

On Matsuri
  15 to 18 December. This festival, dating back to the Heian period, is held to ensure a bountiful harvest and to ward off disease. It takes place at Wakamiya-jinja Shrine (close to Kasuga Taisha Shrine) and features a procession of people dressed in ancient costume, classical dances, wrestling and performances of Nō.

Places to Stay

Although Nara is favoured as a day trip from Kyoto, accommodation can still be packed out for festivals, holidays and at weekends, so try and make reservations in advance if you plan to visit at these times. The Nara City Tourist Centre can help with reservations and has extensive lists of hotels, minshuku, pension, ryokan and shukubō.

Youth Hostels *Seishōnen Kaikan Youth Hostel* (tel 0742-22-5540) is of nondescript, concrete character, but cheap at Y1900 per person per night and the staff are helpful. Breakfast (Y350) and dinner (Y650) fill the gut, rather than whet the appetite. For late arrivals or those on a low budget, there's a pot-noodle machine in the dining hall (Y140).

It's a 30 minute uphill walk from the centre of town to the hostel. From JR Nara station you can take bus No 21 (in the direction of the Dreamland amusement park's south entrance) and get off at the Sahoyama-mae bus stop which is opposite the hostel. Buses run about twice an hour between 7 am and 9 pm.

Nara Youth Hostel (tel 0742-22-1334) is close to Kōno-ike Pond which is a short walk from the other youth hostel. This is a ritzier hostel which *only* takes guests with a hostel membership card and charges Y2100 per person per night. It tends to be booked out and is often swarming with schoolkids on excursions. From Nara Kintetsu station, take a bus in the direction of Dreamland, Kamo or Takanohara and get off at the Yakyujo-mae stop which is in front of a baseball stadium beside the hostel.

Ryokan *Ryokan Seikan-sō* (tel 0742-22-2670) has wooden architecture and a pleasant garden. It's a 15 minute walk from Nara Kintetsu station, close to Sarusawa-no-ike Pond. Prices for a Japanese-style room without bath start at Y3500/7000 for singles/doubles.

A 10 minute walk from the city centre is the quaintly named *Cotton Hyakupasento* or 'Cotton 100%' (tel 0742-22-7117). Most of the rooms are Western style, but the place has a bright atmosphere. Prices per person start around Y5000 without meals.

Ryokan Hakuhoh (tel 0742-26-7891) is in the centre of town, just a five minute walk from JR Nara station. Prices for a Japanese-style room without bath start at Y4500/8500 for singles/doubles.

Ryokan Matsumae (tel 0742-22-3686) is close to Nara-kōen Park, just south of Sarusawa-no-ike Pond. Prices for a Japanese-style room without bath start at Y4500/8000 for singles/doubles.

Edo-san (tel 0742-26-2662) is a ryokan that pulls out all the stops in traditional Japanese style. The accommodation consists of refined huts in a garden setting. Prices start around Y15,000 for a double including delectable meals served in your hut.

Shukubō The Nara City Tourist Centre has a list of temples offering lodgings. *Shin-Yakushi-ji Temple* (tel 0742-22-3736), which is in a quiet area near Nara-kōen Park, offers lodging and breakfast from Y4000 per person per night.

Expensive Hotels There are several top-flight establishments dotted around Nara-kōen Park. *Nara Hotel* (tel 0742-26-3300) is renowned for its tastefully faded elegance and its more recent annexe. Prices for singles/doubles start around Y8000/15,000.

Places to Eat
Nara is known for the full-course delights of kaiseki cuisine which start at about Y5000 for a basic version. This usually includes the local delicacy called 'narazuke' which consists of tart vegetables pickled in saké.

Whilst staying with a farming family in the region, I was introduced at breakfast to another local dish called *chagayu* – a watery rice gruel mixed with green tea – certainly a novel way to start the day.
Robert Strauss

There are plenty of inexpensive restaurants and fast-food places around both the stations. Opposite Kintetsu station are *Lotteria* and *Mister Donut* outfits which do cheap set breakfasts for about Y350. On the streets leading south from Kintetsu station are restaurants offering teishoku (set lunches) around Y1200. For a more expensive meal in garden surroundings you could try *Yanagi-chaya* which is a sophisticated old teahouse in Nara-kōen Park, just east of Kōfuku-ji Temple. Bentō (boxed lunches) start around Y3500 and kaiseki set menus at around Y6000.

The staff at the Nara City Tourist Centre happily make suggestions to match your budget to a local eatery.

Things to Buy
Nara has a long tradition for producing handicrafts such as Nara-shikki (lacquerware), *kogaku-men* (ancient masks), elaborate Nara round-fans, calligraphy materials and dolls made with the *itto-bori* (one chisel) carving technique. Tea utensils such as *akahada-yaki* ceramics and *chasen* (tea whisks) are also popular handicraft items. If you fancy a permanent souvenir of the deer in the park, you could buy *tsuno zaiku* (carved antlers) which

are sawn off during the annual deer antler cutting ceremony. The uses for these would seem limited – perhaps as a weapon to fend off the deer when you're eating your lunch in the park!

A good place to look for handicrafts is the Naramachi area, a short walk south of Sarusawa-no-ike Pond in Nara-kōen Park.

Getting There & Away

Air Nara is served by Osaka Itami Airport. From there you can travel by bus to Osaka or Kyoto and then continue by rail to Nara – there is no direct connection with the airport.

Train *Nara to Kyoto* Unless you have a Japan Rail Pass, the best option is the Kintetsu line linking Kyoto and Nara (Kintetsu Nara station) in 33 minutes by direct limited express (Y900 one way). If you take a local or express train on this line, the ticket price drops to Y500 for the 45 minute ride, but you will need to change at Yamato-Saidaiji which is a five minute ride from Nara Kintetsu station. The JR Nara line connects Kyoto with JR Nara station (Y740 one way, one hour).

Nara to Osaka The Kintetsu Nara line connects Osaka (Kintetsu Namba station) with Nara (Nara Kintetsu station) in half an hour by limited express (Y880). Express and local trains take about 40 minutes and cost Y460.

The JR Kansai line links Osaka (Tennō-ji station) and Nara (JR Nara station) via Hōryu-ji (Y750, 40 minutes by express).

Bus There is an overnight bus service between Tokyo and Nara which costs Y8240 one way or Y14,830 return. The bus leaves Nara at 10.30 pm and reaches Tokyo next day at 6.20 am. The bus from Tokyo leaves at 11 pm and arrives in Nara next day at 6.50 am. Check with the Nara City Tourist Office or the Tokyo TIC for further details.

Getting Around

Bus Nara has an excellent bus system geared to tourists and most of the buses have taped announcements in English. Outside Kintetsu station there's even a machine which gives advice in English for your destination. Just push the right destination button to find out your boarding terminal, bus number, ticket cost and departure time for the next bus.

Most of the area around Nara-kōen Park is covered by two circular bus routes. Bus No 1 runs counter-clockwise and bus No 2 runs clockwise. There's a Y130 flat fare. You can easily see the main sights in the park on foot and use the bus as an option if you are pushed for time or get tired of walking.

The most useful buses for western and south-western Nara (Tōshōdai-ji Temple, Yakushi-ji Temple and Hōryū-ji Temple) are Nos 52 and 97 which have taped announcements in English and link all three destinations with Kintetsu station and JR station. Buses run about every 30 minutes between 8 am and 5 pm, but are much less frequent outside these times.

From Kintetsu station, allow about 20 minutes and a fare of Y200 for the trip to Tōshōdai-ji Temple and Yakushi-ji Temple; add another 30 minutes and an extra Y400 if you continue to Hōryū-ji Temple.

Taxi Taxis are plentiful, but expensive. From JR station to either of the youth hostels costs about Y750.

Bicycle Nara is a convenient size for getting around on a bicycle. The Kintetsu Rent-a-Cycle Centre (tel 0742-24-3528) is close to the Nara City Tourist Centre. From the centre, walk east down the main street to the first intersection, turn left into Konishi-dōri St and walk about 70 metres until you see Supermarket Isokawa on your right. Opposite the supermarket is a small sidestreet on your left – the bicycle rental centre is at the bottom of this street. Prices start at Y720 for four hours or Y1030 for the day. There's a discount for two day rental.

Southern Nara-ken
奈良県の南部

The southern region of Nara prefecture was the birthplace of imperial rule and is rich in historical sights which are easily accessible as day trips from Nara or Kyoto – providing you make an early start.

The Tourist Division of Nara Prefectural Government publishes an excellent, detailed map called *Japan: Nara Prefecture*. The front page has a photo of two deer on a hillside. The Nara City Tourist Centre should have copies of this map which gives an overall view of the prefecture and has insets providing precise locations for temples and other sights.

Sakurai and Yamato-Yagi are two cities which are easily reached by rail and useful as transport hubs for visiting sights in the surrounding region. Travelling from Nara to Yamato-Yagi station you will need to go west to Yamato-Saidaiji first, then change to the southbound Kintetsu Kashihara line. The JR Sakurai line runs direct between Nara and Sakurai.

SAKURAI   桜井
Sakurai can be reached direct from Nara on the JR Sakurai line. To reach Sakurai via Yamato-Yagi (for example, from Kyoto or Osaka), take the Kintetsu Osaka line.

Omiwa-jinja Shrine
This shrine is just north of Sakurai and can be reached by bus from Sakurai station. You can also walk to the shrine from Miwa station which is one stop north of Sakurai on the JR Sakurai line. Omiwa-jinja boasts the highest torii in Japan (32.2 metres) and attracts all those interested in booze because it enshrines the god of liquor. Mt Miwa-yama is considered sacred because it is the abode of the shrine's kami (spirit gods) and there is a trail for pilgrims to hike up the wooded slopes.

Tanzan-jinja Shrine
Tanzan-jinja lies south of Sakurai, and can be reached in about 30 minutes by bus from Sakurai station. It is tucked away in the forests of Mt Tōnomine, famous for their autumn foliage colours, and the central structure of the shrine is an attractive 13 storeyed pagoda. There's a hiking trail from the shrine leading down through the forests in less than two hours to Asuka (Ishibutai Kofun Tomb).

Hase-dera Temple
Two stops east of Sakurai on the Kintetsu Osaka line is Hasedera station which is a 20 minute walk from Hase-dera Temple. After a long climb up endless steps, you enter the main hall and are rewarded with a splendid view from the gallery which juts out on stilts over the mountainside.

MURO-JI TEMPLE   室生寺
To visit Murō-ji Temple, you should return to Hasedera station and continue two stops further east down the Kintetsu Osaka line to Murōguchi-Ono station. From there, it's a 15 minute ride by bus. The temple was founded in the 9th century and has strong connections with Esoteric Buddhism. Unlike other temples, women were never excluded from the precincts here. It's a peaceful, secluded place in thick forest and well worth a visit.

YAMATO-YAGI   大和八木
On the south-western edge of Yamato-Yagi, is the small town of Imai-chō which – an extreme rarity for Japan – has preserved its houses virtually intact from the Edo period. To get there, take a train one stop south from Yamato-Yagi to Yagi-Nishiguchi. The town is a 10 minute walk south-west of the station.

KASHIHARA   橿原
Three stops south of Yamato-Yagi, on the Kintetsu Kashihara line, is Kashihara-jingū-mae station. There are a couple of interesting sights within easy walking distance, north-west of of this station.

The Nara Prefectural Museum
This museum, which houses the Kashihara

Archaeological Institute, is a must for archaeology buffs interested in the rich pickings from digs in the region. The full name is a mouthful – just ask for the Kōko Hakubutsukan.

Kashihara-jingū Shrine

This shrine placed now at the foot of Mt Unebi-yama, dates back to 1889 when many of the buildings were moved here from the Kyoto Imperial Palace. The vast, park-like grounds are pleasant for a stroll. The shrine is five minutes on foot from Kashihara-jingū-mae station.

ASUKA 飛鳥

One stop further south on the Kintetsu Kashihara line is Asuka station. You can rent bicycles here and head east to explore the area's temples, palace remains, tombs and strange stones. Alternatively, you can take a bus from Kashihara-jingū-mae station which makes stops within walking distance of many of the sights.

Two tombs worth seeing are Takamatsuzuka Kofun and Ishibutai Kofun. The former (excavated in 1972) cannot be entered, but has a museum (which is open from 9 am to 4.30 pm) displaying a copy of the frescos. The Ishibutai Kofun can be entered, but has no frescos.

The best museum in the area is Asuka Shiryōkan (Asuka Historical Museum) which has exhibits from regional digs. If you have time, take a look at Asuka-dera Temple which dates from 596 and houses the oldest remaining image of Buddha in Japan – after more than 1300 years of venerable existence, you'll have to excuse its decidedly tatty appearance.

YOSHINO 吉野

History

In early times the remote mountainous regions around Yoshino were considered the mysterious abode of the kami (spirit gods) and later became a centre for Shugendō, a somewhat off-beat Buddhist school which incorporated ancient Shamanistic rites, Shinto beliefs and ascetic Buddhist traditions. The founder was En no Gyōja, to whom legendary powers of exorcism and magic are ascribed.

In 1185, the first Kamakura shogun (Minamoto Yoritomo) turned on his brother Yoshitsune who made a quick exit and used Yoshino as a hideout.

In 1333, Emperor Go-Daigo successfully toppled the Kamakura Shogunate with the help of disgruntled generals. The return to imperial rule, known as the Kemmu Restoration, only lasted three years. Go-Daigo failed to reward his supporters adequately and he was ousted in a revolt by one of his generals, Ashikaga Takauji, who set up a rival emperor.

Go-Daigo beat a hasty retreat to the remote safety of Yoshino where he set up a rival court. Rivalry between the two courts continued for 60 years, known as Nanbokuchō (Northern & Southern Courts period), until the Ashikaga made a promise (which was not kept) that the imperial lines would alternate.

Nowadays, Yoshino is Japan's top cherry blossom wonder. For a few weeks in spring, thousands of cherry trees form a floral carpet gradually ascending the mountainsides. It's definitely a sight worth seeing, but the narrow streets of Yoshino become jammed tight with thousands of visitors and you'll have to be content with a day trip unless you've booked accommodation long in advance. Early morning or late afternoon on a weekday is a good time to escape the crowds. Another severe impediment to enjoyment of the peaceful setting is an irritating loudspeaker system which relentlessly pursues you with a Mickey Mouse voice turned up at full pitch and volume to reverberate across the valley.

Orientation & Information

To walk from the top cablecar station to Kimpu-jinja, should take about 75 minutes at an easy pace. Allow a couple of extra hours to see the sights or take a picnic for a lazy afternoon under the cherry trees and stay longer.

The village is often clogged with traffic

inching its way through the narrow streets past souvenir shops and restaurants, many of which have dining areas on balconies overlooking the valley. Two local specialities are *kuzu* (arrowroot starch) and washi (handmade paper).

For information, you can try the tourist booth on your right as you exit the station, or ask at a similar booth which is in front of the top cablecar station. The official tourist information office is about 400 metres further up the street, on your right just after the Zaō-dō Hall.

Things to See

As you walk up the main street, you pass through Kuro-mon Gate and should then veer slightly to the right up some stone steps to Ni-ō-mon Gate. This brings you to the massive, wooden structure of the Zaō-dō Hall which is the main building of Kimpusen-ji Temple. For many centuries Kimpusen-ji has been one of the major centres for Shugendō.

Tōnan-in Temple, on your right just beyond the tourist office, has an attractive pagoda parked in the garden.

About 500 metres further up the street you pass Katte-jinja Shrine on your right. The road forks uphill to the right, but keep to the left and follow the road until it twists up a hill to some shops. On your left, opposite the shops, there's a steep path leading up the mountain to Kimpu-jinja Shrine. Just past the shops, there's a bus stop (with infrequent buses to Kimpu-jinja) to your left on the Yoshino-ōmine driveway – good for motorised transport, but uninteresting as a walk.

There are plenty of streets or flights of steps leading off the main street to small temples and shrines. A short walk beyond the Kizō-in Temple Youth Hostel is the Chikurin-in Temple which provides expensive lodgings; you can pay to visit the garden only with its ornamental pond and fine view across the valley.

Yoshimizu-jinja Shrine, on a sidestreet opposite the tourist office, has a good platform for blossom viewing.

My view of the blossoms at Yoshimizu-jinja was obscured and my attention diverted by a young Japanese who was wearing a jacket with a curious English slogan on his back:

Lack of affectation
Social Disease
Person's Club
Calm Ocean
Leaves Trembling in the Wind
The Moon Looked down and laughed.

I wonder what Go-Daigo would have made of that?
Robert Strauss

Festivals

On 7 July, there's the bizarre Kaeru Tobi Festival which commemorates the story of a man who insulted a yamabushi (literally 'mountain priest') of the Shugendō school and was turned into a frog. Don't be surprised if you see a man dressed as a frog parading around the village.

Places to Stay & Eat

The tourist information office in the centre of the village can organise accommodation or you can use the information booths outside Yoshino station or at the top cablecar station. Many of the temples offer lodgings, but you'll be looking at a minimum of Y10,000 including meals. A slightly cheaper alternative is provided by several minshuku.

The cheapest option, at Y1900 per person per night, is *Kizō-in Temple* (07463-2-3014) which doubles as the local youth hostel and is an excellent way to stay in a temple if you don't want the full ryokan treatment. The traditional, wooden architecture is pleasant and several of the hostel rooms look out across the valley.

There's no need to worry if you hear strange noises outside – like cats being strangled. It's just the resident peacocks attempting some melodious partying at about 1 am. The temple dinner consists of tasty vegetable matter but the breakfast of pickles and soggy tōfu may be less appealing.

Kizō-in Temple is easy to find. Just after Katte-jinja Shrine, the road divides. Take the right hand fork up the steep hill for about 300 metres until you reach the imposing temple gate at the crest of the hill on your left.

The main street has dozens of restaurants and coffee shops. The former tend to close early after the day-trippers have left.

Getting There & Away

All rail connections to and from Yoshino run via Yoshino-yama station. From the station you can reach the centre of Yoshino by simply walking uphill for 25 minutes or by taking a five minute cablecar ride (Y460 return).

From Kyoto you can take the train south on the Kintetsu Kyoto line to Saidai-ji (Y440, 30 minutes) and then change to the Kintetsu Kashihara line to Kashihara-jingū-mae (Y270, 20 minutes). From there you change to the Kintetsu Yoshino line which takes you to Yoshino station (Y310, 40 minutes).

From Nara take the train to Saidai-ji and then continue on the Kintetsu Kashihara line as described above from Kyoto.

From Osaka (Abenohashi station) you can take the direct train on the Kintetsu line to Yoshino (Y800, one hour 20 minutes).

For rail connections to or from Wakayama Prefecture (for example, Mt Kōya-san) you can join the JR Wakayama line at Yoshino-guchi station.

MT OMINE-SAN 金峰山

From Kimpu-jinja Shrine in Yoshino, there's a Shugendō pilgrimage trail running all the way via the ranges of sacred Mt Omine-san to Kumano. During the Heian period, the pilgrimage became immensely popular with pilgrims and yamabushi (Shugendō priests) trekking from as far as Kyoto and undergoing austere rites en route. Pilgrims who contravened the rules or lacked sufficient faith were given a gentle lesson by being hung over a precipice by their heels. Between May and September many pilgrims still hike this route.

Women were originally barred from the entire route. Today, there are still points at either end of the route beyond which women

definitely may not pass; any who do try are met with fierce resistance.

Wakayama-ken
和歌山県

This remote and mountainous prefecture is on the south-western side of the Kii Peninsula. In the south, the Kumano region has several interesting Shinto shrines. In the north, the temple complex of Kōya-san is one of the major centres of Buddhism in Japan and merits a visit. The eastern parts consist of rocky coastlines and on the western side there are sandy beaches around Shirahama. Transport can be slow and infrequent, whether chugging along the coastline by rail or bussing through the remote, mountainous regions.

JNTO publishes a leaflet called *Shirahama & Wakayama Prefecture* which gives concise details about sights and transport. The International Exchange Section (tel 0734-32-4111) of Wakayama Prefectural Government publishes *Your Passport to Wakayama* which has detailed mapping and information.

There are some curious festivals in this prefecture. On 14 August, the town of Shimotsu celebrates the Grey Mullet Fishing Dance or you could wait until 10 October and choose between the Laughter Festival at Kawabe and the Crying Babies Sumō Festival in Shimotsu.

SHINGU 新宮

This town is nothing exceptional to look at, but functions as a useful transport hub for access to the three major Shinto shrines (Kumano Hayatama Taisha, Kumano Hongū Taisha and Nachi Taisha), known collectively as Kumano Sanzan. There's an information office at the station where you can get tourist information, pick up maps and check bus or train schedules.

If you are killing time between trains or buses, you could visit the gaudy Kumano

Hayatama Taisha Shrine which is a 15 minute walk north-west of Shingū station. The shrine's Boat Race Festival takes place on 15 and 16 October. The nearby Shinpokan Museum houses treasures accumulated by the shrine.

Kamikura Shrine is famous for its Oto Matsuri Festival on 6 February when over a thousand men carrying torches ascend the slope to the shrine. The shrine is a 15 minute walk west of the station.

If you need a place to stay, you could try the *Shingū Hayatama Youth Hostel* (tel 0735-22-2309) which is a 15 minute walk from the station, close to Kumano Hayatama Taisha Shrine.

Getting There & Away

The JR Kisei line connects Shingū with Nagoya and Osaka. The fastest trip by limited express in either direction takes about four hours.

There are buses from Shingū to Shiko (45 minutes) which is the boat dock for trips through the Doro-kyō Gorge. Buses on this route continue via Hongū or the spa towns of Kawayu and Yunomine all the way through the Yoshino-Kumano National Park to Gōjō; some continue east to Nara or west to Hashimoto. The bus passes through spectacular scenery, but you need to allow over five hours for the journey from Shingū to Gōjō.

DORO-KYO GORGE   どろきょう

Glass-roofed boats depart from the dock at Shiko for the dramatic two hour trip on the Kitayamakawa River through what is generally considered to be Japan's most outstanding gorge. The fare is Y3280 and boats operate at regular intervals from 8 am to 2.50 pm during the summer and from 9 am to 2.15 pm between November and February. Buses connect Shiko with Shingū and are co-ordinated with boat times (Y960 one way, 42 minutes).

The glass-roofed boats ply the relatively tranquil lower end of the gorge as far as Doro-hatchō. If you want a less tranquil, wetter and more expensive ride you can shoot the rapids on rafts further upstream, but you will have to approach the gorge from the north and take a bus from Kumano station to Kitayama-mura. Check the latest details and timings with the TIC in Kyoto or Tokyo or make a toll-free call to the Japan Travel-Phone service. At the last check, rafts from Kitayama-mura operated on Saturdays, Sundays and national holidays in May, June and September and from Fridays to Mondays in July and August. The trips departed at 10.40 am (whole course – two hours and 50 minutes), 11.50 am (lower course – one hour and 20 minutes) and 1 pm (upper course – not operated in May – one hour and 20 minutes). The cost for the whole course was Y8000 and for the other two, Y5000 each.

HONGU   本宮

The three sacred shrines of Kumano Sanzan have been the object of pilgrimages attracting yamabushi (Shugendō priests) and other pilgrims to the Kii Peninsula since ancient times. One of these shrines, Kumano Hongū Taisha, is close to the town of Hongū. The approach to the shrine follows a tree-lined avenue which leads to the shrine's pleasant forest setting.

The old passes connecting Hongū and Takijiri along a 40 km pilgrim trail are still in use. An interesting option if you have time for an extended hike and can connect with the infrequent bus services (three buses a day).

Hongū is 70 minutes by bus from Shingū station. There is also a bus connection (three hours) to Tanabe on the western side of the Kii Peninsula.

YUNOMINE & KAWAYU ONSEN
湯の峰、川湯温泉

Yunomine and Kawaya onsen are two ancient spa towns popular with hot-spring enthusiasts.

Yunomine consists of a narrow main street with the river and hot springs running down the middle. There are numerous hotels and minshuku on the wooded slopes either side of the street. Yunomine is on a bus route

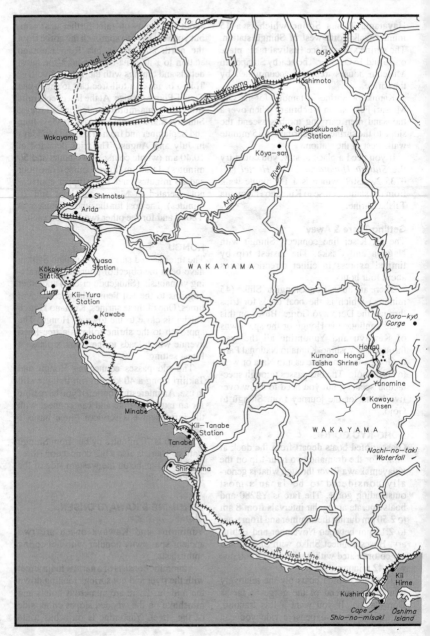

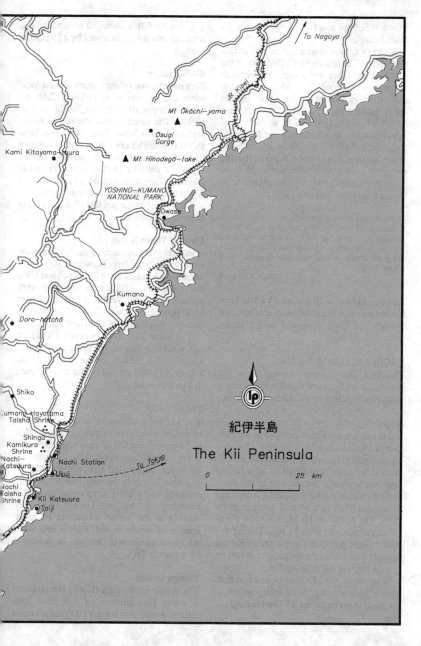

To Nagoya

JR Kisei Line

Mt Ōkōchi-yama ▲

● Osugi Gorge

Kami Kitayama-mura ●

▲ Mt Hinodegō-take

YOSHINO-KUMANO NATIONAL PARK

Owase

Kumano

● Doro-hatchō

Shiko

Kumano Hayatama Taisha Shrine

Shingu
Kamikura Shrine
Nachi-Katsuura

Nachi Station

Ukui

To Tokyo

Nachi Taisha Shrine

● Kii Katsuura

● Taiji

紀伊半島

The Kii Peninsula

0   25 km

between Shingū and Gōjō, only 10 minutes from Hongū.

Kawayu Onsen is in a flatter, less attractive valley. The hot springs bubble out of the riverbed and there are numerous makeshift rotemburo (outdoor, hot-spring baths) dug out of the stones. However, these are not really worth a special visit – Yunomine is a better choice. Apart from a variety of minshuku and hotels, there's the *Kajika-sō* (tel 07354-2-0518) which is a combined youth hostel and minshuku. It's drab, but the cheapest option at Y1900 per night (plus Y100 onsen tax) and it's just a couple of minutes from the bus stop.

I spent several minutes labouring in broken Japanese to explain the concept of a bus stop to the hostel manager. Suddenly, his face lit up and he exclaimed 'Aaaah...basū stoppu', before pointing 30 metres down the street. A long linguistic diversion for a simple thing!

Robert Strauss

Kawayu Onsen is 20 minutes by bus from Hongū and is on the same bus routes between Shingū and Gōjō described earlier in the section on Shingū.

NACHI-KATSUURA 普賢岳

This is a district, close to the tip of the peninsula, with several sights reached either from Nachi station or Kii-Katsuura station.

Nachi

Nachi has several sights grouped around the sacred Nachi-no-taki Waterfall, Japan's highest waterfall, which has a drop of 133 metres. It's also considered to be a Shinto god. Nachi Taisha Shrine, one of the three great shrines of the Kii Peninsula, is adjacent to the waterfall as a natural homage to its kami. The Nachi-no-Hi Matsuri (Fire Festival) takes place here on 14 July. During this lively event portable shrines (mikoshi) are brought down from the mountain and met by groups bearing flaming torches.

Seiganto-ji Temple is next to the shrine. This temple is still popular with pilgrims as the starting point for the 33 Temple Pilgrimage.

The waterfall is about 10 minutes by bus from Nachi station, followed by a 20 minute walk.

Kii-Katsuura

This resort town offers cruises around local islets and the renowned Boki-dō Cave spa which was popular with nobility in the Edo period. The catch is that the spa is inside Japan's largest hotel – the expensive Urashima Hotel. The cave spa is open to visitors from 10 am to 2 pm. Admission costs Y1500. There's a cheaper (Y1000) open-air spa at Katsuura Gyoen ryokan which is open from 5 to 9 am, and from 3 pm to midnight.

The tourist office (tel 07355-2-5311) is in front of the station.

Getting There & Away

A leisurely way of reaching the Kii Peninsula from Tokyo is the ferry between Tokyo Ferry Terminal (Ariake Pier in Toyocho) and Ukui Port close to Nachi. There's one sailing every second day (from Y8800, 13 hours). There is a connecting bus (Y400, 20 minutes) between Nachi station and Ukui Port.

The same ferry runs between Ukui Port and Kōchi on Shikoku in about eight hours. Fares start at Y5400 for this section of the trip or Y13,400 for the whole trip between Tokyo and Kōchi.

TAIJI 太地

The earliest methods of capturing whales in Japan consisted simply of capturing whales that had become beached on the shore or trapped in bays. At the beginning of the 17th century, Taiji was one of the first communities to organise its whale hunting into a full-scale industry using hand harpooning and later resorting to net whaling. The rest of the story leading to the virtual extinction of many species of whale is well known and those who love whales will certainly be saddened by a visit to Taiji.

Things to See

The Whale Beach Park (Kujira Hama-kōen) is about five minutes by bus from Taiji station. Admission costs Y1000 and it's open from 8.30 am to 5 pm. The entry ticket admits you to the Whale Museum, Whalers Museum, Marine Aquarium and Tropical Botanical Garden.

When questioned about the impending extinction of whales and the Japanese government's stance on whaling, many Japanese trot out the facile reply that whaling is a part of their culture. If this is true, then it must be obvious that the present government policy should serve to protect the rapidly dwindling population of whales – otherwise whale meat will disappear from restaurants and the only whales to be found in Japanese culture will be those in museums.

The International Exchange Section (tel 0734-32-4111) of Wakayama Prefectural Government publishes *Your Passport to Wakayama*, a glossy brochure which includes, amongst other things, a section on marine products and local foods. The last line of this section reads: 'Whale meat dishes are also popular in the ancient whaling town of Taiji'. No thanks, I'd like to preserve Japanese culture. See the aside on Japan & Ecology in the Facts About the Country chapter for more details.

Robert Strauss

Places to Stay
The *Taiji Youth Hostel* (tel 07355-9-2636) is three km from the station; 45 minutes on foot or nine minutes by bus.

KUSHIMOTO 串本
This town is at the entrance to Cape Shio-no-misaki, the southernmost point of Honshū. A short ferry ride connects with O-shima Island. If you like weird rock formations, take a look at the Hashi-kui-iwa (rock columns) between Kushimoto station and Kii-Hime station. They have been imaginatively compared to a 'line of hooded monks' heading towards O-shima Island. For local information contact the Kushimoto Tourist Association (tel 07356-2-3171).

There are two youth hostels almost next to each other, on the tip of Cape Shio-no-misaki. *Shio-no-Misaki Youth Hostel* (tel 07356-2-0570) is slightly cheaper than *Misaki Lodge Youth Hostel* (tel 07356-2-1474). The bus ride from the station takes 20 minutes.

Kushimoto is one hour from Shirahama by JR limited express.

SHIRAHAMA 白浜
Shirahama is one of Japan's top, hot-spring resorts and comes complete with acres of swish hotels, golf courses, cabarets, an Adventure World and so forth. This probably makes it rather more interesting for Japanese than for most foreigners. The wonders of Shirahama are some distance from the station so you'll need to take a bus or rent a bicycle if you arrive by rail. The bus ride to the centre takes 17 minutes.

The Shirahama tourist information office (tel 0739-42-2900) is in the station and open from 8.30 am to 5 pm. It's closed on Thursday. You could also try the Shirahama Tourist Association (tel 0739-43-5511).

If you want to be independent, there's a bicycle rental place at the station – charges are Y300 per hour or Y1000 for the day.

Things to See & Do
Sakino-yu hot springs might appeal if you like the idea of taking a bath in the open air close to the sea. Take the bus from Shirahama station to Yuzaki bus stop (17 minutes), then walk for 10 minutes to the segregated baths which are beside the sea. Admission is free. Sakino-yu is open from 7 am to 7 pm in the summer and from 8 am to 5pm in the winter but is closed on Wednesdays. The springs are said to be good for all sorts of things ranging from constipation to the ailments of women.

Sandanbeki Cliffs can be reached by bus (20 minutes) from the station. Get off at the Sandanbeki-mae bus stop and admire all the souvenir stands before taking the elevator down to the Pirate's Cave at the foot of the cliffs. Various pirate items are displayed from the times when local pirates plundered passing shipping.

Close to these cliffs is Hama Blanca (Costa Branca) which promises the intriguing combination of laser lights, tropical theatre, a botanical garden and cabaret. Look out for the Jumbo Tomato Tree. Admission costs Y1000 and it's open from 8 am to 5 pm.

Energy Land, close to Sakino-yu Hot Springs, has displays devoted to alternative energy sources.

At Tsubaki Onsen, two stops south of

Shirahama on the JR line, there's the Tsubaki Monkey Park. The monkeys, some 250 of them, are described as being 'popular with visitors' and 'humorous'. You'd *have* to be humorous if you wanted to live there, deal with all the crowds and stay sane.

Places to Stay

If you don't mind staying outside the town of Shirahama, the cheapest option is *Ohgigahama Youth Hostel* (tel 0739-22-3433), which is close to some good beaches. The hotel is 10 minutes on foot from Kii-Tanabe station which is three stops (15 minutes) north of Shirahama station, or 30 minutes by bus from Shirahama station.

In Shirahama itself, there are several kokuminshukusha and minshuku which charge around Y5500 per person for accommodation and two meals.

Getting There & Away

There are twice daily flights between Shirahama and Tokyo. The Kuroshio limited express on the JR Kisei line links Osaka (Tennōji station) with Shirahama in just over two hours.

There is a bus service from Kii-Tanabe station which runs inland to Hongū via Yunomine and Kawayu in three hours. It follows the Nakaheji road which has been used by pilgrims for centuries.

MINABE 南部

If you are passing through in early February, Minabe is famous for its 300,000 plum trees which blossom at this time.

GOBO 御坊

Gobo is famous for the nearby white, sandy beach of Enjuga-hama. Just beyond the western end of the beach, there's the America-mura Village, so called because thousands of the locals emigrated from here to North America in the past and the place has now taken on the architectural style of their adopted homeland.

While you're in the area, you might like to see Dōjō-ji Temple which is close to Dōjō-ji station, one stop south of Gobo station.

There is a legend associated with the temple which has become a popular subject for Japanese drama:

A farmer's daughter took a shine to Anchin, a young priest of the temple, who often came by her farmhouse on errands. Eventually, she mustered enough courage to tell Anchin of her love for him. The priest promised he'd come back that evening and reciprocate her love. After giving the matter considerable thought, Anchin decided it would be best to ditch the lady and returned immediately to his temple. The farmer's daughter, who was called Kiyohime, soon realised she had been jilted and flew into such a rage that she turned into a dragon and took off in hot pursuit of the priest. Anchin raced around in terror looking for a safe place to hide. He suddenly had the bright idea of slipping under the temple bell which had not yet been hoisted into position. Kiyohime quickly guessed his hide-out and promptly enveloped the bell with her red-hot, dragon anatomy until the bell was superheated. The next morning, the bell was lifted to reveal the frazzled ashes of Anjin. Hell hath no fury like a woman scorned!

YURA 由良

Close to Kii-Yura station is Kōkoku-ji Temple. The founder, Hotto Kokushi, is revered in culinary circles as the man believed to have introduced soy sauce to Japan from China. The town of Yuasa, just north of the temple, is famed for its home-made soy sauce. Avid foodies can see the sauce being produced and there's even a soy sauce museum.

ARIDA 有田

Cormorant fishing takes place on the Arida River from 1 June to 31 August. The standard method of cormorant fishing requires the use of a boat, but the people who fish on the Arida River wade in with a blazing torch in one hand and a cormorant on a leash in the other. The *mikan* (oranges) from the Arida area are highly prized among Japanese for their flavour.

Arida Youth Hostel (tel 0737-62-4536) is reached via Yuasa station. From the station take a bus (10 minutes) then walk for three minutes.

WAKAYAMA 和歌山

This is the prefectural capital, a place of little

Nature

Love Hotels (TW)

interest to travellers beyond its function as a transport hub en route to other parts of the prefecture and beyond. The new Kansai International Airport, scheduled for completion in 1993, will be only 20 km to the north of Wakayama.

If you have time to kill in the city, it's only a 20 minute walk from Wakayama-shi station to Wakayama-jō Castle. The original castle was built in 1585 by Hideyoshi Toyotomi and razed by bombing in WW II. The present structure is a passable postwar reconstruction.

Getting There & Away

Osaka is connected by rail with Wakayama via the Nankai Honsen line (70 minutes) and the JR Hanwa line (55 minutes).

To visit Kōya-san from Wakayama you can go by rail on the JR Wakayama line to Hashimoto (Y780, one hour and 20 minutes) and then continue on the Nankai Dentetsu line express to Gokurakubashi station (Y320, 40 minutes)

From Wakayama Port, there's a ferry service to Komatsushima on Shikoku. From Fuke Port, just north of Wakayama, there are ferries to Sumoto (Awaji-shima Island) and Tokushima on Shikoku.

MT KOYA-SAN & KOYA-SAN　高野山

Mt Kōya-san is a raised tableland covered with thick forests and surrounded by eight peaks in the northern region of Wakayama Prefecture.

The major attraction on this tableland is the monastic complex, known as Kōya-san, which is the headquarters of the Shingon school of Esoteric Buddhism. It's one of the most rewarding places to visit in Japan if you are interested not only in scenery and atmosphere, but also in staying inside temples and observing Japanese religion in action.

Over one million visitors come here annually so you should be prepared for congestion during peak holiday periods or festivals. Summer is a popular time to visit and escape from the lowland heat to the cool of this mountain. You can miss large crowds by getting up really early for a stroll around

the area before returning to take part in the morning religious service usually held around 6 am. Similarly, late-night strolls are most enjoyable for the peace and quiet. Apart from the obvious attractions of spring and autumn foliage, some hardy visitors like to wander round Kōya-san, mingling with skiers and pilgrims in the winter snow.

Although you could visit Kōya-san in a day, it's much better to reduce the travel stress and allow two days. This is one of the best places in Japan to treat yourself and splurge on a stay at a shukubō (temple lodging).

History

The founder of the Shingon school of Esoteric Buddhism, Kūkai (known after his death as Kōbō Daishi), established a religious community here in 816. Kōbō Daishi travelled as a young priest to China and returned after two years to found the school. He is one of Japan's most famous religious figures and is revered as a Boddhisattva, scholar, inventor of the Japanese kana syllabary and as a calligrapher. He is believed to be simply resting in his tomb, not dead but meditating, until the arrival of Miroku (Maitreya – Buddha of the Future).

Over the centuries, the temple complex grew in size and also attracted many followers of the Jōdo (Pure Land) school of Buddhism. During the 11th century, it became popular amongst the nobility and commoners to leave hair or ashes from deceased relatives close to Kōbō Daishi's tomb in handy proximity for his reawakening. This practice continues to be very popular today and accounts for the thousands of tombs around Okuno-in Temple.

In the 16th century, Oda Nobunaga asserted his power by massacring large numbers of monks at Kōya-san. The community subsequently suffered confiscation of lands and narrowly escaped invasion by Toyotomi Hideyoshi. At one stage, Kōya-san numbered over 1500 monasteries and many thousands of monks. The members of the community were divided into three groups: clergy (gakuryō), lay priests

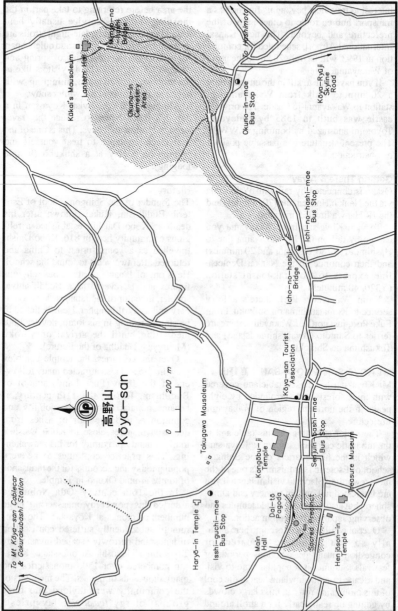

高野山
Kōya-san

0   200 m

To Mt Kōya-san Cablecar
& Gokurakubashi Station

Haryō-in Temple

Isshi-guchi-mae
Bus Stop

Main
Hall

Dai-tō
Pagoda

Sacred Precinct

Henjōson-in Temple

Treasure Museum

Sejuin-bashi-mae
Bus Stop

Kongōbu-ji
Temple

Tokugawa Mausoleum

Kōya-san Tourist
Association

Ichō-no-hashi
Bridge

Ichi-no-hashi-mae
Bus Stop

Kōya-Ryūji
Skyline Road

Okuno-in Bus Stop

To Hashimoto

Okuno-in Cemetery
Area

Lantern Hall

Kūkai's Mausoleum

Mieidō-no-hashi
Bridge

(gyōnin)) and followers of Pure Land Buddhism *(hijiri)*.

In the 17th century, the Tokugawa Shogunate smashed the economic power of the lay priests who managed considerable estates in the region. Their temples were destroyed, their leaders banished and the followers of Pure Land Buddhism were bluntly pressed into the Shingon school. During the Edo period, the government favoured the practice of Shinto and confiscated the lands that supported Kōya-san's monastic community. Women were barred from entry to Kōya-san until 1872.

Today, Kōya-san is a thriving centre of Japanese Buddhism with 120 temples remaining and a population of 7000. As the headquarters of the Shingon school, it numbers over 10 million members and presides over nearly 4000 temples all over Japan.

Orientation & Information

At the top cablecar station there's a tourist information office which doles out information and makes reservations for temple lodgings.

The Kōya-san Tourist Association (tel 0736-56-2616) has an office in the centre of town in front of the Senjuin-bashi-mae bus stop. Some English is spoken and a detailed brochure and maps are provided. Both tourist offices are open from 8.30 am to 5.30 pm in summer and from 9 am to 4.30 pm in winter. If enlightenment is imminent and you'd like to tell the folks abroad, there's an international phone booth beside the office.

The precincts of Kōya-san are divided into the Garan (Sacred Precinct) in the west and Okuno-in Temple with its vast cemetery in the east.

Okuno-in Temple

Anybody worth their salt in Japan has had their remains or just a lock or two of hair interred here to ensure pole position when the Buddha of the Future and Kūkai return to the world.

The Tōrō-dō (Lantern Hall) houses hundreds of lamps including two believed to have been burning for over 900 years. Behind the hall you can see the closed doors of the Gobyō, Kūkai's mausoleum.

On my first visit, I walked out of the Tōrō-dō and joined several hundred elderly pilgrims, dressed in white and clutching staffs with jingling bells, standing outside in complete silence. Just as thick flakes of snow started to fall through the trees onto the heads of the assembly, one of the leaders gave a signal and everyone began a long session of chanting.

On my second visit, the atmosphere was completely ruined by a construction crew busy with their pile-drivers and mobile diggers roaring away next to Kūkai's tomb!

Robert Strauss

As you walk away from the Lantern Hall, you will recross the Mimyo-no-hashi Bridge. Worshippers ladle water from the river and pour it over the Jizō statues as an offering for the dead. The inscribed wooden plaques in the river have been placed there in memory of aborted babies or for those who have met a watery death. Just below the Jizō statues there's a hall with a kitchen at the back where you can join tired, bedraggled pilgrims and brew your own tea.

Return along the main path for about 10 minutes, then take the path to the left and continue wandering through more acres of tombs. Just before you reach the giant car park and Okuno-in bus terminal, take a look on your left at the spaceship tomb dedicated to the employees of an aerospace company.

The best way to approach Okuno-in Temple is to walk or take the bus east to Ichi-no-hashi-mae bus stop. From here you cross Ichi-no-hashi Bridge and enter the cemetery grounds along a winding, cobbled path lined by tall cypress trees and thousands of tombs. As the trees close in and the mist swirls, it's a ghostly feeling to wander past all the monuments to shades from Japan's past. Fortunately, the stone lanterns are lit at night.

Buses return to the centre of town from the terminus just across from the concrete, restaurant and souvenir shop complex.

Kongōbu-ji Temple

This is the headquarters of the Shingon

school and the residence of Kōya-san's abbot. The present structure dates from the 19th century and is definitely worth seeing.

The Ohiro-ma Room has ornate screens painted by Kanō Tanyu in the 16th century. The Yanagi-no-ma (Willow Room) has equally pretty screen paintings of willows, but the rather grisly distinction of being the place where Toyotomi Hideyoshi committed seppuku (ritual suicide).

Another room displays photos of a visit by Hirohito, the previous emperor, and even shows the meal he was given. The kitchens are equipped on a massive scale to feed hundreds of monks.

Admission costs Y350 and includes a cup of tea and rice cakes served beside the stone garden. It's open from 8 am to 5 pm in the summer and from 8.30 am to 4.30 pm in the winter.

Danjogaran

This is a temple complex with several halls and pagodas. The most important buildings are the Dai-tō (Great Pagoda) and Kondō (Main Hall). Admission to these costs Y100 each.

Treasure Museum

The Reihōkan (Treasure Museum) has a compact display of Buddhist works of art, all collected in Kōya-san. There are some fine statues, painted scrolls and mandalas. Admission costs Y500 and it's open from 8.30 am to 5 pm during the summer but closes at 4.30 pm in the winter.

Tokugawa Mausoleum

Admission to the Tokugawa-ke Reidai (Tokugawa Mausoleum) costs Y100 and your view is from behind densely barred doors. It's not worth a special detour.

Festivals

Aoba-Matsuri is a festival held on 15 June to celebrate the birth of Kōbō Daishi.

Mandō-Kuyoe (Candle Festival) is held on 13 August. In remembrance of dead relatives, thousands of mourners light candles along the approaches to Okuno-in Temple.

Places to Stay

There are over 50 temples offering lodgings and meals. Many of them have superb gardens and architecture. Prices range from Y7500 to Y11,000 per person per night and include two meals. The temples double as business concerns, enjoying a monopoly on accommodation in Kōya-san, and have pitched their prices accordingly.

During high season and holidays you should make advance reservations through the Kōya-san Tourist Association or direct with the temples. The two temples mentioned here charge a bit less than the standard prices.

Henjōson-in Temple (tel 0736-56-2434) now functions as a standard temple lodging – no longer as a youth hostel – and has increased its prices accordingly. A room for the night and two meals now costs Y6000. For this you get a pleasant room with a garden view, tatami furnishings, an excellent vegetarian dinner served in your room and the use of a terrific, wooden (smooth cedar) tub in the men's bathroom. There's even a temple bar and barmaid! The temple is close to the treasure museum and if you take the bus you should get off at Reihōkan-mae bus stop.

All in all, this represents excellent value: Henjōson-in is slightly cheaper than the other temple lodgings and its spiffier and more atmospheric than Haryō-in Temple which is a kokuminshukusha.

Haryō-in Temple (tel 0736-56-2702) functions as a kokuminshukusha and is a couple of minutes on foot from the Isshiguchi-mae bus stop. A room for the night and two meals costs Y4800.

The Haryō-in was a little rundown, but – despite the above comment – I liked the faded feel of the place and the friendly staff. When I left, I was embarrassed to find the entire crew out in the rain, down on their knees, bowing deeply in farewell until I'd passed out of the gate. Did somebody lose their contact lenses?
Robert Strauss

Places to Eat

The culinary speciality of Kōya-san is shōjin ryōri (vegetarian food) – no meat, fish, onions or garlic – which you can sample by ordering your evening meal at your temple lodgings. Two tasty tōfu specialities are 'goma-tōfu' (sesame tōfu) and 'koya-tōfu' (local tōfu).

There are various coffee shops dotted around town for breakfast – a convenient one is at the main crossroads close to the tourist office.

Opposite Okuno-in-mae bus stop and the adjoining monstrosity of a car park, there's a large restaurant and souvenir shop. For lunch you could try the restaurant on the 2nd floor which serves a variety of dishes (choose from the window display and buy a ticket at the desk) including 'san-cai rāmen' (mountain vegetables with noodles) for Y700. Mountain vegetable dishes are a local speciality available at restaurants all over town – tasty and nutritious.

Entertainment

Nightlife is restricted to walks in the graveyard, a couple of nondescript pubs and a pachinko parlour just across the road from the tourist office. Beer and saké are freely available in shops and in the temple lodgings – no religious quibbles about grain or rice.

Getting There & Away

All rail connections to and from Mt Kōya-san run via Gokurakubashi which is at the base of the mountain. A cablecar provides frequent connection between the base and the top of the mountain (Y320, five minutes). Buses run on two routes from the top cablecar station via the centre of town to Ichi-no-hashi Bridge and Okuno-in Temple. The fare to Okuno-in is Y360.

From Osaka (Namba station) you can go direct by ordinary express on the Nankai Dentetsu line to Gokurakubashi station (Y770, one hour and 30 minutes). You can also buy a combined rail and cablecar ticket to Kōya-san for Y1020. For the slightly faster, limited express service with reserved seats you pay a supplement almost equal to the ordinary express fare.

From Wakayama you can go by rail on the JR Wakayama line to Hashimoto (Y780, one hour and 20 minutes) and then continue on the Nankai Dentetsu express to Gokurakubashi station (Y320, 40 minutes).

If you are heading into the Kii Peninsula, you should take the train from Gokurakubashi to Hashimoto and then backtrack by rail to Gōjō (10 minutes). There are two buses a day between Gōjō and Shingū (Y3900, 5½ hours).

For rail connections to Yoshino, you must first travel from Mt Kōya-san (via Gokurakubashi) to Hashimoto and then continue on the JR Wakayama line to Yoshino-guchi station where you can change to the Yoshino Kintetsu line for a short trip to Yoshino station.

Getting Around

Apart from Okuno-in Temple, which is 40 minutes on foot from the centre of town, all the other sights in the Garan area are conveniently reached from the centre on foot. As you walk, look out for the street drain covers; they have a temple motif!

Bicycles are available for hire at Y350 per hour or Y1050 for the day. The Kōya-san Tourist Association Office has more details.

There are three convenient bus services. One links the cablecar station with Ichi-no-hashi Bridge; another runs between the cablecar station and Okuno-in; and one more runs between the cablecar station and Daimon Gate. The stop opposite the tourist office in the centre of town is called Senjuin-bashi-mae.

Northern Mie-ken
三重県の北部

The Mie Prefecture stretches across the eastern side of the Kii Peninsula. The southern half consists of densely forested mountains which have a reputation for frequent and heavy rainfall. The northern half consists of two plains divided by a low ridge of mountains.

The main attractions, easily accessible

from Osaka, Kyoto and Nagoya are Ise-jingū Shrine on the Ise Plain, pearl cultivation at Toba and the coastal scenery of Shima-hantō Peninsula and Ise-Shima National Park. Transport is less frequent in Yoshino-Kumano National Park – a wild, mountainous region which would appeal to those prepared to hike way off the beaten track.

IGA-UENO 伊賀一上野

This rather drab town, dominated by a castle, was once a base for ninja who were trained in martial and spiritual skills. The town also derives considerable literary and touristic clout from being the birthplace of Bashō, Japan's most celebrated haiku poet. In response to popular demands, the city elders have considerately installed a drop-in box for visitors' haiku poetry.

Orientation & Information

The sights are contained in Ueno-kōen Park – the castle is visible from the station – which is a 12 minute walk from Ueno-shi station. Use the subway under the tracks, cross the road and continue uphill into the park.

There's an information office with maps and English leaflets just outside Ueno-shi station. If you have a large backpack which won't fit the lockers, you can pay Y260 to deposit it at a luggage check beside the ticket window and save yourself the trouble of lugging your load around the park.

The area around Iga-Ueno is famous as a ceramics centre which produced classic items for the tea ceremony. There's a pottery museum, Iga Shigaraki Kotōkan, right next to Ueno-shi station.

Iga is also famous for producing virtually all of Japan's *kumihimo*, braided cords made from silk as adornments for swords and, in modern times, as classy kimono accessories.

Ninja Yashiki House

The house originally belonged to a village leader and was moved here from Takayama village in the Iga district.

Pink-suited *kunoichi* (ninja girls) go through a quick and wooden routine demonstrating how to slip through revolving doors. The group of visitors is then handed over to an old man who reveals a concealed cupboard and continues with perhaps the most impressive display when he deftly flips up a fake floorboard and retrieves a hidden sword in one rapid movement.

In the basement of the house is a museum with uniforms, martial implements and information in Japanese about ninjutsu (the

---

Ninjutsu

Those who have read *Shogun* by James Clavell, watched a few martial arts movies or taken an interest in the Teenage Mutant Ninja Turtles will know about this martial art. Although the Japanese claim it as their own, it's more probable that it was adapted in ancient times from the Sonshi, a Chinese tactical manual, used in Shugendō for training yamabushi.

Ninjutsu (the art of stealth) was perfected after the 13th century as a means for the practitioners (ninja) to serve their lords with mayhem such as assassination, stealthy thievery, sabotage and spying.

Two schools flourished during the 14th and 15th centuries: the Iga and Koga. Training took place in small family units. At one stage nearly 50 of these were active. Trainee ninja were taught the spiritual and physical skills of both overt and clandestine action along the lines of the Chinese theory of Yin and Yang. They developed tremendous agility in climbing, jumping and swimming, and could even sprint sideways or backwards.

To facilitate their spying and killing, they dressed in black for night operations and used a variety of gadgets. These included a collapsible bamboo stick for scaling walls, metal throwing stars *(shuriken)* and nasty little items called caltrops *(tennenbishi)* which had four spikes arranged to skewer the feet of pursuing enemies. ■

art of ninja). Presumably, this place will become a mecca for modern fans of a weird, pizza-addicted mutation of ninja: the 'Teenage Mutant Ninja Turtles'.

Admission costs Y300 and it's open from 9 am to 5 pm but closed from 29 December to 1 January.

Ueno-jō Castle

This castle was built on the remains of a temple in 1608 by the lord of Iga and Ise, Todo Takatora. The present structure is a reconstruction from 1935. As you climb up steep stairs, there are exhibits of pottery, paintings, armour and ninja paraphernalia on each floor. It's worth a quick visit, particularly in the cherry blossom season and in combination with the Ninja House.

Admission to the castle costs Y300. It's open from 9 am to 5 pm but closed from 29 December to 1 January.

Bashō Memorial Museum

The Bashō Ou Kinekan (Bashō Memorial Museum), is a brick and concrete building displaying some of Bashō's literary works. Unless you are a Bashō fan, you can safely skip this.

Those interested in curious literary trivia might like to know that Bashō is also the name for the Japanese banana tree and the poet was given his name after a disciple had planted one as a present at the gate of his retreat.

Admission costs Y150 and it's open from 8.30 am to 5 pm daily except Mondays, Thursday afternoons and days following a national holiday.

Festivals

Ninja Matsuri takes place on the first Sunday in April in the park.

Ueno Tenjin Matsuri takes place at Sugiwara-jinja Shrine between 23 and 25 October. Dating from the 16th century, the festival features a parade of mikoshi (portable shrines) on ornate floats which are accompanied by fearsomely attired demons.

Getting There & Away

The closest station for Ueno-kōen Park is Ueno-shi which lies between the stations of Iga-Kanbe to the south and Iga-Ueno to the north. It's a short trip to Ueno-shi (25 minutes from Iga-Kanbe; seven minutes from Iga-Ueno) but services are infrequent. You may prefer to take a taxi.

Ise is 90 minutes by normal express train from Iga-Kanbe on the Kintetsu Osaka line. Nara is one hour by express from Iga-Ueno on the JR Kansai line which also connects with Nagoya.

Shima-hantō Peninsula
志摩半島

The Ise-Shima National Park on the Shima-hantō Peninsula has Japan's most sacred Shinto shrine and offers a variety of seascapes with narrow inlets and bays dotted with oyster rafts and seaweed poles. It's easily reached from Nagoya, Kyoto or Osaka and is worth a two day visit.

JNTO publishes *Ise-Shima*, a leaflet providing basic mapping and concise information for the area.

Festivals

The Hatsumōde Festival celebrates the new year between 1 and 3 January. Millions of worshippers pack the area and accommodation is booked out for months in advance.

The Kagurai-sai Festival is celebrated on 5 and 6 April at Ise-jingū Grand Shrine. This is a good chance to see performances of kagura (sacred dance), bugaku (sacred dance and music), Nō and Shinto music.

Those in search of strange festivals might like to be around for the Hamajima Lobster Festival on 6 June when local folks prance around a giant paper lobster. Or else drop in on the Nakiri Waraji Festival which takes place in September (during the typhoon season). An enormous *waraji* (straw sandal) is floated out to sea to protect the locals. It's not surprising that this monstrous footwear is also claimed to scare off the sea monster.

Accommodation & Food

Ise and Toba are prime tourist centres so there's plenty of accommodation, but it's probably preferable to stay in quieter, more attractive places in the Ise-Shima area such as Kashikojima or Futamigaura which are within easy reach of Ise by train.

There are a couple of fast-food places – *Lotteria* and *Mister Donut* – next to Ise-shi station which do budget breakfasts and lunches. Naturally, seafood is a speciality of the area and the dinners offered at youth hostels and ryokan are a good way to sample the local fare without busting your budget.

Youth Hostels *Youth Hostel Taikōji* (tel 05964-3-2283) is a temple hostel in Futamigaura. Take a four minute bus ride from the station, then walk for five minutes. The price is Y1700 per night.

Ise-Shima Youth Hostel (tel 05995-5-0226) is close to Anagawa station (two stops north of Kashikojima) – seven minutes on

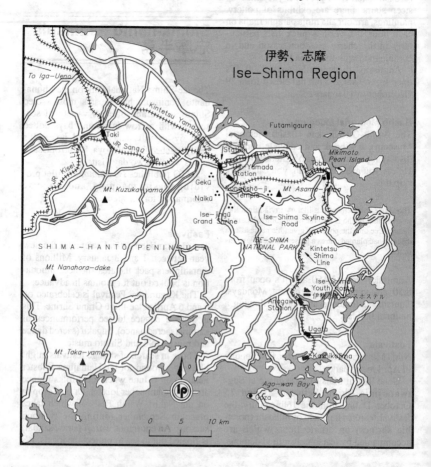

foot. You must be a member and the price is Y1500 per night but a reduction may be given for foreign hostellers.

Ryokan *Hoshide-kan* (tel 0596-28-2377) is a quaint, wooden ryokan with some nice traditional touches, seven minutes on foot from Ise-shi station. It's a member of the Japanese Inn Group and the friendly owners offer vegetarian or macrobiotic food. Singles/doubles cost Y3000/5600. Dinner varies in price (Y500 to Y2500), depending on what you order. Breakfast costs Y500, but it didn't quite match the standard of dinner.

Ishiyama-sō (tel 0599-52-1527) is a member of the Japanese Inn Group on an island in Ago Bay. The owner picks you up at Kashikojima Pier in his boat and spurts you back in a couple of minutes to the ryokan. Singles/doubles cost Y4000/8000. Some rooms have sliding doors less than a metre above the water. You can dip your toes in the water and watch the boats crisscrossing the bay. Dinner is good value at Y1500 for a large spread of seafood.

Business Hotels *Town Hotel Ise* (tel 0596-23-4621) is a couple of minutes on foot from Uji-Yamada station. Singles/doubles cost Y3800/6800.

Business Hotel Danke (tel 0596-22-1849) is a couple of minutes on foot from either Ise-shi station or Uji-Yamada station. Singles/doubles cost Y3800/6800.

Shima Kankō Hotel (tel 0599-43-1211) sits above Kashikojima, commanding a panoramic view across Ago Bay and its prices are commensurate with the view. Doubles start around Y12,000 and Japanese-style rooms start a bit lower at Y11,000. There are no single rooms. The hotel has Japanese and Western restaurants offering fine seafood and nouvelle cuisine respectively.

Getting There & Away
Ise is well endowed with direct rail connections for Nagoya, Osaka and Kyoto. The most convenient direct routings are on private lines. Japan Rail Pass users will have to be prepared to make several time-consum-

ing changes before reaching their destination.

From Nagoya, the limited express on the Kintetsu line takes 80 minutes to Uji-Yamada station, one stop south of Ise, and takes another half hour to reach its terminus at Kashikojima. The fare is expensive (Y2020 one way), but this is the quickest route. If you opt for JR services, your best bet is an express from Nagoya which takes up to two hours and requires a change at Taki for the short ride to Ise-shi station.

From Osaka (Namba station), the limited express on the Kintetsu line takes about 1¾ hours to Uji-Yamada station and the one-way fare is Y2420. There are also limited expresses on the same line, departing from Osaka (Uehon-machi station) and continuing via Ise-shi station to Toba in a total journey time of about two hours.

From Kyoto, the limited express takes two hours to Ise-shi station and continues for about an hour to reach its terminus at Kashikojima. The one-way fare from Kyoto to Ise-shi station costs Y2830.

ISE-JINGU GRAND SHRINE
伊勢神宮

This shrine, dating back to the 3rd century, is the most highly venerated Shinto shrine in Japan. Shinto tradition has dictated for centuries that the shrine buildings (over 200 of them) are replaced every 20 years with exact imitations built on adjacent sites according to ancient techniques – no nails, only wooden dowels and interlocking joints. The present structures date from 1973 and are due for replacement in 1993 at a cost likely to exceed Y5 billion.

Although you cannot enter the buildings, it's possible to peek at their exterior architecture which is interesting because it represents classic Japanese style before the arrival of Chinese influence in the 6th century.

To be fair, foreign visitors may find the place visually unexciting, but you should go there anyway if only to see why the place has such an attraction for the Japanese who come here in their millions every year to pay homage to their spiritual roots.

There are two parts to the shrine: Gekū (Outer Shrine) and Naikū (Inner Shrine) which are six km apart and linked by a frequent bus service. There are over 100 other shrines associated with the Grand Shrine.

No admission is charged and the shrines are open from sunrise to sunset. There are restrictions on photography and smoking.

Gekū

The Gekū (Outer Shrine) dates from the 4th century and is dedicated to the Goddess of Agriculture, Toyouke-Omikami.

A stall at the entrance to the shrine provides a leaflet in English with a map. The main hall is approached along an avenue of tall trees and surrounded by closely fitted wooden fences which hide most of the buildings from sight. Only the emperor and imperial emissaries can enter.

From Ise-shi station, it's a 12 minute walk down the main street to the shrine entrance. Frequent buses leave from stop No 11 opposite the shrine entrance and run to Naikū (Inner Shrine) and Toba. A similar bus service operates to and from Uji-Yamada station.

Naikū

The Naikū (Inner Shrine) is claimed to date from the 4th century BC and is dedicated to the sun goddess, Amaterasu-Omikami, who is considered the ancestral goddess of the imperial family and the guardian deity of the Japanese nation. Since Naikū also houses the sacred mirror, one of the Three Sacred Treasures of the emperor, it is held in even higher reverence than Gekū.

Entrance to the shrine precincts is via Uji-bashi Bridge. One path leads to the left and passes Mitarashi, a place for pilgrims to purify themselves in the Isuzugawa River. The obese carp here slither around with their slobbery lips permanently raised out of the water for yet more food. The path continues along a tree-lined avenue to the main hall. Photos are only allowed from the foot of the

stone steps. Here too, you can only catch a glimpse of the interior; and wooden fences obstruct the surrounding view. On your return to the bridge, take the path to your right and visit the sacred white horse which seems a little bored with its easy life: comfortable accommodation and plenty of fodder in return for a couple of monthly appearances at the shrine.

From the shrine there are buses (Y1000, 45 minutes) to Toba which run along the Ise-Shima Skyline Road via Kongōshō-ji Temple on the top of Mt Asama-yama. If you have time, take a look around the temple which is famous for its Moon Bridge, a footprint of Buddha – he seems to have left plenty around Asia – and eerie rows of memorial poles adorned with paraphernalia from the deceased. It makes a pleasant break from the bus trip with its obnoxious commentary including wailing songs, drumming and a quacking ditty extolling the virtues of the Kashikojima area to the south.

FUTAMIGAURA　二見浦

If you take the train from Ise towards Toba on the JR line, you might want to stop at Futamigaura for an hour. The big attractions – certainly for Japanese who view them at dawn – are the Meota-iwa (Wedded Rocks). These two rocks are considered to be male and female and have been joined in matrimony by sacred ropes (shimenawa) which are renewed each year in a special festival on 5 January.

The rocks are a 20 minute walk from the station. The small town is packed with places to stay, restaurants and souvenir shops.

My visit included the bizarre sight of a funeral complete with a gleaming, gold-trimmed Rolls Royce hearse and a meeting with a long-distance cyclist from Hokkaidō. The elderly cyclist sported two gold fangs and, whilst telling me a great deal about perilous traffic conditions between Hokkaidō and Kyoto which I did not understand, insisted on sharing her punnets of strawberries.

Robert Strauss

TOBA　鳥羽

Unless you have a strong interest in pearls or

enjoy a real tourist circus, you can safely give this place a miss. The information office at the station has a map in English. You can dump your packs here or in the lockers at the aquarium or at Mikimoto Pearl Island. Storage charges are about Y200.

Buses run between Toba and Ise via Naikū and Gekū shrines. The JR line runs from Ise-shi station via Futamigaura to Toba and then on to Kashikojima.

There are ferry connections from Toba Port to Irako on the Atsumi Peninsula in Aichi Prefecture. The trip takes an hour and costs about Y1030.

Mikimoto Pearl Island

This is the place to go if you want to know more about pearls than you ever wanted to know. There are copious explanations in English – a relative rarity in Japan.

The establishment is a monument to Kokichi Michimoto who devoted his life to producing cultured pearls and, after irritating a lot of oysters with a variety of objects, finally succeeded in 1893.

The demonstration halls show all the oyster tricks from growing and seeding to selection, drilling and threading of the finished product. The demonstrators' English vocabulary is limited to their set piece. It must be a weirdly repetitive job, both threading pearls and reciting a text which has been learned by rote.

The Mikimoto Memorial Hall gives minute detail on Mikimoto's path through life and his pearls of wisdom.

The Pearl Museum shows what you can do with pearls. The Liberty Bell pearl is one-third the size of the original and required over 12,000 pearls for its construction.

If you feel hungry, there's an expensive coffee shop selling sandwiches and cheese-cake but no oysters.

There is a separate lounge and observation room for foreigners to watch the diving displays which take place at 45 minute intervals. A nice thought in chilly or windy weather. From here you can watch a boat putter into view and drop off the lady divers in their white outfits. There are several thou-sand *ama* (women divers) still operating in these coastal areas but despite valiant efforts by regional tourist organisations to make you think they're after pearls, they are actually after shellfish or seaweed.

After the divers in the demonstration have retrieved their shells, notice how they surface with a whistling sound to catch their breath again. There is a taped commentary in English which tells you all about the divers and their watery ways. Just ask if you'd like the attendant to put in a tape in another language.

Admission costs Y850 and it's open from 8.30 am to 5 pm in the summer and from 9 am to 4 pm in the winter.

Toba Aquarium

There seems little appeal in paying a large wad of yen to see this cutesy collection of sea creatures in cramped quarters. Those on view include sea otters, Baikal seals, one distinctly dead looking eel lying on its back, a distressed dugong being chased by a diver, a sea-lion show and three common seals in a pathetically tiny cage with a large basin, about as big as a bathtub, as their sole source of water.

Admission costs a whopping Y1400 and it's open from 8 am to 5 pm from 21 March to 30 November; during the rest of the year it is open from 8.30 am to 4.30 pm.

Brazil Maru

This former passenger liner that carted passengers, mostly peasant emigrants, between Japan and South America has been converted into a floating entertainment and shopping centre. The restaurants specialise in exotic South American dishes.

AGO-WAN BAY & KASHIKOJIMA
あご湾、賢島

With its heavily indented coastline, sheltered inlets and small islands, Ago Bay is a pleasant spot to visit. Kashikojima is the terminus of the Kintetsu line, only 40 minutes from Ise, and a good base for exploration of Ago Bay. There's an information office at the station which has a map of the area in Japanese.

From the station, it's a three minute walk down to the pier. A ferry runs between Kashikojima and Goza. The 25 minute ride spins you past oyster rafts along the coast.

Goza is a sleepy fishing community where the main attractions are a fish market and elderly ama, dressed in wetsuits and white headcloths, waddling on and off boats in the harbour. There are bus connections between Goza and Ugata, which is close to Kashikojima, but the bus follows a new road which is boring and bypasses the previous scenic coastal road.

Shirahama campground is on a beach close to Goza.

SOUTH FROM KASHIKOJIMA

If you want to continue down the Kii Peninsula, avoiding the tortuous road, the easiest way is to backtrack to Ise and then go by rail on the JR Kisei line.

The regions around Owase and Kumano offer good opportunities for hiking, but you should check locally for information on facilities and trails before you go into these remote areas.

From Kumano, the railway crosses into Wakayama-ken and continues down to Shingū on its way round the Kii Peninsula.

Owase

The spectacular Osugi Gorge lies to the north of Owase, between Mt Hinodega-take and Mt Okōchi-yama.

Business Hotel Phoenix (tel 05972-2-8111) and *City Hotel Mochizuki* (tel 05972-2-0040) are two business hotels close to Owase station – five minutes on foot. The Phoenix is the cheaper of the two with singles/doubles at Y3800/6300.

Kumano

Kumano can be used as a base to do the white-water raft trip from Kamikitayama-mura to Doro-atchō via the Doro-kyō Gorge. The *Kumano Seinen-no-ie Youth Hostel* (tel 05978-9-0800) is cheap at Y1600 per night

and is only an eight minute walk from the station.

Shiga-ken　滋賀県

This prefecture is dominated by Lake Biwa-ko, Japan's largest lake, which was formed by the same earthquake that created Fuji-san.

The lake has a variety of attractions easily visited as day trips from Kyoto or as stop-offs when travelling to or from Tokyo. Otsu and Hikone are the major sightseeing centres. Mt Hiei-zan and Enryaku-ji Temple are covered under Northern Kyoto in the earlier Kyoto section of this chapter.

JNTO publishes a leaflet entitled *Lake Biwa, Otsu & Hikone* which has useful mapping and concise information. The Kyoto TIC has more detailed information on transport, sights and events in this region.

If you want to stay overnight in the region rather than staying in Kyoto, the main centres for accommodation are Omi-hachiman, Otsu and Hikone. There are youth hostels dotted around the lake, for example, at Omi-imazu (tel 0740-25-3018), Omi-hachiman (tel 0748-32-2938) and Otsu (tel 0775-22-8009).

OTSU　大津

In ancient times this city was a major station for roads between eastern and western Japan. In the late 7th century, Otsu functioned as the national capital for five years. It is now the capital of the prefecture. Otsu-e paintings are part of a tradition dating back to the Edo period when pilgrims were sold vivid Buddhist pictures. They are still popular local souvenirs.

The information office (tel 0755-22-3830) at the JR Otsu station is open from 8.45 am to 5 pm daily.

Mii-dera Temple

Mii-dera Temple, also known as Onjō-ji Temple, is a 10 minute walk from Hama-ōtsu station. The temple, founded in 674, was repeatedly damaged as a result of rivalry

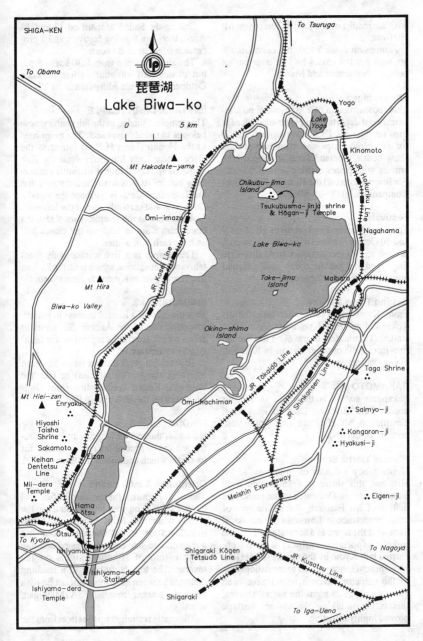

SHIGA-KEN

To Obama

To Tsuruga

琵琶湖
Lake Biwa-ko

0   5 km

Lake Yogo

Yogo

Kinomoto

Mt Hakodate-yama

Chikubu-jima
Island

Tsukubusma-jinja shrine
& Hōgan-ji Temple

Nagahama

JR Hokuriku Line

Ōmi-imazu

Lake Biwa-ko

Take-jima
Island

Maibara

Mt Hira

Biwa-ko Valley

Hikone

JR Kosei Line

Okino-shima
Island

Taga Shrine

Mt Hiei-zan

Enryaku-ji

Hiyoshi
Taisha
Shrine

Sakamoto

Eizan

Keihan
Dentetsu
Line

Mii-dera
Temple

Hama-
ōtsu

Ōtsu

Ishiyama

Omi-hachiman

JR Tōkaidō Line

JR Shinkansen Line

Saimyo-ji

Kongoron-ji

Hyakusi-ji

Meishin Expressway

Eigen-ji

To Kyoto

Ishiyama-dera
Station

Ishiyama-dera
Temple

Shigaraki Kōgen
Tetsudō Line

JR Kusatsu Line

To Nagoya

Shigaraki

To Iga-Ueno

with the monks of Enryaku-ji Temple on Mt Hiei-zan.

Admission costs Y450. It's open from 8 am to 5 pm but closes half an hour earlier between November and March.

The Michigan
This reconstruction of a Mississippi paddle-wheel boat departs from Hama-ōtsu Pier for trips on the lake. Fares start around Y2000 for 90 minute trips and there are special show-boat (Dixieland Jazz) and night-boat cruises with prices starting around Y5000. For reservations call the Biwa-ko Kisen Boat Company (tel 0775-24-5000).

Festivals
The Otsu Matsuri Festival takes place on 9 and 10 October at Tenson-jinja Shrine which is close to JR Otsu station. Ornate floats are displayed on the first day and paraded around the town on the second.

Getting There & Away
From Kyoto, you can either take the JR Tōkaidō line from Kyoto station to Otsu station (10 minutes) or travel on the Keihan line from Keihan-sanjō station in Kyoto to Hama-ōtsu station (25 minutes).

SAKAMOTO 坂本
Sakamoto station is the main station for access from Biwa-ko Lake to Enryaku-ji Temple on Mt Hiei-zan (see the Kyoto section for details).

Hiyoshi Taisha Shrine
If you fancy a detour on your visit to Mt Hiei-zan, this shrine is a 15 minute walk from the station. Dedicated to the protective deities of Mt Hiei-zan, the shrine was of great importance to the monks of Enryaku-ji Temple. Displayed in a separate hall are the mikoshi (portable shrines) which were carried into Kyoto by the monks of Mt Hiei-zan whenever they wished to make demands of the emperor. Since it would have been gross sacrilege to harm the sacred shrines, this tactic of taking the shrines hostage proved highly effective.

During the Sannō Matsuri on 13 and 14 April, there are fighting festivals and a procession of mikoshi on boats.

The shrine is open from 8.30 am to 5 pm but closes half an hour earlier between October and March; admission costs Y300.

ISHIYAMA-DERA TEMPLE 石山寺
This temple, founded in the 8th century, now belongs to the Shingon sect. The room next to the Hondō (Main Hall) is famed as the place where Lady Murasaki wrote the *Tale of the Genji*. Local tourist literature masterfully hedges its bets with the statement that the Tale of the Genji is 'perhaps the world's first novel and certainly one of the longest'.

Admission to the temple costs Y350. It's open from 8 am to 5.30 pm but closes half an hour earlier in winter.

The temple is a five minute walk from Ishiyama-dera station which is on the Keihan line running from Kyoto via Hama-ōtsu.

SHIGARAKI 信楽
This town, with a limited interest to pottery lovers, is one of the Ancient Six Kilns of Japan which acquired a reputation for high-quality stoneware.

To reach Shigaraki, either take a bus from Ishiyama station (70 minutes) or take the Shigaraki Kogen Tetsudō line from Omi-hachiman on the JR Tōkaidō line.

HIKONE 彦根
Hikone is the second largest city in the prefecture and of special interest to visitors for its castle which dominates the town.

Orientation & Information
There is a tourist information office (tel 0749-22-2954) on your left as you leave the station which has helpful maps and literature. The *Street Map & Guide to Hikone* has a map on one side and a suggested one-day bicycle tour of Hikone's sights on the reverse. The tour is outlined in a teaching dialogue between a Japanese girl, an English girl and a teacher from the USA (Michigan, actually).

The castle is straight up the street from the

station – about 10 minutes on foot. There's another tourist office (Hikone Sightseeing Association Office) just before you enter the castle grounds.

Hikone-jō Castle

The castle was completed in 1622 by the Ii family who ruled as daimyō over Hikone. It is rightly considered one of the finest remaining castles in Japan – much of it is original – and there is a great view from the upper storeys across the lake. The castle is surrounded by more than a thousand cherry trees which are famed for their spring blossom.

Admission costs Y300 and includes entry to Genkyū-en Garden. Remember to hang onto your ticket if you plan to visit the garden. It's open from 8.30 am to 5 pm but closes half an hour earlier from November to March.

Next to the main gate of the castle is Hikone-jō Hakubutsukan (Hikone Castle Museum). Items on display came from the Ii family and include armour, Nō costumes, pottery and calligraphy. Admission costs Y300 and it's open from 9 am to 4 pm.

Genkyū-en Garden below the castle is an attractive stroll garden. Buy yourself a bag of fish food for Y20 at the gate and copy the other visitors who save the bloated carp the effort of movement by lobbing morsels straight into their blubbery lips. It's a tough life being an ornamental carp in Japan! Entry to this garden is included in the admission ticket for the castle.

Other Attractions

If you have more time in Hikone, you can follow the cycling route in the *Street Map & Guide to Hikone*. The route passes through the old town to the west of the castle, then south-west via Ichiba (Market Street) to Kawaramachi where you can take a look at a candle-maker's shop (this is also the bar and nightlife district for Hikone) and then crosses to the other side of the Seri River.

From there, you can cross the town and visit a couple of Zen temples in the south-east. The most interesting of these is Ryotan-ji Temple which has a fine Zen garden. Admission to the temple costs Y200 and it's open from 9 am to 5 pm but closes an hour earlier between December and February.

Cruises

There are twice-daily departures from Hikone to the island of Chikubu-jima (Y3260, 2½ hours). There are also several daily departures to the island of Take-jima (Y1700, 30 minutes).

Festivals

Hikone-jō Matsuri takes place at the castle on 3 November. Children dress up in the costume of feudal lords and parade around the area.

Visit Hikone & Find Out About Michigan

If you've never been to Michigan, USA or you have been there and wondered where everybody had gone, a visit to Hikone will inform you on both counts. You will soon find out that Hikone is twinned with Michigan. This accounts for droves of Michigan students from the Japan Centre for Michigan Studies, tourist literature written with a Michigan twist, and a paddle steamer called the Michigan, operating out of Hama-ōtsu Port.

Arriving at Hikone, in a train packed with Japanese, I noticed a lone Westerner purposefully striding towards the exit and thought she might speed my orientation around the city. We walked towards the castle chatting about Japan and I asked her what she was doing in Hikone and where she came from. Yes, you guessed it, she was studying Japanese and came from...Michigan.

Robert Strauss ■

Getting There & Away

Hikone is only 50 minutes from Kyoto on the JR Tōkaidō line. If you take the shinkansen, the best method is to ride from Kyoto to Maibara (25 minutes) and then backtrack from there on the JR Tōkaidō line to Hikone (10 minutes).

MAIBARA 米原

This town is useful to travellers as a major rail junction for the JR Tōkaidō line, JR Hokuriku line and JR shinkansen line.

NAGAHAMA 長浜

Nagahama's main claim to fame is the Nagahama Hikiyama Matsuri held from 14 to 26 April. Costumed children perform Hikiyama kyōgen (comic drama) on top of a

dozen festival floats which are decked out with elaborate ornamentation.

Nagahama is a 10 minute ride north of Maibara on the JR Hokuriku line. From Nagahama there are frequent boats making the 25 minute trip to Chikubu-jima Island.

CHIKUBU-JIMA ISLAND 竹生島

This tiny island is famed for its Tsuku-busuma-jinja Shrine and the Hōgon-ji Temple which is one of those included on the Kansai Kannon temple pilgrimage.

The island is connected by boat with Hama-ōtsu, Hikone, Nagahama and Omi-imazu. Prices and departure times tend to vary so check them with the Kyoto TIC or the Hikone tourist information office.

Western Honshū is also known as Chūgoku. There are three main routes from the Kinki District through the western end of Honshū to the island of Kyūshū. Most visitors choose the southern route through the San-yō region. This is a heavily industrialised and densely populated area with a number of important and interesting cities including Kurashiki and Hiroshima. The island-dotted waters of the Inland Sea, sandwiched between Honshū and Shikoku, the fourth major island, are also reached from ports on the San-yō coast. As an additional reason for choosing this route, the Tokyo–Kyoto–Osaka–Hakata shinkansen rail route also runs along the San-yō coast.

The usual alternative to this route is the northern San-in coast. By Japanese standards, the north coast is comparatively uncrowded and rural. Although there are not as many large cities as on the southern route, the north coast route takes you to the historically interesting town of Hagi. Matsue, Izumo and Tsuwano are also interesting towns worth a stop. Despite the lower population density, travel along the San-in coast is likely to be slower as the train services are less frequent and not so fast. Road travel, too, may be slower, as there are not the long stretches of expressway found along the southern coast. Still, as the traffic is lighter, the San-in coast is an excellent part of Japan to visit using your own transport.

Finally, there is the central route, a fast road route between Kyoto or Osaka and Shimonoseki at the western end of Honshū. The Chūgoku Expressway runs the full length of Western Honshū, more or less equidistant from the north and south coasts. Attractions along this route are comparatively limited and can usually be visited as side trips from the north or south coast routes. Some of these central excursions, particularly the one to the mountain town of Takahashi, are well worth the trip.

Although Himeji is really in the San-yō region and should be the first important city, it is so easy to day-trip there from Kyoto that it is included in the Kinki District chapter.

GETTING THERE & AWAY

Although there are flights to a number of cities in the region and ferry services link major ports with other islands, the shinkansen is the main means of getting to and through Western Honshū. Getting from one end of the region to the other takes less than three hours by shinkansen.

Okayama-ken 岡山県

Okayama Prefecture includes the twin towns of Okayama and Kurashiki along with numerous other interesting towns and tourist attractions. The Seto-ōhashi Bridge forms the main road and rail link from Honshū to Shikoku.

In a brave attempt to attract foreign visitors to the less frequently visited areas of the country, the Okayama Prefectural Government has established six International Villas scattered around the prefecture. They're small and well equipped and rooms cost Y3500/6000 for singles/doubles on the first night and Y3000/5500 on subsequent nights (Y500 less per person for students). The villas have kitchen and cooking facilities, instructions in English on where to shop locally or where to find local restaurants, and even bicycles for visitors' use.

The villas are located in the mountain village of Fukiya; in Koshihata and Hattoji (where the villas are restored thatched-roof farm cottages); in Ushimado, overlooking the Inland Sea; in Kasaoka, also near the coast; and in Takebe, to the north of Okayama city. For more information contact the international exchange section of the prefectural government office on 0862-24-2111, extension 2805. Members of the staff

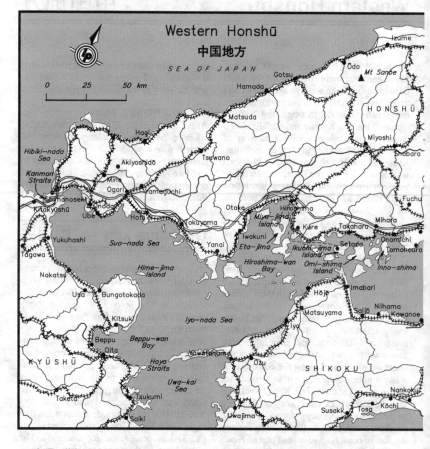

Western Honshū
中国地方

speak English and they can be faxed on 0862-23-3615.

OKAYAMA 岡山

Okayama is so close to the smaller, but touristically more attractive, town of Kurashiki that it's very easy to stay in one town and day-trip to the other. Although Okayama is not as interesting as Kurashiki, there are a number of important places to visit including one of Japan's 'big three' gardens.

Orientation & Information

The town's main street, Momotarō-dōri, leads directly from the station to Okayama-jō Castle and Kōraku-en Garden. Tram lines run down the middle of the street.

JR Okayama station has a tourist information counter and the staff are helpful. Okayama and Kurashiki publish excellent information in English but not all of it may be available at the same time or in the same place. In particular, look for the *Okayama-Kurashiki – New Sites of Discovery* brochure.

The Kinokuniya (5th floor) and Maruzen (2nd floor) bookshops both have good English-language sections. Note the Zap!!

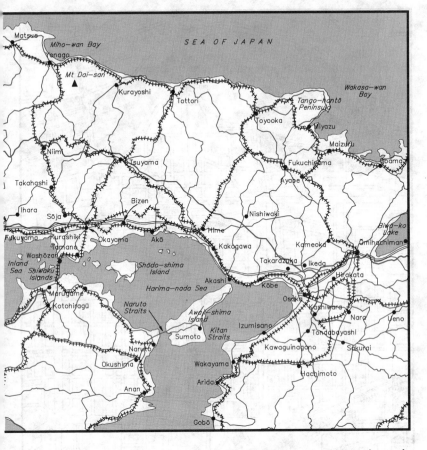

Life Museum among the shops across from the station.

Kōraku-en Garden

The Japanese penchant for rating and numbering things is apparent once again at this park, which is said to be one of the three finest in Japan. The other official members of the big three are the Kairaku-en Garden in Mito (Northern Honshū) and Kenroku-en Garden in Kanazawa (Central Honshū).

Constructed between 1687 and 1700, the Kōraku-en is a stroll garden. Part of its attraction in crowded Japan is the expanse of flat lawn but there are also attractive ponds, a hill in the centre, a curious tiny tea plantation and rice paddy and a neatly placed piece of 'borrowed scenery' in the shape of Okayama-jō Castle. Look for the Nō stage, the pretty little Ryuten building where poetry composing contests were once held, and the nearby Yatsu-hashi zig-zag bridge. *Kōraku-en* means 'the garden for taking pleasure later', taken from the Chinese proverb that 'the lord must bear sorrow before the people and take the pleasure after them'.

Opening hours are from 7.30 am to 6 pm in summer and from 8 am to 5 pm in winter.

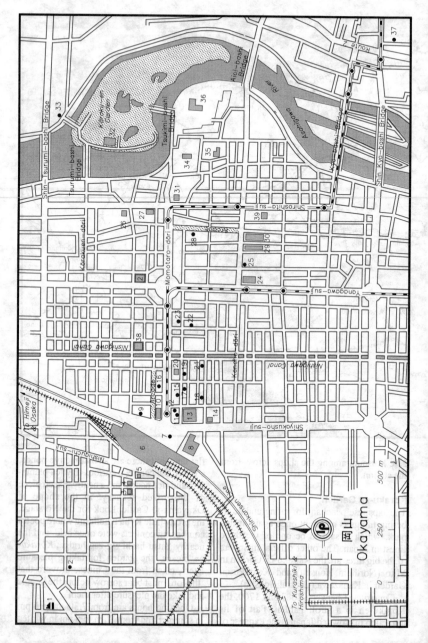

Okayama
岡山

Okayama

1	Okayama Seinen-kaikan Youth Hostel
2	NTT
3	Matsunoki Hotel
4	New Station Hotel
5	Dai Ichi Hotel
6	JR Okayama Station
7	Bus Station
8	Okayama Terminal Hotel
9	Post Office
10	New Okayama Hotel
11	Hitomi-sō Hotel
12	McDonald's
13	Takashimaya Department Store
14	Okayama Castle Hotel
15	Pizza & Salad St Moritz
16	Mister Donut
17	Mura Ichiban Robatayaki
18	Le Pont Neuf II Restaurant
19	Tokyo Inn Okayama
20	Washington Hotel
21	Okayama Business Hotel Annex
22	Peparoncini Italian Restaurant
23	Sunshine Hotel
24	Main Post Office
25	Kinokuniya Bookshop
26	Prefectural Museum of Art
27	Okayama Orient Museum
28	Maruzen Bookshop
29	Tenmaya Bus Station
30	Tenmaya Department Store
31	Chisan Hotel Okayama
32	Prefectural Museum
33	Yumeji Art Museum
34	NHK
35	Hayashibara Museum of Art
36	Okayama-jō Castle
37	Tōko-en Garden
38	Okabiru Market
39	Uno Bus Station

Okayama

1	岡山青年会館
2	NTT
3	まつのき旅館
4	ニューステーションホテル
5	第一ホテル
6	JR 岡山駅
7	バスセンター
8	岡山ターミナルホテル
9	郵便局
10	ホテルニュー岡山
11	ホテル瞳荘
12	マクドナルド
13	高島屋百貨店
14	岡山キャッスルホテル
15	ピザとサラドセイントモリツ
16	ミスタードーナツ
17	村一番ろばと焼
18	Le Pont Neuf II Restaurant
19	東京イン岡山
20	ワシントンホテル
21	岡山ビジネスホテルアネクス
22	Peparoncini Italian Restaurant
23	サンシャインホテル
24	中央郵便局
25	伊国屋書店
26	県立美術館
27	オリエント美術館
28	丸善書店
29	天満屋バスセンター
30	天満屋百貨店
31	ちさんホテル岡山
32	県立博物館
33	夢二郷土美術館
34	NHK
35	林原美術館
36	岡山城
37	東湖園
38	おかびる市場
39	宇野バス本社

Entry is Y250 (see the 'combined entry' note in the Okayama-jō Castle section). An excellent English brochure describing the garden's attractions is available. You can rent rowboats and swan-shaped paddle boats in the river channel between the garden and the castle.

From the station take the Higashi-yama tram to the Shiroshita stop for the garden or castle. Alternatively take an Okaden bus from stand 9 at the station to the Kōrakuen-mae bus stop.

Okayama-jō Castle

U-jō (Crow Castle) was built in 1597 and it is said that its striking black colour was a daimyō's jest at Himeji's pristine 'White Egret Castle'. Like so many other great castles in Japan, U-jō was destroyed in WW II; only the small Tsukima-yagura (Moon-Viewing Turret) survived the wartime destruction. It was rebuilt in 1966, a modern reinforced concrete construction like most of the postwar reconstructions. Nevertheless, there is an interesting display inside and much of it is labelled in English. At the Ote-mon Gate entrance at the south-western corner of the moat, note the interesting sign about the prestige derived from building castle walls with 'big' stones.

Entrance to the castle costs Y250 but you can get combined tickets to the castle plus the Orient Museum for Y350; the castle plus Kōraku-en Garden for Y400; or the castle, the garden and the Hayashibara Museum for Y550. The castle is open from 9 am to 5 pm daily. See the Kōraku-en Garden section for information on getting to the castle.

Museums

Close to the castle's back entrance, near the corner of the moat, the Hayashibara Museum of Art houses a private collection of Japanese and Chinese artefacts. It's open from 9 am to 5 pm and entry is Y300. Beside the main entrance to the Kōraku-en Garden is the Okayama Prefectural Museum which has displays connected with local history. It's open Tuesday to Sunday and entry is Y150.

Just north of the Kōraku-en Garden is the Yumeji Art Museum, displaying work by artist Yumeji Takehisa.

Just north of the end of Momotarō-dōri, where the tram line turns south, is the excellent Okayama Orient Museum. The small collection of Middle Eastern art is beautifully displayed although the absence of any non-Japanese description can be very annoying: one is left wondering where these intriguing-looking places are. Entry is Y200 and it's closed on Mondays. Behind this museum is the Okayama Prefectural Museum of Art; entry is Y300.

Other Attractions

Only a block east of the station, the canal-like Nishigawa River, flanked by its gardens and sculptures, makes for a pleasant short stroll.

South-east of central Okayama is the Tōko-en Garden, which is easy to overlook in a town with one of the 'big three' gardens. It's worth trundling out on the tram to visit this small, attractive early 17th century garden just beyond the river. The garden is centred around a large pond. It actually pre-dates the Kōraku-en Garden by 70 years. Entry is Y300. Beyond the Tōko-en Garden is the Sogen-ji Temple, which also has a noted garden.

Festivals

The Saidai-ji Eyō (Naked Festival) takes place from midnight on the third Saturday in February at the Kannon-in Temple in the

---

Momotarō – the Peach Boy

Okayama-ken and neighbouring Kagawa-ken on the island of Shikoku are linked with the legend of Momotarō, the tiny 'Peach Boy' who emerged from the stone of a peach and, backed up by a monkey, a pheasant and a dog, defeated a three-eyed, three-toed, people-eating demon. There are statues of Momotarō at JR Okayama station and the main road of the town is named after him. Another statue of the boy stands at the end of the Kōraku-en Garden island in Okayama. Mega-shima Island, off Takamatsu in Shikoku, is said to be the site of the clash with the demon. Momotarō may actually have been a Yamato prince who was deified as Kibitsuhiko. His shrine, the Kibitsu-jinja, is visited on the Kibi Plain bicycle ride described in the Around Okayama section. ■

Saidai-ji area. A large crowd of near-naked men fight for two sacred wooden sticks *(shingi)* while water is poured over them!

Places to Stay

Youth Hostels *Okayama Seinen-kaikan Youth Hostel* (tel 0862-52-0651) is west of the railway station and costs Y1900.

Business Hotels There's the usual collection of business hotels around the station. *Hitomi-sō* (tel 0862-25-2371) is a very plain little business hotel where singles/doubles cost from Y4400/8400. It's in front of the station and on the smaller street parallel to Momotarō-dōri. The rooms are relatively large and quite OK except for the worn-looking carpets, but there is no lift which can mean a five floor climb to a top-floor room. There is a snack bar downstairs, with a restaurant above it and the hotel reception above that.

The *Okayama Castle Hotel* (tel 0862-33-311) is one of the more expensive hotels east of the station. Singles/doubles cost from Y5700/9800. The *Okayama Terminal Hotel* (tel 0862-33-3131) is beside the station and has singles at Y6000 to Y7000, doubles and twins at Y10,600 to Y12,200, plus a 10% service charge. At the top of Momotarō-dōri, opposite the station, is the expensive *New Okayama Hotel* (tel 0862-23-8211); further down is the *Washington Hotel* (tel 0862-31-9111). Another hotel is the *Okayama Business Hotel Annex* (tel 0862-24-4111).

In the quieter area west of the station, there are more hotels only a few minutes walk from the centre of things. The *Matsunoki Hotel* (tel 0862-53-4111) is a pleasant, newish place where Japanese-style rooms with bathroom cost Y5200/9000 per night, room only, for singles/doubles. Breakfast costs Y700, dinner Y1300 and there's a cheaper annex which has rooms without bathrooms. A few steps back towards the station is the *New Station Hotel* (tel 0862-53-6655) which charges Y4600/8300 for singles/doubles. There are a number of other cheaper small hotels in the same area as well as the more expensive *Dai Ichi Hotel*.

Places to Eat

Okayama has a familiar collection of eating places in and around the railway station including a *Mister Donut* and a *McDonald's* on Momotarō-dōri. The small street parallel to and immediately south of Momotarō-dōri has a varied collection of places to eat, including the popular *Mura Ichiban Robatayaki* (fully illustrated menu) on the 2nd floor of the Communication building, the *Pizza & Salad St Moritz* and many others.

Peparoncini is a neat little Italian restaurant just off Momotarō-dōri. In Japanese, the name reads 'Akatogarashi' (hot pepper), but a sign in Italian announces that it's an 'Italiano Ristorante'. It offers good pasta at around Y900, pizzas, other Italian dishes and a lunch-time teishoku. This restaurant is known to local expats as the 'Italian place near the silver gorilla' after a silver King Kong figure which scales a building a block to the south. More expensive European food can be found at the French *Le Pont Neuf II Restaurant*, nearer the station, where set meals cost from Y3000 to Y5000.

In summer, there's a beer garden on the roof of the *New Okayama Hotel*, which is just in front of the station. Take the elevator to floor R; a fully illustrated menu of snacks to go with your beer is provided. In the arcade behind the hotel is the *Sushi Land – Marine Polis* rotating sushi restaurant.

Getting There & Away

All Nippon Airways (ANA) fly to Okayama from Tokyo several times daily; the airport is about 40 minutes from the city by bus. Okayama is on the main shinkansen line, unlike nearby Kurashiki. By shinkansen it only takes about an hour to get from Osaka to Okayama. Himeji is about halfway between the two cities.

See the Kurashiki section for travel between Okayama and Kurashiki. When travelling west, it's quicker to transfer from the shinkansen at Okayama than at Shin-Kurashiki. You also change trains at Okayama if you're heading to the island of Shikoku, across the Seto-ōhashi Bridge.

Buses run from in front of the station, from

the Tenmaya bus station in the Tenmaya department store and from the nearby Uno bus station.

Getting Around

Getting around Okayama is a breeze since the Higashi-yama tram route will take you to all the main attractions. There are only two tram routes, both starting from directly in front of the station. With your back to the station, the Higashi-yama tram route is the one on the right, the easily recognised *yama* 山 is the second character on the front. Trams charge a standard Y140 anywhere in town.

AROUND OKAYAMA 岡山の附近

There are a number of places of interest in the Okayama-Kurashiki area including the pottery centre of Bizen, the Inland Sea, the Seto-ōhashi Bridge lookout at Washūzan and, best of all, the enjoyable Kibi Plain bicycle route.

Kibi Plain Bicycle Route

An excellent way to spend a half day seeing a less visited part of Japan is to follow the Kibi Plain bicycle route. The route follows bicycle paths for most of its length and visits a number of temples, shrines and other sites. You can rent a bicycle (*jitensha*) at one JR station along the route and leave it at another.

Take a local JR Kibi line train from Okayama three stops to Bizen Ichinomiya, ride 15 km to Sōja and from there take a JR Hakubi/San-yō line train back through Kurashiki to Okayama. It's easier travelling in that direction because the bicycle path is not so easy to pick up leaving Sōja, a fairly big town. Bicycles cost Y300 for two hours, Y200 for each additional hour or Y800 for a day. Officially they're available from 9 am, but you can actually start earlier.

From the JR Bizen Ichinomiya station turn right, right again to cross the railway line and in just 300 metres you reach the Kibitsuhiko-jinja Shrine, which fronts a large pond. From here you soon pick up the bicycle path following a canal through the fields until it rejoins the road just before the Fudenkai Temple. Ignore this red herring, as it's not a temple of much interest: only 200 metres further is the Kibitsu-jinja Shrine, a large shrine with a commensurately large car park.

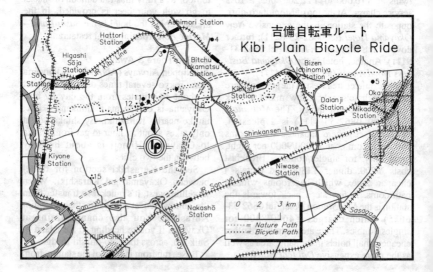

Kibi Plain Bicycle Ride	
1	Hōfuku-ji Temple
2	Sō-ja Shrine
3	Sesshu's Birthplace
4	Takamatsu-jō Castle Site
5	Ikeda Zoo
6	Kibitsuhiko-jinja Shrine
7	Kibitsu-jinja Shrine
8	Koikui-jinja Shrine
9	Tsukuriyama Burial Mound
10	Bitchū Kokubun-niji Convent
11	Kibiji Archaeological Museum
12	Bitchū Kokubun-ji Temple
13	Kōmorizuka Burial Mound
14	Sumotoriyama Burial Mound
15	Anyo-ji Temple

Kibi Plain Bicycle Ride	
1	宝福寺
2	総社宮
3	雪舟誕生の地
4	高松城址
5	吉備動物園
6	吉備津彦神社
7	吉備津神社
8	鯉喰神社
9	造山古墳
10	備中国分尼寺跡
11	吉備路郷土館
12	備中国分寺
13	こうもり塚古墳
14	作山古墳
15	安養寺

A wide flight of steps leads up to this attractive hilltop shrine. Have your fortune told (in English) for Y100 by the serve-yourself oracle in the courtyard. The shrine, built in 1425, is unusual in having both the oratory and main sanctum topped by a single roof. The legendary peach boy Momotarō (see the beginning of the Okayama-ken section) is connected with the shrine.

Pedalling on, you pass the uninteresting-looking Koikui-jinja Shrine, also connected with the legendary figure Kibitsuhiko, and you reach the huge 5th century Tsukuriyama Kofun (Tsukuriyama Burial Mound), rising like a rounded hill from the surrounding plain. You really need to be in a hot-air balloon or a helicopter to appreciate that it's really a 350 metre long keyhole-shaped mound, not a natural hill. Just north of here is the birthplace of Sesshū (1420-1506), the famous artist. He was once a novice monk at the Hōfuku-ji Temple, which is three km north-west of JR Sōja station.

Finally, there are the foundation stones of the Bitchū Kokubun-niji Convent, the nearby Kibiji Archaeological Museum (closed Mondays), the excavated Kōmorizuka Burial Mound and the Bitchū Kokobun-ji Temple with its picturesque five storeyed pagoda. From here it's a few more kilometres into Sōja.

There are countless drink-vending machines along the way, and occasionally the bicycle path passes close enough to a main road to divert for food. If you start early you can arrive in Sōja in time for lunch, or buy a sandwich from the *Little Mermaid* bakery near the station and eat on the train on your way back. If this bicycle ride appeals to you, you can easily plot others on the network of tracks that cover the area. A walking path also runs very close to the bicycle route.

Takamatsu-jō Castle & Ashimori

Places of interest on the Kibi Plain, but not on the bicycle route, include the site of Takamatsu-jō Castle where Hideyoshi defeated the Lord of Shimizu. Hideyoshi hastened the siege by flooding the castle and the remains of the great dykes can still be seen.

North-west of the Takamatsu Castle site is Ashimori, with its well-preserved samurai residence and the Omizu-en Garden, another stroll garden in the Enshū style. The castle is near Bitchū Takamatsu station on the JR Kibi line but the samurai residence and the garden are some distance north of Ashimori station. Take a Tamachi bus for Oi from stand No 18 outside JR Okayama station and get off at Nakanocho.

Although there is little to be seen at the site of Takamatsu-jō Castle, the castle played a crucial part in the finale to the chaotic 'Country at War' century. In 1582, Hideyoshi besieged the castle on behalf of the ruthless Oda Nobunaga and agreed to allow the castle's defenders to surrender on condition that their commander, Lord Shimizu, committed suicide. On the very eve of this event, word came from Kyoto that Oda Nobunaga had been assassinated. Hideyoshi contrived to keep this news from the castle garrison and in the morning his unfortunate opponent killed himself. Hideyoshi then sprinted back to Kyoto and soon assumed command himself.

Imbe & Bizen
East of Okayama, on the JR Akō line, is Imbe, the 700 year old pottery village renowned for its unglazed bizen-yaki pottery. High-quality examples of this pottery, much prized by tea ceremony connoisseurs, are produced in wood-fired kilns and are very expensive. The ceramics museum, near the JR Imbe station, has pottery displays, a pamphlet in English and a map showing local kilns and shops.

North of Bizen, the town east of Imbe, is the Shizutani Gakkō school which was established in 1670. Picturesquely sited and encircled by a beautiful wall, it was one of the first schools established specifically for commoners. It is not easy to reach by public transport.

Kojima, Washūzan & Seto-ōhashi Bridge
From the peninsula south of Kurashiki and Okayama, the Seto-ōhashi Bridge connects Honshū (the biggest island) with Shikoku (the fourth largest). The bridge (or more correctly bridges, since there are six of them stepping from island to island across the strait) was opened in 1988 and has considerably shortened travel time to Shikoku. The long span at the Honshū end is the world's longest double-level suspension bridge carrying both road and rail traffic.

The Washū-zan Hill, near the end of the peninsula, was long renowned as a lookout point over the Inland Sea. Now it looks out over the bridge as well. To really appreciate the bridge you can take a boat tour around it from Kojima. At Kojima you can also visit the Seto-ōhashi Memorial Bridge Museum.

Buses run to Kojima from Kurashiki and Okayama and the JR Seto-ōhashi line from Okayama to Shikoku runs through Kojima station before crossing the bridge. Buses run from Kojima station to Washūzan, but only once or twice an hour. There's also the Shimotsui Narrow Gauge Railway which runs from Kojima (near the Seto-ōhashi Memorial Museum) at one end, via Washūzan station to Shimotsui station at the other. Shimotsui is an interesting little fishing port and ferries cross from here to Marugame on Shikoku. *Washūzan Youth Hostel* (tel 0864-79-9280) is below the hill, right at the end of the peninsula.

Also near Kojima is the old house of a salt merchant named Nozaki. Entry is Y500 and the house is closed on Mondays. To the north-east is the Rendai-ji Temple which dates back to the 8th century and is dedicated to the god who protects sea travellers. The Fujito-ji Temple is further north towards Okayama and has a beautiful painted screen showing a battle between the Genji and Heike families.

KURASHIKI　倉敷
Kurashiki's claim to fame is a small quarter of picturesque buildings around a stretch of moat. There are a number of old black-tiled warehouses which have been converted into an eclectic collection of museums. Bridges arch over, willows dip into the river and the whole effect is quite delightful – it's hardly surprising that the town is a favourite with tourists. Kurashiki means 'warehouse' *(kura)* 'village' *(shiki)*.

In the feudal era, the warehouses were used to store rice brought by boat from the surrounding rich farmlands. As this phase of Kurashiki's history faded, the town's importance as a textile centre increased and the Kurabō Textile Company expanded. Ohara Keisaburō, the owner of the company, gathered together a significant collection of European art and, in the 1920s, opened the

Ohara Museum to display it. It was the first of a series of museums which have become the town's principal attraction and is still one of the finest.

Orientation & Information

As in so many other Japanese towns, the main street leads straight out from the railway station. It's about one km from the station to the old canal area; Ivy Square is just beyond the canal. A number of shops along the main street, Kurashiki Chūō-dōri, sell bizen-yaki pottery.

The staff at the station's information counter will make accommodation bookings, and there is also a helpful tourist information office near the bend in the canal. Most of the museums and galleries are closed on Monday and the number of visitors drops dramatically, so Monday is a good time to enjoy Kurashiki without the crowds.

Around the Canal

The museums and galleries which are the town's major attraction are concentrated along the banks of the canal. At times, the canal area can seem like rush hour at Tokyo station, so, if you want to see how pleasant the area looks without throngs of tour groups, you should wander the canal banks early in the morning or on a Monday. It's not necessary to visit all (or indeed any) of the museums; some are definitely more interesting than others.

Ohara Museum of Art This is undoubtedly Kurashiki's number one museum, housing the predominantly European art collection of the textile magnate Ohara Keisaburō. Rodin, Matisse, Picasso, Pissarro, Monet, Cézanne, Renoir, El Greco, Toulouse-Lautrec, Gauguin, Dégas and Munch are all represented here. The museum's neo-classical facade is Kurashiki's best known landmark, to which the constant procession of tour groups being photographed outside attests. Entry is Y600; opening hours are from 9 am to 5 pm and it's closed on Mondays.

Your ticket also takes you to the museum's folk art and Chinese art collections and to the

contemporary art collection, housed in a new building behind the main one. You have to exit the old building and walk down the street to enter the new gallery where you will find works by Pollock, Rothko, Miró, de Kooning, Henry Moore and others.

Kurashiki Ninagawa Museum Between the Ohara Museum and the tourist office is the interesting Kurashiki Ninagawa Museum which houses a collection of Greek, Etruscan and Roman antiquities, together with more modern European marbles and other items. Entry is Y600 and it's open from 8.30 am to 5 pm daily.

Kurashiki Museum of Folkcraft The folkcraft museum's collection is mainly Japanese but also includes furniture and other items from many other countries. The collection is housed in an attractive complex of linked kura (warehouses). Entry is Y500 and it's open from 9 am to 4.15 pm (December to February) or 5 pm (March to November). It's closed on Mondays.

Japan Rural Toy Museum This interesting museum displays folkcraft toys from Japan and around the world. Japanese rural toys are also on sale. Entry is Y310 and it's open from 8 am to 5 pm daily.

Kurashiki Archaeological Museum Directly across the canal from the tourist office, this museum is strictly for the archaeology buffs and those interested in bits of ancient pottery – it's very dry! There are finds from burial mounds from the Kibi Plain and an Inca room with some pre-Columbian pottery from Peru but even this isn't very interesting. Entry is Y300 and it's open Tuesday to Sunday from 9 am to 4.30 pm.

Other Museums If you've not had your fill of museums there's also the Kurashiki City Museum of Natural History (Y100, open from 9 am to 5 pm, closed Mondays) and the Kurashiki City Art Museum (Y200, same opening hours).

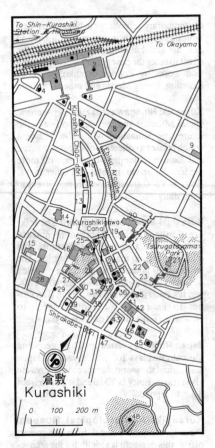

Ivy Square

The Kurabō textile factories have moved on to more modern premises and their fine old Meiji-era red-brick factory buildings (dating from 1889) now house a hotel, restaurants, shops and yet more museums. Ivy Square, with its ivy-covered walls and open-air café, is the centre of the complex.

The Torajirō Kojima Museum displays work by the local artist who helped Ohara establish his European collection, along with some fine pieces from the Middle East in the associated Orient Museum. The museums are open Tuesday to Sunday from 9 am to 5 pm and admission is Y300.

The museum in the Kurabō Memorial Hall

Kurashiki

1	JR 倉敷駅	25	エルグレコ
2	三越百貨店	26	大原美術館
3	倉敷ターミナルホテル	27	大原美術館分館
4	ヤーングイン	28	市立美術館
5	国民旅館おうぐま	29	水島鷲羽山バス停
6	マドナルド	30	イデイスホテル
7	倉敷ステーションホテル	31	倉敷民芸館
8	天満屋百貨店	32	倉敷蟲川博物館
9	郵便局	33	旅館鶴形
10	ドミノカフェイ	34	倉敷考古館
11	ダーンキンドナツ	35	かまいずみレストラン
12	バラタパスバー	36	倉敷旅館
13	レンテンチイ・タリアンレストラ	37	観光案内所
14	大橋家	38	日本郷土玩具館
15	自然史博物館	39	エルパソイン
16	倉敷国際ホテル	40	かわかみ旅館
17	きゆうていステイキハウス	41	児島虎次郎記念館
18	大原家	42	倉紡記念館
19	誓願寺	43	特産館民宿
20	観龍寺	44	アイビースクエア
21	阿智神社	45	倉敷アイビースクエアホテル
22	本栄寺	46	アイビー学館
23	カモ井民宿	47	小島鷲羽山バス停
24	カモ井レストラン	48	倉敷ユースホステル

tells the story of Kurashiki's growth as a textile centre. It's open daily from 9 am to 5 pm and entry costs Y100.

The curious Ivy Academic Hall (Ivy Gakkan) tries to trace the development of Western art through reproductions of notable paintings. The hall is open from 9 am to 5 pm daily and entry costs Y100.

Ohashi House

The Ohashi family were retainers to the Toyotomi family, who were on the losing side of the upheavals leading to the establishment of the Tokugawa Shogunate. The Ohashi family abandoned its samurai status and eventually ended up in Kurashiki, where they became wealthy merchants and built this house in 1796. In its heyday it would

have been a fine example of an upwardly mobile merchant's residence but today it's very worn and shabby. Entry is Y300 and it's open from Tuesday to Sunday from 9 am to 5 pm.

Shrines & Temples

The Achi-jinja Shrine tops Tsurugatayama Park, overlooking the old area of town. The Honei-ji Temple, Kanryū-ji Temple and the Seigan-ji Temple are also found in the park.

Places to Stay

Kurashiki is a good town for staying in a traditional Japanese inn. Although there's a good selection of minshuku and ryokan, business hotels are not as well represented as in other towns.

Youth Hostels *Kurashiki Youth Hostel* (tel 0864-22-7355) is south of the canal area and costs Y2100 per night. It's a long climb to its hilltop location, but the view is great and the staff are friendly.

Minshuku & Ryokan There are several good-value minshuku conveniently close to the canal. The *Tokusan Kan* (tel 0864-25-3056) is near Ivy Square and offers a room-only price as well as a room and two meals at Y5500 per person. Right by the canal near the toy museum the small *Kawakami Minshuku* (tel 0864-24-1221) is slightly cheaper.

The *Kamoi Minshuku* (tel 0864-22-4898) is easy to find (at the bottom of the steps to the Achi-jinja Shrine) and conveniently close to the canal area. Although this minshuku is new, it looks quite traditional: an atmosphere enhanced by the antiques throughout the building. The cost per person, including two good meals in this very pleasant minshuku, is Y5000. The food should be good, as the Kamoi also has a popular restaurant by the canal.

There are also more expensive ryokan around the canal. The canal-side *Tsuragata Inn Kurashiki* (tel 0864-24-1635) is operated by the Kokusai Hotel. The building dates from 1744 and nightly charges in this tasteful ryokan start from close to Y20,000 per person. The ryokan's restaurant also serves outsiders, mainly at lunch time, and there is a café.

Also by the canal, the *Kurashiki Ryokan* (tel 0864-22-0730) is old, elegant and expensive, costing slightly less than the Tsuragata. Either of these ryokan would make a good introduction to staying at a fine traditional inn.

Most of the traditional ryokan and minshuku are around the canal area, an exception being the *Kokumin Ryokan Ohguma* (tel 0864-22-0250) which is near the station. It's to the right as you leave the station, down the small arcade which angles off the main road. Prices fall closer to the minshuku than the ryokan level and you can choose to have meals included.

Hotels – Canal Area Part of the Ivy Square complex, the *Kurashiki Ivy Square Hotel* (tel 0864-22-0011) has singles at Y6000 or Y8000 with bath. Doubles and twins range from Y9000 to Y10,500 without bath, Y11,500 to Y15,000 with bath. Rooms without a bath or shower have a toilet and sink only – there are large communal baths and showers. For all the prices at Ivy Square, add a 10% then 3% surcharge.

Backing on to the Ohara Museum is the expensive *Kurashiki Kokusai Hotel* (tel 0864-22-5141), with singles/doubles from Y8000/12,000. There are also more expensive Japanese-style rooms in this popular and attractive hotel.

Also close to the canal is the stylish *El Paso Inn* (tel 0864-21-8282) where singles/doubles cost from Y5500/9900. A real oddity in the canal area is the *Lady's Hotel* (tel 0864-22-1115); the sign announces this in English. It's a hotel aimed specifically at young OLs (office ladies), which seems to involve painting the rooms pink or a lurid shade of green and dotting stuffed toys around the place.

Hotels – Station Area The JR operated *Hotel Kurashiki* (tel 0864-26-6111) is inside the station building and has singles from Y7000, rooms for two from Y10,000. The *Kurashiki Terminal Hotel* (tel 0864-26-1111) is immediately to the right as you come out of the station and the entrance is on the 9th floor. It's a typical business hotel with singles at Y5800 to Y6700, singles for two at Y8300 or Y8700 and twins or doubles from Y11,300.

The *Young Inn* (tel 0864-25-3411), behind the Terminal Hotel, has singles/doubles without bath for Y4000/7000. There are also slightly more expensive rooms with bathroom in this vaguely hostel-like hotel.

The *Kurashiki Station Hotel* (tel 0864-25-2525) is a short distance along Kurashiki Chūō-dōri towards the canal. The entrance is around the side of the building, with reception on the 5th floor. The rooms in this older but cheaper business hotel are minute and utterly straightforward; singles cost from

Y4400 to Y5000, and doubles from Y7500 to Y10,000.

Places to Eat

If you plan to eat out in the canal area of Kurashiki, don't leave it too late. Many of the restaurants you may notice at lunch time will be closed by early evening. The hordes of day-trippers will have disappeared by then and many of the visitors actually staying in Kurashiki will be eating in their ryokan or minshuku.

El Greco, right by the canal and close to the Ohara Museum, is a fashionable place to stop for a snack. The menu, in English on one side, offers ice cream for Y400, cake for Y200 and a drink for about Y400. It's closed on Mondays.

Also beside the canal is the *Kamoi Restaurant*, run by the same people as the popular Kamoi Minshuku. Plastic meals are on display and the restaurant closes early in the evening as well as all day on Mondays. At the northern end of the canal is *Kiyū-tei*, a steakhouse in an old traditional Japanese house. The fixed evening meal of soup, salad, steak, bread and coffee costs Y2500.

Just back from the canal is *Kama Izumi*, a pleasant, modern restaurant with plastic meals in the window and a fully illustrated menu. You can get good tempura and noodles for Y1400 and the restaurant stays open until at least 8 pm. There's a snack bar in Ivy Square and several restaurants in and near the square.

The familiar selection of restaurants and fast-food outlets can be found around the station including a *McDonald's* and a *Dunkin' Donuts*. Numerous other restaurants can be found along Kurashiki Chūō-dōri. *Domino*, labelled the 'Human's Café', is a neat little place, popular with young OLs, where you can get a good teishoku lunch for Y400 to Y600. A typical meal would be spaghetti, salad and a drink for Y550.

A little further along, *Barra Tapas* (serving beer and South American snacks) and *Etoile* (offering expensive French food and a menu in Japanese and French) are in the same building. The *Rentenchi Italian Restaurant* is another opportunity to have a break from Japanese cuisine.

Getting There & Away

Kurashiki, only 16 km from Okayama, is not on the shinkansen line. Travelling westwards, it's usually faster to disembark at Okayama and take a San-yō line local train to Kurashiki. These operate several times an hour; the trip takes just over 15 minutes and costs Y470. If you're eastbound, get off at the Shin-Kurashiki station, two stops on the San-yō line from Kurashiki.

To get to Washūzan and Shikoku from Kurashiki, you can either travel by train to Okayama and change trains there for Washūzan or take a bus (from outside the station or from the canal area stops shown on the map) direct to Kojima or Washūzan.

Getting Around

Walk – it's only 15 minutes on foot from the station to the canal area where everything is within a few minutes stroll.

TAKAHASHI 高梁

This small town, midway between Kurashiki and the central Chūgoku Expressway, gets few Western visitors even though it has a temple with a very beautiful Zen garden and is overlooked by an atmospheric, even spooky, old castle.

Orientation & Information

The Raikyu-ji Temple is in the town itself but the Matsuyama-jō Castle is about five km out of town, up a steep hillside. The tourist information counter at the railway station has helpful staff and useful information in English.

Raikyu-ji Temple

The classic Zen garden in this small temple is said to be the work of the master designer Kobori Enshū in 1604. It contains all the traditional elements of this style of garden including stones in the form of turtle and crane islands, a series of topiary hedges to represent waves on the sea and it even incorporates Mt Atago in the background as 'borrowed scenery'. Entry is Y300 and it is open from 9 am to 5 pm daily.

Matsuyama-jō Castle

High above Takahashi stands the highest castle in Japan, a relic of an earlier period of castle construction when fortresses were designed to be hidden and inaccessible, unlike the later, larger constructions designed to protect the surrounding lands. The road winds up the hill to a car park from where you have a steep climb to the castle itself. On a dark and overcast day you can almost feel the inspiration for a film like Kurosawa's *Throne of Blood*. Entry to the castle is Y200 but this is no tourist castle – you'll probably have to rouse the caretaker from his hut and you may even have the place all to yourself.

The castle was originally established in 1240 and in the following centuries was enlarged until it finally covered the whole mountain top. The castle fell into disrepair after the Meiji Restoration, but the townspeople took over its maintenance from 1929 and it was finally completely restored in the 1950s.

Other Attractions

Takahashi has some picturesque old samurai streets with traditional walls and gates. The Shoren-ji Temple has fine terraced stone walls. Monkeys can be seen in Mt Gagyu Natural Zoological Park.

Places to Stay

There are ryokan and minshuku in the town and the *Takahashi-shi Cycling Terminal* (tel 0866-22-0135) is a 20 minute bus trip from the JR station at the Wonderland amusement park. Accommodation at the terminal, including meals, is less than Y5000 but it's closed on Tuesdays. You can rent bicycles from the terminal but think twice before setting out to ride up to the castle!

Getting There & Away

Although Takahashi is not on any of the regular tourist routes through Western Honshū, it would not take a great effort to

include it in an itinerary. The town is about 50 km north of Okayama or 60 km from Fukuyama. It's on the JR Hakubi line so a stop could be made when travelling between Okayama on the south coast and Yonago (near Matsue) on the north coast. For those travelling by car on the Chūgoku Expressway, a visit would entail about 30 km extra, leaving the expressway at Nimi and rejoining it at Hokubo, or vice versa.

FUKIYA 吹屋

The beautifully situated village of Fukiya, north-west of Takahashi, was once a rich copper mining centre and has many attractive buildings from the latter years of the Edo period and the first years after the Meiji Restoration. One of the prefecture's International Villas is in the village. To get to Fukiya, take a JR limited express (tokkyū) from Okayama to Bitchū-Takahashi station, from there it is about an hour by bus.

Hiroshima-ken 広島県

FUKUYAMA 福山

Fukuyama is a modern industrial town of little interest to the tourist but its convenient situation on the Osaka-Hakata shinkansen route makes it a good jumping-off point to the pretty fishing port of Tomo no Ura or to Onomichi, which in turn is a jumping-off point for Inland Sea cruises. If you do have a few hours to spend in Fukuyama, you can visit the art gallery and museum and the reconstructed castle.

Orientation & Information

Most of the places of interest as well as the hotels and restaurants are close to the station. Route 2 runs parallel to the railway line, about half a kilometre south. There is a tourist information and accommodation booking counter in the busy, modern railway station.

Fukuyama-jō Castle

Fukuyama Castle was built in 1619, torn

福山
Fukuyama

0   125   250 m

Route 2

To Auto & Clock Museum

To Kumashiki & Okayama

To Hiroshima

Fukuyama

1 ごこく神社
2 福山グランドホテル
3 ふくやま美術館
4 広島県立歴史博物館
5 福山城
6 福山キャッスルホテル
7 オリエンタルホテル
8 福山ホテル
9 福山駅
10 福山ニュー国際ホテル
11 ニューキャッスルホテル
12 福山東武ホテル
13 スモゥドベイカーレストラン
14 NTT
15 マクドナルド
16 福山郵便局

Fukuyama

1 Gokoku Shrine
2 Fukuyama Grand Hotel
3 Fukuyamam Museum of Art
4 Hiroshima Prefectural History Museum
5 Fukuyama-jō Castle
6 Fukuyama Castle Hotel
7 Oriental Hotel
8 Fukuyama Hotel
9 JR Fukuyama Station
10 Fukuyama New Kokusai Hotel
11 New Castle Hotel
12 Fukuyama Tobu Hotel
13 Studebaker Restaurant
14 NTT
15 McDonald's
16 Main Post Office

down during the 'one realm, one castle' period, and reconstructed in 1966. It overlooks the railway station which is only a couple of minutes walk away. As well as the imposing donjon of the castle itself, there are turrets, the fine Sujigane-Go-mon Gate and a bathhouse. The castle contains the usual collection of samurai armour and similar artefacts. Entry is a hefty Y500. The castle may be nothing special inside but it looks wonderful at night.

Art Gallery & History Museum

Immediately to the west of the castle hill are Fukuyama's Museum of Art (open from 9.30 am to 5 pm, entry Y300) and the Hiroshima Prefectural History Museum.

Auto & Clock Museum

The Fukuyama Auto & Clock Museum, north of the town centre, charges an exorbitant Y900 entry fee but the strange little collection makes an interesting change from the usual feudal artefacts. Anything old is a little strange in modern Japan so the 1950 Mazda motorcycle taxi looks particularly curious. The 1961 Datsun Fairlady sports car would have been no competition at all for a British sports car of that period – 30 years on how things have changed! The museum also houses waxwork figures of US Presidents Lincoln and Washington, James Dean, Elvis Presley, General MacArthur and a very dissolute looking Commodore Perry!

The information office's map identifies the museum as the 'Automobile Clock Museum', which conjures up wonderful visions of Japanese obsessiveness – 'This is the digital clock from a 1987 Toyota, and this is...'

Places to Stay

There are lots of business hotels close to the railway station. Two of the cheaper ones are the *Fukuyama Kokusai Hotel* (tel 0849-24-2411) behind the station and the *Fukuyama New Kokusai Hotel* (tel 0849-24-7000) in front. The New Kokusai only has single rooms at Y5000, including service charges and tax. At the Fukuyama Kokusai there are singles from Y5000 to Y6000 and doubles at Y8800 to Y10,000.

Immediately in front of the station is the *Fukuyama Tobu Hotel* (tel 0849-25-3181) with singles at Y6500 and doubles from Y9000 to Y11,000. Nearby is the *New Castle Hotel* (tel 0849-22-2121), at the top of the Fukuyama hotel price range with rooms from Y8200/10,200.

The *Fukuyama Castle Hotel* (tel 0849-25-2111), directly behind the station, has singles at Y6500 to Y7500; doubles from Y10,500 to Y14,000. Also behind the station is the cheaper *Oriental Hotel* (tel 0849-27-0888) with singles from Y4700 to Y5000 and doubles from Y8000 to Y9000. The *Fukuyama Grand Hotel* (tel 0849-21-5511) has singles from Y6000 to Y9000, doubles from Y12,000 up.

Places to Eat

The full complement of fast-food places can be found immediately south of the railway station. *Studebaker* is a Japanese-Italian restaurant curiously named after a US car manufacturer which went belly up in the early '60s. The menu features nine types of spaghetti, none of them bolognese or napolitana, but the food is good.

The entertainment area is a kilometre or so south-east of the station, just south of Route 2.

Getting There & Away

Fukuyama is on the main railway lines along the San-yō coast. If you are travelling between Fukuyama and Kurashiki, it's usually quicker to stick to the San-yō line all the way rather than travel from Fukuyama to Shin-Kurashiki station by shinkansen and transfer to the San-yō line there.

Buses run from the Fukuyama station area to Tomo no Ura.

TOMO NO URA　鞆の浦

The delightful fishing port of Tomo no Ura, with its numerous interesting temples and shrines, is just half an hour by bus south of Fukuyama. Although gaijin visitors are infrequent, an excellent English map and brochure is available and explanatory signs are dotted all around town. If you set aside a day to travel from Kurashiki to Hiroshima you can spend a pleasant morning exploring Tomo no Ura, get back to Fukuyama for lunch and visit Onomichi in the afternoon before continuing to Hiroshima. The Tai-ami Sea Bream Fishing Festival takes place during the entire month of May.

Four km beyond Tomo no Ura is the Abuto Kannon Temple with superb Inland Sea views.

Bicycle Tour

Bicycles (jitensha) are available at the ferry building and cost just Y100 for two hours. The map shows an interesting circuit of the main attractions. Right across the road from the ferry landing is the Muronoki Song Monument with a sad poem composed by a Korean emissary whose wife had died en route to Tomo no Ura. Climb the headland to the ruins of Taigashima Castle where you will also find the Enpuku-ji Temple and a monument to the haiku poet Basho.

Cross the headland to the harbour and continue until you reach the steps leading to the Museum of History (Y150). It's open

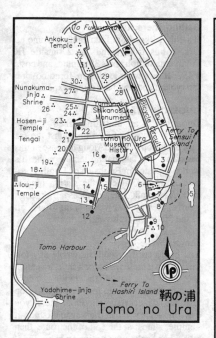

Tomo No Ura

1 Post Office
2 Bus Terminal
3 Taichōrō
4 Fukuzen-ji Temple
5 Benten Island
6 Josen-ji Temple
7 Muronoki Song Monument
8 Ferry Landing
9 Basho Haiku Monument
10 Enpuku-ji Temple
11 Taigashima Castle Ruins
12 Old Lighthouse
13 Iroha-Maru Museum
14 Shichikyō-ochi Ruins
15 Marine Equipment Shop
16 Tomo Castle Ruins
17 Ji-zōin Temple
18 Myoen-ji Temple
19 Amida-ji Temple
20 Nanzenbo-ji Temple
21 Pine Tree
22 Sasayaki Bridge
23 Jokan-ji Temple
24 Myoren-ji Temple
25 Kensyo-ji Temple
26 Komatsudera-ji Temple
27 Daikan-ji Temple
28 Kogarasu-jinja Shrine
29 Zengyo-ji Temple
30 Hongan-ji Temple
31 Ji-tokuin Temple
32 Shobo-ji Temple

Tomo No Ura

1 郵便局
2 バスタミナル
3 対潮楼
4 福禅寺
5 弁天島
6 浄泉寺
7 むろの木歌碑
8 渡船場
9 芭蕉の句碑
10 円福寺
11 大可島城跡
12 常夜灯
13 いろは丸展示館
14 鞆七郷落遺跡
15 マリン店
16 鞆城跡
17 地蔵院
18 明円寺
19 阿弥陀寺
20 南禅坊
21 天蓋の松
22 ささやき橋
23 静観寺
24 妙蓮寺
25 顕政寺
26 小松寺
27 大観寺
28 小鳥神社
29 善行寺
30 本願寺
31 慈徳院
32 正法寺

from 9 am to 4.30 pm or 5 pm. This interesting and well-presented museum features a great model of the sea bream fishing festival. Back on the road, have a look in the nautical equipment shop on the corner and then head down towards the harbour to the Shichikyō-ochi Ruins. This one-time saké shop isn't a ruin at all but played a small part in the Meiji Restoration when a fleeing anti-shogunate group paused here long enough for one member of the group to compose a waka (31 syllable poem) extolling the virtues of the shop's saké.

Continue towards the Iou-ji Temple – although it's easier to park your bike at the bottom of the steep hill and walk up. From the temple, steep steps lead to a fine view over the town from the Taishiden Hill. Back on your bike, continue to the Hosen-ji Temple, originally founded in 1358. The Tengai pine tree in the grounds spreads to cover 600 sq metres. Just beyond the temple, the Sasayaki (Whispering Bridge) commemorates an illicit romance which, according to a local tourist brochure, resulted in the lovers being 'drowned into the sea'. Beside the bridge is the Yamanaka Shikanosuke Monument, where, after a failed vendetta, the hapless Shikanosuke had had his 'head severed for inspection'.

The Nunakuma-jinja Shrine is actually dedicated to two different gods and has a Nō stage which it is claimed Hideyoshi used to take around with him so that he could enjoy performances during sieges! The Ankoku-ji Temple (entry Y100) dates from 1270 and houses two wooden statues which are national treasures. It has a slightly tatty kare-sansui (waterless stream garden) which was relaid in 1599.

From here you head back towards your starting point, pausing to take in 'eastern Japan's most scenic beauty' on the way. The title was awarded by a Korean visitor to the view from the Taichōrō in 1711. The Taichōrō Guest House, built in 1690 for visitors from Korea, is in the Fukuzen-ji Temple compound and the cheerful priest will usher you in and let you sit to admire the view of Kōgō, Benten and Sensui islands.

Getting There & Away

It's only 14 km from Fukuyama to Tomo no Ura; a bus from stand No 2 outside JR Fukuyama station takes 30 minutes and costs Y450. If you want to stay in Tomo no Ura, the ryokan and hotel are rather expensive.

ONOMICHI 尾道

Onomichi is an undistinguished looking industrial town, hemmed in against the sea by a backdrop of hills. Along the base of this backdrop is a fascinating temple walk. It's well signposted in English, and English brochures are available at the station inquiry desk. The walk itself is pleasant although there is no way you would want to visit all of the 30-odd temples and shrines.

Temple Walk

You could easily spend the whole day following the temple walk; for a shorter version take a bus from outside the station and continue for three stops to the Nagaeguchi stop near the cablecar station. From there, you can follow the walk all the way to the Jōdo-ji Temple, almost at the end of the route, then take a bus back to the station from the Jōdo-ji-shita bus stop.

The cablecar (Y270 one way) ascends to the top of Senkō-ji Hill where there is a museum and fine views over the town. As you ride the cablecar up, you can look down on the Senkō-ji Temple, then walk down to it along the Path of Literature where poets and authors have their works immortalised in stones beside the path. The temple, founded in 806, also has fine views over the town and sea. From the temple, you can continue downhill past the three storeyed Tennei-ji Temple. It was originally built with five storeys in 1388 but rebuilt with three in 1692.

The walk continues past the Fukuzen-ji Temple with its impressive gates carved with cranes and (look up) a dragon. The Saikoku-ji Temple is entered through the Nio-mon Gate, which is hung with gigantic two metre long straw sandals. From there, a steep flight of steps leads up to the temple, overlooked by a red three storeyed pagoda.

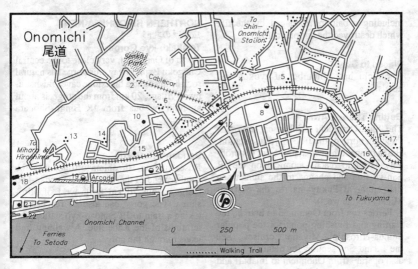

Onomichi

1 Saikoku-ji Temple
2 Senkō-ji Hill Lookout & Museum
3 Jikan-ji Temple
4 Fukuzen-ji Temple
5 Jyōsen-ji Temple
6 Senkō-ji Temple
7 Cablecar Station
8 Rakutenjiguchi Bus Stop
9 Bōjiguchi Bus Stop
10 Memorial Hall of Literature
11 Tennei-ji Temple
12 Nagaeguchi Bus Stop
13 Jikō-ji Temple
14 Kōmyō-ji Temple
15 Kibitsuhiko-jinja Shrine
16 Jōdoji-shita Bus Stop
17 Jōdo-ji Temple
18 JR Onomichi Station
19 Tsuchidōshita Bus Stop
20 Watashibadōri Bus Stop
21 Bus Terminal
22 Onomichi Pier

Onomichi

1 西国寺
2 千光寺博物館
3 慈観寺
4 福善寺
5 浄泉寺
6 千光寺
7 ロープウェイ乗場
8 楽天地口バス停
9 防地口バス停
10 文学記念堂
11 天寧寺
12 長江口バス停
13 持光寺
14 光明寺
15 吉備津彦神社
16 浄土寺下バス停
17 浄土寺
18 JR尾道駅
19 土堂下バス停
20 渡場通リバス停
21 バス乗場
22 尾道桟橋

The Jōdo-ji Temple has an unusual two storeyed temple in its compound and a fine garden (entry Y300) and teahouse moved here from Fushimi Castle. The temple houses a number of important art works including a painting damaged by the fire which destroyed the temple in 1325.

Places to Stay

Onomichi has a number of ryokan and hotels.

Getting There & Away

The Shin-Onomichi shinkansen station is three km north of the JR San-yō line station. Buses connect the two stations but it's probably easier to reach Onomichi on the JR San-yō line and change to the shinkansen line either at Fukuyama (to the east) or Mihara (to the west).

Ferries run from Onomichi to Setoda, the starting and finishing point for the popular Setoda-Hiroshima-Miyajima cruises. (See the Inland Sea section for details.) Ferries also operate from Onomichi to Imabari and Matsuyama, both on Shikoku.

ONOMICHI TO HIROSHIMA
尾道至広島
Mihara

Mihara is on the San-yō shinkansen line and is a convenient departure or arrival point for Setoda on Ikuchi-jima, other islands of the Inland Sea and for Shikoku, but otherwise is of no particular interest.

Takehara

Takehara is on the coastal JR San-yō line or can be reached by boat from Omi-shima Island. It was an important centre for salt production in the Edo period and still retains some interesting old houses.

Kure

The giant battleship *Yamato*, sunk off Nagasaki on a suicide mission to Okinawa during WW II, was just one of the many naval vessels built in Kure. The town, virtually a suburb of Hiroshima, is still an important shipbuilding centre and there is a naval museum on nearby Eta-jima Island – although it takes a long time to get there. The Nikyu Gorge is 15 km north-east of Kure.

NORTHERN HIROSHIMA-KEN
広島県の北部
Taishaku-kyō Gorge

North of Onomichi, very close to the central Chūgoku Expressway, this gorge has natural rock bridges and a limestone cave. Taishaku-mura Village, 20 km from the gorge, is about an hour by bus from JR Bingo-Shobara station.

Sandan-kyō Gorge

Buses run from Hiroshima to Togouchi at the southern end of the 16 km long Sandan-kyō Gorge, about 70 km north-west of Hiroshima. The gorge can also be reached by taking a train to JR Sandan-kyō station, the terminus of the Kabe line. A walking trail leads through the gorge.

HIROSHIMA 広島

Although it's a busy, prosperous, not unattractive industrial city, visitors would have no real reason to leave the shinkansen in Hiroshima (population 1,070,000) were it not for that terrible instant on 6 August 1945 when the city became the world's first atomic bomb target. Hiroshima's Peace Memorial Park is a constant reminder of that tragic day and attracts a steady stream of visitors from all over the world.

The city's history dates back to 1589 when the feudal lord Terumoto Mohri named the city and established his castle.

Orientation & Information

Hiroshima (*hiro* 'broad' *shima* 'island') is a city built on a series of sandy islands on the delta of the Otagawa River. JR Hiroshima station is east of the city centre and, although there are a number of hotels around the station, the central area, with its very lively entertainment district, is much more interesting. Peace Memorial Park and most of the atomic bomb reminders are at the northern end of an island immediately west of the city centre.

Hiroshima's main east-west avenue is

Heiwa-dōri Blvd (Peace Blvd), but the busiest road with the main tram lines from the station is Aioi-dōri Ave, which runs parallel to Heiwa-dōri. Just south of Aioi-dōri, and again parallel to it, is the busy Hon-dōri shopping arcade.

There is an information office in JR Hiroshima station where the staff will make accommodation bookings. For the benefit of those arriving by sea, Ujina, Hiroshima's port, also has an information counter. More comprehensive information can be obtained from the helpful tourist office in the Peace Memorial Park. Hiroshima is a major industrial centre with a Mitsubishi heavy industries plant and the main Mazda (Matsuda in Japanese) car plant. Inquire at the tourist office about factory visits.

The big department stores are Mitsukoshi (closed on Mondays), Tenmaya (closed Tuesdays), Fukuya (closed Wednesdays) and Sogo (closed Thursdays).

Books English-language books can be found in the Kinokuniya bookshop on the 6th floor (through the men's department) of the Sogo department store or in the Maruzen bookshop, nearby in the shopping arcade and opposite Andersen's Restaurant.

John Hersey's *Hiroshima* is still the classic reporter's account of the bomb and its aftermath. It was written in 1946 and in 1985 a new edition, available in paperback, followed up the original protagonists. Eleanor Coerr's children's book *Sadako & the Thousand Paper Cranes* tells the sad but inspiring story of a 12 year old girl's death from leukaemia, contracted due to exposure to the bomb's radiation.

The Hiroshima Bomb

Prior to the atomic bomb explosion, Hiroshima had not been bombed at all. This was a highly unusual situation, given that so many Japanese cities had been virtually flattened by repeated raids, and it is speculated that this was a deliberate policy in order to measure exactly how much damage the atomic bomb had done.

Dropped from the USAF B-29 *Enola Gay*, the bomb exploded at 8.15 am and approximately 75,000 people were killed almost immediately by the blast and subsequent fires. In comparison, all the bombing in WW II killed about 30,000 people in London and about another 30,000 in the rest of Britain. The Hiroshima death toll has probably reached 200,000 by now as people continue to die from the radiation aftereffects. Even today certain types of cancers still occur among Hiroshima's population in greater numbers than other comparable cities.

The first atomic explosion, the testing of a plutonium bomb, had taken place less than three weeks previously in the USA. The Hiroshima bomb used uranium while the bomb dropped on Nagasaki three days later on 9 August was plutonium. On 2 September the Japanese surrendered. Ever since these events, there has been speculation as to whether it was necessary to drop the bomb, whether a demonstration of its capabilities could have prompted the Japanese surrender and whether a warning should have been given. Whether the Japanese would have resorted to using atomic weapons if they had invented them first has raised less speculation.

What is certain is that two bombs equivalent to a total of 38 kilotons of TNT brought Japan to its knees, despite a history of spectacular suicides which had shown that death was very often preferable to surrender. Also, the horrendous carnage at Okinawa had clearly shown that an invasion of the Japanese mainland was not going to be an easy task.

Today, nuclear weapons can have an explosive power equivalent to 50 megatons of TNT, over 1000 times greater than the Hiroshima and Nagasaki bombs combined. Given the devastating effects achieved by two relatively small nuclear bombs, why on earth do we need thousands of enormous ones just a button's push away?

Tony Wheeler ■

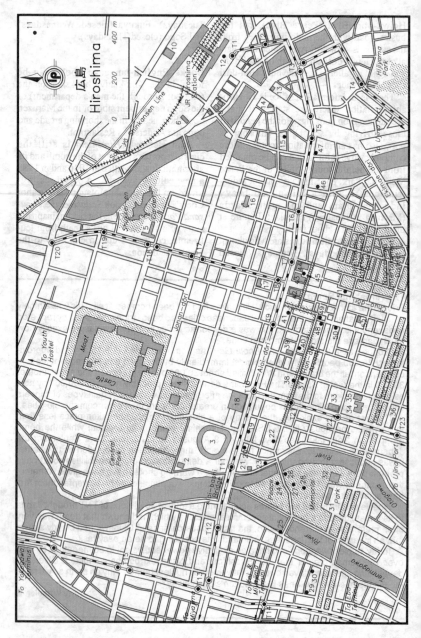

広島
Hiroshima

Hiroshima

1	Hiroshima-jō Castle	40	Denen Italian Restaurant
2	Science & Culture Museum for Children	41	Suishin Restaurant
3	Hiroshima Carp's Baseball Stadium	42	Fukuya Department Store
4	Hiroshima Museum of Art	43	Tenmaya Department Store
5	Prefectural Art Museum	44	Mitsukoshi Department Store
6	Hotel New Hiroden	45	Tokugawa Okonomayaki Restaurant
7	Hiroshima Ekimae Green Hotel	46	Hiroshima Central Hotel
8	Hotel Sun Palace	47	Hotel Union Hiroshima
9	Hotel Yamato	48	Hiroshima T&K Italian Restaurant
10	Hiroshima Terminal Hotel	49	Hobson's Ice Cream
11	Pagoda of Peace	50	Moti Indian Restaurant
12	Hiroshima Station Hotel	51	Tokugawa Okonomayaki Restaurant
13	Hiroshima Century City Hotel	52	Sera Bekkan Ryokan
14	Hiroshima City Hotel		
15	Mikawa Ryokan		**TRAM STOPS**
16	World Peace Memorial Cathedral		
17	Hotel Silk Plaza	T1	Hiroshima ekimae
18	Sogo Department Store (Sogo Bus Centre, Kinokuniya Bookshop)	T2	Enkobashi
		T3	Matoba-cho
19	KDD (International Telephone)	T4	Danbara Ohata-cho
20	ANA	T5	Inarimachi
21	A-Bomb Dome	T6	Kanayama-cho
22	Hiroshima Green Hotel	T7	Ebisu-cho
23	Atomic Bomb Epicentre	T8	Hatchobori
24	Children's Peace Memorial	T9	Tatemachi
25	Korean A-Bomb Memorial	T10	Kamiya-cho
26	Tourist Information Office	T11	Genbaku Domu-mae (A-Bomb Dome)
27	Peace Flame	T12	Honkawa-cho
28	Cenotaph	T13	Tokaichimachi
29	Laundromat	T14	Dobashi
30	Minshuku Ikedaya	T15	Teramachi
31	Peace Memorial Museum	T16	Betsuin-mae
32	Peace Memorial Hall	T17	Jogakuin-mae
33	Former Bank of Japan Building	T18	Shukkeien-mae
34	ANA Hiroshima Hotel	T19	Katei Saibansho-mae
35	Hokke Club Hotel	T20	Hakushima Line Terminus
36	Hiroshima Tōkyū Inn	T21	Hon-dōri
37	Andersen's Bakery & Restaurant	T22	Fukuromachi
38	Maruzen Bookshop	T23	Chuden-mae
39	Hiroshima Kokusai Hotel		

The A-Bomb Dome

Hiroshima's modern symbol is the A-Bomb Dome (Genbaku Dōmu) just across the river from Peace Memorial Park. The building was the Industrial Promotion Hall until the bomb exploded almost directly above it. Its propped up ruins have been left as an eternal reminder of the tragedy, floodlit at night and fronted with piles of the colourful origami cranes which have become a symbol of Hiroshima's plea that nuclear weapons should never again be used. The actual epicentre of the explosion was just south of the A-Bomb Dome, and is marked by a small park.

The easiest way to get to the dome is to take a No 2, No 6 or Miyajima tram from the station and get off at the Genbaku Dōmu-mae stop, right beside the dome. I think it's better to get off the tram a few stops earlier and approach it by the shopping arcade parallel to Aioi-dōri Ave. Walking down the busy arcade you pass bookshops, boutiques and a McDonald's restaurant: all the comfortable symbols of modern, prosperous Japan. Just before the river there's the Hiroshima

Hiroshima

1	広島城	40	テネンイタリャン料理
2	こどこ文化科学館	41	酔心レストラン
3	広島市民球場	42	福屋百貨店
4	広島市美術館	43	天満屋百貨店
5	広島県立美術館	44	三越
6	ホテルニューヒロデン	45	徳川おこのみやきレストラン
7	広島駅前グリーンホテル	46	広島セントラルホテル
8	ホテルサンパラス	47	ホテルユニオン広島
9	ホテルやまと	48	広島TK イタリレストラン
10	広島ターミナルホテル	49	ホブソン
11	平和塔	50	モテイ
12	広島ステイションホテル	51	徳川おこのみやきレストラン
13	広島センチュリーシティホテル	52	セラ別館旅館
14	広島シティホテル		
15	三河旅館		
16	世界平和記念聖堂		**TRAM STOPS**
17	ホテルシルクプルザ		
18	そごう百貨店	T1	広島駅前
19	KDD（国際電話）	T2	猿猴橋
20	ANA	T3	的場町
21	原爆ドーム	T4	段原大畑町
22	広島グリーンホテル	T5	稲荷町
23	広島市道路元標	T6	銀山町
24	原爆の子の像	T7	胡町
25	韓国人原爆犠牲者慰霊碑	T8	八丁堀
26	観光案内所	T9	立町
27	平和灯	T10	紙屋町
28	原爆慰霊碑	T11	原爆ドーム前
29	洗衣店	T12	本川町
30	民宿池田屋	T13	十日市町
31	平和記念資料館	T14	土橋
32	平和記念館	T15	寺町
33	以前の日本銀行ビル	T16	別院前
34	広島全日空ホテル	T17	女学院前
35	法華クラブ	T18	縮景園前
36	広島東急イン	T19	家庭裁判所前
37	アンデルセン	T20	白島
38	丸善本店	T21	本通
39	広島国際ホテル	T22	袋町
		T23	中電前

Green Hotel then the arcade ends and you cross the road into a small park and *bang*, there you are, on the spot where the world ended for the people of Hiroshima.

Tony Wheeler

The A-Bomb Dome is the only blast survivor left in ruins, but some damaged buildings were repaired and still stand. On Rijo Ave, just 380 metres south-east of the epicentre, the former Bank of Japan building looks rock solid; however, although the shell survived intact, the interior was totally destroyed and all 42 people in the bank at the time were killed. Nevertheless, it was back in limited business two days later.

Peace Memorial Park

From the A-Bomb Dome you cross the T-shaped Aioi-bashi Bridge to the Peace Memorial Park (Heiwa-kōen). It is thought that the T-shape may have been the actual aiming point used by the bombardier. If so, his aim was acute. The park is dotted with memorials including the cenotaph which contains the names of all the known victims of the bomb and frames the A-Bomb Dome across the river. The eternal flame burning beneath the arched cenotaph is not designed to be eternal – when the last nuclear weapon on earth has been destroyed it will be turned off.

Nearby is what for many is the most poignant memorial in the park – the Children's Peace Memorial inspired by leukemia victim Sadako. When she developed leukemia at 10 years of age she decided to fold 1000 paper cranes, the symbol of longevity and happiness in Japan, convinced that if she could achieve that target she would recover. She died having completed her 644th crane but children from her school folded another 356 with which she was buried. Her story inspired a nationwide bout of paper crane folding which continues to this day. Around the memorial are heaped not thousands but millions of cranes, regularly delivered by the boxload from schools all over Japan.

Just across the river from the park is a memorial to the bomb's Korean victims.

Great numbers of Koreans were shipped from their homeland to work as slave labourers in Japanese factories during WW II, and more than one in 10 of those killed by the bomb was a Korean. The Korean memorial, erected long after the war (in 1970), carries a bitter reminder that no prayers were said for the Korean victims, and that despite the plethora of A-bomb monuments, not one had been erected in their memory.

A-Bomb Museum

Like its equivalent in Nagasaki, the bomb museum will win no awards for architectural inspiration but its simple message is driven home with sledgehammer force. The exhibits tell the story of the bomb and the destruction it wrought on Hiroshima and its people. A model showing the town after the blast highlights the extent of the damage – seeing this, you might ponder what an insignificant little squib this bomb was, compared to the destructive potential of modern atomic weapons. The museum is open from 9 am to 6 pm (May to November), or 5 pm (December to April). Entry is Y50.

Hiroshima-jō Castle

Also known as 'Carp Castle', Hiroshima-jō was originally constructed in 1589 but much of it was dismantled following the Meiji Restoration, leaving only the donjon, main gates and turrets. The remainder was totally destroyed by the bomb and rebuilt in modern ferro-concrete in 1958. There are some interesting displays including an informative and amusing video with some three dimensional laser embellishments about the construction of the castle. It's open from 9 am to 4.30 pm (October to March) and closes an hour earlier between April and September; entry costs Y300.

Shukkei-en Garden

Modelled after a lake garden in Hangzhou, China, the Shukkei-en Garden dates from 1620 but was badly damaged by the bomb. The garden's name literally means 'shrunk' or 'miniature scenery' and, although not one of the classic gardens, it makes a pleasant stroll if you have time to spare. Entry is Y200 and it's open from 9 am to 5 or 6 pm.

Other Attractions

Hiroshima Museum of Art (Y500, closed Mondays) and the Science & Culture Museum for Children (free except for the planetarium) are both in Central Park just west of the castle. Hijiyama Park, directly south of JR Hiroshima station, is noted for its cherry blossoms in spring. The Hiroshima City Museum of Contemporary Art (Y300) is also in the park. To get to Hijiyama Park, take a No 5 tram from the station towards Ujina (Hiroshima's port) and get off at the Hijiyama-bashi stop.

Fudō-in Temple, directly north of the station and about half a kilometre beyond the youth hostel, is one of the few old structures in Hiroshima which survived the bomb blast. Mitaki-ji Temple is north-west of the town centre.

Festivals

On 6 August paper lanterns are floated down the Otagawa River towards the sea in memory of the bomb blast.

Places to Stay

Youth Hostels Hiroshima Youth Hostel (tel 082-221-5343) is about two km north of the town centre; take a bus from platform 22 in front of the JR station or from platform 29 behind it. The hostel is very clearly marked; the nightly cost for members is Y2090.

Budget Accommodation There are two Japanese Inn Group places in Hiroshima. The Mikawa Ryokan (tel 082-261-2719) is a short stroll from the JR Hiroshima station and has singles/doubles at Y3300/6000, room only. Although the ryokan is convenient for train travellers, and staff are friendly, the rooms are very cramped and gloomy.

In contrast, the Minshuku Ikedaya (tel 082-231-3329) is modern, bright and cheerful. Singles/doubles are Y4000/7000, room only. The helpful manager speaks excellent English and if your dirty washing is piling

up, there's a laundromat on the corner of the road. The Ikedaya is on the other side of Peace Memorial Park in a quiet area but an easy walk via the park from the town centre. To get there, take tram No 6 or a Miyajima tram from the station and get off at the Dobashi stop.

There are a number of other budget places in the vicinity plus a compact enclave of colourful love hotels including one rejoicing in the name 'Hotel Adult'.

Hotels – Station Area The Hiroshima Station Hotel (tel 082-262-3201) is right in the station building and costs from Y6100/10,000 for singles/doubles. Hotel Yamato (tel 082-263-6222) is slightly cheaper at Y5700/10,700 and is close to the station, overlooking the river. Next to it is the Hotel Sun Palace (tel 082-264-6111) which is cheaper at Y4800/8000. Also near the station is the Hiroshima Ekimae Green Hotel (tel 082-264-3939) with rooms at Y5000/8500.

The expensive Hiroshima Terminal Hotel (tel 082-262-1111), directly behind the station, has singles/doubles from Y9500/15,000. Other typical business hotels around the station area include the Hotel New Hiroden (tel 082-263-3456), the River Side Hotel (tel 082-227-1111), the Hiroshima Central Hotel (tel 082-243-2222), the Hiroshima Union Hotel (tel 082-263-7878) and the Hiroshima City Hotel (tel 082-263-5111).

Hotels – Central Hiroshima The Hiroshima Kokusai Hotel (tel 082-248-2323) is right in the city centre and has rooms from Y6900/11,500 for singles/doubles. The Hiroshima Green Hotel (tel 082-248-3939) is on the edge of the city centre and close to the riverside and Peace Memorial Park. Costs are from Y5500/9500.

The Hokke Club Hotel (tel 082-248-3371) has rooms which are small, even by cramped business hotel standards but the 12 noon check-in/checkout is a good deal compared to the usual late check-in and early checkout of Japanese hotels. Singles/doubles cost from Y5900/9900.

Directly behind the Hokke Club, on Heiwa-dōri, is the expensive *ANA Hotel Hiroshima* (tel 082-241-1111) with singles from Y9000, twins and doubles from Y15,000. It's probably the city's best hotel and during the summer there's a rooftop beer garden. Across the avenue from the ANA Hotel the *Hiroshima Tōkyū Inn* (tel 082-244-0109) is part of the popular chain and has rooms from Y6100/10,000.

Hiroshima does have traditional Japanese ryokan but they're in modern, anonymous buildings. The *Sera Bekkan* (tel 082-248-2251) is central and costs from Y12,000 per person including two meals. All rooms have bathrooms.

Places to Eat

Hiroshima is noted for its seafood, particularly oysters. The familiar assortment of fast-food outlets including *Shakey's Pizza*, *McDonald's* and *Mister Donut* can be found in the Hon-dōri shopping arcade. *Andersen's* on Hon-dōri is a popular restaurant complex with an excellent bakery section – a good place for an economical breakfast watching the world pass by from the tables in the front window. There are a variety of other restaurant sections in the Andersen's complex.

The *Moti Indian Restaurant*, only a couple of blocks south of Hon-dōri, is associated with the Motis in Akasaka and Roppongi in Tokyo. Dishes include an excellent-value lunch-time teishoku for Y800 plus a wide variety of curry dishes, typicallly around Y1100, or tandoori dishes and vegetarian thalis. The menu is in English.

On the same street, but back towards the arcade, is the *Hiroshima T&K Italian Restaurant* which also offers an economical fixed-price lunch. Although the menu is in Japanese only, there are some illustrations and a couple of plastic models of the food downstairs. *Hobson's*, across the road, has terrific ice cream.

Just north of the Hon-dōri arcade, near the Kokusai Hotel, more Italian food can be found in *Denen* where there's a downstairs

'lounge' and upstairs 'trattoria' with pizza, good pasta at Y800 and you can even get a glass of wine for Y300. A couple of blocks east, *Yo-rono Taki* is a reasonable robatayaki and across the road is *Rally's* steakhouse. Nearby is *Suishin*, a traditional restaurant with many local specialities.

There are two *Tokugawa* okonomiyaki restaurants in the centre – one behind the Mitsukoshi department store and the other on the edge of the Shintenchi entertainment district. Okonomiyaki is a sort of cook-it-yourself omelette. Each table has a hotplate in the centre, you're provided with whatever ingredients you select and cook your omelette yourself! The plastic meal displays show you what ingredients you get.

The entertainment districts of Nagarekawa and Shintenchi have more than 4000 restaurants, bars and nightclubs.

Getting There & Away

There are connections between Hiroshima and Tokyo, Sapporo, Kagoshima and Okinawa.

Hiroshima has long been an important railway junction, one of the factors which led to it being the prime atomic bomb target in WW II. Today it is an important stop on the Tokyo-Osaka-Hakata shinkansen route, with some services originating or terminating in Hiroshima. By shinkansen, it takes about five hours to reach Hiroshima from Tokyo, 1½ to two hours from Kyoto and slightly less from Hakata.

Hiroshima is also an important port with a variety of Inland Sea cruises as well as connections to other cities. The Hiroshima to Matsuyama ferry and hydrofoil services are a popular way of getting to or from Shikoku. (See the Matsuyama section in the Shikoku chapter for details.) Ferries also operate to Beppu on Kyūshū and to Imabari on Shikoku.

As well as the buses at the JR station, there's a bus centre on the 3rd floor of the Sogo department store.

Getting Around

Hiroshima has an easy-to-use tram (streetcar) service which will get you pretty well anywhere you want to go for a flat Y130 (Y90 on the short No 9 route). There is even a tram which runs all the way to the Miyajima Port – this trip is more expensive. The diagram shows the tram routes. Note that the colours have no connection with the routes, it's popularly rumoured that Hiroshima ended up with their rainbow variety of trams by buying up other cities' old trams as they closed down their tram services. If you have to change trams to get to your destination you should ask for a transfer ticket *(norikaeken)* as you leave the tram and pay an additional Y50.

Buses are more difficult to use as they are not numbered and the names are in kanji, but the stands outside the station are clearly numbered. Take a bus from stand No 1 to the airport, No 2 to the port.

MIYA-JIMA ISLAND 宮島

Correctly known as Itsuku-shima, Miyajima Island is easily reached from Hiroshima. The famous 'floating' torii of the Itsukushima-jinja Shrine is one of the most photographed tourist attractions in Japan, and with the island's Mt Misen as a backdrop is classified as one of Japan's 'three best views'. The other two are the sandspit at Amanohashidate (northern coast of Western Honshū) and the islands of Matsushima-wan Bay (near Sendai, Northern Honshū). Apart from the shrine, the island has some other interesting temples, some good walks and remarkably tame deer which even wander the streets of the small town.

Orientation & Information

There's an information counter in the ferry building. Turn right as you emerge from the building and follow the waterfront to get to the shrine and the centre of the island's small town. The shopping street, packed with souvenir outlets, is a block back from the waterfront.

Itsukushima-jinja Shrine

The shrine, which gives the island its real name, dates from the 6th century and in its

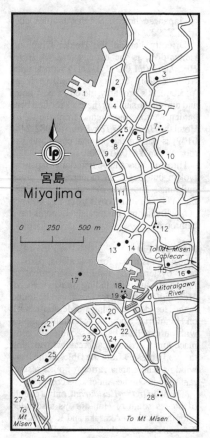

present form from 1168. Its pier-like construction is a result of the island's holy status. Commoners were not allowed to set foot on the island and had to approach the shrine by boat, entering through the floating torii out in the bay. Much of the time, however, the shrine and torii are surrounded not by water but by mud. The view of the torii immortalised in thousands of travel brochures requires a high tide!

The shrine is open from 6 am to sunset and entry is Y200. On one side of the floating shrine is a floating Nō stage built by a Mōri lord. The orange torii, dating from 1875 in

	Miyajima
1	Miyajima Pier
2	Hall of Industrial Traditions (Handicraft Display)
3	Temple
4	Miyajima Royal Hotel
5	Zonko-ji Temple
6	Pension Miyajima
7	Temple
8	Castle Ruins
9	Kamefuku Hotel
10	Temple
11	Kinsuikan Hotel
12	Temple
13	Senjō-kaku Pavilion
14	Five Storeyed Pagoda
15	Miyajima Grand Hotel
16	Iwasō Ryokan
17	Floating Torii
18	Itsukushima-jinja Shrine
19	Nō Stage
20	Daigan-ji Temple
21	Kiyomori Shrine
22	Treasure House
23	Miyajima History & Folklore Museum
24	Taho-tō Pagoda
25	Aquarium
26	Kokuminshukusha Miyajima Lodge
27	Omoto Shrine
28	Daisho-in Temple

	Miyajima
1	宮島港
2	伝統産業会館
3	寺
4	宮島ロイヤルホテル
5	存光寺
6	ペンション宮島
7	寺
8	城跡
9	ホテルかめ福
10	寺
11	きんすいかんホテル
12	寺
13	千畳閣
14	千畳閣五重塔
15	宮島グランドホテル
16	岩惣旅館
17	大鳥居
18	厳島神社
19	能台
20	大願寺
21	清盛神社
22	宝物館
23	歴史民俗資料館
24	多宝塔
25	水族館
26	国民宿舎宮島ロッジ
27	大元神社
28	大聖院

its present form, is often floodlit at night. A 'son et lumière' is sometimes performed from 8.30 to 9 pm, particularly in summer. You can hear it on headphones in English as well as Japanese for Y300.

The treasure house, west of the shrine, is open from 8 am to 5 pm and entry is Y250. The collection of painted sutra scrolls dating from the 12th century are not usually on display and the exhibits are not of great interest except, perhaps, to the scholarly.

Temples & Other Buildings
Topping the hill immediately east of the Itsukushima Shrine is the Senjō-kaku (Pavilion of 1000 Mats) built in 1587 by Hideyoshi. This huge and atmospheric hall (entry Y50) is constructed with equally massive timber pillars and beams and the ceiling is hung with paintings. It looks out on a colourful five storeyed pagoda dating from 1407. The Senjō-kaku should have been painted to match but was left unfinished when Hideyoshi died.

Miyajima has numerous other temples including the Daigan-ji just west of the shrine, which is dedicated to the god of music and dates from 1201. The colourful and glossy Daisho-in Temple is just behind the town and can be visited on the way down Mt Misen. This is a temple with everything – statues, gates, pools, carp, you name it. The rituals performed at the main Itsukushima Shrine are also administered by the Daigan-ji. West of Itsukushima Shrine is the picturesque Taho-tō Pagoda.

Miyajima History & Folklore Museum

This interesting museum combines a 19th century merchant's home with exhibits concerning trade in the Edo period, a variety of displays connected with the island and a fine garden. The museum is open from 8.30 am to 5 pm and there's an excellent and informative brochure in English. Entry is Y250.

Mt Misen & Other Walks

The ascent of 530 metre Mt Misen is the island's finest walk; the uphill part of the round trip can be avoided by taking the two stage cablecar for Y800 one way, Y1400 return. It leaves you about a 15 minute walk from the top. Around the cablecar station there are monkeys as well as deer. On the way to the top look for the giant pot said to have been used by Kōbō Daishi (774-835) and kept simmering ever since! It's in the smaller building beside the main temple hall, also said to have been used by the founder of the Shingon sect.

There are superb views from the summit and a variety of routes leading back down. The descent takes a good hour and walking paths also lead to other high points on the island, or you can just follow the gentle stroll through Momiji-dani (Maple Valley) which leads to the cablecar station.

Other Attractions

There's an aquarium, a popular beach, a seaside park and, across from the ferry landing, a display of local crafts in the Hall of Industrial Traditions.

Festivals

Island festivals include fire-walking rites by the island's monks on 15 April and 15 November, a fireworks display on 14 August and the Kangensai Boat Festival on 16 June.

Places to Stay & Eat

There is no cheap accommodation on Miyajima Island although the *Miyajima-guchi Youth Hostel* (tel 0829-56-1444) is near the ferry terminal and JR Miyajima-guchi station on the mainland.

If you can afford to stay on the island, it's well worthwhile: you'll be able to enjoy the island in the evening, minus the day-trip hordes. The *Kokuminshukusha Miyajima Lodge* (tel 0829-44-0430) is west of the shrine and has rooms with bathroom for Y5500 per person including meals. At the large and pleasant *Iwasō Ryokan* (tel 0829-44-2233) or at the *Miyajima Grand Hotel* (tel 0829-44-2411) you can count on at least Y16,000 to Y20,000 per person with meals. There are a number of fairly expensive hotels and ryokan along the waterfront including the *Kamefuku Hotel* (tel 0829-44-2111), the *Kinsuikan Hotel* (tel 0829-44-2133) and the *Miyajima Royal Hotel* (tel 0829-44-2191).

A more moderately priced alternative is the friendly and very pleasant *Pension Miyajima* (tel 0829-44-0039) which is just back from the ferry landing. Rooms with bathroom cost Y5500 per person and there's superb food at Y3000 for dinner, Y1000 for breakfast. Although there are many restaurants and cafés on Miya-jima Island most of them cater to the day-trippers and close early in the evening.

Getting There & Away

The mainland ferry terminal for Miyajima is near the Miyajima-guchi station on the JR San-yō line between Hiroshima and Iwakuni. Miyajima trams from Hiroshima terminate at the Hiroden-Miyajima stop by the ferry terminal. The tram (50 minutes, Y250) takes longer than the train (25 minutes) but runs more frequently and can be boarded in central Hiroshima. On some trams you may have to transfer at the Hiroden-Hiroshima stop.

From the terminal, ferries shuttle across to Miyajima in just 10 minutes for Y170. One of the ferries is operated by JR so Japan Rail Pass holders should make sure they use this one. Ferry services also operate to Miyajima direct from Hiroshima. High speed ferries (Y1120) take just over 20 minutes from Hiroshima's Ujina Port. The SKK (Seto Naikaikisen) Inland Sea cruise on the

Akinada starts and finishes at Miyajima; the Miyajima to Hiroshima leg costs Y1480.

Getting Around

Bicycles can be rented from the ferry building or you can walk. A free bus operates from in front of the Iwasō Ryokan to the Mt Misen cablecar station.

Southern Yamaguchi-ken
山口県の南部

IWAKUNI 岩国

The five arched Kintai-kyō Bridge is Iwakuni's major attraction although the town also has a US military base and a number of points of interest in the Kikko-kōen Park.

Orientation & Information

Iwakuni has three widely separated areas, which can, at first, be somewhat confusing for visitors. To the far west of the town centre is the Shin-Iwakuni shinkansen railway station, totally separate from the rest of town. In the central area is the old part of town with the bridge, the samurai quarter, the castle and all the other tourist attractions. To the east, in the modern part of town, is the JR Iwakuni station, as well as hotels, restaurants, bars and other conveniences. Tune your radio to 1575 AM for the US military radio station.

Kintai-kyō Bridge

Also known as the 'Brocade Sash Bridge', the Kintai-kyō Bridge was built in 1673 and washed away by a flood in 1950. It was authentically rebuilt in 1953, albeit with some cunningly concealed steel reinforcements. The bridge is immediately recognisable by the five extremely steep arches. In the feudal era only samurai could use the bridge, which connected their side of the river with the rest of the town; commoners had to cross the river by boat. Today visitors have to pay a Y210 toll to walk across and back.

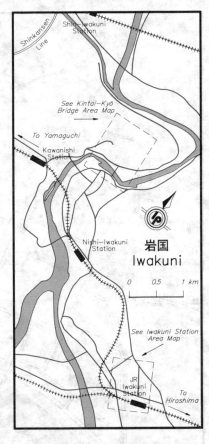

Samurai Quarter & Nishimura Museum

Some traces remain of the old samurai quarter by the bridge. The area is overlooked by Iwakuni-jō Castle and, beside the castle cablecar, is the Nishimura Museum with its extensive collection of samurai armour and equipment. It's said to be one of the best collections in Japan, but since only a small part of it is displayed at one time (and very little is labelled in English) it is unlikely to impress those already suffering from feudal-artefact overload. Entry is an expensive Y500 and it's open from 8 am to 6 pm.

The old samurai quarter is now part of

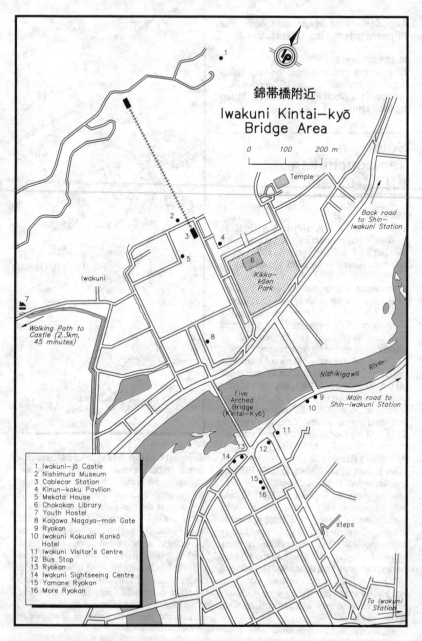

錦帯橋附近

Iwakuni Kintai-kyō Bridge Area

0   100   200 m

Temple

Back road to Shin-Iwakuni Station

Iwakuni

6 Kikko-kōen Park

7

Walking Path to Castle (2.3km, 45 minutes)

8

Nishikigawa River

Five Arched Bridge (Kintai-Kyō)

Main road to Shin-Iwakuni Station

9

10

11

13

12

14

steps

15

16

To Iwakuni Station

1 Iwakuni-jō Castle
2 Nishimura Museum
3 Cablecar Station
4 Kinun-kaku Pavilion
5 Mekata House
6 Chokokan Library
7 Youth Hostel
8 Kagawa Nagaya-mon Gate
9 Ryokan
10 Iwakuni Kokusai Kankō Hotel
11 Iwakuni Visitor's Centre
12 Bus Stop
13 Ryokan
14 Iwakuni Sightseeing Centre
15 Yamane Ryokan
16 More Ryokan

Iwakuni Kintai-kyō Bridge Area

1 岩国城
2 にしむら博物館
3 山麓駅
4 きんうん亭
5 目加田家屋敷
6 ちょこかん図書館
7 ユスホステル
8 香川家長屋門
9 旅館
10 岩国国際観光ホテル
11 岩国観光センタ
12 バスの停
13 旅館
14 観光センタ
15 山根旅館
16 旅館

Kikko-kōen Park and includes some picturesque moats and remnants of the feudal buildings such as the Kagawa Nagaya-mon Gate, a fine old samurai gateway. Beside the moat, close to the cablecar station, is the Kinun-kaku Pavilion. Look for the swan houses in the moat. Also beside the cablecar car park is the Mekata House, a fine old samurai home. The Chokokan Library houses documents from the samurai period.

Iwakuni-jō Castle

The original castle was built between 1603 and 1608 but stood for only seven years before the daimyō was forced to dismantle it and move down to the riverside. It was rebuilt in 1960 during Japan's great castle reconstruction movement; but modern Japanese castles were built for tourism, not warfare, so it now stands photogenically on the edge of the hillside, a short distance in front of its former hidden location. The well beside the path indicates where it was originally built.

You can get to the castle by cablecar or by the road (walking only) from beside the youth hostel. The cablecar costs Y300 one

way or you can get a round-trip ticket with entry to the castle for Y820.

Festivals

Traditional cormorant fishing (ukai) takes place at the Kintai-kyō Bridge every night from June to August except when rain makes the water muddy or on full-moon nights. Sightseeing boats operate on the Nishikigawa River during the fishing.

Places to Stay

Youth Hostels The *Iwakuni Youth Hostel* (tel 0827-43-1092) is close to most of the attractions on the samurai side of the bridge. There are 106 beds and costs per night are Y1700 or Y1900, depending on the season.

Ryokan Iwakuni's ryokan are clustered on the city side of the Kintai-kyō Bridge and typically cost from around Y7000 including breakfast and dinner.

Hotels The *Ogiya Station Hotel* at Shin-Iwakuni shinkansen station has rooms at Y5000/10,000 but is a long way from anywhere. Around JR Iwakuni station, there's a choice of business hotels. The *Iwakuni Kinsui Hotel* is right beside the station. *City Hotel Andoh* (tel 0827-22-0110) is only a couple of minutes walk from the station and has singles/doubles from Y5000/8000. The *A-1 Hotel* (tel 0827-21-2244) is not much further away and has clean, tidy, well-equipped rooms from Y4300/7000 for singles/doubles.

Places to Eat

There are some small restaurants and cafés around the bridge and a wide variety of restaurants, bars and fast-food outlets around the station area including *Mos Burger*, *Lotteria* and the inevitable *Mister Donut*.

Getting There & Away

Iwakuni is only 44 km from Hiroshima, connected by shinkansen to the Shin-Iwakuni station or regular JR San-yō line trains (about 50 minutes) to the central JR Iwakuni station.

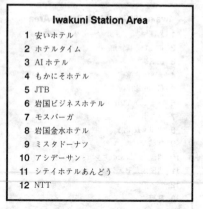

Iwakuni Station Area

1 安いホテル
2 ホテルタイム
3 AIホテル
4 もかにそホテル
5 JTB
6 岩国ビジネスホテル
7 モスバーガ
8 岩国金水ホテル
9 ミスタドーナツ
10 アシデーサン・
11 シティホテルあんどう
12 NTT

months in Yamaguchi on his way to the imperial capital but quickly returned to the safety of this provincial centre when he was unable even to find the emperor in Kyoto! In the following centuries, Yamaguchi took turns with Hagi as the provincial capital and, like Haji, Yamaguchi played an important part in the Meiji Restoration. Today it's a pleasantly peaceful town with a number of interesting attractions.

Orientation & Information
Eki-dōri is the main shopping street, running straight up from the station and crossing the main shopping arcade before it reaches Route 9. There's an information counter in the railway station.

Xavier Memorial Chapel
The Xavier Memorial Chapel overlooks the town centre from a hilltop in Marugame Park; this church was built in 1952 to commemorate the 400th anniversary of Francis Xavier's visit to the city.

Art Gallery & Historical Museum
At the foot of the hill stands the Yamaguchi Prefectural Art Museum (open from 9 am to 4.30 pm, closed Mondays) where frequent special exhibitions are held. Just north is the

Getting Around
The Kintai-kyō Bridge is almost equidistant from the two main stations, about five km from either. Buses shuttle back and forth between Iwakuni station and the bridge (Y170) and Shin-Iwakuni station and the bridge (Y160).

YAMAGUCHI　山口
During the tumultuous Muromachi (Country at War) period from 1467 to 1573, Yamaguchi prospered as an alternative capital to chaotic Kyoto. In 1550, the Jesuit Missionary Francis Xavier paused for two

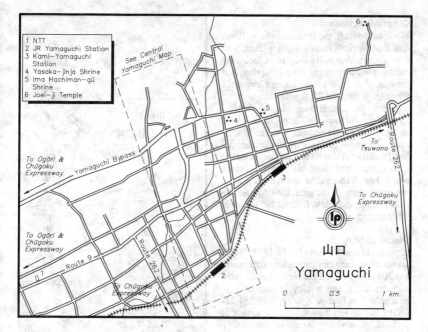

Yamaguchi

1　NTT
2　JR 山口駅
3　上山口駅
4　八坂神社
5　今八幡宮
6　常栄寺

Yamaguchi Historical Museum which has similar opening hours.

Kozan Park & Five Storeyed Pagoda

Further north again from the town centre is Kozan Park where the five storeyed pagoda, dating from 1404, is picturesquely sited beside a small lake. A small museum has photos and details of all 40 Japanese five storeyed pagodas, plus a map indicating where they're located. Entry is Y200 but this is strictly for five storeyed pagoda aficionados!

The Ruriko-ji Temple, with which the pagoda is associated, is also in the park and was moved here from a small village. The park's teahouse was also moved here – the Yamaguchi daimyō held secret talks in the house under the pretext of holding a tea ceremony. The park is also the site of the Toshun-ji Temple and the graves of the Mori lords.

Joei-ji Temple

The Joei-ji Temple, four km north-east of the JR station, was originally built as a house and is notable for its beautiful Zen garden designed by the painter Sesshū. Visitors bring bentō (boxed lunches) and sit on the verandah to eat while admiring the garden. Entry to the garden is Y200; it's open daily from 8 am to 5.30 pm.

Other Attractions

North of Route 9, the Ichinosakakawa River has a particularly pretty stretch lined with cherry trees. Naturally they're at their best during the blossoming time in spring, but they're also lovely on summer evenings when large fireflies flit through the trees.

During the annual Gion Matsuri Festival in late July, the Sagi-mai Egret Dance is held in the Yasaka-jinja Shrine. The Ima Hachiman-gū is an interesting shrine with a unique local architectural style that encompasses the gate, oratory and main hall under the same roof. The Yamaguchi Dai-jingū was a western branch of the great Ise-jingū Shrine near Nara in the Kinki District but is somewhat neglected today.

Places to Stay

Yamaguchi Youth Hostel (tel 0839-28-0057) is about four km from the railway station and has 30 beds at Y1900 per night. You can rent bicycles there and a bicycle tour map is available. The *Fukuya Ryokan* (tel 0839-22-0531), just up Eki-dōri St from the station, is popular, conveniently central and reasonably priced at Y5000 per person with two meals.

There's the usual assortment of modern business hotels around the station area including the *Hotel Sun Route Yamaguchi* (tel 0839-23-3610) which has rooms from Y5600/10,000 for singles/doubles. Cheaper hotels are on Eki-dōri St near the station.

Yuda Onsen, a 10 minute bus trip from the station, has a number of traditional ryokan including the expensive but historically interesting *Matsudaya Hotel* (tel 0839-22-0125) which has rooms from Y15,000 per person with meals.

Places to Eat

The arcade off Eki-dōri has lots of restaurants, coffee bars and a *Lotteria* fast-food place in the arcade. Just a couple of doors down from the Fukuya Ryokan is *Yamabuki* (tel 0839-22-1462), a pleasant old soba shop where you can eat well for Y500. It's closed on the 1st and 15th of each month.

There are a number of good places along Eki-dōri. *Mama No Ki*, close to the station is

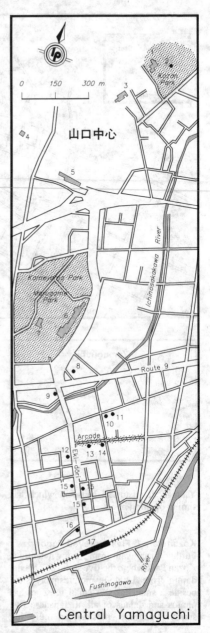

山口中心

Central Yamaguchi

Central Yamaguchi

1. Ruriko-ji Temple
2. Five Storeyed Pagoda
3. Toshun-ji Temple
4. Yamaguchi Dai-jingū Shrine
5. Yamaguchi Historical Museum
6. Yamaguchi Prefectural Art Museum
7. Xavier Memorial Chapel
8. Hotel Sun Route Yamaguchi
9. Green Park Restaurant
10. JTB
11. Lotteria (Fast Food)
12. Jardin Patisserie
13. Fukuya Ryokan
14. Yamabuki Noodle Shop
15. Hotels
16. Mama No Ki Coffee Shop
17. JR Yamaguchi Station

Central Yamaguchi

1. 瑠璃光寺
2. 国宝五重塔
3. 洞春寺
4. 山口大神宮
5. 山口博物館
6. 山口県立美術館
7. サビエル記念堂
8. ホテルサンルート山口
9. グリンパークレストラン
10. JTB
11. ロッテリア
12. ジャーデイン
13. ふくや旅館
14. やまぶき
15. ホテル
16. ままのきコーヒー店
17. JR 山口駅

a pleasant *kissaten* (coffee shop) with a bargain-priced Y330 morning setto (set-menu meal); notice how the regulars have their own cups and saucers (all different) pigeonholed behind the counter. Further up is *Jardin*, a good little bakery/patisserie, while at the top of the road, the *Green Park* restaurant is worth a try.

Getting There & Away
Yamaguchi is only 15 minutes by train from the main shinkansen line station at Ogōri.

Getting Around
Bicycles can be rented from the railway station and since the town's attractions are somewhat scattered (it's eight km just to the Joei-ji Temple and back) and the traffic is not too chaotic, this is a good idea. The first two hours cost Y310 or it's Y820 for a day.

AROUND YAMAGUCHI　山口の附近
Ogōri
Ogōri, only 10 km south-west of Yamaguchi, is of no particular interest except as a place to change trains. It's at the junction of the San-yō Osaka-Hakata shinkansen line with the JR Yamaguchi line, which continues to Tsuwano and Masuda on the San-in coast.

Hofu
The Matsuzaki Tenjin Shrine has impressively large and colourful buildings while the Mōri Hontei Villa dates from the Meiji era and has a famous Sesshū painting on display. It's open from 9 am to 4 pm.

Chōmon-kyō Gorge
The Chōmon-kyō Gorge is on the Abugawa River, and extends about 10 km north from Chōmon-kyō station, about 20 km north-east of Yamaguchi.

SHIMONOSEKI　下関
Shimonoseki (population 270,000) is yet another featureless, modern Japanese city, but for travellers it's also an important cross-roads, a place through which many people pass and few pause. At the extreme western tip of Honshū only a narrow strait separates Shimonoseki from the island of Kyūshū. The expressway crosses the Kanmon Straits by the Kanmon Bridge, while another road, the shinkansen railway line and the JR railway line all tunnel underneath. The town is also an important connection to South Korea, with a daily ferry service to and from Pusan. Despite Shimonoseki's reputation as a place

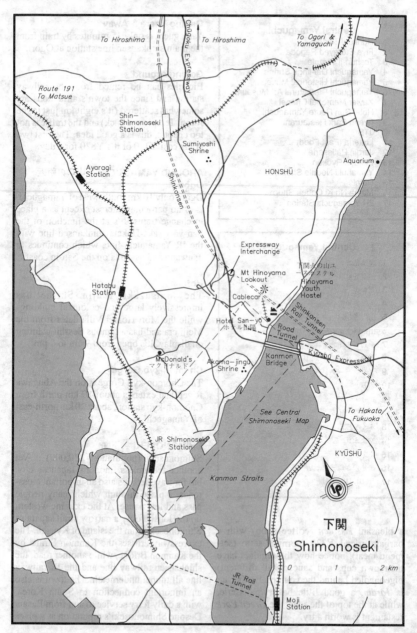

To Hiroshima

To Hiroshima

Chūgoku Expressway

To Ogori &
Yamaguchi

Route 191
To Matsue

Shin-
Shimonoseki
Station

Sumiyoshi
Shrine

Aquarium

HONSHŪ

Ayaragi
Station

Shinkansen

Expressway
Interchange

Mt Hinoyama
Lookout

関火の山ユ
ースホステル
Hinoyama
Youth
Hostel

Cablecar

Hatabu
Station

Shinkansen
Rail Tunnel

Hotel San-yō
ホテル山陽

Road
Tunnel

Kyūshū Expressway

McDonald's
マクドナルド

Akama-jingū
Shrine

Kanmon
Bridge

To Hakata
Fukuoka

See Central
Shimonoseki Map

JR Shimonoseki
Station

KYŪSHŪ

Kanmon Straits

下関
Shimonoseki

0   1   2 km

JR Rail
Tunnel

Moji
Station

to pass through as rapidly as possible, there are a number of points of interest.

Information

There's a tourist information office in the JR Shimonoseki station. Beside the station is the large Sea Mall Shimonoseki shopping centre.

If you're arriving from Korea, note that the bank in the ferry terminal is only open from 9 to 9.30 am after the ferry arrival, but there are branches of the Bank of Tokyo and the Yamaguchi Bank near the station. If you need a visa for Korea, the Korean consulate is about a km south of the station, beyond the ferry terminal.

Akama-jingū Shrine

The bright red/orange Akama Shrine is dedicated to the child-emperor Antoku who died in 1185 in the naval battle of Dan no Ura. The battle took place in the Kanmon Straits which are overlooked by the shrine. In the Hoichi Hall stands a statue of 'Earless Hoichi', hero of a traditional ghost story retold by Lafcadio Hearn. The shrine is about three km north of the station, en route to Mt Hino-yama. Get off the bus at the Akamajingu-mae bus stop.

Mt Hino-yama

About five km north-east of JR Shimonoseki station there are superb views over the Kanmon Straits from the top of 268 metre Mt Hino-yama. The km-long Kanmon Bridge is right at your feet, ships shuttle back and forth through this narrow but important waterway and at night, the views of the city are wonderful. You can walk, drive or travel by cablecar to the top. The cablecar costs Y200 one way, Y400 return. Take a Ropeway-mae bus to the Mimosusogawa bus stop near the cablecar station or a Kokuminshukusha-mae bus right to the top – these depart hourly from stand No 3 at the station.

Sumiyoshi-jinja Shrine

The Sumiyoshi Shrine, dating from 1370, is north of Mt Hino-yama, near the Shin-

Shimonoseki station. It's open from 9 am to 4 pm daily but closed from 8 to 15 December.

Aquarium

Shimonoseki's aquarium may or may not be the 'largest in the far east' as claimed in the aquarium's tourist brochure, but if it wasn't in Japan, it would just be another crummy Third World aquarium. There's a dolphin show and some of the fish, penguins and other sea creatures, are crammed into tanks or enclosures far too small for them. An unfortunate giant leatherback turtle is squeezed into a small circular pool into which visitors toss coins; perhaps it can eventually buy its freedom.

On the hilltop overlooking the complex, a concrete 'whale' houses exhibitions showing all the reasons the Japanese give for slaughtering whales. The aquarium is south of the centre, just past the big Ferris wheel marking Marine Leisureland. In Japanese, aquarium is *suizokukan* and buses run from the station to the Suizokukan-mae bus stop. The aquarium is open from 9 am to 5 pm (6 pm in August) and entry is Y500.

Chōfu

Just north of the aquarium is Chōfu, the old castle town area. Little remains of the old coastal castle itself, but there are old earth walls and samurai gates in Chōfu along with a museum and some important temples and shrines. The Kōzan-ji Temple has a Zen-style hall dating from 1327 and the Chōfu Museum is also in the temple grounds. Other interesting temples and shrines include the Kakuon-ji Temple, the Iminomiya Shrine and the Nogi Shrine. Get off the bus at Torii-mae bus stop for the Chōfu area.

Other Attractions

Across the road from the Grand Hotel in central Shimonoseki and by the Karato bus stop, is the Meiji-era former British consulate building of 1906. The Shimonoseki City Art Museum is opposite the aquarium.

Places to Stay

Youth Hostels The *Hinoyama Youth Hostel*

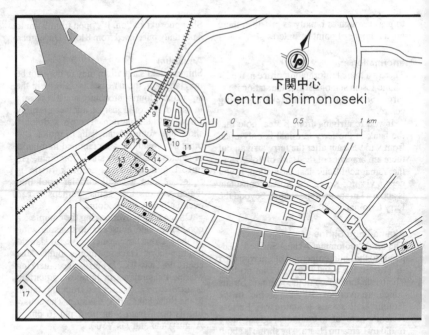

下関中心
Central Shimonoseki

0   0.5   1 km

Central Shimonoseki

1　下関火の山ユースホステル
2　山陽ホテル
3　赤間神宮
4　びぜんや旅館
5　旧英国領事館
6　下関グランドホテル
7　サンテイサンジョリパスタ
8　下関ステーションホテル
9　よかホテル
10　ホテル38下関
11　下関グリーンホテル
12　JR下関駅
13　シーモール下関
14　山口銀行
15　下関東急インと東京銀行
16　下関港国際ターミナル
17　大韓民国領事館

(tel 0832-22-3753) is at the base of Mt Hino-yama, only 100 metres from the lower cablecar station. There are 52 beds at Y1800 or Y1950 depending on the time of year. Take a Hinoyama bus from the station; you can't miss the huge 'YH' sign on top of the building.

Budget Accommodation The *Bizenya Ryokan* (tel 0832-22-6228), 3-11-7 Kami-tanakamachi, is part of the Japanese Inn Group. It's a basic place with rooms from Y3000 to Y4000 per person and is somewhat hidden away at the end of a narrow alley about two km from the centre of town. To get there, take a bus from JR Shimonoseki station (bus stop No 6) or Shin-Shimonoseki station (bus stop No 1) to the Nishinohashi bus stop. There are two petrol stations virtually side by side at this point.

Hotels A number of business hotels can be found close to the station including the *Hotel*

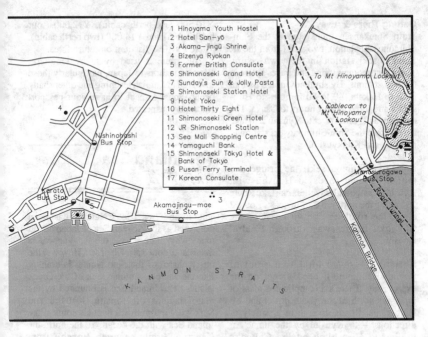

1 Hinoyama Youth Hostel
2 Hotel San-yō
3 Akama-jingū Shrine
4 Bizenya Ryokan
5 Former British Consulate
6 Shimonoseki Grand Hotel
7 Sunday's Sun & Jolly Pasta
8 Shimonoseki Station Hotel
9 Hotel Yoka
10 Hotel Thirty Eight
11 Shimonoseki Green Hotel
12 JR Shimonoseki Station
13 Sea Mall Shopping Centre
14 Yamaguchi Bank
15 Shimonoseki Tōkyū Hotel & Bank of Tokyo
16 Pusan Ferry Terminal
17 Korean Consulate

Thirty Eight (tel 0832-23-1138), only a couple of minutes walk away with singles from Y4000 to Y6000, doubles from Y5800 to Y7000. Close by is the *Shimonoseki Station Hotel* (tel 0832-32-3511) with singles/doubles from Y4500/6800.

Continue a little further down the road opposite the station and you come to the small *Hotel Yoka* (tel 0832-22-2707), a basic place with singles/doubles at Y3200/5800. Or cross the road from the station and turn right to reach the *Shimonoseki Green Hotel* (tel 0832-31-1007) with rooms at Y4900/7300. Right next to the station is the *Shimonoseki Tōkyū Inn* (tel 0832-23-0285) with singles at Y5700 to Y6200, doubles at Y10,500 to Y11,500.

A couple of km from the JR station, the *Shimonoseki Grand Hotel* (tel 0832-31-5000) has a wide variety of Western and Japanese-style singles from Y4000 to Y6000 and doubles from Y7000 to Y10,000. Reception is on the 8th floor and there are superb views over the strait from this 7th, 8th and 9th floor hotel. Even further from the station, just below the cablecar car park, you'll find the *Hotel San-yō* (tel 0832-32-8666). It has great views and rooms at Y6000/10,000 for singles/doubles.

Places to Eat

There are lots of fast-food places and restaurants with plastic meal displays around the station area including a good *Vie de France* patisserie and café, a *Lotteria*, *Kentucky Fried Chicken* and others. Between the station and the Grand Hotel there's a big *Sunday's Sun/Jolly Pasta* restaurant complex.

For fugu fish fans, Shimonoseki is reputed to be an excellent place to dine on this deadly delicacy; around the station giant plastic fugu fish perch on top of the phone boxes.

Getting There & Away

Train Shinkansen trains stop at the Shin-Shimonoseki station, two stops from the JR Shimonoseki station in the town centre. There are frequent trains and buses between the two stations. By shinkansen, it's half an hour to Hakata, 40 to 80 minutes to Hiroshima and three to four hours to Osaka. The easiest way to cross over to Kyūshū is to take a train from the Shin-Shimonoseki station to Moji-ko and Kitakyūshū.

Car From Shimonoseki, the bridge and tunnel connect roads in Honshū with Kyūshū. Eastbound travellers can take Route 191 along the northern San-in coast, Route 2 along the southern San-yō coast or the Chūgoku Expressway through Central Honshū.

Hitching If you're hitchhiking out of Shimonoseki, you'll need to get on the expressway. There's a complicated mass of junctions north of the youth hostel and Mt Hino-yama. Roads diverge in a variety of directions – to Kyūshu by the tunnel or bridge, to Hiroshima by the Chūgoku Expressway and to Yamaguchi by routes 2 and 9.

Ferry *Japan* Ferries run regularly from early morning to late at night from the Karato area of Shimonoseki to Moji-ko on Kyūshū. From Kokura in Kitakyūshū there are ferries to Kōbe, Osaka and Tokyo on Honshū and to Matsuyama on Shikoku.

Korea The Kampu Ferry Service (tel 0832-24-3000) operates the Shimonoseki-Pusan ferry service from the terminal a few minutes walk from the station. There are daily departures with the *Kampu* or the *Pukwan* at 5 pm from Shimonoseki and Pusan, arriving at the other end at 8.30 am (the next morning). You can board from 2 pm. Bookings close on sailing day at 3.30 pm and you must be boarding by 4.30 pm when customs and immigration close. One-way fares start from Y6800 for students and continue up through Y8500 for an open, tatami-mat area,

Y10,500 (six berth cabin), Y12,000 (four berth cabin) and Y14,000 (two berth cabin). There's a 10% discount on return fares.

This route is used by many long-term Western visitors to Japan, particularly those involved in English teaching and other shady occupations! Expect to have your passport rigorously inspected.

The Inland Sea
瀬戸内海

The Inland Sea (Seto Naikai) has been described as the Aegean Sea of Japan and in many ways it does have the same appeal as that island-dotted stretch of sea. However the misty charm of the Seto Naikai is nothing like the sharper, angular look of the Greek islands. The Inland Sea is bounded by the major islands of Honshū, Kyūshū and Shikoku. Four narrow channels connect the Inland Sea with the ocean. To the north the Kanmon Straits separate Honshū from Kyūshū and leads to the Sea of Japan; to the south, leading to the Pacific, the Hoya Straits separate Kyūshū from Shikoku; at the other end of Shikoku the Naruto Straits and Kitan Straits flow each side of Awaji Island, which almost connects Shikoku to Honshū.

For the visitor, the most interesting area of the Inland Sea is the island-crowded stretch from Hiroshima east to Takamatsu and Okayama. There are said to be more than 3000 islands, depending on what you define as an island! There are a number of ways of seeing the Inland Sea. One is to simply travel through it as there are numerous ferry services criss-crossing the sea or even running its full length, such as the service from Osaka on Honshū to Oita, near Beppu, on Kyūshū. Alternatively, but more expensively, there are Inland Sea cruises ranging from short day trips to longer overnight cruises. Also, you can visit single islands in the Inland Sea for a first-hand experience of a part of Japan which, though rapidly changing, is still quite different from the fast-moving metropolitan centres.

Information

Brochures, maps and general tourist information are readily available but Donald Richie's *The Inland Sea*, originally published in 1971 and now available in paperback, makes an excellent introduction to the region. Although much of the Inland Sea's slow moving and easy-going atmosphere has disappeared since his book was published, and indeed he emphasised its rapidly changing nature even at that time, it still provides some fascinating insights. Highpoints of the book include his encounter with a yakuza priest at the Oyamazumi Shrine on Omi-shima Island, his demolition job of the Kōsan-ji Temple at Setoda, the amusing search for a stone cat on Kitagishima and the wistful tale of the prostitutes of Kinoe on Osakikami-jima.

Getting Around

Miyajima to Setoda Cruise The popular SKK (Seto Naikaikisen) line cruise from Miyajima to Setoda on Ikuchi-jima Island is one of the easiest and most popular ways of seeing one of the finest stretches of the Inland Sea. *Popular* is the operative word; this is a very touristy trip. The ship *Akinada* leaves Miyajima at 8.30 am, stops at Hiroshima at 9 am and continues past Kure, through the 70 metre wide Ondo Strait separating Kurahashi-jima Island from Honshū, on through Neko (Cat) Strait, past Greenpia Yasuura then stops at Omi-shima Island to visit the Oyamazumi Shrine and Museum. After that two hour stop it continues to Setoda, arriving at 1.25 pm. From there you can take one of the regular ferries across to Mihara or Onomichi on Honshū and continue by train.

Meanwhile the ship does the same trip in reverse, departing from Setoda at 1.35 pm, reaching Hiroshima at 5.15 pm and Miyajima at 5.38 pm. The trip is shorter in this direction as the Omi-shima Island stop doesn't include a lunch break. From Miyajima or Hiroshima to Setoda costs

Y6380. Lunch and all museum, temple and other entry charges are extra. The cruises operate from 1 March to 30 November.

Other Cruises There are shorter and longer cruises. The Japan Travel Bureau (JTB) and other tour operators have a variety of overnight cruises from Osaka. SKK have numerous other ships operating including day cruises from Hiroshima to Eta-jima, Miya-jima and Eno-shima islands.

OMI-SHIMA ISLAND 大三島

This hilly rather than mountainous island boasts the mountain god's Oyamazumi-jinja Shrine which once commanded much respect from the Inland Sea's pirates. In actual fact, the pirates were more like a local navy than real pirates but, until Hideyoshi brought them to heel, they wielded real power in these parts. Along the way, an armour collection was built up in the shrine's treasure house, including more than half the armour in Japan: a national treasure. Entry to the treasure house is Y800 but despite the importance of the collection it's just more weapons and armour unless you're interested in the fact that something belonged to *the* shogun.

In an adjacent building is a boat used by Emperor Hirohito in his marine science investigations, together with a somewhat tatty natural history exhibit. The shrine's history is actually one of the most ancient in Japan, ranking with the shrines at Ise and Izumo.

Miyaura Port is a 15 minute walk from the shrine. The *Omi-shima Suigun* restaurant is near the shrine.

Getting There & Away

The *Akinada* cruise from Hiroshima visits Omi-shima but you can also get there by ferry service from Onomichi, Mihara or Setoda on the neighbouring island of Ikuchijima, and also from Takehara, further west on the Honshū coast.

IKUCHI-JIMA ISLAND 生口島

At Setoda, the main town on the island,

Ikuchi-jima is actually linked to neighbouring Takane-jima by a bridge. The town is noted for the Kōsan-ji Temple, a wonderful exercise in kitsch. Local steel-tube magnate Kanemoto Kōzō devoted a large slab of his considerable fortune from 1935 on to recreating numerous important temples and shrines all in this one spot and all in grateful homage to his mother. If you haven't got time to visit the originals, this is an interesting substitute.

Entry is Y800 which includes the 1000 Buddhas Cave, the art museum and the treasure house. It costs another Y200 to visit Kanemoto Kōzō's mother's quarters. The extraordinary 1000 Buddhas Cave includes an introductory 'hell', very Tiger balm-like with its tableaux of the damned being mangled, chopped, fried and generally hard done by. From there you follow winding tunnels and spiral stairs lined with 1000 Buddhas. One sour note at this temple is the poor Australian emu penned up in far too small an enclosure by the main entrance.

To get to the temple, turn right as you leave the boat landing then left up the shop-lined 600 metre long street. The Setoda History & Folklore Museum is at the start of this street. Halfway up the same street you can turn left towards a temple on the hillside; around the back of this temple and much further up the hill is the Kōjō-ji Temple, dating from 1403, with a three storeyed pagoda and fine views over the island. You can also get there by turning left from the pier (towards the bridge) and heading straight up the hill.

Places to Stay

The *Setoda Youth Hostel* (tel 08452-7-0244) costs Y1700 and is a short walk from the dock. There's also the *Ikuchi-jima Tarumi Youth Hostel* (tel 08452-7-3137) at the same price. The *Setoda Hotel* (tel 08452-7-0010) is right across from the dock; it's part of the Japanese Inn Group and has rooms from Y4800/7500.

Getting There & Away

You can get to Ikuchi-jima Island by the regular cruise from Hiroshima or by ferries from Mihara or Onomichi on Honshū. A high-speed ferry to Mihara costs Y1260.

INNO-SHIMA ISLAND　因島

Inno-shima Island is connected by bridge to Mukai-shima Island and on to Onomichi. The island has a pirate castle.

SHIWAKU ISLANDS　塩飽諸島

North of Marugame, on Shikoku are the scattered Shiwaku Islands, once the haunt of daring pirates and seafarers. Hon-jima is a larger island just west of the Seto-ōhashi Bridge with some fine old buildings and interesting sites.

SHODO-SHIMA ISLAND　小豆島

Shōdo-shima Island is easily reached from Honshū or Shikoku, offers a number of interesting places to visit and makes an enjoyable short escape from big-city Japan. Although the second-largest island in the Inland Sea, Shōdo-shima is still small enough to explore quite easily. The island even has a miniature version of neighbouring Shikoku's 88 Temple Circuit, though since Shōdo-shima can't muster 88 temples, the itinerary is padded out with a number of other notable sites.

Orientation & Information

Tonoshō, at the western end of the island, is the usual arrival point from Takamatsu, Uno or Okayama and makes a good base from which to explore the island. Fukuda in the north-east and Sakate in the south-east are other busy ports. If you arrive on Shōdo Island from Takamatsu (the most popular jumping-off point) you'll find an information office just inside the ferry building.

Coastal Area

The island's olive-growing activities are commemorated at Olive Park on the south coast. Nearby is the Shōdo-shima Folk Museum (Y300). The end of the peninsula to the south of Ikeda is marked by the Jizōzaki Lighthouse and offers fine views over the Inland Sea. Just north of Sakate is

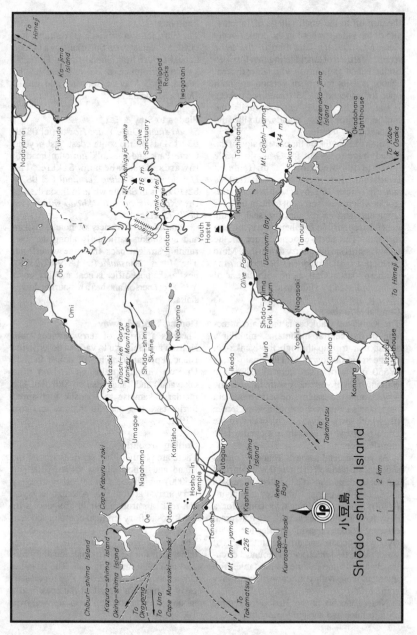

Shōdo-shima Island

小豆島

0   1   2 km

the turn-off to the small village of Tanoura, site of the village school in the book *Twenty Four Eyes* and the later film of the same name. There's a distinct feeling that this was Shōdo Island's sole brush with fame; the real school and its movie set version are both open for inspection (Y350 combined ticket). A statue of the teacher and her pupils (the movie version) also stands outside the Tonoshō ferry terminal.

South of Fukuda, on the eastern side of the island, huge rocks cut for Osaka-jō Castle now lie jumbled down a cliffside at Iwagatani. The rocks are classified as *zanseki* (rocks left over) or *zannen ishi* (rocks which were sorry not to be in time for shipment) and each bears the seal of the general responsible for their quarrying and dispatch. The north-eastern corner of the island is still one big quarry to this day. More unshipped castle rocks can be seen on the northern coast at Omi, along with the site of a shipyard used by Hideyoshi.

Central Mountains
The Kanka-kei Cablecar is the main attraction in the central mountains, making a spectacular trip up through the Kanka-kei Gorge in the shadow of Mt Hoshigajō-yama (Y550 one way, Y980 return). There's a walking track if you really want to walk one way. Around the eastern side of the mountain the island's tenuous connection with Greece (they both grow olives) is celebrated in the Olive Sanctuary where there's even a fake mini-Parthenon.

As you descend towards Tonoshō (rented scooters are allowed to travel down this road but not up it; perhaps it's too steep) you pass the Choshi-kei Gorge's 'monkey mountain' (Y360) where wild monkeys come for a daily feed. Beside the car park is a restaurant offering 'somen nagashi' noodles for Y450. (A bowl of noodles are dropped into a sort of water racetrack which swirls around a circular channel in the middle of the table. You intercept them with your chopsticks as they come by!)

Near Tonoshō is the Hosho-in Temple with its huge and ancient juniper tree.

Festivals
The Shikoku-mura Village at Yashima, just outside Takamatsu on Shikoku, has a village kabuki theatre from Shōdo-shima. Farmers' kabuki performances are still held on the island: on 3 May at Tonoshō and on 10 October at Ikeda.

Places to Stay & Eat
Shōdo-shima Olive Youth Hostel (tel 0879-82-6161) is on the south coast, just beyond Olive Park and the folk museum heading towards Kusakabe and Sakate. The *Uchinomi-chō Cycling Terminal* (tel 0879-82-1099) is in Sakate while in Ikeda there is the *Kokuminshukusha Shōdo-shima* (tel 0879-75-1115).

Tonoshō has a variety of hotels, ryokan and minshuku, particularly along the road running straight back from the waterfront. The *Maruse Minshuku* (tel 0879-62-2385), next to the post office is neat and tidy, costs Y3500 per person and has a restaurant downstairs.

Getting There & Away
There is a variety of ferry services from Honshū and Shikoku to various ports on the island. Popular jumping-off points include Uno on Honshū (trains go to Uno from Okayama) and Takamatsu on Shikoku. The regular Takamatsu to Tonoshō high-speed ferries take less than 30 minutes and cost Y1000.

Getting Around
There are plenty of bus services around the island and a host of bus tours (Y3000 to Y5000) which seem to set off with every ferry arrival at Tonoshō. Alternatively, you can rent cars from a couple of agencies by the Tonoshō ferry terminal or motor scooters from Ryōbi Rent-a-Bike (tel 0879-62-6578). The scooter agency operates out of a container near the ferry terminal; the daily hire cost is Y2990 including fuel. The island is small enough to explore in a day if you start early, although a circuit of the coast and a mountain excursion will clock up well over 100 km.

Top: Seto-ōhashi Bridge from Washūzan (TW)
Middle: Doga-shima Island from Izu-hantō Peninsula (CT)
Bottom: Floating torii, Miya-jima Island (JW)

Top: Himeji from Himeji-jō Castle (JW)
Middle: Approach to Zenkō-ji Temple, Nagano (RS)
Bottom: Ginza, Tokyo (CT)

AWAJI-SHIMA ISLAND 淡路島

Awaji-shima Island, the Inland Sea's largest island, forms the region's eastern boundary and almost connects Honshū with Shikoku. At the Shikoku end, the Naruto-ōhashi Bridge spans the Naruto Straits across the well-known Naruto Whirlpools to connect Shikoku with Awaji Island. (See the Around Tokushima section of the Shikoku chapter.) At the other end of the island, a tunnel is planned to connect the island with Honshū near Kōbe.

The island is densely populated, relatively flat and has some good beaches. It was the original home for the *ningyō jōruri* puppet theatre which preceded the development of bunraku theatre. Short performances are given several times daily in the small puppet theatre in Fukura. The island has many minshuku.

Wakasa Bay Area
宮津湾

The area around Wakasa Bay, the eastern end of the San-in coast, takes in parts of three prefectures: Fukui, Kyoto and Hyogo-ken.

WAKASA BAY 宮津湾

At the eastern end of the bay, the Mikatago-ko Lakes (Mikata Five Lakes) are joined to the sea. Obama is a port town with the ruins of Obama-jō Castle and a number of interesting old temples including the Myōtsū-ji, the Mantoku-ji and the Jingū-ji. Tour buses operate from the JR Obama station and there are also boat trips around the picturesque Sotomo coastline with its inlets, arches and caves, just north of Obama. The town has a variety of accommodation including the *Obama Youth Hostel* (tel 0770-52-2158).

Continuing around the bay, more interesting coastal scenery can be reached by boat trips from Wakasa-Takahama. From Maizuru there are regular ferry services to Otaru in Hokkaidō. Ferries also run to Otaru from Tsuruga, at the other end of Wakasa Bay (see the Fukui-ken section of the Central Honshū chapter).

AMANOHASHIDATE 天橋立

Amanohashidate (Bridge to Heaven) is rated as one of Japan's 'three great views', along with Miya-jima Island (near Hiroshima) and the islands of Matsushima-wan Bay (near Sendai). The 'bridge' is really a 'pier', a tree-covered sandspit 3½ km long with just a couple of narrow channels preventing it from cutting off the top of Miyazu Bay as a separate lake.

The town of Amanohashidate consists of two separate parts, one at each end of the spit. At the southern end there are a number of hotels, ryokan, restaurants, a popular temple and the JR Amanohashidate station. At the other end, a funicular railway (Y260 one way) and a chair lift run up the hillside to the Kasamutsu-kōen Park vantage point from where the view is reputed to be most pleasing. From here, incidentally, you're supposed to view the sandspit by turning your back to it, bending over and observing it framed between your legs! There's another hilltop viewpoint at the southern end of the spit.

A bridge and swing bridge cross the two channels at the southern end of the spit and cycling along the spit is a popular activity.

Places to Stay

There's an information counter at the railway station. The *Amanohashidate Youth Hostel* (tel 07722-7-0121) is at Ichinomiya, close to the funicular to the lookout point. To get there take a Tankai bus from the JR Amanohashidate station and get off at the Jinja-mae bus stop, from where it's a 10 minute walk. The nightly cost is Y2150 or Y2350 depending on the season. The *Amanohashidate Kankōkaikan Youth Hostel* (tel 07722-7-0046) is also near the park.

There are a number of ryokan and hotels, generally fairly expensive, near the station at the other end of the 'bridge'. The *Toriko Ryokan* (tel 07722-2-0010) costs Y10,000 per person including two meals. The *Shoehino Ryokan* is similarly priced. Other places include the *Hotel Taikyo* and the *Hotel Monju-sō*.

Getting There & Away

The coastal JR Miyazu line connects Obama with Amanohashidate and on to Toyooka where you change to the JR San-in line for Tottori. It takes about three hours by limited express from Kyoto, half an hour longer by tour bus.

Getting Around

You can cross the 'bridge to heaven' on foot, bicycle or on a motorcycle of less than 125 cc capacity. Bicycles can be hired at a number of places for Y400 for two hours or Y1600 a day. Tour boats also operate across Miyazu Bay.

TANGO-HANTO PENINSULA
丹後半島

Travelling westward, Amanohashidate marks the start of the Tango-hantō Peninsula, jutting north into the Sea of Japan. A coast road runs around the peninsula passing a number of small scenic fishing ports. The village of Ine, on a perfect little bay, is particularly interesting, with houses built out right over the water and boats drawn in under them as if in a carport. There's a large commercial fishing operation just beyond the village.

At the end of the peninsula, a large car park and restaurant marks the start of the one hour round-trip walk to the Cape Kyōgasaki Lighthouse. There are some pleasant coastal views but the lighthouse itself is nothing special.

TOYOOKA 豊岡

The road around the Tango Peninsula rejoins the main coast before Toyooka. The Genbu-dō Caves are five km north of the town, right by the Maruyama River and across from JR Genbudō station. Amanohashidate to Toyooka takes about 1½ hours on the JR Miyazu line.

TOTTORI 鳥取

Tottori (population 140,000) is a large, busy

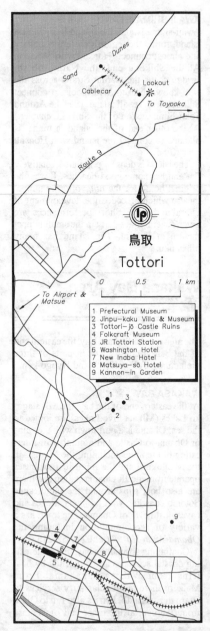

鳥取
Tottori

0   0.5   1 km

1 Prefectural Museum
2 Jinpu–kaku Villa & Museum
3 Tottori–jō Castle Ruins
4 Folkcraft Museum
5 JR Tottori Station
6 Washington Hotel
7 New Inaba Hotel
8 Matsuya–sō Hotel
9 Kannon–in Garden

Tottori

1 県立博物館
2 仁風閣
3 鳥取城跡
4 民芸美術館
5 JR 鳥取駅
6 ワシントンホテル
7 ニューいなばホテル
8 松屋荘ホテル
9 観音院庭

town some distance back from the coast. The main coast road passes through Tottori's northern fringe in a blizzard of car dealers, pachinko parlours and fast-food outlets. The town's main attraction is its famous sand dunes.There's a helpful tourist information booth inside the station.

The Dunes

Used as the location for Teshigahara Hiroshi's classic 1964 film *Woman in the Dunes*, the Tottori sand dunes are a couple of km east of the city. There's a viewing point on a hillside overlooking the dunes along with a huge car park and the usual assortment of tourist amenities. The dunes stretch for over 10 km along the coast and, at some points, can be a couple of km wide. The section where the dunes are highest is popular with parachutists who stand at the edge of the dune, fill their chutes with the incoming seabreezes and leap off the dune top to sail down the dune facing towards the sea. Buses run out to the dunes from Tottori; you can rent bicycles at the dunes and ride along the coast road to escape the main crowds.

Other Attractions

Tottori's other attractions are mainly concentrated in a compact little group about 1½ km north-east of the station. Only the foundations remain of Tottori-jō Castle, which overlooked the town from the hillside. Below the castle walls is the European-style

Jinpu-kaku Villa, dating from 1906-07. The villa is now used as a museum; entry is Y150 and it's open from 9 am to 5 pm, closed on Mondays. Across from this building is the modern Tottori Prefectural Museum (entry Y800). Tottori also has an interesting little Folkcraft Museum near the JR station (closed Wednesdays) and the 17th century Kannon-in Garden.

Dune-parachuting is not the only seaside sporting activity around Tottori. A few km west of the town there's a popular surfing break, packed with Japanese surfies on weekends. There are other breaks along this coast.

Places to Stay & Eat

Hotels around the station area include the *Matsuya-sō Hotel* (tel 0857-22-4891) which has spacious, though basic Japanese-style rooms at Y2000 per person. There's no sign in English.

The *Tottori Green Hotel – Hotel Morris* (tel 0857-22-2331) has rooms at Y4500 to Y7800. The *Hotel New Inaba* has rooms at Y5000 per person. The *Tottori Washington Hotel* (tel 0857-27-8111), next to the railway station, has singles at Y6000 to Y6500 and doubles or twins from Y12,000 to Y13,000.

There are plenty of restaurants (with the usual plastic food displays) around the station including *Mister Donut* and a big selection of fast-food operators along Route 9, the main road through town.

Getting There & Away

The coastal JR San-in line runs through Tottori and it takes about 1½ hours from Toyooka. The JR Inbi line connects with Tsuyama and on to Okayama, nearly three hours away on the south coast.

Tottori has an airport and ANA has flights from Osaka and Tokyo.

TOTTORI TO MATSUE
Mt Daisen

A glance at a map of this region shows an enormous number of roads running up the slopes of 1729 metre Mt Daisen, its summit only about 10 km from the coast. Although it's not one of Japan's highest mountains it looks very impressive because it rises straight from sea level. The popular climb up the volcano cone is a six to seven hour round trip from the ancient Daisen-ji Temple. Bring plenty of water and take care on the final narrow ridge to the summit. From the summit there are fine views over the coast and, in perfect conditions, all the way to the Oki Islands. Buses run to near the temple from Yonago and take about 50 minutes. The mountain snags the north-west monsoon winds in the winter, bringing deep snow and difficult conditions for winter climbers.

Yonago

Yonago is an important railway junction connecting the north and south coasts and, as such, is a place to pass through rather than visit. From Yonaga Airport, there are flights to and from Osaka and Tokyo and on to the Oki Islands.

Shimane-ken   島根県

MATSUE   松江

Matsue (population 140,000) straddles the Ohashi River which connects Shinji-ko Lake to the Nakanoumi-ko Lake and then the sea. A compact area in the north of the town includes almost all of Matsue's important sites: an original castle, a fine example of a samurai residence, the former home of writer Lafcadio Hearn and a delightful teahouse and garden.

Information

The tourist information office at the JR station (on the left as you leave the station, just past Mister Donut) has a surprising amount of information in English and the staff are helpful.

Matsue-jō Castle

Matsue's castle is not huge or imposing but it is original, dating from 1611. Modern Japan has so many rebuilt castles, externally authentic-looking but internally totally modern, that it can almost be a shock to step inside one where the construction is real wood, not modern concrete. Entry is Y310 and it's open from 8.30 am to 5 pm.

The regional museum (Matsue Kyodokan) is within the castle precincts. The road alongside the moat on the north-eastern side of the castle is known as the Shiomi Nawate, at one time a narrow lane through the old samurai quarter. The high tile-topped walls still remain from that era and there are a number of places of interest. A No 1 or 2 bus from outside the JR station will get you to the castle.

Lafcadio Hearn Residence

At the northern end of the samurai street is the Lafcadio Hearn Memorial Museum and next to it is his former home. Hearn was a British writer (although he was born in Greece in 1850, educated in France and Britain and lived in the USA from 1869) who came to Japan in 1890 and was to remain there for the rest of his life. His first book on Japan, *Glimpses of Unfamiliar Japan*, is a classic, providing an insight into the country at that time. The Japanese have a great interest in the outsider's view of their country so Hearn's pretty little house is an important attraction, despite the fact that he only lived in Matsue for just over a year. Hearn's adopted Japanese name is Koizumi Yakumo. While you're admiring the garden you can read his essay *In a Japanese Garden*, describing how it looked a century ago. Entry to the house is Y205 and it's open from 9 am to 12.30 pm and 1.30 to 4.30 pm, closed on Wednesdays and from 13 to 16 August.

Lafcadio Hearn Memorial Museum

Next to the writer's home is his museum (the Koizumi Yakumo Memorial Museum) with displays about his life, his writing and his residence in Matsue. Entry is Y150 and the museum is open from 8.30 am to 5 pm. The museum has an English brochure and map showing various points of interest around the town mentioned in his writings.

Tanabe Art Museum
This museum principally displays family items from the many generations of the region's Tanabe clan, particularly tea bowls and other tea ceremony paraphernalia. Opening hours are 9 am to 5 pm, closed Monday. Entry is Y515.

Buke Yashiki Samurai Residence
The Buke Yashiki is a well-preserved middle Edo period samurai residence built in 1730. There's a good English description leaflet of the various rooms and their uses in this large but somewhat spartan residence. This was not the home of a wealthy samurai! Entry is Y205 and opening hours are from 8.30 am to 5 pm.

Meimei-an Teahouse
A little further south is the turn-off to the Meimei-an Teahouse with its well-kept gardens and fine views to Matsue Castle. The teahouse was built in 1779 and was moved to its present site in 1966 (it had been moved once before in 1928). Look for the steep steps up from the road to the thatched-roof building. Entry is Y200 and it's open from 9 am to 5 pm.

Other Attractions
The Kanden-an Teahouse is about 20 minutes drive north-east of the centre. It dates from 1792 and is one of the finest teahouses in Japan. It's open from 9.30 am to 4 pm, closed Thursdays.

About a km west of the castle is the Gessho-ji Temple, which was converted from an ordinary temple to a family temple for Matsue's Matsudaira clan in 1664 but dismantled during the Meiji Restoration. The graves of nine generations of the clan remain and family effects are displayed in the treasure house.

Matsue has its own onsen (hot-spring) area, just north of the lake near Matsue-onsen station on the Ichihata-Dentetsu line. There are a number of hotels and ryokan in the area and a popular 'hell', a very hot spring known as the O-Yu-Kake Jizō. The sunset views over Shinji-ko Lake are very fine and best appreciated from the Matsue-ōhashi Bridge. The Matsue Folk Art Centre, across from the Ichihata Hotel in the onsen area by the lake, displays regional crafts. The Matsue Prefectural Product & Craft Centre is another regional craft centre, just south of the castle in the town centre.

Places to Stay
Youth Hostels *Matsue Youth Hostel* (tel 0852-36-8620) is about five km from the centre of town in Kososhimachi, on the northern side of the lake at the first station you come to along the Ichihata line from Matsue-onsen station. There are 80 beds at Y2100 a night.

Budget Accommodation The *Pension Tobita* (tel 0852-36-6933) in Hamasadamachi is in the same direction as the youth hostel and has Japanese and Western-style rooms at Y4000 per person with breakfast only, Y4600 to Y5500 with dinner as well.

As usual, there are a lot of business hotels around the station including the unbusinesslike *Business Ishida* (no English sign) (tel 0852-21-5931) in Teramachi, a simple Japanese-style hotel with tatami-mat rooms and shared bathrooms at Y3000 per person. It's good value and conveniently close to the station: just continue walking past the tourist information office through the bicycle and car parks and it's right beside the elevated railway lines, just past the first road you cross.

Other possibilities, all with public bathrooms, include the *Business Daiei* (tel 0852-24-1515) in Wadamimachi at Y3500 or the nearby *Ohabaya* at Y3000. Or there's the *Kiraku Ryokan* (tel 0852-21-5549) at Y3500. It's also immediately north of the station but in Isemiyamachi; English is spoken here. *Hotel Matsuekan* (tel 0852-21-4679) in Asahimachi is just to the left of the station and has rooms at Y4000.

Hotels More expensive hotels include the *Matsue Tōkyū Inn* (tel 0852-27-0109) just across the road from the station. This popular

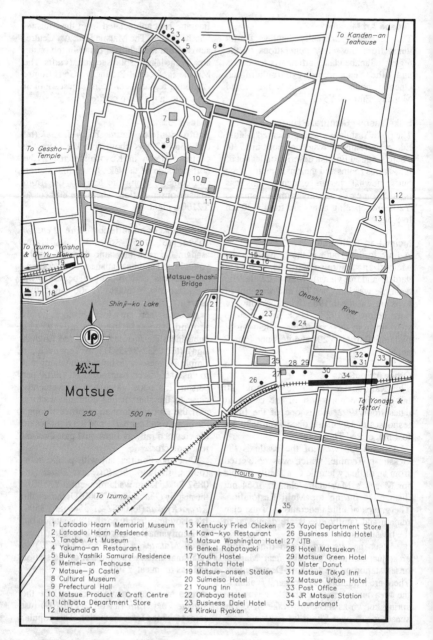

松江

Matsue

1 Lafcadio Hearn Memorial Museum	13 Kentucky Fried Chicken	25 Yayoi Department Store
2 Lafcadio Hearn Residence	14 Kawa–kyo Restaurant	26 Business Ishida Hotel
3 Tanabe Art Museum	15 Matsue Washington Hotel	27 JTB
4 Yakumo–an Restaurant	16 Benkei Robatayaki	28 Hotel Matsuekan
5 Buke Yashiki Samurai Residence	17 Youth Hostel	29 Matsue Green Hotel
6 Meimei–an Teahouse	18 Ichibata Hotel	30 Mister Donut
7 Matsue–jō Castle	19 Matsue–onsen Station	31 Matsue Tōkyū Inn
8 Cultural Museum	20 Suimeiso Hotel	32 Matsue Urban Hotel
9 Prefectural Hall	21 Young Inn	33 Post Office
10 Matsue Product & Craft Centre	22 Ohabaya Hotel	34 JR Matsue Station
11 Ichibata Department Store	23 Business Daiei Hotel	35 Laundromat
12 McDonald's	24 Kiraku Ryokan	

Matsue

1 小泉八雲記念館	19 松江温泉駅
2 小泉八雲旧居	20 水明荘
3 田部美術館	21 ヤングイン
4 やくもあん	22 大市屋ホテル
5 武家屋敷	23 ビジネス大栄ホテル
6 明々庵	24 きらく旅館
7 松江城	25 やよいデパート
8 松江郷土館	26 ビジネス石田ホテル
9 島根県庁	27 JTB
10 島根県物産観光館	28 ホテル松江館
11 一畑デパート	29 松江グリンホテル
12 マクドナルド	30 ミスタードーナツ
13 ケンタッキーフライドチキン	31 松江東急イン
14 かわきょうレストラン	32 松江アーバンホテル
15 松江ワシントンホテル	33 郵便局
16 弁慶	34 JR 松江駅
17 松江ユースホステル	35 洗濯
18 一畑ホテル	

chain hotel has singles from Y6000 to Y7100, doubles and twins at Y12,000 to Y14,000. Also in front of the station, the *Matsue Green Hotel* has singles/doubles at Y5250/9500. The *Matsue Urban Hotel* is a cheaper place behind the Tōkyū Inn with singles from Y4400.

The *Matsue Washington Hotel* (tel 0852-22-4111) is across the river from the JR station but still convenient to the town centre. Singles are Y5800 to Y6500, doubles Y11,400 to Y17,000. The *Ichihata Hotel* (tel 0852-22-0188) is near the Matsue-onsen station and has singles at Y5000 to Y7000, doubles and twins from Y12,000 to Y18,000.

Places to Eat

If you're wandering the Shiomi Nawate, the old samurai street in the shadow of the castle, pause for lunch at the *Yakumo-an Restaurant*, next to the samurai house. It's a delightfully genteel noodle house with a pond full of very healthy-looking carp. Noodle dishes range from Y500 to Y750 for

Niku udon or Niku soba. Warigo-style noodles cost Y550; they're a local speciality, a dish of buckwheat noodles over which you pour broth.

Matsue's *kyodo ryōri* or regional cuisine includes 'seven exotic dishes from Lake Shinji'. They are:

Suzuki or *hosho yaki* – steam baked, paper-wrapped bass
Shirauo – whitebait tempura or sashimi
Amasagi – smelt tempura or teriyaki
Shijimi – tiny shellfish in miso soup
Moroge ebi – steamed shrimp
Koi – baked carp
Unagi – broiled freshwater eel

Kawa-kyo, near the Washington Hotel north of the river, offers these seven local specialities on an English menu with prices from Y250 (shijimi) to Y1500 (hosho yaki).

There are a number of *Benkei* yakitori (grilled-food restaurants) around town: there's a particularly good one with an illustrated menu near the Washington Hotel in Higashihonmachi. The tourist office at the station can give you a list of good local restaurants including numerous Izumo soba (regional noodle dish) specialists.

Restaurants with plastic meal replicas and the usual fast-food places can be found in the station area. There's a *Mister Donut* in the station and a *Dom Dom* burger place in the nearby Yayoi department store where there's also an excellent basement supermarket.

Getting There & Away

Matsue is on the JR San-in line which runs along the north coast. It takes a little over 2½ hours to travel via Yonago to Kurashiki on the south coast. See the Izumo section which follows for information on the two railway lines running west from Matsue. Matsue is also a jumping-off point for the Oki Islands (see the Oki Islands section of this chapter for details).

Yonago is the airport for Matsue. There are ANA flights to Tokyo and JAS flights to the Oki Islands.

Getting Around

Airport buses run between Matsue-onsen station and the airport, taking about 40 minutes. Tour buses leave from stand No 8 in front of JR Matsue station. Other bus routes include Matsue-onsen (No 1), Kaga (No 4), Izumo (No 6) and Yonago (No 7). You pick up a ticket on entering the bus and the relevant fare for your starting point is displayed as you leave.

Matsue is a good place to explore by bicycle: these can be hired at the Matsue and Matsue-onsen stations for Y500 for two hours or Y1000 per day.

AROUND MATSUE & IZUMO
松江、出雲の附近

There are a number of places of interest in the vicinity of Matsue and neighbouring Izumo.

Shinji-ko Lake

Sunset over the Yomega-shima islet in Shinji-ko Lake is a photographer's favourite

and the lake also provides the region's seven favourite local delicacies (see Matsue's Places to Eat section). At the western end of the lake, the garden in the Gakuen-ji Temple in Hirata is noted for its autumn colours.

At the south-western corner of the lake, the town of Shinji has the *Yakumo Honjin* (tel 0852-66-0136), one of the finest ryokan in Japan. Parts of the inn are 250 years old but if you stay here (from Y15,000 per night) ask for the old wing or you'll end up in the modern air-conditioned one. Casual visitors can have a look around for Y300.

Shimane-hantō Peninsula

North of Matsue, the coastline of the Shimane Peninsula has some spectacular scenery, particularly around Kaga, where Kaga no Kukedo is a cave you can enter by boat.

Fudoki no Oka & Shrines

Five km south of Matsue, around the village of Yakumo-mura, there are interesting shrines and important archaeological finds. Fudoki Hill is a 1st century AD archaeological site with finds displayed in the Fudoki no Oka Shiryōkan (Archaeological Museum) which is open from 9 am to 5 pm, closed Mondays. Nearby is the Okadayama Tumuli, an ancient burial mound. Haniwa pottery figures were found here, similar to those of Miyazaki on Kyūshū.

West of Fudoki no Oka is the ancient Kamosu-jinja Shrine, dedicated to Izanami, the mother of the Japanese archipelago. The shrine's Honden (Main Hall) dates from 1346. A little further west is the Yaegaki-jinja Shrine which is dedicated to the gods of marriage and commemorates a princess's rescue from an eight-headed serpent. The events are illustrated in fine 12th century wall paintings and the shrine sells erotic amulets to ensure fruitful marriages! There's a pretty little wood with shrines and ponds close by.

Fudoki no Oka is best visited on the way back from Bessho if you're going there. Get

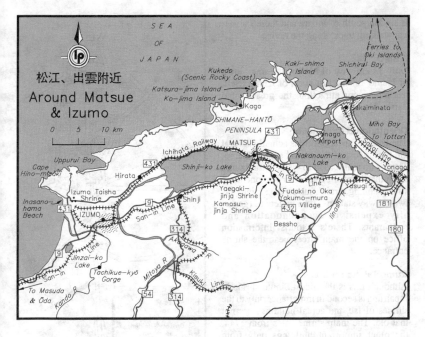

off at the Fudoki no Oka Iriguchi bus stop, walk to the archaeological centre and on to the two shrines then take another bus to Matsue from the Yaegaki-danchi Iriguchi bus stop, north of the Yaegaki-jinja Shrine.

Bessho

About 15 minutes south of Fudoki no Oka is Bessho, which features the Abe Eishiro Museum, dedicated to the craftsman credited with revitalising the making of paper by hand. The museum is open from 9 am to 4.30 pm and you can also visit paper-making workshops in the village. A bus from stand No 3 at the JR Matsue station will get you to Bessho; it stops at Fudoki no Oka on the way back.

Yasugi

East of Matsue on the Nakanoumi-ko Lake is Yasugi. The Kiyomizu Temple has a beautiful three storeyed pagoda and an important 11-faced statue of Kannon, the goddess of

mercy. The Adachi Art Museum in Yasugi has a beautiful garden.

Tachikue-kyō Gorge

Immediately south of Izumo is this km long, steep-sided gorge. It takes 30 minutes by rail to the gorge station from Izumo.

Mt Sanbe-san

Mt Sanbe is inland from Oda and reaches 1126 metres; its four separate peaks are known as the Father, the Mother, the Child and the Grandchild. It's part of the Daisen-Oki National Park and a popular skiing centre during the winter. Buses leave for Oda from Izumo.

It takes about an hour to climb Mt Sanbe from Sanbe Onsen. Buses regularly make the 20 km run from Oda to Sanbe Onsen. Ukinunonoike Lake is near the hot springs.

If you follow the Gogawa River southwest from Mt Sanbe, the Dangyo-kei Gorge is six km south of Inbara and there's a four km walking track along the ravine.

IZUMO 出雲

Only 33 km west of Matsue the small town of Izumo Taisha, just north of Izumo itself, has one major attraction, the great Izumo Taisha Shrine.

Orientation & Information

The Izumo Taisha Shrine is actually several km north-west of the central area of Izumo. There's no real reason to visit central Izumo since the shrine area, more or less one main street running straight up to the shrine, has two railway stations and a variety of (generally expensive) accommodation and restaurants. There's a tourist information office on the main street near the shrine entrance.

Izumo Taisha Shrine

Although this is the oldest Shinto shrine in Japan and is second in importance only to the shrines of Ise, the actual buildings are not that old. The main shrine dates from 1744, the other important buildings only from 1874. Nevertheless, the wooded grounds are pleasant to wander through and the shrine itself enjoys the 'borrowed scenery' of the Yakumo Hill as a backdrop. Okuninushi, to whom the shrine is dedicated, is kami (spirit god) of, among other things, marriage. So visitors to the shrine summon the deity by clapping four times rather than the normal two – twice for themselves and twice for their partner or partners to be.

The Haiden (Hall of Worship) is the first building inside the entrance torii and huge shimenawa (twisted straw ropes) hang over the entry. The main building is the largest shrine in Japan but the Honden (Main Hall) cannot be entered. The shrine compound is flanked by *jūku-sha*, long shelters where Japan's eight million kami (Shinto spirit gods) stay when they make their annual visit to Izumo.

On the south-eastern side of the compound is the Shinko-den (Treasure House) (open from 8 am to 4.30 pm) which has a

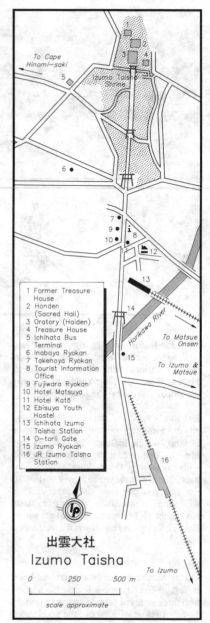

1 Former Treasure House
2 Honden (Sacred Hall)
3 Oratory (Haiden)
4 Treasure House
5 Ichihata Bus Terminal
6 Inabaya Ryokan
7 Takenoya Ryokan
8 Tourist Information Office
9 Fujiwara Ryokan
10 Hotel Matsuya
11 Hotel Katō
12 Ebisuya Youth Hostel
13 Ichihata Izumo Taisha Station
14 O—torii Gate
15 Izumo Ryokan
16 JR Izumo Taisha Station

出雲大社
Izumo Taisha

0   250   500 m

scale approximate

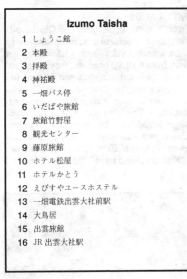

collection of shrine paraphernalia. Behind the main shrine building in the north-western corner is the former Shōkokan (Treasure Hall) with a large collection of images of Okuninushi in the form of Daikoku, a cheerful chubby character standing on two or three rice bales with a sack over his shoulder and a mallet in his hand. Usually his equally happy son Ebisu stands beside him with a fish tucked under his arm.

Cape Hino-misaki
It's less than 10 km from the Izumo Taisha Shrine to Cape Hinomisaki where you'll find a picturesque lighthouse, some fine views and an ancient shrine. On the way, you pass the pleasant Inasano-hama Beach, a good swimming beach just two km from Izumo Taisha station on the private Ichihata line. Buses run regularly from the station out to the cape, via the beach, taking just over half an hour to get to the cape.

The Hinomisaki-jinja Shrine is near the cape bus terminus. From the cablecar park, coastal paths lead north and south offering fine views, particularly from the top of the lighthouse (open from 8.30 am to 4 pm, entry Y100). Beyond the cape is Owashihama and then Uryū, two picturesque little fishing villages where you can stay in minshuku.

Festivals
The lunar calendar month corresponding to October is known throughout Japan as Kami-nazuki (Month without Gods). In Izumo, however, it is known as Kami-arizuki (Month with Gods) for this is the month when all the Shinto gods congregate for an annual get-together at the Izumo Shrine. An important festival takes place here from 11 to 17 October. The month of October is also a popular time for weddings at the shrine.

Places to Stay & Eat
There's no imperative reason to stay overnight in Izumo Taisha since it's easy to day-trip there from Matsue or simply pause there while travelling along the coast. If you do want to stop, there are a host of places along the main street of Izumo Taisha, which runs down from the shrine to the two railway stations.

The *Ebisuya Youth Hostel* (tel 0853-53-2157) is just off the main street and costs Y2100. On the street nearby is *Hotel Katō* (tel 0853-53-2214) with Japanese-style rooms at Y7000 per person including excellent meals. Other places along the main street include *Hotel Matsuya* at Y5000, the *Inabaya Ryokan*, the classy *Takenoya Ryokan* at Y10,000 and the *Fujiwara Ryokan* at Y8000.

Izumo's soba (noodles) get high praise, particularly in the dish known as warigo, buckwheat noodles over which you pour a broth. There are a number of noodle shops along the main street.

Getting There & Away
Izumo Taisha has two railway stations, the JR one at the end of the street leading down from the shrine and the private Ichihata line station about halfway up the street. The Ichihata line starts from Matsue-onsen

station in Matsue and runs on the northern side of Shinji-ko Lake to Izumo Taisha station. The JR line runs from JR Matsue station to JR Izumo station, where you transfer to an Izumo Taisha train. The private-line service also requires a change of train, at Kawato, but is more frequent (more than 20 services a day) and also takes you closer to the shrine. The private-line trip takes less than an hour and passes by rows of trees grown as windbreaks.

Izumo has an airport with JAS flights to and from Tokyo.

OKI ISLANDS 隠岐諸島

Directly north of Matsue, the Oki Islands with their spectacular scenery and steep cliffs are strictly for those who want to get away from it all. At one time, they were used to exile political prisoners and daimyō (on one occasion the emperor himself) who came out on the losing side of political squabbles. The islands consist of the larger Dōgo Island and the three smaller Dōzen Islands plus associated smaller islands. The seven km long cliffs of the Oki Kuniga coast of Nishino-shima Island, at times falling 250

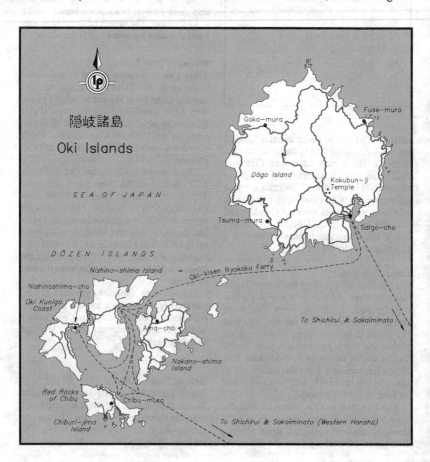

metres sheer into the sea, are particularly noteworthy. The Kokobun-ji Temple on Dōgo Island dates from the 8th century. Bullfights are an attraction during the summer months on Dōgo Island.

Places to Stay
On Dōgo Island the *Okino-shima Youth Hostel* (tel 08512-7-4321) costs Y2050 or Y2300 per night depending on the season. On Chibu Island the *Chibu Youth Hostel* (tel 08514-8-2355) costs Y1900 a night as does the *Takuhi Youth Hostel* (tel 08514-6-0860). The islands also have numerous minshuku and other accommodation.

Getting There & Away
There are ferry services to the Oki Islands from Shichirui or Sakaiminato. From Matsue, it's an hour by bus to Shichirui then 2½ hours by ferry. JAS flights operate to the islands from Yonago, Izumo and Osaka.

MASUDA 益田
Masuda is a modern industrial town with two temples, the Mampuku-ji and the Iko-ji. Both have notable gardens said to have been designed by the famed painter Sesshū, whose tomb is also in the vicinity. The temples are both about 10 minutes by bus from the JR station.

Masuda is the junction for the JR Yamaguchi line, which runs between Ogōri, Yamaguchi, Tsuwano and Masuda, and the JR San-in line, which runs from Shimonoseki, through Hagi and Masuda before continuing along the coast. Masuda is about 30 minutes from Tsuwano, one hour from Higashi-Hagi and two hours and 10 minutes from Izumo.

TSUWANO 津和野
Inland from Masuda is Tsuwano, a pleasant and relaxing mountain town with a fine castle, some interesting old buildings and a wonderful collection of carp swimming in the roadside water channels. The town is noted as a place to get to by the superb old steam-train service from Ogōri and as a place

to get around by bicycle, of which there are quite a phenomenal number for rent.

Orientation & Information
Tsuwano is a long, narrow town wedged into a north-south valley. The steep sides of the valley rise on either side of the town. The Tsuwanokawa River, JR Yamaguchi line and main road all run down the middle of the valley. The staff at the tourist information office by the railway station are very helpful. The number of souvenir shops around town are a clear indicator of just how popular Tsuwano is as a tourist destination.

Tsuwano-jō Castle
The ruins of Tsuwano-jō Castle seem to brood over the valley, the broken stone walls draping along the ridge. The castle was originally constructed in 1325 and remained in use until the Meiji Restoration. A chair lift takes you up the hillside for Y410 (return trip), from where there's a further 15 minute walk to the castle ruins. You can also walk up all the way from the Taikodani-Inari Shrine or directly from the valley floor, but the views from the chair lift are superb.

Taikodani-Inari Shrine
Just below the castle chair-lift station is this brightly painted shrine. You can walk up to it from the main road through a 'tunnel' created by over 1100 red torii gates. Festivals are held here on 15 March and 15 November each year. The annual Sagi Mai Festival (Heron Dance Festival) is performed on 20 and 27 July at the Yasaka-jinja Shrine, near the start of the torii tunnel.

Tonomachi District, Yorokan & Kyōdokan
Only the walls and some fine old gates remain from the former samurai quarter of Tonomachi. 'Ditches' (the word used in the local tourist brochure) is too harsh a word to apply to the water channels that run along-side this picturesque road: the crystal-clear water in the channels is home to numerous large and healthy carp. It's said that these goldfish were bred to provide a potential

source of food should the town ever be besieged. The feared attack never came and the fish have thrived.

At the northern end of the street is the Catholic church, a reminder that Nagasaki Christians were once exiled here. At the other end of Tonomachi, just north of the river, is the Yorokan. This was a school for young samurai in the late Edo period, a relatively innovative idea at that time. The building now houses an interesting small local museum with all sorts of farming and cooking equipment. It's open from 8.30 am to 5.30 pm daily and entry is Y160.

Across the river is the Kyōdokan, now a small local history museum with some displays concerning the Christian exiles. Hours are from 8.30 am to 5 pm and entry is Y310, but it's not of great interest.

Chapel of St Mary

The tiny Maria-Seido Chapel dates from 1948 when a German priest built it as a memorial to the exiled Catholics who died in the final period of Christian persecution before the anti-Christian laws were repealed in 1872. Tsuwano's own Via Dolorosa leads along the side of the valley from the chapel with markers for the stations of the cross. At the end of this winding pathway through the forest, a road leads down by the Yomei-ji Zen Temple which dates from 1420. The tomb of Mori Ogai (see Other Attractions section) is at the temple.

Other Attractions

The former homes of Mori Ogai, a highly regarded novelist, and Nishi Amane, who played an important part in the Meiji Restoration Government, are in the south of the town. Nearby is the Sekishukan, also known as the Washi Kaikan, a museum relating to washi (handmade paper) where you can watch the process of paper making. Entry is free.

The Dento Kogeisha centre also has paper-making displays. Across the road from it is the Jingasa with a museum of old items and costumes used in the annual Heron Dance Festival. The Tsuwano Industry

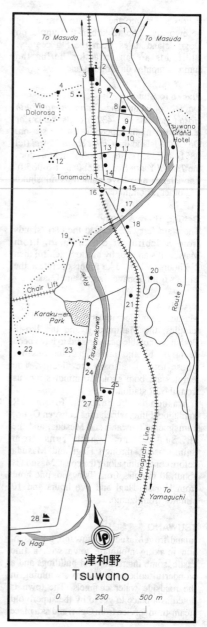

津和野
Tsuwano

0   250   500 m

Tsuwano	
1	Hotel Sun Route
2	Tourist Information Office
3	JR Tsuwano Station
4	Chapel of St Mary
5	Komyo-ji Temple
6	Tsuwano Industry Museum
7	Hoshi Ryokan
8	Post Office
9	Hiroshimaya Minshuku
10	Meigetsu Ryokan
11	Minshuku Mitsuwa
12	Yomei-ji Zen Temple
13	NTT
14	Hotel Kankō
15	Catholic Church
16	Bus Station
17	Yorokan Museum
18	Kyōdokan Museum
19	Taikodani-Inari Shrine
20	Aonesanso People's Lodge
21	Wakasagi no Yado Minshuku
22	Tsuwano-jō Castle Ruins
23	Dento Kogeisha Paper-Making Centre
24	Jingasa Museum
25	Washi Kaikan Museum
26	Mori Ogai House
27	Nishi Amane House
28	Tsuwano Youth Hostel

Tsuwano	
1	ホテルサンルート
2	観光案内所
3	JR 津和野駅
4	マリア聖堂
5	光明寺
6	産業資料館
7	ほし旅館
8	郵便局
9	広島屋民宿
10	明月旅館
11	みつわ民宿
12	永明寺
13	NTT
14	ホテルかんこ
15	カトリック教会
16	バスセンター
17	藩校養
18	郷土館
19	太鼓谷稲荷
20	国民宿合青野山荘
21	民宿若さぎの宿
22	津和野城跡
23	紙すき場
24	じんかさ博物館
25	紙会館
26	森鴎外旧居
27	西周旧居
28	津和野ユースホステル

Museum is right by the station and displays local crafts including paper making and saké brewing. It's open daily. South of the town is the Washibara Hachiman-gū Shrine, about four km from the station. Archery contests on horseback are held here on 2 April.

Festivals
The Sagi Mai (Heron Dance) Festival is a major annual festival held in July. Lighted lanterns are floated down the river in August.

Places to Stay
The information counter at the railway station will help with bookings at the town's many minshuku and ryokan.

Youth Hostels The *Tsuwano Youth Hostel* (tel 08567-2-0373) has 44 beds at Y2100 per night and is a couple of km south of the station.

Minshuku & Ryokan The *Wakasagi no Yado Minshuku* (tel 08567-2-1146) is not in the town centre but it's a pleasant, friendly and frequently recommended place at Y5500 per person with two meals. Other similarly priced minshuku and ryokan include the *Hoshi Ryokan, Hiroshimaya Minshuku* and *Minshuku Mitsuwa*. All are centrally located (see the map) and include two meals. The *Meigetsu Ryokan* (tel 08567-2-0685) is a traditional and more expensive ryokan with costs from Y7000 to Y15,000. This is a place where you may get to try Tsuwano's famine food – carp!

Across the river and away from the centre is the government-run *Aonesanso People's Lodge* (a kokuminshukusha) costing Y5310 including two meals.

Hotels Hotels include the *Sun Route* (tel 08567-2-3232), a bland modern hotel overlooking the town from the eastern slope of the valley with rooms at Y7500/11,000 for singles/doubles. *Hotel Kankō* is right in the centre of town while the *Tsuwano Grand Hotel* is also on the eastern valley side, by Route 9.

Places to Eat
If you're not eating at a minshuku or ryokan there are restaurants and cafés around town, some specialising in the local san-cai (mountain vegetable) dishes.

Getting There & Away
The JR Yamaguchi line runs from Ogōri on the south coast through Yamaguchi to Tsuwano and on to Masuda on the north coast. It takes about one hour 15 minutes by limited express from Ogōri to Tsuwano and about 30 minutes from Masuda to Tsuwano. A bus to Tsuwano from Hagi takes nearly two hours.

During the late April to early May Golden Week holiday, from 20 July to 31 August and on certain other Sundays and national holidays, a steam locomotive service operates between Ogōri and Tsuwano. It takes two hours each way and you should book well ahead.

Getting Around
Tsuwano is packed with bicycle rental places; at the height of the tourist season the town must be one enormous bicycle jam. Rental rates start from Y400 for two hours, with a maximum of Y800 for a day.

Northern Yamaguchi-ken 山口県の北部

Yamaguchi Prefecture, marking the western end of Honshū, straddles both the southern San-yō coast and the northern San-in coast. The northern stretch includes the historically important town of Hagi.

HAGI 萩
If there were a single reason for travelling along the northern coast of Western Honshū it would have to be Hagi, with its interesting combination of temples and shrines, a fascinating old samurai quarter, some picturesque castle ruins and fine coastal views. Hagi also has important historical connections with the events of the Meiji Restoration. It is ironical that the town's claim to fame is its role in propelling Japan directly from the feudal to the modern era while its attractions are principally its feudal past. Hagi is also noted for its fine pottery.

History
Hagi in Honshū and Kagoshima in Kyūshū were the two centres of unrest which played the major part in the events leading up to the Meiji Restoration. Japan's long period of isolation from the outside world under Tokugawan rule had, by the mid-19th century, created tensions approaching breaking point. The rigid stratification of society had resulted in an oppressed peasantry, while the progressive elements of the nobility realised Japan had slipped far behind the rapidly industrialising European nations and the USA. The arrival of Commodore Perry brought matters to a humiliating head as the 'barbarians' simply dictated their terms to the helpless Japanese.

Japan could not stand up against the West if it did not adopt Western technology, and this essential modernisation could not take place under the feudal shogunate. Restoring the emperor to power, even if only as a figurehead, was the route the progressive samurai chose and Yoshida Shōin of Hagi was one of the leaders in this movement. On the surface, he was also a complete failure. In 1854, in order to study the ways of the West first hand, he attempted to leave Japan on Perry's ship, only to be handed over to the authorities and imprisoned in Edo (Tokyo).

When he returned to Hagi he hatched a plot to kill a shogunate official, but talked about it so much that word leaked out to his enemies. He was arrested again and in 1859, at the age of 29, he was executed. Fortunately, while Shōin was a failure when it came to action he was a complete success when it came to inspiration and in 1865 his followers led a militia of peasants and samurai which overturned the Chōshū Government of Hagi. The Western powers supported the new blood in Hagi and Kagoshima and when the shogunate army moved against the new government in Hagi, it was defeated. That the downfall of the shogunate had come at the hands of an army, not just of samurai but of peasants as well, was further proof of the changes taking place.

In late 1867, the forces of Kagoshima and Hagi routed the shogunate, the emperor was restored to nominal power and in early 1868, the capital was shifted from Kyoto to Tokyo, as Edo soon became known. To this day, Hagi remains an important site for visitors interested in the history of modern Japan and Yoshida Shōin 'lives on' at the Shōin-jinja Shrine.

Orientation & Information

Hagi consists of three parts: western and central Hagi are effectively an island created by the Hashimotogawa and Matsumotogawa rivers, while eastern Hagi (with the major JR station, Higashi-Hagi) lies on the eastern bank of the Matsumotogawa River.

The main road through central Hagi starts from JR Hagi station and runs north, past the bus station in the centre of town. There's a wide variety of shops along Tamachi arcade, close to the bus station. West of this central area is the old samurai quarter of Jokamachi,

with its picturesque streets and interesting old buildings. More interesting old buildings can be found in Horiuchi to the north-west and Teremachi to the north-east of Jokamachi.

Hagi's tourist information office is a little difficult to find. On the main road through town, just south of the bus station, is a Ringer Hut, an outlet of the Japanese fast-noodle chain which looks a bit like a New England church building. Across the road from it is a bank-type building and the tourist office is in the back of that building. There's also an information counter at Higashi-Hagi station.

Hagi Pottery & Kilns

Connoisseurs of Japanese pottery rank Hagi-yaki, the pottery of Hagi, second only to Kyoto's raku-yaki. As in other pottery centres in Japan, the craft came from Korea when Korean potters were brought back after Hideyoshi's unsuccessful invasion in the late 1500s. There are a number of shops and kilns where you can see the pottery being made and browse through the finished products. Hagi-yaki is noted for its fine glazes and delicate pastel colours. The small notch in the base of each piece is also a reminder of the pottery's long history. In the feudal era only samurai were permitted to use the pottery, but by cutting a tiny notch in some pieces, the potters 'spoilt' their work and this pottery could then be used by the common folk.

The Shizuki Kiln in Horiuchi has particularly fine pieces. The western end of Hagi has several interesting pottery kilns near Shizuki-kōen Park. Hagi-yaki pottery can also be inspected in the Hagi-yaki Togei Kaikan Museum near the park; there's a big souvenir area downstairs.

Castle Ruins & Shizuki-kōen Park

There's not much of the old Hagi-jō Castle to see, apart from the typically imposing outer walls and its surrounding moat. The castle was built in 1604 but dismantled in 1874 during the Meiji Restoration; since Hagi played a leading part in the end of the feudal era and the downfall of the shogunate,

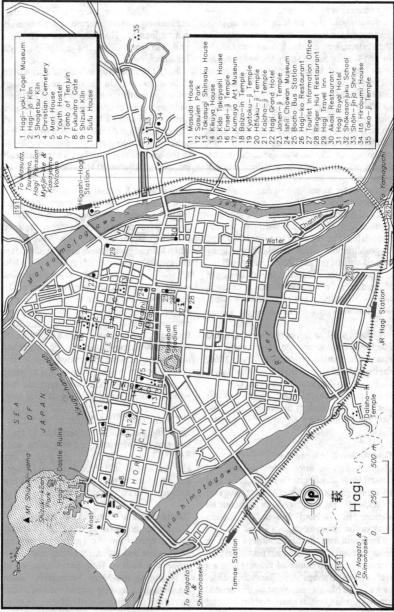

1 Hagi-yaki Togei Museum
2 Hagi-jō Kiln
3 Shogetsu Kiln
4 Christian Cemetery
5 Mori House
6 Youth Hostel
7 Tomb of Tenjun
8 Fukuhara Gate
9 Shizuki Kiln
10 Sufu House

11 Masuda House
12 Sosuien Park
13 Takasugi Shinsaku House
14 Kikuya House
15 Kido Takayoshi House
16 Ensei-ji Temple
17 Kumaya Art Museum
18 Baizo-in Temple
19 Kyotoku-ji Temple
20 Hōfuku-ji Temple
21 Kaicho- Temple
22 Hagi Grand Hotel
23 Jonen-ji Temple
24 Ishii Chawan Museum
25 Bocho Bus Station
26 Hagi-ko Restaurant
27 Tourist Information Office
28 Ringer Hut Restaurant
29 Hagi Travel Inn
30 Akasi Restaurant
31 Hagi Royal Hotel
32 Shōkasonjuku School
33 Shōin-jinja Shrine
34 Itō Hirobumi House
35 Toko-ji Temple

Hagi 萩

Hagi

1 萩焼陶芸会館
2 萩焼窯元
3 松月窯元
4 キリシタン墓地
5 厚狭毛利家長屋
6 萩指月ユースホステル
7 天樹院墓所
8 旧福原家萩屋敷門
9 指月窯元
10 旧周布家長屋門
11 益田家老長屋
12 そすい園
13 高杉晋作旧宅
14 菊屋家
15 木戸孝允旧宅
16 円政寺
17 熊谷美術館
18 梅蔵院
19 本行寺
20 保福寺
21 海潮寺
22 萩グランドホテル
23 じょうぬん寺
24 石井茶碗美術館
25 防長バスセンター
26 萩こレストラン
27 観光案内所
28 リンガーハット
29 萩トラベルイン
30 明石レストラン
31 萩ロヤルホテル
32 松下村塾
33 松陰神社
34 伊藤博文旧宅
35 東光寺

ruins you can climb the hillside to the 143 metre peak of Mt Shizuki-yama. Entry to the castle is Y200 and the entry ticket also covers the Mori House. Also in the park is the small Hagi Shiryokan Museum, open daily.

Mori House

South of the park is Mori House, a row (terrace) house where samurai soldiers were once barracked. It's open daily and the same ticket covers entry to the castle ruins. There's an interesting Christian cemetery to the south of the samurai house.

Jokamachi, Horiuchi & Teremachi

Between the modern town centre and the moat that separates western Hagi from central Hagi is the old samurai residential area with many streets lined by whitewashed samurai walls. This area is fascinating to wander around and there are a number of interesting houses and temples, particularly in the area known as Jokamachi. Teremachi is noted particularly for its many fine old temples.

Kikuya House The Kikuya family were merchants rather than samurai but their wealth and special connections allowed them to build a house well above their station. The house dates from 1604 and has a fine gate, attractive gardens and there are numerous examples of construction details and materials which would normally have been forbidden to the merchant class. Entry to the house is Y370 and it is open from 9 am to 5 pm.

Other Houses Nearby is Kido Takayoshi House (open from 9 am to 5 pm) and Takasugi Shinsaku House which is still a private residence. Takasugi was a student of Shōin Yoshida and played a key role in the events leading up to the Meiji Restoration. Interesting houses in the Horiuchi area include the Masuda and Sufu houses.

Kumaya Art Museum The art museum in Jokamachi has a small and not terribly exciting collection including tea bowls, screens

it was appropriate that the town also led the way in the removal of feudal symbols.

Now the grounds are a pleasant park with the Shizukiyama-jinja Shrine, Hananoe Teahouse and other buildings. From the castle and other items in a series of small warehouses dating from 1768. The Kumaya family handled the trading and commercial operations of Hagi's ruling Mori family. Opening hours are from 8.30 am to 5.30 pm; from 8 am to 5 pm from December to February inclusive. Entry is an expensive Y500.

Other Buildings The Horiuchi and Teremachi areas are dotted with temples and shrines: if you wander around the area you will pass by many of them. The Fukuhara Gate is one of the finest of the samurai gates in Horiuchi. Nearby is the Tomb of Tenjuin, dedicated to Terumoto Mori, the founder of the Mori dynasty. There are numerous old temples in the Teremachi area including the two storeyed Kaicho-ji Temple, the Hōfuku-ji with its Jizō statues (the Buddha for travellers and the souls of departed children), the Jonen-ji Temple with its gate carvings and the Baizo-in Temple with its Buddha statues. The large Kyotoku-ji Temple has a fine garden.

Tea-bowl enthusiasts may find the Ishii Chawan Museum in the central Tamachi shopping arcade interesting. The museum is upstairs in the building at the far eastern end at the end of the arcade. It's closed on Tuesdays and for much of December–January.

Toko-ji Temple
East of the river stands this pretty temple with the tombs of five Mori lords. The odd-numbered lords (apart from number one) were buried here; the even-numbered ones at the Daisho-in Temple. The stone walkways on the hillside behind the temple are flanked by almost 500 stone lanterns erected by the lord's servants. Entry is Y100.

Shōin-jinja Shrine
West of the Toko-ji Temple is this Meiji era shrine to Shōin Yoshida, an important force in the Meiji Restoration. Events from his life are illustrated in the nearby Shōin Yoshida Rekishikan (Shōin Yoshida History Hall) which is open from 9 am to 5 pm daily. Just south of the shrine is the Itō Hirobumi House, the early home of the four-term prime minister who was a follower of Shōin Yoshida and later drafted the Meiji Constitution. There are a number of other places connected with Shōin Yoshida in the vicinity including his tomb near the Toko-ji Temple and his school (the Shōkasonjuku) in the shrine grounds.

Daisho-in Temple
South of the centre, near the JR Hagi station, this funerary temple was the resting place for the first two Mori generations and after that, all even-numbered generations of the Mori lords. Like the better known and more visited Toko-ji Temple, it has pathways lined by stone lanterns erected by the Mori lord's faithful retainers. The original Mori lord's grave is accompanied by the graves of seven of his principal retainers, all of whom committed seppuku (ritual suicide) after their lord died. An eighth grave is that of a retainer to one of the retainers who also joined in the festivities. The shogunate quickly banned similar excessive displays of samurai loyalty. Entry to the temple is Y100.

Myōjin-ike Pond & Kasayama Volcano
A couple of km east of the town, the Myōjin-ike Pond is actually connected to the sea and shelters a variety of saltwater fish. The road beside this small lagoon continues to the top of Kasayama, a small extinct volcano cone from where there are fine views along the coast.

Other Attractions
At the south-eastern end of the Hagi 'island', carp can be seen swimming in the roadside Aiba water channel. East of the town and close to the main road to Masuda, is the Hagi Hansharo, an old reverberating furnace dating from 1858 which was used to make gun and ship parts.

Places to Stay
Hagi Youth Hostel (tel 0838-22-3558) is south of the castle at the western end of the town, has 100 beds at Y2100 per night and has rental bicycles. Tamae is the nearest JR station.

Pension Hagi (tel 0838-28-0071) is a pleasant, modern pension 10 km east of town in the fishing port of Nagato-Ohi (pronounced *oy*). The pension is just back from the main road and costs Y4000 per person including breakfast. JR Nagato-Ohi station is two stops from Higashi-Hagi and the pension's owner, Eukio Yamazaki, who learnt his excellent English in Papua New Guinea, will meet you at the station. Hagi also has a number of ryokan and minshuku and a people's lodge (kokuminshukusha).

The *Hagi Royal Hotel* (tel 0838-25-9595) is right by the Higashi-Hagi station and has rooms at Y7000/14,000. There are cheaper business hotels in town like the *Hagi Travel Inn* (tel 0838-25-2640) just across the river from the Higashi-Hagi station, with rooms at Y5000/10,000.

Places to Eat

There are numerous restaurants in the central area around the bus station, including a couple of nice cake and pastry places – *Kobeya* and *Gateaux Koube*. Just south-west of the station is *Hagi-ko*, a cheerful and bright place with lots of plastic meals to help you make your selection – spaghetti, noodles and other dishes cost Y320 to Y500 and a beer is Y500.

Akasi is east of the centre, on the main through route, and is a better restaurant with good teishoku meals. There are some fast-food specialists including one of the *Ringer Hut* noodle restaurants (except here it's called *Pao*) across from the building with the tourist office.

Getting There & Away

The JR San-in line runs along the north coast through Tottori, Matsue, Masuda and Hagi to Shimonoseki. The faster expresses take four hours to or from Matsue

JR buses to Hagi take 1½ hours from Ogōri, south of Hagi on the Tokyo-Osaka-Hakata shinkansen line. The buses go via Akiyoshi-dai and there are also buses from Yamaguchi. Buses also operate between Tsuwano and Hagi, taking a little under two hours.

Getting Around

Hagi is a good place to explore on a bicycle and there are plenty of bicycle rental places including one at the youth hostel and several around the castle and JR Higashi-Hagi station. Bocho Bus Company tour buses operate from the Bocho bus station.

HAGI TO SHIMONOSEKI 萩至下関

There's some good coastal scenery, small fishing villages and interesting countryside along the coast road between Hagi and Shimonoseki, at the western extremity of Honshū.

Omi-shima Island, with its scenic, rocky coast, is immediately north of Nagato (population 28,000) and connected to the mainland by a bridge. The island is part of the Kita Nagato Coastal Park which extends eastwards beyond Hagi.

AKIYOSHI-DO CAVE 秋芳洞

The rolling Akiyoshi-dai tablelands are

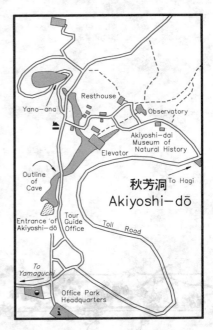

about halfway between Yamaguchi on the southern San-yō coast and Hagi on the northern San-in coast. The green fields are dotted with curious rock spires and beneath this picturesque plateau are hundreds of limestone caverns, the largest of which, Akiyoshi-dō, is open to the public.

The Akiyoshi-dō (*dō* means 'cave') is of interest principally for its size; the stalagmites and stalactites are not particularly noteworthy. In all, the cave extends about 10 km, a river flows through it and a pathway runs through the cave for about a km. At the mid-point of the cave walk you can take an elevator up to the surface where there is a lookout over the surrounding country. There are entrances to the cave at both ends of the pathway as well as at the elevator, and buses run between the two ends if you do not want to retrace your steps. The cave is open from 8.30 am to 4.30 pm daily; entry is Y 1030.

The Akiyoshi-dai Museum of Natural History has exhibits concerning the cave and the surrounding area.

Places to Stay

The *Akiyoshi-dai Youth Hostel* (tel 0837-62-0341) is close to the cave entrance and has 120 beds at Y1900. There is also the *Rest House* and a variety of accommodation around the cave area including the *Kokusai Kankō Hotel Shuhokan* (tel 0837-62-0311) and the *Wakatakesanso Kokuminshukusha* (tel 0837-62-0126).

Getting There & Away

It takes a little over an hour by bus from Yamaguchi or Hagi to the cave. Buses also run to the cave from Ogōri, Shimonoseki and other centres.

Shikoku　　　　　　　　　四国

In Japan's feudal past the island of Shikoku was divided into four *(shi)* regions *(koku)*, which today, have become four prefectures. Although Shikoku is Japan's fourth largest island, it's predominantly rural and very much off the tourist track. Apart from scenery, the Ritsurin-kōen Garden in Takamatsu and four castles (Kōchi, Marugame, Matsuyama and Uwajima) which managed to survive the Meiji Restoration and WW II, there are no overwhelming attractions. The construction of the Seto-ōhashi Bridge linking Shikoku with Honshū has made the island much more accessible.

THE 88 TEMPLE CIRCUIT

Japan's best known pilgrimage is Kōbō Daishi's 88 Temple Circuit of Shikoku. Kūkai (774-835), who became Kōbō Daishi after his death, is the most revered of Japan's saints. He founded the Shingon Buddhist sect in 807 after a visit to China. Shingon is related to Tantric Buddhism with its mystic rituals and multi-armed deities.

Kōbō Daishi was born in Shikoku, and it is said he personally selected the 88 temples which make up the circuit. Today, most pilgrims on the circuit travel by tour bus but some still walk – set aside six weeks and be prepared to walk over 1000 km if you want to join them. Some of the temples are only a few hundred metres apart and you can walk to five or six in a day. However, at the other extreme, it can be 100 km between two temples. Oliver Statler's book *Japanese Pilgrimage* follows the temple circuit.

Individually, none of the temples is particularly interesting; it's the whole circuit that counts. The pilgrims, known as *henro*, wear white robes *(hakui)*, carry a staff *(otsue)* and often top the ensemble with a straw hat *(kasa)*. Temple circuiters stamp their robes with the temples' red seals.

GETTING THERE & AWAY

Air services connect major cities in Shikoku with Tokyo, Osaka and other centres on Honshū. Numerous ferries ply the waters of the Inland Sea, linking Shikoku with the Inland Sea islands and with ports on the San-yō coast of Honshū. Takamatsu and Matsuyama are particularly busy Shikoku ports, though there are many others. The opening of the road and rail Seto-ōhashi Bridge in 1988 has considerably simplified access to the island and there are frequent train services from Okayama to both Takamatsu and Matsuyama.

Kagawa-ken　　　香川県

TAKAMATSU　　高松

Takamatsu (population 330,000) was founded during the rule of Hideyoshi as the castle town of the feudal lord of Kagawa. At that time, Takamatsu was known as Sanuki. The town was virtually destroyed in WW II but rapidly rebounded after the war. The completion of the Seto-ōhashi Bridge has reinforced Takamatsu's importance as a major arrival point on Shikoku. Despite the new rail link, it remains an important port for Inland Sea ferry services, particularly to popular Shōdo-shima Island. The town has an important garden, the nearby Shikoku-mura Village Museum and the very popular Kotohira-gū Shrine is an easy day trip.

Orientation & Information

JR Takamatsu station seems to have a surfeit of tourist offices and information counters. Walk outside the station, through the car park to the six-sided tourist information office by the roadside.

The station is close to the waterfront and beside the ferry terminal buildings. Chūō-dōri, the main road in Takamatsu, leads out from the station with the private Kotoden

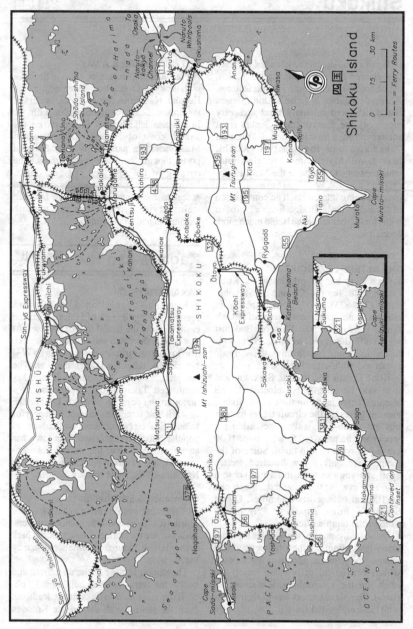

Shikoku Island

四国

0   15   30 km

---- = Ferry Routes

Continued on Inset

Chikko station almost immediately on the left. A busy shopping arcade extends across Chūō-dōri Rd and then runs parallel to it, passing through the entertainment district. The main shopping area is further south around the Kotoden Kawaramachi station area. Takamatsu is surprisingly sprawling, it's a long walk (two km) to the Ritsurin-kōen Garden from the station.

Ritsurin-kōen Garden

Although not one of Japan's 'big three' gardens, Ritsurin-kōen could easily be a contender for that list. The garden, which was first constructed in the mid-1600s, winds around a series of ponds with lookouts, tea-rooms, bridges and islands. The garden actually took more than a century to complete and was used as a villa garden for over 200 years prior to the Meiji Restoration. In one direction, Mt Shiun forms a backdrop to the garden but in the other direction, there is some much less impressive 'borrowed scenery' in the form of dull modern buildings.

In the garden, the Sanuki Folkcraft Museum displays local crafts. The old Kikugetsu-tei Teahouse, also known as the Chrysanthemum Moon Pavilion, is a feudal-era teahouse. Entry to the garden is Y310 and it's open from sunrise to sunset. There's an extra charge for the teahouse. You can get there by Kotoden, JR train or by bus from platform No 2 at the JR station.

Takamatsu-jō Castle

There's very little left of Takamatsu Castle which is just a stone's throw from the JR and Kotoden stations. The castle grounds, which now form the pleasant Tamamo Park, are only one-ninth their original size. When the castle was constructed in 1588, the moats on three sides were filled with sea water while the sea itself formed the fourth side of the castle. Entry is only Y100, and it's open from 8.30 am to 6 pm.

Yashima

The 292 metre high table-top plateau of Yashima stands five km from the centre of Takamatsu. Today, it's the site for the Yashima-ji Temple (No 84 on the temple circuit) and offers fine views over the surrounding countryside and the Inland Sea, but in the 12th century it was the site for titanic struggles between the Genji and Heike clans. The temple treasure house's collection relates to the battle. Just behind the treasure house is the Pond of Blood, where the victorious warriors washed the blood from their swords, staining the water red.

A funicular railway runs up to the top of Yashima Hill from the left of the shrine at the bottom. The cost is Y510 one way or Y1010 return. At the top you can rent a bicycle (Y300 plus Y1000 deposit) to pedal around the attractions – it's a long walk otherwise.

You can get to Yashima by private Kotoden train or, less frequently, by JR train which also drops you a bit further from the base of the hill. It takes about 20 minutes and costs Y190 by JR, slighty less by Kotoden. Buses also run directly to the top of the hill.

Shikoku-mura Village

At the bottom of Yashima Hill is an excellent village museum with old buildings brought from all over Shikoku and neighbouring islands. There are explanations in English of the many buildings and their history. Highlights include a traditional suspension bridge (the vines are actually reinforced with steel cables but it certainly looks the part). There is only one authentic bridge left in Shikoku, across the Iyadani-kei Gorge, and villagers came from there to construct this replica. (See the Iyadani-kei Gorge section in this chapter.)

Shōdo-shima Island is still famed for its traditional farmers' kabuki performances and the fine village kabuki stage came from that island. Other interesting buildings include a border guardhouse from the Tokugawa era when travel was tightly restricted and a bark steaming hut which was used in the paper-making process. There's also a water-powered rice hulling machine and a fine old stone storehouse. Entry is Y500; the small museum in the village costs an extra Y100 and you can safely skip it. The

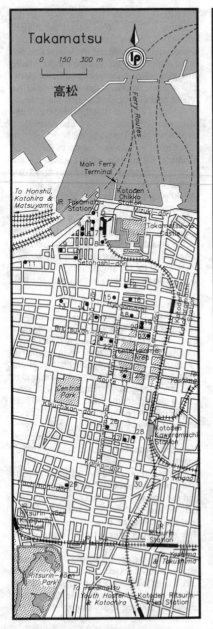

Takamatsu

1 Tourist Information Office
2 Mister Donut
3 Station Hotel
4 Pearl Hotel
5 Urban Hotel
6 ANA
7 Takamatsu Grand Hotel
8 JAL
9 New Getukōen Hotel
10 Hotel New Frontier
11 Century Hotel
12 McDonald's
13 Tenkatsu Restaurant
14 Takamatsu Tōkyū Inn
15 Post Office
16 Mitsukoshi Department Store
17 Hotel Rich
18 Hotel Kawaroku
19 Kawa-Huko Restaurant
20 Grill Yama
21 Public Art Gallery
22 Italian Tomato Restaurant
23 Kamaizumi Restaurant
24 Takamatsu Washington Hotel
25 Royal Park Hotel
26 McDonald's
27 Tokiwa Honkan Ryokan
28 Mister Donut
29 Keio Plaza Hotel
30 NTT

village is open from 8.30 am to 4.30 or 5 pm.
See the Takamatsu Places to Eat section for
information about the popular noodle restaurant just outside Shikoku-mura.

Other Attractions
Just offshore from Yashima is Megi-jima
Island, also known as Oniga-shima or
'Demon Island'. It was here that Momotarō,
the legendary 'Peach Boy', met and conquered the horrible demon. You can tour the
caves where the demon was said to have
hidden. See the Okayama-ken section in the
Western Honshū chapter for the Momotarō
story.

Places to Stay
Hostel The *Takamatsu-shi Youth Hostel* (tel
0878-85-2024) is some distance south of
Takamatsu, and can be reached via the

Takamatsu

1 高松市観光案内所
2 ミスタドナツ
3 ステーションホテル
4 パールホテル
5 アーバンホテル
6 ANA
7 高松グランドホテル
8 JAL
9 ニュー月光園ホテル
10 ホテルニューフロンティア
11 センチュリーホテル
12 マクドナルド
13 天勝本店
14 高松東急イン
15 郵便局
16 三越百貨店
17 ホテルリッチ
18 ホテル川六
19 川富本店
20 やまグリル
21 高松市美術館
22 イタリアントマトレストラン
23 かまいずみレストラン
24 高松ワシントンホテル
25 ロヤルパークホテル
26 マクドナルド
27 常盤本店
28 ミスタドナツ
29 京王プラザホテル
30 NTT

Kotoden line to Kotohira. The hostel charges Y1740 per night. The *Yashima-Sansō Youth Hostel* (tel 0878-22-3656), near the Shikoku-mura Village at Yashima, costs Y1900 per night.

Hotels There are a number of budget business hotels a stone's throw from the station. The *Pearl Hotel* (tel 0878-22-3382), though small, is clean and quite acceptable with rooms at Y4200 to Y5200 for singles and Y8500 to Y10,500 for doubles or twins. Next door is the *Urban Hotel* (tel 0878-23-3001) with singles/doubles from Y4400/8200. Also very close to the station is the *Station Hotel* (tel 0878-21-6989) with singles from Y5500 to Y7000, and doubles or twins from Y11,000 to Y13,000.

A few minutes walk away from the station is the *New Getukōen Hotel* (tel 0878-22-0953) which is definitely at the grotty end of the business hotel spectrum. Singles with sink and toilet but no bath (these rooms are upstairs and more-or-less on the roof) are Y3200. The beds are clean and neat, but otherwise it's well worn, shabby and cheap.

The *Hotel New Frontier* (tel 0878-51-1088) is among the better (and more expensive) hotels; it charges from Y7000/10,000 for singles/doubles. The *Takamatsu Grand Hotel* (tel 0878-51-5757), on top of the Kotoden Chikko station, overlooks the Takamatsu Castle grounds and is conveniently situated only a few steps from the JR station. Singles/doubles cost from Y5300/11,000 plus a 10% surcharge.

The *Takamatsu Tōkyū Inn* (tel 0878-21-0109) is a popular chain hotel on Chūō-dōri Rd, just beyond the arcade. Singles cost from Y6200 to Y7600, doubles from Y12,600. The *Hotel Rich* (tel 0878-22-3555), on the opposite side of Chūō-dōri Rd, has singles from Y6000 to Y7500, doubles and twins from Y12,000 to Y20,000. Much further down Chūō-dōri, almost at the Ritsurin Garden, is the *Keio Plaza Hotel* (tel 0878-34-5511) with singles from Y6600 to Y9000 and twins from Y9000 to Y20,000.

The *Royal Park Hotel* (tel 0878-23-2222) has singles/doubles from Y7000/9000. A few steps away is the *Takamatsu Washington Hotel* (tel 0878-22-7111).

Ryokan Takamatsu has a couple of expensive but centrally located ryokan. *Hotel Kawaroku* (tel 0878-21-5666) is south of the shopping arcade, just off Chūō-dōri Rd. Rooms cost from around Y7000/12,000 for singles/doubles without meals and from around Y15,000 per person with meals.

Near the Kotoden Kawaramachi station and close to the shopping arcade is the traditional *Tokiwa Honkan* (tel 0878-61-5577) which costs from Y12,000 to Y20,000 per person including meals.

Places to Eat

Every larger railway station in Shikoku seems to have an *Andersen's* bakery, also known as *Willie Winkie*. The one at JR Takamatsu station is good for an economical breakfast. Across the road is a *Mister Donut* and there are a number of other restaurants nearby. The Kotoden Kawaramachi station is also a centre for a variety of cheap eats.

The best selection of restaurants is found along the shopping arcade in the entertainment district. *Kawa-Huko* is a pleasant restaurant offering good Sanuki noodles, tempura and other dishes; plastic meals are also on display. Just beyond Kawa-Huko is the *Grill Yama* which offers a variety of grilled meat dishes. The *Kamaizumi Restaurant*, a block east on Ferry-dōri Ave, specialises in Sanuki noodles – you may see them being made in the window. On Bijutsukan-dōri there's a branch of the popular *Italian Tomato* restaurant chain.

Backtracking along the arcade across Chūō-dōri Rd and continuing a few doors beyond the end of the arcade, you'll find *Tenkatsu*, a popular restaurant with a central bar around a large fish tank. (You know the fish is fresh, you see it die.)

If you're out at Yashima at lunch time, head for the restaurant with a water wheel, right beside the Shikoku-mura Village car

park. For Y350, you get a hearty bowl of Sanuki udon and a bowl of soup which you spice up with chopped spring onions and then dip the noodles in.

Getting There & Away

Air Japan Air Systems (JAS) have flights to and from Fukuoka and Tokyo; All Nippon Airways (ANA) flies to and from Osaka and Tokyo.

Train The Seto-ōhashi Bridge has brought Takamatsu much closer to the main island of Honshū. From Tokyo, you can take the shinkansen to Okayama, change trains there and be in Takamatsu in five hours. The Okayama-Takamatsu section takes about an hour.

From Takamatsu, the JR Kotoku line runs south-east to Tokushima and the JR Yosan line runs west to Matsuyama. The Yosan line branches off at Tadotsu and becomes the Dosan line, turning south-west to Kotohira and Kōchi. The private Kotoden line also runs direct to Kotohira.

Bus Direct buses also operate between Tokyo and Takamatsu: the 'Hello Bridge' service costs Y10,300 one way.

Ferry Takamatsu is also an important ferry terminus with services to ports in the Inland Sea, and on Honshū including Kōbe (4½ hours) and Osaka (5½ hours). Prior to the construction of the bridge, Uno, to the south of Okayama, was the main connection point to Takamatsu. It's still a quick way to make

---

Cruel Cuisine

Being cruel to your food is a Japanese tradition – you know the fish is fresh if it squeals when you eat it – and Takamatsu is certainly a centre for it. Sugata-zukuri is a prized dish here, sea bream sliced seconds before it's placed in front of you. If you're quick with the chopsticks you can get the first mouthfuls down before it dies. I ate one night at Tenkatsu, where the bar encloses a large tank of fish and other sea life. When a customer ordered octopus, the unfortunate creature was scooped out of the tank and four tentacles were hacked off. Then, still living, but less than complete, the octopus was tossed back into the tank to crawl forlornly off to a corner.

Tony Wheeler ∎

the Honshū-Shikoku trip since Uno-Okayama trains connect with the ferry departures. Takamatsu is also the easiest jumping-off point for visiting attractive Shōdo-shima Island. Takamatsu's ferry terminal buildings are right beside the JR station.

Getting Around

Takamatsu Airport is 16 km from the city and the bus, which departs from outside JR Takamatsu station, takes about half an hour.

Takamatsu has a local bus service but for most visitors, the major attractions, principally the Ritsurin-kōen Garden and Yashima can easily be reached on the JR Kotoku line or the more frequent Kotoden line service. The main Kotoden junction is Kawaramachi although the line ends at the Chikko station, just across from the JR Takamatsu station.

Takamatsu seems to have an amazing number of cyclists, most of whom (sensibly) use the sidewalks rather than the road. Inevitably, there seem to be many collisions; even late at night in the almost deserted arcades, Takamatsu cyclists contrive to run into one another.

WEST FROM TAKAMATSU
Sakaide

Sakaide, a port city on the JR Yosan line, has nothing of interest for the traveller; it's at the southern end of the Seto-ōhashi Bridge. See the Around Okayama section in the Western Honshū chapter for more information on this important bridge.

Marugame

On the JR Yosan line, just 25 minutes west of Takamatsu and close to the southern end of the Seto-ōhashi Bridge, there are some remains of the 1597 Marugame-jō Castle with its impressive stepped stone walls. The ruins are about a km south of the JR station. The Shiwaku Islands (see the Inland Sea section of the Western Honshū chapter) are reached from Marugame.

Tadotsu

At Tadotsu, the JR Dosan line to Kotohira

and Kōchi branches off from the Yosan line to Matsuyama. The Toryo-kōen Park has a magnificent display of cherry trees (sakura) during the blossoming season.

Zentsū-ji

The Zentsū-ji Temple, No 75 on Kōbō Daishi's 88 Temple Circuit, is said to have been founded in 813 AD. This was Kōbō Daishi's birthplace so it has particular importance. The temple is one station north of Kotohira on the JR Dosan line.

Kanonji

Kanonji (population 145,000) is noted for the Zenigata, the 350 metre diameter outline of a square-holed coin dating from the 1600s. The coin's outline and four kanji characters are formed by trenches which, it is said, were dug by the local population as a warning to their feudal lord not to waste the taxes they were forced to pay to him. The huge coin is beside the sea, at the foot of Kotohiki Hill in Kotohiki Park, 1½ km north-west of the station. The Kanonji Temple is also at the foot of the hill while the Kotohiki Hachiman Shrine is in the park.

KOTOHIRA 琴平

The Kompira-san Shrine at Kotohira is one of Shikoku's major attractions but is also another of Japan's curiously misplaced shrines. On Omi-shima Island in the Inland Sea, the Oyamazumi-jinja Shrine is dedicated to the mountain god. Here a mountaintop shrine is venerated by seafarers!

Orientation & Information

Kotohira is small enough to make orientation quite straightforward. The busy shopping arcade continues on until it reaches the shrine entranceway, lined with the inevitable souvenir shops.

Kompira-san Shrine

Kompira-san or, more correctly, Kotohira-gū, was originally a temple dedicated to the guardian of mariners but became a shrine after the Meiji Restoration. Its hilltop posi-

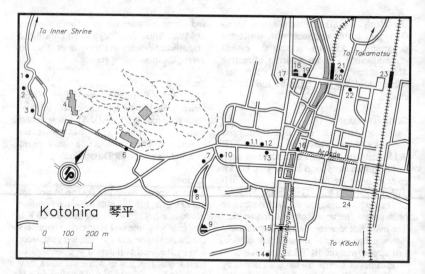

Kotohira 琴平

0   100   200 m

Kotohira

1   Kompira-san Main Hall
2   Ema-dō Pavilion
3   Asahino Yashiro - Sunrise Hall
4   Shoin Building
5   Treasure House
6   Dai-mon Gate
7   Kotohira Grand Hotel
8   Kanamaru-za Kabuki Playhouse
9   Kotohira Seinen-no-Ie Youth Hostel
10 Marine Museum
11 Shikishimakan Ryokan
12 Saké Museum
13 Bizenya Ryokan
14 Kotohira Kadan Ryokan
15 Saya-bashi Bridge
16 Kotobuki Minshuku
17 Kotohira Royal Hotel
18 Post Office
19 Hotel Maruya
20 Kotoden Kotohira Station
21 Fire Tower
22 KDD
23 JR Kotohira Station
24 Bus Station

tion gives superb views over the surrounding country and there are some interesting reminders of its maritime connections.

An enormous fuss is made about how strenuous the climb is to the top but, if you've got this far in Japan, you've probably seen a few long ascents to shrines already: this one isn't the most horrific to be found. If you really blanch at the thought of climbing all those steps (nearly 800 of them) you can be carried up in a palanquin – the carriers wait at the bottom. The countless tour guides are worse than the steps – bawling out over their megaphones, the noise totally spoils the tranquil atmosphere of the shrine.

The first notable landmark on the long climb is the Dai-mon Gate. Just to the right beyond the gate, the rather dull treasure house is open from 8 am to 6 pm in summer, 9 am to 5 pm in winter; entry is Y200. A little further uphill is the reception hall known as the Shoin with the same Y200 entry fee and similar opening hours to the treasure house. Built in 1659, it has some interesting screen paintings and a small garden.

Continuing the ascent, you eventually reach the large Asahino Yashiro also known as the Sunrise Hall. The hall, built in 1837 and dedicated to the sun goddess Amaterasu, is noted for its ornate woodcarving. From here, the short final ascent brings you to the

Kotohira

1 金刀比羅宮本館
2 絵馬堂
3 旭社
4 書院
5 宝物館
6 大門
7 琴平グランドホテル
8 金丸座
9 YH琴平青年の家
10 海の科学館
11 しきしまかん族館
12 酒の博物館
13 備前屋
14 琴平花壇族館
15 鞘橋
16 ことぶき民宿
17 琴平ロイヤルホテル
18 郵便局
19 旅館まるや
20 ことごんことひら駅
21 高灯籠
22 KDD
23 JR琴平駅
24 バスの駅

Gohonsha (Main Hall) and the Ema-dō Pavilion, the latter crowded with suitably maritime offerings. Exhibits range from pictures of ships, both old and new, to models and even modern ship engines. The views from this level extend right down to the coast but incurable climbers can continue another 600-odd steps up to the inner shrine.

Kanamaru-za Kabuki Playhouse

Near the base of the steps is the Kyū Kompira Oshibai or Kanamaru-za, a fine old Kabuki playhouse from the Edo period. It was built in 1835 and became a cinema before being restored to its current elegance in 1976. Inside, you can wander backstage and around the changing rooms, and admire the revolving stage. Entry is Y300 and it's open from 9 am to 5 pm, closed Tuesdays.

Other Attractions

At the bottom of the shrine steps there's a Marine Museum (entry Y300) with a variety of ship models and exhibits. There's also a Saké Museum along the shrine entranceway. At the southern end of the town, past the bus station and just before the Kotohira Kadan Ryokan, is the wooden Saya-bashi covered bridge. Note the curious fire tower beside the Kotoden Kotohira station.

Places to Stay

Kotohira has expensive hotels, very expensive ryokan, some moderately priced minshuku and a youth hostel.

Youth Hostel The *Kotohira Seinen-no-Ie Youth Hostel* (tel 0877-73-3836) costs Y1500 and is near the kabuki playhouse.

Minshuku & Budget Hotels *Kotobuki Minshuku* (tel 0877-73-3872) is right by the riverside on the shopping arcade. It's conveniently situated, clean, comfortable and serves good food. The nightly cost per person with dinner and breakfast is Y6000.

The *Hotel Maruya* (tel 0877-75-2241), next to the post office, is similarly priced but nowhere near as friendly as the Kotobuki.

Ryokan & Expensive Hotels Kotohira has some expensive but very tasteful ryokan, particularly along the entranceway to the shrine steps. Costs per person, including dinner and breakfast, will probably be in the Y12,000 to Y20,000 range. The *Bizenya Ryokan* (tel 0877-75-4131) and the *Shikishimakan Ryokan* (tel 0877-75-5111) are both on the entranceway, while the *Kotohira Kadan Ryokan* (tel 0877-75-3232) is just beyond the Saya-bashi Bridge.

Hotels include the *Kotohira Grand Hotel* (tel 0877-75-3232) near the bottom of the steps up to the shrine and the grand and glossy *Kotohira Royal Hotel* (tel 0877-75-1000) near the Kotoden Kotohira station and the post office.

Places to Eat

Many of the restaurants in Kotohira cater for day-trip visitors and close early. Several places along the shrine entranceway specialise in local Sanuki udon noodles but they're rather expensive.

Getting There & Away

The JR Dosan line branches off the Yosan line at Tadotsu and continues through Kotohira and south to Kōchi. There is also a direct Takamatsu to Kotohira private Kotoden line. On either line, the journey takes between 45 minutes and an hour from Takamatsu.

Tokushima-ken　徳島県

TOKUSHIMA　徳島

Tokushima (population 225,000), on Shikoku's east coast, is a pleasant enough modern city, but offers few attractions in its own right. Apart from the annual Awa Odori Festival, the only real reason for a visit is if you are in transit to somewhere else.

Orientation & Information

Orientation in Tokushima is very easy since it's neatly defined by two hills. One, with the castle ruins, rises up directly behind the station. From in front of the station, the main street, Shinmachibashi-dōri Rd, heads south across the river to the cablecar station at the base of Mt Bizan. The entertainment area and main shopping arcade is south of the river and east of the main street.

There's an information counter just inside the station and an international phone box by the counter.

Bizan

A broad avenue with a central parade of palm trees runs south-west from the station to the foot of Mt Bizan, also known as Mt Otaki. There's a cablecar (Y400 one way, Y620 return) and a four km toll road to the 280 metre high summit from where there are fine views over the city and the Inland Sea. You can walk down in 15 minutes.

Bizan Park also has a 25 metre Peace Pagoda, erected in 1958 as a memorial to the dead of WW II, and a Wenceslão de Morães Museum. Morães, a Portuguese naval officer, lived in Tokushima from 1893 until his death in 1929. He married a Japanese woman and wrote a multi-volume study of Japan.

Tokushima Park

Less than half a km north-east of the railway station, the ruins of Tokushima-jō Castle, built in 1586, stand in Tokushima Park. In the park you will also find the attractively landscaped Senshukaku Garden, which dates from the Momoyama period.

Other Attractions

Just north of the river, near the entertainment district, is the dancing clock, a curious contraption which pops up out of an otherwise undistinguished looking bus stop. You can rent rowboats on the Shinmachigawa River.

Festivals

The annual Awa Odori Festival from 15 to 18 August brings the citizens out into the streets in their traditional costumes and the dancing lasts almost all night. The town is also noted for its puppet theatres – performances are traditionally made by farmers before planting and after harvesting. You might catch a puppet performance at the beginning of June or in mid-August

Places to Stay

Hostel *Tokushima Youth Hostel* (tel 0886-63-1505) is by the beach some distance out of town and costs Y2100.

Hotels Hotels close to the railway station include the *Station Hotel* (tel 0886-52-8181) with singles/doubles at Y4900/9300; the *Astoria Hotel* (tel 0886-53-6151) and *Aivis Hotel*. There are also more expensive places like the *AWA Kankō Hotel* (tel 0886-22-5161) with rooms from Y6200/13,000; the *Grand Palace* (tel 0886-26-1111); the *Park*

Shrines & Temples

Modes of Transport

	Tokushima
1	Wenceslão de Morães Museum
2	Peace Pagoda
3	Cablecar Station
4	JAS
5	Washington Hotel
6	Dancing Clock
7	Boat Rental
8	City Hotel Hamaya
9	Marston Green Hotel
10	Post Office
11	Tōkyū Inn
12	Sogo Department Store
13	Mister Donut
14	Grand Palace Hotel
15	JR Tokushima Station
16	Bus Station
17	AWA Kankō Hotel
18	Station Hotel
19	Astoria Hotel
20	Aivis Hotel
21	Gokoku Shrine
22	Tokushima Castle Garden
23	Park Hotel

	Tokushima
1	モラエス館
2	平和記念堂パゴダ
3	ロープウエイのりば
4	JAS
5	ワシントンホテル
6	阿波およりカラクリ時計
7	Boat Rental
8	ホテルはまや
9	ホテルマーストングリーン
10	郵便局
11	東急イン
12	そうご百貨店
13	ミスタドナツ
14	グランドパラスホテル
15	JR 徳島駅
16	バス駅
17	阿波観光ホテル
18	ステーションホテル
19	アストリアホテル
20	エイビスホテル
21	護国神社
22	旧徳島城表御殿庭園
23	パークホテル

Hotel (tel 0886-25-3311) and the *Tōkyū Inn* (tel 0886-26-0109) with rooms from Y6700/12,700.

Close to the river, in a pleasant and quieter area of town, you'll find the *City Hotel*

Hamaya (tel 0886-22-3411). Although a member of the Japanese Inn Group, it's really just a small business hotel. Singles/doubles with bathroom cost from Y5500/9100, or from Y4500/8100 without bathroom. Nearby is the glossy *Marston Green Hotel* (tel 0886-25-2220) which really does have a green-tiled exterior. Singles/doubles start from Y5800/10,500, and in summer, there's a beer garden on the 9th floor. Also nearby are a number of other cheaper hotels, some fancy ryokan and a scattering of love hotels including one topped by a large sign announcing 'Soap'. (Soapland is a Japanese euphemism for sex and associated activities.) Across the river, on the edge of the entertainment district, is the *Washington Hotel* (tel 0886-22-7781).

Places to Eat
Fast-food places can be found around the station and include an *Andersen's* bakery and a nearby *Lotteria*. The arcade south of the river has a selection of fast-food outlets including a *McDonald's, Mister Donut, Andersen's* and *Kentucky Fried Chicken*.

The hotel area just north of the riverbank has a good selection of restaurants and red-lantern (aka-chochin) bars.

Getting There & Away
Air JAS connect Tokushima with Osaka and Tokyo.

Train & Bus Tokushima is less than 1½ hours from Takamatsu by limited express train (tokkyū). There are also railway lines westward to Ikeda on the JR Dosan line (which runs between Kotohira and Kōchi) and south along the coastal Mugi line as far as Kaifu from where you will have to take a bus to continue to Kōchi.

Ferry Ferries connect Tokushima with Tokyo, Osaka and Kōbe on Honshū, with Kokura on Kyūshū and with various smaller ports. It only takes two hours to Kōbe by hydrofoil.

Getting Around
It's easy to get around Tokushima on foot; from the railway station to the Mt Bizan cablecar station is only 700 metres. Bicycles can be rented from the underground bicycle park in front of the station.

AROUND TOKUSHIMA 徳島附近
Naruto Whirlpools
At the change of tide, the water whisks through the narrow Naruto Channel with such velocity that ferocious whirlpools are created. Boats venture out into the channel, which separates Shikoku from nearby Awaji-shima Island, and travel under the modern Naruto-ōhashi Bridge to inspect the whirlpools close up. A brochure on the boat trips (Y1300) is available at the JR Tokushima station information counter and it details tide times.

There's a fine view over the channel from Naruto Park at the Shikoku end of the bridge and you can save the walk up to the top of the lookout by taking a long, Y200 escalator ride. Getting to the bridge by public transport can be very time consuming although it's not a great distance. From Tokushima, take a train to JR Naruto station (Y310, 40 minutes) and an infrequent bus from there to the bridge (Y300, 20 minutes). It might be better to take a bus directly from Tokushima bus station. Ferries also run to the park from Awaji-shima Island.

Dochū Sand Pillars
About 35 km directly west of Tokushima is Dochū, where erosion has formed curious sand pillars standing about 15 metres high. It's reached via JR Anabuki station.

Mt Tsurugi-san
'Sword' peak (Mt Tsurugi-san) is actually gently rounded rather than sharp edged but, at 1955 metres, it is still the second highest mountain in Shikoku. A chair lift takes you to a point which is a 40 minute walk from the summit.

South of Tokushima
The JR Mugi line runs south as far as Kaifu

from where you can continue by bus to Cape Muroto-misaki and on to Kōchi. There are good views of offshore islands from Anan, while further south at Hiwasi, turtles come ashore to lay their eggs in the Ohama-kōen Park in late July and early August.

KOTOHIRA TO KOCHI 琴平至高知

Although Kotohira is in Kagawa-ken and Kōchi is in Kōchi-ken, most of the distance between the two towns is in Tokushima-ken. The railway and road follow the Yoshino River Gorge much of the way and the scenery is often spectacular.

Koboke & Oboke

The eight km stretch of the Yoshino River between these two rock formations is particularly spectacular. Boat trips are made down the rapids to Koboke from a starting point near Oboke.

Iyadani-kei Gorge

If you've seen the vine suspension bridge (steel reinforced) at the Shikoku-mura Village near Takamatsu, you might be interested in seeing the real thing: the Kazura-bashi Bridge which crosses the Iyadani-kei Gorge. From the Oboke JR station, it's 12 km to the bridge, but buses are infrequent and take an hour. At one time, many river gorges in the mountainous interior of Shikoku were crossed by similar bridges. However, the vines on the bridge have to be totally replaced every three years, and today the Kazura-bashi Bridge is the only one left. There's a miniature replica on the platform at Oboke station.

Jōfuku-ji & Buraku-ji Temples

Further south towards Kōchi, and actually in Kōchi-ken, the Jofuku-ji Temple has a *Youth Hostel* (tel 0887-74-0301) where visitors sometimes make long stays. On the JR Toyonaga station platform, there's a sign in English directing people to the hostel. The next stop is Otaguchi from where it's a 40 minute walk to the Buraku-ji Temple. The main hall there dates from 1151 AD.

Kōchi-ken 高知県

KOCHI 高知

Kōchi (population 270,000) was the castle town of what used to be known as the Tosa Province, and the small but original castle still stands. Like Kagoshima in Kyūshū and Hagi in Western Honshū, the town can lay claim to having played an important role in the Meiji Restoration.

Ryōma Sakamoto

Although it was the progressive samurai of Kagoshima and Hagi who played the major part in the dramatic events of the Meiji Restoration, the citizens of Kōchi claim it was their boy, Ryōma Sakamoto, who brought the two sides together. Unhappy with the rigid class structure institutionalised under Tokugawa rule, Sakamoto sought exile in Nagasaki where he ran a trading company and helped build the powerful alliances which prompted the collapse of the shogunate. His assassination in Kyoto in 1867, when he was just 32 years old, cemented his romantic/tragic image and he appears, looking distinctly sour, on countless postcards and other tourist memorabilia in Kōchi. There's a notable statue of Sakamoto at Katsura-hama Beach.

Dogs & Roosters

The Kōchi area is noted for its fighting dogs and long-tailed roosters. The mastiff-like dogs are ranked like sumō wrestlers and even wear similar aprons! You can see demonstration fights at Katsura-hama Beach, and buy toy fighting dogs from the souvenir shops. Breeders have persuaded the long-tailed rooster to produce tail feathers up to 10 metres long! You can see them at the Nagaodori Centre in the Oshino area of Nankoku City, out towards Kōchi Airport. The JR Gomen station, five stops west of Kōchi, is nearby.

Orientation & Information

The main street in Kōchi, with a tram line

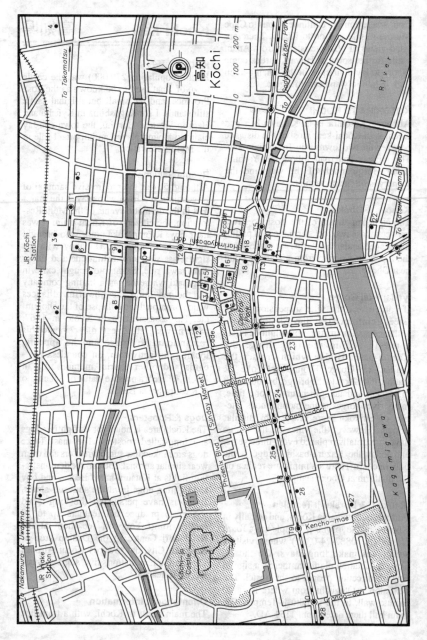

高知
Kōchi

0   100   200 m

To Takamatsu

To Sōgū Sen-kōen Park

To Ōtsuki nama Beach

JR Kōchi Station

JR Iwoke Station

To Nakamura & Uwajima

River

Kagamigawa

Harimayabashi-dori

Ōhashi-dori

Nakanohashi-dori

Phoenix Blvd (Sunday Market)

Kencho-mae

Grabō-dori

Central Park

Kōchi-ō Castle

Kōchi

1	Anraku-ji Temple (No 30 on Circuit)	21	Katsurahama Bus Stop
2	Main Post Office	22	Aki Hotel
3	Bus Station (to Katsura-hama Beach & Matsuyama)	23	Hotel Tosa
		24	Kōchi Sunrise Hotel
4	Kōchi Ekimae Youth Hostel	25	Post Office
5	Dai-Ichi Hotel	26	Hotel New Hankyu
6	Kōchi Hotel	27	Sansuien Ryokan
7	Sun Route Hotel	28	Orient Hotel Kōchi
8	Tosa Gyoen Ryokan		
9	Hotel Takasago		**TRAM STOPS**
10	Kōchi Green Hotel		
11	Prefectural Museum	T1	Kōchi-eki
12	Washington Hotel	T2	Hasuike-machi
13	Café Mousse	T3	Harimaya-bashi
14	Murasaki Robatayaki	T4	Umenotsuji
15	Okonomiyaki Yakisoba Hakobe	T5	Toden-Seibu
16	Tsukasa Restaurant (3 Branches)	T6	Horizume
17	Daimuru Department Store	T7	Ohashi-dōri
18	Harimaya-bashi Bridge	T8	Kochijō-mae
19	Seibu Department Store	T9	Kencho-mae
20	Toden Bus Station	T10	Grando-dōri

Kōchi

1	安楽寺	22	民宿ビジネスあき
2	中央局	23	ビジネスホテル土佐
3	バスの駅	24	高知サンライズホテル
4	YH 高知駅前	25	郵便局
5	第一ホテル	26	新阪急ホテ
6	高知ホテル	27	三翠園ホテル
7	ホテルサンルート	28	オリエントホテル高知
8	ホテル土佐御苑		
9	ホテル高砂		**TRAM STOPS**
10	高知グリーンホテル		
11	郷土文化会館	T1	高知駅
12	ワシントンホテル	T2	はすいけまち
13	カフェイムース	T3	はりまやばし
14	むりさきろばと焼	T4	うめのつじ
15	お好み焼焼そばはこべ	T5	とでんせいぶまえ
16	つかさレストラン	T6	ほりづめ
17	大丸百貨店	T7	おおはしどうり
18	播磨屋橋	T8	こうちじょうまえ
19	西武百貨店	T9	けんちょうまえ
20	とでんバスの駅	T10	グラルドどうり
21	かつらはまバスの駅		

down the centre, runs directly south, crossing the main shopping arcade and the other main street near Harimaya-bashi Bridge. The bridge (apart from some purely visual railings) has long gone but the citizens of Kōchi still recall a famous ditty about a bald monk buying a hair band at the bridge, presumably for a female friend. Apart from the castle, Kōchi's other attractions are all some distance from the town centre.

If you're in Kōchi on Sunday, visit the popular and colourful street market along Phoenix Blvd, the road which leads to Kōchi-jō Castle. The market supplies everything from fruit, vegetables and goldfish to large stones for use in gardens.

The information office at JR Kōchi station is just outside the station and to the left. There are excellent brochures in English, and there is usually a helpful staff member around who speaks good English.

Kōchi-jō Castle

Kōchi's castle may not be one of the great castles of Japan but it is a real survivor, not a post-war concrete reconstruction. Although a construction on the site dates back to the 14th century, the present castle was built between 1601 and 1611, burnt down in 1727 and rebuilt in 1753. By this time, the peace of the Tokugawa period was well established and castles were scarcely necessary except as a symbol of a feudal lord's power. The Kōchi lord therefore rebuilt the castle with his living quarters (the Kaitokukan) on the ground floor, with doors opening into the garden. Kōchi-jō, therefore, is not a gloomy castle, as those which were strongly fortified against enemy attack tended to be.

At the bottom of the castle hill is the well-preserved Ote-mon Gate. Inside the castle there is a small museum with exhibits relating to Ryōma Sakamoto and from the castle, a fine view over the town. The castle is open from 9 am to 5 pm and entry is Y300. There's a very informative brochure on the castle available in English. The Kōchi History Museum is at the base of the hill but is not really worth the Y220 entry fee.

Godaisan-kōen Park & Chikurin-ji Temple

The hilltop Chikurin-ji Temple and Kōchi's botanical garden are both in Godaisan-kōen Park, several km from the town centre. The temple is No 31 on the Shikoku temple circuit, and there's an attractive five storeyed pagoda at the top of the hill. The temple's treasure house has an interesting collection of old statues, some of them looking very Indian or Tantric, and is worth a look. The Y200 entry fee also covers the temple garden, behind another building. On the other side of the car park is the Makino Botanical Garden and greenhouse, admission is Y300.

To get to the park and temple take a bus, marked to the temple, from the Toden Seibu bus station next to the Seibu department store which is at the Harimaya-bashi junction. The journey takes about 20 minutes and the bus stops outside the temple steps. Buses run about once an hour until 5 pm and the fare is Y300.

Katsura-hama Beach

Only the Japanese could make a big deal out of a beach which is liberally dotted with large and permanent looking signs proclaiming 'No Swimming'. Nevertheless, Katsura-hama Beach is a popular 13 km excursion from Kōchi. Apart from the sand, there's a well-known statue of local hero Ryōma Sakamoto, an aquarium, a shell display and demonstration dog fights which are held in the Tosa Tōken Centre.

Buses run from Kōchi bus station to Katsurahama every 20 minutes; there's also a bus stop outside the Seibu department store, just beyond the Harimaya-bashi junction. The trip takes about 35 minutes and costs Y580.

Places to Stay

Youth Hostel *Kōchi Ekimae Youth Hostel* (tel 0888-83-5086) is only a few minutes walk east of the railway station and costs Y2100.

Budget Hotels The *Aki Hotel* (tel 0888-32-

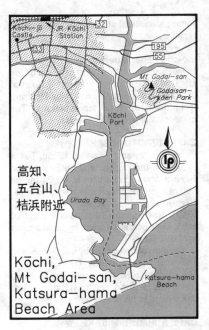

高知、
五台山、
桔浜附近

Kōchi,
Mt Godai—san,
Katsura—hama
Beach Area

3222), just south of the river, can be reached by tram – get off at the first stop beyond the bridge. Behind the main building is a separate annex with simple tatami-mat rooms costing Y2800 for a single. The rooms are utterly without pretensions, but you do get a washbasin, coin TV and air-con.

Back on the town centre side of the river, the *Hotel Tosa* (tel 0888-25-3332) is another economy hotel with rooms starting at Y3850. The *Kōchi Green Hotel* (tel 0888-22-1800) is also another straightforward, cheaper hotel.

Expensive Hotels The *Washington Hotel* (tel 0888-23-6111), on Phoenix Blvd, is conveniently central and close to the castle. Rooms cost from Y7000/14,000 for singles/doubles.

The pleasant *Orient Hotel Kōchi* (tel 0888-22-6565) is south of the castle and on the tram line. Rooms for one cost from Y5500, for two from Y9000. The *Kōchi*

Sunrise Hotel (tel 0888-22-1281) charges from Y5300/10,000 for singles/doubles, while the glossy *Hotel New Hankyū* (tel 0888-73-1111) charges from Y8000/15,000.

Ryokan The large *Sansuien Ryokan* (tel 0888-22-0131), due south of the castle, includes some old buildings from the Kōchi daimyō's grounds. Costs per person with meals are in the Y12,000 to Y16,000 range. Just north of the river, near the station is the *Hotel Takasago* (tel 0888-22-1288), a smaller ryokan in a similar price bracket.

Places to Eat
Kōchi's best restaurants are clustered around the Daimaru department store near the Harimaya-bashi Bridge end of the shopping arcade. Here you'll find at least three branches of *Tsukasa*, a popular Japanese restaurant displaying plastic meals from tempura to sashimi, and offering fixed-price specials and friendly service.

On the 2nd and 3rd floors of a building just off the arcade, there's a branch of the *Murasaki Robatayaki*, easily recognisable by its thatched house motif. *Café Mousse* has snacks, cakes, ice cream and interesting desserts; look for the British Mini crashing out of the 2nd floor of the building around the corner. *Okonomiyaki Yakisoba Hakobe* offers the popular 'cook it yourself' omelette dish known as okonomiyaki.

Getting There & Away
Air ANA connects Kōchi with Osaka, Tokyo and Miyazaki in Kyūshū. Air Nippon Koku (ANK) also fly between Kōchi and Osaka while JAS fly to Fukuoka, Nagoya and Osaka.

Train Kōchi is on the JR Dosan line which runs from the north coast of Shikoku through Kotohira. It takes about 2½ hours by limited express from Takamatsu. From Kōchi, rail services continue westward to just beyond Kubokawa where the line splits south-west to Nakamura and north-west to Uwajima. From Uwajima, you can continue north to

Matsuyama but this is a long and circuitous route.

Bus Travel between Kōchi and Matsuyama is faster by bus. These depart hourly from outside the bus station near the JR Kōchi station. If you want to travel right around the southern coast, either westward around Cape Ashizuri-misaki to Uwajima or eastward around Cape Muroto-misaki to Tokushima you will have to travel by bus as the railway lines do not extend all the way.

Ferry Kōchi is connected by ferry to Osaka and Tokyo.

Getting Around

The tram service running north-south from the station intersects the east-west tram route at the Harimaya-bashi junction. Ask for a *norikaeken* (transfer ticket) if you have to transfer there. You can easily reach the castle on foot, though for the other town attractions, you must take a bus.

AROUND KOCHI   高知の附近

Apart from Katsura-hama Beach, there are a number of other interesting places easily reached from Kōchi.

Ryōma History Museum

You can find out all about local hero Ryōma Sakamoto at this museum which tells his life story in miniature dioramas. It's in Noichi, east of Kōchi towards the Ryūga-dō Cave.

Ryūga-dō Cave

This limestone cavern (one of the three best in Japan!) has typical stalactites and stalagmites plus traces of prehistoric habitation. A bus bound for Odochi will get you to the cave in about an hour, entry is Y850.

Aki

Further east is Aki, a slow-moving town where Yatarō Iwasaki, founder of the giant Mitsubishi conglomerate, was born in 1834. His thatched-roof house is preserved, phone 0887-34-1111 if you want to see it. There are some old samurai streets around the castle remains.

Ino-cho Paper Museum

In Ino, just four stations west of Kōchi on the JR line, the Ino-cho Paper Museum demonstrates the traditional manufacturing techniques for Tosa paper making. The museum is closed on Mondays.

CAPE MUROTO-MISAKI   室戸岬

Cape Muroto, south-east of Kōchi, has a lighthouse topping its wild cliffscape. The Higashi-dera Temple here is No 24 on the Shikoku temple circuit and also houses the *Higashi-dera Youth Hostel* (tel 0887-22-0366). Just north of Muroto is a chain of black-sand beaches known by local surfers as 'Little Hawaii'.

You can reach the cape by bus from Kōchi and you can continue right round to Tokushima on the east coast. The JR Mugi line runs around the east coast from Tokushima as far as Kaifu.

CAPE ASHIZURI-MISAKI   足摺岬

South-west of Kōchi, Cape Ashizuri, like Cape Muroto, is a wild and scenic promontory ending with a lighthouse. As well as the coastal road, there's also a central Skyline Road. Cape Ashizuri also has a temple (the Kongōfuku-ji, No 38 on the temple circuit) which, like the temple at Cape Muroto, also has its own youth hostel (tel 0880-88-0038).

From Tosashimizu, at the northern end of the cape, ferries operate to Kōbe on Honshū. From Kōchi, there is a railway as far as Nakamura; travel from Nakamura around the cape and on to Uwajima is by bus.

NORTH-WEST TO UWAJIMA

From Tosashimizu, the road continues around the southern coast of Shikoku to Uwajima in Ehime-ken. The scenery is particularly attractive through Tatsukushi where there is a coral museum and a shell museum. Sightseeing boats and glass-bottom boats operate from the town.

Sukumo has a fine harbour and the *Sukumo Youth Hostel* (tel 0880-64-0233).

You can take boats out to remote Okinoshima Island from Sukumo.

Sukumo is less than an hour by bus from Nakamura by the direct road although much longer around the coast via the cape. On to Uwajima takes about two hours. From Sukumo, ferries make the three hour crossing several times daily to Saeki on Kyūshū.

Ehime-ken 愛媛県

MATSUYAMA 松山
Shikoku's largest city, Matsuyama, is a busy north coast town (population 400,000) and an important transport hub with frequent ferry links to Hiroshima. Matsuyama's major attractions are its castle, one of the finest survivors from the feudal era, and the Dōgo Onsen (hot springs) area with its magnificent old public bath.

Orientation & Information
The JR Matsuyama station is west of the town centre and the castle hill. The town centre is immediately south of the castle and close to the Matsuyama City station (Shieki) of the private Iyo-tetsu line. The Ichiban-cho tram stop and the Mitsukoshi department store by the busy Okaidō shopping arcade, are important landmarks in the town centre. Dōgo Onsen is east of town while the port at Takahama is north of the town centre and the JR station.

English-language books can be found on the 4th floor of the Kinokuniya bookshop near the Matsuyama City station. Matsuyama is noted for its deep-blue textiles known as Iyo-kasuri. Tobe-yaki is a locally produced pottery.

Information counters can be found at the JR Matsuyama station and at the ferry terminal for arrivals from Hiroshima. The Dōgo Onsen also has an information centre: beside the tram terminus, at the entrance to the arcade which leads to the old public bath.

Matsuyama-jō Castle
Picturesquely sited atop a hill which virtu-ally erupts in the middle of the town, Matsuyama-jō Castle is one of the finest original surviving castles. It only squeaks in with the 'original' label as it was restored just before the end of the Edo period. In the early years of the Meiji Restoration, rebuilding feudal symbols was definitely not a high priority.

The castle was built in 1602-03 with five storeys, but burnt down and was rebuilt in 1642 with three storeys. In 1784, it was struck by lightning and burnt down again, though, in those peaceful and slow-moving Edo years, it took until 1820 for a decision to be made to rebuild it and until 1854 for the reconstruction to be completed! It was completely restored between 1968 and 1986.

You don't even have to climb the steep hill up to the castle, a cablecar and/or chair lift will whisk you up there for Y160 one way or Y310 return. Entry to the castle costs Y260.

Shiki-dō
Just south of the Matsuyama City station (Shi-eki) and in the grounds of the Shoshu-ji Temple, is a replica of the house of haiku poet Shiki Masaoka (1867-1902). The Shiki Memorial Museum in Dōgo Park is also dedicated to the poet; Matsuyama claims to be the capital city of Haiku poetry.

Dōgo Onsen
This popular spa centre, a couple of km east of the town centre, is easily reached by the regular tram service which terminates at the start of the spa's shopping arcade. The arcade leads to the front of Dōgo Onsen Honkan.

Dōgo Onsen Honkan
A high priority for any visitor to Matsuyama should be a bath at this rambling old public bathhouse which dates from 1894. Apart from the various baths, there's also the Yūshinden, a private bathing suite built for an imperial visit in 1899, and the Botchan Room, since a character in the novel *Botchan* was a frequent visitor to the baths.

Dōgo Onsen Honkan is another place where the correct sequence of steps can be a little confusing. Pay your money outside –

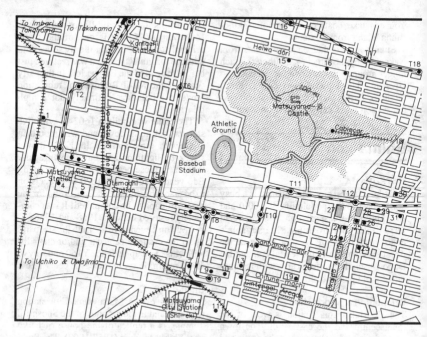

Matsuyama

1 Hotel Sun Route Matsuyama
2 Hotel New Kajiwara
3 City Hotel New American
4 Central Hotel
5 Hotel Nisshin
6 Tokyo Dai Ichi Hotel
7 Mister Donut
8 ANA & JAS
9 New Grand Building
10 Munchen Beer Hall
11 Shiki-do
12 Kirin City Pub
13 Kinokuniya Bookshop
14 Chateau-tel Matsuyama Hotel
15 Hotel Heiwa
16 Business Hotel Taihei
17 Business Hotel New Kashima
18 Cablecar Station
19 JAL
20 Post Office
21 Restaurant Goshiki

22 Yakitori (Several Restaurants)
23 Murasaki Restaurant
24 Murasaki Restaurant
25 Murasaki Restaurant
26 Pound House Coffee Bar
27 ANA Hotel Matsuyama
28 Mitsukoshi Department Store
29 Tandoor Restaurant
30 Matsuyama International Hotel
31 Hotel Top Inn
32 Dōgo Onsen Information Office
33 Dōgo Onsen Honkan Bathhouse
34 Isaniwa-jinja Shrine
35 Municipal Shiki Memorial Museum
36 Matsuyama Youth Hostel
37 Minshuku Miyoshi
38 Ishite-ji Temple

TRAM STOPS

T1 Komachi
T2 Miyato-cho
T3 Kokutetsu-ekimae
T4 Otemachi-ekimae
T5 Nishi-horibata
T6 Honmachi 3-chome
T7 Honmachi 5-chome
T8 Minami-horibata
T9 Shieki-mae
T10 Shiyakusho-mae
T11 Kencho-mae
T12 Ichiban-cho
T13 Katsuyama-cho
T14 Keisatsusho-mae
T15 Kamiichiman
T16 Shimizu-machi
T17 Teppō-cho
T18 Sekijuji Byōin-mae
T19 Minami-machi
T20 Dōgokōen-mae
T21 Dōgo Onsen

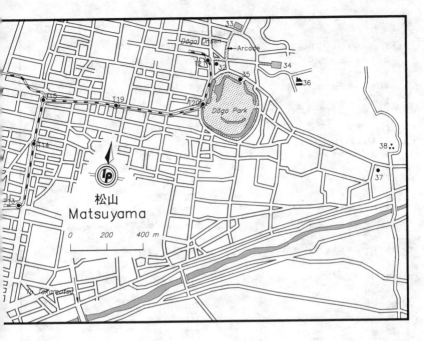

Y250 for a basic bath; Y620 for a bath followed by tea and a snack; Y1200 for the private 'Bath of the Spirits' followed by the tea and snack – enter and leave your shoes in a locker. If you've paid Y250, go to the 'Bath of the Gods' changing room. The changerooms are signposted in English so you won't wander into the wrong one and shock anybody, though if you're male, you may be slightly surprised to find matronly ladies looking after the male changing room. You'd be even more surprised if you took the wrong exit when heading for the bath as in summer, only a cane blind separates the changing room from the street!

If you've paid Y620 or Y1200, first go upstairs to the balcony and get your yukata (dressing gown), then return to the appropriate changing room. You can leave valuables upstairs in the charge of the attendants who dispense the yukata, though it's hard to see why, since there are lockers in the changing room.

After your bath, those destined for upstairs can don their yukata and retire to the verandah to sip tea and look down on onsen visitors clip-clopping by in yukata and geta.

Isaniwa-jinja Shrine

A few minutes walk from the Dōgo Onsen bathhouse, a long flight of steps leads up to the 1667 AD Hachiman Isaniwa-jinja Shrine.

Municipal Shiki Memorial Museum

In Dōgo Park, this museum is dedicated to the memory of local literary figure Shiki Masaoka.

Ishite-ji Temple

It's quite a long walk (more than a km) east from the spa area to this temple, No 51 on the temple circuit. The temple dates from 1318, is noted for its fine Kamakura architecture, has a three storeyed pagoda and is overlooked by a Buddha figure high up on

Matsuyama

1	ホテルサンルート松山	32	道後温泉観光案内所
2	ホテルニューカジワラ	33	道後温泉本館
3	シチホテルニューアメリカン	34	伊佐爾波神社
4	セントラルホテル	35	子規記念博物館
5	ホテル日進	36	YH 神泉園
6	東京第一ホテル	37	みよし民宿
7	ミスタドナツ	38	石手寺
8	ANA & JAS		
9	ニューグランドビル	**TRAM STOPS**	
10	ムンチエンビールホール		
11	子規堂	T1	古町
12	キリンシチパーブ	T2	宮田町
13	紀ノ国屋本店	T3	松山駅前
14	ホテルシャトーテル松山	T4	大手町駅前
15	ホテル平和	T5	西堀端
16	ビジネスホテルニュー泰平	T6	本町三丁目
17	ビジネスホテルかしま	T7	本町四丁目
18	ロープウェイ駅	T8	南堀端
19	JAL	T9	市駅前
20	郵便局	T10	市役所前
21	五志喜	T11	県庁前
22	焼鳥	T12	大街道
23	むらさきレストラン	T13	勝山町
24	むらさきレストラン	T14	警察署前
25	むらさきレストラン	T15	上一万
26	パウンドハウス松山	T16	清水町
27	松山全日空ホテル	T17	鉄砲町
28	三越百貨店	T18	日赤病院前
29	タンドーレストラン	T19	南町
30	松山国際ホテル	T20	道後公園前
31	ホテルトップイン	T21	道後温泉

the hill. The name means 'stone hand', from a legend about a Matsuyama lord born with a stone in his hand.

At the entranceway to the temple is a 'pilgrim's supply shop'. If you're planning on making the pilgrimage around all 88 temples on the Shikoku circuit, the shop can supply maps, guidebooks, pilgrim's attire, hats, bells and staffs, in fact everything for the complete pilgrim. Matsuyama has seven other circuit temples.

Places to Stay

Matsuyama has three accommodation areas – around the JR station (business hotels); around the centre (business hotels and more expensive hotels); and at Dōgo Onsen (ryokan and Japanese-style hotels).

Youth Hostel *Matsuyama Youth Hostel* (tel 0899-33-6366), near the Isaniwa Shrine in Dōgo Onsen, costs Y2100 a night.

Hotels – Matsuyama Station Area The *Central Hotel* (tel 0899-41-4358/59) is a cheaper business hotel with singles/doubles from Y3800/7000.

Other hotels within a stone's throw of the station include the *Hotel New Kajiwara* (tel 0899-41-0402) with singles/doubles from Y4500/7500 and the similarly priced *City Hotel New American* (tel 0899-33-6660) which is next door.

Slightly more expensive station area hotels include the *Hotel Sun Route Matsuyama* (tel 0899-33-2811) where singles cost from Y6000 and doubles or twins from Y9500. The featureless *Hotel Nisshin* (tel 0899-46-3111) is a slightly longer walk from the station and has singles/doubles from Y5500/9000.

Hotels – Central Matsuyama The *Tokyo Dai Ichi Hotel* (tel 0899-47-4411) is on the station side of the town centre and has singles from Y5500, doubles or twins from Y9500. Rooms at the *Chateau-tel Matsuyama* (tel 0899-46-2111) are almost identical in price.

The expensive *ANA Hotel Matsuyama* (tel 0899-33-5511) is near the Ichiban-cho tram stop and the Mitsukoshi department store which mark the town centre. Also right in the centre of things is the modern *Hotel Top Inn* (tel 0899-33-3333) with singles/doubles from Y5300/8500.

Immediately north of the castle hill is a quieter area, conveniently connected to the town centre by a tram line. One of the hotels in this area is the curiously old-fashioned *Business Hotel Taihei* (tel 0899-43-3560), with rooms from Y4500/8000; others are the *Hotel Heiwa* and the *Business Hotel New Kashima*.

Hotels & Ryokan – Dōgo Onsen Area For Japanese tourists, Dōgo Onsen, east of the town centre, is the big attraction and there are numerous Japanese-style hotels and ryokan in the area. They're usually rather expensive, even overpriced, but *Minshuku Miyoshi* (tel 0899-77-2581), behind the petrol station near the Ishite Temple, is an exception at around Y4000 to Y4500 per person. The *Funaya Ryokan* (tel 0899-47-0278) is one of the best of the onsen ryokan but count on around Y20,000 per person, including meals.

Places to Eat
The long Gintengai and Okaidō shopping arcade in central Matsuyama has *McDonald's, Kentucky Fried Chicken* and *Mister Donut*. There's another *Mister Donut* near the Matsuyama City station. The arcade leading from the Dōgo Onsen tram stop to the Dōgo Onsen Honkan bathhouse also has a number of restaurants with plastic meal replicas.

Next to the post office in the town centre, *Restaurant Goshiki* offers sōmen noodles and other dishes. Although there are plastic models in the window and an illustrated menu showing the multi-coloured noodles, this is another place where the artistically scrawled sign looks nothing like the printed kanji. Sōmen and tempura costs Y850 and you can buy noodles in packets (one colour or mixed) to take home.

Close to the Okaidō arcade is the small *Tandoor* Indian restaurant offering various curries from Y750 to Y1000, thali dinners at Y2000 and tandoori dinners at Y2500 – there is a menu in English. There are also several branches of *Murasaki* near the shopping arcade: look for the thatched-house motif. The food is nothing special in these chain restaurants, but the atmosphere is cheerful and the menus illustrated.

The *Pound House* is a coffee bar with a delicious selection of cakes at Y300. For a cold beer, there are several places near the Matsuyama City station. *Kirin City Pub*, looking pseudo-pubbish, is near the Kinokuniya bookshop. Directly opposite the station is *Munchen*, a beer hall looking pseudo-German, plus there's a rooftop beer garden on the *New Grand Building* (that is, if the *ding* in 'Building' has been replaced; if not, look for the *New Grand Buil*). The *ANA Hotel* and the *Hotel Sun Route* both have rooftop beer gardens in the summer.

Getting There & Away

Air ANA connect Matsuyama with Osaka, Nagoya and Tokyo (both Narita International Airport and Haneda Airport). JAS have connections to Fukuoka, Miyazaki and Kagoshima, all in Kyūshū. JAL also fly to Tokyo while South-West Airlines (SWAL) have direct flights between Matsuyama and Naha in Okinawa.

Train & Bus The north coast JR Yosan line connects Matsuyama with Takamatsu and there are also services across the Seto-ōhashi Bridge to Honshū. Another line runs southwest from Matsuyama to Uwajima and then east to Kōchi, though this is a rather circuitous route – it's much faster to take a bus directly to Kōchi.

Ferry There are frequent ferry and hydrofoil connections with Hiroshima. Take the Iyotetsudō private railway line from Matsuyama City (Shi-eki) or Otemachi station right to the end of the line at Takahama (Y440 from Otemachi). From Takahama, a connecting bus whisks you the remaining distance to Matsuyama Kankō port. The hydrofoils zip across to Hiroshima in one hour for Y4950 but there's not much to see en route – the view is much better from the regular ferries. Some services go via Kure, south-west of Hiroshima. The ferry takes from 2¾ to three hours depending on the port in Matsuyama and costs Y3710 1st class and Y1850 2nd class to Hiroshima from Matsuyama Kankō.

Other ferries operate to and from Matsuyama and Beppu, Kokura and Oita on Kyūshū as well as Iwakuni, Kure, Mihara, Onomichi and Yanai in Honshū, but check which of the Matsuyama ports services will operate from. From Matsuyama Kankō, a hydrofoil zips across to Ocho (Y2660), Kinoe (Y3070), Omishima (Y3310), Setoda (Y4530) and Onomichi (Y4950).

Getting Around

Matsuyama has the private Iyo-tetsudō railway line and a tram service. The railway line is mainly useful for getting to and from the port for Hiroshima ferries.

The tram services cost a flat Y150 anywhere in town. There's a loop line and major terminuses at Dōgo Onsen and outside the Matsuyama City station. The Ichiban-chō stop outside the Mitsukoshi department store and ANA Hotel is a good central stopping point. Tram numbers and routes are:

Tram No	Route
1 & 2	The Loop
3	Matsuyama City Station (Shi-eki)-Dōgo Onsen
5	JR Matsuyama Station-Dōgo Onsen
6	Kiya-chō-Dōgo Onsen

AROUND MATSUYAMA　松山の附近
Mt Ishizuchi-san

Mt Ishizuchi-san (1982 metres), the highest mountain in Shikoku (indeed in all western Japan), is easily reached from Matsuyama. It's also a holy mountain and many pilgrim climbers make the hike, particularly during the July-August climbing season. In winter it's snow-capped.

From Matsuyama, you can take a bus to Tsuchi Goya, south-east of the mountain. Alternatively, you can take a bus from the Iyo Saijō station on the Matsuyama-Takamatsu line to the Nishi-no-kawa cablecar station on the northern side. This route passes through the scenic Omogo-kei Gorge, an attraction in its own right. Out of season, bus services to the mountain are infrequent. You can climb up one way and down the other or even make a complete circuit from Nishi-no-kawa to the summit, down to Tsuchi Goya and then back to Nishi-no-kawa. Allow all day and an early start for the circuit.

The cablecar takes about five hours straight up and down and costs Y800 one way or Y1500 return. The ride is followed by an optional chair lift (Y200 one way, Y350 return) which slightly shortens the walk to Jōju where there is a good view of the mountain from the Ishizuchi-jinja Shrine. From Jōju, it's 3½km to the top, first gently downhill through forest, then uphill through forest, across a more open area and finally a steep and rocky ascent. Although there's a path, and often steps, all the way to the top, the fun way to make the final ascent is up a series of *kusari*, heavy chains draped down the very steep rock faces. Clambering up these chains is the approved pilgrimage method. The actual summit, reached by climbing along a sharp ridge, is a little beyond the mountain hut on the top.

Imabari
This industrial city is of no particular interest apart from its position beside the most island-crowded area of the Inland Sea. At this point, whirlpools rather like those at Naruto (see the Around Tokushima section earlier) form in the narrow channel separating Shikoku from O-shima Island.

There are numerous ferry services connecting Imabari with ports on Honshū including Hiroshima, Kōbe, Mihara, Nigata, Onomichi, Takehara and various ports on islands of the Inland Sea.

UCHIKO 内子
Midway between Matsuyama and Uwajima, and on the JR Yosan line, the small town of Uchiko has a street lined with old buildings dating from the last years of the Edo period and the early years following the Meiji Res-

Uchiko

1 高昌寺
2 大森和ろうそく店
3 石燈
4 寺
5 上芳我邸
6 民芸店
7 本芳我邸
8 民芸店
9 町家資料館
10 あまざけ茶屋
11 酒醸造所
12 バスターミナル
13 八幡神社
14 内子座
15 JR 内子駅

1 Kōsho-ji Temple
2 Ōmori Rōsoku Candle Maker
3 Stone Lantern
4 Small Shrine
5 Kami Hagi-tei House
6 Small Craft Shop With Teahouse
7 Hon Hagi-tei House
8 Craft Shop
9 Machi-ya Shiryōkan Museum
10 Amazake Chaya Teahouse
11 Saké Brewery
12 Bus Station
13 Hachiman Shrine
14 Uchiko-za Kabuki Theatre
15 JR Uchiko Station

toration. At that time, Uchiko was an important centre for the production of the vegetable wax known as *rō*, and some of the houses along Yōkaichi, the town's old street, belong to merchants who made their fortunes from producing rō.

Orientation & Information
Many of the places on Yōkaichi seem to shut on Monday, although Wednesday is supposed to be the official day of closure. There's a map with *some* English outside the JR station but nothing else in Uchiko is labelled in English.

Yōkaichi
Uchiko's picturesque old street, which extends for about a km, has a number of interesting old buildings along with souvenir shops, craft shops and teahouses. At the start of the street is an old saké brewery across from which is the Amazake Chaya Teahouse (*amazake* is a sweet saké). A little further along the street is the Machi-ya Shiryōkan Museum and then the Hon Hagi-tei House, a fine example of a wealthy merchant's private home. The Kami Hagi-tei across the road (closed Wednesdays) is a wax merchant's house with a storehouse. At the end of the street the house of Omori Rōsoku (closed Mondays) is still engaged in traditional candle production, and you can see and buy these rō wax candles.

Uchiko-za Theatre
The Uchiko-za is an old kabuki theatre, originally built in 1915 and restored in the mid-80s. Entry is Y210 and it's closed on Mondays.

Getting There & Away
Uchiko can be reached by bus or train from Matsuyama and Uwajima. You need a couple of hours at least to explore Yōkaichi.

Getting Around
Yōkaichi is just over a km from the JR Uchiko station; if you're stopping off on the train and your time is limited, consider

taking a taxi. The bus station is closer to Yōkaichi.

UCHIKO TO UWAJIMA　内子至宇和島
Only 10 km south-west of Uchiko, there are more interesting old houses and shops near the river in Ozu, including the Garyū-sansō (closed Tuesdays), a wealthy trader's house built early this century. Traditional cormorant fishing (ukai) takes place in the river during the summer months. The *Ozu Kyōdokan Youth Hostel* can be contacted on 0893-24-2258.

Twenty km south-west of Ozu is Yawatahama from where ferry services operate to Beppu and Usuki on Kyūshū – the crossing to either port takes about three hours. Cape Sada-misaki extends 50 km towards Kyūshū, and from Misaki, near the end of the cape, ferries make the crossing to Saganoseki, near Oita and Beppu, in just over an hour (Y600).

UWAJIMA　宇和島
Uwajima is a relatively quiet and peaceful place with a small but original castle, the shabby remnants of a fine garden, some pleasant temples and a notorious sex shrine. It makes an interesting pause between Kōchi and Matsuyama although an afternoon or a morning is long enough for a reasonable look around.

Orientation & Information
The JR Uwajima station information office is not actually in the station building; leave the station and cross the road to find it. The staff are very helpful and the office also rents bicycles but it doesn't open until 9 am. Uwajima is a centre for cultured pearls: the tourist information office can tell you about shops dealing in them.

Uwajima-jō Castle
Uwajima-jō was never a great castle but it's an interesting 'little' three storeyed one and, dating from 1665, is an original, not a reconstruction. It once stood by the sea and although land reclamation has moved the sea well back, there are still good views over the

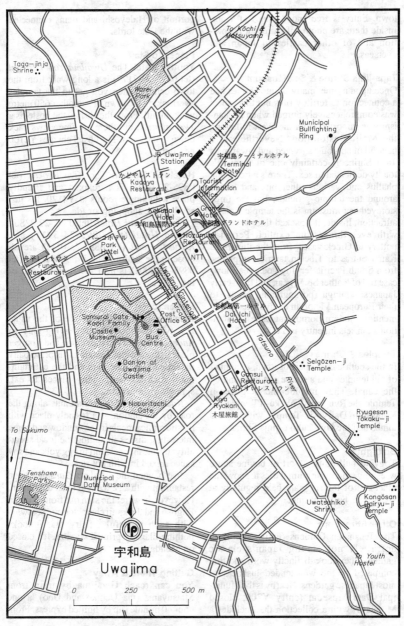

To Kōchi &
Matsuyama

Taga–jinja
Shrine

Warei
Park

Municipal
Bullfighting
Ring

JR Uwajima
Station

宇和島ターミナルホテル
Terminal
Hotel

カドヤレストラン
Kadoya
Restaurant

Tourist
Information
Office

Kokusai
Hotel
宇和島国際ホテル

Grand
Hotel
宇和島グランドホテル

パークホテル
Park
Hotel

Hozumitei
Restaurant

NTT

船平レストラン
Funahei
Restaurant

Uwajima Gintengai Arcade

Samurai Gate
Kaori Family
Castle
Museum

Post
Office

Bus
Centre

宇和島第一ホテル
Dai-Ichi
Hotel

Donjon of
Uwajima Castle

Seigōzen–ji
Temple

Gansui
Restaurant
がんすいレストラン

Tatsuno River

Noboritachi
Gate

Kiya
Ryokan
木屋旅館

Ryugesan
Tōkaku–ji
Temple

To Sukumo

Tenshaen
Park

Municipal
Date Museum

Kongōsan
Dairyu–ji
Temple

Uwatsuhiko
Shrine

宇和島
Uwajima

To Youth
Hostel

0   250   500 m

town. Entry is free and it opens at 9 am. Inside there are photos of its recent restoration and of other castles in Japan and overseas.

Taga-jinja Shrine & Sex Museum

Once upon a time, many Shinto shrines had a connection to fertility rites but this aspect was comprehensively purged when puritanism was imported from the West following the Meiji Restoration. Nevertheless, a handful of holdouts survived and Uwajima's Taga Shrine is certainly one of them: it's totally dedicated to sex. There's a tree trunk phallus and various other bits and pieces around the temple grounds, but the three storeyed sex museum is the temple's major attraction. Inside, it's packed floor to ceiling with everything from explicit Peruvian pottery to Greek vases, from the illustrated Kama Sutras to Tibetan tantric sculptures, from South Pacific fertility gods to a showcase full of leather S&M gear, and from early Japanese shunga (pornographic prints) to their European Victorian equivalents, not to mention modern porno magazines. Saturation soon sets in; entry is Y600.

Temples & Shrines

In the south-eastern part of town, a number of old temples and a shrine can be found by the canal. They include the Seigōzen-ji Temple, the Ryugesan Tōkaku-ji Temple, the Kongōsan Dairyū-ji Temple with its old tombs and the Uwatsuhiko-jinja Shrine.

Bullfights

Tōgyūjō bullfights, a sort of bovine sumō wrestling where one animal tries to shove the other out of the ring, are held regularly at Uwajima's bullfight ring.

Other Attractions

The Tensha-en Gardens (entry Y200) are definitely not among Japan's classic gardens, they look distinctly worn and thin compared to the well-tended lushness of most Japanese gardens. Nearby is the Municipal Date Museum (entry Y200, closed Mondays) with a collection that includes a portrait of Hideyoshi and items connected with the Date lords.

Places to Stay

Youth Hostel The *Uwajima Youth Hostel* (tel 0895-22-7177) is a long walk from the town centre: when you get to the temples overlooking the town, it's another 650 metre walk, uphill. From the shrine, the hostel is a 1¼ km walk, but there are fine views back down to the town. The hostel charges Y2100 per night.

Hotels & Ryokan The *Kiya Ryokan* (tel 0895-22-0101) is a relaxed and friendly place with single rooms at Y4120. It's just south of the shopping arcade.

The *Terminal Hotel* (tel 0895-22-2280), *Grand Hotel* (tel 0895-24-3911) and *Kokusai Hotel* (tel 0895-25-0111) are all close to the station. The *Dai Ichi Hotel* (tel 0895-25-0001) is near the southern end of the arcade.

Places to Eat

Remarkably, Uwajima is free of the usual US-style fast-food chains, having only an *Andersen's* bakery in the station and a burger place in the arcade. The arcade is principally inhabited by coffee bars and the entertainment district, with many places to eat, sprawls on both sides.

Kadoya, one of the restaurants along the road by the station, is a friendly place with plastic replica meals in the window and some interesting dishes including the local speciality 'tai-meshi', sashimi in egg yolk and soy sauce mixed in with hot rice.

Just beyond the arcade is *Gansui*, a large restaurant with an excellent local reputation. However, beware: the sign out front is not in English and the kanji characters are scrawled with such graceful artistry that it looks nothing like any printed version. It's closed on Mondays.

Getting There & Away

You can reach Uwajima by train from Matsuyama (via Uchiko and Uno), a one hour 40 minute trip by limited express. From

Kōchi, it takes 3¾ to 4½ hours by limited express via Kubokawa, where you change trains. If you want to head further south and on to Cape Ashizuri-misaki, you'll have to resort to buses as the railway line from Kōchi terminates at Nakamura.

Direct bus services operate to Honshū from Uwajima, and there is also a ferry con-

nection to Beppu on Kyūshū which travels via Yawatahama.

Getting Around

Uwajima is a good place to explore by bicycle since it's quiet and the traffic is not too bad. The tourist office across from the station rents bicycles for Y100 an hour.

Kyūshū is the furthest south of the four major islands of Japan and, although somewhat isolated from the events of Central Honshū, it has been an important entry point for foreign influence and culture. Kyūshū is the closest island to Korea and China and it was from Kyūshū that the Yamato tribe extended their power to Honshū. Some of the earliest evidence of Japanese civilisation can be seen at the archaeological excavations around Miyazaki and at the many ancient stone carvings in the Usuki area. More recently Kyūshū was for many centuries the sole link to European civilisation. During the long period of isolation from the West, the Dutch settlement at Nagasaki in Kyūshū was Japan's only connection to the outside world.

For visitors, one of Kyūshū's prime attractions would be Nagasaki with its European-influenced history and its atomic tragedy. In the north, Fukuoka/Hakata is a major international arrival point and the terminus for the shinkansen line from Tokyo. In the centre of the island there is the massive volcanic caldera of Mt Aso while more volcanic activity can be witnessed in the south at Sakurajima. Larger towns like Kagoshima and Kumamoto offer fine gardens and magnificent castles while Beppu is one of Japan's major hot-spring centres. There are some good walking opportunities, particularly along the Kirishima volcano chain.

The climate is milder than other parts of Japan and the people of Kyūshū are reputed to be hard drinkers and outstandingly friendly – a visit to a local bar may provide proof of both theories!

GETTING THERE & AWAY
Air
See the introductory Getting Around chapter for details of fares and routes. There are major airports at Beppu/Oita, Fukuoka, Kagoshima, Kumamoto, Miyazaki and Nagasaki. Fukuoka is the major international gateway for Kyūshū. There are also flights to islands off the coast of Kyūshū and to the islands south-west from Kagoshima down to Okinawa.

Train
The shinkansen line from Tokyo and Osaka crosses to Kyūshū from Shimonoseki and terminates in Fukuoka/Hakata. The major cities in Kyūshū are all connected by railway but not by high-speed shinkansen service.

Road and railway tunnels connect Shimonoseki at the western end of Honshū with Kitakyūshū on Kyūshū.

Ferry
There are numerous sea connections to Kyūshū; some of the more interesting ones are dealt with in more detail in the relevant sections of this chapter. Routes include:

Beppu or Oita to Hiroshima, Kōbe, Matsuyama, Osaka, Takamatsu, Uwajima and Yawatahama
Fukuoka/Hakata to Okinawa
Hyuga to Kawasaki and Osaka
Kagoshima to Okinawa and Osaka
Kokura to Hitakatsu, Izumiotsu, Kōbe, Matsuyama, Osaka, Pusan, Tokushima and Tokyo
Kunisaki to Tokuyama
Saeki to Sukumo
Saganoseki to Misaki
Shibushi to Osaka
Takedazu to Tokuyama
Usuki to Yawatahama

In addition local ferry services operate between Kyūshū and islands off the coast.

Fukuoka-ken

福岡県

The northern prefecture of Fukuoka will be the arrival point for most visitors to Kyūshū whether they cross over from Shimonoseki at the western end of Honshū or fly straight into Fukuoka city's conveniently central international airport.

KITAKYUSHU 北九州

Kitakyūshū, literally 'North Kyūshū City', is a place you simply pass through; this industrial conurbation sprawling along the north-eastern corner of the island is unlikely to be anybody's favourite Japanese city. In actual fact it consists of five separate cities – Wakamatsu, Yahata, Tobata, Kokura and Moji – which have gradually merged together into one enormous traffic jam.

Curiously, one of the cities in the Kitakyūshū cluster would be a familiar name today worldwide were it not for a cloudy day in 1945. Kokura would have been the world's second atomic bomb target, but cloud obscured the city and the mission was diverted to Nagasaki.

Kitakyūshū has achieved pre-eminence in Japanese semiconductor manufacture but this is scarcely a reason to hang around. If you do have time to waste in Kitakyūshū, the reconstructed Kokura-jō Castle is about half a km west of JR Kokura station. The superb Kitakyūshū Municipal Art Museum is 20 minutes by road from the railway station; it's closed on Mondays. The Hiraodai Plateau south of Kokura is reached via Ishihara and is somewhat similar to Akiyoshidai in Western Honshū with rolling fields dotted with strange rock outcrops and the limestone Senbutsu Cave as well.

Places to Stay

The *Kitakyūshū Youth Hostel* (tel 093-681-8142) near JR Yahata station has beds at Y2100. The Japanese Inn Group has the *Town House Matsuya* (tel 093-661-7890) at 2-8-3 Nishihonmachi, Yahata-higashi-ku, also near Yahata station. Singles/doubles are Y4000/6400.

The *Kitakyūshū Dai Ichi Hotel* (tel 093-551-7331) is a cheaper business hotel with singles from Y4800 to Y5000, doubles at Y6600 and twins at Y8200. *Kokura Tōkyū Inn* (tel 093-521-0109) and *Kokura Washington Hotel* (093-531-3111) are among the other popular business hotels in the town centre.

Getting There & Away

Train The simplest means of getting from Kitakyūshū to Shimonoseki in Honshū, or vice versa, is to take a JR train through the tunnel under the Kanmon Straits. The first railway station on the Kitakyūshū side is Moji but Kokura is a more central location.

Hitching Kitakyūshū is one long, sprawling urban mess, unpleasant to drive through and near impossible to hitch out of. Travellers hitchhiking to Honshū can either try the Kanmon tunnel entrance near JR Moji station or cross to Shimonoseki on the Honshū side and start from there. Hitching further into Kyūshū is probably best accomplished by getting well out of Kitakyūshū before you start.

Ferry There are regular ferry services between Kokura and Kōbe, Matsuyama, Osaka, Tokyo and other Honshū ports.

FUKUOKA/HAKATA 福岡、博多

Fukuoka/Hakata (population 1.2 million) is a somewhat confusing city as the airport is always referred to as Fukuoka, and the shinkansen terminus as Hakata. Today it is the biggest city in Kyūshū but it was originally two separate towns – the lordly Fukuoka to the west of the Naka River and the common folks' Hakata to the east. When the two merged in 1889, the label Fukuoka was applied to both towns, but subsequent development has chiefly been in Hakata and many residents refer to the town by that name.

Although there are no compelling tourist attractions in Fukuoka it's a pleasant city and easy to get around. The city gives a real impression of energy and movement. It feels very cosmopolitan and, comparatively speaking, there seem to be many gaijin. Nearby areas of interest include the fine coastal scenery beyond Karatsu to the west and the interesting temples and shrines of Dazaifu, only a few km south.

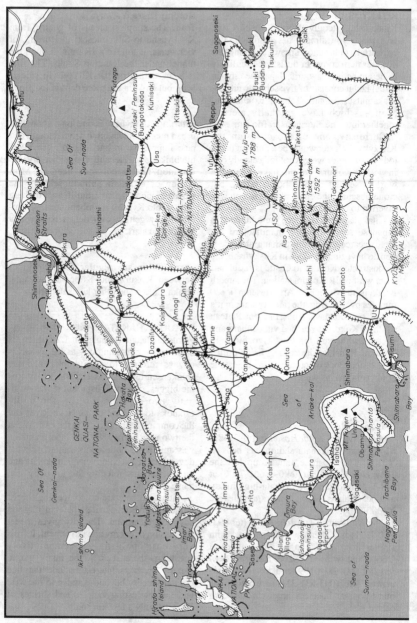

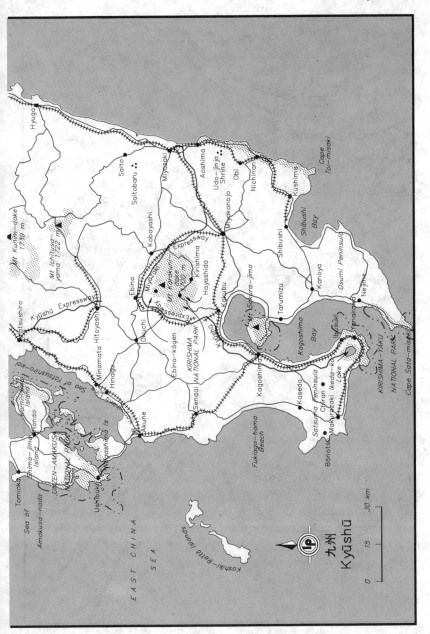

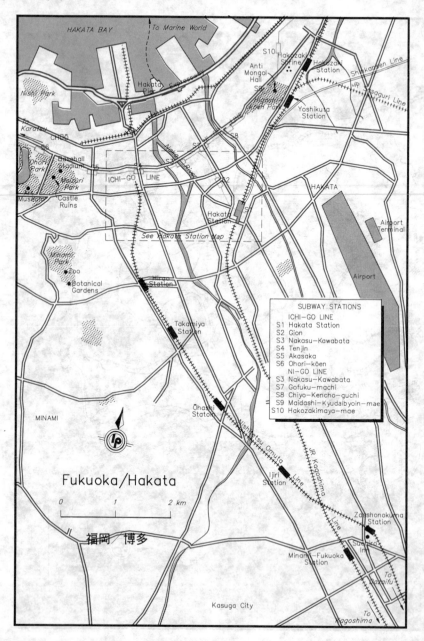

HAKATA BAY

To Marine World

S10 Hakozaki Shrine
Anti Mongol Hall
Hakozaki Station
JR Sasaguri Line

Shinkansen Line

Nishi Park

Hakata Pier

S9

Yoshikuta Station

Karatsu

CBD

S6

Ohori Park

Baseball Stadium
S5
Maizuri Park
S4

Museum

Castle Ruins

ICHI-GO LINE

S3

S2

HAKATA

Airport Terminal

Hakata Station
S1

See Hakata Station Map

Airport

Minami Park
Zoo
Botanical Gardens

Hirao Station

Takamiya Station

SUBWAY STATIONS
ICHI-GO LINE
S1 Hakata Station
S2 Gion
S3 Nakasu-Kawabata
S4 Tenjin
S5 Akasaka
S6 Ohori-kōen
NI-GO LINE
S3 Nakasu-Kawabata
S7 Gofuku-machi
S8 Chiyo-Kencho-guchi
S9 Maidashi-Kyudaibyoin-mae
S10 Hakozakimaya-mae

MINAMI

Ōhashi Station

Nishitetsu Omuta Line

JR Kagoshima Line

Fukuoka/Hakata

0   1   2 km

福岡 博多

Ijiri Station

Zasshonokuma Station

Sueoko Inn

Minami-Fukuoka Station

To Dazaifu

Kasuga City

To Kagoshima

Orientation & Information

There are two important areas in central Fukuoka – Hakata and Tenjin. JR Hakata station is the transport terminus for the city and is surrounded by hotels and offices. The railway station is flanked by the Fukuoka Kōtsū bus centre on one side and the Hakata post office on the other.

West of Hakata is Tenjin, the business and shopping centre, which is focused along Tenjin-nishi-dōri. Underneath this busy street is Tenjin-chika-gai, a crowded underground shopping mall which extends for 400 metres. The Tenjin bus centre here is close to the terminus of the private Nishitetsu Omuta line.

Sandwiched between JR Hakata station and the shopping centre on an island in the Naka River, is Nakasu, the entertainment centre of the city. The name literally means 'sandbank in the middle of the Naka River'!

The tourist information office in JR Hakata station is open from 9 am to 7 pm and has information and maps in English. The station is large and confusing at first but the office is more or less in the centre of the main floor. For travellers going on to South Korea there's a Korean consulate (tel 092-771-0461) west of Tenjin, very near the Akasaka

subway station. There's also a British consulate (tel 092-476-2525) and a US consulate (tel 092-751-9331).

Rainbow is a monthly English-language newsletter produced for Fukuoka-area gaijin and available from Rainbow Plaza (tel 092-733-2220) which is on the 8th floor of the IMS building in Tenjin. Rainbow also has videos on Japan, books, magazines and a noticeboard with events, accommodation and jobs. The Kinokuniya bookshop on the 6th floor of the Tenjin Core building has an excellent selection of English-language books. There's also a Maruzen bookshop just off Daihaku-dōri St, north of JR Hakata station.

Shrines & Temples

The Shōfuku-ji Temple is a Zen temple originally founded in 1195 by the priest who first introduced Zen doctrines to Japan and who is also credited with introducing tea. The temple was badly damaged during WW II and only occupies a quarter of its former area. It's within walking distance of JR Hakata station; don't confuse it with the Sōfuku-ji Temple, a little further away.

Also within walking distance of JR Hakata station is the Sumiyoshi-jinja Shrine, one of the oldest in Kyūshū; the main shrine was restored in 1623.

Fukuoka-jō Castle

Only the walls of Fukuoka-jō Castle remain in what is now Maizuri Park but the castle's hilltop site provides fine views of the city. The Ohori-kōen Park is adjacent to the castle grounds and has a traditional (though recently constructed) Japanese garden on its southern side. The Fukuoka City Art Museum is also in the park and is open from 9.30 am to 5.30 pm daily except Mondays; admission is Y150. You can get to the castle site by bus No 13 from Tenjin or by the subway to Ohori-kōen station.

Other Attractions

The red-brick building on Showa-dōri St, close to the river coming from Tenjin, is of English design and dates from 1909. It used

博多駅附近／天神

Hakata Station & Tenjin Areas

0   150   300 m

1 Akasaka Subway Station
2 Korean Consulate
3 Matsuya Ladies
4 Main Post Office
5 Former Historical Museum
6 Hakata Tōkyū Hotel
7 ANA
8 Tenjin Subway Station
9 Iwataya Department Store
10 Tenjin Core
11 NHK
12 NTT
13 Solaria Plaza
14 Tenjin Bus Centre
15 Kego Park
16 Kego-jinja Shrine
17 Daimaru Department Store
18 Yakuin Station
19 Sumiyoshi Bridge
20 Food Stalls
21 Haruyoshi Bridge
22 Tamaya Department Store
23 Nakasu Subway Station
24 JAL
25 Shōfuku-ji Temple
26 Tocho-ji Temple
27 Gion Subway Station
28 Kushida Shrine
29 Capsule Inn Hakata
30 Capsuleland Fukuoka
31 Sumiyoshi-jinja Shrine
32 Hokke Club Hakata
33 Chisan Hotel Hakata
34 Mitsui Urban Hotel
35 Business Hotel Royal
36 Hakata Business Hotel
37 Meiji Park
38 ANA Hotel Hakata
39 Hakata Post Office
40 ANA
41 JAS
42 British Consulate
43 Fukuoka Kōtsū Bus Centre
44 JR Hakata Station
45 Green Hotel 2
46 Green Hotel 1
47 Sun Life Hotel 1
48 Hotel Centraza & Gourmet City
49 Sun Life Hotel 2
50 Hotel Clio Court
51 NTT

Hakata Station & Tenjin Areas

1	赤坂地下鉄駅	27	祇園地下鉄駅
2	朝国領事館	28	櫛田神社
3	松屋レイテイズ	29	カプセルイン博多
4	中央郵便局	30	カプセルランド福岡
5	歴史博物館	31	住吉神社
6	博多東急ホテル	32	法華クラブ博多
7	ANA	33	ちさんホテル福岡
8	天神地下鉄駅	34	三井アーバンホテル
9	岩田屋	35	ビジネスホテルローヤル
10	天神コー	36	ハカタビジネスホテル
11	NHK	37	明治公園
12	NTT	38	ANA
13	ソラリアプラザ	39	博多郵便局
14	天神バスセンター	40	ANA
15	警固公園	41	JAS
16	警固神社	42	英国領事館
17	大丸	43	福岡交通バスセンター
18	薬院駅	44	JR 博多駅
19	住吉橋	45	グリーンホテル、2.
20	たべもの売店	46	グリーンホテル、1.
21	春吉橋	47	サンライフホテル、1.
22	玉屋店	48	ホテルセントラザ
23	中洲地下鉄駅	49	サンフイフホテル、2.
24	JAL	50	ホテルクリオコート
25	聖福寺	51	NTT
26	とちょ寺		

to house the Fukuoka City Historical Museum, which is now in a new building west of the town centre.

The Kushida Shrine near the Hakata River opposite the southern end of Nakasu Island on the Hakata side is the starting point for the Hakata Yamagasa float race in July. The Hakozaki Shrine has a stone anchor retrieved from the Mongol invasion attempt. To get there, take the Ni-go subway line to Hakozakimaya-mae.

Higashi-kōen Park is north-east of JR Hakata station, en route to the Hakozaki Shrine. The Genkō Historical Museum (entry Y300), also known as the Anti-Mongol Hall, displays items related to the abortive Mongolian invasions. To get there, take a JR train one stop from Hakata to Yoshizuka or take the subway towards Kaizuka and get off at the Maidashi-Kyudai-byoin-mae stop. Between Yoshizuka station and the museum is a large statue of Nichiren (1222-84) who predicted the invasion.

Fukuoka's zoo and botanical gardens are south of the castle in Minami Park. To get there, take a bus No 56 (for Hibaru-eigyosho) or bus Nos 41 or 43 (for Dobutsu-en-yuki) from stop No 10 in the Tenjin bus centre. Marine World Umi-no-Nakamichi is a seaside amusement park and swimming pool reached by ferry across Hakata Bay from Hakata Pier.

Festivals

The Hakata Yamagasa Festival, the city's major annual event, is held from 1 to 15 July; seven groups of men race through the city carrying huge floats which weigh about a ton. The floats are displayed around the city from 1 to 14 July.

A major sumō tournament is held in Kyūshū in mid-November and, in early December, the Fukuoka Marathon is one of the world's most important marathon races, attracting world-class runners from many countries.

Places to Stay

Budget Accommodation Fukuoka itself has no youth hostel, but there is one in nearby Dazaifu, within easy commuting distance of the city (see the Dazaifu Places to Stay section). The information counter in JR Hakata station has a list of inexpensive hotel accommodation in Fukuoka and can make reservations.

The Japanese Inn Group's *Suehiro Inn* (tel 092-581-0306) is a popular place with rooms from Y4000/7300 for singles/doubles and from Y9300 for triples. The inn, at 2-1-9 Minamihonmachi, is directly across the road from the Nishitetsu Zasshonokuma railway station, about seven km from the city centre; it's easy to get there on the regular suburban railway services.

If you've wanted to try a capsule hotel (for which you have to be male) then head for *Capsuleland Fukuoka* (tel 092-291-1009) which is north of Hakata and near the Nakasu Island entertainment district. A sign outside also announces 'Daiwa Club' in English. Your very own capsule costs Y3300 for the night and there's a large bath, sauna, massage room, restaurant, bar, TV room and other amenities. Just around the corner is the *Capsule Inn Hakata* (tel 092-281-2244).

Hotels There are numerous business hotels around the city centre, particularly around JR Hakata station. The *Green Hotel 1* and *Green*

Hotel 2 (tel 092-451-4111) are two of about 10 hotels directly behind the railway station. No 1 has singles/doubles from Y5500/7200, while the newer and slightly better No 2 has singles from Y8000.

Other hotels behind the station include two *Sun Life* hotels – No 1 (tel 092-473-7111) and No 2 (tel 092-473-7112). Both are standard business hotels with rooms from Y5800/ 9000. The *Hotel Clio Court* (tel 092-472-1111) is a glossier and more expensive hotel with singles from Y7000 to Y9000, doubles and twins from Y8000 to Y18,000. Facing the Clio Court is the *Hotel Centraza Hakata* (tel 092-461-0111) which is also in the more expensive category: prices here are from Y8000/11,000 for singles/doubles .

The *Mitsui Urban Hotel* (tel 092-451-5111), five blocks from JR Hakata station along Daihaku-dōri, has singles/doubles from Y6000/10,000; the rooms are typically minute. Next door is the similarly priced *Chisan Hotel Hakata* (tel 092-411-3211). The smaller *Hakata Business Hotel* (tel 092-431-0737) has rooms from Y5500/8500 and the *Business Hotel Royal* (tel 092-411-3300), near the Chisan and Mitsui Urban hotels, has rooms from Y4400/6600 for singles/doubles.

The *ANA Hotel Hakata* (tel 092-471-7111) on the left as you leave JR Hakata station, is one of the best places in town with singles/doubles from Y10,000/14,000. A little beyond it, close to the Sumiyoshi-jinja Shrine, is the *Hokke Club Hakata* (tel 092-271-3171), a member of the popular Hokke Club business hotel chain; rooms without bathroom are Y4500/8000 including breakfast. The *Hakata Tōkyū Hotel* (tel 092-781-7111) is part of the major Tōkyū hotel chain and is next to the Naka River, close to the northern end of Nakasu Island.

Places to Eat

As the western terminus of the shinkansen line from Tokyo, the busy JR Hakata station offers a great number of places to eat including a full assortment of fast-food restaurants, department stores and other places offering eating possibilities. Behind the railway station under the Hotel Centraza is *Gourmet City* with two basement floors of restaurants offering Chinese, Japanese and European food and desserts. At lunch time there are lots of teishoku bargains and it's open until 11 pm. The Green Hotel's *Ginroku* restaurant is good value while the Hotel Clio Court has a series of restaurants known as the *Clio Seven*. There are plenty of restaurants, bars, shops and bakeries around the Sueiro Inn.

The underground shopping mall at Tenjin has numerous eating places. Try *Art Coffee* for a Y200 cup of coffee, a good Y380 setto (set breakfast) or a great selection of hot dogs or sandwiches from Y250 to Y450. Entrances from the mall lead into various department-store food basements. In particular, the Daimaru basement has a fantastic selection of food including sandwiches, pizza slices, bentō (boxed lunches) or whatever else you fancy. You can take your fast food across the road and eat it in the Kego Park beside the Kego-jinja Shrine.

The Nakasu Island entertainment district, between Hakata and Tenjin, has many restaurants and a variety of fast-food outlets including a *McDonald's* and a *Mister Donut*. Along the western bank of the island at night, you'll find a collection of snack stands offering noodles, kebabs and other quick meals which you can enjoy while watching the lights across the Naka River.

Entertainment

Nakasu Island is one of the busiest entertainment districts in Japan with several thousand bars, restaurants and clubs. During the summer evenings from mid-April to August there's a beer garden on top of the Izutsuya department store above JR Hakata station.

Things to Buy

Clay Hakata dolls depicting women, children, samurai and geisha are a popular Fukuoka craft. Hakata *obi*, the silk sashes worn with a kimono, are another typical craft of the region. Try the Iwataya department store in Tenjin for these and other items.

Getting There & Away

Air Fukuoka is an international gateway to Japan with flights to and from Australia, Hong Kong, South Korea, the Philippines, Taiwan and the USA. There are also internal flights to other centres in Japan including more than 20 flights a day to Tokyo (Y25,350, one hour and 45 minutes); almost all of these go to Haneda Airport rather than Narita International Airport. Flights to Osaka (Y14,400) take just over an hour.

Train & Bus JR Hakata station is the western terminus of the 1177 km Tokyo-Osaka-Hakata shinkansen service. There are approximately 15 services a day to or from Tokyo (Y21,300, six to seven hours), 30 to or from Osaka (Y14,310, three to four hours) and 50 from Hiroshima (Y8530, 1½ to two hours).

JR lines also fan out from Hakata to other centres in Kyūshū. The Nippō line runs through Hakata, Beppu, Miyazaki and Kagoshima; the Kagoshima line through Hakata, Kumamoto, Yatsushiro and Kagoshima; and both the Nagasaki and Sasebo lines from Hakata to Saga and Sasebo or Hakata to Nagasaki. From Tenjin railway station the Nishitetsu line operates through Tenjin, Dazaifu, Kurume, Yanagawa and Omuta. You can also travel by road or train to Karatsu and continue from there to Nagasaki by train.

Buses depart from the Kōtsū bus centre near JR Hakata station and from the Tenjin bus centre.

Ferry The Hakata-Nagasaki Holland Village boat service would be an interesting way to get to Nagasaki (see the Nagasaki Holland Village section later). There are also services from Fukuoka to Okinawa, to Iki-shima Island and other islands off Kyūshū.

Getting Around

To/From the Airport Fukuoka Airport is conveniently close to the city centre, a complete contrast with the airport in Tokyo. Airport buses take about 15 minutes to JR Hakata station (Y240) or 30 minutes to

Tenjin (Y270). Transfer tickets on to the subway system can be bought from ticket-vending machines at the airport. The airport bus departs from platform No 12 at the Kōtsū bus centre (next to JR Hakata station). Taxis between the airport and city centre cost from around Y1000. The airport has three terminals – No 3 is for international flights, No 2 is for JAL and JAS flights to Tokyo (both Haneda and Narita airports) and to Okinawa, and No 1 is for all other domestic flights.

Train There are two subway lines in Fukuoka. Line 1 (Ichi-go line) operates from JR Hakata station through Tenjin and out to Meinohama; from there trains continue west on the JR Chikuhi line. Line 2 (Ni-go line) operates from the Nakasu-Kawabata station (the junction subway station between Tenjin and Hakata) out to Kawabata and Kaizuka.

Bus City and long-distance bus services operate from the Kōtsū bus centre at JR Hakata station and the Tenjin bus centre at Tenjin. The Nishitetsu bus company covers most tourist attractions around the city within its Y140 fare zone and you can get a Y700 one-day pass.

DAZAIFU   太宰府
Dazaifu, with its great shrine and interesting temples, is almost close enough to be a suburb of Fukuoka. You could take a day trip to Dazaifu or even stay there and skip Fukuoka altogether.

Information
The information office outside Nishitetsu Dazaifu station, near the entranceway to the Tenman-gū Shrine, has helpful staff and an excellent English brochure and map.

Tenman-gū Shrine
The poet and scholar Sugawara Michizane was an important personage in the Kyoto court until he fell foul of political intrigue and was exiled to distant Dazaifu where he died two years later. Subsequent disasters which struck Kyoto were blamed on his unfair dismissal and he became deified as Tenman Tenjin or Kankō, the god of culture and scholars. His great shrine and burial place attracts countless visitors.

The brightly painted orange shrine is entered via a picturesque arched bridge and behind the shrine building is the Kankō Historical Museum (entry Y200) with dioramas showing events in Tenjin's life. The treasure house has artefacts connected with his life and the history of the shrine. The shrine's Honden (Main Hall) was rebuilt in 1583.

Kōmyō-ji Temple
In this small temple the Ittekikaino-niwa Garden is a breathtakingly beautiful example of a Zen garden and a peaceful contrast to the crowds and hype in the nearby shrine.

Kaidan-in & Kanzeon-ji Temples
Now a Zen Buddhist temple the Kaidan-in dates from 761 AD and was one of the most important monasteries in Japan. The adjacent Kanzeon-ji Temple dates from 746 AD but only the great 697 AD bell, said to be the oldest in Japan, remains from the original construction.

Tenman-gū Treasure Hall
This treasure hall has a wonderful collection of statuary, most of it of wood, dating from the 10th to 12th centuries and of impressive size. The style of some of the pieces is more Indian or Tibetan than Japanese. The display is open from 9 am to 5 pm and entry is Y400.

Other Attractions
The Dazaifu Exhibition Hall displays finds from local archaeological excavations and is open daily from 9 am to 4.30 pm except Mondays. Nearby are the Tofurō Ruins, foundations of the buildings from the era when Dazaifu governed all of Kyūshū. Enoki-sha is where Sugawara Michizane died and from here his body was transported to its burial place, now the shrine, on the ox cart which appears in so many local depictions. The Kyūshū Historical Museum near the shrine is open from 9.30 am to 4.30 pm daily except Mondays; admission is free.

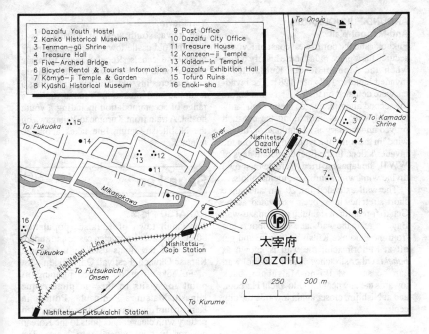

1 Dazaifu Youth Hostel
2 Kankō Historical Museum
3 Tenman-gū Shrine
4 Treasure Hall
5 Five-Arched Bridge
6 Bicycle Rental & Tourist Information
7 Kōmyō-ji Temple & Garden
8 Kyūshū Historical Museum
9 Post Office
10 Dazaifu City Office
11 Treasure House
12 Kanzeon-ji Temple
13 Kaidan-in Temple
14 Dazaifu Exhibition Hall
15 Tofurō Ruins
16 Enoki-sha

太宰府
Dazaifu

0   250   500 m

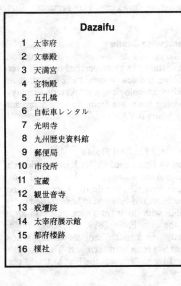

Dazaifu

1 太宰府
2 文華殿
3 天満宮
4 宝物殿
5 五孔橋
6 自転車レンタル
7 光明寺
8 九州歴史資料館
9 郵便局
10 市役所
11 宝蔵
12 観世音寺
13 戒壇院
14 太宰府展示館
15 都府楼跡
16 榎社

Places to Stay

The *Dazaifu Youth Hostel* (tel 092-922-8740) is actually in one of the Dazaifu temples; it has only 24 beds and charges Y2100 per night. Ryokan and other accommodation can be found in the nearby town of Futsukaichi Onsen.

Getting There & Away

Train & Bus A Nishitetsu line train will take you to Futsukaichi railway station from Tenjin in Fukuoka in 20 to 30 minutes. From Futsukaichi, you'll have to change for the two-station ride to Nishitetsu-Dazaifu railway station. Alternatively, you can take a JR train from JR Hakata station to Kokutetsu-Futsukaichi (the JR station) and then a bus to Nishitetsu-Futsukaichi.

Getting Around

Bicycles can be rented from the information office next to Dazaifu railway station.

AROUND FUKUOKA-KEN
Anti-Mongol Wall

Fukuoka and the north-west coast of Kyūshū secured their place in Japanese history books when the Mongol leader Kublai Khan invaded Japan in 1274 and 1281. The invaders were defeated on their first try and before the second attempt, a three metre high 'anti-Mongol wall' was built along the coast. It proved unnecessary as a kamikaze or 'divine wind' in the form of a typhoon wiped out the invader's fleet. In the final desperate days of WW II, the Japanese tried to create their own divine wind with kamikaze suicide pilots.

The wall extended for 20 km and some short stretches have been excavated at the Genkō fort north of Imajuku near Imazu-wan Bay. To get to the wall, take a Nishinoura bus from the Fukuoka Kōtsū bus centre and get off at Midōrimachi; the wall is known as *boheki*. Other stretches of anti-Mongol wall can be seen at Iki-no-Matsubara, back towards the city near the Odo Yacht Harbour, and at Nishijin, closer again towards the city centre.

Genkai Quasi-National Park

The Genkō fort wall at Imajuku is in the Genkai Quasi-National Park and the nearby Obaru beach offers surprisingly good swimming although there are even better beaches further west. Keya-no-Oto (Great Cave of Keya) is at the western end of the Itoshima Peninsula. It's a popular tourist attraction and buses run there directly from the Kōtsū bus centre in Hakata, taking about 1½ hours.

Kurume

The town of Kurume, south of Dazaifu, is noted for its crafts including paper making, bamboo work and tie-dyed textiles. Pottery is also produced in nearby towns. The Ishibashi Bunka Centre is a Bridgestone sponsored art museum (open from 10 am to 5 pm daily except Mondays) and the town also has the Bairin-ji Temple and the Suitengū Shrine. It takes about half an hour to get to Kurume from Fukuoka, either on the JR line or the Nishitetsu railway line.

Yanagawa

Yanagawa, south-west of Kurume, is a peaceful old castle town noted for its many moats and canals. Regular canal trips are made around the waterways. The town has some interesting old buildings including a teahouse and museum. Yanagawa has a range of accommodation including a youth hostel. A train from Kurume to Yanagawa on the Nishitetsu-Omuta line takes about 20 minutes.

Saga-ken　　佐賀県

KARATSU　唐津

The small town of Karatsu (population 80,000) has a reconstructed castle and superb display of the floats used in the annual Karatsu Okunchi Festival. Only 50 km west of Fukuoka, it makes a good jumping-off point for visits to the the picturesque Higashi-Matsuura Peninsula. Potters in Karatsu turn out primitive but well-respected pottery with clear connections to the Korean designs first introduced into Japan. The sandy beach east of Karatsu at Niji-no-Matsubara draws crowds in summer.

Karatsu-jō Castle

Although it's just a modern reconstruction, the castle looks great, perched on a hill overlooking the sea. Inside, there's a museum with archaeological and pottery displays; opening hours are from 9 am to 5 pm and admission is Y300.

Okunchi Festival Floats

The 14 floats used in the Karatsu Okunchi Festival are displayed in the Festival Float Exhibition Hall beside the Karatsu Shrine. The festival is believed to have started in the 1660s with floats from each of the 17 areas of the city. From 1819, the design of the floats was standardised; previously a new float had been built each year. The Aka-jishi (Red Lion) float was the first to take a per-

Temples & Pagodas

Castles

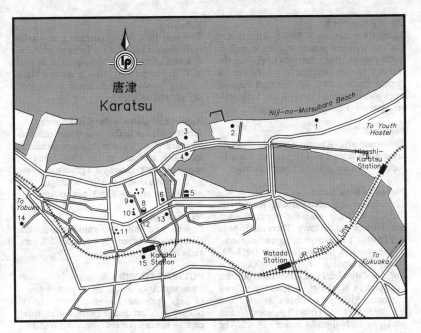

漢津
Karatsu

Niji-no-Matsubara Beach

To Youth Hostel

Higashi–Karatsu Station

To Yobuko

Karatsu Station

Watada Station

JR Chikuhi Line

To Fukuoka

Karatsu

1 Kokuminshukusha
2 Ryokan Yoyokaku
3 Karatsu-jō Castle
4 Car Park
5 Main Post Office
6 NTT
7 Karatsu Shrine
8 Showa Bus Station
9 Festival Float Exhibition Hall
10 Tourist Information Centre
11 Kinsho-ji Temple
12 France's Bakery
13 Karatsu Green Hotel
14 Kojiro Kiln
15 Karatsu City Hotel

Karatsu

1 国民宿舎
2 旅館洋々閣
3 唐津城
4 駐車場
5 中央郵便局
6 NTT
7 唐津神社
8 昭和バスセンター
9 ひき山展示場
10 観光案内所
11 近松寺
12 フランスベイカリ
13 唐津グリーンホテル
14 小次郎窯
15 唐津シティホテル

manent design. Others include a turtle, samurai helmets, strange fish, a dragon and a chicken. The display, which includes a video about the festival parade, is open from 9 am to 5 pm and entry is Y200.

Other Attractions

There are a number of pottery kilns where you can see local potters at work as well as pottery shops along the street between the railway station and the town centre. A popular cycling track cuts through the pine trees planted behind the five km long Niji-no-Matsubara Beach.

Festivals

The wonderful Karatsu Okunchi Festival takes place from 2 to 4 November when 14 superb floats are drawn through the town.

Places to Stay & Eat

The *Niji-no-Matsubara Youth Hostel* (tel 0955-72-4526) is near the popular beach resort just east of the town. There are 56 beds at Y1840 or Y1990 depending on the season.

The *Karatsu Green Hotel* (tel 0955-73-6289) has rooms at Y4000/6000. The *Karatsu City Hotel* (tel 0955-72-1100) is a big, modern hotel right behind the railway station. Singles/doubles start from Y5500/10,000. Most other hotels and ryokan are along the Niji-no-Matsubara Beach. The Kinsho-ji Temple is near the centre.

Getting There & Away

From Fukuoka take the No 1 (Ichi-go) subway line from Hakata or Tenjin to the end of the line and continue on the JR Chikuhi line. It takes about one hour 20 minutes to reach Karatsu. You can continue from Karatsu to Nagasaki on the JR Karatsu line to Saga and on the JR Nagasaki line from there.

Getting Around

Bicycles can be rented from JR Karatsu station, the youth hostel or from Seto Cycle, just across the bridge from the castle towards Niji-no-Matsubara Beach. A circuit of the Higashi-Matsuura Peninsula would make a good day trip from Karatsu in a rental car.

HIGASHI-MATSUURA PENINSULA
東松浦半島

Karatsu is at the base of the Higashi-Matsuura Peninsula with its dramatic coastline and interesting little fishing ports.

Yobuko

This busy little fishing port has a wonderful early-morning market for fish and produce. A series of ryokan, charging from around Y7000 per person, line a narrow lane running beside the waterfront; rooms look straight out onto the bay.

Hatomizaki Underwater Observatory

A pier leads out to this underwater observatory where you can see different species of local fish attracted to the observatory by regular feeding! Nearby is a government-run kokuminshukusha (people's lodge) with rooms from around Y3500 per person.

Nagoya Castle

It was from this now ruined castle that Hideyoshi launched his unsuccessful invasions of Korea.

POTTERY TOWNS

Imari and Arita are the major pottery towns of Saga Prefecture. From the early 1600s, pottery was produced in this area using captive Korean potters. The work was done in Arita and Okawachiyama and the Korean experts were zealously guarded so that the secrets of their craft did not slip out. Pottery from this area, with its brightly coloured glazes, is still highly esteemed in Japan.

Imari

Although Imari is the name commonly associated with the pottery from this area, it is actually produced in Okawachiyama and Arita. Okawachiyama, where 20 pottery kilns operate today, is a 15-minute bus ride from JR Imari station. The nearby Nabeshima Hanyō-kōen Park shows the techniques and living conditions in a feudal-era pottery. Imari is about an hour by bus from Karatsu, a little less by train on the JR Chikuhi line.

Arita

It was at Arita that kaolin clay was discovered in 1615, permitting the manufacture of fine porcelain for the first time. It's a sprawling town, less interesting than Imari, but you can visit the Kyūshū Ceramic Museum (open from 9 am to 4.30 pm daily except Mondays) and Korean potter Ri Sanpei's original kaolin quarry. The Rekishi Minzoku Shiryōkan (Historical Museum) is by the quarry and the Arita Tōji Bijutsukan (Arita Ceramic Art Museum) is also nearby; both have the same opening hours as the Kyūshū Ceramic Museum. Pottery connoisseurs will find the Imaizumi Imaemon Gallery (open from 9 am to 5 pm daily except Sundays), the Sakaida Kakiemon Kiln (open from 9 am to 5 pm) and the Genemon Kiln (open Monday to Saturday from 8 am to 5.30 pm) very interesting.

Islands off Kyūshū's North-West Coast

Five larger and many smaller islands lie to the north-west of Kyūshū and are accessible from Fukuoka, Sasebo and Nagasaki. Tsu-shima, the largest of the group, is in the strait midway between Japan and Korea and is actually closer to Pusan than to Fukuoka. These are islands strictly for those who want to get far away from it all, foreign visitors are very rare. Some of the islands are part of Saga-ken Prefecture, others part of Naga-saki-ken.

Accommodation
There are youth hostels and many minshuku and ryokan on Tsu-shima, Hirado-shima and Fukue-jima islands.

Getting There & Away
Air There are a number of local air services to the islands. ANK flies between Fukuoka and Iki-shima for Y5210, Fukuoka and Tsu-shima for Y7960, Fukuoka and Fukue-jima for Y10,430 and Nagasaki and Fukue-jima for Y6410.

Ferry Ferry services operate from Fukuoka to Tsu-shima and Iki-shima islands, from Yobuko to Iki-shima Island, from Sasebo to

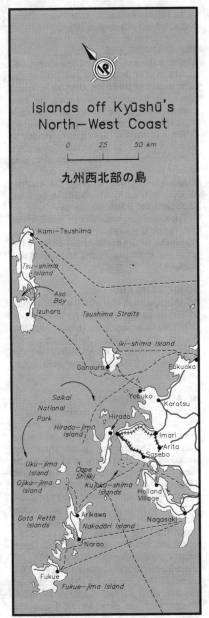

Islands off Kyūshū's North—West Coast

0   25   50 km

九州西北部の島

Nakadōri Island and from Nagasaki to
Nakadōri and Fukue-jima islands.

TSU-SHIMA ISLAND

The mountainous island of Tsu-shima, 682
sq km in area, is actually two islands; the
narrow neck of land connecting the two parts
was channelled through during the 16th
century. The port of Izuhara is the island's
main town and has a fort originally built by
Toyotomi Hideyoshi during an expedition to
Korea in 1592. The island has seen a more
recent conflict when the Czar's fleet was
utterly routed by the Japanese during the
Russo-Japanese War in 1905. The conflict
took place in the Tsushima Straits, between
Tsu-shima and Iki-shima islands.

Tsu-shima has a number of small towns
and a road runs most of its length. Aso Bay,
the almost totally enclosed bay between the
north and south islands, has many islets and
inlets.

IKI-SHIMA ISLAND

Iki-shima, with an area of 138 sq km, is south
of Tsu-shima and much closer to Fukuoka.
Iki-shima is an attractive island with fine
beaches; it's also relatively flat and a good
place for cycling. Gonoura is the main port
and Toyotomi Hideyoshi also built a fort
there.

HIRADO-SHIMA ISLAND

The island of Hirado-shima, close to Sasebo
and actually joined to Kyūshū by a bridge
from Hirado-guchi, has had an interesting
European history. Portuguese ships first
landed on Hirado-shima in 1549 and, a year
later, St Francis Xavier paid a visit to the
island (after his expulsion from Kagoshima).

It was not until 1584 that the Portuguese
formally established a trading post on the
island but they were soon followed by the
Dutch (in 1609) and the British (in 1613).
Relations between the British and Dutch
became so acrimonious that in 1618, the
Japanese had to restore law and order on the
island. In 1621, the British abandoned Japan
and turned their full attention to India.
Things were not easy for the Europeans

during the anti-Christian period in Japan and
today there is very little trace of the European
trading operations. The main town, Hirado,
was burnt down in 1906.

Hirado-shima has some older buildings
including a museum in the residence of the
Matsuura, who ruled the island from the 11th
to the 19th centuries. There are fine views
over the Gotō Rettō Islands from Cape
Shijiki-zaki and the western coast of the
island is particularly attractive. From
Kashimae, half an hour by bus from Sasebo,
regular boats operate to Hirado-shima via the
Kujukū-shima Islands.

GOTO RETTO ISLANDS

Fukue and Nakadōri are the two main islands
in the Gotō Rettō group but there are three
other medium-sized islands, squeezed
between the two large ones, plus over 100
small islands and islets. At one time, the
islands were a refuge for Japanese Christians
fleeing the Edo government's anti-Christian
repression; today the main attraction is the
natural beauty of the mountainous islands.

Fukue, the fishing port on the island of the
same name, is the main town in the group.
The Ishida-jō Castle in the town was burnt
down in 1614 and rebuilt in 1849. Along
with Hirado-shima and a strip of the Kyūshū
coast, the Gotō Rettō Islands are part of the
Saikai National Park.

KUJUKU-SHIMA ISLANDS

Between Hirado-shima and the Kyūshū
coast are the 170-odd Kujukū-shima Islands;
the name actually means '99 islands'. Cruise
boats operate around the islands from
Sasebo.

Nagasaki-ken　長崎県

NAGASAKI　長崎

Nagasaki is a busy and colourful city (population 450,000) but its unfortunate fate as the
second atomic bomb target quite obscures its
fascinating early history of contact with the
Portuguese and Dutch. Even after Commo-

dore Perry's historic visit to Japan, Nagasaki remained one of the major contact points with the West. Despite the popular image of Nagasaki as a totally modern city rising from an atomic wasteland, there are many reminders of its earlier history and European contact. The bomb itself actually missed its intended target towards the south of the city and scored a near direct hit on the largest Catholic church in Japan.

History

Nagasaki has the most varied history of any city in Japan, much of it tied up with the dramatic events of the 'Christian Century'. The accidental arrival of an off-course Portuguese ship at Tanega-shima Island in 1542 signalled the start of Nagasaki's long period as Japan's principal connection with the West.

The first visitors were soon followed by the great missionary St Francis Xavier in 1560 and although his visit was also brief, these Portuguese contacts were to have far-reaching effects. The primitive guns introduced by the Portuguese soon revolutionised warfare in Japan, forcing the construction of new and stronger castles and bringing to an end the anarchy and chaos of the 'Country at War' century.

Among the first Japanese to be converted to Christianity by the visitors was a minor daimyō in north-western Kyūshū. As a result of his conversion, the daimyō's new port of Nagasaki, established in 1571, soon became the main arrival point for Portuguese trade ships. Although the Portuguese principally acted as intermediaries between China and Japan, the trade was mutually profitable and Nagasaki quickly became a fashionable and wealthy city.

The growing influence of Christianity soon began to worry the Japanese and by 1587, Hideyoshi had decided to kick out the troublesome Jesuit missionaries and take direct control from Kyoto. By the end of the century, there were so many Christians in Japan and so much fear that their allegiance might lie outside the country that persecution became a serious business. The crucifixion of 26 European and Japanese Christians in Nagasaki in 1597 epitomised this new attitude and in 1614 the religion was completely banned. Suspected Christians were rounded up, tortured and killed, the Japanese wives and children of foreigners were deported, and the Catholic Portuguese and Spanish traders were expelled in favour of the Protestant Dutch, who were perceived as being more interested in trade and less in religion.

Finally, a bloody rebellion in 1637 brought the Christian Century to a dramatic close and ushered in Japan's two centuries of near complete isolation from the West. On the Shimabara-hantō Peninsula near Nagasaki, the peasantry rose up against the oppressive nobility and ran rings around the local armies. The peasantry held out for 80 days in a siege of Hara-jō Castle, but were finally wiped out by the local armies who had called in the support of the Dutch.

The shogun then banned all foreigners from Japan and no Japanese were allowed to travel overseas. The one small loophole in this ruling was the closely watched Dutch enclave at De-jima Island near Nagasaki. Through this small outpost a trickle of Western science and progress continued to filter into Japan and from 1720, when Dutch books were once again permitted to enter the country, Nagasaki became an important scientific and artistic centre. When Nagasaki reopened to the West in 1859, it quickly re-established itself as a major economic force, particularly for shipbuilding, and it was this industry which made Nagasaki an atomic target in the closing days of WW II.

Orientation & Information

The Hamanomachi arcade and the Maruyama entertainment area form the focus of Nagasaki's central city area, about a km south of the railway station. Further south are the Chinatown, Dutch Slopes and Glover Garden areas. Nagasaki is relatively compact and it's quite feasible to walk from the central area all the way south to Glover Garden. The atom bomb epicentre is in the

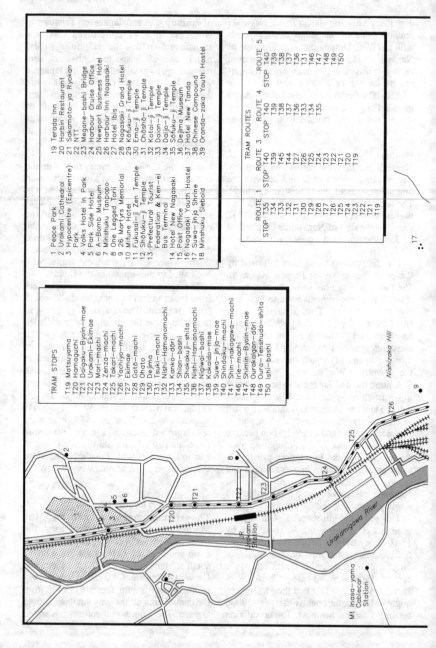

TRAM STOPS

T19 Matsuyama
T20 Hamaguchi
T21 Daigaku–Byoin–mae
T22 Urakami–Ekimae
T23 Mori–machi
T24 Zenzo–machi
T25 Takari–machi
T26 Yachiyo–machi
T27 Ekimae
T28 Gotō–machi
T29 Ohato
T30 Dejima
T31 Tsuki–machi
T32 Nishi–Hamanomachi
T33 Kanko–dōri
T34 Shian–bashi
T35 Shokakuji–shita
T36 Nishi–Hamanomachi
T37 Nigiwai–bashi
T38 Kokaido–mae
T39 Suwa–jinja–mae
T40 Shindaiku–machi
T41 Shin–nakagawa–machi
T46 Irie–machi
T47 Shimin–Byoin–mae
T48 Ourakaigan–dōri
T49 Oura–Tenshudo–shita
T50 Ishi–bashi

1 Peace Park
2 Urakami Cathedral
3 Hypocentre (Epicentre)
  Park
4 Volks Hotel In Park
5 Park Side Hotel
6 A–Bomb Museum
7 Minshuku Tanpopo
8 One Legged Torii
9 26 Martyrs Memorial
10 Mifune Hotel
11 Fukusai–ji Zen Temple
12 Shōfuku–ji Temple
13 Prefectural Tourist
   Federation & Ken–ei
   Bus Terminal
14 Hotel New Nagasaki
15 Post Office
16 Nagasaki Youth Hostel
17 Suwa–jinja Shrine
18 Minshuku Siebold

19 Terada Inn
20 Harbin Restaurant
21 Sakamoto–ya Ryokan
22 NTT
23 Megane–bashi Bridge
24 Harbour Cruise Office
25 Newport Business Hotel
26 Harbour Inn Nagasaki
27 Hotel Ibis
28 Nagasaki Grand Hotel
29 Kōfuku–ji Temple
30 Enma–ji Temple
31 Chōshō–ji Temple
32 Kotai–ji Temple
33 Daion–ji Temple
34 Daijo–ji Temple
35 Sōfuku–ji Temple
36 Dejima Museum
37 Hotel New Tanda
38 Chinese Compound
39 Oranda–zaka Youth Hostel

TRAM ROUTES

	ROUTE 1	ROUTE 3	ROUTE 4	ROUTE 5
STOP T40	STOP T35	STOP T40	STOP T40	STOP T40
	T34	T39	T39	T39
	T33	T45	T38	T38
	T32	T44	T37	T37
	T31	T27	T37	T36
	T30	T26	T36	T31
	T29	T25	T35	T46
	T28	T24	T34	T47
	T27	T23		T48
	T26	T22		T49
	T25	T21		T50
	T24	T20		
	T23	T19		
	T22			
	T21			
	T19			

Nishizaka Hill

Urakamigawa River

JR Urakami Station

Mt Inasa–yama Cablecar Station

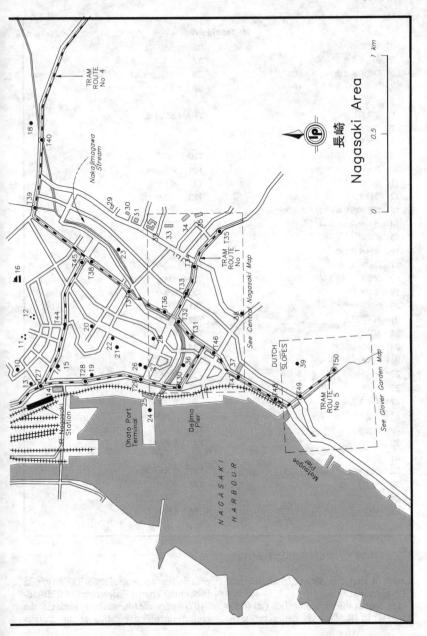

長崎

Nagasaki Area

TRAM ROUTE No 4

Nakajimagawa Stream

TRAM ROUTE No 1

See Central Nagasaki Map

DUTCH SLOPES

TRAM ROUTE No 5

See Glover Garden Map

JR Nagasaki Station

Ohato Port Terminal

Dejima Pier

Matsugoe Pier

NAGASAKI HARBOUR

0   0.5   1 km

Nagasaki Area

1	平和公園	36	出島資料館
2	浦上天主堂	37	ホテルニュータンダ
3	原爆中心公園	38	新地町(中華街)
4	フォルクスホテルインパーク	39	オランダザカユースホステル
5	パークサイドホテル		
6	原爆福祉会館	**TRAM STOPS**	
7	民宿タンポポ		
8	片足鳥居	T19	松山
9	二十六聖人殉教地	T20	浜口
10	みふめホテル	T21	大学病院前
11	福済寺	T22	浦上駅前
12	聖福寺	T23	茂里町
13	観光案内所/県営バスタミナル	T24	銭座町
14	ホテルニュー長崎	T25	宝町
15	郵便局	T26	八千代町
16	長崎青少年館	T27	駅前
17	諏訪神社	T28	五島町
18	民宿シーボルト邸	T29	大波止
19	テラダイン	T30	出島
20	ハビンレストラン	T31	築町
21	坂本屋旅館	T32	西浜町
22	NTT	T33	観光通
23	眼鏡橋	T34	思案橋
24	観光船大波止発着所	T35	正覚寺下
25	ニューポートビジネスホテル	T36	西浜町
26	ハーバーイン長崎	T37	賑橋
27	ホテルアイビス	T38	公会堂前
28	長崎グランドホテル	T39	諏訪神社前
29	興福寺	T40	新大工町
30	えま寺	T41	新中川町
31	長照寺	T46	入江町
32	皓台寺	T47	市民病院前
33	大音寺	T48	大浦海岸通
34	大光寺	T49	大浦天主堂下
35	崇福寺	T50	石橋

suburb of Urakami, about 2½ km north of JR Nagasaki station.

The tourist information office (tel 0958-23-3631) in JR Nagasaki station can assist with finding accommodation. The Nagasaki Prefectural Tourist Federation (tel 0958-56-9407) is opposite (the walkway leads into the prefectural office building at the upstairs level, through the exhibition of local crafts and manufactures). An information computer in the station displays information (Japanese and English) about attractions, hotels and restaurants and even prints out a map.

There is a great deal to see in Nagasaki and it's easy to spend a couple of days there.

A-Bomb Site

Urakami, the epicentre of the atomic explosion, is today a prosperous, peaceful suburb with modern shops, restaurants, cafés and even a couple of love hotels just a few steps from the epicentre. Nuclear ruin seems a long way away. The Matsuyama tram stop, the eighth stop north of JR Urakami station on tram routes 1 or 3, is near the site.

The Epicentre The Hypocentre Park has a black stone column marking the exact point above which the bomb exploded. Nearby are bomb-blasted relics including a section of the wall of the Urakami Cathedral and a buckled water tower.

A-Bomb Museum The Kokusai Bunka

Kaikan (International Cultural Hall) as the museum is curiously named, is an ugly and badly designed building overlooking the Hypocentre Park. The four floors of photographs, reports, equipment and displays telling the story of the blast are quite enough to leave most visitors decidedly shaken. After that it's worth remembering that Nagasaki's A-bomb packed only a tiny fraction of the destructive power of the countless nuclear weapons we are so lucky to possess today. Entry to the museum is Y50 and it is open from 9 am to 6 pm (April to October) and from 9 am to 5 pm (November to March). Behind the museum is the Nagasaki Municipal Museum; entry is Y100.

Peace Park North of the Hypocentre Park is the Heiwa-kōen (Peace Park) presided over by the Nagasaki Peace Statue. At the time of the explosion, the park was the site of the Urakami Prison and every occupant of the prison – prisoners and warders – was killed instantly. An annual antinuclear protest is held at the park on 9 August.

Urakami Cathedral The original Urakami

The Atomic Explosion

When the USAF B-29 bomber 'Bock's Car' set off from Tinian in the Marianas on 9 August 1945 to drop the second atomic bomb on Japan the target was Kokura on the north-eastern coast of Kyūshū. Fortunately for Kokura it was a cloudy day and, despite flying over the city three times, the bomber's crew could not sight the target, so a course was set for the secondary target, Nagasaki.

The B-29 arrived over Nagasaki at 10.58 am but again visibility was obscured by cloud. When a momentary gap appeared in the cloud cover, the Mitsubishi Arms Works, not the intended Mitsubishi shipyard, was sighted and became the target. The 4.5 ton 'Fat Man' bomb had an explosive power equivalent to 22 kilotons of TNT, far more than the 13 kilotons of Hiroshima's 'Little Boy'. Afterwards, the aircraft turned south and flew to Okinawa, arriving there with its fuel supply almost exhausted.

The explosion took place at 11.02 am, at an altitude of 500 metres, completely devastating the Urakami suburb of northern Nagasaki and killing 75,000 of Nagasaki's 240,000 population. Another 75,000 were injured and it is estimated that that number again have subsequently died as a result of the blast. Anybody out in the open within two km of the epicentre suffered severe burns from the heat of the explosion; even four km away exposed bare skin was burnt. Everything within a one km radius of the explosion was destroyed and the resultant fires burnt out almost everything within a four km radius. A third of the city was wiped out. ∎

Cathedral, the largest church in the East, was completed in 1914 and flattened in 1945. Relics from the cathedral are displayed in the Hypocentre Park. The replacement cathedral was completed in 1959.

Other Relics The 'One-legged Torii' is 850 metres south-east of the epicentre. The blast knocked down one side of the entrance arch to the Sanno Shinto-gū Shrine but the other leg still stands to this day.

Dr Nagai Takashi devoted himself to the treatment of bomb victims until he himself died in 1951 from the bomb aftereffects; his small hut is preserved as a memorial.

Nagasaki Railway Station Area

26 Martyrs Memorial Only a couple of minutes walk from JR Nagasaki station on Nishizaka Hill is a memorial wall with reliefs of the 26 Christians crucified in 1597. In this, Japan's most brutal crackdown on Christianity, six of those crucified were Spanish friars, the other 20 were Japanese and the two youngest were boys of just 12 and 13 years of age. The memorial dates from 1962 and behind it is an interesting museum with displays about Christianity in the area; entry is Y250. The museum is open from 9 am to 6 pm and closes an hour earlier from December to February.

Fukusai-ji Zen Temple Although the Fukusai-ji is not on any list of architectural or cultural gems, this unique construction, also known as the Nagasaki Kannon Universal Temple shouldn't be missed. In fact you can't miss it, since the temple building is in the form of a huge turtle, carrying on its back an 18 metre high figure of the goddess Kannon. It faces JR Nagasaki station from near the 26 Martyrs Memorial. Inside, a Foucault Pendulum (a device which demonstrates the rotation of the earth on its tilted axis) hangs from near the top of the hollow statue. Only Leningrad and Paris have larger examples of these pendulums.

The original temple was built in 1628 but was completely burnt down by the A-bomb fire. The replacement, totally unlike the orig-

inal of course, was built in 1979. A bell tolls from the temple at 11.02 am daily, the exact time of the explosion. Entry to this somewhat bizarre temple is Y200.

Shōfuku-ji Temple The Shōfuku-ji, not to be confused with the important Sōfuku-ji, is near the Nagasaki Youth Hostel and JR Nagasaki station. The temple gardens are particularly pleasant and contain an arched stone gate dating from 1657 and moved here from the old Jingū-ji Temple outside the city in 1886. The main building, of typical Chinese style, was reconstructed in 1715. Almost adjacent to the temple is the Kanzan-ji Temple with the biggest camphor tree in Nagasaki.

Suwa-jinja Shrine

The Okunchi Festival (7-9 October) with its dragon dance, is Nagasaki's most important annual celebration and is centred at this shrine. The Suwa-jinja Shrine was originally established in 1555, and although it is mostly new, its wooded hilltop setting is attractive. Tram lines 3, 4 and 5 all run to the Suwa-jinja-mae stop, close to the shrine.

Sōfuku-ji Temple

One of Nagasaki's most important temples, the Sōfuku-ji, dates from 1629 and has a fine gateway which was built in China and brought to Japan for reassembling in 1696. Inside the temple, you can admire a great bell from 1647 and a huge cauldron used to prepare food for victims of a famine in 1680. The temple is open from 8 am to 5 pm and entry is Y150.

Temple Row

The path from the Sōfuku-ji to the Kōfuku-ji is lined with a series of lesser temples which you can visit en route between the two major temples. Just down the road from the Sōfuku-ji, steep steps lead up to the Daijo-ji, behind the huge Kowloon Restaurant. The entrance is the most interesting part; it's now used as a preschool.

Almost at the bottom of the road turn right a few steps to the Hosshin-ji Temple bell;

cast in 1483, it's the oldest temple bell in Nagasaki. Climb up the stairs to the large Kuroganemochi tree at the entrance to the Daion-ji Temple. Follow the road to the left of the temple to the grave of Matsudaira Zushonokami. He had been magistrate of Nagasaki for a year when, in 1808, the British warship HMS *Phaeton* sailed into Nagasaki Harbour and seized two Dutch hostages. The British and Dutch were on opposite sides in the Napoleonic War at that time. Unable to oppose the British, Zushonokami capitulated to their demands for supplies, then committed seppuku.

A short distance further on, turn down the path to the Kotai-ji Temple; it's a favourite with local artists and has a notable bell dating from 1702. Again, the grounds are used by a preschool. Continuing towards the Kōfuku-ji, you come to the Chosho-ji and the Ema-ji, both pleasant escapes from the hustle of modern Japan. Nagasaki's temple row does not end with the Kōfuku-ji, there are several temples beyond it. Only the major temples at the beginning and end of the row charge admission.

Kōfuku-ji Temple

The final temple along the temple-row walk dates from the 1620s and has always had strong Chinese connections. The temple is noted for its lawns and cycad palms and for the Chinese-influenced architecture of the main hall. Like the Sōfuku-ji, it is an Obaku Zen temple and entry is Y200; opening hours are from 8 am to 5 pm.

Megane-bashi Bridge & Nakajimagawa Stream

Parallel to the temple row is the Nakajimagawa Stream, crossed by a picturesque collection of bridges. At one time, each bridge was the distinct entranceway to a separate temple. The best known of the bridges is Megane-bashi (Spectacles Bridge) so called because if the water is at the right height, the arches and their reflection in the water together create a 'spectacles' effect. The double arched stone bridge was built in 1634 but in 1982 a typhoon flood washed away all the bridges along the stream. The Megane-bashi has been meticulously rebuilt.

Maruyama Area

The Shian-bashi tram stop marks the site of the Shian-bashi Bridge over which pleasure seekers would cross into the Maruyama quarter. The bridge and the elegant old brothels are long gone but this is still the entertainment area of Nagasaki. During Japan's long period of isolation from the West, the Dutch, cordoned off at their Dejima trading post, were only allowed contact with Japanese trading partners and courtesans. It's said that fortunes were made as much from smuggling as from the world's oldest profession!

In between the bars, restaurants and clubs Maruyama still has a few reminders of those old days. A walk up from Shian-bashi to where the first road forks, leads to Fukusaya, an old *kasutera* (sponge cake) shop where the cake recipe is said to have come from the Portuguese. An elegantly wrapped package of this traditional Nagasaki delicacy costs from Y600.

Turn left at this junction, pass the police post and you come to the driveway entrance to Kagetsu, now an elegant and expensive restaurant, but at one time an even more elegant and expensive brothel.

Dejima Museum

The old Dutch trading enclave is long gone, swallowed up by new buildings and land reclamation to the point where it is now well inland from the sea. From the mid-1600s until 1855, this small isolated community was Japan's only contact with the Western world and fortunes were made by traders here in the exchange of Japanese crafts for Western medicine and technology. The small museum near the old site of Dejima has exhibits on the Dutch and other foreign contact with Nagasaki. It's open from 9 am to 5 pm daily except Mondays; entry is free. Across the road in the museum yard is an outdoor model of Dejima. Attempts to reconstruct the trading post have fallen foul of local landowners.

Chinatown Area

Theoretically, during Japan's long period of seclusion, Chinese traders were just as circumscribed in their movements as the Dutch, but in practice, they were relatively free to come and go from their compound. Only a couple of buildings remain from the old area but Nagasaki has an energetic Chinese community which has had a great influence on Nagasaki's culture, festivals and cuisine.

Dutch Slopes

The gently inclined flagstoned streets known as the Dutch Slopes or 'Oranda-zaka' were once lined with wooden Dutch houses. To reach them, take a tram to the Shimin-Byoin-mae stop or walk there from the Dejima Museum or Glover Garden.

Confucian Shrine & Historical Museum of China

Behind the gaudily coloured Confucian Shrine is the Historical Museum of China with exhibits on loan from the Beijing Museum of History. The original building dates from 1893 but was destroyed in the fires following the A-bomb explosion. The shrine, near the Dutch slopes, is also known as the Koshibyo-tojinkan; entry is Y515.

Glover Garden

At the southern end of Nagasaki, a number of the former homes of the city's pioneering Meiji-period (1868-1912) European residents have been reassembled in this hillside garden. The series of moving stairways up the hill, plus the fountains, goldfish and announcements, give it the air of a cultural Disneyland but the houses are attractive, the history is interesting and the views across Nagasaki are superb.

The garden takes its name from Thomas Glover (1838-1911), the best known of the expatriate community. This amazingly energetic Scot seemed to have time to dabble in half a dozen fields at once. Glover's arms-importing operations played an important part in the Meiji Restoration; he built the first railway line in Japan and he even helped

establish the first modern shipyard from which Nagasaki's Mitsubishi shipyard is a direct descendant.

The best way to explore the hillside garden is to take the walkways to the top and then walk back downhill. At the top of the park is the Mitsubishi No 2 Dock building with displays about the city's important shipyard. Going down the hill you come to the Walker House, the Ringer and Alt houses and finally the Glover House.

Halfway down the hill, above the Glover House, is the renowned statue of the Japanese opera singer Miura Tamaki. The statue is

Glover Garden Area

1 Museum of History & Folklore
2 Telegraph Office Museum Annexe
3 Shikairo Restaurant
4 Nagasaki Tōkyū Hotel
5 Confucian Shrine & Historical Museum of China
6 Oranda-zaka Youth Hostel
7 Oura Catholic Church
8 Nagasaki Traditional Performing Arts Museum
9 Glover House
10 Walker House
11 Ringer House
12 Alt House
13 Mitsubishi No 2 Dock Building

Glover Garden Area

1 民俗資料館
2 郵電局
3 四海楼レストラン
4 長崎東急ホテル
5 孔子廟/中国歴代博物館
6 オランダ坂ユースホステル
7 大浦天主堂
8 十六番館
9 グラバー邸
10 ワーカ邸
11 リンガ邸
12 オルト邸
13 ミツビシ第二港ビル

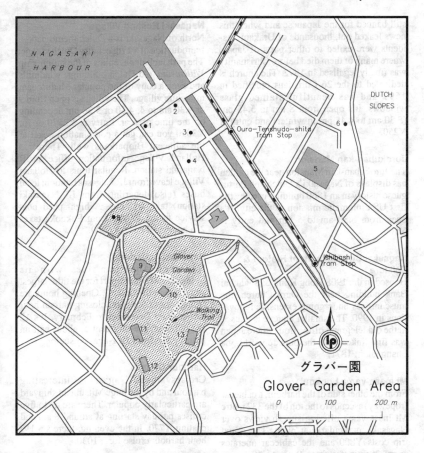

グラバー園

Glover Garden Area

0   100   200 m

NAGASAKI HARBOUR

DUTCH SLOPES

Oura-Tenshudo-shita Tram Stop

Ishibashi Tram Stop

Glover Garden

Walking Trail

often referred to as Madame Butterfly although, of course, she was a purely fictitious character. Puccini, the Italian composer of *Madame Butterfly*, is also honoured here with a relief made, so the caption goes, of Italian marbles. You exit the garden through the Nagasaki Traditional Performing Arts Museum with a display of dragons and floats used in the colourful Okunchi Festival.

Entry is Y600 and the park is open from 8 am to 6 pm (March to November) and from 8.30 am to 5 pm (December to February). Glover Garden, the Historical Museum of China and the Oura Church are all near the

end of tram route 5, get off at the Oura-Tenshudo-shita tram stop.

Oura Catholic Church

Just below Glover Garden is this prettily situated church, built between 1864 and 1865 for Nagasaki's new foreign community. Soon after its opening, a group of Japanese came to the church and announced that Christianity had been maintained amongst the Urakami community throughout the 250 years it had been banned in Japan. Unfortunately, despite Japan's newly opened doors to the West, Christianity was still banned for the Japanese and when this news leaked out, thousands of Urakami residents were exiled to other parts of Japan, where many of them died before Christianity was finally legalised in 1872. The church is dedicated to the 26 Christians crucified in 1597 and has beautiful stained-glass windows. It's open from 8 am to 5.45 pm (8.30 am to 4.45 pm in winter) and entry is Y250.

Jurokuban-kan Mansion

The Jurokuban-kan Mansion near the garden has displays of Nagasaki's Dutch and Portuguese history in an 1860 building used by the first US diplomatic mission to the city. It's open from 8.30 am to 5 pm and entry is Y500.

Nagaskai City Museum of History & Folklore

Housed in the 1908 Hong Kong & Shanghai Bank building near the Oura Church, the museum was undergoing extensive renovations in 1990. The smaller annexe is housed in the old telegraph office from where Japan was first linked with the outside world, via Shanghai, in 1871.

Mt Inasa-yama Lookout

From the other side of the harbour, a cablecar (ropeway) ascends to the top of the 332 metre Mt Inasa-yama offering superb views over Nagasaki, particularly at night. The round trip costs Y800 and the cablecar operates every 20 minutes from 9 am to 10 pm in summer and from 9 am to 5 pm in winter. Bus Nos 3 or 4 leave from outside JR Nagasaki station; get off at the Ropeway-mae stop. For the return trip, take a No 30 or No 40 bus.

Siebold House

Near the Shin-Nakagawamachi tram stop is the site of Dr Siebold's House. The doctor is credited with being an important force for the introduction of Western medicine and scientific learning to Japan between 1823 and 1829.

Nagasaki Holland Village

North of Nagasaki is a Dutch theme park, a reproduction of a 17th century Dutch village. The park includes a replica of the sailing ship *Willemstad*, old Dutch buildings, windmills and even a copy of the popular Madurodam miniature village. The village is open from 9 or 9.30 am to 4, 4.30 or 5.30 pm depending on the time of year. Entry is Y2570 or for Y3090 you can get a combination ticket to the adjacent Biopark as well. There's a Holland Village information office at JR Nagasaki station. Regular tours to Holland Village leave from JR Nagasaki station; local buses (also departing from JR Nagasaki station) take an hour. A high-speed boat service to the village from Fukuoka takes 2¼ hours and costs Y6800.

Nagasaki Aquarium

Nagasaki Aquarium vies with its Shimonoseki counterpart for the title 'largest aquarium in the Orient'. Opening hours are from 9 am to 5.30 pm, closing half an hour earlier from December to February. It's 12 km out from the city centre, about half an hour by bus from JR Nagasaki station.

Harbour Cruises

Cruises around Nagasaki's interesting harbour and by the huge Mitsubishi shipyard are particularly popular. There are up to five cruises per day starting at around 8 am and costing Y770. In the evening, there's a 1½ hour harbour cruise for Y1030.

Festivals

Nagasaki's major annual event is the Okunchi Festival (7-9 October), featuring Chinese-influenced dragon dances and parades. The festival centres around the Suwa-jinja Shrine (although tourists are not allowed in there) and there are displays concerning the festival at the Glover Garden.

Places to Stay

Youth Hostels There are four youth hostels in Nagasaki. The *Nagasaki Youth Hostel* (tel 0958-23-5032) has 132 beds at Y2100 and is within walking distance of JR Nagasaki station; it's well signposted in English.

The *Oranda-zaka Youth Hostel* (tel 0958-22-2730) is south of the centre on the hilly Dutch Slopes street and can be reached by tram No 5; get off at the Shimin-Byoin-mae stop. Beds are Y2100.

The other two youth hostels are inconveniently located about 20 minutes by bus from JR Nagasaki station. They are the *Nanpoen Youth Hostel* (tel 0958-23-5526) in Hamahira-cho and the *Uragami-ga-Oka Youth Hostel* (tel 0958-47-8473) in Miyoshimachi.

Minshuku & Ryokan *Minshuku Tanpopo* (tel 0958-61-6230), a Japanese Inn Group member, is at 21-7 Hoeicho, north of JR Nagasaki station and near the A-bomb site. Get off at the Matsuyama tram stop or JR Urakami station, cross the river, and walk to the street with a petrol station. Follow that street, turn left at the first junction and take the right side of the fork. Rooms are Y3300 (singles) or Y3000 per person in double or triple rooms.

Minshuku Siebold (tel 0958-22-5623) at 1-2-11 Sakurababa is a small place with just five rooms from Y3500 per person without meals. To get there, take tram No 3 from JR Nagasaki station, beyond the Suwa-jinja-mae stop to Shindaikumachi. Follow the road left from the tram stop and take the first right.

South of JR Nagasaki station in the central city area, the *Sakamoto-ya Ryokan* (tel 0958-26-8211) at 2-13 Kanayamachi is an old and very well-kept place with costs from around Y14,000 to Y30,000 per person including meals. In the same area, the *Terada Inn* (tel 0958-22-6178) is a cheaper and simpler ryokan with costs from Y3500 to Y5000 per person excluding meals. It's only a short walk from JR Nagasaki station, just beyond the Gotōmachi tram stop.

Hotels *North of the Station* The *Park Side Hotel* (tel 0958-45-3191) is at 14-1 Heiwamachi right beside the A-Bomb Museum and overlooking the epicentre park. It's a pleasantly quiet location with singles/doubles from Y6000/10,000. In summer there's a beer garden on the roof.

Just below the Park Side Hotel and beside the Hypocentre park are three discreet love hotels. Somehow the idea of making love only metres away from the epicentre seems a little curious but, as usual with love hotels, if you can wait until late (which usually means 10 pm) you can get an interesting room for the night from around Y6500. The hotels in this cluster are the *Volks Hotel In Park* (tel 0958-43-2900), the *Hotel Seagull* (tel 0958-48-0008) and the *Hotel Palette*.

Nagasaki Station Area There are numerous business hotels around the station area, although they are also dotted around other areas of Nagasaki as well. The small *Mifune Hotel* (tel 0958-22-0233) is conveniently close to the railway station and although the corridors look threadbare the rooms are tiny but comfortable. Singles/doubles cost from Y4500/8000.

The expensive *Hotel New Nagasaki* (tel 0958-26-8000) at 14-5 Daikokumachi has singles from Y12,000 to Y18,000, doubles and twins from Y19,000 to Y21,000. Opposite the station, the *Nishikyūshū Dai Ichi Hotel* (tel 0958-21-1711) charges from around Y5000/9000 for singles/doubles.

Central Nagasaki In the Maruyama entertainment area of central Nagasaki, the *Holiday Inn* (tel 0958-28-1234) at 6-24 Dozamachi, has singles/doubles from Y7500/9500. The *Nagasaki Grand Hotel* (tel 0985-23-1234) is also close to the central entertainment and business areas and has singles from Y7000 to Y9000, doubles and twins from Y10,000 to Y16,000 as well as a very popular beer garden.

A little further back towards the harbour is the *Harbour Inn Nagasaki* (tel 0958-27-1111) at 8-17 Kabashimamachi. This is a comfortable modern business hotel with singles/doubles from Y4900/8000. Next door is the *Hotel Ibis* (tel 0958-24-2171), another economical business hotel with singles/doubles at Y4900/8000. Closer again to the harbour and overlooking the harbour

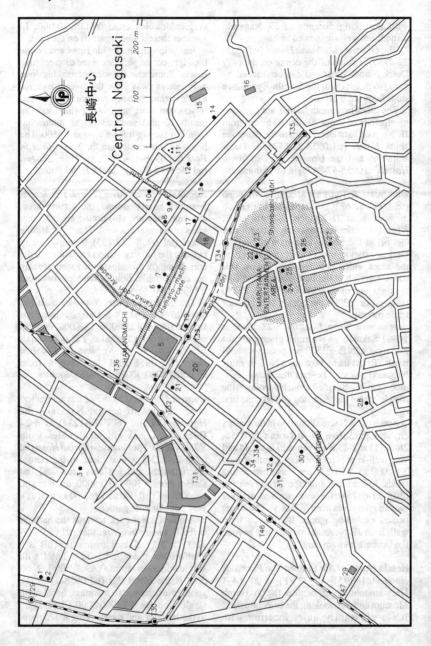

Central Nagasaki

長崎中心

0   100   200 m

HAMANOMACHI

Kanko-dori Arcade

Hamano-machi Arcade

Kanko-dori

Shianbashi-dori

MARUYAMA
ENTERTAINMENT
AREA

CHINATOWN

Central Nagasaki

1 Harbour Inn Nagasaki
2 Hotel Ibis
3 Nagasaki Grand Hotel
4 Lotteria
5 Daimaru Department Store
6 Tivoli Restaurant
7 Kobundo Bookshop
8 Garde Pizza House
9 Juraka Restaurant
10 Ginrei Restaurant
11 Hosshin-ji Temple Bell
12 Hamakatsu Restaurant
13 Bharata Restaurant
14 Kowloon Restaurant
15 Daion-ji Temple
16 Sōfuku-ji Temple
17 Mister Donut
18 With Nagasaki
19 Kentucky Fried Chicken
20 Holiday Inn
21 McDonald's
22 Italian Tomato
23 Kento's Nightclub
24 Obinata Restaurant

25 Fukusaya Castella Cake Shop
26 Police Post
27 Kagetsu Restaurant
28 Chinese Compound
29 Hotel New Tanda
30 Kozanro Restaurant
31 Chukaen Restaurant
32 Saiko Restaurant
33 Kyokaen Restaurant
34 Nagasaki Washington Hotel

TRAM STOPS

T29 Ohato
T30 Dejima
T31 Tsuki-machi
T32 Nishi-Hamanomachi
T33 Kanko-dōri
T34 Shian-bashi
T35 Shokaku-ji-shita
T36 Nishi-Hamanomachi
T46 Irie-machi
T47 Shimin-Byoin-mae

Central Nagasaki

1 ハーバーイン長崎
2 ホテルアイビス
3 長崎グランドホテル
4 ロッテリア
5 大丸デパート
6 ティボリレストラン
7 こぶんど書店
8 ガーデピーサハウス
9 じゅらかレストラン
10 銀嶺レストラン
11 ほっしん寺の鈴
12 はまかつレストラン
13 バラタレストラン
14 九龍レストラン
15 大音寺
16 崇福寺

17 ミスタドナツ
18 ウーイフ長崎
19 ケンタキフライドチケン
20 ホリデイイン
21 マクドナルド
22 イタリアントマト
23 けんとナイトクラブ
24 おびなたレストラン
25 ふくさやカステラケイキショップ
26 交番
27 花月レストラン
28 唐人屋敷跡
29 ホテルニュータンダ
30 こざんろレストラン
31 中華園レストラン
32 さいこレストラン

33 きよかえんレストラン
34 長崎ワシントンホテル

TRAM STOPS

T29 大波止
T30 出島
T31 築町
T32 西浜町
T33 観光通り
T34 思案橋
T35 正覚寺下
T36 西浜町
T46 入江町
T47 市民病院前

cruise dock, is the *Newport Business Hotel* (tel 0958-21-0221) with singles from Y4500 to Y4600, doubles and twins from Y8000 to Y8500. Reception is on the 4th floor.

South of the Holiday Inn, where the enter-

tainment area merges into the Chinatown area, is the *Nagasaki Washington Hotel* (tel 0958-28-1211) at 9-1 Shinchimachi. Rooms cost from Y7000 to Y12,000 in this more expensive business hotel.

Glover Garden Area South of the centre, below the Dutch Slopes, is the *Hotel New Tanda* (tel 0958-27-6121). It's at 2-24 Tokiwamachi and has singles from Y6900 to Y8500, doubles and twins from Y13,500 to Y16,000 and a popular rooftop beer garden in summer.

Nagasaki Tōkyū Hotel (tel 0958-25-1501) is at 1-18 Minami-yamatemachi, just below Glover Garden, and is typical of the more expensive hotels in the Tōkyū chain. Singles cost from Y9800 to Y11,000, doubles from Y17,500 to Y21,000.

Places to Eat

Nagasaki's local speciality is *shippoku*, a multi-dish meal which illustrates the city's diverse Chinese, European and Japanese influences. You generally need a group of two or more people to try shippoku. Another local speciality is the thick Chinese noodle known as 'champon', usually served as a soup. 'Sara-udon' is like a drier version of this noodle dish.

Nagasaki's European influence can be seen in a number of excellent Western restaurants.

The railway station area has a selection of restaurants with plastic meal displays and fast-food places but Nagasaki's restaurant centre is around the Hamanomachi arcade and Maruyama entertainment area. For a cheap, quick breakfast in the railway station try the *Train D'Or* bakery.

Closing days for Nagasaki restaurants seem to vary, so check first.

Hamanomachi There are a number of restaurants along the Hamanomachi arcade itself including the popular *Tivoli Restaurant* which serves vaguely Italian food. The *Garde Pizza House*, a block north of the arcade, has no less than 54 varieties of pizza on offer – all at Y700/1050/1400 for small/medium/large. Pasta and other dishes are also available. The restaurant has an English menu and you can buy wine by the glass (Y500) or by the bottle. It closes at 9 pm.

Also in this central area is *Bharata Res-*

taurant, an upstairs Indian restaurant in the Yasaka St building. It can be a little hard to find although the name is in English outside. It offers excellent South Indian thalis for Y1250 or tandoori and curry dishes from Y800. Bharata is closed on Mondays.

Nearby, on Kajiyamachi, is *Juraka Restaurant*, a 'beer and barbecue' hall where you can try shabu-shabu and other 'cook it yourself' dishes. Upstairs from Juraka is *Pietro*, with Italian and other dishes from Y650 to Y1200. Also on Kajiyamachi is *Ginrei Restaurant*, a relatively expensive Western-style restaurant, instantly identifiable from its ivy-covered frontage. It specialises in steaks and a variety of dishes are illustrated at the entrance.

The *Hamakatsu Restaurant* at 6-50 Kajiyamachi serves a variety of local specialities including a relatively inexpensive shippoku, although that still means a cost of about Y4500 per person. There's an illustrated menu and the downstairs area is cheaper than upstairs. A little further up the street is the huge Chinese *Kowloon Restaurant*.

There are plenty of fast-food places in this area as well. A *Mister Donut* can be found at the Kajiyamachi end of the Hamanomachi arcade while along Kankō-dōri you can choose from *Kentucky Fried Chicken*, *McDonald's* and *Lotteria*.

Maruyama If you cross Kankō-dōri by the Shian-bashi tram stop, you enter the Maruyama entertainment area. In amongst the pachinko parlours and bars along Shianbashi-dōri you'll find an *Italian Tomato* pasta specialist (dishes from Y1000) and the *Yagura-chaya* robatayaki next to Kento's nightclub.

At the end of Shianbashi-dōri the road forks; turn left, walk past the police post and at the far end of the square is the entrance road to *Kagetsu Restaurant*, a shippoku restaurant with a history stretching back over 300 years. At one time it was a high-class brothel and today its prices are as high as its history is long; count on Y20,000 per person!

Take the other fork at the end of

Shianbashi-dōri and you find the *Obinata Restaurant* at 3-19 Funadaikumachi with an interesting and imaginative Western menu, a wide selection of wines and fairly reasonable prices.

Chinatown South from Maruyama is Nagasaki's Chinatown area. During Japan's long period of isolation from the West, Nagasaki was a conduit not only for Dutch trade and culture but also for the trade and culture of the Chinese. Today that influence can be seen in the city's many Chinese-style temples and Chinese restaurants.

Popular Chinese restaurants around the Nagasaki Washington Hotel include *Saiko*, *Kyokaen*, *Chukaen* and *Kozanro*. There are many other economical places around Chinatown.

The *Shikairo Restaurant* at 4-5 Matsugae-cho is a Nagasaki institution; it's a huge building able to accommodate over 1000 diners on five floors. The restaurant claims to be the creator of the popular champon noodles. There's an English menu but last orders are taken at 8 pm.

Other Areas There are a number of interesting possibilities in other areas of the city particularly between Hamanomachi and JR Nagasaki station. *Zac's*, upstairs in the building by the Megane-bashi Bridge, suggests that by eating there you can 'produce a fashionable life'. You can choose from no less than 60 varieties of pizza from Y730 to Y880, though choosing can be tricky as the menu board is all in Japanese. At lunch time a small pizza, salad and drink costs Y580.

If you'd like a change from Japanese food then *Harbin Restaurant* at 2-27 Kozenmachi is a wonderful place to make your escape. This Russian/French restaurant has an English menu, white tablecloths, heavy cutlery, dark wood and excellent food. At lunch time you can select from a long menu offering a starter, main course, bread and butter and tea or coffee all for Y1300 to Y1600 – a real bargain. At night, main courses cost from Y1700 to Y5000.

The *Sakamoto-ya Ryokan* at 2-13 Kanaya-machi, also between the JR Nagasaki station and central areas, is a good place for traditional shippoku dishes.

Entertainment

There are plenty of bars, clubs and pachinko parlours around the Maruyama entertainment area. Try *Kento's* on Shianbashi-dōri; It specialises in live '50s and '60s pop music, everything from *Peppermint Twist* and *Hippy Hippy Shake* to *Hound Dog* and *Johnny Angel*! There's a Y1500 entry charge plus you must buy at least one drink and one food item from their reasonably priced menu – good fun from around Y3000.

There are plenty of other bars, pubs and clubs in this very busy area. *With Nagasaki*, just across Kankō-dōri, is a nine storeyed building completely devoted to clubs and bars. On Kajiyamachi, above the Juraka Restaurant, *Goody Goody* has excellent live jazz and a Y2000 entry charge. The beer garden at the *Nagasaki Grand Hotel* is a popular place for a drink in summer. The *Hotel New Tanda*, near the Dutch Slopes, has a rooftop beer garden.

Things to Buy

There are displays of local crafts and products directly opposite JR Nagasaki station on the same floor as the prefectural tourist office. You'll find lots of shops along the busy Hamanomachi shopping arcade. For Japanese visitors, the Portuguese-influenced kasutera sponge cake is *the* present to take back from Nagasaki and Fukusaya is the place to buy it – see Maruyama in Nagasaki's Places to Eat section for details.

Please ignore Nagasaki's tortoise-shell crafts: turtles need their shells more than humans do.

Getting There & Away

Air There are flights between Nagasaki and Kagoshima, Tokyo (Haneda Airport), Osaka and Okinawa as well as flights to and from a variety of lesser locations.

Train By local train, it takes about 2½ to three hours from Hakata to Nagasaki on the

JR Nagasaki line for Y2470; add Y2060 if you want to travel by limited express (tokkyū). Kyoto to Nagasaki by shinkansen takes about six hours. To get to Kumamoto from Nagasaki, take a JR Nagasaki main line train north to JR Tosu station (two hours) and a Kagoshima main line train from there (one hour).

Bus Regular buses operate between Nagasaki and Kumamoto, the four hour trip costs about Y2750 but note the following section about the interesting route via the Shimabara-hantō Peninsula. From the Ken-ei bus terminal opposite JR Nagasaki station, buses go to Unzen from stand No 3 (express buses from stand No 2), Shimabara from stand No 5, Sasebo from stand No 6 (bus S) or stand No 9 (bus E), Fukuoka from stand No 8, Kumamoto from stand No 11 and sightseeing buses from stand No 12.

Hitching Hitching out of Nagasaki is easier if you take a train or bus to Isahaya and start from there.

Getting Around
To/From the Airport Nagasaki's airport is about 40 km from the city and is situated on an artificial island. Buses to the airport (one hour, Y1150) operate from stand No 4 in the Ken-ei bus terminal opposite JR Nagasaki station.

Tram The best way of getting around Nagasaki is on the excellent and easy to use tram service. There are four colour-coded routes numbered 1, 3, 4 and 5 (there's no No 2 for some reason). Most stops are signposted in English. It costs Y100 to travel anywhere in town or you can get a Y500 all-day pass for unlimited travel. The passes are available from the shop beside the station information centre, from the prefectural tourist office across the road or from major hotels. On a one-ride ticket, you can only transfer to another line at the Tsukimachi stop. The trams stop around 11 pm at night.

Bus Buses cover a greater area (reaching more of the sights) but are, of course, much harder to decipher than the trams. Nagasaki is compact enough to explore on foot.

Shimabara-hantō Peninsula 島原半島

A popular route to or from Nagasaki is to travel via the Shimabara Peninsula and take the regular car ferry service between Shimabara and Misumi, south of Kumamoto. Bus services connect with the ferry timetable and tour buses (No 262) also operate directly between Nagasaki and Kumamoto. The major attractions on the peninsula are Unzen with its hot springs and walks in the nearby Unzen National Park and Shimabara itself.

It was the uprising on the Shimabara Peninsula (1637-38) which led to the suppression of Christianity in Japan and the country's subsequent two centuries of seclusion from the West. The peasant rebels made their final valiant stand against overwhelm-

ing odds (37,000 versus 120,000) at Hara-jō Castle, almost at the southern tip of the peninsula. The warlords even chartered a Dutch man-of-war to bombard the hapless rebels who held out for 80 days but were eventually slaughtered. Little remains of the castle.

In June 1991, 1369 metre Mt Unzen-dake erupted after laying dormant for 199 years. The explosion resulted in the deaths of at least 38 people. Nearby villages were evacuated and the lava flow reached the outskirts of the town of Shimabara.

UNZEN 雲仙

The Japanese enthusiasm for hot springs runs riot once again in this onsen town. Unfortunately the bubbling and spurting 'hells' or *jigoku* are rather spoilt by the spaghetti tangle of pipes running back and forth, taking the hot water to the various hotels and spas. (Jigoku are hot springs for looking at rather than bathing in.) A few centuries ago, the boiling hot water was put to a much more sinister use: in the era when Christianity was banned, dropping Christians into a boiling pool was a favourite method of execution.

Later, Unzen was a popular resort for Western visitors from Hong Kong and Shanghai and its much acclaimed golf course dates from that time. From the town there are popular walks to Mt Kinugasa, Mt Takaiwa and Mt Ya-dake. Outside the town, reached via the Nita Pass, is Mt Fugen, part of the Unzen-dake range, with its popular hiking trail.

Information

There's a visitor's centre with displays about the vicinity and an information centre opposite the post office.

Places to Stay

Unzen has numerous hotels and ryokan and two people's lodges (kokuminshukusha) with nightly costs from around Y5250 including dinner and breakfast. They are the *Seiun-sō* (tel 0957-73-3273) and the *Yurin-sō* (tel 0957-73-3355).

Getting There & Away

Bus Direct buses between Nagasaki and Unzen take less than 2½ hours and cost about Y2000. From Unzen, it takes another 50 minutes by bus to Shimabara. The bus to Nita Pass, the starting point for the Mt Fugen walk, operates regularly from the Unzen bus terminal (Y300, half an hour). There's a Y700 toll fee for cars. The No 262 Nagasaki-Kumamoto tour bus goes via Unzen.

MT FUGEN WALK 普賢岳

The circular walk to Mt Fugen starts with the cablecar ascent of 1333 metre Mt Myoken. Ask for a one-way *(katamichi)* ticket for Y500, though nearly everybody gets a return *(ōfuku)*. From the summit, it's a 20 minute ridge walk to 1347 metre Mt Kunimi, the final stretch leaves the Mt Fugen path and scrambles steeply to the summit.

After returning to the main trail, the path drops steeply down the ridge line to a saddle between Mt Kunimi and Mt Fugen. From here, you can continue around the northern side of Mt Fugen to Kazaama and Watoana or around the southern side through the Azami Valley. For the full experience, con-

Mt Fugen Walk
普賢岳

tinue the ascent for another half an hour to the 1359 metre summit. This is a good place for lunch and there are superb views all the way to Mt Aso on a clear day.

The descent on the eastern side is more gradual and eventually meets the circular trail just a couple of minutes south of the Fugen Pond or north of the Fugen Shrine. From the shrine, the trail drops again, cutting across the southern side of the mountain. Ignore the south-east turn-off and you'll eventually reach the Azami Valley trail junction where you'll find a trail map, bird chart, entrance torii and benches for a final sit and relax. From there, it's an easy stroll back to the base of the cablecar run. The walk takes 2½ to three hours at an easy pace. Another possibility is to follow the trail in a counterclockwise direction, finishing up at the top of the cablecar run – from there you could take the cablecar back down or simply walk on the trail beneath it.

SHIMABARA 島原
Shimabara is the port for ferries to Misumi, south of Kumamoto, and has a rebuilt castle and other attractions. The ferry terminal has an information desk.

Shimabara-jō Castle
The castle, originally built in 1624, played a part in the Shimabara Rebellion in 1637 and was rebuilt in 1964 during Japan's nationwide spate of castle reconstruction. It houses a museum of items connected with the Christian uprising. There's also a small sculpture museum in the watch tower with works by Seibo Kitamura who sculpted the Nagasaki Peace Statue. Entry is Y300.

Other Attractions
In the Teppocho district north-west of the castle is the Bukeyashiki, a small stretch of samurai walled street. Just south of the town centre, near the Shimamtetsu bus station, are carp streams with lots of colourful goldfish. Also south of the town centre in the Koto-ji Temple is the Nehan Zō or 'Nirvana Statue', the longest reclining Buddha statue in Japan, though by Thai or Burmese reclining-

Buddha standards, eight metres isn't all that long.

Places to Stay

Shimabara has the *Shimabara Youth Hostel* (tel 0957- 62-4451/6107) which costs Y2100 per person. There's also a variety of hotels.

Getting There & Away

Train & Bus You can reach Shimabara from Nagasaki by bus via Unzen or by rail via Isahaya. The JR trains on the Nagasaki line run to Isahaya, where you connect with the private Shimabara Tetsudō railway line to Shimabara. Shimabara Tetsudō railway station is within walking distance from the castle.

Ferry Ferries run 13 to 17 times a day to Misumi and take about an hour. The fare is Y830 per person or Y2370 to Y4840 for a car and driver. From Misumi it's 50 minutes by train or 1½ hours by bus to Kumamoto. Ferries also run to the Amakusa Islands from Shimabara.

Kumamoto-ken　熊本県

KUMAMOTO　熊本

Kumamoto (population 565,000) has one of Japan's finest reconstructed (as opposed to original) castles plus a contender for Japan's 'best garden' title. Add a few lesser temples and shrines, a very active entertainment area and a convenient location whether you're travelling up, down or across the island then a pause in Kyūshū's third largest city becomes a very worthwhile proposition.

Orientation & Information

The JR station is some distance south of Kumamoto's concentrated town centre where you'll find not only offices, banks, hotels, restaurants and the entertainment area but also the big Kumamoto Kōtsū bus centre, the castle and other attractions.

The tourist information office is in a small building in front of JR Kumamoto station.

There is a good map and brochure in English in which you'll find information about Kumamoto's unique Kobori swimming style – 'the art of swimming in the standing posture attired in armor and helmet'! Kinokuniya and Nagasaki Books are good bookshops in the central arcades. The Nippon Telegraph & Telephone (NTT) office, for long-distance phone calls, is beside the Kumamoto Kōtsū bus centre.

Kumamoto-jō Castle

Kumamoto's castle dominates the centre of town and, like many other castles in Japan, it looks superb at night. Also like many others, Kumamoto is a modern reproduction but the lack of authenticity is compensated for by the castle's sheer size and the numerous interesting exhibits and displays. These include a section of the ceremonial boat in which a daimyō and his followers made their regular voyage to the court of Edo.

Kumamoto-jō, built between 1601 and 1607, was once one of the great castles of feudal Japan. Its architect, Kato Kiyomasa, was considered a master of castle design and some of his ingenious engineering, including slots for dropping stones and other missiles onto attackers, can be seen in the reconstruction. In its prime, the castle had 120 wells, 49 turrets, 18 turret gates, 29 castle gates and a circumference around the outer walls of more than five km!

The extremely steep outer walls with their backward curve were known as *musha-gaeshi* or *nezumi-gaeshi* which meant that not even a mouse could climb them. The main donjon was entered through the *kuragari mon ato* or 'gate of dark passage'. Nevertheless, in 1877, during the turmoil of the Satsuma Rebellion, a postscript to the Meiji Restoration, the castle was besieged and burnt in one of the final stands made by the samurai warriors against the new order. The rebel samurai held out for 55 days before finally being overcome. (See the Kagoshima section for more on the rebellion and its leader, Saigō Takamori.)

Entry to the castle grounds is Y200, plus another Y300 for entry into the castle itself.

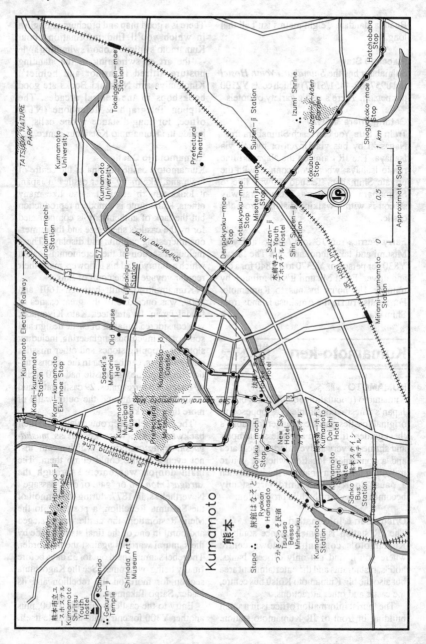

Kumamoto
熊本

It's open from 8.30 am to 5.30 pm in summer and from 8.30 am to 4.30 pm in winter.

Museums
Beyond the castle are the Kumamoto Prefectural Art Museum and the Kumamoto Municipal Museum. The art gallery is open from 9.30 am to 5 pm daily except Mondays and although entry to the general gallery is free, most of the building is used for special exhibits. The museum is open from 9 am to 5 pm daily except Mondays and entry is Y100. The museum has a three-dimensional relief map of part of southern Kyūshū. It's interesting to see the configuration of Mt Fugen on the Shimabara-hantō Peninsula, Mt Aso and the many other peaks.

Suizen-ji-kōen Garden
This fine and relatively expansive garden originated with a temple in 1632. The Momoyama or 'stroll' garden's design is supposed to follow the 53 stations of the Tōkaidō and the miniature Mt Fuji is certainly instantly recognisable. The Kokin Denju no Ma Teahouse was moved here from Kyoto in 1912 and although the building itself is somewhat shoddy, the views across the ornamental lake show the garden at its finest. Turn the other way and you will see the garden at its worst: the Japanese ability to see beauty in small portions and ignore the ugliness around the corner is well illustrated here where one side of the garden is lined by the usual rampant collection of souvenir and refreshment stalls.

The garden is open from 7.30 am to 6 pm in summer and from 8.30 am to 5 pm in winter; entry is Y200. The garden actually remains open after hours and entry is then free but only the north gate is open. A route 2 tram will take you there from JR Kumamoto station or you can take a route 2 or 3 tram from the central area. Get off at the Suizen-ji-kōen-mae stop.

Honmyō-ji Temple
To the north-west of the centre, on the hills sloping up from the river, is the temple and mausoleum of Kato Kiyomasa, the architect of Kumamoto's great castle. A steep flight of steps lead up to the mausoleum which was designed to be at the same height as the castle's keep. There's a treasure house with exhibits concerning Kiyomasa (open from 9 am to 4.30 pm daily except Mondays). Steps continue up the hill to another temple and then a final steep flight leads to the very top from where there are good views over the town.

Writers' Homes
Right in the centre of town, behind the Tsuruya department store, is the former home of writer Lafcadio Hearn (Koizumi Yagumo). Entry is free but it's not as interesting as his first Japanese residence in Matsue (see Matsue in the Western Honshū chapter). The Meiji era novelist Natsume Soseki's former home is preserved as the Soseki Memorial Hall. It's just north of the castle and the Traditional Crafts Centre.

Tatsuda Natural Park
The Tatsuda Natural Park with the 1646 Taisho-ji Temple and a famous teahouse is north-east of the centre. The grave of Hosokawa Gracia (1563-1600) is in the temple grounds. She was an early convert to Christianity but her husband had her killed to prevent his enemies from capturing her. To get there, take a Kusunoki-danchi-Musashigaoka-danchi line bus from platform 28 at the Kotsū bus centre to the Tatsuda Shizen-kōen-iriguchi stop.

The International Folk Art Museum is half an hour by bus from central Kumamoto or 15 minutes beyond the Tatsuda Park and displays crafts from all over the world.

Other Attractions
Continue up the hill beyond the cheap ryokan and minshuku near JR Kumamoto station, past the large collection of love hotels and you eventually reach the pagoda topping the hill. The effort of the climb is rewarded with superb views over the town. Also on this side of town, north of the stupa

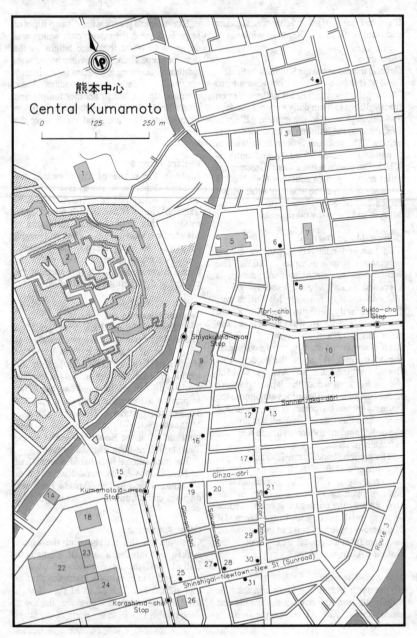

熊本中心
Central Kumamoto

0   125   250 m

4

3

1

5   6   7

2

8

Tori-cho
Stop

Suido-cho
Stop

Shiyakusho-mae
Stop

9   10

11

Sonenzaka-dori

12   13

16

17

15

Ginza-dori

Kumamotojo-mae
Stop

19   20   21

14

Shintori-dori

18

29

Route 3

23

27   28   30

22

25

24

31

Shinshigai-Newtown-New St (Sunroad)

Karashima-cho
Stop

26

Central Kumamoto

1	Traditional Crafts Centre	17	Kinokuniya Bookshop
2	Kumamoto-jō Castle	18	NTT
3	Maruko Hotel	19	Kumamoto Nightlife Information Board
4	Ryokan Saekya	20	Kento's Nightclub
5	Kumamoto Castle Hotel	21	Foremost Blue Seal Ice Cream
6	Nagasaki Books	22	Kumamoto Kōtsū Bus Centre
7	Tsukasa Honten Hotel	23	Kumamoto Kōtsū Centre Hotel
8	Mister Donut	24	Iwataya Isetan Department Store
9	Municipal Office/City Hall	25	Lotteria
10	Tsuruya Department Store	26	Kumamoto Tōkyū Inn
11	Lafcadio Hearn House	27	Higokko Robatayaki
12	Maharao Restaurant	28	Cheap Noodle Shop
13	Swiss Restaurant	29	Sanesu Steakhouse
14	Kumamoto Kankō Hotel	30	McDonald's
15	JAL	31	Kentucky Fried Chicken
16	Muraichiban Restaurant		

Central Kumamoto

1	県伝統工芸館	17	尹国屋書店
2	熊本城	18	NTT
3	丸小旅館	19	熊本ナイトライフ案内所
4	栄屋旅館	20	けんとズナイトクラブ
5	熊本ホテルキャッスル	21	フオモストブルーシルアイスクリーム
6	長崎本店	22	熊本交通バスセンター
7	司本店ホテル	23	熊本センタホテル
8	ミスタドーナツ	24	岩田屋伊勢丹
9	熊本市役所	25	ロッテリア
10	鶴屋デパート	26	熊本東急イン
11	小泉八雲旧居	27	ひごっころばと焼
12	まはらおレストラン	28	ラーメン
13	スイスレストラン	29	さめすステイキハウス
14	熊本観光ホテル	30	マクドナルド
15	JAL	31	ケンターキフライドヒケン
16	村一番レストラン		

and south of the Honmyō-ji Temple, is the privately owned Shimada Art Museum (open from 9 am to 5 pm daily except Wednesdays).

Places to Stay

Accommodation in Kumamoto is scattered: you'll find places around the railway station, the town centre and many others between the two locales.

Youth Hostels Kumamoto has two hostels. The *Suizen-ji Youth Hostel* (tel 096-371-9193) is about halfway between the town centre and Suizen-ji Garden and costs Y2100 per night. The Misotenjin-mae stop on tram routes 2 or 3 is close by. The *Kumamoto-Shiritsu Youth Hostel* (tel 096-352-2441) is west of town, across the Iserigawa River, and costs Y1600 or Y1800 depending on the time of year. A bus from platform 36 at the

Kumamoto Kōtsū bus centre will take you there.

Ryokan & Minshuku The Japanese Inn Group's representative in Kumamoto is bigger and more expensive than most of its other hotels. The *Maruko Hotel* (tel 096-353-1241) at 11-10 Kamitori-cho is in the town centre, north-east of the castle, and has 46 rooms, nearly all of them Japanese style, at Y6500/12,000 for singles/doubles with bathroom. From JR Kumamoto station, take a route 2 tram and get off at the Tetori-Honcho stop. There's a prominent sign from the covered arcade. One block north of the Maruko Hotel is the pleasant *Ryokan Saekya* (tel 096-353-5181).

The *Tsukasa Besso Minshuku* (tel 096-354-3700) at 1-12-20 Kasuga has rooms at Y3500 or from Y6000 with meals. To get there from JR Kumamoto station, turn left onto the road by the railway tracks, not onto the main road at the front of the railway station car park.

A 10 minute walk north of the station (crossing the railway lines, walking up the hill and taking the right fork in the road twice) brings you to *Ryokan Hanasato* (tel 096-354-9445) which costs Y3000 per person for a Japanese-style room with toilet and washbasin. The road continues beyond the ryokan up the hill to the pagoda at the top and passes a varied collection of love hotels on the way. Generally, the hotels cost between Y2500 and Y3600 for a short 'rest' (a strange description for what is supposed to go on there!) or Y4000 to Y6000 for overnight 'lodging'. The *Minshuku Higogi* (tel 096-352-7860/354-9812), also along the road, costs Y3000 for a room or Y5000 with two meals.

Hotels The *Kumamoto Station Hotel* (tel 096-325-2001) is about two minutes walk from the station, just across the first small river. It's a typical modern business hotel with Japanese and Western-style rooms from Y5200/9000 for singles/doubles.

The *Hokke Club Hotel* (tel 096-322-5001), between the railway station and the centre, is another typical business hotel with singles from Y5250 to Y6200 and doubles or twins from Y7200 to Y11,000. The *Kumamoto Kōtsū Centre Hotel* (tel 096-354-1111) is centrally located right above the Kumamoto Kōtsū bus centre and has singles/doubles at Y5900/9500. Reception is on the 3rd floor. Also in the centre of town, the *Kumamoto Tōkyū Inn* (tel 096-322-0109) is part of the popular Tōkyū chain and has singles/doubles from Y7000/8500.

More expensive hotels include the *New Sky Hotel* (tel 096-354-2111) about midway between the railway station and the town centre. This efficiently run and well-equipped modern hotel has both Japanese and Western-style rooms which cost from Y7500/14,000 for singles/doubles. Overlooking the castle, the *Kumamoto Castle Hotel* (tel 096-326-3311) has singles from Y8000 to Y10,000 and doubles from Y12,000 to Y13,500.

Places to Eat

The somewhat isolated railway station area doesn't have a wide selection of eating places, though, for a quick breakfast, there's a big *Mister Donut* inside the station. The central arcades have the usual selection of restaurants with plastic food displays and fast-food places: *McDonald's, Kentucky Fried Chicken, Mister Donut, Lotteria* and even *Foremost Ice Cream* are all represented.

Just off the Shinshigai arcade is the *Higokko Robatayaki* where you can sit at the bar and select from a wide range of kebabs. The chef will grill the kebabs right in front of you and pass them over the counter on a long paddle, rather like the one used for removing pizzas from a pizza oven. Each spit costs around Y300 to Y500. At the corner of the arcade and Sakae-dōri St is a good, cheap noodle shop.

Also in the town centre, *Muraichiban Restaurant* is a crowded, popular robatayaki with a huge square bar in the centre and tables around the edge. The well-illustrated menu shows everything including beers for Y400, salads at Y350 to Y400 and most dishes (kebabs, pizzas, noodles, sashimi, etc) for Y200 to Y600. There are even colour pictures of 13 different cocktails!

Places to eat along the Simotori arcade include *Sanesu Steakhouse*, a basement steakhouse with steaks from around Y2000. Also at basement level, *Maharao Restaurant* offers a variety of curry and rice dishes from Y800 to Y2000. The *Swiss Restaurant* serves coffee, cakes, ice cream and light lunches.

For the gourmet, Kumamoto's local specialities are raw horsemeat (ba-sashi) and fried lotus root (karashi-renkon).

Entertainment

The *Kumamoto Castle Hotel* operates a beer garden from May to August while the *Kumamoto Kōtsū Centre Hotel* on top of the bus station has a popular rooftop beer garden which also serves snacks like french fries, chicken kebabs, sushi and so on for Y200 to Y1000. You order and pay for food as you enter and there's a display cabinet showing what's available. A big mug of beer is Y600.

The Kumamoto Nightlife Information Board (see map) shows what's on where (all in Japanese of course) but there are also pictures of many of the bars, so you can see if it's respectable boozing or scantily clad bargirls on offer. A video even shows the exciting activity in some of the bars – that means scantily clad bargirls! There's a branch of the popular *Kento's* 'live house' for '50s rock & roll fans.

Things to Buy

The Traditional Crafts Centre displays local crafts and shows how they're made. *Higo zogan*, black steel with silver and gold inlaid patterns, is a renowned local craft. Entry to the downstairs shop area is free but it costs Y160 to see the upstairs exhibits. The tourist office map identifies the centre as the *Industrial Art Museum*; it's just north of the Kumamoto Castle Hotel.

Getting There & Away

There are flights to Kumamoto from Tokyo, Osaka, Nagoya and Naha (Okinawa). The JR Kagoshima line between Hakata and Nishi-Kagoshima runs through Kumamoto and there is also a JR line to Miyazaki on the south-eastern coast. Buses depart from the Kōtsū bus centre for Hakata, taking just over 1½ hours. The cost is Y1850 for the basic futsū (local train) fare, add Y1750 for limited express service.

See the Shimabara-hantō Peninsula section for details on travel to Nagasaki via Misumi, Shimabara and Unzen. Kumamoto is a popular gateway to Mt Aso (see that section for transport details and the Beppu section for travel across Kyūshū via Mt Aso to Beppu).

Getting Around

To/From the Airport The airport bus service takes nearly an hour between the airport and JR Kumamoto station.

Tram Kumamoto has an effective tram service which will get you to most places of interest. On boarding the tram you take a ticket with your starting tram stop number, when you finish your trip a display panel at the front indicates the fare for each starting point. From the railway station to the castle/town centre costs Y140. Alternatively you can get a Y500 one-day pass for unlimited travel.

There are two tram routes. Route No 2 starts from near JR Kumamoto station, runs through the town centre and out past the Suizen-ji-kōen Garden. Route No 3 starts to the north, near Kami-Kumamoto station and merges with route No 2 just before the centre. Services are frequent, particularly on route No 2.

MT ASO AREA 阿蘇山

In the centre of Kyūshū, halfway from Kumamoto to Beppu, is the gigantic Mt Aso volcano caldera. There have been a series of eruptions over the past 30 million years but the explosion which formed the outer crater about 100,000 years ago must have been a

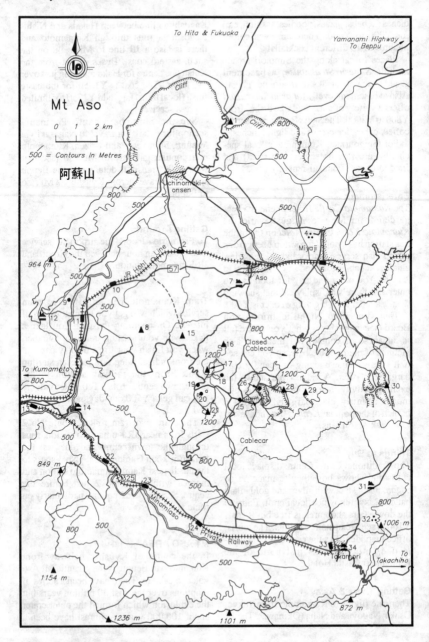

Mt Aso

0   1   2 km

500 = Contours In Metres

阿蘇山

To Hita & Fukuoka

Yamanami Highway
To Beppu

Cliff

Cliff

Cliff

800

500

Ichinomaki-
onsen

500

800

500

964 m

JR Hōhi Line

57

500

800

10

9

12

8

15

500

To Kumamoto

800

800

500

849 m

22

325

23

Minamiaso

800

500

Private Railway

24

Miyaji

4

3

7

Aso

6

16

1200

17

Closed Cablecar

27

18

19

26

28

29

30

20

21

25

1200

Cablecar

1200

31

800

32   1006 m

33   34

Takamori

To Takachiho

1154 m

1236 m

1101 m

872 m

Mt Aso

1	Mt Daikanbo & Lookout	18	Ski Field
2	JR Uchinomaki-onsen Station	19	Aso Volcanic Museum
3	JR Aso Station	20	Kusasenri Meadow
4	Aso-jinja Shrine	21	Mt Eboshi-dake
5	Lookout	22	Choyo Station
6	JR Miyaji Station	23	Aso-shimoda Station
7	Aso Youth Hostel	24	Nakamatsu Station
8	Mt Janoo	25	Aso-nishi Cablecar Station
9	Akamizu Hot Springs	26	Mt Naka-dake Crater
10	JR Ichinokawa Station	27	Sensui-kyō
11	JR Akamizu Station	28	Mt Naka-dake
12	YMCA & Youth Hostel Aso Camp	29	Mt Taka-dake
13	Tateno Station	30	Mt Neko-dake
14	Tochinoki Pension Village	31	Takamori Pension Village
15	Mt Komezuka	32	Pagoda
16	Mt Ojo-dake	33	Takamori Station
17	Mt Nishima-dake	34	Murataya Ryokan Youth Hostel

Mt Aso

1	大観峰	18	スキー場
2	内牧温泉駅	19	炭山博物館
3	阿蘇駅	20	草千里
4	阿蘇神社	21	鳥帽子岳
5	ルーカオト	22	ちよよ駅
6	宮地駅	23	阿蘇下田駅
7	阿蘇ユースホステル	24	中松駅
8	Mt Janoo	25	阿蘇西ロープウェイのり場
9	Akamizu Hot Springs	26	岳火口
10	市川駅	27	仙酔峡
11	赤水駅	28	中岳
12	YMCA & ユースホステル	29	高岳
13	立野駅	30	根十岳
14	とちのきペンション村	31	高森ペンション村
15	米塚	32	塔
16	往生岳	33	高森駅
17	林島岳	34	むらたや旅館ユースホステル

big one. Depending on who is doing the measuring it's 20 km to 30 km across the original crater from north to south, 15 km to 20 km east to west and 80 km to 130 km in circumference. Inside this huge outer crater there are towns, roads, railways, farms, 100,000 people and a number of smaller volcanoes, some of them still active.

Orientation & Information

Highway route Nos 57, 265 and 325 make a circuit of the outer caldera and the JR Hōhi line runs across the northern section. Aso is the main town in the crater but there are other towns including Takamori on the southern side. All the roads running into the centre of the crater and to the five 'modern' peaks within the one huge, ancient, outer peak, are toll roads. There's a very helpful and informative tourist office at JR Aso station.

Five Mountains of Aso

Aso-gogaku (Five Mountains of Aso) are the five smaller mountains within the outer rim. They are Mt Eboshi-dake (1337 metres), Mt Nishima-dake (1238 metres), Mt Naka-dake (1216 metres), Mt Neko-dake (1408 metres) and Mt Taka-dake (1592 metres). Mt Naka-dake is currently the active volcano in this group. Mt Neko-dake, furthest to the east, is instantly recognisable from its craggy peak but Mt Taka-dake, between Neko-dake and Naka-dake, is the highest.

Mt Naka-dake

Recently Mt Naka-dake has been very active indeed. The cablecar to the summit of Naka-dake was closed from August '89 to March '90 due to eruptions and it had only been opened for a few weeks when the volcano erupted again in April '90, spewing dust and ash over a large area to the north.

In 1958, when a totally unexpected eruption killed 12 onlookers, concrete 'bomb shelters' were built around the rim for sightseers to take shelter in an emergency. Nevertheless, an eruption in 1979 killed three visitors over a km from the cone in an area which was thought to be safe. This eruption destroyed the cablecar which used to run up the north-eastern slope of the cone, and, although the supports still stand, the cablecar has never been replaced.

When Mt Naka-dake is not misbehaving, the cablecar whisks you up to the summit in just four minutes (Y410 one way or Y820 return). There are departures every eight minutes. The walk to the top takes less than half an hour. The 100 metre deep crater varies in width from 400 metres to 1100 metres and there's a walk around the southern edge of the crater rim.

Mt Aso Walks

There are plenty of interesting walks around Mt Aso. You can walk all the way to the Aso-nishi cablecar station from the Aso

Youth Hostel in about three hours. From the top of the cablecar run you can walk around the crater rim to the peak of Mt Naka-dake and on to the top of Mt Taka-dake. From there you can descend either to Sensui-kyō, the bottom station of the old cablecar run on the north-eastern side of Naka-dake, or to the road which runs between Taka-dake and Neko-dake. Either road will then take you to Miyaji, the next railway station east from Aso. The direct descent to Sensui-kyō is very steep, so it's easier to continue back from Taka-dake to the Naka-dake rim and then follow the old cablecar route down to Sensui-kyō.

Allow four or five hours from the Aso-nishi cablecar station to Sensui-kyō. Buses down to Miyaji are irregular and the downhill walk takes about 1½ hours.

Shorter walks include the interesting ascent of Mt Nishima-dake from the Aso Volcanic Museum. From the top you can descend to the top of the ski lift on the ski field just east of the museum. You can also climb to the top of Mt Eboshi-dake and any of these peaks offer superb views over the whole Aso area. The outer rim of the ancient crater also gives good views from a number of points. Shiroyami-tempodai, a lookout on the Yamanami Highway as it leaves the crater, is one good point; Daikanbo near Uchinomaki Onsen is another.

Aso Volcanic Museum

Despite the usual shortage of non-Japanese labelling, the Aso Volcanic Museum will undoubtedly fill a few gaps in the average person's knowledge of volcanoes. There are displays, models and natural history exhibits. An entertaining selection of videos shows various volcanoes around the world strutting their stuff while another film shows what the Aso volcano can do along with scenes of the Aso region through the seasons and local festivals. The museum is open from 9 am to 5 pm daily and admission is Y820.

Kusasenri & Mt Komezuka

In front of the museum is the Kusasenri, a grassy meadow in the flattened crater of an

Left: Boats, Hiroshira River (TW)
Right: Cemetery, Onomichi (TW)
Bottom: Taga-jinja phallus, Uwajima (TW)

Top: Ueno-koen Park, Tokyo (TW)
Middle: Sensō-ji Temple, Asakusa, Tokyo (TW)
Bottom: Paper cranes, Peace Memorial Park, Hiroshima (TW)

ancient volcano. There are two lakes in the meadow. Just off the road which runs from the museum down to the town of Aso is the perfectly shaped small cone of Mt Komezuka, another extinct volcano. The name means 'rice mound', because that's exactly the shape it is.

Aso-jinja Shrine

Aso-jinja Shrine is a 20 minute walk north of JR Miyaji station and is dedicated to the 12 gods of Mt Aso.

Places to Stay & Eat

There are over 50 places to stay around Mt Aso including a youth hostel, a collection of places (many of them pensions) at Uchinomaki Onsen, north of Aso, and pensions at Tochinoki Onsen (to the west of the caldera) and the village of Takamori (to the south).

Aso The *Aso Youth Hostel* (tel 0967-34-0804) is a 15 to 20 minute walk or a three minute bus ride from JR Aso station and costs Y1800 or Y1950 depending on the time of year. There's a campground further along the road from the hostel. *Aso No Fumoto* (tel 0967-32-0264) is a good minshuku, conveniently close to JR Aso station which costs Y5000 per person. There's also a good little restaurant with an English menu in the station.

Takamori The *Murataya Ryokan Youth Hostel* (tel 0967-62-0066) costs Y2100 and is right in Takamori. The *Minami Aso Kokumin Kyūkamura* (tel 0967-62-2111), a national vacation village, costs from Y4500 per person without meals; it's crowded in July and August.

Just outside Takamori, on the southern side of the ancient crater, is a *pension mura* (pension village) with prices around Y7000 per person including dinner and breakfast. Pensions include the *Wonderland* (tel 0967-62-3040), *Cream House* (tel 096-762-3090) and *Flower Garden* (tel 0967- 62-3021). (The others don't have their names in

English but they're all in one convenient little clump.)

Just out of Takamori towards the kokumin kyūkamura is *Dengaku no Sato* an old farmhouse restaurant where you cook your own kebab-like 'dengaku' on individual hibachi barbecues. The restaurant closes at 7.30 pm and the set meal teishoku is good value for around Y1600.

Other Places The *YMCA/Youth Hostel Aso Camp* (tel 0967-35-0124) is near JR Akamizu station, the third stop west of JR Aso station. The cost per night is Y1900. *Minami Aso Kokuminshukusha* (tel 0967-67-0078) is a people's lodge near the Aso-shimoda private railway station, the third stop west of Takamori. Rooms cost from Y3000 without meals.

Getting There & Away

The JR Hōhi line operates between Kumamoto and Beppu via Aso. From JR Aso station there are buses to the Aso-nishi cablecar station. From Kumamoto to Aso, local trains take from one to 1½ hours and cost from Y1000. The Beppu-Aso limited express service costs Y2800 and takes 2½ hours. To get to Takamori on the southern side of the crater transfer from the JR Hōhi line to the Minamiaso private railway line at Tateno.

From March to November the 'Aso Boy' steam train makes a daily run from Kumamoto to Aso, terminating at Miyaji railway station. The one-way fare is Y1730.

Bus No 266 starts from the Sanko bus terminal at JR Kumamoto station, stops at the Kumamoto Kōtsū bus centre then continues right across Kyūshū with an excursion to the Aso volcanic peaks and then along the Yamanami Highway to Beppu. The trip takes seven hours including a short photo stop at the Kusasenri meadow in front of the Aso Volcanic Museum and costs from Y7500. Buses from Beppu to Aso take 2½ to three hours and cost Y3000, plus another Y1100 for the services that continue to the Aso-nishi cablecar station.

From Takamori, buses continue south to

the mountain resort of Takachiho, a 1½ hour trip along a very scenic route.

Getting Around

Buses operate approximately hourly from JR Aso station via the Aso Youth Hostel to the Aso-nishi cablecar station on the slopes of Mt Naka-dake. The trip takes 40 minutes up, 30 minutes down and costs Y600. There are less frequent services between Miyaji and Sensui-kyō on the northern side of Mt Naka-dake.

Buses also operate between Aso and Takamori. Cars can be rented at Aso and at Uchinomaki Onsen, one stop west from JR station.

SOUTH OF KUMAMOTO

Yatsushiro

The castle town of Yatsushiro, directly south of Kumamoto, was where Hosokawa Tadoki retired. The powerful daimyō is chiefly remembered in Japan for having his Christian wife killed to stop her falling into the hands of his enemies. Near the castle ruins is the 1688 Shohinken house and garden. The town's Korean-influenced Koda-yaki pottery is admired by pottery experts.

Hinagu & Minamata

Further south along the coast at Hinagu there are fine views out towards the Amakusa Islands. South again is the port of Minamata which became infamous in the late '60s and early '70s when it was discovered that the high incidence of illnesses and birth defects in the town were caused by mercury poisoning. A local factory had dumped waste containing high levels of mercury into the sea and this had contaminated the fish eaten by local residents. The company's ruthless efforts to suppress the story focused worldwide attention on the town.

Hitoyoshi

Directly south of Yatsushiro towards the Kirishima volcano chain, the town of Hitoyoshi is noted for the 18 km boat trip down the rapids of the Kumagawa River. There are a variety of trips taking from about

2½ hours, ending at Osakahama and costing from Y2400 per person. The boat departure point is about 1½ km from the railway station, directly across the river from the ruins of Hitoyoshi Castle.

Getting There & Away From Kumamoto it's half an hour on the JR Kagoshima line to Yatsushiro then one hour on the JR Hisatsu line to Hitoyoshi. From Hitoyoshi, it's a little over 1½ hours on the Hisatsu line and then the JR Kitto line to Kobayashi from where buses run to Ebino in the Kirishima National Park.

AMAKUSA ISLANDS
天草海中公園

South of the Shimabara-hantō Peninsula are the Amakusa Islands. The islands were a stronghold of Christianity during Japan's Christian Century and the grinding poverty here was a major factor in the Shimabara Rebellion in 1637. It's still one of the more backward regions of Japan.

Hondo is the main town on the islands and has a museum relating to the Christian era. Tomioka, where the Nagasaki ferries berth, has castle ruins and a museum. This west coast area is particularly interesting.

There are ferry services from various places in Nagasaki-ken (including Mogi near Nagasaki and Shimabara on the Shimabara Peninsula) and from the Kumamoto-ken coast (including Yatsushiro and Minamata). In addition, the Amakusa Five Bridges link the island directly with Misumi, south of Kumamoto.

Kagoshima-ken
鹿児島県

Kyūshū's southernmost prefecture has the large city of Kagoshima, overlooked by the ominous, smoking volcano of Sakurajima across Kinko-wan Bay. South of Kagoshima is the interesting Satsuma Peninsula while to

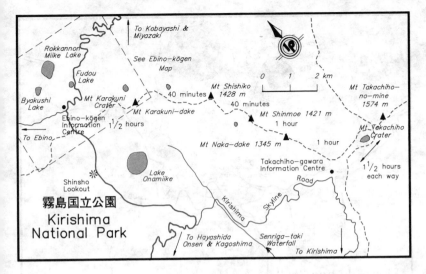

the north is the Kirishima National Park with its superb volcanoes.

KIRISHIMA NATIONAL PARK
霧島国立公園

The day walk from the village on the Ebino-kōgen Plateau to the summits of a string of volcanoes is one of the finest volcanic hikes in Japan. It's about 15 km from the summit of Mt Karakuni-dake to the summit of Mt Takachiho-no-mine and there's superb scenery all the way. If your time or energy is limited there are shorter alternatives such as a pleasant lake stroll on the plateau or a walk up and down Mt Karakuni-dake or Mt Takachiho. The area is also noted for its spring wildflowers and has fine hot springs and the impressive 75 metre Senriga-taki Waterfall.

Orientation & Information

There are tourist information centres with maps and some information in English at Ebino-kōgen Village and at Takachiho-gawara, the two ends of the volcano walk. There are restaurant facilities at both ends of the walk as well but Ebino-kōgen has most of the hotels, camping facilities and the like.

Kobayashi to the north and Hayashida, just to the south, are the main towns near Ebino-kōgen.

Ebino-kōgen Walk

The Ebino-kōgen lake circuit is a pleasantly relaxed stroll around a series of volcanic lakes – Rokkannon Miike Lake has the most intense colour, a deep blue-green. Across the road from Fudou Lake, at the base of Mt Karakuni-dake, is a steaming jigoku (hot spring). From there you can make the stiff climb to the 1700 metre summit of Mt Karakuni-dake, skirting the edge of the volcano's deep crater before arriving at the high point on the eastern side. There are good views back over Ebino-kōgen Plateau, but the view to the south is superb, taking in the perfectly circular caldera lake of Onamiike, the rounded Mt Shinmoe-dake and the perfect cone of Mt Takachiho-no-mine. On a clear day, you can see right down to Kagoshima and the smoking cone of Sakurajima.

Longer Walks

The views across the almost lunar landscape from any of the volcano summits is other-

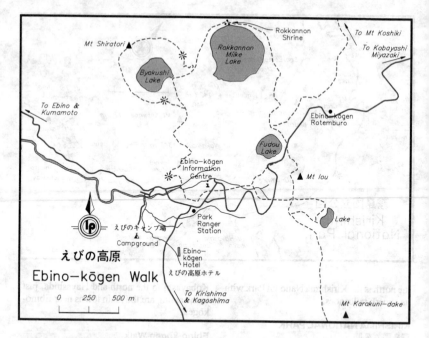

えびの高原
Ebino-kōgen Walk

0   250   500 m

worldly. If you have time you can continue from Mt Karakuni-dake to Mt Shishiko, Mt Shinmoe-dake, Mt Naka-dake and Takachiho-gawara, from where you can make the ascent of Mt Takachiho-no-mine. Close up Takachiho is a decidedly ugly looking volcano with a huge, gaping crater. Legends relate that Ninigi-no-mikoto, a descendant of the sun goddess, arrived in Japan on the summit of this mountain.

Places to Stay
Ebino-kōgen Village has a good choice of accommodation including the *Ebino-kōgen Hotel* (tel 0984-33-1155) and a kokumin-shukusha (tel 0984-33-0161) with accommodation from Y5250 per person including two meals. Just north-east of the centre is the *Ebino-kōgen Rotemburo* with basic but cheap huts around a popular series of open-air hot-spring baths. There's also a campground. More accommodation can be

found at Hayashida Onsen, between Ebino-kōgen and the Kirishima-jinja Shrine.

Getting There & Away
JR Kobayashi station to the north of Ebino-kōgen and Kirishima-jinja station to the south are the main railway junctions. From Miyazaki or Kumamoto take a JR Ebino-go limited express train to Kobayashi on the JR Kitto line, from where buses operate to Ebino. From Kagoshima (around one hour) or Miyazaki (1½ hours) you can take a JR Nippō limited express to Kirishima-jinja railway station. From there buses operate to Takachiho-gawara (about 45 minutes) and Ebino-kōgen.

Buses arrive and depart from Ebino-kōgen (the village on the Ebino Plateau, not to be confused with the town of Ebino down on the plains). You can arrive there from Kobayashi to the north, Miyazaki to the east or Kagoshima to the south and continue on another service. From Nishi-Kagoshima railway station in Kagoshima, buses depart for Kirishima Shrine and Hayashida Onsen at least hourly and some continue on to Ebino-kōgen. It takes about 2½ hours to Hayashida Onsen.

There are good views of the volcano scenery from buses driving along the Kirishima Skyline road.

KIRISHIMA-JINJA SHRINE　霧島神宮

The bright orange Kirishima Shrine is colourful and beautifully located, with fine views down towards Kagoshima and the smoking cone of Sakurajima, but otherwise is not of great interest. It originally dates from the 6th century although the present shrine was built in 1715 and is dedicated to Niniginomikoto who made his legendary arrival in Japan on the summit of Mt Takachiho.

The shrine can be visited en route to the park from Kagoshima; see the preceding Kirishima National Park section for transport details. The shrine is about 15 minutes by bus from Kirishima-jinja railway station and it's another 50 minutes by bus to the Ebino-kōgen Plateau.

KAGOSHIMA　鹿児島

Kagoshima (population 530,000) is the southernmost major city in Kyūshū and a warm, sunny and relaxed place – at least, it is as long as Sakurajima is behaving itself and the wind is blowing in the right direction. Only a stone's throw away from Kagoshima, across Kinkō-wan Bay, is Sakurajima's huge cone. When this very active volcano spits out great clouds of dust and ash, and the wind carries it across the bay and dumps it on the streets of Kagoshima, the city is not so sunny and relaxed at all! 'Dustfall' brings out the umbrellas just as frequently as rainfall.

History

Kagoshima's history has been dominated by a single family, the Shimazu clan who held sway there for 29 generations and nearly 700 years until the Meiji Restoration. The Kagoshima region, known as Satsuma, was always receptive to outside contact and for many years was an important centre for trade with China. St Francis Xavier first arrived here in 1549, making Kagoshima one of Japan's earliest contact points with Christianity and the West.

The Shimazu family's interests were not confined to trade, however. In the 16th century their power extended throughout Kyūshū and they also gained control of the islands of Okinawa, where they treated the people so oppressively that the Okinawans have regarded the mainland Japanese with suspicion ever since.

During the 1800s, as the Tokugawa Shogunate was becoming more and more out of touch, the Shimazu were already looking further afield: in the 1850s, the Shimazu established the country's first Western-style manufacturing operation. Then, in 1865 the family smuggled 17 young men out of the country to study Western technology firsthand in Britain. In conjunction with the Mori

---

Saigō Takamori

Although the 'Great Saigō' had played a leading part in the Meiji Restoration in 1868, in 1877 he changed his mind, possibly because he felt the curtailment of samurai power and status had gone too far, and led the ill-fated Satsuma or Seinan Rebellion. Kumamoto's magnificent castle was burnt down during the rebellion but when defeat became inevitable, Saigō eventually retreated to Kagoshima and committed seppuku. Despite his mixed status as both a hero and villain of the restoration, Saigō is still a great figure in Satsuma's history and indeed in the history of Japan. His square-headed features and bulky appearance are instantly recognisable and Kagoshima has a famous Saigō statue, as does Ueno-kōen Park in Tokyo. ■

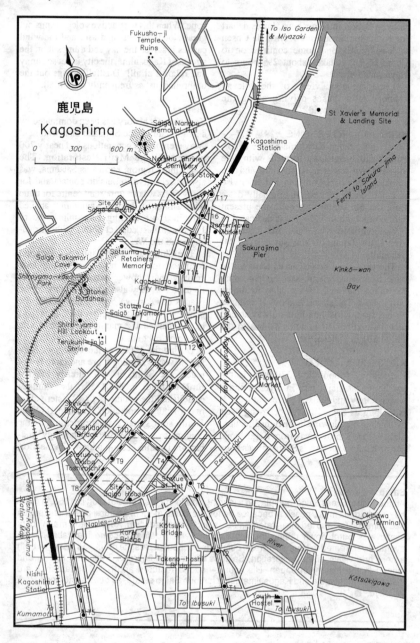

鹿児島
Kagoshima

0   300   600 m

Fukusho-ji Temple Ruins
To Iso Garden & Miyazaki
Saigō Nanshū Memorial Hall
Nanshū Shrine & Cemetery
Bus Stop
Kagoshima Station
St Xavier's Memorial & Landing Site
Site of Saigō's Death
T17
T16
Hamerikawa Market
T15
Ferry to Sakura-jima Island
Saigō Takamori Cave
Satsuma Loyal Retainers Memorial
T14
Sakurajima Pier
Shiroyama-köen
Kagoshima City Hall
Statue of Saigō Takamori
Kinkō-wan Bay
Stone Buddhas
T13
Shiro-yama Hill Lookout
Terukuni-jinja Shrine
T12
Flower Market
T11
Shinkan Bridge
Nishida Bridge
T10
T9
T4
Pedi-dōri
Statue of Okubo Toshimichi
Statue of Hat
T8
Site of Saigō House
T6
Okinawa Ferry Terminal
T7
Naples-dōri
Kōra Bridge
Kōtsuki Bridge
Takeno-hashi Bridge
River
T2
Kōtsukigawa
See Nishi-Kagoshima Station Map
To Kumamoto
Nishi-Kagoshima Station
T3
T5
T1
Youth Hostel
To Ibusuki
To Ibusuki

Kagoshima

TRAM STOPS:

Route 1

T1	Kōtsū-kyoku
T2	Takenohashi
T3	Shinyashiki
T4	City Hospital

Route 2

T5	Nakasu-dōri
T6	Miyako-dōri
T7	Nishi Kagoshima Station
T8	Takamibashi
T9	Kajya-machi

Route 1 & 2

T10	Takami-baba
T11	Tenmonkan-dōri
T12	Izuro-dōri
T13	Asahi-dōri
T14	City Hall
T15	Prefectural Office
T16	Sakurajima Sanbashi-dōri
T17	Kagoshima Station

Kagoshima

TRAM STOPS

Route 1

T1	交通局前
T2	武之橋
T3	新屋敷
T4	市立病院前

Route 2

T5	中洲通
T6	都通
T7	西鹿児島駅前
T8	高見橋
T9	加治屋町

Routes 1 & 2

T10	高見馬場
T11	天文館通
T12	いづろ通
T13	朝日通
T14	市役所前
T15	県庁前
T16	桜島桟橋通
T17	鹿児島駅前

clan of Hagi (see the Hagi section in the Western Honshū chapter) the Shimazu played a leading part in the Meiji Restoration.

Orientation & Information

Kagoshima sprawls north-south along the bayside and has two major JR stations, Nishi-Kagoshima to the south and Kagoshima to the north. The town centre is between the two stations but most accommodation is near the Nishi-Kagoshima station. The Iso-teien Garden, the town's principal attraction, is north of Kagoshima station but most other things to do are around the centre, particularly on the hillside that forms a backdrop to the city. While these hills provide one clear landmark, the city's other great landmark, the smoking Sakurajima volcano, is even more evident.

The tourist information office (tel 0992-53-2500) in the Nishi-Kagoshima station car park is open from 8.30 am to 5 pm and has a surprising amount of information in English, if you ask for it. Also in front of the station

is the curious stepped column with 17 people perched on it, commemorating the 17 Kagoshima students who defied the 'no going overseas' rules. The main post office is right beside the station.

The Tenmonkan-dōri tram stop, where the Tenmonkan-dōri shopping arcade crosses the tram lines, marks the town centre. There's another tourist office (tel 0992-22-2500) at JR Kagoshima station, and the Kagoshima Prefectural Tourist Office (tel 0992-23-5771), 4th Floor Sangyo Kaikan Building, 9-1 Meizan-cho, is between the centre and JR Kagoshima station. Kagoshima Airport also has a tourist office.

Iso-teien Garden

The Shimazu family not only dominated Kagoshima's history, they also left the city

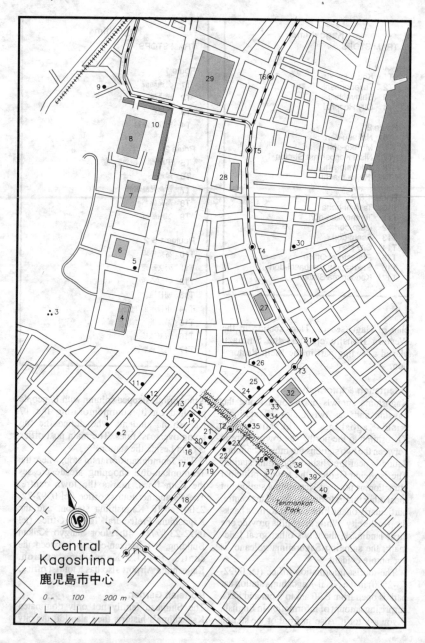

Central
Kagoshima
鹿児島市中心

0   100   200 m

Central Kagoshima

1	St Francis Xavier Church	16	Kentucky Fried Chicken	32	Mitsukoshi Department Store
2	St Francis Xavier Memorial	17	JAL	33	Kentucky Fried Chicken
3	Terukuni-jinja Shrine	18	Kagoshima Washington Hotel	34	Business Hotel
4	Kagoshima Prefectural Museum	19	ANA	35	Toit-vert Patisserie
5	Saigō Takamori Statue	20	Hayashida Kagoshima Hotel	36	Boulangerie
6	City Art Museum	21	JTB	37	Mujaki Family Restaurant
7	Prefectural Library	22	Vie de France Bakery	38	Bali Bali Yakiniku House
8	Reimeikan Museum of Culture	23	Lotteria	39	Kagoshima Kankō Hotel
9	Satsuma Loyal Retainers Memorial	24	Mister Donut	40	Akachochi Robatayaki
10	Tsurumaru Castle Site	25	McDonald's		
11	Kumasotei Restaurant	26	Dom Dom		TRAM STOPS
12	Le Ciel de Paris Patisserie	27	Yamakataya Department Store & Bus Terminal	T1	Takamibaba
13	Early Steakhouse	28	City Hall	T2	Tenmonkan-dōri
14	Wakana Restaurant	29	Prefectural Office	T3	Izuro-dōri
15	Roman Yakata Restaurant	30	Kagoshima Prefectural Tourist Office	T4	Asahi-dōri
		31	Izuro (Stone Lantern)	T5	City Hall
				T6	Prefectural Office

Central Kagoshima

1	ザビエル教堂	18	鹿児島ワーシントンホテル	35	Toit-vert Patisserie
2	ザビエル滞鹿記念	19	ANA	36	ブランジェリ
3	照国神社	20	林田鹿児島ホテル	37	むじゃきフアミリレストラン
4	県立博物館	21	JTB	38	バリバリ焼肉ハウス
5	西郷隆盛銅像	22	ビーデフランスベーカリ	39	鹿児島観光ホテル
6	市立美術館	23	ロッテリア	40	あかちょちろばた焼
7	県立図書館	24	ミスタドーナツ		
8	黎明館	25	マクドナルド		TRAM STOPS
9	薩摩義士碑	26	ドムドム	T1	高見馬場
10	鶴丸城跡	27	山形屋デパート	T2	天文館通
11	くまそていレストラン	28	市役所	T3	いづろ通
12	レシエルデパリレストラン	29	県庁	T4	朝日通
13	エーリスティキハウス	30	県観光案内所	T5	市役所前
14	わかなレストラン	31	石燈篭	T6	県庁前
15	ロマンヤカタレストラン	32	三越デパート		
16	ケンターキフライドチキン	33	ケンタキフライドチキン		
17	JAL	34	ビジネスホテル		

its principal attraction, the beautiful bayside Iso Garden. The 19th Shimazu lord laid the garden out in 1660 incorporating one of the most impressive pieces of 'borrowed scenery' to be found anywhere in Japan – the fuming cone of Sakurajima!

Although the garden is not as well kept and immaculate as tourist literature would have you believe, it is pleasant to wander through. Look for the stream where the 21st Shimazu lord once held poem parties – the participants had to compose a poem before the next cup of saké floated down the stream to them!

The garden contains the Shimazu Villa, the family home of the powerful Shimazu clan. Above the garden and reached by a cablecar (Y280 one way) is the Isoyama recreation ground, which has great views over the city. Look for the large rock on the hillside overlooking the garden, into which are carved two Chinese characters proclaiming it 'a huge rock'!

The garden is north of the centre (10 minutes by Hayashida line bus No 11 from the stop outside JR Kagoshima station) and open from 8.30 am to 5.30 pm, except in winter, when it closes half an hour earlier. Entry is Y720.

Shōko Shuseikan Museum
This museum, adjacent to Iso Garden, shows items relating to the Shimazu family and is housed in the building established in the 1850s as Japan's first factory. At one time the factory employed 1200 workers. Exhibits relate to the Shimazu family and to the factory's activities but only a few items are labelled in English. Entry is included in the garden admission fee and opening hours are the same.

Other Museums
The City Art Museum (Kagoshima Shiritsu Bijutsukan) has a small permanent collection principally dedicated to the works of local artists but also including paintings by European impressionists. Entry is Y200 and there are also regular special exhibits. Nearby, the Kagoshima Prefectural Museum of Culture (Reimeikan) is on the former site of Tsurumaru-jō Castle: the walls and the impressive moat are all that remain of the 1602 castle. The museum has displays on Kagoshima's history with special emphasis on the Satsuma period and entry is Y250. The gallery and the museum are both open from 9 am to 5 pm daily except Mondays.

The Kagoshima Prefectural Museum covers natural history and science and has an interesting exhibit on the Sakurajima volcano, tracing its history and eruptions. Entry is Y200.

Saigō Takamori
There are numerous reminders of Saigō Takamori's importance in Kagoshima including the large statue of him near the City Art Museum. In true Japanese fashion, there's a sign showing you where to stand in order to get yourself and the statue in the same photograph! The cave where he hid and the place where he eventually committed suicide are on Shiro-yama Hill. Further north there is the Nanshu Shrine, the Saigō Nanshu Memorial Hall (where displays tell of the failed rebellion) and the Nanshu-bochi Cemetery, which contains the graves of more than 2000 of Saigō's followers.

St Francis Xavier
There are a number of memorials to St Francis Xavier around the city, including a church and a memorial park near the city centre. Near the waterfront, north of JR Kagoshima station and towards the Iso Garden, is a memorial at his supposed landing spot.

Kōtsukigawa River
Kagoshima enjoys twin-city status with Naples in Italy and Perth in Australia. The street running perpendicular to the Nishi-Kagoshima station starts as Naples-dōri Ave and changes to Perth-dōri Ave after it crosses the Kotsukigawa River. There's a very pleasant riverside walk from near the station. Start at the attractive 18th century stone Nishida Bridge and walk south: there are four other attractive bridges along the way.

The statue of Okubo Toshimich, another important local personage in the events of the Meiji Restoration (he became the prime minister in the new government) is by the tramline road. Further south is the site of Saigō's home and the 'Statue of Hat', actually named after the statue's only item of apparel!

Other Attractions

Behind the prefectural museum is the Ter-ukuni-jinja Shrine, dedicated to Shimazu Nariakira, the 28th Shimazu lord who was responsible for building Japan's first factory and introducing modern Western technology to the area. He also designed Japan's rising sun flag. Continue up the hillside behind the shrine and you eventually reach the lookout in Shiroyama-kōen Park, which has fine views over the city and across to Sakurajima. An alternative route up the hill from behind the Reimeikan Museum starts from beside the Satsuma Loyal Retainers' Memorial.

North of the memorial are the remains of the Fukusho-ji Temple, once the Shimazu family temple. Iso-hama Beach, near the Iso Garden, is the town's popular summer getaway. The Ijinkan or 'foreigners' residence', also near Iso Garden, was used by British engineers brought to Japan to help set up the factory at Shōko Shuseikan. Tagayama Park, between Iso Garden and Kagoshima station, has a noted statue of Admiral Togo, who defeated the Czar's fleet in the Russo-Japanese war of 1905.

Some distance south of Kagoshima is the Hirakawa Zoological Park, which has a koala collection.

Festivals

One of Kagoshima's more unusual events is the late July umbrella burning festival. Boys burn umbrellas on the banks of the Kotsukigawa River in honour of the Soga brothers, though why they do this isn't exactly clear!

Places to Stay

The *Fujin-Kaikan Youth Hostel* (tel 0992-51-1087) is at 2-27-12 Shimoarata, towards the waterfront east of Nishi-Kagoshima station. The hostel is in a large old house and the nightly cost is Y1700 or Y1900, depending on the time of year. The hostel is a short walk from the Kōtsū-kyoku stop on tram route 1.

To get to the *Sakurajima Youth Hostel* you have to take the ferry across the bay (see the following Sakurajima section for details).

There's a good selection of business hotels in the Nishi-Kagoshima station area. The *Business Hotel Gasthof* (tel 0992-52-1401) at 7-3 Chūō-cho, has good, low-priced rooms at Y3800/6600; ones without bathrooms are even cheaper. Across the road from the Gasthof, right on the corner, is the small *Tkuba* hotel, which is also very low priced: rooms without bathroom cost from Y2500.

Across the road from the Nishi-Kagoshima station, the *Station Hotel New Kagoshima* (tel 0992-53-5353) has singles at Y5000 to Y6500 and doubles and twins from Y8000 to Y11,000. Opposite and by the riverside is the *Kagoshima Tōkyū Inn* (tel 0992-53-3692) with singles/doubles from Y6200/11,600.

The *Hotel Taisei Annex* (tel 0992-57-1111), opposite the Station Hotel, is a modern business hotel with singles at Y5000 and doubles and twins at Y7500 and Y8000.

Other station-area hotels a few minutes walk further away include the good-value *Silk Inn Kagoshima* (tel 0992-58-1221), where singles/doubles cost from Y4500/8000. Or turn left immediately out of the station, pass the post office and take the first left across the railway tracks to the *Union Hotel* (tel 0992-53-5800). It's a friendly place with rooms at Y5000/8000 but definitely at the tatty and worn-out end of the business hotel spectrum and for emergency accommodation only. Nearby is the *Business Hotel Kagoshima* (tel 0992-58-0331), with rooms at Y3600/7200.

Although most hotels are around Nishi-Kagoshima station, there are also some in the centre of town. By the tramline and close to the Tenmonkan-dōri shopping arcade, the *Hayashida Kagoshima Hotel* (tel 0992-24-4111) is an important central meeting point and has singles/doubles from Y6800/9500. The hotel features a large central garden atrium. Across the road is the *Kagoshima Washington Hotel* (tel 0992-25-6111), a hotel in the popular high-class business hotel chain. Singles range from Y5250 to Y7000, and doubles or twins from Y9750 to Y11,000.

On the other side of the Tenmonkan-dōri arcade, the *Business Hotel* (tel 0992-23-3434) is fairly basic but in a very central location; singles/doubles cost from Y5000/7500. A few blocks down Tenmonkan-dōri St, but still close to the town centre, the *Kagoshima Kankō Hotel* (tel 0992-24-3111) is another typical business hotel.

Places to Eat
The main restaurant area is in the town centre but there's also a good selection around the Nishi-Kagoshima station area including an old railway carriage converted into a restaurant called the *Vesuvio* (an appropriate name, given the Naples-Vesuvius versus Kagoshima-Sakurajima connections). Pizza and spaghetti feature heavily on the menu. There are also quite a few Italian-style restaurants around town.

There are various fast-food places around the station, including the inevitable *Mister Donut*, though for real Satsuma food try the *Satsuma*, across the road from the station. It's a tiny place, though there's more space upstairs, and the menu features tonkotsu (pork ribs) and other traditional Satsuma dishes; look for the red lanterns out front.

The town centre has a wide variety of fast-food outlets, bakeries and restaurants with plastic meal displays, particularly around the Tenmonkan-dōri arcade area. The streets to the south-west of the arcade feature a number of the town's more interesting restaurants including *Kumasotei* (tel 0992-22-6356) at 6-10 Higashisengoku-cho,

Nishi-Kagoshima Station Area
1 Union Hotel
2 Vesuvio Restaurant
3 17 Young Pioneers Statues
4 Tourist Information Office
5 Post Office
6 Akachochi Robatayaki
7 Italian Tomato Restaurant
8 Hotel Taisei Annex
9 Mister Donut
10 Satsuma Restaurant
11 Station Hotel New Kagoshima
12 Tkuba Hotel
13 Kagoshima Tōkyū Inn
14 Business Hotel Gasthof
15 Morning Market
16 Silk Inn

BUS STOPS & BUS COMPANIES

B1 Kagoshima Kōtsū & City Bus (Sightseeing Buses)
B2 JR Bus (Sakurajima)
B3 Hayashida Sangyo Kōtsū (Ebino, Kirishima)
B4 Kagoshima Kōtsū (Chiran, Ibusuki)
B5 City Bus (Kagoshima City)
B6 Hayashida Sangyo Kōtsū (Kirishima), Minami Kyūshū Kosoku (Miyazaki)

TRAM STOPS

T7 Nishi-Kagoshima Station
T8 Takamibashi

which is a favourite for its Satsuma cuisine. There is an English menu (although English-speaking visitors seem to be so infrequent that the owners often have trouble finding

---

Kagoshima's cuisine speciality is known as Satsuma, the food of the Satsuma region. Satsuma dishes include *tonkotsu*, which is pork ribs seasoned with miso and black sugar then boiled until they're on the point of falling apart; *kibinago*, a sardine-like fish which is usually prepared as sashimi with vinegared miso sauce; *satsuma-age*, a fried fish sausage; *satsuma jiru*, a chicken miso soup; *torisashi*, which is raw chicken with soy sauce; *katsuo no tataki*, which is sliced bonito; *katsuo no shiokar*, which is salted bonito intestines and *sakezushi*, a mixed seafood sushi.

Kagoshima ramen is the region's renowned noodle dish. *Shōchū*, the Kagoshima firewater, comes in many forms, including *imo-shōchū*, made from sweet potatoes. There's also a local sweet-potato ice cream. ■

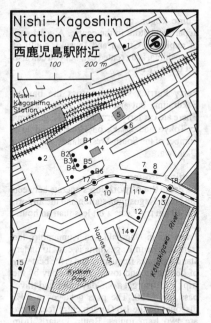

Nishi-Kagoshima
Station Area
西鹿児島駅附近
0   100   200 m

Nishi-Kagoshima Station

it!) which offers a variety of set dinners at Y3000, Y4800 and Y6000 (including tax and service). More exotic dishes are, of course, much more expensive. The Y4000 dinner gives you a taste of all the most popular Satsuma specialities.

Other places in this central area include *Early* for steak and hamburgers, *Wakana* with a variety of meals (all with plastic versions on display), *Roman Yakata* for Italian dishes, *La Sei* for French dishes and *Le Ciel de Paris*, a pleasant little patisserie/coffee bar.

There are numerous fast-food places along the tramline road and a variety of cheaper restaurants south of this road. Further down Tenmonkan-dōri, *Akachochi* is a robatayaki of wildly exaggerated cheerfulness – the welcomes are bawled out so loudly that new arrivals reel back at the door. The menu is in Japanese only, though some dishes are illustrated and most are in the Y250 to Y500 range. Look for the octopus over the entrance. There's another branch of this popular robatayaki near the Nishi-Kagoshima station.

Nishi-Kagoshima Station Area

1	ユーニョンホテル
2	ベスビオレストラン
3	若き薩摩の群像
4	観光案内所
5	中央郵便局
6	あかちょちろぽと焼
7	イタリャントマトレストラン
8	ホテルタイセイアネックス
9	ミスタドーナツ
10	くまそていレストラン（さつま料理）
11	ステションホテルニュー鹿児島
12	トクバホテル
13	鹿児島東急イン
14	ビジネスホテルガストフ
15	朝市場
16	シルクイン鹿児島

BUS STOPS & BUS COMPANIES

B1	鹿児島交通市営バス（定期観光バス）
B2	JR バス（桜島）
B3	林田産業交通（えびの、霧島）
B4	鹿児島交通（川辺、知覧）
B5	市営バス（市内）
B6	林田産業交通
	南九州高速

TRAM STOPS

T7	西鹿児島駅前
T8	高見橋

Things to Buy

Oshima pongee silk items and the fiery drink known as shōchū are local products of interest but Satsuma pottery is the best known and comes in two forms – black for the common folk, white for the nobility. A number of potteries can be visited.

Local crafts are displayed in the same building as the Kagoshima Prefectural Tourist Office (see the Orientation & Information section for its location). Mitsukoshi, Yamakataya and Takashimaya are the main department stores and Kagoshima also has busy morning markets (asa-ichi) near the two main stations.

Getting There & Away

Air Kagoshima's airport has overseas connections as well as domestic flights to Tokyo, Osaka, Nagoya and a variety of other places in Honshū and Kyūshū. Kagoshima is the major jumping-off point for flights to the South-West Islands and also has connections with the Kagoshima-ken islands and Naha on Okinawa. (See the Okinawa & the South-West Islands chapter for more details.)

Train Both the Nishi-Kagoshima and Kagoshima stations are arrival and departure points for other areas of Japan. While the Nishi-Kagoshima station is close to a greater choice of accommodation, the Kagoshima station is closer to Iso-teien Garden and the Sakurajima ferry. The stations are about equal distance north and south of the town centre.

It takes about five hours by train from Fukuoka/Hakata via Kumamoto to Kagoshima on the JR Kagoshima line. The local train fare is Y5150; add Y2470 for the limited express service. The JR Nippō line connects Kagoshima with Kokura on the north-eastern tip of Kyūshū for Y7210, plus Y2780 for limited express. Nippō line trains operate via Miyazaki and Beppu.

Trains also run south from Kagoshima to the popular hot-spring resort of Ibusuki, taking about one hour 10 minutes.

Bus Hayashida buses to Kirishima and Ebino-kōgen go from the Takashimaya department store in the centre. A good way of exploring Chiran and Ibusuki, south of Kagoshima, is by rented car, but you can also get there by bus.

Ferry Ferries shuttle across the bay to Sakurajima but also operate further afield. There are car ferry services from Kagoshima to Tokyo and Osaka on Honshū and to a number of the South-West Islands, including Okinawa.

Getting Around

To/From the Airport Buses operate between the Nishi-Kagoshima station and the airport; the 40 km trip takes a bit less than an hour.

Tram As in Nagasaki and Kumamoto, the tram service in Kagoshima is easy to understand, operates frequently and is the best way of getting around town. You can pay by the trip (Y150) or get a one-day unlimited travel pass for Y500. The pass gets you a 20% discount on the Iso Garden entry fee. There are two tram routes. Route 1 starts from Kagoshima station, goes through the centre and on past the suburb of Korimoto to Taniyama. Route 2 follows the same route through the centre, then diverges at Takamibaba to Nishi-Kagoshima station and terminates at Korimoto.

Bus Bus tours operate twice daily from the Nishi-Kagoshima station and cost about Y2000.

SAKURAJIMA 桜島

Dominating the skyline from Kagoshima is the brooding cone of this decidedly overactive volcano. In fact, Sakurajima is so active that the Japanese differentiate between its mere eruptions (since 1955 there has been an almost continuous stream of smoke and ash) and real explosions, which have occurred in 1914, 1915, 1946, 1955 and 1960. The most violent erruption was in 1914, during which the volcano poured out over three billion tons of lava, overwhelming numerous villages and converting

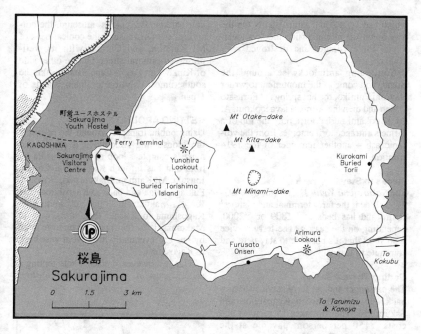

桜島
Sakurajima

Sakurajima from an island to a peninsula. The flow totally filled in the 400 metre wide and 70 metre deep strait which had separated the volcano from the mainland and extended the island further west towards Kagoshima.

Sakurajima actually has three peaks – Kita-dake (1117 metres), Naka-dake (1060 metres) and Minami-dake (1040 metres) – but at present only Minami is active. While some parts of Sakurajima are covered in deep volcanic ash or crumbling lava, other places have exceptionally fertile soil and huge radishes weighing up to 35 kg are grown. Sakurajima is also known for its tiny oranges, only three cm in diameter.

Sakurajima Visitors' Centre

The visitors' centre near the ferry terminal has a variety of exhibits about the volcano, its eruptions and its natural history. The working model showing the volcano's growth over the years is the centre's main

attraction. The centre is open from 9 am to 5 pm daily except Mondays and entry is free.

Lookouts

Although visitors are not permitted to climb the volcano there are several good lookout points. The Yunohira lookout is high on the side of the volcano and offers good views up the forbidding, barren slopes and down across the bay to Kagoshima. The Arimura lava lookout is east of Furusato Onsen; there are walkways across a small corner of the immense lava flow and the lookout points offer a glimpse of the immense outpouring that linked the island to the mainland in 1914. The An-ei lava flow lies to the west, the 1914 Taisho flow to the east.

Other Attractions

A complete circuit of the volcano is 38 km. Just south of the visitors' centre is 'buried Torishima Island', where the 1914 Taisho lava flow totally engulfed the small island which had been a half km offshore. On the way down the mountainside the lava swallowed three villages and destroyed over 1000 homes.

Continuing anticlockwise around the island, you come to the monument to writer Hayashi Fumiko, the hot springs at Furusato Onsen and then the Arimura lava lookout. At the Kurokami buried torii, only the top of a shrine's entrance torii emerges from the volcanic ash – another reminder of the 1914 eruption.

Places to Stay
The *Sakurajima Youth Hostel* (tel 0992-93-2150) is near the ferry terminal and visitors' centre and has beds at Y1800 or Y2000, depending on the season. The ferry service is so short that it's possible to stay here and commute to Kagoshima.

Getting There & Away
The passenger and car ferry service shuttles back and forth between Kagoshima and Sakurajima. The trip takes 15 minutes and costs Y150 per person, payable at the Sakurajima end. From Kagoshima station or the Sakurajima Sanbashi-dōri tram stop, the ferry terminal is a short walk through the Nameriwaka market area.

Getting Around
Getting around Sakurajima without your own transport can be difficult. You can rent bicycles from near the ferry terminal but a complete circuit of the volcano would be quite a push, even without the climbs to the various lookouts. Three-hour sightseeing bus tours operate several times daily from the ferry terminal and cost Y1500.

Satsuma Peninsula & Cape Sata-misaki
薩摩半島、佐多岬

The Satsuma Peninsula, south of Kagoshima, has fine rural scenery, an unusual kamikaze pilots' museum, the hot-spring resort of Ibusuki, the conical peak of Mt Kaimon, and Chiran, with its well-preserved samurai street. On the other side of Kinkō-wan Bay is Cape Sata-misaki, the southernmost point on the main islands of Japan.

GETTING AROUND
Using public transport around the region is time-consuming although it is possible to make a complete loop of the peninsula by train and bus through Kagoshima, Chiran, Ibusuki, Mt Kaimon, Makurazaki, Bōnotsu, Fukiage-hama and back to Kagoshima. The Ibusuki-Makurazaki JR line runs south from Kagoshima to Ibusuki then turns west to Makurazaki. You can continue on from there by bus and eventually make your way back to Kagoshima.

This is, however, a place where renting a car can be useful. Alternatively, there are tour

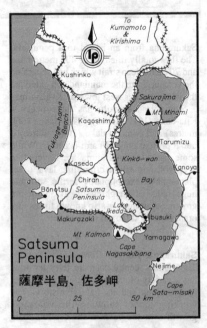

buses which operate from Kagoshima via Chiran to Ibusuki and from Ibusuki back to Kagoshima via Chiran and Tarumizu on the opposite side of the bay. There's a Yamakawa-Nijeme ferry service across the southern end of the bay.

CHIRAN 知覧

South of Kagoshima, Chiran is a worthwhile place to pause en route to Ibusuki. This inter- esting little town has a well-preserved samurai street with a fine collection of samurai houses and gardens, plus a fascinat- ing memorial and museum to WW II's kamikaze pilots. Chiran was one of the major bases from which the hapless pilots made

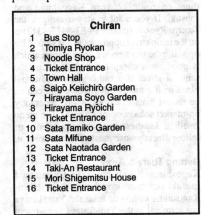

Chiran

1 Bus Stop
2 Tomiya Ryokan
3 Noodle Shop
4 Ticket Entrance
5 Town Hall
6 Saigō Keiichirō Garden
7 Hirayama Soyo Garden
8 Hirayama Ryōichi
9 Ticket Entrance
10 Sata Tamiko Garden
11 Sata Mifune
12 Sata Naotada Garden
13 Ticket Entrance
14 Taki-An Restaurant
15 Mori Shigemitsu House
16 Ticket Entrance

Chiran

1 バスの停
2 富屋旅館
3 ラメン
4 クーポン券取扱処
5 役場
6 西郷恵一郎庭園
7 平山ソヨ
8 平山亮一
9 クーポン券取扱処
10 佐多民子庭園
11 佐多美舟氏庭園
12 佐多直忠氏庭園
13 クーポン券取扱処
14 多喜庵レストラン
15 森重堅氏庭園
16 クーポン券取扱処

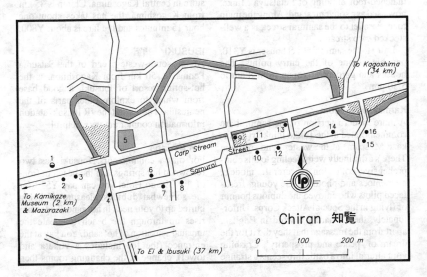

their suicidal and less than totally successful attacks on Allied shipping.

Samurai Street

The seven houses along Chiran's samurai street are noted for their finely preserved gardens, where you'll find all the standard features of formal garden design. Look for the use of 'borrowed scenery', particularly in No 6 (the houses are numbered on the brochure you pick up at the street entry point) where the garden is not so impressive but the 'borrowed' hill is focused wonderfully. Notice how each garden features a 'mountain', backed by a tall hedge and always in the left corner when viewed with the house to your back; this feature is particularly evident in Nos 1, 4 and 5.

Traditionally, the outhouses were placed just inside the front gate, where an occupant could eavesdrop on comments from passersby. House No 3 has a good example of this. The water features are always imitated by sand or gravel except in No 7, the Mori Shigemitsu House, where real water is used. The Mori Shigemitsu House is particularly well preserved and dates from 1741.

Between houses No 3 and No 4/5 is the thatched-roof building of Futatsuya Minke, now used as a souvenir stand. Along the main road, parallel to the samurai street, is a well-stocked carp stream.

Entry to the samurai street houses is Y310, payable at one of the entry points. The houses and gardens are open from 8 am to 5.30 pm.

Kamikaze Museum

A more modern version of the samurai are commemorated in the Tokko Ihinkan (Kamikaze Museum) at the western end of town. There's a distinctly weird feeling to this comprehensive collection of aircraft, models, mementoes and photos of the young, fresh-faced pilots who enjoyed the dubious honour of flying in the Special Attack Corps. Unfortunately, there's hardly a word in English, apart from the message that they did it for the dream of 'peace and prosperity'. Crashing your aircraft into a battleship seems a strange way of ensuring peace and prosperity but the bare statistics indicate that, far from achieving the aim of 'a battleship for every aircraft', only minor ships were sunk at the cost of over 1000 aircraft and, of course, their pilots. The museum is open from 9 am to 4.30 pm and entry is Y310.

Places to Stay & Eat

Most visitors take a day trip to Chiran or stop there en route between Kagoshima and Ibusuki. If you want to stay overnight, the *Tomiya Ryokan* (tel 09938-83-8417/4313) is on the main street opposite the bus stop. Also opposite the bus stop is a noodle shop which is good for a cheap lunch. *Taki-An* on the samurai street is a rather more traditional place with a nice garden where you can sit on tatami mats to eat a bowl of pleasantly up-market soba noodles at Y600. The menu is all in Japanese but there are plenty of fellow diners whose meals you can point at.

Getting There & Away

Kagoshima Kōtsū buses to Chiran and Ibusuki run from stop No 4 at the Nishi-Kagoshima station or from the Yamakataya bus terminal at the Yamakataya department store in central Kagoshima. Chiran is 35 km from Kagoshima, the bus takes about one hour 15 minutes and the fare is about Y800.

IBUSUKI   指宿

At the south-western end of the Satsuma Peninsula, 50 km from Kagoshima, is the hot-spring resort of Ibusuki, a good base from which to explore other parts of the peninsula. The staff at the JR Ibusuki station information counter are very helpful.

Hot Springs

For onsen connoisseurs, Ibusuki has two renowned hot springs. On the beach in front of the Ginsho Hotel you can pay Y510 for the somewhat dubious pleasure of being buried up to your neck in hot sand. The steam rises up through the beach to create the unusual sensation of hot sand. You pay at the entrance (the fee includes a yukata and towel), change in the changing rooms then

Ibusuki
1. Kokumin Kyūkamura (Vacation Village)
2. Minshuku Sakura-sò
3. Baseball Stadium
4. Hakusuikan Hotel
5. Seaside Hotel
6. Post Office
7. Youth Hostel
8. Bus Station
9. Supermarket
10. Restaurant
11. Minshuku Marutomi
12. Youth Hostel
13. Ginshō Hotel & Sand Bath
14. Ryokan Syūsuien
15. Ibusuki Art Galleries
16. Ibusuki Kankō Hotel & Jungle Bath
17. Ginshō Pottery

Ibusuki
1. 指宿国民休暇村
2. 国民桜荘
3. 野球場
4. 指宿白水館
5. シーサイドホテル
6. 郵便局
7. ユースホステル
8. バスタミナル
9. スーパマーケット
10. レストラン
11. 民宿まるとみ
12. ユースホステル
13. 旅館吟松
14. 秀水園旅館
15. 指宿美術館
16. 指宿観光ホテル
17. 吟松窯

wander down to the beach where the burial ladies are waiting, shovel in hand. Those unused to real onsen heat may find the experience too hot to bear and quickly retreat to the baths to wash the sand off. You can take part in this ritual between 8.30 am and 9 pm from April to October and between 8.30 am and 8 pm from November to March.

The other unusual hot spring is the huge Jungle Bath at the Ibusuki Kankō Hotel, which is actually a host of different hot-spring pools surrounded by tropical vegetation. The Jungle Bath costs Y620 and operates from 6 am to 10 pm.

Other Attractions

The town's modern art gallery is also next to the Kankō Hotel and is open from 8 am to 5.30 pm daily. There are fine views over Ibusuki and along the coast from the 214 metre summit of Mt Uomi-dake.

Places to Stay & Eat

Ibusuki has two hostels. The *Ibusuki Youth Hostel* (tel 0993-22-2758/2271) is just north of the station and costs Y1900 or Y2100, depending on the season. The ryokan-style *Tamaya Youth Hostel* (tel 0993-22-3553) at 5-27-8 Yunohama is near the sand baths and costs Y1700 or Y1900.

Minshuku Marutomi (tel 0993-22-5579) at 5-24-15 Yunohama is a small but popular place, close to the town centre and just a stone's throw from the sand baths. The cost per person, including two meals, is Y5000. *Minshuku Sakura-sō* (tel 0993-23-3590) is 2½ km from town, directly below Mt Uomi-dake, and costs Y5000 per person including two meals. The owner speaks good English, the rooms are comfortable, the food is good and there's an outdoor bath.

The other side of Uomi-dake is the *Kokumin Kyūkamura* (tel 0993-22-3211), a large people's lodge that charges Y3200 to Y4300 per person (less for students) for room only; meals are extra.

More expensive hotels and ryokan include *Ryokan Syūsuien* (tel 0993-23-4141) at 5-27-27 Yunohama, which has a restaurant with a very high reputation and a nightly price tag from Y16,000 per person. Although many visitors eat at the ryokan's restaurant, Ibusuki has many other restaurants to choose from, especially around the JR station. There is also a good supermarket on the road leading straight out from the station.

Getting There & Away

See the Chiran section for details about bus transport from Kagoshima: Ibusuki is about 1½ hours from Kagoshima by bus, slightly less by train.

OTHER SATSUMA PENINSULA ATTRACTIONS

Lake Ikeda-ko, west of Chiran, is a beautiful volcanic caldera lake inhabited by giant eels weighing up to 15 kg. Heading west along the coast you come to Cape Nagasakibana from where the offshore islands, including the smoking cone of Iwo-jima, can be seen on a clear day. Mt Kaimon-dake's beauti-fully symmetrical 922 metre cone can be climbed in about two hours from the Kaimondake bus stop.

At the south-western tip of the peninsula is Makurazaki, a busy fishing port and the terminus for the railway line from Kagoshima. Just beyond Mazurazaki is Bōnotsu, a pretty little fishing village which was an unofficial trading link with the outside world via Okinawa during Japan's two centuries of seclusion. North of Bōnotsu is Fukiage-hama, where the long beach is used for an annual summer sand castle construction competition. The *Fukiage-hama Youth Hostel* (tel 0992-92-3455) costs Y1700 or Y1900, depending on the season.

CAPE SATA-MISAKI 佐多岬

The southernmost point on the main islands of Japan is marked by the oldest lighthouse in Japan. You can reach Cape Sata from the Kagoshima side of Kinkō Bay either by going around the northern end of the bay, taking the ferry from Kagoshima to Sakurajima or by taking the ferry from Yamakawa, south of Ibusuki, to Nejime, near Cape Sata. An eight km bicycle track leads down to the end of the cape.

Miyazaki-ken 宮崎県

OBI 飫肥

Only five km from the coast, the pretty little castle town of Obi has some interesting buildings around its old castle site. From 1587, the wealthy Ito clan ruled from the castle for 14 generations, surviving the 'one kingdom one castle' ruling in 1615. The clan eventually moved out in 1869 when the Meiji Restoration ended the feudal period.

Obi Castle

Although only the walls of the actual castle remain, the grounds contain a number of interesting buildings. The Y300 entry fee includes all these buildings and Yoshokan House just outside the castle entrance. Opening hours are from 9.30 am to 5 pm.

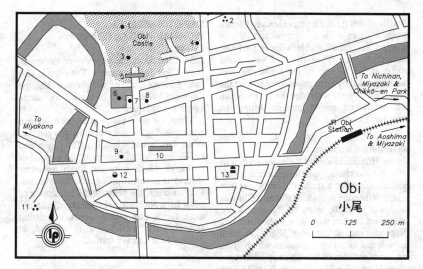

Obi

1 Matsuo-no-Maru House
2 Tanoue Hachiman-jinja Shrine
3 Obi Castle Museum
4 Shintokudo School
5 Ote-mon Gate
6 Yoshokan House
7 Restaurant
8 Noodle Shop
9 Merchant's Museum
10 Carp Stream
11 Ioshi-jinja Shrine
12 Bus Station
13 Post Office

Obi

1 松尾の丸
2 田上八幡神社
3 資料館
4 振徳堂
5 大手門
6 豫章館
7 レストラン
8 ラーメン店
9 商家資料館
10 鯉遊泳
11 いおし神社
12 バスターミナル
13 郵便局

Yoshokan House When the Obi lord was forced to abandon his castle after the Meiji Restoration, he moved down the hill to the Yoshokan, formerly the residence of the clan's chief retainer. It stands just outside the castle entrance and has a large garden incorporating Mt Atago as 'borrowed scenery'. Beyond this house you enter the castle proper through the impressive Ote-mon Gate.

Obi Castle Museum The castle museum has a collection relating to the Ito clan's long rule over Obi and includes everything from weapons and armour to clothing and household equipment.

Matsuo-no-Maru House Matsuo-no-Maru, the lord's private residence, has been reconstructed and there's an excellent descriptive leaflet of this quite extensive house. There's even a room with a window specifically placed for comfortable viewing of the autumn moon. When the lord visited the toilet at the far end of the house, he was accompanied by three pages – one to lead the way, one to carry water for the lord to wash his hands and one to fan him during the summer months!

Merchant's Museum

In the Honmachi area of the town, traditionally the merchants' quarters, there's a carp stream alongside a section of one street (see map). When the main road through Obi was widened in 1980, many of the town's old merchant houses were demolished but one fine building, dating from 1866, has been rebuilt as a merchant's museum which gives an excellent idea of what a shop of that era would have been like. It's open from 9.30 am to 5 pm and entry is Y100.

Other Attractions

The Shintokudo, adjacent to the castle, was established as a samurai school in 1801. Up the hill behind the Shintokudo is the Tanoue Hachiman-jinja Shrine, shrouded by trees and reached by a steep flight of steps. On the western side of the river, the Ioshi-jinja Shrine has a pleasant garden and the Ito family mausoleum. The Chikkō-en Park is on the eastern side of town, near the railway station.

Places to Eat

The entranceway to the castle is flanked by a restaurant and a noodle shop. The noodle shop has a menu with pictures of all its dishes.

Getting There & Away

The JR Nichinan line runs through Obi and Aoshima to Miyazaki – about a one hour trip. Route 222 from Miyakono to Obi and Nichinan on the coast is a superb mountain road, twisting and winding as it climbs over the hills.

CAPE TOI-MISAKI & NICHINAN-KAIGAN COAST
都井岬、日南海岸

Like Cape Sata, the views over the ocean from Cape Toi are superb. The cape is also famed for its herds of wild horses although the word 'wild' has to be treated with some suspicion in Japan!

There's a good beach at Ishinami-kaigan where, during the summer only, you can stay in old farmhouse minshuku. The tiny island of Kō-jima, just off the coast, has a group of monkeys which were the focus for some interesting anthropological discoveries. Further north, the beautiful 50 km stretch of coast from Nichinan to Miyazaki offers stunning views, pretty little coves, interesting stretches of 'washboard' rocks and, at holiday times, heavy traffic.

Udo-jinja Shrine

The coastal shrine of Udo-jinja is brightly painted in orange and has a wonderful setting. If you continue through the shrine to the end of the path, you'll find yourself in an open cavern overlooking some weird rock formations at the ocean's edge. A popular sport is to buy five round clay pebbles for Y100 and try to get them into a shallow depression on top of one of the rocks. Succeeding at this task is supposed to make your wish come true.

Aoshima

This popular beach resort about 10 km south of Miyazaki is a real tourist trap famed for the small island covered in betel palms, fringed by 'washboard' rock formations and connected to the mainland by a causeway. Due to the prevailing warm currents, the only place you'll find warmer water in Japan is much further south in the Okinawa Islands.

Places to Stay The *Aoshima Youth Hostel* (tel 0985-65-1657) is near the railway tracks and costs Y1800 or Y2000, depending on the season. *Minshuku Také* (tel 0985-65-1420) is part of the Japanese Inn Group and costs Y3000/5600 for singles/doubles. The *Aoshima Kokuminshukusha* (tel 0985-65-1533) is a people's lodge with Japanese-style rooms starting from Y3500. Aoshima also has a wide variety of hotels.

Getting There & Away Aoshima is on the JR Nichinan-Miyazaki line and less than half an hour away from Miyazaki station by train.

MIYAZAKI　宮崎
Miyazaki (population 290,000) is a reasonably large city with an important shrine and a pleasant park. Due to the warm offshore currents, the town has a balmy climate. The area around Miyazaki played an important part in early Japanese civilisation and some interesting excavations can be seen in Saitobaru, 27 km north.

Orientation & Information
JR Miyazaki station is immediately to the east of the town centre and the restaurant and entertainment area. Most hotels and the youth hostel are reasonably close to the station and even the more expensive hotels (mainly along the riverside) are still quite close to the station area. The bus station is south of the Oyodo River while the town's two principal attractions – the Miyazaki-jinja Shrine and the Heiwadai-kōen Park – are several km north.

There's a tourist information office in JR Miyazaki station and one in the prefectural office where you will also find a display of local products. The prefectural tourist office is just off Tachibana-dōri, the main street through town.

Miyazaki-jinja Shrine & Prefectural Museum
The Miyazaki Shrine is dedicated to the Emperor Jimmu, the semimythological first emperor of Japan and founder of the Yamoto court. At the northern end of the shrine grounds is the Miyazaki Prefectural Museum with displays relating to local history and archaeological finds. Entry to the museum is Y155 and it's open from 9 am to 4.30 pm daily except Mondays.

The shrine is about 2½ km north of JR Miyazaki station or a 15 minute walk from the Miyazaki-jinja station, one stop north. Bus No 1 also runs to the shrine.

Heiwadai-kōen Park
The *heiwa* or 'peace' park has as its centrepiece a 36 metre high tower constructed in 1940, a time when peace in Japan was about

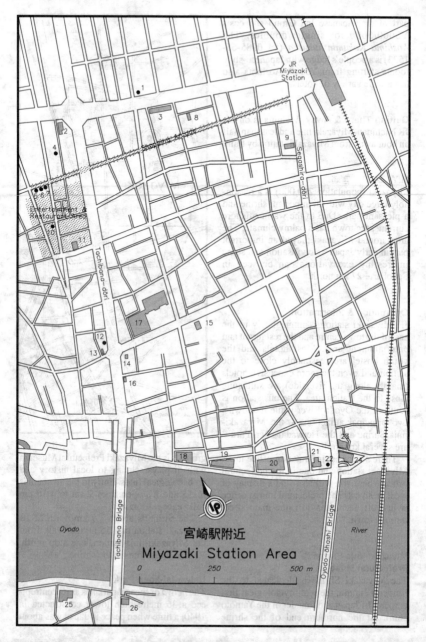

JR
Miyazaki
Station

Sadashira-dori

Tachibana-dori

Entertainment &
restaurant area

1
3
8
2
4
9
5
6
7
17
15
12
13
14
16
18
19
21
22
23
24
20
25
26

Oyodo

Tachibana Bridge

Oyodo-ōhashi Bridge

River

宮崎駅附近
Miyazaki Station Area

0   250   500 m

Miyazaki Station Area

1	Main Post Office	14	Hotel Bigman
2	ANA/JAS	15	Fujin Kaikan Youth Hostel
3	NTT	16	Business Hotel Tachibana
4	Italian Tomato Restaurant	17	Prefectural Office
5	Kentucky Fried Chicken	18	Kandabashi Hotel
6	Foremost Ice Cream	19	Miyazaki Plaza Hotel
7	Mister Donut	20	Miyazaki Kankō Hotel
8	Mimikan Minshuku	21	Ronkotei Hotel
9	Miyazaki Oriental Hotel	22	KKR Hotel
10	Restaurant with Train Front	23	Miyazaki Grand Hotel
11	Miyazaki Washington Hotel	24	Phoenix Hotel
12	Mos Burgers	25	Konanso Hotel
13	Suginoko Restaurant	26	Sun Route Hotel

Miyazaki Station Area

1	中央郵便局	14	ホテルビッグマン
2	ANA/JAS	15	YH 宮崎県婦人会館
3	NTT	16	ビジネスホテルたちばな
4	イタリアントマトレストラン	17	県庁
5	ケンタキフライドチケン	18	ホテル神田橋
6	フォーモストアイスクリーム	19	ホテルプラザ宮崎
7	ミスタドーナツ	20	宮崎観光ホテル
8	耳川荘	21	ホテル臨江亭
9	宮崎オリエンタルホテル	22	KKR Hotel ホテル
10	はか盛	23	宮崎グランドホテル
11	宮崎ワシントンホテル	24	ホテルフェニックス
12	モスバーガ	25	ホテル江南荘
13	すぎのこレストラン	26	ホテルサンルート宮崎

to disappear. Standing in front of the tower and clapping your hands produces a strange echo.

The Haniwa Garden in the park is dotted with reproductions of the curious clay *haniwa* figures which have been excavated from burial mounds in the region. You can buy small and large examples of these often rather amusing figures from a shop in the Haniwa Garden or from the park's main shopping complex. Small figures cost as little as Y800 but the large ones are in the Y10,000 to Y20,000 bracket.

The Haniwa Garden is about 1½ km north of the Miyazaki Shrine but the museum, in

the northern corner of the shrine grounds, is only a couple of minutes walk from the southern corner of the park. Bus No 8 runs to the park from outside JR Miyazaki station.

Places to Stay

The *Fujin Kaikan Youth Hostel* (tel 0985-24-5785) is within walking distance of Miyazaki station and costs Y1800 or Y2000, depending on the time of year.

Walk straight out from the station, cross Segashira-dōri St, take the third road to the left then the first right and you'll reach the small *Mimikan Minshuku* (tel 0985-22-2623), which has rooms from Y2500 per person. *Miyako* (tel 0985-29-7070) is another minshuku in the station area and its rooms cost from Y2800.

Across the road from the station, the *Miyazaki Oriental Hotel* (tel 0985-27-3111) is a straightforward business hotel with singles from Y4800 to Y6900 and doubles and twins from Y7500 to Y12,700.

Hotel Bigman (tel 0985-27-2111) (what a great name!) is further west along the road from the youth hostel. It's a budget-priced business hotel with singles/doubles from Y4700/7600. When it comes to thinking of good names, the proprietors didn't stop at the hotel title; the Bigman also has the *Realips Coffee Bar*! Just around the corner from the Bigman is the *Business Hotel Tachibana* (tel 0985-27-6868), another low-cost business hotel with singles at Y4800 and doubles and twins from Y7800 to Y8800.

Most of the more expensive hotels are clustered along the riverside between the Tachibana Bridge and the Oyodo-ōhashi Bridge. The *Miyazaki Plaza Hotel* (tel 0985-27-1111/2727) has singles/doubles from Y7000/11,000. Next to it is the *Miyazaki Kankō Hotel* (tel 0985-27-1212) with singles at Y7000 and Y8000 and doubles and twins from Y10,000 to Y17,000. Other riverside hotels include the *Kandabashi Hotel* (tel 0985-25-5511) and the smaller *KKR Hotel* (tel 0985-27-1555). One place outside the riverside hotel strip is the *Miyazaki Washington Hotel* (tel 0985-28-9111) which is in the town centre and entertainment area.

Places to Eat

Fast-food possibilities include *Italian Tomato*, *Kentucky Fried Chicken*, *Mister Donut* and others. There's quite a selection of restaurants in the street south of the Mister Donut. Check out the place with the railway engine emerging from its facade and the adjacent restaurant bedecked with flags and banners for cheap yakitori snacks.

Suginoko (tel 0985-22-5798) at 2-1-4 Tachibana specialises in Miyazaki cuisine with its emphasis on locally grown vegetables. Although the menu is in Japanese only, there is a brief description in English posted

downstairs and simply asking for the teishoku (the set meal of the day) will get you something interesting. A lunch-time 'hanashobu course' (mainly tempura) is Y1500, a 'hamayu course' (mainly sushi) is Y2500. At night the set meals cost from Y3800 to Y6000.

The riverside *Phoenix Hotel* has a rooftop beer garden with good views over the city. The Miyazaki station is known for its 'shiitake ekiben', a boxed lunch featuring a mushroom dish.

Getting There & Away

Miyazaki is connected with Tokyo, Osaka and other centres by air. The JR Nippō line runs from Kokura (5½ hours, Y5360) in the north through Miyazaki to Kagoshima (2½ hours, Y2160) in the west. There are also train connections to Kumamoto and south through Obi to Nichinan.

The Miya-kō City bus station is south of the Oyodo River near JR Minami-Miyazaki station. Take a bus No 10 down the coast to Aoshima and Nichinan or a Cape Toi Express for Cape Toi. Buses also go from here to Ebino-kōgen in the Kirishima National Park, taking about two hours 15 minutes, to Fukuoka, Kagoshima and other centres. Many bus services run along Tachibana-dōri.

There are also ferry services linking Miyazaki with Hiroshima and Osaka in Honshū.

Getting Around

To/From the Airport Miyazaki's airport is conveniently situated only about 20 minutes by bus from JR Miyazaki station.

Bus Although bus services start and finish at the Miya-kō City bus station near JR Minami-Miyazaki station, many of them run along Tachibana-dōri St in the centre, including No 1 to the Miyazaki-jinja Shrine and No 8 to Heiwadai-kōen Park. Miyazaki-Eigyosho, the other bus terminal, is near JR Miyazaki Station.

Tours from the Miya-kō City bus station are operated by the Miyazaki Kōtsū Bus

Company and cover not only the sights in town but sights along the coast to Ao-shima Island and the Udo-jinja Shrine. The all-day tours cost about Y5000.

SAITOBARU 西都原

If the pottery haniwa figures in Miyazaki piqued your interest in the region's archaeology, then head north 27 km to the Saitobaru Burial Mounds Park, where several sq km of fields and forest are dotted with over 300 burial mounds. The 4th to 7th century AD mounds or 'kofun' range from insignificant little bumps to hillocks large enough to appear natural creations. They also vary in shape, some being circular, some square, others a curious keyhole shape. Many are numbered with small signs, though any information is in Japanese. There's an interesting small museum with displays about the burial mounds and the finds that have been made, including swords, armour, jewellery, haniwa pottery figures and much more. Another exhibit shows items from the 18th century Edo period.

Entry to the museum is Y155 and it is open from 9 am to 4.30 pm daily except Mondays. The park area is always open, of course. Buses run to Saitobaru from the Miya-kō City bus station in Miyazaki. Some also depart from the Miyazaki town centre but would be easier to find at the station. If you want to explore the mound-dotted countryside you're either going to need your own transport or plan to walk a lot. Saitobaru is just outside the town of Saito.

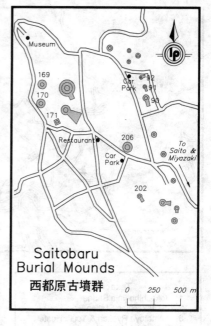

Saitobaru
Burial Mounds
西都原古墳群

0   250   500 m

TAKACHIHO 高千穂

The mountain resort town of Takachiho is about midway between Nobeoka on the coast and Mt Aso in the centre of Kyūshū. It's famed for its beautiful gorge and for a number of interesting shrines. There's a helpful tourist information counter by the tiny train station.

Takachiho Legends

Niniginomikoto, a descendant of the sun goddess Amaterasu, is said to have made landfall in Japan on top of Mt Takachiho in southern Kyūshū. Or at least that's what's said in most of Japan; in Takachiho the residents insist that it was in their town that the sun goddess' grandson arrived, not on top of the mountain of the same name.

They also lay claim to the sites for a few other important mythological events, including Ama no Iwato, the 'boulder door of heaven'. Here Amaterasu hid and night fell across the world. To lure her out another goddess performed a dance so comically lewd that the sun goddess was soon forced to emerge from hiding to find out what was happening. That dance, the 'Iwato Kagura', is still performed in Takachiho today. ■

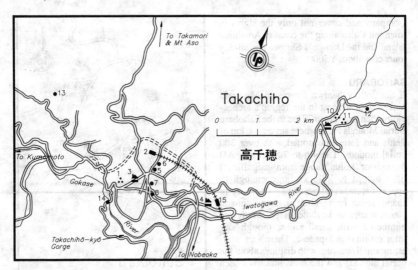

Takachiho	
1	Takachiho-jinja Shrine
2	JR Takachiho Station
3	Yamatoya Ryokan & Youth Hostel
4	Takachiho Youth Hostel
5	Business Hotel Kanaya
6	City Hall
7	Bus Station
8	Folkcraft Ryokan Kaminoya
9	Iwato Furusato Youth Hostel
10	Amano Iwato-jinja Shrine - Nishi Hongu
11	Amano Iwato-jinja Shrine - Higashi Hongu
12	Amano Yasugawara Cave
13	Kunimigaoka Lookout
14	Takachiho-kyō Gorge Bridge
15	Amano-Iwato Station

Takachiho	
1	高千穂神社
2	高千穂駅
3	旅館大和屋ユースホステル
4	高千穂ユースホステル
5	ビジネスホテルかなや
6	市役所
7	バスターミナル
8	民芸旅館かみの家
9	岩戸ふるさとユースホステル
10	天岩神社西本殿
11	天岩神社東本殿
12	天ノ安川原
13	国見が岳
14	高千穂神社
15	天岩戸駅

Takachiho-kyō Gorge

Takachiho's beautiful gorge, with its waterfalls, overhanging rocks and sheer walls, is the town's major attraction. There's a one km walk alongside the gorge, or you can inspect it from below in a rowboat, rented for a pricey Y1000 for 40 minutes. The gorge is about two km from the centre, a Y700 ride by taxi.

Takachiho-jinja Shrine

The Takachiho shrine, about a km from JR Takachiho station, is surrounded by wonderful tall trees. The local Iwato Kagura dances are performed from 8 to 9 pm each evening, and entry is Y300.

Amano Iwato-jinja Shrine

The Iwatogawa River splits the Amano Iwato Shrine into two parts. The main shrine, Nishi Hongu, is on the western bank of the river; while on the eastern bank is Higashi Hongu, at the actual cave where the sun goddess hid and was lured out by the first performance of the Iwato Kagura dance. From the main shrine it's a 15 minute walk to the cave. The shrine is eight km from Takachiho. Buses leave every 45 minutes from the bus station and cost Y310 while a taxi would cost around Y1500.

Amano Yasugawara Cave

A beautiful short walk from the Amano Iwato Shrine alongside a picture-postcard stretch of stream takes you to the Amano Yasugawara cavern. There, it is said, the gods conferred on how they could persuade the sun goddess to leave her hiding place and thus bring light back to the world. Visitors pile stones into small cairns all around the cave entrance.

Kunimigaoka Lookout

From the 'land surveying bluff' overlooking Takachiho, the gods are said to have gazed across the countryside. Today tourists can drive up there to admire the superb view.

Festivals

Important Iwato Kagura festivals are held on 3 May, 23 September and 3 November at the Amano Iwato-jinja Shrine. There are also all-night performances in farmhouses from the end of November to early February and a visit can be arranged by inquiring at the shrine. A short dance performance takes place every night at the Takachiho-jinja Shrine.

Places to Stay

Takachiho has plenty of places to stay: the list at the JR station information counter includes more than 20 hotels, ryokan and pensions and another 20 minshuku. Despite this plethora of accommodation, every place in town can be booked out at peak holiday periods.

There are three youth hostels in the area, each costing Y2100 a night. Right in the town centre, the *Yamatoya Ryokan & Youth Hostel* (tel 0982-72-2243/3808) is immediately recognisable by the huge figure painted on the front. The *Takachiho Youth Hostel* (tel 0982-2-5152) is a couple of km from the centre, near the JR Amano-Iwato station. The *Iwato Furusato Youth Hostel* (tel 0982-74-8254/8750) is near the Amano Iwato Shrine.

The *Folkcraft Ryokan Kaminoya* (tel 0982-72-2111) is a member of the Japanese Inn Group and just down from the bus station, right in the centre of Takachiho. The friendly owner speaks good English and singles/doubles are Y3500/6000.

The *Business Hotel Kanaya* (tel 0982-72-3261), on the corner of the station road and the main road through town, has singles from Y3500. The ryokan part of the *Yamatoya Ryokan & Youth Hostel* costs from Y6000 to Y10,000, including meals. The *Iwato Furusato Youth Hostel* also has a ryokan section, which costs from Y5000.

The minshuku all cost from Y4800 a night – bookings can be made at the JR station information counter.

Places to Eat

Many people will eat in their ryokan or minshuku but Takachiho has plenty of restaurants with plastic meal displays as well as other, higher-class restaurants. If you need a meal you could definitely do worse than *Kencha's*, a cheerful little yakitori (grill restaurant specialising in chicken dishes) marked by a bamboo frontage, banners, flags, signs, lanterns and a cavepeople cartoon across the top. It's opposite the Folkcraft Ryokan, near the bus station.

Getting There & Away

The JR Takachiho line runs inland from Nobeoka on the coast, taking just over 1½ hours. Alternatively, there are bus services to Takachiho: buses take about three hours 15 minutes from Kumamoto, 1½ hours from Nobeoka or less than an hour from Takamori near Mt Aso.

Getting Around

Although you can walk to the gorge and the Takachiho Shrine, the other sites are some distance from town and public transport is a problem. Regular tours leave from the bus station: the 'A Course' (Y1100) covers everything, while the 'B Course' (Y750) misses the Amano Iwato Shrine.

Oita-ken   大分県

The Oita Prefecture offers an insight into the Japanese onsen (hot-spring) mania at both its best (Yufuin) and worst (Beppu). The region also bears traces of Japan's earliest civilisations, particularly on the Kunisaki Peninsula and around Usuki.

BEPPU   別府

Beppu (population 140,000) is the Las Vegas of spa resort towns, a place where bad taste is almost a requisite. If you're trying to develop an appreciation and understanding of the Japanese mania for onsen, you are not going to find it here. Beppu can be fun – just don't take it seriously.

Information

The JR Beppu station concourse has a tourist information counter with maps and other information, but Beppu also has a Foreign Tourist Information Office (tel 0977-23-1119) a few blocks from the station on the 3rd floor of the Kitahama Centre building. The office has information sheets, maps and other useful material in English and usually has helpful personnel on hand who can speak English.

The Beppu station area is very convenient for visitors: facilities include a choice of accommodation, restaurants, banks, travel agencies and, of course, the railway station and other transport facilities. Beppu is, however, a sprawling town and the hot-spring areas are spread out, often some distance from the town centre. The adjacent town of Oita is virtually contiguous with Beppu, and although it lacks any notable attractions, it could be an alternative place to stay.

Hot Springs

Beppu has two sorts of hot springs and there are lots of statistics about the more than 100 million litres of hot water they pump out every day. The jigoku are hot springs for looking at. The onsen are hot springs for bathing in.

The Hells Beppu's most hyped attraction is the 'hells' or jigoku, a collection of hot springs where the water bubbles forth from underground, often with unusual results. Admission to each hell is Y300, or you can get a booklet of tickets for Y1500 which covers all except one hell. The only real reason to visit all of them would be if you had a passion to see Japanese tourism at its absolute worst – car parks overflowing with tour buses, enthusiastic flag-waving visitors, souvenir stands, the full panoply of delights. If this doesn't interest you, save your money: Rotorua in New Zealand has equally interesting and much less spoilt thermal activity. Jigoku tour buses depart regularly from the JR Beppu station bus stop and cost Y2700.

The hells are in two groups: seven at Kannawa, about eight km north-west of the station, and two more several km away. In the Kannawa group, the Umi Jigoku (Sea Hell), with its large expanse of gently steaming blue water, and the Shiraike Jigoku (White Pond Hell) are quite pleasant. Kinryu Jigoku (Golden Dragon Hell) and Kamado Jigoku (Oven Hell) have a dragon figure and a demon figure overlooking the pond... big deal. Skip the Oniyama Jigoku (Devil's Mountain Hell) where crocodiles are kept in miserable concrete pens, and the Yama Jigoku (Mountain Hell), where a variety of animals are kept under miserable conditions.

The smaller group has the Chinoike (Blood Pool Hell) with its photogenically red water, and the Tatsumaki (Waterspout Hell), where a geyser performs regularly. The former is worth a visit, but the latter can be skipped (there's too much concrete and too

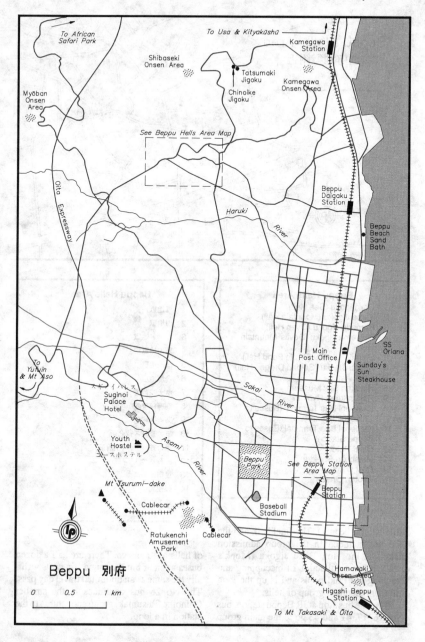

To African Safari Park

To Usa & Kityakūshū →

Kamegawa Station

Shibaseki Onsen Area

Tatsumaki Jigoku

Chinoike Jigoku

Kamegawa Onsen Area

Myōban Onsen Area

Ōita Expressway

See Beppu Hells Area Map

Haruki River

Beppu Daigaku Station

Beppu Beach Sand Bath

Main Post Office

SS Oriana

Sunday's Sun Steakhouse

To Yufuin & Mt Aso

Suginoi Palace Hotel

Sakai River

Youth Hostel
ユースホステル

Asami River

Beppu Park

See Beppu Station Area Map

Beppu Station

Mt Tsurumi-dake

Cablecar

Baseball Stadium

Cablecar

Ratukenchi Amusement Park

Hamawaki Onsen Area

Higashi Beppu Station

Beppu 別府

0   0.5   1 km

To Mt Takasaki & Ōita

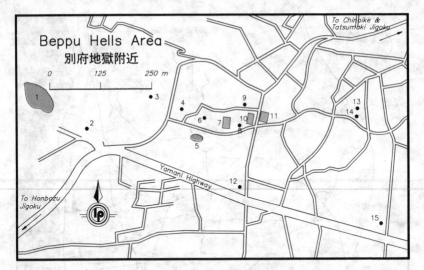

Beppu Hells Area

1 Umi Jigoku (Sea Hell)
2 Yama Jigoku (Mountain Hell)
3 Kamado Jigoku (Oven Hell)
4 Oniyama Jigoku (Devils' Mountain Hell)
5 Shiraike Jigoku (White Pond Hell)
6 Kinryu Jigoku (Golden Dragon Hell)
7 Hotel Ashiya
8 Hinokan Sex Museum
9 Rakurakuen Ryokan
10 Kamenoi Bus Terminal (Buses to Chinoike Jigoku)
11 Kamenoi Bus Terminal (Buses to Beppu Station)
12 Oishi Hotel
13 Minshuku Saekya
14 Post Office
15 Hyotan Onsen

Beppu Hells Area

1 海地獄
2 山地獄
3 カマド地獄
4 鬼山地獄
5 白池地獄
6 金龍地獄
7 ホテル芦屋
8 別府秘宝館
9 楽々園旅館
10 亀の井バス待合所
11 亀の井バス停（別府駅）
12 大石ホテル
13 民宿サカエヤ
14 郵便局
15 ひょたん温泉

little natural beauty). The final hell, and the one not included in the group admission ticket, is the Hon Bozu Jigoku (Monk's Hell). It has a collection of hiccupping and belching hot mud pools and is up the long hill from the main group of hells.

From the bus stop at JR Beppu station, bus Nos 16, 17, 41 and 43 go to the main group of hells at Kannawa. There are half a dozen buses an hour but the round trip costs virtually the same as an unlimited travel day pass. The No 26 bus continues to the smaller Chinoike/Tatsumaki group and returns to the station in a loop.

Onsen Ostensibly, it's sitting back and relaxing in the warm spring water that's Beppu's main attraction (though who can tell how many visitors are also drawn by the hype), and scattered around the town are eight onsen areas. Onsen enthusiasts will spend their time in Beppu moving from one bath to another. Costs range from Y200 to Y600, although some are cheaper and others more expensive. Bring your own soap and towel.

The Beppu onsen area is in the town centre area near Beppu station. Amongst the popular onsen is the Takegawara Onsen (Y600), which dates from the Meiji era and includes a sand bath. Here, the heat from the spring rises up through the sand and patrons lie down in a shallow trench and are buried up to their necks in the super-heated sand.

In the south-western part of town, near the road to Oita, is the Hamawaki onsen area with the popular old Hamawaki Koto Bath. North of the town, the Kannawa onsen area (near the major group of hells) is one of the most popular onsen areas in Beppu. There are also many ryokan and minshuku in this area.

The quieter Shibaseki onsen area is near the smaller group of hells, close to a mountain stream. Also north of Beppu station, near Kamegawa station, is the Kamegawa onsen area where the Hamada Bath is particularly popular. The Beppu Municipal Beach Sand Bath (Y600) is two km south of the Kamegawa onsen area. In the hills northwest of the town centre is the Myōban onsen area.

Suginoi Palace Any tour of Beppu's onsen eventually has to make its way to the Suginoi Palace. On a hill overlooking Beppu, very close to the youth hostel, is the large, deluxe Suginoi Hotel, a favourite of tour groups. The adjacent Suginoi Palace closed down in 1990 for extensive renovations. It had games, night-time entertainment and two huge fantasyland baths, one for males and one for females, which switched each day so patrons could try both over a two day period. Bus Nos 4 and 14 go to the Suginoi Palace.

Bus No 4 leaves from the western exit of Beppu railway station and continues to Kannawa.

Hinokan Sex Museum

All that lolling around in hot water must have some sort of sensual side to it so a sex museum seems just the thing for Beppu. It's in amongst the hells, beside the large Indian Temple Relief opposite the Ashiya Hotel. Inside you'll find a bizarre collection ranging from 'positions' models and illustrations to a large collection of wooden phalluses (some very large indeed). Erotic art on display ranges from Papua New Guinean fertility figures to Tibetan Tantric ones. There are life-size models which plunge into copulatory action at the press of a button, including one of Snow White having a lot of fun with the Seven Dwarfs. Another button lights up the windows of a model apartment building to reveal something happening in every room, including one room with tiny figures of Popeye and Olive Oil on a rotating bed. Entry costs a hefty Y1500 and opening hours are from 9 am to 11 pm.

Mt Takasaki Monkey Park

A couple of km beyond Beppu towards Oita, tribes of monkeys descend to the park at the foot of Mt Takasaki for a daily feed. It's said that the monkeys got into the habit of appearing for a free meal in the 1950s when a local farmer decided that feeding them was more economical than allowing them simply to take his crops. The monkeys are in three distinct tribes: the largest with about 1000 members, the other two with 500 and 400. Each tribe has its own appointed feeding time during the day. Admission to the park is Y500 and Oita Kōtsū buses from the Kitahama bus station operate to the Mt Takasaki park entrance (shared with the Marine Palace Aquarium) every 20 minutes.

The SS Oriana

In the pre-jet era, the British ocean liner SS *Oriana* operated regularly between England and Australia. Later, as the ocean-liner era

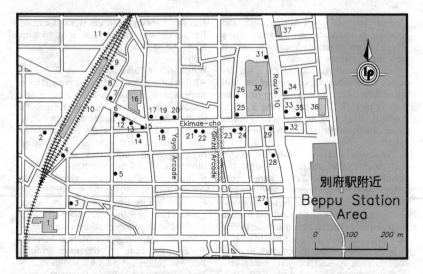

別府駅附近
Beppu Station
Area

Beppu Station Area

1	Kamenoi Hotel	20	Beppu Shinyo Bank
2	Business Hotel Kagetsu	21	Green Hotel
3	Foreign Tourist Information Office	22	Fukuoka City Bank
4	Kentucky Fried Chicken	23	Good Noodle Restaurant
5	Laundry	24	Cinema
6	New Hayashi Hotel	25	Post Office
7	Bentō Shop	26	Oita Bank
8	Beppu Station Bus Stop	27	Takegawara Onsen
9	Car Rental Office	28	JTB
10	JR Beppu Station	29	Pub
11	Hotel Dai Ichi	30	Cosmopia Shopping Centre/Tokiwa Department Store
12	Italian Tomato Restaurant	31	Airport Bus Stop
13	Shimizuso Hotel	32	Royal Host Restaurant
14	Minshuku Kokage	33	Kitahama Bus Station
15	Sundelica Bakery France-kan	34	Kamenoi Bus Station
16	Kintetsu Department Store	35	Daifuku Hotel
17	Bentō Shop	36	Seifu Hotel
18	Cinema	37	Beppu Tower
19	Iyo Bank		

ground to a halt, the *Oriana* became a popular cruise ship. Today the 41,000 ton ship is a floating museum; admission is Y2250.

Other Attractions

West of the station area, there is a cablecar that carries visitors to the 1375 metre summit of Mt Tsurumi-dake but you can also walk to the top. It's a popular jumping-off point for hang-gliders. The 12 km long Yufugawa Ravine is sandwiched between Mt Tsurumi-dake and Mt Yufu-dake (see the Yufuin section). The two mountains rise from the

Beppu Station Area

1	角井ホテル	20	別信
2	ビジネスホテル花月	21	グリーンホテル
3	外国旅客観光案内所	22	福岡シティ銀行
4	ケンタキフライドチケン	23	ラメン店
5	コインランドリー	24	映画館
6	ニューはやしホテル	25	郵便局
7	便當店	26	大分銀行
8	別府駅バス停	27	竹瓦温泉
9	カーレンタル	28	JTB
10	JR 別府駅	29	パープ
11	ホテル第一	30	トキワデパート
12	イタリャントマトレストラン	31	空港バス停
13	しみずぞホテル	32	ロヤルホストレストラン
14	民宿こかげ	33	北浜バス停
15	スンデリカパン屋	34	角井バス停
16	近鉄百貨店	35	大福ホテル
17	便當店	36	セイフホテル
18	映画館	37	別府タワー
19	伊豫銀行		

Tsukahara Plateau, also known as Matsuzuka or 'Pine Mound'.

There's a large African safari park 18 km north-west of Beppu, while the Rakutenchi amusement park is in Beppu. Utopia Shidaka is another amusement park about 12 km out from the town centre. The Marine Palace Aquarium is by the seafront, sharing the same car park as the monkey park at Mt Takasaki.

Places to Stay

Although places to stay are scattered around Beppu, they are concentrated on the Suginoi palace hill, around JR Beppu station and in the Kannawa hot-springs area.

Around Suginoi The huge *Suginoi Hotel* (tel 0977-24-1141), overlooking Beppu from its hillside location, has rooms at Y9500/10,500 for singles/doubles. Nearby is the *New Showaen Hotel* (tel 0977-22-3211), also expensive.

The small *Beppu Youth Hostel* (tel 0977-23-4116) costs Y2100 a night and is very close to the Suginoi Hotel. To get to the hostel, take a No 4 bus (departing hourly, from Beppu station's western exit) or a No 14 bus (departing half hourly) and get off at the Kankaiji-bashi bus stop.

Around Beppu Station The *Minshuku Kokage* (tel 0977-23-1753), a member of the Japanese Inn Group, is at 8-9 Ekimae-cho, just a few minutes walk from Beppu station. It's a particularly friendly minshuku, very used to dealing with the vagaries of gaijin clients, and has rooms at Y3250 per person without bathroom or Y3750 per person with. There's a pleasantly spacious bath upstairs and a laundry costing Y100 each for a load of washing and drying.

Also a few minutes walk from the station is the *Minshuku Sumi* (tel 0977-23-0146) with similarly priced rooms. *Business Hotel Kagetsu* (tel 0977-24-2355) is right behind

JR Beppu station and has rooms at Y2500 per person. The *Hotel Dai Ichi* (tel 0977-24-6311/22-3459), also behind the station, is a pleasant business hotel with singles/doubles at Y3300/6000. Walk straight out from the station and along Ekimae-cho St a short distance to the *New Hayashi Hotel* (tel 0977-24-5252). This is a straightforward business hotel where singles/doubles cost Y3700/6200. A bit further down the same street is the *Green Hotel* (tel 0977-25-2244), with singles/doubles at Y4000/7000.

South of the station is the larger *Kamenoi Hotel* (tel 0977-22-3301), with singles at Y600 and twins from Y8500 to Y12,000. There are a number of hotels along Route 10 through town, at the bottom of the station road.

Kannawa Jigoku Area There are a number of minshuku and ryokan around the Kannawa hot springs, including the big *Hotel Ashiya* (tel 0977-67-7711), which is right in amongst the jigoku.

Also close to the Kannawa jigoku is the *Rakurakuen Ryokan* (tel 0977-67-2682) which costs from Y5000 to Y8000 per person and has a variety of baths to try. Up the road from the jigoku, behind the small post office, is *Minshuku Sakaeya* (tel 0977-66-6234). It costs Y3000 per person (room only) or Y6000 with breakfast and dinner. This popular minshuku is in an interesting old building and your food is cooked using hot-springs heat.

Places to Eat

Beppu is renowned for its freshwater fish, for its fugu (globefish) and for the wild vegetables grown in the mountains further inland. *Morisawa* is a good restaurant for local specialities.

In the station you'll find a *Lotteria*, a *Little Mermaid* (bakery) and a *Kentucky Fried Chicken*. Elsewhere in Beppu you'll find a *McDonald's*, a *Mos Burger*, a *Sunday's Sun* (steakhouse) and other fast-food restaurants. Just down from the station there's a branch of the *Italian Tomato*, with wine, beer, coffee and great cakes from Y300 to Y500 a slice.

Along Ekimae-cho (the road leading from the station) there are lots of restaurants with plastic meals on display; several places offering bentō (boxed lunch) meals; a number of good bakeries; and noodle shops. The popular Minshuku Kokage has the *Kakegi Restaurant*.

Getting There & Away

Air There are flights to Oita Airport from Tokyo, Osaka, Nagoya, Kagoshima and Okinawa.

Train From Fukuoka/Hakata via Kokura in Kitakyūshū it takes about 2½ hours on the JR Nippō line to Beppu. The basic futsū fare is Y3190, while the limited express service costs an additional Y2060. The line continues on down the coast to Miyazaki. The shinkansen from Tokyo runs to Kokura and on to Fukuoka/Hakata. The JR Hōhi line runs from Beppu to Kumamoto via Mt Aso; it takes about 2½ hours to Aso and another hour down to Kumamoto.

Bus The Yamanami Highway bus No 266 links Beppu and Kumamoto with a side trip to Mt Aso. The journey between Beppu and Mt Aso takes about three hours, another hour from Mt Aso to Kumamoto.

Ferry Ferries run to Beppu or Oita from Osaka (Y5870, 15 hours), Kōbe (Y5870, 14 to 15 hours), Hiroshima (Y3600, 5½ to 8½ hours), Takamatsu (Y4700, 11 hours), Matsuyama (Y2400, 4½ hours), Uwajima (Y1900, three hours) and Yawatahama (Y1750, three hours). Late evening boats to Western Honshū should pass through the Inland Sea during daylight hours the next morning.

There's a convenient ferry service from Saganoseki, which travels around the southern side of the bay towards Usuki then on to Misaki on Shikoku. The trip, which takes a little over one hour and costs Y600, is a very convenient route. Other Shikoku services operate from Usuki to Yawatahama (Y1300, two hours) and from Saiki to Sukumo (Y1650, three hours).

Getting Around

To/From the Airport Hovercraft run from Oita and Beppu to Oita Airport, which is 40 km around the bay from Beppu. The airport bus service takes about an hour and leaves from the stop outside the Cosmopolitan shopping centre.

Bus There are four local bus companies, of which Kamenoi is the largest. Most buses are numbered but Oita Kōtsū buses, for the Mt Takasaki monkey park and Oita, are not. An unlimited travel 'My Beppu Free' pass for Kamenoi buses is not free at all; the 'mini pass' version covers all the local attractions, including the hells, for Y800. A 'wide pass' goes further afield: Y1400 for one day or Y2200 for two. The passes are available at the JR Beppu station information counter and at the Beppu Youth Hostel.

A variety of bus tours operate from the Kitahama bus station including tours to the Kannawa hot springs, the African safari park and other attractions.

USUKI 臼杵

About five km from Usuki is a collection of

superb 10th to 13th century Buddha images. There are more than 60 images in a series of niches in a ravine. Some are complete statues while others have only the heads remaining, but many are in wonderful condition, even with paintwork still intact. The Dainichi Buddha head is the most impressive and important of the Usuki images. There are various other stone Buddha images at sites around Oita Prefecture such as Motomachi, Magari and Takase but the Usuki ones are the most numerous and most interesting.

Entry to the ravine is Y520 and it's open from 8.30 am to sunset. There's a choice of restaurants at the site. The town of Usuki is about 40 km south-east of Beppu: trains take a little under one hour and cost Y1400. It's then a 20 minute bus ride to the ravine site; alternatively, you could walk the few km from the Kami-Usuki station.

YUFUIN 湯布院

If Beppu is the hot-spring resort scene at its glitzy worst, then Yufuin is its smaller, more refined relation. About 25 km inland from Beppu, Yufuin makes a pleasant stop between Beppu and Mt Aso and has an inter-

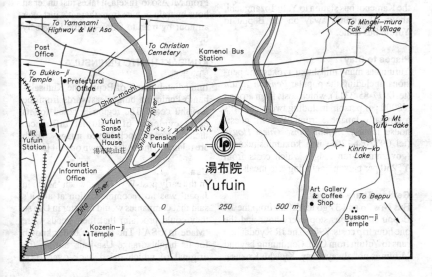

esting variety of baths to sample, including some fine *rotemburo* (open-air baths).

Information

The tourist information office in front of the railway station has some information in English. Change money in Beppu, as there's no place to do it readily in Yufuin. There are onsen festivals in April and May.

Things to See & Do

As in Beppu, making a pilgrimage from one onsen to another is a popular activity in Yufuin. The difference is that in Yufuin it's rural peace which is on offer, not city hype. The Kinrinko and Makinote rotemburo are special attractions. Kinrin-ko Lake is fed by hot springs, so it's warm all year round.

The town has a number of interesting temples and shrines including the Kozenin-ji, Bussan-ji and Bukko-ji temples. Yufuin is also noted for its arts and handicrafts, which can be seen at the Mingei-mura Folk Art Village and in a number of shops and galleries.

The double-peaked 1583 metre Mt Yufu-dake volcano overlooks Yufuin and takes about two hours to climb. Take a bus from the Kamenoi bus station to Yufu Tozanguchi, about 20 minutes away on the Beppu to Yufuin bus route.

Places to Stay

Yufuin has many minshuku, ryokan and pensions, including the popular *Pension Yufuin* (tel 0977-85-3311), which costs from around Y8000 per person, including two meals. It's a typically Japanese 'rural Western' guesthouse fantasy! *Yufuin Sansō Guest House* (tel 0977-84-1205) is a kokuminshukusha (government-run lodge) which costs from Y5250 per person, including two meals.

Getting There & Away

Bus Nos 36 and 37 go to Yufuin from the JR Beppu station bus stop every hour and the one hour trip costs Y900. The JR Kyūdai line runs to Yufuin from Oita. Continuing beyond Yufuin is not always easy. Kyūshū Kokusai

Kankō (KKC) buses go to Mt Aso and Kumamoto but not year round.

BEPPU TO MT ASO
別府至阿蘇山

Yamanami Highway

The picturesque Yamanami Highway extends 63 km from the Mt Aso region to near Yufuin; from there, the Oita Expressway runs to Beppu on the east coast. There's a Y1850 toll to drive along this scenic but tour buses operating between Kumamoto, Aso and Beppu, or the reverse, also use this route. The road crosses a high plateau and passes numerous mountain peaks, including Mt Kujū-san (1788 metres), the highest point in Kyūshū.

Taketa

South of Yufuin, near the town of Taketa, are the Oka-jō Ato Castle ruins, which have a truly magnificent ridge-top position. The ruins are about two km from JR Bungo-Taketa station: take a bus there and walk back into town. There are some interesting old buildings, reminders of the Christian period and a museum. Bungo-Taketa is on the JR Hōhi line between Oita and Mt Aso. From Mt Aso to Taketa, it takes just under an hour by train or bus; from there it's just over an hour by train to Oita – a little longer by bus.

KUNISAKI-HANTO PENINSULA
国東半島

Immediately north of Beppu, the Kunisaki-hantō Peninsula bulges eastwards from the Kyūshū coast. The region is noted for its early evidence of Buddhist influence, including some rock-carved images which are related to the better known ones at Usuki.

Usa

In the early post-WW II era, when 'Made in Japan' was no recommendation at all, it's said that companies would register in Usa so they could proclaim that their goods were 'Made in USA'! The town is better known for its bright orange Usa-jinja Shrine, the original of which dated back over 1000

国東半島
Kunisaki—hantō
Peninsula

Getting Around

The easiest way to tour the peninsula is on the daily five to seven-hour bus tours from Beppu or Nakatsu. Beppu's Oita Airport is on (or rather off!) the peninsula, about 40 km from Beppu.

NORTHERN OITA-KEN
大分県の北部
Yaba-kei Gorge

Further north from the Kunisaki Peninsula, route 212 turns inland from Nakatsu and runs through the picturesque Yaba-kei Gorge. The gorge extends for about 10 km, beginning about 16 km from Nakatsu. The Ao Tunnel or 'Ao no Domon', at the start of the gorge, was originally cut over a 30 year period by a hard-working monk in order to make the Rankan-ji Temple more accessible.

Smaller gorges join the main one, and there are frequent buses up the gorge road from Nakatsu. A 22 km cycling track follows a now disused railway line. You can rent bicycles and stay at the *Yabakei Cycling Terminal* (tel 09795-4-2655). There's also the *Yamaguniya Youth Hostel* (tel 09795-2-2008), which costs Y2100 per night.

Hita & Around

Further inland from the Yaba-kei Gorge is Hita, a quiet country town and onsen resort where cormorant fishing (ukai) takes place in the river from May through October. You can view the operation from tourist boats during the season. Just across the border in Fukuoka-ken you can also see cormorant fishing in Harazura, another hot-spring resort.

North of Hita, towards Koishiwara, is Onta, a small village renowned for its curious pottery. The Onta-yaki Togeikan Museum has a display of the local product. Koishiwara also has a pottery tradition dating back to the era when Korean potters were first brought to Kyūshū.

Hita is on the JR Kyūdai line between Oita (two hours) and Kurume (one hour). By bus it takes about 45 minutes to travel from Hita to Onta.

years. The current shrine is much newer and connected with Hachiman, the god of war.

Other Attractions

The Kunisaki Peninsula is said to have more than half of all the stone Buddhas in Japan. The 11th century Fuki-ji Temple in Bungotakada is the oldest wooden structure in Kyūshū and one of the oldest wooden temples in Japan. Right in the centre of the peninsula, near the summit of Mt Futago-san, is the Futago-ji Temple, dedicated to Fudomyo-o, the god of fire.

Carved into a cliff behind the Taizo Temple, two km south of Maki Odo, are two large Buddha images: the six metre high figure of the Dainichi Buddha and an eight metre high figure of Fudomyo-o. These are known as the Kumano Magaibutsu and are the largest Buddhist images of this type in Japan. Other stone statues, thought to be from the Heian period of 1000 to 1100 AD, can be seen in Maki Odo.

Okinawa & the South-West Islands
沖縄、南西諸島

Nansei means south-west and the South-West (Nansei-shotō) Islands extend for more than 1000 km in that direction from Kagoshima on Kyūshū to Yonaguni Island, which is just over 100 km from the east coast of Taiwan. The islands cross two prefectures: those in the two northern groups fall within the Kagoshima Prefecture while the four southern groups are part of Okinawa Prefecture.

A warm climate, fine beaches, excellent scuba diving and traces of traditional Okinawan culture are the prime attractions. But don't think of these islands as forgotten backwaters with a mere handful of visitors – both ANA and JAL fly tourists to Okinawa from mainland Japan by the 747-load and even the local flights from Okinawa to other islands in the chain are by 737s.

Okinawa is the gateway to the island chain and its key role in the closing months of WW II holds a continuing fascination for visitors. For an insight into Okinawan culture and to enjoy the least spoilt natural aspects of the islands, you must continue on to the *ritō* or 'outer islands'. Kume-jima is famed for its unspoilt beauty, Taketomi-jima is a tiny island with a picture-postcard village, while Iriomote-jima is Japan's last wilderness, cloaked in dense tropical jungle. Prime scuba-diving sites are found around the Kerama Islands and around Iriomote.

The northern half of the Nansei-shotō group falls within Kagoshima-ken and includes the Osumi-shotō Islands and the Amami-shotō Islands.

The southern half of the Nansei-shotō Islands comprises four island groups. The most important islands, and those that attract the most visitors, are the Okinawa or Ryūkū Islands to the north and the Yaeyama Islands to the south. It's only 100 km from the westernmost island of the Yaeyama group to Taiwan so the whole Nansei-shotō chain

forms a bridge all the way from the southern tip of Kyūshū, 1000 km away.

In between the Okinawa Islands and the Yaeyama Islands are the Miyako Islands, while way off to the east are the isolated Daito Islands. Okinawa, the main island, is referred to as the *hontō* while the outer islands are the *ritō*; the outer islands offer a far better insight into Okinawan culture than the main island. Despite having survived centuries of mainland exploitation and then horrific destruction during the closing months of WW II, the traditional ways may not survive the onslaught of mass tourism.

HISTORY
The islands in the chain look like stepping stones from Japan to Taiwan, and they have long been a bridge between Japanese and Chinese culture. For the often unfortunate residents of the islands this has sometimes resulted in their being squeezed and pulled from both sides. More recently Okinawa was the scene for some of the most violent and tragic action in the closing months of WW II.

For centuries the islands formed a border zone between Chinese and Japanese suzerainty. In the 14th century the Chinese influence was felt most strongly in the Okinawa Islands, and the islands' kingdoms maintained strong links with China for 500 years. In the 15th century the whole island of Okinawa was united under the rule of the Shō dynasty and the capital shifted from Urasoe to Shuri, where it was to remain until the Meiji Restoration. The period from 1477 to 1525 is remembered as a golden age of Okinawan history. By the 17th century, however, Japanese power was on the ascendancy and the Okinawans found themselves under a new ruler when the Satsuma kingdom of southern Kyūshū invaded in 1609. The islands were controlled with an

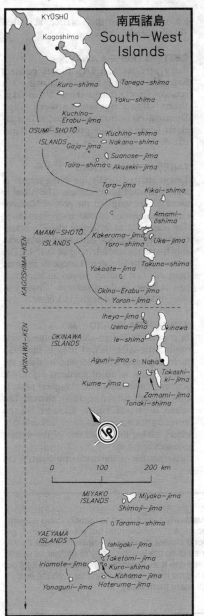

南西諸島
South-West
Islands

KYŪSHŪ

Kagoshima

Kuro-shima
Tanega-shima

Yaku-shima

Kuchino-
Erabu-jima
OSUMI-SHOTŌ
ISLANDS
Kuchino-shima
Nakano-shima
Gaja-jima

Suwanose-jima
Taira-shima
Akuseki-jima

Tara-jima
Kikai-shima

Amami-
ōshima
AMAMI-SHOTŌ
ISLANDS
Kakeroma-jima
Uke-jima
Yoro-shima

Yokoate-jima
Tokuno-shima

Okino-Erabu-jima
Yoron-jima

KAGOSHIMA-KEN

OKINAWA-KEN

Iheya-jima
Izena-jima
Okinawa
Ie-shima

OKINAWA
ISLANDS

Aguni-jima
Naha

Tokashi-
ki-jima

Kume-jima

Zamami-jima
Tonaki-shima

0   100   200 km

MIYAKO
ISLANDS
Miyako-jima

Shimoji-jima

Tarama-shima

YAEYAMA
ISLANDS
Ishigaki-jima

Iriomote-jima
Taketomi-jima
Kuro-shima
Kohama-jima
Yonaguni-jima
Hateruma-jima

iron fist and taxed and exploited so greedily that an anti-mainland resentment continues to this day. The islands were formally made a prefecture under Meiji rule in 1879.

After being treated as foreign subjects by the Satsuma regime, the poor Okinawans were then pushed to become 'real' Japanese. They ended up paying a heavy price for this new role when they were trapped between the relentless American hammer as it smashed down upon the fanatically resistant Japanese anvil in the closing stages of WW II. The war arrived with a fury in October 1944 when US bombing commenced, and on 1 April 1945, US troops landed on the island. The Japanese were prepared to make an all-out stand and it took 82 horrendous days for the island to be captured. Not until 22 June was the conquest complete; by which time 13,000 Americans and, according to some estimates, a quarter of a million Japanese had died. Many of the Japanese deaths were of civilians and there are terrible tales of mass suicides by mothers clutching their children and leaping to their deaths off cliff tops to avoid capture by the foreigners whom, they had been led to believe, were worse than barbarians.

The Japanese commanders committed seppuku (ritual suicide) but a final horror remained. The underground naval headquarters at Tomigusuku were so well hidden they were not discovered until three weeks after the US victory. The underground corridors contained the bodies of 4000 naval officers and men, all of whom had committed suicide.

Even today there's a trace of mistrust against mainland Japan. The Okinawans were exploited by the mainland when they were under Satsuma control and were looked upon as expendable during WW II. The region is still economically backward compared to the mainland and to many main-island Japanese, it is now viewed principally as a place for a beach vacation.

CLIMATE
The climate in the Nansei-shotō Islands is much warmer than that of the Japanese main

islands and Okinawa is virtually a tropical getaway. November to April is considered to be the best season; May and June can bring heavy rain while September and October is the typhoon season. July to August is not only very hot but also very crowded. Although the November to March winter months are cooler the crowds are lighter, and for divers, underwater visibility is at its best.

GETTING THERE & AWAY

Okinawa is the travel centre for the Nansei-shotō chain and there are numerous flights and shipping services to Naha, the main city on Okinawa, from Kagoshima at the southern end of Kyūshū and from many other cities including Tokyo. Some shipping services stop at islands on the way to Okinawa and there are connecting flights and ships from Okinawa to other islands further down the chain. See the individual islands for details.

Travellers who show their YHA membership card when buying boat tickets will get coupons for free meals on board.

Osumi-shotō Islands
大隅諸島

Tanega-shima and Yaku-shima, the two main islands of the group, are less than 100 km from Kagoshima at the southern end of Kyūshū. The islands, one flat and long, the other high and round, are about as unalike as two islands could be. South of these two main islands are the smaller, scattered Tokara Islands.

GETTING THERE & AWAY

Ferry services and JAS flights connect Kagoshima with the two main islands – 3½ hours by ferry to Tanega-shima, 4½ to Yaku-shima. Boats operate between Cape Shimama-zaki at the southern end of Tanega-shima Island and Kamiyaku on Yaku-shima Island.

TANEGA-SHIMA ISLAND   種子島

Tanega-shima Island's low-lying terrain is mainly devoted to agriculture. The island is about 55 km long and the port of Nishino-omote (population 26,000) is the main town. The island has an important place in Japanese history, for this was where a Portuguese ship first made landfall in Japan in 1543. The introduction of modern European firearms from this first contact played an important part in bringing the disastrous 'Country at War' or Muromachi period to a close.

YAKU-SHIMA ISLAND   屋久島

In contrast to Tanega-shima's flatness, volcanic Yaku-shima Island rises to the 1935 metre high peak of Mt Miyanoura-dake, the highest point in all of southern Japan. Mt Kuromi, the island's second highest peak, is only slightly lower at 1836 metres. The island is just 25 km in diameter but the towering terrain catches every inbound rain cloud, giving the island one of the wettest climates in Japan.

Kamiyaku, on the north-east coast, is the

Habu Snakes
Any discussion of the South-West Islands eventually gets around to 'deadly habu snakes'. Perhaps it's a reflection of Japan's severe shortage of real dangers, but you could easily get the impression that the poor habu is the world's most dangerous snake and that they're waiting behind every tree, shrub, bush or bar stool on the islands. They're neither so deadly nor so prolific; in fact the most likely place to see one is at a mongoose versus habu fight put on for tourists. Nevertheless, it's probably not a good idea to go stomping through the bushes barefoot. Do stomp though, the vibrations will scare them away. ■

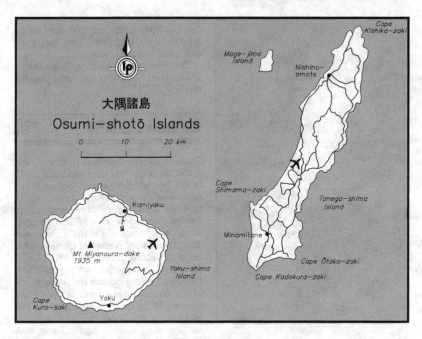

main port; a road runs around the island, passing through Ambo and Yaku. You can take a taxi up the slopes of the mountain and walk past a waterfall and through an ancient cedar forest.

Amami-shotō Islands
奄美諸島

There are five main islands in the Amami-shotō group. From Kagoshima to Amami-ōshima, the largest island in the group, is about 180 km. The islands are predominantly agricultural (producing bananas, papayas, pineapples and sugar cane) and have a warm, sub-tropical climate, clear water and good beaches.

GETTING THERE & AWAY
There are JAS flights from Kagoshima to all five main islands but it's Air Nippon Koku (ANK), which also flies between Kagoshima and Amami-ōshima and Amami-ōshima and Okinawa. South-West Airlines (SWAL) links Yoron-jima with Okinawa. Ferry services stop at Amami-ōshima Island en route from Kagoshima to Okinawa. Kagoshima to Naze on Amami-ōshima takes about 12 hours by ferry; Osaka to Naze takes 25 hours.

AMAMI-OSHIMA ISLAND   奄美大島
This 40 km long island, also known as Oshima Island, has a highly convoluted coastline with the almost enclosed Bay of Setouchi separating it from nearby Kakeroma-jima. Naze is the main port.

OTHER ISLANDS
Kikai-shima is east of Amami-ōshima, while the other three main islands lie like stepping stones in a direct line from Amami-ōshima to Okinawa. In order they are Tokuno-shima, Okino-Erabu-jima and Yoron-jima.

Tokuno-shima is the largest after Amami-ōshima but Okino-Erabu-jima is probably the most interesting island, with its coral reefs and thatched-roof rice barns. The Shonyu-dō Cave stretches for over two km and is one of the most important limestone caves in Japan. China and Wadomari are the main ports on Okino-Erabu-jima. Tiny Yoro-shima also has coral reefs.

There are youth hostels on Okino-Erabu-jima (tel 09979-2-2024) and Yoron-jima (tel 09979-7-2273).

Okinawa Island　　沖縄

Okinawa gives its name to the prefecture and is also the largest and most important island in the Nansei-shotō chain. Okinawa had developed distinct cultural differences to mainland Japan, particularly in architecture, but the destruction of WW II obliterated almost every trace of the old architecture. The USA retained control of Okinawa after the war, handing it back in 1972. The 26 years of US management did a pretty effective job of wiping out any remaining traces of the old Okinawan ways but for good measure the Japanese have turned the island into a major tourist resort. Okinawa is still the biggest US military base in Japan, with 50,000 military and non-military personnel and dependents.

Okinawa's wartime history may have some interest for foreign visitors, but the islands further south will probably offer a more interesting insight into Ryūkyū's history.

The War & Okinawa

The Battle of Okinawa is still a controversial subject. The Okinawans had long felt they'd got a tough deal from mainland Japan. Back in the Satsuma days they were exploited and looked down upon by the mainlanders. In the struggle for Okinawa during WW II they were expendable, a people to be used in order to delay the barbarian invasion of the mainland. The Okinawans paid a terrible price for that delay, as far more Okinawan civilians died than mainland military personnel.

Masahide Ota's *The Battle of Okinawa* (Kume Publishing, 1984) gives some interesting insights into the relentless ferocity of the struggle but I came out of the underground naval headquarters pondering the sheer idiotic futility of it all. What I felt was anger at the stupidity rather than sorrow for the deaths. If you're searching for reasons why the decision was made to nuke Nagasaki and Hiroshima, perhaps what happened in Okinawa will supply some answers.

Tony Wheeler ∎

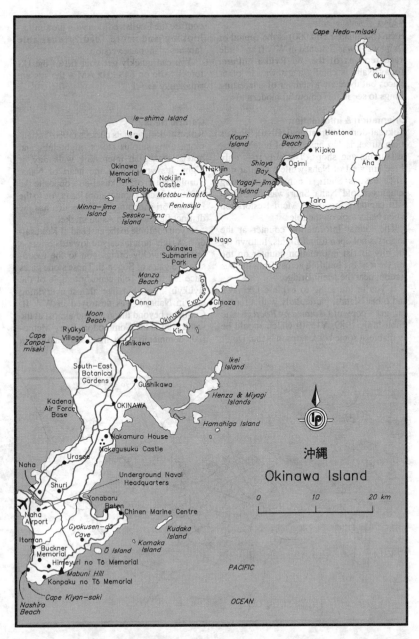

Cape Hedo-misaki

Oku

Ie-shima Island

Ie

Kouri
Island

Okuma
Beach

Hentona

Kijoka

Aha

Okinawa
Memorial
Park

Nakijin
Castle

Nakijin

Shioya Bay

Ogimi

Motobu

Motobu-hantō
Peninsula

Yagaji-jima
Island

Minna-jima
Island

Sesoko-jima
Island

Taira

Nago

Okinawa
Submarine
Park

Manza
Beach

Onna

Ginoza

Moon
Beach

Okinawa Expressway

Ryūkyū
Village

Kin

Cape
Zanpa-
misaki

Ishikawa

South-East
Botanical
Gardens

Ikei
Island

Gushikawa

Henza & Miyagi
Islands

Kadena
Air Force
Base

OKINAWA

Hamahiga Island

沖縄

Okinawa Island

Nakamura House

Makagusuku Castle

0   10   20 km

Urasoe

Naha

Shuri

Underground Naval
Headquarters

Yonabaru

Baten

Chinen Marine Centre

Naha
Airport

Gyokusen-dō
Cave

Kudaka
Island

Itoman

Buckner
Memorial

Ō Island

Komaka
Island

PACIFIC

Himeyuri no Tō Memorial

Mabuni Hill

Konpaku no Tō Memorial

OCEAN

Cape Kiyan-saki

Nashiro
Beach

NAHA 那覇

Naha (population 300,000) is the capital of Okinawa; it was flattened in WW II and little trace remains of the old Ryūkū culture. Today Naha is chiefly a gateway to other places but there are a number of interesting things to see in this colourful modern town.

Orientation & Information

Kokusai-dōri (International Blvd), Naha's main street, is 1½ busy km of hotels, bars, restaurants and shops. The airport is only three km west of Naha while a similar distance east is Shuri, the most interesting remains of 'old' Naha. Shuri was the Okinawan capital prior to the Meiji Restoration when Naha took on the role.

The tourist information counter at the airport is not open for all flights. In town try the city tourist information counter on the 4th floor of the building across from the bus station, near the Meiji Bridge.

If you're intending to explore Okinawa and other islands, particularly with a rented car, get a copy of *Okinawa by Road* (Kume Publishing, 1989, Y1550) which should be available at some bookshops in Naha. Don't confuse the English edition with the similar-looking and more readily available Japanese-language version.

You can quickly get your fill of the US forces radio on 648 kHz AM – the ads are amazingly awful.

Central Naha

Kokusai-dōri, with its curious mix of restaurants, army-surplus stores, nightclubs and hotels, makes an interesting walk day or night. It's very much the heart of Naha. Turning south off Kokusai-dōri opposite the Mitsukoshi department store leads you to the Heiwa-dōri shopping arcade, which has the distinct flavour of an Asian market.

If you continue to the east end of Kokusai-dōri, a right turn takes you towards Shuri, a left turn quickly brings you to the reconstructed gates of Sōgen-ji. These stone gates once led to the 16th century temple of the Ryūkyū kings, but like almost everything else in Naha, it was destroyed in WW II. Continue beyond the gates and almost at the waterfront is the Commodore Perry Memorial, commemorating his 1853 landing in

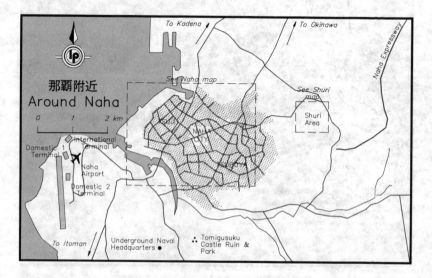

Naha (prior to his arrival in Tokyo). Nearby is a foreigners' cemetery.

Tsuboya Area

Continue along the Heiwa-dōri Ave shopping arcade, taking the left fork at the junction, and a short walk beyond the arcade will bring you to the Tsuboya pottery area. If you miss it simply continue in the same direction until you hit the big Himeyuri- dōri Ave and Tsuboya is across the road from McDonald's.

About 20 traditional pottery workshops still operate in this compact area, a centre for ceramic production since 1682. You can peer into many of the small workshops and there are numerous shops selling popular Okinawan products such as the *shiisā* (lion roof guardians) or the containers for serving *awamori*, the local firewater. The Tsuboya Pottery Centre (Tsuboya Toki Kaikan) is open from 9 am to 6 pm and has items from all the kilns.

Waterfront Temples

Kume-dōri Ave runs straight to the waterfront, where the hilltop Naminoue-gū Shrine and the Gokoku-ji and Kōshi-byō temples are picturesquely sited overlooking the sea and the red-light district! The buildings are unexceptional modern reconstructions and the neat little bay they overlook has been totally ruined by the highway flyover which runs straight across it. Okinawan road building often seems to make no concessions for natural features. The Tsuji entertainment area was once a brothel quarter; now it features clubs, bars and some noted restaurants, together with a collection of colourful love hotels and American-style steakhouses.

Shuri Area

Prior to the Meiji Restoration, Shuri was the capital of Okinawa; that title passed to Naha in 1879. The city's temples, shrines, tombs and castle were all destroyed in WW II. Some reconstructions and repairs have been made but it's a pale shadow of the former city.

Shuri is about 2½ km from the end of Kokusai-dōri. Bus Nos 12, 13, 14, 17 and 25 run by the Okinawa Grand Castle Hotel and past the prefectural museum. Get off at the

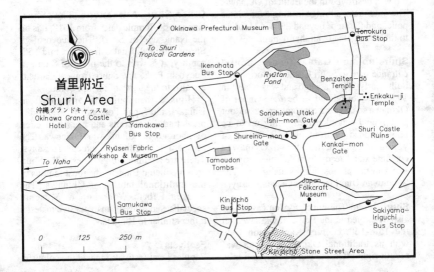

Ikenohata bus stop (immediately before the museum) or the Tonokura stop (right after it). The Ryūtan Pond, directly opposite the museum, is another good landmark. From the museum you can walk around the pond to the other Shuri attractions.

Prefectural Museum The museum's displays are connected with Okinawan lifestyle and culture and include some exhibits on the Battle of Okinawa and a large model of the Shuri Castle. Entry to the museum is Y200 and it's open from 9 am to 5 pm, closed Mondays. The Ryūtan Pond across the road was built in 1427 and was used for dragonboat races.

Benzaiten-dō & Enkaku-ji Temples At the end of the Ryūtan Pond, a wall separates it from another (smaller) body of water, the Enkan Pond. In the centre of this pond, connected to the shore by a bridge, is the Benzaiten-dō Temple. It was originally built in 1502, rebuilt in 1609 after being destroyed and rebuilt again in 1968 after being burnt out during WW II. Cross the road to the rather bedraggled remnants of the Enkaku-ji Temple. The temple dates from 1492 but it too was destroyed in the Battle of Okinawa. The outer gate, a bridge leading over a lotus pond, and the steps beyond the pond leading to the main gate are all that remain.

Shureino-mon Gate The ceremonial entrance gate to Shuri Castle was originally built nearly 500 years ago and was rebuilt in 1958. It's considered to be *the* symbol of Okinawa so there's a constant stream of tour groups and school parties lining up to be photographed in front of it. A couple of young women in traditional Okinawan costume stand ready to make guest appearances in the photos, for a suitable fee. The Sonohiyan Utaki Ishi-mon Gate is nearby.

Shuri Castle The huge wooden castle was also destroyed in the Battle of Okinawa but the 15th-16th century Kankai-mon Gate with its traditional Okinawan design was rebuilt right after the war. The Kyukei-mon

Gate, built in 1508, has also been restored. The third large gate, the Keisei-mon, was originally built in 1546. Reconstruction work is continuing on this and eight smaller gates.

Tamaudon Tombs The war-time destruction did not spare this stone royal mausoleum (also known as Gyokuryo) which dates from 1501, but it has been restored. Bodies were first placed in the central chamber. When the flesh had decayed the bones were then removed, cleaned and permanently interred – kings and queens to the left, princes and princesses to the right. Stone lion figures look down on the courtyard from the central tower and both sides. Entry is Y200 and opening hours are from 8.30 am to 6 pm in summer and from 8.30 am to 5.30 pm in winter.

Kinjōchō Stone Street At one time the 15th century Kinjōchō Ishidatamimichi ran for 10 km from Shuri to the port at Naha. Now there's just one stretch of a couple of hundred metres plus a few side lanes, but the steep and narrow path with its old stone walls and ornate gateways is very picturesque.

Other Shuri Attractions The Shuri Kannon-dō Temple dates from 1618; it is on the Naha side of Shuri. The Sueyoshi-gū Shrine originally dates from the mid-15th century; it is well to the north of Shuri, in Sueyoshi Park. The Shuri Tropical Gardens are also to the north of the museum.

Housed in a building brought from Ishigaki, the Japan Folkcraft Museum displays traditional crafts and has a collection of photographs of pre-war Okinawa. The museum is open daily except Tuesdays. There are a number of factories in the Shuri area producing Bingata, the most famous of the traditional fabrics of Okinawa. The Ryusen Fabric Workshop & Museum specialises in Ryusen, an expensive material rather similar to Bingata.

Festivals
Popular local festivals include the colourful

Geisha Horse Festival (Jiriuma) during which young women ride wooden horses in a parade starting from the Teahouse of the August Moon in the Tsuji entertainment district. The festival usually takes place in March. The Hārii dragon boat races take place in early May, particularly in Itoman and Naha. In August the Tsunahiki Festival takes place in various locations but particularly in Itoman, Naha and Yonabaru – huge teams contest a tug-of-war using a gigantic rope (up to a metre thick).

Places to Stay

The information desk at Naha Airport has a map and hotel list in English and the staff will book accommodation. Okinawa's hotels tend to be scattered around Naha although there are many along Kokusai-dōri.

Youth Hostels Naha has three youth hostels. The *Naha Youth Hostel* (tel 0988-57-0073) is the largest, with room for 100 people at Y2100 a night. It's south of the Meiji Bridge, near the road to the airport in Onoyama.

The other two are both north of the city centre. The *Tamazono-sō Youth Hostel* (tel 0988-67-5377) in Asato has room for 30 people and costs Y1500. It's near the end of Kokusai-dōri, before the Sōgen-ji gates. The *Harumi Youth Hostel* (tel 0988-67-3218/4422), a little further north-west from the Tamazono-sō, towards Route 58, accommodates 38 people at Y2100.

Hotels Just off Kokusai-dōri is *Hotel Sankyo* (tel 0988-67-5041), a basic but comfortable enough business hotel with rooms from Y3600. There are other similar places in the alley directly behind the Sankyo.

The *Air Way Hotel* (tel 0988-61-1122) is another fairly cheap business hotel. It's on Route 58 at 2-3-6 Matsuyama and has singles/doubles at Y5300/9200. *Hotel Maruki* (tel 0988-62- 6135) is next to the JAL office, overlooking the Kumoji River and near Kokusai-dōri. Singles/doubles are from Y5000/9000. *Hotel Yagi* (tel 0988-62-3008) is near the bus station at 1-16-5 Izumizaki and is similarly priced.

There are plenty of moderately priced places along Kokusai-dōri, including the *Hotel Kokusai Plaza* (tel 0988-62- 4243) where singles cost from Y5250. Right behind it is the slightly more expensive *Naha Grand Hotel* (tel 0988-62- 6161) and next door to it is the *Hotel New Okinawa* (tel 0988-67-7200).

More expensive places include the *Okinawa Washington Hotel* (tel 0988-69-2511) which is away from the city centre, halfway between Kokusai-dōri and the waterfront at 2-32-1 Kume. This popular chain hotel has singles/doubles from Y6000/9000. The *Nansei Kankō Hotel* (tel 0988-62-7144) at 3-13-23 Makishi is right on Kokusai-dōri and has rooms from Y6500 per person. The big and glossy *Oceanview Hotel* (tel 0988-53-2112) is on Route 58 and prices start from Y9000/13,000 for singles/doubles. There are many others.

The red-light area near the waterfront has numerous love hotels including the *Wake Hotel* which has a huge mermaid perched on the roof and the imaginatively named *Hotel Joy Box*.

Places to Eat

Perhaps due to the US military presence, Naha has just about every variety of fast-food restaurant available in Japan, many of them in duplicate, triplicate or even more. Along Kokusai-dōri alone you'll find *McDonald's, Kentucky Fried Chicken, Mos Burger, Lotteria, Mister Donut, Shakey's Pizza, A&W Burgers* and probably a few others. Shakey's offers unlimited quantities of pizza from 10 am to 3 pm for Y520.

Among the restaurants along Kokusai-dōri, it's hard to pass by *Rawhide* when the sign outside announces that it specialises in 'Stake & Robster' but the food's just average (and the plastic replicas look awful). Okinawa is said to have the best priced steaks in Japan and there are plenty of steakhouses along Kokusai-dōri although the best of them are in the Tsuji red-light district near the Naminoue-gū Shrine. Here you can choose from *Restaurant George, Jackie's Steakhouse, Restaurant Stateside, Restau-*

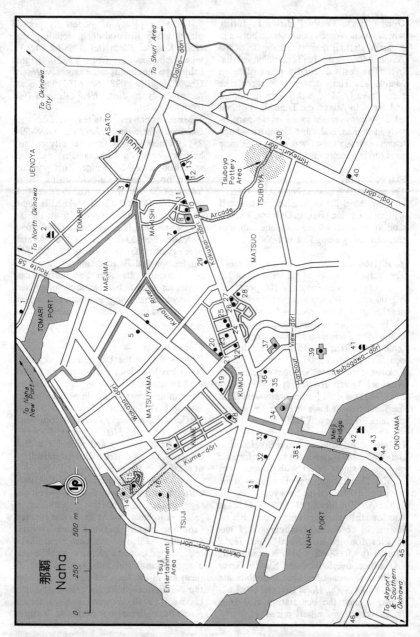

那覇
Naha

Naha

1	Commodore Perry Memorial	16	Teahouse of the August Moon	32	Japaren Rent-a-Car
2	Harumi Youth Hostel	17	Okinawa Washington Hotel	33	KDD (International Telephone Office)
3	Sōgen-ji Gates	18	Oceanview Hotel	34	Bus Station
4	Tamazono-sò Youth Hostel	19	ANA	35	Hotel Yagi
5	Air Way Hotel	20	JAL	36	Naha City Office
6	Nissan Rent-a-Car	21	Hotel Maruki	37	Okinawa Prefectural Office
7	Hotel Sankyo	22	JAS	38	Tourist Office
8	Mitsukoshi Department Store & Naha Tower	23	Farine Patisserie	39	Okinawa Harbourview Hotel
9	Kokusai Shopping Centre	24	Yūnangii Restaurant	40	Immigration Office
10	Ionesk Ice Cream	25	Italian Tomato Restaurant	41	Main Post Office
11	Dinner Bell Pizza	26	Hotel New Okinawa	42	Naha Youth Hostel
12	Rawhide 'Stake & Robster'	27	Hotel Kokusai Plaza	43	Naha Soba Restaurant
13	Nansei Kankò Hotel	28	Naha Grand Hotel	44	Toyota Rent-a-Car
14	Naminoue-gù Shrine	29	Yatakaya Department Store	45	SWAL
15	Gokoku-ji Temple	30	McDonald's	46	US Consulate
		31	Nippon Rent-a-Car		

Naha

1	コモドーペリ記念碑	17	沖縄ワーツントンホテル	33	KDD（国際電話局）
2	春海荘ユースホステル	18	オーシャンビューホテル	34	バスセンター
3	崇元寺石門	19	ANA	35	ホテルやぎ
4	玉園荘ユースホステル	20	JAL	36	那覇市役所
5	ホテルエアウエイ	21	ホテルまるき	37	沖縄県役所
6	ニッサンレンタカー	22	JAS	38	観光案内所
7	ホテルサンキョー	23	フアリーンパティサリー	39	沖縄ハーボービューホテル
8	三越百貨店	24	ゆうなんぎい	40	入国役所
9	国際ショビングセンター	25	イタリアントマトレストラン	41	主要郵便局
10	ネスク	26	ホテルニュー沖縄	42	那覇ユースホステル
11	ディナベルピーザ	27	ホテル国際プラザ	43	那覇そばレストラン
12	Rawhide	28	那覇グランドホテル	44	トヨタレンタカー
13	南西観光ホテル	29	やかたや百貨店	45	南西航空
14	波の上宮	30	マクドナルド	46	アメリカ領事館
15	五国寺	31	日本レンタカー		
16	秋月の茶館	32	ジャパレンレンタカー		

rant Texas, Restaurant 88 and others. These restaurants offer steaks from around Y1000 to Y2500 plus other dishes including pizzas and tacos. The Tsuji area also has some fine traditional restaurants like the *Teahouse of the August Moon*.

Back on Kokusai-dōri the *Italian Tomato* offers good pasta from Y800 to Y1200; it's a real OL hangout, the salarymen clearly don't bother with it. Just off Kokusai-dōri is *Yūnangii*, a pleasant red-lantern (aka-chochin) bar – cheerful, crowded and friendly. There is a great selection of awamori (the local firewater) for Y500 a glass or Y2500 a bottle. You can eat well here for less than Y1000; simply asking for the local specialities works fine.

In the same street as the Yūnangii is *Farine*, a good patisserie. The *Dinner Bell*, further along Kokusai-dōri, is a pizza specialist. Directly opposite is the *Ionesk Ice Cream* parlour. There are also many plastic meal restaurants, rotating sushi restaurants and so on.

Route 58 through town also has numerous restaurants, and steakhouses. Just off Route 58, south of the Meiji Bridge and near the Naha Youth Hostel, is *Naha Soba*, with a reputation for tasty Okinawan noodle dishes.

Things to Buy

Okinawa is renowned for its pottery and its fabrics. Tsuboya pottery owes its origins to Chinese influences, as opposed to the Korean techniques which form the basis of most other Japanese pottery. Much of the pottery is in the form of storage vessels but look for the shiisā (guardian lion figures) which can be seen perched on the rooftops of many traditional Okinawan buildings. Shiisā usually come in pairs, one with the mouth open, the other with the mouth closed.

Okinawa also has its own distinctive textiles, particularly the brightly coloured Bingata fabrics made in Shuri. Other fabrics made on Okinawa or other islands in the chain include Bashōfu (from northern Okinawa), Jōfu (from Miyako), Kasuri (from southern Okinawa), Minsā (from Taketomi), Ryusen and Tsumugi (from Kume). Another popular Okinawan product is awamori, a real firewater with an alcohol content of 30-60%. Drink with care!

Getting There & Away

Air Northwest Orient have direct flights from the USA, Continental from Guam, JAL from Hong Kong and China Airlines from Taipei. JAL, ANA, ANK, JAS and South-West Airlines (SWAL) connect major cities on the main islands with Naha including

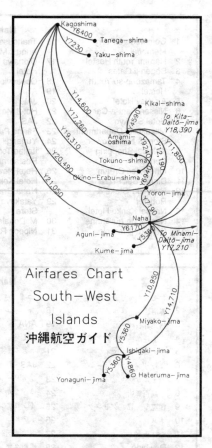

Fukuoka (one hour, Y14,400), Kagoshima (1½ hours, Y21,050), Osaka (two hours, Y29,100), Tokyo (2½ hours, Y34,900) and a number of other centres. SWAL have the most connections to the other South-West Islands. See the South-West Islands airfares chart.

Airline phone numbers in Naha are ANA or ANK (tel 0988-66-5111), JAS (tel 0988-67-8111), JAL (tel 0988-57-5411) and SWAL (tel 0988-57-4961). All the offices can be found in the city centre except for SWAL which is across the Meiji Bridge towards the airport. There are plenty of travel agencies in central Naha which can handle bookings.

Sea Various operators have shipping services from Tokyo, Osaka, Kagoshima and other ports to Naha. The schedules are complex and there is a wide variety of fares. From Tokyo it takes about 50 hours (Y20,000 to Y50,000), from Osaka about 36 hours (Y15,000 to Y40,000) and from Kagoshima about 24 hours (Y12,000 to Y30,000). Shipping companies include Arimura Sangyo, Kansai Kisen, Oshima Unyu, Ryūkyū Kaiun (RKK) and Terukuni Yusen. The frequency of services varies from eight to 10 a month from Tokyo to more than 30 a month from Kagoshima.

From Naha Port boats head south to Ishigaki-jima and Miyako-jima islands, north to Yoron-jima Island and Kagoshima. From Naha New Port there are boats to Fukuoka/Hakata, Kagoshima, Kōbe, Osaka and Tokyo and also to Miyako and Ishigaki islands. From the Tomai Port, boats operate to a number of the smaller islands including Kume, Aguni and the Daito Islands.

The Arimura Sangyo shipping company (tel 0988-68-2191 in Naha, 03-3562-2091 in Tokyo), operates a weekly boat service between Okinawa and Taiwan. Boats depart from Naha Port on Fridays and from Keelung (or sometimes Kaohsiung) in Taiwan on Sundays. From Naha, boats travel via Ishigaki and sometimes Miyako. The trip takes about 36 hours and costs Y16,000 to Y22,000.

Getting Around

To/From the Airport The busy Naha Airport is only three km from the town centre – 10 minutes by taxi for Y800 to Y1100 or 12 minutes by bus Nos 24 or 102 for Y160. The buses run three to six times an hour (7 am to 10 pm) via the main bus station and then down Kokusai-dōri. The airport has three widely spaced terminals: international, domestic 1 (for mainland Japan) and domestic 2 (for the South-West Islands).

Bus The bus system is relatively easy to use.

You collect a ticket showing your starting point as you board and pay the appropriate fare as you disembark; a board at the front shows the various starting numbers and the equivalent fares. Buses run from Naha to destinations all over the island.

There are many bus tours around the island, particularly to the war sites in the south.

Car & Motorcycle Okinawa is a good place to get around in a rented vehicle since the traffic is not too heavy and the northern end of the island is lightly populated and has poor public transport. There are numerous rental companies in Naha with cars from around Y5000 per day plus Y1500 insurance. Convertibles are very popular. Try Japaren (tel 0988-61-3900), Nippon Rent-a-Car (tel 0988-68-4554) or Toyoto Rent-a-Car (tel 0988-57-0100), among others.

A number of places rent scooters and motorcycles. A 50cc scooter costs from Y1500 for three hours to Y3000 for a day; a 250cc motorcycle Y4000 to Y8000. Try Sea Rental Bikes (tel 0988-64-5116) or Trade (tel 0988-63-0908).

SOUTHERN OKINAWA　沖縄の南部

The area south of Naha was the scene of some of the heaviest fighting during the closing days of the Battle of Okinawa. There are a number of reminders of those terrible days as well as some other places of interest in this densely populated part of the island. The initial US landing on Okinawa took place north of Naha at Kadena and Chatan beaches on 1 April 1945. By 20 April US forces had captured the northern part of the island and the area running south from their landing place to Naha. The rest of the island was not captured until 21 June.

Underground Naval Headquarters

About five km directly south of Naha is the underground naval headquarters (described in one Japanese tourist brochure as the 'shelter of the defunct Japanese naval headquarters') where 4000 naval men committed suicide as the battle for Okinawa drew to its prolonged and bloody conclusion. Only 200 metres of the 1.5 km of tunnels is open but you can wander through the underground maze of corridors, see the commander's final words on the wall of his room and inspect the holes and scars in other walls from the grenade blasts which killed many of the men. In Japanese the headquarters are known as 'Kyū Kaigun Shireibugō', though the sign from the main road simply reads 'Kaigungo Park'. Entry is Y410 and it's open from 8.30 am to 5 pm. To get there take bus Nos 33 or 95 from the Naha bus station to the Tomigusuku-kōen-mae stop, a 10 minute walk from the site.

Nearby is the Tomigusuku Park with pleasant views of Naha, though there is very little trace of Tomigusuku Castle, after which the park was named.

Itoman Area

The fisherfolks' Hakugin-dō Shrine is in this port town, 12 km south of Naha. The Kōchi family tombs are here, while just south is Nashiro Beach and the Lieutenant General Buckner Memorial, in memory of the US commander who was killed here by stray shrapnel in the final days of the Battle of Okinawa. The site of Gushikawa Castle at Cape Kiyan-saki is now popular with hang gliders, but in the closing days of the Battle of Okinawa many civilians jumped to their death from the cliffs. Itoman can be reached by bus Nos 32, 33, 34 or 35 from Naha bus station.

War Sites

Around the southern end of the island are a series of sites connected with the final days of the Battle of Okinawa. On 19 June 1945 at Himeyuri no Tō, 200 schoolgirls and their teachers committed suicide in the school grounds rather than fall into the hands of the US military. The memorial to this event is now one of the most popular tourist attractions in Okinawa. Directly south on the coast is the Konpaku no Tō Memorial to 35,000 unknown victims of the fighting who were subsequently buried here.

At Mabuni no Oka (Mabuni Hill), the

remaining Japanese forces were virtually pushed into the sea. In their underground hideaway the commanders committed seppuku (ritual suicide) on 23 June 1945, while above ground the US forces already had complete control of the island. Memorials from every prefecture in Japan dot the hillside and the Peace Memorial Museum tells the gruesome story of the struggle. It's open from 9 am to 4.30 pm, closed Mondays; entry is Y100. Also at this extensive site is the Peace Hall (Y520), a seven sided tower built in 1978 and housing a 16 metre high Buddha statue. Behind the hall is a Peace Art Museum.

Taking public transport to the sites is time consuming. Bus Nos 82, 83 and 85 go there from Itoman; get off at the Komesu stop for Konpaku no Tō or the Kenji no Tō stop for Mabuni Hill. There are frequent bus tours from Naha, which cost about Y4000.

Gyokusen-dō Cave

Japan has plenty of limestone caves but for those who can't get enough of stalactites and stalagmites there are more here. Nearly a km of the cave is open to visitors from 9 am to 5, 5.30 or 6 pm (depending on the time of year). Entry is Y720. When you leave the cave you can continue straight in to the Gyokusendō Habu Park (Y620) and see the unfortunate 'deadly' habu suffering the traditional defeat by a mongoose. Bus No 54 from Naha bus station takes 50 minutes to reach the cave; bus Nos 51 or 52 drop you further from the cave (15 minutes walk versus five minutes) but depart from Naha much more frequently.

Other Attractions

Just beyond the Mabuni Hill memorials is the Okinawa Coral Museum. Coral is much nicer where it belongs – underwater. Continuing north on Route 15, you'll find Himeyuri Park, which specialises in cactus. Turn east on Route 76 to reach Tomori no Ojishi where a large stone shiisā (lion) overlooks a reservoir. This particular shiisā dates back to at least 1689; a popular image from the Battle of Okinawa shows a US soldier sheltering behind it while watching with binoculars.

Tiny O Island is linked to the main island by bridge and has good beaches, as has Nibaru Beach a little further north. Glass-bottom-boat trips are made from the Chinen Marine Leisure Centre and boats also run from here to Kudaka Island and minute Komaka Island, which has a fine beach all the way around. Ferries to Kudaka also operate from Baten Port on the south-eastern coast of Okinawa. There are good views from the sites of Tamagusuku and Chinen castles, which look out towards the islands of O and Kudaka.

CENTRAL OKINAWA 沖縄の中部

Central Okinawa (north of Naha through Okinawa City to Ishikawa City) is heavily populated, but beyond this area the island is much less crowded. The US military bases are principally in the southern part of central Okinawa, the resorts in the northern part. Dotted around this stretch of Okinawa is an amazing number of artificial tourist attractions where many thousands of yen could be squandered on entry fees.

Urasoe

In Urasoe, eight km north of Naha, the Yudori Royal Tombs date back to the 13th century.

Nakagusuku Castle

The hilltop ruins of Nakagusuku Castle have a wonderful position overlooking the coast. The castle was built in 1448, preceding stone construction of this type on the mainland by 80 years. It's much better stonework than that found on the mainland. The castle was destroyed in 1458 in a bizarre episode of feudal manoeuvring known as the Amawari Rebellion. When Gosamaru, the Nakagusuku lord, heard that Amawari, another Okinawan lord, was plotting a rebellion against the king he mobilised his troops. The scheming Amawari then convinced the king that it was Gosamaru who was planning to revolt, so the hapless Nakagusuku ruler committed suicide. There's no sign pointing

out the castle site and an earlier 'pass' sign down the road is a red herring. Look for the entrance gate with a field in front of it and the inevitable tourist activity. To get there by public transport from Naha, take a bus to Futenma and from there a bus No 58. Entry is Y500.

Nakamura House

A half km up the road from the castle is probably the best preserved traditional Okinawan house on the island. The Nakamura family's origins in the area can be traced back to the 15th century, but the foundations of this house date from around 1720. The construction is a typical example of a well-off farming family's residence at that time. Originally, the roof would have been thatched but it was later roofed with traditional red tiles. As you explore this interesting and surprisingly comfortable-looking home, notice the substantial stone pig pens, the elevated storage area (to deter rats) and the trees grown as typhoon windbreaks. The house is open from 9 am to 6 pm and entry is Y300. It's a 10 minute walk up from Nakagusuku Castle; bus No 58 passes by the house.

Okinawa City

Okinawa City is the US military centre on Okinawa, centred around the Kadena Air Force Base which was the initial target of the US invasion. The pre-war village has mushroomed to a population of over 100,000. The city has all the hallmarks of American influence, from pizzerias to army surplus stores. There's even an *A&W Burgers* outlet where you can order from your car over an intercom and your food is brought out to you – shades of American drive-ins of the '50s. The Tuttle Bookstore at the Plaza House shopping mall is the best English-language bookshop on Okinawa.

Attractions around Okinawa City, some of them decidedly artificial, include the Moromi Folkcraft Museum, the Koza Yaki Pottery Factory, Okinawa Children's Land, the Tonan or South-East Botanical Gardens and the Agena and Katsuren Castle sites.

Bullfights, where one bull tries to push another out of a ring, are held on Sundays at Gushikawa, near Okinawa Children's Land.

Bus Nos 21, 22, 23, 24, 25, 26, 31, 63, 77 and 90 all run to Okinawa City from Naha in a little over one hour.

Okinawa City to Nago

Enthusiasts of castle ruins can find more of them at the Iha Castle site near Ishikawa and at the Zakimi Castle site on the west coast, north of Kadena. In the Zakimi Castle Park the Yomitan Museum displays local farming equipment. The Okinawan resort strip starts from Zanpa Beach on Cape Zanpa-misaki. The Ryūkyū Village offers yet another opportunity to see a re-creation of Okinawan farming life, and yet another snake park where, for the amusement of tourists, those 'deadly' habu lose out to those plucky mongooses. More beach life can be found at the Ramada Renaissance Resort, Moon Beach and Manza Beach, while just before Nago City is the Okinawa Submarine Park, which has an underwater observatory.

As well as the expensive resort hotels along this coast, there is also the *Maedamisaki Youth Hostel* (tel 09896-4-2497) near the Ryūkyū Village. Bus No 20 from Naha runs along the west coast past all these sites to Nago. It takes about one hour 20 minutes to get to the Ryūkyū Village or Moon Beach; one hour 40 minutes to Manza Beach and two hours to the submarine park.

NAGO 名護

If you're spending a couple of days explor-

ing Okinawa then Nago (population 46,000) is a good overnight stop; it's about two-thirds of the way up the island. There are fine views over the town and the coast from the castle hill, although little trace remains of the castle itself. In spring the cherry blossoms on the hill are particularly good. A fine old banyan tree, the Hinpun Gajumara, is a useful landmark in the centre of town. You can find out all about traditional farming (which is fast-disappearing on Okinawa) at the Nago Museum. The museum is close to the banyan tree and is open from 10 am to 6 pm; entry is Y100.

Places to Stay & Eat

The *Nago Castle Hotel* (tel 0980-52-5954) is a clean, pleasant place close to the centre of town, with singles for Y4000 and breakfast available for Y500. The fancier *Hotel Okura* (tel 0980-52-2250) has singles at Y4640 and doubles at Y8240. Both hotels have popular restaurants; the latter does Okinawan specialities while the former has a sign announcing 'pizza'.

Shinzan Shokudō is a good noodle shop near the Okura Hotel. Nago has many fast-food outlets – a *McDonald's* and *A&W Burgers* mark the entry to town. There's also the usual plethora of bars, snack bars and so on in the entertainment area. Two blocks south-east of the Nago Castle Hotel is a big, bright, friendly and busy restaurant (see the Nago map); there's nothing in English but enough food comes over the bar for the 'point and ask' routine to afford success, and you can eat well for Y1000.

Bullfighting

Battles between opposing bulls, where one tries to push the other out of the ring (rather like sumō wrestlers) are known as *tōgyū* in Japan. The custom is found in a long sweep of islands all the way from Indonesia to Japan. There are about a dozen tōgyū stadiums in Okinawa, the most important ones being the Agena Stadium in Gushikawa and the Kankō Stadium in Okinawa City. The most important fights are held in May and November, but they take place a couple of times a month year-round. The bulls for Okinawa tōgyū events are bred on Kuro-shima Island, near Iriomote. ■

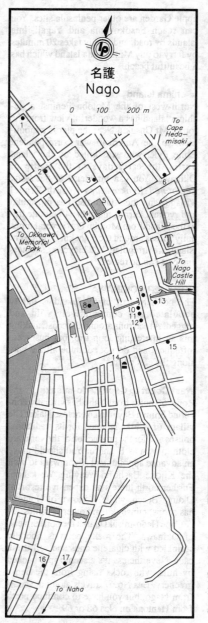

Nago

1	Nago Castle Hotel
2	Restaurant
3	Oki-Mart Supermarket & Bus Stop
4	Dom Dom
5	Market
6	NTT
7	Nago Cross Roads
8	Bowling Alley
9	Banyan Tree
10	Shinzan Shokudō Restaurant
11	Hotel Okura
12	Shiroyama Hotel
13	Futubase Hotel
14	Post Office
15	Museum
16	A & W Burgers
17	McDonald's

Nago

1	名護キャッスルホテル
2	レストラン
3	おきマートスーパマケット
4	ドムドム
5	市場
6	NTT
7	名護十字路
8	北ボーリング場
9	バンヤンの木
10	新山食堂
11	おおくらホテル
12	城山ホテル
13	双苑荘
14	郵便局
15	名護博物館
16	A & W Burgers
17	マクドナルド

Getting There & Away

Nago is the junction town for buses to northern Okinawa or the Motobu-hantō Peninsula. From Okinawa City bus station bus Nos 20 and 21 make the 62 km trip in about 2½ hours for Y1600.

MOTOBU-HANTO PENINSULA
本部半島

Jutting out to the north-west of Nago, the hilly Motobu-hantō Peninsula has several points of interest as well as ferry services to nearby Ie-shima Island.

Okinawa Memorial Park
The site of the 1975 International Ocean Exposition has a cluster of tourist attractions, most of which can be bypassed without any great sacrifice. Entry to the park itself is free, but the individual attractions charge entry fees. The aquarium (Y620) is claimed to be one of the largest in the world and the sharks and rays in the big tank, particularly the huge whale shark, are indeed impressive, although the tank is very crowded.

Aquapolis (Y510) is a rusting and faded vision of a floating city of the future where the main news is that there will still be a demand for tacky souvenirs. There's also the Oceanic Culture Museum (Y150), the Museum of Okinawa (Y150), the Native Okinawan Village (free), the Tropical Dream Centre, with orchid and other flower displays around the curious circular spiral tower (Y620), and a dolphin show (free). The park also has a beach and an amusement park.

The park is open from 9.30 am to 5.30, 6 or 7 pm depending on the season; it's closed on Thursdays. Individual attractions close half an hour earlier. On Sundays and holidays, three No 93 buses run directly from Naha to the park; on other days you will have to take a bus to Nago, and from there take a No 70 bus on the Motobu Peninsula Bise line. Shuttle buses run around the surprisingly sprawling park and cost Y100.

Nakijin Castle Site
Winding over a hilltop, the walls of this fort may not be as neat as Nakagusuku but they look terrific. From the summit of the hill there are superb views out to sea. Entry is Y150; bus No 66 operates from Nago and bus No 65 from the Okinawa Memorial Park.

Other Attractions
The Yambaru Wildlife Park and Izumi Pine-apple Garden are other peninsula sites. You can reach Sesoko-jima and Yagaji-jima islands by road, and it only takes 20 minutes by ferry to tiny Minna-jima Island which has a beautiful beach.

Ie-shima Island
North-west of the Motobu Peninsula, Ie-shima Island has a wonderful view from the top of Mt Gusuku. Near the pier is a monument to the American war correspondent Ernie Pyle, who was killed on the island during the early days of the Battle of Okinawa. You can hire tents at the *Ieson Seishonen Ryoko Mura* (Youth Travel Village) and the island also has minshuku and ryokan. Ferries make the 40 minute trip to the island from Motobu Port several times daily. Buses around the eight km by three km island are irregular, but bicycles, scooters and cars can be rented.

NORTHERN OKINAWA　沖縄の北部
The northern part of the island is lightly populated and comparatively wild and rugged. A road runs around the coast, making this an interesting loop trip, but buses are infrequent and do not continue all the way along the east coast.

West Coast to Cape Hedo-misaki
Route 58 north from Nago has virtually converted Shioya Bay into an enclosed lake. The village of Kijoka is noted for its traditional houses and for the production of the very rare cloth known as Bashōfu. You should make an advance appointment if you want to visit the Kijoka Bashōfu Weaving Workshop. Further north there's an expensive resort at Okuma Beach, while the town of Hentona has shops, minshuku and other facilities.

Cape Hedo-misaki marks the northern end of Okinawa. The rocky point is liberally sprinkled with cigarette ends and soft-drink cans. Nevertheless it's a scenic spot backed by hills, with rocks rising from the dense greenery. Bus No 67 travels along the coast from Nago, but you have to continue north from Hentona on Nos 68 or 69.

East Coast

From Cape Hedo-misaki, the road continues to Oku, the termination point for buses travelling up the west coast via the cape. The English sign 'Hotel' at the beginning of the village leads you in just 50 metres to the cheap and cheerful *Oku Ryokan*. Then, 200 metres further along, another sign 'Wellcomes' you to *Lodging Okuyanbaruso*.

There are good beaches around Oku. For the next 15 km the road stays very close to the coastline, with more fine-looking beaches but frequent warnings of current and tide dangers for swimmers, divers and snorkellers. Aha is a picturesque village which still has some traditional thatched-roof houses.

ISLANDS AROUND OKINAWA

Apart from the islands just a stone's throw from the Okinawan coast, there are three other island groups a little further away.

Iheya-jima & Izena-jima Islands

North of Okinawa, these two islands have good beaches and snorkelling and a number of hotels and minshuku. A daily ferry runs from Motobu's port to Izena (1½ hours) and to Iheya (another 20 minutes).

Kerama Islands

There are about 20 islands in this group west of Okinawa, only four of them inhabited. The islands have fine beaches, some good walks, great lookouts and some of the best scuba diving in Japan. Ferries from Naha take one to 1½ hours; flights are also available.

Kume Island

Further west from the Kerama Islands is beautiful Kume Island, with its superb scenery, excellent beaches and the long curving sweep of sandbank at Sky Holiday Reef, just east of the island. The Uezu House is a samurai-style home dating from 1726. There are ryokan and minshuku on the island, particularly near Eef Beach where there is also a small resort hotel. Day trips can be made from Eef Beach to Sky Holiday Reef.

From Naha, ferries to the island take about 3½ hours, and SWAL have regular daily flights, taking 35 minutes at a cost of Y5360. You can get around the island by rented car, scooter or bicycle.

Miyako Islands
宮古列島

About 300 km south-west of Okinawa, directly en route to the Yaeyama Islands, is the small Miyako group, comprising Miyako itself and, a few km to the west, Irabu-jima and Shimoji-jima Islands, plus a scattering of smaller islands.

MIYAKO-JIMA ISLAND　宮古島

Like the other Okinawa-ken islands, Miyako offers beaches and diving, and, since it escaped the destruction rained down upon Okinawa itself, some traces of Ryūkū culture and architecture remain. One thing it does not offer is the poisonous habu snake which seems to engender so much fear and loathing throughout the South-West Islands. Miyako is the Ireland of the Nansei-shotō chain – no snakes here!

Orientation & Information

Hirara, the main town on Miyako-jima Island, is compact and easy to get around. Each year the very low spring tide reveals the huge Yaebishi reef, north of Ikema Island. Japanese triathletes flock to Miyako Island in April each year for the Strongman Challenge, which involves a three km swim, a 136 km bicycle race and a 42 km marathon.

Hirara

There are a few minor attractions in Hirara (population 33,000). Near the waterfront, just north of the ferry terminal, is the Nakasone Toimiyā, a large mausoleum to a 15th century Miyakoan hero who not only conquered the Yaeyama Islands to the south

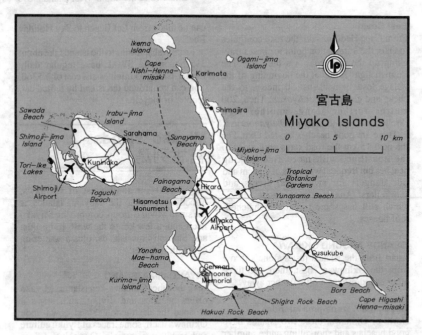

Ikema Island

Ogami-jima Island

Cape Nishi-Henna-misaki

Karimata

宮古島

Miyako Islands

0   5   10 km

Sawada Beach

Irabu-jima Island

Shimajira

Shimoji-jima Island

Sarahama

Sunayama Beach

Miyako-jima Island

Tori-Ike Lakes

Kuninaka

Shimoji Airport

Toguchi Beach

Painagama Beach

Hirara

Tropical Botanical Gardens

Yunapama Beach

Hisamatsu Monument

Miyako Airport

Yonaha Mae-hama Beach

Gusukube

German Schooner Memorial

Ueno

Kurima-jima Island

Bora Beach

Shigira Rock Beach

Cape Higashi Henna-misaki

Hakuai Rock Beach

but also prevented an invasion from the north. There's another impressively large mausoleum cut into the hillside just beyond it.

Continuing north along the coast road you'll find the Jintōzeiseki, a 1.4 metre high stone more or less plonked down in someone's front garden. During the heavy-handed rule of the Satsumas (the Satsuma Kingdom invaded from Kagoshima on Kyūshū in the 15th century), anyone taller than this stone was required to pay taxes.

Other sights in the town include the Kaiser Wilhelm or Hakuai Monument, presented to the island in 1878 as a gesture of gratitude for the rescue of the crew of a typhoon-wrecked German merchant ship. The Harimizu Utaki Shrine is close to the ferry terminal.

Beaches & Diving

Miyako-jima Island has its share of good beaches and diving spots. Try the beaches along the southern and northern coasts or Yonaha Mae-hama Beach on the south-west coast, reputed to be the finest beach in Japan, where the Tōkyū Resort is located. Kurima-jima Island can be reached by ferry from Yonaha Maehama Port in just 10 minutes. Immediately north of Hirara is Sunayama (Sand Mountain) Beach. Ikema Island is two km off Cape Nishi-Henna, the northernmost point of Miyako Island, and can be reached by ferry from the town Karimata.

Miyako is a popular scuba-diving centre and there are a number of dive operators on the island.

Cape Higashi-Henna-misaki

At the south-eastern end of the island this long, narrow and quite spectacular peninsula ends with a picturesquely placed lighthouse overlooking the rocky coastline.

Other Attractions

The Hisamatsu-goyushi Monument in the

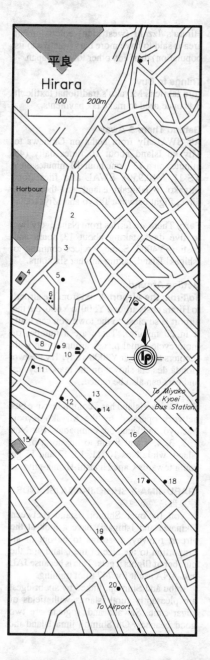

Hirara

1 Tax Stone
2 Mausoleum
3 Nakasone Toimiyā Mausoleum
4 Harbour Terminal
5 Hotel Kyowa
6 Harimizu Shrine
7 Yachiyo Bus Station
8 Port Hotel
9 Kaiser Wilhelm Monument
10 Post Office
11 Hotel Urizun
12 Grand Hotel
13 Tsubohachi Restaurant
14 Mos Burger
15 Market
16 New Marakatsu Hotel
17 Tomihama Motorcycle Rental
18 Normura Restaurant
19 Honey's Donuts
20 Marutama Motorcycle Rental

Hirara

1 人頭税石
2 知利真良豊見親之墓
3 仲宗根豊見親之墓
4 平良港ターミナル
5 ホテル共和
6 漲水御嶽
7 八千代バスセンター
8 ポートホテル
9 ドイツ皇帝博愛記念碑
10 郵便局
11 ホテルうりずん
12 宮古グランドホテル
13 つぼはちレストラン
14 モスバーガー
15 平良市公設市場
16 ホテルニュー丸勝
17 とみはらモータバイクレンタル
18 のむらレストラン
19 ハーニズドーナツ
20 まるたまモータバイクレンタル

village of Hisamatsu, a few km south-west of Hirara, commemorates the fishermen who spotted the Russian fleet steaming north during the Russo-Japanese War of 1904-05. Admiral Tōgō was able to intercept them north of Kyūshū (see the Tsu-shima Island section in the Kyūshū chapter).

The Hirara Tropical Botanical Gardens are four km east of Hirara in Onoyama.

Places to Stay

The *New Marakatsu Hotel* (tel 09807-2-9936) is a rambling, slightly tatty place down an entrance alley from the main road in Hirara. There's no sign in English but look for the big letter 'K' in a circle at the top of the hotel sign. Singles are Y4950.

None of the many other Hirara hotels are easy to locate. Cheaper centrally located hotels with rooms from around Y4000 include the *Port Hotel* (tel 09807-2-9820) and the *Hotel Urizun* (tel 09807-2-4410). The slightly pricier *Grand Hotel* (tel 09807-2-3351) is also right in the centre of town. The new *Hotel Kyowa* is near the waterfront, overlooking the Harimizu Utaki Shrine. There are also numerous ryokan and minshuku around the town.

Elsewhere on the island is the expensive *Tōkyū Resort* (tel 09807-6-2109), on the beautiful Yonaha Mae-hama Beach. There are a few places to stay on neighbouring Irabu-jima Island.

Places to Eat

Tsubohachi is a very mod-con robatayaki (grilled food restaurant); the sign outside proclaims it's a 'Casual House'. Not only does the full-colour menu show all the possibilities, but it also lists the calories for each one! (Not for the beer, thank goodness.) Most dishes are Y300 to Y500.

Fast-food places around the centre of town include a *Mos Burger* and *Honey's Donuts* which serves donuts, noodle dishes and drinks. There are also lots of red-lantern bars and 24 hour coffee shops, the latter good for a set breakfast or 'morning service'. The people of Miyako have a reputation for being outgoing and friendly – to the point where

Hirara's Izzatu (west side) entertainment area is said to have more bars (relative to its population) than any other town in Japan.

Things to Buy

Jōfu fabric is Miyako's traditional textile. It was once used to make tax payments.

Getting There & Away

Air SWAL fly from Naha on Okinawa to Miyako Island about 10 times daily (45 minutes on a 737, one hour 10 minutes on a YS-11, Y10,950). SWAL also flies from Miyako to Ishigaki Island and there is a direct flight between Tokyo and Miyako.

Ferry There are ferries from Naha every two to five days, taking about 13 hours and costing about Y4000. Some services continue to Ishigaki Island, taking another six hours.

Getting Around

To/From the Airport A taxi from the airport to Hirara costs around Y500 to Y600, but the airport is so close to the town you can walk it in 20 minutes. There are a number of motorcycle rental places around town with scooters for hire at Y2000 a day. Try the two Honda dealers shown on the map. Bicycles and cars can also be rented.

Bus Miyako Island has a comprehensive bus network operated by the Miyako Kyoei, Yachiyo, and Ueno bus companies. Bus Nos 1, 2, 3, 4, 7 and 8 run to the north of the island; while Nos 10, 11, 12, 13 and 15 go south towards Cape Higashi-Henna-misaki.

IRABU-JIMA & SHIMOJI-JIMA ISLANDS
伊良部島、下地島

If you fly over Shimoji Island (between Okinawa and Ishigaki) have a look at the airport runway. It seems to be out of all proportion to the size of the island and the number of flights it gets. This is because JAL and ANA use it for 747 pilot training.

Irabu and Shimoji, linked by six bridges, are pleasantly rural islands with fields of sugar cane. Sawada and Toguchi are two good beaches. On Shimoji-jima Island the

Tōri-ike Lakes are linked to the sea by hidden tunnels.

Getting There & Away

SWAL have a daily flight from Naha on Okinawa to Shimoji but most visitors arrive on the regular 15 minute, Y450 ferry crossing between Hirara on Miyako-jima Island and Sarahama on Irabu-jima Island.

Yaeyama Islands
八重山列島

At the far south-western end of the Nansei-shotō chain are the islands of the Yaeyama group, consisting of two main islands (Ishigaki-jima and Iriomote-jima) and a scattering of smaller islands between and beyond the two main ones. There are some fine dive sites around the islands, particularly on Yonaguni-jima Island, the westernmost point in Japan, and Hateruma-jima Island, the southernmost point. Although there are many Japanese visitors to the islands, most of them, in true Japanese fashion, are daytrippers. Come nightfall on Iriomote or Taketomi most of the tourists will have scuttled back to their hotels on Ishigaki.

ISHIGAKI-JIMA ISLAND   石垣島

Ishigaki has the major airport in the Yaeyama group and boat services fan out from its harbour to the other islands. There are a few sights in the town of Ishigaki itself but otherwise its main function is as a jumping-off point to the other islands. Ishigaki is about 400 km south-west of Okinawa Island.

Ishigaki

Orientation & Information Ishigaki's focus is its busy harbour; you can walk to most places around the town in a few minutes. Parallel to the main street are two shopping arcades. If you plan to take supplies to the outer islands you'll find a better choice in the arcades than at the places around the harbour.

Miyara Donchi House Although the South-West Islands never really had samurai, this is essentially a samurai house. It dates from 1819 and is the only one left in the whole island chain. The building itself is run down and the garden is poorly maintained, but it's still nice to see. Entry is Y100; it's closed on Tuesdays.

Torin-ji Temple Founded in 1614, this Zen temple is the most important on the island. 'Sentry' boxes flank the gates and statues dating from 1737 (said to be the guardian deities of the islands) can be seen in the dim interiors. Immediately adjacent to the temple is the 1787 Gongen-dō Shrine. The original shrine was built in 1614 but destroyed in a flood in 1771. The temple is about a 15 minute walk from the harbour.

Other Attractions The small Yaeyama Museum (Shiritsu Yaeyama Hakubutsukan) is very close to the harbour and has various displays relating to the islands, including coffin palanquins or gau, dugout canoes and other old boats. Entry is Y100 and it's open from 9 am to 4.30 pm, closed Mondays.

The Ishigakike-teien Garden follows the regular garden construction conventions, complete with volcanic rocks, but there's not much garden to see. Although it is private, you should be able to see the garden if you ask politely.

Places to Stay Ishigaki is a compact little town and there are plenty of places to stay within a couple of minutes walk of the harbour. Other accommodation can be found scattered around the island.

The *Yashima Youth Hostel* (tel 09808-2-3157) is close to the centre of town and costs Y1900 per night. The *Trek Ishigaki-jima Youth Hostel* (tel 09808-6-8257) is on the east coast of the island and also costs Y1900.

Hotel O-Hara (tel 09808-2-3380) is a business hotel, small and a little tatty but quite OK at Y5000 for singles. (The name comes from the town on Iriomote, not from some wayward Irishman!)

More expensive hotels include the

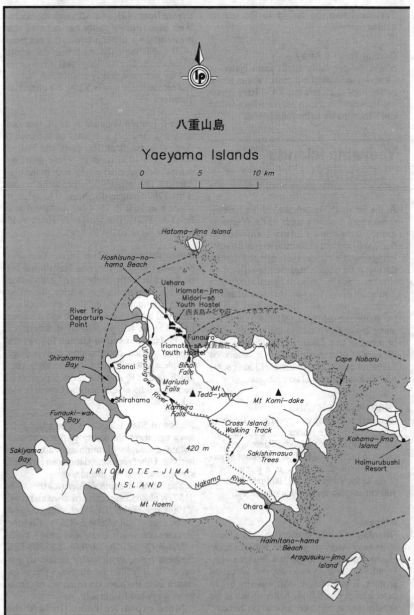

八重山島

Yaeyama Islands

0   5   10 km

Hatoma-jima Island

Hoshisuna-no-hama Beach

Uehara
Iriomote-jima
Midori-sō
Youth Hostel
西表島みどり荘ユースホテル

River Trip
Departure
Point

Funaura
Iriomote-sō 西表島荘ユースホテル
Youth Hostel

Shirahama Bay

Sonai

Binai
Falls

Cape Nobaru

Utsuchigawa River

Mariudo Falls

Mt
Tedō-yama

Mt Komi-dake

Shirahama

Kampira
Falls

Funauki-wan Bay

Cross Island
Walking Track

Kohama-jima
Island

Sakiyama Bay

420 m

Sakishimasuo
Trees

Haimurubushi
Resort

IRIOMOTE-JIMA
ISLAND

Nakama River

Mt Haemi

Ohara

Haimitano-hama Beach

Aragusuku-jima Island

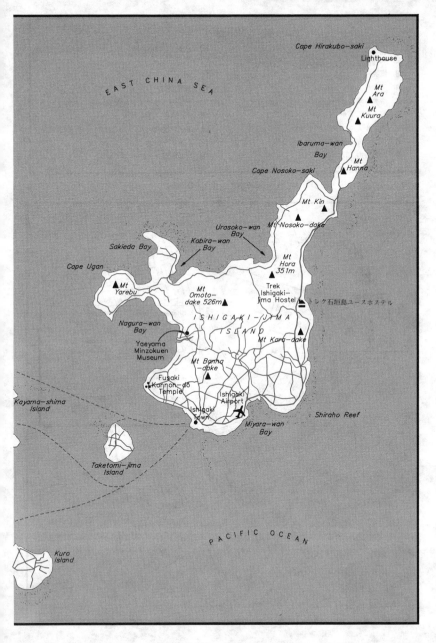

EAST CHINA SEA

Cape Hirakubo-saki
Lighthouse

Mt Ara

Mt Kuura

Ibaruma-wan Bay

Cape Nosoko-saki

Mt Hanna

Mt Kin

Mt Nosoko-dake

Urasoko-wan Bay

Kabira-wan Bay

Sakieda Bay

Mt Hora 351m

Cape Ugan

Trek Ishigaki-jima Hostel

トレク石垣島ユースホステル

Mt Yarebu

Mt Omoto-dake 526m

ISHIGAKI-JIMA ISLAND

Nagura-wan Bay

Yaeyama Minzokuen Museum

Mt Kara-dake

Mt Banna -dake

Fusaki
Kannon-dō Temple

Kayama-shima Island

Ishigaki Airport

Ishigaki Town

Miyara-wan Bay

Shiraho Reef

Taketomi-jima Island

PACIFIC OCEAN

Kuro Island

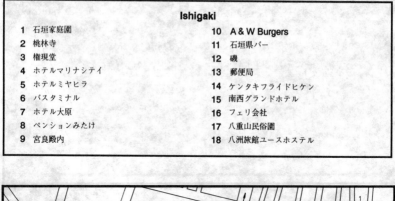

Ishigaki

1	石垣家庭園	10	A & W Burgers
2	桃林寺	11	石垣県バー
3	権現堂	12	磯
4	ホテルマリナシテイ	13	郵便局
5	ホテルミヤヒラ	14	ケンタキフライドヒケン
6	バスタミナル	15	南西グランドホテル
7	ホテル大原	16	フェリ会社
8	ペンションみたけ	17	八重山民俗園
9	宮良殿内	18	八洲旅館ユースホステル

石垣市
Ishigaki

0   125   250 m

To Kariba

To Airport

Inter-Island Harbour

Arcades

1	Ishigakike-teien Garden	11	Ishigaki-sen Bar
2	Torin-ji Temple	12	Iso Restaurant
3	Gongen-dō Shrine	13	Post Office
4	Hotel Marina City	14	Kentucky Fried Chicken
5	Hotel Miyahira	15	Nansei Grand Hotel
6	Bus Station	16	Ferry Company Offices
7	Hotel O-Hara	17	Yaeyama Museum
8	Pension Mitake	18	Yashima Youth Hostel
9	Miyara Donchi House		
10	A&W Burgers		

Ishigaki Grand Hotel (tel 09808-3-6161) right across from the harbour, with rooms from Y9000. Also near the harbour are the *Hotel Miyahira* (tel 09808-2-6111) and the *Hotel Marina City* (tel 09808-2-0088) which has rooms from Y6000.

Three narrow alleyways run parallel to the main road before you come to the two shopping arcades. On the first one is neat little *Pension Mitake* (tel 09808-2-4993) with rooms at Y4000 to Y6000 per person including meals, Y3000 to Y4500 room only.

Places to Eat The arcades have a selection of plastic meal restaurants, an *A&W Burgers* and a *Kentucky Fried Chicken*.

The *Iso Restaurant* (tel 09808-2-7721) serves good food in a bright and cheerful setting; you can even see in from outside! Set meals featuring local specialities are available from Y1000 to Y2000 (you can eat well for Y1500); beers cost Y600. Right across the narrow road from Iso is the pleasant *Ishigaki-sen* (tel 09808-2-8084), a local red-lantern bar.

Getting There & Away *Air* SWAL has more than 10 flights a day between Naha (Okinawa Island) and Ishigaki (one hour, Y14,710) and three between Miyako and Ishigaki islands (30 minutes, Y5360). ANK operate less frequent services between Naha and Ishigaki. SWAL fly from Ishigaki to the tiny Yonaguni-jima and Hateruma-jima islands. There are controversial plans to extend the Ishigaki Airport runway which would result in the destruction of the beautiful coral reefs in the adjacent bay at Shiraho.

Ferry There are ferry services every two to five days directly beween Naha and Ishigaki (13 hours, Y5500) or via Miyako Island. Miyako to Ishigaki takes about six hours and costs Y2000. The Okinawa to Taiwan ferry services operates via Ishigaki.

Ishigaki is the centre for all the Yaeyama Islands' ferry services and the small harbour is a hive of activity. The ferry company offices are along the two sides of the harbour

and there are often several operators, at a variety of prices, to a given destination.

Getting Around A taxi between the airport and town costs about Y700, there is no convenient bus service. Bus services fan out from Ishigaki town, the station is across the road from the harbour. A bus to Kabira costs Y510, to the top end of the island costs Y950. Cars and bicycles can be rented in town.

AROUND ISHIGAKI ISLAND
石垣島の附近
Beaches & Diving
There are a number of popular beaches around the island, including the well-known Kabira-wan Bay with its fine sandy and sheltered beach, collection of places to stay and black-pearl industry. There are a number of dive shops on Ishigaki Island, including Sea Friends (tel 09808-2-0863).

Other Attractions
Mt Omoto-dake (526 metres) in the centre of the island is the highest point in Okinawa. Mt Banna-dake, five km from town, is only 230 metres high but has fine views and a botanical garden. The Fusaki Kannon-dō Temple dates from 1701 and from its hilltop position, about six km north-west of the town, there are good views towards Taketomi and Iriomote islands. At the northern end of the island is Cape Hirakubo-saki and a lighthouse.

There are several small museums in the Kaiyo Minzoku Village which faces Nagura-wan Bay about halfway to Kabira-wan Bay. The Yaeyama Minzokuen Museum will tell you everything you need to know about Yaeyama weaving and Yaeyama pottery. It's about 20 minutes by bus from Ishigaki town. There are a number of outlets for local weaving and black pearls.

TAKETOMI-JIMA ISLAND 竹富島
Only a 10 minute boat ride from Ishigaki is the popular but relaxed little island of Taketomi. It's noted for its beaches and the pretty little flower-bedecked village in the centre of the island.

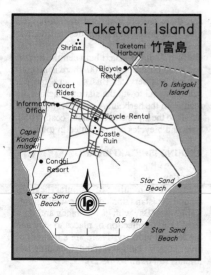

Orientation & Information

Taketomi is a pancake-flat island with its village smack in the middle. From Taketomi Village, the roads fan out to various places around the edge. A perimeter road following the 10 km coastline is on the drawing board and a section has already been constructed around the north-western quadrant. The tourist information office has a coral and shell display.

Taketomi Village

Akayama Oka is a tiny lookout atop an even tinier hillock but, on this otherwise flat island, it offers good views over the red-tiled roofs. Look for the walls of coral and rock and the angry guardian lion figures (shiisā) on the rooftops. The other observation point is the Nbukulu lookout, at the northern end of the village, on top of someone's house. It costs Y100.

The Kihōin Shūshūkan is a small private museum with a diverse collection of local items and a Y300 entry price. Taketomi Mingeikan is a local craft centre where you can see the island's Minsā belts and other local textiles being produced. Opposite the craft centre is the Nishitō Utaki Shrine, ded-

icated to a 16th century ruler of the Yaeyama Islands.

Beaches

Most of the island is fringed with beach, but the water is generally very shallow. At several places you can look for star sand (hoshisuna), tiny grains of sand with a distinctive star shape. They're actually the dried skeletons of tiny creatures. Although you are requested not to souvenir more than a few grains it's sold by the bucketful at shops and at Ishigaki Airport. The map shows good star-sand hunting points. Around Cape Kondoi-misaki on the western side of the island you'll find star sand and the best swimming spot on the island.

Places to Stay & Eat

The Takana Ryokan & Youth Hostel (tel 09808-5-2151) is opposite the post office. Costs per night are Y1900 for the hostel and from Y5000 for the ryokan section. Many of the traditional houses around the island are minshuku or ryokan.

There are also a number of small restaurants and coffee bars. Chirorin-mura, a rustic little snack bar, is a good place for a lunch-time bowl of noodles for Y400. Both beer barrels and tree stumps are used as stools at the tables and bar.

Getting There & Away

There's a regular ferry service from Ishigaki. Fares vary from around Y500 to Y1000 (one way) for the 10 minute trip.

Getting Around

There are numerous bicycle rental places on the island including one near the docks. Bikes cost Y200 an hour, Y1000 a day and are great for exploring the tiny island's sandy roads. You can also hire tandem bicycles and motor scooters. Touring the village streets in a carriage pulled by water buffalo is a popular activity.

IRIOMOTE-JIMA ISLAND 西表島

Dense jungle blankets much of Iriomote, an island which could well qualify as Japan's

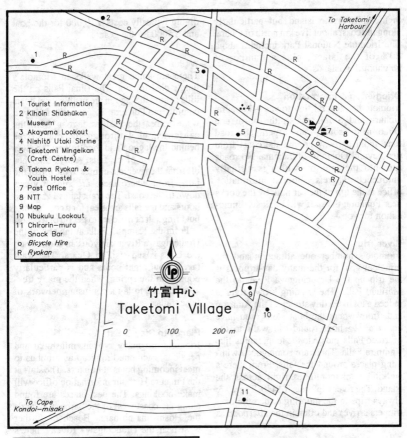

1 Tourist Information
2 Kihōin Shūshūkan Museum
3 Akayama Lookout
4 Nishitō Utaki Shrine
5 Taketomi Mingeikan (Craft Centre)
6 Takana Ryokan & Youth Hostel
7 Post Office
8 NTT
9 Map
10 Nbukulu Lookout
11 Chirorin-mura Snack Bar
o Bicycle Hire
R Ryokan

竹富中心
Taketomi Village

0   100   200 m

To Taketomi Harbour

To Cape Kondoi-misaki

Taketomi Village

1 観光案内所
2 喜宝院蒐集館
3 赤山丘
4 西塘御嶽
5 竹富民芸館
6 高那旅館
7 郵便局
8 NTT
9 地図
10 のぶくるルカアト
11 ちろりん村

last frontier. Trekking through the interior, you may find leeches, which in Japan is probably good enough for the 'wilderness' tag. The island's major attractions are fine beaches, rivers and waterfalls, and the Iriomote wildcat. Similar in size (and appearance) to a domestic cat, the Iriomote wildcat is nocturnal and rarely seen. The picturesque road signs alerting drivers of its possible presence are, however, quite common.

Much easier to find are the curious sakishimasuo trees with their twisting, ribbon-like root buttresses. You will find them all over the island but particularly along the coast about five km north of Ohara. The Iriomote National Park includes about 80% of the island, plus a number of neighbouring islands.

Orientation & Information

Iriomote has several tiny towns – Funaura, Uehara and Shirahama in the north and Ohara in the south – and a perimeter road runs about halfway around the coast from just beyond Ohara to Shirahama. No roads run into the interior, which is virtually untouched. There's a tourist information office at the top of the car park by the docks near Funaura; the staff will book accommodation for you.

River Trip

Iriomote's number one attraction and the principal goal for the many day-trippers is the trip up the Urauchigawa River to the Mariudo Falls. The winding brown river is indeed a lot like a tiny stretch of the Amazon and, from where the boat stops, you have about a 1½ hour round-trip walk to the Mariudo Falls and on to the long, rapids-like Kampira Falls. There are some good swimming places around the falls. From there a walking track continues right across the island. The river trip costs Y1440. There are always trips in the morning (when the day-trippers arrive) and often in the afternoon as well.

Beaches & Diving

There are some fine beaches around the island and star sand can be found at Hoshisuna-no-hama (Star Sand Beach). Sonai, beyond the Urauchigawa River towards Shirahama, also has a pleasant beach and some good places to stay. Haimitano-hama Beach, south of Ohara, is said to be the best beach on the island.

Diving around Iriomote certainly isn't cheap, but there are some fine sites like the famed Manta Way in the straits between Iriomote and Kohama, where you are almost certain to come across manta rays. A day's diving typically costs Y10,000 for the boat and Y5000 for the gear.

Walks

There are some great walks in Iriomote's jungle-clad interior. The Binai Falls on the hills behind the lagoon are visible from boats coming into Funaura. To get to the falls you wade across the shallow lagoon from the causeway, plod through the mangroves behind the lagoon and then follow the river up to the base of the falls. A path branches off from the river and climbs to the top of the falls, from where there are superb views down to the coast. The walk takes 1½ to two hours and the falls are great for a cooling dip, but bring salt or matches to get rid of leeches.

From the Kampira Falls at the end of the Urauchigawa River trip you can continue on the cross-island trail to Ohara. The walk takes about eight hours and is particularly popular in the spring, when the many trekkers manage to lay a confusing network of false trails.

Places to Stay & Eat

Iriomote has many ryokan, minshuku and pensions, each one lining up its minibus to meet incoming boats at Funaura. The staff at the Funaura Harbour information office will make bookings. The best places are found along the coast west of the harbour towards the Hoshisuna-no-hama Beach or further west near the Urauchigawa River. There's also some good accommodation in the small village of Sonai where the *Hoshisuna-sō Minshuku* (tel 09808-5-6411) is particularly good.

The *Iriomote-sō Youth Hostel* (tel 09808-5-6255) has a great hillside location near Funaura Harbour, good facilities, great food and a dive shop. The nightly cost is Y1900. Continuing west along the coast from Funaura you soon come to the *Iriomote-jima Midori-sō Youth Hostel* (tel 09808-5-6525/6253), which costs Y1700 per night.

Robinson's Inn is a pleasant coffee bar on the main junction in Uehara, a km along the road from Funaura Harbour.

Getting There & Away

A variety of boats operate between Ishigaki and Iriomote, most to Funaura rather than Ohara. Occasionally there are services to Shirahama. The fares vary from around Y1750 to Y2400 and the trip typically takes from 40 minutes to one hour on the faster craft. The slower and less frequent ferries are cheaper.

Getting Around

Many of the minshuku and the youth hostels rent bicycles (Y200 per hour, Y1200 per day) and scooters (Y600, Y3000). Cars can also be rented; try Iriomote Rent-a-Car (tel 09808-5-5303). There's a regular bus service between Ohara and Shirahama at the two ends of the island's single road. A bus all the way from one end to the other takes nearly an hour and costs Y960; a bus from Funaura Harbour to the Urauchigawa River costs Y220.

ISLANDS AROUND IRIOMOTE

Directly north of Iriomote, clearly visible from Funaura, tiny Hatoma-jima Island has a handful of minshuku and some very fine beaches and snorkelling.

Close to the east coast of Iriomote the small island of Kohama has minshuku, the expensive Haimurubushi Resort and superb scuba diving, particularly in Manta Way. Boats operate there from Ishigaki. Directly south of Kohama is Kuro Island where bulls are raised for Okinawa's bullfights (tōgyū).

YONAGUNI-JIMA ISLAND 与那国島

Yonaguni Island is 100 km west of Iriomote and Ishigaki islands and only 100 km from the east coast of Taiwan. The hilly island is just 11 km long and there are fine views from the top of 231 metre Mt Urabu. It's said that on a clear day you can see the mountains of Taiwan from Yonaguni. The island is renowned for its strong saké and its jumbo-sized moths known as yonagunisan. Traditional houses on the island have thatched roofs but tiled roofs are becoming the norm.

Sonai, overlooked by Mt Urabu, is the island's main town. From here it's seven km west by road to Kubura Bay and four km east by foot to the unusual rock known as Saninu dai.

Getting There & Away

SWAL fly to Yonaguni-jima Island from Ishigaki twice daily; the 40 minute flight costs Y5360 one way. A ferry operates between the two islands every few days and takes about seven hours at a cost of Y3500.

HATERUMA-JIMA ISLAND ハテルマ島

Directly south of Iriomote Island is tiny Hateruma Island, only five km long and the southernmost point of Japan. Hateruma means 'the end of the coral'. The SWAL flight from Ishigaki takes 20 minutes and costs Y4860. Ferries take about three hours and cost Y2000.

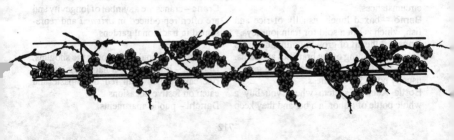

Glossary

Abecu – from *avec*, the French word for 'with' and used by the Japanese to refer to a courting couple. Thus Love Hotels were called *Abecu Hoteru*; this has now fallen out of use and the English is more commonly used.

Aimai – ambiguous and unclear talk, not coming to the point.

Ainu – the original people of Japan, recognisable by their rounded eyes, hirsute appearance and wavy hair; only isolated pockets of pure Ainu remain, in the northern extremes of Hokkaidō.

Aka-chochin – red-lantern bar; working man's pub.

Akirame – to relinquish, resignation.

Amakudari – 'descent from heaven'; a retiring civil servant who then goes to work for a private corporation which he formerly dealt with.

Annaijo – information office.

Arahitogami – living god, the emperor.

Ayu – sweetfish caught during *ukai* (cormorant fishing).

Baito – from *arbeit* the German word for 'work', is a part time job or an illegal immigrant worker.

Bangasa – rain umbrella made from oiled paper.

Banzai – literally '10,000 years', *banzai* means 'hurrah' or 'hurray'; in the West this exclamation is mostly associated with WW II although its modern use is quite peaceful.

Basho – sumō wrestling tournament.

Basho-gara – literally 'the character of a place', fitting to the particular conditions or circumstances.

Bentō – boxed lunch, usually of rice and fish, which is often sold for train journeys.

Bonsai – the art of growing miniature trees by careful pruning of the branches and roots.

Boso-zoku – hot car or motorcycle gangs, usually noisy but harmless.

Bottle Keep – system where you buy a whole bottle of liquor in a bar and they keep it for you to drink on subsequent visits. Real entertainers may have bottles stored at numerous bars around town.

Bugaku – dance pieces played by court orchestras in ancient Japan.

Bunraku – classical puppet theatre using huge puppets to portray dramas similar to *kabuki*.

Burakumin – literally 'village people', the *burakumin* were traditionally outcastes associated with lowly occupations such as leather work.

Bushidō – 'Way of the Warrior', set of values followed by the samurai.

Butsudan – Buddhist altar in Japanese homes.

Carp – carp are considered to be a brave, tenacious and vigorous fish and the *koinobori* carp windsocks are flown in honour of sons whom it is hoped will inherit a carp's virtues. Many towns and villages have carp ponds or channels teeming with colourful ornamental *nishiki-goi* carp.

Chaniwa – tea garden.

Chanoyu – tea ceremony.

Charm – small dish of peanuts or other snack food served, often unrequested, with a drink at a bar and charged for.

Chizu – map.

Cho – city area (for large cities) between a ward *ku* and *chome* in size. Also a street.

Chome – city area of a few blocks.

Chōchin – paper lantern.

Chōnan – oldest son.

Chu – loyalty.

Cinderella Mrs – housewife.

Crane – cranes are a symbol of longevity and are often reproduced in *origami* and represented in traditional gardens.

Daimyō – regional lords under the shoguns.

Daifuku – literally 'great happiness', sticky rice cakes filled with red bean paste and eaten on festive occasions.

Danchi – public apartments.

Dantai – a group such as the ubiquitous Japanese tourist group.

Deru kui wa utareru – 'the nail that sticks up gets hammered down', popular Japanese proverb which is more or less the opposite of the Western 'the squeaky wheel gets the oil'!

Donko – name for local trains in country areas.

Eboshi – black, triangular samurai hat.

Eki – train station.

Ekiben – *bentō* lunch box bought at a railway station.

Ema – small wooden plaques depicting divine steeds; one writes on the back and then hangs it up in a shrine's grounds.

Engawa – traditional verandah from a Japanese house overlooking the garden.

Enka – often referred to as the Japanese equivalent of country & western music, these are folk ballads about love and human suffering that are popular amongst the older generation.

Enryō – individual restraint and reserve.

Ero-guro – erotic and grotesque manga.

Fu – urban prefecture.

Fude – brush used for calligraphy.

Fugu – poisonous blowfish or pufferfish.

Fundoshi – loincloth or breechcloth, traditional male garment consisting of a wide belt and a cloth drawn over the genitals and between the buttocks. Now usually seen only at festivals or on *sumō* wrestlers.

Furigana – Japanese script used to give pronunciation for kanji.

Furii kippu – one day open ticket.

Futon – traditional quilt-like mattress which is rolled up and stowed away during the day.

Fusuma – sliding screen.

Futsū – literally 'ordinary', a basic stopping-all-stations train.

Gagaku – music of the imperial court.

Gaijin – literally 'outside people', foreigners.

Gaman – to endure.

Gasshō-zukuri – 'hands in prayer' architectural style.

Gei-no-kai – the 'world of art and talent', usually refers to TV where there's not much of either.

Geisha – not a prostitute but a 'refined person', a woman versed in the arts and dramas who entertains guests.

Genkan – foyer area where shoes are removed or replaced when entering or leaving a building.

Geta – traditional wooden sandals.

Giri – a person's social obligations.

Giri-ninjō – combination of social obligations and one's personal values; the two are often in conflict.

Go – board game.

Hachimaki – headband worn as a symbol of resolve; kamikaze pilots wore them in WW II, students wear them to exams.

Haiku – 17 syllable poems.

Haitaku – a hired taxi.

Hakurai – literally 'brought by ship', foreign or imported goods.

Hanami – cherry blossom viewing.

Haniwa – earthenware figures found in Kofun period tombs.

Hanko – stamp or seal used to authenticate any document, in Japan your *hanko* carries much more weight than your signature.

Harakiri – belly cutting, common name for *seppuku* or ritual suicide.

Hara-kyū – acupuncture.

Hashi – chopsticks.

Heiwa – peace.

Henro – pilgrims on the Shikoku 88 Temple Circuit.

Higasa – sunshade umbrella.

Hiragana – phonetic syllabary used to write Japanese words.

Ichi-go – square wooden sake 'cups' holding 180 ml.

Ijime – bullying or teasing.

Ikebana – art of flower arrangement.

Irezumi – a tattoo or the art of tattooing. Japanese tattoos are usually much more complex and artistic than their Western counterparts. Traditionally they are worn by *yakuza* (Japanese Mafia members) but in practice carpenters and labourers are just as likely to be tattooed.

Itadakimasu – before-meals expression, literally 'I will receive'.

Ittaikan – feeling of unity, of being one type.

Jiage-ya – specialists used by developers to persuade recalcitrant landowners to sell up.

Jika-tabi – split toe boots traditionally worn by Japanese carpenters and builders, which have recently become fashionable attire.

Jigoku – 'hells' or hot springs for looking at.

Jikokuhyō – the book of timetables.

Jitensha – bicycle.

Jujitsu – martial art from which *judō* was derived.

Juku – cramming schools.

Kabuki – form of Japanese theatre based on popular legends and characterised by elaborate costumes, stylised acting and the use of male actors for all roles.

Kachi-gumi – the 'victory group' who refuse to believe Japan lost WW II.

Kaigo – honorific language used to show respect to elders.

Kaikan – hotel-style accommodation sponsored by government; literally 'meeting hall'.

Kaiseki – Japanese cuisine which obeys very strict rules of etiquette for every detail of the meal and the diner's surroundings.

Kaisha – a company, firm.

Kaisoku – rapid train.

Kaisūken – discount bus tickets.

Kakizome – New Year's resolutions.

Kami – Shinto gods, spirits of natural phenomena.

Kamidana – Shinto altar in Japanese homes.

Kamikaze – 'divine wind'; typhoon that sunk Kublai Khan's 13th century invasion fleet and the name adopted by suicide pilots in the waning days of WW II.

Kampo – Japanese herbalism.

Kana – the two phonetic syllabaries, *hiragana* and *katakana*.

Kanban-musume – 'shop sign girl', girl who stands outside a shop or business to lure customers in.

Kanbu – management.

Kanji – literally 'Chinese script', Chinese ideographic script.

Kannon – Buddhist Goddess of Mercy, adopted by the underground Christians as a substitute Virgin Mary during Japan's long period of isolation from the West.

Kannushi – chief priest of a Shinto shrine.

Kanpai – 'Cheers!'

Karakasa – oiled paper umbrella.

Karaoke – bars where you sing along with taped music (usually mournful folk ballads); literally 'empty orchestra'.

Kasa – umbrella.

Kasekininru – 'fossil breed', ancient form of *kyujinrui*.

Katamichi – one-way ticket.

Katana – Japanese sword.

Katakana – phonetic syllabary used to write foreign words.

Ken – prefecture.

Kendō – oldest martial art; literally 'the way of the sword'.

Ki – life force, will.

Kimono – brightly coloured robe-like traditional outer garment.

Kin-en-sha – nonsmoking carriage.

Kissaten – coffee shop.

Kōban – police box, the officers in this local police station keep a careful eye on their district.

Koinobori – carp banners and windsocks; the colourful fish pennants which wave over countless homes in Japan in late April and early May are for Boys' Day, the final holiday of Golden Week. These days Boys' Day has become Children's Day and the windsocks don't necessarily simply fly in honour of the household sons.

Kokuminshukusha – national vacation village, an inexpensive form of accommodation.

Kokutetsu – Japanese word for JR, literally, 'national line'.

Komeito – clean party government, third largest political party.

Kone – personal connections.

Kotatsu – heated table with a quilt or cover over it to keep the legs and lower body warm.

Koto – 13-stringed instrument that is played flat on the floor.

Kura – mud-walled storehouses.

Kyakuma – drawing room of a home, where guests are met.

Kyōiku mama – education mother, a woman who pushes her kids through the Japanese education process.

Kyujinrui – 'old breed', opposite of *shinjuru*.

Kyūkō – ordinary express train (faster than a *futsū*, only stopping at certain stations).

Live House – nightclub or bar where live music is performed.

Machi – city area (for large cities) between a ku (ward) and chome (area of a few blocks) in size; also street or area.

Maiko – apprentice geisha.

Mama-san – woman who manages a water trade bar or club.

Maneki-neko – beckoning cat figure frequently seen in restaurants and bars, it's supposed to attract customers and trade.

Manga – Japanese comics (contents often include soft porn).

Matsuri – festival.

Meinichi – the 'deathday' or anniversary of someone's death.

Meishi – business card, very important in Japan.

Mentsu – face.

Miai Kekkon – arranged marriage, now rare.

Mibun – social rank.

Miko – shrine maidens.

Mikoshi – portable shrines carried around by hordes of sweaty, half-naked salarymen during festivals.

Minshuku – the Japanese equivalent of a B&B; family-run budget accommodation.

Misoshiru – bean-paste soup.

Mitsubachi – accommodation for motorcycle tourers.

Mizu-shobai – see *water trade*.

Mochi – pounded rice made into cakes and eaten at festive occasions.

Mōfu – blanket.

Morning service – *moningū sābisu*, a light breakfast served until 10 am in many *kissaten*.

Muko – 'over there', anywhere outside Japan.

Mura – village.

My house Mrs – housewife.

Nagashi – folk singers and musicians who wander from bar to bar.

Nagashi somen – flowing noodles.

Nengajo – new year cards.

New humans – the younger generation, brought up in more affluent times than their parents and consequently less respectful of the frugal values of the post-war generation.

Nihonga – term for Japanese-style painting.

Ningyō – Japanese doll.

Ninja – practitioners of *ninjutsu*.

Ninjō – debt, fellow feeling, that which is universally right.

Ninjutsu – 'the art of stealth'.

Nihon or **Nippon** – Japanese word for Japan, literally 'source of the sun'.

Nō – classical Japanese drama performed on a bare stage.

Noren – cloth hung as a sunshade, typically carries the name of the shop or premise, indicates that a restaurant is open for business.

Norikae – to change buses or trains, make a connection.

Norikaeken – transfer ticket (trams and buses).

O- – prefix used to show respect to anything it is applied to. See *san*.

Obāsan – grandmotherly type, an old woman.

Obi – sash or belt worn with a kimono.

O-cha – tea.

Ofuku – return ticket.

O-furo – traditional Japanese bath.

OL – 'office lady', standard female employee of a large firm, usually a clerical worker.

Omake – an extra bonus or premium when you buy something.

Omiai – arranged marriage, almost disappeared in modern Japan.

Omiyaki – the souvenir gifts which Japanese must bring back from any trip.

On – favour.

Onbu – 'carrying on the back', getting someone else to bear the expense, pick up the tab. Also the custom of carrying a baby strapped to the back.

Onnagata – male actor playing a woman's role (usually in *kabuki*).

Onsen – mineral bath/spa area, usually with accommodation.

Origami – art of paper folding.

Oshibori – hot towels provided in restaurants.

Otsumani – bar snacks *charms*.

Oyabun/kobun – teacher/pupil or senior/junior relationship.

Pachinko – vertical pinball game which is a Japanese craze (estimated to take in over 6 trillion yen a year) and a major source of tax evasion, yakuza funds, etc.

Periipeido kaado – 'prepaid card', a sort of reverse credit card; you buy a magnetically coded card for a given amount and it can be used for certain purchases until spent. The prepaid phone cards are the most widespread but there are many others such as Prepaid Highway Cards for use on toll roads.

Pinku saron – 'pink saloon', seedy hostess bars.

Rakugo – Japanese raconteurs, kind of stand-up comics.

Robatayaki – yakitori with a deliberately rustic, friendly, down home atmosphere.

Romaji – Japanese Roman script.

Rōnin – 'masterless samurai', students who must resit university entrance exams.

Rotemburo – open-air baths.

Ryokan – traditional Japanese inn.

Saisen-bako – offering box at Shinto shrines.

Sakazuki – saké cups.

Sakoku – Japan's period of national seclusion.

Sakura – cherry blossoms.

Salaryman – standard male employee of a large firm.

Samurai – warrior class.

San – suffix which shows respect to the person it is applied to, see also *o*, the equivalent prefix. Both can occasionally be used together as *o-kyaku-san*, where *kyaku* is the word for guest or customer.

San-sō – mountain cottage.

Satori – Zen concept of enlightenment.

Seku hara – sexual harassment.

Senpai – one's elder or senior at school or work.

Sensei – generally translates as 'teacher' but has wider reference. Politicians are *sensei* through their power rather than their teaching ability.

Sentō – public baths.

Seppuku – ritual suicide by disembowelment.

Settō – set breakfast.

Shamisen – three-stringed banjo-like instrument.

Shi – city (to distinguish cities with prefectures of the same name).

Shiken-jigoku – 'examination hell', the enormously important and stressful entrance exams to various levels of the Japanese education system.

Shiki – village.

Shikki – lacquerware.

Shinjū – double suicide by lovers.

Shinjuru – 'new species', young people who do not believe in the standard pattern of Japanese life. Opposite of *kyujinrui*.

Shinkansen – ultra fast 'bullet' trains, literally 'new line' since new railway lines were laid for the high speed trains.

Shitamachi – low-lying, less affluent parts of Tokyo.

Shodō – Japanese calligraphy, literally the 'way of writing'.

Shōgi – an Oriental version of chess in which each player has 20 pieces and the object is to capture your opponent's king.

Shogun – military ruler of old Japan.

Shōji – sliding rice paper screens.

Shōjin ryori – vegetarian meals (especially at temple lodgings).

Shūji – the 'practice of letters', a lesser form of *shodō*.

Shukubō – temple lodgings.

Shunga – explicit erotic prints, literally 'spring pictures'.

Shunto – spring labour offensive, an annual 'strike'.

Shūyū-ken – excursion train ticket.

Soba – noodles.

Soapland – Japanese euphemism for sex and associated activities.

Sogo Shosha – integrated trading houses, like the old *zaibatsu*.

Sokaiya – Yakuza who specialise in ensuring that company general meetings go smoothly.

Soroban – an abacus.

Sukebe – lewd in thought and deed, can be a compliment in the right context (among male drinking partners for example).

Sumi-e – black ink brush paintings.

Sumō – Japanese wrestling.

Suzuki – the most common Japanese family name, equivalent to Smith in English.

Tabi – split-toed Japanese socks used when wearing *geta*.

Tadaima – 'now' or 'present', a traditional greeting called out when one returns home.

Tako – kites.

Talentu – Western rock band.

Tanin – outsider, stranger, someone not connected with the current situation.

Tanka – poems of 31 syllables.

Tanuki – racoon or dog-like folklore character frequently represented in ceramic figures.

Tachishōben – men urinating in public are a familiar sight in Japan. It's the cause of some academic discussion over Japanese concepts of private places (strict rules apply) and public ones (anything goes), insiders (your friends don't care) and outsiders (whether they care doesn't matter) and even rural environments (we're all farmers at heart) versus urban ones (even in the city).

Tatami – tightly woven floor matting on which shoes are never worn. Traditionally room size is defined in number of tatami mats.

Tatemae – 'face', how you act in public, your public position.

Teikiken – discount commuter passes.

Teishoku – set lunch.

Tekito – suitable or appropriate.

Tennō – heavenly king, the emperor.

To – metropolis.

Tokkuri – saké flask.

Tokkyū – limited express, faster than an ordinary express (kyūkū) train.

Tokonoma – alcove in a house in which flowers may be displayed or a scroll hung.

Tokuko – red light district.

Torii – entrance gate to a Shinto shrine.

Tsukiai – after work socialising by salarymen.

Tsunami – huge 'tidal' waves caused by an earthquake.

Uchi – literally one's own house but has other meanings relating to belonging and being part of.

Ukai – fishing with trained cormorants.

Ukiyo-e – wood-block prints, literally 'pictures of the floating world'.

Umeboshi – Japanese flag.

Wa – harmony, team spirit or the old word for Japan as in *wafuku*.

Wabi – enjoyment of peace and tranquillity.

Wafuku – Japanese-style clothing.

Waka – 31 syllable poem.

Wanko – lacquerware bowls.

Warabashi – lacquered chopsticks.

Warikan – custom of sharing the bill (among good friends).

Washi – Japanese paper.

Water Trade – entertainment, bars, prostitution, etc.

Yakitori – chicken kebabs.

Yakitori-ya – restaurant specialising in *yakitori*.

Yakuza – Japanese mafia.

Yamabushi – mountain priests (Shugendō Buddhism practitioners).

Yama-goya – mountain huts.

Yamato damashi – Japanese spirit.

Yamato-e – traditional Japanese-style painting.

Yasaiya – Zen vegetable shops.

Yatai – festival floats.

Yenjoy girl – unmarried woman with time and cash to spare.

Yōfuku – Western-style clothing.

Yomiuri Giants – *the* Japanese baseball team; although there are 12 big league teams over 50% of the population back the Giants.

Yukata – rather like a dressing gown, worn for lounging or casual use; standard issue for bathing in ryokan.

Zabuton – small cushions for sitting on (used in *tatami* rooms).

Zaibatsu – industrial conglomerates; the term arose pre-WW II but the Japanese economy is still dominated by huge firms like Mitsui, Marubeni or Mitsubishi which are involved in many different industries.

Index

TEXT

Map references are in **bold** type

Patterns

Signs & Symbols

People

Patterns
Food & Drink
Architechture
Statues & Sculptures
Advertising, Japanese style
Nature
Shrines & Temples
Modes of Transport
Temples & Pagodas
Castles

Patterns – facing page 193

a. Votive wooden plaques (RS)
b. Japanese garden, Kyoto (CT)
c. Shrine & miniature torii, Fushimi Inari Shrine,
   Kyoto (RS)
d. Japanese cemetery (CT)
e. Akihabara, Tokyo (CT)
f. Souvenir Nakasendō hats (RS)
g. Ginza, Tokyo (CT)
h. Abandoned bicycles, Fukuyama (TW)
i. Koinobori (carp banners) (TW)

Food & Drink – facing page 224

a. Drying fish (TW)
b. Drying octopus, Amanohashidate (TW)
c. Fishmongers (CT)
d. Traditional rice bales (RS)
e. Eggs cooking on a sulphur vent (RS)
f. Drying fish (TW)
g. Plastic food display (CT)
h. Saké barrels, Hiraizumi (RS)
i. Melons, Ginza, Tokyo (CT)

Signs & Symbols – facing page 225

a. 'Surprise Attack', Okinawa (TW)
b. Bar sign, Kōchi (TW)
c. 'The Route of Seeing' (RS)
d. Small boys only! (TW)
e. 'Yellow Dick', Okinawa (TW)
f. 'Lassie Planet II' (TW)
g. 'Pretty Roman' club (TW)
h. Fortune teller, Asakusa, Tokyo (TW)
i. 'Think Potato' (RS)
j. 'Apex Brain Co Ltd' (RS)
k. Billboard, Tokyo (CT)

People – facing page 320

a. Taraibuné boat woman, Ogi (RS)
b. Market lady, Takayama (RS)
c. Divers, Ago-wan Bay (RS)
d. School children (CT)
e. Street procession, Autumn Festival,
   Takayama (AE)
f. Young girls (CT)
g. Face in the crowd (CT)

Architecture – facing page 321

a. Screened entrance (CT)
b. Yasukuni-jinja Shrine, Tokyo (CT)
c. Shop front, Tokyo (CT)
d. Shin-kyō Bridge, Nikkō (CT)
e. Tokyo tower (CT)
f. Kintai-kyō Bridge, Iwakuni (TW)
g. Genbaku Dōmu, Hiroshima (JW)
h. Kara-mon Gate, Nishi Hongan-ji Temple,
   Kyoto (TW)
i. Pachinko parlour (TW)

Statues & Sculptures – facing page 353

a. Jūroku Rakan statue, Morioka (RS)
b. Roadside guardian statue (dōsojin), Hotaka
   (RS)
c. Bronze statue detail (CT)
d. Statue with saxophone, Himeji (TW)
e. Statue, Kumamoto (TW)
f. Modern sculpture, Tokyo (CT)
g. Zenkō-ji Temple statue, Nagano (RS)
h. Ninna-ji Temple stone Buddhas, Kyoto (TW)
i. Maneki-neko (beckoning cat), Takayama (RS)

Advertising, Japanese style – facing page 449

a. Fugu phone box, Shimonoseki (DS)
b. Rooster phone box, Katsurahama, Kōchi (TW)
c. Fugu phone box (TW)
d. King Kong, Tokushima (TW)
e. Tree-trunk toilet, Miyako (TW)
f. Karate-chopped building, Naha (TW)
g. Kamikaze building, Nagasaki (TW)
h. Emerging Mini, Kōchi (TW)
i. Rocket tomb, Okuno-in Temple, Mt Kōya-san (RS)

Nature – facing page 480

a. Oirase Valley, near Lake Towado-ko (RS)
b. Stone path, Mt Haguro-san (RS)
c. Rock formation, Lake Towado-ko (RS)
d. Deer with hitchhiking crow, Kinkazan Island (RS)
e. Kegon Falls, Chūzenji-ko Lake, Nikkō (DS)
f. Pinai Falls, Iriomote Island (TW)
g. Captive bear, Noboribetsu Onsen (RS)
h. Siberian fox, Hokkaidō (RS)
i. Hot-spring area, Unzen (TW)

Shrines & Temples – facing page 576

a. Saikoku-ji Temple, Onomichi (TW)
b. Shinto priest, Meiji-jingū Shrine, Tokyo (CT)
c. Burning incense, Buddhist temple (CT)
d. Shimenawa (plaited ropes), Nagasaki (TW)
e. Gong rope, Shinto shrine (RS)
f. Shimenawa at shrine entrance (CT)
g. Temple gate, Nikkō (TW)
h. Kannon-ji Temple, Nagasaki (TW)
i. Haniwa-jinja Shrine, Matsuyama (TW)

Modes of Transport – facing page 577

a. Taraibuné (wooden tubs) at Ogi, Sado-ga-shima Island (RS)
b. Abandoned bicycles, Fukuyama (TW)
c. Rickshaw, Takayama (RS)
d. Shin-Hotaka cablecar (ropeway), Japan Alps (RS)
e. Tracks, Ueno station (CT)
f. Lotus 7, Yamaguchi (TW)
g. Nagasaki line train, Fukuoka (TW)
h. Car park, Tokushima (TW)
i. Swan pedal boats, Lake Towada-ko (RS)

Temples & Pagodas – facing page 608

a. Five storeyed pagoda from Kijukaku Pavilion, Miyajima (TW)
b. Five storeyed pagoda Ruriko-ji, Yamaguchi (TW)
c. Chikurin-ji, Kōchi (TW)
d. Five storeyed pagoda, Mt Haguro-san (CT)
e. Tennō-ji, Onomichi (TW)
f. Two storeyed pagoda, Kyoto (CT)
g. Ninna-ji, Kyoto (TW)
h. Kōsani-ji, Setoda (TW)
i. Kōjō-ji, Setoda (TW)

Castles – facing page 609

a. Matsumoto-jō, Central Honshū (RS)
b. Himeji-jō, Western Honshū (CT)
c. Kumamoto-jō, Kyūshū (TW)
d. Osaka-jō, Kinki District (CT)
e. Momotaro (Peach Boy) statue and Okayama-jō, Honshū (TW)
f. Karatsu-jō, Kyūshū (TW)
g. Matsuyama-jō, Shikoku (TW)
h. Kōchi-jō, Shikoku (TW)
i. Takamatsu-jō, Shikoku (TW)

THANKS

Writers (apologies if we've misspelt your names) to whom thanks must go include:

Ria & Peter Andeweg (Nl), Elizabeth Arndt (UK), Barbara Aylon (J), Peter Bailey (J), Bruce Barrett (USA), Yves Bartholome (B), Dale Bay (C), E M Benjamin (NZ), Steve Benz (USA), Tom Birdwell (USA), J C Bithell, Sophie Blackmore (USA), Rachel Boyd (J), Jan Brown (Aus), Ainslie Bruneau (USA), Glenn Burns (Aus), David Carter (UK), F Chevassus (Fr), John Chudleigh (Aus), Ann Collins (USA), Cynthia Connolly (USA), Robert Cordre (Thai), Carol Crump, Sylvie Dewit (B), E A Duncan (UK), Brian Durrans (UK), Leanne Eamen, Glenna Eshlesman (USA), Lawrence Fordyce (Aus), Samuel Freeman (USA), Tania Friedman (Aus), Maria Gilbert (J), Ken Gillow (J), John D C Gorick (UK), Michael Gower (UK), Alan & Lee Grant (Aus), Zavier Grau (Sp), Shannon Hanzek, Darlene Hardy (C), Andrew Holder (Aus), Lina Hoshino (USA), Jeff Ibbotson (Aus), Ruth & Leslie Isaacs (UK), Ron Keehn (USA), Janet Kehelly (Ire), Tim Lange (Aus), John R Lange (USA), Christy Lanzl (USA), Keith Liker (USA), Rob Lober (UK), John Malotte (J), Marion McDonald (J), Manuel Metzler (D), Hiroshi Mine (J), Inge Nielsen (Dk), Mrs C Noble (J), Elizabeth Nua (Phil), Rick Olderman (J), Danny R Olsen (USA), Gwy'an Rhabyt (USA), Steve Rogers (USA), Tomas Rohlin (HK), Sumner M Rosen (USA), Uwe Schlokat (A), Jane Schneider (USA), Caroline Schofield, Karmel Schreyer (USA), Simon Sostaric (Aus), Peter Sprigg (Aus), John E Stein (USA), Antje Steinwachs (D), Gisela and Dani Sulgerbuel (CH), Sean Sweeney (Aus), Elisa Ai Takao (J), Junichi Tamura (J), Joanne Thorburn (J), Gene Trabich (USA), James Trainor (USA), Heidi Truman (UK), Fiona Tyrrell (UK), Anita Ulrich (Dk), Jan Vydra (D), Margaret Wade (USA), Tracy Weatherby (USA), Tim Willian (J), Patricia Yodan (USA) and Liz Yourman (J).

A – Austria, Aus – Australia, B – Belgium, CH – Switzerland, D – Germany, Dk – Denmark, Fr – France, HK – Hong Kong, Ire – Ireland, J – Japan, Nl – Netherlands, NZ – New Zealand, Phil – Philippines, Sp – Spain, Thai – Thailand, UK – United Kingdom, USA – United States of America

Where Can You Find Out.........

HOW to get a Laotian visa in Bangkok?

WHERE to go birdwatching in PNG?

WHAT to expect from the police if you're robbed in Peru?

WHEN you can go to see cow races in Australia?

In the Lonely Planet Newsletter!

Every issue includes:

- *a letter from Lonely Planet founders Tony and Maureen Wheeler*
- *a letter from an author 'on the road'*
- *the most entertaining or informative reader's letter we've received*
- *the latest news on new and forthcoming releases from Lonely Planet*
- *and all the latest travel news from all over the world*

Guides to North-East Asia

North-East Asia on a shoestring
Concise information for independent low-budget travel in China, Hong Kong, Japan, Macau, South Korea and Taiwan, plus short notes on North Korea.

Hong Kong, Macau & Canton - a travel survival kit
This practical guide had all the travel facts on these three diverse cities, linked by history, culture and geography.

China - a travel survival kit
This book is the recognised authority for independent travellers in the People's Republic. With essential tips for avoiding pitfalls, and comprehensive practical information, it will help you to discover the real China.

Tibet - a travel survival kit
The fabled mountain-land of Tibet was one of the last areas of China to become accessible to travellers. This guide has full details on this remote and fascinating region, including the border crossing to Nepal.

Korea - a travel survival kit
The second edition of this comprehensive guide includes an exclusive chapter on North Korea, one of the world's most reclusive countries – finally opening its doors to independent travellers.

Also available:
China phrasebook, *Korean* phrasebook, *Tibet* phrasebook, and *Japanese* phrasebook.

Lonely Planet Guidebooks

Lonely Planet guidebooks cover every accessible part of Asia as well as Australia, the Pacific, South America, Africa, the Middle East and parts of North America and Europe. There are four series: *travel survival kits*, covering a single country for a range of budgets; *shoestring guides* with compact information for low-budget travel in a major region; *walking guides*; and *phrasebooks*.

Australia & the Pacific
Australia
Bushwalking in Australia
Islands of Australia's Great Barrier Reef
Fiji
Micronesia
New Caledonia
New Zealand
Tramping in New Zealand
Papua New Guinea
Papua New Guinea phrasebook
Rarotonga & the Cook Islands
Samoa
Solomon Islands
Sydney
Tahiti & French Polynesia
Tonga
Vanuatu

South-East Asia
Bali & Lombok
Burma
Burmese phrasebook
Indonesia
Indonesia phrasebook
Malaysia, Singapore & Brunei
Philippines
Pilipino phrasebook
Singapore
South-East Asia on a shoestring
Thailand
Thai phrasebook
Vietnam, Laos & Cambodia

North-East Asia
China
Chinese phrasebook
Hong Kong, Macau & Canton
Japan
Japanese phrasebook
Korea
Korean phrasebook
North-East Asia on a shoestring
Taiwan
Tibet
Tibet phrasebook

West Asia
Trekking in Turkey
Turkey
Turkish phrasebook
West Asia on a shoestring

Indian Ocean
Madagascar & Comoros
Maldives & Islands of the East Indian Ocean
Mauritius, Réunion & Seychelles

Mail Order

Lonely Planet guidebooks are distributed worldwide and are sold by good bookshops everywhere. They are also available by mail order from Lonely Planet, so if you have difficulty finding a title please write to us. US and Canadian residents should write to Embarcadero West, 112 Linden St, Oakland CA 94607, USA and residents of other countries to PO Box 617, Hawthorn, Victoria 3122, Australia.

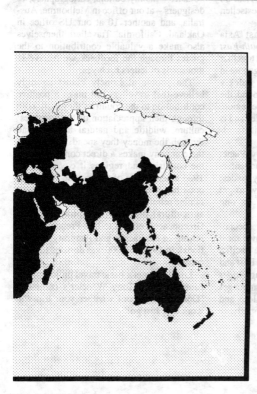

Europe
Eastern Europe on a shoestring
Iceland, Greenland & the Faroe Islands
Trekking in Spain

Indian Subcontinent
Bangladesh
India
Hindi/Urdu phrasebook
Trekking in the Indian Himalaya
Karakoram Highway
Kashmir, Ladakh & Zanskar
Nepal
Trekking in the Nepal Himalaya
Nepal phrasebook
Pakistan
Sri Lanka
Sri Lanka phrasebook

Africa
Africa on a shoestring
Central Africa
East Africa
Kenya
Swahili phrasebook
Morocco, Algeria & Tunisia
Moroccan Arabic phrasebook
West Africa

North America
Alaska
Canada
Hawaii

Mexico
Baja California
Mexico

Central America
Costa Rica
La Ruta Maya

Middle East
Egypt & the Sudan
Egyptian Arabic phrasebook
Israel
Jordan & Syria
Yemen

South America
Argentina
Bolivia
Brazil
Brazilian phrasebook
Chile & Easter Island
Colombia
Ecuador & the Galápagos Islands
Latin American Spanish phrasebook
Peru
Quechua phrasebook
South America on a shoestring

The Lonely Planet Story

Lonely Planet published its first book in 1973 in response to the numerous 'How did you do it?' questions Maureen and Tony Wheeler were asked after driving, bussing, hitching, sailing and railing their way from England to Australia.

Written at a kitchen table and hand collated, trimmed and stapled, *Across Asia on the Cheap* became an instant local bestseller, inspiring thoughts of another book.

Eighteen months in South-East Asia resulted in their second guide, *South-East Asia on a shoestring*, which they put together in a backstreet Chinese hotel in Singapore in 1975. The 'yellow bible' as it quickly became known to backpackers around the world, soon became *the* guide to the region. It has sold well over ½ million copies and is now in its 6th edition, still retaining its familiar yellow cover.

Today there are over 80 Lonely Planet titles – books that have that same adventurous approach to travel as those early guides; books that 'assume you know how to get your luggage off the carousel' as one reviewer put it.

Although Lonely Planet initially specialised in guides to Asia, they now cover most regions of the world, including the Pacific, South America, Africa, the Middle East and Eastern Europe. The list of *walking guides* and *phrasebooks* (for 'unusual' languages such as Quechua, Swahili, Nepalese and Egyptian Arabic) is also growing rapidly.

The emphasis continues to be on travel for independent travellers. Tony and Maureen still travel for several months of each year and play an active part in the writing, updating and quality control of Lonely Planet's guides.

They have been joined by over 50 authors, 40 staff – mainly editors, cartographers, & designers – at our office in Melbourne, Australia, and another 10 at our US office in Oakland, California. Travellers themselves also make a valuable contribution to the guides through the feedback we receive in thousands of letters each year.

The people at Lonely Planet strongly believe that travellers can make a positive contribution to the countries they visit, both through their appreciation of the countries' culture, wildlife and natural features, and through the money they spend. In addition, the company makes a direct contribution to the countries and regions it covers. Since 1986 a percentage of the income from each book has been donated to ventures such as famine relief in Africa; aid projects in India; agricultural projects in Central America; Greenpeace's efforts to halt French nuclear testing in the Pacific and Amnesty International. In 1991 $68,000 was donated to these causes.

Lonely Planet's basic travel philosophy is summed up in Tony Wheeler's comment, 'Don't worry about whether your trip will work out. Just go!'